THE MILITARY BALANCE

2013

published by

Routledge
Taylor & Francis Group

for

The International Institute for Strategic Studies

ARUNDEL HOUSE | 13–15 ARUNDEL STREET | TEMPLE PLACE | LONDON | WC2R 3DX | UK

THE **MILITARY BALANCE** 2013

The International Institute for Strategic Studies
ARUNDEL HOUSE | 13–15 ARUNDEL STREET | TEMPLE PLACE | LONDON | WC2R 3DX | UK

This publication has been prepared by the Director-General and Chief Executive of the Institute and his Staff, who accept full responsibility for its contents. The views expressed herein do not, and indeed cannot, represent a consensus of views among the worldwide membership of the Institute as a whole.

FIRST PUBLISHED March 2013

ISBN 978-1-85743-680-8
ISSN 0459-7222

Cover images: USMC/Tommy Lamkin; Stuart Price/AFP/Getty Images; European External Action Service; Piotr Butowski; Adek Berry/AFP/Getty; ChinaFotoPress/Getty.

The *Military Balance* (ISSN 0459-7222) is published annually by Routledge Journals, an imprint of Taylor & Francis, 4 Park Square, Milton Park, Abingdon, Oxfordshire OX14 4RN, UK. The 2013 annual subscription rate is: UK£197 (individual rate), UK£304 (institution rate) UK£266 (online only); overseas US$327 (individual rate), US$531 (institution rate), US$465 (online only).

A subscription to the institution print edition, ISSN 0459-7222, includes free access for any number of concurrent users across a local area network to the online edition, ISSN 1479-9022.

Dollar rates apply to subscribers in all countries except the UK and the Republic of Ireland where the pound sterling price applies. All subscriptions are payable in advance and all rates include postage.

Journals are sent by air to the USA, Canada, Mexico, India, Japan and Australasia. Subscriptions are entered on an annual basis, i.e. January to December. Payment may be made by sterling cheque, dollar cheque, international money order, National Giro, or credit card (Amex, Visa, Mastercard).

Please send subscription orders to: USA/Canada: Taylor & Francis Inc., Journals Department, 325 Chestnut Street, 8th Floor, Philadelphia, PA 19106, USA. UK/Europe/Rest of World: Routledge Journals, T&F Customer Services, T&F Informa UK Ltd., Sheepen Place, Colchester, Essex, CO3 3LP, UK.

The print edition of this journal is printed on ANSI conforming acid-free paper by Bell & Bain, Glasgow, UK.

CONTENTS

Index of **TABLES**

Index of **FIGURES**

Index of **MAPS**

The Military Balance 2013
Editor's Foreword

The Military Balance 2013 is a comprehensive and independent assessment of global military capabilities and defence economics. It is also a reference work on developments in global military and security affairs.

The strategic consequences of the Arab Spring and the brutal conflict in Syria again dominated headlines throughout 2012. Syria increasingly preoccupied policy planners in the Middle East and Europe, given the impact of the war on Syrian civilians and its destabilising effect on the immediate region. At time of writing, the prospects for direct military intervention from abroad seemed remote. For defence analysts, however, Syria added to the increasingly complex global military and security environment in 2012. China's rise manifested itself in new ways, particularly in growing maritime capabilities. Western defence budgets continued to contract, with increased pressure on defence planners to balance financial priorities with the requirement to hedge against longer-term strategic risks.

In the Middle East, the insurgency in Syria showed increasing characteristics of a civil war. The UN estimated that over 30,000 people had died by September 2012, and resolution of the conflict appeared distant. By late 2012, ethnic and sectarian faultlines had deepened. It was likely that, over time, the balance of forces would shift to the rebels, given that their capability and external support would rise. But government forces could still tactically defeat the rebels if the latter abandoned their guerrilla approach and tried to hold urban areas: if President Bashar al-Assad could not win, the rebels could still lose. Iran sent supplies and personnel to aid the regime, but most states backed the rebels politically, while some sent material supplies. Though a notionally unified Syrian opposition emerged after November talks in Qatar, concern persisted about the number of rebel groups, their aims, and the presence of jihadists. In Libya, over one year after the fall of Muammar Gadhafi, many rebel groups had still to disarm; there will be similar concerns over Syria, and fears that regime collapse could lead to a wider bureaucratic disintegration.

Elsewhere in the region, a Muslim Brotherhood member, Muhammad Morsi, was elected president of the most populous Arab country, Egypt, and recalibrated relations with the country's military leadership. Renewed conflict between Israel and Hamas briefly drove Syria from the headlines in November. Israel launched attacks on Hamas military and civil infrastructure in Gaza, while Hamas continued rocket attacks on Israel, for the first time using the Iranian-origin *Fajr*-5 rocket and bringing Tel Aviv and Jerusalem within range of the Gaza Strip. As part of its response, Israel deployed its *Iron Dome* point-defence missile batteries, and the results will have been carefully studied by both the Israeli military and Hamas, as well as Hizbullah in Lebanon. Missile defence dominated procurements in the Gulf, where states see Iran as the main threat to regional stability, notably through its ballistic-missile and nuclear programmes. The US continued to maintain substantial deployments in the region and to play a coordinating role in regional defence cooperation.

US dispositions in the Middle East also remain vital to Washington's presence in Afghanistan. There, NATO and the Afghan government are engaged in a race against the clock to improve security, grow the Afghan National Security Forces (ANSF), develop state capacity, reduce corruption and persuade reconcilable insurgents to disarm, all in time for Afghan forces to assume the security lead and for NATO to withdraw from combat operations by the end of 2014. On the current trend, it is likely that the ANSF will reach full strength and improve its capability. But, the most likely situation in 2015 is rather like today's – a security patchwork with the ANSF suppressing insurgent activity in many areas but with others, particularly in eastern Afghanistan, probably subject to insurgent influence.

With the withdrawal of combat forces from Afghanistan approaching, US forces were, according to US Defense Secretary Leon Panetta, at a 'strategic turning point'. The pending end of a decade of complex wars centred on the land environment gave the US a chance to reassess force structures, roles and inventories. That US forces were going to become smaller was not in doubt. January 2012's new strategic guidance stated that forces would no longer be sized 'to conduct large scale, prolonged stability operations'. This force reduction was in part made necessary by sustained pressure on defence expenditure. But how the US interprets the experience of the last 11 years of war will have implications for force development and modernisation. It remains to be seen whether the US will try to institutionalise adaptations made in the conduct of recent wars or turn away from recent experience, as it did after Vietnam.

Most attention focused on Panetta's statement that US forces would 'of necessity rebalance towards the Asia-Pacific'. Force reductions announced for Europe were significant. But as far as Asia was concerned, there was less to this rebalance than first appeared. Capabilities in Guam had been built up in the 2000s, and the new military deployments announced were limited. Indeed, the rebalance could also be seen as a way for Washington to rebuild capabilities, denuded since 9/11, with the operational demands of Iraq and Afghanistan. Asian states were, meanwhile, trying to discern what was new in the US rebalance. Indeed, it is as much a signal to allies (and potential rivals) that the US will be increasingly engaged in regional security. This reflects not just US economic ties to the region but also the emergence of China as a regional competitor in terms of both commerce and military capability.

There was a continued shift in the relative balance of military power to Asia, notably in terms of budgets and expenditures – and new capability acquisitions. China's rise, and its growing strategic reach, was illustrated by the commissioning of its first aircraft carrier in September 2012, and the first at-sea carrier landing of its J-15 combat aircraft two months later. However, this does not yet constitute a fully developed combat capability. China is still learning how to operate carriers, the J-15 remains largely developmental, and the People's Liberation Army Navy's ability to carry out integrated carrier task group operations is embryonic. But the capacity of China's defence industry to produce advanced capabilities is gradually transforming the PLA. In 1992, China's air force, for example, had around 5,000 combat aircraft; by 2012, this had reduced to 1,900, but this smaller force was more capable and increasingly equipped with fourth-generation multi-role fighters with associated air-to-air and air-to-surface weapons. But as well as giving Beijing military forces that would allow it to project power over distance, these figures are a reminder that China's force modernisation is, in a way, just that.

China's defence developments are fuelled by continuing spending increases, with an 8.3% increase in real defence spending between 2011 and 2012. In Asia as a whole, real defence spending rose by 2.44% in 2011, and the pace accelerated to 4.94% in 2012. Indeed, 2012 saw Asian defence spending (at current prices and exchange rates, and excluding Australia and New Zealand) overtake that of NATO European states for the first time. The biggest decline in defence spending was in North America, although much of this reflects lower levels of funding for US operations in Afghanistan. This reduction also has to be balanced against the continuing sheer size of the overall US budget: in 2012, the US accounted for just under half of global defence spending (45.3%) and still outstrips that of the next 14 countries combined.

The 2012 reduction in real spending in Europe was 1.63% (on top of a 2.52% decline in 2011). In the context of existing regional European budgets, this is a more severe contraction than North America's. In 2012, real defence spending fell in 60% of European states. European governments' defence planning was again dominated by the dilemmas prompted by budget woes. Discussion focused on what defence capabilities and ambitions states should retain, and whether it was possible to generate economies of scale across NATO or the EU, in terms of capability development and equipment holdings. Declining defence budgets continued to lead to force reductions in many countries. Those states in Europe seeing the toughest cuts were having to consider the effect these would have on their ability to sustain even reduced levels of capability. Some countries, meanwhile, saw demonstrations by service personnel against the impact of cuts on their pay and conditions. While NATO and the EU might try to develop 'smart defence', or pooling and sharing, and this might lead to some rationalisation, this would probably be more in support and training, rather than combat capability. In the main, states continued to act according to national imperatives, and capability reductions were largely uncoordinated.

In NATO states, some defence ministries and armed forces have seriously examined the challenges that austerity will pose for their capabilites after Afghanistan. Some, such as the US and UK, have used the Afghanistan drawdown as an opportunity to start rebuilding expeditionary capability, though on a lower level than before and with adjusted strategic focus. Others have reduced their capabilities for contingent operations after 2015. Many new capabilities, such as UAVs and counter-IED, have applications beyond the campaigns for which they were bought. Defence ministries face hard choices about which capabilities procured for recent operations they should maintain or discard, and which should enter core defence budgets. Many Western militaries, including those which actively participated in the wars of the last decade, will field smaller, though potentially more capable, forces. But while they might envision these taking part in fewer enduring land-focused operations, it must be remembered that Western forces did not initially foresee staying in Iraq for eight years. Conflicts evolve in response to military engagements and local dynamics that can themselves change in response to intervening states' political and military activity. Flexibility, agility and scaleability of forces will be central to addressing future contingencies. While doing more with less is a challenge, sometimes numbers count.

Chapter One
Conflict Analysis and Conflict Trends

Armed conflict continued around the world in 2012. Many are captured on the *2013 Chart of Conflict* included with this volume, and further details can be found in the *IISS Armed Conflict Database*. In a section new to *The Military Balance* this year, the IISS examines the wars in Afghanistan and Syria, analysing the course of both wars from November 2012 to November 2013. Both involve conflict between insurgents and governments, but with varying degrees of external assistance to all warring parties. A short concluding analytical essay compares the role of key military factors in both conflicts, offering some general conclusions about modern insurgency and counter-insurgency.

THE WAR IN AFGHANISTAN

NATO and the Afghan government are racing against the clock to improve security, grow the Afghan National Security Forces (ANSF), develop the capacity of the Afghan state, reduce corruption, and persuade 'reconcilable' insurgents to lay down their arms, all in time to allow Afghan authorities to assume the lead for security across the country and for NATO to withdraw from combat operations by the end of 2014. This does not require elimination of the insurgency but it does need to be reduced sufficiently so as to no longer pose an existential threat to the Afghan state and to be containable by Afghan security forces without NATO's combat power.

Security transition

At its May 2012 Chicago Summit, NATO declared that 'the Afghan security forces are well on track to take full security responsibility across the country by the end of 2014'. Pledges of military and financial assistance made at Chicago and subsequently at Tokyo were designed to reassure Afghans that the country would continue to receive political, development and financial support after 2014. The additional 33,000 US 'surge' troops deployed from 2009 had withdrawn by October, leaving 68,000 US troops alongside 28,000 troops from other nations. After Washington and Kabul agreed that Afghans would assume the lead for special operations and would take over the US prison

and detainees at Bagram, a US–Afghan strategic partnership agreement was signed in May, which led the US to designate Afghanistan a major non-NATO ally.

Since the surge began in 2009, security has improved. Improved intelligence and special forces capabilities caused significant attrition of insurgent leaders inside Afghanistan. Three tranches of districts and provinces across the country, including most of Kabul, entered the security-transition process. Two further tranches are due to do so next year. Transition does not mean that NATO-led forces withdrew from these areas, but rather that their role shifted to providing mentoring and support.

Despite insurgent ambitions to stage a counter-offensive, security gains made in the surge have not been rolled back. In September 2012, the UN assessed that 'there has been no significant deterioration of public order or security in areas in which the transition has taken place'. NATO claimed that violence was being held at arm's length from much of the Afghan population, and displayed cautious optimism that the improving confidence and capability of the ANSF meant improvements in security would endure. Evidence suggested that ISAF and the ANSF were gaining an advantage over the Taliban: NATO statistics showed an 8% reduction in insurgent attacks during 2011, while the UN assessed a 30% decrease in security incidents in the first nine months of 2012, and NATO claimed a 38% drop in its casualties in the same period. There was evidence that insurgents had difficulties in acquiring IED components and credible reports of local popular uprisings against the Taliban in Ghazni Province and elsewhere. The Afghan reintegration programme has persuaded over 5,000 insurgents to lay down their arms, although this has yet to have strategic effect.

Countervailing trends

Targeted killings of civilians (especially Afghan government officials) continued with, for example, over 230 people killed between May and July 2012 alone. Most were believed to be victims of Taliban assassinations. There were also reports of a small but steady stream of defections from the ANSF to the Taliban as well as indications of some local accommodations between the ANSF and insurgents. And there has been less military progress in southeastern Afghanistan, including the provinces bordering North Waziristan, the heartland of the Haqqani network in Pakistan. US Defense Secretary Leon Panetta told Congress that 'in eastern Afghanistan the topography, the cultural geography and the continuing presence of safe havens in Pakistan give the insurgents advantages they have lost elsewhere in the country'.

Kabul was the location of only 1% of security incidents, but it was the focus of concerted efforts by the Haqqani network to launch spectacular attacks, mostly by infiltrating from Pakistan into eastern Afghanistan, through the border provinces of ISAF's Regional Command-East. NATO and Afghan forces claimed to have pre-empted many attacks on the city; citing the lack of any such successful attacks after April 2012. Earlier attacks that got through were successfully contained by Afghan forces and then counter-attacked by Afghan commandos, with ISAF support limited to helicopters and military advisers. But, as 'propaganda of the deed', such attacks had some success in portraying the transition as failing and eroding confidence within NATO nations. Meanwhile, an attack on Camp Bastion that destroyed six US Marine Corps AV-8B aircraft showed that well-planned attacks by determined insurgents are likely to continue.

Pakistan

In 2011 Congressional testimony, outgoing US Chairman of the Joint Chiefs of Staff General Mike Mullen criticised support provided to the insurgents by Pakistan's Inter-Services Intelligence agency (ISI), claiming that the Haqqani network acted as a 'veritable arm of ISI', though a January 2012 leaked NATO report contained evidence that both parties distrusted each other.

A deterioration in US–Pakistani relations, especially after the killing of Osama bin Laden and accidental killing of 24 Pakistani troops by US forces, halted cooperation and closed NATO's supply lines. Although Pakistan eventually re-opened these supply lines, air-strikes against Pakistani targets from armed US UAVs continued to stoke Pakistani resentment of the US and contaminate attitudes towards ISAF.

It is not clear that Pakistan has sufficient civilian and military security capacity to further suppress Afghan insurgent safe havens, at the same time as countering its domestic militants. But the challenge to the state posed by the Pakistan Taliban may have changed attitudes of some securocrats who see a Taliban victory in Afghanistan as encouraging Pakistan's insurgents. This may have been reinforced by popular and military shock at the October Pakistan Taliban attack on a teenaged schoolgirl.

The ANSF

The planned expansion of ANSF strength to 157,000 Afghan National Police (ANP) officers and 195,000 Afghan National Army (ANA) personnel by the end of 2012 was ahead of schedule. An estimated 146,000 police officers and 185,000 army personnel were in place by October. NATO's training mission, therefore, shifted its efforts from increasing force size to building support and logistic capabilities. NATO and Afghan initiatives sought to reduce attrition and absence rates, including initiatives to improve troop rotation and leave schedules.

By April 2012, some 40% of operations were led by the ANSF, with only 10% conducted solely by ISAF. Brigade-level operations were being mounted in Helmand by the Afghan army with little ISAF assistance, reflecting a considerable improvement in its capability. NATO was especially confident about the rapidly maturing capabilities of Afghan army and police special forces.

Until the surge the ANP was a lower international priority. But its capability development subsequently received more international support. As a result, attrition in the ANP fell below the 16.8% annual target. However, delivering results to ordinary Afghans depends on corresponding improvements in the whole machinery of justice, including courts, lawyers and prisons, as much as it did on bolstering police capacities. These areas lagged even further behind, as shown by NATO's refusal to send detainees to Afghan prisons betraying evidence of human-rights abuses. The Afghan Local Police, small self-defence forces in villages that have opted to resist the Taliban, are mentored by embedded teams of US special-operations forces. The UN assessed that 'by mid-August, more than 16,266 personnel were operating at 71 validated sites. While these local security forces have contributed to stability in several areas, concerns remain about issues of impunity, vetting, lack of clear command and control, and the potential re-emergence of ethnically or politically biased militias.'

There are ambitious plans to provide the Afghan Air Force with a robust fixed- and rotary-wing airlift capability, as well as attack helicopters and light turboprop attack aircraft. They may achieve an initial casualty evacuation capability in 2013. But personnel

Map 1 **Afghanistan**

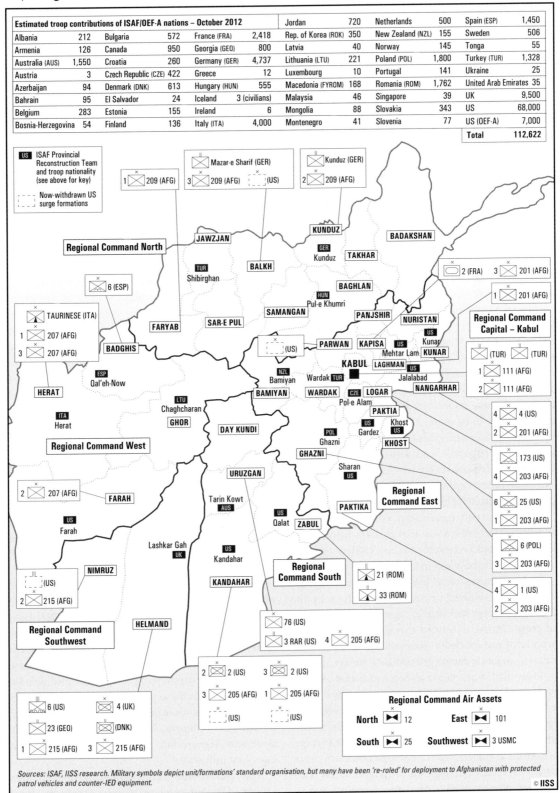

Estimated troop contributions of ISAF/OEF-A nations – October 2012									Jordan	720	Netherlands	500	Spain (ESP)	1,450
Albania	212	Bulgaria	572	France (FRA)	2,418			Rep. of Korea (ROK)	350	New Zealand (NZL)	155	Sweden	506
Armenia	126	Canada	950	Georgia (GEO)	800			Latvia	40	Norway	145	Tonga	55
Australia (AUS)	1,550	Croatia	260	Germany (GER)	4,737			Lithuania (LTU)	221	Poland (POL)	1,800	Turkey (TUR)	1,328
Austria	3	Czech Republic (CZE)	422	Greece	12			Luxembourg	10	Portugal	141	Ukraine	25
Azerbaijan	94	Denmark (DNK)	613	Hungary (HUN)	555			Macedonia (FYROM)	168	Romania (ROM)	1,762	United Arab Emirates	35
Bahrain	95	El Salvador	24	Iceland	3 (civilians)			Malaysia	46	Singapore	39	UK	9,500
Belgium	283	Estonia	155	Ireland	6			Mongolia	88	Slovakia	343	US	68,000
Bosnia-Herzegovina	54	Finland	136	Italy (ITA)	4,000			Montenegro	41	Slovenia	77	US (OEF-A)	7,000
												Total	**112,622**	

Sources: ISAF, IISS research. Military symbols depict unit/formations' standard organisation, but many have been 're-roled' for deployment to Afghanistan with protected patrol vehicles and counter-IED equipment.

© IISS

shortages and presence of a criminal patronage network in the air force make December 2017 the earliest it can achieve full capability. The Border Police are similarly challenged.

Friction and insider attacks

2012 saw increasing friction between Afghans and ISAF. A particular incident was the mistaken burning of copies of the Koran by US forces at Bagram, reports of which led to nationwide riots. In general, these were successfully contained by Afghan police forces, as were protests in September against the provocative 'Innocence of Muslims' web video.

Attacks on ISAF by Afghan troops and police have occurred since at least 2006, but greatly increased in 2012. Some 56 ISAF troops were killed between January and October 2012, 40% more than in the whole of 2011. NATO and the Afghan authorities announced initiatives to improve security against Taliban infiltration as well as drives to improve vetting and counter-intelligence. A spike in these attacks in late 2012, together with the tension resulting from the 'Innocence of Muslims' video, led ISAF to order a 'reduction in low level tactical partnering with the Afghan forces below battalion level'. As of October 2012, it was unclear when these restrictions would be lifted, but the impending US election meant they were unlikely to be relaxed in the short term. While suspending partnering could affect security provision, some in the ANSF would welcome the increased authority and responsibility this suspension provides as long as their troops do not suffer major reversals in combat, which could affect confidence.

Insurgents will have taken comfort from this. It will reinforce the view that despite heavy attrition, they should continue to attack ISAF in order to exploit NATO and Western states' casualty aversion.

Insider attacks were invariably claimed by the Taliban. But evidence, including an analysis by the Pentagon, suggested that a significant proportion of these attacks is instead carried out by Afghans who have unexpectedly 'snapped', often as a result of an apparently minor grievance or provocation. It is likely that war fatigue and accumulated Afghan resentment of the NATO presence are major motivating factors and, as a consequence, improved security measures may not have a decisive effect; such attacks will probably continue until NATO troops withdraw completely. But they have become a major threat to NATO's strategic narrative and to the political commitment of all troop-contributing nations.

Plans and prospects for 2013–15

From 2012–14, NATO plans to adjust its force 'from a combat force with advisors, to an advisory force with combat capabilities'. In March 2012, US defence official James Miller summarised plans for transition: 'at some point in 2013, the ANSF will be in the lead for providing security across Afghanistan. At that time, US and Coalition forces will be in a support role ... This includes US and coalition forces partnered with Afghan units ... and it will include the smaller footprint associated with US and coalition forces in a train, advise and assist role.' While NATO Secretary-General Anders Fogh Rasmussen has made great efforts to portray NATO nations as united in the transition strategy, national approaches to force reductions have diverged. Further US reductions will probably be at least matched by similar troop reductions by other ISAF nations.

There is little evidence that military efforts are having sufficient coercive effect to bring insurgents to the conference table, let alone generate an acceptable deal. Meanwhile, it is far from clear that there will be sufficient improvement in Afghan governance and reduction in corruption to neutralise the root causes of the insurgency, even in areas that have been 'cleared and held'. Transition may have proceeded as planned at the military level, but the UN assesses that, despite improvements in the security situation, 'these gains have not ... generated public perceptions of greater security and do not reflect improvements to the institutional structures required for longer-term stability. Little has changed in the underlying dynamics to mitigate a deep-seated cycle of conflict. Furthermore, a diminished international presence will have a significant financial impact in many areas that, at least in the short term, may even exacerbate predatory behaviour, with a reduced flow of money encouraging criminality.'

On present trend, it is likely that the ANSF will reach full strength and will improve its capability. So as NATO reduces, they will, for example, likely hold onto those areas in southern Afghanistan now clear of insurgents. But the outcome most likely in 2015 is a situation much like today – a security patchwork with the ANSF suppressing much insurgent activity in many areas. In these places, the insurgency would probably have a residual presence, and an ability to mount limited attacks. But, other areas, particularly in eastern Afghanistan, will probably remain under insurgent influence.

The end of the surge makes it unlikely that further major offensive operations will be mounted to clear more areas of Helmand and Kandahar. As ISAF reduces in size, the troops available to train and mentor the ANSF will reduce, unless contributing nations choose to reinvest in these areas. The US drawdown makes it far less likely that Haqqani network strongholds in southeast Afghanistan can be cleared, let alone 'held and built'. However, if ISAF and the ANSF make insufficient military progress in eastern Afghanistan, the insurgents' ability to mount 'spectacular' attacks in Kabul will continue to pose a strategic threat to NATO's narrative, creating in Afghanistan and internationally an impression of un-governability and failure of the transition process.

SYRIA

By the end of 2012, the conflict in Syria was a full-fledged insurgency, showing increasing elements of sectarian civil war. The UN estimated that as of October 2012, 30,000 people had died, over 2.5 million Syrians needed humanitarian assistance within the country, and over 340,000 had fled into neighbouring countries. The rebels sought to depose the regime of President Bashar al-Assad through either military defeat or forcing him to cede power. To prevent this, Assad and his forces sought to contain the insurgency, then progressively neutralise the rebels, whilst re-establishing political control.

The war so far

Civil protests erupted against the Assad regime in March 2011. In the absence of meaningful reform, protests increased and a 'security solution' was implemented from July 2011. Syrian security forces' heavy-handed efforts at repression were broadcast internationally by traditional media as well as social media and YouTube, rapidly giving the opposition information dominance in Western and Arab media. With both sides increasingly radicalising, and the opposition joined by self-organising armed groups, attacks on government forces gradually increased throughout 2011. By early 2012, the 'security solution' had failed, as had an Arab League peace initiative and monitoring mission. The regime then pursued a 'military solution'.

The first major government offensive focused on Homs, and particularly the Baba Amr district. The army surrounded and then shelled the area, causing significant destruction and loss of life. At the end of the operation, the armed opposition and most civilians had fled. This provided the model for subsequent government offensives: first, ring the area with checkpoints, and then engage with coordinated artillery, rocket and tank fire complemented by attacks from helicopters and fighter aircraft. The army appeared to forgo using combined arms tank/infantry tactics to mount close assaults on rebel positions and it displayed no capability to counter improvised explosive devices (IEDs). Once bombardment was judged to have neutralised most opposition, troops would enter, often accompanied by snipers and the pro-government Shabbiha militia, to conduct house-to-house searches, often detaining (and allegedly executing many) young men of military age who had not fled. There was no meaningful reconstruction by the government.

Fighting intensified through the year with the armed opposition increasing in strength and effectiveness, and absorbing some defectors from regime forces. The rebels increasingly employed all the methods of modern insurgency including hit-and-run attacks, ambushes, assassinations and suicide bombings. They destroyed armoured vehicles using rocket-propelled grenades, land mines and IEDs, and learned to shoot down low-flying regime aircraft with small arms, anti-aircraft artillery, and possibly man-portable missiles. Weapons were largely seized from regime forces, or purchased in Libya, Iraq, Lebanon and Turkey. Attacks against air force bases sought to reduce regime airpower and capture anti-aircraft weapons.

The Russian–Chinese veto of a UN Security Council Resolution in February emboldened the regime to increase repression in Homs, Aleppo and Damascus. A subsequent UN peace plan, ceasefire and monitoring mission was used by both sides as an opportunity to regroup.

The regime's strategy was to secure loyalists and loyalist areas, and repress the opposition, while keeping level of conflict below that which would trigger international intervention. Assad's narrative was that the uprising was a conspiracy of dark forces including al-Qaeda, Western states and other Arab nations. At the operational level, the regime sought to secure the Alawite heartland in western Syria, the road from Aleppo to the Jordanian border and those running southeast into Iraq, as well as the energy infrastructure and agricultural areas in the eastern Euphrates valley. But over time, the regime increasingly abandoned efforts to control much of the countryside and withdrew from most of Syrian Kurdistan, providing a significant boost to PKK insurgents fighting in Turkey.

The only common objective of the opposition groups was to remove the Assad regime. There was no evidence of any effective higher-level command or direction at the operational or strategic level. Some groups operated under the umbrella of the Free Syrian Army (FSA), some autonomously. In some provinces, notably Idlib, rebel Provincial Military Councils coordinated activities by disparate rebel groups. Tensions emerged between the local population and the rebels, and between military defectors and armed civilians. Defectors brought military skills, but could be resented by those who switched sides earlier. There was some inflow of foreign fighters, many of whom were jihadis, some claiming membership of al-Qaeda. Home-grown radical factions such as Jabhat as-Nusra embraced terrorist tactics. Rebel forces committed atrocities, including killing prisoners, though in response to resulting outrage in Syria and abroad, prominent rebel brigades issued a code of conduct and pledged to uphold international law.

Concurrent with an 18 July bomb attack on Assad's security council, there was a major uprising in Damascus and attacks on government border posts increased. But rebel limitations were exposed in the summer fighting around Aleppo. This showed strategic overreach, as well as a lack of coordination and tactical and logistical shortcomings. The rush to liberate the city clashed with previously successful guerrilla tactics aimed at securing the countryside, harassing supply lines and complicating the movement of regime forces. Aleppo residents, including opposition sympathisers, failed to rally behind the rebel operation.

On several other occasions, rebel groups took over key urban areas, only to be subject to counter-attacks forcing eventual withdrawal. Provided government forces concentrated in sufficient strength, the rebels could not avoid eventual eviction. But these offensives caused such destruction that they reduced government support, while each counter-offensive served to weaken government control elsewhere. The rebels were waging a modern guerrilla war – although less effectively than if they had a unified political–military strategy, campaign plan and a central military command.

Nonetheless, the rebels could, by October 2012, move freely in much of the countryside. They controlled significant parts of Idlib and Aleppo provinces bordering Turkey, and part of Damascus province, as well as several border-crossing points. The regime controlled the Alawite heartland of Latakia province and much of Damascus and Aleppo, but they could not prevent repeated uprisings by the rebels in and around those key cities.

By October, it also became apparent that the government forces were over-extended and no longer had the military capability to re-assert control over the whole country. The regime lost control over several army and air force installations. There was evidence of exchanges of prisoners and of local cease-fires between rebel and regime commanders, for example in Ain al-Fijeh, a village with natural springs that provided water to Damascus.

The Syrian Air Force and Navy suffered few casualties, but the army's combat power considerably reduced, losing up to 20–30 killed daily, more during intense fighting, with probably two or three times as many seriously wounded. Strength was also sapped by the steady stream of defections. Reserves were mobilised, but only half reported for duty. Despite its notional strength of 220,000 troops, the effective strength of the army was by autumn 2012 probably about half that. Perhaps half of these could be trusted with routine security duties, such as guarding installations, manning checkpoints and escorting convoys. In sum, the regime could only be certain of the loyalty and fighting effectiveness of the mainly Alawite Special Forces, Republican Guard, and the elite 3rd and 4th divisions – perhaps 50,000 troops in total.

External factors

The government continued to receive military equipment from Russia and there were reports of Iranian expert, financial and material assistance, including credible rebel claims to have captured Iranian Revolutionary Guards posing as pilgrims. Media reports suggested that at least one member of Lebanon's Hizbullah had been killed fighting for the regime. Rebels, meanwhile, drew support and recruits from the refugees in Turkey, Lebanon and Jordan. Some groups benefitted from foreign expertise, including from Libyans who fought against Muammar Gadhafi, but the best financed and armed appeared to be Islamist groups.

As well as providing financial support and reportedly some material assistance of unknown type, Gulf states and Saudi Arabia have allowed discreet fundraising on their soil. Western governments feared that weapons would end up in the hands of radical groups, including al-Qaeda affiliates, so they limited assistance to non-lethal equipment such as communications sets. They also tried to vet Syrian groups before providing assistance, and there were reports

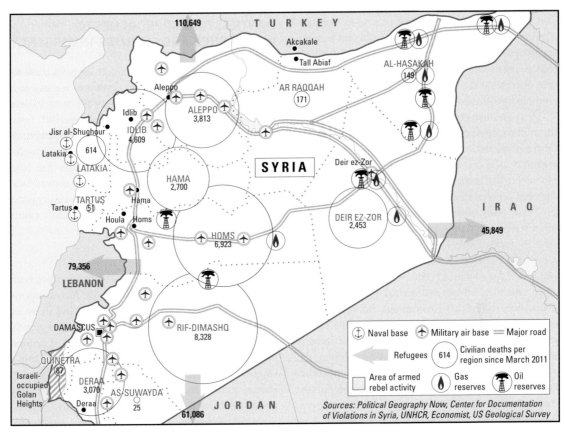

Map 2 **Conflict in Syria**

that Western officials offered rebel groups modern weapons on the condition that they unite under a single leadership. There was evidence that Western states provided intelligence to select rebel groups, and encouraged regime defections. Covert coordination centres were established in Turkey to manage foreign assistance, notably salary payments to FSA fighters. But this effort suffered from infighting among rebel groups and between donor countries, especially Turkey, Qatar and Saudi Arabia.

Syria sought to deter external intervention. Politically, it relied on Russia and China to block UN Security Council initiatives by the UK, the US and France. Meanwhile, the regime was aware of foreign concern over its conventional and unconventional military capabilities, and sought to highlight uncertainty. Regime officials declared that its hitherto unacknowledged chemical and biological capabilities would not be used against the rebels, but did constitute a deterrent against intervention or attack. Israel was deeply concerned about surface-to-air missiles, chemical or biological weapons and ballistic missiles falling into the hands of Hizbullah or other extremist groups.

Neighbouring countries were all affected. As of October 2012, Syrian refugees in Lebanon had exceeded 100,000, while an estimated 170,000 were in Turkey, 105,000 in Jordan and 42,000 in Iraq, placing strains on the receiving governments. Syrian shells fell on Jordanian territory. Lebanon saw regular cross-border fire, shelling and incursions, as well as abductions by Syrian intelligence. It suffered greatly increased tension and outbreaks of inter-communal fighting sparked by the conflict. In June, a Turkish RF-4 jet, which may have been on a reconnaissance mission, was shot down by Syria after briefly violating its airspace; in September and October, Syrian shelling of Turkish territory prompted heavier counter fire by Turkish artillery. This may have been a deliberately disproportionate tactical response to deter further incidents.

Neither intervention nor peace deal likely

Citing its difficulties in handling Syrian refugees, Turkey advocated a no-fly zone and safe areas, as did France, though both countries may have calculated the prospects of UN authority for such initiatives as remote. The practical challenges of a no-fly zone and a ground 'safe area', the two most-discussed humanitarian options, not least those posed by Syrian air and coastal defences, are considerable. Experts assessed that Syria's air-defence network still constituted a credible threat.

Most Western countries showed little enthusiasm for military intervention, though US President Barack Obama indicated in August that the use or transfer of chemical weapons would constitute a clear red line. However, the complexity of the crisis, its potential regional repercussions, deadlock at the UN and the projected costs of any military operations deterred other states. A UN mandate for action seemed impossible to obtain given Russian and Chinese refusal to accept the premise of Western and certain regional states that Assad should cede power.

In late 2012, ethnic and sectarian faultlines were deepening, with pro-government fighters sympathetic to the ruling Alawite minority ranged against mainly Sunni rebels. Although the regime retained the loyalty of a significant number of Sunnis and non-Alawite minority groups, and the armed opposition included many Sunni secular and non-Sunni fighters, the sectarian narrative was increasingly shaping perceptions and actions. The increasingly bitter fighting served to increase polarisation and mutual hatred, making the chances of a peace deal remote, as shown by the collapse of UN efforts to broker a late October ceasefire during the festival of Eid.

If both sides continued the approaches employed up to October 2012, rebel capability and internal and external support would probably grow, whilst government capability and support would reduce. Short of using chemical weapons against rebels, with attendant risk of international intervention, it was difficult to see how Assad could reverse this trend. So the balance of forces would, over time, likely shift to the rebels. However, should they abandon their guerrilla approach and attempt to permanently hold urban areas before such a tipping point is reached, government forces could tactically defeat them: if Assad could not win, the rebels could still lose. And without authoritative political and military leadership, competition between rebel groups over territory and resources could increase, carrying with it the potential for inter-factional fighting. This could see the country descend into a civil war with the government just the strongest faction amongst many, increasing the chance of regional destabilisation.

CONTRASTING APPROACHES TO INSURGENCY AND COUNTER-INSURGENCY

The wars in Afghanistan and Syria are both contests between insurgents and government forces, and in each case both sides are supported by a variety of external actors. Insights can be derived from comparing both conflicts against two key principles of all military operations: unity of effort; and legitimacy and operating in accordance with the law. Further insights can also result from comparison against two key principles of counter-insurgency: intelligence and focusing on the population's needs and security.

Unity of effort
Both wars reinforced the value of unity of effort, both politically and militarily. In Syria, the Assad regime directly controlled its political strategy and its security forces. Meanwhile, the Syrian rebels were greatly handicapped by an almost complete lack of unified political authority and strategy; they also lacked a single overall military command and displayed only partial local tactical military coordination. All this greatly reduced their military effectiveness.

In Afghanistan, the Taliban-led insurgency achieved a degree of political and military unity of effort, although it was unclear if there was sufficient common ground between the various groupings that share the Taliban's banner for an over-arching ceasefire to be implemented. On the government side, achieving unity of effort within the Afghan political arena appeared to be a major part of President Hamid Karzai's approach in balancing various power brokers and factions, though as a result, some egregious corruption may have been tolerated.

At the strategic level, there appeared to be limited effective international coordination of reconstruction and development, but at the tactical level, Provincial Reconstruction Teams had some effect in achieving unity of international civilian effort at provincial and district level. Security operations gained unity of effort from a single NATO–Afghan campaign plan: *Operation OMID*. At the tactical level, considerable unity of effort was achieved by NATO's 'partnering' of Afghan units and formations, and by embedding teams of advisers. This means that combined Afghan–NATO tactical operations had become well coordinated, providing few opportunities for the insurgents to exploit boundaries or seams between Afghan and NATO units.

Legitimacy and the law

Both wars also showed the importance of achieving legitimacy and operating in accordance with the law. Syrian government forces, through repeated human-rights abuses including torture, rapidly forfeited their legitimacy with the civilian unarmed opposition, with the Sunni majority and with many Arab and Western states. This was reinforced by the pursuit of a military solution which saw overwhelming force used against rebel strongholds, with no apparent constraints on the use of force or attempts to reduce civilian casualties. Indeed, the overwhelming use of indiscriminate force appeared to be a deliberate attempt to intimidate actual and potential opposition supporters.

Despite international legal legitimacy conferred by numerous UN Security Council resolutions, NATO and Afghan government operations in Afghanistan have sometimes struggled to achieve legitimacy, particularly at a local level, where NATO found it difficult to understand complex tribal dynamics. But recognising that collateral damage and civilian casualties both eroded legitimacy and acted as powerful recruiting sergeants for the insurgents, NATO sought to use force with precision and discrimination. This has included highly restrictive rules of engagement and increased use of precision weapons, including guided missiles and precision artillery.

In both wars, legitimacy has also been an issue for anti-government forces. Taliban propaganda and statements have emphasised the importance of minimising Afghan civilian casualties, although the conspicuous contradiction between these sentiments and the many civilian deaths from IEDs and suicide attacks rendered this message almost irrelevant. Credible evidence of human-rights abuses sufficiently threatened the credibility of Syrian rebel forces to cause several rebel groups to issue codes of conduct.

Intelligence

Both wars have emphasised the importance of intelligence. During the Syrian government's security-solution phase, state security forces enjoyed some success in disrupting networks of protesters through arrest and detention operations. This probably benefitted from extensive background information gathered over many years, as well as tutelage by Iranian experts who had learned from the experience of repressing civil protest in 2009. But the Syrian Army's subsequent operations appeared to be indiscrimi-nate, whilst some rebel attacks, such as the July 2012 bombing of the security headquarters, appeared to be very well-informed, possibly by insiders.

Security operations in Afghanistan, by contrast, have been increasingly well-informed by intelligence. A decade-long international effort to develop the Afghan National Directorate of Security is bearing fruit. And following the winding down of the Iraq War, large numbers of US intelligence and surveillance systems were shifted to Afghanistan. Combined with new techniques of data fusion and analysis, this greatly increased the effectiveness of intelligence-led operations, particularly the attack of insurgent networks by special forces.

Focus on the people

This allowed NATO and Afghan forces to increasingly focus on the security and other needs of the general population. In security terms, this saw them implement the direction of former US General David Petraeus, borne of experience in Iraq, to 'protect the population'. And as security improved, civilian development efforts increasingly sought to meet the needs of the Afghan population, connecting the government to the people at village and precinct level.

In Syria, by contrast, the government appeared to have effectively abandoned efforts to protect the majority Sunni population, providing opportunities for the rebels to gain legitimacy. It attempted to protect its core Alawite supporters, but it appeared that extensive use of irregular militias stoked the flames of ethno-religious sectarian tension. And the government seemed to largely abandon efforts to provide government services to the majority of the Syrian population.

Both wars can be compared against many other principles of war, and specific principles of insurgency and counter-insurgency. But the greatest contrast is in the attitude to the use of force. NATO and Afghan operations in Afghanistan seemed overwhelmingly conditioned by a desire to use force proportionately and precisely, minimising unintended casualties and damage, and in conjunction with all the other levers of state governance. The Syrian government's approach appeared to be the antithesis of NATO's, apparently regarding force as a means and end in itself and a tool of repression and deterrence, accepting that this would result in considerable civilian casualties and collateral damage. In doing so, they conceded many opportunities to the rebels that NATO and Afghan forces seek to deny to the Taliban.

Trends in defence capability

FUTURE INTELLIGENCE, SURVEILLANCE AND RECONNAISSANCE

For Western armed forces, the dilemmas highlighted in recent editions of *The Military Balance* continue. Budget pressures are forcing states to conduct defence reviews that in many cases are leading to reductions in military organisations, inventories and capabilities. A key element of this challenge will be to decide which capabilities to keep, and in what scale and number, and even whether these should be retained on a national basis.

Intelligence, surveillance and reconnaissance (ISR) capacities, sometimes costly and in recent years often procured by using funding for specific military campaigns, are central to this debate. At the same time, a reduction in overseas operations and a consequently smaller global 'footprint' will test the effectiveness of ISR-relevant ties established in recent campaigns with allies, other partner states and even other national agencies. The requirement to maintain deployable armed forces is unlikely to diminish in the near future. The places into which these forces are deployed might not, however, resemble the theatres of operation of recent decades. Judging what ISR capabilities and organisations to maintain, both technically and operationally, will be the challenge.

In the recent conflicts in Iraq and Afghanistan, joint operations have increasingly been enabled by advanced ISR capabilities. Including mid- and low-tier unmanned aerial vehicles (UAVs) and the accompanying command-and-control networks that integrate these and their output into force structures, these capabilities have developed beyond recognition since the 9/11 terrorist attacks prompted the Western intervention in Afghanistan. The use of ISR capabilities ranging from space-based and unattended ground sensors, as well as sensors on manned and unmanned aircraft, combined with pre-existing capacities such as signals, electronic and human intelligence, have given Western armed forces key information advantages in later stages of these recent campaigns.

After early failures in information collection, analysis and intelligence dissemination, the picture improved in Iraq and Afghanistan. This was particularly true for US forces, after then-defence secretary Robert Gates, in April 2008, expressed his frustration at failures in intelligence collection, analysis and dissemination in Iraq and Afghanistan, and moved to fast-track innovative approaches to fielding new capabilities. For British forces in Iraq's Multi-national Division South East, until *Operation Charge of the Knights* in Basra in March 2008, there had not been enough available ISR capabilities to support intelligence-led strike operations or maintain a counter-IED roadwatch.

Many of these new technical capabilities are now filtering down to non-Western armed forces. Differences between Western states and newer users lie more in the scale and ambition of use and coordination, and the technological complexity of the capabilities employed. New users will have to be mindful of the challenges ISR capabilities bring, such as the supply of ever greater amounts of information, as well as the benefits. That said, the effect on new users of the challenges identified by Western states may be limited by the range of capabilities they can afford.

ISR matures, slowly

In their broadest sense, ISR capabilities have been used by armed forces for centuries: intercepts of written communications would have been familiar to the armies of antiquity, while technical means rapidly developed in response to advances in telegraphy, telephony and wireless communications from the late nineteenth century. It was during the Cold War that their use was considered to have matured.

However, the 'persistence' of present-day ISR platforms is a new development. Designed to loiter for hours, days, or longer in the case of some space-based systems, such platforms conduct an ever-expanding amount of persistent surveillance (perhaps better termed data accumulation and assisted by technical advances in computer storage and processing power) on the ground and in cyberspace, and in both civilian and military domains.

Information-gathering capabilities used in Iraq ranged from strategic-level satellite reconnaissance and U-2 over-flights to, after the situation received top-level attention in the spring of 2008, relatively low-cost airframes fitted with ISR suites like the MC-12 *Liberty*, as well as ground sensors. The campaign also saw ISR capabilities devolve down to small-unit levels: hand-launched UAVs, such as the *Raven*, *Desert Hawk* and *Skylark*, gave ground troops direct access to real-time imagery without the relatively time-consuming need to route tasking orders through a higher formation, and thus presumably waiting for other assets to be deployed, in the midst of a fast-moving environment. Though equipment such as this did improve timeliness, troops had first to be on the ground in sufficient numbers to either launch such assets, develop 'local knowledge' and language skills, or gather information from interactions with local communities.

As the wars in Iraq and Afghanistan evolved into counter-insurgency campaigns, Western armed forces rediscovered the value of cadres of linguists and analysts capable of liaising with the local population or extracting information from prisoners. Information gathered from these multiple sources, including human intelligence and from ISR platforms or other methods such as email and mobile intercepts, was often combined in an analytic process termed 'fusion'. In this, analysis centres would use sophisticated methodologies to fuse different kinds of intelligence into actionable mission packages that would then be disseminated in a timely manner, as noted in IISS *Strategic Survey 2012* (pp. 36–7). This could then enable, where required, targeting by assets such as aircraft, ground troops or special-forces teams. Persistent surveillance from UAVs and improvements in communications also permitted real-time monitoring of such operations, with damage assessments carried out near-concurrently.

Too much information?

As the amount of information requiring analysis has increased, so too have the challenges of aggregating, collating and analysing it. This problem is exacerbated in 'conditions of high operational tempo such as exist in Afghanistan [where] huge volumes of data … need to be analysed and packaged in something close to real time. At present the capacity to do this is severely limited' (*Ibid*.). If anything, this is still a growing problem. Greater volumes of information are now accessible, for instance through cyberspace, giving the collection agencies ever more targets and potential sources to assess, and likely more collection

priorities. Additional analytical complications arise from the increased likelihood of circular reporting in digital sources (where a story is repeated by many sources creating a false impression that information has been corroborated) – something clear to any regular Internet user.

In operational theatres, one way that Western states have sought to overcome challenges to collation and analysis is by increasing intelligence staffs. Another is by formalising fusion centres and putting these at the disposal of commands in peacetime, as well as war. In these centres, all-source analysis and information exploitation (and sometimes collection) is carried out by co-located civilian and military staff from a range of countries and agencies in a bid to avoid duplication of the collection and analysis effort, and in an attempt to enable more effective command and control of friendly forces and targeting of hostile forces. These groups are working in addition to national and multinational intelligence cells and command-and-control networks. Meanwhile, the means that national and multinational organisations employ to analyse data have also evolved, with the emergence of technical tools to filter and analyse information. But still, 'the ability of intelligence agencies to collect data far outstrips their capacity to analyse it' (*Ibid*.). While using technical means can help in tasks like filtering large amounts of data, making sense of the information still requires analysts exercising reasoned judgements.

Operations draw down, and budgets contract

NATO forces in Afghanistan are to withdraw from a combat role by the end of 2014, with the transition to Afghan security control. This reduction in resources, coupled with the increasing pressure on Western defence budgets because of the financial crisis, means that many Western armed forces now see themselves at a turning point, where reassessments of defence priorities and armed-forces structures and holdings will be necessary.

In relation to ISR, defence ministries will be considering which capabilities will form part of future military structures. This process is fraught with problems, as it requires states to make choices on national defence priorities and attempt to predict likely strategic challenges. Western armed forces will need to retain sufficient flexibility to respond to unforeseen crises, possibly including international disputes which might precipitate armed conflict between states. Changes in the strategic landscape, such as in the Middle East and North Africa, may also make it more difficult for Western states to assume that they will be able to rely on the assistance of regional partners in the same way as before. Meanwhile, the ability to field theatre- and tactical-level technical ISR assets may also be limited by factors such as a lack of launching sites or sensitivity about overflights.

Operating in new environments

Difficult decisions about which ISR capabilities to reduce and which to retain, while ensuring a similar level of coverage, analytical capability and timeliness, are unavoidable for Western armed forces. Though the operational environments of both Iraq and Afghanistan were eventually information-rich, the more recent Libyan campaign provided a rather different experience in ISR terms.

The NATO-led *Operation Unified Protector* implemented a no-fly zone and arms embargo over Libya, and NATO-led forces conducted air- and naval strikes against regime forces judged to be threatening to attack, or attacking, Libyan civilians. In October, rebel forces finally ousted Colonel Muammar Gadhafi from power. NATO deemed its operation a success, but it was a campaign generated from a cold start in terms of the availability of ISR assets, as well as up-to-date intelligence on Libyan force structures, dispositions and capabilities. A key challenge for NATO-led air forces and targeting staffs was the adaptation by Gadhafi's forces to their loss of airspace control. They went on to use camouflage and dispersal to their advantage. The gradual development of rebel forces' combat capability, the provision to them of secure communications devices and the incremental development of allied ISR coverage – together with a suitable array of low-yield air-launched weapons – helped in targeting and dismantling Gadhafi's forces. However, the campaign highlighted the difficulties that Western forces would face in entering a fresh environment without an adequate understanding of it or the mature ISR architecture to which they have become accustomed.

In information-poor environments such as these, forces looking to intervene can of course generate new information sources or deploy whatever ISR assets are at their disposal. However, given recent experiences in coalition warfare, in which forces from NATO states have become used to operating in multinational environments and drawing on multi-national ISR assets and analytical capacities, another approach may be to try to replicate these institutional partnership networks using differing groups of states. This could be one way of maintaining more comprehensive ISR capacities, but trusted networks suitable for high degrees of information exchange – like NATO's fusion centres – are likely to take a long time to establish, if they are at all feasible, given the levels of classification probably applied to some ISR output.

Widening the availability of low-level ISR capabilities to friendly nations – such as the small hand-launched RQ-11 *Raven* UAVs provided to Uganda and Burundi by the US in 2011 – could also help to maintain 'visibility', or 'access without presence', though doubts over whether such states would have the technical capacity to combine the output of each system into an effective information-sharing network might mean some residual involvement for Western states; this is, of course, assuming that states remain on friendly terms and that classification levels permit effective collaboration. That said, a number of non-Western states, such as Brazil, India, South Korea and Singapore, possess or are purchasing theatre-level UAV assets that could feed information into such networks or even assume command-and-control functions for themselves.

Cooperation could also include common procurement or operation of ISR assets. Discussions continue among NATO and EU member states over the pooling and sharing of assets, and there has been progress on NATO's Alliance Ground Surveillance initiative. Cooperation is easier among countries with established military-to-military ties, but concerns over sovereign control of capabilities and intelligence mean that it is not straightforward.

Enduring truths

With the withdrawal from relatively benign ISR environments in Iraq and Afghanistan, limitations on information obtained through technical methods mean that, unless the information gathered is judged sufficiently reliable, human intelligence will remain vital in discerning intent. It is also apparent that Western armed forces' platforms will be fewer in the future and personnel numbers will also decline. So as well as assessing what lessons should be learned from joint operations over the past decade, Western military planners will be keen to examine which ISR capabilities represent the best value and are discriminate in terms of the level of information they generate, so that smaller teams of analysts are not swamped by information. The risk remains that any capabilities shelved now may be precisely those required in the future. Specialist analysts will also have to be retained, even if in smaller numbers, as will deployable intelligence specialists from military and civilian agencies. Useful capabilities are not simply military ones. Developments in civilian forensic technology have been applied in tracking bomb-makers, while biometrics technology – widely fielded by US forces – enables the effective collection of security-relevant information on civilians or prisoners that is capable of integration with database systems.

Meanwhile, defence establishments, and security authorities more broadly, will need to be far-sighted in maintaining their investment in language training for intelligence specialists and other force members who are likely to come into day-to-day contact with locals, along with core training for military intelligence staffs down to battalion level, to ensure that the skills accumulated in past campaigns do not atrophy. While financially attractive, focusing language training on a core set of 'approved' languages runs the risk of limiting both the pool of current expertise as well as the capacity to 'surge' the training provision in minor languages as required. Civilian agencies, meanwhile, need to consider how to retain the links with armed forces that have further developed in the past decade, and to remain aware of these forces' intelligence requirements in large- and small-scale contingencies, while ensuring that the support they can offer is scaleable, and can be increased in size if required. Above all, the lessons learned from campaigns relating to useful assets, analytical techniques and capabilities need to be institutionalised within armed forces, at the tactical as well as operational levels, so that capabilities endure even as forces may shrink. Developing assets, information and analysis into an effective ISR architecture takes time; the challenge lies in keeping that time to an affordable minimum.

Though the barriers to accessing certain parts of the world may well rise, the requirement for Western armed forces to exert influence and perhaps establish a presence internationally will remain; doing so will require accurate and timely information, within an increasingly information-rich environment. For states wishing to preserve the ability to project force at speed in unfamiliar environments, the shape of future ISR capabilities will remain a key preoccupation.

LAND: COUNTERING THE THREAT OF IMPROVISED EXPLOSIVE DEVICES

Improvised explosive devices (IEDs) have been the weapon of choice for insurgents in the recent wars in Iraq and Afghanistan. With the raw materials often costing less than $20, these devices are cheap, often 'home-made', simple to use and effective, serving as an asymmetric counter to advanced armies' technological advantage.

Initially overlooked by many Western military planners and advocates of the 'Revolution in Military Affairs', these devices are now estimated to have been responsible for nearly 70% of military casualties in Iraq and Afghanistan. By sowing fear, lowering troop morale, limiting freedom of movement and undermining public support, they have high impact at the tactical, operational and strategic levels. Tens of billions of dollars have been spent in trying to neutralise the IED threat. Yet, they remain likely to create further problems in future.

IEDs are not new, and in recent decades have been used by non-state groups in Colombia, India, Iran, Lebanon, Mexico, Nigeria, Pakistan, Somalia and Thailand. During its conflict with the UK, the IRA made extensive use of IEDs, which greatly restricted the mobility of security forces, nearly succeeded in killing then-prime minister Margaret Thatcher and inflicted the majority of military, police and civilian casualties.

The unexpectedly heavy casualties inflicted by IEDs in Iraq and Afghanistan greatly contributed to the growing unpopularity of these wars in the US and other NATO countries. This was a strategic shock that had significant consequences for Western policy, tactics and procurement. As the operation in Afghanistan winds down, the US and its allies may find it difficult to retain expertise in countering IEDs. However, the increasing use of IEDs elsewhere means that the counter-IED capabilities developed in recent years will remain vital for armies and police forces.

Challenge in Iraq

Following the US-led invasion of Iraq in 2003, insurgents used large amounts of ammunition abandoned by the disbanded Iraqi Army in order to manufacture IEDs. Aided by Internet-based learning, their capabilities improved rapidly and by August 2003, US casualties caused by IEDs overtook those caused by small arms and rocket-propelled grenades. By the end of the year, IEDs were responsible for two-thirds of US deaths. UK forces in southern Iraq quickly applied the tactical approaches that they had used to counter IEDs in Northern Ireland, though the British Army was slow to recognise the vulnerability of its lightly armoured *Snatch* Land Rovers, with the resultant British casualties undermining popular support for the war.

US forces did not have the benefit of this experience, but the problem was quickly recognised by commanders in Iraq. In December 2003, CENTCOM's commander at the time, General John Abizaid, asked Defense Secretary Donald Rumsfeld to commission a major cross-governmental response to the threat, along the lines of the Second World War Manhattan Project to develop the atomic bomb. The Pentagon's initial response was slow and under-resourced. But by 2006, the 12-strong Joint IED Defeat Task Force had evolved into Joint IED Defeat Organisation (JIEDDO) with several thousand dedicated government, military and contract personnel. Countering the new threats not only required an array of armoured vehicles, electronic jammers and remote-controlled robots, it also required close cooperation between intelligence and operations staff, scientists and industry, placing demands on the flexibility and agility of armies, military-procurement bodies and defence ministries of all the coalition nations.

Initially, much of the US response focused on improving physical protection, such as personal body armour, and reinforcing existing tanks and armoured fighting vehicles. But support and logistics units had few, if any, armoured vehicles. So in the first two years of the war, these troops resorted to desperate expedients, such as adding makeshift armour, made from scrap metal, to 'soft-skinned' vehicles. Although many armoured high-mobility multi-purpose wheeled vehicles (or 'humvees') were fielded in 2004–05, they were quickly overmatched by improved insurgent IEDs and it was not until November 2006 that the requirement was identified for the more heavily armoured mine-resistant ambush-protected (MRAP) vehicle. Some 28,000 MRAPs had been procured by US and NATO forces by August 2012.

But despite the application of sophisticated intelligence, scientific, industrial and military resources to the problem, an 'action–reaction' relationship evolved between insurgent bombers and coalition troops, scientists and engineers. The many ways of configuring bombs and the complex technology required to counter them meant that it could often take six to 12 months between the emergence of a new type of IED and the fielding of a sufficient technical countermeasure by trained troops.

Operational approach

In Iraq, the US military moved from a strategy of addressing the IED itself and its consequences (more armour and better medical care) to preventing insurgent networks from building and laying IEDs in the first place. Based on British doctrine, a common counter-IED approach was applied by all coalition troops in Iraq and, later, in Afghanistan. This

---

Case study: explosively formed projectiles

An example of the IED challenge and response was the fielding of explosively formed projectile (EFP) devices against British forces in southern Iraq from 2005–09. There was nothing new about the technology, in which explosives detonating behind a disc-shaped charge mould it into a high-energy metal slug that is capable of punching through even tank armour with lethal results. Indeed, during the Cold War the British stockpiled French-manufactured EFP mines for use against Warsaw Pact armour. But drawing on expertise from Hizbullah and with a supply of EFP components from Iran, Shia militias used EFP devices to great effect against coalition vehicles.

Initially the British had no technical countermeasures and could only reduce the threat by adapting tactics. This included rigorous control of road movement and devoting considerable resources to force protection. This so reduced the available combat power of the British brigade that both its operational effect and its ability to train Iraqi forces were reduced. It was months before additional armour and other countermeasures to protect against EFPs were fielded. It was only in the aftermath of the 2008 Iraqi forces' surge in Basra, *Operation Charge of the Knights*, that the level of security forces on the streets in Basra City was sufficient to disrupt the emplacement of EFPs.

In the UK, the issue had political significance as many British lightly armoured *Snatch* Land Rover 4×4 patrol vehicles were destroyed by EFPs, causing well-publicised casualties. This produced considerable criticism that the reaction of the government, Ministry of Defence and army had been too slow.

saw three lines of action: 'defeat the device'; 'attack the network'; and 'train the force' at all levels of command. All needed to be integrated by rapid information exchange across forces, so that counter-IED action could quickly be initiated.

Defeat the device

Detecting technologies included hand-held devices, sniffer dogs and sophisticated search techniques and equipment, while electronic jammers were fitted to vehicles and carried by troops, to block trigger signals sent to bombs. Considerable effort was also devoted to the development of explosive ordnance disposal (EOD) technologies that would help in neutralising devices detected before detonation and recovering them for forensic analysis.

These measures were complemented by attempts to disrupt the laying of IEDs, principally by imposing more rigorous control over road movements and with more patrols on the ground, though these depended on there being sufficient troops to dominate an area. Air movement alleviated the threat, although some transport aircraft and helicopters struck IEDs placed on landing sites. And while many countries bought more helicopters and isolated units were supplied by parachute, not even the US could move sufficient troops and supplies by air. Therefore, previously soft-skinned trucks also had armour and jammers added.

Attack the network

In Iraq, extra intelligence resources were deployed to identify insurgents involved in IED construction and supply, as well as those planning attacks and planting and operating the devices. Airborne surveillance, particularly from long-endurance manned and unmanned aircraft, proved particularly useful in identifying insurgent teams planting devices. These could then be attacked, or in the case of those making or moving bombs, followed. The preference was to detain insurgents and seize devices and bomb-making material for forensic and technical analysis and the development of further intelligence. Biometric technology fielded by US forces greatly improved their ability to link bomb components to bomb-makers.

Train the force

Troops would ideally train with the specialist counter-IED equipment they would use in theatre. However, there was often insufficient equipment for pre-oper-ational training, and troops had to learn on the job, with all of the attendant risks. In the case of British forces in Iraq, casualties tended to be suffered during the first weeks of tours of duty as troops learned on operations, until sufficient equipment was provided for pre-deployment training.

IEDs in Afghanistan

The dominant IED in Iraq was the explosively formed projectile (see box, p. 20), which coupled a highly engineered warhead with civilian infrared control technology, optimised against armoured vehicles. The typical IED in Afghanistan has been a much simpler home-made bomb initiated by a so-called 'victim-operated' pressure plate. But these IEDs have been laid even more widely. In the southern provinces of Helmand and Kandahar, the density of IEDs has approached that of minefields previously laid in state-on-state warfare. In 2009, 9,304 IED explosions were recorded, but this rose to 15,225 in 2010 and peaked at 16,554 in 2011.

Techniques used to attack IED networks in Iraq have been refined. Combined with improved countermeasures and pre-tour training, these techniques have resulted in fewer troops being killed or injured by roadside bombs; the US has claimed a 40% reduction in IED casualties in Afghanistan during 2011–12. JIEDDO assesses that with adequate numbers of UAV-borne sensors to detect IEDs, the number of bombs found before they explode has increased to 64%, after stubbornly hovering around 50% for years. However, experts repeatedly say that the best tools remain sniffer dogs with handlers, a well-trained soldier's eye and information from a supportive local population. Using these tools, NATO foot patrols in Afghanistan currently achieve an average 80% detection rate. But insurgent IEDs remain the single-largest source of civilian deaths in Afghanistan, killing nearly 1,000 in Afghanistan in 2011, according to the United Nations.

In early 2010, at the height of *Operation Moshtarak* in Helmand and Kandahar Provinces, US and British forces used heavy engineer tanks to clear routes through these dense belts of IEDs by firing rocket-propelled explosive hoses. Later that year, the British Army fielded its *Talisman* system: a dedicated group of armoured vehicles and expert personnel with powerful surveillance systems, small UAVs/ground robots and the *Buffalo*, an armoured vehicle with a remotely operated arm. The US has similar 'route-opening detachments'. Both teams also include high-mobility JCB armoured excavators to repair damage caused by IED blasts. Dedicated surveillance systems have been fielded, including specially modified surveillance aircraft.

Increased protection has saved lives, but has reduced the effectiveness of NATO forces. Soldiers have to carry heavy loads – body armour, jamming equipment and mine detectors – meaning that their mobility is correspondingly reduced. In addition, the large numbers and types of protected vehicles create logistical challenges, reducing both operational flexibility and NATO troops' ability to interact with the Afghan people.

Beyond Iraq and Afghanistan

In 2011, almost 600 IED incidents per month occurred in countries outside Iraq and Afghanistan. Anti-government forces have made increasing use of them in Syria, in roadside bombs and suicide car bombs, and in assassination attempts. The Syrian government claimed that there were over 700 IED incidents in May 2012 alone. By August 2012, it was clear that not only were Syrian rebels successfully destroying government tanks and armoured vehicles with IEDs, but also that government forces appeared greatly handicapped by an apparent lack of tactical counter-IED capability.

Armed forces of countries that may have to fight Western forces will have observed the advantages that IEDs have given to insurgents in Iraq and Afghanistan. They are likely to see the overlapping characteristics of IEDs and conventional sea- and landmines. So countering both IEDs and conventional landmines will remain a core requirement for land forces.

In an age of austerity, the absence of major operations will make keeping knowledge and expertise alive difficult. A relevant example is British tactical intelligence in Iraq, where hard-won tactical intelligence skills and capabilities that had been developed in Northern Ireland and used to great effect against IRA bombers were allowed to atrophy as the campaign there wound down, to the consequent disadvantage of operations in Basra. The British managed to regenerate these capabilities in time to have an impact in Afghanistan. This shows how difficult it can be to retain the intellectual capital and understanding to regenerate idle military capabilities. The recently announced 'Army 2020' reorganisation of the British Army provides for the retention of sniffer dog, search and EOD capabilities in a specialist brigade.

Speaking at IISS in February 2012, the JIEDDO chief argued that the threat is an 'enduring and global' one that cannot be solved by any single 'silver bullet'. JIEDDO has proposed that institutionalising counter-IED capabilities requires continued investment in relevant research and development as well as forensic capabilities, retaining current techniques to fuse operational information and intelligence, continuing to train service personnel in counter-IED tactics, and a 'whole-of-government' response as part of wider security efforts. To counter this widening threat, greater national and international cooperation will be required among intelligence agencies, police and security forces, scientists and the defence and security industries. However, funding for such efforts could be under pressure as NATO troops withdraw from Afghanistan: future armies may well, therefore, merge counter-IED efforts with broader counter-mine capabilities.

MARITIME: SUBMARINE CAPABILITY IMPROVEMENTS

A key trend in maritime procurements is the rapid development of submarine fleets. States with existing fleets are developing the capabilities of their vessels while a number of states, particularly in the Asia-Pacific, are fielding submarines in their inventories for the first time.

Submarines offer the ability to project power at range and with stealth. They are the most expensive type of naval vessel, tonne for tonne, but are affordable for an increasing number of states. Most states opt for conventionally powered submarines, but even the list of countries operating nuclear-powered submarines (SSNs) is expanding: India commissioned its first SSN in more than 20 years in April 2012, while Brazil is developing an SSN capability.

Submarine capabilities are also developing. Air-independent propulsion systems have been widely adopted in conventionally powered submarines; these systems increase cruising times and reduce acoustic signatures. Weaponry has also improved: many submarines now have the capacity to launch varying types of missiles beyond the ballistic systems long seen in nuclear ballistic-missile submarines, while torpedoes have become faster and more accurate, with better guidance systems and on-board sensors. This will only heighten the imperative for states to improve anti-submarine warfare (ASW) capabilities.

Table 1 **Germany's Type-209 submarine and successor types: world operators**

	209/1100	209/1200	209/1300	209/1400	209/1500	214
Argentina	1 (1)					
Brazil				5		
Chile				2		
Colombia		2				
Ecuador			2			
Egypt				2 (in negotiation)		
Greece	3 (1)	4				4 (2)
India					4	
Indonesia			2	3 (*Chang Bogo*)		
South Korea		9 (*Chang Bogo*)				3 (6)
Peru	2	4				
Portugal						2
South Africa				3		
Turkey		6		8		6
Venezuela			2			
Total	**6 (2)**	**25**	**6**	**18 (3+2)**	**4**	**9 (14)**

The Type-209 submarine is the most popular exported boat in the sub-surface sector. Thus far, the 209, in its various guises, has been exported to 13 countries, with a 14th in negotiation, while its successor the 214 has already been exported to four with a fifth contracted. The remarkable success of German manufacturer HDW's submarine types, which have now seen 68 vessels exported, is owing to a number of factors: their modular designs allow for incremental improvements and various options tailored to the client; their size and adaptability makes them appealing to a wide range of countries; and the initial development of the 209 occurred as many countries were looking to update ageing pre-Second World War submarine designs. The above figures do not include the six Type-210 (*Ula*-class) supplied to Norway, the four *Dolphin*-class boats delivered to Israel and the Type-212A design that has also been procured by Italy.

Expanding conventional fleets

While fleets are being developed in Europe, the Middle East and North Africa, and Latin America, a raft of submarine purchases in the Asia-Pacific has provoked more concern, given that Asian defence-modernisation programmes often reflect efforts to hedge against the assumed motives of others. As noted in *The Military Balance 2012* (p. 208), 'this risks destabilising interaction between defence strategies, doctrines and capability-development programmes.' It means that there is increased potential for action–reaction procurements.

The growth in China's submarine fleet has encouraged this view. Over the past two decades, its fleet has grown from 46 to 66. In 1992, the majority comprised outdated, 1950s-era *Romeo*-class diesel-electric submarines. Twenty years later, and particularly after the creation of the South Sea Fleet's 72nd submarine flotilla in the early 2000s, China could boast 12 *Kilos* imported from Russia, and the indigenously designed and constructed *Song*- and *Yuan*-class, with the older *Ming*-class now slowly being decommissioned.

Other regional states are ordering new boats, some for the first time, others are updating ageing fleets, and still others are increasing the number of hulls in service in a concerted effort to expand their sub-surface capabilities. Countries such as Malaysia, Singapore, Vietnam, Indonesia, South Korea, Australia, Japan, India and Pakistan are all expanding their existing fleets or creating new ones. For states surrounding the South China Sea – the location of a number of disputes over territory or maritime boundaries – or those perceived as potential regional rivals to China, these procurements are a reaction to Beijing's growing surface and sub-surface fleet. Procurements of these advanced capabilities may also spring from a desire to improve military capabilities in the wake of economic growth, while there are a number of sub-regional rivalries and military competitions that also go some way to explaining procurements.

Beyond East Asia, other states are also expanding or improving their fleets of conventional submarines, particularly in the Middle East. Israel took delivery of its fourth *Dolphin*-class (German Type-212 variant) submarine in May 2012, as part of its plan to double the size of its three-boat fleet. Algeria similarly doubled its two-boat fleet with two improved *Kilos* in 2010. Iran continues to maintain its three-vessel *Kilo*-class fleet, with one of the boats having been repaired after a lengthy refit in early 2012, but it is also expanding its midget submarine fleet through the indigenous *Qadir*-class to offer asymmetric sub-surface capabilities in the crowded and often shallow Persian Gulf.

In Latin America, Chile received two *Scorpene*-class boats in 2005, adding to its existing fleet of two Type-209s, while Brazil has ordered four *Scorpene*-class boats to be received in the latter half of this decade.

In Europe, a number of replacement programmes are currently in train. Germany has commissioned four modern Type-212 submarines – two are in build – and has exported four of the class to Italy, of which two are already in service. Greece has received four Type-214s (the export variant of the 212), and, despite its financial troubles, has agreed to complete a six-boat deal with Germany. Turkey has ordered a further six Type-214s, to replace the six oldest Type-209s in its 14-boat fleet.

After a long hiatus, Russia has once again started to produce conventional submarines, with two classes, the *Lada* and the *Varshavyanka*, being separate, improved variants of the original *Kilo* design. One *Lada* was commissioned in 2010 and two more are in build, while six *Varshavyanka* are apparently to be built and transferred to the Black Sea Fleet.

Improved technological capabilities

The proliferation of air-independent propulsion (AIP) systems signifies a substantial improvement in conventional submarine stealth. Originally, AIP systems were confined to Europe and Russia, but these are now in use in Pakistan, Malaysia, Singapore, South Korea, Japan and China. The Vietnamese *Kilos* and Indian and Brazilian *Scorpenes* will all have AIP technology.

AIP allows boats to remain submerged for extended periods, perhaps up to three weeks, without the need to 'snorkel' for air, making it more difficult for surface and aerial forces to track them. A benefit of current AIP systems is that some can be retrofitted into existing vessels; the Swedish Stirling cycle AIP system, for example, can be inserted into a boat by extending the hull. Until recently, conventional AIP technology was produced exclusively by Germany, France, Spain, Sweden and Russia. However, with the *Yuan*-class submarine, China has also begun to produce and deploy AIP-equipped vessels, and will co-produce with Pakistan AIP technology for Islamabad's future submarines.

For countries with relatively poor ASW capabilities, AIP-equipped submarines compound the problems raised by submarine proliferation more generally; that is, assuming that the countries in possession of these systems are able to operate them to best effect. So the decision in various East Asian capitals to purchase submarines can be seen from two perspectives. On the one hand, as a tacit admission that some states are unable to compete with the modernisation of China's surface fleet and as a result are adopting sea-denial rather than sea-control capabilities. On the other hand, these submarine procurements can be viewed as an attempt to exploit the People's Liberation Army Navy's perceived weakness in ASW. The corollary of this is, of course, that it will only encourage China to develop its ASW capabilities to counteract this perceived weakness, as evidenced by an increased focus on improving ASW capabilities in, for instance, the new Type-056 corvette. These requirements will only increase now that China has commissioned its first aircraft carrier, where ASW escorts will be crucial to ensure its survival. The development of the Y-8X maritime patrol aircraft, currently in service, and in particular the prototype ASW variant with a magnetic anomaly detector, will be another significant step forward for China's ASW capabilities.

Weapons are also improving. Torpedoes have become quieter, faster and able to operate at greater depths. Like submarines, torpedoes are manufactured by a relatively small number of countries, meaning various states will use the same type. In the heavyweight torpedo market, for example, Raytheon's Mk 48 is now in service in 29 countries officially (and unofficially in China as the unlicensed, reverse-engineered Yu-6/Yu-7) and Atlas Elektronik's DM2A4 is in service in Germany, Spain, Pakistan, Turkey, Greece and Israel.

Propellers have largely been phased out in favour of quieter propulsors, while sound-isolation techniques, exhaust muffling and 'body damping' have all aided acoustic quieting. Sensors and guidance systems have improved, notably in terms of target acquisition and discrimination. Torpedoes are also increasingly incorporating active/passive sonars to detect and track targets, while wake-homing torpedoes, a technology developed in the 1960s in the Soviet Union, are now utilised in Atlas Elektronik's DM2A4. Supercavitation, the technology that allows torpedoes to greatly increase their speeds up to 250 miles per hour, remains limited to the Russian VA-111 *Shkval*, in service since the early 1970s; torpedoes reportedly exported to China lacked fire-control systems, limiting their utility. In the US, a programme funded by the Defense Advanced Research Projects Agency is examining the uses of supercavitation, though the noise created by the process, as currently understood, limits its attractiveness. An Iranian claim that it tested its first supercavitating torpedo in 2006 has not been verified.

Television images of *Tomahawk* land-attack cruise missiles (LACM) exiting US and UK submarines in recent campaigns, such as against Muammar Gadhafi's regime in Libya in 2011, highlight another developing sub-surface capability: to launch an increasing number of guided weapons from submarines. Though only six states can currently launch LACM from submarines, shorter-range submarine-launched guided missiles are proliferating. France has supplied the *Exocet* to Pakistan and India, while the US submarine-launched *Harpoon* is in service with 11 navies. Introducing such technology is not simply a matter of fitting missiles to existing torpedo tubes. Some boats have bespoke vertical launch systems fitted to enable missile-launch capability, while others have specially widened torpedo tubes or the ability to launch missiles from canisters. But while costly complications may thus be introduced in design, manufacture and also on-board weapons storage and handling, these are outweighed by the resulting capability improvements.

More nuclear power

Though the first operational nuclear-powered submarine, USS *Nautilus*, was launched in 1954, until 2009, only the five members of the UN Security Council had constructed and launched SSNs. While the cost and expertise required to operate nuclear submarines has hitherto proven an effective barrier to entry, this situation is now changing. India and Brazil are both developing SSNs, in moves that some have ascribed as much to each state's great-power aspirations as to military necessity. India previously operated a Soviet *Skat*-class (*Charlie* I) SSN from the late 1980s until 1991, and has recently taken delivery of a Russian *Akula*-class boat, christened INS *Chakra*. India also launched, in 2009, a nuclear-powered ballistic missile submarine, INS *Arihant*, though this boat has yet to enter service, and its missile complement is unclear. Brazil's aspirations are rooted in nuclear-powered boats. France's DCNS, involved in the construction of Brazil's four *Scorpenes*, is also assisting in the design and construction of the non-nuclear portions of Brazil's nuclear submarine.

SSNs are attractive due to their duration, range and speed relative to conventional counterparts. The largest SSNs in the world, the Russian *Typhoon*-class ballistic-missile boats, can theoretically remain submerged on patrol for six months. As such, nuclear power is necessary for an effective continuous at-sea nuclear-deterrent capability. However, nuclear submarines tend to be noisier than conventionally powered boats as certain systems such as reactor pumps must constantly operate; a situation exacerbated as conventional boats become quieter. Furthermore, substantial technical expertise is required to maintain and sustain SSNs, with land-based infrastructure also required for fuel management and storage. Decommissioning nuclear submarines is also problematic and costly because of the need to dismantle and store the reactor safely.

Future submarine market

Developments in submarine technologies, as well as a wider set of operators, will likely encourage further investment in ASW capabilities, from depth charges to sonar, frigates to ASW aviation. This will only be reinforced if other technological advances make submarines and their weapons systems more effective. At the same time, submarines are likely to be used for a wider range of roles. Intelligence gathering, special-forces insertion, mine-laying and land-attack are but four, while it should not be forgotten that submarines are also a key part of ASW capabilities themselves. The North Korean attack on the *Cheonan* in 2010 demonstrated the difficulties that even advanced navies can have in tracking and sensing potentially hostile submarines. Given this inherent advantage, submarine proliferation is likely to continue as more navies seek to exploit the range of capabilities that these boats offer.

MILITARY AEROSPACE: FASTER TARGET ENGAGEMENTS BECKON

Advances in guidance technologies are providing world air forces with the capacity to engage targets with a high degree of accuracy in all weathers, day or night. In the West, precision-guided air-launched munitions have been broadly adopted in the last ten years. The 2011 NATO-led operation in Libya underscored the ability of certain participating air forces to engage targets with near sub-metric accuracy. Now, if a static target can be found and identified, and it is determined that it falls within the rules of engagement, an air force can, if it has the material resources, almost always hit the target. This does not eliminate, however, the possibility of air-strikes having unintended consequences: hardware or software failures can occur, as can human error, and civilian deaths and friendly-fire casualties still occur as a result of target misidentification.

To use airborne munitions effectively, targets have to be identified and, if multiple targets present themselves, discriminated amongst, while complying with the rules of engagement. But achieving military effect is not just reliant on hitting a specific target; timeliness is also an issue. Some targets may only offer fleeting engagement opportunities or may be time-sensitive, such as engaging a hostile ballistic-missile launch, disrupting an air-defence command-and-control centre, or defeating a mobile surface-to-air missile system.

For targets like these, there is a desire to compress the engagement cycle. To reduce the 'sensor-to-shooter' time, improvements can be made to ISR technologies, command-and-control systems, guidance technologies, as well as weapons payloads. Air-launched munitions can also be made faster. While not a panacea, using faster munitions to reduce launch-to-strike times offers decision-makers more time for their deliberations. They can also deliver advantages in terms of penetration, either through surface-to-air missile defences, or in attacking hard and deeply buried targets.

The impetus of velocity

Research and development work is taking place into both supersonic (Mach 1-5) and hypersonic (Mach 5+) cruise-missile technology. High-speed weapons research is not new. During the Cold War, research into hypersonic 'air-breathing' weapons was driven by concerns over the survivability of existing, slower, air-launched nuclear-capable systems. Research now continues on air-breathing technologies. Relying on the intake of air for fuel combustion, these can operate with lighter fuel loads and over greater ranges than munitions relying solely on solid rocket propellants. However, complex technological issues and high costs have so far limited hypersonic research, while the same factors mean potential operators will likely be restricted to a handful of nations.

Research into high-speed air-breathing propulsion has mainly been carried out by the US and Russia. France, China, India and Brazil have also funded hypersonic-propulsion research, as has Japan, with an eye to space launch. Washington is principally interested in using conventionally armed hypersonic cruise missiles in the tactical role. High-speed weapons could potentially be of use in strike missions in anti-access/area-denial environments. Steven Walker, deputy assistant secretary for science, technology and engineering in the US Department of the Air Force, said in February 2012 that 'we are planning to initiate a technology demonstration effort in Fiscal Year 2013 to demonstrate a high speed capability option. If successful, this High Speed Strike weapon technology demonstration will be representative of an air-breathing hypersonic missile system with the capability to engage fixed and relocatable targets at extended ranges and survive the most stringent environments presented to us in the next decade.'

Two of Washington's most recent efforts are the air force's X-51A *Waverider* and the HIFiRE project, which also involves Australia's Defence Science and Technology Organisation. The X-51 programme, managed by the Air Force Research Laboratory, is an air-launched vehicle intended to explore hypersonic propulsion in free flight. Test results are so far mixed, with one out of its three flights seeing its air-breathing supersonic combustion ramjet (scramjet) take the vehicle to speeds over Mach 5. HIFiRE uses a ground-launched vehicle to examine basic technologies required for hypersonic flight.

The attraction of hypersonic cruise missiles can be gauged by considering the approximate fly-out times of a subsonic and a Mach 5-class weapon. Most land-attack cruise missiles fly at around Mach 0.7 and would take approximately an hour to travel 500 miles. By comparison, a Mach 5 missile would cover a similar distance in under ten minutes. The time advantage is considerably less against a comparatively high-speed supersonic missile, though with a higher velocity hypersonic weapon the gap widens. Along with hypersonic work, Washington is also supporting technologies applicable to supersonic cruise-missile development: Walker also noted the 'Supersonic Turbine Engine for Long Range' project intended to develop propulsion technology for a next-generation cruise missile. The US Navy's 'Revolutionary Approach to Long Range Time Critical Strike' project explored a turbojet-powered missile capable of cruise speeds in excess of Mach 3.

Russian efforts

Russian Deputy Prime Minister Dmitry Rogozin has lamented the US 'lead' in hypersonics, and in 2012, moved to create a 'national competitor' by further consolidating Russia's guided-weapons industry: NPO Mashinostroyenia is being folded into the Tactical Missile Corporation (which already includes most Russian guided-weapons manufacturers including the Raduga design bureau).

Rogozin delivered his comments during a visit to the Raduga design bureau in Dubna, north of Moscow. Towards the end of the Soviet era, Raduga had started developing the Kh-90 high-speed strategic cruise missile, which may have had an intended design speed of Mach 5. Flight hardware was tested using a Tu-95 *Bear* as the launch aircraft, though with mixed results. The collapse in Russian defence expenditure during the 1990s led to the programme being shelved.

Raduga and NPO Mashinostroyenia had both previously conducted high-speed cruise-missile research, though Raduga is likely to lead any work on hypersonic cruise-missile technology within the Tactical Missile Corporation, given its experience on the Kh-90. NPO's general director, Aleksandr Leonov, suggested in February 2012 that the company was working on a hypersonic weapon for naval applications. He indicated the project was part of the Russian defence ministry's 2011–20 funding programme.

Leonov did not say whether this effort was related to joint work between Russia and India to develop a successor to the supersonic *BrahMos* missile (*BrahMos* is a variant of the NPO Mashinostroyenia 3M55 *Onyx* [SS-N-26 *Strobile*]). *BrahMos* II, as the project is dubbed, is intended to develop a scramjet-powered missile capable of hypersonic flight. *BrahMos* uses ramjet propulsion, engine technology best suited to flight between Mach 2 to around Mach 5. Beyond Mach 5, ramjets face increasing problems in slowing the intake of air to the subsonic speeds required in the combustion chamber. Conversely, scramjet propulsion requires speeds of Mach 5 and above for efficient combustion. In parallel to its work with Russia, India is also pursuing independent research into hypersonic systems through its Defence Research and Development Organisation. Its hypersonic technology demonstrator vehicle is intended to begin to explore scramjet propulsion at Mach 6.5.

European ambitions

Russia features in one of Europe's main hypersonic demonstrator projects: MBDA France's LEA programme. France dominates European research into air-breathing hypersonic technology, which is in part a legacy of its strategic air-launched cruise-missile programmes. Paris has been cultivating its ties with Moscow over the past two decades, motivated by a pragmatic interest in using Russian research infra-

structure. In the case of LEA, an MBDA-designed air vehicle and engine will be dropped from a Tu-22M *Backfire* bomber; the test item will then be boosted to the required transition speed for scramjet propulsion using a modified Kh-22 (AS-4 *Kitchen*) missile. Telemetry support from the Russian test range will be provided by an Il-76PP telemetry aircraft. A key aim of the LEA programme is to examine aero-propulsive balance: the drag environment of the hypersonic flight regime is such that there is a risk that, even if the engine operates, it will not generate positive thrust and the missile will slow, even with an operational engine. Flight tests are planned for 2013 to 2015, with the air vehicle being flown at speeds between Mach 4 and Mach 8. The flight trials are also intended to support the predictive methodology MBDA is using with regard to the performance of the LEA.

France and the UK also began study work at the end of 2011, looking at technology options for a next-generation cruise missile. Initially, up to a dozen design alternatives were to be considered before selecting perhaps three for fuller exploration. Subsonic and supersonic designs will be looked at, though whether the study will also encompass any hypersonic candidates is uncertain. The UK Ministry of Defence had earlier shelved its own sustained hypersonic flight experiment.

Technical challenges

There are substantial engineering challenges to sustained hypersonic flight. These include the design and close integration of the airframe and engine, guidance and control, and the thermal environment.

The heat from air friction can result in surface temperatures of 1,200 degrees Fahrenheit at Mach 4, more than double this temperature at Mach 6, and near four times at Mach 8. At speeds up to Mach 6, the use of advanced materials alone may not be enough to provide the required structural integrity. At any greater speed, active cooling would also likely be required, such as using fuel as the airframe's heat-sink. Airframe control is a challenge given the stresses of the air environment, exacerbated by high speeds, while effective terminal guidance at hypersonic speeds could also pose problems. Technologies currently used for both radio frequency and infrared transparency are not capable of withstanding the thermal stresses of sustained flight in excess of Mach 4.5. Research is under way into a range of ceramic materials that could meet sensor window requirements, possibly in combination with an active cooling system. Another possibility could lie in minimising the time the window is also directly exposed to the air flow, while providing adequate time for the inputs needed for high accuracy.

The promise of air-breathing high-speed weaponry has remained simply that for several decades. Though criticism continues that these systems are perhaps more driven by the demands of research laboratories than battlefield practicalities, the nature of future threat environments seems to have led to a redoubling of interest, as well as efforts, mainly in the US and Russia. The effect of Chinese efforts remain unknown. To fully exploit the benefits of hypersonic technologies, however, the weapons-targeting process needs to be more responsive. Hypersonic weapons will need to be nested within a networked environment capable of supporting a rapid targeting cycle from target search and identification, planning, and engagement; one which could also include near real-time battle-damage assessment.

Anti-access/Area denial: Washington's response

Since the end of the Cold War, the United States has been able to deploy its considerable military capacity to operational theatres unopposed, and once in theatre has faced little if any opposition in key areas of its own asymmetric advantage, such as air and space power, and the ability to engage targets with precision weaponry at extended ranges. However, the Department of Defense (DoD) has recognised since the late 1990s that freedom of manoeuvre cannot be assumed indefinitely. An erosion of the previously overwhelming US technological edge compounds this challenge.

Recent doctrinal and equipment developments demonstrate the Pentagon's focus on countering what it calls anti-access/area-denial (A2/AD) capabilities, which threaten to restrict US and allied forces' movement to and within potential theatres. Anti-ship missiles, submarines, mines and cyber capabilities are high among US armed forces' concerns regarding the inventories of potential adversaries.

The Pentagon has to address these issues, and adopt new strategies, while undergoing what Chairman of the Joint Chiefs of Staff General Martin Dempsey has called three transitions: firstly, a move from a military 'generally focused on deploying for combat into one that can perform missions besides counter-insurgency'; secondly, a transition in personnel strength, with notable reductions in the US Army and Marine Corps; and thirdly, doing this within an increasingly tight fiscal environment.

Improving military technology

The US and its allies are now challenged by the priority placed by a growing number of states, including potential adversaries, on developing and acquiring conventional precision weapons systems increasingly comparable in accuracy and reach to their own. Such technologies, deployed by China, Iran and North Korea among others, and offered for export by Russia, could constrain deployments by the US and its allies. These systems include medium- and extended-range surface-to-air missile systems; long-range land attack cruise missiles; medium- and long-range anti-ship missiles; and the associated targeting infrastructure using airborne (and in some cases space-based) sensors in combination with advanced command-and-control systems. The development and spread of such systems has encouraged the development of revised operational concepts to sustain US freedom of action; an early iteration was the US Air Force's Global Strike Task Force concept of 2001, intended to start addressing 'access challenges'.

Concerns about precision-guided munitions and longer-range missiles persist, and are now compounded by other emerging technologies. Cyber operations and, in particular, the consistent attacks on targets in the US and other countries, some of which may have originated in China, highlight the US armed forces' increasing reliance on the digital domain. Use of such non-kinetic tactics raises questions about how to attribute such incidents, as well as how to deter and, if necessary, respond to such threats. Among other effects, offensive cyber operations could disable command-and-control capabilities. They could also, in conjunction with electronic warfare, be used for jamming. Digital vulnerabilities are also underscored by the more kinetic options available to some states, such as the use of anti-satellite weaponry, of which China's rudimentary but effective anti-satellite missile test in 2007 was a reminder. North Korea's use of GPS jamming devices, which hampered civilian air and maritime traffic in and out of South Korea in April–May 2012, also highlighted the potential vulnerability of digital navigation systems.

Notional adversary states need not rely solely on expensive technologies to complicate access or freedom of action; innovative tactics using low-technology weaponry may also cause problems. For instance, mines are a tried-and-tested means of attempting to deny large areas of sea or land to an adversary and, during *Operation Unified Protector* in waters off Libya in 2011, gave NATO planners pause for thought. Mines introduce an element of risk to force-deployment calculations and remain useful defensive weapons.

In the face of the proliferation of both high- and low-technology systems to a larger number of potential adversaries, and these states' presumed development of relevant doctrines, the Pentagon has started to formulate and formalise thinking aimed at ensuring continued access and freedom of action, notably in its Air–Sea Battle (ASB) concept, a descendent of the Global Strike Task Force. Air–Sea Battle merited one paragraph when it was first publicly aired in the 2010 Quadrennial Defense Review (QDR). Two years on, it contributes to the conceptual foundations of the US armed forces' shift in geographical focus, enshrined in the government's revised strategic guidance of January 2012. The 'rebalance toward the Asia-Pacific' was intended to signal to allies and potential rivals alike that the US will be increasingly engaged in the security of the region, reflecting its economic interests and – though this is not made explicit – China's emergence as a potential peer competitor.

The Air–Sea Battle concept

After several years of classified work, the US began to brief some of its closest allies on Air–Sea Battle during the course of 2012, indicating its importance not only to the US armed forces, but also as a tool for reassuring partners in Asia. The limited official material available on the concept does not identify any specific state as a threat, but rather sets out capabilities that an adversary could possess. But the strategy was almost certainly conceived as a signal to China that the US is noting developments in its military capability, and is taking what it considers appropriate measures in response.

Discussing ASB in May 2012, then-US Air Force Chief of Staff General Norton Schwartz said that, for Washington, 'the ultimate goal is interoperable air and naval forces that can execute networked, integrated attacks-in-depth to disrupt, destroy, and defeat enemy anti-access area denial capabilities … sustaining the deployment of US joint forces'. To achieve this, the US is looking to boost inter-service capabilities, allowing the air force and navy to communicate more quickly, efficiently and at various levels of command, accompanied by close coordination to enable cross-domain operations. Exactly how this improvement in communications will be achieved remains unclear, although an exercise in November 2011 gives some indication. It involved communications between a fifth-generation fighter aircraft, a forward-deployed command-and-control facility, a floating maritime-operations centre and a nuclear-powered submarine that launched a *Tomahawk* cruise missile against a target located and identified by the aircraft.

Attacking in depth implies prompt targeting of adversaries' high-value assets well behind front lines, rather than attempting to 'roll back' layers of defences.

These networked, integrated air–sea forces would be expected to 'disrupt, destroy and defeat' – disrupt the C4ISR (command, control, communications, computers, intelligence, surveillance and reconnaissance) networks of an adversary, destroy weapons-delivery platforms, and defeat incoming munitions and platforms before they can threaten US forces.

Essentially, the ASB is designed to preserve freedom of access and manoeuvre by destroying or neutralising adversaries' networks and weapons platforms from the start of any conflict. This could involve attacking territory rather than targeting only ships and submarines at sea or missiles and aircraft in flight. The intention is for the ASB to inform national strategy, force posture and budgets, but not to act as a specific proposal for a particular scenario. Indeed, thinking regarding Air–Sea Battle is still comparatively immature and has yet to produce many specifics. Although the idea was discussed before and during the 2010 QDR, the Air–Sea Battle Office was only created in August 2011 and, as of mid-2012, only employed around 15 people from the air force, navy and marine corps.

The primary aim of ASB is to encourage operational integration between these three services, though the Pentagon has stressed that the concept affects all five domains (land, sea, air, space and cyberspace). Aware that there will be interest in the future role of ground forces, as US forces transition from the land-focused campaigns of the 2000s, DoD has said that ASB allows for the more effective insertion of land and amphibious forces into contested space, and hence benefits all services. To that end, while the Pentagon's Joint Operational Access Concept (JOAC) notes that the defence secretary 'directed the Department of the Navy and the Department of the Air Force to develop the Air–Sea Battle Concept', it continues by saying that the 'intent of Air–Sea Battle was to improve integration of air, land, naval, space, and cyberspace forces'. March 2012 saw the army and marine corps publish a concept document entitled 'Gaining and Maintaining Access', describing 'the US Army and Marine Corps contribution towards defeating area-denial capabilities within the larger context of the joint force effort to gain and maintain operational access'. Having said this, the army and marines will likely struggle against any tendency to define the problem of – and concepts relating to – future conflict in a way that regards technology as decisive, particularly if there is an attempt to paint recent wartime experiences as aberrational. These services, and particularly the army, function primarily on land where geography, people, politics and culture complicate military operations and limit the effects of technology. Unless ASB and related strategies to counter A2/AD can rule out the use of land forces in such scenarios, these concerns will persist in some quarters.

Making it happen

The Joint Operational Access Concept was released within two weeks of the official announcement of the 'rebalance' to Asia in January 2012. Intended to provide the 'overarching concept under which we can nest other concepts dealing with more specific aspects of anti-access/area-denial challenges, such as the Air–Sea Battle', JOAC stresses the need for 'cross-domain synergy'. This translates as a closer working relationship between the different services, including the use of dispersed forces in several bases to operate on 'multiple, independent lines of operations', and bringing these forces together to 'manoeuvre directly against key operational objectives from strategic distance'. These ideas were reflected in the Pentagon's proposals for new forward deployments, including the six-monthly rotation of up to 2,500 marines through Australia, the placing (although not basing) of up to four littoral combat ships in Singapore and an increased presence in Guam. At its simplest, JOAC can be seen as a framing document for addressing the 'anti-access' part of A2/AD, but it does not focus on how subsequently to maintain the fight by countering the adversary's area-denial methods.

This realignment of US forces throughout the Asia-Pacific is a clear signal that the Air–Sea Battle concept is intended to be a guiding principle for future US joint service planning: the US aims to complicate any adversary's potential A2/AD operations, offering multiple lines of attack that would be more difficult to counter. But perhaps the greatest impact of the concept will be how it relates to regional dynamics. Though the official material available on the concept does not identify any specific state as a threat, rather

setting out potential adversaries' capabilities, by focusing on anti-access/area-denial capabilities, the ASB essentially alerts potential rivals – particularly China – to the willingness and ability of the US armed forces to adapt to challenges it perceives they might offer. For example, one scenario could involve the US escalating early in a crisis by attacking targets on an adversary's home territory and dismantling A2/AD networks and capabilities. In this way it would maintain freedom of access and manoeuvre, and hope to assume dominance of the battlespace. The DoD's March 2012 joint doctrine on 'Countering Air and Missile Threats' stresses that offensive counter-air operations 'are most effective against missiles prior to their launch'.

Concerns about anti-access/area-denial capabilities resonate beyond the Asian theatre. In the Middle East, the accelerated refitting of USS *Ponce* as a floating forward-staging base in early 2012, and its deployment to the Persian Gulf in July 2012, reflected continuing US concern over Iran's anti-access/area-denial forces. The *Ponce* is designed to act as a 'lily pad' for mine-countermeasure forces, acting in a logistical role for the mine hunters stationed in Bahrain and a platform for MH-53 helicopters. Though not ostensibly connected to the Air–Sea Battle concept, the *Ponce's* refit and deployment is a clear sign of increasing US focus on planning and capabilities that might be required to counter A2/AD strategies. A host of easily envisaged scenarios might require the US to overcome A2/AD, which is testament to the difficulties presented by technologies such as cyber, precision-guided munitions and even low-tech but innovatively deployed capacities, and the relatively cost-effective deterrent they can provide. As such, developing the concepts, plans and equipment necessary to counter A2/AD capabilities globally is likely to continue to occupy the Pentagon for many years, as potential adversaries expand their own capabilities and develop doctrines aimed at complicating the military options of the US and its partners.

Global trends in defence economics

GLOBAL DEMAND

Macroeconomics

Global economic growth slowed from 5.1% in 2010 to 3.8% in 2011 and an estimated 3.3% in 2012, as advanced economies continued to struggle with high levels of sovereign, bank and household indebtedness. Heightened financial contagion emanating from the eurozone – the 17 countries using the euro as a common currency – adversely affected European growth, while the unwinding of various domestic stimulus packages enacted in Asia in the aftermath of the 2008 financial crisis served to limit the extent to which Asia was able to drive global demand. High oil prices, an anaemic US economic recovery, and the lagged effects of incremental monetary tightening instituted across Asia and Latin America throughout 2011 acted as further constraints to 2012 activity.

Despite the global downshift, emerging economies in Asia, the Middle East and Latin America are projected to maintain steady rates of growth, while advanced economies continue to address the weakness of their public finances. According to the International Monetary Fund's April 2012 *World Economic Outlook,*

> Gross debt-to-GDP ratios will rise further in many advanced economies, with a particularly steep increase in the G7 economies, to about 130% by 2017. Without more action than currently planned, debt ratios are expected to reach 256% in Japan, 124% in Italy, close to 113% in the US and 91% in the euro area over the forecast horizon. … In a striking contrast, many emerging and developing economies will see a decline in debt-to-GDP ratios, with the overall ratio for the group dropping to below 30% by 2017.

Defence spending 2011–12

Reflecting these macroeconomic trends, global defence spending fell in real terms for a second year running in 2012. After a 1.5% real reduction in 2011, real defence spending declined by a further 2.05% in 2012 (constant 2010 prices and exchange rates).

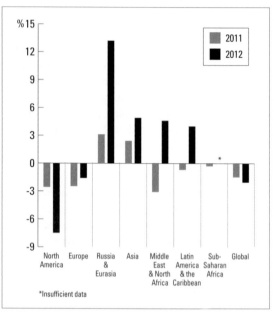

Figure 1 **Real global defence spending changes 2011–12 (%)**

Despite the overall reduction, defence spending trends varied considerably across regions. Real defence spending rose in Asia by 2.44% in 2011, before accelerating to 4.94% in 2012. In a similar vein, real defence spending in Russia and Eurasia grew by 3.11% in 2011, before rising by 13.28% in 2012. In Latin America, after a 0.71% real reduction in 2011 regional spending (caused in part by higher-than-expected rates of inflation), real defence spending grew in 2012 by 4.0%. Similarly, after high oil prices in 2011 contributed to greater-than-anticipated inflation in the Middle East and North Africa, real defence spending is estimated to have fallen by 3.06% in 2011, before rising by an estimated 4.57% in 2012.

Meanwhile, defence austerity in Europe saw real defence spending in Europe decline in both 2011 and 2012, falling by 2.52% in 2011 and by a further 1.63% in 2012. In North America, real military spending declined by 2.6% in 2011, and a further 7.5% in 2012. Sub-Saharan Africa saw a 0.3% real decline in 2011 spending (2012 trend unavailable at time of publication due to incomplete data availability), and continued to account for just 1% of global defence spending. (Note: real figures used here are measured at constant 2010 prices and exchange rates, see Figure 1 for further details.) See also 'Comparative Defence Statistics', pp. 41–2.

Asian and European spending converges

These general macroeconomic and defence-spending trends illustrate a broader shift in the underlying balance of global defence spending. This is highlighted by the convergence between Asian and NATO European defence-spending levels since the onset of the financial crash of 2008. As shown in Figure 2, between 2005 and 2007 (i.e. prior to the 2008 financial crisis), nominal defence spending in Asia (excluding Australia and New Zealand) rose from around US$148.1 billion to US$178.4bn, an average annual rate of increase of 9.8%. Nominal defence spending in NATO Europe rose at a broadly similar rate over the same period – from US$252.7bn in 2005 to US$298.5bn in 2007, an average annual rate of increase of 8.8%.

However, after the 2008 financial crisis, a marked convergence began between Asian and NATO European spending levels. Nominal NATO European defence spending fell from a peak of US$305.6bn in 2008 to a post-crisis low of US$262.7bn in 2012, declining by an average of 3.6% per annum in each of the four years since the crisis. By contrast, nominal Asian defence spending post-2008 has continued to rise at just under pre-crisis rates, with spending increasing from US$207.4bn in 2008 to US$287.4bn in 2012, equivalent to an average annual growth rate of 8.6%. In the process, nominal Asian spending overtook that of NATO Europe, with the former rising from US$268.8bn in 2011 to US$287.4bn in 2012, while the latter fell from US$290.0bn in 2011 to US$262.7bn in 2012.

Indeed, the increase in Asian spending has been so rapid, and the defence austerity pursued by European states so severe, that in 2012 nominal Asian spending (US$287.4bn) exceeded total official defence spending not just in NATO Europe, but across all of Europe, including spending by non-NATO European states. These convergence trends would be more pronounced if military pensions (a more significant proportion of defence spending in many European states than in Asian countries) were excluded from European totals.

Of course, the above trends refer to nominal spending levels at current prices and exchange rates, and therefore do not account for either exchange-rate fluctuations or variations in inflation rates between

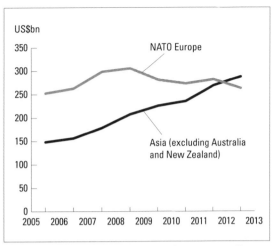

Figure 2 **Asia–NATO Europe defence spending convergence 2006–12**

Asia and Europe. Additionally, defence spending per capita in European states remains significantly higher than in Asian states. Nonetheless, these nominal trends are indicative of the underlying shift in the distribution of real global defence spending.

Nominal NATO European defence spending now hovers at around 2006 levels (with spending in both 2006 and 2012 amounting to around $262.7bn), although the real decline in spending is substantially more than this nominal level would suggest, as the price inflation that has occurred since 2006 means that a similar amount of spending in 2012 purchases less than it did in 2006. In real terms, 2012 NATO European defence-spending levels are around 11% lower than in 2006 (at constant 2010 exchange rates and prices).

GLOBAL SUPPLY

Governments and defence industries in advanced economies have adopted three main approaches to mitigate the contraction in Western defence markets described above. Firstly, there have been tentative moves towards consolidating defence industries and increasing collaboration between defence firms, in order to improve market access, realise economies of scale, and pool fixed costs such as R&D expenses. A second trend has been towards removing impediments to defence trade, particularly barriers to market entry, and relaxing export regulations. Thirdly, defence firms have sought to diversify their activities across a wider range of countries and sectors, in order to reduce their reliance on particular markets.

Defence-industrial consolidation and collaboration

Attempts at industrial consolidation have been strongest in Europe, which saw several proposals for consolidation during 2011 and 2012. As part of the November 2010 Anglo-French defence cooperation agreement, BAE Systems entered into collaboration with France's Dassault Aviation to study the viability of jointly developing unmanned aerial systems (UAS). In June 2012, France and Germany signed a letter of intent to explore potential cooperation in acquiring and developing a range of weapons platforms, including air- and missile-defence systems, UAS and space systems. Then, in September 2012, Paris and Berlin announced that they would work to establish a common operational requirement for a Medium Altitude, Long Endurance (MALE) UAV, with a view to developing an interim solution to their capability gaps in this area. Also, in September 2012,

it was announced that BAE Systems and pan-European defence conglomerate EADS were engaged in merger negotiations (see p. 37). Earlier, in January 2012, German firms Cassidian (the defence arm of EADS) and Rheinmetall said they would merge their tactical and MALE UAS activities to enable access to a greater resource pool for R&D. In the land-systems arena, in October 2012, Renault Trucks Defense (RTD) announced its acquisition of France's specialist armoured-vehicle manufacturer Panhard General Defense.

Russia has also sought to expand the scope of its collaborative defence-industrial activities. Following a bilateral accord with France in January 2011 to supply *Mistral*-class amphibious assault vessels (with Russia's United Shipbuilding Corporation assisting DCNS with construction), Rosoboronexport approached EADS in 2012, as well as Spain's Indra Sistemas and Navantia, to explore opportunities for

Regulating the global arms trade

On 27 July 2012, the Arms Trade Treaty (ATT) Diplomatic Conference concluded a month of tough negotiations without producing a treaty. Those drafting the treaty hoped for two outcomes: firstly, to 'establish the highest possible common standards' regulating the global conventional arms trade; and secondly, to tackle the illicit trade in conventional arms and 'their diversion to the illicit market or for unauthorised end use'.

Although the conference functioned by consensus and states pursued different objectives during negotiations, it was widely held that the president of the conference, Argentina's Ambassador Roberto Garcia Moritán, had succeeded in crafting a workable compromise document. However, on the final day of proceedings, the US delegation asked for more time to consider the text, prompting many analysts to speculate about the influence on the process of US domestic politics and the impending US presidential and congressional elections in November.

Civil society organisations have long campaigned for an arms trade treaty, but realistic prospects for agreement first emerged when the UK came on-board in 2005. UN Resolution 61/87 in 2006 – co-authored by Argentina, Australia, Costa Rica, Finland, Japan, Kenya and the UK – paved the way for negotiations. Before the 2012 Diplomatic Conference, a Group of Governmental Experts was established to assess the feasibility of a treaty and four Preparatory Committee meetings were held.

The main faultline in negotiations was between countries promoting human-security concerns and those

seeking to privilege state security interests. But other fissures emerged. A core group of sceptical states – Cuba, Iran, North Korea, Syria and Venezuela – offered opposition throughout, while a second layer of countries, including Russia and Ukraine, maintained relatively muted but constant opposition. A third group, which included China and India, were sceptical but flexible – except when it came to certain issues. China categorically opposed explicit reference to gifts and loans; India insisted on including a clause stipulating that the arms trade treaty could not void 'contractual obligations under defence cooperation agreements'.

The coalition of states advocating for a treaty with strong humanitarian components – mostly African, Caribbean Community, EU, Latin American and Pacific states – also had clusters of countries with differing priorities. For instance, African and Caribbean Community states prioritised the inclusion of ammunition in the treaty's scope while Australia, France and the UK emphasised the importance of US, Chinese and Russian consent on this issue.

The US holds a distinct position outside the two main camps. The Obama administration overturned its predecessor's opposition to the ATT in 2009, but insistently opposed the inclusion of ammunition or any reference to non-state actors.

While less robust than many states and civil society organisations had wished, the draft treaty text delivered on the penultimate day of the Diplomatic Conference covers establishing defence-industrial relations. In July 2012, Rosoboronexport reached agreement with Navantia to explore means of integrating Russian weapons systems with Navantia's patrol boats for export markets – a collaboration that could generate greater market access for both companies to countries that had previously purchased equipment from the other. Earlier, in November 2011, Rosoboronexport signed an MoU with Indra Sistemas over technological cooperation; in December 2011, it said it was seeking further collaborative partnerships with countries in Asia, such as Brunei, Cambodia and the Philippines.

Defence trade facilitation

States have also been trying to reduce barriers to trade in defence markets. For example, with the volume of US Department of Defense domestic contracts set to decline relative to the past decade, and as defence firms based in the United States seek to expand their

global footprint, the US administration has sought to reform US arms-export-control regulations and procedures, particularly those applying to close allies. Priorities have been the transfer of thousands of restricted items on the State Department's US Munitions List (USML, where all items on the list are subject to the same restrictions) to the Department of Commerce's more flexible Commerce Control List (CCL, where export-licence restrictions are calibrated according to the nature of the item). The idea is to create a Single Control List consisting of only the most sensitive defence technologies. The administration also began streamlining the procedures by which the Department of State notifies Congress of proposed transfers from the USML to the CCL and of proposed Foreign Military Sales (FMS). Unbounded informal consultation periods built into the current FMS procedure allow a single lawmaker to delay the entire process, with the result that notifications to

---

'at a minimum' items included in the seven categories of the UN Register of Conventional Arms (battle tanks, armoured combat vehicles, large-calibre artillery systems, combat aircraft, attack helicopters, warships, and missiles and missile launchers), as well as small arms and light weapons (SALW). The scope of activities includes exports, imports, brokering, transit and transhipment. There are also robust prohibitions and national risk assessments to guide arms-transfer decisions, including references to international human rights and humanitarian law.

Yet fundamental weaknesses remain with the draft treaty. Firstly, the clause stipulating that defence cooperation agreements take precedence over the arms trade treaty has caused considerable concern. It means, for instance, that Russian arms transfers to the Assad regime in Syria – which are delivered under such defence cooperation agreements – would remain outside the treaty's remit. (Some legal experts, however, question whether this clause carries legitimacy, given that it privileges private international law over public international law.)

Secondly, ammunition, weapons parts and components are only partially covered by the draft text: not all risk criteria apply to these items and only their export is regulated (leaving out their brokering, import, transit and transhipment). African and Caribbean Community states had strongly argued for ammunition and munitions to be subject to robust regulations, but they lost out to the US position.

Thirdly, the text does not adequately address the threat of arms being diverted from the legal to the illicit market or unauthorised end-users, making it optional for states

to act on such concerns in their national risk assessments. Given that most uncontrolled or illicit SALW and ammunition are diverted from legal transfers, this point is seen by experts as highly problematic.

If the text had been agreed, it would not necessarily have prevented Western states from arming the Libyan rebels, armaments finding their way to the Free Syrian Army, or Russian arms transfers to the Syrian government. Any arms trade treaty would not be able to absolutely prevent arms transfers, like the arms embargoes authorised by the UN Security Council do. Instead, it would provide a forum for discussion through reporting requirements, regular meetings of state parties and dispute-resolution mechanisms that would force states to justify their decisions with regard to arms transfers. If a critical body of opinion deemed the transfer(s) in question to be contrary to the treaty's rules, diplomatic pressure could subsequently be applied.

An ATT's utility rests predominantly on its long-term application, with its intervention aimed at mitigating the risks posed by arms transfers before violent situations escalate. Although the July 2012 Diplomatic Conference failed, the pursuit of an ATT has not ended. States met to discuss the treaty at the First Committee on Disarmament and International Security (DISEC) in October and passed a resolution in November allowing a two-week extension of the Diplomatic Conference in March 2013. Were this also to fail, some states have shown willingness to force a vote at the UN General Assembly, either shortly after the March 2013 conference or at the DISEC later in the year.

Congress are often withheld to prevent the stalling of other legislative items. This causes lengthy delays that diminish the United States' reputation as a reliable arms supplier. According to the State Department, it takes 90–95 days on average to obtain approval for a major arms sale, and an average of 215 days to move an item from the USML to the CCL.

Specific bilateral arrangements between the US and its close allies to expedite export approval and reduce delivery times for defence items also came into effect in 2012. The Defence Trade Cooperation Treaty with the United Kingdom (first signed in 2007 and ratified by the US Senate in 2010) to reduce export-licence and ITAR (International Traffic in Arms Regulations) approval requirements came into effect in April 2012. A similar defence trade cooperation treaty signed with Australia (in 2007, ratified in 2010) was implemented in November 2012 with the passage of the Defence Trade Controls Bill in Canberra.

In late 2011, Japan also eased its long-standing defence-export regulations and restrictions on the participation of its domestic defence industry in collaborative international defence-industrial programmes. In June 2012, Japan signed an MoU with the United Kingdom that included an undertaking to cooperate on joint R&D and defence-equipment production. Later, in September 2012, Japan announced a similar bilateral agreement with Australia, which aimed to expand defence research ties and exchange information on areas of defence technology of common interest.

Elsewhere, European Union Directive 2009/81/EC on Defence and Security Procurement came into force in August 2011, attempting to unify Europe's fragmented defence markets, thereby encouraging greater defence trade across the region.

Geographic and sectoral diversification

Economic turbulence in developed markets has made it more important for defence firms in advanced economies to have a strong portfolio of foreign orders. These companies have correspondingly put increasing emphasis on emerging markets, particularly in Asia, the Middle East and Latin America. In Asia, maritime territorial disputes have seen an expansion in the market for intelligence, surveillance and reconnaissance (ISR) systems, while procurement budgets in Indonesia, the Philippines, Bangladesh and India have also increased. India remains one of the largest defence markets for foreign suppliers, importing some 70% of its equipment requirements. The Middle East continues to spend record amounts on defence, as countries upgrade their combat-aircraft fleets, radar and missile-defence systems. Meanwhile, Latin American states have increased spending on border-defence systems, training aircraft, light helicopters, naval patrol vessels and UAS.

Foreign defence companies seeking to penetrate regional markets have increased their engagement with domestic defence industries and research institutions to better meet offset requirements and secure contracts. In other cases, foreign firms have entered into partnership agreements with, or taken direct stakes in, local defence firms, in order to take advantage of lower manufacturing costs, improve market access and their regional presence. Many emerging market governments have themselves placed considerable emphasis on the establishment of industrial partnerships with advanced suppliers in order to accelerate their own defence-industrial transformation and to raise their defence production capacity. These trends are explored in depth in the Latin American and the Caribbean chapter (see pp. 422–3).

Europe's defence industrial base: consolidation stymied, for the time being

Merger talks between Europe's two largest arms manufacturers, BAE Systems and EADS, were revealed in September 2012. In the end, no agreement could be reached, but the talks brought uncomfortable facts about Europe's defence industrial base into the open. It seems unwise to rule out the possibility of such a deal at some point in the future. However, even if no BAE–EADS merger ever eventuates, change seems likely to be on the way.

A merged group would have been centred on Airbus, the world's largest civil aircraft builder, and would also have had a substantial defence arm – a structure which, like that of Boeing of the United States, would have made it more resilient to economic and budget cycles. The global reach of Airbus, which is owned by EADS, could have helped to give a stronger foundation to the defence businesses of BAE. This would have been beneficial because shrinking defence budgets mean that Europe's weapons manufacturers face an uncertain future. The two companies' chief executives, in entering into talks, were recognising hard market realities and seeking to insulate themselves against them.

A proposal for a merger on such a scale, involving sensitive technologies, inevitably provoked strong opinions. While the companies argued that the rationale for a deal was founded firmly on commercial logic, they could not escape obvious political issues. These centred on sovereignty, the role of governments in the proposed group and jobs. EADS has 133,000 employees, including 48,400 in France, 47,000 in Germany, 13,500 in the United Kingdom, 10,700 in Spain and 2,800 in the United States. BAE employs 93,500 people, including 37,300 in the United States, 34,800 in the UK, 5,800 in Saudi Arabia and 5,600 in Australia.

A group with 226,500 employees would be a substantial one, important as a leading European manufacturer and as a developer of new technologies. However, the merger would not have created a 'monster' company by global standards. For example, its combined annual sales revenues of around $100 billion would be larger than those of Boeing or Lockheed Martin, the US defence contractors, but smaller than those of many companies in the energy, automotive and electronics sectors. Ranked by market capitalisation, EADS came 235th in the FT Global 500 list produced by the *Financial Times* in mid-2012, and BAE was outside the top 500. Putting the two companies' market value at that time together, a combined group would have come about 140th, below Boeing (125th) and well below the aerospace and defence company United Technologies (80th) and automotive manufacturer Daimler (97th), which controls 22.5% of EADS. Neither EADS nor BAE is a global giant.

Issues of sovereignty proved to be the most important barrier to the merger. Germany in particular had concerns of this nature; France and the United Kingdom also had sensitivities, though these appeared to be overcome during negotiations. Their reservations were ironic given that the governments of France, Germany and the United Kingdom had, 15 years earlier, jointly demanded that such a conglomerate be created. Arguably, the reasons that were cited then in support of a mega-merger apply even more strongly today.

Previous attempt at consolidation

In December 1997, the leaders of France, Germany and the UK called on the main aerospace and defence companies to unite into a combined group. French President Jacques Chirac, German Chancellor Helmut Kohl and British Prime Minister Tony Blair said a restructuring of the industry 'should embrace civil and military activities in the field of aerospace, and should lead to European integration based on balanced partnership'. The background to their statement was the rapid consolidation that had taken place in the American defence industry at the Department of Defense's instigation, following a 'last supper' meeting between officials and company executives in 1993. The Pentagon's call resulted in the mergers of Northrop and Grumman in 1994, Lockheed and Martin Marietta in 1995, and Boeing and McDonnell Douglas in 1997, as well as many other transactions.

At the time, European governments and defence contractors worried that rationalisation of the US defence sector would lower American companies' cost base and increase their market power to such an extent that governments would in future have no choice but to buy equipment from American companies rather than from their much-smaller European competitors. Just as in the US, European defence budgets had shrunk since the end of the Cold War, sharply reducing the business available to contractors. The European defence industry, however, was still largely organised along national lines. All sides could see that this was no longer sustainable and that cross-border consolidation was essential. Hence the government leaders' unusual joint move.

Things did not, however, turn out as they envisaged. British Aerospace (BAe) embarked on merger talks with its German counterpart, Daimler Benz Aerospace (known as DASA), with a plan to incorporate France's Aerospatiale and Matra later, once privatisation and a merger were completed. Meanwhile, GEC of the UK was in discussions with Thomson-CSF of France. However, GEC then decided to exit the defence sector and executed a clever corporate play that resulted in an all-British merger of its Marconi defence business with BAe to create BAE Systems. This upset their continental interlocutors. In retaliation, DASA, Aerospatiale Matra and their Spanish counterpart merged to create EADS, and Thomson-CSF (renamed Thales) bought Racal of the UK. Finmeccanica of Italy bought Westland, the UK helicopter company.

It was this industrial structure that prevailed in Europe for more than a decade, though with some adjustments, especially in the field of naval shipbuilding. As governments had demanded, there had indeed been some cross-border consolidation. But BAE headed in a different direction, seeking to build its US business through a series of acquisitions of second-tier defence-systems suppliers. It also expanded its armoured vehicle and shipbuilding businesses. While BAE did retain important European interests, including its stakes in the consortium building the Eurofighter *Typhoon* and in the missiles joint-venture MBDA, it sold EADS its minority shareholdings in Airbus and the space subsidiary Astrium. EADS, meanwhile, sought to build a large defence business but struggled to reach critical mass.

Renewed impetus

The BAE–EADS talks signalled that this period of relative calm was coming to an end. Some of the same factors that had worried the industry in the 1990s were reasserting themselves. European defence spending fell still further (see pp. 92–6), and the decline seems set to continue with a programme of cuts already announced in the UK and Germany, and expected in France. Though European factories have been busy with contracts won some years ago, prospects for new projects seem much more limited, especially for military aircraft. No manned European combat aircraft is planned after production ends of *Typhoon*, the French *Rafale* and the Swedish *Gripen*. Many European companies will be employed instead as subcontractors on the US F-35 *Lightning* fighter, which is to be bought by several European governments. Lockheed Martin is the prime contractor for the F-35.

Additional factors point to an uncertain future for the supplier base. Firstly, after the late-1990s round of consolidation, there has been little further effort to rationalise the European industry. This means that companies are not ideally placed to withstand reductions in equipment spending. Secondly, the defence manufacturers' customers – governments – have made little progress in long-demanded efforts to harmonise and coordinate their equipment requirements. This makes it difficult for European companies to achieve the economies of scale – and hence better value for taxpayers – that should come from operating across borders. Europe's defence industry, like that of the United States, is characterised by a few large players, and a much longer list of medium-sized suppliers, many of which have a national focus. The four largest companies – all with a multinational spread – are BAE, EADS, Finmeccanica and Thales.

Table 2 **Companies with defence sales in 2011 of between $1bn and $5bn**

Rolls-Royce	UK
DCNS	France
Safran	France
Saab	Sweden
Rheinmetall	Germany
Babcock International	UK
Serco	UK
Cobham	UK
Qinetiq	UK
Kongsberg	Norway
GKN	UK
Krauss-Maffei Wegmann	Germany
Dassault Aviation	France
Nexter	France
Chemring	UK
Fincantieri	Italy

Source: *Defence News*

In the next tier are companies with defence sales in 2011 of between $1bn and $5bn (using figures from the Top 100 ranking published annually by *Defense News*). These are shown in Table 2.

For some of these companies – engine makers Rolls-Royce of the UK and Safran of France are the best examples, along with Serco of the UK – defence makes up a minority of their revenues, and so they are well-placed to withstand shocks. Some have a primarily domestic focus, while others have built up international interests, especially through acquisitions in the US. Together, they span the range of products and services, from aircraft, armoured vehicles, shipbuilding and sub-systems of many kinds to provide support to armed forces.

The entire supplier base, from large companies to small, seems bound to be negatively affected by the decline in military spending on both sides of the Atlantic (see pp. 59–66, and pp. 92–6). The trend is already clear. According to data compiled by the IISS, the number of procurement projects under way in Europe with a value exceeding €1bn fell from 41 in 2008 to 31 in 2012 (see IISS Strategic Dossier, *European Military Capabilities: Building Armed Forces for Modern Operations*, 2008, pp. 104–6, and *The Struggle for Value in European Defence* in *Survival* 54:1, February–March 2012, pp. 71–2). While some of these still have life for years to come, like the F-35 and the A400M military airlifter, others will complete production relatively soon.

Collaborative projects intrinsically provide contractors with longer-lasting and more secure business, with sufficient demand to enable them to achieve economies. But between 2008 and 2012, no new collaborative project of this scale was initiated. In addition, the projects that offer scope for retaining and building a skills base are those involving development of new technologies. But there has been a clear trend towards 'off-the-shelf' purchases – a sensible choice for governments seeking to limit cost and project risk.

An absence of future substantial production orders, limited development of new technologies, and for some companies, over-dependence on defence – these surely are signals that a new round of consolidation of Europe's defence industrial base will be needed. Thus it was that discussions between BAE and EADS, which began in an analysis of why India had opted to buy the French *Rafale* rather than the *Typhoon*, quickly turned into merger talks. (*Typhoon* is assembled in BAE and EADS factories, while *Rafale*

is produced by Dassault, in which EADS has a 46% passive stake).

BAE was already seeing a decline in revenues. It had built a strong and profitable transatlantic defence business. However, the boom that BAE had experienced in constructing armoured vehicles for US forces in Iraq and Afghanistan was coming to an end. Partly because of this, the company's total sales fell 14% in 2011 to £19.1bn, though its profitability improved. In the first half of 2012, sales were down 10% on the same period in 2011, and the company noted that 'the risk of further reductions in US defence budgets remains'.

For its part, EADS has recorded steady growth in revenues, reaching €49bn in 2011, with Airbus responsible for about two-thirds of sales. By the end of 2011, the group's order backlog was €541bn, of which 91% belonged to Airbus. Sales of the other main subsidiaries, Cassidian (defence), Eurocopter (helicopters) and Astrium (space), have been steady without recording spectacular growth.

Thomas Enders and Ian King, chief executives of EADS and BAE respectively, argued in the *Financial Times* on 30 September 2012 that a merger was not a necessity, and that each company was strong. 'Together, we would become a business with a global footprint and a wider customer base,' the two men wrote. 'We would be better able to ride the cycles of civil aviation demand and defence spending. And we would be a business with the scale and stability to invest more in research and development, and a force for greater competition and growth. All of this would deliver tangible benefits to our customers in each of the defence, aerospace and security worlds.'

Dissenting voices

However, not all their major customers agreed. The German government, although owning no shares in EADS, viewed the matter essentially as one to be resolved between governments. Chancellor Angela Merkel apparently feared that German influence over the combined group would be unacceptably low.

Since the formation of EADS – in which governments had a major hand – German and French interests in EADS have been equal: on the German side, controlled by Daimler, and on the French side, a combination of the state and the Lagardère group. Daimler, however, wished to sell its 15% direct holding, and negotiations had been under way on a sale to the German government.

Following the announcement of merger talks, negotiations between the German and French governments produced a possible deal under which each would own 9% each of the future group. An 18% combined state holding would probably have been enough to satisfy the British government that the governments would not exert undue influence over the future company, though the US authorities would also have had to be persuaded on this point. But Berlin was reportedly concerned that the French government might later increase its stake by buying additional shares from Lagardère. The precise rationale prevailing in Berlin was obscure, but its effect was not. Merkel vetoed the deal and the companies had no option but to call it off.

However, the logic driving the industry towards further consolidation – as well as towards close collaboration between governments, as customers – will persist. And if it is compelling for manufacturers as large as BAE and EADS, it seems likely to be even more so for companies with smaller defence businesses, especially if they are particularly reliant on their military custom. Rationalisation among second- and third-tier defence suppliers therefore seems likely. While market factors will put considerable pressure on chief executives, these factors also offer opportunities to build, through mergers and acquisitions, new companies that can provide a stronger foundation for government customers and better long-term value for customers and shareholders. When budget pressures ease and governments can again afford to invest in new projects, both the companies and taxpayers would then be able to derive the benefits of rationalisation.

With the halting of the BAE–EADS talks, the first move was stymied. But market factors that argue for large-scale mergers could well prevail in the end over political constraints. Change has merely been postponed.

Chapter Two
Comparative defence statistics

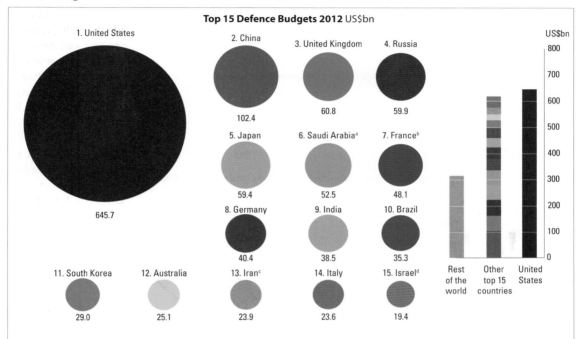

Top 15 Defence Budgets 2012 US$bn

1. United States — 645.7
2. China — 102.4
3. United Kingdom — 60.8
4. Russia — 59.9
5. Japan — 59.4
6. Saudi Arabia[a] — 52.5
7. France[b] — 48.1
8. Germany — 40.4
9. India — 38.5
10. Brazil — 35.3
11. South Korea — 29.0
12. Australia — 25.1
13. Iran[c] — 23.9
14. Italy — 23.6
15. Israel[d] — 19.4

US$bn: 800, 700, 600, 500, 400, 300, 200, 100, 0

Rest of the world / Other top 15 countries / United States

[a] Estimated spending; [b] Figures based on 2012 'credits de paiement', the French public-accounting definition for the actual level of financial resources allocated for 2012, as distinct from the higher 'autorisation d'engagement' figure (US$50.6bn), which includes funding permitted to be disbursed in future years; [c] Based on Iranian official Rial–US dollar exchange rate (see p. 359); [d] Includes US Foreign Military Assistance.

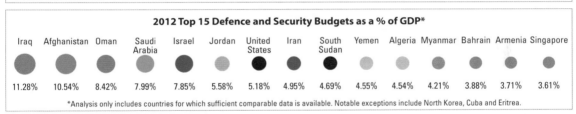

2012 Top 15 Defence and Security Budgets as a % of GDP*

Iraq	Afghanistan	Oman	Saudi Arabia	Israel	Jordan	United States	Iran	South Sudan	Yemen	Algeria	Myanmar	Bahrain	Armenia	Singapore
11.28%	10.54%	8.42%	7.99%	7.85%	5.58%	5.18%	4.95%	4.69%	4.55%	4.54%	4.21%	3.88%	3.71%	3.61%

*Analysis only includes countries for which sufficient comparable data is available. Notable exceptions include North Korea, Cuba and Eritrea.

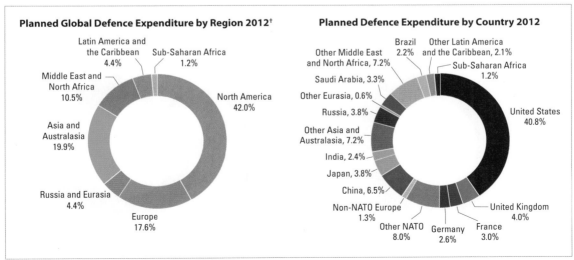

Planned Global Defence Expenditure by Region 2012†

- Latin America and the Caribbean 4.4%
- Sub-Saharan Africa 1.2%
- Middle East and North Africa 10.5%
- North America 42.0%
- Asia and Australasia 19.9%
- Russia and Eurasia 4.4%
- Europe 17.6%

Planned Defence Expenditure by Country 2012

- Brazil 2.2%
- Other Latin America and the Caribbean, 2.1%
- Other Middle East and North Africa, 7.2%
- Sub-Saharan Africa 1.2%
- Saudi Arabia 3.3%
- Other Eurasia, 0.6%
- Russia, 3.8%
- United States 40.8%
- Other Asia and Australasia, 7.2%
- India, 2.4%
- Japan, 3.8%
- China, 6.5%
- Non-NATO Europe 1.3%
- United Kingdom 4.0%
- Other NATO 8.0%
- Germany 2.6%
- France 3.0%

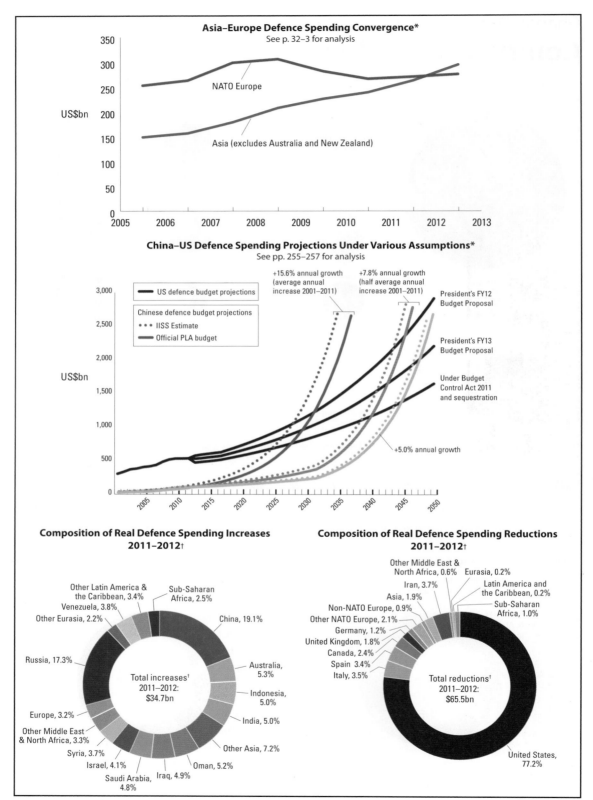

Asia–Europe Defence Spending Convergence*
See p. 32–3 for analysis

China–US Defence Spending Projections Under Various Assumptions*
See pp. 255–257 for analysis

Composition of Real Defence Spending Increases 2011–2012†

Composition of Real Defence Spending Reductions 2011–2012†

*At current prices and exchange rates †At constant 2010 prices and exchange rates

Selected C-130H *Hercules* operators

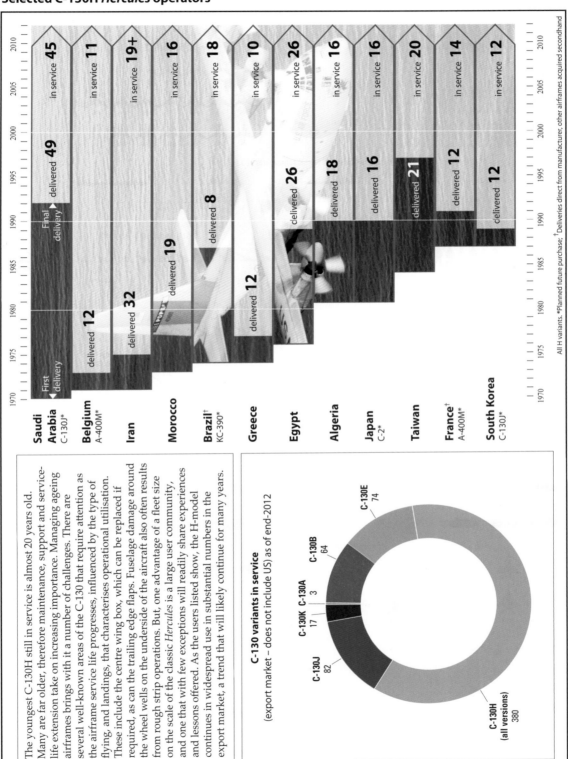

Saudi Arabia C-130J* First delivery · Final delivery · delivered **49** · in service **45**

Belgium A-400M* delivered **12** · in service **11**

Iran delivered **32** · in service **19+**

Morocco delivered **19** · in service **16**

Brazil[†] KC-390* delivered **8** · in service **18**

Greece delivered **12** · in service **10**

Egypt delivered **26** · in service **26**

Algeria delivered **18** · in service **16**

Japan C-2* delivered **16** · in service **16**

Taiwan delivered **21** · in service **20**

France[†] A-400M* delivered **12** · in service **14**

South Korea C-130J* delivered **12** · in service **12**

All H variants. *Planned future purchase; [†] Deliveries direct from manufacturer, other airframes acquired secondhand

The youngest C-130H still in service is almost 20 years old. Many are far older, therefore maintenance, support and service-life extension take on increasing importance. Managing ageing airframes brings with it a number of challenges. There are several well-known areas of the C-130 that require attention as the airframe service life progresses, influenced by the type of flying, and landings, that characterises operational utilisation. These include the centre wing box, which can be replaced if required, as can the trailing edge flaps. Fuselage damage around the wheel wells on the underside of the aircraft also often results from rough strip operations. But, one advantage of a fleet size on the scale of the classic *Hercules* is a large user community, and one that with few exceptions will readily share experiences and lessons offered. As the users listed show, the H-model continues in widespread use in substantial numbers in the export market, a trend that will likely continue for many years.

C-130 variants in service
(export market – does not include US) as of end-2012

C-130E — 74
C-130B — 64
C-130A — 3
C-130K — 17
C-130J — 82
C-130H (all versions) — 380

Key defence statistics

Strategic

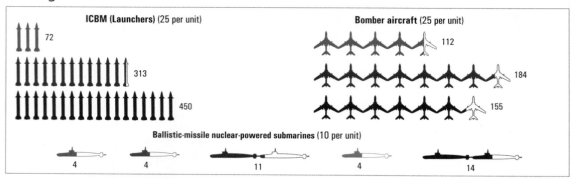

ICBM (Launchers) (25 per unit)   72   313   450

Bomber aircraft (25 per unit)   112   184   155

Ballistic-missile nuclear-powered submarines (10 per unit)   4   4   11   4   14

Manoeuvre

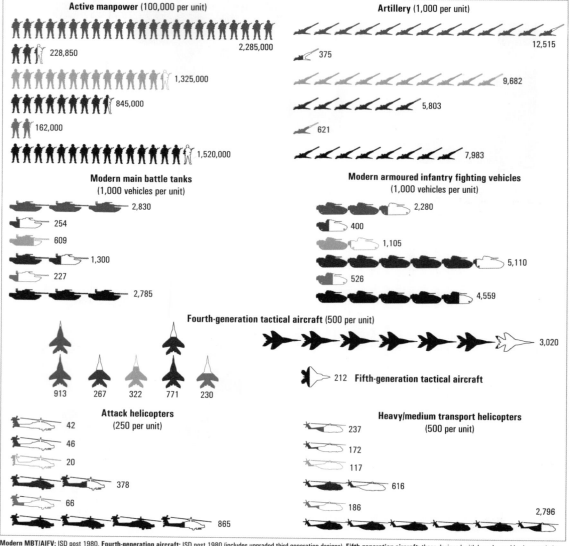

Active manpower (100,000 per unit)
2,285,000
228,850
1,325,000
845,000
162,000
1,520,000

Artillery (1,000 per unit)
12,515
375
9,682
5,803
621
7,983

Modern main battle tanks (1,000 vehicles per unit)
2,830
254
609
1,300
227
2,785

Modern armoured infantry fighting vehicles (1,000 vehicles per unit)
2,280
400
1,105
5,110
526
4,559

Fourth-generation tactical aircraft (500 per unit)
913   267   322   771   230
3,020

212 **Fifth-generation tactical aircraft**

Attack helicopters (250 per unit)
42
46
20
378
66
865

Heavy/medium transport helicopters (500 per unit)
237
172
117
616
186
2,796

Modern MBT/AIFV: ISD post 1980. **Fourth-generation aircraft:** ISD post 1980 (includes upgraded third-generation designs). **Fifth-generation aircraft:** those designed with low-observable characteristics as a fundamental design driver

Projection

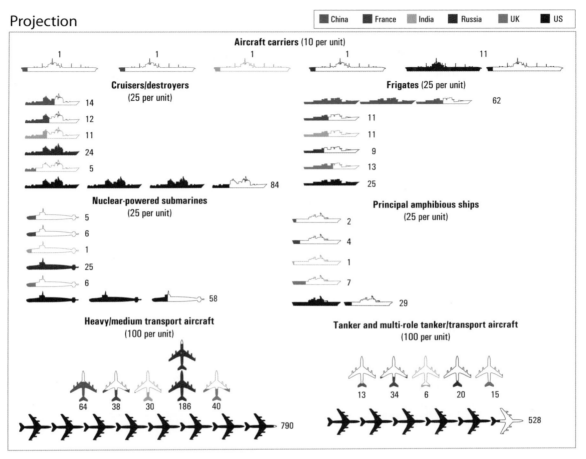

Aircraft carriers (10 per unit)

China 1 · France 1 · India 1 · Russia 1 · UK 11 · US

Cruisers/destroyers (25 per unit)
- 14
- 12
- 11
- 24
- 5
- 84

Frigates (25 per unit)
- 62
- 11
- 11
- 9
- 13
- 25

Nuclear-powered submarines (25 per unit)
- 5
- 6
- 1
- 25
- 6
- 58

Principal amphibious ships (25 per unit)
- 2
- 4
- 1
- 7
- 29

Heavy/medium transport aircraft (100 per unit)
- 64
- 38
- 30
- 186
- 40
- 790

Tanker and multi-role tanker/transport aircraft (100 per unit)
- 13
- 34
- 6
- 20
- 15
- 528

ISTAR

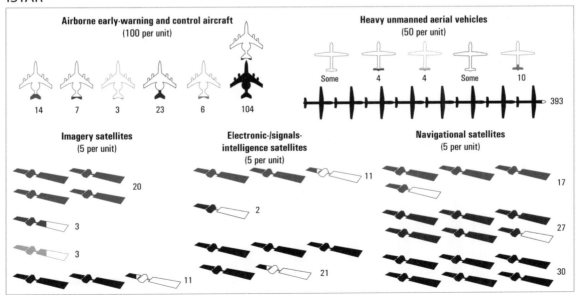

Airborne early-warning and control aircraft (100 per unit)
- 14
- 7
- 3
- 23
- 6
- 104

Heavy unmanned aerial vehicles (50 per unit)
- Some
- 4
- 4
- Some
- 10
- 393

Imagery satellites (5 per unit)
- 20
- 3
- 3
- 11

Electronic-/signals-intelligence satellites (5 per unit)
- 11
- 2
- 21

Navigational satellites (5 per unit)
- 17
- 27
- 30

IEDs and the rise of the MRAP

This graphic shows the number of IED attacks in Iraq and Afghanistan from 2004–2011 and the number of mine-resistant ambush protected (MRAP) vehicles fielded by US and other forces in the same time period. The bottom graph shows US, Coalition and NATO fatalities in the same period. In Iraq, the US surge reduced IED attacks and the introduction of the MRAP reduced Coalition fatalities. The deployment of the MRAP to Afghanistan from 2009 onwards means that, despite a rise in IED attacks, US and NATO fatalities were less than they might have been and, in 2011, started to fall.

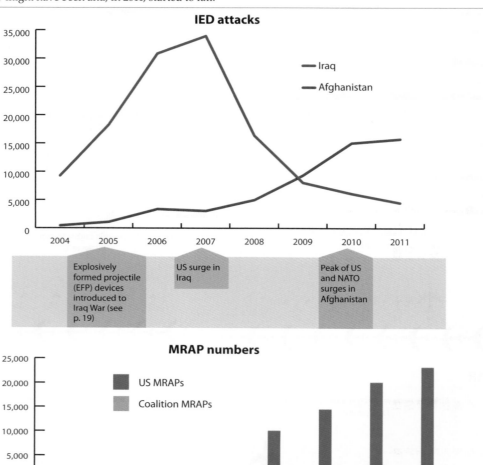

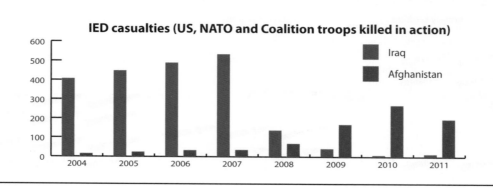

Sea-denial capabilities for selected countries in East Asia

Over the past 20 years, East Asia has witnessed significant changes in the weaponry fielded by regional states, moving towards more technologically advanced guided missiles and submarine-launched torpedoes.

Ship-based anti-ship missile launchers

While anti-ship missile launchers stayed relatively stable for much of the 1990s and 2000s, this was largely owing to the retirement of Soviet-era equipment in China. In recent years, China has developed more modern surface combatants with more advanced missiles, such as the Type-022 fast-attack craft, each of which carries eight tubes. At the same time, other governments have started to adopt such technology in greater numbers.

Heavyweight (533 mm) torpedo tubes

As with anti-ship missiles, torpedo tubes dropped off significantly in the early 1990s, as Soviet-era torpedo craft were phased out in countries such as China, North Korea and Vietnam. However, since then, more states have developed submarines, a key trend in current naval procurement, and hence the number of tubes available has levelled out. As further submarines are delivered, for instance with six *Kilo*-class en route to Vietnam and three Type 209s to Indonesia, these numbers are likely to increase further.

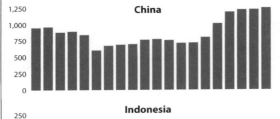

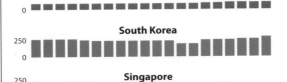

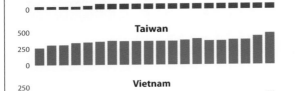

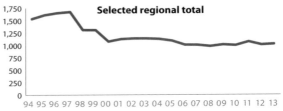

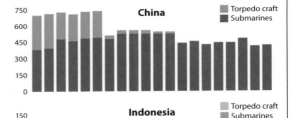

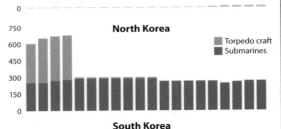

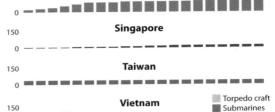

Sea-based anti-ship missile types in service: **2013: China** YJ-82*, YJ-1*, 3M54 *Klub**, 3M80/82, YJ-83, YJ-62, SY-1, HY-1, HY-2; **Indonesia** RGM-84A *Harpoon*, 3M55 *Yakhont*, MM-38 *Exocet*, MM-40 *Exocet* Block II, C-705; **Japan** UGM-84C *Harpoon**, SSM-1B, RGM-84C *Harpoon*; **North Korea** P-15 *Termit*; **South Korea** RGM-84C *Harpoon*, MM-38 *Exocet*; **Malaysia** MM-40 *Exocet*, MM-38 *Exocet*, *Otomat* Mk2; **Singapore** RGM-84C *Harpoon*; **Taiwan** RGM-84C/L *Harpoon*, *Hsiung Feng* II/III; **Vietnam** 3M24 *Uran*, P-15 *Termit*, KN-01; **1994: China** YJ-81*, HY-2; **Indonesia** RGM-84A *Harpoon*, MM-38 *Exocet*; **Japan** UGM-84C *Harpoon**, RGM-84C *Harpoon*, SSM-1B; **North Korea** P-15 *Termit*; **South Korea** RGM-84C *Harpoon*, MM-38 *Exocet*; **Malaysia** MM-38 *Exocet*; **Singapore** RGM-84C *Harpoon*; **Taiwan** *Hsiung Feng* I/II, RGM-84C *Harpoon*; **Vietnam** P-15 *Termit*
*Denotes may be/is submarine-launched

Revamping China's tactical air power

China's air force (PLAAF) and naval aviation arm are undergoing modernisation with significant changes in equipment and operational doctrine. Twenty years ago, the PLAAF was in effect a large but poorly equipped force intended only for homeland air defence, only just beginning to introduce modern combat aircraft types. In 1992 it had a combat aircraft strength just under 5,000; in 2012 this had been reduced to 1,900. It is now a smaller but far more capable force, equipped increasingly with fourth-generation multi-role fighters and associated air-to-air and air-to-surface weapons. China now also has at least two low-observable combat aircraft in development, the J-20 and J-21/31, and other still classified projects could yet come to light.

The PLAAF is benefitting from an increasingly capable inventory of air-to-surface weapons, with domestically developed systems now complementing previously acquired Russian missiles and guided bombs. Two decades ago, its air-to-ground weaponry was dominated by free-fall unguided bombs. The air force now fields a variety of electro-optical, radar, laser-guided and satellite-navigation augmented weaponry. The KD-88 family of stand-off air-to-surface missiles is now in service, as is the YJ/KD-63 land-attack cruise missile. An air-launched variant of the DH/CJ-10 is at least on the brink of being brought into the inventory, to provide the H-6 bomber with a 1,500km+ range cruise missile.

The air force's indigenous active radar-guided air-to-air missile is the PL-12. This is generally held to be a capable medium-range weapon, and is likely the basis also for a number of ongoing developments, including a compressed airframe design for internal carriage. The basic PL-12 entered service around 2005. During the 1990s, the only beyond-visual-range weapons likely available to the air force were provided by Russia, with the semi-active R-27 (AA-10A/C *Alamo*). Prior to the PL-12, national efforts to develop beyond-visual-range air-to-air missiles were less successful. The basic PL-12 also uses Russian subsystems.

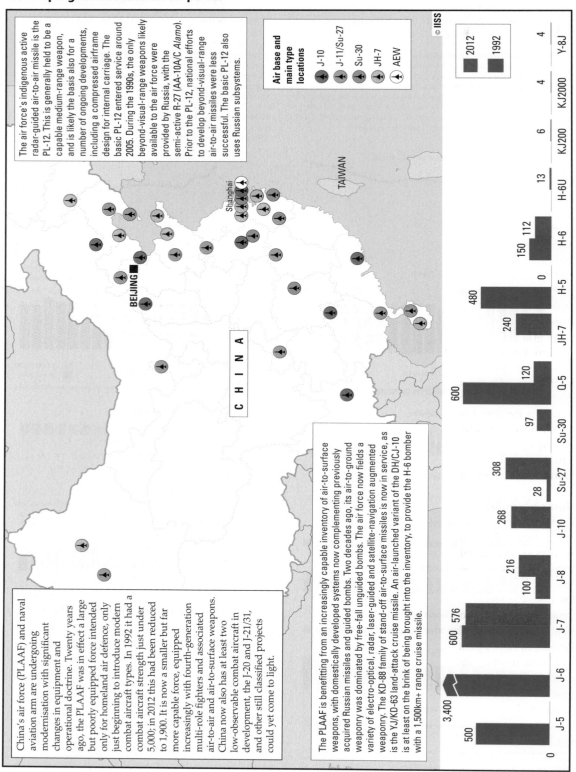

Air base and main type locations

J-10
J-11/Su-27
Su-30
JH-7
AEW

2012
1992

TAIWAN

Shanghai

BEIJING

C H I N A

© IISS

	J-5	J-6	J-7	J-8	J-10	Su-27	Su-30	Q-5	JH-7	H-5	H-6	H-6U	KJ2000	KJ200	Y-8J
2012	500	3,400	576	216	268	308	97	600	240	480	150	13	4	6	4
1992			600	100	28			120		0	112				

Chapter Three
North America

THE UNITED STATES

Washington began 2012 by unveiling new strategic guidance and ended the year with the last of its 'surge' forces exiting Afghanistan. Many of the remaining 68,000 will leave by the end of 2014 as the US withdraws from a combat role. It is, then, little wonder US Secretary of Defense Leon Panetta said the US armed forces were at a 'strategic turning point', with the pending transition to Afghan security control by the end of 2014 following the final withdrawal of US deployments to Iraq in late 2011. After a decade of complex wars centred on the land environment, the timeline for US disengagement provides the US Department of Defense (DoD) with the chance to reassess force structures, roles, and inventories, in part necessitated by sustained funding pressure on defence expenditure. The 2011 Budget Control Act required that the DoD axe US$487 billion from its spending plans over ten years – reflected in the president's FY2013 budget proposal – while also including the threat of sequestration. Though this is, in Panetta's view, a 'crazy, nutty tool', the possibility of sequestration coming into force nonetheless introduces unwelcome uncertainty with regard to future defence spending.

New strategies

That US forces were going to become smaller was not in doubt. They had been expanded since 2001, as the attacks on Afghanistan and Iraq turned into long-term missions. But new strategic guidance issued in January ('Sustaining US Global Leadership: Priorities for 21st Century Defense') said forces would no longer be sized 'to conduct large-scale, prolonged stability operations'. The aim was rather, according to Panetta, to have a joint force that was smaller, leaner, agile and flexible, able to work within a range of operational concepts and environments. The services would be expected to retain the expertise of a decade of war, including training coalition forces in counter-insurgency, and they would be 'able to reconstitute quickly or grow capabilities as needed'. How the US interprets the experience of the last 11 years of war will have implications for force development and force modernisation. It remains to be seen if the US will try to institutionalise adaptations made in the conduct of recent wars or turn away from recent experience, as it did after Vietnam.

One sentence in the strategic guidance document attracted particular attention: 'while the US military will continue to contribute to security globally, *we will of necessity rebalance towards the Asia-Pacific*' (p. 2). The Pentagon said this was driven by a number of considerations, including links between US economic and security interests and the Asia-Pacific. But the 'rebalance' was also intended to signal to allies and potential rivals alike that the US will be increasingly engaged in the security of the region, a reflection of the interests noted above and of the emergence of China as a regional competitor in terms of both commerce and its growing military capability. Europe, meanwhile, where most countries were now 'producers of security than consumers of it', was to see a slightly reduced presence. In the Middle East, the objective was to counter 'violent extremists and destabilizing threats, as well as upholding our commitment to allies and partner states'. Maintaining and developing security partnerships was seen as a way of 'sharing the costs and responsibilities of global leadership'. While a multinational approach to security problems is clearly essential, the experience of the wars in Afghanistan and Iraq have highlighted the limits of working through proxy forces as well as the limits of coalition warfare.

Over time, rebalancing does seem likely to be significant, fuelled by Washington's interests in Asia, as well as its concerns over anti-access and area-denial (A2/AD) strategies that might be employed by potential regional competitors. But it will be a long-term process: for example, the funding for a new long-range bomber will take many years to bear fruit; its in-service date is due in the 2020s. Additionally, some of these moves have actually been under way for some time: the US was building up its base in Guam, with additions to Andersen Field air base and the island's submarine facilities, long before the rebalance was announced, and also long before it became apparent that marines relocating from Okinawa would find a home there (see map p. 267). At the same time, much of the rebalance was diplomatic, with officials stressing that renewed US attention to allies in the Asia-Pacific had already bolstered their confidence and restored a psychological balance in relation to Beijing.

The administration of US President Barack Obama was starting to redraw a world role for the US that it saw as more sustainable, though still robust and assertive. But the strategy depended on having capable partner states, and as the IISS *Strategic Survey 2012* puts it, 'the strategic weight of the European partner was now in doubt' (p. 91). Meanwhile, the death of Osama bin Laden in 2011, as well as the continued campaign to target remaining al-Qaeda command structures, underscored 'that Obama's strategic retrenchment and earlier efforts at diplomatic conciliation in no way indicate a less robust defence of core US interests. "There's a name", wrote the respected analyst Peter Beinert, "for the strategy the Obama administration is increasingly pursuing from the Persian Gulf to the South China Sea: offshore balancing."'

For all the talk of the military rebalancing to Asia, the steps taken towards this in the FY2013 budget, issued on 13 February 2012, were modest. Troop numbers in Europe were slated to drop by 10,000 to about 70,000, while marines were to be deployed to Australia and Littoral Combat Ships to Singapore. In the Middle East, the number of troops deployed will be significantly below their peak level, but substantial assets remain in Kuwait and other locations such as Bahrain (US Fifth Fleet and NAVCENT HQ) and Qatar (home to a Combined Air Operations Center and a USAF Central Command forward-deployed headquarters). Since its themes had been foreshadowed in previous announcements, the main interest in the budget was in the detail of the many cuts proposed for the military and its equipment programmes. But the budget's publication was the beginning rather than the end of the process: it shifted battles about specific reductions beyond the Pentagon hierarchy and into the political arena.

With the re-election of Obama in November 2012, it is likely that, barring a strategic shock, the course

Service specifics

Over the next six years the US Army will contract from 570,000 to 490,000 regulars, while the marines will reduce from 202,000 to 182,000. Eight out of the army's 45 regular Brigade Combat Teams (BCTs) will be disbanded, including two of the four currently based in Europe. *Stryker* BCT numbers will remain at six. Funding for the army's Ground Combat Vehicle (to replace the *Bradley*) amounts to $640 million for R&D. However, some army and marine corps capabilities will see a moderate rise in funding: the number of active combat aviation brigades will increase from 12 to 13, and the fleet of unmanned aerial vehicles (UAVs) will grow, as will army special operations forces and cyber capabilities. The marines will lose one of their nine infantry regiment HQs and four regular infantry battalions. They will retain an amphibious fleet of large vessels, though in lower numbers than originally intended.

The US Navy was to decommission seven *Ticonderoga*-class cruisers and two *Whidbey Island*-class dock landing ships early. *Ticonderoga*-class vessels *Cowpens*, *Anzio*, *Vicksburg* and the BMD-capable *Port Royal* will decommission in FY2013, with the remainder, along with the *Whidbey Island*-class vessels, in FY2014. Some shipbuilding programmes will be delayed: construction of the second *Ford*-class aircraft carrier will now take six years rather than four; the second *America*-class amphibious assault ship will be delayed by one year; and

the *Ohio*-class submarine replacement – the SSBN(X) – will be delayed by two years.

Purchasing plans for the F-35 were scaled down and decelerated, partly reflecting technical problems encountered in the aircraft's development. The level of simultaneous development within the programme has magnified technical problems. The air force will take delivery of 166 F-35As by FY2017, rather than the previously planned 264. The navy will acquire 69 fewer F-35Bs and Cs over the FY2013–17 period than previously projected. It will instead purchase 41 F-35B short take-off and vertical landing aircraft and 37 F-35C carrier variants over this five-year period. The marines will proceed with plans to acquire the F-35B, which had previously been in question. Slowing delivery of the F-35 for the three services will save $15.1bn between 2013 and 2017. However, as a result, up to 350 of the air force's F-16s will be put through a life-extension programme. Air Mobility Command will see the decommissioning of 27 C-5A *Galaxy* strategic transport and 65 C-130H *Hercules* tactical transport aircraft, as well as all 38 planned C-27J *Spartan* intra-theatre-transport airlifters, reflecting the drawdowns in Iraq and Afghanistan, as well as the reduction in strength of the army and marines. The scrapping of 11 RC-26s, one E-8 JSTARS and 18 RQ-4 Block 30 *Global Hawk* UAVs will have an impact on intelligence, surveillance and reconnaissance fleets.

for defence capability development and spending will remain set. The rhetorical atmosphere in Congress is unlikely to improve, but the chance for compromise over issues such as sequestration may, paradoxically, have increased: before the November elections, neither side had an incentive to back down or make concessions. Planned reductions in the US armed forces, however, need to be put into context. Compared to total inventories, reductions are fairly modest, while defence capability more broadly does not simply stem from the number of platforms a country possesses. It may be true that, as former Defense Secretary Robert Gates said in 2011, 'a smaller military, no matter how superb, will be able to go fewer places and be able to do fewer things', but US forces will still be the most technologically capable, well-equipped combat experienced and globally deployable in the world.

Developing the Joint Force 2020

Much attention was paid, earlier in 2012, to concepts such as the Joint Operational Access Concept (JOAC) and ideas around the Air–Sea Battle (ASB). As discussed in the essay on pp. 29–31, ASB is designed to preserve freedom of access and manoeuvre by countering adversaries' networks and weapons platforms from the start of any conflict. The intention is for the ASB to inform national strategy, force posture, and budgets, but not to act as a specific proposal for a particular scenario. The JOAC was released within two weeks of the official announcement of the 'rebalance' to Asia, and is intended to provide the 'overarching concept under which we can nest other concepts dealing with more specific aspects of anti-access/area-denial challenges, such as the Air–Sea Battle'. Essentially, this means a closer working relationship between the services, including the use of dispersed forces in several bases to operate on 'multiple, independent lines of operations', and bringing these forces together to 'manoeuvre directly against key operational objectives from strategic distance'. The concepts seem appropriate and important as far as they go, but beg the question of access for what. It seems that the next step will be to determine how ASB fits in to an overarching concept that addresses the fundamental political and military sources of national-security threats – sources that are land-based and pose complicated problems that are unlikely to be solved solely through the application of military force onto land from the aerospace and maritime domains.

> **Joint Force Missions:**
> - Counter-terrorism and irregular warfare
> - Deter and defeat aggression
> - Project power despite A2/AD challenges
> - Counter WMD
> - Operate effectively in cyberspace and space
> - Maintain a safe, secure, and effective nuclear deterrent
> - Defend the homeland and provide support to civil authorities
> - Provide a stabilising presence
> - Conduct stability and counter-insurgency operations
> - Conduct humanitarian, disaster relief and other operations

The Capstone Concept for Joint Operations: Joint Force 2020 (CCJO), released by the Joint Chiefs of Staff in September 2012, aimed 'to establish a bridge from the new strategic guidance to subordinate concepts, force development guidance, and follow-on doctrine'. It looks wider than ASB and JOAC, trying to address, according to the document's introduction, a paradox that while 'the world is trending toward greater stability overall, destructive technologies are available to a wider and more disparate range of adversaries'. CCJO proposes an ambitious concept of 'globally integrated operations' where forces, positioned around the globe, can quickly combine with other services or partner nations, across domains, at differing echelons, in different areas.

The Joint Force is tasked with ten primary missions, including counter-terrorism and irregular warfare, projecting power despite A2/AD challenges, countering weapons of mass destruction (WMD) and operating in outer space and cyberspace. The requirement to conduct stability and counter-insurgency operations remains. These will be conducted in the face of trends (seen by DoD as continuities) such as WMD proliferation, the rise of modern competitor states and competition for resources. Differences include a certain levelling of the ground across geographies and among adversaries: 'the diffusion of advanced technology in the global economy means that middleweight militaries and non-state actors can now muster weaponry once available only to superpowers; while the proliferation of cyber and space weapons, precision munitions, ballistic missiles, and anti-access and area denial capabilities will grant more adversaries the ability to inflict devastating losses.'

This concept is written with lessons of recent wars and strategic shifts – such as those in the Middle East and North Africa – firmly in mind. Adversaries will, it says, 'continue to explore asymmetric ways to employ both crude and advanced technology to exploit US vulnerabilities', while the growth and importance of cyberspace and the diffusion of advanced technologies across states and to individuals can mean a reduction in the importance of geographic boundaries in the growth and escalation of potential threats. Meanwhile, military actions 'will receive intense media scrutiny, a dynamic that potentially invests otherwise inconsequential actions with strategic importance'. DoD envisages a 'globally postured Joint Force' meeting the challenges of this security environment through 'globally integrated operations'. Flexible, prepositioned or forward deployed, 'networks of forces and partners will form, evolve, dissolve, and reform in different arrangements in time and space with significantly greater fluidity than today's Joint Force'. With the Pentagon having to choose carefully what capabilities to retain and which to reduce, DoD is in the meantime working to adopt concurrent strategies such as the drives to mobilise influence through partner states and to integrate effectively across the whole of government.

Arrangements like these globally postured forces might seem like a way of maximising value in an environment of increasingly complex threats, but they are costly in other ways: investments in equipment storage and maintenance, in intelligence specialists in a broad range of areas – including technical and cultural expertise – and, perhaps more fundamentally, in the required level of training for personnel – will be substantial. The latter is vital to ensure operations with partners work as seamlessly as possible, and also to ensure the endurance of the principle of mission command. Cyber and global strike are identified as options in 'rapidly bring combat power to bear' and while 'massed formations will remain an option ... increasingly they will not be the option of choice'. The document does seem to point to a developing role for technology-focused capabilities: the final page says that it 'plans for cyberspace, space, special operations, global strike, and global intelligence, surveillance and reconnaissance capabilities to play a more pronounced role in future joint operations'. But at the same time, it references real-world lessons: operations need to be increasingly discriminate to minimise unintended consequences (difficult though this may be to ensure), while the increasing ability

of adversaries to disrupt friendly-force technical capacities means training has to be conducted in '"worst case" degraded environments'.

Some within the armed services, notably in the army and marine corps, are concerned that budgetary pressures may encourage a return of late 1990s defence theories (such as the 'Revolution in Military Affairs') that emerging technologies will revolutionise warfare and permit the 'smaller and leaner' forces called for in the January 2012 strategic guidance to prevail in future conflicts through 'technological, joint, and networked advantage'. One lesson of the wars since 9/11 is that conflicts evolve in response to military engagements but also to local dynamics that themselves can change in response to intervening states' political and military activity, among other factors. Flexibility, agility and scalability of forces will be central to addressing future contingencies and, while doing more with less is a challenge, sometimes numbers count. The Capstone Concept tries to balance all these imperatives, and it 'recognizes that much of the nature of conflict in the world is enduring ... Even when waged with increasingly sophisticated technologies, the conduct of military operations remains a fundamentally human enterprise.' Within DoD, another challenge will be actually developing the new concepts of operation that have been advanced to cope with an increasingly complex global environment, including those that advocate increasingly deep cooperation across the armed services.

Army and Marine Corps

The US Army and US Marine Corps are confronting an environment dominated by fiscal pressure and a new national defence strategy. The active US Army plans a gradual reduction from 570,000 to 490,000 troops, while the active marine corps is reducing from 202,000 to 182,000 by 2016. Leaders in both services are concerned that further reductions may render the services too small for future contingencies and, as noted above, might encourage a return of technology-centric theories of conflict. The army and marine corps primarily operate on land, where geography, people, politics and culture complicate military operations and limit the effects of technology, and these services are likely to struggle against a tendency to define the problem of future conflict in a way that regards technology as decisive and recent wartime experiences as aberrational. During the past decade, the army and marine corps have adapted their doctrine, training, organisation and force modernisation efforts to the demands of wars in Afghanistan and Iraq. Both services, which have seen the growth of a combat-proven generation of soldiers, are engaged in what seems to be the final stages of their involvement in direct combat in Afghanistan and are endeavouring to consolidate relevant lessons of the last 11 years of war whilst preparing for future contingencies.

Doctrine

The services published joint counter-insurgency doctrine in October 2009 and are working on a revised manual. The army has published new doctrine on army operations, mission command and army leadership and all army tactical doctrine is due to be revised in the next two years. Those manuals will reveal which lessons of recent conflicts the army intends to institutionalise. The first of these are driving a renewed focus on leader development and education. Perhaps most significant in the emerging doctrine is renewed emphasis in both services on disciplined initiative at lower levels and the conduct of decentralised operations based on mission orders.

Training

Both services continue to conduct mission-rehearsal exercises to prepare units for combat and advisory duty in Afghanistan, but recent training exercises such as the army's brigade-sized exercises in its training centres have been designed to improve proficiency in major combat operations, or what the army is calling 'decisive action scenarios'. With more forces returning to the US, the army is in the process of determining how to conduct effective training at 'home stations' using combinations of live exercises, virtual reality and constructive simulations, and computer-based games. With an eye to their amphibious role, and a desire to return to an 'afloat posture' after recent land-focused operations, marine corps exercises have emphasised brigade-sized amphibious operations. Though recent attention has focused on presumed future roles for the air force and navy, both the army and marine corps are also focused on defeating, as part of a broader joint-force effort, A2/AD threats. In March 2012, the two services published a joint concept entitled 'Gaining and Maintaining Access'. Army and special-operations exercises are designed around forcible entry scenarios such as airfield seizures. The marine corps, in addition to over-the-horizon amphibious assaults, is focusing on ship-to-objective manoeuvres to envelop enemy forces and then clear backwards to a beach or port facility. Both services are keen to retain innovations in individual training, particularly in the areas of small-arms marksmanship and cognitive skills such as the army's advanced situational awareness and comprehensive soldier fitness training and the marine corps' combat hunter programme.

Organisation

Leaders of both services have pledged not to allow them to become hollow as they reduce the strength of their active forces. The army will retain a mix of heavy, medium and light brigade combat teams. Active duty brigades will be reduced from the current total of 43, but will bolster capabilities as armoured and infantry brigades will add a third manoeuvre battalion. While some have argued that the mix of active duty brigades should include fewer armoured brigades and more light infantry brigades, recent combat experience and the anticipated need for mobile protected firepower in future contingency operations argue, other experts say, in favour of retaining more armoured brigades in the active force. Moreover, while lighter organisations appear attractive due to speed and ease of deployment, those organisations often lack the mobility, firepower and protection to accomplish the mission. Operations in Iraq during and after 2003, for example, proved the continued utility of the tank. And while the army's armoured brigades have demonstrated the ability to 'lighten up' for operations, it is recognised that lighter forces would not have the capability to easily 'heavy up' for contingencies requiring mobility and protection. For these reasons, and because the training requirements for an armoured brigade make it difficult for reserve forces to maintain proficiency, the army is likely to retain at least ten armoured brigades in its active force. In the coming year, focus will likely sharpen on the division and corps level, with the army considering options to enhance its ability to conduct multiple brigade operations in a new theatre during contingency operations. Emphasis is likely to be on operating as part of a joint and multinational force, deployment, logistics and reconnaissance and security operations. The marine corps is emphasising retaining critical enablers across its air–ground–logistics task forces as it reduces numbers of infantry battalions, artillery battalions, logistics battalions and tactical air squadrons to a level slightly below that which it maintained prior to September 2001.

Force modernisation

In recent years force modernisation was driven by the immediate demands of combat in Iraq and Afghanistan: large and expensive programmes such as the army's Future Combat System and the marine corps' Expeditionary Fighting Vehicle were cancelled. The numbers of unmanned aerial vehicles and specialised technical intelligence capabilities have proven critical to conducting counter-insurgency operations against elusive enemy organisations. Countering the enemy in Iraq and Afghanistan and, in particular, the threat of improvised explosive devices, also required new armoured vehicles, jammers, robots, detection devices and a broad range of intelligence and surveillance capabilities (see essay, p. 16). Both services added protection to existing armoured vehicles and procured, after 2007, heavily armoured mine-resistant ambush-protected vehicles (MRAPs). The MRAP programme will have delivered approximately 28,000 vehicles by the end of 2014. Both services are now working to integrate many of the adaptations and innovations of the last decade, as well as decide which capabilities to retain and how to structure forces accordingly, whilst modernising their forces in preparation for future contingencies.

Army modernisation priorities include its tactical communications network and the Ground Combat Vehicle (GCV). The army is seeking to replace analogue radios with digital systems that can be periodically upgraded and to field those systems to dismounted squads as well as place them on combat vehicles. The GCV, an infantry fighting vehicle, is meant to transport a nine-soldier infantry squad under protection with sufficient precision direct firepower to overwhelm enemy forces in encounter actions. MRAPs have improved protection for soldiers, but the vehicles cannot carry sufficient numbers of infantry, are largely road bound (and therefore travel on predictable routes), and cannot provide precision direct firepower. The army's wheeled *Stryker* infantry carrier, although it can move a full infantry squad, is significantly limited in firepower, protection and off-road mobility. The *Bradley* fighting vehicle has been continuously improved since it entered service in the mid-1980s, but requires dismounted squads to link up on the ground, is vulnerable to underbelly attack, and seems to be at its capacity for further electronic and digital enhancements. The GCV programme, therefore, is seen by the army as critical to preserving its advantages in close combat combined-arms operations. The army is also advancing a broad range of capabilities to improve the combat effectiveness of its dismounted squads. These include a new counter-defilade weapon, the XM-25, and over 90 improvements to weapons, optics and equipment. A major effort is underway to lighten the combat load: the heavy weights that soldiers now carry have reduced their agility and endurance.

The army and marine corps are both funding the Joint Light Tactical Vehicle (JLTV) programme as a replacement for the HMMWV. And the marine corps is increasingly focused on developing 'connectors' to accomplish amphibious assaults and sustain combat inland with tanks, artillery and engineers. The success of army and marine corps modernisation programmes depends, in large measure, on convincing their own defence officials that the improved capability justifies the expense. While ground-force modernisation programmes are not as expensive as many aircraft and ship modernisation programmes, a critical challenge for army and marine corps officials is to communicate the relevance of these desired capabilities to defence officials, with renewed scrutiny on the importance of ground forces as a component of joint forces in future conflicts.

Navy and Coast Guard

Navy capabilities are key to both the rebalance to Asia and emerging doctrines and concepts related to A2/AD capabilities. They were central to Defense Secretary Panetta's speech concerning the US rebalance to Asia at the 2012 IISS Shangri-La Dialogue in Singapore. Panetta said that 'the navy will reposture its forces from today's roughly 50/50 split between the Pacific and the Atlantic to about a 60/40 split between those oceans'. But when examined in detail, the only addition to capacity in East Asia will be the four Littoral Combat Ships to be deployed to Singapore, with three amphibious vessels rotated through the region and two Joint High-speed Vessels (JHSVs) deployed there. A stronger presence on the US Pacific coast through SOUTHCOM, with ten patrol craft, two Littoral Combat Ships and two JHSVs replacing two cruisers/destroyers, one amphibious vessel and one frigate leads to a higher hull count, but not necessarily an increase in warfighting capability.

The navy's rebalance to Asia started more than a decade ago. The forward deployment of three nuclear-powered submarines to Guam, a process that began in 2002 and was completed by 2007, signalled the growing weight of naval forces in the region. Guam has come to assume a greater importance in

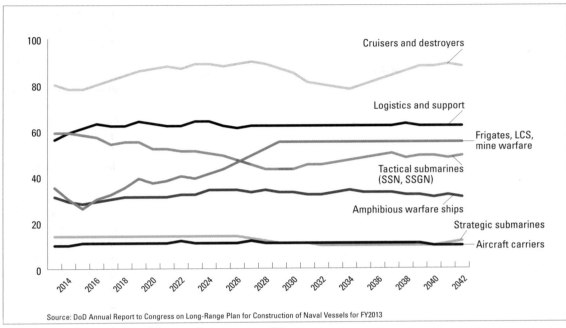

Figure 3 **US Navy: planned future fleet composition**

the Pentagon's Pacific strategy, a fact highlighted by the agreement to shift to the island more than half of the 9,000 marines relocating from Okinawa.

Another reason that the increase in capability in the Pacific is rather modest stems from the requirement to station vessels in other, possibly unstable regions, as well as from the limited projected growth of the fleet in coming years. A plan to field a combat fleet of 313 ships was first announced in 2006. The 313 plan has never formally been dropped but now seems highly improbable given successive cuts to shipbuilding and early retirement schedules for vessels, most recently in the FY2013 budget that proposed the early retirement of seven *Ticonderoga*-class cruisers. The current planned peak is 307 vessels, only to be reached by 2041 (see Figures 3–4).

Within this total, the proportion of smaller surface combatants will increase significantly, due to ambitions for a fleet of 55 Littoral Combat Ships. In the future, these could comprise around one-sixth of the entire fleet, reflecting current concerns over brown-water operations and maritime-security roles suitable for smaller, more flexible vessels. The two classes of LCS vessel, the *Freedom* and the *Independence*, are both multi-role ships with modular designs allowing the vessels' role to be modified by swapping mission packages. The third LCS was commissioned in September 2012, four years after the first.

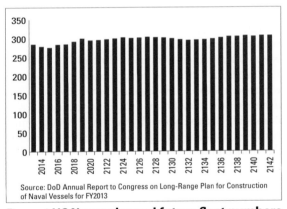

Figure 4 **US Navy: planned future fleet numbers**

Various problems have beset the programme. The first vessel that will be deployed, the *Freedom*, will have an additional 20 berths because the minimal-manning concept, which relied on just 40 core crew (plus a further 35 to 40 sailors to operate embarked aircraft and mission packages), proved problematic to introduce, with concerns over safety and operational effectiveness. The same vessel suffered 16 cracks, damaging on-board equipment, in its first 30 months after launch; then, in March–April 2012, it had to be laid up to fix a broken shaft seal that had caused minor flooding. Meanwhile, the second LCS, the *Independence*, suffered 'aggressive galvanic corrosion pitting within all four of the water jet tunnels and water jet cone assemblies', according to a June 2011 navy statement.

Initially, it was intended that the ships' modular mission packages would be able to change over in a matter of days, but press reports in July 2012 suggested the process may instead take weeks. Assessments in mid-2012 also reportedly judged that the LCS was unable to fulfil three of six core missions: forward presence, sea control and power projection. The cancellation of the Non-line of Sight Launch System (NLOS-LS) was also a significant setback for the LCSs' weapons package. The navy released an information paper in August 2012 refuting or explaining all of these alleged problems, specifically stating that, for instance, mission packages could be installed within 96 hours, but the programme has nonetheless suffered from poor media relations.

The costs of the vessel have also ballooned. In 2006, a cost cap of US$220m each was introduced from the fifth and sixth vessels; this was raised to US$460m in January 2008 for vessels procured in FY2008 and after; the cost cap was deferred for two years in October 2008; and finally was increased to US$480m per vessel with certain costs excluded and with a proviso that the secretary of the navy could waive the cap under certain conditions.

The LCS is not the only programme to suffer from controversy over affordability: the *Zumwalt*-class destroyer was in 1998 costed at US$35.5bn for 32 ships, or roughly US$1bn apiece. By the time the programme had been cut to the now planned three vessels in 2009, the costs had fallen, but only to US$10.6bn, or more than US$3bn apiece. In addition, development costs rose from US$2.3bn to US$10.4bn; including these raises the price tag for each ship to US$7bn. Further construction of *Zumwalt*-class destroyers is possible, but given their cost, size (roughly 50% larger than *Arleigh Burke*-class destroyers) and limitations (including a lack of anti-ballistic missile radars), the class does not fit easily into the navy's current view of requirements. It is feasible that a less expensive alternative may follow, in much the same way as the *Virginia*-class attack submarines followed the larger and more expensive *Seawolf*-class in the 2000s, but this appears to counter the current trend for smaller, flexible ships. For similar budgetary and applicability reasons, the CG(X) programme was cancelled in 2010; the *Arleigh Burke*-class has been extended and Flight III will be upgraded to act in a ballistic-missile-defence role.

In contrast, submarine procurement has recently increased in an attempt to avoid a shortfall in fleet numbers. In FY2011, the construction rate for *Virginia*-class submarines was augmented to two boats per year. Even with this increase (currently, FY2014 is budgeted for just one submarine build, but all other years up to FY2018 are budgeted for two boats), the total number of nuclear-powered attack submarines is currently projected to fall to 43 between 2028 and 2030 (not including the four modified *Ohio*-class submarines, classified as SSGN rather than SSN in the US Navy) – less than half the 1987 peak of 97. To some extent, this drop in numbers may be compensated by an enlarged *Virginia*-class submarine from FY2019, with an additional mid-section 'Virginia Payload Module' that can add four further vertical-launch tubes to the boat and allow for 28 additional *Tomahawk* cruise missiles (taking the figure from 37 to about 65). Additional vertical-launch systems could be crucial around FY2028–2030, as this is the period in which the four modified *Ohio*-class submarines, each equipped with 24 vertical-launch tubes and the capacity to carry 154 *Tomahawks* per boat, will retire.

Naval aviation

Regardless of the delays to the F-35 programme – the navy and marines are buying the F-35C and F-35B respectively – the average age of the navy's aircraft fleet will actually fall over the next ten years as legacy types are replaced. The navy will, however, have to manage a tactical aircraft shortfall projected for the 2020s, while also securing longer than initially planned flying hours from its F/A-18E/F *Super Hornet* fighter fleet.

In 2010, the navy calculated it would be around 100 below its target strength for strike fighter aircraft. The FY2013 budget will, the navy believes, reduce this figure to less than 65 aircraft. 'The net effect of the … budget, which includes restructuring the F-35B/C ramp, along with the impact of reduced operational rates and force structure requirements put the [navy's] projected shortfall at a manageable level', Vice Admiral Mark Skinner, principal military deputy, assistant secretary of the navy (R&D and acquisition), told the Senate Armed Services Committee in May 2012.

While the navy now appears more sanguine about the shortfall it will face in the 2020s, there is more concern over USMC airframe numbers during the same period, primarily driven by an overall eight-year delay in the service's transition plan. In FY2011 the USMC AV-8B *Harrier* squadrons were scheduled to re-equip with the F-35B by 2022. In FY2012, this was moved to 2026, and in FY2013 this was extended further, to 2030. The latest move results from a reduction in the F-35 production rate in the early years of its manufacture, coupled with the *Harrier* fleet retaining more flight hours than the marines' legacy F/A-18 *Hornets*. The corps is also closely monitoring projected through-life costs for the F-35, which Skinner said remained a 'concern'.

The navy also continues to recapitalise its special mission fleets. The service will withdraw the last of its EA-6B electronic-warfare aircraft in 2015, as the type is replaced by the EA-18G. Some of the aircraft withdrawn from navy units will be transferred to the USMC until the type is retired in 2019. The FY2013 budget requested funding for a further 13 P-8A *Poseidon* maritime patrol aircraft. An initial operational capability is due in late 2013, with the last of the P-3C *Orions* due to be replaced during FY2018. Vertical lift recapitalisation continued with the USMC's MV-22 *Osprey* and the CH-53K *Sea Stallion* heavy-lift helicopter. A further 17 MV-22s were ordered as part of FY2013. The CH-53K is intended to replace the CH-53D/E. 2013 should be significant for the navy's Unmanned Combat Air System Carrier Demonstration (UCAS-D) project. Two air vehicles are now involved in the test programme, with carrier launch and recovery of the unmanned systems planned for 2013. The FY2013 budget, however, did see the Medium Range Maritime Unmanned Aerial System deferred 'indefinitely'.

Coast Guard

The US Navy is not the only maritime service to be suffering from budgetary concerns. The US Coast Guard is facing a flat budget for FY2013 of approximately US$6.79bn. This will allow the service to continue to replace its 12 ageing *Hamilton*-class cutters with the larger *Legend*-class cutters, with the fourth currently in production out of a total eight planned. The USCG is also prioritising the Arctic in its 2013 strategy. Despite lacking sufficient ice-strengthened hulls for Arctic operations, the USCG stated in 2012 that it would forward deploy to the region in anticipation of drilling in the High North. The budget for FY2013 includes the procurement of a new *Polar*-class icebreaker and investment in Alaskan infrastructure to sustain operations. However, as of September 2012, the USCG had only three icebreakers in service, with one, the USCG *Polar Star*, in reserve pending reactivation in 2013 and a second, the USCG *Polar Sea*, in reserve and slated for decommissioning.

Developments in American airpower

The 2014 drawdown in Afghanistan offers little respite for the US Air Force as it faces financial, operational and procurement challenges. Credited, with marine airpower, for playing a decisive role in helping remove the regimes in Afghanistan and Iraq, the air force was seen by some as slow to adapt when the situations in these theatres deteriorated and when an expanded set of capabilities, such as improved ISR, was required. There were tensions, for instance,

Towards the long-range bomber

The USAF is looking to increase five-fold the size of its stealthy long-range bomber force, beginning with the introduction of a new aircraft planned presently for the mid-2020s.

The ability to operate in a contested air environment at significant range from deployed bases is a core element of the broad requirement. The project, referred to as Long Range Strike-Bomber (LRS-B), is intended to bolster the USAF's ability to counter A2/AD tactics and technologies. Unlike previous bomber developments dating back beyond the B-52, the aircraft is being designed primarily for a conventional, rather than a nuclear, attack role. The aircraft will have a secondary nuclear capability. Michael Donley, Secretary of the Air Force, said 'we are building this airplane for conventional long-range strike. It will be nuclear capable ... but the focus ... is not the nuclear mission.'

Beyond its existence and basic budgetary data, the project is classified as a Special Access Programme, which is indicative of the sensitivity regarding some of the technology liable to be under consideration, along with possible demonstrator projects, and other still classified designs the bomber development could draw upon. Active stealth along with passive low observable techniques are likely being examined. Development will also explore the potential of the LRS-B being optionally crewed; this could include an uninhabited variant potentially for longer-endurance intelligence, surveillance and reconnaissance missions. The air force has a target unit cost of $550m per aircraft.

Complementing the bomber in meeting long-range strike missions, the air force is also pursuing a next-generation air-launched cruise missile to replace the AGM-86B.

Falcon fights on

The F-35A was originally intended to reach an initial operating capability with the USAF around the end of the first quarter of 2013, but delays have forced the service to plan on extending the life of its F-16s.

In an effort to cover a shortfall in combat aircraft caused by planned retirements and the F-35 delay, the air force aims to upgrade at least 300 F-16 Block 40/42 and 50/52 aircraft to sustain their combat capability and ensure the airframe remains structurally sound. The first Block 40 and 42 aircraft were delivered in 1989–90.

A combat avionics programmed extension suite (CAPES) includes equipping the aircraft with an active electronically scanned array (AESA) radar, improved cockpit displays and enhanced electronic warfare (EW) system, while a service life-extension programme (SLEP) is aimed at ensuring a minimum of a further 2,000 flight hours for the upgraded aircraft. The F-16 is certified presently for 8,000 flight hours. The SLEP will cover replacement or reworking of airframe structures liable otherwise to contribute to fatigue damage. For instance, bulkhead cracks have been identified in over two-thirds of the Block 40/52 fleet. CAPES will result in either a Raytheon or Northrop Grumman AESA being fitted to the F-16, similar to upgrade projects which have already been implemented to parts of the Air Force's F-15 fleet, and the navy's F/A-18E/F. AESA technology provides greater detection range and additional functionality and reliability compared to mechanically-scanned array radar. Better reliability will significantly reduce the through-life costs associated with radar maintenance and repair. The integration of a version of the ALQ-213 EW management system is intended to improve the aircraft's survivability in the threat environment envisaged to 2025 and beyond. The FY13 budget allocated $1.4 billion in the Future Years Defense Program toward sustaining the F-16 to 2025 and beyond.

---

between former Defense Secretary Robert Gates and the service over the initial pace of unmanned aerial vehicle (UAV) surveillance. The air force was also seen as not shouldering its share of the burden on the ground in Iraq and Afghanistan. In both these areas improvements occurred in time, but the air force's reputation suffered. This could affect the debate on defence resources in Washington, particularly as the air force finds itself in a position to appeal for more resources.

Future planning

Secretary of the Air Force Michael Donley and former chief of staff General Norton Schwartz might well be judged as having moved the air force back in support of the wars, as well as correcting nuclear security concerns. Their focus, arguably of necessity, was on the near term, but this may have been to the detriment of future planning. As Schwartz said in an interview prior to leaving post in August 2012, 'maybe we de-emphasised innovation more than we should have. We had some things to do early on, and we never really came back to pushing that innovative culture.'

Schwartz said he expected his successor, General Mark Welsh, to be more focused on fostering a culture of innovation; to restore a sense within the air force that the institution is engaged in helping shape the larger national-security debate as well as responding to it.

The Obama administration's new strategic guidance, and notably the rebalance to the Asia-Pacific, gives the force an opportunity to demonstrate that air power, in combination with other capabilities and forces, can help address important strategic challenges. The speed and reach of air force capabilities are ostensibly well-suited to the revised strategic guidance. However, to meet the demands of the rebalance, the air force will need to be able to accommodate and manage change in a cash-poor environment. It also needs to manage ageing fighter fleets with continuing uncertainty as to when it will begin to receive replacements, try to keep a future bomber programme within budget and schedule, and manage the changing relationship between active and reserve components. 'A smaller air force at a higher state of readiness' was how the outlook for the service was characterised by Lieutenant-General Janet Wolfenbarger, the military deputy within the office of the assistant secretary of the air force.

An emerging core doctrinal element of the rebalancing is the Air–Sea Battle (see p. 29). This is intended to more closely combine air and maritime domain operations to counter A2/AD capabilities, but the air force has yet to elaborate in detail, at least in public, the implications of such an approach.

Equipment issues

Commentators have pointed to the disparity in the air force's fighter, attack and bomber fleets, with too many short-range and too few long-range assets to give adequate reach in the Asia-Pacific. This could point to a need to invest in long-range capabilities such as the new bomber (see box, p. 57), even if it ultimately means fewer fighter or attack assets such as the F-35.

Other areas that will require further consideration in light of the rebalance include the air force's comparative lack of intelligence, surveillance and reconnaissance assets that can operate in the face of advanced air defences, as the suite of capabilities that has evolved over the past ten years has largely operated in a benign environment. Moreover, US space assets are relatively vulnerable to rudimentary attack. High levels of investment, however, continue in some mobility assets, not least due to the boost to these capabilities in recent decades to meet operational requirements.

As part of the planned reduction in defence expenditure, the air force is to reduce seven combat squadrons: five A-10 units, one F-16 and one F-15 aggressor squadron. F-16s will, however, remain in the inventory longer than originally foreseen as a result of the delays to the F-35. The aircraft will remain in service well beyond 2025, while the F-15C/D will be retained until 2030–35 and the F-15E, beyond 2035. As of mid-2012, the average age of US fighter aircraft was 22 years.

Such ageing fleets will place considerable demands on the systems required to support them, including suppliers in industry, and will increase pressure on the air force as it makes annual decisions about supporting legacy aircraft, buying F-35s and purchasing other needed capabilities. If few believe the air force will ultimately purchase its intended total of 1,763 F-35s, fewer still are prepared to venture how many it will actually buy.

The air force also needs to become accustomed to operating with less money. Even after the spending cuts that are now being implemented, the US defence budget is at an all-time high. The air force share of spending has declined from earlier eras and the service may make the case that its spending share should grow as missions expand, but it should still assume that it will have less funding than currently planned (see below). Were sequestration to come into effect, the air force would have to review its procurement programme fundamentally.

The new chief of staff, General Mark Welsh, will make the case that his air force, like that of earlier generations, has credible answers to the strategic challenges of this era, but those answers will have to be balanced with ideas linked closely to broader national strategy, particularly in the area of supporting key allies and partners, followed by focused investments in necessary capabilities, and perhaps most importantly by a willingness to make changes to the air force itself.

DEFENCE ECONOMICS

Macroeconomics

After initial signs of improving economic conditions in late 2011 and early 2012, the US economy lost momentum towards the middle of the year. This was in part caused by the deteriorating external environment (an escalating eurozone debt crisis, as well as slower than expected growth in emerging market economies), resulting in fears of contagion via trade channels and a consequent decline in risk appetite and asset prices. US households remain highly indebted. With the economy operating with a sizeable output gap, and with well-anchored long-term inflation expectations, the Federal Reserve continued monetary easing, focusing on reducing long-term interest rates. In June 2012, it announced a US$267bn expansion to the Maturity Extension Program ('Operation Twist'), originally designed for September 2011–July 2012, purchasing up to US$400bn in US Treasury securities with remaining maturities of 6–30 years, and selling an equivalent amount of US Treasury securities with maturities of three years or less. Additionally, in mid-September 2012 the Fed announced it would undertake a third, open-ended round of quantitative easing (QE3), which unlike previous episodes of QE did not have a defined end date and would continue indefinitely until the labour market outlook improved, provided that inflation levels remained low. Earlier, in January 2012, it extended by 18 months (through to mid-2014) its commitment to extraordinarily low interest rates.

The collapse in property prices – a quarter of households are still in negative equity and considerable excess supply remains – and resultant deterioration in household wealth continued to sap aggregate demand, business confidence and investment. Unemployment remained above 8%, and there were increased concerns over a rise in long-term unemployment. Overall, while the International Monetary Fund expects the US economy to grow by a moderate 2% in 2012, risks remained significant over much of the year. Additionally, the long-running

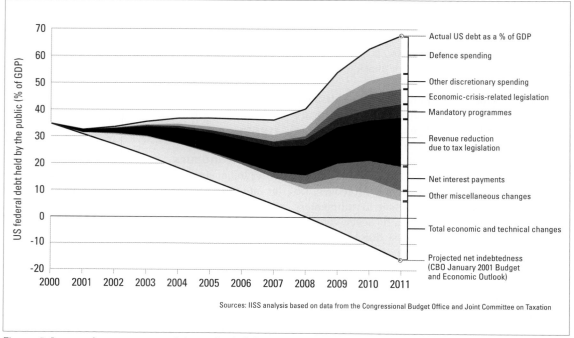

Figure 5 **Approximate composition of US debt increases 2001–2011 (% of GDP)**

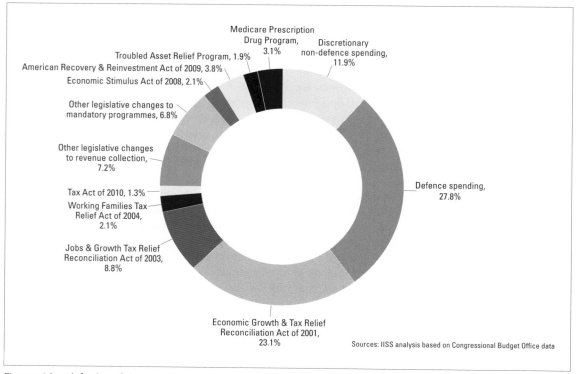

Figure 6 **Legislative drivers of recent increases in US public debt 2001–2011**

Figure 6 represents the approximate shaded areas of the legislative items contained in Figure 5.

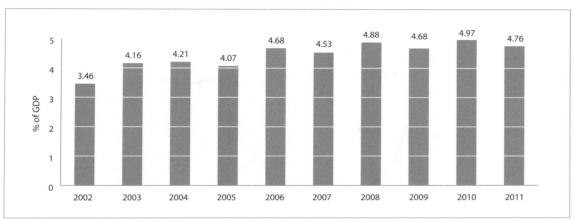

Figure 7 **US Defence Expenditure (Budget Authority)** as % of GDP

standoff between the Democrats and Republicans over the future trajectory of US debt and fiscal policy raised fears that a severe 'fiscal cliff' could be triggered in January 2013, casting further doubts over the sustainability of the modest recovery.

Defence spending in the context of rising US debt

Bipartisan support for legislative fiscal restraint has declined in the last ten years. The budget rules characteristic of the 1990s were ignored by both major parties, with an atmosphere in Congress characterised by increased political polarisation, with Republicans endeavouring to lower taxes and Democrats reluctant to countenance corresponding reductions in entitlement spending. Higher discretionary spending on defence was prioritised to fund military operations in Afghanistan and Iraq – indeed, real defence-spending levels since 2003 have been higher than at any point since the Second World War. Thus, with increased spending and lower tax revenue, the US government has run budget deficits every year since 2001, with each year's deficit adding incrementally to overall US public debt. By 2009, total federal revenues had reached their lowest levels as a proportion of GDP since FY1950 (15.1% of GDP, and down from 20.6% in 2000), while total federal expenditure as a proportion of GDP simultaneously reached its highest levels since FY1945 (25.2% of GDP, and up from 18.2% in 2000). Overall, a cumulative US$6.72 trillion was added to US public debt over a ten-year period, which by the end of FY2011 had tripled to US$10.1tr (67.7% of GDP).

These increases have been driven mainly by legislation enacted since 2001 – the last year in which the US government ran a budget surplus (of 1.3% of GDP). The key legislative drivers underlying the increase in US public debt between 2001 and 2011 are shown in Figures 5 and 6. After discounting for economic fluctuations, technical factors and rises in net interest payments, legislation mandating increased defence spending – including operations in Iraq and Afghanistan – accounted for over a quarter (27.8%) of this increase. Without this increased discretionary military expenditure, US public debt at the end of FY2011 would be about 53.9% of GDP, some 12.8% percentage points lower than its actual level. Overall, the largest driver of US public debt has been the revenue-reduction measures authorised by the Bush-era tax cuts of 2001 and 2003 – which were extended in 2010, by two years, as an economic stimulus measure. These tax measures, and other legislative changes to revenue projections, accounted for 42.6% of the total legislation-driven increase in public debt over 2001–2011. Together, increased defence spending and lower tax collection contributed to 70.4% of the increase. Indeed, US military operations in Iraq and Afghanistan marked the first time in US history that a US administration waged war whilst simultaneously cutting taxes (in the past, high levels of military spending were financed mainly by higher taxes rather than debt issuance).

Dealing with debt – defence spending and fiscal policy

The long-term unsustainability of the imbalance between federal revenues and expenditures is demonstrated by the Congressional Budget Office's 'Extended Alternative Fiscal Scenario' projection (Figure 8). This shows that, should current policies

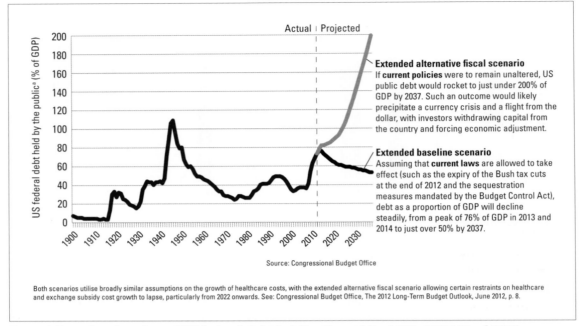

Figure 8 **Actual and projected US federal debt held by the public, 1900–2037 (% of GDP)**

[a] US public debt is all federal debt held outside the US government and the Federal Financing Bank. This could be held by individuals, corporations, state or local governments, foreign governments and other entities. Public debt does not include intra-governmental holdings such as debt held in government trust funds, revolving funds, special funds and Federal Financing Bank securities. The sum of these intra-governmental holdings (US$4.78tr as of 30 August 2012) and public debt (US$11.21tr as of 30 August 2012) makes up total US federal debt (which stood at US$15.99tr, or 102.4% of projected 2012 US GDP, as of 30 August 2012).

– such as high defence-spending levels, the Bush-era tax cuts and other tax-revenue reducing measures – be allowed to continue unaltered (instead of expiring at the end of 2012, as many of the tax measures would under current law), US public debt will be set to rocket to just under 200% of GDP by 2037. By contrast, if scheduled policy changes written into existing legislation (e.g. the expiry of tax breaks at the end of 2012, and the budget sequestration set to occur on 2 January 2013 under the Budget Control Act of 2011) come into effect, the CBO's current law baseline projection (see the 'Extended Baseline Scenario' in Figure 8) indicates that a considerable improvement in the US debt outlook would occur – with US public debt-to-GDP forecast to peak at 76% of GDP in 2013 and 2014, before falling back to just over 50% of GDP by 2037. However, for this to happen, a combination of laws mandating revenue increases and spending reductions must be allowed to come into force.

The expiry in December 2012 of the two-year extension to the Bush-era tax cuts would help federal tax revenues improve significantly, reaching a projected 24% of GDP by 2037, considerably higher

than in much of the recent past. (Between 1972 and 2011, federal revenues averaged 17.9% of GDP.) On the expenditure side, the Budget Control Act of 2011 was designed to restrain recent spending increases by cutting US$2.1tr in federal expenditure between FY2012 and FY2021.

This US$2.1tr in savings was to be achieved in two stages. Annual nominal budgetary appropriations for areas of federal government expenditure such as defence and other domestic discretionary programmes would firstly be capped between FY2012 and FY2021; excluded were major mandatory federal spending programmes such as social security and healthcare, debt-interest payments and unavoidable discretionary allocations such as emergency spending and disaster relief. These spending caps would reduce total discretionary spending by around US$900bn over the next ten years. Of this, US$486.9bn was to be cut from base defence-budget projections contained in the FY2011 Presidential Budget Request, with US$259.4bn of this being cut over the five years between FY2013 and FY2017. (See footnote to Figure 9 for definitions of budgetary terms, including that of the base defence budget.)

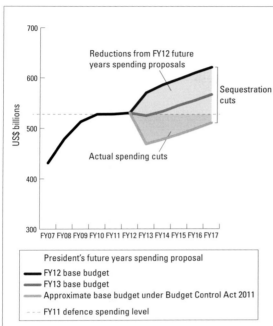

US$ billions

700

600

500

400

300

Reductions from FY12 future
years spending proposals

Sequestration
cuts

Actual spending cuts

FY07 FY08 FY09 FY10 FY11 FY12 FY13 FY14 FY15 FY16 FY17

President's future years spending proposal

━━ FY12 base budget
━━ FY13 base budget
━━ Approximate base budget under Budget Control Act 2011

--- FY11 defence spending level

Sources: IISS analysis based on Department of Defense and Congressional Budget Office data

The base defence budget provides funds for all non-war military activities that keep the Department of Defense in readiness throughout the year. Additional expenses associated with operational military activities, such as the wars in Iraq and Afghanistan, are financed under the overseas contingency operations (OCO) supplemental allocation.

The fiscal year 2013 (FY13) runs from 1 October 2012 to 30 September 2013. The legislative process on the FY13 budget commenced in February 2012, when the White House's Office of Management & Budget (OMB) submitted the president's FY13 budget request to Congress. The House and Senate Budget Committees (along with the relevant sub-committees) amend the budget request and draft budget resolutions to be voted on the floor of the House and Senate. Once the budget resolutions are passed, the House and Senate Appropriations Committees each draft Appropriation Bills, which are then voted on by both chambers. When passed, a Conference Committee resolves difference between the House and Senate bills, and a final Conference Bill is passed by both chambers before it is sent to the president. Once approved, a budget request is known as a budget authority.

Figure 9 **US defence spending trajectory under various proposals**

Secondly, a 'sequestration trigger' was incorporated into the legislation, mandating that, unless a bipartisan supercommittee could reach agreement on US$1.5tr of expenditure reductions by 23 November 2011 (with legislation enacted by 13 January 2012), an across-the-board spending reduction process (sequestration) for the remaining US$1.2tr in cuts required by the act would start automatically on 2 January 2013, unless subsequent legislation preventing this was passed. Up to half of these additional spending reductions were to be achieved by cuts to defence spending. As the supercommittee failed to reach bipartisan agreement by the stipulated date (the committee announced it had reached an impasse and concluded its negotiations on 21 November 2011), the US$1.2tr in sequestration cuts were set to go ahead, unless new legislation which revised the provisions of the Budget Control Act before its 2 January 2013 implementation

date was enacted. Thus, up to an additional US$600bn over the next ten years will need to be cut from the US base defence budget (see Figure 9).

The politics of the FY13 Defense Authorization Bill

As a result of the Budget Control Act, and with presidential and congressional elections set for 6 November, defence spending played a central role in political debates in 2012. While all sides agreed that the act should be replaced with a bipartisan deal over deficit and debt reduction, there was little political will to compromise. Leading Republicans strongly advocated reversing or amending the defence-related provisions of the act. During the presidential campaign, Republican candidate Mitt Romney even argued that defence spending should not be allowed to fall below 4% of US GDP – which, if instituted, would lead to defence-spending levels in excess of US$750bn by 2017, according to IMF *World Economic Outlook* US GDP projections. But Obama and the Democrats maintained that any agreement to lower defence-spending reductions was conditional on enacting measures to increase revenues. Republicans countered that cuts to rising entitlement expenditure (and in particular, healthcare) should be made instead.

With elections forthcoming in November 2012, neither side had an incentive to back down and make concessions. The stalemate that ensued was exacerbated by legislative deadlock, where bills acceptable to the Republican-controlled House of Representatives would have been stymied by the Democratic-controlled Senate and White House. As each side waited for the other to 'blink' over the impasse, the resulting stalemate meant that for much of the year, there was considerable uncertainty over the eventual funding levels that defence would receive.

With a variety of counter-proposals advocated by all sides, little effort was made to meet the actual defence-related provisions of the Budget Control Act. In February 2012, the base defence-budget funding allocation contained in the president's FY2013 budget request was US$525.4bn (before this was revised upward to US$526.9bn by the CBO, as the original estimate did not account for certain military construction expenditures). This was approximately US$56.7bn higher than base defence-budget funding levels envisaged under the act's sequestration trigger. Additionally, while the FY2013 base budget request

Table 3 **US National Defense Budget Function[1] and Other Selected Budgets[2] 1992, 2003–2013**

(US$bn)	National Defense Budget Function		Department of Defense		Atomic Energy Defense Activities	Department of Homeland Security	Veterans Administration	Total Federal Government Outlays	Total Federal Budget Surplus/ Deficit
FY	BA	Outlay	BA	Outlay	BA	BA (Gross)	BA		
1992	295.1	298.3	282.1	286.9	10.6	n.a.	33.9	1,381	-290
2003	456.2	404.9	437.9	387.3	16.4	30.8	59.1	2,160	-377
2004	490.6	455.9	471.0	436.5	16.8	31.6	60.5	2,293	-412
2005	505.7	495.3	483.9	474.1	17.9	100.7	69.2	2,472	-318
2006	617.1	521.8	593.7	499.3	17.4	32.4	71.0	2,655	-248
2007	625.8	551.2	602.9	528.6	17.2	39.7	79.5	2,728	-160
2008	696.3	616.1	674.7	594.6	16.6	50.6	88.3	2,982	-458
2009	697.8	661.0	667.5	631.9	22.9	45.3	96.9	3,517	-1,412
2010	721.3	693.6	695.6	666.7	18.2	45.8	124.4	3,456	-1,293
2011	717.4	705.6	691.5	678.1	18.5	45.1	123.1	3,603	-1,300
2012 est.	676.7	716.3	650.5	688.3	18.4	49.6	124.6	3,796	-1,327
2013 est.	647.4	701.8	620.3	672.9	19.4	48.7	137.7	3,803	-901

Notes

FY = Fiscal Year (1 October–30 September)
[1] The National Defense Budget Function subsumes funding for the DoD, the Department of Energy Atomic Energy Defense Activities and some smaller support agencies (including Federal Emergency Management and Selective Service System). It does not include funding for International Security Assistance (under International Affairs), the Veterans Administration, the US Coast Guard (Department of Homeland Security), nor for the National Aeronautics and Space Administration (NASA). Funding for civil projects administered by the DoD is excluded from the figures cited here.
[2] Early in each calendar year, the US government presents its defence budget to Congress for the next fiscal year, which begins on 1 October. The government also presents its Future Years Defense Program (FYDP), which covers the next fiscal year plus the following five. Until approved by Congress, the Budget is called the Budget Request; after approval, it becomes the Budget Authority.

Sources: US National Defence Budget Estimates for FY2013 – Office of the Under Secretary of Defense (Comptroller), Department of Homeland Security FY2013 Budget in Brief, Budget of the US Government, FY2013.

indicated reduced military personnel funding levels (by 4.7% relative to FY2012), much of this stemmed from re-routing personnel payroll allocations for some 49,700 soldiers and 15,200 marines through the overseas contingency operations (OCO) budget account – which is also subject to the act's spending caps and sequester, but where large reductions in operations and maintenance, procurement and research and development expenditures between FY2012 and FY2013 had enabled the military personnel component to increase by 24.5% relative to FY2012 levels. Overall, the FY2013 OCO funding request still declined by 23.1% relative to FY2012, to US$88.5bn, while the total FY2013 defence-budget request was US$613.9bn.

Subsequently, in May 2012, the House Armed Services Committee added funds to the FY2013 base defence-budget request for several platforms that the DoD had planned to retire, such as A-10 and F-16 combat aircraft, C-27 and C-23 transport aircraft, and RQ-4 Block 30 *Global Hawk* UAVs. Congress also refused to countenance cuts to the Air National Guard, and provided additional funds for 12 MQ-9 *Reaper* UAVs, as well as for three of the four cruisers that the US Navy planned to retire in 2013. Increased funding was also allocated towards upgrading the radio and networking systems of M2 *Bradley* infantry fighting vehicles, modernising *Humvees* for the Army National Guard, and to prevent the US Army's planned three-year temporary closure of General Dynamic Land Systems M1 *Abrams* tank-production facilities. Mark-ups to the FY2013 budget request in the Senate had much in common with those instituted in the House (for example, the provision of funds for C-27 *Spartan* military transport aircraft, RQ-4 Block 30 *Global Hawk* UAVs and for continued M1 *Abrams* tank-production facilities), but overall these were less extensive than the House measures.

With the additional funds allocated by the House Armed Services Committee, the FY13 base defence budget rose to US$529.7bn, before US$10.6bn in military construction funding was reallocated under a separate bill, enabling the House Appropriations Committee to recommend to the House a FY2013 base defence budget of US$519.1bn (on 19 July 2012). The House subsequently revised this down to US$518.1bn. Without the reallocation of military construction funding, the base defence budget would have been US$1.8bn higher than the FY2013 budget request, and around US$10bn higher than base defence-spending levels permitted by the Budget Control Act spending cap. Overall, House allocations for the budget

Table 4 **US National Defense Budget Authority FY2011–FY2013**

(US$million)	2011	2012			2013 Request		
		Base	Overseas Contingency Operations	Total	Base	Overseas Contingency Operations	Total
Military Personnel	158,389	147,194	11,293	158,488	142,062	14,060	156,122
Operations & Maintenance	305,235	198,111	86,776	284,886	209,672	63,986	273,658
Procurement	131,898	104,527	16,052	120,580	98,823	9,687	108,511
R, D, T & E	76,687	71,376	526	71,902	69,408	246	69,653
Military Construction	15,991	11,367	0	11,367	9,572	0	9,572
Family Housing	1,833	1,690	0	1,690	1,651	0	1,651
Other	1,436	1,135	435	1,570	589	503	1,093
Total Department of Defense	**691,471**	**535,400**	**115,083**	**650,483**	**531,778**	**88,482**	**620,260**
Department of Energy (defence-related)	18,534			18,430			19,419
Other (defence-related)	7,416			7,774			7,742
Total National Defense	**717,421**			**676,687**			**647,421**

Sources: US National Defence Budget Estimates for FY2013 – Office of the Under Secretary of Defense (Comptroller) March 2012

category 'national defence' (which includes defence-related funding allocated to the Department of Energy and other agencies) exceeded the US$546bn spending cap on national defence allocations by US$6.3bn. On 31 July, the Senate Defense Appropriations Subcommittee approved a US$511bn base defence budget (a figure within the spending cap for the base defence budget), reallocating some US$5bn under the OCO budget line and including military construction expenditure under a separate appropriations bill.

Sequestration

Meanwhile, DoD refused to assume that sequestration would occur, with officials stating that sequestration planning would not commence unless directed by the White House's Office of Management and Budget (OMB). Kathleen Hicks, Deputy Undersecretary of Defense for Policy, stated in mid-July that 'we do not have a Plan B'. In late September, Defense Department Comptroller Robert Hale said that the DoD was only just beginning to accept that such plans may be necessary.

In part, this was due to the very lack of flexibility that the legislation was intended to produce. At the account level, in line with the original sequestration legislation, the Budget Control Act mandated that uniform percentage cuts be enacted across all accounts, with only the president allowed to exempt military personnel accounts. This exemption was announced on 1 August 2012, and meant that sequestration would not cause either the layoff of any military personnel or any reductions to military pay,

allowances or bonuses (military healthcare would be subject to sequestration unless Congress approved its reprogramming, as military healthcare is funded out of the operations & maintenance account, rather than the military personnel account). The exemption of the military personnel account from sequestration meant that the same US$56.7bn in base-budget spending reductions required by the act would have to be spread, in uniform percentage terms, across fewer accounts. The result was that funding allocated to all other accounts would need to be reduced by around 10.5% relative to the original FY2013 budget request, some 2.2% more than would have been the case had the military personnel account not been exempted. The exact, final percentage reduction required would only be established in late December 2012, after the remaining unobligated funds in agency accounts were calculated by the OMB.

In late July 2012, Frederick Vollrath, acting assistant secretary of defense for readiness and force management, revealed that Defense Secretary Panetta had not yet ordered a review of DoD activities, to identify both spending priorities and areas that should be cut if sequestration was in fact to occur, despite the fact that such a review would require several months. In reality, the sequestration legislation and the exemption of military personnel accounts limited the DoD's room for manoeuvre. At the programme level, the Budget Control Act required uniform, across-the-board funding reductions for each 'program, project and activity' line item in defence appropriation bills, thereby preventing the cancellation of particular programmes or the reallocation, or 'reprogramming', of resources to fulfil the funding needs of priority programmes. While Section 258B of the Balanced Budget and Emergency Deficit Control Act of 1985 grants the president authority to seek Congressional approval for a joint resolution allowing the reallocation of resources across programmes (provided that there is no net increase in budget authority and outlays), there was legal uncertainty as to whether this provision was applicable to the 2011 act.

In the absence of a joint resolution enabling the reallocation of resources, policy options, should sequestration be enacted, could include planning for the renegotiation and modification of supplier contracts to purchase reduced quantities of the same items; and where this is not possible (for example, naval programmes such as the LCS, the DDG-51 *Arleigh Burke* destroyer, or the CVN-78 aircraft carrier), delaying acquisition timetables. Additionally, DoD has to plan on how it would cope with significant reductions to its civilian workforce, with up to an estimated 108,000 out of 791,000 civilian personnel potentially losing their jobs as a result of sequestration. This could prove to be one of the more significant challenges, as the need to pay high termination costs may offset some of the cost savings achieved by civilian payroll reductions. The fact that sequestration would commence three months into the fiscal year (which starts on 1 October) exacerbates the problem, as the cost reductions would have to be achieved in nine rather than 12 months.

Without a bipartisan compromise on a comprehensive deficit reduction plan, and absent a detailed DoD plan for dealing with sequestration, Senate majority leader Harry Reid and House Speaker John Boehner announced on 31 July 2012

that agreement over a continuing resolution had been reached. (Continuing resolutions are a type of appropriation legislation that fund government agencies if a formal appropriation bill has not been enacted in time for the new fiscal year.)

A final continuing resolution was passed by the Senate on 22 September. This fixed defence spending for all programmes at their FY2012 levels until 27 March 2013, providing temporary certainty and room to negotiate during the lame-duck session of Congress following the November elections, and enabling the government to continue functioning into FY2013 year without disruption. However, the resolution rendered redundant the work done over the course of the year by the House and Senate Appropriations Committees on the FY2013 budget. Also, with fixed funding levels from the previous year maintained, new programmes are unable to start and older programmes are unable to wind down.

Additionally, simply passing a continuing resolution does not prevent sequestration from occurring. To achieve this, legislation specifically amending the provisions of the Budget Control Act must be passed. In the absence of such legislation, OMB would have to produce a report applying the spending cap and sequestration within 15 days of the end of the 112th Congress on 3 January 2013 – an action which would invalidate the continuing resolution. On 2 January 2013, the president would have to issue an order informing government agencies of the final sequestration cuts required. This would commence a gradual process of sequestration, with the OMB processing and approving departmental plans to reduce expenditure over the following weeks. If sequestration was to go ahead on 2 January 2013, the new Congress would have up to 20 days to modify its terms.

Sequestration: after the elections

Following the US elections on 8 November 2012, negotiations commenced over avoiding the 'fiscal cliff' and the onset of sequestration on 2 January 2013. With the Democrats winning the White House and the Senate, and the Republicans retaining their overall majority in the House of Representatives, the elections did little to alter the political gridlock seen during the pre-election period. There were three potential outcomes to the intervening 'lame duck' session of the outgoing congress: a deal could be reached over the balance between tax increases and spending reductions to be instituted, both sides

could agree to delay sequestration, or no agreement may be reached at all.

After a series of fraught negotiations, an eleventh-hour deal to delay sequestration by two months was finally reached on 1 January 2013. This meant that the Pentagon did not need to immediately begin cancelling contracts or issuing layoff and furlough notices. Nevertheless, the failure to fully resolve the impasse meant that further negotiations over the debt ceiling, spending cuts and sequestration awaited the incoming 113th Congress, and that delays to the FY2014 budget cycle were likely to occur.

CANADA

The past year saw continued implementation of the 2008 *Canada First Defence Strategy*, particularly the shipbuilding programme detailed in previous editions of *The Military Balance*. This National Shipbuilding Procurement Strategy has two key elements. A combat component includes between six and eight ice-capable offshore patrol vessels able to operate in the High North and Canada's EEZs in the Atlantic and Pacific. It also includes construction of the Canadian Surface Combatant vessels, designed to replace capabilities provided by the current fleet of *Iroquois* and *Halifax* classes. The non-combat ship package includes offshore science vessels for the coast guard and an icebreaker. Shipyards were selected in late 2011, and February 2012 saw the government announce umbrella agreements with them: Nova-Scotia-based Irving Shipbuilding Inc. for the combat package, and Vancouver Shipyards for the non-combat ships. According to the Department of Public Works and Government Services, the next stage in the process is the negotiation of individual project contracts, with the ice-capable offshore patrol vessels due first. *Operation Nanook* – Ottawa's northern sovereignty operation – saw its sixth and latest iteration in August. This is another aspect of the Canada First strategy. The 2012 operation took place in new areas, involving 1,250 personnel from the armed forces as well as personnel from the coast guard and Royal Canadian Mounted Police.

Debates over future aircraft fleets highlighted in last year's *Military Balance* (p. 49) continued in 2012, with the Spring Report of the Auditor General of Canada recommending that the government 'refine its estimates for the full life-cycle costs of the F-35 and make those estimates public'. The F-35 is slated as the replacement for Canada's fleet of CF-18 combat aircraft. In response, the government in April adopted a seven-pronged response: freeze the 'funding envelope' allocated for the F-35 purchase; establish a new F-35 secretariat, to play a lead coordinating role in the replacement of the CF-18s; the Department of National Defence (DND), through the secretariat, to provide annual updates to parliament; continue to evaluate options to

sustain a fighter capacity; prior to project approval, commission an independent review of the acquisition and sustainment project assumptions and potential costs for the F-35; Treasury Board secretariat to also review the acquisition and sustainment costs; and continue to identify opportunities for industry to participate in the project. Canada remains a partner in the F-35 programme, but the DND made clear in 2012 that 'Canada has not signed a contract to purchase any aircraft', and that 'Canada will not sign a contract to purchase any aircraft until [the seven steps noted above] are completed and developmental work is sufficiently advanced'.

Last year's *Military Balance* noted the CF2020 Transformation Initiative report submitted on July 2011 by Lieutenant-General Andrew Leslie, intended to propose 'organizational changes that are appropriately balanced and aligned across [the department] and Canadian Forces' and designed so that Canada's military can 'streamline ourselves while maintaining the required operational focus' (p. 49). A major development was announced by the DND in May 2012, when a revision of the operational command and control structure saw the creation of a single command, the Canadian Joint Operations Command (CJOC), to be implemented over a period of months. Ottawa has said that the move was prompted by a 'logical evolution' of the 2006 transformation initiative that saw the creation of Canada Command, Canadian Expeditionary Force Command, Canadian Special Operations Forces Command and Canadian Operational Support Command. It was also prompted by the lessons of domestic and overseas operations, including in Afghanistan. According to DND, 'the revised structure will reduce the number of CF Officers in strategic headquarters by up to 25 per cent and will make more efficient use of administrative resources'. Meanwhile, Canada's Afghanistan deployments continue. *Operation Attention* constitutes Canada's participation in the NATO Training Mission–Afghanistan, with around 900 Canadian personnel deployed to train the Afghan National Army, Afghan National Air Force and the Afghan National Police. Canada had earlier, in July 2011, ended its combat deployments to Afghanistan.

Canada CAN

Canadian Dollar $		2011	2012	2013
GDP	C$$	1.72tr	1.78tr	
	US$	1.74tr	1.77tr	
per capita	US$	50,729	51,603	
Growth	%	2.41	1.94	
Inflation	%	2.89	1.79	
Def exp [a]	C$$	23.4bn		
	US$	23.7bn		
Def bdgt	C$$	19.9bn	18.4bn	
	US$	20.1bn	18.4bn	
US$1= CAN$		0.99	1.00	

Population   34,300,083

[a] NATO definition

Age	0–14	15–19	20–24	25–29	30–64	65 plus
Male	8.0%	3.2%	3.5%	3.4%	24.3%	7.2%
Female	7.6%	3.1%	3.3%	3.3%	24.0%	9.1%

Capabilities

Canada can deploy and sustain its armed forces on demanding long-duration missions. From 2006 until 2011, Canadian forces in Afghanistan engaged in sustained combat operations. They showed considerable adaptation in combat, including rapidly procuring tanks, UAVs and other equipment. Now withdrawn from a combat role (a training team remains), Canadian forces are refurbishing equipment and rebuilding expeditionary capability. Strategic and Operational command and control is to be rationalised by merging three existing HQs into a single Canadian Joint Operations Command (CJOC), responsible for all operational force employment in Canada and worldwide, apart from special forces. Its armed forces are able to meet national-security requirements. The size of the country and its economic dependence on the US means that Homeland Security and enforcing sovereignty is a major driver for defence-capability development. Canada is improving its ability to operate in its High North, including improved basing and rebuilding Arctic capabilities. The National Shipbuilding Procurement Strategy includes ice-capable offshore patrol vessels capable of operating in the High North. The defence budget is now to be reduced by 13% over three years. Although withdrawal from a combat role in Afghanistan will produce savings, capability reductions have already begun, with the elimination of anti-air and anti-armour missiles from the army and withdrawal from NATO surveillance programmes. It still plans to improve its equipment, including modernising army vehicles and a politically controversial plan to replace F/A-18A/B *Hornets* with 65 F-35As. But reductions in numbers procured are likely.

ACTIVE 66,000 (Army 34,800 Navy 11,300 Air Force 19,900)

CIVILIAN 4,500 (Coast Guard 4,500)

RESERVE 30,950 (Army 23,150, Navy 5,450, Air 2,350)

ORGANISATIONS BY SERVICE

Army 34,800

FORCES BY ROLE
COMMAND
1 Task Force HQ
MANOEUVRE
Mechanised
1 (1st) mech bde gp (1 armd regt, 2 mech inf bn, 1 lt inf bn, 1 arty regt, 1 cbt engr regt)
2 (2nd & 5th) mech bde gp (1 armd recce regt, 2 mech inf bn, 1 lt inf bn, 1 arty regt, 1 cbt engr regt)
COMBAT SUPPORT
1 AD regt
1 engr/cbt spt regt
3 int coy
3 MP pl
COMBAT SERVICE SUPPORT
3 log bn
3 med bn

EQUIPMENT BY TYPE
MBT 120: 40 *Leopard* 2A6M; 80 *Leopard* 2A4; (61 *Leopard* 1C2 in store)
RECCE 201 LAV-25 *Coyote*
APC 1,220
  APC (T) 332: 64 Bv-206; 235 M113; 33 M577
  APC (W) 810: 635 LAV-III *Kodiak* (incl 33 RWS); 175 MILLAV *Bison* (incl 10 EW, 32 amb, 32 repair, 64 recovery)
  PPV 78: 68 RG-31 *Nyala*; 5 *Cougar*; 5 *Buffalo*
ARTY 295
  TOWED 190 **105mm** 153: 27 C2 (M101); 98 C3 (M101); 28 LG1 MK II; **155mm** 37 M777
  MOR 81mm 100
    SP 81mm 24 *Bison*
AT
  MSL 493
    SP 33 LAV-TOW
    MANPATS 460: 425 *Eryx*; 35 TOW-2A/ITAS
  RCL 84mm 1,075 *Carl Gustav*; M2/M3
AD
  SAM • SP 33 ADATS
    MANPAD *Starburst*
ARV 2 BPz-3 *Büffel*
UAV • ISR • Light *Skylark*

Reserve Organisations 23,150

Canadian Rangers 4,300 Reservists

The Canadian Rangers are a Reserve sub-component of the Canadian Forces, which provide a limited military presence in Canada's northern, coastal and isolated areas. They have sovereignty, public-safety and surveillance roles.

FORCES BY ROLE
MANOEUVRE
Other
5 (patrol) ranger gp (165 patrols)

Army Reserves
Most units have only coy sized establishments.

FORCES BY ROLE
COMMAND
10 bde gp HQ
MANOEUVRE
Reconnaissance
18 armd recce regt
Light
51 inf regt
COMBAT SUPPORT
14 fd arty regt
2 indep fd arty bty
1 cbt engr regt
7 engr regt
3 indep engr sqn
1 EW sqn
4 int coy
6 sigs regt
16 indep sigs sqn
COMBAT SERVICE SUPPORT
10 log bn
14 med coy
4 med det
4 MP coy

Royal Canadian Navy 11,300
EQUIPMENT BY TYPE
SUBMARINES SSK 4
4 *Victoria* (ex-UK *Upholder*) with 6 single 533mm TT with
Mk48 *Sea Arrow* HWT (2 currently operational)
PRINCIPAL SURFACE COMBATANTS 15
DESTROYERS • DDHM 3 mod *Iroquois* with 1 Mk41
VLS with SM-2MR SAM, 2 triple 324mm ASTT with
Mk46 LWT, 1 76mm gun, (capacity 2 SH-3 (CH-124) *Sea
King* ASW hel)
FRIGATES • FFGHM 12 *Halifax* with 2 quad lnchr with
RGM-84 Block II *Harpoon* AShM, 2 octuple Mk48 lnchr
with RIM-7P *Sea Sparrow* SAM/RIM-162 ESSM SAM, 2
twin 324mm ASTT with Mk46 LWT, (capacity 1 SH-3
(CH-124) *Sea King* ASW hel) (rolling modernisation
programme until 2017)
**MINE WARFARE • MINE COUNTERMEASURES •
MCO** 12 *Kingston*
LOGISTICS AND SUPPORT 31
AORH 2 *Protecteur* with 3 SH-3 (CH-124) *Sea King* ASW
hel
AGOR 1
AX 9: **AXL** 8 *Orca;* **AXS** 1
YDT 6 (2 MCM spt; 4 diving tender/spt)
YTB 8
YTL 5

Reserves 5,430 reservists
FORCES BY ROLE
MANOEUVRE
Other
24 navy div (tasked with crewing 10 of the 12 MCO,
harbour defence & naval control of shipping)

Royal Canadian Air Force (RCAF) 19,900 (plus 2,350 Primary Reservists integrated within total Air Force structure)
FORCES BY ROLE
FIGHTER/GROUND ATTACK
3 sqn with F/A-18A/B *Hornet* (CF-18AM/BM)
ANTI-SUBMARINE WARFARE
3 sqn with SH-3 *Sea King* (CH-124)
MARITIME PATROL
3 sqn with P-3 *Orion* (CP-140 *Aurora*)
SEARCH & RESCUE/TRANSPORT
4 sqn with AW101 *Merlin* (CH-149 *Cormorant*); C-130E/
H//H-30/J-30 (CC-130) *Hercules*
1 sqn with DHC-5 (CC-115) *Buffalo*
TANKER/TRANSPORT
1 sqn with A310/A310 MRTT (CC-150/CC-150T)
1 sqn with KC-130H
TRANSPORT
1 sqn with C-17A (CC-177)
1 sqn with CL-600 (CC-144B)
1 (utl) sqn with DHC-6 (CC-138) *Twin Otter*
TRANSPORT HELICOPTER
5 sqn with Bell 412 (CH-146 *Griffon*)
3 (cbt spt) sqn with Bell 412 (CH-146 *Griffon*)
1 (Spec Ops) sqn with Bell 412 (CH-146 *Griffon* –
OPCON Canadian Special Operations Command)
ISR UAV
1 unit with *Heron* (CU-170)
RADAR
1 (NORAD Regional) HQ located at Winnipeg;
1 Sector HQ at North Bay with 11 North Warning
System Long Range Radar; 36 North Warning System
Short Range Radar; 4 Coastal Radar; 2 Transportable
Radar
EQUIPMENT BY TYPE
AIRCRAFT 95 combat capable
FGA 77: 59 F/A-18A (CF-18AM) *Hornet*; 18 F/A-18B (CF-
18BM) *Hornet*
ASW 18 P-3 *Orion* (CP-140 *Aurora*)
TKR/TPT 7: 2 A310 MRTT (CC-150T); 5 KC-130H
TPT 58: **Heavy** 4 C-17A (CC-177) *Globemaster*; **Medium**
35: 10 C-130E (CC-130) *Hercules*; 6 C-130H (CC-130)
Hercules; 2 C-130H-30 (CC-130) *Hercules*; 17 C-130J-30
(CC-130) *Hercules* **Light** 10: 6 DHC-5 (CC-115) *Buffalo*;
4 DHC-6 (CC-138) *Twin Otter* **PAX** 9: 3 A310 (CC-150
Polaris); 6 CL-600 (CC-144B)
TRG 4 DHC-8 (CT-142) *Nav Trainer*
HELICOPTERS
ASW 28 SH-3 (CH-124) *Sea King*
MRH 78 Bell 412 (CH-146 *Griffon*) (incl 10 spec ops)
TPT 20 **Heavy** 6 CH-47D (CH-147D) *Chinook* **Medium** 14
AW101 *Merlin* (CH-149 *Cormorant*)
UAV • ISR • Heavy 5 *Heron* (CU-170) (leased for 3 yrs)

RADARS 53
  AD RADAR • NORTH WARNING SYSTEM 47: 11
  Long Range; 36 Short Range
  STRATEGIC 6: 4 Coastal; 2 Transportable
MSL
  ASM AGM-65 *Maverick*
  AAM • IR AIM-9L *Sidewinder* **SARH** AIM-7M *Sparrow*
  ARH AIM-120C AMRAAM
BOMBS
  Conventional: Mk 82; Mk 83; Mk 84
  Laser-Guided: GBU-10/GBU-12/GBU-16 *Paveway* II;
  GBU-24 *Paveway* III

NATO Flight Training Canada

EQUIPMENT BY TYPE
AIRCRAFT
  TRG 45: 26 T-6A *Texan* II *(CT-156 Harvard* II); 19 *Hawk*
  115 (CT-155) (advanced wpns/tactics trg)

Contracted Flying Services – Southport

EQUIPMENT BY TYPE
AIRCRAFT
  TPT • Light 7 Beech C90B *King Air*
  TRG 11 G-120A
HELICOPTERS
  MRH 9 Bell 412 (CH-146)
  TPT • Light 7 Bell 206 *Jet Ranger* (CH-139)

Canadian Special Operations Forces Command 1,500

FORCES BY ROLE
SPECIAL FORCES
  1 SF regt (Canadian Special Operations Regiment)
  1 SF unit (JTF2)
MANOEUVRE
  Aviation
  1 sqn, with Bell 412 (CH-146 *Griffon* – from the RCAF)
COMBAT SERVICE SUPPORT
  1 CBRN unit (Canadian Joint Incidence Response Unit
  – CJIRU)
EQUIPMENT BY TYPE
RECCE 4 LAV *Bison* (NBC)
HEL • MRH Bell 412 (CH-146 *Griffon)*

Canadian Operational Support Command 2,000

FORCES BY ROLE
COMBAT SUPPORT
  1 engr spt coy
  1 (joint) sigs regt
COMBAT SERVICE SUPPORT
  3 (spt) log unit
  4 (movement) log unit
  1 med bn
  1 (close protection) MP coy

Canadian Coast Guard 4,500 (civilian)

Incl Department of Fisheries and Oceans; all platforms are
designated as non-combatant.

PATROL AND COASTAL COMBATANTS 69
  PSO 2: 1 *Leonard J Cowley*; 1 *Sir Wilfred Grenfell*
  PCO 7: 2 *Cape Roger*; 1 *Dumit*; 1 *Eckaloo*; 1 *Gordon Reid*; 1
  Nahidik; 1 *Tanu*
  PCC 4: 1 *Arrow Post*; 1 *Harp*; 2 *Louisbourg*
  PB 55: 4 *Point Henry*; 3 *Post*; 1 *Quebecois*; 1 *Tembah*; 1 *Vakta*;
  4 Type-100; 10 Type-300A; 31 Type-300B
AMPHIBIOUS • LANDING CRAFT • LCAC 4
LOGISTICS AND SUPPORT 49
  ABU 9
  AG 8
  AGB 15
  AGOR 8 (coastal and offshore fishery vessels)
  AGOS 9
HELICOPTERS • TPT 22 **Medium** 1 S-61 **Light** 21: 3 Bell
206L *Long Ranger*; 4 Bell 212; 14 Bo-105

Cyber

Canada published its Cyber Security Strategy in October
2010. The White Paper said that the Communications
Security Establishment Canada, the Canadian Security
Intelligence Service and Royal Canadian Mounted Police
will all investigate incidents according to their relevant
mandates. Meanwhile, the armed forces will strengthen
their capacity to defend their own networks. The Canadian
Forces Network Operation Centre, meanwhile, is the
'national operational Cyber Defence unit', permanently
assigned tasks to support Canadian Forces operations.

DEPLOYMENT

AFGHANISTAN
NATO • ISAF (NTM-A) • *Operation Attention* 529

ARABIAN SEA & GULF OF ADEN
Combined Maritime Forces • CTF-150: 1 FFGHM

CYPRUS
UN • UNFICYP (*Operation Snowgoose*) 1

DEMOCRATIC REPUBLIC OF THE CONGO
UN • MONUSCO (*Operation Crocodile*) 8 obs

EGYPT
MFO (*Operation Calumet*) 28

GERMANY
NATO (ACO) 287

HAITI
UN • MINUSTAH (*Operation Hamlet*) 5

JAMAICA
Operation Jaguar 65 (providing SAR spt)

MIDDLE EAST
UN • UNTSO (*Operation Jade*) 8 obs

SERBIA
NATO • KFOR • *Joint Enterprise* (*Operation Kobold*) 5

SIERRA LEONE
IMATT (*Operation Sculpture*) 10

SOUTH SUDAN

UN • UNMISS (*Operation Soprano*) 5; 5 obs

UNITED STATES

US CENTCOM (*Operation Foundation*) 12

US NORTHCOM/NORAD/NATO (ACT) 303

FOREIGN FORCES

United Kingdom 420; 2 trg unit; 1 hel flt with SA341 *Gazelle*
United States 135

United States US

United States Dollar $		2011	2012	2013
GDP	US$	15.08tr	15.65tr	
per capita	US$	48,049	49,865	
Growth	%	1.81	2.17	
Inflation	%	3.14	1.97	
Def Exp [a] National Def Budget	US$	732bn		
BA	US$	717.4bn	676.7bn	647.4bn [b]
Outlay	US$	705.6bn	716.3bn	701.8bn [b]

[a] NATO definition

[b] Figures for 2013 uncertain due to debate over sequestration – see p. 59–66

Population	313,847,465

Age	0–14	15–19	20–24	25–29	30–64	65 plus
Male	10.21%	3.45%	3.60%	3.45%	22.69%	5.87%
Female	9.79%	3.29%	3.46%	3.34%	23.19%	7.66%

Capabilities

The US is the world's pre-eminent military power, with highly-trained armed forces capable of large-scale sustained high-intensity full-spectrum operations around the world. In January 2012, the administration issued revised strategic guidance that increased emphasis on the Asia-Pacific, while budget proposals including force-structure cuts were unveiled by the Pentagon in February. These are intended to cope with funding reductions of US$450 billion over a ten year period; the threat of sequestration (See p. 65) was an additional complication for Pentagon planners. Washington is in the process of disengaging most of its forces from Afghanistan by the end of 2015. While the strain of prolonged conflicts in Afghanistan and Iraq may have led to some 'war weariness', morale and motivation within the military is good, though continuing uncertainty over the threat of further funding cuts, as a result of sequestration, are unwelcome. The build-up of land forces over the past decade is being reversed, with the army to be cut from 570,000 to 490,000 over a six-year period. The USMC takes a 10% cut in size, with personnel to fall to 182,000. There were cuts to the size of air force tactical aviation, while the navy will also lose some ships earlier than previously planned. The force-structure reductions are intended to sustain the Pentagon's future procurement

programme in a period of relative financial constraint. In the procurement arena, the F-35 *Lightning* II combat aircraft remains a focus. The Pentagon proposals slowed the pace of procurement, and also reduced aircraft numbers being bought in the period to FY2017.

ACTIVE 1,520,100 (Army 600,450 Navy 332,800 Air Force 346,100 US Marine Corps 199,550 US Coast Guard 41,200)

CIVILIAN 14,000 (US Special Operations Command 6,400 US Coast Guard 7,600)

RESERVE 810,350 (Army 514,850 Navy 95,150 Air Force 154,900 Marine Corps Reserve 37,350 US Coast Guard 8,100)

ORGANISATIONS BY SERVICE

US Strategic Command

HQ at Offutt AFB (NE). Five missions: US nuclear deterrent; missile defence; global strike; info ops; ISR

US Navy

EQUIPMENT BY TYPE
SUBMARINES • STRATEGIC • SSBN 14 *Ohio* (mod) SSBN with up to 24 UGM-133A *Trident* D-5 strategic SLBM, 4 single 533mm TT with Mk48 *Sea Arrow* HWT

US Air Force • Global Strike Command

FORCES BY ROLE
MISSILE
   9 sqn with LGM-30G *Minuteman* III
BOMBER
   6 sqn (incl 1 AFRC) with B-52H *Stratofortress*
   2 sqn with B-2A *Spirit*

EQUIPMENT BY TYPE
BBR 91: 19 B-2A *Spirit*; 72 B-52H *Stratofortress*
MSL • STRATEGIC
   ICBM 450 LGM-30G *Minuteman* III (capacity 1-3 MIRV Mk12/Mk12A per missile)
   ALCM AGM-86B; AGM-129A

Strategic Defenses – Early Warning

North American Aerospace Defense Command (NORAD), a combined US–CAN org.

EQUIPMENT BY TYPE
SATELLITES (see Space)
RADAR
   NORTH WARNING SYSTEM 15 North Warning System Long Range (range 200nm); 40 North Warning System Short Range (range 80nm)
   OVER-THE-HORIZON-BACKSCATTER RADAR (OTH-B) 2: 1 AN/FPS-118 *OTH-B* (500–3,000nm) located at Mountain Home AFB (ID); 1 non-operational located at Maine (ME)
   STRATEGIC 2 Ballistic Missile Early Warning System *BMEWS* located at Thule, GL and Fylingdales Moor, UK; 1 (primary mission to track ICBM and SLBM; also used to track satellites) located at Clear (AK)

SPACETRACK SYSTEM 11: 8 Spacetrack Radar located at Incirlik (TUR), Eglin (FL), Cavalier AFS (ND), Clear (AK), Thule (GL), Fylingdales Moor (UK), Beale AFB (CA), Cape Cod (MA); 3 Spacetrack Optical Trackers located at Socorro (NM), Maui (HI), Diego Garcia (BIOT)
USN SPACE SURVEILLANCE SYSTEM *NAV SPASUR* 3 strategic transmitting stations; 6 strategic receiving sites in southeast US
PERIMETER ACQUISITION RADAR ATTACK CHARACTERISATION SYSTEM *PARCS* 1 at Cavalier AFS, (ND)
PAVE PAWS 3 at Beale AFB (CA), Cape Cod AFS (MA), Clear AFS (AK); 1 (phased array radar 5,500km range) located at Otis AFB (MA)
DETECTION AND TRACKING RADARS Kwajalein Atoll, Ascension Island, Antigua, Kaena Point (HI), MIT Lincoln Laboratory (MA)
GROUND BASED ELECTRO OPTICAL DEEP SPACE SURVEILLANCE SYSTEM *GEODSS* Socorro (NM), Maui (HI), Diego Garcia (BIOT)
STRATEGIC DEFENCES – MISSILE DEFENCES
SEA-BASED: *Aegis* engagement cruisers and destroyers
LAND-BASED: 21 ground-based interceptors at Fort Greeley, (AK); 3 ground-based interceptors at Vandenburg, (CA)

Space
SATELLITES 107
COMMUNICATIONS 32
2 AEHF; 8 DSCS-III; 2 *Milstar*-I; 3 *Milstar*-II; 1 MUOS; 1 PAN-1 (P360); 4 SDS-III; 7 UFO; 4 WGS SV2
NAVIGATION/POSITIONING/TIMING 31: 9 NAVSTAR Block II/IIA; 3 NAVSTAR Block IIF; 19 NAVSTAR Block IIR
METEOROLOGY/OCEANOGRAPHY 6 DMSP-5
ISR 11: 2 FIA *Radar*; 4 *Improved Crystal* (visible and infrared imagery, resolution 6 inches); 2 *Lacrosse* (*Onyx* radar imaging satellite); 1 ORS-1; 1 *TacSat*-3; 1 *TacSat*-4;
ELINT/SIGINT 21: 3 *Mentor* (advanced *Orion*); 3 Advanced *Mentor*; 2 *Mercury*; 1 *Trumpet*; 2 *Trumpet*-2; 10 SBWASS (Space Based Wide Area Surveillance System); Naval Ocean Surveillance System
SPACE SURVEILLANCE 1 SBSS (Space Based Surveillance System)
EARLY WARNING 5: 4 DSP; 1 SBIRS *Geo*-1

US Army 552,100; 32,050 active ARNG; 16,300 active AR (total 600,450)
FORCES BY ROLE
Sqn are generally bn sized and tp are generally coy sized
COMMAND
4 (I, III, V & XVIII AB) corps HQ
SPECIAL FORCES
(see USSOCOM)
MANOEUVRE
Reconnaissance
2 (2nd & 3rd CR) cav regt (1 recce sqn, 3 mech sqn, 1 arty sqn, 1 AT tp, 1 engr tp, 1 int tp, 1 sigs tp, 1 CSS sqn)
3 (BfSB) surv bde

Armoured
1 (1st) armd div (2 (2nd & 4th HBCT) armd bde (1 armd recce sqn, 2 armd/armd inf bn, 1 SP arty bn, 1 cbt spt bn, 1 CSS bn); 1 (1st SBCT) mech bde (1 armd recce sqn, 3 mech inf bn, 1 arty bn, 1 AT coy, 1 engr coy, 1 int coy, 1 sigs coy, 1 CSS bn); 1 (3rd IBCT) lt inf bde (1 recce sqn, 2 inf bn, 1 arty bn, 1 cbt spt bn, 1 CSS bn); 1 log bde)
1 (1st) cav div (4 (1st–4th HBCT) armd bde (1 armd recce sqn, 2 armd/armd inf bn, 1 SP arty bn, 1 cbt spt bn, 1 CSS bn); 1 (cbt avn) hel bde; 1 log bde)
1 (1st) inf div (2 (1st & 2nd HBCT) armd bde (1 armd recce sqn, 2 armd/armd inf bn, 1 SP arty bn, 1 cbt spt bn, 1 CSS bn); 2 (3rd & 4th IBCT) lt inf bde (1 recce sqn, 2 inf bn, 1 arty bn, 1 cbt spt bn, 1 CSS bn); 1 (cbt avn) hel bde; 1 log bde)
2 (3rd & 4th) inf div (3 (1st–3rd HBCT) armd bde (1 armd recce sqn, 2 armd/armd inf bn, 1 SP arty bn, 1 cbt spt bn, 1 CSS bn); 1 (4th IBCT) lt inf bde; (1 recce sqn, 2 inf bn, 1 arty bn, 1 cbt spt bn, 1 CSS bn); 1 (cbt avn) hel bde; 1 log bde)
1 (172nd) armd inf bde (1 armd bn, 2 armd inf bn, 1 cbt engr bn, 1 CSS bn, 1 recce tp, 1 SP arty bty)
Mechanised
1 (2nd) inf div (1 (1st HBCT) armd bde (1 armd recce sqn, 2 armd/armd inf bn, 1 SP arty bn, 1 cbt spt bn, 1 CSS bn); 3 (2nd–4th SBCT) mech bde (1 armd recce sqn, 3 mech inf bn, 1 arty bn, 1 AT coy, 1 engr coy, 1 int coy, 1 sigs coy, 1 CSS bn); 1 (cbt avn) hel bde; 1 log bde)
1 (25th) inf div (2 (1st & 2nd SBCT) mech bde (1 armd recce sqn, 3 mech inf bn, 1 arty bn, 1 AT coy, 1 engr coy, 1 int coy, 1 sigs coy, 1 CSS bn); 1 (3rd IBCT) inf bde (1 recce sqn, 2 inf bn, 1 arty bn, 1 cbt spt bn, 1 CSS bn); 1 (4th AB BCT) AB bde (1 recce bn, 2 para bn, 1 arty bn, 1 cbt spt bn, 1 CSS bn); 1 (cbt avn) hel bde; 1 log bde)
Light
1 (10th Mtn) inf div (4 (1st–4th IBCT) lt inf bde (1 recce sqn, 2 inf bn, 1 arty bn, 1 cbt spt bn, 1 CSS bn); 1 (cbt avn) hel bde; 1 log bde)
Air Manoeuvre
1 (82nd) AB div (4 (1st–4th AB BCT) AB bde (1 recce bn, 2 para bn, 1 arty bn, 1 cbt spt bn, 1 CSS bn); 1 (cbt avn) hel bde; 1 log bde)
1 (101st) air aslt div (4 (1st–4th AB BCT) AB bde (1 recce bn, 2 para bn, 1 arty bn, 1 cbt spt bn, 1 CSS bn); 2 (cbt avn) hel bde; 1 log bde)
1 (173rd AB BCT) AB bde (1 recce bn, 2 para bn, 1 arty bn, 1 cbt spt bn, 1 CSS bn)
Aviation
2 indep (cbt avn) hel bde
Other
1 (11th ACR) trg armd cav regt (OPFOR) (2 armd cav sqn, 1 CSS bn)
COMBAT SUPPORT
7 arty bde
1 civil affairs bde
5 engr bde
2 EOD gp (2 EOD bn)
5 AD bde

5 int bde
1 int regt
2 int gp
4 MP bde
2 NBC bde
3 (strat) sigs bde
5 (tac) sigs bde
3 (Mnv Enh) cbt spt bde
COMBAT SERVICE SUPPORT
3 log bde
3 med bde

Reserve Organisations

Army National Guard 358,200 reservists (incl 32,050 active)

Normally dual funded by DoD and states. Civil emergency responses can be mobilised by state governors. Federal government can mobilise ARNG for major domestic emergencies and for overseas operations.

FORCES BY ROLE
COMMAND
8 div HQ
SPECIAL FORCES
(see USSOCOM)
MANOEUVRE
Reconnaissance
3 recce sqn
7 (BfSB) surv bde
Armoured
7 (HBCT) armd bde (1 armd recce sqn, 2 armd/armd inf bn, 1 SP arty bn, 1 cbt spt bn, 1 CSS bn)
3 armd/armd inf bn
Mechanised
1 (SBCT) mech bde (1 armd recce sqn, 3 mech inf bn, 1 arty bn, 1 AT coy, 1 engr coy, 1 int coy, 1 sigs coy, 1 CSS bn)
Light
20 (IBCT) lt inf bde (1 recce sqn, 2 inf bn, 1 arty bn, 1 cbt spt bn, 1 CSS bn)
11 lt inf bn
Aviation
2 (cbt avn) hel bde
5 (theatre avn) hel bde
COMBAT SUPPORT
7 arty bde
2 AD bde
7 engr bde
1 EOD regt
1 int bde
3 MP bde
1 NBC bde
2 sigs bde
16 (Mnv Enh) cbt spt bde
COMBAT SERVICE SUPPORT
10 log bde
17 (regional) log spt gp

Army Reserve 205,000 reservists (incl 16,300 active)

Reserve under full command of US Army. Does not have state emergency liability of Army National Guard.

FORCES BY ROLE
SPECIAL FORCES
(see USSOCOM)
MANOEUVRE
Aviation
1 (theatre avn) hel bde
COMBAT SUPPORT
4 engr bde
4 MP bde
2 NBC bde
2 sigs bde
3 (Mnv Enh) cbt spt bde
COMBAT SERVICE SUPPORT
9 log bde
11 med bde

Army Standby Reserve 700 reservists
Trained individuals for mobilisation

EQUIPMENT BY TYPE
MBT 2,338 M1A1/A2 *Abrams* (ε3,500 more in store)
RECCE 1,940: 361 M7A3 BFIST; 577 M1127 *Stryker* RV; 134 M1128 *Stryker* MGS; 166 M1131 *Stryker* FSV; 141 M1135 *Stryker* NBCRV; 465 M1200 *Armored Knight*; 96 Tpz-1 *Fuchs*
AIFV 4,559 M2A2/A3 *Bradley*/M3A2/A3 *Bradley* (ε2,000 more in store)
APC 23,866
  APC (T) 3,901 M113A2/A3 (ε9,000 more in store)
  APC (W) 2,548: 1,794 M1126 *Stryker* ICV; 337 M1130 *Stryker* CV; 150 M1132 *Stryker* ESV; 267 M1133 *Stryker* MEV
  PPV 17,417: 11,658 MRAP (all models); 5,759 M-ATV
ARTY 6,477
  SP 155mm 969 M109A1/A2/A6 (ε500 more in store)
  TOWED 1,836: **105mm** 821 M119A2 **155mm** 1,015: 656 M198; 359 M777A1/2
  MRL 227mm 1,189: 359 M142 HIMARS; 830 M270/M270A1 MLRS (all ATACMS-capable)
  MOR 2,483: **81mm** 990 M252 **120mm** 1,493: 1,076 M120/M121; 417 M1129 *Stryker* MC
AT • MSL
  SP 2,119: 1,379 HMMWV TOW; 626 M901; 114 M1134 *Stryker* ATGM
  MANPATS *Javelin*
AMPHIBIOUS 124
  LCU 45: 11 LCU-1600 (capacity either 2 MBT or 350 troops); 34 LCU-2000
  LC 79: 6 *Frank Besson* (capacity 32 *Abrams* MBT); 73 LCM-8 (capacity either 1 MBT or 200 troops)
AIRCRAFT
  ISR 49: 37 RC-12D/H/K *Guardrail*; 12 RC-12P/Q *Guardrail*
  ELINT 9: 3 *Dash-7* ARL-M (COMINT/ELINT); 3 *Dash-7* ARL-1 (IMINT); 3 *Dash-7* ARL-C (COMINT)
  TPT 196 **Light** 194: 113 Beech A200 *King Air* (C-12 *Huron*); 28 Cessna 560 *Citation* (UC-35); 11 SA-227 *Metro* (C-26); 42 Short 330 *Sherpa* (C-23A/B) **PAX** 2 Gulfstream (C-20)
HELICOPTERS
  ATK 697: 16 AH-64A *Apache*; 681 AH-64D *Apache*
  MRH 326 OH-58D *Kiowa Warrior*
  ISR 120 OH-58A/C *Kiowa*
  SAR 26 HH-60L *Black Hawk*

TPT 2,903 **Heavy** 372: 221 CH-47D *Chinook,* 151 CH-47F *Chinook* **Medium** 2,072: 885 UH-60A *Black Hawk;* 747 UH-60L *Black Hawk;* 440 UH-60M *Black Hawk* **Light** 305: 240 EC145 (UH-72A *Lakota*); 65 UH-1H/V *Iroquois*
TRG 154 TH-67 *Creek*

UAV • ISR 304

Heavy 68: 3 *I-Gnat;* 26 MQ-1C *Grey Eagle;* 20 RQ-5A *Hunter;* 4 *Sky Warrior;* 15 *Warrior*
Medium 236 RQ-7A *Shadow*

AD • SAM 1,281+

SP 798: 703 FIM-92A *Avenger* (veh-mounted *Stinger*); 95 M6 *Linebacker* (4 *Stinger* plus 25mm gun)
TOWED 480 MIM-104 *Patriot*/PAC-2/PAC-3
MANPAD FIM-92A *Stinger*

RADAR • LAND 251: 98 AN/TPQ-36 *Firefinder* (arty); 56 AN/TPQ-37 *Firefinder* (arty); 60 AN/TRQ-32 *Teammate* (COMINT); 32 AN/TSQ-138 *Trailblazer* (COMINT); 5 AN/TSQ-138A *Trailblazer*

AEV 250 M9 ACE

ARV 1,108+: 1,096 M88A1/2 (ε1,000 more in store); 12 Pandur; some M578

VLB 60: 20 REBS; 40 *Wolverine* HAB

MW *Aardvark* JSFU Mk4; Hydrema 910 MCV-2; M58/M59 MICLIC; M139; *Rhino*

US Navy 322,700; 10,100 active reservists (total 333,248)

Comprises 2 Fleet Areas, Atlantic and Pacific. All combatants divided into 5 Fleets: 3rd – Pacific, 4th – Caribbean, Central and South America, 5th – Indian Ocean, Persian Gulf, Red Sea, 6th – Mediterranean, 7th – W. Pacific; plus Military Sealift Command (MSC); Naval Reserve Force (NRF); for Naval Special Warfare Command, see US Special Operations Command element.

EQUIPMENT BY TYPE
SUBMARINES 72

STRATEGIC • SSBN 14 *Ohio* (mod) opcon US STRATCOM with up to 24 UGM-133A *Trident* D-5 strategic SLBM, 4 single 533mm TT with Mk48 *Sea Arrow* HWT

TACTICAL 58

SSGN 44:

4 *Ohio* (mod) with total of 154 *Tomahawk* LACM , 4 single 533mm TT with Mk48 *Sea Arrow* HWT
8 *Los Angeles* with 1 12-cell VLS with *Tomahawk* LACM; 4 single 533mm TT with Mk48 *Sea Arrow* HWT/UGM-84 *Harpoon* AShM
23 *Los Angeles* (Imp) with 1 12-cell VLS with *Tomahawk* LACM, 4 single 533mm TT with Mk48 *Sea Arrow* HWT/UGM-84 *Harpoon* AShM
9 *Virginia* with 1 12-cell VLS with *Tomahawk* LACM, 4 single 533mm TT with Mk48 ADCAP mod 6 HWT (3 additional vessels in build)

SSN 14:

11 *Los Angeles* with 4 single 533mm TT with Mk48 *Sea Arrow* HWT/UGM-84 *Harpoon* AShM
3 *Seawolf* with 8 single 660mm TT with up to 45 *Tomahawk* LACM/UGM-84C *Harpoon* AShM, Mk48 *Sea Arrow* HWT

PRINCIPAL SURFACE COMBATANTS 112
AIRCRAFT CARRIERS • CVN 11:

1 *Enterprise* with 3 octuple Mk29 GMLS with RIM-7M/P *Sea Sparrow* SAM, 2 Mk49 GMLS with RIM-116 SAM (typical capacity 55 F/A-18 *Hornet* FGA ac; 4 EA-6B *Prowler*/EA-18G *Growler* EW ac; 4 E-2C/D *Hawkeye* AEW ac; 4 SH-60F *Seahawk* ASW hel; 2 HH-60H *Seahawk* SAR hel); (to decommission Dec 2012)
10 *Nimitz* with 2–3 octuple Mk29 lnchr with RIM-7M/P *Sea Sparrow* SAM, 2 Mk49 GMLS with RIM-116 SAM (typical capacity 55 F/A-18 *Hornet* FGA ac; 4 EA-6B *Prowler*/EA-18G *Growler* EW ac; 4 E-2C/D *Hawkeye* AEW ac; 4 SH-60F *Seahawk* ASW hel; 2 HH-60H *Seahawk* SAR hel)

CRUISERS • CGHM • 22 *Ticonderoga* (*Aegis* Baseline 2/3/4) with *Aegis* C2, 2 quad lnchr with RGM-84 *Harpoon* AShM, 2 61-cell Mk41 VLS with SM-2ER SAM/*Tomahawk* LACM, 2 127mm gun (capacity 2 SH-60B *Seahawk* ASW hel); (extensive upgrade programme scheduled from 2006–2020 to include sensors and fire control systems; major weapons upgrade to include *Evolved Sea Sparrow* (ESSM), SM-3/SM-2 capability and 2 Mk45 Mod 2 127mm gun - 4 to decommission Mar 2013)

DESTROYERS 62

DDGHM 34 *Arleigh Burke* Flight IIA with *Aegis* C2, 2 quad lnchr with RGM-84 *Harpoon* AShM, 1 32-cell Mk41 VLS with ASROC/SM-2ER SAM/*Tomahawk* (TLAM) LACM, 1 64-cell Mk41 VLS with ASROC ASsW/SM-2 ER SAM/*Tomahawk* LACM, 2 triple 324mm ASTT with Mk46 LWT, 1 127mm gun, (capacity 2 SH-60B *Seahawk* ASW hel), (additional ships in build)
DDGM 28 *Arleigh Burke* Flight I/II with *Aegis* C2, 2 quad lnchr with RGM-84 *Harpoon* AShM, 1 32-cell Mk41 VLS with ASROC/SM-2ER SAM/*Tomahawk* LACM, 1 64-cell Mk 41 VLS with ASROC/SM-2 ER SAM/*Tomahawk* LACM, 2 Mk49 RAM with RIM-116 RAM SAM, 2 triple 324mm ASTT with Mk46 LWT, 1 127mm gun, 1 hel landing platform

FRIGATES 17

FFHM 3:

2 *Freedom* with 1 21 cell Mk99 lnchr with RIM-116 SAM, (capacity 2 MH-60R/S *Seahawk* hel or 1 MH-60 with 3 MQ-8 *Firescout* UAV)
1 *Independence* with 1 11-cell SeaRAM lnchr with RIM-116 SAM, (capacity 1 MH-60R/S *Seahawk* hel and 3 MQ-8 *Firescout* UAV)

FFH 14 *Oliver Hazard Perry* with 2 triple 324mm ASTT with Mk46 LWT, 1 76mm gun, (capacity 2 SH-60B *Seahawk* ASW hel)

PATROL AND COASTAL COMBATANTS 41
PCF 13 *Cyclone*
PBF 12
PBR 16

MINE WARFARE • MINE COUNTERMEASURES 9
MCO 9 *Avenger* with 1 SLQ-48 MCM system, 1 SQQ-32(V)3 Sonar (mine hunting)

COMMAND SHIPS • LCC 2:
2 *Blue Ridge* (capacity 3 LCPL; 2 LCVP; 700 troops; 1 med utl hel)
AMPHIBIOUS
PRINCIPAL AMPHIBIOUS SHIPS 29
LHD 8 *Wasp* with 2 octuple Mk29 GMLS with RIM-7M/RIM-7P *Sea Sparrow* SAM, 2 Mk49 GMLS with RIM-116 RAM SAM (capacity: 5 AV-8B *Harrier* II FGA; 42 CH-46E *Sea Knight* hel; 6 SH-60B *Seahawk* hel; 3 LCAC(L); 60 tanks; 1,890 troops)
LHA 1 *Tarawa* with 2 Mk49 GMLS with RIM-116 RAM SAM (capacity 6 AV-8B *Harrier* II FGA ac; 12 CH-46E *Sea Knight* hel; 9 CH-53 *Sea Stallion* hel; 4 LCU; 100 tanks; 1,900 troops)
LPD 8:
2 *Austin* (capacity 6 CH-46E *Sea Knight* hel; 2 LCAC(L)/LCU; 40 tanks; 788 troops)
6 *San Antonio* with 2 21 cell Mk49 GMLS with RIM-116 SAM (capacity 1 CH-53E *Sea Stallion* hel or 2 CH-46 *Sea Knight* or 1 MV-22 *Osprey*; 2 LCAC(L); 14 AAAV; 720 troops) (5 additional vessels in build)
LSD 12:
4 *Harpers Ferry* with 1–2 Mk 49 GMLS with RIM-116 SAM, 1 hel landing platform (capacity 2 LCAC(L); 40 tanks; 500 troops)
8 *Whidbey Island* with 2 Mk49 GMLS with RIM-116 SAM, 1 hel landing platform (capacity 4 LCAC(L); 40 tanks; 500 troops)
AMPHIBIOUS CRAFT 269+
LCU 34 LCU-1600 (capacity either 2 M1-A1 *Abrams* MBT or 350 troops)
LCVP 8
LCPL 75
LCM 72
LCAC 80 LCAC(L) (capacity either 1 MBT or 60 troops; (undergoing upgrade programme))
SF 6 DDS opcon USSOCOM

Navy Reserve Surface Forces
PRINCIPAL SURFACE COMBATANTS 8
FFH 8 *Oliver Hazard Perry* with 2 triple 324mm ASTT with Mk46 LWT, 36 SM-1 MR SAM, 1 76mm gun, (capacity 2 SH-60B *Seahawk* ASW hel)
MINE WARFARE • MINE COUNTERMEASURES 5
MCO 5 *Avenger* with 1 SLQ-48 MCM system, 1 SQQ-32(V)3 Sonar (mine hunting)
INSHORE UNDERSEA WARFARE 45 HDS/IBU/MIUW

Naval Reserve Forces 105,250 (incl 10,100 active)

Selected Reserve 62,500

Individual Ready Reserve 42,750

Naval Inactive Fleet
Under a minimum of 60–90 days notice for reactivation; still on naval vessel register
PRINCIPAL SURFACE COMBATANTS 2
AIRCRAFT CARRIERS 1 **CV**
FRIGATES 1 **FFH**

AMPHIBIOUS 12
2 **LHA**
5 **LPD**
5 **LKA**
LOGISTICS AND SUPPORT 1 ATF

Military Sealift Command (MSC)

Combat Logistics Force
LOGISTICS AND SUPPORT 33
AEH 1 *Kilauea*
AO 15 *Henry J. Kaiser*
AOE 4 *Supply*
AKEH 13 *Lewis and Clark* (1 additional vessel in build)

Maritime Prepositioning Program
LOGISTICS AND SUPPORT 30
AOT 1 *Champion*
AG 1
AK 7
AKR 13: 3; 2 *Bob Hope*; 8 *Watson*
AKRH 5
AVB 2
AP 1 HSV

Strategic Sealift Force
(At a minimum of 4 days readiness)
LOGISTICS AND SUPPORT 18
AOT 3 (long-term chartered)
AK 3
AKR 9: 5 *Bob Hope*; 2 *Gordon*; 2 *Shughart*
AP 3 HSV

Special Mission Ships
LOGISTICS AND SUPPORT 16
AGM 4: 1 *Howard O. Lorenzen*; 1 *Invincible*; 1 *Observation Island*; 1 Sea-based X-band Radar
AGOS 5: 1 *Impeccable*; 4 *Victorious*
AGS 7: 6 *Pathfinder*; 1 *Waters*

Service Support Ships
LOGISTICS AND SUPPORT 14
ARS 4 *Safeguard*
AFSB 1 *Ponce* (modified *Austin*-class LPD)
AH 2 *Mercy*, with 1 hel landing platform
ARC 1 *Zeus*
AS 2 *Emory S Land*
ATF 4 *Powhatan*

US Maritime Administration Support • National Defense Reserve Fleet
LOGISTICS AND SUPPORT 34
AOT 4
ACS 3 *Keystone State*
AFS 1
AGOS 3
AGS 3
AK 16: 4; 12 T-AK (breakbulk)
AKR 2
AP 2

Ready Reserve Force

Ships at readiness up to a maximum of 30 days

LOGISTICS AND SUPPORT 48:

  ACS 6 *Keystone State*

  AK 6: 2 T-AK (breakbulk); 4 T-AK (heavy lift)

  AKR 35: 1 *Adm WM M Callaghan*; 8 *Algol*; 26 *Cape Island*

  AOT 1 *Petersburg*

Augmentation Force

COMBAT SERVICE SUPPORT

  1 (active) Cargo Handling log bn

  12 (reserve) Cargo Handling log bn

Naval Aviation 98,600

10 air wg. Average air wing comprises 8 sqns: 4 each with 12 F/A-18 (2 with F/A-18C, 1 with F/A-18E, 1 with F/A-18F), 1 with SH-60B/MH-60R, 1 with EA-6B/EA-18G, 1 with E-2C/D; 1 with MH-60S

FORCES BY ROLE

FIGHTER/GROUND ATTACK

  1 sqn with F/A-18A+ *Hornet*

  12 sqn with F/A-18C *Hornet*

  12 sqn with F/A-18E *Super Hornet*

  10 sqn with F/A-18F *Super Hornet*

ANTI-SUBMARINE WARFARE

  3 sqn with HH-60H *Seahawk*; SH-60F *Seahawk*

  6 sqn with MH-60R *Seahawk*

  7 sqn with SH-60B *Seahawk*

ELINT

  1 sqn with EP-3E *Aries* II

ELINT/ELECTRONIC WARFARE

  7 sqn with EA-6B *Prowler*

  6 sqn with EA-18G *Growler*

MARITIME PATROL

  12 (land-based) sqn with P-3C *Orion*

AIRBORNE EARLY WARNING & CONTROL

  10 sqn with E-2C/D *Hawkeye*

COMMAND & CONTROL

  2 sqn with E-6B *Mercury*

MINE COUNTERMEASURES

  2 sqn with MH-53E *Sea Dragon*

TRANSPORT

  2 sqn with C-2A *Greyhound*

TRAINING

  1 (FRS) sqn with EA-18G *Growler*

  1 (FRS) sqn with E-2C *Hawkeye*

  1 (FRS) sqn with E-6B *Mercury*

  2 (FRS) sqn with F/A-18A/A+/B/C/D *Hornet*; F/A-18E/F *Super Hornet*

  1 (FRS) sqn (forming) with F-35C *Lightning* II

  1 (FRS) sqn with MH-60S *Knight Hawk*; HH-60H *Seahawk*; SH-60F *Seahawk*

  1 (FRS) sqn with MH-60R *Seahawk*

  1 sqn with P-3C *Orion*

  1 (FRS) sqn with P-3C *Orion*; P-8A *Poseidon*

  1 (FRS) sqn with SH-60B *Seahawk*

  4 sqn with T-6A/B *Texan* II

  1 sqn with T-39G/N *Sabreliner*; T-45C *Goshawk*

  2 sqn T-34C *Turbo Mentor*

  1 sqn with T-44A *Pegasus*

  4 sqn with T-45A/C *Goshawk*

  1 sqn with TC-12B *Huron*

  2 hel sqn with TH-57B/C *Sea Ranger*

TRANSPORT HELICOPTER

  13 sqn with MH-60S *Knight Hawk*

EQUIPMENT BY TYPE

AIRCRAFT 964 combat capable

  FGA 817: 33 F/A-18A/A+ *Hornet*; 24 F/A-18B *Hornet*; 268 F/A-18C *Hornet*; 41 F/A-18D *Hornet*; 201 F/A-18E *Super Hornet*; 250 F/A-18F *Super Hornet*

  ASW 152: 147 P-3C *Orion*; 5 P-8A *Poseidon*

  EW 167: 92 EA-6B *Prowler*; 75 EA-18G *Growler*

  ELINT 11 EP-3E *Aries* II

  ISR 4: 2 RC-12F *Huron*; 2 RC-12M *Huron*

  AEW&C 66 E-2C/D *Hawkeye*

  C2 16 E-6B *Mercury*

  TPT 92: **Medium** 3: 2 LC-130F *Hercules*; 1 LC-130R *Hercules*; **Light** 80: 4 Beech A200 *King Air* (C-12C *Huron*); 21 Beech A200 *King Air* (UC-12B *Huron*); 35 C-2A *Greyhound*; 1 Cessna 560 *Citation Encore* (UC-35D); 1 *Sabreliner* (CT-39G); 2 DHC-2 *Beaver* (U-6A); 7 SA-227-BC *Metro* III (C-26D); 4 UP-3A *Orion*; 5 VP-3A *Orion* **PAX** 9: 1 Gulfstream III (C-20A); 2 Gulfstream III (C-20D); 5 Gulfstream IV (C-20G); 1 Gulfstream V (C-37);

  TRG 647: 47 T-6A *Texan* II; 2 T-6B *Texan* II; 269 T-34C *Turbo Mentor*; 9 T-38 *Talon*; 1 T-39D *Sabreliner*; 8 T-39G *Sabreliner*; 15 T-39N *Sabreliner*; 55 T-44A *Pegasus*; 74 T-45A *Goshawk*; 144 T-45C *Goshawk*; 21 TC-12B *Huron*; 2 TE-2C *Hawkeye*

HELICOPTERS

  MRH 219 MH-60S *Knight Hawk* (Multi Mission Support)

  ASW 255: 35 MH-60R *Seahawk*; 148 SH-60B *Seahawk*; 72 SH-60F *Seahawk*

  MCM 28 MH-53E *Sea Dragon*

  ISR 3 OH-58A *Kiowa*

  SAR 36 HH-60H *Seahawk*

  TPT 37 **Heavy** 18: 9 CH-53D *Sea Stallion*; 9 CH-53E *Sea Stallion* **Medium** 14: 9 UH-46D *Sea Knight*; 3 UH-60L *Black Hawk*; 2 VH-3A *Sea King* (VIP) **Light** 5: 1 UH-1N *Iroquois*; 4 UH-1Y *Iroquois*;

  TRG 132: 44 TH-57B *Sea Ranger*; 82 TH-57C *Sea Ranger*; 6 TH-6B

UAV 53

  Heavy 18: 14 MQ-8B *Fire Scout* (under evaluation and trials); 4 RQ-4A *Global Hawk* (under evaluation and trials)

  Medium 35 RQ-2B *Pioneer*

MSL

  AAM • IR AIM-9 *Sidewinder*; **IIR** AIM-9X *Sidewinder* II, **SARH** AIM-7 *Sparrow*; **ARH** AIM-120 AMRAAM

  ASM AGM-65A/F *Maverick*; AGM-114B/K/M *Hellfire*; AGM-84E SLAM/SLAM-ER LACM; AGM-154A JSOW; **AShM** AGM-84D *Harpoon*; AGM-119A *Penguin* 3; **ARM** AGM-88 HARM

BOMBS

  Conventional: BLU-117/Mk 84 (2,000lb); BLU-110/Mk 83 (1,000lb); BLU-111/Mk 82 (500lb); Mk 46; Mk 50; Mk 54

Laser-Guided: *Paveway* II; *Paveway* III (fits on Mk 82, Mk 83 or Mk 84)

INS/GPS guided: JDAM (GBU-31/32/38); Enhanced *Paveway* II

Naval Aviation Reserve

FORCES BY ROLE

FIGHTER/GROUND ATTACK
  1 sqn with F/A-18A+ *Hornet*

ANTI-SUBMARINE WARFARE
  1 sqn with HH-60H *Seahawk*
  1 sqn with SH-60B *Seahawk*

ELECTRONIC WARFARE
  1 sqn with EA-6B *Prowler*

MARITIME PATROL
  2 sqn with P-3C *Orion*

TRANSPORT
  4 log spt sqn with B-737-700 (C-40A *Clipper*)
  2 log spt sqn with Gulfstream III/IV (C-20A/D/G); Gulfstream V/G550 (C-37A/C-37B)
  5 tactical tpt sqn with C-130T *Hercules*
  1 log spt sqn with DC-9 (C-9B *Skytrain* II)

TRAINING
  2 (aggressor) sqn with F-5F/N *Tiger* II
  1 (aggressor) sqn with F/A-18C *Hornet*

TRANSPORT HELICOPTER
  2 sqn with HH-60H *Seahawk*

EQUIPMENT BY TYPE

AIRCRAFT 68 combat capable
  FTR 32: 2 F-5F *Tiger* II; 30 F-5N *Tiger* II
  FGA 24: 12 F/A-18A+ *Hornet*; 12 F/A-18C *Hornet*
  ASW 12 P-3C *Orion*
  EW 4 EA-6B *Prowler*
  AEW&C 6 E-2C *Hawkeye* (being withdrawn)
  TPT 50: **Medium** 19 C-130T *Hercules*; **Light** 5 Beech A200C *King Air* (UC-12B *Huron*); **PAX** 26: 12 B-737-700 (C-40A *Clipper*); 4 DC-9 *Skytrain* II (C-9B); 6 Gulfstream III/IV (C-20A/D/G); 1 Gulfstream V (C-37A); 3 Gulfstream G550 (C-37B)

HELICOPTERS
  ASW 6 SH-60B *Seahawk*
  MCM 8 MH-53E *Sea Stallion*
  SAR 24 HH-60H *Rescue Hawk*

US Marine Corps 197,300; 2,250 active reservists (total 199,550)

3 Marine Expeditionary Forces (MEF), 3 Marine Expeditionary Brigades (MEB), 7 Marine Expeditionary Units (MEU) drawn from 3 div. An MEU usually consists of a battalion landing team (1 SF coy, 1 lt armd recce coy, 1 recce pl, 1 armd pl, 1 amph aslt pl, 1 inf bn, 1 arty bty, 1 cbt engr pl), an aviation combat element (1 medium lift sqn with attached atk hel, FGA ac and AD assets) and a composite log bn, with a combined total of about 2,200 men. Composition varies with mission requirements.

FORCES BY ROLE

MANOEUVRE
  Reconnaissance
  3 MEF recce coy

Amphibious
  1 (1st) mne div (2 (LAV-25) lt armd recce bn, 1 recce bn, 1 armd bn, 3 inf regt (4 inf bn), 1 amph aslt bn, 1 arty regt (4 arty bn), 1 cbt engr bn)
  1 (2nd) mne div (1 lt armd recce bn, 1 recce bn, 1 armd bn, 3 inf regt (4 inf bn), 1 amph aslt bn, 1 arty regt (3 arty bn), 1 cbt engr bn)
  1 (3rd) mne div (1 recce bn, 1 inf regt (3 inf bn), 1 arty regt (2 arty bn), 1 cbt spt bn (1 lt armd recce coy, 1 amph aslt coy, 1 cbt engr coy))

COMBAT SERVICE SUPPORT
  3 log gp

EQUIPMENT BY TYPE

MBT 447 M1A1 *Abrams*
RECCE 252 LAV-25 *Coyote* (25mm gun, plus 189 variants)
AAV 1,311 AAV-7A1 (all roles)
APC • PPV 4,059: 2,380 MRAP; 1,679 M-ATV
ARTY 1,506
  TOWED 832: **105mm:** 331 M101A1; **155mm** 501 M777
  MRL 227mm 40 HIMARS
  MOR 634 **81mm** 585: 50 LAV-M; 535 M252 **120mm** 49 EFSS
AT
  MSL 2,299
    SP 95 LAV-TOW
    MANPATS 2,204: 1,121 *Predator*; 1,083 TOW
AD • SAM • MANPAD FIM-92A *Stinger*
UAV • Light 100 BQM-147 *Exdrone*
RADAR • LAND 23 AN/TPQ-36 *Firefinder* (arty)
AEV 42 M1 ABV
ARV 185: 60 AAVRA1; 45 LAV-R; 80 M88A1/2
VLB 6 Joint Aslt Bridge

Marine Corps Aviation 34,700

3 active Marine Aircraft Wings (MAW) and 1 MCR MAW

Flying hours   365 hrs/year on tpt ac; 248 hrs/year on ac; 277 hrs/year on hel

FORCES BY ROLE

FIGHTER
  1 sqn with F/A-18A/A+ *Hornet*
  6 sqn with F/A-18C *Hornet*
  5 sqn (All Weather) with F/A-18D *Hornet*

FIGHTER/GROUND ATTACK
  7 sqn with AV-8B *Harrier* II

ELECTRONIC WARFARE
  4 sqn with EA-6B *Prowler*

COMBAT SEARCH & RESCUE/TRANSPORT
  1 sqn with Beech A200/B200 *King Air* (UC-12B/F *Huron*); Cessna 560 *Citation Ultra/Encore* (UC-35C/D); DC-9 *Skytrain* (C-9B *Nightingale*); Gulfstream IV (C-20G); HH-1N *Iroquois*; HH-46E *Sea Knight*

TANKER
  3 sqn with KC-130J *Hercules*

TRANSPORT
  11 sqn with MV-22B *Osprey*

TRAINING
  1 sqn with AV-8B *Harrier* II; TAV-8B *Harrier*
  1 sqn with F/A-18B/C/D *Hornet*
  1 sqn with F-35B *Lightning* II

1 sqn with MV-22A *Osprey*
1 hel sqn with AH-1W *Cobra*; AH-1Z *Viper*; HH-1N
Iroquois; UH-1N *Iroquois*; UH-1Y *Venom*
1 hel sqn with CH-46E *Sea Knight*
1 hel sqn with CH-53E *Sea Stallion*

ATTACK HELICOPTER
3 sqn with AH-1W *Cobra*; UH-1N *Iroquois*
4 sqn with AH-1W *Cobra*; UH-1Y *Venom*
1 sqn with AH-1W *Cobra*; AH-1Z *Viper*; UH-1Y *Venom*
1 sqn with AH-1Z *Viper*; UH-1Y *Venom*

TRANSPORT HELICOPTER
4 sqn with CH-46E *Sea Knight*
8 sqn with CH-53E *Sea Stallion*
1 (VIP) sqn with CH-46E *Sea Knight*; VH-3D *Sea King*;
VH-60N *Presidential Hawk*

ISR UAV
3 sqn with RQ-7B *Shadow*

AIR DEFENCE
2 bn with FIM-92A *Avenger*; FIM-92A *Stinger* (can
provide additional heavy calibre support weapons)

EQUIPMENT BY TYPE
AIRCRAFT 380 combat capable
  FGA 380: 16 F-35B *Lightning* II; 43 F/A-18A/A+ *Hornet*;
  2 F/A-18B *Hornet*; 83 F/A-18C *Hornet*; 94 F/A-18D
  Hornet; 125 AV-8B *Harrier* II; 17 TAV-8B *Harrier*
  EW 29 EA-6B *Prowler*
  TKR 47 KC-130J *Hercules*
  TPT 19 **Light** 16: 9 Beech A200/B200 *King Air* (UC-
  12B/F *Huron*); 7 Cessna 560 *Citation Ultra/Encore* (UC-
  35C/D); **PAX** 3: 2 DC-9 *Skytrain* (C-9B *Nightingale*); 1
  Gulfstream IV (C-20G);
  TRG 3 T-34C *Turbo Mentor*
TILTROTOR 180
  20 MV-22A *Osprey*; 160 MV-22B *Osprey*
HELICOPTERS
  ATK 156: 127 AH-1W *Cobra*; 29 AH-1Z *Viper*
  SAR 9: 5 HH-1N *Iroquois*; 4 HH-46E *Sea Knight*
  TPT 408 **Heavy** 179: 34 CH-53D *Sea Stallion*; 145 CH-
  53E *Sea Stallion*; **Medium** 109: 90 CH-46E *Sea Knight*;
  8 VH-60N *Presidential Hawk* (VIP tpt); 11 VH-3D *Sea
  King* (VIP tpt); **Light** 120: 50 UH-1N *Iroquois*; 70 UH-1Y
  Iroquois
UAV • ISR • Medium 32 RQ-7B *Shadow*
AD
  SAM • SP some FIM-92A *Avenger*
    MANPAD some FIM-92A *Stinger*
MSL
  AAM • IR AIM-9M *Sidewinder*; **IIR** AIM-9X; **SARH**
  AIM-7 *Sparrow*; **ARH** AIM-120 AMRAAM
  ASM AGM-65F IR *Maverick*/AGM-65E *Maverick*;
  AGM-114 *Hellfire*; AGM-175 *Griffin* **AShM** AGM-84
  Harpoon; **ARM** AGM-88 HARM
BOMBS
  Conventional: CBU-59; CBU-99; MK-82 (500lb);
  MK-83 (1,000lb)
  Laser-Guided: GBU 10/12/16 *Paveway* II (fits on Mk
  82, Mk 83 or Mk 84)
  INS/GPS Guided: JDAM

Reserve Organisations

Marine Corps Reserve 39,600 (incl 2,250 active)
FORCES BY ROLE
MANOEUVRE
  Reconnaissance
  2 MEF recce coy
  Amphibious
  1 (4th) div (3 inf regt (3 inf bn), 1 arty regt (4 arty bn),
  1 (LAV-25) lt armd recce bn, 1 recce bn, 1 amph aslt
  bn, 1 cbt engr bn)
COMBAT SERVICE SUPPORT
  1 log gp

Marine Corps Aviation Reserve 11,592 reservists
FORCES BY ROLE
FIGHTER
  1 sqn with F/A-18A/A+ *Hornet*
TANKER
  2 sqn with KC-130T *Hercules*
TRAINING
  1 sqn with F-5F/N *Tiger* II
ATTACK HELICOPTER
  1 sqn with AH-1W *Cobra*; UH-1N *Iroquois*
TRANSPORT HELICOPTER
  2 sqn with CH-46E *Sea Knight*
  1 det with CH-53E *Sea Stallion*
ISR UAV
  1 sqn with RQ-7B *Shadow*
EQUIPMENT BY TYPE
AIRCRAFT 27 combat capable
  FTR 12: 1 F-5F *Tiger* II; 11 F-5N *Tiger* II
  FGA 15 F/A-18A/A+ *Hornet*
  TKR 28 KC-130T *Hercules*
  TPT • Light 7: 2 Beech A200 *King Air* (UC-12B *Huron*);
  5 Cessna 560 *Citation Ultra/Encore* (UC-35C/D)
HELICOPTERS
  ATK 12 AH-1W *Cobra*
  TPT 44 **Heavy** 6 CH-53E *Sea Stallion*; **Medium** 26 CH-
  46E *Sea Knight*; **Light** 12 UH-1N *Iroquois*
UAV • ISR • Medium 4 RQ-7B *Shadow*

Marine Stand-by Reserve 700 reservists
Trained individuals available for mobilisation

US Coast Guard 43,600 (military); 7,650 (civilian)
Comprises Force Readiness Command (FORCECOM); and
Operational Command (OPCOM). 9 districts (4 Pacific, 5
Atlantic). 2 (1 Atlantic, 1 Pacific) Maintenance and Logistics
Command Atlantic (MLCA)
PATROL AND COASTAL COMBATANTS 156
  PSOH 25: 1 *Alex Haley*; 13 *Famous*; 8 *Hamilton*; 3 *Legend*
  PCO 17: 14 *Reliance*; 3 *Sentinel*
  PCC 41 *Island*
  PBI 73 *Marine Protector*
LOGISTICS AND SUPPORT 384
  ABU 16 *Juniper*
  AGB 4: 1 *Mackinaw*; 1 *Healy*; 2 *Polar Icebreaker*
  AX 1 *Eagle*
  WLI 4

WLIC 13
WLM 14 *Keeper*
WLR 18
WTGB 9 *Bay*-class
YAG 177: 107 *Response*; 70 Utility Boat
YP 117
YTM 11

US Coast Guard Aviation
AIRCRAFT
   MP 14: 3 HU-25A *Guardian*; 6 HU-25C+; 5 HU-25D
   SAR 27: 21 HC-130H *Hercules* (additional 4 in store); 6 HC-130J *Hercules*
   TPT 16 **Light** 14 CN-235-200 (HC-144A); **PAX** 2 Gulfstream V (C-37A)
HELICOPTERS
   SAR 125: 35 MH-60J/T *Jayhawk* (additional 7 in store); 90 AS366G1 (HH-65C/MH-65C/D) *Dauphin* II (additional 11 in store)

US Air Force (USAF) 328,900; 14,300 active ANG; 2,900 active AFR (total 346,100)
Flying hours Ftr 189, bbr 260, tkr 308, airlift 343

Almost the entire USAF (plus active force ANG and AFR) is divided into 10 Aerospace Expeditionary Forces (AEF), each on call for 120 days every 20 months. At least 2 of the 10 AEFs are on call at any one time, each with 10,000–15,000 personnel, 90 multi-role Ftr and bbr ac, 31 intra-theatre refuelling aircraft and 13 aircraft for ISR and EW missions.

Global Strike Command (GSC)
2 active air forces (8th & 20th); 6 wg
FORCES BY ROLE
MISSILE
   9 sqn with LGM-30G *Minuteman* III
BOMBER
   5 sqn (inlc 1 trg) with B-52H *Stratofortress*
   2 sqn with B-2A *Spirit*

Air Combat Command (ACC)
2 active air forces (9th & 12th); 15 wg. ACC numbered air forces provide the air component to CENTCOM, SOUTHCOM and NORTHCOM.
FORCES BY ROLE
BOMBER
   4 sqn with B-1B *Lancer*
FIGHTER
   3 sqn with F-22A *Raptor*
FIGHTER/GROUND ATTACK
   4 sqn with F-15E *Strike Eagle*
   5 sqn with F-16C/D *Fighting Falcon*
GROUND ATTACK
   3 sqn with A-10C *Thunderbolt* II
ELECTRONIC WARFARE
   1 sqn with EA-6B *Prowler*; EA-18G *Growler* (personnel only – USN aircraft)
   2 sqn with EC-130H *Compass Call*
ISR
   1 sqn with Beech 350ER *King Air* (MC-12W *Liberty*)

5 sqn with OC-135/RC-135/WC-135
2 sqn with U-2S
AIRBORNE EARLY WARNING & CONTROL
   5 sqn with E-3B/C *Sentry*
COMMAND & CONTROL
   1 sqn with E-4B
COMBAT SEARCH & RESCUE
   6 sqn with HC-130J/N/P *King*; HH-60G *Pave Hawk*
TRAINING
   2 sqn with A-10C *Thunderbolt* II
   1 sqn with Beech 350ER *King Air* (MC-12W *Liberty*)
   2 sqn with F-15E *Strike Eagle*
   1 sqn with RQ-4A *Global Hawk*; TU-2S
   1 UAV sqn with MQ-1B *Predator*
   3 UAV sqn with MQ-9A *Reaper*
COMBAT/ISR UAV
   4 sqn with MQ-1B *Predator*
   1 sqn with MQ-1B *Predator*/MQ-9A *Reaper*
   1 sqn with MQ-1B *Predator*/RQ-170 *Sentinel*
   2 sqn with MQ-9 *Reaper*
ISR UAV
   2 sqn with RQ-4B *Global Hawk*

Pacific Air Forces (PACAF)
Provides the air component of PACOM, and commands air units based in Alaska, Hawaii, Japan and South Korea. 3 active air forces (5th, 7th, & 11th); 8 wg
FORCES BY ROLE
FIGHTER
   2 sqn with F-15C/D *Eagle*
   2 sqn with F-22A *Raptor* (+1 sqn personnel only)
FIGHTER/GROUND ATTACK
   5 sqn with F-16C/D *Fighting Falcon*
GROUND ATTACK
   1 sqn with A-10C *Thunderbolt* II
AIRBORNE EARLY WARNING & CONTROL
   2 sqn with E-3B/C *Sentry*
COMBAT SEARCH & RESCUE
   1 sqn with HH-60G *Pave Hawk*
TANKER
   1 sqn with KC-135R (+1 sqn personnel only)
TRANSPORT
   1 sqn with B-737-200 (C-40B); Gulfstream V (C-37A)
   2 sqn with C-17A *Globemaster*
   1 sqn with C-130H *Hercules*
   1 sqn with Beech 1900C (C-12J); UH-1N *Huey*
TRAINING
   1 (aggressor) sqn with F-16C/D *Fighting Falcon*

United States Air Forces Europe (USAFE)
Provides the air component to both EUCOM and AFRICOM. 1 active air force (3rd); 5 wg
FORCES BY ROLE
FIGHTER
   1 sqn with F-15C/D *Eagle*
FIGHTER/GROUND ATTACK
   2 sqn with F-15E *Strike Eagle*
   3 sqn with F-16C/D *Fighting Falcon*
GROUND ATTACK
   1 sqn with A-10C *Thunderbolt* II

COMBAT SEARCH & RESCUE
    1 sqn with HH-60G *Pave Hawk*
TANKER
    1 sqn with KC-135R *Stratotanker*
TRANSPORT
    1 sqn with C-130J *Hercules*
    2 sqn with Gulfstream III/IV (C-20); Gulfstream V (C-37); Learjet 35A (C-21)

Air Mobility Command (AMC)

Provides strategic and tactical airlift, air-to-air refuelling and aero medical evacuation. 1 active air force (18th); 13 wg and 1 gp

FORCES BY ROLE
TANKER
    4 sqn with KC-10A *Extender*
    7 sqn with KC-135R/T *Stratotanker* (+1 sqn with personnel only)
TRANSPORT
    1 VIP sqn with B-737-200 (C-40B); B-757-200 (C-32A)
    1 VIP sqn with Gulfstream III/IV (C-20)
    1 VIP sqn with VC-25 *Air Force One*
    2 sqn with C-5B/C/M *Galaxy*
    11 sqn with C-17A *Globemaster* III
    6 sqn with C-130H/J *Hercules* (+2 sqn personnel only)
    1 sqn with Gulfstream V (C-37A)
    4 sqn with Learjet 35A (C-21)

Air Education and Training Command

1 active air force (2nd), 10 active air wgs

FORCES BY ROLE
TRAINING
    1 sqn with C-17A *Globemaster* III
    1 sqn with C-21 Learjet
    2 sqn with C-130H/J *Hercules*
    6 sqn with F-16C/D *Fighting Falcon*
    1 sqn with F-22A *Raptor*
    1 sqn with F-35A *Lightning* II
    1 sqn with KC-135R *Stratotanker*
    5 (flying trg) sqn with T-1A *Jayhawk*
    10 (flying trg) sqn with T-6A *Texan* II
    12 (flying trg) sqn with T-38C *Talon*
    1 UAV sqn with MQ-1B *Predator*

EQUIPMENT BY TYPE
AIRCRAFT 1,430 combat capable
    BBR 139: 64 B-1B *Lancer* (2 more in test); 19 B-2A *Spirit* (1 more in test); 56 B-52H *Stratofortress* (4 more in test; 18 in store)
    FTR 279: 112 F-15C *Eagle*; 10 F-15D *Eagle*; 157 F-22A *Raptor*
    FGA 826: 211 F-15E *Strike Eagle*; 480 F-16C *Fighting Falcon*; 116 F-16D *Fighting Falcon*; 19 F-35A *Lightning* II
    ATK 186 A-10C *Thunderbolt* II
    EW 14 EC-130H *Compass Call*
    ISR 76: 37 Beech 350ER *King Air* (MC-12W *Liberty*); 2 E-9A; 2 OC-135B *Open Skies*; 28 U-2S; 5 TU-2S; 2 WC-135 *Constant Phoenix*
    ELINT 22: 8 RC-135V *Rivet Joint*; 9 RC-135W *Rivet Joint*; 3 RC-135S *Cobra Ball*; 2 RC-135U *Combat Sent*
    AEW&C 32 E-3B/C *Sentry* (1 more in test)

C2 4 E-4B
TKR 170: 140 KC-135R *Stratotanker*; 30 KC-135T *Stratotanker*
TKR/TPT 59 KC-10A *Extender*
CSAR 22 HC-130J/N/P *Combat King/Combat King* II
TPT 431 **Heavy** 228: 33 C-5B *Galaxy*; 2 C-5C *Galaxy*; 3 C-5M *Galaxy*; 190 C-17A *Globemaster* III **Medium** 140 C-130H/J *Hercules*; **Light** 39: 4 Beech 1900C (C-12J); 35 Learjet 35A (C-21) **PAX** 24: 2 B-737-700 (C-40B); 4 B-757-200 (C-32A); 5 Gulfstream III (C-20B); 2 Gulfstream IV (C-20H); 9 Gulfstream V (C-37A); 2 VC-25A *Air Force One*
TRG 1,130: 179 T-1A *Jayhawk*; 405 T-6A *Texan* II; 546 T-38A *Talon*
HELICOPTERS
    CSAR 81 HH-60G *Pave Hawk*
    TPT • Light 62 UH-1N *Huey*
UAV 215
    Cbt ISR • Heavy 191: 101 MQ-1B *Predator*; 90 MQ-9 *Reaper*
    ISR • Heavy 24+: 23 RQ-4B *Global Hawk*; 1+ RQ-170 *Sentinel*
MSL
    AAM • IR AIM-9 *Sidewinder* **IIR** AIM-9X *Sidewinder* II **SARH** AIM-7M *Sparrow* **ARH** AIM-120B/C AMRAAM
    ASM AGM-86B (ALCM) LACM (strategic); AGM-86C (CALCM) LACM (tactical); AGM-86D LACM (penetrator); AGM-130A; AGM-158 JASSM; AGM-65A *Maverick*/AGM-65B *Maverick*/AGM-65D *Maverick*/AGM-65G *Maverick*; AGM-175 *Griffin* **ARM** AGM-88A/AGM-88B HARM; **EW** MALD/MALD-J
    MANPAD FIM-92 *Stinger*
BOMBS
    Conventional: BLU-109/Mk 84 (2,000lb); BLU-110/Mk 83 (1,000lb); BLU-111/Mk 82 (500lb)
    Laser-guided: *Paveway* II, *Paveway* III (fits on Mk82, Mk83 or Mk84)
    INS/GPS guided: JDAM (GBU 31/32/38); GBU-15 (with BLU-109 penetrating warhead or Mk 84); GBU-39B Small Diameter Bomb (250lb); GBU-43B; GBU-57A/B; Enhanced *Paveway* III

Reserve Organisations

Air National Guard 101,600 reservists (incl 14,300 active)

FORCES BY ROLE
BOMBER
    1 sqn with B-2A *Spirit* (personnel only)
FIGHTER
    5 sqn with F-15C/D *Eagle*
    1 sqn with F-22A *Raptor* (+1 sqn personnel only)
FIGHTER/GROUND ATTACK
    13 sqn with F-16C/D *Fighting Falcon*
GROUND ATTACK
    5 sqn with A-10C *Thunderbolt* II
ISR
    3 sqn with E-8C J-STARS (mixed active force and ANG personnel)
COMBAT SEARCH & RESCUE
    9 sqn with HC-130 *Hercules*/MC-130P *Combat Shadow*; HH-60G *Pave Hawk*

TANKER
  16 sqn with KC-135R *Stratotanker* (+2 sqn with personnel only)
  3 sqn with KC-135T *Stratotanker*

TRANSPORT
  1 sqn with B-737-700 (C-40C); Gulfstream G100 (C-38A)
  2 sqn with C-5A *Galaxy*
  2 sqn with C-17A *Globemaster* (+2 sqn personnel only)
  3 sqn with C-27J *Spartan*
  12 sqn with C-130H *Hercules* (+1 sqn personnel only)
  1 sqn with C-130H/LC-130H *Hercules*
  2 sqn with C-130J *Hercules*
  4 sqn with Learjet 35A (C-21A)
  1 sqn with WC-130H *Hercules*

TRAINING
  1 sqn with C-130H *Hercules*
  1 sqn with F-15C/D *Eagle*
  4 sqn with F-16C/D *Fighting Falcon*

COMBAT/ISR UAV
  4 sqn with MQ-1B *Predator*
  1 sqn with MQ-9A *Reaper*

EQUIPMENT BY TYPE
AIRCRAFT 615 combat capable
  FTR 150: 108 F-15 *Eagle*; 22 F-15D *Eagle*; 20 F-22A *Raptor*
  FGA 359: 314 F-16C *Fighting Falcon*; 45 F-16D *Fighting Falcon*
  ATK 106 A-10C *Thunderbolt* II
  ISR 17 E-8C J-STARS
  ELINT 11 RC-26B *Metroliner* (being withdrawn)
  CSAR 9 HC-130P/N *King*
  TKR 160: 136 KC-135R *Stratotanker*; 24 KC-135T *Stratotanker*
  TPT 240 **Heavy** 35: 18 C-5A *Galaxy*; 17 C-17A *Globemaster* III; **Medium** 174: 15 C-27J *Spartan* (being withdrawn); 119 C-130H *Hercules*; 20 C-130J *Hercules*; 10 LC-130H *Hercules*; 4 MC-130P *Combat Shadow*; 6 WC-130H *Hercules*; **Light** 26 Learjet 35A (C-21A); **PAX** 5: 3 B-737-700 (C-40C); 2 Gulfstream G100 (C-38A)
  HELICOPTERS • CSAR 17 HH-60G *Pave Hawk*
  UAV • Cbt ISR • Heavy 56: 42 MQ-1B *Predator*; 14 MQ-9A *Reaper*

Air Force Reserve Command 70,500 reservists (incl 2,900 active)

FORCES BY ROLE
BOMBER
  1 sqn with B-52H *Stratofortress* (personnel only)
FIGHTER
  2 sqn with F-22A *Raptor* (personnel only)
FIGHTER/GROUND ATTACK
  2 sqn with F-16C/D *Fighting Falcon* (+2 sqn personnel only)
GROUND ATTACK
  2 sqn with A-10A *Thunderbolt* II
ISR
  1 (Weather Recce) sqn with WC-130H/J *Hercules*
AIRBORNE EARLY WARNING & CONTROL
  1 sqn with E-3 *Sentry* (personnel only)

COMBAT SEARCH & RESCUE
  3 sqn with HC-130P/N *Hercules*; HH-60G *Pave Hawk*
TANKER
  4 sqn with KC-10A *Extender* (personnel only) 6 sqn with KC-135R *Stratotanker* (+2 sqn personnel only)
TRANSPORT
  1 (VIP) sqn with B-737-700 (C-40C)
  3 sqn with C-5A/B/M *Galaxy* (+2 sqn personnel only)
  2 sqn with C-17A *Globemaster* (+9 sqn personnel only)
  10 sqn with C-130H/J *Hercules*
  1 (Aerial Spray) sqn with C-130H *Hercules*
TRAINING
  2 sqn with A-10A *Thunderbolt* II
  1 sqn with A-10A *Thunderbolt* II; F-15 *Eagle*; F-16 *Fighting Falcon*
  1 sqn with B-52H *Stratofortress*
  1 sqn with C-5A *Galaxy*
  1 sqn with F-16C/D *Fighting Falcon*
  5 (flying training) sqn with T-1A *Jayhawk*; T-6A *Texan* II; T-38C *Talon*
COMBAT/ISR UAV
  1 sqn with MQ-1B *Predator*/MQ-9A *Reaper* (personnel only)
ISR UAV
  1 sqn with RQ-4B *Global Hawk* (personnel only)

EQUIPMENT BY TYPE
AIRCRAFT 106 combat capable
  BBR 16 B-52H *Stratofortress*
  FGA 48: 46 F-16C *Fighting Falcon*; 2 F-16D *Fighting Falcon*
  ATK 42 A-10A *Thunderbolt* II
  ISR 10 WC-130J *Hercules* (Weather Recce)
  CSAR 5 HC-130P/N *King*
  TKR 64 KC-135R *Stratotanker*
  TPT 142 **Heavy** 44: 14 C-5A *Galaxy*; 14 C-5B/M *Galaxy*; 16 C-17A *Globemaster* III; **Medium** 94: 84 C-130H *Hercules*; 10 C-130J *Hercules*; **PAX** 4 B-737-700 (C-40C)
  HELICOPTERS • CSAR 13 HH-60G *Pave Hawk*

Civil Reserve Air Fleet
Commercial ac numbers fluctuate
AIRCRAFT • TPT 37 carriers and 1,376 aircraft enrolled, including 1,273 aircraft in the international segment (990 long-range and 283 short-range), plus 37 national, 50 aeromedical evacuation segments and 4 aircraft in the Alaskan segment.

Air Force Stand-by Reserve 16,858 reservists
Trained individuals for mobilisation

US Special Operations Command (USSOCOM) 60,200; 6,400 (civilian)
Commands all active, reserve and National Guard Special Operations Forces (SOF) of all services based in CONUS

Joint Special Operations Command
Reported to comprise elite US SF including Special Forces Operations Detachment Delta ('Delta Force'), SEAL Team 6 and integral USAF support.

US Army Special Operations Command
32,400

FORCES BY ROLE
SPECIAL FORCES
   5 SF gp (3-4 SF bn, 1 spt bn)
   1 ranger regt (3 ranger bn; 1 cbt spt bn)
MANOEUVRE
   Aviation
   1 (160th SOAR) regt (4 avn bn)
COMBAT SUPPORT
   1 civil affairs bde (5 civil affairs bn)
   2 psyops gp (3 psyops bn)
COMBAT SERVICE SUPPORT
   1 (sustainment) log bde (1 sigs bn)
EQUIPMENT BY TYPE
APC • PPV 640 M-ATV
HELICOPTERS
   MRH 50 AH-6M/MH-6M *Little Bird*
   TPT 123 **Heavy** 61 MH-47G *Chinook*; **Medium** 62 MH-60K/L/M *Black Hawk*
UAV 57
   ISR • **Light** 29: 15 XPV-1 *Tern*; 14 XPV-2 *Mako*;
   TPT • **Heavy** 28 CQ-10 *Snowgoose*

Reserve Organisations

Army National Guard
FORCES BY ROLE
SPECIAL FORCES
   2 SF gp (3 SF bn)

Army Reserve
FORCES BY ROLE
COMBAT SUPPORT
   2 psyops gp
   4 civil affairs comd HQ
   8 civil affairs bde HQ
   36 civil affairs bn (coy)

US Navy Special Warfare Command 9,500

Naval Special Warfare Command (NSWC) is organised around eight SEAL Teams and two SEAL Delivery Vehicle Teams. These components deploy SEAL Teams, SEAL Delivery Vehicle Teams, and Special Boat Teams worldwide to meet the training, exercise, contingency and wartime requirements of theatre commanders. Operationally, up to two of the eight SEAL Teams are deployed at any given time.

FORCES BY ROLE
SPECIAL FORCES
   8 SEAL team (total: 48 SF pl)
   2 SEAL Delivery Vehicle team
EQUIPMENT BY TYPE
SF 6 DDS

Naval Reserve Force
SPECIAL FORCES
   8 SEAL det
   10 Naval Special Warfare det
   2 Special Boat sqn
   2 Special Boat unit
   1 SEAL Delivery Vehicle det

US Marine Special Operations Command (MARSOC) 3,000

FORCES BY ROLE
SPECIAL FORCES
   1 SF regt (3 SF bn)
COMBAT SUPPORT
   1 int bn
COMBAT SERVICE SUPPORT
   1 spt gp

Air Force Special Operations Command (AFSOC) 15,300

FORCES BY ROLE
GROUND ATTACK
   2 sqn with AC-130H/U *Spectre*
TRANSPORT
   1 sqn with An-26; C-130E *Hercules*; Mi-8 *Hip*; UH-1N *Iroquois*
   1 sqn with C-130 *Hercules*/MC-130P *Combat Shadow*
   2 sqn with CV-22A *Osprey* (+2 sqn personnel only)
   1 sqn with DHC-8
   3 sqn with MC-130H *Combat Talon*
   1 sqn with MC-130J *Commando II*
   1 sqn with MC-130P *Combat Shadow*
   1 sqn with MC-130W *Combat Spear*
   3 sqn with PC-12 (U-28A)
TRAINING
   2 sqn with CV-22A *Osprey*
   1 sqn with MC-130J *Commando II*
   1 sqn with MC-130H *Combat Talon II*; MC-130P *Combat Shadow*
   1 sqn with Bell 205 (TH-1H *Iroquois*)
   1 sqn with HH-60G *Pave Hawk*; UH-1N *Huey*
COMBAT/ISR UAV
   1 sqn with MQ-1B *Predator*
   1 sqn with MQ-9 *Reaper*
EQUIPMENT BY TYPE
AIRCRAFT 25 combat capable
   ATK 25: 8 AC-130H *Spectre*; 17 AC-130U *Spectre*
   CSAR Some HC-130P/N *King*
   TPT 62+ **Medium** 62+: Some C-130 *Hercules*; 20 MC-130H *Combat Talon II*; 7 MC-130J *Commando II*; 23 MC-130P *Combat Shadow*; 12 MC-130W *Combat Spear*; **Light** Some An-26 *Curl*; Some DHC-8; Some PC-12 (U-28A)
TILT-ROTOR 29 CV-22A *Osprey* (3 more in test)
HELICOPTERS
   CSAR Some HH-60G *Pave Hawk*
   TPT • **Medium** Some Mi-8 *Hip*; **Light** Some Bell 205 (TH-1H *Iroquois*); Some UH-1N *Huey*
   UAV • **CISR** • **Heavy** 39: 29 MQ-1B *Predator*; 10 MQ-9 *Reaper*

Reserve Organisations

Air National Guard
FORCES BY ROLE
ELECTRONIC WARFARE
   1 sqn with C-130J *Hercules*/EC-130J *Commando Solo*

TRANSPORT
1 flt with B-737-200 (C-32B)

EQUIPMENT BY TYPE
AIRCRAFT
EW 3 EC-130J *Commando Solo*
TPT 5 **Medium** 3 C-130J *Hercules*; **PAX** 2 B-757-200 (C-32B)

Air Force Reserve
FORCES BY ROLE
TRANSPORT
1 sqn with MC-130E *Combat Talon*
1 sqn with PC-12 (U-28A) (personnel only)
COMBAT/ISR UAV
1 sqn with MQ-1B *Predator* (personnel only)
EQUIPMENT BY TYPE
AIRCRAFT
TPT • **Medium** 10 MC-130E *Combat Talon* I

Cyber

Each arm of the US military is developing cyber capacity. US Army Cyber Command (ARCYBER) is mandated to 'plan, coordinate, integrate, synchronize, direct, and conduct network operations and defense of all Army networks'. The 24th Air Force manages cyber for the air force, which, in October 2010, issued a doctrine entitled 'Cyberspace Operations'. Fleet Cyber Command (the US 10th Fleet) delivers 'integrated cyber, information operations cryptologic and space capabilities' for the navy. Marine Force Cyber Command was established in 2009. These service groups are commanded by US Cyber Command (itself under US Strategic Command, and co-located with the NSA). DoD's November 2011 'Cyberspace Policy Report' report said that 'the Department has the capability to conduct offensive operations in cyberspace to defend our Nation, Allies and interests. If directed by the President, DoD will conduct offensive cyber operations in a manner consistent with the policy principles and legal regimes that the Department follows for kinetic capabilities, including the law of armed conflict.' According to the Cyber Command chief, in March 2012 the command element had 937 staff (with an FY2013 budget request of US$182m), while service cyber staff totalled over 12,000. For Cyber Command, the government's January 2012 Defense Strategic Guidance 'means we must pay attention to the ways in which nations and non-state actors are developing asymmetric capabilities to conduct cyber espionage – and potentially cyber attacks as well – against the United States'. In October 2012, President Barack Obama signed Presidential Policy Directive 20, the purpose of which was to establish clear standards for US federal agencies in confronting threats in cyberspace. The terms of the directive are secret but are thought to include an explicit distinction between network defence and offensive cyber operations.

DEPLOYMENT

AFGHANISTAN
NATO • ISAF 68,000; 1 corps HQ; 2 div HQ; 2 mech inf SBCT; 4 lt inf IBCT; 2 AB IBCT; 3 cbt avn bde; 1 ARNG IBCT HQ; 1 USMC MEF HQ with 1 RCT

US Central Command • *Operation Enduring Freedom – Afghanistan* (OEF-A) ε7,000
EQUIPMENT BY TYPE (ISAF and OEF-A)
M1A1 *Abrams*; *Stryker*; MRAP; M-ATV; M119; M198; M777; F-15E *Strike Eagle*; F-16C/D *Fighting Falcon*; A-10 *Thunderbolt* II; AV-8B *Harrier*; EC-130H *Compass Call*; C-130 *Hercules*; MV-22B Osprey; KC-130J *Hercules*; AH-64 *Apache*; OH-58 *Kiowa*; CH-47 *Chinook*; UH-60 *Black Hawk*; HH-60 *Pave Hawk*; AH-IW *Cobra*; CH-53 *Sea Stallion*; UH-1 *Iroquois*; RQ-7B *Shadow*; MQ-1 *Predator*; MQ-9 *Reaper*

ANTIGUA AND BARBUDA
US Strategic Command • 1 detection and tracking radar at Antigua Air Station

ARABIAN SEA
US Central Command • Navy • 5th Fleet (5th Fleet's operating forces are rotationally deployed to the region from 2nd and/or 3rd Fleet)
EQUIPMENT BY TYPE
2 CVN; 2 CGHM; 2 DDGHM; 3 DDGM; 5 PCO; 1 LHD; 1 LPD; 1 LSD; 1 AOE
Combined Maritime Forces • TF 53: 1 AE; 2 AKE; 1 AOH; 3 AO
Combined Maritime Forces • CTF-150: 1 DDGHM

ARUBA
US Southern Command • 1 Forward Operating Location at Aruba

ASCENSION ISLAND
US Strategic Command • 1 detection and tracking radar at Ascension Auxiliary Air Field

ATLANTIC OCEAN
US Northern Command • US Navy
EQUIPMENT BY TYPE
6 SSBN; 23 SSGN; 2 SSN; 4 CVN; 8 CGHM; 10 DDGHM; 13 DDGM; 11 FFH; 8 PCO; 3 LHD; 2 LPD; 5 LSD

AUSTRALIA
US Pacific Command • 180; 1 SEWS at Pine Gap; 1 comms facility at Pine Gap; 1 SIGINT stn at Pine Gap

BAHRAIN
US Central Command • 2,100; 1 HQ (5th Fleet)

BELGIUM
US European Command • 1,200

BRITISH INDIAN OCEAN TERRITORY
US Strategic Command • 290; 1 Spacetrack Optical Tracker at Diego Garcia; 1 ground-based electro optical deep space surveillance system (*GEODSS*) at Diego Garcia
US Pacific Command • 1 MPS sqn (MPS-2 with equipment for one MEB) at Diego Garcia with 5 logistics and support ships; 1 naval air base at Diego Garcia, 1 support facility at Diego Garcia

CANADA
US Northern Command • 135

COLOMBIA
US Southern Command • 60

CUBA

US Southern Command • 950 at Guantánamo Bay

DEMOCRATIC REPUBLIC OF THE CONGO

UN • MONUSCO 3 obs

DJIBOUTI

US Africa Command • 1,200; 1 naval air base

EGYPT

MFO 700; 1 ARNG inf bn; 1 spt bn

EL SALVADOR

US Southern Command • 1 Forward Operating Location (Military, DEA, USCG and Customs personnel)

ETHIOPIA

US Africa Command • some MQ-9 Reaper

GERMANY

US Africa Command • 1 HQ at Stuttgart

US European Command • 50,500; 1 Combined Service HQ (EUCOM) at Stuttgart–Vaihingen

US Army 35,200

FORCES BY ROLE

1 HQ (US Army Europe (USAREUR)) at Heidelberg; 1 cav SBCT; 1 armd inf bde; 1 cbt avn bde; 1 engr bde; 1 int bde; 1 MP bde; 2 sigs bde; 1 spt bde; 1 (APS) armd HBCT eqpt set (transforming)

EQUIPMENT BY TYPE

M1 Abrams; M2/M3 Bradley; Stryker; M109; M777; M270 MLRS; AH-64 Apache; CH-47 Chinook; UH-60 Black Hawk

US Navy 485

USAF 14,450

FORCES BY ROLE

1 HQ (US Air Force Europe (USAFE)) at Ramstein AB; 1 HQ (3rd Air Force) at Ramstein AB; 1 ftr wg at Spangdahlem AB with 1 ftr sqn with 24 F-16CJ Fighting Falcon; 1 atk sqn with 18 A-10C Thunderbolt II; 1 tpt wg at Ramstein AB with 16 C-130E/J Hercules; 2 C-20 Gulfstream; 9 C-21 Learjet; 1 C-40B

USMC 365

GREECE

US European Command • 380; 1 naval base at Makri; 1 naval base at Soudha Bay; 1 air base at Iraklion

GREENLAND (DNK)

US Strategic Command • 120; 1 ballistic missile early warning system (BMEWS) at Thule; 1 Spacetrack Radar at Thule

GUAM

US Pacific Command • 4,300; 1 air base; 1 naval base

EQUIPMENT BY TYPE

2 SSGN; 1 SSN; 1 MPS sqn (MPS-3 with equipment for one MEB) with 4 Logistics and Support vessels

GULF OF ADEN & SOMALI BASIN

NATO • Operation Ocean Shield 1 FFH

HAITI

UN • MINUSTAH 8

HONDURAS

US Southern Command • 360; 1 avn bn with CH-47 Chinook; UH-60 Black Hawk

ISRAEL

US European Command • 1 AN/TPY-2 X-band radar at Nevatim

ITALY

US European Command • 7,800

US Army 200 (1 AB IBCT currently deployed to AFG)

US Navy 3,300; 1 HQ (US Navy Europe (USNAVEUR)) at Naples; 1 HQ (6th Fleet) at Gaeta; 1 MP sqn with 9 P-3C Orion at Sigonella

USAF 4,200; 1 ftr wg with 2 ftr sqn with 21 F-16C/D Fighting Falcon at Aviano

USMC 100

JAPAN

US Pacific Command • 36,700

US Army 2,500 1 HQ (9th Theater Army Area Command) at Zama

US Navy 6,750; 1 HQ (7th Fleet) at Yokosuka; 1 base at Sasebo; 1 base at Yokosuka

EQUIPMENT BY TYPE

1 CVN; 2 CGHM; 3 DDGHM; 4 DDGM; 1 LCC; 4 MCO; 1 LHD; 1 LPD; 2 LSD

USAF 12,500

FORCES BY ROLE

1 HQ (5th Air Force) at Okinawa – Kadena AB; 1 ftr wg at Okinawa – Kadena AB with 2 ftr sqn with 18 F-16C/D Fighting Falcon at Misawa AB; 1 ftr wg at Okinawa – Kadena AB with 1 AEW&C sqn with 2 E-3B Sentry, 1 CSAR sqn with 8 HH-60G Pave Hawk, 2 ftr sqn with 24 F-15C/D Eagle; 1 tpt wg at Yokota AB with 10 C-130H Hercules; 3 Beech 1900C (C-12J); 1 Special Ops gp at Okinawa – Kadena AB

USMC 14,950

FORCES BY ROLE

1 Marine div (3rd); 1 ftr sqn with 12 F/A-18D Hornet; 1 tkr sqn with 12 KC-130J Hercules; 2 tpt hel sqn with 12 CH-46E Sea Knight; 1 tpt hel sqn with 12 MV-22B Osprey; 3 tpt hel sqn with 10 CH-53E Sea Stallion

KOREA, REPUBLIC OF

US Pacific Command • 28,500

US Army 19,200

FORCES BY ROLE

1 HQ (8th Army) at Seoul; 1 div HQ (2nd Inf) located at Tongduchon; 1 armd HBCT; 1 cbt avn bde; 1 arty bde; 1 AD bde

EQUIPMENT BY TYPE

M1 Abrams; M2/M3 Bradley; M109; M270 MLRS; AH-64 Apache; CH-47 Chinook; UH-60 Black Hawk; MIM-104 Patriot/FIM-92A Avenger; 1 (APS) HBCT set

US Navy 250

USAF 8,800

FORCES BY ROLE

1 (AF) HQ (7th Air Force) at Osan AB; 1 ftr wg at Osan AB with 1 ftr sqn with 20 F-16C/D Fighting Falcon; 1 ftr sqn with 24 A-10C Thunderbolt II; 1 ISR sqn at Osan AB with U-2S; 1 ftr wg at Kunsan AB

with 1 ftr sqn with 20 F-16C /D *Fighting Falcon*; 1 Special Ops sqn
USMC 250

KUWAIT
US Central Command • 23,000; 1 HBCT; 1 ARNG cbt avn bde; 1 ARNG spt bde; 2 AD bty with 16 PAC-3 *Patriot*; elm 1 (APS) HBCT set

LIBERIA
UN • UNMIL 6; 4 obs

MARSHALL ISLANDS
US Strategic Command • 1 detection and tracking radar at Kwajalein Atoll

MEDITERRANEAN SEA
US European Command • US Navy • 6th Fleet
EQUIPMENT BY TYPE
2 DDGM; 1 LCC

MIDDLE EAST
UN • UNTSO 2 obs

NETHERLANDS
US European Command • 400

NORWAY
US European Command • 1 (APS) SP 155mm arty bn set

PACIFIC OCEAN
US Pacific Command • US Navy • 3rd Fleet
EQUIPMENT BY TYPE
8 SSBN; 19 SSGN; 8 SSN; 5 CVN; 11 CGHM; 18 DDGHM; 6 DDGM; 9 FFH; 3 FFHM; 2 MCO; 3 LHD; 1 LHA; 3 LPD; 4 LSD
US Southern Command • US Navy • 4th Fleet
EQUIPMENT BY TYPE
1 FFH

PERSIAN GULF
Combined Maritime Forces • CTF-152: 8 MCO; 1 AFSB

PHILIPPINES
US Pacific Command • 180

PORTUGAL
US European Command • 700; 1 spt facility at Lajes

QATAR
US Central Command • 600; elm 1 (APS) HBCT set

SAUDI ARABIA
US Central Command • 270

SERBIA
NATO • KFOR • *Joint Enterprise* 764; 1 ARNG cbt spt bde

SEYCHELLES
US Africa Command • some MQ-9 *Reaper* UAV

SINGAPORE
US Pacific Command • 150; 1 log spt sqn; 1 spt facility

SOUTH SUDAN
UN • UNMISS 5

SPAIN
US European Command • 1,480; 1 air base at Morón; 1 naval base at Rota

THAILAND
US Pacific Command • 120

TURKEY
US European Command • 1,500; MQ-1B *Predator* UAV at Incirlik; 1 air base at Incirlik; 1 support facility at Ankara; 1 support facility at Izmir
US Strategic Command • 1 Spacetrack Radar at Incirlik

UNITED ARAB EMIRATES
US Central Command • 175: 2 bty with MIM-104 *Patriot*

UNITED KINGDOM
US European Command • 9,300
FORCES BY ROLE
1 ftr wg at RAF Lakenheath with 1 ftr sqn with 24 F-15C/D *Eagle*, 2 ftr sqn with 23 F-15E *Strike Eagle*; 1 ISR sqn at RAF Mildenhall with OC-135/RC-135; 1 tkr wg at RAF Mildenhall with 15 KC-135R *Stratotanker*; 1 Spec Ops gp at RAF Mildenhall with 5 MC-130H *Combat Talon* II; 5 MC-130P *Combat Shadow*; 1 C-130E *Hercules*
US Strategic Command • 1 ballistic missile early warning system (BMEWS) and 1 Spacetrack Radar at Fylingdales Moor

FOREIGN FORCES

Canada 3 USCENTCOM; 303 NORTHCOM (NORAD)
Germany Air Force: trg units at Goodyear AFB (AZ)/ Sheppard AFB (TX) with 40 T-38 *Talon* trg ac; 69 T-6A *Texan* II; 1 trg sqn Holloman AFB (NM) with 24 *Tornado* IDS; NAS Pensacola (FL); Fort Rucker (AL) • Missile trg located at Fort Bliss (TX)
United Kingdom Army, Navy, Air Force ε480

Table 5 **Selected Arms Procurements and Deliveries, North America**

Designation	Type	Quantity	Contract Value	Prime Nationality	Prime Contractor	Order Date	First Delivery Due	Notes
Canada (CAN)								
LAV III	APC (W) upgrade	550	CAN$1bn (US$859.7m)	US	General Dynamics (GDLS)	2009	2012	Focus on weapons and mobility systems. Part of FLCV upgrade and procurement project worth CAN$5bn
M1117 *Guardian* ASV	Recce	500	CAN$603m	US	Textron Systems	2012	2014	Tactical Armoured Patrol Vehicle programme. Option for 100 more. Delivery to be complete in 2016
Single Class Surface Combatant Project	DDGHM/ FFGHM	15	see notes	CAN	Irving Shipyard	2011	2016	Part of CAN$25bn contract, including 8 PSOH. Intended to replace *Iroquois*-class DDGHM and *Halifax*-class FFGHM
Halifax-class	FFGHM upgrade	12	CAN$3.1bn (US$2.9bn)	CAN	Halifax Shipyard/ Victoria Shipyards	2007	2010	SLEP. *Halifax*-class HCM/FELEX project. To be fitted with *Sea Giraffe* 150 HC surv radar. Final delivery due 2017
Hero-class	PSOH	9	CAN$194m	CAN	Halifax Shipyard	2009	2012	For coast guard. First vessel launched May 2012. Delivery to be complete in 2013
Arctic Patrol Ship Project	PSOH	8	n/k	CAN	Irving Shipyard	2011	n/k	For navy. Based on NOR coast guard *Svalbard*-class
Joint Support Ship	AG	2	see notes	CAN	Vancouver Shipyards	2011	n/k	For navy. Option on a third vessel. Part of CAN$8bn contract including one *Diefenbaker*-class AGB and four AGOR
John G. Diefenbaker-class	AGB	1	see notes	CAN	Vancouver Shipyards	2011	2017	Polar Class Icebreaker Project. For coast guard. Part of CAN$8bn contract including 2 Joint Support Ships and four AGOR
F-35A *Lightning II*	FGA ac	65	CAN$9bn (US$8.5bn)	US	Lockheed Martin	2010	2016	To replace F/A-18 *Hornet* fleet. First aircraft in 2017, with deliveries continuing until 2022
CH-148 *Cyclone*	Tpt Hel	28	US$5bn	US	UTC (Sikorsky)	2004	2010	Programme continues to suffer delay. Handover of 6 interim standard ac due by end-2012
CH-47F *Chinook*	Tpt Hel	15	US$1.15bn	US	Boeing	2009	2013	For army use
United States (US)								
Stryker	APC (W)	4,292	US$14.4bn	US	General Dynamics (GDLS)	2001	2002	Incl multiple variants; incl DVH (Double V-Hull) versions
M119A2	105mm towed arty	443	US$524m	US	Rock Island Arsenal	2005	2006	New-build programme to fully equip new modular army structure
M777	155mm towed arty	421	US$1.3bn	UK	BAE Systems	2005	2006	Replacing M198s
M777	155mm towed arty	511	US$1.9bn	UK	BAE Systems	2003	2004	Replacing M198s. Final delivery due by end-2013
M142 HIMARS	MRL	375	US$1.7bn	US	Lockheed Martin	2003	2004	Final delivery due mid-2013
FGM-148 *Javelin*	MANPATS	27,172	US$4.5bn	US	Lockeed Martin/ Raytheon	1994	1996	Production continues
Gerald R Ford-class	CVN	2	US$15.4bn	US	Huntingdon Ingalls Industries	2008	2015	Keel of lead ship laid in 2009. Total cost for the 2 vessels is currently estimated at US$23.7bn
Virginia-class	SSN	18	US$49bn	US	General Dynamics (Electric Boat)	1998	2004	Nine currently in service

Table 5 **Selected Arms Procurements and Deliveries, North America**

Designation	Type	Quantity	Contract Value	Prime Nationality	Prime Contractor	Order Date	First Delivery Due	Notes
Zumwalt-class (DDG-1000)	CGHM	3	US$11bn	US	General Dynamics (BIW)/ Huntingdon Ingalls Industries	2008	2014	First delivery due Jul 2014
Arleigh Burke-class	DDGHM	68	US$68.2bn	US	General Dynamics (BIW)/ Huntingdon Ingalls Industries	1985	1991	62 vessels in service
Freedom/ Independence-class (Littoral Combat Ship)	FFHM	16	US$7.3bn	AUS/US	Austal (Austal USA)/ Lockheed Martin	2005	2008	2 competing designs for vessels; at least 12 of each design to be built. 3 currently in service; 6 currently in build
America-class	LHA	2	US$6.5bn	US	Huntingdon Ingalls Industries	2007	2013	First vessel under construction
San Antonio-class	LPD	11	US$18.4bn	US	Huntingdon Ingalls Industries	1996	2002	Enduring problems and delays with class. 7 vessels currently in service; 2 more launched
Spearhead-class (Joint High-Speed Vessel)	AG/LSL	10	εUS$1.9bn	US	Austal (Austal USA)	2008	2012	First commissioned in Aug 2012. Possible future contracts for total 23 in class. Planned army vessels transferred to navy in 2011
Mountford Point-class	AG	3	US$919m	US	General Dynamics (NASSCO)	2010	2013	Mobile Landing Platform programme. Fourth vessel may be ordered
F/A-18E/F Super Hornet	FGA	552	US$43bn	US	Boeing	1997	1998	Deliveries ongoing
F-35A Lightning II	FGA	87	US$17.3bn	US	Lockheed Martin	2007	2011	CTOL variant. 19 delivered as of late 2012
F-35B Lightning II	FGA	44	εUS$9.7bn	US	Lockheed Martin	2008	2011	STOVL variant; first delivered Dec 2011
F-35C Lightning II	FGA	22	εUS$5.6bn	US	Lockheed Martin	2010	2012	CV variant
P-8A Poseidon	ASW ac	37	US$8.7bn	US	Boeing	2011	2012	First delivered Mar 2012
EA-18G Growler	EW ac	114	US$8.9bn	US	Boeing	2003	2009	Deliveries ongoing
E-2D Hawkeye	AEW&C ac	64	US$8.1bn	US	Northrop Grumman	2004	2010	
C-130J Hercules	Med Tpt ac	88	US$7bn	US	Lockheed Martin	1995	1999	Deliveries continue; additional ac expected in FY13 & FY14
CV-22 Osprey	Tilt Rotor ac	47	US$4bn	US	Textron (Bell)/Boeing	2002	2006	29 delivered as of late 2012
MV-22 Osprey	Tilt Rotor ac	262	US$23bn	US	Textron (Bell)/Boeing	1997	1999	
AH-1Z Viper	Atk Hel	27	US$1bn	US	Textron (Bell)	2010	2013	New build; first delivery due May 2013
CH-47F/MH-47G Chinook	Hvy Tpt Hel	413	εUS$10.4bn	US	Boeing	2000	2004	227 new-build hel and 186 remanufactured
UH-60M Black Hawk	Med Tpt Hel	504	εUS$9.7bn	US	Sikorsky	2004	2006	
EC145 (UH-72A Lakota)	Lt Tpt Hel	305	US$1.9bn	Int'l	EADS (EADS North America)	2006	2006	
MH-60R Seahawk	ASW Hel	201	US$8.6bn	US	Sikorsky	2000	2006	
MH-60S Knight Hawk	MRH Hel	249	US$6.2bn	US	Sikorsky	1999	2002	

Table 5 **Selected Arms Procurements and Deliveries, North America**

Designation	Type	Quantity	Contract Value	Prime Nationality	Prime Contractor	Order Date	First Delivery Due	Notes
MQ-1C *Grey Eagle*	Hvy CISR UAV	103	US$2bn	US	General Atomics/ASI	2010	2011	First delivered Dec 2011
MQ-8 *Fire Scout*	Hvy ISR UAV	41	US$637m	US	Northrop Grumman	2006	2008	
MQ-9 *Reaper*	Hvy CISR UAV	231	US$3.9bn	US	General Atomics	2001	2002	Deliveries continue. 114 delivered by late 2012
RQ-4 *Global Hawk*	Hvy ISR UAV	45	US$4.7bn	US	Northrop Grumman	1995	1997	Block 40 numbers reduced to fund upgrade of earlier production models
AGM-158A JASSM	ASM	1,590	US$1.4bn	US	Lockheed Martin	1998	2000	1,200 delivered by late 2012
AGM-158B JASSM-ER	ASM	100	US$0.2bn	US	Lockheed Martin	2011	2012	First delivered Sep 2012

Chapter Four
Europe

Cuts and cooperation

In 2012, closer defence cooperation remained at the top of the agenda within both NATO and the EU. Budget pressures continued to drive defence-policy decisions in member-state capitals, and leaders began to ask how armed forces that have grown used to operating together will maintain interoperability in the future. This is particularly pressing given the possibility that the operational tempo will decrease after the combat element of the NATO-led ISAF mission in Afghanistan, by far the largest commitment for most European nations, ends in 2014.

NATO's May 2012 Chicago summit focused on an agenda largely defined two years earlier at the Lisbon summit. In Chicago, leaders committed to create 'modern, tightly connected forces equipped, trained, exercised and commanded so that they can operate together and with partners in any environment'. NATO will look to generate such forces, *NATO Forces 2020*, through prioritisation, cooperation, and specialisation – the building blocks of what has become known as 'smart defence'. In Chicago, it was suggested that 'smart defence is at the heart' of *NATO Forces 2020* and represents 'a changed outlook, the opportunity for a culture of cooperation in which mutual collaboration is given new prominence as an effective option for developing critical capability'.

Leaders adopted a package consisting of some 20 smart-defence projects covering, for example, the pooling of maritime patrol aircraft and improving the availability of precision weapons. Each project will be taken forward by a volunteer lead nation. The list of active projects is slowly growing as individual proposals mature in a wider pool of some 150 potential projects. Outgoing Supreme Allied Commander Transformation (SACT) General Stéphane Abrial suggested that total projects might increase to more than 30 by the end of 2012. He said 'NATO must continue to provide the framework and be a catalyst for multinational projects … but also serve [to promote] coherence and a source of strategic advice, to help inform national decision making'. On the capability side, NATO leaders highlighted progress in developing an interim missile-defence capability, progress on the Alliance Ground Surveillance system,

and an agreement to extend Allied air policing in the Baltic member states, saying these were flagship smart-defence projects. While these do implement some principles common to those advanced under the smart-defence banner, they have all been under way for some years and are unlikely to serve as a lasting inspiration for the smart-defence concept.

In addition to smart defence, NATO is looking to improve its forces' interoperability through the so-called Connected Forces Initiative, even though the content of this proposal, put forward by NATO Secretary-General Anders Fogh Rasmussen in early

NATO: missile-defence plans proceed

At the Chicago summit, NATO declared an interim missile-defence capability. NATO heads of state had agreed at the 2010 Lisbon summit that NATO should have a missile-defence system covering all of NATO's territory, due to a perceived threat from ballistic missiles to NATO member states' populations, territories and deployed personnel. The US decision to make available its national assets as the backbone of NATO's system made the agreement possible. Russia continues to object to the missile-defence system, having earlier proposed other ideas including an integrated NATO–Russian missile-defence system. However, in September 2012, Deputy Secretary-General Alexander Vershbow said that 'NATO will continue to seek closer cooperation with Russia on missile defence … But irrespective of the progress we make with Russia in this area, we will push ahead with our own NATO missile defence capability as planned.' Under phase 1 of this plan (initial capability), US *Aegis* vessels with BMD capability have deployed to the Mediterranean (four will eventually be based at Rota), with a C2 cell at Ramstein, while Turkey has agreed to host a land-based early-warning radar at Kürecik. Phase 2 will include land-based SM-3 interceptors at Deveslu air base in Romania. November 2011 saw the Netherlands announce plans to upgrade the SMART-L radars on four frigates with longer-range BMD-suitable capability. Phase 3 of the plan is due to see another SM-3 facility developed in Poland. According to the Pentagon, phase 4 will see the US deploy more advanced interceptors potentially capable of engaging longer-range missiles.

2012, remains sketchy. During a press briefing on 12 September 2012, Abrial said that the initiative was designed to be 'the framework for unified efforts to make sure [NATO] forces, and those of our partners, are optimized for working collectively and also that [NATO] forces maintain the strong coherence that they have developed during operations'. Thus, in a post-ISAF environment, the Connected Forces Initiative is likely to concentrate on combat effectiveness, in particular by focusing on training and exercises.

Lessons from Libya

The Libya intervention, authorised by UNSCR 1973 on 17 March 2011, which initially began as *Operation Odyssey Dawn* using US, British and French assets, was taken over by NATO on 31 March 2011 under the name *Operation Unified Protector*. On 31 October 2011, *Unified Protector* officially ended after the fall of the Gadhafi regime. NATO officials were quick to develop a narrative that *Unified Protector* had been a wholly successful operation, underlining NATO's enduring value in a changing security environment. During a visit to Jordan in June 2012, NATO Deputy Secretary-General Alexander Vershbow said that *Unified Protector* underlined that NATO was at the service of the wider international community: 'The events in Libya last year showed just how much the security of countries across the Mediterranean region is now linked to the security of NATO. But it also showed how much we can achieve together if we act with determination and persistence to do what is right.' Cooperative security was a core task for NATO, according to the 2010 Strategic Concept. In July 2012, Rasmussen struck a similar note in London: 'We can launch and sustain complex joint operations in a way that no one else can. We can work effectively with partners in a way that no one else can…From Afghanistan to the Balkans, and last year over Libya, our partners have played a vital role in the operational outcome and the political legitimacy of our missions…We need an alliance that is globally aware. Globally connected. And globally capable.' Libya did demonstrate that NATO can work with partners and successfully conduct and conclude a military operation, but it also highlighted the limitations of Europe's military capabilities. In particular, enabling capabilities in the field of intelligence, surveillance and reconnaissance (ISR) and logistics were stretched, and Europeans had to heavily rely on US assets, while certain countries' stocks of precision weapons ran low. The Libya experience suggests that Alliance cohesion during operations of this nature is heavily dependent on the risks to Allied forces and civilians on the ground being successfully minimised.

EU: civilian missions predominate

In the European Union, there has been sharpened focus on the level of operational ambition for its Common Security and Defence Policy (CSDP). Military ambitions, in particular, remain unclear and operations initiated in 2012 support the view that CSDP is gradually being limited to civilian missions at the soft end of security. On 12 December 2011, a crisis-management concept was approved for a regional maritime capacity-building mission in the Horn of Africa and Western Indian Ocean. This would be coordinated with the EU Naval Force Somalia (*Operation Atalanta*) and the EU Training Mission Somalia, which trains Somali security forces at Uganda's Bihanga training camp. A technical assessment team deployed to the region in February 2012 and, subsequently, EUCAP *Nestor* was officially established on 16 July 2012. *Nestor*, a 176-strong civilian mission augmented with military expertise, is due to reach full operational capability during autumn 2012 and is mandated for two years. Key objectives include improving the capacity of regional governments to control territorial waters with a view to fighting piracy. In the case of Somalia, this will include training a coastal police force and the training and protection of judges. It is also intended to strengthen the maritime capacities of Djibouti, Kenya, Tanzania, Mozambique, the Seychelles, Mauritius and Yemen. As part of the planning process for *Nestor*, the EU activated its Operations Centre for the first time in March 2012. Created in 2003, it will stay activated for at least two years and will coordinate the activities of the three EU operations in the area (*Operation Atalanta*, EUTM Somalia, EUCAP *Nestor*).

A second new civilian-dominated CSDP operation began in August 2012 in the Sahel region. EUCAP Sahel Niger is intended to boost the capacities of Niger's security forces in combating terrorism and organised crime. Focus is on the Gendarmerie, National Police and National Guard, though some military personnel will deploy to liaise with Niger's armed forces. The mission is, initially, mandated for two years, and staff will be posted to Niamey (headquarters) with liaison detachments in Bamako and Nouakchott. According to the EU, its 'strategy for security and development in the Sahel, of which the mission is part, focuses initially on Mali, Mauritania, Niger and Algeria'.

A third mission, EUAVSEC South Sudan, was approved by the Council on 18 June 2012, after an invitation from the South Sudan government to help strengthen airport security at Juba international airport, to prevent its use by criminal and terrorist networks, and to enable it to contribute to economic development. This small 64-strong advisory, mentoring and technical assistance mission started in September 2012, and has been mandated to last up to 19 months. Meanwhile, in the midst of continuing concern over the political and security situation in Mali, EU foreign ministers in October considered support for security-sector capacity-building in Mali, and support to related ECOWAS and AU initiatives. The European Council requested planning to take place for a possible CSDP mission in Mali, with a focus on reorganising and training Mali's armed forces.

The three latest missions strengthen an observed tendency whereby CSDP deployments are focused primarily on Africa-based civilian crisis-management activities. However, more expansive ambitions are being advanced in corridors of Brussels, more in line with the overall ambition for CSDP agreed by EU leaders. The EU's engagement in the Horn of Africa is cited as an example. Brussels considers its civilian–military approach as finally coming of age in this case, and that integrated civil–military crisis-management operations are close to becoming a reality. The EU hopes that its version of a comprehensive approach to crisis management and conflict prevention will soon bear fruit, underlining the added value of the EU as a global security actor. Certainly, the EU has invested vast resources in trying to bolster security and development in the Horn of Africa: by the end of 2013 it will have spent some €1.6 billion in the region over five years. In November 2011, the EU adopted a Strategic Framework to guide its engagement with the region and an EU Special Representative for the Horn of Africa was appointed on 1 January 2012. Since 2009, the EU has made funding available through diverse mechanisms, including the Instrument for Stability and the European Development Fund, to launch a variety of maritime-security initiatives supporting regional strategies and actors. The CSDP operations, EUTM Somalia, EUCAP *Nestor* and EUNAVFOR *Atalanta,* are supported by the EU Operations Centre and the Operations Headquarters at Northwood, UK. Additionally, the EU gives financial support to the African Union Mission in Somalia – some €325 million at the time of writing – and provides other assistance through its humanitarian aid department.

Ultimately, implementing this ambition will also depend on progress in developing military capabilities. In the EU, an agenda similar to NATO's 'smart defence' is being pursued, called pooling and sharing. The idea goes back some years (see *The Military Balance 2011*, p. 77), and was articulated by the EU's Foreign Affairs Council in March 2012: 'European cooperation on pooling and sharing military capabilities represents a common response to European capability shortfalls, aiming at enhancing operational effectiveness in a context of financial austerity and a changing security environment.' The impetus for the process was highlighted in September 2012 by General Håkan Syrén, then-chairman of the EU Military Committee. Recent budget cuts had made matters worse. The fundamental problem was that defence was becoming more costly, 'that our efforts are spread too thinly to be really efficient and most important that our decisions are taken in 27 different national contexts. The potential for generating a greater capability output is substantial if we are able to coordinate our efforts better.'

On 30 November 2011, the EDA steering board endorsed a list of 11 projects, to be developed after 2012. Satellite communications (SATCOM) is one area that has progressed. A European Satellite Communication Procurement Cell was set up to explore how pooling European SATCOM demand could realise savings. On 28 September 2012, the EDA signed an agreement with Astrium, a commercial provider, pooling demand from France, Italy, Poland, Romania and the UK. The three-year contract will, according to Astrium, allow the members 'to pool their needs, purchase, and even switch satellite communication capacity between themselves'. According to EDA figures, pooling demand in this way produced 10% savings over national procurement processes. Existing military satellite communications systems in Europe will need replacement in the 2020–2025 timeframe, according to the EDA; a European framework for developing and procuring new capabilities could lead to further significant costs savings. Other projects include: helicopter and pilot training; air-to-air refueling; smart munitions; and ISR.

EUROPE DEFENCE ECONOMICS

Macroeconomics

The heightened financial contagion from the euro-zone periphery in late 2011 – principally Greece, Italy and Spain – continued to affect Europe's economies in 2012. The widespread perception, in financial markets, that policy responses at the national and European levels were inadequate, led to persistent fears over the willingness of the European Central Bank (ECB) and European Financial Stability Facility (EFSF)/European Stability Mechanism (ESM) to respond should the crisis deepen. Fears also grew over the ability of peripheral European states to implement fiscal consolidation and structural adjustments. These fears led to episodic panic in the financial markets, particularly in the final quarter of 2011 and the second quarter of 2012, with banks, insurers and firms withdrawing liquidity from peripheral eurozone states. As funding pressures heightened, sovereign bond yields and risk premiums rose, causing balance-sheet deleveraging (where banks reduce the percentage of their balance sheets made up of debt) to accelerate across Europe, particularly in parts of Central and Eastern Europe, and resulting in a bank credit supply shock to the private sector – further damaging business confidence and resulting in the stagnation of investment expenditure across the region. High levels of household debt due to the pre-crisis housing boom (particularly in Ireland, Spain, Denmark and the UK) continued to restrict consumption, while governmental priorities to reduce budget deficits constrained the extent to which states were able to support demand.

The ECB reacted to these developments by providing emergency liquidity assistance – mainly to banks in Italy, Spain, France, Greece and Ireland – through its three-year Long Term Refinancing Operations (LTROs). While this averted an immediate liquidity crisis, stresses to sovereign funding markets resumed in the second quarter of 2012, as uncertainty mounted over the potential for a Greek exit from the eurozone following the May 2012 elections. In response, at a summit on 29 June 2012, eurozone leaders agreed to begin moves towards establishing a banking union with a single bank supervisory mechanism – a framework which would enable the ESM to hold direct equity stakes in banks. Subsequently, Spain accepted financing of up to €100bn to restructure its banking sector. Then, in September 2012, the ECB announced it would consider Outright Monetary Transactions (OMTs) to purchase government securities for countries in an adjustment or precautionary programme with the EFSF or ESM. Nonetheless, European economic activity stagnated in 2012. The IMF projected that the euro area would contract by 0.4% in 2012, before growing by an anaemic 0.16% in 2013. By end-2012, even Germany – hitherto one of the most resilient economies in the region – was set for an economic slowdown.

Defence spending

As discussed in *The Military Balance 2012* (pp. 73–76), with rising debt-to-GDP ratios across the continent, defence-budget austerity in Europe between 2008 and 2010 mirrored the downward trajectory in European growth rates. Broadly, these trends continued between 2010 and 2012, although European defence spending (at current prices and exchange rates) first rose from US$293.16bn in 2010 to US$304.02bn in 2011, a nominal increase of 3.71%; before falling by 7.01% in 2012 to US$282.72bn. The unexpected increase in 2011 nominal defence-spending levels was mainly the product of exchange-rate movements, as the euro appreciated relative to the US dollar by an average of 4.8% across the year – serving to lift total European defence spending in 2011, in US dollar terms. With heightened economic uncertainty and financial contagion across Europe from late 2011, the euro depreciated strongly in 2012 (by around 9.9% relative to its 2011 average), contributing to the 7.01% nominal reduction in US dollar defence spending seen in 2012. (Although the euro depreciated in 2012, its value relative to the US dollar remained around the levels seen in 2006 and 2007, indicating that while exchange-rate movements contributed to the large decline in nominal US dollar spending levels in 2012, they were not so drastic that the 2012 nominal US dollar spending total should be regarded as an outlier when compared to previous years.)

After discounting for these exchange-rate effects, and after factoring in the effects of inflation, real defence spending in Europe declined in both 2011 and 2012, falling by 2.52% in 2011, and by a further 1.63% in 2012 (constant 2010 prices and exchange rates). In general, defence spending across Europe has fallen at a faster rate than the contraction in European economies, with the result that defence spending as a percentage of European GDP fell from 1.63% in 2010 to 1.53% in 2012 (Figure 10), although the 2.52% real reduction in 2011 and the 1.63% fall in 2012 seem to

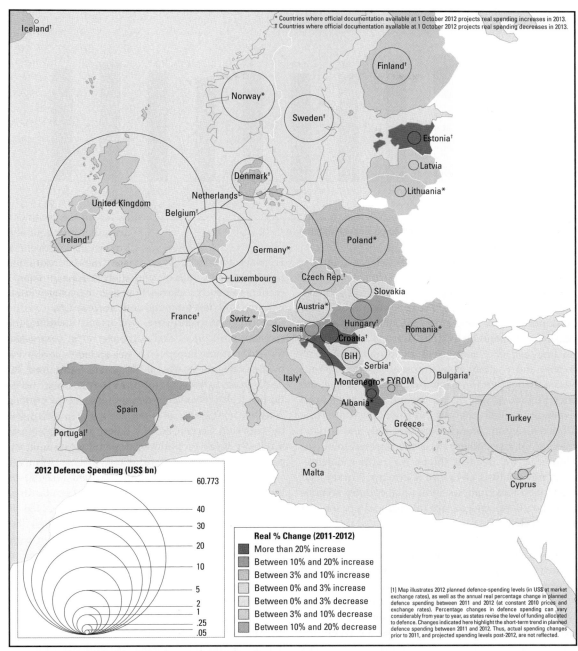

Europe

Map 3 **Europe Regional Defence Spending**[1]

Sub-regional groupings referred to in defence economics text: Central Europe (Austria, Czech Republic, Germany, Hungary, Poland, Slovakia and Switzerland), Northern Europe (Denmark, Estonia, Finland, Latvia, Lithuania, Norway and Sweden), Southern Europe (Cyprus, Greece, Italy, Malta, Portugal and Spain), Southeastern Europe (Bulgaria, Romania and Turkey), the Balkans (Albania, Bosnia & Herzegovina, Croatia, FYROM, Montenegro, Serbia and Slovenia) and Western Europe (Belgium, France, Iceland, Ireland, Luxembourg, the Netherlands and the United Kingdom).

indicate that the rate of European defence-spending reductions may be decelerating (by contrast, real defence expenditure in NATO European countries fell by an average of 3.7% annually between 2008 and 2010 – see *The Military Balance 2012*, Table 8 – NATO

Europe Gross Government Debt and Real Defence Expenditure 2008–2010, p. 74).

Defence spending in NATO Europe continued to dominate regional totals, accounting for almost 93% of defence spending across Europe. Similar to the

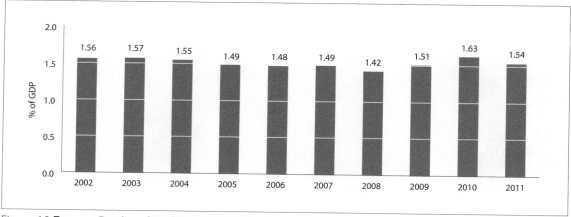

Figure 10 **Europe Regional Defence Expenditure** as % of GDP

overall trend in Europe, nominal defence spending in NATO Europe increased from $273.04bn in 2010 to $281.96bn in 2011 (an increase of 3.27%), before falling by 6.82% in 2012 to $262.74bn. As above, after accounting for exchange rate and inflationary effects, real defence spending in NATO Europe continued the decline seen since 2008 – real spending fell by 2.60% in 2011 and 1.54% in 2012. In common with previous years, the top ten European defence-spending countries in 2012 accounted for around 85% of planned expenditure, with the top five spending states (the United Kingdom, France, Germany, Italy and Turkey) making up just under 70% of the regional total (see Figure 11 for details). (Note: for further defence-economic analysis of France, Germany, Turkey and the United Kingdom, see individual country sections on pp. 97–8, pp. 99–100, pp. 101–104 and pp. 109–111 respectively.)

In 2012, real defence spending fell in 60% of European states, with the largest real reductions occurring in Spain (-17.6%), Hungary (-16.7%) and Slovenia (-16.1%), as governments in these countries sought to narrow their budget deficits and reduce their public-debt burdens. Significant real cuts to defence also occurred in Cyprus (-9.6%), where the banking sector had been heavily exposed to Greek sovereign-debt write-downs, and where the government implemented austerity measures in 2012 as it sought alternative sources of finance to recapitalise its banks from a variety of potential lenders, including the EU/IMF, Russia and private markets. By contrast, large spending increases in 2012 were seen in Albania (11.8%), Croatia (12.6%) and Estonia (17.8%). Significant real spending increments also occurred in Poland (6.1% in 2011 and 4.7% in 2012), and spending

is projected to rise by a further 6.6% in 2013 (in nominal terms), with expanded allocations for equipment repair and modernisation, facilities construction, research and development, and medical care.

Between 2010 and 2012, real defence spending (at constant 2010 prices and exchange rates) contracted most in Southern Europe (-11.19%, see below), followed by the Balkans (-5.6%, although spending rose by 0.48% in 2012). Western Europe experienced a -3.28% decline (relatively evenly distributed over the period, -1.84% in 2011 and -1.46% in 2012), while spending fell by -2.45% in Central Europe. These reductions were markedly more pronounced if spending on military pensions was excluded from the analysis. Planned expenditure remained roughly constant (-0.07%) in the relatively healthy economies of Northern Europe, but even here, real defence spending in 2012 fell in Norway (-2.1%) and Finland (-3.5%), although the former was set for a 4.2% nominal increase in 2013 as procurement funding was boosted to finance the purchase of the F-35 Joint Strike Fighter. (For analysis of developments in Europe's defence-industrial base, see essay on p. 37.) Despite strong domestic economic fundamentals, further cuts are anticipated in Finland in 2013, particularly to the equipment budget, although personnel expenditure is set to rise as salaries are revised upwards and conscript allowances are increased. Overall, Southeastern Europe was the only sub-region to experience a real increase, of 1.06%, buoyed by a 4.5% increase in Romania and an estimated 1.2% increase in Turkey.

Defence austerity in Southern Europe

Since 2008, Southern European countries have frequently been at the heart of Europe's economic

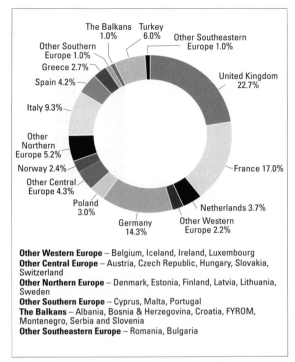

Other Western Europe – Belgium, Iceland, Ireland, Luxembourg
Other Central Europe – Austria, Czech Republic, Hungary, Slovakia, Switzerland
Other Northern Europe – Denmark, Estonia, Finland, Latvia, Lithuania, Sweden
Other Southern Europe – Cyprus, Malta, Portugal
The Balkans – Albania, Bosnia & Herzegovina, Croatia, FYROM, Montenegro, Serbia and Slovenia
Other Southeastern Europe – Romania, Bulgaria

Figure 11 **Europe Defence Spending by Country and Sub-Region 2012**

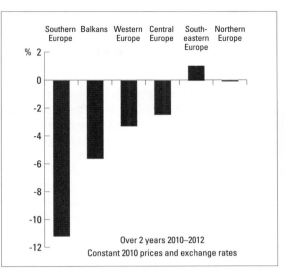

Figure 12 **Europe Real Defence Spending Changes 2010–2012 by Sub-Region (%)**

turbulence. As governments across the sub-region undertake fiscal consolidation to tackle rising budget deficits and public debt ratios, planned defence spending has correspondingly fallen by the highest percentages in Europe – with real defence spending (at constant 2010 prices and exchange rates) cut by 7.59% in 2011 and by a further 3.90% in 2012. The largest real-terms percentage reduction in planned defence allocations across Europe in 2012 occurred in Spain, where spending fell by around 17.6% as additional defence cuts (as compared to the original 2012 budget) were announced in January 2012. Personnel expenditure was restrained by cutting civilian posts at the Ministry of Defence and there has been talk of reducing manpower levels; while operational expenses were set to be cut by reducing overseas deployments. The Spanish presence in the UN mission in Lebanon was earmarked to decline by 50% by the end of 2012 (as opposed to the 20% reduction originally planned), and suggestions for an accelerated withdrawal schedule from Afghanistan were made over the course of the year. Research and development funding has also been reduced. In terms of equipment procurement, Spain announced in September 2012 that it had delayed to 2015 the

delivery of 15 *Typhoon* aircraft initially contracted for delivery between 2012 and 2014. The MoD was also negotiating additional delivery delays for other procurement programmes, such as the A400M transport aircraft.

Defence spending in Italy has also fallen substantially, by around 18% in real terms between 2010 and 2012. Following a real reduction of 10.5% in 2011, planned defence spending (not including pensions) fell by a further 6.6% in 2012, as the technocratic government led by Mario Monti set about dealing with the fiscal deficit to signal to financial markets that the government was serious about reducing national debt (gross government debt was projected by the IMF to be 126% of GDP in 2012). Major cuts to personnel and equipment programmes were announced in February 2012, with reductions of some 34,000 military personnel and 10,000 civilian employees envisaged by 2024, and a reduction in brigades from 11 to nine. This 20% cutback in manpower would be extended to senior military staff, where it was announced that up to 30% of senior admirals and generals would be axed. Around a third of all Italian military bases would be closed within five years, and between 26 and 28 naval vessels would be withdrawn from service over the next five to six years (including reductions to the number of submarines, offshore patrol vessels and mine-countermeasure vessels operated). Large savings (of at least €5bn), due to be achieved by a decrease in the planned number of F-35s to be purchased from Lockheed Martin (from an initial requirement of 131 aircraft in 2002, down to 90), enabled additional reductions in planned procurement expenditure. To reduce operational costs, a significant number of armoured vehicles and army helicopters would also be retired, although funding for armoured-vehicle programmes has in general been more generous than other equipment platforms, as the 2012 budget prioritises improvements to force protection.

In 2012, real defence spending fell by 2.6% in Greece and by 1.1% in Portugal, though both countries experienced larger real spending declines in 2011 (21.3% and 11.0% respectively). In order to rationalise limited available resources, in July 2012, Portugal suspended its participation in the multinational NH90 helicopter programme, cancelling its order for ten helicopters. After several months of negotiations with General Dynamics European Land Systems, in October 2012, Portugal terminated its order for *Pandur* II 8×8 armoured vehicles. The implementation of EU/IMF austerity measures in Greece has meant that the Ministry of National Defence will see a 22.3% reduction in its budget appropriations by 2015, relative to 2011 levels. Although defence spending will remain one of the largest areas of Greek government spending, budgetary allocations for personnel wages are being cut by 14.7%, operational expenses trimmed by 24.9%, and equipment procurement allocations reduced by 33.3%.

FRANCE

The Hollande administration

While it is unlikely that the tone of France's defence policy and posture will change significantly after the change of government in May 2012, the effects of the financial crisis will affect defence ambitions, planning and procurement. Defence policy played little part in the presidential campaign, with the exception of François Hollande's pledge to end France's combat role in Afghanistan by December 2012 (an option with which Sarkozy himself had toyed). Indeed, the appointment of Hollande's friend Jean-Yves Le Drian as minister of defence was a clear statement that there would be continuity with the past. Le Drian was formerly the ranking socialist on the defence commission of the National Assembly and Hollande's adviser on defence issues during the electoral campaign.

For much of the past three decades, there has been a virtual consensus on defence issues across the French political divide. Sarkozy's 2009 decision to return to NATO's integrated command structure did provoke debate for a time, though a report by Hubert Védrine on France's relationship with NATO, commissioned by Hollande and unpublished at time of writing, was likely to lay any remaining controversy to rest. Future policy will be dictated in large part by the ongoing economic and budgetary crisis and by the requirements of coalition operations, whether mounted by the UN, NATO or the EU. Hollande made clear during the presidential campaign that the French nuclear deterrent would remain sacrosanct.

Livre Blanc

At time of writing, a new *Livre Blanc* (White Book) on defence and national security was being prepared by a high-ranking commission presided over by Jean-Marie Guehenno. The commission was due to report in early 2013. The rationale behind the new White Paper was reportedly the transformed world order which has emerged since the last such exercise in 2008: the global economic crisis, the Arab Spring, the US rebalance to the Asia-Pacific, the apparent stalling of the European security and defence project, the emergence of new zones of instability and the shifting nature of crisis and conflict (such as failing states, UAVs and cyber warfare). France's deterrent was ring-fenced. Though this effectively meant that the deterrent would not explicitly be part of the White Paper process, it might in practical terms have the effect of cramping other defence sectors, particularly when defence finances tighten. The commission was given an explicit 'steer' both by Le Drian and Hollande, who during his 14 July National Day address noted threats from the effects of the economic crisis and increasing military spending outside Europe, and continuing threats from WMD proliferation and terrorism. Four main priorities were identified: ensuring coherence between force sizes and aspirations for military missions; develop intelligence capacities (likely those noted in the last White Paper under the term 'connaissance et anticipation'), including some emphasis on cyber capabilities; industrial and research policy; and recruitment, training and personnel management. Given that key themes have already been decided, and since the commission is expected rapidly to conclude its work by the end of 2012, there are unlikely to be any major surprises. The presence on the commission, of two high-profile European members, the UK ambassador to France, Sir Peter Ricketts, and the chair of the Munich Security Conference and former German ambassador to the US, Wolfgang Ischinger, underscores Hollande's determination to situate French defence thinking within a European context.

In a keynote speech to the Institut des Hautes Etudes de Défense Nationale on 5 October 2012, Le Drian made the government's expectations clear regarding the overall framework for French defence policy through to 2025, without anticipating the precise recommendations of the White Paper Commission. (Le Drian was unable to attend in person; the speech was instead delivered by M. Kader Arif, minister for defence veterans.)

Foreseeing an 'updated strategic mission', the speech highlighted the geographical zone running from the Atlantic coast of Africa to the Indian Ocean, refocusing attention on the Sahel. The relaunch of the European defence project (CSDP) was seen as both a necessity and a much needed opportunity, a 'real shared political priority', for all 27 member states. There are four main reasons spurring this European focus. The first is the US rebalance to the Asia-Pacific, which will oblige the EU to become a 'producer of defence' rather than a 'consumer of security', assuming ever greater regional and international responsibility to its south and east. Secondly, the new threats to which Europe is exposed demand the comprehensive toolkit of instruments which only the EU can offer. Thirdly, in terms of military capacity, Europe is seen as being at a critical juncture where there are only two alternatives: pooling or abandonment of entire military equipment programmes. Finally, the speech resurrected the political ambition to pursue further integration: European defence would lay the final stone of a peaceful Europe. In order to achieve these objectives, a new, genuine, European Security Strategy had to be crafted, so that a new document (replacing the 2003 version) would constitute a common strategy backed by serious force-projection assets. A European mind-set for pooling and sharing had to develop from concrete bilateral projects extensible to all member states. Additionally, a genuine European defence-industrial base should be developed. Areas of 'industrial synergy' that allow the development of competitive advantage should be considered (Arif went on to cite EADS as a good example in the aeronautical context), while intiatives could also be developed to better coordinate R&D activity, and secure European-level funding for such initiatives.

Budgeting, operations and policy

The *Commission du Livre Blanc* is unlikely to make radical suggestions on defence equipment. This will be the MoD's job when it produces, in spring 2013, a new military programme law to cover the period 2014–19. Although the target defence budget figure for 2013, some €31.4bn, technically holds spending at the 2012 level (before inflation), when set within the broader framework of the 2009–14 military programme law established by Sarkozy, the 2013 figure amounts to a basic 1% cut, which will be further aggravated by a predicted 7% cut in the operating budget and by the postponement of some €5.5bn in new equipment orders. Defence spending is now more or less tied to the evolution of the wider state budget. Currently, significant proportions of projected government savings are due to come from tax rises; if this situation changes in future years and savings accrue more directly from spending cuts, then defence may suffer further.

The spending projected from the 2008 White Paper up to 2020 (€377bn) is currently predicted to show a shortfall of between €15bn and €30bn. According to the chief of defence staff, Admiral Edouard Guillaud, key provisions of the 2008 White Paper are already beyond reach, such as the ambition for the simultaneous deployment of 30,000 troops on a major overseas operation, 10,000 on an internal operation and 5,000 on alert. Helicopter pilots currently fly only 170 hours per year instead of the 200 hours envisaged. Army leaders, meanwhile, are reportedly feeling particularly vulnerable. When all combat troops are withdrawn from Afghanistan in December 2012, there will be fewer than 10,000 French soldiers deployed overseas – against a 2011 figure of 13,500 and an average of 12,600 over the past 20 years. This is not to say that the army is looking for missions that do not present themselves, but there is a generalised concern that France will simply not be able to afford the same level and scale of overseas operations seen in recent years. Having built up, since 2000, an impressively trained and equipped professional force, some French military leaders are lamenting the prospect, widely hawked in certain circles, of that force being essentially confined to barracks. The morale of France's armed forces in general, and of the army in particular, is considered to be on 'alert' status, with this perhaps compounded by dissatisfaction over problems with new technical systems designed to pay military salaries.

Above all, the first challenge set by President Hollande to the *Commission du Livre Blanc* – that of spending and procurement coherence – seems to many specialists a daunting one. Given that the nuclear deterrent is ring-fenced (at €3.5bn), there seem to be only two choices to some: cuts in one entire sector (such as frigates, or armoured brigades, or cruise missiles); or the emergence of what is referred to as a 'sampler armed force' – featuring single units of each main category of equipment. Neither option is considered by defence experts as acceptable or even viable, but then the alternative – pooling and sharing at the EU level – is seen by many as equally problematic. The decision taken decades ago not to commit resources to the suppression of enemy air defences role, on the grounds that this amounted duplication of US assets available via NATO, is now perceived in some quarters as a strategic mistake given European dependence on US systems in Libya in 2011. France remains psychologically committed to sovereignty in defence policy and is loath to engage in 'specialisation', but cannot afford or cannot accept politically any of the available options.

Relations with NATO are set to evolve. Hollande's electoral promise to bring back French combat troops from Afghanistan by the end of 2012 was quietly endorsed by his NATO partners at the Chicago summit in May 2012. French forces in Kapisa Province were, by late 2012, replaced by a mix of US and Afghan forces. But the semantic distinction between 'combat troops' and 'non-combat troops' is a fudge; 1,200 French troops will remain in Afghanistan in 2013 to help train the Afghan army, and if they are required by the US for combat duty, will be available. Four hundred French troops will remain alongside their allies until the final withdrawal date of December 2014. A French general has assumed command of ISAF forces guarding Kabul airport. During his election campaign, Hollande criticised the NATO ballistic-missile-defence project, largely on the doctrinal grounds that this could be read as calling into question France's firm belief in nuclear deterrence. However, in Chicago, he gave his consent to the project. More generally, post-ISAF, relations between CSDP and NATO will rise to the top of the Alliance's agenda. Hollande will be unlikely to favour Georgian membership of the Alliance, which Washington is now pursuing. But Le Drian has made it clear that CSDP and NATO have no alternative but to engage in ever deeper cooperation.

GERMANY

Germany continued to implement its wide-ranging defence-reform initiative (see *The Military Balance 2012*, p. 79). This is due to be complete by 2017. Key elements included the suspension of universal conscription in summer 2011, manpower reductions and a reorganised force posture. This process is taking place against the background of reducing defence budgets, a protracted debate about future capability priorities, demographic challenges for recruitment, and controversial arms-export requests. Defence-spending cuts have so far been modest compared to other European NATO members. When the government decided, in June 2010, to reduce spending significantly, it was realised that the reforms necessary to enable these savings in the long term (such as force restructuring) would likely cost more up front. It is estimated that cuts will likely accelerate in the 2014–16 period.

Policy developments

Like most European states, Germany is trying to grapple with the long-term planning challenges of a highly unpredictable security environment, as well as declining resources for defence. These financial constraints impose limits on the number of contingencies for which armed forces can prepare. At the same time, uncertainty about future missions prevents the development of a strategy that would rely on capabilities designed for certain scenarios. Forces have to be able to adjust, so a key principle of the reform effort has been to maintain as broad a spectrum of capabilities as possible. But there has been a trade-off with sustainability, as a focus on breadth effectively means less depth. This decision was influenced by the belief that a country of Germany's size and economic weight should have to be able to provide the broad spectrum of capability necessary to exert political influence, including in NATO. The armed forces' level of ambition has been set as being able to provide up to 10,000 troops for sustainable overseas deployments. Germany also intends to maintain capability that enables it to serve as a framework nation for two simultaneous land operations and one maritime operation.

A central element of the restructuring is to move to a smaller, all-volunteer force consisting of 170,000 contracted and professional personnel, and up to 12,500 short-term volunteers and 2,500 active reservists. The total of 185,000 compares to a total strength of approximately 220,000 in May 2011, including 188,000 contracted and professional soldiers, when the reform plans were announced. The number of civilian staff is set to decline from 75,000 to 55,000. The personnel reductions led to a decision, published on 26 October 2011, to close some 30 bases throughout Germany; this leaves just over 260 bases in service.

When it was first announced, the decision to suspend universal conscription drew criticism. Commentators suggested the Bundeswehr would find it difficult to recruit adequate numbers of men and women to fill its posts and that the link between the armed forces and society at large would weaken. Unfavourable demographic trends mean that the armed forces will have to compete with other potential employers for shrinking cohorts of young Germans. It is too early, just one year after the suspension, to draw firm conclusions on whether these dangers can be avoided. However, initial data on what has been dubbed 'voluntary conscription' – essentially short-term service contracts with a duration of up to 23 months – provides some evidence for the conclusion that the Bundeswehr is an attractive option for a significant part of society. The Ministry of Defence aims to attract between 5,000 and 15,000 voluntary conscripts annually. In the first 12 months after universal conscription was suspended, some 35,000 applied and the Bundeswehr employed some 12,500 of them for an average contract length of 15 months. In socio-economic terms, those that signed up were a reasonable cross-section of German society. However, about 25% of those engaged on such contracts left during the initial months, which gives a sense of the long-term challenges ahead. The ministry hopes that 'voluntary conscripts' of sufficient calibre will be attracted to full-time positions.

Another challenge for the political and military leadership emerged in September 2012, when opinion polls among military and civilian Bundeswehr members revealed that a majority of those polled do not believe the reform process is being implemented successfully. The majority of respondents also consider that reform is failing to make the Bundeswehr into a more attractive employer and a more capable force. In part, such results are to be expected in the context of the wide-ranging restructuring initiated in 2011. Some of the scepticism might be ameliorated through better communication and participatory information campaigns. Speaking in September, Defence Minister Thomas de Maizière acknowledged that the speed of the reform process could be one cause of dissatisfaction, as well as the uncertainty that it can foster among defence staff. However, if those who ultimately have to make the new structure and posture work, the military and civilian personnel, do not understand what the vision for the new force looks like, implementation is likely to remain difficult.

Defence economics, the services, and procurement

The 2012 defence budget was set at €31.87bn. Spending on personnel (including pensions) amounted to some 47% in 2012, down from 52.5% in 2011. At the same time, spending on defence investment (equipment procurement plus research and development) increased slightly to 20.1% in 2012, from 19.7% in 2011. The medium-term outlook, based on the five-year advance planning cycle for the federal budget, gives an indication of future developments. In June 2012, the cabinet approved budget parameters for the period up to 2016. According to these decisions, the defence budget is set to rise to €33.28bn in 2013, with de Maizière in September saying that this increase owed much to pay increases in January 2012 and those scheduled for January 2013. Cuts in absolute terms are scheduled to begin in 2014, a year for which the planning documents foresee a defence budget of just under €33bn. The budget for 2015 and 2016 is currently fixed at just under €32.5bn for both years.

The services have had to plan for the future within these fluctuating, but generally downward, defence-budget trends. The army's overall goal is to generate more front-line capability available, and aims to provide 5,000 troops for sustainable deployments. Major equipment holdings will be reduced to 70–80% of current totals. Units on operations, preparing for operations or covering national contingencies will be fully equipped but the equipment available for basic training will be reduced so that fewer overall systems need to be maintained. The brigade will be the core unit for operations and each of the two mechanised divisions will have three largely identical brigades. These six brigades will each have dedicated logistics and engineering support as well as reconnaissance battalions. The combat element in each brigade will be provided by at least two battalions. Given their similar composition, these brigades will be able to replace each other, more or less directly, on operations that require such rotations. Additional capability will be provided through the Franco-German brigade and an airborne special-forces brigade.

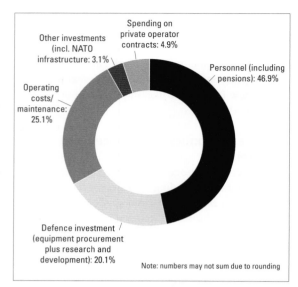

Figure 13 Germany: 2012 Defence Spending Breakdown

The navy will further develop its multi-crew concept to support the ambition to use existing equipment more intensively and sustain vessels at sea for longer periods of time. For example, up to eight crews will be allocated to Germany's four F125 frigates to enable crew swaps. The navy aims to be able to sustain deployments of up to 1,000 sailors. For the air force, a key objective will be to provide the core of a Joint Forces Air Component Headquarters for operations lasting up to six months, running up to 350 sorties per day. This has been defined as the air force contribution to Germany's framework-nation capability. Its future A400M transport fleet of 40 planes will be concentrated at Wunstorf air base. The air force expects deliveries to begin in the last quarter of 2014. Germany's complete Eurofighter fleet, pending corresponding funding decisions, is to gain multi-role capability from 2016 onwards.

The debate about future air force capabilities became controversial when the issue of unmanned combat air vehicles (UCAV) was discussed. De Maizière indicated, in August 2012, that Germany might require a UCAV capability. Lieutenant-General Karl Müllner, chief of the air force, has indicated that a UCAV capability would be desirable to provide faster close air support to troops engaged in ground operations. Presently, Germany only uses unarmed reconnaissance UAVs and intends to terminate its *Heron*-1 leasing arrangement in 2014. While Germany hopes that its requirements post-2020 can be met through

a product developed by Europe's defence industry, funding has been earmarked in the 2013 budget to procure a stop-gap solution for the period 2014–2020. The public debate on this question remained oddly removed from the question of actual military requirements and centred on ethical questions, morality, and international law. The US practice of using armed UAVs for the targeted killing of individual terrorists has sparked concerns among some commentators that Germany might pursue similar policies once it has the means to do so. However, it is also possible that the UCAV debate might be stimulated by concerns within the ministry over what combat air platform Germany will operate in the years after *Tornado* and Eurofighter; as yet there is, at least publicly, no European manned fighter programme in development.

TURKEY

Policy matters

Long-standing NATO member Turkey's relations with other NATO states were strained in 2012, when Ankara chose to consider Russian and Chinese bids, as well as Western bids, for its US$4bn Long-Range Air and Missile Defence System (LORAMIDS) project. In some areas, Turkey remains heavily dependent on foreign purchases and Ankara has traditionally sourced most of its requirements from other NATO members, particularly the US.

The decision to deploy LORAMIDS was consistent with Turkey's determination to establish itself as a regional military power. As of September 2012, Ankara was considering bids from Rosoboronexport of Russia, offering the S-300, and the China Precision Machinery Export–Import Company (CPMIEC) with its HQ-9, in addition to bids from a US partnership of Raytheon and Lockheed Martin with the *Patriot* system and the SAMP/T *Aster* 30 of the Italian–French Eurosam. Although it appears likely to choose the US or European option, Turkey's decision to consider the Russian and Chinese systems has further tested its already strained ties with its NATO allies, who have expressed concern about potential compromise of NATO procedures.

Tensions between Turkey and its NATO allies were partly alleviated by the ruling Justice and Development Party's (AKP) announcement, on 2 September 2011, that it had agreed to deploy an AN/TPY-2 X-band early-warning radar at Kürecik in eastern Anatolia, as part of the first phase of NATO's

Ballistic Missile Defence (BMD) system (see p. 89). Although located on a Turkish air force installation, the system is operated by US personnel and will run in parallel to LORAMIDS. Initially, incoming missiles detected by the NATO system will be targeted by *Standard Missile*-3 (SM-3) interceptors based on US warships in the eastern Mediterranean, although land-based SM-3s are later expected to be deployed in Romania and Poland. On 17 January 2012, Turkish officials announced that the radar at Kürecik had become operational.

The early-warning radar's deployment further soured relations with Tehran, which maintained that the system's location 450 miles from the Turkish–Iranian border indicated that it was primarily directed against Iran. Iranian officials also claimed that the radar could be used to support a US or Israeli military strike against the country's nuclear programme. The charges were rejected by Turkey, which insisted on the exclusion of any reference by NATO to Iran as a potential threat, as a precondition for agreeing to the system's deployment at Kürecik. Turkish officials have publicly pledged that they will prevent any data from the radar being shared with Israel. Ankara's hostility towards Israel remains one of several factors that continue to strain Turkey's relations within NATO. The AKP has repeatedly threatened to use its veto to block any cooperation between the Alliance and Israel. In addition, Ankara's long-standing refusal to recognise the government of Cyprus has meant that Turkey has also continued to prevent meaningful cooperation between NATO and the EU.

Since mid-2011, there has been a convergence between Turkey and NATO in terms of attitudes towards the Assad regime in Damascus. But by September 2012, there was a growing gap in terms of preferred response. Frustrated by NATO's reluctance to take action, Turkey has increasingly pushed for a multilateral military intervention to establish a no-fly zone and create a 'safe haven' to enable those displaced by the civil war to return and be supplied with humanitarian aid inside Syria. By September 2012, an estimated 100,000 Syrian refugees had fled to Turkey. After a Turkish RF-4E *Phantom* crashed off the Syrian coast on 22 June 2012, downed by Syrian air defences, Turkey deployed additional forces and started conducting military exercises in border areas. It also increased its support to the Free Syrian Army (FSA).

Yet, in October 2012 – even after incidents of Syrian artillery fire landing on Turkish territory, and a swift Turkish military response in kind –, there appeared little prospect of Turkey staging a unilateral military intervention in Syria. In November, Turkey requested the deployment of NATO *Patriot* missiles to boost air-defence capacity. Turkish officials remained wary of being dragged into the sectarian strife which they feared would follow the eventual overthrow of Assad. There were also concerns that any unilateral military involvement in northern Syria, where most of the country's Kurdish minority is located, could exacerbate Turkey's own Kurdish insurgency. An upsurge in PKK attacks in summer 2012 forced the Turkish security forces onto the defensive and left them struggling to assert control over large areas of the predominantly Kurdish southeast. In addition, the morale of military officers was depressed, and internal command structures disrupted, by a string of court cases alleging that military personnel were plotting to overthrow the government. No convincing evidence has yet been produced to support the charges, which critics claim have been fabricated by Islamist sympathisers in order to damage the traditionally secular officer corps. Nevertheless, at one point in early August 2012, 399 serving military personnel were being held in prison pending trial, including 125 serving colonels and 68 (nearly one in five) of the country's 362 serving generals and admirals. Forty of the imprisoned generals and admirals were forced to take compulsory early retirement at the end of August 2012.

Defence economics

Turkey's official defence budget was L18.23bn (US$10.06bn) in 2012, an increase over the 2011 allocation of L16.98bn (US$10.13bn). Over the last decade, strong GDP growth has led to an increase in resource allocations to the defence ministry. However, despite a growth in absolute terms, official defence spending has not kept pace with GDP growth, declining both as a percentage of GDP (from 2.2% to 1.3% in the 2003–12 period), and as a proportion of governmental outlays (from 6.9% to 5.4% in the same period). The single largest share of the defence budget for 2012, some L8.2bn (US$4.5bn) is earmarked for salaries (45.1% of the budget, up from 42.6% in 2010). This showed a 10% nominal increase from 2011, when L7.5bn was allocated. Approximately 21% of planned defence outlays (amounting to L4bn, or US$2.3bn) will cover armed forces' modernisation programmes – only a minor increase compared to available 2011 figures (L3.76bn (US$2.24bn)). The overall data

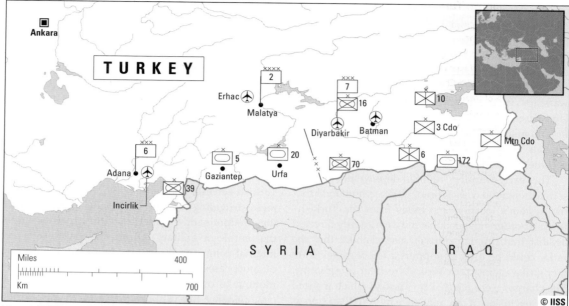

Map 4 **Military Dispositions in Southern Turkey**

omit both the budget allocated for the Gendarmerie General Command (L4.9bn (US$2.7bn) for FY2012, a 7.5% nominal increase from 2011), as this is formally under the authority of the Ministry of Interior, as well as a significant part of resources allocated for defence procurement. This is because these are made available to the Undersecretariat for Defence Industries (SSM) through a different source – the Defence Industry Support Fund (SSDF) – on which official figures are not available. When these additional elements are taken into account, it is estimated that Turkey's defence expenditure rises to around L30bn (US$16.6bn) in 2012 (see Table 6).

Procurement programmes

Several important procurement programmes are currently under way, mostly as part of the ambitious goal of making Turkey self-sufficient in defence procurement requirements before 2023. One of the most ambitious programmes is the *Altay* main battle tank project developed by Turkish firm Otokar with the technical support of the South Korean company Rotem. Armaments, armour and related systems will be manufactured by Turkey's Aselsan, Roketsan and MKEK. The Turkish government signed the agreement in 2007, allocating US$500m for the design and production of four prototypes to be delivered by Otokar in 2015. Tests on the first prototype are expected to start by the end of 2012. According to

the planned schedule, delivery should begin by 2017, and Turkey is expected to purchase a first batch of 250–300. Progress in the development of Turkey's missile-defence capabilities proceeds at a slower pace. In early 2011, Aselsan received governmental funds to develop both the 'T-Laladmis' (low-altitude missile-defence system) and the 'T-Maladmis' (medium-altitude system) projects; final designs are due by the end of 2016. The Defence Industry Executive Committee has yet to select a firm to provide the LORAMIDS system. Production of the T-155 *Firtina*, a self-propelled 155mm howitzer, is currently at an advanced stage: 150 units were already delivered in 2011, and Turkey is expected to purchase more in the coming years.

Two main projects are aimed at boosting the navy's anti-submarine and littoral-warfare capabilities. Since 2004, Istanbul Naval Shipyards Command has so far delivered two of eight *Ada*-class ASW corvettes along with four F-100-class frigates as part of the MILGEM project (the remaining six *Adas* will be built in different shipyards by 2016). The 'TF-2000' project will give the navy six TF-2000-class anti-air warfare frigates, the first of which is planned to be commissioned by 2018. Turkish firms have been awarded several other contracts in the last few years. The Istanbul-based Dearsan Shipyard is building 16 *Tuzla*-class patrol boats under a €402m contract signed in 2007, with the last boat to be delivered in

Table 6 **Turkey Defence Expenditure Estimate 2010–2012 (Lbn)**

	2010	2011	2012
GDP (Lbn)	1,099	1,298	1,419
GDP Growth	9.2%	8.5%	3.0%
Total Official Defence Budget	**15.12**	**16.98**	**18.23**
Nominal % Change	9.8%	4.1%	11.9%
% of Total Outlays	5.6%	5.3%	5.4%
% of GDP	1.4%	1.3%	1.3%
(Breakdown of Official Defence Budget:)			
Personnel Salaries & Benefits	6.44	7.51	8.23
Pensions & Social Security Payments	1.28	1.45	1.58
Equipment Repair & Modernisation	3.56	3.76	3.91
Other Expenditures[1]	3.84	4.26	4.52
Non-MoD Elements of Turkish Defence Expenditure	**11.18**	**11.62**	**12.49**
Estimated Procurement Expenditure (DISF)	6.31	6.75	7.22
Gendarmerie General Command	4.56	4.56	4.90
Coast Guard Command	0.316	0.316	0.375
Estimated Total Defence Spending	**26.3**	**28.6**	**30.7**
% of GDP	2.4%	2.2%	2.2%

[1]Includes transfers and other capital expenditures.

2015. Under a €2bn contract from 2009, which came into effect in July 2011, the navy will receive its first Type-214 SSK submarine by 2015; six were purchased in total. Turkish firms are to design and produce the vessels' electronics and weapon systems.

Turkey is a Level 3 Partner in the F-35 *Lightning II* project, which it joined in 2002. Turkish Aerospace Industries (TAI) is part of the consortium in charge of producing, among other elements, the F-35's centre fuselage. Due to a disagreement with the United States over technology sharing, and despite an initial informal agreement for 100 aircraft, Turkey has put its order on hold, confirming the purchase of only two units. Turkey is also trying to develop its own fighter, and TAI is currently working on the design and development of a jet engine in cooperation with Tusas Engine Industries (TEI). Helicopters have long been a procurement priority, not least because of the continuing Partiya Karkeren Kurdistan (PKK) insurgency. After two years of negotiations, in 2011, Turkey eventually signed a US$3.5bn deal with Sikorsky for the production of 109 S-70 *Blackhawk* helicopters, with TAI and other Turkish companies in charge of manufacturing several key components. Also, in late 2011, the US Congress approved the sale of three AH-1W *Super Cobra* attack helicopters in a US$111m Foreign Military Sale to Turkey. In the meantime, Turkey is also working on an indigenous attack helicopter project, on which AgustaWestland and TAI are collaborating, based upon AgustaWestland's

A129 *Mangusta*. The first prototype of the T129 *Atak* successfully completed its first flight in August 2011, and deliveries are planned to start by 2013. TAI is also developing the *Anka*, a medium-altitude, long-endurance UAV that will likely replace Turkey's Israeli Aerospace Industries (IAI)-manufactured *Heron* fleet.

The *Anka* UAVs are expected to be used primarily against the PKK insurgency. Turkey took delivery of its 10 *Heron* UAVs in 2010 and also leased two *Aerostar* UAVs from Israel. But the deterioration in bilateral political ties resulted in the withdrawal of Israeli technicians and trainers from Turkey, hampering the effective use of the UAVs and complicating maintenance and repair. In December 2011, four US MQ-1B *Predator* UAVs were relocated from Iraq to the air base at Incirlik in southern Turkey, operated by US personnel. Although the locally produced *Anka* UAV is expected to become operational in 2014, its effectiveness is still unclear. Indeed, privately, members of the Turkish military have expressed concern that the government's emphasis on local input is delaying the completion of co-production projects and that wholly domestically manufactured products are sometimes technically inferior to imported ones.

Defence industry

Turkey's defence industry has grown steadily in the last decade. The annual turnover increased from US$1.1bn to US$4.4bn between 2002 and 2011. The volume of defence-industry exports was relatively small until the end of the 1990s. Despite setbacks in the 2000s, exports increased from US$123m in 2000 to US$817m in 2011. If civil-aviation sales finalised by defence industries are included, export values for 2011 reach about US$1.1bn. R&D investments have grown accordingly, from US$367m in 2007 to US$672m in 2011 (+83%): for 2011, 33% of R&D funds were allocated directly by industries, while the largest share (67%) was raised through projects depending on external funds. In 2011, several important international contracts were signed. A US$600m agreement signed between FNSS and the Malaysian government constituted the biggest contract a Turkish defence firm had ever obtained with a foreign country. Additional contracts with Pakistan and Azerbaijan, and potential collaborations with Gulf states, are bolstering Turkey's efforts to boost the profile and activity of its defence industry.

New strategic plan

In March 2012, Ankara announced an ambitious five-year Strategic Plan for 2012–16 which aims to make the country's defence industry one of the ten largest in the world by 2016, with total annual turnover of US$8bn and exports of US$2bn. Since the AKP first came to power in November 2002, it has sought to maximise the proportion of the Turkish military's defence-industry needs that are met from domestic sources, increasing the share from 25% in 2003 to 54% in 2011. The main reason has been to reduce Turkey's vulnerability to purchases from the US and Europe being delayed or blocked for political reasons, such as concerns over the country's human-rights record and its often fractious relationships with its neighbours. However, the 2012–2016 Strategic Plan also reflects the AKP's broader ambition to transform Turkey into the pre-eminent political and military power in its region.

The main projects in the 2012–16 Strategic Plan which will be wholly or predominantly locally produced include:

- completion of the prototype of the *Altay* MBT by 2015, leading eventually to the production of 1,000 tanks;
- completion of the prototype of an infantry rifle for use by the Turkish army;
- completion of the conceptual design for a domestic fighter aircraft and jet trainer by 2014 (this will be in addition to the planned eventual purchase of around 100 F-35s);

- launch of a radar observation satellite by 2016;
- completion of the design for a general-purpose light helicopter.

The 2012–16 Strategic Plan also foresees the completion of a number of ongoing projects, including:

- delivery of nine T-129 attack helicopters, which are being co-produced by AgustaWestland and the TAI, by 2013 (the wider *Atak* procurement stands);
- delivery of the first of what will eventually be four B-737 airborne early-warning and control (AEW&C) aircraft in early 2013;
- inclusion of the locally produced *Anka* UAVs in the Turkish military's inventory by 2014.

THE UNITED KINGDOM

Defence reform continues

The UK government continues to implement the far-reaching defence modernisation, reform and restructuring process analysed in last year's *Military Balance* (pp. 81–7). Plans to reduce the size of the Ministry of Defence (MoD) and delegate considerable budgetary and management authority to the services have constituted the most radical changes in the UK management of defence for 50 years. Meanwhile, the October 2010 UK Strategic Defence and Security Review (SDSR) reduced the defence budget by about 8%, leading to a 20–30% reduction in the UK armed forces' operational ambition and deployable capability. Increases of resources were confined to improving the support to special forces and £650m for an increased UK cyber capability.

Lord Levene's independent Defence Reform report of 2011 recommended that senior military and civil-service posts be reduced; a 25% reduction in these posts, to begin after April 2013, was announced by Defence Secretary Philip Hammond in August 2012. Meanwhile, the Defence Equipment and Support (DE&S) organisation (responsible for procuring all MoD equipment and materiel) has, by insisting on rigorous and honest costing of defence programmes, played a major role in moves to balance the defence budget. Considerable work went on behind the scenes to develop new management models for DE&S, including a Government Owned

Contractor Operated (Go–Co) model. Although there was much press and industry speculation regarding the future structure of DE&S, no announcement was forthcoming.

Modest reductions in UK commitments to Afghanistan are allowing the forces to begin rebuilding their contingent capability for expeditionary operations. The Royal Navy in 2012 deployed around a dozen vessels on its second annual 'Response Force Task Group' deployment. Meanwhile, both the navy's commando brigade and the army air-assault brigade exercised in their amphibious and airborne roles. The need for reactive defence capability was demonstrated in July. A military contribution to security of the London 2012 Olympics, including around 7,500 army, naval, air and special-forces personnel, had been long planned and was rehearsed in May. But unforeseen requirements, including the unplanned failure of G4S, a civilian security company, to deliver sufficient civilian security staff resulted in the armed forces having to provide almost 10,000 more troops, many at short notice. In the event, this deployment proceeded flawlessly and led to the armed forces' contribution being widely praised, giving a boost to British military self-confidence, previously dented by the unpopularity and apparent intractability of the Iraq and Afghan wars.

Balancing the books

The MoD continued efforts to bring resources and budget into balance. Though then-Defence Secretary Liam Fox claimed in July 2011 that 'for the first time in a generation, the MoD will have brought its plans and budget broadly into balance'. He announced an increase in spending of 1% per annum in the equipment and procurement budget. The MoD then announced funding for three *Rivet Joint* electronic-intelligence aircraft, 14 *Chinook* helicopters (down from 22 announced by the previous government), an armoured-vehicle modernisation programme, a mid-life update to the *Warrior* infantry fighting vehicle, initial funding for the Joint Strike Fighter, fitting catapults to the future aircraft carriers and development funds for a new Global Combat Ship to replace Royal Navy frigates.

After Fox's resignation, further work was required to complete the balancing of the defence budget, the outcome of which was announced in spring 2012 (see p. 109). But the MoD has not yet identified which additional equipment purchased as 'Urgent Operational Requirements' for the Afghanistan war

were to be taken into its core programme, and which were to be abandoned. Many of these, such as the *Brimstone* dual-mode missile used to great success in Libya, have a much wider utility. For example, the army is assuming that the *Jackal*, *Mastiff* and *Foxhound* vehicles will be retained in service after 2015.

Joint Forces Command

Lord Levene's report concluded that important joint military capabilities and functions, such as medical services, training and education, intelligence and cyber abilities, were 'not organised and managed as coherently or effectively as they could be', as they had 'generally not been seen as core to single service outputs' and therefore 'not given sufficient priority'.

As a result, Joint Forces Command was created to manage the increasing number of joint organisations, including Defence Intelligence, the new Defence Cyber Operations Group, the high-readiness Joint Force HQ and Joint Force Logistics HQ, UK Special Forces (itself a joint command of special forces drawn from all UK forces), joint training units, the joint medical command, Permanent Joint Headquarters (PJHQ) and joint operating bases in Gibraltar, Cyprus, Diego Garcia and the Falkland Islands. It is also to act as institutional advocate for joint warfare. This includes ensuring that lessons learned on operations are applied quickly, which often proved problematic for UK forces in the early stages of both the Iraq and Afghan wars.

The chiefs of staff have gone out of their way to welcome the Joint Forces Command. Speaking at the IISS in January 2012, British Army Chief General Sir Peter Wall said: 'We shall be forging a close relationship with the newly formed Joint Forces Command, another defence-reform innovation, which will be the proponent and conscience for joint coherence across the board, as well as for critical joint enablers such as intelligence and information systems and surveillance.'

Army 2020

The MoD initially envisaged that the army would not greatly reduce while British operations continued in Afghanistan. But by July 2011, the ministry's efforts to balance its budget required greater reduction in the army's size by 20%; from 102,000 to 82,000 regular personnel over the next 5 years. UK Defence Secretary Phillip Hammond's summer 2012 announcement of 'Army 2020' saw five regular infantry battalions and two cavalry regiments as well as artillery, engineer and logistic units identified for disbandment, as part of an ambitious programme of reorganisation re-equipment, restructuring and rebasing.

The redesign exercise sought to better position the army for the 'age of austerity', the ability to partner with and train overseas armies. It also drew on many of the lessons of the Iraq and Afghan wars, as well as on thinking about the nature of future conflict. This includes the considerable challenges of fighting 'hybrid' opponents, such as Hizbullah, combining the characteristics of both a conventional army and a guerrilla force. It concluded that the evolutionary approach initially envisaged by the SDSR should be replaced by a much more radical redesign.

The high readiness echelon of the army is termed the 'Reaction Force'. Its main combat power will be a division of three armoured-infantry brigades containing a mixture of *Challenger* tanks and armoured infantry in *Warrior* infantry fighting vehicles, intended for hard fighting against both conventional and 'hybrid' enemies, including in urban areas, as well as the most challenging peace-enforcement missions. The Air Assault Brigade will continue to have its unique mixture of paratroops and *Apache* attack helicopters, although it will reduce in size.

There will be a complementary 'Adaptable Force' of partnered regular and reserve infantry and 'light cavalry' regiments organised in seven infantry brigades. Given sufficient warning it would be capable of generating up to two combined-arms light brigades to follow on from Reaction Force brigades in any enduring stabilisation operations. The army sees it as the primary tool for delivering UK military assistance and training to other countries, as well as support in case of UK civil emergencies.

The army will become more 'modular', seeing regular and reserve supporting capabilities, such as engineers, artillery, intelligence, logistics and medical, grouped as a division of 'Force Troops' spanning both the reaction and adaptable force structures. Within the Force Troops, previously disparate UAV and intelligence-gathering units will be grouped into a single new intelligence and surveillance brigade. Signals units will be radically redesigned, to deliver network and broadband access to battlefield units in new ways. A new Security Assistance Group keeps alive the lessons on training, mentoring and partnership learned from developing Iraqi and Afghan forces, and will also to be the army's focus for overseas engagement, by acting a repository of reconstruction, language and cultural experts.

As the regular army reduces, it intends to make much greater use of its reserves: the Territorial Army (TA) and the 'regular reserve' of former soldiers. For example, future stabilisation operations could see one-third of troops come from the reserves. Although the army's reserves have contributed up to 10% of the troops on recent operations in the Balkans, Iraq and Afghanistan and have provided a complete battalion to the UN peacekeeping force in Cyprus, they were relatively neglected in the previous decade. So Army 2020 requires the TA's trained strength to double to 30,000. An additional £1.8bn (US$2.8bn) is allocated to this, including for overseas training. This may be difficult for many of the reserves' employers to accept. And there are particular problems for reserves who work in small businesses. But the levels of commitment shown by UK Special Forces reserves and the US, Canadian and Australian reserves indicate that a quantum leap of capability can be made. But there will have to a significant cultural change among employers, the reserves and the regular army, as well as new legislation.

Although Defence Secretary Hammond and his CDS General Sir David Richards are bullish about the initiative, it is one of the greatest risks to the Army 2020 project, and the new TA organisation has yet to be designed. The reorganisation of the regular army and reserves are both dependent on the yet to be announced plan for the rebasing of the army to support the new structure, as well as the withdrawal of all British troops from Germany. And although the SDSR had signalled increased army basing and training in Scotland, investing in extra army facilities there must be in doubt until after the 2014 referendum on Scottish independence.

The other significant risk concerns personnel. Although a redundancy programme has started, most of those who would volunteer for redundancy have already done so. It is likely that at least 10,000 more people will be made compulsorily redundant over the next few years, at a time of uncertain UK economic prospects and while the army still has to finish its war in Afghanistan. Despite a generous redundancy and retraining package, this has, unsurprisingly, proven unpopular. But given the ministry's target of a 20% reduction in regular army size, senior leaders see little alternative.

Army 2020 is perhaps the most radical reorganisation of the army since the end of conscription in 1960. Taken together these measures have the poten-

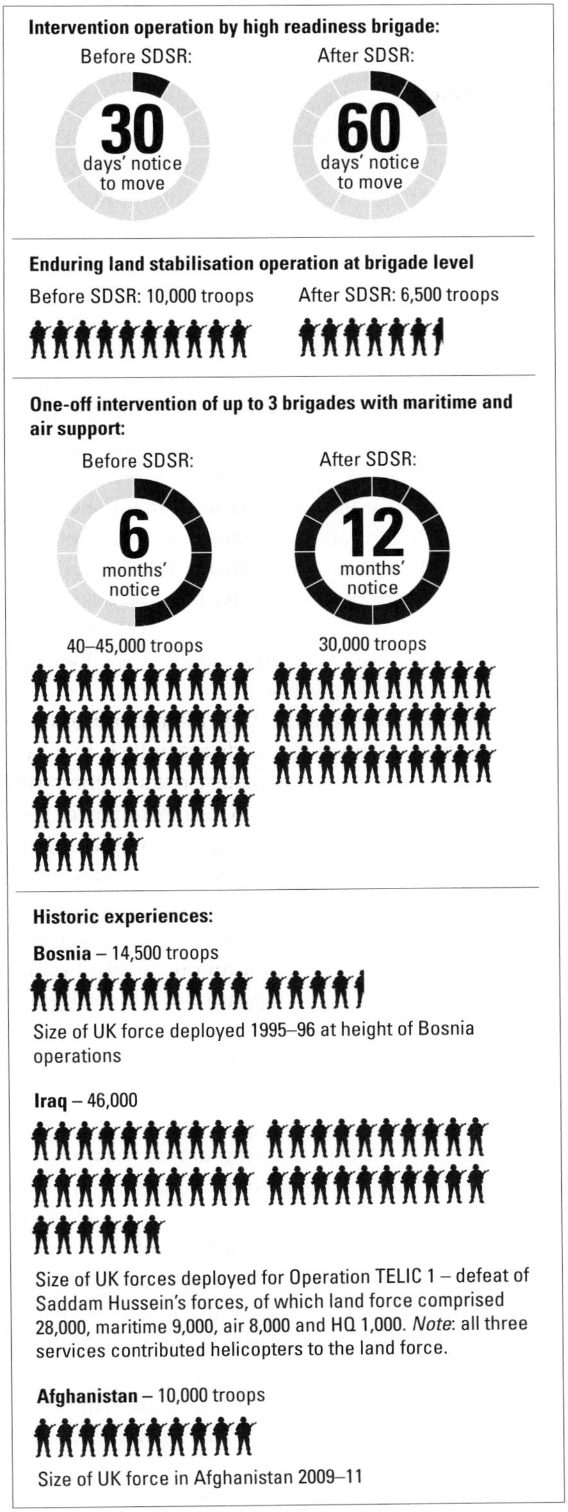

Intervention operation by high readiness brigade:

Before SDSR:	After SDSR:
30 days' notice to move	**60** days' notice to move

Enduring land stabilisation operation at brigade level

Before SDSR: 10,000 troops   After SDSR: 6,500 troops

One-off intervention of up to 3 brigades with maritime and air support:

Before SDSR:	After SDSR:
6 months' notice	**12** months' notice
40–45,000 troops	30,000 troops

Historic experiences:

Bosnia – 14,500 troops

Size of UK force deployed 1995–96 at height of Bosnia operations

Iraq – 46,000

Size of UK forces deployed for Operation TELIC 1 – defeat of Saddam Hussein's forces, of which land force comprised 28,000, maritime 9,000, air 8,000 and HQ 1,000. *Note*: all three services contributed helicopters to the land force.

Afghanistan – 10,000 troops

Size of UK force in Afghanistan 2009–11

Figure 14 **UK Military Ambitions: Before and After SDSR 2010**

Table 7 **Army 2020**

The current ORBAT of 17 regular and ten regional brigades will be reduced to four Reaction Forces, seven Adaptable Forces and seven Force Troops brigades. Total reductions of 27 to 18 brigade HQs.

Arm		Regular Units	
	Now	A2020	% Change
Infantry	36	31	-14%
Royal Armoured Corps	11	9[1]	-18%
Royal Artillery	14	12	-14%
Royal Engineers	15	11	-27%
Royal Signals	12	11	-8%
Royal Logistics Corps	18	12	-33%
REME (equipment maintenace)	8	7	-13%

(Changes to TA ORBATs have yet to be announced.)
[1]The regular RAC will reduce from 11 regiments to nine by the amalgamation of four regiments into two.

tial to transform army capability, provided that this programme of change is properly led, managed, resourced and politically supported. But the fact remains that the British Army of 2020 will, in concert with the navy and air force, be smaller overall than when the process started, and have reduced operational ambition, a smaller set of operational capabilities and be much more dependent on reserves.

The navy

The Royal Navy continues to see personnel and hull numbers fall as it attempts to manage the reductions outlined in SDSR 2010. Many naval cuts were front-loaded in the SDSR, including the retirement of the aircraft carrier HMS *Ark Royal* in 2011. Vessels decommissioned in 2012 were replaced either on a one-for-one basis or by more capable vessels: the nuclear-powered submarine HMS *Turbulent* paid off in July 2012 and will be replaced by HMS *Ambush* in 2013; while the Type-42 destroyers HMS *Liverpool* and HMS *York* were decommissioned in March and September 2012 respectively, and HMS *Dragon* was commissioned in April 2012, as the former 12-strong destroyer force is replaced by the six-ship Type-45 fleet.

The navy has a delicate task in managing the reduced assets at its disposal (beyond the decommissioned vessels, HMS *Albion* is also now on extended readiness, leaving just one landing platform dock available for operations) and the lack of a fixed-wing carrier strike capability. Paradoxically, an embarrassing volte-face over the choice of aircraft variant for the future carriers actually presented the navy with an opportunity. In May 2012, the MoD announced that an earlier decision to overturn the previous government's choice of the short take-off and vertical landing variant of the F-35 (F-35B) in favour of the conventional carrier variant F-35C was itself being overturned, reverting back to the F-35B. It had emerged that the cost of fitting a carrier with the EMALS catapult launch system would be close to £2bn, more than double the initial estimate of £920m at the time of the SDSR. For the navy, this means that the decision in SDSR 2010 to re-equip one of the planned two *Queen Elizabeth*-class carriers with the catapult and arrestor equipment necessary for the F-35C, and to leave the fate of the second hull undecided, has itself been brought into question. With the construction of two hulls that could theoretically operate the F-35B, the possibility now exists that both carriers could be retained in service.

Other funding decisions in 2012 suggested a continuation of key defence commitments. The October 2012 announcement of £315m (US$495m) for BAE Systems and £38m (US$59.7m) for Babcock to continue work on the successor class of ballistic-missile submarines indicated the likelihood of a like-for-like replacement of the UK's nuclear deterrent. Although a main gate decision has been delayed until 2016, £1.1bn (US$1.7bn) of funding for reactor cores for the remaining *Astute*-class and successor-class SSBNs was awarded to Rolls Royce in June 2012. Earlier, in May, an initial tranche of £350m (US$550m) was awarded to BAE Systems for successor-class designs, indicating a growing financial commitment to the project, despite the absence of a final decision. Given the decision to base all navy submarines in Faslane by 2017, it also indicates confidence that the Scottish independence referendum will not lead to secession from the union, with the resulting potential for an independent Scotland to reject the basing of *Trident* north of the border. The successor class is currently expected to replace *Vanguards* from 2028. Before then, the navy will see further cuts to its fleet, as HMS *Illustrious* is retired in 2014. With cuts to personnel continuing, the navy will have to operate as a smaller, less capable force for much of the next decade.

Air force

The government's May 2012 decision to revert to the F-35B short take-off and vertical landing variant of the Joint Strike Fighter was perhaps the main air power development of 2012 in the UK. As part of the SDSR 2010, the UK had opted to buy the carrier variant F-35C intended for the US Navy. The C-version offers greater range and payload, but

required that the UK revise the design of its new aircraft carriers to introduce catapults and arrestor gear. The SDSR also indicated that one of the two aircraft carriers would be mothballed on completion. The government attributed the latest change of heart to the increasing cost estimated to be associated with the required ship-modification programme and the resulting delay in its introduction into service. The modifications, according to the government, would have pushed the initial operational capability from 2020 to 2023.

The Royal Air Force, which will operate the F-35B in a joint force with the Royal Navy, is trying to manage its combat-aircraft numbers while some types are withdrawn from service and others are due for upgrades to broaden combat capability or extend service lives. The last of the RAF's *Tornado* GR4 ground-attack aircraft is planned to be withdrawn from service in 2019, with the *Typhoon* taking on more of the air-to-surface role to provide this capability until the F-35B is introduced into service in significant numbers, and to complement it beyond this. There were also suggestions that *Typhoon* Tranche 1 aircraft might be retained longer than previously planned.

The planned withdrawal of UK forces from Afghanistan by the end of 2014 is a near-term focus for the air force, underlining the importance of the air bridge at a time when its airlift and tanker transport fleets are being revamped. The Airbus A330 *Voyager* will replace the VC10 and *Tristar* tankers. The last of the VC10s are due to be retired at the end of the first quarter of 2013 with the *Tristars* to be withdrawn by around the turn of that year.

Assessment

The UK continues to have the fourth-largest defence budget in the world, and the top leadership of defence has shown public determination to more efficiently manage defence funding. In this they have been more successful than many of their recent predecessors, although they have been aided by clear political leadership and the UK deficit-reduction strategy. But the influential House of Commons Defence Committee and many UK defence analysts express scepticism that defence spending will prove sufficient to fully fund the Future Force 2020 set out in the SDSR. And both balancing the books and regenerating land and air expeditionary capability are dependent on successful British drawdown in Afghanistan.

UK defence economics

Defence cuts

UK defence continues to undergo fundamental reform, as noted above and in last year's *Military Balance* (pp. 81–7). Two principal objectives have been implementing the cuts necessary to achieve the 8% real-terms reduction in the defence budget by FY2014/15 envisaged in the October 2010 SDSR, and plugging the £38bn (US$58.7bn) 'unfunded liabilities' gap in the MoD's equipment-acquisition programme for the ten years from FY2011/12 to FY2020/21. Progress towards both these objectives commenced with the approximately £20bn (US$30.9bn) in reductions to planned equipment spending announced during the 2010 SDSR, which were increased by £5.2bn (US$8.3bn) during Planning Round 2011 (PR11). Cuts were further expanded in July 2011 by the '3-Month Review', which outlined an additional £6.6bn (US$10.6bn) in reductions weighted heavily towards the 2015–20 period, and targeted funding decreases particularly for armoured-vehicle programmes. Also in July 2011, the then-Secretary of State for Defence, Liam Fox, announced that a 1% real-terms uplift in the equipment-procurement budget between 2015–20 – cumulatively amounting to around £3bn (US$4.8bn) – had been negotiated with the UK Treasury. (This refers to a 1% real uplift in the equipment procurement budget, rather than in the overall defence budget post-2015, funding levels for which will only be determined after parliamentary elections scheduled for May 2015.)

These measures notwithstanding, by end-2011, the defence budget and equipment programme were only 'broadly in balance', as a procurement overhang of around £2–3bn (US$3.2bn–4.8bn) still remained. In part, this overhang persisted due to the higher costs associated with retrofitting catapults and arrestor gear onto one of the two new aircraft carriers (see above). It subsequently emerged that the cost of this would be close to £2bn (US$3.2bn) – more than double the initial estimate of £920m (US$1.4bn) at the time of the SDSR.

With the need for a further £2–3bn in cost reductions to be achieved in Planning Round 2012 (PR12), in January 2012, it was announced that an additional 3,000 more civilian staff at the MoD would be made redundant (bringing the total number of military and civilian job cuts at the MoD between 2011–14 to 45,000, of which 28,000 were civilian positions), while in early May 2012 the decision was taken to revert to the F-35B, enabling savings of an additional £2bn (US$3.1bn). A further £1bn (US$1.6bn) in C4ISR efficiencies was also achieved. These measures led to the announcement, on 14 May 2012, that for the first time in a decade, the much-publicised £38bn (US$58.7bn) 'black hole' had finally been plugged. In addition to balancing the budget, £8bn (US$12.6bn) in unallocated funds were set aside for future equipment requirements (type unspecified) not in the current acquisition programme; while a £4bn (US$6.3bn) contingency reserve fund was created to meet any unexpected cost overruns in current acquisitions. As a result, Defence Secretary Phillip Hammond claimed, in May 2012, that the UK could now definitely fund its armed forces modernisation plan between 2012 and 2020.

However, in October 2012, Hammond said, at a defence conference, that there remained 'an issue around cash spikes in the 2020s and 2030s' concerning the UK's nuclear deterrent. A final decision on replacing the *Trident* nuclear deterrent will only be made during the next parliament, likely after May 2015. Earlier, in a November 2011 report, the Public Accounts Committee claimed that 80% of the cost savings the MoD had made to the *Queen Elizabeth*-class aircraft carrier and JSF programmes had been achieved by deferring costs to the post-2020 period, raising the prospect that the MoD equipment budget after 2020 may require rationalisation.

Structure of Defence Equipment & Support

Reforms in other areas of the MoD have yet to be fully addressed or implemented. A key question that remains unresolved is the future organisational structure of Defence Equipment & Support (DE&S) – the agency responsibility for equipment acquisition and through-life support. DE&S had previously been heavily criticised for extensive delays and cost overruns in the MoD's equipment procurement programme – with average costs on key projects 40% higher than original estimates, and time to in-service dates around 80% longer than initially envisaged. A central reform issue has been the question of whether to restructure DE&S as a government-owned, contractor-operated (Go–Co) entity (where a private-sector management team is brought in to run the organisation separately from the MoD, similar to the UK's naval dockyards and the Atomic Weapons Establishment). This proposal is favoured by MoD Chief of Defence Material Bernard Gray. An alternative proposal is for DE&S to be run as an Executive

Non-Departmental Public Body (ENDPB/SP, similar to the Nuclear Decommissioning Authority), which would operate at arm's length from government departments in collaboration with a strategic private-sector partner. A third option was to establish DE&S as a trading fund, similar to the Defence Science and Technology Laboratory (DSTL).

Bernard Gray's October 2009 independent report recommended the establishment of a 'Go-Co', in order to bring in private-sector expertise to address areas of MoD weakness – in such areas as commercial negotiations, programme management for complex projects, finance and budgeting, and supply-chain management. Also, it was deemed that the MoD's routine practice of rotating both its civilian and military staff into and out of DE&S on a short-term basis did not help through-life project management, the development of specialised expertise and the retention of corporate memory. In addition, both Liam Fox and Philip Hammond have argued that a private-sector management company running DE&S would have greater flexibility to pay higher salaries than those permitted by public-sector pay scales, thereby enabling DE&S to better attract and retain specialist talent with the requisite commercial skill sets.

Having determined that the 'Go-Co' option would be the most suitable, it was hoped that this proposal would be adopted for the Material Strategy by the Defence Board (the MoD's highest decision-making authority) in June 2012. However, the Treasury requested further value-for-money testing of the 'Go-Co' proposal, due to the potentially high management fees charged by the private contractors operating the new entity, as well as the redundancy and pension costs associated with down-scaling the current DE&S staff structure – which by 2015 would have halved to 14,500, down from 29,000 in 2007. Earlier, in April 2012, private companies were invited to submit ideas and proposals for potential future commercial involvement in DE&S. Should the results of this value-for-money testing conclude that the 'Go-Co' option is indeed superior to the ENDPB/SP and trading-fund proposals, a decision to pursue this option would be made in late 2012. Subsequently, the proposal would undergo an investment appraisal and, over the course of 2013, a competition would be run to identify a commercial partner to operate the new entity. These delays mean that any final decision on DE&S's eventual restructuring is unlikely to occur before 2014 and could even run into 2015.

UK defence industry

Following a decade of elevated defence-expenditure levels to fund an ambitions equipment-procurement programme as well as military operations in Iraq and Afghanistan, the UK defence sector is now facing the prospect of a sustained period of contraction as overseas combat operations (and hence Urgent Operational Requirement funding for particularly land and air equipment) wind down and pressure on public finances forces domestic fiscal retrenchment. The delayed 'National Security through Technology' defence-industrial White Paper, eventually published in January 2012, reiterated the MoD's preference for open-competition, off-the-shelf procurement, although where necessary the MoD would continue resorting to single-source procurement. In general, the document bore considerable similarity to the 'Equipment, Support and Technology for UK Defence & Security' consultation paper which preceded it in December 2010, with little by way of new policies on export facilitation or increased involvement of small and medium-sized enterprises in defence supply chains.

The impending drawdown in operations in Afghanistan, the reduction in the army and broader defence austerity in Europe, has seen the UK's domestic land defence-industrial sector hard hit. As orders for armoured vehicles dry up, and after BAE Systems' Land & Armaments division lost out to both General Dynamics UK and Lockheed Martin UK on contracts to produce the UK's next generation of armoured vehicles (FRES SV) and the £1bn *Warrior* upgrade respectively, the company announced, in May 2012, it would close its land-systems plant in Newcastle-upon-Tyne by end-2013, after it completes production of its *Terrier* route-clearing vehicle. As a result, BAE will no longer manufacture armoured fighting vehicles in the UK, having earlier consolidated its armoured vehicle maintenance and support activities at its Telford plant. BAE has also repeatedly warned that it may have to close one of its three naval shipyards, a development that may result in the loss of a further 1,500 jobs. Overall, since the financial crisis broke in 2008, BAE has cut some 22,000 jobs worldwide – although the company still employs some 38,000 people in the UK and remains the country's largest manufacturing employer. BAE also continued to divest itself of non-core assets, announcing in May 2012 that it had reached an agreement to sell its Safariland business (which produces protective equipment for civilian law-enforcement agencies) for around US$200m.

These factors have spurred UK defence firms to look overseas. As arms-importing countries look to ensure that their domestic defence-manufacturing firms develop indigenous capabilities, overseas industrial collaboration, local partnerships and technology-transfer agreements have all become significantly more important to ensure that the high-value defence-engineering expertise developed by UK defence industries is not lost. For example, in January 2012, BAE Systems was able to win its first major naval contract in Brazil, in part due to its willingness to provide the Brazilian navy with manufacturing and design instructions to enable a Brazilian firm to construct five out of eight vessels; BAE will make three. BAE Systems and the UK government have also sought out international partners to share in the development costs of the Type-26 Global Combat Ship, reportedly approaching Australia, Brazil, Canada, India, Malaysia, New Zealand and Turkey to explore options for collaboration, although by mid-2012 it appeared that only Brazil remained as a serious proposition.

The UK continued strengthening its defence-industrial relationships with Asian states in 2012, following on from the accords it signed with Malaysia and Vietnam in 2011. In February 2012, it was announced that Daewoo Shipbuilding & Marine Engineering (DSME) had won the US$710m contract to construct, in Korea, four naval refuelling ships (the Military Afloat Reach & Sustainability programme) for operation by the Royal Fleet Auxiliary. The vessels are based on British designs and UK companies will supply key components, systems and support services through associated contracts with DSME. This arrangement enabled UK defence industries to utilise and develop their technological capabilities whilst simultaneously allowing the MoD to take advantage of the lower production costs in South Korea. In June 2012, an official visit to Korea by the UK's then-Minister for Defence Equipment, Support and Technology Peter Luff coincided with the announcement that South Korea would acquire MT30 gas turbine engines from Rolls-Royce for its new frigate. In July 2012, South Korea selected BAE Systems over Lockheed Martin to act as systems integrator for its won1.3tr (US$1.14bn) F-16 upgrade programme. Earlier, in February 2012, British ground surveillance radar manufacturer Plextek Ltd and South Korea's Nuriplan Co. Ltd announced the signing of a Memorandum of Understanding in which the latter would assist in the manufacture, marketing and technical customer support of the former's *Blighter* radars for the South Korean market. During the year, the UK also signed defence-cooperation agreements with Indonesia, Japan and the UAE, in theory paving the way for increased cooperation in research and development, investment and defence production.

Overall, UK defence firms have been seeking overseas partnerships to diversify their portfolios and assist with foreign market access. In June 2012, UK countermeasures group Chemring entered the Indian defence market, forming a joint venture with a holding company of India's Hinduja Group, Aasia Enterprises. The joint venture company (49% of which is owned by Chemring), Chemring Aasia Services, would provide support services for Chemring's Indian customer base and assist in managing the group's international supply chain. A second joint venture between the two to manufacture countermeasures in India (including electronic warfare, pyrotechnics, energy materials and munitions) is currently awaiting Indian government approval. In August 2012, UK defence electronics and communications firm Cobham Aviation Services set up a Brazilian subsidiary (Cobham do Brasil Ltda), to boost its presence in the country and better enable it to develop business opportunities there. This followed Embraer's selection, in September 2011, of the UK firm to provide wing-mounted aerial refuelling pods for its KC-390 aircraft.

Albania ALB

Albanian Lek		2011	2012	2013
GDP	lek	1.32tr	1.35tr	
	US$	13bn	12.4bn	
per capita	US$	4,329	4,129	
Growth	%	3.00	0.50	
Inflation	%	3.43	2.01	
Def exp [b]	lek	19.9bn		
	US$	196m		
Def bdgt [a]	lek	21.6bn	24.7bn	27.1bn
	US$	212m	226m	
FMA (US)	US$	3.99m	3m	3m
US$1=lek		101.67	109.31	

[a] Excludes military pensions

[b] NATO definition

Population   3,002,859

Age	0–14	15–19	20–24	25–29	30–64	65 plus
Male	10.9%	5.1%	5.0%	4.1%	19.4%	5.0%
Female	9.7%	4.8%	5.0%	4.3%	21.1%	5.6%

Capabilities

A NATO member since 2009, Albania sustains limited military capability predicated on internal security and disaster relief. Efforts continue to reform its armed forces and upgrade mainly obsolete equipment, though these are constrained by limited funding. As well as wider ties with fellow NATO members, Albania is trying to develop bilateral regional ties, and, in 2011, carried out a small-scale naval exercise with Slovenia. The army, the largest of the three services, is equipped mainly with obsolete Chinese-origin equipment. It has provided troops to ISAF in Afghanistan – both to Kabul and on surveillance and force-protection duties in RC-W – and troops, including an EOD team to *Operation Althea*, in Bosnia. The small air brigade operates only rotary and light liaison aircraft, and the country depends on NATO Allies for air defence. The armed forces have no strategic lift. Albania is engaged in revising its national military strategy.

ACTIVE 14,250 (Joint Force Comd 8,150, Support Command 4,300, TRADOC 1,000, MoD and General Staff 800) **Paramilitary 500**

Terms of service conscription 12 months

ORGANISATIONS BY SERVICE

Joint Forces Command (JFC) 8,150

Consists of a Land Element (comprising a Rapid Reaction Bde, Cdo Regt, Regional Spt Bde, Log Bn and Comms Bn), an Air Bde and Naval Bde. JFC units are intended to conduct and support international peace-support and humanitarian operations, and other crisis management tasks.

Land Element

FORCES BY ROLE
SPECIAL FORCES
1 cdo regt
MANOEUVRE
Light
1 (rapid reaction) lt inf bde
COMBAT SUPPORT
1 arty bn
1 cbt spt bde
1 sigs bn
COMBAT SERVICE SUPPORT
1 log bn
EQUIPMENT BY TYPE
MBT 3 Type-59
APC (T) 6 Type-5310
ARTY
TOWED 18 **152 mm**
MOR 81: **82mm** 81
AD • GUNS 42 **37mm** M-1939/S 60
ARV T-54/T-55
MW *Bozena*

Navy Element

The Albanian Navy Brigade, under the command of JFC, is organised into two naval flotillas with additional hydrographic, logistics, auxiliary and training support services.
EQUIPMENT BY TYPE
PATROL AND COASTAL COMBATANTS • PB 3: 2 *Po-2†* (FSU Project 501); 1 *Shanghai* II† (PRC) with two single 533mm TT
MINE WARFARE • MINE COUNTERMEASURES • MSO 1 T-43† (FSU Project 254)
LOGISTICS AND SUPPORT • ARL 1

Coast Guard

FORCES BY ROLE
The Albanian Coast Guard (Roja Bregdetare) is under the command of the Navy Brigade's Coastal Defence Command.
EQUIPMENT BY TYPE
PATROL AND COASTAL COMBATANTS 32
  PBF 12: 8 V-4000; 4 *Archangel* (1 additional vessel to be delivered)
  PB 7: 2 *Iluria* (Damen Stan 4207 - 2 additional vessels to be delivered); 3 Mk3 *Sea Spectre*; 2 (other)
  PBR 13: 4 Type-227; 1 Type-246; 1 Type-303; 7 Type-2010

Air Element

Flying hours at least 10–15 hrs/year.
EQUIPMENT BY TYPE
HELICOPTERS
  TPT • Light 21: 1 AW109; 5 Bell 205 (AB-205); 7 Bell 206C (AB-206C); 8 Bo-105

Support Command (SC) 4,300

Consists of the Logistics Brigade, GS Support Regiment, Infrastructure Regiment, Personnel and Recruiting Centre, Military Hospital, Systems Development Centre and Military Police Battalion.

FORCES BY ROLE
COMBAT SUPPORT
  1 MP bn
COMBAT SERVICE SUPPORT
  1 log bde (1 spt regt (tpt, EOD & maint)
  1 fd hospital

Training and Doctrine Command (TRADOC)
1,000

Consists of the Defense Academy, Military University, NCO Academy, Basic Training Brigade, the consolidated Troops School, Centre for Defense Analysis and Training Support Centre.

Paramilitary ε500

DEPLOYMENT

Legal provisions for foreign deployment:
Constitution: Codified constitution (1998)
Decision on deployment of troops abroad: By the parliament upon proposal by the president (Art.171 II)

AFGHANISTAN
NATO • ISAF 212; 1 inf coy

BOSNIA-HERZEGOVINA
EU • EUFOR • *Operation Althea* 11

SERBIA
NATO • KFOR 9

FOREIGN FORCES

Italy 18 (Delegazione Italiana Esperti)

Austria AUT

Euro €		2011	2012	2013
GDP	€	301bn	309bn	
	US$	418bn	391bn	
per capita	US$	50,853	47,568	
Growth	%	2.70	0.92	
Inflation	%	3.55	2.34	
Def exp [a]	€	2.45bn		
	US$	3.41bn		
Def bdgt [a]	€	2.47bn	2.5bn	
	US$	3.43bn	3.16bn	
US$1=€		0.72	0.79	

[a] Includes military pensions

Population 8,219,743

Age	0–14	15–19	20–24	25–29	30–64	65 plus
Male	7.1%	3.0%	3.1%	3.1%	24.8%	7.8%
Female	6.8%	2.8%	3.0%	3.1%	24.8%	10.7%

Capabilities

The armed forces are configured to provide territorial defence, and also generate units capable of being deployed as part of multinational peacekeeping missions. The lack of a significant number of transport aircraft indicates a reduced ability to independently project power at range, though the armed forces do maintain a high readiness element; Rapid Deployment Units, made up of career soldiers, have been generated to deploy at short notice to conduct full-spectrum crisis-management operations. Nonetheless, the armed forces have had to manage a reduction in force equipment fleets in recent years, notably in armoured vehicles and artillery. Austria's level of ambition for participation in international missions has been reduced with the decision to give up, until 2016, the aim to be able to deploy a framework brigade. Priorities include Eurofighter upgrades, MLUs for transport helicopters, and acquisitions to ensure interoperable units for EU Battlegroups. Training levels are high, including as part of multinational exercises. Austria anticipates increased international cooperation and burden-sharing. This, as well as a shift in focus to new risks and emerging challenges, is reflected in the drafts of Austria's revised National Security Strategy. A new Defence White Paper is anticipated in 2013.

ACTIVE 23,250 (Army 11,500; Air 2,750; Support 9,000)

RESERVE 176,450 (Joint structured 26,100; Joint unstructured 150,350)

Terms of service 6 months recruit trg, 30 days reservist refresher trg for volunteers; 90–120 days additional for officers, NCOs and specialists. Authorised maximum wartime strength is 55,000; Some 66,000 reservists a year undergo refresher trg in tranches.

ORGANISATIONS BY SERVICE

Joint Command – Land Forces 11,500

FORCES BY ROLE
MANOEUVRE
  Mechanised
    1 (3rd) bde (1 recce/SP arty bn, 1 armd bn, 1 mech inf bn, 1 inf bn, 1 cbt engr bn, 1 CBRN defence coy, 1 spt bn)
    1 (4th) bde (1 recce/SP arty bn, 1 armd bn, 1 mech inf bn, 1 inf bn, 1 CBRN defence coy, 1 spt bn)
  Light
    1 (6th) bde (3 inf bn, 1 cbt engr bn, 1 CBRN defence coy, 1 spt bn)
    1 (7th) bde (1 recce/arty bn, 3 inf bn, 1 cbt engr bn, 1 CBRN defence coy, 1 spt bn)

EQUIPMENT BY TYPE
MBT 56 *Leopard* 2A4
RECCE 12 CBRN *Dingo*
AIFV 112 *Ulan*
APC 94
  APC (W) 71 *Pandur*
  PPV 23 *Dingo* II
ARTY 156
  SP • 155mm 40 M109A5ÖE
  MOR • 120mm 105 M-43 (80 more in store)
AT • MSL • MANPATS PAL 2000 BILL
ARV 48: 38 4KH7FA-SB; 10 M88A1
MW 6 AID2000 Trailer

Joint Command - Air Force 2,750

The Air Force is part of Joint Forces Comd and consists of 2 bde; Air Support Comd and Airspace Surveillance Comd

Flying hours 160 hrs/year on hel/tpt ac; 110 hrs/year on ftr

FORCES BY ROLE

FIGHTER
  2 sqn with *Typhoon*

ISR
  1 sqn with PC-6B *Turbo Porter*

TRANSPORT
  1 sqn with C-130K *Hercules*

TRAINING
  1 trg sqn with Saab 105Oe*
  1 trg sqn with PC-7 *Turbo Trainer*

TRANSPORT HELICOPTER
  2 sqn with Bell 212 (AB-212)
  1 sqn with OH-58B *Kiowa*
  1 sqn with S-70A *Black Hawk*
  2 sqn with SA316/SA319 *Alouette* III

AIR DEFENCE
  2 bn
  1 radar bn

EQUIPMENT BY TYPE

AIRCRAFT 37 combat capable
  FTR 15 Eurofighter *Typhoon* Tranche 1
  TPT 11: **Medium** 3 C-130K *Hercules*; **Light** 8 PC-6B *Turbo Porter*
  TRG 34: 12 PC-7 *Turbo Trainer*; 22 Saab 105Oe*

HELICOPTERS
  MRH 24 SA316/SA319 *Alouette* III
  ISR 11 OH-58B *Kiowa*
  TPT 32: **Medium** 9 S-70A *Black Hawk*; **Light** 23 Bell 212 (AB-212)

AD
  SAM 24 *Mistral* (12 more in store)
  GUNS • **35mm** 24 Z-FIAK system (29 more in store)
MSL • **AAM** • **IIR** IRIS-T

Joint Command – Special Operations Forces

FORCES BY ROLE

SPECIAL FORCES
  1 SF gp

Support 9,000

Support forces comprise Joint Services Support Command and several agencies, academies and schools. The agencies include intelligence, security, defence technology, medical and personnel whilst the academies and schools comprise training elements and schools including The National Defence and NCO Academies.

Cyber

The MoD is developing a national-level Cyber Attack Information System (CAIS) with the goal of strengthening resilience and increasing survivability and reliability of IT structures. The MoD constitutes one of four main strands in Austria's 'Strategy for Cyber Security'. At the end of 2012, these are due to merge into a 'Cyber Security Strategy AUT' under the aegis of the Federal Chancellery. The MoD's primary goal is 'cyber defence', by ensuring national defence in cyberspace as well as securing MoD ICT. The Military Cyber Emergency Readiness Team (milCERT) will be expanded to improve situational awareness and develop Computer Network Operations capabilities. These will constitute nationally available ICT technological capabilities as well as providing cyber forensics. MoD adopted a mil.ICT umbrella concept in 2011. MoD concepts on Computer Network Operations and Computer Network Defence – Information Assurance are due to be finalised by end-2012.

DEPLOYMENT

Legal provisions for foreign deployment:
Constitution: incl 'Federal Constitutional Law' (1/1930)
Specific legislation: 'Bundesverfassungsgesetz über Kooperation und Solidarität bei der Entsendung von Einheiten und Einzelpersonen in das Ausland' (KSE-BVG, 1997)
Decision on deployment of troops abroad: By government on authorisation of the National Council's Main Committee; simplified procedure for humanitarian and rescue tasks (Art. 23j of the 'Federal Constitutional Law'; § 2 of the KSE-BVG)

AFGHANISTAN
NATO • ISAF 3

BOSNIA-HERZEGOVINA
EU • EUFOR • *Operation Althea* 321; 1 inf bn HQ; 1 recce pl; 1 inf coy

CYPRUS
UN • UNFICYP 4

DEMOCRATIC REPUBLIC OF THE CONGO
EU • EUSEC RD Congo 1

LEBANON
UN • UNIFIL 151; 1 log bn

MIDDLE EAST
UN • UNTSO 6 obs

SERBIA
NATO • KFOR 535; elm 1 recce coy; 1 mech inf coy; 1 tpt coy

SYRIA/ISRAEL
UN • UNDOF 374; elm 1 inf bn

WESTERN SAHARA
UN • MINURSO 2 obs

Belgium BEL

Euro €		2011	2012	2013
GDP	€	369.8bn	376.6bn	
	US$	514.6bn	476.8bn	
per capita	US$	49,299	45,678	
Growth	%	1.78	0.04	
Inflation	%	3.47	2.79	
Def exp[b]	€	3.97bn		
	US$	5.52bn		
Def bdgt [a]	€	3.82bn	3.77bn	3.82bn
	US$	5.31bn	4.77bn	
US$1=€		0.72	0.79	

[a] Includes military pensions
[b] NATO definition

Population   10,438,353

Age	0–14	15–19	20–24	25–29	30–64	65 plus
Male	8.1%	2.9%	3.1%	3.1%	24.1%	7.7%
Female	7.7%	2.8%	3.0%	2.9%	23.9%	10.7%

Capabilities

As a result of reductions in Belgian military expenditure, all forces will reduce in size in terms of personnel and equipment; most of this reduction will be complete by end-2013. The armed forces plan to further develop deployable and flexible forces. They exercise jointly on a regular basis and also participate in a broad range of multinational training exercises. Belgian forces have deployed to ISAF since 2003. Belgium maintains a quick reaction force, and the military has a limited ability to project force, although only as part of a multinational deployment, such as *Operation Unified Protector* in 2011. The land component has been transformed into a wheeled medium brigade and an airborne-capable light brigade. The naval component focuses on escort and mine countermeasures for littoral and blue-water operations. The air component faces a significant change in inventory around the end of this decade when it will need to replace its F-16s; for now Belgium's most pressing procurement concerns are replacement anti-tank missiles and patrol craft.

ACTIVE 32 ,650 (Army 11,950 Navy 1,500 Air 5,450 Medical Service 1,750 Joint Service 12,000)

RESERVE 1,400

ORGANISATIONS BY SERVICE

Land Component 11,950

FORCES BY ROLE
SPECIAL FORCES
  1 SF gp
MANOEUVRE
  Reconnaissance
  1 ISTAR gp (2 ISTAR coy, 1 surv coy)
  Mechanised
  1 (med) bde (4 mech bn)
  Light
  1 (lt) bde (1 cdo bn, 1 lt inf bn, 1 para bn)
COMBAT SUPPORT
  1 arty gp (1 arty bty, 1 mor bty, 1 AD bty)
  2 engr bn (1 cbt engr coy, 1 lt engr coy, 1 construction engr coy)
  1 EOD unit
  1 CBRN coy
  1 MP coy (with 1 pl dedicated to EUROCORPS)
  3 CIS sigs gp
COMBAT SERVICE SUPPORT
  3 log bn

Reserves 1,400

Territorial Support Units
FORCES BY ROLE
MANOEUVRE
  Light
  11 inf unit
EQUIPMENT BY TYPE
MBT 30 *Leopard* 1A5
AIFV 39: 19 *Piranha* III-C DF30; 14 *Piranha* III-C DF90; 6 AIFV-B-C25 (25mm)
APC 298
  APC (W) 78: 64 *Piranha* III-C; 14 *Piranha* III-PC
  PPV 220 *Dingo*
ARTY 105
  TOWED 105mm 14 LG1 MK II
  MOR 91: **81mm** 39; **120mm** 52
AD • SAM 45 *Mistral*
AEV 6 *Leopard* 1
ARV 27: 14 *Leopard* 1; 9 M113; 4 *Pandur*
VLB 4 *Leguan*

Naval Component 1,500
EQUIPMENT BY TYPE
PRINCIPAL SURFACE COMBATANTS 2
  FRIGATES • FFGHM 2 *Karel Doorman* each with 2 quad lnchr with *Harpoon* AShM, 1 16-cell Mk48 VLS with RIM-7P *Sea Sparrow* SAM, 4 single 324mm Mk 32 MOD 9 ASTT with Mk 46 MOD 5 HWT, 1 76mm gun, (capacity 1 med hel)
PATROL AND COASTAL COMBATANTS • PBR 1 *Liberation* (in reserve)
MINE WARFARE • MINE COUNTERMEASURES • **MHC** 5 *Flower* (*Tripartite*)
LOGISTICS AND SUPPORT 9
  AG 1 *Stern*
  AGFH 1 *Godetia* (log spt/comd)
  AGOR 1 *Belgica*
  AXS 1 *Zenobe Gramme*
  YTL 3 *Wesp*
  YTM 2

Naval Aviation
HELICOPTERS • MRH 3 SA316B *Alouette* III (part of the Air Component); (to be replaced by 2 NH90 NFH on order, delivery expected from mid-2013)

Air Component 5,450

Flying hours 165 hrs/yr on cbt ac. 500 hrs/yr on tpt ac. 300 hrs/yr on hel; 200 hrs/yr for trg purposes

FORCES BY ROLE

FIGHTER/GROUND ATTACK/ISR
4 sqn with F-16AM/BM *Fighting Falcon*

SEARCH & RESCUE
1 sqn with *Sea King* Mk48

TRANSPORT
1 sqn with A330; ERJ-135 LR; ERJ-145 LR; *Falcon* 20 (VIP); *Falcon* 900B
1 sqn with C-130H *Hercules*

TRAINING
1 unit with F-16AM/BM *Fighting Falcon*
1 sqn with SF-260D/MB
1 BEL/FRA unit with *Alpha Jet**
1 OCU with AW109

TRANSPORT HELICOPTER
2 sqn with AW109 (ISR)

ISR UAV
1 sqn with RQ-5A *Hunter* (B-*Hunter*)

EQUIPMENT BY TYPE

AIRCRAFT 88 combat capable
FTR 59: 49 F-16AM *Fighting Falcon*; 10 F-16BM *Fighting Falcon*
TPT: 19 **Medium** 11 C-130H *Hercules*; **Light** 4: 2 ERJ-135 LR; 2 ERJ-145 LR; **PAX** 4: 1 A330; 2 *Falcon* 20 (VIP); 1 *Falcon* 900B
TRG 61: 29 *Alpha Jet**; 9 SF-260D; 23 SF-260MB

HELICOPTERS
MRH 3 SA316B *Alouette* III opcon Navy
SAR 4 *Sea King* Mk48 (to be replaced by 2 NH90 NFH, delivery expected from mid-2013)
TPT • Light 20 AW109 (ISR) (4 NH90 TTH on order, delivery from mid-2013)
UAV • ISR • Heavy 13 RQ-5A *Hunter* (B-*Hunter*)

MSL
AAM • IR AIM-9M/N *Sidewinder*; **ARH** AIM-120B AMRAAM

BOMBS
Conventional: Mk 84, Mk 82
INS/GPS guided: GBU-31 JDAM; GBU-38 JDAM
Laser-Guided: GBU-10/GBU-12 *Paveway* II; GBU-24 *Paveway* III

PODS Infrared/TV: 12 *Sniper*

Cyber

A consolidated national cyber-security strategy is being drafted. At the national level, several services are active, notably the Federal Computer Crime Unit (FCCU), which combats organised ICT crime, and CERT.be, the federal cyber emergency team. The MoD has a limited cyber capacity within the General Intelligence & Security service. Belgian defence is following and supporting the initiatives by NATO and the EU on cyber security.

DEPLOYMENT

Legal provisions for foreign deployment:
Constitution: Codified constitution (1831)

Specific legislation: 'Loi relatif à la mise en oeuvre des forces armées, à la mise en condition, ainsi qu'aux périodes et positions dans lesquelles le militaire peut se trouver' (1994)

Decision on deployment of troops abroad: By the government (Federal Council of Ministers) and the minister of defence (1994 law, Art. 88, 106, 167 of constitution)

AFGHANISTAN
NATO • ISAF 283; 6 F-16 *Fighting Falcon*

DEMOCRATIC REPUBLIC OF THE CONGO
EU • EUSEC RD Congo 4
UN • MONUSCO 21; 4 obs; 1 avn flt with 1 C-130

FRANCE
NATO • Air Component 28 *Alpha Jet* located at Cazeaux/Tours

LEBANON
UN • UNIFIL 100; 1 engr coy

MIDDLE EAST
UN • UNTSO 2 obs

NORTH SEA
NATO • SNMCMG 1: 1 MHC; 1 AGFH

UGANDA
EU • EUTM 6

FOREIGN FORCES

United States US European Command: 1,200

Bosnia–Herzegovina BIH

Convertible Mark		2011	2012	2013
GDP	mark	25.5bn	25.6bn	
	US$	18.1bn	16.6bn	
per capita	US$	4,666	4,279	
Growth	%	1.26	0.00	
Inflation	%	3.70	2.20	
Def exp	mark			
	US$			
Def bdgt	mark	346m	352m	
	US$	246m	228m	
FMA (US)	US$	4.49m	4.5m	4.5m
US$1=mark		1.41	1.54	

Population 3,879,296

Age	0–14	15–19	20–24	25–29	30–64	65 plus
Male	7.4%	3.1%	3.7%	3.8%	25.8%	4.9%
Female	7.0%	2.9%	3.5%	3.7%	26.4%	7.8%

Capabilities

The Bosnian armed forces are an uneasy amalgam of troops from all three formerly warring entities. Considerably reduced to a size that the country can afford, they likely have little capability to mount combat operations. They are capable of making contributions to international operations, and have identified an infantry company, military police platoon and EOD platoon as possible contributions. Bosnia has deployed forces to Iraq and Afghanistan, and has been a NATO member since 2009.

ACTIVE 10,550 (Joint 500 Army 9,200, AF/AD 850)

ORGANISATIONS BY SERVICE

Joint 500 (Joint Staff 250; Joint Operational Command 150; Support Command 100)

Army 9,200

1 ops comd; 1 cbt spt comd; 1 trg comd; 1 log comd

FORCES BY ROLE
MANOUEVRE
  Light
  3 inf bde
COMBAT SUPPORT
  1 cbt spt bde
  1 EOD bn
  1 CBRN coy
COMBAT SERVICE SUPPORT
  1 log bde (5 log bn)
EQUIPMENT BY TYPE
MBT 316: 50 AMX-30; 45 M60A1/A3; 71 M-84; 150 T-54/T-55
RECCE 3: 1 BDRM-1; 2 BDRM-2
AIFV 137: 25 AMX-10P; 112 BVP M-80
APC 127
  APC (T) 98: 18 M-60P; 80 M113A2
  APC (W) 29: 4 BOV-M; 21 BOV-VP; 4 BTR-60
ARTY 1,521
  SP **122mm** 24 2S1 *Carnation*
  TOWED 730: **105mm** 161: 36 L-118 Light Gun; 101 M-56; 24 M101/M101A1; **122mm** 268 D-30 **130mm** 74: 61 M-46; 13 M-82 **152mm** 30: 13 D-20; 17 M-84 **155mm** 197: 3 M-59; 194 M114/M114A2
  MRL 153: **107mm** 28 VLR Type-63; **122mm** 43: 37 APRA 40; 5 BM-21; 1 *Kacusa*; **128mm** 77: 21 M-63; 21 M-77; 35 M-91; **262mm** 5 M-87
  MOR 614: **82mm** 81 MB M-69; **120mm** 538: 23 2B11 (UK-2); 11 HADID; 7 KROM; 1 M-38; 1 M-43; 460 M-74/M-75; 30 UBM-52
AT
  MSL
    SP 60: 8 9P122 *Malyutka*; 9 9P133 *Malyutka*; 32 BOV-1; 11 M-92
    MANPATS 641: 508 9K11 *Malyutka* (AT-3 *Sagger*); 76 9K111 *Fagot* (AT-4 *Spigot*); 1 9K115 *Metis* (AT-7 *Saxhorn*); 51 HJ-8; 5 *Milan*
  GUNS 175:
    SP • **82mm** 20 M-60PB
    TOWED • **100mm** 155 MT-12/T-12
AD
  SAM
    SP 27: 1 *Strela*-10M3 (SA-13 *Gopher*); 20 2K12 *Kub* (SA-6 *Gainful*); 6 *Strela*-1 (SA-9 *Gaskin*)

  MANPAD 9K34 *Strela*-3 (SA-14 *Gremlin*); 9K310 (SA-16 *Gimlet*)
  GUNS 764
    SP 169: **20mm** 9 BOV-3 SPAAG; **30mm** 154: 38 M53; 116 M-53-59; **57mm** 6 ZSU 57/2
    TOWED 595: **20mm** 468: 32 M-55A2, 4 M38, 1 M55 A2B1, 293 M55 A3/A4, 138 M75; **23mm** 38: 29 ZU-23, 9 GSh-23; **30mm** 33 M-53; **37mm** 7 Type-55; **40mm** 49: 31 L60, 16 L70, 2 M-12
VLB MTU
MW Bozena

Air Wing 850
FORCES BY ROLE
HELICOPTER
  3 sqn with Bell 205; Mi-8 *Hip*; Mi-8MTV *Hip*; Mi-17 *Hip* H; SA342L *Gazelle* (H-45/HN-45M)
EQUIPMENT BY TYPE
AIRCRAFT 19 combat capable
  FGA 7 J-22 *Orao*
  ATK 9: 6 J-1 (J-21) *Jastreb*; 3 TJ-1(NJ-21) *Jastreb*
  ISR 2 RJ-1 (IJ-21) *Jastreb**
  TRG 1 G-4 *Super Galeb* (N-62)*
HELICOPTERS
  MRH 16: 2 Mi-8MTV *Hip*; 1 Mi-17 *Hip* H; 1 SA-341H *Gazelle* (HN-42); 7 SA-341H/SA-342L *Gazelle* (HN-42M/HN-45M); 5 SA-342L *Gazelle* (H-45)
  TPT 26 **Medium** 11 Mi-8 *Hip* **Light** 15 Bell 205 (UH-1H *Iroquois*)
  TRG 1 Mi-34 *Hermit*

DEPLOYMENT

Legal provisions for foreign deployment: Constitution: Codified constitution within Dayton Peace Agreement (1995)
Specific legislation: 'Law on participation of military, police, state and other employees in peacekeeping operations and other activities conducted abroad'
Decision on deployment of troops abroad: By the members of the Presidency (2003 'Defence Law' Art. 9, 13)

AFGHANISTAN
NATO • ISAF 54

DEMOCRATIC REPUBLIC OF THE CONGO
UN • MONUSCO 5 obs

FOREIGN FORCES

Part of EUFOR – *Operation Althea* unless otherwise stated.
Albania 11
Austria 321; 1 inf bn HQ; 1 recce pl; 1 inf coy; 3 SA316 *Allouette* III
Bulgaria 10
Chile 22
Czech Republic 2
Estonia 1
Finland 10
France 11
Germany 2

Greece 25
Hungary 162; 1 inf coy
Ireland 40
Italy 3
Luxembourg 1
Macedonia, Former Yugoslav Republic of 12
Netherlands 5
Poland 47
Portugal 6
Romania 59
Slovakia 34
Slovenia 14
Spain 13
Sweden 1
Switzerland 20
Turkey 288; 1 inf coy
United Kingdom 4

Bulgaria BLG

Bulgarian Lev L		2011	2012	2013
GDP	L	75.3bn	77.5bn	
	US$	53.6bn	50.8bn	
per capita	US$	7,616	7,218	
Growth	%	1.67	1.00	
Inflation	%	3.39	1.89	
Def exp [b]	L	1.07bn		
	US$	758m		
Def bdgt [a]	L	1.01bn	1bn	1bn
	US$	720m	657m	
FMA (US)	US$	9.48m	8.5m	7.8m
US$1=L		1.41	1.52	

[a] Excludes military pensions
[b] NATO definition

Population	7,037,935

Age	0–14	15–19	20–24	25–29	30–64	65 plus
Male	7.2%	2.5%	3.2%	3.6%	23.9%	7.5%
Female	6.8%	2.3%	3.0%	3.4%	25.5%	11.1%

Capabilities

The armed forces continue to transition from Soviet-era to modern force structures commensurate with the country's national-defence needs and NATO membership. The intent is to field smaller but more capable armed forces, and to replace Soviet-era equipment. A White Paper in late 2010 set out Bulgaria's plans for a force-structure review, which would lead to a reduction in army size, though with the expanded ability to carry out such tasks as CIMIC. The armed forces are due to transition to a modified force structure by 2014. Funding shortages have curtailed or delayed some procurement. Air Force ambitions to acquire a more modern fighter type to replace Soviet-era aircraft have yet to bear fruit. The armed forces exercise regularly at the national level, and also participate in NATO exercises. Bul-

garia contributes to ISAF and, in 2011, sent naval forces as part of *Operation Unified Protector*.

ACTIVE 31,300 (Army 16,300 Navy 3,450 Air 6,700 Central Staff 4,850) Paramilitary 16,000

RESERVE 303,000 (Army 250,500 Navy 7,500 Air 45,000)

ORGANISATIONS BY SERVICE

Army 16,300
Forces are being reduced in number.
FORCES BY ROLE
SPECIAL FORCES
  1 SF bde
MANOEUVRE
  Reconnaissance
  1 recce bn
  Mechanised
  2 mech bde
COMBAT SUPPORT
  1 arty regt
  1 engr regt
  1 NBC regt
COMBAT SERVICE SUPPORT
  1 log regt
EQUIPMENT BY TYPE
MBT 80 T-72
RECCE *Maritza* NBC
AIFV 160: 90 BMP-1; 70 BMP-2/3
APC 127
  APC (T) 100 MT-LB
  APC (W) 27: 20 BTR-60; 7 M1117 ASV
ARTY 311
  SP • 122mm 48 2S1 *Carnation*
  TOWED • 152mm 24 D-20
  MRL 122mm 24 BM-21
  MOR 120mm 215 2S11 SP *Tundzha*
AT
  MSL
    SP 24 9P148 *Konkurs* (AT-5 *Spandrel*)
    MANPATS 236 9K111 *Fagot* (AT-4 *Spigot*)/9K113 *Konkurs* (AT-5 *Spandrel*); (200 9K11 *Malyutka* (AT-3 *Sagger*) in store)
  GUNS 126: **100mm** 126 MT-12; **85mm** (150 D-44 in store)
AD
  SAM • SP 24 9K33 *Osa* (SA-8 *Gecko*)
  MANPAD 9K32 *Strela* (SA-7 *Grail*)
  GUNS 400 **100mm** KS-19 towed/**57mm** S-60 towed/**23mm** ZSU-23-4 SP/ZU-23 towed
RADARS • LAND GS-13 *Long Eye* (veh); SNAR-1 *Long Trough* (arty); SNAR-10 *Big Fred* (veh, arty); SNAR-2/-6 *Pork Trough* (arty); *Small Fred/Small Yawn* (veh, arty)
AEV MT-LB
ARV T-54/T-55; MTP-1; MT-LB
VLB BLG67; TMM

Navy 3,450

EQUIPMENT BY TYPE
PRINCIPAL SURFACE COMBATANTS 4
  FRIGATES 4
    FFGM 3 *Drazki* (BEL *Wielingen*) with 2 twin lnchr with MM-38 *Exocet* AShM, 1 octuple Mk29 GMLS with RIM-7P *Sea Sparrow* SAM, 2 single 533mm ASTT with L5 HWT, 1 sextuple 375mm MLE 54 *Creusot-Loire* A/S mor, 1 100mm gun
    FFM 1 *Smeli* (FSU *Koni*) with 1 twin lnchr with 2 *Osa*-M (SA-N-4 *Gecko*) SAM, 2 RBU 6000 *Smerch* 2, 2 twin 76mm gun
PATROL AND COASTAL COMBATANTS 6
    PCFGM 1 *Mulnaya* (FSU *Tarantul* II) with 2 twin lnchr with P-15M *Termit*-M (SS-N-2C *Styx*) AShM, 2 quad lnchr with *Strela*-2 (SA-N-5 *Grail*) SAM, 1 76mm gun
    PCM 2 *Reshitelni* (FSU *Pauk* I) with 1 *Strela*-2 (SA-N-5 *Grail)* SAM, 4 single 406mm TT, 2 RBU 1200, 1 76mm gun
    PBFG 3 *Osa* I/II† (FSU) each with 4 P-15/P-15U *Termit* (SS-N-2A/B *Styx*) AShM
MINE COUNTERMEASURES 6
    MHC 1 *Tsibar* (*Tripartite* – BEL *Flower*)
    MSC 3 *Briz* (FSU *Sonya*)
    MSI 2 *Olya*, less than 100 tonnes (FSU)
AMPHIBIOUS 1
    LCU 1 *Vydra*
LOGISTICS AND SUPPORT 17: 1 **AORL**; 2 **AOL**; 1 **ARS**; 2 **APT**; 2 **AT**; 2 **YTR**; 1 **AX**; 3 **AGS**; 1 **ADG**; 2 **ADT**

Naval Aviation
  HELICOPTERS • **ASW** 3 AS565MB *Panther*

Air Force 6,700

Flying hours   30–40 hrs/yr

FORCES BY ROLE
FIGHTER/ISR
    1 sqn with MiG-21bis/UM *Fishbed*
    1 sqn with MiG-29A/UB *Fulcrum*
FIGHTER/GROUND ATTACK
    1 sqn with Su-25K/UBK *Frogfoot*
TRANSPORT
    1 sqn with An-30 *Clank*; C-27J *Spartan*; L-410UVP-E; PC-12M
TRAINING
    1 sqn with L-39ZA *Albatros*
    1 sqn with PC-9M
ATTACK HELICOPTER
    1 sqn with Mi-24D/V *Hind* D/E
TRANSPORT HELICOPTER
    1 sqn with AS532AL *Cougar*; Bell 206 *Jet Ranger*; Mi-17 *Hip* H

EQUIPMENT BY TYPE
AIRCRAFT 42 combat capable
    FTR 16: 12 MiG-29A *Fulcrum*; 4 MiG-29UB *Fulcrum*
    FGA 12: 10 MiG-21bis *Fishbed*; 2 MiG-21UM *Mongol* B (to be wirhdrawn by end-2014)
    ATK 14: 10 Su-25K *Frogfoot*; 4 Su-25UBK *Frogfoot* (to be withdrawn by end-2014)
    ISR 1 An-30 *Clank*

TPT 7: **Medium** 3 C-27J *Spartan*; **Light** 4: 1 An-2T *Colt*; 2 L-410UVP-E; 1 PC-12M
TRG 12: 6 L-39ZA *Albatros*; 6 PC-9M (basic)
HELICOPTERS
    ATK 6 Mi-24D/V *Hind* D/E
    MRH 6 Mi-17 *Hip* H
    TPT 18: **Medium** 12 AS532AL *Cougar*; **Light** 6 Bell 206 *Jet Ranger*
UAV • **EW** *Yastreb*-2S
AD
    SAM S-300 (SA-10 *Grumble*); S-75 *Dvina* (SA-2 *Guideline* towed); S-125 *Pechora* (SA-3 *Goa*); S-200 (SA-5 *Gammon*); 2K12 *Kub* (SA-6 *Gainful*)
MSL
    AAM • **IR** R-3 (AA-2 *Atoll*)‡ R-73 (AA-11 *Archer*) **SARH** R-27R (AA-10 *Alamo* A)
    ASM Kh-29 (AS-14 *Kedge*); Kh-23 (AS-7 *Kerry*)‡; Kh-25 (AS-10 *Karen*)

Paramilitary 16,000

Border Guards 12,000
Ministry of Interior
FORCES BY ROLE
Paramilitary 12 regt

EQUIPMENT BY TYPE
PATROL AND COASTAL COMBATANTS 20
    PB 20: 9 *Grif* (FSU *Zhuk*); 3 *Nesebar* (FSU *Neustadt*); 8 (other)

Security Police 4,000

DEPLOYMENT

Legal provisions for foreign deployment:
Constitution: Codified constitution (1991)
Decision on deployment of troops abroad: By the president upon request from the Council of Ministers and upon approval by the National Assembly (Art. 84 XI)

AFGHANISTAN
NATO • ISAF 572; 1 mech inf coy

BOSNIA-HERZEGOVINA
EU • EUFOR • *Operation Althea* 10

LIBERIA
UN • UNMIL 2 obs

SERBIA
NATO • KFOR 19

Croatia CRO

Croatian Kuna k		2011	2012	2013
GDP	k	334bn	337.8bn	
	US$	62.4bn	57.5bn	
per capita	US$	13,928	12,835	
Growth	%	-0.01	-1.14	
Inflation	%	2.26	2.99	
Def exp [a]	k	5.18bn		
	US$	969m		
Def bdgt	k	4.15bn	4.78bn	4.43bn
	US$	776m	814m	
FMA (US)	US$	3.49m	2.5m	2.5m
US$1=k		5.35	5.87	

[a] NATO definition

Population   4,480,043

Age	0–14	15–19	20–24	25–29	30–64	65 plus
Male	7.6%	3.2%	3.1%	3.4%	24.1%	6.8%
Female	7.2%	3.0%	3.0%	3.4%	24.9%	10.4%

Capabilities

Croatia continues to work on the long-term goals laid out in its 2005 defence review and the associated 2006–2015 long-term development plan. Croatia joined NATO in 2009 and defence-policy focus is directed at further integration into NATO structures and planning processes. Military tasks cover national sovereignty, the defence of Croatia and allies, the ability to participate in crisis-response operations overseas, and support to civil institutions. The country contributes to ISAF in Afghanistan and also provides support to a number of UN missions. It has declared reaction forces to NATO and EU missions, which can deploy within Europe. Force modernisation and re-equipment plans have been hampered by the economic downturn. Perhaps the most high profile of the projects affected is the air force's need to replace its obsolescent MiG-21s with a modern combat aircraft, which has likely been delayed by several years. But modernisation of its army continues, with new Patria APCs delivered in 2012, while the government announced, in September, a decision to procure five coastal patrol vessels, to be planned for budgets in the 2013–18 timeframe.

ACTIVE 18,600 (Army 11,400 Navy 1,850 Air 3,500 Joint 1,850) Paramilitary 3,000

RESERVE 21,000 (Army 18,500 Navy 250 Air 2,250)

ORGANISATIONS BY SERVICE

Joint 1,850 (General Staff)

Army 11,400

FORCES BY ROLE
SPECIAL FORCES
  1 SF bn

MANOEUVRE
  Armoured
  1 armd bde
  Light
  1 mot inf bde
  Other
  3 gd regt (org varies)
COMBAT SUPPORT
  1 MRL regt
  1 AT regt
  1 ADA regt
  1 engr regt
  1 int bn
  1 MP regt
  1 NBC bn
  1 sigs regt
EQUIPMENT BY TYPE
MBT 72 M-84
AIFV 103 M-80
APC 138
  APC (T) 16 BTR-50
  APC (W) 106: 9 BOV-VP; 13 LOV OP; 84 Patria AMV
  PPV 16: 4 *Cougar* HE; 12 *Maxxpro*
ARTY 1,436
  SP 122mm 8 2S1 *Carnation*
  TOWED 416: **105mm** 165: 89 M-2A1 **122mm** 95: 53 D-30 **130mm** 78: 44 M-46; 34 M-46H1 **152mm** 41: 20 D-20; 18 M-84; 3 M 84H; **155mm** 18 M-1H1; **203mm** 19 M-2
  MRL 42
    SP 42: **122mm** 39: 1 SVLR M 96 *Typhoon*, 7 M91 *Vulkan* 31 BM-21 *Grad*; **128mm** 2 LOV RAK M91 R24; **262mm** 1 M-87 *Orkan*
  MOR 790: **82mm** 475: 339 LMB M96; **120mm** 315: 310M-75; 5 UBM 52
AT
  MSL 603+
    SP 43 POLO BOV 83
    MANPATS 560+: 418 9K11 *Malyutka* (AT-3 *Sagger*); 81 9K111 Fagot (AT-4 *Spigot*); 23 9K115 Metis (AT-7 *Saxhorn*); 38 9K113 Konkurs (AT-5 *Spandrel*); *Milan* (reported)
  RL 90mm M-79
  GUNS 100mm 133 T-12
AD
  MANPADS 619: 539 9K32M *Strela* 2M (SA-7 *Grail*); 80 9K38 *Igla* (SA-18 *Grouse*)
  GUNS 463
    SP 62: **20mm** 45: 44 BOV-3 SP **30mm** 17 BOV-3
    TOWED 401: **20mm** 390: 177 M55 **40mm** 11
ARV M84A1; WZT-3
VLB 3 MT-55A
MW Bozena; 1 *Rhino*

Navy 1,600; 250 conscript (total 1,850)

Navy Central Command HQ at Split. Two naval districts, NAVSOUTH and NAVNORTH
EQUIPMENT BY TYPE
SUBMARINES • SDV 3: 1 R-1; 2 R-2 *Mala*
PATROL AND COASTAL COMBATANTS 6
  PCGF 1 *Koncar* with 2 twin lnchr with RBS-15B AShM
  PCGM 2 *Helsinki* with 4 twin lnchr with RBS-15M AShM

PCG 2 *Kralj* with 2–4 twin lnchr with RBS-15B AShM
PBR 1 OB 93
MINE WARFARE • MINE COUNTERMEASURES •
MHI 1 *Korcula*
AMPHIBIOUS 6
LCT 2 *Cetina*
LCVP 4: 3 Type-21; 1 Type-22
LOGISTICS AND SUPPORT 12:
AKL 2; AXS 1 *Kraljica Mora*; YDT 2; YFU 5; YTM 2

Coastal Defence

FORCES BY ROLE
COMBAT SUPPORT
21+ arty bty
3 AShM bty with RBS-15K
EQUIPMENT BY TYPE
MSL • TACTICAL • AShM RBS-15K

Marines

FORCES BY ROLE
MANOEUVRE
Amphibious
2 indep mne coy

Coast Guard

FORCES BY ROLE
The Croatian Coast Guard is a command under the navy.
It retains two divisions, headquartered in Split (1st div)
and Pula (2nd div).

EQUIPMENT BY TYPE
PATROL AND COASTAL COMBATANTS • PB 6: 4
Mirna; 2 other
LOGISTICS AND SUPPORT • AX 2

Air Force and Air Defence 3,500

Flying hours   50 hrs/year

FORCES BY ROLE
FIGHTER/GROUND ATTACK
2 (mixed) sqn with MiG-21bis/UMD *Fishbed*
TRANSPORT
1 sqn with An-32 *Cline*
TRAINING
1 sqn with PC-9M; Z-242L
1 hel sqn with Bell 206B *Jet Ranger* II
FIRE FIGHTING
1 sqn with AT-802FA *Fire Boss*; CL-415
TRANSPORT HELICOPTER
2 sqn with Mi-8MTV *Hip* H; Mi-8T *Hip* C; Mi-171Sh

EQUIPMENT BY TYPE
AIRCRAFT 10 combat capable
FGA 10: 6 MiG-21bis *Fishbed*; 4 MiG-21UMD *Fishbed*
TPT • Light 3: 2 An-32 *Cline*; 1 AT-802F Air Tractor
TRG 25: 20 PC-9M; 5 Z-242L
FF 11: 5 AT-802FA *Fire Boss*; 6 CL-415
HELICOPTERS
MRH 11 Mi-8MTV *Hip* H
TPT 21 **Medium** 13: 3 Mi-8T *Hip* C; 10 Mi-171Sh **Light** 8
Bell 206B *Jet Ranger* II

UAV *Hermes* 450 (ISR)
AD • SAM
SP S-300 (SA-10 *Grumble*); 9K31 *Strela*-1 (SA-9 *Gaskin*)
MANPAD 9K34 *Strela*-3 (SA-14 *Gremlin*); 9K310 *Igla*-1
(SA-16 *Gimlet*)
RADAR 8: 5 FPS-117; 3 S-600
MSL • AAM • IR R-3S (AA-2 *Atoll*)‡; R-60 (AA-8 *Aphid*)

Paramilitary 3,000

Police 3,000 armed

DEPLOYMENT

Legal provisions for foreign deployment:
Constitution: Codified constitution (2004)
Decision on deployment of troops abroad: By the parliament (Art. 7 II); simplified procedure for humanitarian aid and military exercises

AFGHANISTAN
NATO • ISAF 260

CYPRUS
UN • UNFICYP 2

INDIA/PAKISTAN
UN • UNMOGIP 8 obs

LEBANON
UN • UNIFIL 1

LIBERIA
UN • UNMIL 2

SERBIA
NATO • KFOR 19

SYRIA/ISRAEL
UN • UNDOF 95; 1 inf coy

WESTERN SAHARA
UN • MINURSO 7 obs

Cyprus CYP

Cypriot Pound C£		2011	2012	2013
GDP	C£	17.8bn	17.7bn	
	US$	24.7bn	22.5bn	
per capita	US$	21,703	19,770	
Growth	%	0.48	-2.25	
Inflation	%	3.49	3.10	
Def bdgt	C£	221m	204m	
	US$	308m	258m	
US$1=C£			0.72	0.79

Population   1,138,071

Age	0–14	15–19	20–24	25–29	30–64	65 plus
Male	8.2%	4.0%	4.8%	5.0%	24.4%	4.6%
Female	7.7%	3.4%	3.9%	4.1%	23.7%	6.0%

Capabilities

The country's national guard is predominantly a land force supplemented by small air and maritime units. It is intended to act as a deterrent to any possible Turkish incursion, and to provide enough opposition until military support can be provided by its primary ally, Greece. The air wing has a small number of rotary- and fixed-wing utility platforms, perhaps most notably the Mi-35 attack helicopters. Key procurements include SAR helicopters and T-80U MBTs. But readiness and morale are not thought to be high. Expeditionary deployments have been limited to a few officers joining UN and EU missions. It is possible that Cyprus's economic fragility may depress capability.

ACTIVE 12,000 (National Guard 12,000)
Paramilitary 750

Terms of service conscription, 24 months, then reserve to age 50 (officers dependent on rank; military doctors to age 60)

RESERVE 50,000 (National Guard 50,000)

ORGANISATIONS BY SERVICE

National Guard 1,300 regular; 10,700 conscript (total 12,000)

FORCES BY ROLE
SPECIAL FORCES
1 comd (regt) (1 SF bn)
MANOEUVRE
Armoured
1 lt armd bde (3 armd bn)
Mechanised
2 (1st & 2nd) mech inf div (3 mech inf bn)
Light
1 (4th) bde (2 lt inf regt)
COMBAT SUPPORT
1 arty comd (8 arty bn)
COMBAT SERVICE SUPPORT
1 (3rd) spt bde
EQUIPMENT BY TYPE
MBT 164: 82 T-80U; 30 AMX-30G; 52 AMX-30B2
RECCE 124 EE-9 *Cascavel*
AIFV 43 BMP-3
APC 294
 APC (T) 168: 168 *Leonidas*
 APC (W) 126 VAB (incl variants)
ARTY 522+
 SP 155mm 24: 12 Mk F3; 12 *Zuzana*
 TOWED 104: 100mm 20 M-1944; 105mm 72 M-56; 155mm 12 TR-F-1
 MRL 22: 122mm 4 BM-21; 128mm 18 M-63 *Plamen*
 MOR 372+: 81mm 240+: 70+ M1/M-9 in store; 170 E-44; 107mm 20 M2/M30; 120mm 112 RT61
AT
 MSL
 SP 33: 15 EE-3 *Jararaca* with *Milan*; 18 VAB with HOT
 MANPATS 115: 70 HOT; 45 *Milan*
 RCL 153: 106mm 144 M40A1; 90mm 9 EM-67
 RL 1,000: 112mm 1,000 APILAS

AD
 SAM 48
 SP 6 9K322 *Tor* (SA-15 *Gauntlet*); *Mistral*
 STATIC 12 *Aspide*
 MANPAD 30 *Mistral*
 GUNS • TOWED 60: 20mm 36 M-55; 35mm 24 GDF-003 (with *Skyguard*)
ARV 2 AMX-30D; 1 BREM-1

Maritime Wing

FORCES BY ROLE
COMBAT SUPPORT
1 (coastal defence) AShM bty with MM-40 *Exocet* AShM
EQUIPMENT BY TYPE
PATROL AND COASTAL COMBATANTS 6
 PBF 4: 2 *Rodman* 55; 2 *Vittoria*
 PB 2: 1 *Esterel*; 1 *Kyrenia* (GRC *Dilos*)
MSL • AShM 24 MM-40 *Exocet*

Air Wing

AIRCRAFT
TPT • Light 2: 1 AT-802F *Air Tractor*; 1 BN-2B *Islander*
TRG 1 PC-9
HELICOPTERS
ATK 11 Mi-35P *Hind*
MRH 7: 3 AW139 (SAR); 4 SA342L1 *Gazelle* (with HOT for anti-armour role)
TPT • Light 2 Bell 206L-3 *Long Ranger*

Paramilitary 750+

Armed Police 500+

FORCES BY ROLE
MANOEUVRE
Other
1 (rapid-reaction) paramilitary unit
EQUIPMENT BY TYPE
APC (W) 2 VAB VTT
HELICOPTERS • MRH 2 Bell 412 SP

Maritime Police 250

PATROL AND COASTAL COMBATANTS 10
 PBF 5: 2 *Poseidon*; 1 *Shaldag*; 2 *Vittoria*
 PB 5 SAB-12

DEPLOYMENT

Legal provisions for foreign deployment:
Constitution: Codified constitution (1960)
Decision on deployment of troops abroad: By parliament, but president has the right of final veto (Art. 50)

LEBANON
UN • UNIFIL 2

UGANDA
EU • EUTM 1

FOREIGN FORCES

Argentina UNFICYP 265; 2 inf coy; 1 avn pl

Austria UNFICYP 4
Brazil UNFICYP 1
Canada UNFICYP 1
Chile UNFICYP 15
China UNFICYP 2
Croatia UNFICYP 2
Greece Army: 950; ε200 (officers/NCO seconded to Greek-Cypriot National Guard)
Hungary UNFICYP 77; 1 inf pl
Paraguay UNFICYP 14
Serbia UNFICYP 46
Slovakia UNFICYP 159; elm 1 inf coy; 1 engr pl
United Kingdom Army 1,710; 2 inf bn; **Navy** 30; **Air Force** 880; 1 hel sqn with 4 Bell 412 *Twin Huey* •
UNFICYP 266: 1 inf coy

TERRITORY WHERE THE GOVERNMENT DOES NOT EXERCISE EFFECTIVE CONTROL

Data here represent the de facto situation on the northern half of the island. This does not imply international recognition as a sovereign state.

Capabilities

ACTIVE 3,500 (Army 3,500) **Paramilitary 150**
Terms of service conscription, 24 months, then reserve to age 50.

RESERVE 26,000 (first line 11,000 second line 10,000 third line 5,000)

ORGANISATIONS BY SERVICE

Army ε3,500

FORCES BY ROLE
MANOEUVRE
Light
7 inf bn
EQUIPMENT BY TYPE
ARTY
MOR • 120mm 73
AT
MSL • MANPATS 6 *Milan*
RCL • 106mm 36

Paramilitary

Armed Police ε150

FORCES BY ROLE
SPECIAL FORCES
1 (police) SF unit

Coast Guard

PATROL AND COASTAL COMBATANTS 6
PCC 5: 2 SG45/SG46; 1 *Rauf Denktash*; 2 US Mk 5
PB 1

FOREIGN FORCES

TURKEY
Army ε43,000
1 army corps HQ, 1 armd bde, 2 mech inf div, 1 avn comd
EQUIPMENT BY TYPE
MBT 348: 8 M48A2 (trg); 340 M48A5T1/2
APC (T) 627: 361 AAPC (T) (incl variants); 266 M-113 (T) (incl variants)
ARTY
SP 155mm 90 M-44T
TOWED 102: **105mm** 72 M101A1; **155mm** 18 M-114A2; **203mm** 12 M115
MRL 122mm 6 T-122
MOR 450: **81mm** 175; **107mm** 148 M-30; **120mm** 127 HY-12
AT
MSL • MANPATS 114: 66 *Milan*; 48 TOW
RCL 106mm 192 M40A1; **90mm** M67
AD • GUNS
TOWED 20mm Rh 202; **35mm** 16 GDF-003; **40mm** 48 M-1
AIRCRAFT • TPT • Light 3 Cessna 185 (U-17)
HELICOPTER • TPT 4 Medium 1 AS532UL *Cougar* **Light** 3 Bell 205 (UH-1H *Iroquois*)
PATROL AND COASTAL COMBATANTS 1 PB

Czech Republic CZE

Czech Koruna Kc		2011	2012	2013
GDP	Kc	3.81tr	3.86tr	
	US$	215.2bn	193.5bn	
per capita	US$	21,145	19,013	
Growth	%	1.66	-1.01	
Inflation	%	1.93	3.40	
Def exp [b]	Kc	43.3bn		
	US$	2.45bn		
Def bdgt [a]	Kc	44.4bn	43.3bn	42.1bn
	US$	2.51bn	2.17bn	
FMA (US)	US$	5.99m	5m	5m
US$1=Kc		17.70	19.95	

[a] Includes military pensions
[b] NATO definition

Population   10,177,300

Age	0–14	15–19	20–24	25–29	30–64	65 plus
Male	6.9%	2.6%	3.2%	3.4%	25.8%	6.8%
Female	6.5%	2.5%	3.1%	3.2%	25.7%	10.2%

Capabilities

Following its accession to NATO, the capability of the Czech armed forces has increased as a result of military reform and restructuring, equipment improvements, and operational experience in Kosovo, Afghanistan and Iraq. Maintaining this capability in the face of budget cuts may prove challenging. The 2011 Defence White Paper, noting that the MoD had a budget deficit of Kc80–90 billion, concluded that personnel numbers would have to fall further and that not all procurement projects were affordable. The ministry said that measures would include 'limitation of some military capabilities', and have put 124 surplus T-72 MBTs up for sale. For now, delivery of *Pandur* vehicles continues, as do plans for a soldier modernisation project including new small arms. The ten-year lease of *Gripen* continues until 2015, and the air force also has plans to modernise its Mi-171Sh helicopters. It is understood that a new Defence Strategy will replace the existing Military Strategy document in 2013.

ACTIVE 23,650 (Army 14,000, Air 4,800, Other 4,850) Paramilitary 3,100

ORGANISATIONS BY SERVICE

Army 14,00; 2,500 civilian
FORCES BY ROLE
SPECIAL FORCES
  1 SF gp
MANOEUVRE
  Reconnaissance
  1 recce bn
  Armoured
  1 (7th) mech bde (1 armd bn, 2 armd inf bn, 1 mot inf bn)
  Mechanised
  1 (4th) rapid reaction bde (2 mech bn; 1 mot inf bn; 1 AB bn)
COMBAT SUPPORT
  1 (13th) arty bde (2 arty bn)
  1 engr bde (3 bn)
  1 EOD gp
  1 EW bn
  1 CBRN bde (2 CBRN bn)
  1 sigs bn
  1 CIMIC pl
COMBAT SERVICE SUPPORT
  1 log bde

Active Reserve
FORCES BY ROLE
COMMAND
  14 (territorial defence) comd
MANOEUVRE
  Armoured
  1 armd coy
  Light
  14 inf coy (1 per territorial comd) (3 inf pl, 1 cbt spt pl, 1 log pl)
EQUIPMENT BY TYPE
MBT 40: 10 T-72 (86 more in store); 30 T-72M4CZ
AIFV 466: 139 BMP-1; 181 BMP-2; 64 BPzV; 55 *Pandur* II
APC 99:
  APC (T) 24 OT-90
  APC (W) 54: 20 OT-64; 34 *Pandur* II
  PPV 21 *Dingo* 2
ARTY 105:

SP 152mm 57 M-77 *Dana* (7 trg); (50 more in store)
MRL 122mm (19 RM-70 in store)
MOR 120mm 48: 40 M-1982; 8 SPM-85; (42 more in store)
AT • MSL 196
  SP 21 9P148 *Konkurs*
  MANPATS 175 9K111 *Fagot* (AT-4 *Spigot*)
RADAR • LAND 3 ARTHUR
ARV MT-72; VT-72M4CZ; VPV-ARV; WPT-TOPAS
VLB AM-50; MT-55A
MW *Belarty* UOS-155

Air Force 4,800; 700 civilian
Principal task is to secure Czech airspace. This mission is fulfilled within NATO Integrated Extended Air Defence System (NATINADS) and, if necessary, by means of the Czech national reinforced air-defence system. The air force also provides CAS for the army SAR, and performs a tpt role.

Flying hours   120hrs/yr cbt ac 150 for tpt ac

FORCES BY ROLE
FIGHTER/GROUND ATTACK
  1 sqn with *Gripen* C/D
  1 sqn with L-39ZA*
  1 sqn with L-159 ALCA/L-159T
TRANSPORT
  2 sqn with A319CJ; C-295M; CL-601 *Challenger*; L-410 *Turbolet*; Yak-40 *Codling*
ATTACK HELICOPTER
  1 sqn with Mi-24/Mi-35 *Hind*
TRANSPORT HELICOPTER
  1 sqn with Mi-17 *Hip* H; Mi-171Sh
  1 sqn with Mi-8 *Hip*; Mi-17 *Hip* H; PZL W-3A *Sokol*
AIR DEFENCE
  1 (25th) SAM bde (2 AD gp)
EQUIPMENT BY TYPE
AIRCRAFT 47 combat capable
  FGA 14: 12 *Gripen* C (JAS 39C); 2 *Gripen* D (JAS 39D)
  ATK 24: 20 L-159 ALCA; 4 L-159T
  TPT 17: **Light** 14: 4 C-295M; 8 L-410 *Turbolet*; 2 Yak-40 *Codling*; **PAX** 3: 2 A319CJ; 1 CL-601 *Challenger*
  TRG 26: 1 EW-97 *Eurostar*; 8 L-39C *Albatros*; 9 L-39ZA*; 8 Z-142C
HELICOPTERS
  ATK 24: 6 Mi-24 *Hind* D; 18 Mi-35 *Hind* E
  MRH 8 Mi-17 *Hip* H
  TPT 30: **Medium** 20: 4 Mi-8 *Hip*; 16 Mi-171Sh (med tpt); **Light** 10 PZL W3A *Sokol*
AD
  SAM 9K35 *Strela*-10 (SA-13 *Gopher*); 2K12 *Kub* (SA-6 *Gainful*); RBS-70; 9K32 *Strela*-2 (SA-7 *Grail*) (available for trg RBS-70 gunners)
MSL
  AAM • IR AIM-9M *Sidewinder*; **ARH** AIM-120 AMRAAM
BOMBS
  Conventional: GBU Mk 82; Mk 84
  Laser-guided: GBU *Paveway*

Joint Forces Support Units

FORCES BY ROLE

COMBAT SUPPORT
1 engr bde (3 engr bn; 2 (rescue) engr coy)
1 CIMIC/psyops coy (1 CIMIC pl; 1 psyops pl)
1 CBRN bde (2 CBRN bn)

COMBAT SERVICE SUPPORT
1 (14th) bde (1 spt bn; 1 supply bn)

Other Forces

FORCES BY ROLE

MANOEUVRE

Other
1 (presidential) gd bde (2 bn)
1 (presidential) gd coy

COMBAT SUPPORT
1 int gp
1 (central) MP comd
3 (regional) MP comd
1 (protection service) MP comd

Paramilitary 3,100

Border Guards 3,000

Internal Security Forces 100

Cyber

In 2011, a National Security Authority was established to, among other tasks, supervise the protection of classified information and perform tasks related to communications and information-systems security. A Cyber Security Strategy was published in 2011, with the intent to coordinate government approaches to network security and create a framework for legislative developments, international cooperative activity and the development of technical means, as well as promoting network security. It also announced the creation of a national CERT agency.

DEPLOYMENT

Legal provisions for foreign deployment:
Constitution: Codified constitution (1992), Art. 39, 43
Decision on deployment of troops abroad: External deployments require approval by the parliament. As an exception, such as urgent cases, the government can decide on such a deployment for up to 60 days with the aim of fulfilling international treaty obligations concerning collective defence.

AFGHANISTAN
NATO • ISAF 422
UN • UNAMA 1 obs

BOSNIA-HERZEGOVINA
EU • EUFOR • *Operation Althea* 2

DEMOCRATIC REPUBLIC OF THE CONGO
UN • MONUSCO 3 obs

EGYPT
MFO 3

LITHUANIA
NATO • Baltic Air Policing 4 *Gripen* C

SERBIA
NATO • KFOR 7
UN • UNMIK 1 obs

Denmark DNK

Danish Krone kr		2011	2012	2013
GDP	kr	1.78tr	1.82tr	
	US$	332bn	309bn	
per capita	US$	59,890	55,741	
Growth	%	0.77	0.51	
Inflation	%	2.76	2.60	
Def exp [b]	kr	24.3bn		
	US$	4.52bn		
Def bdgt [a]	kr	24.3bn	25.7bn	25.6bn
	US$	4.52bn	4.37bn	
US$1=kr		5.37	5.89	

[a] Includes military pensions
[b] NATO definition

Population   5,543,453

Age	0–14	15–19	20–24	25–29	30–64	65 plus
Male	8.9%	3.4%	3.1%	2.7%	23.3%	7.8%
Female	8.5%	3.2%	3.1%	2.8%	23.4%	9.8%

Capabilities

Denmark's forces are geared towards, and well-practised in, participation in international missions. They also conduct domestic tasks, including SAR, counter-piracy, airspace defence and surveillance. Acquisition of the C-130J will aid tactical mobility, and Denmark is a partner in the F-35 programme, as it considers replacements for its F-16s. Notwithstanding equipment reductions, such as in long-range ATGW, the ground force has benefitted from combat experience in Afghanistan. Denmark has maintained a battalion-plus deployment to ISAF in Afghanistan (though numbers are reducing and the eventual aim is a 1:1 combat-to-training ratio), as well as a number of UN peacekeeping missions. Denmark plans to have no combat troops in Afghanistan by 2014. Due to Denmark's 'no' vote to the Maastricht Treaty in 1992, Denmark cannot participate in EU-led military operations or the development of EU military capabilities.

ACTIVE 16,450 (Army 7,950 Navy 3,000 Air 3,050 Joint 2,450)

Terms of service 4–12 months

RESERVES 53,500 (Army 40,800 Navy 4,500 Air Force 5,300 Service Corps 2,900)

ORGANISATIONS BY SERVICE

Army 6,450; 1,500 conscript (total 7,950) 210 civilian

Div and bde HQ are responsible for trg only; if necessary, can be transformed into operational formations

FORCES BY ROLE
COMMAND
  1 div HQ
  2 bde HQ
SPECIAL FORCES
  1 SF unit
MANOEUVRE
  Reconnaissance
  1 recce bn
  1 ISTAR bn
  Armoured
  1 tk bn
  Mechanised
  5 armd inf bn
COMBAT SUPPORT
  1 SP arty bn
  1 cbt engr bn
  1 EOD bn
  1 MP bn
  1 sigs regt (1 sigs bn, 1 EW coy)
COMBAT SERVICE SUPPORT
  1 construction bn
  1 log regt (1 spt bn, 1 log bn, 1 maint bn, 1 med bn)

EQUIPMENT BY TYPE
MBT 60: 55 *Leopard* 2A4/5; 5 *Leopard* 1A5
RECCE 113: 22 *Eagle* 1; 91 *Eagle* IV
AIFV 45 CV9030 Mk II
APC 590
  APC (T) 439 M113 (incl variants); (162 more in store awaiting disposal)
  APC (W) 111 *Piranha* III (incl variants)
  PPV 40 *Cougar*
ARTY 44
  SP 155mm 24 M109
  MRL 227mm (12 MLRS in store awaiting disposal)
  MOR • TOWED 120mm 20 K6B1 *Soltam*
AT
  MSL • MANPATS 20 TOW
  RCL 84mm 349 *Carl Gustav*
AD • SAM • MANPAD FIM-92A *Stinger*
RADAR • LAND ARTHUR
ARV 11 *Bergepanzer* 2
VLB 10 *Biber*
MW 14 910-MCV-2

Navy 2,850; 150 conscript (total 3,000) 300 civilian

EQUIPMENT BY TYPE
PRINCIPAL SURFACE COMBATANTS 5
  DESTROYERS • DDGHM 1 *Iver Huitfeldt* with 1-2 octuple lnchr with RGM-84 *Harpoon* Block II AShM, 1 32-cell Mk41 VLS with SM-2 IIIA SAM, 2 12-cell Mk56 VLS with RIM-162 SAM, 2 twin 324mm TT, 2 76mm guns (2 additional vessels under construction; expected ISD 2013–14)
  FRIGATES • FFH 4 *Thetis* with 2 twin lnchr with *Stinger* SAM, 1 76mm gun, (capacity 1 *Super Lynx* Mk90B)
PATROL AND COASTAL COMBATANTS 9
  PSO 2 *Knud Rasmussen* with 1 hel landing platform
  PCC 7: 1 *Agdlek*; 6 *Diana*
MINE WARFARE • MINE COUNTERMEASURES 7:
  MCI 4 MSF MK-I
  MHD 1 *Sav*
  MSD 2 *Holm*
LOGISTICS AND SUPPORT 22
  ABU 2 (primarily used for MARPOL duties)
  AE 1 *Sleipner*
  AG 2 *Absalon* (flexible support ships) with 2 octuple VLS with RGM-84 Block 2 *Harpoon* 2 AShM, 4 twin lnchr with *Stinger* SAM, 3 12-cell Mk 56 VLS with RIM-162B *Sea Sparrow* SAM, 2 twin 324mm TT, 1 127mm gun (capacity 2 LCP, 7 MBT or 40 vehicles; 130 troops)
  AGB 3: 1 *Thorbjørn*; 2 *Danbjørn*
  AGE 1 *Dana*
  AGS 4 *Ska 11*
  AGSC 2 *Holm*
  AKL 2 *Seatruck*
  AX 1 *Søløven* (used as diving trainer)
  AXL 2 *Holm*
  AXS 2 *Svanen*

Air Force 2,950; 100 conscript (total 3,050) 120 civilian

Flying hours   165 hrs/yr

Tactical Air Comd

FORCES BY ROLE
FIGHTER/GROUND ATTACK
  2 sqn with F-16AM/BM *Fighting Falcon*
ANTI-SUBMARINE WARFARE
  1 sqn with *Super Lynx* Mk90B
SEARCH & RESCUE/TRANSPORT HELICOPTER
  1 sqn with AW101 *Merlin*
  1 sqn with AS550 *Fennec* (ISR)
TRANSPORT
  1 sqn with C-130J-30 *Hercules*; CL-604 *Challenger* (MP/VIP)
TRAINING
  1 unit with MFI-17 *Supporter* (T-17)

EQUIPMENT BY TYPE
AIRCRAFT 45 combat capable
  FTR 45: 35 F-16AM *Fighting Falcon*; 10 F-16BM *Fighting Falcon* (30 operational)
  TPT 7: **Medium** 4 C-130J-30 *Hercules*; **PAX** 3 CL-604 *Challenger* (MP/VIP)
  TRG 27 MFI-17 *Supporter* (T-17)
HELICOPTERS
  ASW 7 *Super Lynx* Mk90B (transferred from naval aviation)
  MRH 8 AS550 *Fennec* (ISR) (4 more non-operational)
  TPT • Medium 14 AW101 *Merlin* (8 SAR; 6 Tpt)
MSL
  AAM • IR AIM-9L; **IIR** AIM-9X; **ARH** AIM-120 AMRAAM

ASM AGM-65 *Maverick*
BOMBS
  LGB/INS/GPS-guided: GBU-31 JDAM; EGBU-12/GBU-24 *Paveway* LGB

Control and Air Defence Group

1 Control and Reporting Centre, 1 Mobile Control and Reporting Centre. 4 Radar sites. No SAM.

Reserves

Home Guard (Army) 40,800 reservists (to age 50)
FORCES BY ROLE
MANOEUVRE
  Light
  2 regt cbt gp (3 mot inf bn, 1 arty bn)
  5 (local) def region (up to 2 mot inf bn)

Home Guard (Navy) 4,500 reservists (to age 50) organised into 30 Home Guard units
EQUIPMENT BY TYPE
PATROL AND COASTAL COMBATANTS 30
  PB 30: 18 MHV800; 12 MHV900

Home Guard (Air Force) 5,300 reservists (to age 50)

Home Guard (Service Corps) 2,900 reservists

Cyber

Denmark lacks a cyber-defence strategy, but has a national CERT. Within the army, the 3rd Electronic Warfare Company is in charge of exploiting and disrupting enemy communications. The planning of a cyber-warfare unit within the Defence Intelligence Service is underway with the aim of protecting military technology from cyber attack. Denmark is a member of the Nordic Resource Network aimed at strengthening cyber defences.

DEPLOYMENT

Legal provisions for foreign deployment:
Constitution: Codified constitution (1849)
Decision on deployment of troops abroad: On approval by the parliament (Art. 19 II)

AFGHANISTAN
NATO • ISAF 613; 1 mech BG (1 tk pl, 2 mech inf coy); 4 *Leopard* 2A5; 11 CV9030 MkII; 23 M113; 12 *Piranha* III; 6 K6B1 120mm mor; 1 C-130J-30
UN • UNAMA 1 obs

DEMOCRATIC REPUBLIC OF THE CONGO
UN • MONUSCO 2 obs

GULF OF ADEN & SOMALI BASIN
NATO • *Operation Ocean Shield* 1 CL-604 (MP)

LEBANON
UN • UNIFIL 151; 1 log bn

LIBERIA
UN • UNMIL 2; 3 obs

MIDDLE EAST
UN • UNTSO 11 obs

SERBIA
NATO • KFOR 35
UN • UNMIK 1 obs

SOUTH SUDAN
UN • UNMISS 10; 12 obs

Estonia EST

Euro € [a]		2011	2012	2013
GDP	€	16bn	16.9bn	
	US$	22.2bn	21.4bn	
per capita	US$	17,416	16,788	
Growth	%	7.64	2.45	
Inflation	%	5.12	4.41	
Def exp [a]	€	280m		
	US$	389m		
Def bdgt	€	280m	341m	354m
	US$	389m	432m	
FMA (US)	US$	2.70m	2.4m	2.4m
US$1=€		0.72	0.79	

[a] NATO definition

Population   1,274,709

Age	0–14	15–19	20–24	25–29	30–64	65 plus
Male	7.9%	2.7%	3.8%	3.8%	21.6%	5.9%
Female	7.4%	2.5%	3.6%	3.8%	25.0%	12.0%

Capabilities

While its conscript-based armed forces are small, Estonia's government sees NATO membership as guaranteeing the nation's security against external threats. Estonia contributes personnel to ISAF, as well as to UN peacekeeping operations, and is a member of the Nordic Battlegroup. Estonia possesses no aircraft capable of airspace defence, and relies on a NATO Air Policing Mission for this task. Following Estonia's experience of cyber attack in 2007, Tallinn is the location for NATO's Cooperative Cyber Defence Centre of Excellence. This conducts training (theoretical and practical) for member states' personnel. Major procurement plans centre around the development of an air-defence system and radars. A Defence Development Plan (for the period 2013–22) is under consideration and should be signed by the end of 2012. Economic issues have meant that not all of the anticipated funding will now be available, likely requiring procurement ambitions to be revisited.

ACTIVE 5,750 (Army 5,300 Navy 200 Air 250)
Defence League 12,000

RESERVE 30,000 (Joint 30,000)

Terms of service 8 months, officers and some specialists 11 months. (Conscripts cannot be deployed.)

ORGANISATIONS BY SERVICE

Army 2,800; 2,500 conscript (total 5,300)

4 def region. All units except Scouts bn are reserve based

FORCES BY ROLE

MANOEUVRE

Reconnaissance

1 recce bn

Light

1 (1st) bde (2 inf bn, 1 CSS bn)

3 indep inf bn

COMBAT SUPPORT

1 arty bn

1 AD bn

1 engr bn

1 sigs bn

COMBAT SERVICE SUPPORT

1 log bn

Defence League 12,000

15 Districts

EQUIPMENT BY TYPE

APC 130

APC (W) 117: 56 XA-180 *Sisu*; 40 XA-188 *Sisu*; 21 BTR-80

PPV 13: 6 *Maxxpro*; 7 *Mamba*

ARTY 334

TOWED 98: **105mm** 32 H 61-37; **122mm** 42 D-30 (H 63); **155mm** 24 FH-70

MOR 230: **81mm** 51: 41 B455; 10 NM 95; **120mm** 179: 14 2B11; 165 41D

AT

MSL • MANPAT *Milan*; IMI MAPATS

RCL 160 **106mm**: 30 M40A1; **90mm** 130 PV-1110

AD • SAM • MANPAD *Mistral*

Navy 200

EQUIPMENT BY TYPE

PATROL AND COASTAL COMBATANTS • PB 1 (FIN *Rista Rihtniemi*)

MINE WARFARE • MINE COUNTERMEASURES 4

MCD 1 *Tasuja* (DNK *Lindormen*)

MHC 3 *Admiral Cowan* (UK *Sandown*)

LOGISTICS AND SUPPORT • AGF 1 *Admiral Pitka* with 1 76mm gun

Air Force 250

Flying hours   120 hrs/year

FORCES BY ROLE

TRANSPORT

1 sqn with An-2 *Colt*

TRANSPORT HELICOPTER

1 sqn with R-44 *Raven* II

EQUIPMENT BY TYPE

AIRCRAFT • TPT • Light 2 An-2 *Colt*

HELICOPTERS • TPT • Light 4 R-44 *Raven* II

Paramilitary

Border Guard

The Estonian Border Guard is subordinate to the Ministry of the Interior. Air support is provided by the Estonian Border Guard Aviation Corps.

EQUIPMENT BY TYPE

PATROL AND COASTAL COMBATANTS 20

PB 9: 1 *Maru* (FIN *Viima*); 8 (other)

PBR 11

AMPHIBIOUS • LANDING CRAFT • LCU 2

LOGISTICS & SUPPORT • AGF 1 *Balsam*

AIRCRAFT • TPT • Light 2 L-410

HELICOPTERS • TPT • 3 AW139

Cyber

Estonia established CERT-ee in 2006 and has further developed its cyber-security infrastructure after the cyber attacks of 2007. It adopted a national Cyber Security Strategy in 2008. This strategy is due to be updated in 2013. In 2011, the Ministry of Economic Affairs and Communication was given overall responsibility for cyber security which it addresses through the Estonian Informatics Centre and the Department of State Information System. As well as domestic capacities, Tallinn hosts the NATO Cooperative Cyber Security Centre of Excellence, established in 2008 to enhance NATO's cyber-defence capability.

DEPLOYMENT

Legal provisions for foreign deployment:

Constitution: Codified constitution (1992)

Decision on deployment of troops abroad: By parliament (Art. 128). Also, International Military Cooperation Act stipulates conditions for deployment abroad. For the collective defence purposes, ratification of the North Atlantic Treaty is considered a parliamenary decision that would allow Cabinet to deploy troops. The president, chairman of the parliament and chairman of the parliament's State Defence Commission shall be immediately informed of such decision. For other international operations, a separate parliamentary decision is necessary: the Ministry of Defence prepares a draft legal act and coordinates this with the Ministry of Foreign Affairs and the Ministry of Justice. It also asks the opinion of the chief of defence. The draft is then proposed to cabinet for approval and submission for parliamentary consideration.

AFGHANISTAN

NATO • ISAF 155; 1 mech inf coy with 14 XA-180 *Sisu*; 1 mor det with 3 81mm

BOSNIA-HERZEGOVINA

EU • EUFOR • *Operation Althea* 1

MIDDLE EAST

UN • UNTSO 1 obs

NORTH SEA

NATO • SNMCMG 1: 1 MHC

SERBIA

NATO • KFOR 1

Finland FIN

Euro €		2011	2012	2013
GDP	€	189.4bn	195.2bn	
	US$	263.5bn	247.2bn	
per capita	US$	50,067	46,970	
Growth	%	2.74	0.19	
Inflation	%	3.32	2.90	
Def exp	€	2.7bn		
	US$	3.76bn		
Def bdgt	€	2.86bn	2.84bn	2.78bn
	US$	3.98bn	3.6bn	
US$1=€		0.72	0.79	

Population	5,262,930

Age	0–14	15–19	20–24	25–29	30–64	65 plus
Male	8.1%	3.1%	3.2%	3.2%	23.7%	7.7%
Female	7.8%	3.0%	3.0%	3.0%	23.4%	10.8%

Capabilities

The armed forces' primary role is to act as a guarantor of national sovereignty by providing territorial defence, and its combination of a conscript/reserve-based structure with a modern equipment inventory is shaped to support this aim. All the armed services exercise regularly, with an increasingly joint emphasis, and the air force and navy particularly participate in multinational exercises. There are no planned changes to the key premises of Finland's defence policy, such as territorial defence, non-alignment and general conscription. However, Finland has embarked on a wide-ranging defence reform process in a bid to reconcile defence priorities with funding and demographics (the number of available conscripts is reducing), with the process planned to complete by 2015. Current plans call for the disbandment of a Jaeger brigade, an engineer regiment, a coastal artillery battalion and two air force training wings in 2013 and 2014. In addition, currently independent signals, air defence and artillery formations will be merged with existing manoeuvre brigades. The number of command levels will reduce from four to three, and the military provinces will cease to exist, with tasks divided between army command and regional offices. A new report on Finnish security and defence policy was expected by end-2012.

ACTIVE 22,200 (Army 16,000 Navy 3,500 Air 2,700) **Paramilitary 2,800**

General Conscription terms of Service 6–9–12 months (12 months for officers NCOs and soldiers with special duties. 25,000 reservists a year do refresher training: total obligation 40 days (75 for NCOs, 100 for officers) between conscript service and age 50 (NCOs and officers to age 60). From early 2013, concscript service will reduce by 15 days. Reserve total reducing to 340,000.

RESERVE 354,000 (Army 285,000 Navy 31,000 Air 38,000) **Paramilitary 11,500**

ORGANISATIONS BY SERVICE

Army 5,000; 11,000 conscript (total 16,000); civilian 3,000

FORCES BY ROLE

Finland's army maintains a mobilisation strength of about 285,000. In support of this requirement, two conscription cycles, each for about 15,000 conscripts, take place each year. After conscript training, reservist commitment is to the age of 60. Reservists are usually assigned to units within their local geographical area. All service appointments or deployments outside Finnish borders are voluntary for all members of the armed services. All brigades are reserve based.

Reserve Organisations

60,000 in manoeuvre forces and 225,000 in territorial forces

FORCES BY ROLE
SPECIAL FORCES
  1 SF bn
MANOEUVRE
  Armoured
  2 armd BG (regt)
  Mechanised
  2 (Karelia & Pori Jaeger) mech bde
  Light
  3 (Jaeger) bde
  6 lt inf bde
  Aviation
  1 hel bn
COMBAT SUPPORT
  1 arty bde
  1 AD regt
  7 engr regt
  3 sigs bn
COMBAT SERVICE SUPPORT
  Some log unit

EQUIPMENT BY TYPE
MBT 100 *Leopard* 2A4
RECCE 34 BMP-1TJ
AIFV 212: 110 BMP-2; 102 CV90
APC 613
  APC (T) 142: 40 MT-LBU; 102 MT-LBV
  APC (W) 471: 260 XA-180/185 *Sisu*; 101 XA-202 *Sisu*; 48 XA-203 *Sisu*; 62 AMV (XA-360)
ARTY 678
  SP 122mm 36 2S1 *Carnation* (PsH 74)
  TOWED 354: **122mm** 234 D-30 (H 63); **130mm** 36 K 54; **155mm** 54 K 83/K 98
  MRL 227mm 22 M270 MLRS
  MOR 120mm 265: 261 KRH 92; 4 XA-361 AMOS
AT • MSL 100 *Spike*; TOW 2
HELICOPTERS
  MRH 7: 5 Hughes 500D; 2 Hughes 500E
  TPT • Medium 15 NH90 TTH
UAV • ISR • Medium 11 ADS-95 *Ranger*

Europe

AD • SAM
SP 36 +: 16 ASRAD (ITO 05); 20 *Crotale* NG (ITO 90);
9K37 *Buk*-M1 (ITO 96)
MANPAD: 86 RBS 70 (ITO 05/05M)
GUNS 23mm; 30mm; 35mm; 57mm
AEV 6 *Leopard* 2R CEV
ARV 12 VT-55A
VLB 15+: BLG-60M2; 6 *Leopard* 2L; 9 SISU *Leguan*
MW *Aardvark* Mk 2; KMT T-55; RA-140 DS

Navy 1,600; 1,900 conscript (total 3,500); civilian 500

FORCES BY ROLE
Naval Command HQ located at Turku; with two
subordinate Naval Commands (Gulf of Finland and
Archipelago Sea); 1 Naval bde; 3 spt elm (Naval Materiel
Cmd, Naval Academy, Naval Research Institute)

EQUIPMENT BY TYPE
PATROL AND COASTAL COMBATANTS 8
PBG 4 *Rauma* with 6 RBS-15SF3 (15SF) AShM, 1
sextuple *Sadral* lnchr with *Mistral* SAM
PCG 4 *Hamina* with 4 RBS-15 (15SF) AShM, 1 octuple
VLS with *Umkhonto* SAM
MINE WARFARE 17
MINE COUNTERMEASURES 11
MHSO 1 *Katanpää* (2 further vessels in build;
expected ISD 2013)
MSI 10: 7 *Kiiski*; 3 *Kuha*
MINELAYERS • ML 6:
2 *Hameenmaa* with 1 octuple VLS with *Umkhonto* SAM,
2 RBU 1200, up to 100–120 mines
3 *Pansio* with 50 mines
1 *Pohjanmaa* with up to 100–150 mines
AMPHIBIOUS • LANDING CRAFT 51
LCU 1 *Kampela*
LCP 50
LOGISTICS AND SUPPORT 35:
AG 3: 1 *Louhi*; 2 *Hylje*
AGB 7 (Board of Navigation control)
AKSL 10: 2 *Hauki*; 3 *Hila*; 5 *Valas*
AX 5: 3 *Fabian Wrede*; 2 *Lokki*
YFB 8
YTM 2 *Haukipaa*

Coastal Defence
ARTY • COASTAL 118: **130mm** 102: 30 K-53tk (static);
72 K-54 RT **100mm** 16 tank turrets
MSL • TACTICAL • 4 RBS-15K AShM

Air Force 1,950; 750 conscript (total 2,700); civilian 1,000
3 Air Comds: Satakunta (West), Karelia (East), Lapland
(North)

Flying hours   90–140 hrs/year

FORCES BY ROLE
FIGHTER/GROUND ATTACK
3 sqn with F/A-18C/D *Hornet*
ISR
1 (survey) sqn with *Learjet* 35A

TRANSPORT
1 flt with C-295M
4 (liaison) flt with L-90 *Redigo*; PC-12NG
TRAINING
1 sqn with *Hawk* Mk50/51A/66* (air defence and ground
attack trg)
1 unit with L-70 *Vinka*

EQUIPMENT BY TYPE
AIRCRAFT 109 combat capable
FGA 62: 55 F/A-18C *Hornet*; 7 F/A-18D *Hornet*
MP 1 F-27-400M
ELINT 1 C-295M
TPT • Light 11: 2 C-295M; 3 *Learjet* 35A (survey; ECM
trg; tgt-tow); 6 PC-12NG
TRG 83: 29 *Hawk* Mk50/51A*; 18 *Hawk* Mk66*; 8 L-90
Redigo; 28 L-70 *Vinka*
MSL • AAM • IR AIM-9 *Sidewinder*; **IIR** AIM-9X
Sidewinder; **ARH** AIM-120 AMRAAM

Paramilitary

Border Guard 2,800
Ministry of Interior. 4 Border Guard Districts and 2 Coast
Guard Districts

FORCES BY ROLE
MARITIME PATROL
1 sqn with Do-228 (maritime surv); AS332 *Super Puma*;
Bell 412 (AB-412) *Twin Huey*; Bell 412EP (AB-412EP)
Twin Huey;AW119KE *Koala*

EQUIPMENT BY TYPE
PATROL AND COASTAL COMBATANTS 54
PCC 3: 2 *Tursas*; 1 *Merikarhu*
PBO 3 *Telkaa*
PB 48
AMPHIBIOUS • LANDING CRAFT • LCAC 7
AIRCRAFT • TPT • Light 2 Do-228
HELICOPTERS
MRH 5: 4 Bell 412 (AB-412) *Twin Huey*; 1 Bell 412EP
(AB-412EP) *Twin Huey*
TPT 7: **Medium** 3 AS332 *Super Puma*; **Light** 4
AW119KE *Koala*

Reserve 11,500 reservists on mobilisation

Cyber

Finland has a national CERT, is involved in informal CERT
communities and is a member of the European government
CERTs Group (ECG). A national cyber strategy is expected
by the end of 2012, and the country has announced the
establishment of a common secure network in 2013 to
protect military, police, border guard and government
confidential networks.

DEPLOYMENT

Legal provisions for foreign deployment:
Constitution: Codified constitution (2000)
Specific legislation: 'Act on Peace Support Operations'
(2000); 'Act on Military Crisis Management (211/2006)'.

Decision on deployment of troops abroad: By president upon proposal by government (Art. 129 of constitution) and after formal consultation of parliamentary Foreign Affairs Committee ('Act on Peace Support Operations', Ch. 1, Section 2; 'Act on Military Crisis Management (211/2006)').

AFGHANISTAN
NATO • ISAF 136

BOSNIA-HERZEGOVINA
EU • EUFOR • *Operation Althea* 10

INDIA/PAKISTAN
UN • UNMOGIP 6 obs

LEBANON
UN • UNIFIL 177; 1 inf coy
Liberia UN • UNMIL 2

MIDDLE EAST
UN • UNTSO 17 obs

SERBIA
NATO • KFOR 22

UGANDA
EU • EUTM 7

France FRA

Euro €		2011	2012	2013
GDP	€	2.0tr	2.04tr	
	US$	2.78tr	2.58tr	
per capita	US$	42,358	39,311	
Growth	%	1.69	0.12	
Inflation	%	2.14	1.92	
Def exp [b]	€	38.4bn		
	US$	53.5bn		
Def bdgt [a]	€	37.4bn	38bn	38.2bn
	US$	52.1bn	48.1bn	
US$1=€		0.72	0.79	

[a] Includes military pensions. All defence budget figures reflect Crédits de Paiement (CP) fiscal accounting. 2011 and 2012 reflect CP figures from the Loi de Finances Initiale, while figure for 2013 reflects CP figures from the Projet de Loi de Finances.

[b] NATO definition

Population	65,630,692					
Age	0–14	15–19	20–24	25–29	30–64	65 plus
Male	9.6%	3.0%	3.1%	3.1%	22.7%	7.4%
Female	9.1%	2.9%	3.0%	3.0%	23.0%	10.1%

Capabilities

A new *Livre Blanc* will be published in 2013, which will reassess France's security environment and defence priorities. Cuts in personnel levels and procurement are likely, as are improvements in areas such as intelligence and cyber, but details remain unknown. France will remain one of the two pre-eminent defence powers in Europe, maintaining rapidly deployable armed forces, capable of self-sustainment and operation across the full spectrum of combat activity. The nuclear deterrent continues to be revamped with the introduction of the M51 SLBM and the ASMPA nuclear-armed cruise missile. An improved version of the M51, the 51.2, is due for entry into service in 2015. Significant procurement programmes continue for the army, navy and air force. Strategic airlift will be strengthened with the eventual delivery of the A400M, while the air force is also planning a future strategic tanker aircraft. The introduction of these platforms will support France's ability to continue to project power on a global scale. France's combat participation in ISAF was due to draw to a close at the end of 2012, but France continues to maintain substantial overseas deployments in Africa and Lebanon. All of the services exercise regularly and jointly at the national level, while also participating in a broad range of international exercises.

ACTIVE 228,850 (Army 122,500 Navy 38,650 Air 49,850, Other Staffs 17,850) **Paramilitary 103,400**

RESERVE 29,650 (Army 16,000, Navy 5,500, Air 4,750, Other Staffs 3,400) **Paramilitary 40,000**

ORGANISATIONS BY SERVICE

Strategic Nuclear Forces

Navy 2,200
SUBMARINES • STRATEGIC • SSBN 4
  3 *Le Triomphant* with 16 M45 SLBM with 6 TN-75 nuclear warheads, 4 single 533mm TT with F17 Mod 2 HWT/SM-39 *Exocet* AShM
  1 *Le Triomphant* with 16 M51 SLBM with 6 TN-75 nuclear warheads, 4 single 533mm TT with F17 Mod 2 HWT/SM-39 *Exocet* AShM
AIRCRAFT • FGA 20 *Rafale* M F3 with ASMP-A msl

Air Force 1,800

Air Strategic Forces Command
FORCES BY ROLE
STRIKE
  1 sqn with *Mirage* 2000N with ASMP/ASMP-A msl
  1 sqn with *Rafale* B F3 with ASMP/ASMP-A msl
TANKER
  1 sqn with C-135FR; KC-135 *Stratotanker*

EQUIPMENT BY TYPE
AIRCRAFT 45 combat capable
  FGA 45: 25 *Mirage* 2000N; 20 *Rafale* B F3
  TKR/TPT 11 C-135FR
  TKR 3 KC-135 *Stratotanker*

Paramilitary

Gendarmerie 40

Space
SATELLITES 7
  COMMUNICATIONS 2 *Syracuse*-3 (designed to integrate with UK *Skynet* & ITA *Sicral*)
  ISR 3 *Helios* (1A/2A/2B)
  EARLY WARNING 2 *Spirale*

Army 122,500 (incl 7,300 Foreign Legion; 12,800 Marines)

Regt and BG normally bn size

FORCES BY ROLE

COMMAND

2 (task force) HQ

MANOEUVRE

Reconnaissance

1 ISR bde (1 recce regt, 1 UAV regt, 2 EW regt, 1 int bn)

Armoured

1 armd bde (2 armd regt, 2 armd inf regt, 1 SP arty regt, 1 MLRS regt, 1 AD regt, 1 engr regt)

1 armd bde (2 armd regt, 2 armd inf regt, 1 SP arty regt, 1 engr regt)

Mechanised

1 lt armd bde (1 armd cav regt, 2 mech inf regt, 1 SP arty regt, 1 engr regt)

1 (FRA/GER) mech bde (1 armd cav regt, 1 mech inf regt)

2 mech inf bde (1 armd cav regt, 1 armd inf regt, 1 mech inf regt, 1 SP arty regt, 1 engr regt)

1 mech BG (UAE)

2 mech regt (Djibouti & New Caledonia)

Light

2 regt (French Guiana)

1 regt (French West Indies)

1 regt (Polynesia)

1 bn (French West Indies)

1 bn (Mayotte)

Air Manoeuvre

1 AB bde (1 armd cav regt, 4 para regt, 1 arty regt, 1 engr regt, 1 spt regt)

1 AB regt (Réunion)

1 AB bn (Gabon)

Amphibious

1 lt armd bde (1 armd cav regt, 2 mech inf regt, 1 SP arty regt, 1 engr regt)

Mountain

1 mtn bde (1 armd cav regt, 3 mech inf regt, 1 arty regt, 1 engr regt)

Aviation

3 avn regt

Other

4 SMA regt (French Guiana, French West Indies & Indian Ocean)

5 SMA coy (French Polynesia & New Caledonia)

COMBAT SUPPORT

1 CBRN regt

1 sigs bde (5 sigs regt)

COMBAT SERVICE SUPPORT

1 log bde (5 tpt regt; 1 log regt; 1 med regt)

3 trg regt

Special Operation Forces 2,200

FORCES BY ROLE

SPECIAL FORCES

2 SF regt

MANOEUVRE

Aviation

1 avn regt

Reserves 16,000 reservists

Reservists form 79 UIR (Reserve Intervention Units) of about 75 to 152 troops, for 'Proterre' – combined land projection forces bn, and 23 USR (Reserve Specialised Units) of about 160 troops, in specialised regt.

EQUIPMENT BY TYPE

MBT 254 *Leclerc*

RECCE 2,050: 256 AMX-10RC; 160 ERC-90F4 *Sagaie*; 40 VAB Reco NBC; 1,594 VBL M-ll

AIFV 731: 331 AMX-10P/PC; 400 VBCI

APC 3,659

  APC (T) 53 BvS-10 being delivered

  APC (W) 3,586: 3,500 VAB; 60 VAB BOA; 26 VAB NBC

  PPV 20: 15 *Aravis*; 5 *Buffalo*

ARTY 375

  SP 155mm 114: 37 AU-F-1; 77 CAESAR

  TOWED 155mm 43 TR-F-1

  MRL 227mm 26 MLRS

  MOR 120mm 192 RT-F1

AT • MSL

  SP 325: 30 VAB HOT; 110 VAB *Milan*; 185 VAB *Eryx*

  MANPATS 550 *Milan*

AIRCRAFT • TPT • Light 16: 5 PC-6B *Turbo-Porter*; 8 TBM-700; 3 TBM-700B

HELICOPTERS

  ATK 46: 39 EC665 *Tiger* HAP; 7 EC665 *Tiger* HAD

  MRH 172 SA341F/342M *Gazelle* (all variants)

  TPT 162: **Heavy** 8 EC725AP *Caracal* (CSAR); **Medium** 118: 23 AS532UL *Cougar*; 2 NH90 TTH; 93 SA330 *Puma*; **Light** 36 EC120B *Colibri*

UAV • ISR • Medium 20 SDTI (*Sperwer*)

AD • SAM 897

  TOWED 15 MIM-23B I-HAWK

  MANPAD 882 *Mistral*

RADAR • LAND 66: 10 *Cobra*; 56 RASIT/RATAC

AEV 71 AMX-30 EBG

ARV 20+: AMX-1-ECH; 134 AMX-30D; 20 *Leclerc* DNG; VAB-EHC

VLB 67: 39 EFA; 18 PTA; 10 SPRAT (being delivered)

MW AMX-30 B/B2; 20 *Minotaur*

Navy 38,650 (incl 2,200 opcon Strategic Nuclear Forces)

EQUIPMENT BY TYPE

SUBMARINES 10

  STRATEGIC • SSBN 4:

    3 *Le Triomphant* opcon Strategic Nuclear Forces with 16 M45 SLBM with 6 TN-75 nuclear warheads, 4 single 533mm TT with F17 Mod 2 HWT/SM-39 *Exocet* AShM (currently undergoing modernisation programme to install M51 SLBM; expected completion 2018)

    1 *Le Triomphant* opcon Strategic Nuclear Forces with 16 M51 SLBM with 6 TN-75 nuclear warheads, 4 single 533mm TT with F17 Mod 2 HWT/SM-39 *Exocet* AShM

  TACTICAL • SSN 6:

    6 *Rubis* with 4 single 533mm TT with F-17 HWT/SM-39 *Exocet* AShM

PRINCIPAL SURFACE COMBATANTS 24
AIRCRAFT CARRIERS 1:
  CVN 1 *Charles de Gaulle* with 4 octuple VLS with *Aster* 15 SAM, 2 sextuple *Sadral* lnchr with *Mistral* SAM (capacity 35–40 *Super Etendard/Rafale* M/E-2C *Hawkeye/AS365 Dauphin*)
DESTROYERS • DDGHM 12:
  2 *Cassard* with 2 quad lnchr with MM-40 *Exocet* Block 2 AShM, 1 Mk13 GMLS with SM-1MR SAM, 2 sextuple *Sadral* lnchr with *Mistral* SAM, 2 single 533mm ASTT with L5 HWT, 1 100mm gun, (capacity 1 AS565SA *Panther* ASW hel)
  2 *Forbin* with 2 quad lnchr with MM-40 *Exocet* Block 3 AShM, 1 48-cell VLS with *Aster* 15/*Aster* 30 SAM, 2 sextuple *Sadral* lnchr with *Mistral* SAM, 2 twin 324mm ASTT with MU-90, 2 76mm gun, (capacity 1 NH90 TTH hel)
  1 *Georges Leygues* with 2 twin lnchr with MM-38 *Exocet* AShM, 1 octuple lnchr with *Crotale* SAM, 2 twin *Simbad* lnchr with *Mistral* SAM, 2 single 533mm ASTT with L5 HWT, 1 100mm gun, (capacity 2 *Lynx* hel)
  1 *Georges Leygues* with 2 twin lnchr with MM-38 *Exocet* AShM, 1 octuple lnchr with *Crotale* SAM, 2 sextuple *Sadral* lnchr with *Mistral* SAM, 2 single 533mm ASTT with L5 HWT, 1 100mm gun, (capacity 2 *Lynx* hel)
  2 *Georges Leygues* with 2 quad lnchr with MM-40 *Exocet* AShM, 1 octuple lnchr with *Crotale* SAM, , 2 sextuple *Sadral* lnchr with *Mistral* SAM, 2 single 533mm ASTT with L5 HWT, 1 100mm gun, (capacity 2 *Lynx* hel)
  3 *Georges Leygues* (mod) with 2 quad lnchr with MM-40 *Exocet* AShM, 1 octuple lnchr with *Crotale* SAM, 2 twin *Simbad* lnchr with *Mistral* SAM, 2 single 324mm ASTT with MU90 LWT, 1 100mm gun, (capacity 2 *Lynx* hel)
  1 *Tourville* with 6 single lnchr with MM-38 *Exocet* AShM, 1 octuple lnchr with *Crotale* SAM, 2 single 533mm ASTT with L5 HWT, 2 100mm gun, (capacity 2 *Lynx* hel)
FRIGATES • FFGHM 11:
  6 *Floreal* with 2 single lnchr with MM-38 *Exocet* AShM, 1 twin *Simbad* lnchr with *Mistral* SAM, 1 100mm gun, (capacity 1 AS565SA *Panther* hel)
  5 *La Fayette* with 2 quad lnchr with MM-40 *Exocet* Block 2 AShM, 1 octuple lnchr with *Crotale* SAM, (space for fitting 2 8-cell VLS lnchr for *Aster* 15/30), 1 100mm gun, (capacity 1 AS565SA *Panther*/SA321 *Super Frelon* hel) (to be upgraded with MM-40 *Exocet* Block 3 AShM by 2013)
PATROL AND COASTAL COMBATANTS 20
  FSG 9
    7 *D'Estienne d'Orves* with 2 single or twin lnchr with MM-40 *Exocet* AShM, 4 single ASTT, 1 100mm gun
    2 *D'Estienne d'Orves* with 4 single ASTT, 1 100mm gun
  PCC 7: 4 *L'Audacieuse* (all deployed in the Pacific or Caribbean); 3 *Flamant*
  PCO 3: 1 *Lapérouse*; 1 *Le Malin*; 1 *Gowind* (owned by priate company DCNS; currently operated by French Navy)
  PSO 1 *Albatros*
MINE WARFARE • MINE COUNTERMEASURES 18

MCS 7: 3 *Antares* (used as route survey vessels); 4 *Vulcain* (used as mine diving tenders)
MHO 11 *Éridan*
AMPHIBIOUS
PRINCIPAL AMPHIBIOUS SHIPS 4
  LHD 3 *Mistral* (capacity mixed air group of up to 16 NH90/SA330 *Puma*/AS532 *Cougar*/EC665 *Tiger* hel; 2 LCAC or 4 LCM; 60 AFVs; 450 troops)
  LPD 1 *Foudre* (capacity 4 AS532 *Cougar*; either 2 LCT or 10 LCM; 22 tanks; 470 troops)
LANDING SHIPS • LST 3 *Batral* (capacity 12 trucks; 140 troops)
LANDING CRAFT 42:
  LCT 6: 1 Edic 700; 1 CDIC; 4 EDA-R
  LCM 11 CTMS
  LCVP 25
LOGISTICS AND SUPPORT 148
  ABU 1 *Telenn Mor*
  AE 1 *Denti*
  AFS 1 *Revi*
  AG 4: 1 *Lapérouse* (used as trials ships for mines and divers); 3 *Chamois*
  AGE 1 *Corraline*
  AGI 1 *Dupuy de Lome*
  AGM 1 *Monge*
  AGOR 2: 1 *Pourquoi pas?* (used 150 days per year by Ministry of Defence; operated by Ministry of Research and Education otherwise); 1 *Beautemps-beaupré*
  AGS 3 *Lapérouse*
  AORH 4 *Durance* with 1-3 twin *Simbad* lnchr with *Mistral* SAM (capacity 1 SA319 *Alouette* III/AS365 *Dauphin*/*Lynx*)
  ATA 2 *Malabar*
  AXL 12: 8 *Léopard*; 2 *Glycine*; 2 *Engageante*
  AXS 4: 2 *La Belle Poule*; 2 other
  YAG 2 *Phaéton* (towed array tenders)
  YD 5
  YDT 10: 1 *Alize*; 9 *VIP 21*
  YFB 2 *VTP*
  YFL 12: 9 *V14*; 3 *Nymphea*
  YFRT 2 *Athos*
  YFU 8
  YGS 7 *VH8*
  YTB 3 *Bélier*
  YTL 34: 4 *RP10*; 4 *PSS10*; 26 *P4*
  YTM 21: 3 *Maïto*; 16 *Fréhel*; 2 *Esterel*
  YTR 5: 3 *Avel Aber*; 2 *Las*

Naval Aviation 6,500

Flying hours 180–220 hrs/yr on strike/FGA ac

FORCES BY ROLE
STRIKE/FIGHTER/GROUND ATTACK
  2 sqn with *Rafale* M F3
FIGHTER/GROUND ATTACK
  1 sqn with *Super Etendard Modernisé*
ANTI-SURFACE WARFARE
  1 sqn with AS565SA *Panther*
ANTI-SUBMARINE WARFARE
  2 sqn (forming) with NH90 NFH
  1 sqn with Lynx Mk4

MARITIME PATROL
2 sqn with *Atlantique* 2
1 sqn with Falcon 20H *Gardian*
1 sqn with Falcon 50M

AIRBORNE EARLY WARNING & CONTROL
1 sqn with E-2C *Hawkeye*

SEARCH & RESCUE
1 sqn with AS365N/F *Dauphin* 2
1 sqn with EC225

TRAINING
1 sqn with SA319B *Alouette* III
1 unit with *Falcon* 10 M
1 unit with CAP 10; EMB 121 *Xingu*; MS-880 *Rallye*

EQUIPMENT BY TYPE
AIRCRAFT 78 combat capable
  FGA 68: 34 *Rafale M* F3; 34 *Super Etendard Modernisé*
  ASW 15 *Atlantique* 2 (10 more in store)
  AEW&C 3 E-2C *Hawkeye*
  TPT 27: **Light** 11 EMB-121 *Xingu*; **PAX** 16: 6 *Falcon* 10MER; 5 *Falcon* 20H *Gardian*; 5 *Falcon* 50M
  TRG 16: 7 CAP 10; 9 MS-880 *Rallye**
HELICOPTERS
  ASW 32: 25 *Lynx* Mk4; 7 NH90 NFH
  MRH 52: 9 AS365N/F *Dauphin* 2; 2 AS365N3; 16 AS565SA *Panther*; 25 SA319B *Alouette* III
  TPT • Medium 3 EC225 *Super Puma*
MSL
  AAM • IR R-550 *Magic* 2; **IIR** *Mica* IR; **ARH** *Mica* RF
  AShM AM-39 *Exocet*
  ASM ASMP-A; AS-30 *Laser*; AASM

Marines 2,500

Commando Units
FORCES BY ROLE
MANOEUVRE
  Reconnaissance
  1 recce gp
  Amphibious
  3 aslt gp
  1 atk swimmer gp
  1 raiding gp
COMBAT SERVICE SUPPORT
  1 spt gp

Fusiliers-Marin 1,600
FORCES BY ROLE
MANOEUVRE
  Other
  9 (force protection) sy unit
  14 (Naval Base) sy gp

Public Service Force
Naval personnel performing general coast guard, fishery protection, SAR, anti-pollution and traffic surveillance duties. Command exercised through Maritime Prefectures (Premar): Manche (Cherbourg), Atlantique (Brest), Méditerranée (Toulon)

FORCES BY ROLE
MARITIME PATROL
  1 sqn with *Falcon* 50M; *Falcon* 200 *Gardian*

EQUIPMENT BY TYPE
PATROL AND COASTAL COMBATANTS 6
  PSO 1 *Albatros*
  PCO 1 *Arago*
  PCC 4: 3 *Flamant*; 1 *Grèbe*
  AIRCRAFT • MP 9: 4 *Falcon* 50M; 5 *Falcon* 200 *Gardian*
  HELICOPTERS • MRH 4 AS365 *Dauphin* 2

Reserves 5,500 reservists

Air Force 49,850

Flying hours 180 hrs/year

Strategic Forces
FORCES BY ROLE
STRIKE
  1 sqn with *Mirage* 2000N with ASMP/ASMP-A msl
  1 sqn with *Rafale* B F3 with ASMP/ASMP-A msl
TANKER
  1 sqn with C-135FR; KC-135 *Stratotanker*

EQUIPMENT BY TYPE
AIRCRAFT 45 combat capable
  FGA 45: 25 *Mirage* 2000N; 20 *Rafale* B F3
  TKR/TPT 11 C-135FR
  TKR 3 KC-135 *Stratotanker*

Combat Brigade
FORCES BY ROLE
FIGHTER
  1 sqn with *Mirage* 2000-5
  1 sqn with *Mirage* 2000B/C
FIGHTER/GROUND ATTACK
  3 sqn with *Mirage* 2000D
  1 (composite) sqn with *Mirage* 2000C/D (Djibouti)
  2 sqn with *Rafale* B/C F3
  1 sqn with *Rafale* B/C F3 (UAE)
ISR
  1 sqn with *Mirage* F-1CR *
ELECTRONIC WARFARE
  1 flt with C-160G *Gabriel* (ESM)
TRAINING
  1 OCU sqn with *Mirage* 2000D
  1 OCU sqn with *Rafale*
  1 (agressor) sqn with *Alpha Jet**
  4 sqn with *Alpha Jet**
ISR UAV
  1 sqn with *Harfang*

EQUIPMENT BY TYPE
AIRCRAFT 336 combat capable
  FTR 73: 22 *Mirage* 2000-5; 12 *Mirage* 2000B; 39 *Mirage* 2000C
  FGA 143: 61 *Mirage* 2000D; 6 *Mirage* F-1B; 22 *Mirage* F-1CT; 17 *Rafale* B F3; 37 *Rafale* C F3
  ISR 29 *Mirage* F-1CR*
  ELINT 2 C-160G *Gabriel* (ESM)
  TRG 91 *Alpha Jet**
UAV • ISR • Heavy 4 *Harfang*
MSL
  AAM • IR R-550 *Magic* 2; **IIR** *Mica* IR; **SARH** *Super* 530D; **ARH** *Mica* RF

ASM ASMP-A; AS-30L; *Apache*; AASM
LACM SCALP EG
BOMBS
  Laser-guided: GBU-12 *Paveway* II

Air Mobility Brigade
FORCES BY ROLE
SEARCH & RESCUE/TRANSPORT
  5 sqn with C-160 *Transall*; CN-235M; DHC-6-300 *Twin
  Otter*; SA330 *Puma*; AS555 *Fennec* (Djibouti, French
  Guiana, Gabon, Indian Ocean & New Caledonia)
TANKER/TRANSPORT
  2 sqn with C-160NG *Transall*
TRANSPORT
  1 sqn with A310-300; A330; A340-200 (on lease)
  3 sqn with C-130H/H-30 *Hercules*; C-160 *Transall*
  2 sqn with CN-235M
  1 sqn with EMB-121
  1 sqn with *Falcon* 7X (VIP); *Falcon* 50 (VIP); *Falcon* 900
  (VIP); *Falcon* 2000
  3 flt with TBM-700A
  1 (mixed) gp with AS532 *Cougar*; C-160 *Transall*; DHC-
  6-300 *Twin Otter*
TRAINING
  1 OCU sqn with SA330 *Puma*; AS555 *Fennec*
  1 OCU unit with C-160 *Transall*
TRANSPORT HELICOPTER
  2 sqn with AS555 *Fennec*
  2 sqn with AS332C/L *Super Puma*; SA330 *Puma*; EC725
  Caracal
EQUIPMENT BY TYPE
AIRCRAFT
  TKR/TPT 20 C-160NG *Transall*
  TPT 115: **Medium** 38: 5 C-130H *Hercules*; 9 C-130H-30
  Hercules; 24 C-160 *Transall*; **Light** 63: 19 CN-235M-100;
  5 CN-235M-300 (3 more due for delivery by early
  2013); 5 DHC-6-300 *Twin Otter*; 25 EMB-121 *Xingu*;
  9 TBM-700; **PAX** 14: 3 A310-300; 1 A330; 2 A340-200
  (on lease); 2 *Falcon* 7X; 3 *Falcon* 50 (VIP); 2 *Falcon* 900
  (VIP); 1 *Falcon* 2000
HELICOPTERS
  MRH 37 AS555 *Fennec*
  TPT 43: **Heavy** 11 EC725 *Caracal*; **Medium** 32: 3
  AS332C *Super Puma*; 4 AS332L *Super Puma*; 3 AS532
  Cougar (tpt/VIP); 22 SA330 *Puma*

Air Space Control Brigade
FORCES BY ROLE
SPACE
  1 (satellite obs) sqn with *Helios*
AIRBORNE EARLY WARNING & CONTROL
  1 (Surveillance & Control) sqn with E-3F *Sentry*
AIR DEFENCE
  3 sqn with *Crotale* NG; SAMP/T
  2 sqn with SAMP/T
EQUIPMENT BY TYPE
SATELLITES *see* Space
AIRCRAFT• AEW&C 4 E-3F *Sentry*
AD
  SAM *Crotale* NG; SAMP/*T*

GUNS 20mm 76T2
SYSTEMS STRIDA (Control)

Security and Intervention Brigade
FORCES BY ROLE
MANOEUVRE
  Other
  24 protection units
  30 fire fighting and rescue scn
  3 intervention paratroop cdo

Air Training Command
FORCES BY ROLE
TRAINING
  3 sqn with CAP 10; Grob G120A-F; TB-30 *Epsilon*
EQUIPMENT BY TYPE
AIRCRAFT
  TRG 48: 5 CAP 10; 18 Grob G120A-F; 25 TB-30 *Epsilon*
  (incl many in storage)

Reserves 4,750 reservists

Paramilitary 103,400

Gendarmerie 103,400; 40,000 reservists
EQUIPMENT BY TYPE
LT TK 28 VBC-90
APC (W) 153 VBRG-170
ARTY MOR 157+ **60mm**; 81mm
PATROL AND COASTAL COMBATANTS 39
  PCO 1 *Fulmar*
  PB 38: 4 *Géranium*; 2 VSC 14; 24 VSCM; 8 EBSLP
HELICOPTERS • TPT • Light 35: 20 EC135; 15 EC145

Customs (Direction Générale des Douanes et Droits Indirects)
EQUIPMENT BY TYPE
PATROL AND COASTAL COMBATANTS 30
  PBO 2: 1 *Jacques Oudart Fourmentin*; 1 *Kermovan*
  PB 28: 7 *Plascoa* 2100; 7 *Haize Hegoa*; 2 *Avel Gwalarn*; 1
  Rafale; 1 *Arafenua*; 1 *Vent d'Amont*; 1 *La Rance*; 8 others

Coast Guard (Direction des Affaires Maritimes)
EQUIPMENT BY TYPE
PATROL AND COASTAL COMBATANTS 25
  PBO 2: 1 *Themis*; 1 *Iris*
  PB 23: 4 *Callisto*; 19 others
LOGISTICS AND SUPPORT • AG 7

Cyber

The French Network and Information Security Agency
(ANSSI), under the authority of the prime minister and attached to the office of the secretary-general for national security and defence, was established in 2009 to conduct surveillance on sensitive government networks and respond to
cyber attacks. The 2008 French Defence White Paper placed
emphasis on cyber threats, calling for programmes in offensive and defensive cyber-war capabilities. The White
Paper noted that part of the offensive capability 'will come

under the Joint Staff and the other part […] developed within specialised services'. CALID (Analysis and Combat Centre for Computer Defence) monitors military networks and counters intrusions in coordination with ANSSI. In July 2011, the MoD produced a classified Joint Cyber Defence Concept. Ahead of the new *Livre Blanc*, the general secretariat on defence and national security (SGDSN) released a preparatory document stressing the strategic dimension of cyber threats and confirming the development of technical capabilities to control access to cyberspace. In addition, France is strengthening bilateral relations with strategic partners and through EU and NATO frameworks France has a national CERT, is involved in informal CERT communities, and is a member of the European government CERTs Group (ECG).

DEPLOYMENT

Legal provisions for foreign deployment:
Constitution: Codified constitution (1958)
Specific legislation: 'Order of 7 January 1959'
Decision on deployment of troops abroad: De jure: by the minister of defence, under authority of the PM and on agreement in council of ministers ('Order of 7 January 1959', Art. 16, Art.20-1 of constitution)

AFGHANISTAN

NATO • ISAF/OEF-A 2,418; 1 armd bde HQ; 2 inf regt; 1 hel bn; 1 log bn; 8 AMX 10 RC; 10 VBCI; 449 VAB APC; 76 VBL; 4 EC665 *Tiger*; 2 AS532 *Cougar*; 2 EC725AP *Caracal*; 3 *Harfang* UAV

BOSNIA-HERZEGOVINA

EU • EUFOR • *Operation Althea* (*Operation Astrée*) 11

CENTRAL AFRICAN REPUBLIC

ECCAS • MICOPAX 7
Operation Boali 230; 1 inf coy; 1 spt det

CHAD

Operation Epervier 950; 1 mech inf BG; 1 air unit with 3 *Mirage* 2000D; 1 *Mirage* F1-CR; 1 C-130H *Hercules*; 1 C-160 *Transall*; 1 C-135FR; 1 hel det with 4 SA330 *Puma*

CÔTE D'IVOIRE

Operation Licorne 450; 1 AB BG; 1 C-160 *Transall*; 1 AS555 *Fennec*
UN • UNOCI 6

DEMOCRATIC REPUBLIC OF THE CONGO

EU • EUSEC RD Congo 10
UN • MONUSCO 5 obs

DJIBOUTI

Army 1,050; 1 (Marine) combined arms regt with (1 engr coy, 1 arty bty, 2 recce sqn, 2 inf coy); 1 hel det with 4 SA330 *Puma*; 2 SA342 *Gazelle*
Navy: 100; 1 LCT
Air Force: 250; 1 FGA sqn with 7 *Mirage* 2000C/D; 1 SAR/tpt sqn with 1 C-160 *Transall*; 2 SA330 *Puma*; 1 AS555 *Fennec*

EGYPT

MFO 2

FRENCH GUIANA

Army 1,619 1 (Foreign Legion) inf regt; 1 (Marine) inf regt; 1 SMA regt
Navy 150; 1 PCC
Air Force 1 tpt unit; 1 DHC-6; 6 SA330 *Puma*; 3 AS555 *Fennec*
Gendarmerie 3 coy; 1 AS350 *Ecureuil*

FRENCH POLYNESIA

Army 429 (incl Centre d'Expérimentation du Pacifique); 1 (Marine) inf regt; 3 SMA coy
Navy 710; 1 HQ at Papeete; 1 FFGHM; 1 AOT; 3 Falcon 200 *Gardian*
Air Force 1 SAR/tpt sqn with 3 CN-235M; 1 AS332 *Super Puma*; 1 AS555 *Fennec*

FRENCH WEST INDIES

Army 607; 1 (Marine) inf regt; 1 (Marine) inf bn; 2 SMA regt
Navy 450; 2 FFGHM; 1 PCC; 1 LST: 1 naval base at Fort de France (Martinique)
Gendarmerie 4 coy; 2 AS350 *Ecureuil*

GABON

Army 762; 1 recce pl with ERC-90F1 *Lynx*; 1 (Marine) inf bn
Air Force 1 SAR/tpt sqn with 4 SA330 *Puma*

GERMANY

Army 2,800 (incl elm Eurocorps and FRA/GER bde (2,500)); 1 (FRA/GER) army bde (1 army HQ, 1 armd cav regt, 1 mech inf regt)

GULF OF ADEN & INDIAN OCEAN

EU • *Operation Atalanta* 2 FFGHM

GULF OF GUINEA

Operation Corymbe 1 LPD

HAITI

UN • MINUSTAH 3

INDIAN OCEAN

Army 988 (incl La Réunion and TAAF); 1 (Marine) para regt; 1 (Foreign Legion) inf det; 1 SMA regt
Navy 1 base at Dzaoudzi (Mayotte), 1 HQ at Port-des-Galets (La Réunion); 1 FFGHM; 1 PSO; 1 LST
Air Force 1 SAR/tpt sqn with 2 C-160 *Transall*; 2 AS555 *Fennec*
Gendarmerie 5 coy; 1 SA319 *Alouette III*

LEBANON

UN • UNIFIL 902; 1 armd cav BG; *Leclerc*; AMX-10P; VBCI; PVP; VAB; CAESAR; AU-F1 155mm; *Mistral*

LIBERIA

UN • UNMIL 1

MIDDLE EAST

UN • UNTSO 2 obs

NEW CALEDONIA

Army 757; 1 (Marine) mech inf regt; 2 SMA coy; 6 ERC-90F1 *Lynx*
Navy 510; 1 FFGHM; 2 PCC; 1 LST; 1 base with 2 *Falcon* 200 *Gardian* at Nouméa

Air Force 1 tpt unit; 3 CN-235 MPA; 4 SA330 *Puma*; 1 AS555 *Fennec*

Gendarmerie 4 coy; 2 AS350 *Ecureuil*

SENEGAL

Army/Navy/Air Force 350; 1 *Atlantique*; 1 C-160 *Transall*

SERBIA

NATO • KFOR 335; 1 armd cav sqn; 1 log coy

UAE

800: Army: 1 (Foreign Legion) BG (2 recce coy, 2 inf coy, 1 arty bty, 1 engr coy)

Air Force: 1 FGA sqn with 6 *Rafale* F3, 1 KC-135F

UGANDA

EU • EUTM 23

WESTERN SAHARA

UN • MINURSO 14 obs

FOREIGN FORCES

Belgium Air Force: 29 *Alpha Jet* trg ac located at Cazaux/Tours

Germany Army: 209 (GER elm Eurocorps)

Singapore Air Force: 200; 1 trg sqn with 5 A-4SU *Super Skyhawk*; 11 TA-4SU *Super Skyhawk*

Germany GER

Euro €		2011	2012	2013
GDP	€	2.59tr	2.66tr	
	US$	3.61tr	3.37tr	
per capita	US$	44,400	41,448	
Growth	%	3.10	0.94	
Inflation	%	2.48	2.15	
Def exp [b]	€	34.6bn		
	US$	48.2bn		
Def bdgt [a]	€	32bn	31.9bn	33.3bn
	US$	44.5bn	40.4bn	
US$1=€		0.72	0.79	

[a] Includes military pensions

[b] NATO definition

Population 81,305,856

Age	0–14	15–19	20–24	25–29	30–64	65 plus
Male	6.8%	2.6%	3.0%	3.0%	24.8%	8.9%
Female	6.4%	2.4%	2.9%	3.0%	24.4%	11.8%

Capabilities

The armed forces are undergoing a period of restructuring, and substantial down-sizing, as defence cuts announced in 2010 and the reform agenda announced in September 2011 are implemented. Personnel numbers will fall, and conscription has been 'suspended'. Land forces will be restructured to provide three divisions rather than the previous five, with brigades down from eleven to eight. Up to 20,000 civilian posts are also being cut. The air force is being reorganised around operational-unit and support-unit commands, replacing its divisional structure, with the navy similarly being organised into capability areas. There will be base closures in Germany and reductions in equipment holdings, including battlefield helicopters. The armed forces are deployed to ISAF, though numbers are reducing as transition progresses. While the armed forces remain constrained politically in terms of out-of-area operations, they will increasingly have the ability for power projection, supported by the eventual introduction into service of the A400M military airlifter. Although there have been very slight increases to the defence budget in 2011 and 2012, there is evidence that another budgetary crunch will come in the period 2014–2016.

ACTIVE 196,000 (Army 70,050 Navy 15,850 Air 33,450 Joint Support Service 48,250 Joint Medical Service 20,000 Other 8,400)

Terms of service Mandatory conscription indefinitely suspended 1 July 2011; voluntary conscripts can serve up to 23 months.

RESERVE 40,320 (Army 15,350 Navy 1,850 Air 4,900 Joint Support Service 12,850 Joint Medical Service 4,950 MoD 420)

ORGANISATIONS BY SERVICE

Space

SATELLITES 7

COMMUNICATIONS 2 COMSATBw (1 & 2)

ISR 5 SAR-*Lupe*

Army 70,050

The German army is currently divided into response forces (RF) and stabilisation forces (StF).

FORCES BY ROLE

MANOEUVRE

Armoured

1 (1st) armd div (RF) (1 armd bde (1 armd recce coy, 2 armd bn, 1 armd inf bn, 1 SP arty bn, 1 engr coy, 1 log bn); 1 armd bde (1 recce coy, 1 armd bn, 1 armd inf bn, 1 SP arty bn, 1 engr coy, 1 log bn); 1 armd recce bn; 1 arty regt; 1 engr regt; 1 sigs bn; 1 NBC bn; 1 log bn)

1 (10th) armd div (StF) (1 armd bde (1 recce bn, 1 armd bn, 2 armd inf bn, 1 engr bn, 1 sigs bn, 1 log bn); 1 mtn inf bde (1 recce bn, 3 mtn inf bn, 1 engr bn, 1 sigs bn, 1 log bn))

1 (13th) mech div (StF) (2 mech bde (1 recce bn, 1 armd bn, 2 armd inf bn, 1 engr bn, 1 sigs bn, 1 log bn))

Light

2 bn (GER/FRA bde)

Air Manoeuvre

1 spec ops div (RF) (1 SF bde, 2 AB bde (1 recce coy, 2 para bn, 1 engr coy, 1 log bn), 1 AD coy, 1 sigs bn)

1 air mob div (RF) (1 air mob bde (1 air mob inf regt, 2 atk hel bn, 1 tpt hel bn); 1 cbt spt bde with (1 arty regt, 1 NBC regt); 2 tpt hel regt, 1 lt tpt hel regt, 1 sigs bn)

COMBAT SUPPORT
1 arty bn (GER/FRA bde)
1 engr coy (GER/FRA bde)
COMBAT SERVICE SUPPORT
1 log bn (GER/FRA bde)
EQUIPMENT BY TYPE
MBT 322 Leopard 2A6
RECCE 340: 221 Fennek (incl 24 engr recce, 19 fires spt); 94 Tpz-1 Fuchs (CBRN); 25 Wiesel (16 recce; 9 engr)
AIFV 528: 420 Marder 1A2/A3; 5 Puma (test); 103 Wiesel (with 20mm gun)
APC 1,650
  APC (T) 473: 177 Bv-206D/S; 296 M113 (inc variants)
  APC (W) 907: 51 Boxer; 856 TPz-1 Fuchs (incl variants)
  PPV 270 APV-2 Dingo II
ARTY 272
  SP • 155mm 130 PzH 2000
  MRL • 227mm 55 MLRS
  MOR • 120mm 87 Tampella
AT • MSL 463
  SP 120 Wiesel (TOW)
  MANPATS 343 Milan
AMPHIBIOUS 30 LCM (river engr)
HELICOPTERS
  ATK 23 EC665 Tiger
  MRH/ISR 97 Bo-105M/Bo-105P PAH-1 (with HOT)
  TPT 144 **Medium** 16 NH90; **Light** 128: 76 Bell 205 (UH-1D Iroquois); 38 Bo-105; 14 EC135
UAV • ISR 15 **Medium** 6 KZO; **Light** 9 LUNA
RADARS 101: 8 Cobra; 76 RASIT (veh, arty); 17 RATAC (veh, arty)
AEV 185: 149 Dachs; 36 Leopard A1
ARV 77: 75 Büffel; 2 M88A1
VLB 169: 104 Biber; 30 M3; 35 Panzerschnellbrücke 2
MW 124+: 100 Area Clearing System; 24 Keiler; Minelayer 5821; Skorpion Minelauncher

Navy 19,180

Previous Type Comds have been merged into two Flotillas. Flotilla I combines SS, MCM, PBF and SF whilst Flotilla II comprises 2 FF and Aux squadrons.

EQUIPMENT BY TYPE
SUBMARINES • TACTICAL • SSK 4:
  4 Type-212A with 6 single 533mm TT with 12 A4 Seehecht DM2 HWT (2 further vessels on order)
PRINCIPAL SURFACE COMBATANTS 19
  DESTROYERS • DDGHM 7
    4 Brandenburg with 2 twin lnchr with MM-38 Exocet AShM, 1 16-cell Mk41 VLS with RIM-7M/P, 2 Mk49 GMLS with RIM-116 RAM SAM, 2 twin 324mm ASTT with Mk 46 LWT, 1 76mm gun, (capacity 2 Sea Lynx Mk88A ASW hel)
    3 Sachsen with 2 quad Mk141 lnchr with RGM-84F Harpoon AShM, 1 32-cell Mk41 VLS with SM-2MR/RIM-162B Sea Sparrow SAM, 2 21-cell Mk49 GMLS with RIM-116 RAM SAM, 1 76mm gun, (capacity; 2 Sea Lynx Mk88A ASW hel)
  FRIGATES 12
    FFGHM 7 Bremen (of which 1 laid up for decommissioning in early 2013) with 2 quad

Mk141 lnchr with RGM-84A/C Harpoon AShM, 1 octuple Mk29 GMLS with RIM-7M/P Sea Sparrow SAM, 2 Mk49 GMLS with RIM-116 RAM SAM, 2 twin 324mm ASTT with Mk46 LWT, 1 76mm gun, (capacity 2 Sea Lynx Mk88A ASW)
    FFGM 5 Braunschweig (K130) (of which 3 vessels are launched but not commissioned owing to technical problems) with 2 twin lnchr with RBS-15 AShM, 2 Mk49 GMLS each with RIM-116 RAM SAM, 1 76mm gun, 1 hel landing platform
PATROL AND COASTAL COMBATANTS • PCGM 8
  8 Gepard with 2 twin lnchr with MM-38 Exocet AShM, 1 Mk49 GMLS with RIM-116 RAM SAM, 1 76mm gun
MINE WARFARE • MINE COUNTERMEASURES 36:
  MHO 13: 10 Frankenthal (1 used as diving support; 1 more scheduled for conversion); 3 Kulmbach
  MSO 5 Ensdorf
  MSD 18 Seehund
AMPHIBIOUS 2
  LCU 2 Type-520
LOGISTICS AND SUPPORT 58
  AFH 3 Berlin Type-702 (capacity 2 Sea King Mk41 hel; 2 RAMs)
  AG 5: 2 Schwedeneck Type-748; 3 Stollergrund Type-745
  AGI 3 Oste Type-423
  AGOR 1 Planet Type-751
  AO 2 Walchensee Type-703
  AOR 6 Elbe Type-404 (2 specified for PFM support; 1 specified for SSK support; 3 specified for MHC/MSC support)
  AOT 2 Spessart Type-704
  APB 3: 1 Knurrhahn; 2 Ohre
  AT 5
  ATR 1 Helgoland
  AXS 1 Gorch Fock
  YAG 2 (used as trials ships)
  YDT 5 Wangerooge
  YFD 5
  YFRT 4 Todendorf Type-905
  YPC 2 Bottsand
  YTM 8 Vogelsand

Naval Aviation 2,200

AIRCRAFT 8 combat capable
  ASW 8 AP-3C Orion
  TPT • Light 2 Do-228 (pollution control)
HELICOPTERS
  ASW 22 Lynx Mk88A with Sea Skua
  SAR 21 Sea King Mk41
MSL AShM Sea Skua

Air Force 33,450

Flying hours   140 hrs/year (plus 40 hrs high-fidelity simulator)

Air Force Command

FORCES BY ROLE
FIGHTER
  1 wg (2 sqn with F-4F Phantom II)
  2 wg (4 sqn with Eurofighter Typhoon)

FIGHTER/GROUND ATTACK
1 wg (2 sqn with *Tornado* IDS)
1 wg (2 sqn with Eurofighter *Typhoon*)
ISR
1 wg (1 ISR sqn with *Tornado* ECR/IDS; 1 UAV sqn (ISAF only) with *Heron*)
AIR DEFENCE
1 wg (3 SAM gp) with *Patriot*
1 AD gp with ASRAD *Ozelot*; C-RAM MANTIS
3 (tac air ctrl) radar gp

EQUIPMENT BY TYPE
AIRCRAFT 209 combat capable
FTR 119: 91 Eurofighter *Typhoon*; 28 F-4F *Phantom* II (OSD Jul 2013)
FGA 69 *Tornado* IDS
EW/FGA 21 *Tornado* ECR*
UAV • ISR • Heavy 3 *Heron*
AD • SAM
SP 30 ASRAD *Ozelot* (with FIM-92A *Stinger*)
TOWED 16: 14 *Patriot* PAC-3, 2 C-RAM MANTIS
MSL
AAM • IR AIM-9L/Li *Sidewinder*; **IIR** IRIS-T; **ARH** AIM 120A/B AMRAAM
LACM KEPD 350 *Taurus*
ARM AGM-88B HARM
BOMBS
LGB: GBU-24 *Paveway* III, GBU-54 JDAM

Transport Command
FORCES BY ROLE
TANKER/TRANSPORT
1 (special air mission) wg (3 sqn with A310 MRT; A310 MRTT; A340; AS532U2 *Cougar* II; Global 5000)
TRANSPORT
4 wg (total: 2 sqn with CH-53G *Stallion*; 4 sqn with C-160D *Transall*; 1 sqn forming with NH90)

EQUIPMENT BY TYPE
AIRCRAFT
TKR/TPT 4 A310 MRTT
TPT 70: **Medium** 60 C-160D *Transall*; **PAX** 10: 2 A310 MRT; 2 A340 (VIP); 2 A319; 4 Global 5000
HELICOPTERS • TPT 90: **Heavy** 82 CH-53G *Stallion*; **Medium** 8: 4 AS532U2 *Cougar* II (VIP); 4 NH90

Training Command
FORCES BY ROLE
TRAINING
1 sqn located at Holloman AFB (US) with *Tornado* IDS
1 unit (ENJJPT) located at Sheppard AFB (US) with T-6 *Texan* II; T-38A
1 hel unit located at Fassberg
1 AD unit located at Fort Bliss (US) with ASRAD *Ozelot*; C-RAM MANTIS; *Patriot*

EQUIPMENT BY TYPE
AIRCRAFT 14 combat capable
FGA 14 *Tornado* IDS
TRG 109: 69 T-6 *Texan* TII, 40 T-38A
AD • SAM ASRAD *Ozelot*; C-RAM MANTIS; *Patriot*

Joint Support Services 48,250
FORCES BY ROLE
COMBAT SUPPORT
6 MP bn
3 sigs regt
COMBAT SERVICE SUPPORT
1 log bde
2 log regt

Joint Medical Services 20,000
FORCES BY ROLE
COMBAT SERVICE SUPPORT
9 med regt (1 rapid)
5 fd hospital

Paramilitary

Border Guard 500
EQUIPMENT BY TYPE
PATROL AND COASTAL COMBATANTS 15
PCO 6: 3 *Bad Bramstedt*; 1 *Bredstedt*; 2 *Sassnitz*
PB 9: 3 *Vogtland*; 5 *Prignitz*; 1 *Rettin*

Cyber
Germany established a Department of Information and Computer Network Operations in 2009 under the guidance of the then-chief of the Bundeswehr's Strategic Reconnaissance Command. Bundeswehr units maintain organic IT monitoring capability: a Bundeswehr CERT team (CERTBw) is available. Germany issued a Cyber Security Strategy in February 2011. A National Cyber Response Centre, involving police, customs, the Federal Intelligence Service and the Bundeswehr, began operations on 1 April 2011. It reports to the Federal Office for Information Security. A National Cyber Security Council has also been established, with high-level representatives from government and, as associate members, businesses.

DEPLOYMENT
Legal provisions for foreign deployment:
Constitution: Codified constitution ('Basic Law', 1949)
Specific legislation: 'Parlamentsbeteiligungsgesetz' (2005)
Decision on deployment of troops abroad: a) By parliament: in general and in the case of military intervention; b) by government: in urgent cases of threat or emergency (parliamentary consent a posteriori), or for preparatory measures or humanitarian interventions; c) simplified procedure for 'missions of low intensity' or if the government seeks an extension of parliamentary approval (§§ 1–5 of the 2005 law).

AFGHANISTAN
NATO • ISAF 4,737; 1 div HQ; 2 inf BG; *Marder* AIFV; *Fennek* (Recce); *Boxer* APC; TPz-1 *Fuchs* APC; *Dingo* II PPV; PzH 2000 155mm SP arty; *Wiesel* (TOW) SP AT; KZO UAV; LUNA UAV **Air Force:** 6 *Tornado* ECR (SEAD); CH-53 tpt hel; C-160 tpt ac; *Heron* UAV
UN • UNAMA 1 obs

BOSNIA-HERZEGOVINA
EU • EUFOR • Operation Althea 2

DEMOCRATIC REPUBLIC OF THE CONGO

EU • EUSEC RD Congo 3

FRANCE

Army 400 (incl GER elm Eurocorps)

GULF OF ADEN & INDIAN OCEAN

EU • *Operation Atalanta* 1 DDGHM; 1 P-3C

LEBANON

UN • UNIFIL 153; 2 PC; 1 SPT

MEDITERRANEAN SEA

NATO • SNMG 2: 1 DDGHM

NATO • SNMCMG 2: 1 MHO

NORTH SEA

NATO • SNMCMG 1: 1 MHO

POLAND

Army 67 (GER elm Corps HQ (multinational))

SERBIA

NATO • KFOR 1,330; 1 NBC bn HQ; elm 1 MP coy; 2 NBC coy; 1 sigs coy; 1 spt bn; 1 med unit; elm 1 hel gp; 16 TPz-1 *Fuchs*; 7 UH-1D *Iroquois*

SOUTH SUDAN

UN • UNMISS 8; 8 obs

SUDAN

UN • UNAMID 10

UGANDA

EU • EUTM 21

UNITED STATES

Air Force: trg units at Goodyear AFB (AZ)/Sheppard AFB (TX) with 40 T-38 *Talon* trg ac; 69 T-6A *Texan* II; 1 trg sqn Holloman AFB (NM) with 14 *Tornado* IDS; NAS Pensacola (FL); Fort Rucker (AL) • Missile trg located at Fort Bliss (TX)

UZBEKISTAN

NATO • ISAF 106

FOREIGN FORCES

Canada NATO 226

France Army: 1 (FRA/GER) army bde (1 army HQ, 1 armd cav rgt, 1 mech inf regt); 1,776

United Kingdom Army 16,240; 1 armd div (2 armd bde); 1 hel regt (2 sqn with *Lynx* AH7/9); **Royal Navy** 40; **Air Force** 210

United States

US Africa Command: **Army**; 1 HQ at Stuttgart

US European Command: 50,500; 1 combined service HQ (EUCOM) at Stuttgart-Vaihingen

   Army 35,200; 1 HQ (US Army Europe (USAREUR) at Heidelberg; 1 cav SBCT; 1 armd inf bde; 1 cbt avn bde; 1 engr bde; 1 int bde; 1 MP bde; 2 sigs bde; 1 spt bde; 1 (APS) armd HBCT eqpt. set (transforming); M1 *Abrams*; M2/M3 *Bradley*; *Stryker*; M109; M777; M270 MLRS; AH-64 *Apache*; CH-47 *Chinook*; UH-60 *Black Hawk*

   Navy 485

USAF 14,450; 1 HQ (US Airforce Europe (USAFE)) at Ramstein AB; 1 HQ (3rd Air Force) at Ramstein AB; 1 ftr wg at Spangdahlem AB with (1 atk sqn with 18 A-10C *Thunderbolt* II; 1 ftr sqn with 24 F-16CJ *Fighting Falcon*); 1 airlift wg at Ramstein AB with 16 C-130E/J *Hercules*; 2 C-20 Gulfstream; 9 C-21 Learjet; 1 C-40B

USMC 365

Greece GRC

Euro €			2011	2012	2013
GDP		€	215.1bn	201.4bn	
		US$	299.3bn	254.9bn	
per capita		US$	27,796	23,765	
Growth		%	-6.91	-6.00	
Inflation		%	3.33	0.94	
Def exp[b]		€	4.62bn		
		US$	6.43bn		
Def bdgt [a]		€	6.12bn	6.02bn	
		US$	8.52bn	7.62bn	
US$1=€			0.72	0.79	

[a] Includes military pensions

[b] NATO definition

Population	10,767,827					
Age	**0–14**	**15–19**	**20–24**	**25–29**	**30–64**	**65 plus**
Male	7.3%	2.5%	2.6%	3.1%	24.7%	8.7%
Female	6.9%	2.3%	2.5%	3.1%	25.1%	11.2%

Capabilities

The armed forces are tasked with assuring the territorial integrity of Greece and support to Cyprus, as well as contributing to international peacekeeping and peace-support initiatives. Regional tensions with Turkey and (FYR) Macedonia remain. A National Defence Policy was adopted in 2011 which emphasised deterrence, internal cooperation and enhanced situational awareness, as well as primary security tasks. The armed forces have little organic ability to deploy other than regionally. Significant procurement plans have been shelved as a result of the country's economic problems – which have led to a significant reduction in defence spending – while cuts in military salaries, and significant reductions in training and exercises, will have depressed capability and morale.

ACTIVE 144,350 (Army 86,150, Navy 20,000 Air 26,600, Joint 11,600) **Paramilitary 4,000**

Terms of service: Conscripts in all services up to 9 months

RESERVE 216,650 (Army 177,650 Navy 5,000, Air 34,000)

ORGANISATIONS BY SERVICE

Army 48,450; 37,700 conscripts (total 86,150)

Units are manned at 3 different levels – Cat A 85% fully ready, Cat B 60% ready in 24 hours, Cat C 20% ready in 48 hours (requiring reserve mobilisation). 3 military regions.

FORCES BY ROLE
COMMAND
  4 corps HQ (incl NDC-GR)
  1 armd div HQ
  3 mech inf div HQ
  1 inf div HQ
  1 log corps HQ
SPECIAL FORCES
  1 comd (1 amph bde, 1 cdo/para bde)
MANOEUVRE
  Reconnaissance
  5 recce bn
  Armoured
  4 armd bde (2 armd bn, 1 mech inf bn, 1 SP arty bn)
  Mechanised
  8 mech inf bde (1 armd bn, 2 mech bn, 1 SP arty bn)
  Light
  2 inf div
  7 inf bde (1 armd bn, 3 inf regt, 1 arty regt)
  Air Manoeuvre
  1 air mob bde
  Amphibious
  1 mne bde
  Aviation
  1 avn bde (1 hel regt with (2 atk hel bn), 2 tpt hel bn, 4 hel bn)
COMBAT SUPPORT
  1 arty regt (1 arty bn, 2 MRL bn)
  3 AD bn (2 with I-HAWK, 1 with *Tor* M1)
  3 engr regt
  2 engr bn
  1 EW regt
  10 sigs bn
COMBAT SERVICE SUPPORT
  1 log div (3 log bde)

EQUIPMENT BY TYPE
MBT 1,462: 170 *Leopard* 2A6HEL; 183 *Leopard* 2A4; 526 *Leopard* 1A4/5; 208 M60A1/A3; 375 M48A5
RECCE 229 VBL
AIFV 398 BMP-1
APC 1,883
  APC (T) 1,872: 89 *Leonidas* Mk1/2; 1,685 M113A1/A2; 98 M577
  PPV 11 *Maxxpro*
ARTY 3,353
  SP 547: **155mm** 442: 418 M109A1B/A2/A3GEA1/A5; 24 PzH 2000; **203mm** 105 M110A2
  TOWED 410: **105mm** 281: 263 M101; 18 M-56; **155mm** 129 M114
  MRL 147: **122mm** 111 RM-70 *Dana*; **227mm** 36 MLRS (incl ATACMS)
  MOR 2,249: **81mm** 1,629; **107mm** 620 M-30 (incl 231 SP)
AT
  MSL 1,108
    SP 528: 196 9M133 *Kornet-E* (AT-14); 290 M901; 42 *Milan* HMMWV
    MANPATS 580: 262 9K111 *Fagot* (AT-4 *Spigot*); 248 *Milan*; 70 TOW
  RCL 3,927:
    SP 106mm 581 M40A1

  MANPATS 3,346 **84mm** 2,000 *Carl Gustav*; **90mm** 1,346 EM-67
AIRCRAFT • TPT • Light 26: 2 Beech 200 *King Air* (C-12R/AP *Huron*); 24 Cessna 185 (U-17A/B)
HELICOPTERS
  ATK 29: 19 AH-64A *Apache*; 10 AH-64D *Apache*
  TPT 132: **Heavy** 15: 9 CH-47D *Chinook*; 6 CH-47SD *Chinook*; **Medium** 8 NH90 TTH; **Light** 108: 95 Bell 205 (UH-1H *Iroquois*); 13 Bell 206 (AB-206) *Jet Ranger*
UAV • ISR • Medium 2 *Sperwer*
AD
  SAM 614
    SP 113: 21 9K331 *Tor*-M1 (SA-15 *Gauntlet*); 38 9K33 *Osa*-M (SA-8B *Gecko*); 54 ASRAD HMMWV
    TOWED 42 I-HAWK
    MANPAD 459 FIM-92A *Stinger*
  GUNS • TOWED 727: **20mm** 204 Rh 202; **23mm** 523 ZU-23-2
RADAR • LAND 76: 3 ARTHUR, 5 AN/TPQ-36 *Firefinder* (arty, mor); 8 AN/TPQ-37(V)3; 40 BOR-A; 20 MARGOT
ARV 268: 12 *Büffel*; 43 *Leopard* 1; 95 M88A1; 113 M578
VLB 12+: 12 *Leopard* 1; *Leguan*
MW *Giant Viper*

National Guard 33,000 reservists

Internal security role
FORCES BY ROLE
MANOEUVRE
  Light
  1 inf div
  Air Manoeuvre
  1 para regt
  Aviation
  1 avn bn
COMBAT SUPPORT
  8 arty bn
  4 AD bn

Navy 16,900; 3,100 conscript; (total 20,000)

EQUIPMENT BY TYPE
SUBMARINES • TACTICAL • SSK 8:
  4 *Poseidon* (GER T-209/1200) (of which 1 modernised with AIP technology) with 8 single 533mm TT with SUT HWT
  3 *Glavkos* (GER T-209/1100) with 8 single 533mm TT with UGM-84C *Harpoon* AShM/SUT HWT
  1 *Papanikolis* (GER T-214) with 8 single 533mm TT with UGM-84C *Harpoon* AShM/SUT HWT (5 additional vessels in build)
PRINCIPAL SURFACE COMBATANTS 14
  FRIGATES • FFGHM 14:
    4 *Elli* Batch I (NLD *Kortenaer* Batch 2) with 2 quad Mk141 lnchr with RGM-84A/C *Harpoon* AShM, 1 octuple Mk29 GMLS with RIM-7M/P *Sea Sparrow* SAM, 2 twin 324mm ASTT with Mk46 LWT, 1 76mm gun, (capacity 2 Bell 212 (AB-212) hel)
    2 *Elli* Batch II (NLD *Kortenaer* Batch 2) with 2 quad Mk141 lnchr with RGM-84A/C *Harpoon* AShM, 1 octuple Mk29 GMLS with RIM-7M/P *Sea Sparrow* SAM, 2 twin 324mm ASTT with Mk46 LWT, 2 76mm gun, (capacity 2 Bell 212 (AB-212) hel)

4 *Elli* Batch III (NLD *Kortenaer* Batch 2) with 2 quad Mk141 lnchr with RGM-84A/C *Harpoon* AShM, 1 octuple Mk29 lnchr with RIM-7M/P *Sea Sparrow* SAM, 2 twin 324mm ASTT with Mk46 LWT, 1 76mm gun, (capacity 2 Bell 212 (AB-212) hel)

4 *Hydra* (GER MEKO 200) with 2 quad lnchr with RGM-84G *Harpoon* AShM, 1 16-cell Mk48 Mod 5 VLS with RIM-162 ESSM SAM, 2 triple 324mm ASTT each with Mk46 LWT, 1 127mm gun, (capacity 1 S-70B *Seahawk* ASW hel)

PATROL AND COASTAL COMBATANTS 33

CORVETTES • FSGM 5 *Roussen* (*Super Vita*) with 2 quad lnchr with MM-40 *Exocet* AShM, 1 Mk49 GMLS with RIM-116 RAM SAM, 1 76mm gun (2 additional vessels in build)

PCFG 12:

5 *Kavaloudis* (FRA *La Combattante* II, III, IIIB) with 6 RB 12 *Penguin* AShM, 2 single 533mm TT with SST-4 HWT, 2 76mm gun

4 *Laskos* (FRA *La Combattante* II, III, IIIB) with 4 MM-38 *Exocet* AShM, 2 single 533mm TT with SST-4 HWT, 2 76mm gun

1 *Votsis* (FRA *La Combattante*) with 2 twin Mk-141 lnchr with RGM-84C *Harpoon* AShM, 1 76mm gun

2 *Votsis* (FRA *La Combattante* IIA) with 2 twin MM-38 *Exocet* AShM, 1 76mm gun

PCO 8:

2 *Armatolos* (DNK *Osprey*) with 1 76mm gun

2 *Kasos* with 1 76mm gun

4 *Machitis* with 1 76mm gun

PB 8: 4 *Andromeda* (NOR *Nasty*); 2 *Stamou*; 2 *Tolmi*

MINE COUNTERMEASURES 7

MHO 4: 2 *Evropi* (UK *Hunt*); 2 *Evniki* (US *Osprey*)

MSC 3 *Alkyon* (US MSC-294)

AMPHIBIOUS

LANDING SHIPS • LST 5:

5 *Chios* (capacity 4 LCVP; 300 troops) with 1 hel landing platform (for med hel)

LANDING CRAFT 7

LCU 4

LCAC 3 *Kefallinia* (*Zubr*) (capacity either 3 MBT or 10 APC (T); 230 troops)

LOGISTICS AND SUPPORT 48:

ABU 2

AG 2 *Pandora*

AGS 2: 1 *Strabon*; 1 *Naftilos*

AOR 2 *Axios* (ex-GER *Luneburg*)

AORH 1 *Prometheus* (ITA *Etna*)

AOT 4 *Ouranos*

AWT 6 *Kerkini*

AXS 5

YFU 4

YNT 1 *Thetis*

YPT 3 *Evrotas*

YTM 16

Naval Aviation

FORCES BY ROLE

ANTI-SUBMARINE WARFARE

1 div with S-70B *Seahawk*; Bell 212 (AB-212) ASW; SA319 *Alouette* III

EQUIPMENT BY TYPE

AIRCRAFT • ASW (5 P-3B *Orion* in store)

HELICOPTERS

ASW 19: 8 Bell 212 (AB-212) ASW; 11 S-70B *Seahawk*

MRH 2 SA319 *Alouette* III

MSL

ASM AGM-119 *Penguin*, AGM-114 *Hellfire*

Air Force 22,050; 4,550 conscripts (total 26,600)

Tactical Air Force

FORCES BY ROLE

FIGHTER/GROUND ATTACK

1 sqn with A-7E/H *Corsair* II; TA-7C *Corsair* II

2 sqn with F-4E *Phantom* II

3 sqn with F-16CG/DG Block 30/50 *Fighting Falcon*

3 sqn with F-16CG/DG Block 52+ *Fighting Falcon*

1 sqn with F-16C/D Blk 52+ ADV *Fighting Falcon*

1 sqn with *Mirage* 2000-5EG/BG Mk2

1 sqn with *Mirage* 2000EG/BG

ISR

1 sqn with RF-4E *Phantom* II

AIRBORNE EARLY WARNING

1 sqn with EMB-145H *Erieye*

EQUIPMENT BY TYPE

AIRCRAFT 282 combat capable

FGA 234: 34 F-4E *Phantom* II; 70 F-16CG/DG Block 30/50 *Fighting Falcon*; 56 F-16CG/DG Block 52+; 30 F-16 C/D Block 52+ ADV *Fighting Falcon*; 20 *Mirage* 2000-5EG Mk2; 5 *Mirage* 2000-5BG Mk2; 17 *Mirage* 2000EG; 2 *Mirage* 2000BG

ATK 28 20 A-7E/H *Corsair* II; 8 TA-7C *Corsair* II

ISR 15 RF-4E *Phantom* II*

AEW 4 EMB-145AEW (EMB-145H) *Erieye*

MSL

AAM • IR AIM-9L/P *Sidewinder*; R-550 *Magic* 2 **IIR** IRIS-T; *Mica* IR; **SARH** Super 530; **ARH** AIM-120B/C AMRAAM; *Mica* RF

ASM AGM-65A/B/G *Maverick*

LACM SCALP EG

AShM AM 39 *Exocet*

ARM AGM-88 HARM

BOMBS

Conventional: Mk81; Mk82; Mk83; Mk84; GBU-8B HOBOS; AGM-154C JSOW; GBU-31 JDAM

Laser-guided: GBU-12/GBU-16 *Paveway* II; GBU-24 *Paveway* III

Air Defence

FORCES BY ROLE

AIR DEFENCE

6 sqn/bty with PAC-3 *Patriot* (MIM-104 A/B SOJC/D GEM)

2 sqn/bty with S-300PMU-1 (SA-10C *Grumble*)

12 bty with *Skyguard/Sparrow* RIM-7/guns; *Crotale* NG/GR; *Tor* M-1 (SA-15 *Gauntlet*)

EQUIPMENT BY TYPE

AD

SAM • TOWED 61+: 36 PAC-3 *Patriot*; 12 S-300 PMU-1 (SA-10C *Grumble*); 9 *Crotale* NG/GR; 4

9K331 *Tor*-M1 (SA-15 *Gauntlet*); some *Skyguard/Sparrow*
GUNS 35+ 35mm

Air Support Command

FORCES BY ROLE
SEARCH & RESCUE/TRANSPORT HELICOPTER
1 sqn with AS332C *Super Puma* (SAR/CSAR)
1 sqn with AW109; Bell 205A (AB-205A) (SAR); Bell 212 (AB-212 - VIP, tpt)
TRANSPORT
1 sqn with C-27J *Spartan*
1 sqn with C-130B/H *Hercules*
1 sqn with EMB-135BJ *Legacy*; ERJ-135LR; Gulfstream V
FIRE FIGHTING
2 sqn with CL-215; CL-415

EQUIPMENT BY TYPE
AIRCRAFT
TPT 26: **Medium** 23: 8 C-27J *Spartan*; 5 C-130B *Hercules*; 10 C-130H *Hercules*; **Light** 2: 1 EMB-135BJ *Legacy*; 1 ERJ-135LR; **PAX** 1 Gulfstream V
FF 21: 13 CL-215; 8 CL-415
HELICOPTERS
TPT 31: **Medium** 11 AS332C *Super Puma*; **Light** 20: 13 Bell 205A (AB-205A) (SAR); 4 Bell 212 (AB-212) (VIP, Tpt); 3 AW109

Air Training Command

FORCES BY ROLE
TRAINING
2 sqn with T-2C/E *Buckeye*
2 sqn with T-6A/B *Texan* II
1 sqn with T-41D

EQUIPMENT BY TYPE
AIRCRAFT • TRG 104: 5 T-2C *Buckeye*; 35 T-2E *Buckeye*; 20 T-6A *Texan* II; 25 T-6B *Texan* II; 19 T-41D

Paramilitary • Coast Guard and Customs
4,000

EQUIPMENT BY TYPE
PATROL AND COASTAL COMBATANTS 122: **PCC** 3; **PBF** 54; **PB** 65
LOGISTICS AND SUPPORT • YPC 4
AIRCRAFT • TPT • Light 4: 2 Cessna 172RG *Cutlass*; 2 TB-20 *Trinidad*

DEPLOYMENT

Legal provisions for foreign deployment:
Constitution: Codified constitution (1975/1986/2001)
Specific legislation: 'Law 2295/95' (1995))
Decision on deployment of troops abroad: By the Government Council on Foreign Affairs and Defence

AFGHANISTAN
NATO • ISAF 12

BOSNIA-HERZEGOVINA
EU • EUFOR • *Operation Althea* 25

CYPRUS
Army 950 (ELDYK army); ε200 (officers/NCO seconded to Greek-Cypriot National Guard) (total 1,150)
1 mech bde (1 armd bn, 2 mech inf bn, 1 arty bn); 61 M48A5 MOLF MBT; 80 *Leonidas* APC; 12 M114 arty; 6 M110A2 arty

LEBANON
UN • UNIFIL 51; 1 PB

MEDITERRANEAN SEA
NATO • *Operation Active Endeavour* 1 FFGHM

SERBIA
NATO • KFOR • *Joint Enterprise* 152; 1 mech inf coy

FOREIGN FORCES
United States US European Command: 380; 1 naval base at Makri; 1 naval base at Soudha Bay; 1 air base at Iraklion

Hungary HUN

Hungarian Forint f		2011	2012	2013
GDP	f	28.15tr	29.31tr	
	US$	140.3bn	128.8bn	
per capita	US$	14,089	12,934	
Growth	%	1.70	-1.02	
Inflation	%	3.90	5.60	
Def exp [b]	f	277bn		
	US$	1.38bn		
Def bdgt [a]	f	267bn	234bn	238bn
	US$	1.33bn	1.03bn	
FMA (US)	US$	0.998m	0.9m	0.9m
US$1=f		200.67	227.45	

[a] Excludes military pensions
[b] NATO definition

Population	9,958,453

Age	0–14	15–19	20–24	25–29	30–64	65 plus
Male	7.7%	3.0%	3.2%	3.2%	24.2%	6.3%
Female	7.2%	2.8%	3.1%	3.1%	25.4%	10.8%

Capabilities

Since the end of the Cold War, Hungary's armed forces have transitioned from a conscript-based to a professional structure, with a much smaller order of battle but better-equipped and -trained troops. However, with defence expenditure under pressure, budgetary constraints have curtailed procurement plans. Hungary's defence policy provides for deployed operations under NATO and the EU. It has contributed troops to ISAF operations in Afghanistan. The armed forces conduct regular training exercises with bilateral and multinational partners. The country is host to the Stategic Airlift Capability's C-17 unit. It has agreed with Sweden a ten-year extension to its lease of *Gripen* fighter aircraft.

ACTIVE 26,500 (Army 10,300, Air 5,900 Joint 10,300) **Paramilitary 12,000**

RESERVE 44,000 (Army 35,200 Air 8,800)

ORGANISATIONS BY SERVICE

Hungary's armed forces have reorganised into a joint force.

Land Component 10,300 (incl riverine element)

FORCES BY ROLE
SPECIAL FORCES
 1 SF bn
MANOEUVRE
 Mechanised
 2 mech inf bde (total: 4 mech inf, 1 lt inf, 1 mixed bn, 2 log bn)
COMBAT SUPPORT
 1 engr regt
 1 EOD/rvn regt
 1 CBRN bn
 1 sigs regt
COMBAT SERVICE SUPPORT
 1 spt bde (1 log regt)
EQUIPMENT BY TYPE
MBT 30 T-72
RECCE 24 K90 CBRN Recce; PSZH-IV CBRN Recce
AIFV/APC (W) 380 BTR-80/BTR-80A
ARTY 68
 TOWED 152mm 18 D-20
 MOR 82mm 50
AT • MSL • MANPATS 130: 30 9K111 *Fagot* (AT-4 *Spigot*); 100 9K113 *Konkurs* (AT-5 *Spandrel*)
PATROL AND COASTAL COMBATANTS • PBR 2
AEV BAT-2
ARV BMP-1 VPV; T-54/T-55; VT-55A
VLB BLG-60; MTU; TMM

Air Component 5,900

Flying hours 50 hrs/yr

FORCES BY ROLE
FIGHTER/GROUND ATTACK
 1 sqn with *Gripen* C/D
TRANSPORT
 1 sqn with An-26 *Curl*
TRAINING
 1 sqn with Yak-52
ATTACK HELICOPTER
 1 sqn with Mi-24 *Hind*
TRANSPORT HELICOPTER
 1 sqn with Mi-8 *Hip*; Mi-17 *Hip* H
AIR DEFENCE
 1 regt (9 bty with *Mistral*; 3 bty with 2K12 *Kub* (SA-6 *Gainful*))
 1 radar regt
EQUIPMENT BY TYPE
AIRCRAFT 14 combat capable
 FGA 14: 12 *Gripen* C; 2 *Gripen* D

TPT • Light 4 An-26 *Curl*
TRG 8 Yak-52
HELICOPTERS
 ATK 11 3 Mi-24D *Hind* D; 6 Mi-24V *Hind* E; 2 Mi-24P *Hind* F
 MRH 7 Mi-17 *Hip* H
 TPT • Medium 10 Mi-8 *Hip*
AD • SAM 61
 SP 16 2K12 *Kub* (SA-6 *Gainful*)
 MANPAD 45 *Mistral*
 RADAR: 3 RAT-31DL, 6 P-18: 6 SZT-68U; 14 P-37
MSL
 AAM • IR AIM-9 *Sidewinder*; R-73 (AA-11 *Archer*)
 SARH R-27 (AA-10 *Alamo* A); **ARH** AIM-120C AMRAAM
 ASM 250: 20 AGM-65 *Maverick*; 150 3M11 *Falanga* (AT-2 *Swatter*); 80 9K113 *Shturm*-V (AT-6 *Spiral*)

Paramilitary 12,000

Border Guards 12,000 (to reduce)

Ministry of Interior
FORCES BY ROLE
MANOEUVRE
 Other
 1 (Budapest) paramilitary district (7 rapid reaction coy)
 11 (regt/district) paramilitary regt
EQUIPMENT BY TYPE
APC (W) 68 BTR-80

Cyber

There is no dedicated cyber organisation, but IT network management contains INFOSEC and cyber-defence elements. In February 2012, the government adopted a National Security Strategy, noting an intent to prevent and avert cyber attacks. The MoD has also developed a Military Cyber Defence concept.

DEPLOYMENT

Legal provisions for foreign deployment:
Legislation: Fundamental Law (2011)
Decision on deployment of troops abroad: Government decides on cross-border troop movements or employment, in the case of NATO. (Paragraph 2.) For operations not based on NATO or EU decisions, the Fundamental Law gives parliament the prerogative to decide on the employment of Hungarian armed forces or foreign forces in, or from, Hungarian territory.
AFGHANISTAN
NATO • ISAF 555; 1 lt inf coy

BOSNIA-HERZEGOVINA
EU • EUFOR • *Operation Althea* 162; 1 inf coy

CYPRUS
UN • UNFICYP 77; 1 inf pl

DEMOCRATIC REPUBLIC OF THE CONGO
EU • EUSEC RD Congo 2

EGYPT
MFO 42; 1 MP unit

LEBANON
UN • UNIFIL 4

SERBIA
NATO • KFOR 194; 1 inf coy (KTM)

UGANDA
EU • EUTM 4

WESTERN SAHARA
UN • MINURSO 7 obs

Iceland ISL

Icelandic Krona Kr		2011	2012	2013
GDP	Kr	1.63tr	1.74tr	
	US$	14.1bn	13.6bn	
per capita	US$	45,022	43,425	
Growth	%	3.05	2.86	
Inflation	%	4.01	5.64	
Sy Bdgt [a]	Kr	4.02bn	4.41bn	4.64bn
	US$	35m	34m	
US$1=Kr		116.04	129.46	

[a] Iceland has no armed forces. Budget is mainly for coast guard.

Population   313,183

Age	0–14	15–19	20–24	25–29	30–64	65 plus
Male	10.1%	3.7%	3.8%	3.4%	23.0%	5.9%
Female	9.9%	3.6%	3.7%	3.4%	22.5%	7.0%

Capabilities

The country has no armed forces, though there is a coast guard that operates ships, fixed-wing and rotary aircraft. A NATO member, the country is reliant on other Alliance partners for air policing and air defence.

ACTIVE NIL Paramilitary 180

ORGANISATIONS BY SERVICE

Paramilitary

Iceland Coast Guard 180
EQUIPMENT BY TYPE
PATROL AND COASTAL COMBATANTS • PSOH: 2 *Aegir*
PSO 1 *Thor*
LOGISTICS AND SUPPORT • AGS 1 *Baldur*
AIRCRAFT • TPT • **Light** 1 DHC-8-300
HELICOPTERS
   TPT • **Medium** 3 AS332L1 *Super Puma*

FOREIGN FORCES

NATO • Iceland Air Policing: Aircraft and personnel from various NATO members on a rotating basis.

Ireland IRL

Euro €		2011	2012	2013
GDP	€	159bn	161.7bn	
	US$	221.2bn	204.7bn	
per capita	US$	46,844	43,350	
Growth	%	1.43	0.35	
Inflation	%	1.19	1.40	
Def exp [a]	€	692m		
	US$	963m		
Def bdgt [a]	€	725m	679m	688m
	US$	1.3bn	1.13bn	
US$1=€		0.72	0.79	

[a] Excludes military pensions.

Population   4,722,028

Age	0–14	15–19	20–24	25–29	30–64	65 plus
Male	10.9%	3.0%	3.1%	3.8%	23.8%	5.4%
Female	10.4%	2.9%	3.1%	3.9%	23.4%	6.4%

Capabilities

The armed forces' primary task is to 'defend the state against armed aggression'. It also participates in peace-support, crisis-management and humanitarian-relief operations. Military forces are also routinely called upon to conduct EOD operations within Ireland due to paramilitary activity. The army is the largest service, supported by a small air corps and naval service. Ireland's armed forces have been further trimmed as a result of Dublin's economic difficulties, while some procurement programmes are being extended over a longer period to spread costs. The armed forces have been asked to cut 15% (US$146.5 million) from their spending plans from 2011–14 as part of a broader package of government-funding reductions. This has reduced participation in overseas operations.

ACTIVE 8,900 (Army 7,200 Navy 950 Air 750)

RESERVE 4,930 (Army 4,550 Navy 300 Air 80)

ORGANISATIONS BY SERVICE

Army ε7,200
FORCES BY ROLE
SPECIAL FORCES
   1 ranger coy
MANOEUVRE
   Reconnaissance
   1 armd recce sqn
   Mechanised
   1 mech inf coy
   Light
   2 inf bde (1 cav recce sqn, 4 inf bn, 1 arty regt (3 fd arty bty, 1 AD bty), 1 fd engr coy, 1 sigs coy, 1 MP coy, 1 log bn)
COMBAT SUPPORT
   Some EOD teams

COMBAT SERVICE SUPPORT
1 construction engr coy

EQUIPMENT BY TYPE
LT TK 14 *Scorpion*
RECCE 52: 15 *Piranha IIIH*; 18 AML-20; 19 AML-90
APC 94
  APC (W) 67: 65 *Piranha III*; 2 XA-180 *Sisu*
  PPV 27 RG-32M
ARTY 495
  TOWED 24: **105mm** 24 L-118 Light Gun
  MOR 495: **81mm** 400; **120mm** 95
AT
  MSL • MANPATS 57: 36 *Javelin*; 21 *Milan*
  RCL 84mm 444 *Carl Gustav*
AD
  SAM • MANPAD 7 RBS-70
  GUNS • TOWED 40mm 32 L/70 each with 8 *Flycatcher*
MW *Aardvark* Mk 2

Reserves 4,550 reservists (to reduce to 3,800)

FORCES BY ROLE
SPECIAL FORCES
1 SF coy (2 aslt pl, 1 spt pl)
MANOEUVRE
  Reconnaissance
  3 (integrated) cav tp
  Light
  3 (non integrated) inf bde (1 cav recce sqn, 3 inf bn, 1
    fd arty regt (2 fd arty bty), 1 fd engr coy, 1 log bn)
  9 (integrated) inf coy
COMBAT SUPPORT
  3 (integrated) arty bty
  3 AD bty
COMBAT SERVICE SUPPORT
  1 log bn

Navy 950

EQUIPMENT BY TYPE
PATROL AND COASTAL COMBATANTS 8
  PSOH 1 *Eithne*
  PSO 2 *Roisin* with 1 76mm gun
  PCO 5: 3 *Emer*; 2 *Orla* (UK *Peacock*) with 1 76mm gun
LOGISTICS AND SUPPORT 6
  AXS 2
  YFL 3
  YTM 1

Air Corps 750

2 ops wg; 2 spt wg; 1 comms and info sqn
EQUIPMENT BY TYPE
AIRCRAFT
  MP 2 CN-235 MPA
  TPT 8: **Light** 7: 1 BN-2 *Defender* 4000 (police spt); 5
  Cessna FR-172H; 1 Learjet 45 (VIP); **PAX** 1 Gulfstream
  GIV
  TRG 8 PC-9M
HELICOPTERS:
  MRH 6 AW139
  TPT • Light 2 EC135 P2 (incl trg/medevac; 1 non-
  operational)

DEPLOYMENT

Legal provisions for foreign deployment:
Constitution: Codified constitution (1937)
Specific legislation: 'Defence (Amendment) Act' 2006
Decision on deployment of troops abroad: a) By
parliament; b) by government if scenario for deployment
corresponds with conditions laid out in Art.3 of 2006
'Defence (Amendment) Act' which exempts from
parliamentary approval deployments for purposes of
participation in exercises abroad; monitoring, observation,
advisory or reconnaissance missions; and 'humanitarian
operations 'in response to actual or potential disasters or
emergencies.

AFGHANISTAN
NATO • ISAF 6

BOSNIA-HERZEGOVINA
EU • EUFOR • *Operation Althea* 40

CÔTE D'IVOIRE
UN • UNOCI 2 obs

DEMOCRATIC REPUBLIC OF THE CONGO
UN • MONUSCO 3 obs

LEBANON
UN • UNIFIL 354; 1 mech inf bn(-)

MIDDLE EAST
UN • UNTSO 11 obs

SERBIA
NATO • KFOR 12

UGANDA
EU • EUTM 10

WESTERN SAHARA
UN • MINURSO 3 obs

Italy ITA

Euro €		2011	2012	2013
GDP	€	1.58tr	1.56tr	
	US$	2.20tr	1.98tr	
per capita	US$	35,912	32,321	
Growth	%	0.43	-2.29	
Inflation	%	2.90	3.01	
Def exp[b]	€	21.7bn		
	US$	30.3bn		
Def bdgt [a]	€	20.2bn	18.7bn	19.1bn
	US$	28.1bn	23.6bn	
US$1=€		0.72	0.79	

[a] Includes military pensions
[b] NATO definition

Population	61,261,254

Age	0–14	15–19	20–24	25–29	30–64	65 plus
Male	7.1%	2.4%	2.6%	2.8%	24.7%	8.7%
Female	6.8%	2.4%	2.6%	2.8%	25.4%	11.8%

Capabilities

The armed forces' primary role is territorial defence and participation in NATO operations, with the ability for extended deployment as part of a multinational force. The belated arrival of its air-to-air refuelling aircraft will help in this role, which is also supported by the navy's amphibious capability. Italian forces participate in ISAF, though troops are due to start reducing after the end of 2012. Funding pressure continued to be exerted on the defence ministry as the government implemented fiscal-reform packages intended to alleviate debt concerns. The armed forces have been undergoing a process of reform for over a decade involving force reductions and modernised capabilities. Planned defence spending from 2012–14 had already been reduced before an additional package of cuts was announced in August 2011.

ACTIVE 181,450 (Army 105,900 Navy 33,000 Air 42,550) Paramilitary 186,100

Terms of service all professional

RESERVES 18,300 (Army 13,400 Navy 4,900)

ORGANISATIONS BY SERVICE

Space
SATELLITES 6
    COMMUNICATIONS 2 *Sicral*
    IMAGERY 4 *Cosmo* (*Skymed*)

Army 105,900
FORCES BY ROLE
COMMAND
  1 (NRDC-IT) corps HQ (1 sigs bde, 1 spt regt)
SPECIAL FORCES
  1 spec ops regt (4th *Alpini paracadutisti*)
MANOEUVRE
  Mechanised
    1 (*Mantova*) div (1st FOD) (1 (*Ariete*) armd bde (3 tk regt, 2 mech inf regt, 1 arty regt, 1 engr regt, 1 log bn); 1 (*Pozzuolo del Friuli*) cav bde (3 cav regt, 1 amph regt, 1 arty regt); 1 (*Folgore*) AB bde (1 SF regt, 1 SF RSTA regt, 3 para regt, 1 cbt engr regt); 1 (*Friuli*) air mob bde (1 cav regt, 1 air mob regt, 2 avn regt))
    1 (*Acqui*) div (2nd FOD) (1 (*Pinerolo*) mech bde (1 tk regt, 3 mech inf regt, 1 SP arty regt, 1 cbt engr regt); 1 (*Granatieri*) mech bde (1 cav regt, 2 mech inf regt, 1 SP arty regt); 1 (*Garibaldi Bersaglieri*) mech bde (1 cav regt, 1 tk regt, 2 hy mech inf regt, 1 SP arty regt, 1 cbt engr regt); 1 (*Aosta*) mech bde (1 cav regt, 3 mech inf regt, 1 SP arty regt, 1 cbt engr regt); 1 (*Sassari*) lt mech bde (2 mech inf regt, 1 cbt engr regt))
  Mountain
    1 (*Tridentina*) mtn div (1 (*Taurinense*) mtn bde (1 cav regt, 3 mtn inf regt, 1 arty regt, 1 mtn cbt engr regt, 1 spt bn); 1 (*Julia*) mtn bde with (3 mtn inf regt, 1 arty regt, 1 mtn cbt engr regt, 1 spt bn); 1 mtn inf trg regt))
  Aviation
    1 avn bde (3 avn regt, 1 avn sqn)

COMBAT SUPPORT
  1 arty comd (1 hy arty regt, 2 arty regt, 1 psyops regt, 1 NBC regt)
  1 AD comd (2 (HAWK) AD regt, 2 (SHORAD) AD regt)
  1 engr comd (3 engr regt, 1 CIMIC regt)
  1 EW/sigs comd (1 EW/ISTAR bde (1 ISTAR bn, 1 EW bn, 1 (HUMINT) int bn); 1 sigs bde with (6 sigs bn))
COMBAT SERVICE SUPPORT
  1 log comd (4 (manoeuvre) log regt, 4 tpt regt)
  1 spt regt
EQUIPMENT BY TYPE
MBT 320: 200 C1 *Ariete*; 120 *Leopard* 1A5
RECCE 314: 300 B-1 *Centauro*; 14 VAB-RECO NBC
AIFV 308: 200 VCC-80 *Dardo*; 108 VBM 8×8 *Freccia*
APC 2,974
  APC (T) 2,404: 237 Bv-206; 396 M113 (incl variants); 1,771 VCC-1 *Camillino*/VCC-2
  APC (W) 560 *Puma*
  PPV 10: 4 *Buffalo*; 6 *Cougar*
AAV 16: 14 AAVP-7; 1 AAVC-7; 1 AAVR-7
ARTY 953
  SP 155mm 186: 124 M109L; 62 PzH 2000
  TOWED 155mm 164 FH-70
  MRL 227mm 22 MLRS
  MOR 581: **81mm** 253; **120mm** 328: 183 Brandt; 145 RT-F1
AT
  MSL • MANPATS 1,032: 32 *Spike*; 1,000 *Milan*
  RCL 80mm 482 *Folgore*
  RL 110mm 2,000 Pzf 3 *Panzerfaust* 3
AIRCRAFT • TPT • Light 6: 3 Do-228 (ACTL-1); 3 P-180 *Avanti*
HELICOPTERS
  ATK 59: 9 AW129A *Mangusta*; 50 AW129CBT *Mangusta*
  MRH 18 Bell 412 (AB-412) *Twin Huey*
  TPT 138: **Heavy** 18 CH-47C *Chinook*; **Medium** 17 NH90 TTH; **Light** 103: 18 AW109; 57 Bell 205 (AB-205); 12 Bell 206 *Jet Ranger* (AB-206); 18 Bell 212 (AB-212)
AD
  SAM 108
    TOWED 44: 12 MIM-23 HAWK; 32 *Skyguard/Aspide*
    MANPAD 64 FIM-92A *Stinger*
  GUNS • SP 25mm 64 SIDAM
AEV 40 *Leopard* 1; M113
ARV 137 *Leopard* 1
VLB 64 *Biber*
MW 2 *Miniflail*

Navy 33,000
EQUIPMENT BY TYPE
SUBMARINES • TACTICAL • SSK 6:
  4 *Pelosi* (imp *Sauro*, 3rd and 4th series) with 6 single 533mm TT with Type-A-184 HWT
  2 *Salvatore Todaro* (Type-U212A) with 6 single 533mm TT with Type-A-184 HWT/DM2A4 HWT (2 additional vessels under construction)
PRINCIPAL SURFACE COMBATANTS 18
  AIRCRAFT CARRIERS • CVS 2:
    1 *G. Garibaldi* with 2 octuple *Albatros* lnchr with *Aspide* SAM, 2 triple 324mm ASTT with Mk46 LWT,

(capacity mixed air group of either 12–18 AV-8B *Harrier* II; 17 SH-3D *Sea King* or AW101 *Merlin*)

1 *Cavour* with 1 32-cell VLS with *Aster* 15 SAM, 2 76mm guns, (capacity mixed air group of 18–20 AV-8B *Harrier* II; 12 AW101 *Merlin*)

DESTROYERS • DDGHM 4:

2 *Andrea Doria* with 2 quad lnchr with *Otomat* Mk2A AShM, 1 48-cell VLS with *Aster* 15/*Aster* 30 SAM, 2 twin 324mm ASTT with MU-90 LWT, 3 76mm gun, (capacity 1 AW101 *Merlin*/NH90 hel)

2 *Luigi Durand de la Penne* (ex-*Animoso*) with 2 quad lnchr with *Milas* AS/*Otomat* Mk 2A AShM, 1 Mk13 GMLS with SM-1MR SAM, 1 octuple *Albatros* lnchr with *Aspide* SAM, 2 triple 324mm ASTT with Mk46 LWT, 1 127mm gun, 1 76mm gun (capacity 1 Bell 212 (AB-212) hel)

FRIGATES • FFGHM 12:

4 *Artigliere* with 8 single lnchr with *Otomat* Mk 2 AShM, 1 octuple *Albatros* lnchr with *Aspide* SAM, 1 127mm gun (capacity 1 Bell 212 (AB-212) hel)

8 *Maestrale* with 4 single lnchr with *Otomat* Mk2 AShM, 1 octuple *Albatros* lnchr with *Aspide* SAM, 2 triple 324mm ASTT with Mk46 LWT, 1 127mm gun (capacity 2 Bell 212 (AB-212) hel)

PATROL AND COASTAL COMBATANTS 22

CORVETTES 8

FSM 4 *Minerva* with 1 octuple *Albatros* lnchr with *Aspide* SAM, 1 76mm gun

FS 4 *Minerva* with 1 76mm gun

PSOH 6:

4 *Comandante Cigala Fuligosi* with 1 76mm gun, (capacity 1 Bell 212 (AB-212)/NH90 hel)

2 *Comandante Cigala Fuligosi* (capacity 1 Bell 212 (AB-212)/NH-90 hel)

PCO 1 *Cassiopea* with 1 76mm gun (capacity 1 Bell 212 (AB-212) hel)

PB 4 *Esploratore*

MINE WARFARE • MINE COUNTERMEASURES 12

MHO 12: 8 *Gaeta*; 4 *Lerici*

AMPHIBIOUS

PRINCIPAL AMPHIBIOUS SHIPS • LPD 3:

2 *San Giorgio* with 1 76mm gun (capacity 3-5 AW101/NH90/SH3-D/Bell 212; 1 CH-47 *Chinook* tpt hel; 3 LCM 2 LCVP; 30 trucks; 36 APC (T); 350 troops)

1 *San Giusto* with 1 76mm gun (capacity 4 AW101 *Merlin*; 1 CH-47 *Chinook* tpt hel; 3 LCM 2 LCVP; 30 trucks; 36 APC (T); 350 troops)

LANDING CRAFT 30: 17 **LCVP**; 13 **LCM**

LOGISTICS AND SUPPORT 130

ABU 5 *Ponza*

AFD 19

AGE 2: 1 *Vincenzo Martellota*; 1 *Raffaele Rosseti*

AGI 1 *Elettra*

AGOR 1 *Leonardo* (coastal)

AGS 3: 1 *Ammiraglio Magnaghi*; 2 *Aretusa* (coastal)

AKSL 6 *Gorgona*

AORH 3: 1 *Etna* (capacity 1 AW101/NH90 hel); 2 *Stromboli* (capacity 1 AW101/NH90 hel)

AOT 7 *Depoli*

ARS 1 *Anteo*

ATS 7 *Prometeo*

AT 9 (coastal)

AWT 7: 1 *Bormida*; 2 *Simeto*; 4 *Panarea*

AXL 3 *Aragosta*

AXS 8: 1 *Amerigo Vespucci*; 1 *Palinuro*; 1 *Italia*; 5 *Caroly*

YDT 2 *Pedretti*

YFT 1 *Aragosta*

YFU 2 *Men 215*

YPT 2 *Men 212*

YTB 9 *Porto*

YTM 32

Naval Aviation 2,200

FORCES BY ROLE

FIGHTER/GROUND ATTACK

1 sqn with AV-8B *Harrier* II; TAV-8B *Harrier*

ANTI-SUBMARINE WARFARE/TRANSPORT

5 sqn with AW101 ASW *Merlin*; Bell 212 ASW (AB-212AS); Bell 212 (AB-212); NH90 NFH

MARITIME PATROL

1 flt with P-180

AIRBORNE EARLY WANRING & CONTROL

1 flt with AW101 *Merlin* AEW

EQUIPMENT BY TYPE

AIRCRAFT 16 combat capable

FGA 16: 14 AV-8B *Harrier* II; 2 TAV-8B *Harrier*

MP 3 P-180

HELICOPTERS

ASW 34: 10 AW101 ASW *Merlin*; 14 Bell 212 ASW; 10 NH90 NFH

AEW 4 AW101 *Merlin* AEW

TPT 14: **Medium** 8 AW101 *Merlin* **Light** 6 Bell 212 (AB-212)

MSL

AAM • IR AIM-9L *Sidewinder*; **ARH** AIM-120 AMRAAM

ASM AGM-65 *Maverick*

AShM *Marte* Mk 2/S

Marines 2,000

FORCES BY ROLE

MANOEUVRE

Amphibious

1 mne regt (1 SF coy, 1 aslt bn, 1 log bn)

1 landing craft gp

COMBAT SERVICE SUPPORT

1 log regt (1 log bn)

EQUIPMENT BY TYPE

APC (T) 40 VCC-2

AAV 18 AAV-7

ARTY • MOR 12: **81mm** 8 Brandt; **120mm** 4 Brandt

AT • MSL • MANPATS 6 *Milan*

AD • SAM • MANPAD FIM-92A *Stinger*

ARV 1 AAV7RAI

Air Force 42,550

4 Commands – Air Sqn Cmd (air defence, attack, recce, mobility, support, force protection, EW ops); Training; Logistics; Operations (national and international exercises)

FORCES BY ROLE

FIGHTER

4 sqn with Eurofighter *Typhoon*

FIGHTER/GROUND ATTACK
  2 sqn with AMX *Ghibli*
  1 (SEAD/EW) sqn with *Tornado* ECR
  2 sqn with *Tornado* IDS
FIGHTER/GROUND ATTACK/ISR
  1 sqn with AMX *Ghibli*
MARITIME PATROL
  1 sqn (opcon Navy) with BR1150 *Atlantic*
TANKER/TRANSPORT
  1 sqn with KC-767A; G-222/G-222VS (EW)
COMBAT SEARCH & RESCUE/SEARCH & RESCUE
  3 sqn with HH-3F *Pelican*; AW139 (HH-139A)
SEARCH & RESCUE
  1 det with Bell 212 (AB-212)
TRANSPORT
  2 (VIP) sqn with A319CJ; AW139; *Falcon* 50; *Falcon* 900 *Easy*; *Falcon* 900EX; SH-3D *Sea King*
  2 sqn with C-130J/C-130J-30/KC-130J *Hercules*
  1 sqn with C-27J *Spartan*
  1 (calibration) sqn with P-166-DL3; P-180 *Avanti*
TRAINING
  1 sqn with Eurofighter *Typhoon*
  1 sqn with MB-339PAN (aerobatic team)
  1 sqn with MD-500D/E (NH-500D/E)
  1 sqn with Bell 212 (AB-212)
  1 sqn with HH-3F *Pelican*
  1 sqn with *Tornado*
  1 sqn with AMX-T *Ghibli*
  1 sqn with MB-339A
  1 sqn with MB-339CD*
  1 sqn with SF-260EA
TRANSPORT HELICOPTER
  1 sqn with AB-212 SAR ICO
ISR UAV
  1 sqn with MQ-9 *Reaper*; RQ-1B *Predator*
AIR DEFENCE
  6 bty with *Spada* towed SAM
EQUIPMENT BY TYPE
AIRCRAFT 234 combat capable
  FTR 64 Eurofighter *Typhoon*
  FGA 127: 55 *Tornado* IDS; 64 AMX *Ghibli*; 8 AMX-T *Ghibli*
  EW/FGA 15 *Tornado* ECR*
  ASW 6 BR1150 *Atlantic*
  EW 1 G-222VS
  TKR/TPT 6: 4 KC-767A; 2 KC-130J *Hercules*
  TPT 74: **Medium** 33: 9 C-130J *Hercules*; 10 C-130J-30 *Hercules*; 12 C-27J *Spartan*; 2 G-222; **Light** 30: 5 P-166-DL3; 15 P-180 *Avanti*; 10 S-208 (liaison) **PAX** 10: 3 A319CJ; 2 *Falcon* 50 (VIP); 2 *Falcon* 900 *Easy*; 3 *Falcon* 900EX (VIP)
  TRG 103: 3 M-346; 21 MB-339A; 28 MB-339CD*; 21 MB-339PAN (aerobatics); 30 SF-260EA
HELICOPTERS
  MRH 58: 10 AW139 (HH-139A/VH-139A) (Delivery by end 2012); 2 MD-500D (NH-500D); 46 MD-500E (NH-500E)
  SAR 20 HH-3F *Pelican*;
  TPT 31: **Light** 29 Bell 212 (AB-212)/AB-212 SAR ICO (of which 26 for SAR); **Medium** 2 SH-3D *Sea King* (liaison/VIP)
UAV • ISR • Heavy 9: 4 MQ-9 *Reaper* (2 more to be delivered); 5 RQ-1B *Predator*

AD • SAM
  TOWED *Spada*
MSL
  AAM • IR AIM-9L *Sidewinder*; **IIR** IRIS-T; **ARH** AIM-120 AMRAAM
  ARM AGM-88 HARM
  LACM SCALP EG/*Storm Shadow*
BOMBS
  Laser-guided/GPS: Enhanced *Paveway* II; Enhanced *Paveway* III

Joint Special Forces Command (COFS)

Army
FORCES BY ROLE
SPECIAL FORCES
  1 SF regt (9th *Assalto paracaduisti*)

Navy (COMSUBIN)
FORCES BY ROLE
SPECIAL FORCES
  1 SF gp (GOI)
  1 diving gp (GOS)

Air Force
FORCES BY ROLE
SPECIAL FORCES
  1 sqn (17th *Stormo Incursori*)

Paramilitary

Carabinieri
FORCES BY ROLE
SPECIAL FORCES
  1 spec ops gp (GIS)

Paramilitary 186,100

Carabinieri 106,800
The Carabinieri are organisationally under the MoD. They are a separate service in the Italian Armed Forces as well as a police force with judicial competence.

Mobile and Specialised Branch
FORCES BY ROLE
MANOEUVRE
  Aviation
  1 hel gp
  Other
  1 (mobile) paramilitary div (1 bde (1st) with (1 horsed cav regt, 11 mobile bn); 1 bde (2nd) with (1 (1st) AB regt, 2 (7th & 13th) mobile regt))
EQUIPMENT BY TYPE
APC 37
  APC (T) 25: 10 VCC-1 *Camillino*; 15 VCC-2
  APC (W) 12 *Puma*
AIRCRAFT • TPT • Light: 1 P-180 *Avanti*
HELICOPTERS
  MRH 24 Bell 412 (AB-412)
  TPT • Light 19 AW109

Customs 68,100

(Servizio Navale Guardia Di Finanza)
PATROL AND COASTAL COMBATANTS 213
  PCF 1 *Antonio Zara*
  PBF 181: 19 *Bigliani*; 24 *Corrubia*; 9 *Mazzei*; 35 V-600;
  62 V-2000; 32 V-5000/V-6000
  PB 31: 23 *Buratti*; 8 *Meatini*

Coast Guard 11,200

(Guardia Costiera – Capitanerie Di Porto)
PATROL AND COASTAL COMBATANTS 226
  PCO 2 CP 920
  PCC 17: 1 *Saettia*; 4 200-class; 12 400-class
  PB 207: 14 300-class; 75 500-class; 12 600-class; 12
  700-class; 94 800-class
  LOGISTICS AND SUPPORT • AX 1 (ex-US *Bannock*)
    AIRCRAFT MP 4: 3 ATR-42 MP *Surveyor*, 1 P-180GC
  HELICOPTERS • MRH 13: 4 AW139; 9 Bell 412SP (AB-412SP *Griffin*)

Cyber

Overall responsibility for cyber security rests with the presidency of the Council of Ministers and, more specifically, the Inter-Ministerial Situation and Planning Group which includes, among others, representatives from the defence, interior and foreign affairs ministries. A Joint Integrated Concept on Computer Network Operations was approved in 2009. In 2011, an Inter-Forces Committee on Cyberspace (CIAC) was established to advise the chief of defence staff. In January 2012, an Inter-Forces Policy Directive was approved to provide a vision for both operational management (under the C4 Defence Command, the Inter-Forces Intelligence Centre and individual armed forces) and strategic direction (under the chief of defence staff (CDS) and CIAC). CDS established the Computer and Emergency Response Team (CERT-Defence) to promote the security of IT networks and share knowledge on cyber threats and cyber defence including through the collaboration with national and international CERTs.

DEPLOYMENT

Legal provisions for foreign deployment:
Constitution: Codified constitution (1949)
Decision on deployment of troops abroad: By the government upon approval by the parliament.

AFGHANISTAN

NATO • ISAF 4,000; 1 mtn inf bde HQ; 3 mtn inf regt;
AIFV *Dardo*; A-129 *Mangusta*; CH-47; NH90; *Tornado*;
C-130
UN • UNAMA 1 obs

ALBANIA

Delegazione Italiana Esperti (DIE) 18

BOSNIA-HERZEGOVINA

EU • EUFOR • *Operation Althea* 3

EGYPT

MFO 84; 4 coastal patrol unit

GULF OF ADEN & INDIAN OCEAN

EU • *Operation Atalanta* 1 LPD

INDIA/PAKISTAN

UN • UNMOGIP 3 obs

LEBANON

UN • UNIFIL 1,150; 1 armd bde HQ; 1 armd recce bn; 1
hel sqn; 1 sigs coy; 1 CIMIC coy(-)

MALTA

Air Force 22; 2 Bell 212 (AB-212)

MEDITERRANEAN SEA

NATO • SNMG 2: 1 FFGHM
NATO • SNMCMG 2: 1 MHO

MIDDLE EAST

UN • UNTSO 7 obs

SERBIA

NATO • KFOR 869; 1 AD BG HQ; 1 engr unit; 1 hel unit; 1
sigs unit; 1 CSS unit; 1 Carabinieri regt

SOUTH SUDAN

UN • UNMISS 1

UGANDA

EU • EUTM 11

WESTERN SAHARA

UN • MINURSO 5 obs

FOREIGN FORCES

United States US European Command: 7,800
  Army 200; (1 AB IBCT currently deployed to AFG);
  some M119; some M198
  Navy 3,300; 1 HQ (US Navy Europe (USNAVEUR)) at
  Naples; 1 HQ (6th Fleet) at Gaeta; 1 MP Sqn with 9 P-3C
  Orion at Sigonella
  USAF 4,200; 1 ftr wg with (2 ftr sqn with 21 F-16C/D
  Fighting Falcon) at Aviano
  USMC 100

Latvia LVA

Latvian Lat L		2011	2012	2013
GDP	L	14.16bn	15.09bn	
	US$	28.3bn	27.2bn	
per capita	US$	12,913	12,411	
Growth	%	5.47	4.45	
Inflation	%	4.22	2.40	
Def exp [b]	L	145m		
	US$	289m		
Def bdgt [a]	L	149m	143m	
	US$	297m	257m	
FMA (US)	US$	2.794m	2.25m	2.25m
US$1=L		0.50	0.56	

[a] Includes military pensions
[b] NATO definition

Population   2,191,580

Age	0–14	15–19	20–24	25–29	30–64	65 plus
Male	7.0%	2.5%	4.0%	4.1%	23.2%	5.5%
Female	6.7%	2.4%	3.8%	4.1%	25.2%	11.4%

Capabilities

Latvia's small army is essentially a light infantry force, supported by a small number of utility aircraft. The navy operates a handful of patrol and mine-countermeasures vessels, and there are plans for multi-purpose patrol vessels. Other procurement plans include air surveillance radars and SHORAD. Latvian forces completed structural reforms in 2009–10, and now plan to improve education, supply and maintenance, as well as to develop international cooperation. Budget plans for 2013 and 2014, however, could be affected by the economic downturn. Latvia participates in NATO and EU missions, and the country has deployed personnel with ISAF. Forces train regularly with NATO partners and in other multilateral exercises. NATO provides substantial assurance of the country's security from external threat, and air policing is provided by NATO states on a rotational basis, although Latvia has a long-term ambition to address this requirement in concert with Estonia and Lithuania.

ACTIVE 5,350 (Army 1,400 Navy 550 Air 300 Joint Staff 2,500 National Guard 600)

RESERVE 7,800 (National Guard 7,800)

ORGANISATIONS BY SERVICE

Joint 2,500
FORCES BY ROLE
SPECIAL FORCES
  1 SF unit
COMBAT SUPPORT
  1 MP bn

Army 1,400
FORCES BY ROLE
MANOEUVRE
  Light
  1 inf bde (2 inf bn, 1 cbt spt bn HQ, 1 CSS bn HQ)

National Guard 600; 7,800 part-time (8,400 in total)
FORCES BY ROLE
MANOEUVRE
  Light
  11 inf bn
COMBAT SUPPORT
  1 arty bn
  1 AD bn
  1 engr bn
  1 NBC bn
COMBAT SERVICE SUPPORT
  3 spt bn
EQUIPMENT BY TYPE
MBT 3 T-55 (trg)
APC • PPV 8 Cougar (on loan from US)
ARTY 56
  TOWED 100mm 26 K-53
  MOR 54: 81mm 24 L16; 120mm 30 M120
AT
  MANPATS 12 Spike-LR
  GUNS 90mm 132
AD
  SAM • MANPAD 27 RBS-70
  GUNS • TOWED 40mm 22 L/70

Navy 550 (incl Coast Guard)
1 Naval HQ commands a Naval Forces Flotilla separated into two squadrons: an MCM squadron and a Patrol Boat squadron. LVA, EST and LTU have set up a joint Naval unit* BALTRON with bases at Liepaja, Riga, Ventspils (LVA), Tallinn (EST), Klaipeda (LTU). *Each nation contributes 1–2 MCMVs

EQUIPMENT BY TYPE
PATROL AND COASTAL COMBATANTS 6
  PB 6: 3 Storm (NOR) with 1 76mm gun; 3 Skrunda (GER Swath) (2 more vessels in build)
MINE WARFARE • MINE COUNTERMEASURES 6
  MHO 5 Imanta (NLD Alkmaar/Tripartite)
  MCCS 1 Vidar (NOR)
LOGISTICS AND SUPPORT 2
  AXL 1 Varonis (C3 and support ship, ex-Buyskes, NLD)

Coast Guard
Under command of the Latvian Naval Forces.
PATROL AND COASTAL COMBATANTS
PB 6: 1 Astra; 5 KBV 236 (SWE)

Air Force 300
Main tasks are air space control and defence, maritime and land SAR and air transportation.
FORCES BY ROLE
AIR DEFENCE
  1 AD bn
  1 radar sqn (radar/air ctrl)

AIRCRAFT • TPT • Light 4 An-2 *Colt*
HELICOPTERS
  MRH 4 Mi-17 *Hip* H
  TPT • Light 2 PZL Mi-2 *Hoplite*

Paramilitary

State Border Guard

PATROL AND COASTAL COMBATANTS
PB 3: 1 *Valpas* (FIN); 1 *Lokki* (FIN); 1 *Baltic Patrol* 24

DEPLOYMENT

Legal provisions for foreign deployment:
Constitution: Codified constitution (1922)
Specific legislation: 'Law on Participation of the National Armed Forces of Latvia in International Operations' (1995) (Annex of 21 Jan 2009 allows Latvian armed forces to take part in quick response units formed by NATO/EU)
Decision on deployment of troops abroad: a) By parliament (Section 5 I of the 1995 'Law on Participation', in combination with Art. 73 of constitution); b) by cabinet, for rescue or humanitarian operations (Section 5 II of the 1995 law) or military exercises in non-NATO states (Section 9 of the 1995 law); c) by defence minister for rescue and humanitarian aid operations in NATO/EU states. Latvian units can be transferred under the control of an international organisation or another country to conduct international operations for a limited time frame only in compliance with and under conditions defined by a Parliamentary decree.

Afghanistan NATO • ISAF 40

Lithuania LTU

Lithuanian Litas L		2011	2012	2013
GDP	L	106bn	112.3bn	
	US$	42.7bn	41.2bn	
per capita	US$	12,111	11,685	
Growth	%	5.87	2.74	
Inflation	%	4.12	3.15	
Def exp [b]	L	872m		
	US$	351m		
Def bdgt [a]	L	874m	870m	1.12bn
	US$	352m	319m	
FMA (US)	US$	2.994m	2.55m	2.55m
US$1=L		2.48	2.73	

[a] Includes military pensions
[b] NATO definition

Population 3,525,761

Age	0–14	15–19	20–24	25–29	30–64	65 plus
Male	7.0%	3.0%	3.9%	4.0%	23.4%	5.7%
Female	6.6%	2.9%	3.7%	3.9%	24.9%	10.9%

Capabilities

Like its Baltic neighbours Estonia and Latvia, Lithuania is a NATO member with small armed forces. The army is by far the largest of the three, supported by smaller air and naval arms. Reform and re-equipment programmes, intended to provide deployable land forces drawn from a motorised infantry brigade, are underway, but continue to be slowed by funding constraints, which have also restricted training. Discussions continued during the first half of 2012 on the formation of the Lithuanian–Polish–Ukrainian trilateral army brigade. This was first proposed in 2009 and was intended to be operational during 2013. The air force provides a light transport capability while the naval focus is on mine countermeasures. Lithuania contributes troops to ISAF.

ACTIVE 11,800 (Army 7,350 Navy 650 Air 1,100 Joint 2,700) **Paramilitary 11,550**
Terms of service 12 months.

RESERVE 6,700 (Army 6,700)

ORGANISATIONS BY SERVICE

Army 3,200; 4,150 active reserves (total 7,350)
FORCES BY ROLE
MANOEUVRE
  Mechanised
  1 mech bde (3 mech inf bn, 1 arty bn)
  Light
  3 mot inf bn
COMBAT SUPPORT
  1 engr bn
COMBAT SERVICE SUPPORT
  1 trg regt
EQUIPMENT BY TYPE
APC (T) 128 M113A1
ARTY 83
  TOWED 105mm 18 M101
  MOR 120mm 65: 16 2B11; 9 M/41D; 40 M113 with Tampella
AT • MSL
  SP 10 M1025A2 HMMWV with *Javelin*
  MANPATS *Javelin*
RCL 84mm *Carl Gustav*
AD • SAM • MANPAD *Stinger*
AEV 10 MT-LB
ARV 4 M113

Reserves

National Defence Voluntary Forces 4,150 active reservists
FORCES BY ROLE
MANOEUVRE
  Other
  6 (territorial) def unit

Navy 650
LVA, EST and LTU established a joint naval unit BALTRON with bases at Liepaja, Riga, Ventpils (LVA), Tallinn (EST), Klaipeda (LTU), HQ at Tallinn
EQUIPMENT BY TYPE
PATROL AND COASTAL COMBATANTS 4

PCC 3 *Standard Flex 300* (DNK *Flyvefisken*) with 1 76mm
    gun
PB 1 *Storm* (NOR)
MINE WARFARE • MINE COUNTERMEASURES 5:
    MHC 4: 2 *Sūduvis* (GER *Lindau*); 2 *Skulvis* (UK *Hunt*)
    MCCS 1 *Vidar* (NOR)
LOGISTICS AND SUPPORT 4
    AAR 1 *Sakiai*
    YAG 1 *Lokys* (DNK)
    YGS 1
    YTL 1 (SWE)

Air Force 1,100

Flying hours   120 hrs/year

FORCES BY ROLE
AIR DEFENCE
    1 AD bn
EQUIPMENT BY TYPE
AIRCRAFT
    TPT 5: **Medium** 3 C-27J *Spartan*; **Light** 2 L-410 *Turbolet*
    TRG 2 L-39ZA *Albatros*
HELICOPTERS • TPT • Medium 9 Mi-8 *Hip* (tpt/SAR)
AD • SAM • MANPAD FIM-92A *Stinger*; RBS-70

Special Operation Force

FORCES BY ROLE
SPECIAL FORCES
    1 SF gp (1 CT unit; 1 Jaeger bn, 1 cbt diver unit)

Joint Logistics Support Command 1,300

FORCES BY ROLE
COMBAT SERVICE SUPPORT
    1 log bn

Joint Training and Doctrine Command (TRADOC) 800

FORCES BY ROLE
COMBAT SERVICE SUPPORT
    1 trg regt

Other Units 600

FORCES BY ROLE
COMBAT SUPPORT
    1 MP bn

Paramilitary 11,550

Riflemen Union 7,550

State Border Guard Service 4,000
Ministry of Internal Affairs

Coast Guard 530
PATROL AND COASTAL COMBATANTS • PB 3: 1
Lokki (FIN); 1 KBV 041 (SWE); 1 KBV 101 (SWE)
AMPHIBIOUS • LANDING CRAFT • UCAC 2
Christina (*Griffon* 2000)

Cyber

A National Electronic Information Security (cyber-security) Strategy was approved by the government in 2011. Earlier, a Cyber Security Strategy for National Defence was adopted in 2009, and is currently being implemented. To help this process, the MoD established a cyber-security division under its Communication and Information System Service the same year. Lithuania is a sponsor nation of the NATO Cooperative Cyber Defence Centre of Excellence (CCD COE) in Estonia. In 2010, Lithuania signed an MOU with NATO on cooperation in cyber defence.

DEPLOYMENT

Legal provisions for foreign deployment:
Constitution: Codified constitution (1992)
Decision on deployment of troops abroad: By Parliament (Art. 67, 138, 142) According to legislation, the defence minister has the authority to establish the exact amount or size of contingent to be deployed, and the duration of the deployment, not exceeding the limits set out by the Parliament.

AFGHANISTAN
NATO • ISAF 221

FOREIGN FORCES

Czech Republic NATO Baltic Air Policing 4 *Gripen* C

Luxembourg LUX

Euro €		2011	2012	2013
GDP	€	42.8bn	43.7bn	
	US$	59.6bn	55.3bn	
per capita	US$	117,075	108,629	
Growth	%	1.56	0.17	
Inflation	%	3.73	2.47	
Def exp [a]	€	201m		
	US$	280m		
Def bdgt	€	201m	204m	
	US$	279m	258m	
US$1=€		0.72	0.79	

[a] NATO definition

Population   509,074
Foreign citizens: ε124,000

Age	0–14	15–19	20–24	25–29	30–64	65 plus
Male	9.3%	3.2%	3.2%	3.2%	24.0%	6.3%
Female	8.7%	3.1%	3.1%	3.2%	23.9%	8.8%

Capabilities

Luxembourg maintains a small army, with no air or naval capacity. In 2011, the government funded a private company to operate two Fairchild SW3A *Merlin* maritime patrol aircraft out of the Seychelles in support of EU NAV-FOR counter-piracy missions. Luxembourg is also part of the SALIS consortium to meet shortfalls in NATO airlift capacities.

ACTIVE 900 (Army 900) **Paramilitary 610**

ORGANISATIONS BY SERVICE

Army 900

FORCES BY ROLE
MANOEUVRE
  Reconnaissance
  2 recce coy (1 to Eurocorps/BEL div, 1 to NATO pool of
    deployable forces)
  Light
  1 lt inf bn
EQUIPMENT BY TYPE
APC • PPV 48 *Dingo* II
ARTY • MOR 81mm 6
AT • MSL• MANPATS 6 TOW

Paramilitary 610

  Gendarmerie 610

DEPLOYMENT

Legal provisions for foreign deployment:
Constitution: Codified constitution (1868)
Specific legislation: 'Loi du 27 juillet 1992 relatif à la
participation du Grand-Duché de Luxembourg à des
opérations pour le maintien de la paix (OMP) dans le cadre
d'organisations internationales'.
Decision on deployment of troops abroad: By government after formal consultation of relevant parliamentary
committees and the Council of State (Art. 1–2 of the 1992
law).

AFGHANISTAN
NATO • ISAF 11

BOSNIA-HERZEGOVINA
EU • EUFOR • *Operation Althea* 1

DEMOCRATIC REPUBLIC OF THE CONGO
EU • EUSEC RD Congo 1

LEBANON
UN • UNIFIL 3

SERBIA
NATO • KFOR 22

Macedonia, Former Yugoslav Republic FYROM

Macedonian Denar d		2011	2012	2013
GDP	d	463.4bn	476.9bn	
	US$	10.6bn	10.2bn	
per capita	US$	5,090	4,898	
Growth	%	3.11	0.96	
Inflation	%	3.90	2.00	
Def bdgt	d	5.67bn	6.18bn	
	US$	130m	132m	
FMA (US)	US$	3.992m	3.6m	3.6m
US$1=d		43.54	46.77	

Population   2,082,370

Age	0–14	15–19	20–24	25–29	30–64	65 plus
Male	9.4%	3.7%	3.8%	4.0%	23.9%	5.1%
Female	8.8%	3.4%	3.6%	3.8%	23.8%	6.7%

Capabilities

Ambitious reform plans spelled out in the 2003 Defence
Concept, and reiterated in the 2005 Defence White Paper,
have so far only partly been realised, though the armed
forces have been reorganised. The services, as of 2006,
moved from a conscript-based to a professional structure.
The 2003 Defence Concept calls for armed forces to support territorial integrity, regional stability, peace-support
missions and deployed operations. The country continues to aspire to NATO membership, having joined the
NATO Membership Action Plan in 1999. The impasse with
Greece over the state's name is one element that hinders
full NATO status. While it deploys forces to ISAF in Afghanistan, the armed forces have a small air arm consisting mainly of transport and armed support helicopters,
but have no organic fixed-wing airlift. Although forces deployed to ISAF and the EU in Bosnia are mission-capable,
only a small proportion of the remaining forces are likely
operationally ready.

ACTIVE 8,000 (Joint 8,000)

RESERVE 4,850

ORGANISATIONS BY SERVICE

Joint Operational Command 8,000

Army
FORCES BY ROLE
COMMAND
  2 corps HQ (cadre)
SPECIAL FORCES
  1 (Special Purpose) SF unit (1 SF bn; 1 Ranger bn)
MANOEUVRE
  Armoured
  1 tk bn
  Mechanised
  2 mech inf bde (with 1 engr coy each)

COMBAT SUPPORT
1 (mixed) arty regt
1 AD coy
1 engr bn
1 MP bn
1 NBC coy
1 sigs bn

Logistic Support Command

FORCES BY ROLE
COMBAT SUPPORT
1 engr bn (1 active coy)
COMBAT SERVICE SUPPORT
3 log bn

Reserves

FORCES BY ROLE
MANOEUVRE
  Light
  1 inf bde
EQUIPMENT BY TYPE
MBT 31 T-72A
RECCE 51: 10 BRDM-2; 41 M1114 HMMWV
AIFV 11: 10 BMP-2; 1 BMP-2K
APC 200
  APC (T) 47: 9 *Leonidas*; 28 M113A; 10 MT-LB
  APC (W) 153: 57 BTR-70; 12 BTR-80; 84 TM-170
  Hermelin
ARTY 126
  TOWED 70: **105mm** 14 M-56; **122mm** 56 M-30 M-1938
  MRL 17: **122mm** 6 BM-21; **128mm** 11
  MOR 39: **120mm** 39
AT • MSL • MANPATS 12 *Milan*
RCL 57mm; **82mm** M60A
AD
  SAM 8 9K35 *Strela*-10 (SA-13 *Gopher*)
  MANPAD 5 9K310 *Igla*-1 (SA-16 *Gimlet*)
  Guns 40mm 36 L20

Marine Wing

PATROL AND COASTAL COMBATANTS 7:
  PCC 1 *Matsilo*
  PB 6
AMPHIBIOUS • LC • LCM 1 *EDIC*
LOGISTICS AND SUPPORT 4:
  YTB 1 *Trozona*
  YTM 3

Air Wing

Air Wg is directly under Joint Operational Cmd
FORCES BY ROLE
TRANSPORT
  1 (VIP) sqn with An-2 *Colt*
TRAINING
  1 sqn with Bell 205 (UH-1H *Iroquois*)
  1 sqn with Z-242
ATTACK HELICOPTER
  1 sqn with Mi-24K *Hind* G2; Mi-24V *Hind* E
TRANSPORT HELICOPTER
  1 sqn with Mi-8MTV *Hip*; Mi-17 *Hip* H

EQUIPMENT BY TYPE
AIRCRAFT
  TPT • **Light** 1 An-2 *Colt*
  TRG 5 Z-242
HELICOPTERS
  ATK 4 Mi-24V *Hind* E (10: 2 Mi-24K *Hind* G2; 8 Mi-24V *Hind* E in store)
  MRH 6: 4 Mi-8MTV *Hip*; 2 Mi-17 *Hip* H
  TPT • **Light** 2 Bell 205 (UH-1H *Iroquois*)

Paramilitary

Police 7,600 (some 5,000 armed)

incl 2 SF units

EQUIPMENT BY TYPE
APC BTR APC (W)/M-113A APC (T)
HELICOPTERS 3
  MRH 1 Bell 412EP *Twin Huey*
  TPT • **Light** 2: 1 Bell 206B (AB-206B) *JetRanger* II; 1 Bell 212 (AB-212)

DEPLOYMENT

Legal provisions for foreign deployment of armed forces:
Constitution: Codified constitution (1991)
Specific legislation: 'Defence Law' (2005)
Decision on deployment of troops abroad: a) by the government is deployment is for humanitarian missions or military exercises; b) by the parliament if for peacekeeping operations ('Defence Law', Art. 41).

AFGHANISTAN
NATO • ISAF 168

BOSNIA-HERZEGOVINA
EU • EUFOR • *Operation Althea* 12

LEBANON
UN • UNIFIL 1

Malta MLT

Maltese Lira ML		2011	2012	2013
GDP	ML	6.4bn	6.7bn	
	US$	8.9bn	8.4bn	
per capita	US$	21,716	20,496	
Growth	%	2.06	1.20	
Inflation	%	2.51	3.48	
Def exp [a]	ML	40m		
	US$	56m		
Def bdgt [a]	ML	40m	41m	
	US$	56m	52m	
FMA (US)	US$	0.399m		
US$1=ML		0.72	0.79	

[a] Excludes military pensions

Population   409,836

Age	0–14	15–19	20–24	25–29	30–64	65 plus
Male	7.9%	3.2%	3.5%	3.6%	24.2%	7.3%
Female	7.5%	3.0%	3.4%	3.4%	23.7%	9.2%

Capabilities

The armed forces consist of a limited number of army personnel supported by small naval and air units. There are plans to procure another maritime surveillance aircraft. Following Malta's accession to the European Union in 2004, there was a renewed focus on the country's armed services to support its ability to participate in any EU-led peace-support or crisis-management deployment. But their ability to do so is limited by the majority of units and personnel being optimised for domestic security tasks. Malta deploys personnel to the headquarters of EU NAVFOR, as well as a ship-protection team; it also deploys personnel to EU FRONTEX activities in Greece.

ACTIVE 1,950 (Armed Forces 1,950)

RESERVE 170 (Emergency Volunteer Reserve Force 120 Individual Reserve 50)

ORGANISATIONS BY SERVICE

Armed Forces of Malta 1,950

FORCES BY ROLE
MANOEUVRE Light
1 (1st) inf regt (2 inf coy, 1 AD/spt coy)
COMBAT SUPPORT
1 (3rd) cbt spt regt (1 engr sqn, 1 EOD sqn, 1 maint sqn)
1 (4th) cbt spt regt (1 CIS coy, 1 sy coy (Revenue Security Corps))

Maritime Squadron

The AFM maritime element is organised into 5 Divisions: Offshore Patrol; Inshore Patrol; Rapid Deployment and Training; Marine Engineering and Logistics.

EQUIPMENT BY TYPE
PATROL AND COASTAL COMBATANTS 8
  PCC 1 Diciotti
  PB 7: 4 Austal 21m; 2 Marine Protector; 1 Bremse (GER)
LOGISTICS AND SUPPORT 2
  AAR 2 Cantieri Vittoria

Air Wing

1 Base Party. 1 Flt Ops Div; 1 Maint Div; 1 Integrated Logs Div; 1 Rescue Section
EQUIPMENT BY TYPE
AIRCRAFT
  TPT • Light 4: 2 Beech 200 King Air (maritime patrol); 2 BN-2B Islander
  TRG 3 Bulldog T MK1
HELICOPTERS
  MRH 3 SA316B Alouette III

DEPLOYMENT

Legal provisions for foreign deployment:
Constitution: Codified constitution (1964)
Decision on deployment of troops abroad: The government decides on a case-by-case basis on the deployment of Maltese military personnel abroad (Malta Armed Forces Act, Chapter 220 of the Laws of Malta).

UGANDA
EU • EUTM 87

FOREIGN FORCES

Italy 22; 2 Bell 212 (SAR) hel

Montenegro MNE

Euro €		2011	2012	2013
GDP	€	3.3bn	3.4bn	
	US$	4.5bn	4.3bn	
per capita	US$	6,845	6,541	
Growth	%	2.45	0.20	
Inflation	%	3.08	3.41	
Def exp [a]	€	57m		
	US$	80m		
Def bdgt [b]	€	37m	40m	47m
	US$	52m	52m	
FMA (US)	US$	1.472m	1.2m	1.2m
US$1=€		0.72	0.78	

[a] Includes military pensions
[b] Excludes military pensions

Population   657,394

Age	0–14	15–19	20–24	25–29	30–64	65 plus
Male	7.5%	2.4%	3.5%	4.5%	26.5%	5.4%
Female	7.9%	2.8%	3.4%	3.8%	24.2%	8.2%

Capabilities

In the wake of its separation from Serbia in 2006, Montenegro shifted from conscript to professional armed services.

Force and organisational changes are underway that will likely see a further reduction in numbers, mainly in the army. The naval capability consists of two patrol boats, while the air element is limited to a small number of fixed-wing and rotary aircraft. Maintenance issues have affected operational availability. The country participates in NATO's Membership Action Plan, with the aim of becoming a member of the Alliance, but its capability is limited to relatively un-demanding internal security missions.

ACTIVE 2,080 (Army 1,500 Navy 350 Air Force 230)
Paramilitary 10,100

ORGANISATIONS BY SERVICE

Army 1,500
FORCES BY ROLE
SPECIAL FORCES
1 SF bde
MANOEUVRE
Reconnaissance
1 recce coy
Light
1 mot inf bde (1 SF coy, 2 inf regt (1 inf bn, 1 mtn bn), 1 arty bty, 1 cbt spt coy, 1 CBRN pl, 1 sig pl)
COMBAT SUPPORT
1 engr coy
3 sigs pl
1 MP coy
EQUIPMENT BY TYPE
APC (W) 8 BOV-VP M-86
ARTY 149
TOWED 122mm 12 D-30
MRL 128mm 18 M63/M94 *Plamen*
MOR 119: **82mm** 76; **120mm** 43
AT
SP 8 BOV-1
MSL • MANPATS 117: 71 9K111 *Fagot* (AT-4 *Spigot*); 19 9K113 Konkurs (AT-5 *Spandrel*); 27 9K114 *Shturm* (AT-6 *Spiral*)

Navy 350
1 Naval Cmd HQ with 4 Operational Naval Units (Patrol Boat; Coastal Surveillance; Maritime Detachment and SAR) with additional Sig, Log and Trg units with a separate Coast Guard Element. Some listed units are in the process of decommissioning.
EQUIPMENT BY TYPE
SUBMARINES • SDV 2 † (*Mala*)
PATROL AND COASTAL COMBATANTS 5
PSO 1 *Kotor* with 1 twin 76mm gun (1 further vessel in reserve)
PCFG 2 *Rade Končar* with 2 single lnchr with P-15 *Termit* (SS-N-2B *Styx*) AShM (missiles disarmed)
PB 2 *Mirna* (Type-140) (Police units)
AMPHIBIOUS • LANDING CRAFT 5
LCU 5: 3 (Type-21); 2 (Type-22)
LOGISTICS AND SUPPORT 3
AOTL 1 *Drina*; **AET** 1 *Lubin*; **AXS** 1 *Jadran*

Air Force 230
Golubovci (Podgorica) air base under army command.
FORCES BY ROLE
TRAINING
1 (mixed) sqn with G-4 *Super Galeb*; Utva-75 (none operational)
TRANSPORT HELICOPTER
1 sqn with SA341/SA342L *Gazelle*
EQUIPMENT BY TYPE
AIRCRAFT • TRG 8: 4 G-4 *Super Galeb* (none serviceable); 4 Utva-75 (none serviceable)
HELICOPTERS
MRH 15 SA341/SA342L *Gazelle* (7 serviceable)
TPT • Medium (1 Mi-8T awaiting museum storage)

Paramilitary ε10,100

Montenegrin Ministry of Interior Personnel ε6,000

Special Police Units ε4,100

DEPLOYMENT

Legal provisions for foreign deployment:
Constitution: Constitution (2007)

Decision on deployment of troops abroad: The Assembly, on the proposal of the Council for Defence and Security, decide on the use of Montenegrin armed forces in international forces (Article 82, item 8).

AFGHANISTAN
NATO • ISAF 41

LIBERIA
UN • UNMIL 2 obs

Multinational Organisations

Capabilities

The following represent shared capabilites held by contributors collectively rather than as part of national inventories.

ORGANISATIONS BY SERVICE

NATO AEW&C Force
Based at Geilenkirchen (GER). 12 original participating countries (BEL, CAN, DNK, GER, GRC, ITA, NLD, NOR, PRT, TUR, USA) have been subsequently joined by 5 more (CZE, ESP, HUN, POL, ROM).
FORCES BY ROLE
AIRBORNE EARLY WARNING & CONTROL
1 sqn with B-757 (trg); E-3A *Sentry* (NATO standard)
EQUIPMENT BY TYPE
AIRCRAFT
AEW&C 17 E-3A *Sentry* (NATO standard)
TPT • PAX 1 B-757 (trg)

Strategic Airlift Capability

Heavy Airlift Wing based at Papa airbase (HUN). 12 particiapting countries (BLG, EST, FIN, HUN, LTU, NLD, NOR, POL, ROM, SVN, SWE, USA)

EQUIPMENT BY TYPE
AIRCRAFT
TPT • **Heavy** 3 C-17A *Globemaster*

Strategic Airlift Interim Solution

Intended to provide strategic airlift capacity pending the delivery of A400M aircraft by leasing An-124s. 14 particiapting countries (BEL, CAN, CZE, DNK, FIN, FRA, GER, HUN, LUX, NOR, POL, ROM, SVK, SVN, SWE, UK)

EQUIPMENT BY TYPE
AIRCRAFT
TPT • **Heavy** 2 An-124-100 (4 more available on 6-9 days notice)

Netherlands NLD

Euro €		2011	2012	2013
GDP	€	602.4bn	608.3bn	
	US$	838.1bn	770.2bn	
per capita	US$	50,094	46,035	
Growth	%	1.09	-0.46	
Inflation	%	2.48	2.22	
Def exp [a]	€	8.16bn		
	US$	11.3bn		
Def bdgt	€	8.38bn	8.24bn	7.78bn
	US$	11.7bn	10.4bn	
US$1=€		0.72	0.79	

[a] NATO definition

Population	16,730,632

Age	0–14	15–19	20–24	25–29	30–64	65 plus
Male	8.8%	3.0%	3.2%	3.1%	24.0%	7.4%
Female	8.4%	2.9%	3.1%	3.0%	23.9%	9.2%

Capabilities

Government spending cuts in 2011 resulted in significant reductions in all three services. The navy saw its mine-hunter and patrol-vessel fleets reduced, while the army lost heavy armour. The air force's F-16 fleet was also reduced. There have also been reductions to spares and activity levels. Although the Netherlands remains in the F-35 project, the Dutch parliament voted against the project mid-year, citing cost concerns, among other factors. In spite of the cuts, some modernisation programmes, such as the army's CV90, *Fennek* and *Boxer* armoured vehicles continued. Naval capability enhancements include some new small-platform additions, and a contract awarded to equip the four destroyers with a new BMD-capable search radar. Fighting in Afghanistan has produced a generation of combat-experienced army commanders, and the armed forces remain a motivated and professional force capable of participating in demanding joint operations in an Alliance context.

ACTIVE 37,400 (Army 20,850; Navy 8,500; Air 8,050)
Military Constabulary 5,900

RESERVE 3,200 (Army 2,700; Navy 80; Air 420)
Military Constabulary 80
Soldiers/sailors to age 35, NCOs to 40, officers to 45

ORGANISATIONS BY SERVICE

Army 20,850

FORCES BY ROLE
COMMAND
elm 1 (GER/NLD) Corps HQ
SPECIAL FORCES
5 SF coy (4 land; 1 maritime)
MANOEUVRE
Reconnaissance
1 ISTAR bn (2 armd recce sqn, 1 EW coy, 1 arty bty, 1 UAV bty)
Mechanised
2 (13th & 43rd) mech bde (1 armd recce sqn, 2 armd inf bn, 1 SP arty bn (2 bty), 1 engr bn, 1 maint coy, 1 medical coy)
Air Manoeuvre
1 (11th) air mob bde (3 air mob inf bn, 1 mor coy, 1 AD coy, 1 engr coy, 1 med coy, 1 supply coy, 1 maint coy)
COMBAT SUPPORT
1 AD comd (3 AD bty)
1 CIMIC bn
1 engr bn
48 EOD teams
1 (CIS) sigs bn
1 CBRN coy
COMBAT SERVICE SUPPORT
1 med bn
5 fd hospital
3 maint coy
2 tpt bn

Reserves 2,700 reservists

National Command
Cadre bde and corps tps completed by call-up of reservists (incl Territorial Comd)
FORCES BY ROLE
MANOEUVRE
Light
3 inf bn (could be mob for territorial def)
EQUIPMENT BY TYPE
RECCE 305: 296 *Fennek*; 9 *Fuchs* Tpz-1 CBRN recce
AIFV 184 CV9035N
APC 169
APC (W) 84: 14 M577A1; 70 XA-188
PPV 85 *Bushmaster* IMV
ARTY 61:
SP 155mm 18 PzH 2000
MOR 43: **81mm** 27 L16/M1 **120mm** 16 Brandt
AT
MSL
SP 40 *Fennek* MRAT

MANPATS 297 *Spike*-MR (*Gil*)
RL 1,381 Pzf
AD
SAM
SP 36: 18 *Fennek* with FIM-92A *Stinger*; 18 MB with FIM-92A *Stinger*
MANPAD 18 FIM-92A *Stinger*
GUNS• SP35mm 60 *Gepard* (in store for sale)
RADAR • LAND 6+: 6 AN/TPQ-36 *Firefinder* (arty, mor); WALS; *Squire*
AEV 35+: 10 *Kodiak*; 25 *Leopard* 1; YPR-806 A1
ARV 77+: 25 *Büffel*; 52 *Leopard* 1; YPR-809
MW Bozena

Navy 8,500 (incl Marines)

EQUIPMENT BY TYPE
SUBMARINES • TACTICAL • SSK 4:
4 *Walrus* with 4 single 533mm TT with Mk48 *Sea Arrow* HWT (equipped for UGM-84C *Harpoon* AShM, but none embarked)
PRINCIPAL SURFACE COMBATANTS 6
DESTROYERS • DDGHM 4:
4 *Zeven Provinciën* with 2 quad Mk141 lnchr with RGM-84F *Harpoon* AShM, 1 40-cell Mk41 VLS with SM-2MR/ESSM SAM, 2 twin 324mm ASTT with Mk46 LWT, 1 127mm gun, (capacity 1 NH-90 hel)
FRIGATES • FFGHM 2:
2 *Karel Doorman* with 2 quad Mk141 lnchr with RGM-84A/C *Harpoon* AShM, 1 Mk48 VLS with RIM-7P *Sea Sparrow* SAM, 2 twin 324mm ASTT with Mk46 LWT, 1 76mm gun, (capacity 1 NH-90 hel)
PATROL AND COASTAL COMBATANTS • PSOH 3
Holland with 1 76mm gun (1 further vessel in build)
MINE WARFARE • MINE COUNTERMEASURES •
MHO 6 *Alkmaar* (*tripartite*)
AMPHIBIOUS
PRINCIPAL AMPHIBIOUS SHIPS • LPD 2:
1 *Rotterdam* (capacity either 4 NH90/AS532 *Cougar* hel; either 6 LCVP or 2 LCU and 3 LCVP; either 170 APC (T) or 33 MBT; 538 troops)
1 *Johan de Witt* (capacity 6 NH90 hel or 4 AW101 *Merlin*/AS532 *Cougar* hel; either 6 LCVP or 2 LCU and 3 LCVP; either 170 APC (T) or 33 MBT; 700 troops)
LANDING CRAFT 17:
LCU 5 Mk9
LCVP 12 Mk5
LOGISTICS AND SUPPORT 31
AGS 2 *Snellius*
AK 1 *Pelikaan*
AORH 1 *Amsterdam* (capacity 2 NH90 hel) with 1 *Goalkeeper* CIWS
AOT 1 *Patria*
ASL 1 *Mercuur*
AXL 1 *Van Kingsbergen*
AXS 1 *Urania*
YDT 5: 4 *Cerberus*; 1 *Someba*
YFL 6
YTM 5 *Linge*
YTL 7 *Breezand*

Marines 2,654 FORCES BY ROLE
MANOEUVRE
Amphibious
2 mne bn (1 integrated with UK 3 Cdo Bde to form UK/NLD Amphibious Landing Force)
COMBAT SUPPORT
1 amph cbt spt bn (some SF units, 1 recce coy, 1 AD pl, 2 amph beach units, 1 (Maritime Joint Effect) bty)
COMBAT SERVICE SUPPORT
1 spt bn (2 spt units, 1 sea-based spt gp, 2 medical facility)
EQUIPMENT BY TYPE
APC (T) 151: 87 Bv-206D; 73 BvS-10 *Viking*
ARTY • MOR 18: **81mm** 12 L16/M1; **120mm** 6 Brandt
AT • MSL • MANPATS 24 MRAT *Gil*
RL 84mm 144 *Pantserfaust* III Dynarange 2000
AD • SAM • MANPAD 4 FIM-92A *Stinger*
ARV 5 BvS-10
MED 4 BvS-10

Air Force 8,050

Flying hours   180 hrs/year

FORCES BY ROLE
FIGHTER/GROUND ATTACK
4 sqn with F-16AM/BM *Fighting Falcon*
ANTI-SUBMARINE WARFARE/SEARCH & RESCUE
1 sqn with NH90 NFH
SEARCH & RESCUE
1 sqn with Bell 412SP (AB-412SP *Griffin*)
TANKER/TRANSPORT
1 sqn with C-130H/C-130H-30 *Hercules*; DC-10/KDC-10; Gulfstream IV
TRAINING
1 sqn with PC-7 *Turbo Trainer*
ATTACK HELICOPTER
1 sqn with AH-64D *Apache*
TRANSPORT HELICOPTER
1 sqn with AS532U2 *Cougar* II
1 sqn with CH-47D/F *Chinook*
AIR DEFENCE
4 sqn (total: 7 AD Team. 4 AD bty with MIM-104 *Patriot* (TMD capable))
EQUIPMENT BY TYPE
AIRCRAFT 72 combat capable
FTR 72 F-16AM/BM *Fighting Falcon*
TKR 2 KDC-10
TPT 6: **Medium** 4: 2 C-130H *Hercules*; 2 C-130H-30 *Hercules*; **PAX** 2: 1 DC-10; 1 Gulfstream IV
TRG 13 PC-7 *Turbo Trainer*
HELICOPTERS
ATK 29 AH-64D *Apache*
ASW 8 NH90 NFH
MRH 7: 3 Bell 412 (AB-412SP *Griffin*); 4 SA316 *Alouette* III
TPT 21: **Heavy** 13: 11 CH-47D *Chinook*; 2 CH-47F *Chinook*; **Medium** 8 AS532U2 *Cougar* II
AD • SAM
TOWED 20 MIM-104 *Patriot* (TMD Capable/PAC-3 msl)
MANPAD FIM-92A *Stinger*

MSL
  AAM • IR AIM-9L/M/N **ARH** AIM-120B AMRAAM
  ASM AGM-114K *Hellfire*; AGM-65D/G *Maverick*
BOMBS
  Conventional Mk 82; Mk 84
  Laser-guided GBU-10/GBU-12 *Paveway* II; GBU-24
  Paveway III (all supported by LANTIRN)

Paramilitary

Royal Military Constabulary 5,900

Subordinate to the Ministry of Defence, but performs
most of its work under the authority of other ministries.

FORCES BY ROLE
MANOEUVRE
  Other
    6 paramilitary district (total: 60 paramilitary 'bde')
EQUIPMENT BY TYPE
AIFV 24 YPR-765

Cyber

In early 2011, the Dutch defence minister indicated that cyber defence would attract some of the Netherlands' declining budget and, between 2011–2015, around €30 million
plus staff would be allocated, with full capability by 2016.
In June 2012, the defence ministry launched a Defence Cyber Strategy to direct military cyber efforts. Among other
elements, the strategy is intended to strengthen cyber defence, and 'develop the military capability to conduct cyber operations (offensive element)'. In developing these,
the document says that 'optimal use will be made of the
expertise and assets of the Defence Intelligence and Security Centre'. While a separate cyber service will not be established by the MoD, 'relevant cyber capabilities will be
incorporated within the Defence Cyber Command, which
will come under the […] management of the […] army'. A
broader National Cyber Security Strategy was published
in 2011, and a Cyber Security Council was established to
coordinate activities and information exchange between
the private and public sector in the context of critical infrastructure. A National Security Centre was launched in
January 2012. The Netherlands has a national CERT, is involved in informal CERT communities, and is a member of
the European government CERTs Group (ECG).

DEPLOYMENT

Legal provisions for foreign deployment:
Constitution: Codified constitution (1815)
Decision on deployment of troops abroad: By the
government (Art. 98)

AFGHANISTAN
NATO • ISAF 500

BOSNIA-HERZEGOVINA
EU • EUFOR • *Operation Althea* 5

DEMOCRATIC REPUBLIC OF THE CONGO
EU • EUSEC RD Congo 3

GULF OF ADEN & SOMALI BASIN
NATO • *Operation Ocean Shield* 1 LPD

MIDDLE EAST
UN • UNTSO 11 obs

NORTH SEA
NATO • SNMCMG 1: 1 MHO

SERBIA
NATO • KFOR 9

SOUTH SUDAN
UN • UNMISS 7; 2 obs

FOREIGN FORCES

United Kingdom Air Force 90
United States US European Command: 400

Norway NOR

Norwegian Kroner kr		2011	2012	
GDP	kr	2.72tr	2.96tr	
	US$	485.4bn	499.8bn	
per capita	US$	103,117	106,176	
Growth	%	1.52	3.06	
Inflation	%	1.30	1.02	
Def exp [a]	kr	40.5bn		
	US$	7.23bn		
Def bdgt	kr	39.2bn	40.5bn	42.2bn
	US$	7bn	6.85bn	
US$1=kr		5.60	5.92	

[a] NATO definition

Population   4,707,270

Age	0–14	15–19	20–24	25–29	30–64	65 plus
Male	9.0%	3.4%	3.4%	3.0%	23.5%	7.2%
Female	8.7%	3.3%	3.3%	2.9%	23.1%	9.2%

Capabilities

Norway maintains small but capable armed forces focused
largely on territorial defence, particularly in the High
North, which ensures that the armed forces possess skills
in cold-weather warfare. Recent acquisitions, including
destroyers, demonstrate an investment in equipment necessary to sustain Norway's presence in the Arctic region.
However, these have also added a new element to the
country's maritime capabilities. During the Cold War, Norway relied on small-attack craft and submarines to pursue
a policy of sea-denial; now, Norway is able to deploy further from its coast with more muscular surface platforms.
Norway places importance on its alliances, particularly
with European states and NATO. Given the small size of
the armed forces, Norway relies on conscription for current personnel levels and reserves for crisis deployment.
Conscripts comprise approximately one-third of the armed
forces at any one point, affecting the level of training and
readiness. Whilst Norway has made significant contribu-

tions to ISAF, this has depressed land-force readiness for other tasks.

ACTIVE 24,450 (Army 8,900, Navy 3,900, Air 3,650, Central Support 7,500, Home Guard 500)

Terms of service: conscription with maximum 18 months of duty. Conscripts initially serve 12 months at the age of 19 to 21, and then up to 4–5 refresher training periods until the age of 35, 44, 55 or 60 depending on rank and function. Numbers above include conscripts during initial service.

RESERVE 45,250 (Army 270, Navy 320, Central Support 350, Home Guard 44,250)

Reserves: readiness varies from a few hours to several days

ORGANISATIONS BY SERVICE

Army 4,500; 4,400 conscript (total 8,900)

The mechanised brigade – Brigade North – trains new personnel of all categories and provides units for international operations. At any time around one-third of the brigade will be trained and ready to conduct operations. The brigade includes one high- readiness mechanised battalion (Telemark Battalion) with combat support and combat service support units on high readiness.

FORCES BY ROLE
SPECIAL FORCES
  1 SF regt
MANOEUVRE
  Reconnaissance
  1 (Border Guard) lt bn (3 coy (HQ/garrison, border control & trg))
  Mechanised
  1 mech inf bde (1 ISTAR bn, 2 mech inf bn, 1 lt inf bn, 1 arty bn, 1 engr bn, 1 MP coy, 1 CIS bn, 1 spt bn, 1 med bn)
  Light
  1 bn (His Majesty The King's Guards)
EQUIPMENT BY TYPE
MBT 52 *Leopard* 2A4
RECCE *Fuchs* tpz 1 CBRN recce
AIFV 104 CV9030N
APC 410
  APC (T) 315 M113 (incl variants)
  APC (W) 75 XA-186 *Sisu*/XA-200 *Sisu*
  PPV 20 *Dingo* II
ARTY 264
  SP 155mm 78: 24 FH77 *Archer* being delivered; 54 M109A3GN
  MOR 186:
    SP 36: 81mm 24 M106A1; 12 M125A2
    81mm 150 L-16
AT
  MANPATS 90 *Javelin*
  RCL 84mm 2,300 *Carl Gustav*
RADAR • LAND 12 ARTHUR
AEV 22 *Alvis*
ARV 3 M88A1; M578; 6 *Leopard* 1
VLB 26 *Leguan*; 9 *Leopard* 1
MW 9 910 MCV-2

Navy 2,450; 1,450 conscripts (total 3,900)

Joint Command – Norwegian National Joint Headquarters. The Royal Norwegian Navy is organised into four elements under the command of the chief of staff of the Navy; the naval units '*Kysteskadren*', the schools '*Sjøforsvarets Skoler*', the naval bases and the coast guard '*Kystvakten*'.

FORCES BY ROLE
SPECIAL FORCES
  1 SF sqn
MANOEUVRE
  Reconnaissance
  1 ISTAR coy (Coastal Rangers)
COMBAT SUPPORT
  1 EOD pl
EQUIPMENT BY TYPE
SUBMARINES • TACTICAL • SSK 6 *Ula* with 8 single 533mm TT with A3 *Seal* DM2 HWT
PRINCIPAL SURFACE COMBATANTS 5
  DESTROYERS • DDGHM 5 *Fridjof Nansen* with 2 quad lnchr with NSM AShM (under acquisition), 1 8-cell Mk41 VLS with ESSM SAM, 2 twin 324mm ASTT with *Sting Ray* LWT, 1 76mm gun, (capacity NH90 hel)
PATROL AND COASTAL COMBATANTS • PCFGM 6 *Skjold* with 8 single lnchr with NSM AShM (under acquisition), 1 twin lnchr with *Mistral* SAM, 1 76mm gun
MINE WARFARE • MINE COUNTERMEASURES 6:
  MSC 3 *Alta*
  MHC 3 *Oksøy*
AMPHIBIOUS • LANDING CRAFT • LCP 16 S90N
LOGISTICS AND SUPPORT 19
  AGI 1 *Marjata*
  AGDS 1 *Tyr*
  AGS 6: 1 *HU Sverdrup II*; 4 *Oljevern*; 1 *Geofjord*
  ATS 1 *Valkyrien*
  AXL 4: 2 *Hessa*; 2 *Kvarnen*
  YAC 1 *Norge*
  YDT 5

Coast Guard

PATROL AND COASTAL COMBATANTS 14
  PSO 8: 3 *Barentshav*; 1 *Svalbard* with 1 hel landing platform; 1 *Harstad*; 3 *Nordkapp* with 1 hel landing platform
  PCO 6: 1 *Aalesund*; 5 *Nornen*

Air Force 2,800; 850 conscript (total 3,650)

Joint Command – Norwegian National HQ

Flying hours   180 hrs/year

FORCES BY ROLE
FIGHTER/GROUND ATTACK
  3 sqn with F-16AM/BM *Fighting Falcon*
MARITIME PATROL
  1 sqn with P-3C *Orion*; P-3N *Orion* (pilot trg)
ELECTRONIC WARFARE
  1 sqn with *Falcon* 20C (EW, Flight Inspection Service)
SEARCH & RESCUE
  1 sqn with *Sea King* Mk43B
TRANSPORT
  1 sqn with C-130J-30 *Hercules*

TRAINING
  1 sqn with MFI-15 SAAB *Safari*
TRANSPORT HELICOPTER
  2 sqn with Bell 412SP *Twin Huey*
  1 sqn with *Lynx* Mk86
AIR DEFENCE
  1 bty(+) with NASAMS II
EQUIPMENT BY TYPE
AIRCRAFT 63 combat capable
  FTR 57: 47 F-16AM *Fighting Falcon*; 10 F-16BM *Fighting Falcon*
  ASW 6: 4 P-3C *Orion*; 2 P-3N *Orion* (pilot trg)
  EW 3 *Falcon* 20C
  TPT • Medium 4 C-130J-30 *Hercules*
  TRG 16 MFI-15 *Safari*
HELICOPTERS
  ASW 6: 5 *Lynx* Mk86 ; 1 NH90 NFH (delivery schedule of all 14 revised to an FOC of 2014)
  SAR 12 *Sea King* Mk43B
  MRH 18: 6 Bell 412HP; 12 Bell 412SP
AD
  SAM
    TOWED NASAMS II
  MSL
    AAM • IR AIM-9L *Sidewinder*; **IIR** IRIS-T; **ARH** AIM-120B AMRAAM
BOMBS
  Laser-guided: EGBU-12 *Paveway* II
  INS/GPS guided: JDAM

Central Support, Administration and Command 6,750; 1,000 conscripts (total 7,750)

Central Support, Administration and Command includes military personnel in all joint elements and they are responsible for logistics and CIS in support of all forces in Norway and abroad.

Home Guard 500 (total 500 with 46,000 reserves)

The Home Guard is a separate organisation, but closely cooperates with all services. The Home Guard can be mobilised on very short notice for local security operations.

Land Home Guard 42,650 with reserves

11 Home Guard Districts with mobile Rapid Reaction Forces (5,000 troops in total) as well as reinforcements and follow-on forces (37,150 troops in total).

Naval Home Guard 1,900 with reserves

Consisting of Rapid Reaction Forces (500 troops), and 17 'Naval Home Guard Areas'. The Naval Home Guard is equipped with 2 vessels of the *Reine*-class and 13 smaller vessels. In addition, a number of civilian vessels can be requisitioned as required.

EQUIPMENT BY TYPE
PATROL AND COASTAL COMBATANTS 15
  PCO 2 *Reine*
  PB 13: 4 *Harek*; 2 *Gyda*; 7 *Alusafe* 1290

Air Home Guard 1,450 with reserves

Provides force protection and security detachments for air bases.

Cyber

In summer 2012, parliament passed a new Long Term White Paper for the Norwegian defence sector highlighting major security challenges, including those in the cyber domain, and announcing the establishment of a Cyber Command, inaugurated on 18 September.

DEPLOYMENT

Legal provisions for foreign deployment:
Constitution: Codified constitution (1814)
Decision on deployment of troops abroad: By royal prerogative exercised by the government (Art. 25, 26).

AFGHANISTAN
NATO • ISAF 145
UN • UNAMA 1 obs

DEMOCRATIC REPUBLIC OF THE CONGO
UN • MONUSCO 1 obs

EGYPT
MFO 3

MIDDLE EAST
UN • UNTSO 12 obs

NORTH SEA
NATO • SNMCMG 1: 1 MHC

SERBIA
NATO • KFOR 3
UN • UNMIK 1

SOUTH SUDAN
UN • UNMISS 12; 4 obs

FOREIGN FORCES

United States US European Command: 1 (APS) 155mm SP Arty bn eqpt set

Poland POL

Polish Zloty z		2011	2012	2013
GDP	z	1.52tr	1.6tr	
	US$	514.5bn	470.4bn	
per capita	US$	13,393	12,245	
Growth	%	4.32	2.35	
Inflation	%	4.27	3.85	
Def exp [b]	z	26.4bn		
	US$	8.91bn		
Def bdgt [a]	z	27.3bn	29.2bn	31.2bn
	US$	9.23bn	8.62bn	
FMA (US)	US$	33.932m	24.165m	20m
US$1=z		2.96	3.39	

[a] Includes military pensions

[b] NATO definition

Population   38,415,284

Age	0–14	15–19	20–24	25–29	30–64	65 plus
Male	7.5%	3.0%	3.5%	4.2%	24.8%	5.4%
Female	7.1%	2.8%	3.4%	4.1%	25.5%	8.6%

Capabilities

Poland continues to restructure its armed forces, with the focus now on capability rather than mass. As such, it is a force in transition, though still able to provide territorial defence and act as a contributor to NATO operations. Quantity has been traded for quality, most notably in the army, which in 20 years has reduced its numerical strength by three-quarters. The 2011 Strategic Defence Review set out the general aims and development of the military over the next 25 years. NATO membership is a key pillar of Polish defence policy, and Poland is a notable participant in NATO and EU operations, including in Afghanistan. Soviet-era equipment is being phased out as part of a broad re-equipment programme, though some projects have already fallen foul of funding pressures. There are 14 major operational programmes in the armed forces' 2012 Technical Modernisation Plan. Within the army, the emphasis is on expanding deployable forces, with increased helicopter support. Mobility is aided by involvement in the Strategic Airlift Capability's C-17 unit, with the air force also operating its own tactical transport aircraft. The navy is presently structured around a fleet of frigates and corvettes, with longer-term plans looking to a multi-role corvette. It is a member of NATO's 11-nation Multinational Corps Northeast, and its armed forces participate in bilateral and multilateral exercises.

ACTIVE 96,000 (Army 45,600, Navy 7,600, Air 16,500, Special Forces 2,200, Joint 24,100) **Paramilitary 22,050**

ORGANISATIONS BY SERVICE

Land Forces Command 45,600

Land Forces Command directly controls airmobile bdes and their avn. Transition to lighter forces is continuing but is hampered by lack of funds.

FORCES BY ROLE
COMMAND
1 (2nd) mech corps HQ
elm 1 (MNC NE) corps HQ
MANOEUVRE
Reconnaissance
3 recce regt
Armoured
1 (11th) armd cav div (2 armd bde, 1 mech bde)
Mechanised
1 (12th) div (2 mech bde, 1 (coastal) mech bde)
1 (16th) div (2 armd bde, 2 mech bde)
1 (21st) mech bde (1 armd bn, 3 mech bn, 1 arty bn, 1 AD bn, 1 engr bn)
Air Manoeuvre
1 (6th) air aslt bde (3 air aslt bn)
1 (25th) air cav bde (2 tpt hel bn, 2 air cav bn, 1 (casevac) med unit)
Aviation
1 (1st) avn bde (4 atk hel sqn with Mi-24D/V Hind D/E, 3 ISR sqn with Mi-2; 1 tpt hel sqn with Mi-2)
COMBAT SUPPORT
3 arty regt
2 engr regt
1 ptn br regt
2 chem regt
3 AD regt

EQUIPMENT BY TYPE
MBT 901: 128 Leopard 2A4; 232 PT-91 Twardy; 541 T-72/T-72M1D/T-72M1
RECCE 358: 227 BRDM-2; 37 BWR; 94 WD R-5
AIFV 1,784: 1,297 BMP-1; 487 Rosomak
APC • PPV 70: 40 Cougar (on loan from US); 30 Maxxpro
ARTY 702
    SP 315: **122mm** 204 2S1 Carnation; **152mm** 111 M-77 Dana
    MRL 122mm 180: 75 BM-21; 30 RM-70; 75 WR-40 Langusta
    MOR 207: **98mm** 98 M-98; **120mm** 109 M120
AT • MSL • MANPATS 289: 43 9K11 Malyutka (AT-3 Sagger); 6 9K111 Fagot (AT-4 Spigot); 240 Spike-LR
AD
    SAM 564
        SP 64 9K33 Osa-AK (SA-8 Gecko)
        MANPAD 480: 91 9K32 Strela-2 (SA-7 Grail); 389 GROM
    GUNS 348
        SP 23mm 32: 17 ZSU-23-4; 15 ZSU-23-4MP Biala
        TOWED 23mm 316; 244 ZU-23-2; 72 ZUR-23-2KG/PG
RADAR • LAND 3 LIWIEC (veh, arty)
HELICOPTERS
    ATK 30 Mi-24D/V Hind D/E
    MRH 28: 9 Mi-17T/U Hip H; 19 PZL Mi-2URP Hoplite
    MRH/TPT 39: 35 PZL W-3A Sokol (med tpt)/W-3W Sokol (MRH); 4 PZL W-3PL Gluszec
    TPT 44: **Medium** 17 Mi-8T/U Hip **Light** 27 PZL Mi-2 Hoplite
AEV IWT; MT-LB

ARV 65+: 10 *Leopard 1*; 15 MT-LB; TRI; WPT-TOPAS; 40 WZT-3
VLB 52: 4 *Biber*; 48 BLG67M2
MW 18: 14 *Bozena*; 4 *Kalina* SUM

Navy 7,600
EQUIPMENT BY TYPE
SUBMARINES • TACTICAL 5:
  SSK 5:
    4 *Sokol* (NOR Type-207) with 8 single 533mm TT
    1 *Orzel* (FSU *Kilo*) with 6 single 533mm TT each with T-53/T-65 HWT
PRINCIPAL SURFACE COMBATANTS 2
  FRIGATES • FFGHM 2 *Pulaski* (US *Oliver Hazard Perry*) with 1 Mk13 GMLS with RGM-84D/F *Harpoon* AShM/ SM-1MR SAM, 2 triple 324mm ASTT with A244 LWT, 1 76mm gun, (capacity 2 SH-2G *Super Seasprite* ASW hel) (1 vessel to be used as training ship; 1 to be refitted)
PATROL AND COASTAL COMBATANTS 6
  CORVETTES • FSM 1 *Kaszub* with 2 quad lnchr with 9K32 *Strela-2* (SA-N-5 *Grail*) SAM, 2 twin 533mm ASTT with SET-53 HWT, 2 RBU 6000 *Smerch* 2, 1 76mm gun
  PCFGM 5:
    3 *Orkan* (GDR *Sassnitz*) with 1 quad lnchr with RBS-15 Mk3 AShM, 1 quad lnchr (manual aiming) with *Strela-2* (SA-N-5 *Grail*) SAM, 1 76mm gun
    2 *Tarantul* with 2 twin lnchr with P-21/22*Termit-M* (SS-N-2C/D *Styx*) AShM, 1 quad lnchr (manual aiming) with 9K32 *Strela-2* (SA-N-5 *Grail*) SAM, 1 76mm gun
MINE WARFARE • MINE COUNTERMEASURES 21:
  MCCS 1 Project 890
  MHI 4 *Mamry*
  MHO 3 *Krogulec*
  MSI 13 *Goplo*
AMPHIBIOUS 8
  LANDING SHIPS • LSM 5 *Lublin* (capacity 9 tanks; 135 troops)
  LANDING CRAFT • LCU 3 *Deba* (capacity 50 troops)
LOGISTICS AND SUPPORT 38
  AGI 2 *Moma*
  AGS 8: 2 *Heweliusz*; 6 (coastal)
  AORL 1 *Baltyk*
  AOL 1 *Moskit*
  ARS 4: 2 *Piast*; 2 *Zbyszko*
  ATF 2
  AX 1 *Wodnik*
  AXS 1 *Iskra*
  YDG 2 *Mrowka*
  YDT 3
  YFB 7
  YPT 1 *Kormoran*
  YTM 5

Naval Aviation 1,300
FORCES BY ROLE
ANTI SUBMARINE WARFARE/SEARCH & RESCUE
  1 sqn with MI-14PL *Haze* A; MI-14PS *Haze* C
  1 sqn with PZL W-3RM *Anakonda*; SH-2G *Super Seasprite*
TRANSPORT
  1 sqn with An-28B1R; An-28E

1 sqn with An-28TD; Mi-17 *Hip* H; PZL Mi-2 *Hoplite*; PZL W-3RM; PZL W-3T
EQUIPMENT BY TYPE
AIRCRAFT
  MP 10: 8 An-28B1R *Bryza*; 2 An-28E *Bryza* (ecological monitoring)
  TPT • Light 2 An-28TD *Bryza*
HELICOPTERS
  ASW 12: 8 Mi-14PL *Haze*; 4 SH-2G *Super Seasprite*
  MRH 2 Mi-17 *Hip* H
  SAR 9: 2 Mi-14PS *Haze* C; 7 PZL W-3RM *Anakonda*
  TPT 3: **Medium** 1 PZL W-3T *Sokol*; **Light** 2 PZL Mi-2 *Hoplite*

Air Force 16,500
Flying hours   160 to 200 hrs/year
FORCES BY ROLE
FIGHTER
  2 sqn with MiG-29A/UB *Fulcrum*
FIGHTER/GROUND ATTACK
  3 sqn with F-16C/D Block 52+ *Fighting Falcon*
FIGHTER/GROUND ATTACK/ISR
  2 sqn with Su-22M-4 *Fitter*
TRANSPORT
  1 sqn with C-130E; PZL M-28 *Bryza*
  1 sqn with C-295M; PZL M-28 *Bryza*
  1 VIP sqn with PZL M-28 *Bryza*
TRAINING
  1 sqn with PZL-130 *Orlik*
  1 sqn with TS-11 *Iskra*; SW-4 *Puszczyk*
TRANSPORT HELICOPTER
  2 sqn with Mi-2; PZL W-3 *Sokol*
  1 sqn with Mi-2; Mi-17
AIR DEFENCE
  1 bde with S-125 *Neva SC* (SA-3 *Goa*); S-200C *Vega* (SA-5 *Gammon*)
EQUIPMENT BY TYPE
AIRCRAFT 106 combat capable
  FTR 32: 26 MiG-29A *Fulcrum*; 6 MiG-29UB *Fulcrum*
  FGA 74: 36 F-16C Block 52+ *Fighting Falcon*; 12 F-16D Block 52+ *Fighting Falcon*; 26 Su-22M-4 *Fitter*
  TPT 36: **Medium** 5 C-130E *Hercules*; **Light** 31: 11 C-295M; 20 M-28 *Bryza* TD
  TRG 72: 28 PZL-130 *Orlik*; 44 TS-11 *Iskra*
HELICOPTERS
  MRH 2 Mi-17 *Hip* H
  TPT 57: **Medium** 25: 8 Mi-8 *Hip*; 17 PZL W-3 *Sokol*; **Light** 32: 8 PZL Mi-2 *Hoplite*; 24 SW-4 *Puszczyk* (trg)
AD • SAM
  SP 17 S-125 *Neva SC* (SA-3 Goa); **STATIC** 1 S-200C *Vega* (SA-5 *Gammon*)
MSL
  AAM • IR R-60 (AA-8 *Aphid*); R-73 (AA-11 *Archer*), AIM-9 *Sidewinder*, R-27T (AA-10B *Alamo*); **ARH** AIM-120C AMRAAM
  ASM AGM-65J/G *Maverick*, Kh-25 (AS-10 *Karen*), Kh-29 (AS-14 *Kedge*)

Special Forces 2,200

FORCES BY ROLE
SPECIAL FORCES
4 SF units (GROM, AGAT, FORMOZA & cdo)
COMBAT SUPPORT/COMBAT SERVICE SUPPORT
1 cbt spt/spt unit

Paramilitary 22,050

Border Guards 14,750
Ministry of Interior and Administration

Maritime Border Guard 1,550
PATROL AND COASTAL COMBATANTS 14:
PCC 2 *Kasper*
PBF 2 *Straznik*
PB 10: 2 *Wisloka*; 2 *Baltic* 24; 6 others
AMPHIBIOUS • LANDING CRAFT • LCAC 2
Griffon 2000TDX

Prevention Units of Police 6,300; 1,000 conscript (total 7,300)
OPP–Ministry of Interior

Cyber

Poland has both national and government CERTs and is involved in informal CERT communities. A national cyber strategy is in the process of being drafted and Poland is an active participant in international cyber exercises.

DEPLOYMENT

Legal provisions for foreign deployment:
Constitution: Codified constitution (1997); Act on Principles of Use or External Deployment of the Polish Armed Forces (17/12/1998)
Decision on deployment of troops abroad: a) By president on request of prime minister in cases of direct threat (Art. 136);
b) in general, specified by ratified international agreement or statute (both must be passed by parliament, Art. 117)

AFGHANISTAN
NATO • ISAF 1,800; 1 AB bde (2 inf BG); 125 *Rosomak*; 103 other IFV; 5 Mi-24 *Hind*; 4 Mi-17 *Hip*
UN • UNAMA 1 obs
Bosnia-Herzegovina EU • EUFOR • *Operation Althea* 47

CÔTE D'IVOIRE
UN • UNOCI 2 obs

DEMOCRATIC REPUBLIC OF THE CONGO
UN • MONUSCO 2 obs

LIBERIA
UN • UNMIL 2 obs

SERBIA
NATO • KFOR 160; 1 inf coy
UN • UNMIK 1 obs

SOUTH SUDAN
UN • UNMISS 2 obs

FOREIGN FORCES

Germany Army: 67 (elm Corps HQ (multinational))

Portugal PRT

Euro €		2011	2012	2013
GDP	€	170.9bn	166.3bn	
	US$	237.8bn	210.6bn	
per capita	US$	22,056	19,534	
Growth	%	-1.67	-3.01	
Inflation	%	3.56	2.79	
Def exp [a]	€	2.6bn		
	US$	3.61bn		
Def bdgt	€	2.07bn	2.05bn	2.09bn
	US$	2.88bn	2.6bn	
US$1=€		0.72	0.79	

[a] NATO definition

Population   10,781,459

Age	0–14	15–19	20–24	25–29	30–64	65 plus
Male	8.4%	3.0%	3.1%	3.4%	23.4%	7.4%
Female	7.7%	2.6%	2.8%	3.0%	24.4%	10.7%

Capabilities

Portugal's military is moderately equipped and bolstered by a substantial force of reserves and the air force retains adequate strike capabilities, but the navy suffers from an ageing surface fleet (the sub-surface fleet has seen an improvement with two new Type-209 submarines commissioned since 2010). The level of joint training and readiness is relatively high, but there is only limited power projection capacity. This would likely make sustaining overseas deployments challenging, unless this operations were conducted within an alliance structure. The country's difficult economic situation means that it will be hard for the government to maintain Portugal's military capabilities. Lisbon withdrew from the co-operative NH90 helicopter programme, in July 2012, for cost-saving reasons, abandoned a programme to procure more than 39,000 assault rifles, pistols and light machine guns in August 2012, and cancelled a contract for a remaining 94 *Pandur* II armoured vehicles in October 2012. The planned modernisation of the armed forces will therefore probably be limited, with other future capabilities such as offshore patrol craft and upgrades likely to come under scrutiny. Siginificant cuts to conditions of service, including heating and hot meals, have resulted in public demonstrations by serving personnel.

ACTIVE 42,600 (Army 25,700 Navy 9,700 Air 7,200)
Paramilitary 47,700

RESERVE 211,950 (Army 210,000 Navy 1,250, Air Force 700)
Reserve obligation to age 35

ORGANISATIONS BY SERVICE

Army 25,700
5 Territorial Comd (2 mil region, 1 mil district, 2 mil zone)
FORCES BY ROLE
SPECIAL FORCES
1 SF unit
MANOEUVRE
Reconnaissance
1 ISTAR bn
Mechanised
1 mech bde (1 cav tp, 1 tk regt, 2 mech inf bn, 1 arty bn.
 1 AD bty, 1 engr coy, 1 sigs coy, 1 spt bn)
1 (intervention) bde (1 cav tp, 1 recce regt, 2 mech inf
 bn, 1 arty bn, 1 AD bty, 1 engr coy, 1 sigs coy, 1 spt
 bn)
Air Manoeuvre
1 (rapid reaction) bde (1 cav tp, 1 cdo bn, 2 para bn, 1
 arty bn, 1 AD bty, 1 engr coy, 1 sigs coy, 1 spt bn)
Other
1 (Madeira) inf gp (2 inf bn, 1 AD bty)
1 (Azores) inf gp (1 inf bn, 1 AD bty)
COMBAT SUPPORT
1 STA bty
1 AD bn
1 engr bn
1 EOD unit
1 ptn br coy
1 EW coy
2 MP coy
1 CBRN coy
1 psyops unit
1 CIMIC coy (joint)
1 sigs bn
COMBAT SERVICE SUPPORT
1 construction coy
1 maint coy
1 log coy
1 tpt coy
1 med unit

Reserves 210,000
FORCES BY ROLE
MANOEUVRE
 Light
 3 (territorial) def bde (on mobilisation)
EQUIPMENT BY TYPE
MBT 113: 37 *Leopard* 2A6; 72 M60A3; 4 M48A5
RECCE 44: 15 V-150 *Chaimite*; 31 ULTRAV M-11
APC 458
 APC (T) 261: 180 M113A1; 34 M113A2; 47 M577 A2
 APC (W) 197: 31 V-200 *Chaimite*; 166 *Pandur* II (all
 variants)
ARTY 360
 SP 155mm 23: 6 M109A2; 17 M109A5
 TOWED 33: **105mm** 33: 19 L-119; 9 M101; 5 M-56
 COASTAL • 150mm 1
 MOR 303: **81mm** 190 (incl 21 SP); **107mm** 53 M30 (incl
 20 SP); **120mm** 60 *Tampella*

AT
 MSL
 SP 28: 18 M113 with TOW; 4 M901 with TOW; 6
 ULTRAV-11 with *Milan*
 MANPATS *Milan*; *Spike* LR; *Spike* MR; TOW
 RCL 182: **106mm** 58 M40; **84mm** 89 *Carl Gustav*; **90mm**
 35
AD
 SAM • MANPAD 58: 32 *Chaparral*; 26 FIM-92A *Stinger*
AEV M728
ARV 6 M88A1, 7 *Pandur*
VLB M48

Navy 9,700 (incl 1,550 Marines)
EQUIPMENT BY TYPE
SUBMARINES • TACTICAL • SSK 2 *Tridente* (GER
Type-209) with 8 533mm TT
PRINCIPAL SURFACE COMBATANTS 5
 FRIGATES • FFGHM 5:
 3 *Vasco Da Gama* with 2 Mk141 quad lnchr with RGM-
 84C *Harpoon* AShM, 1 octuple Mk 29 GMLS with
 RIM-7M *Sea Sparrow* SAM, 2 Mk36 triple 324mm
 ASTT with Mk46 LWT, 1 100mm gun, (capacity 2
 Lynx Mk95 (*Super Lynx*) hel)
 2 *Bartolomeu Dias* (ex-NLD *Karel Doorman*) with 2
 quad Mk141 lnchr with RGM-84C *Harpoon* AShM, 1
 Mk48 VLS with RIM-7M *Sea Sparrow* SAM, 2 Mk32
 twin 324mm ASTT with Mk46 LWT, 1 76mm gun,
 (capacity: 1 *Lynx* Mk95 (*Super Lynx*) hel)
PATROL AND COASTAL COMBATANTS 24
 CORVETTES • FS 7:
 3 *Baptista de Andrade* with 1 100mm gun, 1 hel
 landing platform
 4 *Joao Coutinho* with 1 twin 76mm gun, 1 hel landing
 platform
 PSO 2 *Viana do Castelo* with 1 hel landing platform (2
 additional vessels in build)
 PCC 3 *Cacine*
 PBR 12: 2 *Albatroz*; 5 *Argos*; 4 *Centauro*; 1 *Rio Minho*
AMPHIBIOUS • LANDING CRAFT • LCU 1 *Bombarda*
LOGISTICS AND SUPPORT 13
 ABU 2: 1 *Schultz Xavier*; 1 *Guia*
 AGS 4: 2 *D Carlos* I (US *Stalwart*); 2 *Andromeda*
 AORL 1 *Bérrio* (ex UK *Rover*) with 1 hel landing platform
 (for medium hel)
 AXS 3: 1 *Sagres*; 1 *Creoula*; 1 *Polar*
 YGS 3

Marines 1,550
FORCES BY ROLE
SPECIAL FORCES
1 SF det
MANOEUVRE
 Light
 2 lt inf bn
COMBAT SUPPORT
1 mor coy 1 MP det

EQUIPMENT BY TYPE
ARTY • MOR 30 120mm

Naval Aviation

HELICOPTERS • ASW 5 *Lynx* Mk95 (*Super Lynx*)

Air Force 7,200

Flying hours   180 hrs/year on F-16 *Fighting Falcon*

FORCES BY ROLE

FIGHTER/GROUND ATTACK
  2 sqn with F-16AM/BM *Fighting Falcon*
MARITIME PATROL
  1 sqn with P-3C *Orion*
ISR/TRANSPORT
  1 sqn with C-295M
COMBAT SEARCH & RESCUE
  1 sqn with with AW101 *Merlin*
TRANSPORT
  1 sqn with C-130H/C-130H-30 *Hercules*
  1 sqn with *Falcon* 50
TRAINING
  1 sqn with *Alpha Jet**
  1 sqn with SA316 *Alouette III*
  1 sqn with TB-30 *Epsilon*

EQUIPMENT BY TYPE

AIRCRAFT 42 combat capable
  FTR 30: 27 F-16AM *Fighting Falcon*; 3 F-16BM *Fighting Falcon*
  ASW 5 P-3C *Orion*
  ISR 7: 5 C-295M (maritime surveillance), 2 C-295M (photo recce)
  TPT 14: **Medium** 6: 3 C-130H *Hercules*; 3 C-130H-30 *Hercules* (tpt/SAR); **Light** 5 C-295M; **PAX** 3 *Falcon* 50 (tpt/VIP)
  TRG 23: 7 *Alpha Jet**; 16 TB-30 *Epsilon*
HELICOPTERS
  MRH 12 SA316 *Alouette* III (trg, utl)
  TPT • Medium 12 AW101 *Merlin* (6 SAR, 4 CSAR, 2 fishery protection)
MSL
  AAM • IR AIM-9L/I *Sidewinder*; **ARH** AIM-120 AMRAAM
  ASM AGM-65A *Maverick*
  AShM AGM-84A *Harpoon*
BOMBS
  Enhanced Paveway II; GBU-49; GBU-31 JDAM

Paramilitary 47,700

National Republican Guard 26,100

APC (W): some *Commando* Mk III (*Bravia*)
HELICOPTERS • MRH 7 SA315 *Lama*

Public Security Police 21,600

DEPLOYMENT

Legal provisions for foreign deployment:
Constitution: Codified constitution (1976) (revised in 2005)
Decision on deployment of troops abroad: By government

AFGHANISTAN

NATO • ISAF 141
UN • UNAMA 1 obs

BOSNIA-HERZEGOVINA

EU • EUFOR • *Operation Althea* 6

DEMOCRATIC REPUBLIC OF THE CONGO

EU • EUSEC RD Congo 2

SERBIA

NATO • KFOR 168; 1 inf coy (KTM)
UN • UNMIK 1 obs

TIMOR LESTE

UN • UNMIT 2 obs

UGANDA

EU • EUTM 2

FOREIGN FORCES

United States US European Command: 700; 1 spt facility at Lajes

Romania ROM

New Lei		2011	2012	2013
GDP	lei	578.6bn	607.3bn	
	US$	189.8bn	171.4bn	
per capita	US$	8,687	7,845	
Growth	%	2.45	0.95	
Inflation	%	5.78	2.90	
Def exp [b]	lei	7.26bn		
	US$	2.38bn		
Def bdgt [a]	lei	7.06bn	7.67bn	8.28bn
	US$	2.31bn	2.16bn	
FMA (US)	US$	12.974m	12m	12m
US$1=lei		3.05	3.54	

[a] Includes military pensions
[b] NATO definition

Population   21,848,504

Age	0–14	15–19	20–24	25–29	30–64	65 plus
Male	7.6%	2.7%	3.6%	3.8%	24.9%	6.0%
Female	7.2%	2.6%	3.4%	3.7%	25.5%	8.9%

Capabilities

NATO membership is at the heart of Romania's defence posture, and the country has moved from a conscript to a professional military as it attempts to restructure its armed forces to perform NATO and EU missions. Since 2008, however, modernisation efforts have been hampered by funding difficulties. The army has been restructured to support deployed operations, with Romanian contingents joining NATO, EU and UN missions. An ageing fighter fleet undermines air force combat capability, with the replacement programme constrained by budget shortfalls. As of mid-2012, the favoured option was to acquire second-hand F-16s. There are a small number of tactical airlifters and Romania is a member of the Strategic Airlift Capability's C-17 unit. Romania's armed forces exercise regularly on a national and multinational basis.

ACTIVE 71,400 (Army 42,600, Navy 6,900, Air 8,400, Joint 13,500) Paramilitary 79,900

RESERVE 45,000 (Joint 45,000)

ORGANISATIONS BY SERVICE

Army 42,600

Readiness is reported as 70–90% for NATO-designated forces and 40–70% for other forces

FORCES BY ROLE
COMMAND
3 div HQ (1 NATO designated)
SPECIAL FORCES
1 SF bde
MANOEUVRE
Reconnaissance
3 recce bn
Mechanised
5 mech bde (1 NATO designated)
Light
2 inf bde (1 NATO designated)
Mountain
2 mtn inf bde (1 NATO designated)
COMBAT SUPPORT
1 arty bde
3 arty regt
3 AD regt
1 engr bde
3 engr bn
3 sigs bn
1 CIMIC bn
1 MP bn
3 CBRN bn
COMBAT SERVICE SUPPORT
4 spt bn

EQUIPMENT BY TYPE
MBT 437: 250 T-55; 42 TR-580; 91 TR-85; 54 TR-85 M1
AIFV 124: 23 MLI-84; 101 MLI-84 JDER
APC 1,090
  APC (T) 75 MLVM
  APC (W) 969: 69 B33 TAB *Zimbru*; 31 *Piranha III*; 367 TAB-71; 140 TAB-77; 362 TABC-79
  TYPE VARIANTS 505 APC
  PPV 60 *Maxxpro*
ARTY 899
  SP 122mm 24: 6 2S1 *Carnation*; 18 Model 89
  TOWED 422: **122mm** 72 (M-30) M-1938 (A-19); **152mm** 350: 247 M-1981 Model 81; 103 M-1985
  MRL 122mm 187: 133 APR-40; 54 LAROM
  MOR 120mm 266 M-1982
AT
  MSL • SP 134: 12 9P122 *Malyutka* (AT-3 *Sagger*); 74 9P133 *Malyutka* (AT-3 *Sagger*); 48 9P148 *Konkurs* (AT-5 *Spandrel*). All on BRDM-2
  GUNS 100mm 232: 209 M1977 Gun 77; 23 SU-100 SP
AD • GUNS 66
  SP 35mm 42 *Gepard*
  TOWED • 35mm 24 GDF-203
RADARS • LAND 8 SNAR-10 *Big Fred*
ARV 3 BPz-2

Navy 6,900

EQUIPMENT BY TYPE
PRINCIPAL SURFACE COMBATANTS 3
  DESTROYERS 3:
    DDGH 1 *Marasesti* with 4 twin lnchr with P-15M *Termit-M* (SS-N-2C *Styx*) AShM, 2 triple 533mm ASTT with RUS 53–65 ASW, 2 RBU 6000 *Smerch* 2, 2 twin 76mm gun, (capacity 2 SA-316 (IAR-316) *Alouette* III hel)
    DDH 2 *Regele Ferdinand* (ex UK Type-22), with 2 triple 324mm TT, 1 76mm gun (capacity 1 SA330 (IAR-330) *Puma* - platforms undergoing upgrades)
PATROL AND COASTAL COMBATANTS 21
  CORVETTES 4:
    FSH 2 *Tetal* II with 2 twin 533mm ASTT, 2 RBU 6000 *Smerch* 2, 1 76mm gun, (capacity 1 SA-316 (IAR-316) *Alouette* III hel)
    FS 2 *Tetal* I with 2 twin 533mm ASTT with RUS 53-65 ASW, 2 RBU 2500 *Smerch* 1, 2 twin 76mm gun
  PCFG 3 *Zborul* with 2 twin lnchr with P-15M *Termit-M* (SS-N-2C *Styx*) AShM, 1 76mm gun
  PCR 8:
    1 *Brutar* I with 2 BM-21 MRL, 1 100mm gun
    4 *Brutar* II with 2 BM-21 MRL, 1 100mm gun
    3 *Kogalniceanu* with 2 BM-21 MRL, 2 100mm gun
  PBR 6 VD 141 (ex MSI now used for river patrol)
MINE WARFARE 11
  MINE COUNTERMEASURES 10:
    MSO 4 *Musca* with 2 quad lnchr with *Strela* 2M (SA-N-5 *Grail*) SAM
    MSI 6 VD141 (used for river MCM)
  MINELAYERS • ML 1 *Corsar* with up to 100 mines, 2 RBU 1200 ASROC
LOGISTICS AND SUPPORT 14
  ADG 1 *Magnetica*
  AETL 2 *Constanta*
  AGOR 1 *Corsar*
  AGS 2: 1 *Emil Racovita*; 1 *Catuneanu*
  AOL 3: 1 *Tulcea*; 2 others
  ATF 1 *Grozavu*
  AXS 1 *Mircea*
  YTL 3

Naval Infantry

FORCES BY ROLE
MANOEUVRE
  Light
  1 naval inf bn

EQUIPMENT BY TYPE
APC (W) 14: 11 ABC-79M; 3 TABC-79M

Air Force 8,400

Flying hours 120 hrs/year

FORCES BY ROLE
FIGHTER
  2 sqn with MiG-21 *Lancer* C
FIGHTER/GROUND ATTACK
  1 sqn with MiG-21 *Lancer* A/B

TRANSPORT
1 sqn with An-26 *Curl*; An-30 *Clank*; C-27J *Spartan*
1 sqn with C-130B/H *Hercules*
TRAINING
1 sqn with IAR-99 *Soim**
1 sqn with SA316B *Alouette* III (IAR-316B); Yak-52 (Iak-52)
TRANSPORT HELICOPTER
2 (multirole) sqn with IAR-330 SOCAT *Puma*
3 sqn with SA330 *Puma* (IAR-330)
AIR DEFENCE
1 AD bde
COMBAT SERVICE SUPPORT
1 engr regt
EQUIPMENT BY TYPE
AIRCRAFT 69 combat capable
FGA 36: 10 MiG-21 *Lancer* A; 6 MiG-21 *Lancer* B; 20 MiG-21 *Lancer* C
ISR 2 An-30 *Clank*
TPT 13: **Medium** 10: 5 C-27J *Spartan* (2 more on order); 4 C-130B *Hercules*; 1 C-130H *Hercules*; **Light** 3 An-26 *Curl*
TRG 32: 10 IAR-99 *Soim**; 10 IAR-99C *Soim**; 12 Yak-52 (Iak-52)
HELICOPTERS
MRH 31: 23 IAR-330 SOCAT *Puma*; 7 SA316B *Alouette* III (IAR-316B)
TPT • **Medium** 37: 21 SA330L *Puma* (IAR-330L); 16 SA330M *Puma* (IAR-330M)
AD • **SAM** 14: 6 S-75M3 *Volkhov* (SA-2 *Guideline*); 8 MIM-23 HAWK PIP III
MSL
AAM • **IR** R-73 (AA-11 *Archer*); R-550 *Magic* 2; *Python* 3
ASM *Spike-ER*

Paramilitary 79,900

Border Guards 22,900 (incl conscripts)
Ministry of Interior
EQUIPMENT BY TYPE
PATROL AND COASTAL COMBATANTS 8
PCO 1 *Stefan cel Mare* (Damen OPV 900)
PB 7: 4 *Neustadt*; 3 *Mai*

Gendarmerie ε57,000
Ministry of Interior

Cyber

Romania has a national CERT and is involved in informal CERT communities. A nationwide cyber-security policy is currently being implemented. The private sector is investing heavily in Romania with a number of international firms planning to open cyber-security facilities.

DEPLOYMENT

Legal provisions for foreign deployment:
Constitution: Codified constitution (1991)
Decision on deployment of troops abroad: By parliament (Art. 62); or b) by president upon parliamentary approval (Art. 92).

AFGHANISTAN
NATO • ISAF 1,762; 2 mtn inf bn; TAB-77; TABC-79; *Piranha* IIIC
UN • UNAMA 1 obs

BOSNIA-HERZEGOVINA
EU • EUFOR • *Operation Althea* 59

CÔTE D'IVOIRE
UN • UNOCI 4 obs

DEMOCRATIC REPUBLIC OF THE CONGO
UN • MONUSCO 22 obs

GULF OF ADEN & INDIAN OCEAN
EU • *Operation Atalanta* 1 DDH

LIBERIA
UN • UNMIL 2 obs

SERBIA
NATO • KFOR 89
UN • UNMIK 1 obs

SOUTH SUDAN
UN • UNMISS 2; 4 obs

Serbia SER

Serbian Dinar d		2011	2012	2013
GDP	d	3.18tr	3.36tr	
	US$	43.3bn	37.2bn	
per capita	US$	5,951	5,112	
Growth	%	1.62	-0.48	
Inflation	%	11.15	5.93	
Def bdgt	d	71.2bn	73.9bn	76.6bn
	US$	972m	819m	
FMA (US)	US$	1.896m	1.8m	1.8m
US$1=d		73.30	90.26	

Population   7,276,604

Age	0–14	15–19	20–24	25–29	30–64	65 plus
Male	7.7%	3.0%	3.2%	3.5%	24.6%	6.8%
Female	7.2%	2.8%	3.0%	3.4%	25.0%	9.8%

Capabilities

2011 saw the shift from conscript to professional armed forces as part of a near decade-long restructuring process. Following the conflicts of the 1990s and the political turmoil of the turn of the century, the armed forces have been reduced in size, but with the long-term aim of crafting a capable and modern force. The land forces are built around four combined-arms brigades, supported by an army aviation unit run by the air force. The latter has a small number of combat aircraft in-service, and had been aiming to procure one or two squadrons of a modern multi-role type. Funding constraints have meant that this project has been delayed. Serviceability and platform availability are likely to be a problem for the air force. It also has no long-range transport capacity. There is a very limited coastal and river patrol capability.

ACTIVE 28,150 (Army 13,250, Air Force and Air Defence 5,100, Training Command 3,000, Guards 1,600; Other MoD 5,200)

RESERVE 50,150

Terms of service 6 months (voluntary)

ORGANISATIONS BY SERVICE

Army 13,250

FORCES BY ROLE
SPECIAL FORCES
1 SF bde (1 CT bn, 1 cdo bn, 1 para bn, 1 log bn)
MANOEUVRE
Mechanised
1 (1st) bde (1 tk bn, 2 mech inf bn, 1 inf bn, 1 SP arty bn, 1 MRL bn, 1 AD bn, 1 engr bn, 1 log bn)
3 (2nd, 3rd & 4th) bde (1 tk bn, 2 mech inf bn, 2 inf bn, 1 SP arty bn, 1 MRL bn, 1 AD bn, 1 engr bn, 1 log bn)
COMBAT SUPPORT
1 (mixed) arty bde (4 arty bn, 1 MRL bn, 1 spt bn)
2 ptn bridging bn
1 NBC bn
1 sigs bn
2 MP bn

Reserve Organisations

FORCES BY ROLE
MANOEUVRE
Light
8 (territorial) inf bde
EQUIPMENT BY TYPE
MBT 212: 199 M-84; 13 T-72
RECCE 46: 46 BRDM-2
AIFV 323 M-80
APC 39 BOV VP M-86
ARTY 515
SP **122mm** 67 2S1 *Carnation*
TOWED 204: **122mm** 78 D-30; **130mm** 18 M-46; **152mm** 36 M-84; **155mm** 72: 66 M-1; 6 M-65
MRL 81: **128mm** 78: 18 M-63 *Plamen*; 60 M-77 *Organj*; **262mm** 3 *Orkan*
MOR 163: **82mm** 106 M-69; **120mm** 57: M-74/M-75
AT • MSL
SP 48 BOV-1 (M-83) AT-3 9K11 *Sagger*
MANPATS 168: 99 AT-3 9K11 *Sagger*; 69 AT-4 9K111 *Fagot* (*Spigot*)
RCL 6: **90mm** 6 M-79;
AD • SAM 156
SP 77 2K12 Kub (SA-6 *Gainful*); 12 S-1M (SA-9 *Gaskin*); 5 SAVA S10M
MANPADS 62: 8 S-2M (SA-7 *Grail*); 54 *Šilo* (SA-16 *Gimlet*)
GUNS 36
TOWED **40mm:** 36 L70 Bofors
AEV IWT

ARV M84A1; T-54/T-55
VLB MT-55; TMM

River Flotilla

The Serbian-Montenegrin navy was transferred to Montenegro upon independence in 2006, but the Danube flotilla remained in Serbian control. The flotilla is subordinate to the Land Forces.

EQUIPMENT BY TYPE
PATROL AND COASTAL COMBATANTS • PBR 5: 3 Type-20; 2 others
MINE WARFARE • MINE COUNTERMEASURES • MSI 4 *Nestin*
AMPHIBIOUS • LANDING CRAFT • LCU 5 Type-22
LOGISTICS AND SUPPORT 5:
ADG 1 *Šabac*
AGF 1 *Kozara*
AOL 1
YFD 1
YTL 1

Air Force and Air Defence 5,100

Flying hours: Ftr – 40 per yr
FORCES BY ROLE
FIGHTER
1 sqn with MiG-21bis *Fishbed*; MiG-29 *Fulcrum*
FIGHTER/GROUND ATTACK
1 sqn with G-4 *Super Galeb**; J-22 *Orao*
ISR
2 flt with IJ-22 *Orao* 1*; MiG-21R *Fishbed* H*
TRANSPORT
1 sqn with An-2; An-26; Do-28; Yak-40 (Jak-40); 1 PA-34 *Seneca* V
TRAINING
1 sqn with G-4 *Super Galeb** (adv trg/light atk); SA341/342 *Gazelle*; Utva-75 (basic trg)
ATTACK HELICOPTER
1 sqn with SA341H/342L *Gazelle*; (HN-42/45); Mi-24 *Hind*
TRANSPORT HELICOPTER
2 sqn with Mi-8 *Hip*; Mi-17 *Hip* H
AIR DEFENCE
1 bde (5 bn (2 msl, 3 SP msl) with S-125 *Neva* (SA-3 *Goa*); 2K12 *Kub* (SA-6 *Gainful*); 9K32 *Strela*-2 (SA-7 *Grail*); 9K310 Igla-1 (SA-16 *Gimlet*))
2 radar bn (for early warning and reporting)
COMBAT SUPPORT
1 sigs bn
COMBAT SERVICE SUPPORT
1 maint bn
EQUIPMENT BY TYPE
AIRCRAFT 84 combat capable
FTR 30: 20 MiG-21bis *Fishbed* L & N; 6 MiG-21UM *Mongol* B; 3 MiG-29 *Fulcrum*; 1 MiG-29UB *Fulcrum*
FGA 18 J-22 *Orao* 1
ISR 12: 10 IJ-22R *Orao* 1*; 2 MiG-21R *Fishbed* H*
TPT • Light 10: 1 An-2 *Colt*; 4 An-26 *Curl*; 2 Do-28 *Skyservant*; 2 Yak-40 (Jak-40); 1 PA-34 *Seneca* V
TRG 28: 24 G-4 *Super Galeb**; 11 Utva-75; 3+ Lasta 95 (order for 15 due for completion end 2012)

HELICOPTERS
ATK 2 Mi-24 *Hind*
MRH 51: 2 Mi-17 *Hip* H; 2 SA341H *Gazelle* (HI-42); 34 SA341H *Gazelle* (HN-42)/SA342L *Gazelle* (HN-45); 13 SA341H *Gazelle* (HO-42)/SA342L1 *Gazelle* (HO-45)
TPT • Medium 7 Mi-8T *Hip* (HT-40)
AD
SAM 15: 6 S-125 *Pechora* (SA-3 *Goa*); 9 2K12 *Kub* (SA-6 *Gainful*)
MANPAD 156; 120 9K32 *Strela*-2 (SA-7 *Grail*); 36 9K310 *Igla*-1 (SA-16 *Gimlet*)
GUNS • 40mm 24 L-70 Bofors
MSL
AAM • IR R-60 (AA-8 *Aphid*)
ASM AGM-65 *Maverick*; A-77 *Thunder*

Guards 1,600
MANOEUVRE
Other
1 (ceremonial) gd bde (1 gd bn, 1 MP bn, 1 spt bn)

DEPLOYMENT

Legal provisions for foreign deployment:
Constitution: Codified constitution (2006)
Decision on deployment of troops abroad: By parliament (Art. 140)

CÔTE D'IVOIRE
UN • UNOCI 3 obs

CYPRUS
UN • UNFICYP 46

DEMOCRATIC REPUBLIC OF THE CONGO
UN • MONUSCO 6 (Air Medical Evacuation Team); 2 obs

LEBANON
UN • UNIFIL 5

LIBERIA
UN • UNMIL 4 obs

MIDDLE EAST
UN • UNTSO 1 obs

TERRITORY WHERE THE GOVERNMENT DOES NOT EXERCISE EFFECTIVE CONTROL

Data here represent the de facto situation in Kosovo. This does not imply international recognition as a sovereign state. In February 2008, Kosovo declared itself independent. Serbia remains opposed to this, and while Kosovo has not been admitted to the United Nations, a number of states have recognised Kosovo's self-declared status.

Kosovo Security Force 2,500; reserves 800

The Kosovo Security Force was formed, in January 2009, as a non-military organisation with responsibility for crisis response, civil protection and explosive ordnance disposal. The force is armed with small arms and light vehicles only. A July 2010 law created a reserve force.

FOREIGN FORCES
All under Kosovo Force (KFOR) comd. unless otherwise specified.
Albania 9
Armenia 35
Austria 535; elm 1 recce coy, 1 mech inf coy; elm 1 MP coy
Bulgaria 19
Canada 6
Croatia 19
Czech Republic 7 • UNMIK 1 obs
Denmark 35
Estonia 1
Finland 22
France 335; 1 armd cav sqn; 1 log coy
Germany 1,330; 1 NBC bn HQ; elm 1 MP coy; 2 NBC coy; 1 sigs coy; 1 spt bn; 1 med unit; elm 1 hel gp; 26 C2 *Leopard* MBT; 17 SPz-2 *Luchs* recce; 25 *Marder* 1 AIFV; 21 APC (T); 54 TPz-1 *Fuchs* APC (W); 10 M109A3G 155mm SP; 6 *Wiesel* (TOW) msl; 3 CH-53G *Stallion* hel; 9 UH-1D *Iroquois* hel
Greece 152; 1 mech inf coy
Hungary 194; 1 inf coy (KTM)
Ireland 12
Italy 869; 1 AD regt HQ; 1 engr unit; 1 hel unit; 1 sigs unit; 1 CSS unit; 1 Carabinieri regt
Luxembourg 21
Moldova UNMIK 1 obs
Morocco 168; 1 inf coy
Netherlands 9
Norway 3 • UNMIK 1 obs
Poland 160; 1 inf coy
Portugal 168; 1 inf coy (KTM) • UNMIK 1 obs
Romania 89 • UNMIK 1 obs
Slovenia 323; 2 mot inf coy
Sweden 54
Switzerland 257; 1 inf coy; elm 1 MP coy; elm 1 hel gp
Turkey 402; 1 inf coy; elm 1 MP coy • UNMIK 1 obs
Ukraine 149; 1 inf coy • UNMIK 2 obs
United Kingdom 1
United States 764; 1 ARNG cbt spt bde

Europe

Slovakia SVK

Euro €		2011	2012	2013
GDP	€	69.1bn	72bn	
	US$	96.1bn	91.2bn	
per capita	US$	17,527	16,633	
Growth	%	3.35	2.64	
Inflation	%	4.08	3.62	
Def exp [b]	€	766m		
	US$	1.07bn		
Def bdgt [a]	€	763m	798m	736m
	US$	1.06bn	1.01bn	
FMA (US)	US$	1.397m	1m	1m
US$1=€		0.72	0.79	

[a] Includes military pensions

[b] NATO definition

Population   5,483,088

Age	0–14	15–19	20–24	25–29	30–64	65 plus
Male	8.0%	3.0%	3.6%	4.0%	24.9%	4.9%
Female	7.6%	2.9%	3.5%	3.9%	25.5%	8.2%

Capabilities

The Slovakian armed forces suffer from the twin pressures of low funding and the need to modernise an ageing equipment inventory. A Strategic Defence Review process was begun in late 2010, partly driven by the country's low level of defence expenditure in relation to its perceived defence requirements, but also by the desire to map out a path for Slovak military development. It recommended restructuring the Slovak armed forces, but in 2012, the new government decided not to implement its conclusions. The government has mooted the possibility of merging the existing defence and interior ministries, as well as merging the current civilian and military intelligence organisations. Training remains geared towards meeting core national requirements (such as SAR), Alliance requirements (air defence), or focused on participation in international operations. Discussions were reported to have restarted on the possible provision of an airlift capability. Meanwhile, the year was likely to see modernisation of Slovakia's Mi-17Ms to meet CSAR requirements.

ACTIVE 15,850 (Army 6,250, Air 3,950, Central Staff 2,550, Support and Training 3,100)

Terms of service 6 months

ORGANISATIONS BY SERVICE

Army 6,250

FORCES BY ROLE

MANOEUVRE

Reconnaissance

1 (5th Special) recce regt

Mechanised

1 (1st) mech bde (3 mech inf bn, 1 engr coy, 1 spt bn)

1 (2nd) mech bde (1 ISATR coy, 1 tk bn, 2 mech inf bn, 1 mixed SP arty bn, 1 engr coy, 1 spt bn)

COMBAT SUPPORT

1 MRL bn

1 engr bn

1 MP bn

1 NBC bn

EQUIPMENT BY TYPE

MBT 30 T-72M

AIFV 239: 148 BMP-1; 91 BMP-2

APC 101+

  APC (T) 72 OT-90

  APC (W) 22: 7 OT-64; 15 *Tatrapan* (6×6)

  PPV 7+ RG-32M

ARTY 68

  SP 19: **152mm** 3 M-77 *Dana*; **155mm** 16 M-2000 *Zuzana*

  TOWED 122mm 19 D-30

  MRL 30: **122mm** 4 RM-70; **122/227mm** 26 RM-70/85 MODULAR

AT

  SP 9S428 with *Malyutka* (AT-3 *Sagger*) on BMP-1; 9P135 *Fagot* (AT-4 *Spigot*) on BMP-2; 9P148 (AT-5 *Spandrel*) on BRDM-2

  MANPATS 425 9K11 *Malyutka* (AT-3 *Sagger*)/9K113 *Shturm* (AT-6 *Spandrel*)

AD

  SAM • TOWED

  SP 48 9K35 *Strela*-10 (SA-13 *Gopher*)

  MANPADS 9K32 *Strela*-2 (SA-7 *Grail*); 9K310 *Igla*-1 (SA-16 *Gimlet*)

RADAR • LAND SNAR-10 *Big Fred* (veh, arty)

ARV MT-55; VT-55A; VT-72B; WPT-TOPAS

VLB AM-50; MT-55A

MW Bozena; Belarty UOS-155

Air Force 3,950

Flying hours 90 hrs/yr for MiG-29 pilots (NATO Integrated AD System); 90 hrs/yr for Mi-8/17 crews (reserved for EU & NATO)

FORCES BY ROLE

FIGHTER

1 sqn with MiG-29AS/UBS *Fulcrum*

TRANSPORT

1 flt with An-26 *Curl*

1 flt with L-410FG/T/UVP *Turbolet*

TRANSPORT HELICOPTER

1 sqn with Mi-8 *Hip*; Mi-17 *Hip H*

1 sqn with PZL MI-2 *Hoplite*

TRAINING

1 sqn with L-39CM/ZA/ZAM *Albatross*

AIR DEFENCE

1 bde with 2K12 *Kub* (SA-6 *Gainful*); 9K32 *Strela*-2 (SA-7 *Grail*); S-300 (SA-10 *Grumble*)

EQUIPMENT BY TYPE

AIRCRAFT 20 combat capable

  FTR 20: 10 MiG-29AS *Fulcrum*; 2 MiG-29UBS *Fulcrum*; 8 MiG-29A/UB *Fulcrum*

  TPT • Light 9: 1 An-26 *Curl*; 2 L-410FG *Turbolet*; 2 L-410T *Turbolet*; 4 L-410UVP *Turbolet*

TRG 13: 6 L-39CM *Albatross;* 5 L-39ZA *Albatross;* 2 L-39ZAM *Albatross*
HELICOPTERS
ATK (15: 5 Mi-24D *Hind* D; 10 Mi-24V *Hind* E all in store)
MRH 14 Mi-17 *Hip* H
TPT 7: **Medium** 1 Mi-8 *Hip;* **Light** 6 PZL MI-2 *Hoplite*
AD • SAM
SP S-300 (SA-10B *Grumble*); 2K12 *Kub* (SA-6 *Gainful*)
MANPAD 9K32 *Strela-*2 (SA-7 *Grail*)
MSL
AAM • IR R-60 (AA-8 *Aphid*); R-73 (AA-11 *Archer*);
SARH R-27R (AA-10A *Alamo*)
ASM S5K/S5KO (57mm rockets); S8KP/S8KOM (80mm rockets)

DEPLOYMENT

Legal provisions for foreign deployment:
Constitution: Codified constitution (1992)
Decision on deployment of troops abroad: By the parliament (Art. 86)

AFGHANISTAN

NATO • ISAF 343

BOSNIA-HERZEGOVINA

EU • EUFOR • *Operation Althea* 34

CYPRUS

UN • UNFICYP 159; elm 1 inf coy; 1 engr pl

MIDDLE EAST

UN • UNTSO 2 obs

Slovenia SVN

Euro €		2011	2012	2013
GDP	€	36.2bn	35.9bn	
	US$	50.3bn	45.4bn	
per capita	US$	25,193	22,738	
Growth	%	0.60	-2.22	
Inflation	%	1.83	2.17	
Def exp [b]	€	478m		
	US$	665m		
Def bdgt [a]	€	515m	448m	446m
	US$	717m	567m	
FMA (US)	US$	0.748m	0.45m	0.45m
US$1=€		0.72	0.79	

[a] Includes military pensions
[b] NATO definition

Population 1,996,617

Age	0–14	15–19	20–24	25–29	30–64	65 plus
Male	6.9%	2.5%	3.0%	3.4%	26.1%	6.8%
Female	6.5%	2.4%	2.8%	3.3%	26.0%	10.3%

Capabilities

The military's role is to support territorial integrity and participate in peace-support and stabilisation operations.

A NATO member since 2004, the country has been moving to reshape its armed forces so that they are fully capable of operating within the Alliance. But funding limitations continue to dictate the pace of change, particularly in equipment modernisation. It contributes to both KFOR and ISAF. The air force lacks any fighter aircraft, with air policing supplied by the Italian air force. Aspirations to remedy this are likely to remain unfulfilled in light of the defence budgeting. There is no organic capability to deploy beyond Slovenia's borders.

ACTIVE 7,600 (Army 7,600) Paramilitary 4,500

RESERVE 1,700 (Army 1,600, Air Element 100)

ORGANISATIONS BY SERVICE

Army 7,600
FORCES BY ROLE
SPECIAL FORCES
1 SF unit
MANOEUVRE
Reconnaissance
1 ISTAR bn
Light
3 mot inf bn
COMBAT SUPPORT
1 arty bn
1 engr bn
1 MP bn
1 CBRN bn
1 sigs bn

Reserves
FORCES BY ROLE
MANOEUVRE
Armoured
1 tk bn
Mountain
1 mtn inf bn (6 coy)
EQUIPMENT BY TYPE
MBT 45 M-84
RECCE 10 *Cobra* CBRN
APC (W) 115: 85 *Pandur* 6×6 (*Valuk*); 30 *Patria* 8×8 (*Svarun*)
ARTY 74
TOWED • **155mm** 18 TN-90
MOR **120mm** 56: 8 M-52; 16 M-74; 32 MN-9
AT • MSL
SP 24: 12 BOV-3 9K11 *Malyutka* (AT-3 *Sagger*); 12 BOV-3 9K111 *Fagot* (AT-4 *Spigot*)
MANPATS 9K11 *Malyutka* (AT-3 *Sagger*); 9K111 *Fagot* (AT-4 *Spigot*)
ARV VT-55A
VLB MTU

Army Maritime Element 50
FORCES BY ROLE
MANOEUVRE
Amphibious
1 maritime bn (part of Sp Comd)

EQUIPMENT BY TYPE
PATROL AND COASTAL COMBATANTS 2
PBF 1 *Super Dvora* MkII
PCC 1 *Triglav* III (RUS *Svetlyak*)

Air Element 530
FORCES BY ROLE
TRANSPORT
1 sqn with L-410 *Turbolet*; PC-6B *Turbo-Porter*
TRAINING
1 unit with Bell 206 *Jet Ranger* (AB-206); PC-9; PC-9M*;
Z-143L; Z-242L
TRANSPORT HELICOPTER
1 bn with AS532AL *Cougar*; Bell 412 *Twin Huey* (some
armed)
AIR DEFENCE
1 bn
COMBAT SERVICE SUPPORT
1 maint coy
EQUIPMENT BY TYPE
AIRCRAFT 9 combat capable
TPT • Light 3: 1 L-410 *Turbolet*; 2 PC-6B *Turbo-Porter*
TRG 21: 2 PC-9; 9 PC-9M*; 2 Z-143L; 8 Z-242L
HELICOPTERS
MRH 8: 5 Bell 412EP *Twin Huey*; 2 Bell 412HP *Twin
Huey*; 1 Bell 412SP *Twin Huey* (some armed)
TPT 8: **Medium** 4 AS532AL *Cougar*; **Light** 4 Bell 206 *Jet
Ranger* (AB-206)
AD • SAM 138
SP 6 *Roland* II
MANPAD 132: 36 9K310 *Igla*-1 (SA-16 *Gimlet*); 96 9K38
Igla (SA-18 *Grouse*)

Paramilitary 4,500

Police 4,500 (armed); 5,000 reservists (total 9,500)
PATROL AND COASTAL COMBATANTS • PBF 1 *Ladse*
HELICOPTERS
MRH 2: 1 Bell 412 *Twin Huey*, 1 Bell 212 (AB-212)
TPT • Light 4: 1 AW109; 2 Bell 206 (AB-206) *Jet Ranger*;
1 EC135

DEPLOYMENT
Legal provisions for foreign deployment:
Constitution: Codified constitution (1991)
Decision on deployment of troops abroad: By
government (Art. 84 of Defence Act)

AFGHANISTAN
NATO • ISAF 77

BOSNIA-HERZEGOVINA
EU • EUFOR • *Operation Althea* 14

LEBANON
UN • UNIFIL 14; 1 inf pl

MIDDLE EAST
UN • UNTSO 3 obs

SERBIA
NATO • KFOR 323; 2 mot inf coy

Spain ESP

Euro €		2011	2012	2013
GDP	€	1.06tr	1.06tr	
	US$	1.48tr	1.34tr	
per capita	US$	31,461	28,485	
Growth	%	0.42	-1.54	
Inflation	%	3.05	2.44	
Def exp [b]	€	10.1bn		
	US$	14bn		
Def bdgt [a]	€	10.9bn	9.3bn	
	US$	15.2bn	11.8bn	
US$1=€		0.72	0.79	

[a] Includes military pensions
[b] NATO definition

Population	47,042,984

Age	0–14	15–19	20–24	25–29	30–64	65 plus
Male	7.9%	2.4%	2.7%	3.3%	25.8%	7.3%
Female	7.4%	2.2%	2.5%	3.0%	25.6%	9.9%

Capabilities

Defence spending has suffered significantly since the
global financial crisis, with this likely to have an impact
on Spanish military capabilities. The country maintains
advanced weaponry, and combat experience has been
gained from overseas deployments. In terms of real-terms
percentage reduction in planned defence allocations,
Spain saw the largest fall in 2012. Personnel expenditure
was restrained by cutting civilian posts at the Ministry of
Defence. Operational expenses were set to be cut by reducing overseas deployments. Spain announced, in September 2012, that it had delayed to 2015 the delivery of 15
Typhoon aircraft initially contracted for delivery between
2012 and 2014. Spain also cancelled a bilateral military
satellite programme with Norway in order to save costs.
Five naval vessels were decommissioned or scheduled for
decommissioning in 2012 as the fleet shrinks, and it was
even reported, in May 2012, that the *Principe de Asturias*
aircraft carrier might be mothballed. Research and development funding has also been reduced. Spain provides
one of the six corps-level headquarters for NATO's High
Readiness Forces Land. The Spanish armed forces have
been involved in a variety of multinational coalitions in
recent years, from Afghanistan to the Gulf of Aden, and
regularly participate in peacekeeping operations. The
armed forces are well-versed in combined operations with
other militaries. Spain also retains modest global power-
projection capabilities. As with some other European nations, it lacks strategic transport aircraft, making sizeable
overseas deployments problematic, but the country can
deploy and sustain at least a small brigade-sized unit in
theatre. Spain will continue to retain advanced equipment
but its forces will likely shrink in their capabilities and
may struggle to retain the ability to deploy globally in the
longer term.

ACTIVE 135,500 (Army 70,800 Navy 22,200, Air 21,200 Joint 21,300) **Paramilitary 80,200**

RESERVE 32,000 (Army 17,000 Navy 9,000 Air 6,000)

ORGANISATIONS BY SERVICE

Space
SATELLITES • COMMUNICATIONS 2: 1 *Spainsat*; 1 *Xtar-Eur*

Army 70,800
The Land Forces High Readiness HQ Spain provides one NATO Rapid Deployment Corps HQ (NRDC-SP).

FORCES BY ROLE
Infantry regiments usually comprise 2 bn. Spain deploys its main battle tanks within its armd/mech inf formations, and its armd cav regt

COMMAND
1 corps HQ (CGTAD) (1 int regt, 1 MP bn)
2 div HQ (coordination role)

SPECIAL FORCES
1 comd (3 Spec Ops bn, 1 sigs coy)

MANOEUVRE
Reconnaissance
1 (2nd) bde (3 lt armd cav regt, 1 fd arty regt, 1 AD coy, 1 engr bn, 1 sigs coy, 1 log bn)

Armoured
1 (12th) bde (1 recce sqn, 1 armd inf regt, 1 mech inf regt, 1 SP arty bn, 1 AD coy, 1 engr bn, 1 sigs coy, 1 log bn)

Mechanised
2 (10th & 11th) bde (1 recce sqn, 1 armd inf bn, 1 mech inf regt, 1 SP arty bn, 1 AD coy, 1 engr bn, 1 sigs coy, 1 log bn)

Light
2 (2nd/La Legion & 7th) bde (1 recce bn, 2 inf regt, 1 fd arty bn, 1 AD coy, 1 engr bn, 1 sigs coy, 1 log bn)
1 (5th) bde (2 lt inf regt)

Air Manoeuvre
1 (6th) bde (2 para bn, 1 air mob bn, 1 fd arty bn, 1 AD coy, 1 engr bn, 1 sigs coy, 1 log bn)

Mountain
1 (1st) comd (3 mtn inf regt)

Other
1 (Canary Islands) comd (1 lt inf bde (3 lt inf regt, 1 fd arty regt, 1 engr bn, 1 sigs coy, 1 log bn); 1 spt hel bn; 1 AD regt)
1 (Balearic Islands) comd (1 inf regt)
2 (Ceuta and Melilla) comd (1 cav regt, 2 inf regt, 1 arty regt, 1 engr bn, 1 sigs coy, 1 log bn)

Aviation
1 (FAMET) avn comd (1 atk hel bn, 2 spt hel bn, 1 tpt hel bn, 1 sigs bn, 1 log unit (1 spt coy, 1 supply coy))

COMBAT SUPPORT
1 arty comd (3 arty regt; 1 coastal arty regt)
1 AD comd (5 ADA regt, 1 sigs unit)
1 engr comd (2 engr regt, 1 bridging regt)
1 EW/sigs bde with (1 EW regt, 3 sigs regt)
1 EW regt

1 sigs regt
1 CIMIC bn

COMBAT SERVICE SUPPORT
1 log bde (5 log regt)
1 med bde (1 log unit, 2 med regt, 1 fd hospital unit)
1 NBC regt

EQUIPMENT BY TYPE
MBT 324: 108 *Leopard* 2A4; 216 *Leopard* 2A5E
RECCE 291: 84 B-1 *Centauro*; 207 VEC-3562 *BMR-VEC*
AIFV 144 *Pizarro* (incl 22 comd)
APC 904
  APC (T) 457 M113 (incl variants)
  APC (W) 347 BMR-600/BMR-600M1
  PPV 100 RG-31
ARTY 1,895
  SP 155mm 96 M109A5
  TOWED 314: **105mm** 225: 56 L118 light gun; 169 Model 56 pack howitzer; **155mm** 89: 43 M114; 46 SBT 155/52 SIAC (18 more on order)
  COASTAL 155mm 19 SBT 155/52 APU SBT V07
  MOR 1,466: **81mm** 996; **120mm** 470
AT
  MSL
    SP 187: 113 *Milan*; 74 *TOW*
    MANPATS 500: 39 *Spike*-LR (197 more on order); 335 *Milan*; 126 *TOW*
HELICOPTERS
  ATK 6 EC665 *Tiger* (18 more on order)
  MRH 21 Bo-105 HOT
  TPT 73: **Heavy** 17 CH-47D *Chinook* (HT-17D); **Medium** 33: 16 AS332B *Super Puma* (HU-21); 17 AS532UL *Cougar*; **Light** 23: 13 Bell-205 (HU-10B *Iroquois*); 5 Bell 212 (HU.18); 5 Bo-105
UAV • ISR • Medium 4 *Searcher* Mk II-J (PASI)
AD 360
  SAM 269
    SP 18 *Roland*
    TOWED 71: 42 MIM-23B I-HAWK Phase III; 13 *Skyguard/Aspide*; 8 NASAMS; 8 PAC-2 *Patriot*
    MANPAD 180 *Mistral*
  GUNS • TOWED 35mm 91 GDF-005
RADAR • LAND 6: 4 ARTHUR; 2 AN/TPQ-36 *Firefinder*
AEV 26 CZ-10/25E
ARV 58: 16 *Büffel*; 1 AMX-30; 1 BMR 3560.55; 4 Centauro REC; 22 M47-VR; 2 M578; 12 M113
VLB 19 M60

Reserves 17,000 reservists
Cadre units
FORCES BY ROLE
MANOEUVRE
  Reconnaissance
  1 armd cav bde
  Light
  3 inf bde
COMBAT SERVICE SUPPORT
  1 railway regt

Navy 22,200 (incl Naval Aviation and Marines); 4,000 civilian

HQ located at Madrid

EQUIPMENT BY TYPE
SUBMARINES • TACTICAL • SSK 3:

3 *Galerna* with 4 single 533mm TT with F17 Mod 2/L5 HWT

PRINCIPAL SURFACE COMBATANTS 12

AIRCRAFT CARRIERS • CVS 1 *Principe de Asturias* (capacity: 10 AV-8B *Harrier* II/AV-8B *Harrier* II Plus FGA ac; 8 SH-3 *Sea King* ASW hel; 2 Bell 212 (HU-18) hel)

DESTROYERS • DDGHM 5:

5 *Alvaro de Bazan* with Baseline 5 *Aegis* C2, 2 quad Mk141 lnchr with RGM-84F *Harpoon* AShM, 1 48-cell Mk41 VLS (LAM capable) with SM-2MR/RIM-162B *Sea Sparrow* SAM, 2 twin 324mm ASTT with Mk46 LWT, 1 127mm gun, (capacity 1 SH-60B *Seahawk* ASW hel)

FRIGATES • FFGHM 6:

6 *Santa Maria* with 1 Mk13 GMLS with RGM-84C *Harpoon* AShM/SM-1MR SAM, 2 Mk32 triple 324mm ASTT with Mk46 LWT, 1 76mm gun, (capacity 2 SH-60B *Seahawk* ASW hel)

AMPHIBIOUS

PRINCIPAL AMPHIBIOUS SHIPS 3:

LHD 1 *Juan Carlos I* (capacity 4 LCM; 42 APC; 46 MBT; 700 troops; able to operate as alternate platform for CVS aviation group)

LPD 2 *Galicia* (capacity 6 Bell-212 or 4 SH-3D *Sea King*; 4 LCM or 6 LCVP; 130 APC or 33 MBT; 450 troops)

LANDING SHIPS • LST 1 *Pizarro* (scheduled for decommissioning by end-2012)

LANDING CRAFT 44:

LCM 28: 14 LCM 1E; 14 LCM 6

LCVP 16

LOGISTICS AND SUPPORT 2

AORH 2: 1 *Patino*; 1 *Cantabria*

Navy – Maritime Action Force

PATROL AND COASTAL COMBATANTS 23

PSO 7:

3 *Alboran* each with 1 hel landing platform

4 *Descubierta*

PSOH 4 *Meteoro* (*Buquesde Accion Maritime* – 5 additional vessels on order, of which 3 are PSOH, 1 ASR and 1 AGS)

PCO 4 *Serviola*

PCC 3 *Anaga*

PB 2 *Toralla*

PBR 3

MINE WARFARE • MINE COUNTERMEASURES 6:

MHO 6 *Segura*

LOGISTICS AND SUPPORT 76

AGDS 1 *Neptuno*

AGI 1 *Alerta*

AGOR 2 (with ice-strengthened hull, for polar research duties in Antarctica)

AGS 4: 2 *Malaspina*; 2 *Castor*

AK 2: 1 *Martin Posadillo* (with 1 hel landing platform); 1 *El Camino Espanol*

AP 1 *Contramaestre* (with 1 hel landing platform)

ATF 3: 1 *Mar Caribe*; 1 *Mahon*; 1 *La Grana*

AXL 8: 4 *Contramaestre*; 4 *Guardiamarina*

AXS 7

YO 22

YTM 25

Naval Aviation 800

Flying hours — 150 hrs/year on AV-8B *Harrier* II FGA ac; 200 hrs/year on hel

FORCES BY ROLE
FIGHTER/GROUND ATTACK

1 sqn with AV-8B *Harrier* II; AV-8B *Harrier* II Plus

ANTI-SUBMARINE WARFARE

1 sqn with SH-60B *Seahawk*

AIRBORNE EARLY WARNING

1 sqn with SH-3H AEW *Sea King*

TRANSPORT

1 (liaison) sqn with Cessna 550 *Citation* II; Cessna 650 *Citation* VII

TRAINING

1 sqn with Hughes 500MD8

1 flt with TAV-8B *Harrier*

TRANSPORT HELICOPTER

1 sqn with Bell 212 (HU-18)

1 sqn with SH-3D *Sea King*

EQUIPMENT BY TYPE
AIRCRAFT 24 combat capable

FGA 17: 4 AV-8B *Harrier* II; 12 AV-8B *Harrier* II Plus; 1 TAV-8B *Harrier* (on lease from USMC)

ASW 7 P-3 *Orion*

TPT • Light 4: 3 Cessna 550 *Citation* II; 1 Cessna 650 *Citation* VII

HELICOPTERS

ASW 20: 8 SH-3D *Sea King* (tpt); 12 SH-60B *Seahawk*

MRH 9 Hughes 500MD

AEW 3 SH-3H AEW *Sea King*

TPT • Light 8 Bell 212 (HA-18)

MSL

AAM • IR AIM-9L *Sidewinder*; **ARH** AIM-120 AMRAAM

ASM AGM-65G *Maverick*

AShM AGM-119 *Penguin*

Marines 5,300

FORCES BY ROLE
MANOEUVRE

Amphibious

1 mne bde (1 spec ops unit, 1 recce unit, 1 mech inf bn, 2 inf bn, 1 arty bn, 1 log bn)

5 mne garrison gp

EQUIPMENT BY TYPE
MBT 16 M60A3TTS

APC (W) 35 *Piranha* IIIC (4 more to be delivered)

AAV 18: 16 AAV-7A1/AAVP-7A1; 2 AAVC-7A1

ARTY 18

SP 155mm 6 M109A2

TOWED 105mm 12 M-56 (pack)

AT • MSL • MANPATS 24 TOW-2
  RL 90mm C-90C
AD • SAM • MANPAD 12 *Mistral*
ARV 1 AAVR-7A1

Air Force 21,200; 5,280 civilian

The Spanish Air Force is organised in 3 commands – General Air Command, Combat Air Command and Canary Islands Air Command

Flying hours 120 hrs/year on hel/tpt ac; 180 hrs/year on FGA/ftr

FORCES BY ROLE
FIGHTER
  3 sqn with Eurofighter *Typhoon*
  1 sqn with *Mirage* F-1C (F-1CE)/F-1E (F-1EE)
FIGHTER/GROUND ATTACK
  5 sqn with F/A-18A/B MLU *Hornet* (EF-18A/B MLU)
MARITIME PATROL
  1 sqn with CN-235 MPA
  1 sqn with P-3A/M *Orion*
ELECTRONIC WARFARE
  1 sqn with B-707 *Santiago*; C-212 *Aviocar*; Falcon 20D/E
SEARCH & RESCUE
  1 sqn with AS332B/B1 *Super Puma*; C-212 *Aviocar*
  1 sqn with AS332B *Super Puma*; F-27 *Friendship*
  1 sqn with C-212 *Aviocar*; SA330J/L *Puma* (AS330)
TANKER/TRANSPORT
  1 sqn with B-707/B-707 tkr
  1 sqn with KC-130H *Hercules*
TRANSPORT
  1 VIP sqn with A310; *Falcon* 900
  1 sqn with Beech C90 *King Air*
  1 sqn with C-130H/H-30 *Hercules*
  1 sqn with C-212 *Aviocar*
  2 sqn with C-295
  1 sqn with CN-235
TRAINING
  1 OCU unit with Eurofighter *Typhoon*
  1 OCU sqn with F/A-18A/B (EF-18A/B MLU) *Hornet*
  1 sqn with Beech F33C *Bonanza*
  2 sqn with C-101 *Aviojet*
  1 sqn with C-212 *Aviocar*
  1 sqn with T-35 *Pillan* (E-26)
  2 (LIFT) sqn with F-5B *Freedom Fighter*
  1 hel sqn with EC120 *Colibri*
  1 hel sqn with S-76C
FIRE FIGHTING
  2 sqn with CL-215; CL-415
TRANSPORT HELICOPTER
  1 sqn with AS332M1 *Super Puma*

EQUIPMENT BY TYPE
AIRCRAFT 173 combat capable
  FTR 62: 42 Eurofighter *Typhoon*; 20 F-5B *Freedom Fighter*
  FGA 105: 74 F/A-18A *Hornet* (EF-18A); 12 F/A-18B *Hornet* (EF-18B – 67 EF-18s being given MLU); 19 *Mirage* F-1C (F-1CE)/F-1E (F-1EE)
  ASW 6: 2 P-3A *Orion*; 4 P-3M *Orion*
  MP 8 CN-235 MPA
  EW 6: 1 B-707 *Santiago* (TM.17); 1 C-212 *Aviocar* (TM.12D); 2 Falcon 20D; 2 Falcon 20E

TKR 6: 5 KC-130H *Hercules*, 1 B-707 Tkr
TPT 92: **Medium** 7: 6 C-130H *Hercules*; 1 C-130H-30 *Hercules*; **Light** 66: 4 Beech C90 *King Air*; 22 Beech F33C *Bonanza*; 7 C-212 *Aviocar*; 13 C-295; 14 CN-235 (12 tpt, 2 VIP); 3 Cessna 550 *Citation* V (ISR); 3 F-27 *Friendship* (SAR); **PAX** 9: 2 A310; 2 B-707; 5 Falcon 900 (VIP)
TRG 103: 66 C-101 *Aviojet*; 37 T-35 *Pillan* (E-26)
FF 17: 14 CL-215; 3 CL-415
HELICOPTERS
  TPT 46: **Medium** 23: 11 AS332B/B1 *Super Puma*; 4 AS332M1 *Super Puma*; 2 AS532AL *Cougar* (VIP); 4 SA330J *Puma* (AS330); 2 SA330L Puma (AS330) **Light** 23: 15 EC-120 *Colibri*; 8 S-76C
AD
  SAM *Mistral*; R-530
  TOWED *Skyguard/Aspide*
MSL
  AAM • IR AIM-9L/JULI *Sidewinder*; **IIR** IRIS-T; **SARH** AIM-7P *Sparrow*; **ARH** AIM-120B/C AMRAAM
  ARM AGM-88A HARM
  ASM AGM-65G *Maverick*
  AShM AGM-84C/D *Harpoon*
  LACM *Taurus* KEPD 350
BOMBS
  Conventional: Mk 82; Mk 83; Mk 84; BR-250; BR-500; BRP-250
  Laser-guided: GBU-10/16 *Paveway* II; GBU-24 *Paveway* III; EGBU-16 *Paveway* II; BPG-2000

Emergencies Military Unit (UME)

FORCES BY ROLE
COMMAND
  1 div HQ
FIRE FIGHTING
  2 sqn with CL-215; CL-415 opcon Air Force
MANOEUVRE
  Aviation
  1 hel bn opcon Army
  Other
  5 Emergency Intervention bn

Paramilitary 80,200

Guardia Civil 79,950
9 regions, 56 Rural Comds
FORCES BY ROLE
SPECIAL FORCES
  10 (rural) gp
MANOEUVRE
  Other
  17 (Tercios) paramilitary regt
  6 (traffic) sy gp
  1 (Special) sy bn
EQUIPMENT BY TYPE
APC (W) 18 BLR
HELICOPTERS
  MRH 26 Bo-105ATH
  TPT • Light 12: 8 BK-117; 4 EC-135P2

Guardia Civil Del Mar 750

PATROL AND COASTAL COMBATANTS 72

    PSO 1
    PCC 2
    PBF 40
    PB 29

Cyber

Spain has a national CERT, is involved in informal CERT communities, and is a member of the European government CERTs Group (ECG). No cyber-security strategy has been put in place and at present the national intelligence's CERT (CCN-CERT) is responsible for the coordination of CERTs activities. ICT spending has suffered cuts since 2008 owing to the financial crisis and a change in government (2011).

DEPLOYMENT

Legal provisions for foreign deployment:
Constitution: Codified constitution (1978)
Specific legislation: 'Ley Orgánica de la Defensa Nacional' (2005)
Decision on deployment of troops abroad: a) By the government (Art. 6 of the 'Defence Law'); b) parliamentary approval is required for military operations 'which are not directly related to the defence of Spain or national interests' (Art. 17 of the 'Defence Law')

AFGHANISTAN

NATO • ISAF 1,450; 1 AB bde

BOSNIA-HERZEGOVINA

EU • EUFOR • *Operation Althea* 13

GULF OF ADEN & INDIAN OCEAN

EU • *Operation Atalanta* 1 PSO; 1 LPD; 1 P-3A

LEBANON

UN • UNIFIL 977; 1 mech bde HQ; 1 armd inf bn

UGANDA

EU • EUTM 18

FOREIGN FORCES

United States US European Command: 1,480 1 air base at Morón; 1 naval base at Rota

Sweden SWE

Swedish Krona Skr		2011	2012	2013
GDP	Skr	3.54tr	3.63tr	
	US$	544.7bn	520.3bn	
per capita	US$	59,832	57,152	
Growth	%	3.97	1.25	
Inflation	%	2.96	1.41	
Def exp [a]	Skr	38.8bn		
	US$	5.98bn		
Def bdgt [a]	Skr	40bn	40.4bn	40.6bn
	US$	6.16bn	5.79bn	
US$1=Skr			6.49	6.98

[a] Excludes pensions

Population 9,103,788

Age	0–14	15–19	20–24	25–29	30–64	65 plus
Male	7.9%	3.1%	3.6%	3.2%	22.6%	9.0%
Female	7.5%	3.0%	3.5%	3.1%	22.3%	11.1%

Capabilities

While the army and air force are relatively well-equipped, the navy retains limited capabilities and is unable to operate beyond Sweden's territorial waters and the Baltic Sea. Sweden retains a policy of formal neutrality. The country regularly participates in peacekeeping operations, and has sent troops to participate in the NATO-led coalition in Afghanistan, even though the country remains outside NATO. Nonetheless, the primary role of the armed forces is territorial defence and Sweden's power-projection capabilities are limited. Two *Stockholm*-class corvettes that participated in *Operation Atalanta* in 2009 were transported by a dock ship as they were unable to make the journey independently. The air force has only one tanker to support its aircraft when on operations. Swedish forces are well-trained and professional, with compulsory military service having been formally abolished in July 2010. A reform process since the 1990s has attempted to transform the armed forces into a more agile force, but they would only likely be able to fully mobilise and deploy 2,000–3,000 troops within ten days. Budget cuts are gradually affecting Sweden's procurement programme, with the two-seat JAS39 *Gripen* F element of the combat aircraft development programme cancelled in August 2012, leaving just the delayed single-seat programme. Nevertheless, Sweden's armed forces will likely continue to fulfil one of their main goals of contributing small units and support to multinational coalitions.

ACTIVE 20,500 (Army 5,550 Navy 3,000 Air 3,300 Staff 8,550) **Paramilitary 800 Voluntary Auxiliary Organisations 22,000**

ORGANISATIONS BY SERVICE

Army 5,550

The army has been transformed to provide brigade-sized task forces depending on the operational requirement.

FORCES BY ROLE
COMMAND
1 div HQ (on mobilisation)
2 bde HQ
MANOEUVRE
Armoured
3 armd coy
Mechanised
6 mech bn
COMBAT SUPPORT
2 arty bn
2 AD bn
2 engr bn
COMBAT SERVICE SUPPORT
2 log bn

Reserves

FORCES BY ROLE
MANOEUVRE
Other
40 Home Guard bn
EQUIPMENT BY TYPE
MBT 132: 12 *Leopard* 2A4 (Strv-121); 120 *Leopard* 2A5 (Strv 122)
AIFV 354 CV9040 (Strf 9040)
APC 646
  APC (T) 194 Pbv 302
  APC (W) 192: 24 XA-180 *Sisu* (Patgb 180); 20 XA-202 *Sisu* (Patgb 202); 148 XA-203 *Sisu* (Patgb 203)
  PPV 260 RG-32M
ARTY 311
  SP 155mm 24 *Archer* (being delivered) **TOWED 155mm** 48 FH-77B
  MOR 120mm 239
AT
  MSL • MANPATS RB-55; RB-56 *Bill*
  RCL 84mm *Carl Gustav*
AD
  SAM
    SP 16 RBS-70
    TOWED RBS-90
    MANPAD RBS-70
  GUNS • SP 40mm 30 Strv 90LV
RADAR • LAND ARTHUR (arty); M113 A1GE *Green Archer* (mor)
UAV • ISR • Medium 3 *Sperwer*
AEV *Kodiak*
ARV 40: 14 Bgbv 120; 26 CV90
MW *Aardvark* Mk2; 33 Area Clearing System

Navy 2,150; 850 Amphibious; (total 3,000)

EQUIPMENT BY TYPE
SUBMARINES 6
  TACTICAL • SSK 5:
    3 *Gotland* (AIP fitted) with 2 single 400mm TT with Tp432/Tp 451, 4 single 533mm TT with Tp613/Tp62
    2 *Sodermanland* (AIP fitted) with 6 single 533mm TT with Tp432/Tp451/Tp613/Tp62
  SSW 1 *Spiggen* II

PATROL AND COASTAL COMBATANTS 20
  CORVETTES • FSG 4 *Visby* with 8 RBS-15 AShM, 4 single 400mm ASTT with Tp45 LWT, 1 hel landing plaform; (2 at FOC, 2 at IOC; 1 additional vessel expected ISD 2013)
  PCG 4:
    2 *Göteborg* with 4 twin lnchr with RBS-15 Mk2 AShM, 4 single 400mm ASTT with Tp431 LWT, 4 Saab 601 A/S mor
    2 *Stockholm* with 4 twin lnchr with RBS-15 Mk2 AShM, 4 Saab 601 mortars, 4 single ASTT with Tp431 LWT
  PBR 12 *Tapper*
MINE WARFARE • MINE COUNTERMEASURES 8
  MCC 5 *Koster*
  MCD 2 *Spårö*
  MSD 1 *Sokaren*
AMPHIBIOUS • LANDING CRAFT 164
  LCM 17 *Trossbat*
  LCPL 147 *Combatboat* 90
LOGISTICS AND SUPPORT 43:
  AG 2: 1 *Carlskrona* with 1 hel landing platform (former ML); 1 *Trosso* (spt ship for corvettes and patrol vessels but can also be used as HQ ship)
  AGI 1 *Orion*
  AGS 2 (Government Maritime Forces)
  AK 1 *Loke*
  ARS 1 *Furusund* (former ML)
  AX 7: 5 **AXS**; 2 (other)
  YAG 16 *Trossbat*
  YDT 1 *Agir*
  YPT 1 *Pelikanen*
  YTM 11

Amphibious 850

FORCES BY ROLE
MANOEUVRE
Amphibious
1 amph bn

EQUIPMENT BY TYPE
ARTY • MOR 81mm 12
MSL • SSM 8 RBS-17 *Hellfire*

Air Force 3,300

Flying hours   100–150 hrs/year

FORCES BY ROLE
FIGHTER/GROUND ATTACK/ISR
4 sqn with JAS 39C/D *Gripen*
SIGINT
1 sqn with Gulfstream IV SRA-4 (S-102B)
AIRBORNE EARLY WARNING & CONTROL
1 sqn with S-100B/D *Argus*
TRANSPORT
1 sqn with C-130E/H *Hercules* (Tp-84); KC-130H *Hercules* (Tp-84)
TRAINING
1 sqn with JAS-39A/B *Gripen*
1 OCU sqn with JAS-39A/B/C/D *Gripen*
1 unit with Sk-60
AIR DEFENCE
1 (fighter control and air surv) bn

EQUIPMENT BY TYPE

AIRCRAFT 110 combat capable

FGA 110 JAS39A/B/C/D *Gripen*

ELINT 2 Gulfstream IV SRA-4 (S-102B)

AEW&C 3: 1 S-100B *Argus*; 2 S-100D *Argus*

TKR 1 KC-130H *Hercules* (Tp-84)

TPT 10: **Medium** 7 C-130E/H *Hercules* (Tp-84); **Light** 2 Saab 340 (OS-100A/Tp-100C); **PAX** 1 Gulfstream 550 (Tp-102D)

TRG 80 Sk-60W

UAV • ISR • Medium 8 RQ-7 *Shadow* (AUV 3 *Örnen*)

MSL

ASM AGM-65 *Maverick* (RB-75)

AShM RB-15F

AAM • IR AIM-9L *Sidewinder* (RB-74); **IIR** IRIS-T (RB-98); **ARH** AIM-120B *AMRAAM* (RB-99)

Armed Forces Hel Wing (included in Air Force figures)

FORCES BY ROLE

TRANSPORT HELICOPTER

3 sqn with AS332 *Super Puma* (Hkp-10A/B/D); AW109 (Hkp 15A); AW109M (Hkp-15B); NH90 TTH (Hkp-14A); UH-60M *Black Hawk* (Hkp-16)

EQUIPMENT BY TYPE

HELICOPTERS

TPT 51: **Medium** 31: 9 AS332 *Super Puma* (Hkp-10A/B/D - SAR); 15 UH-60M *Black Hawk* (Hkp-16); 7 NH90 TTH (Hkp-14A); **Light** 20: 12 AW109 (Hkp-15A); 8 AW109M (Hkp-15B)

Paramilitary 800

Coast Guard 800

PATROL AND COASTAL COMBATANTS 28

PSO 3 KBV-001

PCO 1 KBV-181 (fishery protection)

PCC 2 KBV-201

PB 22: 1 KBV-101; 4 KBV-281; 3 KBV-288; 11 KBV-301; 3 KBV-312

AMPHIBIOUS • LANDING CRAFT • LCAC 2 Griffon 2000 TDX (KBV-591)

LOGISTICS AND SUPPORT • AG 12: 8 MARPOL-CRAFT; 4 KBV-031

Air Arm

AIRCRAFT • TPT • Light 3 DHC-8Q-300

Cyber

Sweden has a national CERT, is involved in informal CERT communities, and is a member of the European government CERTs Group (ECG). A national cyber-security strategy has also been adopted. Four ministries have a cyber remit: defence, foreign affairs, justice, and enterprise and industry. The Swedish Civil Contingencies Agency (AMS), which reports to the MoD, is in charge of supporting and coordinating security across society. The Swedish National Defence College and the NATO Cooperative Cyber Defence Centre of Excellence in Estonia have established the informal Nordic-Baltic Hub to provide joint, cross-border education programmes.

DEPLOYMENT

Legal provisions for foreign deployment:

Constitution: Constitution consists of four fundamental laws; the most important is 'The Instrument of Government' (1974)

Decision on deployment of troops abroad: By the government upon parliamentary approval (Ch. 10, Art. 9)

AFGHANISTAN

NATO • ISAF 506

UN • UNAMA 3 obs

BOSNIA-HERZEGOVINA

EU • EUFOR • *Operation Althea* 1

DEMOCRATIC REPUBLIC OF THE CONGO

UN • MONUSCO 5 obs

INDIA/PAKISTAN

UN • UNMOGIP 5 obs

KOREA, REPUBLIC OF

NNSC • 5 obs

MIDDLE EAST

UN • UNTSO 8 obs

SERBIA

NATO • KFOR 54

SOUTH SUDAN

UN • UNMISS 4; 3 obs

UGANDA

EU • EUTM 8

Switzerland CHE

Swiss Franc fr		2011	2012	2013
GDP	fr	587bn	593bn	
	US$	660.8bn	622.9bn	
per capita	US$	83,376	78,594	
Growth	%	1.93	0.85	
Inflation	%	0.23	-0.50	
Def exp [a]	fr	4.42bn		
	US$	4.97bn		
Def bdgt [a]	fr	4.82bn	4.53bn	4.69bn
	US$	5.43bn	4.76bn	
US$1=fr		0.89	0.95	

[a] Includes military pensions

Population 7,925,517

Age	0–14	15–19	20–24	25–29	30–64	65 plus
Male	7.8%	2.9%	3.1%	3.3%	24.8%	7.4%
Female	7.4%	2.7%	3.0%	3.3%	24.6%	9.7%

Capabilities

The Swiss armed forces are almost entirely reliant on conscripts for their active personnel and reserves for full mobilisation, with professional, volunteer personnel comprising just 5% of the total armed forces. With conscripts and reserves serving for short periods of time (the average service time per conscript in 2010 was 260 days), the armed forces lack adaptability and readiness. The only rapid-reaction force is a small (fewer than 100 personnel) army reconnaissance detachment. A referendum that will question whether to end conscription is expected in 2013, which would have significant effects for Switzerland's forces and defence spending. The armed forces' equipment is largely aimed at protecting Switzerland's territorial sovereignty, with limited power-projection capabilities (only light transport aircraft and no tankers). However, Switzerland is neutral, so the armed forces are more than sufficient to fulfil its roles of territorial defence in a benign environment, and international peace-support operations. The size of Switzerland's armed forces is likely to be severely reduced in forthcoming years. Current plans suggest a reduction to 100,000 personnel (still largely conscript and reserves), despite an increasing defence budget in the near term. These extra funds will likely go towards equipment replacement, in particular new fighter aircraft to replace F-5s.

ACTIVE 23,100 (Joint 23,100)

RESERVE 157,100 (Army 107,900, Air 24,050, Armed Forces Logistic Organisation 9,000, Command Support Organisation 16,150)

Civil Defence 76,000

Terms of service 18 weeks compulsory recruit trg at age 19–20 (19,000 (2006)), followed by 7 refresher trg courses (3 weeks each) over a 10-year period between ages 20–30. (189,000 continuation trg (2006)).

ORGANISATIONS BY SERVICE

Joint 3,400 active; 19,700 conscript (187,230 on mobilisation)

Land Forces (Army) 107,900 on mobilisation

4 Territorial Regions. With the exception of military security all units are non-active.

FORCES BY ROLE
COMMAND
4 regional comd (2 engr bn, 1 sigs bn)
MANOEUVRE
Armoured
1 (1st) bde (1 recce bn, 2 armd bn, 2 armd inf bn, 1 sp arty bn, 2 engr bn, 1 sigs bn)
1 (11th) bde (1 recce bn, 2 armd bn, 2 armd inf bn, 1 inf bn, 2 SP arty bn, 1 engr bn, 1 sigs bn)
Light
1 (2nd) bde (1 recce bn, 4 inf bn, 2 SP arty bn, 1 engr bn, 1 sigs bn)
1 (5th) bde (1 recce bn, 3 inf bn, 2 SP arty bn, 1 engr bn, 1 sigs bn)
1 (7th) reserve bde (3 recce bn, 3 inf bn, 2 mtn inf bn, 1 sigs bn)
Mountain
1 (9th) bde (5 mtn inf bn, 1 SP Arty bn, 1 sigs bn)
1 (12th) bde (2 inf bn, 3 mtn inf bn, 1 (fortress) arty bn, 1 sigs bn)

1 (10th) reserve bde (1 recce bn, 2 armd bn, 3 inf bn, 2 mtn inf bn, 2 SP arty bn, 2 sigs bn)
Other
1 sy bde
COMBAT SERVICE SUPPORT
1 armd/arty trg unit
1 inf trg unit
1 engr rescue trg unit
1 log trg unit
EQUIPMENT BY TYPE
MBT 296 *Leopard* 2 (Pz-87 *Leo*)
RECCE 455: 443 *Eagle* II; 12 *Piranha* IIIC CBRN
AIFV 154 CV9030
APC • APC (W) 346 *Piranha* II
AIFV/APC look-a-likes 555: M113/*Piranha* I/II(8×8)/ IIIC(8×8)/CV 9030 CP
ARTY 496
SP 155mm 200 M109
MOR SP 81mm 296 M113 with M72/91
AT
MSL • SP 110 *Piranha* I 6×6 TOW-2
AD • SAM • MANPAD FIM-92A *Stinger*
PATROL AND COASTAL COMBATANTS • PBR 11 *Aquarius*
AEV 12 *Kodiak*
ARV 25 *Büffel*
VLB 14 Brueckenlegepanzer 68/88
MW 46: 26 Area Clearing System; 20 M113 A2

Air Force 24,050 (incl air defence units and military airfield guard units)

Flying hours   200–250 hrs/year

FORCES BY ROLE
FIGHTER
3 sqn with F-5E/F *Tiger* II
3 sqn with F/A-18C/D *Hornet*
TRANSPORT
1 sqn with Beech 350 *King Air*; DHC-6 *Twin Otter*; PC-6 *Turbo-Porter*; PC-12
1 VIP Flt with Beech 1900D; Cessna 560XL *Citation*; *Falcon* 50
TRAINING
1 sqn with PC-7CH *Turbo Trainer*; PC-21
1 sqn with PC-9 (tgt towing)
1 OCU Sqn with F-5E/F *Tiger* II
TRANSPORT HELICOPTER
6 sqn with AS332M *Super Puma*; AS532UL *Cougar*; EC635
ISR UAV
1 sqn with ADS 95 *Ranger*
EQUIPMENT BY TYPE
AIRCRAFT 87 combat capable
FTR 54: 42 F-5E *Tiger* II; 12 F-5F *Tiger* II
FGA 33: 26 F/A-18C *Hornet*; 7 F/A-18D *Hornet*
TPT 22: **Light** 21: 1 Beech 350 *King Air*; 1 Beech1900D; 1 Cessna 560XL *Citation*; 1 DHC-6 *Twin Otter*; 15 PC-6 *Turbo-Porter*; 1 PC-6 (owned by armasuisse, civil registration); 1 PC-12 (owned by armasuisse, civil registration); **PAX** 1 *Falcon* 50
TRG 47: 28 PC-7CH *Turbo Trainer*; 11 PC-9; 8 PC-21

HELICOPTERS

TPT 46: **Medium** 26: 15 AS332M *Super Puma*; 11
AS532UL *Cougar*; **Light** 20 EC635
UAV • ISR • **Medium** 4 ADS 95 *Ranger* systems
MSL • AAM • IR AIM-9P *Sidewinder*; IIR AIM-9X
Sidewinder; ARH AIM-120B AMRAAM

Ground Based Air Defence (GBAD)

GBAD assets can be used to form AD clusters to be
deployed independently as task forces within Swiss
territory.

EQUIPMENT BY TYPE

AD
  SAM
    TOWED *Rapier*
    MANPAD FIM-92A *Stinger*
  GUNS 35mm
  RADARS • AD RADARS *Skyguard*

Armed Forces Logistic Organisation 9,000 on mobilisation

FORCES BY ROLE
COMBAT SERVICE SUPPORT
  1 log bde

Command Support Organisation 16,150 on mobilisation

FORCES BY ROLE
COMBAT SERVICE SUPPORT
  1 spt bde

Civil Defence 80,000
(not part of armed forces)

Cyber

Five major Swiss government organisations maintain an
overview of elements of cyber threats and responses: the
Federal Intelligence Service; the Military Intelligence Service; the Command Support Organisation; Information
Security and Facility Protection; and the Federal Office for
Civil Protection. The government's Reporting and Analysis
Centre for Information Assurance (MELANI) monitors and
reports on intrusion attempts and other cyber and network
attacks. The government published a National Cyber Defence Strategy in June 2012.

DEPLOYMENT

Legal provisions for foreign deployment:
Constitution: Codified constitution (1999)
Decision on deployment of troops abroad:
Peace promotion (66, 66a, 66b Swiss Mil Law): UN.OSCE
mandate. Decision by govt; if over 100 tps deployed or
op over 3 weeks Fed Assembly must agree first, except in
emergency.
Support service abroad (69, 60 Swiss Mil Law): Decision
by govt; if over 2,000 tps or op over 3 weeks Fed Assembly
must agree in next official session

BOSNIA-HERZEGOVINA

EU • EUFOR • *Operation Althea* 20

BURUNDI

UN • BNUB 1 mil advisor

DEMOCRATIC REPUBLIC OF THE CONGO

UN • MONUSCO 4 obs

KOREA, REPUBLIC OF

NNSC • 5 officers

MIDDLE EAST

UN • UNTSO 11 obs

SERBIA

NATO • KFOR 257 (military volunteers); 1 inf coy; elm 1
MP coy; elm 1 hel gp; 2 hel

SOUTH SUDAN

UN • UNMISS 2; 2 obs

Turkey TUR

New Turkish Lira L		2011	2012	2013
GDP	L	1.3tr	1.42tr	
	US$	774.3bn	783.1bn	
per capita	US$	9,709	9,820	
Growth	%	8.50	2.97	
Inflation	%	6.47	8.72	
Def exp [b]	L	24.3bn		
	US$	14.5bn		
Def bdgt [a]	L	28.6bn	30.7bn	
	US$	17.1bn	17bn	
US$1=L		1.68	1.81	

[a] Includes military pensions, procurement spending, as well as
funding for Gendarmerie General Command and the Coast Guard
Command (see p. 103).

[b] NATO definition

Population	79,749,461

Age	0–14	15–19	20–24	25–29	30–64	65 plus
Male	13.4%	4.4%	4.4%	4.4%	20.9%	2.9%
Female	12.8%	4.2%	4.2%	4.3%	20.7%	3.5%

Capabilities

Turkey has capable armed forces intended to meet national-
defence requirements and its NATO obligations. The role
of the armed forces has been recast since the end of the
Cold War, with internal security and regional instability providing challenges, as made apparent by events in
Syria during 2012. The armed forces, and particularly the
army, continue a reform process reflecting changing security concerns. The army is becoming smaller but more
capable with the aim of improving its ability to meet a full
range of NATO missions while providing a highly mobile
force able to fight across the spectrum of conflict. The air
force is well-equipped and -trained, and is introducing
airborne early-warning aircraft. It already operates tanker
aircraft and will bolster its transport fleet with the A400M
airlifter. Rotary-wing procurement projects will benefit
the army's air arm with new light-attack and transport

helicopters in the pipeline. The navy is the smallest of the three services, and operates a mix of frigates, corvettes, fast-attack craft and amphibious vessels. Turkish forces are deployed to ISAF, and Ankara sent ships to take part in *Operation Unified Protector* in 2011. Single and inter-service training is carried out regularly, as is mobilisation training, and the armed forces participate in multination-al exercises with NATO partners. Turkey's relations with Israel, with which it had deepened defence ties during the 1990s and the early part of this century, deteriorated dur-ing 2011. The military has ambitions procurement plans, which will require a significant increase in funding over the period to 2016.

ACTIVE 510,600 (Army 402,000 Navy 48,600 Air 60,000) Paramilitary 102,200

Terms of service 15 months. Reserve service to age of 41 for all services. Active figure reducing.

RESERVE 378,700 (Army 258,700 Navy 55,000 Air 65,000) Paramilitary 50,000

ORGANISATIONS BY SERVICE

Army ε77,000; ε325,000 conscript (total 402,000)

FORCES BY ROLE
COMMAND
  4 army HQ
  9 corps HQ
SPECIAL FORCES
  4 cdo bde
  1 mtn cdo bde
  1 cdo regt
MANOEUVRE
  Armoured
  1 (52nd) armd div (2 armd bde, 1 mech bde)
  7 armd bde
  Mechanised
  2 (28th & 29th) mech div
  14 mech inf bde
  Light
  1 (23rd) mot inf div (3 mot inf regt)
  11 mot inf bde
  Aviation
  4 avn regt
  4 avn bn
COMBAT SUPPORT
  2 arty bde
  1 trg arty bde
  6 arty regt
  2 engr regt

EQUIPMENT BY TYPE
MBT 2,494: 315 *Leopard* 2A4; 170 *Leopard* 1A4; 227 *Leopard* 1A3; 274 M60A1; 658 M60A3; 850 M48A5 T1/T2 (2,000 more in store)
RECCE 320+: ε250 *Akrep*; 70+ ARSV *Cobra*
AIFV 650
APC (T) 3,643: 830 AAPC; 2,813 M113/M113A1/M113A2
ARTY 7,807+

SP 1,088: **105mm** 391: 26 M108T; 365 M-52T; **155mm** 422: 222 M-44T1; ε220 T-155 *Firtina* (K-9 *Thunder*); **175mm** 36 M107; **203mm** 219 M110A2
TOWED 760+: **105mm** 75+ M101A1; **155mm** 523: 517 M114A1/M114A2; 6 *Panter*; **203mm** 162 M115
MRL 146+: **107mm** 48; **122mm** ε36 T-122; **227mm** 12 MLRS (incl ATACMS); **302mm** 50+ TR-300 *Kasirga* (WS-1)
MOR 5,813+
  SP 1,443+: **81mm**; **107mm** 1,264 M-30; **120mm** 179
  TOWED 4,370: **81mm** 3,792; **120mm** 578
AT
  MSL 1,363
    SP 365 TOW
    MANPATS 998: 80 9K123 *Kornet*; 186 *Cobra*; ε340 *Eryx*; 392 *Milan*
  RCL 3,869: **106mm** 2,329 M40A1; **57mm** 923 M18; **75mm** 617
AIRCRAFT
  TPT • Light 38: 5 Beech 200 *Super King Air*; 30 Cessna 185 (U-17B); 3 Cessna 421
  TRG 74: 45 Cessna T182; 25 T-41D *Mescalero*; 4 T-42A *Cochise*
HELICOPTERS
  ATK 40: 18 AH-1P *Cobra*; 12 AH-1S *Cobra*; 6 AH-1W *Cobra*; 4 TAH-1P *Cobra*
  MRH 28 Hughes 300C
  ISR 3 OH-58B *Kiowa*
  TPT 221+: **Medium** 80+: 30 AS532UL *Cougar*; 50+ S-70A *Black Hawk*; **Light** 141: 12 Bell 204B (AB-204B); ε45 Bell 205 (UH-1H *Iroquois*); 64 Bell 205A (AB-205A); 20 Bell 206 *Jet Ranger*
UAV • ISR Heavy some *Falcon* 600/*Firebee*; **Medium** 196+: some CL-89; some *Gnat*; **Light** some *Harpy*
AD
  SAM
    SP 148: 70 *Altigan* PMADS octuple *Stinger*, 78 *Zipkin* PMADS quad *Stinger* lnchr
    MANPAD 935: 789 FIM-43 *Redeye* (being withdrawn); 146 FIM-92A *Stinger*
  GUNS 1,664
    SP 40mm 262 M42A1
    TOWED 1,402: **20mm** 439 GAI-D01; **35mm** 120 GDF-001/GDF-003; **40mm** 843: 803 L/60/L/70; 40 T-1
RADAR • LAND AN/TPQ-36 *Firefinder*
AEV 12 M48; M113A2T2
ARV 150: 12 *Leopard* 1; 105 M48T5; 33 M88A2
VLB 52 Mobile Floating Assault Bridge
MW *Tamkar*

Navy 14,100; 34,500 conscript (total 48,600 including 2,200 Coast Guard and 3,100 Marines)

EQUIPMENT BY TYPE
SUBMARINES • TACTICAL • SSK 14:
  6 *Atilay* (GER Type-209/1200) with 8 single 533mm ASTT with SST-4 HWT
  8 *Preveze/Gür* (GER Type-209/1400) with 8 single 533mm ASTT with UGM-84 *Harpoon* AShM/*Tigerfish* Mk2 HWT

PRINCIPAL SURFACE COMBATANTS 18
  FRIGATES • FFGHM 18:
   2 *Barbaros* (mod GER MEKO 200 F244 & F245) with 2 quad Mk141 lnchr with RGM-84C *Harpoon* AShM, 1 octuple Mk29 lnchr with *Aspide* SAM, 2 Mk32 triple 324mm ASTT with Mk46 LWT, 1 127mm gun, (capacity: 1 Bell 212 (AB-212) hel)
   2 *Barbaros* (mod GER MEKO 200 F246 & F247) with 2 quad Mk141 lnchr with RGM-84C *Harpoon* AShM, 1 8-cell Mk41 VLS with *Aspide* SAM, 2 Mk32 triple 324mm ASTT with Mk46 LWT, 1 127mm gun, (capacity: 1 Bell 212 (AB-212) hel)
   2 *Gaziantep* (ex-US *Oliver Hazard Perry*-class) with 1 Mk13 GMLS with RGM-84C *Harpoon* AShM/SM-1MR SAM, 1 8-cell Mk41 VLS with RIM-162 SAM, 2 Mk32 triple 324mm ASTT with Mk46 LWT, 1 76mm gun, (capacity: 1 S-70B *Seahawk* ASW hel)
   6 *Gaziantep* (ex-US *Oliver Hazard Perry*-class) with 1 Mk13 GMLS with RGM-84C *Harpoon* AShM/SM-1MR SAM, 2 Mk32 triple 324mm ASTT with Mk46 LWT, 1 76mm gun, (capacity: 1 S-70B *Seahawk* ASW hel)
   1 *Muavenet* (ex-US *Knox*-class) with 1 octuple Mk16 lnchr with ASROC/RGM-84C *Harpoon* AShM, 2 twin 324mm ASTT with Mk46 LWT, 1 127mm gun, (capacity: 1 Bell 212 (AB-212) utl hel)
   4 *Yavuz* (GER MEKO 200TN) with 2 quad Mk141 lnchr with RGM-84C *Harpoon* AShM, 1 octuple Mk29 GMLS with *Aspide* SAM, 2 Mk32 triple 324mm ASTT with Mk46 LWT, 1 127mm gun, (capacity: 1 Bell 212 (AB-212) hel)
   1 *Ada* with 2 quad lnchr with RCM-84C *Harpoon* AShM, 1 Mk49 21-cell lnchr with RIM-116 SAM, 2 Mk32 twin 324mm ASTT with Mk46 LWT, 1 76mm gun, (capacity: 1 S-70B *Seahawk* hel) (1 further vessel in build)
PATROL AND COASTAL COMBATANTS 60
  CORVETTES • FSGM 6:
   6 *Burak* (FRA *d'Estienne d'Orves*) with 2 single lnchr with MM-38 *Exocet* AShM, 4 single 533mm ASTT with L5 HWT, 1 100mm gun
  PCFG 19:
   8 *Dogan* (GER *Lurssen*-57) with 2 quad lnchr with RGM-84A/C *Harpoon* AShM, 1 76mm gun
   9 *Kilic* with 2 quad Mk 141 lnchr with RGM-84C *Harpoon* AShM, 1 76mm gun
   2 *Yildiz* with 2 quad lnchr with RGM-84A/C *Harpoon* AShM, 1 76mm gun
  PCC 13: 6 *Tuzla*; 6 *Karamursel* (GER *Vegesack*); 1 *Trabzon*;
  PBFG 8 *Kartal* (GER *Jaguar*) with 4 single lnchr with RB 12 *Penguin* AShM, 2 single 533mm TT
  PBF 4: 2 *Kaan* 20; 2 *MRTP22*
  PB 10: 4 PGM-71; 6 *Turk*
MINE WARFARE • MINE COUNTERMEASURES 28:
  MCM SPT 8 (tenders)
  MHO 11: 5 *Edineik* (FRA *Circe*); 6 *Aydin*
  MSC 5 *Silifke* (US *Adjutant*)
  MSI 4 *Foca* (US *Cape*)
AMPHIBIOUS
  LANDING SHIPS • LST 5:
   2 *Ertugrul* (capacity 18 tanks; 400 troops) (US *Terrebonne Parish*) (with 1 hel landing platform)
   1 *Osman Gazi* (capacity 4 LCVP; 17 tanks; 980 troops) (with 1 hel landing platform)
   2 *Sarucabey* (capacity 11 tanks; 600 troops) (with 1 hel landing platform)
  LANDING CRAFT 49:
   LCT 33: 8 C-151; 12 C-117; 13 C-302
   LCM 16 C-302
LOGISTICS AND SUPPORT 79
  ABU 2
  AGS 3: 2 *Cesme* (US *Silas Bent*); 1 *Cubuklu*
  AKL 1 *Eregli*
  AOR 2 *Akar* with 1 hel landing platform
  AORL 1 *Taskizak*
  AOT 2 *Burak*
  AOL 1 *Gurcan*
  AO 1 (harbour)
  AP 1 *Iskenderun*
  ARS 1 *Isin*
  ASR 1 *Akin*
  ATA 1 *Tenace*
  ATR 1 *Inebolu*
  ATS 2: 1 *Gazal*; 1 *Darica*
  AWT 13: 9; 4 (harbour)
  AXL 8
  AXS 2 *Pasa* (GER *Rhein*)
  YAG 2 *Mesaha*
  YFD 13
  YPB 2
  YPT 3
  YTM 16

Marines 3,100

FORCES BY ROLE
MANOEUVRE
  Amphibious
   1 mne bde (3 mne bn; 1 arty bn)

Naval Aviation

FORCES BY ROLE
ANTI-SUBMARINE WARFARE
   2 sqn with Bell 212 ASW (AB-212 ASW); S-70B *Seahawk*
   1 sqn with CN-235M-100; TB-20 *Trinidad*
EQUIPMENT BY TYPE
AIRCRAFT
  MP 4 CN-235M-100 (2 more on order)
  TPT • Light 5 TB-20 *Trinidad*
HELICOPTERS
  ASW 29: 11 Bell 212 ASW (AB-212 ASW); 18 S-70B *Seahawk*

Air Force 60,000

2 tac air forces (divided between east and west)

Flying hours   180 hrs/year

FORCES BY ROLE
FIGHTER
   1 sqn with F-4E *Phantom* II
   2 sqn with F-16C/D *Fighting Falcon*
FIGHTER/GROUND ATTACK
   2 sqn with F-4E *Phantom* II
   8 sqn with F-16C/D *Fighting Falcon*

ISR
  2 sqn with RF-4E/ETM *Phantom* II
  1 unit with *King Air* 350
AIRBORNE EARLY WARNING & CONTROL
  1 sqn (forming) with B-737 AEW&C
EW
  1 unit with CN-235M EW
SEARCH & RESCUE
  1 sqn with AS532AL/UL *Cougar*
TANKER
  1 sqn with KC-135R *Stratotanker*
TRANSPORT
  1 sqn with C-130B/E/H *Hercules*
  1 sqn with C-160D *Transall*
  1 (VIP) sqn with Cessna 550 *Citation* II (UC-35); Cessna
    650 *Citation* VII; CN-235M; Gulfstream 550
  3 sqn with CN-235M
  10 (liaison) flt with Bell 205 (UH-1H *Iroquois*); CN-235M
TRAINING
  1 sqn with F-4E *Phantom* II; F-16C/D *Fighting Falcon*
  1 sqn with F-5A/B *Freedom Fighter*; NF-5A/B *Freedom
    Fighter*
  1 OCU sqn with F-16C/D *Fighting Falcon*
  1 sqn with SF-260D
  1 sqn with KT-IT
  1 sqn with T-38A/M *Talon*
  1 sqn with T-41D *Mescalero*
AIR DEFENCE
  4 sqn with MIM-14 *Nike Hercules*
  2 sqn with *Rapier*
  8 (firing) unit with MIM-23 *HAWK*
MANOEUVRE
  Air Manoeuvre
  1 AB bde
EQUIPMENT BY TYPE
AIRCRAFT 354 combat capable
  FTR 53: 18 F-5A *Freedom Fighter*; 8 F-5B *Freedom Fighter*;
    17 NF-5A *Freedom Fighter*; 10 NF-5B *Freedom Fighter* (48
    being upgraded as LIFT)
  FGA 301: 70 F-4E *Phantom* II (52 upgraded to *Phantom*
    2020); 213 F-16C/D *Fighting Falcon* (all being upgraded to
    Block 50 standard); 9 F-16C Block 50 Fighting Falcon; 9
    F-16D Block 50 *Fighting Falcon*
  ISR 34+: 33 RF-4E/ETM *Phantom* II; 1+ Beech 350 *King Air*
    (four more due by end-2012)
  EW 2+ CN-235M EW
  AEW&C 1 B-737 AEW&C (3 more on order)
  TKR 7 KC-135R *Stratotanker*
  TPT 86 **Medium** 35: 6 C-130B *Hercules*; 12 C-130E
    Hercules; 1 C-130H *Hercules*; 16 C-160D *Transall*; **Light**
    50: 2 Cessna 550 *Citation* II (UC-35 - VIP); 2 Cessna 650
    Citation VII; 46 CN-235M; **PAX** 1 Gulfstream 550
  TRG 172: 34 SF-260D; 70 T-38A/M *Talon*; 28 T-41D
    Mescalero; 40 KT-IT
HELICOPTERS
  TPT 40 **Medium** 20: 6 AS532AL *Cougar* (CSAR); 14
    AS532UL *Cougar* (SAR) **Light** 20 Bell 205 (UH-1H
    Iroquois)
  UAV • ISR 28: **Heavy** 10 *Heron* **Medium** 18 *Gnat* 750

AD
  SAM *Rapier*
    TOWED: MIM-23 HAWK
    STATIC MIM-14 *Nike Hercules*
MSL
  AAM • IR AIM-9S *Sidewinder*; *Shafrir* 2(‡); **SARH** AIM-
  7E *Sparrow*; **ARH** AIM-120A/B AMRAAM
  ARM AGM-88A HARM
  ASM AGM-65A/G *Maverick*; *Popeye* I
BOMBS
  Conventional BLU-107; GBU-8B HOBOS (GBU-15)
  Laser-guided *Paveway* I; *Paveway* II
PODS Infrared 80: 40 AN/AAQ-14 LANTIRN; 40 AN/
AAQ-13 LANTIRN

Paramilitary

Gendarmerie/National Guard 100,000; 50,000 reservists (total 150,000)

Ministry of Interior; Ministry of Defence in war
FORCES BY ROLE
SPECIAL FORCES
  1 cdo bde
MANOEUVRE
  Other
  1 (border) paramilitary div
  2 paramilitary bde
EQUIPMENT BY TYPE
RECCE *Akrep*
APC (W) 560: 535 BTR-60/BTR-80; 25 *Condor*
AIRCRAFT
  ISR Some O-1E *Bird Dog*
  TPT • Light 2 Do-28D
HELICOPTERS
  MRH 19 Mi-17 *Hip H*
  TPT 36: **Medium** 13 S-70A *Black Hawk*; **Light** 23: 8 Bell
    204B (AB-204B); 6 Bell 205A (AB-205A); 8 Bell 206A
    (AB-206A) *Jet Ranger*; 1 Bell 212 (AB-212)

Coast Guard 800 (Coast Guard Regular element); 1,050 (from Navy); 1,400 conscript (total 3,250)

PATROL AND COASTAL COMBATANTS 106:
  PSOH 2 *Dost* with 1 76mm gun (2 further vessels in
    build; expected ISD 2013)
  PBF 46
  PB 58
AIRCRAFT • MP 3 CN-235 MPA
HELICOPTERS • MRH 8 Bell 412EP (AB-412EP – SAR)

DEPLOYMENT

Legal provisions for foreign deployment:
Constitution: Codified constitution (1985)
Decision on deployment of troops abroad: a) In general,
by parliament (Art. 92); b) in cases of sudden aggression
and if parliament is unable to convene, by president (Art.
92, 104b)

AFGHANISTAN

NATO • ISAF 1,328; 1 inf bde HQ; 2 inf bn
UN • UNAMA 1 obs

ARABIAN SEA & GULF OF ADEN

Combined Maritime Forces • CTF-151: 1 FFGHM

BOSNIA-HERZEGOVINA

EU • EUFOR • *Operation Althea* 288; 1 inf coy

CYPRUS (NORTHERN)

Army ε43,000

1 army corps HQ; 1 armd bde; 2 mech inf div; 1 avn comd; 8 M-48A2 training; 340 M48A5T1/T2; 361 AAPC (incl variants); 266 M113 (incl variants); (towed arty) 102: **105mm** 72 M101A1; **155mm** 18 M114A2; **203mm** 12 M115; (SP) **155mm** 90 M-44T; (MRL) **122mm** 6 T-122; (MOR) 450: **81mm** 175; **107mm** 148 M-30; **120mm** 127 HY-12; (AT MSL) 114: 66 *Milan*; 48 TOW; (RCL) **106mm** 192 M40A1; **90mm** M67; (AD towed) **20mm** Rh 202; **35mm** GDF 16 GDF-003; **40mm** 48 M1; 3 Cessna 185 (U-17) ac; 1 AS532UL *Cougar*; 3 UH-1H *Iroquois* hel; 1 **PB**

LEBANON

UN • UNIFIL 452; 1 engr coy; 1 FFGH

MEDITERRANEAN SEA

NATO • *Operation Active Endeavour* 1 FFGHM
NATO • SNMCMG 2: 1 MHO

SERBIA

NATO • KFOR 402; 1 inf coy; elm 1 MP coy
UN • UNMIK 1 obs

FOREIGN FORCES

United States US European Command: 1,500; 4 MQ-1B *Predator* UAV at Incirlik; 1 spt facility at Izmir; 1 spt facility at Ankara; 1 air base at Incirlik • US Strategic Command: 1 Spacetrack Radar at Incirlik

United Kingdom UK

British Pound £		2011	2012	2013
GDP	£	1.52tr	1.55tr	
	US$	2.43tr	2.43tr	
per capita	US$	38,543	38,543	
Growth	%	0.76	-0.38	
Inflation	%	4.45	2.73	
Def exp [b]	£	39.7bn		
	US$	63.6bn		
Def bdgt [a]	£	39bn	38.7bn	
	US$	62.5bn	60.8bn	
US$1=£		0.62	0.64	

[a] Net Cash Requirement figures. These will differ from official figures based on Resource Accounting & Budgeting. Excludes military pensions covered by the Armed Forces Pension Scheme (AFPS) and the Armed Forces Compensation Scheme (AFCS).

[b] NATO definition

Population   63,047,162

Age	0–14	15–19	20–24	25–29	30–64	65 plus
Male	8.9%	3.2%	3.5%	3.5%	23.3%	7.3%
Female	8.5%	3.1%	3.4%	3.3%	22.9%	9.2%

Capabilities

Many RN and RAF capabilities have reduced by 20–30% as a result of cuts made in the 2010 Strategic Defence and Security Review. Some cuts, such as maritime patrol aircraft and NBC reconnaissance, reduce the overall flexibility of British forces whilst increasing their dependence on NATO and multinational partners. A new Joint Forces Command has taken over strategic intelligence, special forces and other joint strategic capabilities. The Army 2020 programme will likewise reduce the regular British Army's overall capability by 20–30% by 2018 and will greatly increase dependence on reserves. It does, however, retain many of the capabilities specially developed for Iraq and Afghanistan. Although the government has stated an aspiration to rebuild capability after 2015, it is not clear that this can be afforded. Indeed, unless the UK economy improves, sustaining existing capability may prove problematic, particularly if equipment or personnel costs increase beyond current planning assumptions. The regeneration of a capability for contingency operations is planned as force levels in Afghanistan reduce. This has begun with amphibious, air-assault and naval-reaction forces. In the longer term, although the size of the forces has reduced, MoD is still funding some ambitious modernisation programmes for all three services. Overall, the UK armed forces maintain a high standard of training, but the combination of a redundancy programme and new constraints on pay, allowances and pensions could trigger an outflow of experienced staff.

ACTIVE 165,650 (Army 96,850, Navy 32,000 Air 36,800)

RESERVE 80,550 (Regular Reserve ε51,000 (incl 4,850 RAF); Volunteer Reserve 30,550 (Army 26,650; Navy 2,550; Air 1,350)

Includes both trained and those currently under training within the Regular Forces, excluding university cadet units.

ORGANISATIONS BY SERVICE

Strategic Forces 1,000

Armed Forces
RADAR • STRATEGIC 1 Ballistic Missile Early Warning System BMEWS at Fylingdales Moor

Royal Navy
SUBMARINES • STRATEGIC • SSBN 4:
4 *Vanguard* with 4 533mm TT with *Spearfish* HWT, up to 16 UGM-133A *Trident D-5* SLBM (Each boat will not deploy with more than 48 warheads, but each missile could carry up to 12 MIRV, some *Trident* D-5 capable of being configured for sub-strategic role)
MSL • STRATEGIC 48 SLBM (Fewer than 160 declared operational warheads)

Space
SATELLITES • COMMUNICATIONS 7: 1 NATO-4B; 3 *Skynet*-4; 3 *Skynet*-5

Army 93,350; 3,500 Gurkhas (total 96,850)
Regt normally bn size
FORCES BY ROLE
COMMAND
1 (ARRC) corps HQ (1 sigs bde)
MANOEUVRE
Armoured
1 (1st) armd div (2 (7th & 20th) armd bde (1 armd regt, 1 recce regt, 2 armd inf bn, 1 lt inf bn, 1 sigs sqn); 1 cbt spt gp (3 SP arty regt, 1 AD regt, 3 cbt engr regt, 1 ptn br regt, 1 MP regt, 2 log regt, 2 maint regt, 2 med regt); 1 sigs regt)
Mechanised
1 (3rd) div (1 (1st) mech bde (1 armd regt, 1 armd recce regt, 1 armd inf bn, 1 mech inf bn, 2 lt inf bn, 1 sigs sqn); 1 (4th) mech bde (1 armd regt, 1 recce regt, 1 armd inf bn, 1 mech inf bn, 2 lt inf bn, 1 (Gurkha) lt inf bn, 1 sigs sqn); 1 (12th) mech bde (1 armd regt, 1 recce regt, 1 armd inf bn, 1 mech inf bn, 3 lt inf bn, 1 sigs sqn); 1 (19th) lt inf bde (4 lt inf bn, 1 sigs sqn); 1 cbt spt gp (2 SP arty regt, 1 arty regt, 3 cbt engr regt, 2 engr regt, 1 MP regt, 3 log regt, 3 med regt); 1 sigs regt)
Light
5 lt inf bn (3 in London, 2 in Cyprus); 1 (Gurkha) lt inf bn (Brunei)
Other
1 trg BG (based on 1 armd inf bn)

COMBAT SUPPORT
1 arty bde (1 UAV regt, 1 STA regt, 1 MRL regt)
1 (opcon RAF) AD bde (1 AD regt)
1 engr bde (3 EOD regt, 1 air spt bn)
1 int bde
1 sigs bde
COMBAT SERVICE SUPPORT
3 log bde
7 log regt
7 maint bn
1 med bde (3 bn)

Home Service Forces • Gibraltar 200 reservists; 150 active reservists (total 350)

Reserves

Territorial Army 26,650 reservists
The Territorial Army generates individuals, sub-units and some full units.
FORCES BY ROLE
MANOEUVRE
Reconnaissance
2 recce regt
Armoured
2 armd regt
Light
13 lt inf bn
Air Manoeuvre
1 para bn
Aviation
1 UAV regt
COMBAT SUPPORT
3 arty regt
1 STA regt
1 MRL regt
1 AD regt
5 engr regt; 1 engr sqn; 1 (cdo) engr sqn
2 EOD regt
5 sigs regt
COMBAT SERVICE SUPPORT
17 log regt
2 maint bn
EQUIPMENT BY TYPE
MBT 227 *Challenger* 2
RECCE 727: 150 *Jackal*; 110 *Jackal* 2; 140 *Jackal* 2A; 327 *Scimitar*; (8 Tpz-1 *Fuchs* in store)
AIFV 526 *Warrior*
APC 1,936
APC (T) 1,050: 541 *Bulldog* Mk3; 394 FV103 *Spartan*; 115 *Warthog*
PPV 886: 300 *Foxhound*; 304 *Mastiff* (6×6); 157 *Ridgback*; 125 *Wolfhound* (6×6)
ARTY 621
SP 155mm 89 AS90 *Braveheart*
TOWED 105mm 126 L118 Light gun
MRL 227mm 35 M270 MLRS/GMLRS
MOR 371: 81mm SP 11; 81mm 360
AT • MSL • MANPATS *Javelin*
AD • SAM 70
SP 32 FV4333 *Stormer*

TOWED 14 *Rapier* FSC
MANPAD 24 *Starstreak* (LML)
AEV 33+: some *Terrier*; 33 *Trojan*
ARV 256: 75 CRARRV; 4 *Samson*; 177 *Warrior* ARRV
MW 94: 64 *Aardvark*; 30 M139
VLB 71: 38 M3; 33 *Titan*
RADAR • LAND 150: 5–7 *Cobra* (to be withdrawn 2012); 4 *Mamba*; 139 MSTAR
UAV • ISR • Medium 10 *Hermes* 450; *Watchkeeper* (in test – ISD delayed)
AMPHIBIOUS 6 LCVP
LOGISTICS AND SUPPORT 5 RCL

Royal Navy 32,000

EQUIPMENT BY TYPE
SUBMARINES 11
  STRATEGIC • SSBN 4:
    4 *Vanguard*, opcon Strategic Forces with up to 16 UGM-133A *Trident* D-5 SLBM, 4 single 533mm TT each with *Spearfish* HWT, (each boat will not deploy with more than 40 warheads, but each missile could carry up to 12 MIRV; some *Trident* D-5 capable of being configured for sub strategic role)
  TACTICAL • SSN 6:
    5 *Trafalgar* with 5 single 533mm TT with *Spearfish* HWT/*Tomahawk* tactical LACM/UGM 84 *Harpoon* AShM
    1 *Astute* with 6 single 533mm TT with *Spearfish* HWT/ UGM-84 *Harpoon* AShM/*Tomahawk* tactical LACM (4 additional vessels in build; 2 additional vessels on order)
PRINCIPAL SURFACE COMBATANTS 18
  DESTROYERS • DDHM 5:
    4 *Daring* (Type-45) with 1 48-cell VLS with *Sea Viper* SAM, 1 114mm gun, (capacity 1 *Lynx*/AW101 *Merlin* hel – 2 additional vessels in trials)
    1 *Sheffield* (Type-42 Batch 3) with 1 twin lnchr with *Sea Dart* SAM, 1 114mm gun, (capacity 1 *Lynx* hel)
  FRIGATES • FFGHM 13:
    13 *Norfolk* (Type-23) with 2 quad Mk141 lnchr with RGM-84C *Harpoon* AShM, 1 32-cell VLS with *Sea Wolf* SAM, 2 twin 324mm ASTT with *Sting Ray* LWT, 1 114mm gun, (capacity either 2 *Lynx* or 1 AW101 *Merlin* hel)
PATROL AND COASTAL COMBATANTS 22
  PSO 4: 3 *River*; 1 *River* (mod) with 1 hel landing platform
  PB 18: 16 *Archer* (trg); 2 *Scimitar*
MINE WARFARE • MINE COUNTERMEASURES 16:
  MCO 8 *Hunt* (incl 4 mod *Hunt*)
  MHC 8 *Sandown* (1 decommissioned and used in trg role)
AMPHIBIOUS
  PRINCIPAL AMPHIBIOUS SHIPS 4:
    LPD 2 *Albion* (capacity 2 med hel; 4 LCVP; 6 MBT; 300 troops) (1 at extended readiness)
    LPH 2:
      1 *Ocean* (capacity 18 hel; 4 LCU or 2 LCAC; 4 LCVP; 800 troops)
      1 *Invincible* (capacity 22 hel; 600 troops)
  LANDING CRAFT 37: 10 **LCU**; 23 **LCVP**; 4 **LCAC**

LOGISTICS AND SUPPORT 10
  AGB 1 *Protector* (NOR *Polarbjørn*, chartered for three years from April 2011) with 1 hel landing platform
  AGS 3: 1 *Scott*; 2 *Echo* (all with 1 hel landing platform)
  YGS 6: 1 *Gleaner*; 5 *Nesbitt*

Royal Fleet Auxiliary

Support and Miscellaneous vessels are mostly manned and maintained by the Royal Fleet Auxiliary (RFA), a civilian fleet owned by the UK MoD, which has approximately 2,500 personnel with type comd under CINCFLEET.

AMPHIBIOUS • PRINCIPAL AMPHIBIOUS SHIPS 3
  LSD 3 *Bay* (capacity 4 LCU; 2 LCVP; 24 CR2 *Challenger* 2 MBT; 350 troops)
LOGISTICS AND SUPPORT 16
  AORH 3: 2 *Wave*; 1 *Fort Victoria*
  AOR 1 *Leaf*
  AORLH 2 *Rover*
  AFSH 2 *Fort Rosalie*
  ARH 1 *Diligence*
  AG 1 *Argus* (aviation trg ship with secondary role as primarily casualty receiving ship)
  AKR 6 *Point* (not RFA manned)

Naval Aviation (Fleet Air Arm) 5,520

FORCES BY ROLE
ANTI-SUBMARINE WARFARE
  3 sqn with AW101 ASW *Merlin* (HM1)
  1 sqn with *Lynx* HAS3/HMA8
  1 flt with *Lynx* HAS3
AIRBORNE EARLY WARNING
  3 sqn with *Sea King* AEW7
SEARCH & RESCUE
  1 sqn (and detached flt) with *Sea King* HU5
TRAINING
  1 sqn with Beech 350ER *King Air*
  1 sqn with G-115 (op under contract)
  1 OCU sqn with AW101 ASW *Merlin* (HM1)
  1 sqn with *Lynx* HAS3

EQUIPMENT BY TYPE
AIRCRAFT 12 combat capable
  TPT • Light 4 Beech 350ER *King Air*
  TRG 17: 5 G-115 (op under contract); 12 *Hawk* T1*
HELICOPTERS
  ASW 88: 13 *Lynx* HAS3; 33 *Lynx* HMA8; 42 AW101 ASW *Merlin* (HM1/2)
  AEW 13 *Sea King* AEW Mk7
  TPT • Medium 16 *Sea King* HU Mk5
MSL • AShM *Sea Skua*

Royal Marines 6,850

FORCES BY ROLE
MANOEUVRE
  Amphibious
  1 (3rd Cdo) mne bde (1 ISTAR gp (1 EW sqn; 1 cbt spt sqn; 1 sigs sqn; 1 log sqn), 3 cdo; 1 (army) lt inf bn; 1 amph aslt sqn; 1 (army) arty regt; 1 (army) engr regt; 1 log regt)
  3 landing craft sqn opcon Royal Navy

Other

1 Fleet Protestion sy gp

EQUIPMENT BY TYPE

APC (T) 142: 118 BvS-10 *Viking*; 24 BvS-10 Mk2 *Viking*
ARTY 50

TOWED 105mm 18 L-118

MOR 81mm 32

AT • MSL • MANPATS *Javelin*
AMPHIBIOUS • LANDING CRAFT • LCAC 4 Griffon 2400TD
AD • SAM • HVM
RADAR • LAND 4 MAMBA (*Arthur*)

Royal Marines Reserve 600

Royal Air Force 36,800

Flying hours   210/yr on fast jets; 290 on tpt ac; 240 on support hels; 90 on *Sea King*

FORCES BY ROLE
FIGHTER

2 sqn with *Typhoon* FGR4

FIGHTER/GROUND ATTACK

5 sqn with *Tornado* GR4/GR4A

2 sqn with *Typhoon* FGR4

ISR

1 sqn with Beech 350 *Shadow* R1

1 sqn with *Sentinel* R1

AIRBORNE EARLY WARNING & CONTROL

1 sqn with E-3D *Sentry*

SEARCH & RESCUE

2 sqn with *Sea King* HAR-3A

1 sqn with Bell 412EP *Griffin* HAR-2

TANKER/TRANSPORT

1 sqn with *Tristar* C2/C2A/K1/KC1

TANKER

1 sqn with VC-10C1K/K3/K4

TRANSPORT

1 (comms) sqn with AS355 *Squirrel*; AW109E; BAe-125; BAe-146; BN-2A *Islander* CC2

1 sqn with C-17A *Globemaster*

3 sqn with C-130J/J-30/K/K-30 *Hercules*

TRAINING

1 OCU sqn with *Tornado*

1 OCU sqn with *Typhoon*

2 OEU sqn with *Typhoon, Tornado*

1 OCU sqn with E-3D *Sentry*; *Sentinel* R1

1 OEU sqn with E-3D *Sentry*; *Sentinel* R1

1 OCU sqn with *Sea King* HAR-3A

1 sqn with Beech 200 *King Air*

1 sqn with EMB-312 *Tucano* (T Mk1)

3 sqn with *Hawk* T Mk1/1A/1W; *Hawk* 128

3 sqn with *Tutor*

1 hel sqn with Bell 412EP *Griffin* HT1

COMBAT/ISR UAV

2 sqn with MQ-9 *Reaper*

EQUIPMENT BY TYPE

AIRCRAFT 318 combat capable

FGA 230: 134 *Tornado* GR4/GR4A; 98 *Typhoon*

ISR 10: 5 Beech 350 *Shadow* R1; 5 *Sentinel* R1 (Option to be withdrawn from role post-Afghanistan)
AEW&C 6 E-3D *Sentry*
TKR/TPT 15: 1 A330 *Voyager*; 1 Tristar K1; 4 Tristar KC1; 4 VC-10C1K; 4 VC-10K3; 1 VC-10K4
TPT 67: **Heavy** 8 C-17A *Globemaster*; **Medium** 32: 10 C-130J *Hercules*; 14 C-130J-30 *Hercules*; 3 C-130K *Hercules*; 5 C-130K-30 *Hercules*; **Light** 14: 8 Beech 200 *King Air* (on lease); 3 Beech 200GT *King Air* (on lease); 3 BN-2A *Islander* CC2; **PAX** 13: 6 BAe-125 CC-3; 4 BAe-146 MkII; 2 Tristar C2; 1 *Tristar* C2A
TRG 375: 91 EMB-312 *Tucano* T1; 101 G-115E *Tutor*; 28 *Hawk* 128*; 60 *Hawk* T1/1A/1W* (ε60 more in store); 38 T67M/M260 *Firefly*

HELICOPTERS

MRH 5: 1 AW139; 4 Bell 412EP *Griffin* HAR-2
TPT 27 **Medium** 25 *Sea King* HAR-3A; **Light** 3 AW109E
UAV • CBT/ISR • Heavy 10 MQ-9 *Reaper*
MSL

AAM • IR AIM-9L/9L/I *Sidewinder;* **IIR** ASRAAM; **ARH** AIM-120B/C5 AMRAAM

ARM ALARM

ASM *Brimstone; Dual-Mode Brimstone;* AGM-65G2 *Maverick*

LACM Storm Shadow

BOMBS

Conventional Mk 82

Laser-Guided/GPS: *Paveway* II; GBU-10 *Paveway* III; Enhanced *Paveway* II/III; GBU-24 *Paveway* IV

Royal Air Force Regiment

FORCES BY ROLE
COMMAND

3 (tactical Survive To Operate (STO)) sqn

MANOEUVRE

Other

7 field squadron

COMBAT SERVICE SUPPORT

1 (joint) AD trg unit with *Rapier* C

Tri-Service Defence Helicopter School

HELICOPTERS

MRH 11 Bell 412EP *Griffin* HT1
TPT • Light 27: 25 AS350B *Ecureuil*; 2 AW109E

Volunteer Reserve Air Forces

(Royal Auxiliary Air Force/RAF Reserve)
MANOEUVRE

Other

5 field sqn

COMBAT SUPPORT

2 int sqn

COMBAT SERVICE SUPPORT

1 med sqn

1 (air movements) sqn

1 (HQ augmentation) sqn

1 (C-130 Reserve Aircrew) flt

Joint Helicopter Command

Includes Army, Royal Navy and RAF units

Army

FORCES BY ROLE
MANOEUVRE
Air Manoeuvre
1 (16th) air aslt bde (1 recce pl, 2 para bn, 2 air aslt bn, 2 atk hel regt (3 sqn with AH-64D *Apache*), 1 hel regt (3 sqn with *Lynx* AH7/9A), 1 arty regt, 1 engr regt, 1 MP coy, 1 log regt, 1 med regt)
Aviation
1 avn regt (1 sqn with BN-2 *Defender/Islander*; 1 sqn with SA341 *Gazelle*)
1 hel regt (2 sqn with *Lynx* AH7/9A)
1 hel sqn with *Lynx* AH7//9A
1 (test) hel sqn with *Lynx* AH7/9A
1 trg hel regt (1 sqn with AH-64D *Apache*; 1 sqn with AS350B *Ecureuil*; 1 sqn with Bell 212; *Lynx* AH7; SA341 *Gazelle*)
1 hel flt with AS365N3; SA341 *Gazelle*
1 hel flt with Bell 212 (Brunei)
1 hel flt with SA341 *Gazelle* (Canada)

Territorial Army

FORCES BY ROLE
MANOEUVRE
Aviation
1 hel regt

Royal Navy

FORCES BY ROLE
ATTACK HELICOPTER
1 lt sqn with *Lynx* AH7
TRANSPORT HELICOPTER
2 sqn with *Sea King* HC4
TRAINING
1 hel sqn with *Sea King* HC4

Royal Air Force

FORCES BY ROLE
TRANSPORT HELICOPTER
3 hel sqn with CH-47 *Chinook*
2 hel sqn with AW101 *Merlin*
2 hel sqn with SA330 *Puma*

EQUIPMENT BY TYPE
AIRCRAFT • TPT • **Light** 13 8 BN-2T-4S *Defender*; 5 BN-2 *Islander*

HELICOPTERS
ATK 66 AH-64D Apache
MRH 95 : 5 AS365N3; 49 Lynx AH7; 22 Lynx AH9A; 19 SA341 *Gazelle*
TPT 155: **Heavy** 46: 24 CH-47 (HC2/4) *Chinook*; 14 CH-47 (HC2A/4A) *Chinook*; 8 CH-47 (HC3) *Chinook*; **Medium** 101: 28 AW101 *Merlin* (HC3/3A); 34 SA330 *Puma* (HC1) (24 being upgraded to HC2 standard); 37 *Sea King* (HC4); **Light** 17: 9 AS350B *Ecureuil*; 8 Bell 212

UK Special Forces

Includes Army, Royal Navy and RAF units

FORCES BY ROLE
SPECIAL FORCES
1 (SAS) SF regt
1 (SBS) SF regt
1 (Special Reconnaissance) SF regt
1 SF spt gp (based on 1 para bn)
MANOEUVRE
Aviation
1 wg (includes assets drawn from 2 army avn sqn, 1 army hel flt, 1 RAF tpt sqn and 1 RAF hel sqn)
COMBAT SUPPORT
1 sigs regt

Reserve

FORCES BY ROLE
SPECIAL FORCES
2 (SAS) SF regt

Cyber

The Office of Cyber Security & Information Assurance works with the Cyber Security Operations Centre and ministries and agencies to implement cyber-security programmes. CSOC is hosted by GCHQ and was also established in 2009. The UK's October 2010 Strategic Defence and Security Review said that the country would 'establish a transformative national programme to protect ourselves in cyber space'. This 'National Cyber Security Programme' is supported by some £650m – with programme management by OSCIA – and led to a new Cyber Security Strategy, published in November 2011. A UK Defence Cyber Operations Group was set up in 2011 to place 'cyber at the heart of defence operations, doctrine and training'. This group was transferred to Joint Forces Command on this formation's establishment in April 2012.

DEPLOYMENT

Legal provisions for foreign deployment:
Constitution: Uncodified constitution which includes constitutional statutes, case law, international treaties and unwritten conventions
Decision on deployment of troops abroad: By the government

AFGHANISTAN

NATO • ISAF 9,500;
Army: 1 (4th) mech bde (1 recce regt, 1 armd regt, 5 inf bn, 1 cdo bn, 1 arty regt; 1 engr regt); *Jackal; Scimitar; Warrior; Spartan; Mastiff; Ridgback; Warthog Wolfhound;* L-118; GMLRS; AH-64D *Apache; Lynx; Hermes* 450
Royal Navy: *Sea King* HC Mk4
Air Force: *Tornado* GR4/GR4A; C-130 *Hercules;* CH-47 *Chinook;* HC Mk3 *Merlin;* Beech *King Air* 350 *Shadow* R1; MQ-9 *Reaper*

ARABIAN SEA & GULF OF ADEN

Combined Maritime Forces • CTF-150: 1 FFGHM

ARMENIA/AZERBAIJAN
OSCE • Minsk Conference 1

ASCENSION ISLAND
Air Force 20

ATLANTIC (NORTH)/CARIBBEAN
Royal Navy 1 AG

ATLANTIC (SOUTH)
Royal Navy 1 DDHM

BAHRAIN
Royal Navy 20; Air Force 1 BAe-125, 1 BAe-146

BELIZE
Army 10

BOSNIA-HERZEGOVINA
EU • EUFOR • *Operation Althea* 4

BRITISH INDIAN OCEAN TERRITORY
Royal Navy 40; 1 Navy/Marine party at Diego Garcia

BRUNEI
Army 550; 1 (Gurkha) lt inf bn; 1 jungle trg centre; 1 hel flt with 3 Bell 212

CANADA
Army 390; 2 trg units; 1 hel flt with SA341 *Gazelle*; Royal Navy 10: Air Force 20

CYPRUS
Army 1,710; 2 inf bn
Navy 30
Air Force 880; 1 SAR sqn with 4 Bell 412 *Twin Huey*; 1 radar (on det)
UN • UNFICYP 266; 1 inf coy

DEMOCRATIC REPUBLIC OF THE CONGO
EU • EUSEC RD Congo 4
UN • MONUSCO 4 obs

FALKLAND ISLANDS
Army 420; 1 inf coy (+); 1 AD det with *Rapier* FSC
Navy 420; 1 OPV
Air Force 680; 1 ftr flt with 4 *Typhoon* FGR4; 1 SAR sqn with *Sea King* HAR-3/3A; 1 tkr/tpt flt with C-130 *Hercules*; VC-10K3/4

GERMANY
Army 16,240; 1 armd div with (2 armd bde); 1 hel regt (2 sqn with *Lynx* AH-7/9)
Navy 40
Air Force 210

GIBRALTAR
Army 300 (incl 175 pers of Gibraltar regt)

Navy 40
Air Force 70 some (periodic) AEW det

KENYA
Army 170 (trg team)

KUWAIT
Army 30 (trg team)

MEDITERRANEAN SEA
NATO • SNMCMG 2: 1 MHC

NEPAL
Army 280 (Gurkha trg org)

NETHERLANDS
Air Force 90

OMAN
Army 30
Royal Navy 20
Air Force 30: 1 *Sentinel*; 1 *Tristar* tkr

PERSIAN GULF
Combined Maritime Forces • CTF-152: 1 DDHM; 2 MCO; 2 MHC

QATAR
Air Force 4 C-130J

SERBIA
NATO • KFOR 1

SIERRA LEONE
IMATT 21

SOUTH SUDAN
UN • UNMISS 3; 1 obs

UGANDA
EU • EUTM 3

UNITED STATES
Army/Royal Navy/Air Force ε480

FOREIGN FORCES

United States
US European Command: 9,300; 1 ftr wg at RAF Lakenheath with (1 ftr sqn with 24 F-15C/D *Eagle*, 2 ftr sqn with 23 F-15E *Strike Eagle*); 1 ISR sqn at RAF Mildenhall with OC-135/RC-135; 1 tkr wg at RAF Mildenhall with 15 KC-135R *Stratotanker*; 1 Special Ops gp at RAF Mildenhall with 5 MC-130H *Combat Talon* II; 5 MC-130P *Combat Shadow*; 1 C-130E *Hercules*
US Strategic Command: 1 Ballistic Missile Early Warning System (BMEWS) at Fylingdales Moor; 1 *Spacetrack* radar at Fylingdales Moor

Table 8 **Selected Arms Procurements and Deliveries, Europe**

Designation	Type	Quantity (Current)	Contract Value	Prime Nationality	Prime Contractor	Order Date	First Delivery Due	Notes
Albania (ALB)								
AS532AL Cougar	Tpt Hel	5	€78.6m	Int'l	Eurocopter	2009	2012	4 to be delivered in 2012; fifth in 2013. Delivery status unclear; may be delayed following Jul crash
Belgium (BEL)								
Piranha IIIC	APC (W)	242	€700m (US$844m)	US	General Dynamics (MOWAG)	2006	2010	Delivery in progress. Option on further 104
A400M Atlas	Tpt ac	7	n/k	Int'l	EADS (Airbus)	2003	2018	5 flight-test aircraft now in programme. Belgium is now likely to take delivery of its aircraft 2018–19
NH90	ASW/Tpt Hel	8	€293m (US$400m)	Int'l	NH Industries	2007	2013	4 TTH, 4 NFH. Delivery expected to begin mid-2013; option on two more NH90 TTH
Croatia (CRO)								
Patria 8x8	APC (W)	126	€170m (US$218m)	CRO/FIN	Patria	2007	2008	Delivery extended until 2012
Czech Republic (CZE)								
Pandur II 8x8	APC (W)	107	US$828m	US	General Dynamics (GDLS Steyr)	2008	2009	To replace OT-64 SKOT. Reduced from 199 vehicles. Final delivery due 2013
Denmark (DNK)								
Iver Huitfeldt-class	DDG	3	DKK4.3bn (US$471m)	DNK	Odense Staalskibs-værft	2006	2012	Projekt Patruljeskib. First vessel commissioned Feb 2012
Estonia (EST)								
XA-188	APC (W)	80	€20m	NLD	Government transfer	2010	2010	Second-hand Dutch veh. Delivery to be completed in 2015
Finland (FIN)								
Norwegian Advanced Surface-to-Air Missile System (NASAMS)	SAM	n/k	NOK3bn (US$458m)	NOR/US	Kongsberg/ Raytheon	2009	2011	To replace Buk-M1 (SA-11 Gadfly). Expected to be operational by 2015
Katanpaa-class	MCM	3	€244.8m (US$315m)	GER/ITA	Intermarine SpA	2006	2012	Delivery to be completed in 2013
U700-class	LC	12	€34m (US$44m)	FIN	Marine Alutech	2012	2014	Delivery to be completed in 2016
NH90 TTH	Tpt Hel	20	€370m	Int'l	NH Industries	2001	2008	15 delivered by mid-2012
France (FRA)								
VBCI 8x8	AIFV	630	n/k	FRA	Nexter	2000	2008	To replace AMX10P. Final delivery due 2015
Barracuda-class	SSN	6	€8bn (US$10.5bn)	FRA	DCNS	2006	2016	1 SSN to be delivered every 2 years until 2027
Aquitaine-class	FFG	11	US$23.6bn	FRA	DCNS	2002	2012	FREMM. Torpedo trials complete Jul 2012. Final delivery due 2022

Table 8 **Selected Arms Procurements and Deliveries, Europe**

Designation	Type	Quantity (Current)	Contract Value	Prime Nationality	Prime Contractor	Order Date	First Delivery Due	Notes
SCALP Naval	LACM	200	n/k	Int'l	MBDA	2007	2013	To be deployed on *Barracuda*-class SSN (2017) and *Aquitaine*-class FFG (2014)
Rafale F3	FGA ac	180	n/k	FRA	Dassault	1984	2006	Delivery in progress
A400M *Atlas*	Tpt ac	50	see notes	Int'l	EADS	2003	2013	In development. France now expected to receive first 3 of 50 aircraft in 2013
CN-235-300	Tpt ac	8	€225m (US$305m)	Int'l	EADS	2010	2011	Delivery to be complete in early 2013
EC665 *Tiger*	Atk Hel	80	n/k	Int'l	Eurocopter	1999	2005	40 HAD, 40 HAP variant.
NH90 NFH	ASW Hel	27	n/k	Int'l	NH Industries	2000	2010	For navy. Seventh hel delivered Jul 2012. Final delivery due 2019
NH90 TTH	Tpt Hel	34	see notes	Int'l	NH Industries	2007	2012	For army avn. 12 ordered 2007 with 22 more ordered Jan 2009. €1.8bn if all options taken. First delivery in Jul 2012
Harfang	UAV	n/k	see notes	Int'l	EADS	2001	2009	Formerly known as SDIM. Total programme cost: US$1.4bn
Meteor	BVRAAM	200	n/k	Int'l	MBDA	2011	2018	First test firing from *Rafale* in 2012
Germany (GER)								
Puma	AIFV	350	n/k	GER	PSM	2007	2010	To replace *Marder* 1A3/A4/A5 AIFVs. Order reduced from 450 and trial period extended to 2013. To be fitted with *Spike* LR ATGW launcher. Final delivery due 2020
Boxer (8x8)	APC (W)	272	€1.5bn (US$2.1bn)	GER/NLD	ARTEC GmbH	2006	2009	135 APC, 65 CP variants, 72 heavy armoured ambulances.
IRIS-T SLS	SAM	n/k	€123m (US$166m)	GER	Diehl BGT	2007	2012	Surface-launched variant of infrared guided IRIS-T AAM. Secondary msl for army MEADS
Type-212A	SSK	2	n/k	GER	TKMS (HDW)	2006	2013	Due to enter service from 2013
Baden-Württemberg-class	DDGHM	4	€2bn	GER	TKMS	2007	2016	Final delivery due late 2018
Braun-schweig-class	FS	5	n/k	GER	TKMS	2001	2008	Full operational capability now expected 2014
Typhoon	FGA ac	143	n/k	Int'l	Eurofighter GmbH	1998	2003	31 aircraft Tranche 3A order signed in 2009
A400M *Atlas*	Tpt ac	53	see notes	Int'l	EADS (Airbus)	2003	2010	First German aircraft now expected 2014. Original order cut from 60 to 53, further cut to 40 aircraft proposed in late 2011
EC665 *Tiger* (UHT variant)	Atk Hel	80	US$2.6bn	Int'l	Eurocopter	1984	2005	Late 2011 German defence review indicates procurement will be cut to 40
NH90 TTH	Tpt Hel	122	n/k	Int'l	NH Industries	2000	2007	Initial order for 80 (50 for army, 30 for air force) with additional 42 (30 army and 12 air force) ordered in 2007. Total order may be cut to 80
Euro Hawk	ISR UAV	5	€430m (US$559m)	Int'l/US	EADS/ Northrop Grumman	2007	2011	Delivery of first UAV fitted with German SIGINT system due in 2012, with all handed over by 2016
Greece (GRC)								
Katsonis-class	SSK	6	ε€1.67bn	GER	TKMS (HDW)	2000	2010	Type-214. All scheduled to be in service by 2018

Table 8 **Selected Arms Procurements and Deliveries, Europe**

Designation	Type	Quantity (Current)	Contract Value	Prime Nationality	Prime Contractor	Order Date	First Delivery Due	Notes
Roussen/ Super Vita- class	PFM	2	€299m (US$405m)	GRC/UK	Elefsis/BAE Systems (Maritime)	2008	2014	Further order to bring total to seven. Delivery now expected in 2014
NH90 TTH	Tpt Hel	20	€657m	Int'l	NH Industries	2002	2011	16 tac tpt variants and 4 Special Op variants. Option on further 14. Delivery began Jun 2011

Ireland (IRL)

Designation	Type	Quantity (Current)	Contract Value	Prime Nationality	Prime Contractor	Order Date	First Delivery Due	Notes
PV90	PSO	2	US$136m	UK	Babcock International (Babcock Marine)	2010	2014	Keel of first vessel laid in May 2012. Option for a third vessel

Italy (ITA)

Designation	Type	Quantity (Current)	Contract Value	Prime Nationality	Prime Contractor	Order Date	First Delivery Due	Notes
PzH 2000	Arty (155mm SP)	70	n/k	GER/ITA	KMW/Finmeccanica (Oto Melara)	1999	2004	68 delivered by Sep 2012
*Todaro-*class	SSK	2	€915m (US$1.34 bn)	ITA	Fincantieri	2008	2015	Type-212A. Option for second batch exercised from 1996 contract. With AIP
Bergamini- class	FFG	6	€1,628m (US$2,361m)	FRA/ITA	Orizzonte Sistemi Navali	2002	2013	FREMM. Batch 1 (2 vessels) in production. Batch 2 (4 vessels) funding confirmed Mar 2008. Deliveries due 2013–17. Third batch of four vessels may be cut
Typhoon	FGA ac	96	n/k	Int'l	Eurofighter GmbH	1998	2004	21 aircraft Tranche 3A order signed in 2009
Gulfstream G550 CAEW	AEW&C ac	2	US$750m	ISR	IAI	2012	n/k	
ATR-72MP	MP ac	4	€360–400m	ITA	Finmeccanica (Alenia Aeronautica)	2009	2012	To be fitted with long-range surv suite. Final delivery due 2014
M-346 *Master*	Trg ac	6	€220m (US$330m)	ITA	Finmeccanica (Alenia Aeronautica)	2009	2010	Part of agreement for 15. First delivered late 2011
NH90 TTH/ NFH	Tpt/ASW Hel	116	n/k	Int'l	NH Industries	2000	2007	60 TTH for army; 46 NFH & 10 TTH for navy. 20 delivered to army as of late 2012. 10 NFH delivered to navy
CH-47F *Chinook*	Tpt Hel	16	€900m	US	Boeing	2009	2013	For army. Final delivery due 2017

Luxembourg (LUX)

Designation	Type	Quantity (Current)	Contract Value	Prime Nationality	Prime Contractor	Order Date	First Delivery Due	Notes
A400M *Atlas*	Tpt ac	1	see notes	Int'l	EADS (Airbus)	2003	2018	Programme delayed significantly. Luxembourg now to receive ac in 2018–19

NATO

Designation	Type	Quantity (Current)	Contract Value	Prime Nationality	Prime Contractor	Order Date	First Delivery Due	Notes
RQ-4 *Global Hawk* Block 40	ISR UAV	5	€1.3bn (US$1.7bn)	US	Northrop Grumman	2012	2015	To be based at NAS Sigonella ITA. Part of NATO's Alliance Ground Surveillance programme

Netherlands (NLD)

Designation	Type	Quantity (Current)	Contract Value	Prime Nationality	Prime Contractor	Order Date	First Delivery Due	Notes
Boxer (8X8)	APC (W)	200	€595m (US$747m)	GER/NLD	ARTEC GmbH	2006	2013	19 cargo/C2, 27 cargo, 55 CP variants, 58 ambulances and 41 engr. To replace YPR 765
*Walrus-*class	SSK upgrade	4	€50–150m (US$77–232m)	NLD	n/k	2011	2018	SLEP. Incl. combat systems and nav upgrades

Table 8 **Selected Arms Procurements and Deliveries, Europe**

Designation	Type	Quantity (Current)	Contract Value	Prime Nationality	Prime Contractor	Order Date	First Delivery Due	Notes
Holland-class	PSOH	4	€365m	NLD	Damen Schelde	2007	2011	First three commissioned; fourth vessel launched 2011
Karel Doorman-class	AFSH	1	€364m (US$545m)	NLD	Damen Schelde (DSNS)	2009	2014	Joint Logistics Support Ship. To replace HrMS *Zuiderkruis*. Laid down 2011
NH90 NFH/ TTH	ASW/Tpt Hel	20	n/k	Int'l	NH Industries	2000	2010	12 NFH, 8 TTH. First NFH delivered Apr 2010. 8 NFH delivered as of late 2012
CH-47F *Chinook*	Tpt Hel	6	US$335m	US	Boeing	2007	2012	Delivery delayed. First 5 now due mid-late 2012; final hel due early 2013

Norway (NOR)								
Hisnorsat	Sat	24	€300m (US$368m)	ESP	Hisdesat	2010	2013	Military communications satellite
CV90	AIFV/AIFV Upgrade	144	£500m (US$750m)	UK	BAE Systems (Land & Armaments)	2012	2013	41 new-build CV90s and 103 existing CV9030s to be upgraded
FH-77 BW L52 *Archer* 6x6	Arty (155mm SP)	24	£135m (US$200m)	UK	BAE Systems (Land & Armaments)	2010	2011	Contract value is for combined 48 unit NOR/SWE order. Delivery status unclear
Naval Strike Missile (NSM)	AShM	n/k	NOK 2.27bn (US$466m)	NOR	Kongsberg (KDA)	2007	2012	First deliveries Jun 2012. Final delivery due 2014
F-35A *Lightning* II	FGA	2	n/k	US	Lockheed Martin	2012	n/k	To remain in the US for training, and to be followed by 2 more in 2016. Up to 48 more to be based in Norway with deliveries from 2017
NH90 NFH/ TTH	ASW/Tpt Hel	14	n/k	Int'l	NH Industries	2001	2011	6 for ASW, 8 for coast guard. Now expected to enter service in 2012

Poland (POL)								
Rosomak	AIFV	690	US$1.7bn	FIN	Patria	2003	2004	AMV XC-360P. Initial order for 690 in 2003, with additional 200 ordered in 2012. Final delivery due 2018
Spike LR	MANPATS	264	PLN1.487bn (US$512m)	ISR	Rafael	2003	2004	264 launchers and 2,675 msl. Manufactured under licence
Gawron-class	PSO	2	PLN77m (US$24.8m)	POL	SMW	2004	n/k	Project 621. Project cancelled in Feb 2012, and then restarted Sep 2012. Originally to be constructed as FFG, now to be a patrol ship
M-28B/PT *Bryza*	Tpt ac	8	PLN399m	US	UTC (PZL Mielec)	2008	2010	For air force. Order reduced from 12 to 8 ac in 2009 due to budget cuts. Final delivery due 2013
C-295	Tpt ac	5	PLN876m (US$262m)	Int'l	EADS (CASA)	2012	2012	First delivery due by end 2012

Romania (ROM)								
C-27J *Spartan*	Tpt ac	7	€220m (US$293m)	ITA	Fin-meccanica (Alenia Aeronautica)	2006	2010	To replace An-26. Incl. log and trg support. 5 in service by late 2012
F-16AM/ BM *Fighting Falcon*	FGA ac	12	US$600m	PRT	n/a	2012	2016	Second-hand PRT F-16 MLUs

Spain (ESP)								
Paz (Peace) satellite	Sat	2	€160m	ESP / Int'l	Hisdesat/ EADS (CASA)	2008	2012	–

Table 8 **Selected Arms Procurements and Deliveries, Europe**

Designation	Type	Quantity (Current)	Contract Value	Prime Nationality	Prime Contractor	Order Date	First Delivery Due	Notes
Pizarro	AIFV	212	€707m (US$853m)	US	General Dynamics (SBS)	2003	2005	In 5 variants. Delivery status unclear
Piranha IIIC	APC (W)	21	n/k	US	General Dynamics (GDELS/ MOWAG)	2007	2010	For marines. Delivery to be complete by 2013
RG-31	PPV	20	€15.3m	US	General Dynamics (SBS)	2012	2012	To equip ESP forces in AFG and LBN
SBT (V07)	Arty (155mm Towed)	70	€181m (US$216m)	US	General Dynamics	2005	2006	4 155/52 APU SBT (V07) how, plus design and production of 66 how (SIAC). Also retrofit of 12 APU SBT how from V06 to V07 version and 82 towing vehicles
S-80A	SSK	4	n/k	ESP	Navantia	2003	2015	Delivery of first vessel, S-81, delayed until 2015
Typhoon	FGA ac	74	n/k	Int'l	Eurofighter GmbH	1998	2003	21 aircraft Tranche 3A order signed 2009
A400M Atlas	Tpt ac	27	see notes	Int'l	EADS (Airbus)	2003	2015	Spain will begin to take delivery of the type in 2015
EC665 Tiger (HAD)	Atk Hel	24	€1.4bn	Int'l	Eurocopter	2003	2007	First 3 hel delivered May 2007, second 3 by 2008. Status of further deliveries unclear
NH90 TTH	Tpt Hel	45	n/k	Int'l	NH Industries	2007	2012	First flight Dec 2010. Deliveries scheduled to begin in 2012
Sweden (SWE)								
BvS10 Mk II	APC (T)	48	£65m (US$100m)	UK	BAE Systems (Land & Armaments)	2012	2012	First delivery due by end-2012
Armoured Modular Vehicle (AMV)	APC (W)	113	€240m (US$338m)	FIN	Patria	2009	2011	79 APCs and 34 other variants. Further 113 req. To be delivered 2011–13
FH-77 BW L52 Archer 6x6	Arty (155mm SP)	24	£135m (US$200m)	UK	BAE Systems (Land & Armaments)	2010	2011	Contract value is for combined 48-unit NOR/SWE order. Delivery status unclear
NH90	ASW/Tpt Hel	18	n/k	Int'l	NH Industries	2001	2007	13 TTT/SAR hel and 5 ASW variants. Option for 7 further hel. 7 delivered by mid-2012
Turkey (TUR)								
Gokturk	Sat	1	€270m (US$380m)	ITA/FRA	Telespazio/ Thales (Alenia Space)	2009	2013	–
Altay	MBT	250	see notes	TUR	Otokar	2007	n/k	4 initial prototypes by 2014 for approx US$500m. To be followed by an order for 250 units following testing
Firtina 155mm/52-cal	Arty (155mm SP)	350	n/k	ROK	Samsung Techwin	2001	2003	ROK Techwin K9 Thunder. Total requirement of 350. Deliveries ongoing
Type-214	SSK	6	€1.96bn (US$2.9bn)	GER	MFI/TKMS (HDW)	2009	2015	To be built at Golcuk shipyard
Ada-class	FFGHM	8	n/k	TUR	Istanbul Naval Shipyard	1996	2011	Second vessel due for delivery in 2013. Part of Milgem project which incl. requirement for four F-100-class FFG

Table 8 **Selected Arms Procurements and Deliveries, Europe**

Designation	Type	Quantity (Current)	Contract Value	Prime Nationality	Prime Contractor	Order Date	First Delivery Due	Notes
Dost-class	PSOH	4	€352.5m	TUR	RMK Marine	2007	2011	Based on *Sirio*-class PCO design. For coast guard. All 4 vessels to be launched by end-2012
Tuzla-class	PCC	16	€402m (US$545m)	TUR	Dearsan Shipyard	2007	2010	New Type Patrol Boat (NTPB). Six vessels delivered by Aug 2012. Final delivery due 2015
F-16C/D Block 50 *Fighting Falcon*	FGA ac	30	US$1.78bn	US	Lockheed Martin	2009	2011	14 F-16C and 16 F-16D variants. Final assembly in TUR. First delivery May 2011. Final delivery due 2014
ATR-72MP	MP ac	10	€260m	ITA	Finmeccanica (Alenia Aeronautica)	2005	n/k	Programme delayed; seven of 10 MP mission systems delivered by mid-2012
B-737 AEW	AEW&C ac	4	US$1bn	US	Boeing	2002	2012	Peace Eagle programme. Option for a further 2. First aircraft now to be delivered 2012; remaining 3 in 2013.
A400M *Atlas*	Tpt ac	10	see notes	Int'l	EADS (Airbus)	2003	2012	TUK is now due to take the first of its 10 ac in 2013
T129 (AW129 *Mangusta*)	Atk Hel	51	US$3bn	TUR/ITA	TAI/Aselsan/ Finmeccanica (Agusta Westland)	2007	2013	Option on further 41. Serial production planned for 2013
T129 (AW129 *Mangusta*)	Atk Hel	9	€150m (US$208m)	TUR/ITA	TAI/Aselsan/ Finmeccanica (Agusta Westland)	2010	2012	Interim measure to fill capability gap until large-scale production of T129 begins. Four due for delivery 2012
CH-47F *Chinook*	Tpt Hel	6	see notes	US	Boeing	2011	2013	Original aim to acquire 14 for US$1.2bn, but order cut to six, five for the army and one for SF Command
S-70i *Black Hawk* (T-70)	Tpt Hel	109	US$3.5bn	TUR/US	TAI/UTC (Sikorsky)	2011	n/k	–
Anka	ISR UAV	10	n/k	TUR	TAI	2012	2014	–
United Kingdom (UK)								
Ocelot (Foxhound)	PPV	376	£180m	US	General Dynamics (Force Protection)	2010	2011	Initial order for 200 in 2010, with additional orders in 2011 and 2012
Astute-class	SSN	6	see notes	UK	BAE Systems (Maritime)	1994	2010	Second vessel entered sea trials with third outfitting in Sep 2012. Contract awarded for seventh boat reactor
Queen Elizabeth-class	CV	2	£3.9bn (US$8bn)	UK	BAE Systems (Maritime)	2007	2016	ISD delayed until 2017 and 2020. 2010 SDSR decision to convert one carrier to CATOBAR version reversed in May 2012
Daring-class	DDGHM	6	see notes	UK	BAE Systems (Maritime)	2001	2008	Type-45. Overall cost now expected to be £5.9bn. Final two vessels to be commissioned 2013/14
Tide-class	AOT	4	£452m	ROK	Daewoo Shipbuilding and Marine Engineering (DSME)	2012	2016	Military Afloat Reach & Sustainability (MARS) programme
Typhoon	FGA ac	160	n/k	Int'l	Eurofighter GmbH	1998	2004	40 aircraft order as part of Tranche 3A, includes 24 to replace elements of Tranche 2 order diverted to the RSAF as part of Project Salam
F-35B *Lightning* II	FGA ac	3	US$600m	US	Lockheed Martin	2009	2012	Test and trg ac. First 2 delivered by late 2012, will remain in US. Shift from F-35B to C-model reversed

Table 8 **Selected Arms Procurements and Deliveries, Europe**

Designation	Type	Quantity (Current)	Contract Value	Prime Nationality	Prime Contractor	Order Date	First Delivery Due	Notes
Voyager (A330-200)	Tkr / Tpt ac	14	£13bn (US$26 bn)	Int'l	AirTanker Consortium	2008	2011	Delivery in progress
RC-135 *Rivet Joint*	ELINT ac	3	ε£700m (US$1bn)	US	Boeing	2010	2013	First of 3 aircraft to be delivered in 2013
A400M *Atlas*	Tpt ac	22	n/k	Int'l	EADS (Airbus)	2003	2014	UK now due to take first of 22 aircraft in 2014. Original order reduced by three
AW159 *Lynx Wildcat*	MRH Hel	62	£1bn (US$1.8bn)	ITA	Finmeccanica (Agusta Westland)	2006	2012	34 for army, 28 for navy. Option for a further 4 hel. Final delivery due 2015
Hermes 450	ISR UAV	n/k	US$110m	FRA	Thales	2007	2010	Contract incl. trg, log spt and management services
Watchkeeper WK450	ISR UAV	54	£800m (US$1.2bn)	FRA	Thales	2005	n/k	Delivery repeatedly delayed

Chapter Five
Russia and Eurasia

RUSSIA

Efforts by the senior leadership in the Ministry of Defence to reform Russia's armed forces continue. As in previous years, these initiatives ranged in 2012 from the bureaucratic to the practical, such as developing the armed forces' training and exercise regimes. The stated ambition to professionalise the armed forces is intended to be achieved by increasing the number of contract servicemen while retaining a conscript element. The armed forces, however, remain unable to generate sufficient numbers of contract personnel and non-commissioned officers to meet personnel targets, and manpower levels continue to fall. Many junior officers, as in the previous year, remain posted to units as NCOs (see box).

The pattern of the structural reform process generally remains as before: design, test, and then adjust or adapt if required. Some analysts believe that key elements of the reform process are largely complete, such as the initiative to transform the army towards a combined-arms brigade-based structure, though adjustments are still to be made, largely in the internal formation of these units. Some units retain established structures: the Airborne Forces (VDV) remain a divisional-level formation, and the 18th Machine Gun Artillery Division continues to be stationed in the Kuril Islands. There are some outstanding issues: changes in unit-level combat training are still under development; there is a lack of clarity over how the Joint Strategic Commands (see *The Military Balance 2011*, p. 174), which are planned to operate in Military Districts in times of war, will actually work when activated; and the armed forces are still waiting for an integrated and automated command and control (C2) system to emerge. But the army has already changed substantially, while the armed forces in general have become more compact and mobile and have benefitted from improved frequency of training. Whether this translates directly into improved 'readiness' is less clear.

The authorities in Moscow increasingly see rearmament as a second stage in the reform process. The administration maintains its ambitions to field more and newer equipment, though in recent years budgetary problems as well as changing requirements have meant that some programmes have not been realised on schedule, if at all. The latest programme, The State Armaments Programme 2011–2020, was signed by then-President Dmitry Medvedev on 31 December 2010. It saw around R19 trillion ($US610bn) out of the programme's total R20tr allocated to the Ministry of Defence; the remainder going to other forces. Generating the industrial capacity to address new as well as established procurement ambitions remains a major problem (see Defence Economics, p. 205).

Administrative developments

Russia's presidential election in March 2012 did not affect key leadership positions in the MoD. With Vladimir Putin regaining the presidency and Medvedev once again assuming the post of prime minister, there was a significant reshuffle of government portfolios, but Defence Minister Anatoly Serdyukov kept his position. This indicated that Serdyukov, and the reform process he initiated, had high level support at that time. However, the defence reform process continued to be criticised by some in the political and military establishments as hasty, poorly drafted and poorly explained.

In November, in the midst of what was ostensibly a corruption scandal, Serdyukov was sacked and replaced by Sergei Shoigu, who held the military rank of General from a previous post in the Emergencies Ministry. CGS Makarov was also sacked, with Colonel-General Valeriy Gerasimov appointed in his place, even though Makarov had earlier in 2012 had his career extended beyond the normal retirement age. A series of deputy ministers were also sacked. Aleksandr Sukhorokov was dismissed from his post as first deputy minister, and replaced by Colonel-General Arkady Bukhin. Deputy ministers Dmitry Chushkin and Yelena Kozlova were also fired. On taking post, Shoigu halted moves to merge some defence academies and close some military hospitals. Some analysts also expected changes in the systems used for defence outsourcing and in selling real estate; Serdyukov was reportedly sacked after inves-

Cyber

In March 2012, Dmitry Rogozin, the Russian deputy prime minister with responsibility for the defence industry, announced that a Cyber Security Command would be established within the Russian armed forces. This was presented as a response to the creation of similar establishments overseas, with particular reference to the United States. As of December 2012, few reliable details were available on this supposed new entity, with reports suggesting it could take various configurations, including becoming a distinct arm of service or a directorate of the General Staff.

The first official doctrinal statement on the role of the Russian military in cyberspace, the 'Conceptual Views on the Activity of the Russian Federation Armed Forces in Information Space', was released at the end of 2011, and described cyber force tasks which bear little resemblance to those of equivalent commands in the West. The differences from published doctrine in the US or UK are substantial. In particular, the 'Views' contain no mention of the possibility of offensive cyber activity. The document is entirely defensive in tone, and focuses on force protection and prevention of information war, including allowing for a military role in negotiating international treaties governing information security.

At first sight, this would seem a continuation of the pattern whereby offensive cyber activity is not seen as the domain of the military. Following mixed performance in the information aspects of the armed conflict with Georgia in 2008, there was intense discussion of the possible creation of 'Information Troops', whose role would include cyber capability; but this initiative was publicly scotched by the Federal Security Service. Then-CGS Makarov, however, had given a very different picture of the new command's three main tasks in a comment in a briefing in January 2012:

- 'disrupting adversary information systems, including by introducing harmful software;
- defending our own communications and command systems;
- working on domestic and foreign public opinion using the media, Internet and more'.

The reference to 'introducing harmful software' appears to be the first official avowal of an offensive cyber role for a Russian government body, and is more in keeping with overseas concepts of the purpose of cyber commands. At the same time, the third task, influencing public opinion, is a reminder that unlike some other nations with advanced cyber capabilities, Russia deals in cyber warfare as an integral component of overall information warfare.

tigations into real estate transactions. However, while elements of the reform process might be paused or recast, and while some aspects might be subject to greater scrutiny or better explained to defence establishment and industry, it is unlikely that there will be radical change to the overall direction of Russian defence reform.

Recruitment and manning

Official figures have for some time put the total strength of the Russian armed forces at around one million, but examination of demographic statistics, conscript numbers and the continuing low numbers of contract servicemen rendered this position doubtful. In April 2012, a memorandum from State Secretary/Deputy Minister of Defense Nikolay Pankov to Serdyukov was published in the Russian press. According to this document, as of April 2012, the total active strength of the Russian armed forces was 160,100 officers, 317,200 conscripts and 189,700 contract soldiers, for a total of 667,000. The figure rises to around 800,000 when military doctors, cadets and instructors at military academies, officers who were

declared excess and some other categories of military personnel are included.

Russia's armed forces continue to suffer the effects of the sharp demographic collapse from 1987–99, when male births fell by more than 50%; the broad effect of this is that the pool of available personnel will continue to shrink until the 2020s. The demographic situation has negatively affected the aspiration to field increasing numbers of contract servicemen, but its effects are most clearly manifested in a lack of available conscripts. Poor health among recruits continues to prompt concern: just over 67% of conscripts reporting for duty were judged fit for military service during the spring 2012 draft. Additionally, substantial numbers evade the call-up.

In response to concerns about evasion, the defence ministry reportedly considered amending the conscription procedure, doing away with notification by post or courier. Young men of conscription age were, according to Interfax, to be obliged 'to appear in district military committees within two weeks after a presidential decree on conscription is published and receive an enlistment notice. In case

Developing an NCO cadre

Despite early recognition that Russia's plans for reforming its armed forces depend heavily on developing NCOs into more effective junior leaders, administrators and operators, progress in this area appears painfully slow. June 2012 saw the graduation of the first 180 'long-course' NCO cadets from the Institute of Airborne Forces in Ryazan. Initial enrollment in this two-year course was 241. These numbers, and the length of the course, compared with the immediate requirement for tens of thousands of trained and effective NCOs, put the challenge in perspective. Meanwhile, reports in early 2012 suggested that some NCOs were still undergoing the 10-month warrant officer (*praporshchik*) course in order to fill administrative posts, despite the fact that *praporshchiki* had notionally been abolished.

Like plans for recruitment of contract servicemen, the ambitions for redistribution of roles and responsibilities between officers and junior NCOs have been repeatedly adjusted in the light of reality. As noted in *The Military Balance 2012* (p. 185), basic failures of arithmetic in predicting required numbers led to several thousand cadets graduating from military academies as officers, but continuing to serve as NCOs. Another 12,000 junior officers graduated during 2012, with the effective two-year moratorium on officer recruitment still to feed through in reduced numbers completing training. At the same time, there were reports of units being unable to carry out their functions since NCOs or conscripts tasked with carrying out duties previously assigned to officers – as crew chiefs or operators, for example – simply did not have the necessary training or experience. The problem was formally recognised in May 2012, with the announcement that several thousand posts that had been downgraded to be filled by NCOs would revert to requiring commissioned officers. The reported number of posts affected ranged from 5,000–11,000.

In the move to professional NCOs, as with the development of officer manning overall, the Russian military's ambitions appear to have run ahead of the possible without detailed long-term planning and a fundamental cultural shift in the understanding of precisely what effective non-commissioned officers are for, and how to go about creating them. Further readjustment should be expected.

a draftee dodges the draft, he may face criminal charges.' But sanctions on evasion already exist, and the fact remains that the young men will first have to be found before they can be made to appear at a district military committee.

The MoD hopes that the reduction in potential conscripts will be offset by a rise in the number of contract personnel. This process has been under way for some years with limited success. In late 2010, the official number of contract personnel was 150,000. This had risen to 180,000 by 2011, and reached 186,400 by mid-2012. Serdyukov restated in 2012 his aim to have 425,000 contract personnel by 2017. However, confusion in how public and internal MoD figures are calculated means it is difficult to analyse the real recruitment situation. For instance, all officers are technically contract servicemen, and can be added or subtracted from total contract numbers; overall totals can vary according to different assessment criteria by 20,000–30,000.

Contract soldiers currently sign a three-year contract, with the possibility of extension. Officials hope that significant numbers of suitable conscripts will also choose to transfer to a contract basis. But attracting and retaining the right personnel remains a problem, particularly given the roles and services for which contract personnel are seen as suitable; Serdyukov reportedly highlighted the service of contract personnel in the navy, strategic rocket forces and air and space defence troops. Improved accommodation and terms of service would be needed to attract good recruits, as would pay scales competitive with the civilian workplace. Presently, contract soldiers can only serve up to the rank of sergeant; this means that their salaries are significantly lower than those of officers. In November 2011, Medvedev signed a law, which took effect on 1 January 2012, raising military salaries and pensions. Military pensions were increased by 60%, while military salaries were nearly tripled: a contract sergeant is now paid around R34,000 (US$1,092), while a lieutenant receives around R50,000 (US$1,605). Bonuses for time served, trade training and other factors such as particular military skills or postings were also detailed. However, the officers' financial bonus package known as the 'Order 400' scheme will remain. In March, MoD personnel chief Sergei Chvarkov reportedly said that the scheme would be widened to include soldiers and NCOs. Order 400 was thought an interim step to address the salary issue and, while it provided substantial incentives, it also led to some discontent among those left out.

The ministry is also addressing concern over the sensitive issue of housing provision for military personnel. Putin first raised the issue of improving housing provision for servicemen back in 2005, and progress since then has been modest. The president returned to the theme in early 2012, saying that the construction of permanent, individual housing, as well as military housing complexes, should be boosted. A modern service housing fund is scheduled to be set up by 2014, while the problem will also be helped by a simultaneous reduction in the number of servicemen requiring housing. According to Chvarkov, the number has fallen from 170,000 to around 40,000 since 2007. At the same time, the ministry has started to transfer ownership of its real estate, including plots of land, to region and municipal authorities on a cost-free basis. It is estimated that the ministry has more than five million square metres of real estate (i.e military bases and buildings), and around 11 million hectares of land (such as training areas, land within closed bases and garrisons, and even some forests). After 2008, the ministry was allowed to sell real estate at auction, with the resulting R6.6bn from sales invested in social programmes for servicemen. Overall, the number of garrisons is due to fall, mirroring the drop in other defence establishments in recent years. Though the ministry registered 7,500 garrisons on its books in 2012, it intends to reduce that number to 184; by, it is assumed, 2020. Real estate transactions came under greater scrutiny after the November 2012 ministerial changeover.

Army

The ministry unveiled a raft of plans for the army during 2012. Despite the problems with staffing detailed above, 26 new infantry brigades are scheduled to deploy by 2020. The understaffing issue has in some cases led, according to an Interfax article, to motor-rifle and combined-arms brigades ostentibly at full readiness operating with a 30–50% shortfall in personnel. The ministry's response, the article continued, was to form 'reinforced battalions' in these brigades, comprised of contract personnel and combat-experienced troops. The army currently consists of around 100 brigades (40 motor-rifle or tank brigades, with the remainder including artillery, rocket, anti-aircraft brigades, around ten combat service support brigades, NBC troops, and special task brigades, etc.). The ministry is still establishing the 130th Separate Motorised Military Police Brigade (see *The Military Balance 2012*, p. 187).

Each of ten combined-arms armies will have one reconnaissance brigade and one army aviation brigade. The four military districts will each house four extra army aviation brigades and two anti-aircraft brigades. Though army aviation is currently under air force command, the plan is for it to revert to army authority, exercised by military district commanders. The army and airborne troops received more than R2.6 trillion (US$88.5bn) under the State Armaments Programme 2011–2020. Ten *Iskander*-M tactical ballistic-missile brigade units (120 launchers), nine brigade units of S-300V4 air-defence systems, more than 2,300 tanks of varying type and around 2,000 self-propelled guns are planned to enter service by 2020.

The Arctic

Russia plans to establish military installations along the Northern Sea Route for basing naval and coast guard vessels, according to Nikolay Patrushev, secretary of Russia's Security Council, although precise details have yet to emerge. The army will establish a special Arctic brigade. While the location of its headquarters has yet to be decided, the cities of Pechenga and Kandalaksha in Murmansk Oblast, the Yamal-Nenetz autonomous district and the Republic of Yakutia are being considered. In the near term, the brigade will be equipped with MT-LBV vehicles, specially adapted for Arctic terrain, in the APC role. In future, it will be equipped with a combat and support vehicle based on the unified platform discussed opposite. The possibility of such Arctic brigades was noted some years ago, in light of Russia's economic and political interests in the region, and with reference to the 2008 publication of Russia's state policy for the Arctic to 2020 and beyond.

Navy

The State Armaments Programme 2011–2020 allocated R4.4tr (US$150bn), or 23.4% of the total excluding the strategic nuclear forces, for naval rearmament. The ministry hopes to create balanced joint naval forces armed with long-range precision weapons. Eight *Borei*-class nuclear submarines (Class-955, due to carry the *Bulava* missile when it is ready), eight multi-purpose nuclear submarines and eight diesel-electric submarines, and 51 modern surface combat ships (including 15 frigates, up to 25 corvettes and four *Mistral* assault helicopter ships) are planned to enter service by 2020. The first *Mistral* is scheduled for completion by the end of 2014, though the precise

Armour

President Vladimir Putin and Deputy Prime Minister Dmitry Rogozin visited Russian armoured-vehicle manufacturer Uralvagonzavod within days of each other in May 2012, where both were briefed on the progress of the *Armata* project, Moscow's latest effort to develop a next-generation family of heavy armour vehicles.

Main battle-tank development suffered badly as a result of the collapse of the Soviet Union, followed rapidly by that of the Russian economy in the 1990s. The intended successor to the T-90, sometimes referred to as Object 195, was cancelled. A highly ambitious programme, it proved unaffordable.

Armata appears to be the heavy element of a three-tier approach to overhauling the land forces' armoured-vehicle inventory. This parallels in part the army's aim of fielding heavy, medium and light brigades. The replacement for the BMP family of infantry fighting vehicles has been given the name *Kurganets*; it is being designed by Kurganmashzavod. Meanwhile a wheeled vehicle project is known as *Boomerang*, and is to be developed by the Bryansk Motor Vehicle Plant.

The Russian military has released little information on the nature of *Armata*, beyond the name. Rogozin, who has responsibility within the government for overseeing the defence industry, has indicated that the tracked chassis will form the basis of a family of vehicles.

If, as reported, the military technical specifications for the *Armata* project were only concluded in mid-2011, then the timescale is demanding. As of May 2012, Rogozin was stating that 'serial production' should begin in 2015. While Uralvagonzavod builds and continues to upgrade the T-90 MBT, the army's focus is now on the *Armata*; there are no plans to buy further T-90s and in the interim the plant will upgrade T-72s for the military.

During his May visit Putin said a three-year contract worth R19bn (US$613m) had been recently signed that would maintain a full workload for the assembly shops. The company is also receiving state funding to improve its infrastructure as part of a broader drive to make up for years of neglect.

There is speculation that the MBT element of the *Armata* may have a remotely operated gun, with the crew housed in the chassis. What is intended as a modular design could also form the basis of a heavy armoured support vehicle similar to the BMPT, and for a family of combat support vehicles. Hardware for the *Armata* programme is due to begin testing in 2013, with the type intended to be in widespread service by 2020.

---

weapons fit for the vessel remains unclear. R&D work is under way on projects to develop a multi-purpose conventional submarine, a destroyer, a multi-role corvette suitable for littoral waters and an aircraft carrier. There has yet to be discussion on the shape of a prospective air group for the latter. Russia's only current aircraft carrier, the *Admiral Kuznetsov*, dates from the mid-1980s. Based in the Northern Fleet, it is due to be sent for complete overhaul. Meanwhile, the ministry plans to restore, upgrade and put into service its nuclear-powered *Kirov*-class Project 1144 battle cruisers. Only one, the *Pyotr Velikiy*, is on strength with the Northern Fleet; the remaining three are classed as 'in reserve'. The *Admiral Nakhimov* and *Admiral Lazarev* are due to be overhauled and upgraded; the fate of the *Admiral Ushakov* is less clear.

Air force

The reform of Russia's air force, and the reduction in its facilities, has been traced in recent editions of *The Military Balance*. The actual and target numbers of air bases and air fields continue to vary, but analysts now believe that the intention is to have ten main air bases (including two naval aviation bases) and 27 secondary airfields attached to these ten. As of late 2012, there were still 52 airfields in air force use. It is difficult to ascertain precise squadron basing from the available data; aircraft of varying type are assigned to air bases in varying numbers and there seems little standardisation in squadron size across the country. This is perhaps as much a function of the air force still trying to ascertain the best formations and asset-mix for each area of responsibility as much as it is a reflection of ageing equipment.

The plan is for 600 new aircraft and 1,100 helicopters to be put into air force service by 2020. Preliminary estimates are that, if the State Armaments Programme 2011–2020 is completed according to plan, the air force will have up to 2,500 modern and upgraded aircraft and helicopters; R4tr (US$136bn) were allocated for this task. The air force plans to purchase up to 90 Su-35S fighter aircraft, around 28 Su-30s, 80 upgraded Su-25SM ground-attack aircraft, 129 Su-34 strike aircraft, 65 Yak-130 trainers and 60 fifth-generation combat aircraft based on the Sukhoi T-50 prototype. While these plans would be difficult to fulfil, they are not impossible, though industrial capacity would have to significantly improve. Helicopter purchases are slated to include 150 Mi-28N *Night Hunters*, 180 Ka-52 *Alligators*, including up to 40 for the *Mistrals*, and 49 Mi-35s.

Aerospace defence

Some analysts indicate that air-defence units previously incorporated into the air force in 1999 have been reorganised into 11 brigades combining anti-aircraft missile and radio-radar regiments under an Aerospace Defence Command, activated on 1 December 2011. As noted in *The Military Balance 2012*, the command is intended to unify Russia's Space Forces, Air–Space Defence Strategic Command, as well as air force air-defence units under a new organisation, the Aerospace Defence Forces (Vozdushno Kosmicheskaya Oborona, VKO), though it is difficult to precisely assess the structure of this command from the available information. It is likely, however, that the command will be focused on medium- and upper-tier threats, with lower-tier and point-defence remaining the purview of geographically dispersed units. Equipment includes early-warning systems (in two echelons – space and ground), space-tracking systems, Russia's Ballistic Missile Defence System (A-135) and missile systems in the service of AA brigades. The early-warning space echelon presently consists of only three satellites, providing limited surveillance with significant time gaps, a problem due to be solved by the introduction of new satellites.

The ground echelon consists of seven independent radio-radar centres equipped with *Dnepr*, *Daryal*, *Volga* and *Voronezh* over-the-horizon radar stations. These systems can acquire a ballistic target at ranges from 4,000 to 6,000 kilometres. The only gap in the ground echelon's coverage is presently in the northeast, which will be closed when *Voronezh*-DM radars are put into service (possibly in Barnaul, Yeniseisk and Omsk). The A-135 system is deployed around Moscow and has only a 150km operational radius. It consists of a warning and monitoring system, silos of 53T6 *Gazelle* short-range anti-ballistic missiles and 51T6 *Gorgon* long-range anti-ballistic missiles. Though the system is relatively old, no modernisation plans have been announced. Meanwhile, the in-service date of the S-500 missile system, billed as a replacement, has slipped further.

The State Armaments Programme 2011–2020 allocated R4tr (US$136bn) for aerospace defence, and the plan is for around 100 SAM and *Pantsyr-S1* systems, as well as more than 30 *Vityaz* medium-range missile systems, to be in service by 2020. *Vityaz* is currently in development and, according to media reports, will replace some S-300 systems. It is believed that the system uses the 9M96 and 9M100 missiles. Three anti-aircraft brigades were transferred from the air force and are deployed in the central industrial region, with 12 AA regiments (32 batteries in total) mainly armed with the S-300. Two AA regiments,

Russia's nuclear triad

The Russian military continues to revamp its nuclear triad, with all three arms of the services pursuing projects of varying degrees of ambition. The air force was expected to begin to field a new strategic cruise missile during 2012, the navy's Project 955 *Borei*-class SSBN build programme is ongoing, and the Strategic Rocket Forces continue to deploy the solid propellant RS-24 *Yars* and are also pursuing a new liquid-fuelled ballistic missile. Proposals to create a unified strategic forces command, however, appeared to have been shelved as of the fourth quarter of 2012.

The Kh-101/Kh-102 (AS-2X) likely entered service with the Russian air force in 2012, carried on the Tupolev Tu-95MS *Bear* H. The Kh-102 is the nuclear variant of this large cruise missile, with the Kh-101 a conventionally armed derivative. It is not known if the missile also entered service during 2012 with the half-dozen or so Tu-160 *Blackjack* bomber aircraft the air force has operational at any one time.

The Kh-101/102 programme has been under way since at least the latter half of the 1980s. Development was hampered by the collapse in defence expenditure in the 1990s and 2000s, but funding has improved in the last few years. After nearly 20 years in the doldrums the Russian air force now has a fifth-generation fighter in flight-test and also harbours ambitions to introduce a new strategic bomber (PAK-DA) after 2025. Tupolev, the USSR's main bomber design house, was selected in 2009 to develop the aircraft in preference to a bid from Sukhoi. Though the decision may seem obvious in that Tupolev has design history in bomber fleets, it has faired poorly since the collapse of the Soviet Union. Sukhoi, by comparison, has emerged as the country's pre-eminent combat-aircraft manufacturer. The government and industry finally concluded a contract in May 2012 covering the purchase of five Project 955A *Borei* SSBNs following prolonged negotiations over price and the schedule for the delivery of boats.

with two batteries of S-400 in each, are deployed in Electrostal and Dmitrov. Two more S-400 regiments are deployed in the Baltic Fleet AOR and in the city of Nakhodka (Primorsk Territory). A fifth regimental S-400 unit is supposed to be delivered by the end of 2012. By 2015, the plan is for nine regimental S-400 units to be deployed.

Defence economics

The most significant development in recent years has been an appreciable increase in budget expenditure on the military as a share of GDP, due, above all, to the implementation of the highly ambitious State Armaments Programme 2011–2020. That far-reaching modernisation is required is not in dispute; the forces have received little new equipment since the early 1990s. But reduced economic growth following the 2008–09 global financial crisis makes it harder for the country to afford increased spending on defence. The defence industry, meanwhile, will find supplying the required quantities of new weapons on schedule, within budget and to quality standards to be a challenge.

As shown in Table 9, between 2006 and 2008 spending under the budget heading 'National Defence' (essentially MoD outlays on personnel, operations, construction, procurement and R&D; the development and production of nuclear munitions; participation in peacekeeping operations; state programmes of 'military-technical cooperation'; and allocations for maintaining the mobilisation preparedness of the economy) was held at approximately 2.5% of GDP. Following the brief war with Georgia in August 2008, far-reaching military reforms were launched and it was decided to speed up re-equipment of the forces. In 2009, when Russia

was most severely affected by the global economic crisis, defence spending rose to more than 3% of GDP, then fell back to 2.8% in 2009 and 2010 as the economy began to recover. But with the start of the new ten-year state armaments programme, signed off by Medvedev on 31 December 2010, spending began to increase more rapidly.

As of late September 2012, the draft three-year budget for 2013–15 was still being finalised by the Ministry of Finance. Provisional details of spending on 'national defence', however, indicate that its GDP share is set to increase to almost 3.8%. Total military expenditure will exceed 5% of GDP if military-related spending in other chapters of the budget are factored in (military pensions; the armed forces of the Interior Ministry and the security services; some military-related R&D not included under 'National Defence'; and support for the closed cities of the nuclear-weapons industry). The question is whether the country can afford to spend so much at a time of unfavourable growth prospects compared to the pre-crisis period, and with the formidable challenges posed by demographic trends and the urgent need for all-round socio-economic modernisation.

The state armaments programme to 2020 was based on an optimistic pre-crisis forecast of annual GDP growth averaging more than 6%. Total spending under the programme is more than R20tr (US$610bn), of which more than R19tr is for the armed forces under the MoD, the balance for other forces. Of the total funding, 31% is to be disbursed during the five years to 2015, 69% during 2015–20. Whereas the preceding armaments programme to 2015 allocated sizeable shares of funding to R&D and the modernisation and repair of existing arms, the current programme prioritises procurement of

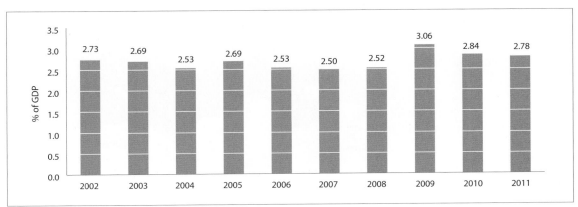

Figure 15 **Estimated Russian Defence Expenditure** as % of GDP

Table 9 **Russia National Defence Expenditure Trends (2005–15)**

Year	GDP (R bn)	Real GDP Change (%)	National Defence Expenditure[1] (R bn)	% Change in Real Defence Expenditure	National Defence as a % of GDP
2005	21,609.8	6.4	581.14	13.3%	2.69%
2006	26,917.2	8.2	681.80	1.8%	2.53%
2007	33,247.5	8.5	831.88	7.2%	2.50%
2008	41,276.8	5.2	1,040.86	6.0%	2.52%
2009	38,807.2	–7.1	1,188.17	12.0%	3.06%
2010	45,172.7	4.2	1,276.51	–3.6%	2.83%
2011	54,585.6	4.3	1,515.96	2.4%	2.78%
2012	61,238.0	3.5	1,864.15	13.4%	3.04%
2013	66,515.0	3.7	2,345.70	20.2%	3.53%
2014	73,993.0	4.3	2,771.60	10.7%	3.75%
2015	82,937.0	4.5	2,864.70	–3.7%	3.45%

Sources: Federal Service of State Statistics (Rosstat), Russian Ministry of Finance, Kremlin Annual Laws on Budget Implementation, 2011 budget and 2012–14 draft budget.

[1]National defence expenditure figures from 2005 to 2011 reflect actual expenditure, figure for 2012 reflects the amended federal budget, and figures for 2013 to 2015 reflect the draft national budget.

new weapons and other military hardware. There is also a parallel ten-year targeted federal programme to develop the defence industry, with total allocated funding to 2020 – not all from the budget – of R3tr (more than US$90bn). This is intended to improve production capacities deemed essential for the manufacture of a new generation of armaments. One indication that strains are mounting is the increasing resort to state-guaranteed credits, instead of direct budget allocations, as a means of maintaining the spending levels set out in the two programmes. This means that tough decisions on spending priorities

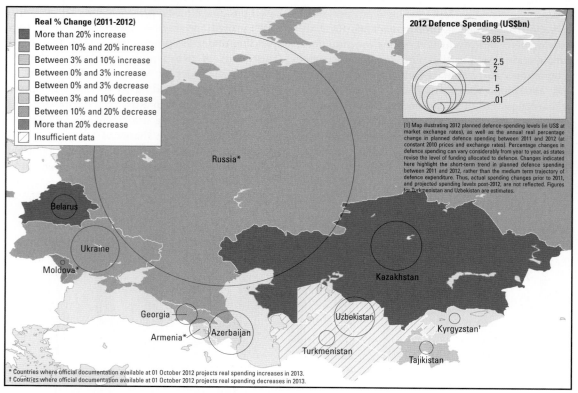

Map 5 **Russia and Eurasia Regional Defence Spending[1]**

Table 10 **Russian Arms Procurement 2010–12 and Approximate State Armaments Programme 2020 Objectives**

	2010		2011		2012		2020
	P	A	P	A	P	A	
ICBMs	30	27	36	30	–	–	400+
Military satellites	11	6	5	2	–	–	100+
Fixed-wing aircraft	28	23	35	28	58	–	600+
Helicopters	–	37	109	82	124	–	1,100+
S-400 air def systems (divisions)	–	–	2	2	2	2	56
Strategic nuclear submarines	2	0	2	0	2	a	8
Multi-role nuclear submarines	1	0	1	0	1	b	7*
Surface combat ships	–	0	6	2	5*	–	50+
Tanks	61	61	0	0	0	0	2,300+

* Estimates
P Procurement plan, according to State Defence Order; **A** Actual; – Insufficient data available
a. *Yurii Dolgorukii* and *Aleksandr Nevskii Borei*-class submarines may be handed over to navy by end 2012, but without full complement of *Bulava* missiles.
b. Handover of *Severodvinsk*, a '*Yasen*-class submarine, may be delayed until 2013.

are delayed and makes Russian military expenditure even less transparent.

The targets of the state armaments programme are highly ambitious (see Table 10). Contracts for these new weapons systems are being concluded within the framework of the annual state defence order. In 2011 and the first half of 2012, this proved an extremely complex process generating considerable tension between the MoD and the defence industry, often requiring intervention by the president and prime minister to resolve. Some disputes related to the specification of new systems and delivery schedules, but the most contentious issue concerned prices. The MoD has frequently challenged the cost estimates presented by contractors, notably for very expensive items such as nuclear submarines, surface ships and strategic missiles, and it has sought to fix prices at a level below that considered acceptable by the industrial producers. Putin has also criticised 'unjustified price hikes' and the practice of 'squeezing money' out of those who place the orders. 'In this particular case', Putin has said, 'the customer is the state itself, through the Defence Ministry'.

The MoD now works to a strict 20+1 rule: prime contractors must work to a rate of profit no higher than 20%, but their suppliers are not permitted to charge more than 1%. This practice has been widely criticised, not least for promoting forms of self-supply, in other words minimising resort to sub-contracting, by prime contractors of a type characteristic of the Soviet defence industry, leading to higher costs. Until recently, most contracts concluded under the state defence order were for a single year but it has now become common to sign contracts extending

over five years or more. According to Serdyukov, in late September 2012, almost all large-scale contracts for major systems up to 2020 had been concluded. An active role in resolving disputes, not always to the benefit of the MoD, has been played by Dmitry Rogozin, deputy prime minister and chair of the government's Military Industrial Commission.

Defence industry

Some new projects appear to have been successful, such as the *Yars* (RS-24/SS-X-29) ICBM and the *Lainer* (R-29RMU2) submarine-launched missile, an upgrade of the *Sineva*. As of late 2012, however, testing of the new *Bulava* missile for the *Borei* strategic-submarine class had not been completed, raising the possibility that the first two boats would not enter service until 2013, though they could enter service without their missile complement.

Meanwhile, the development of the fifth-generation fighter T-50 prototype continues, with three aircraft now being flown. The third aircraft is being flown with a development model of an active electronically-scanned array radar. According to the state armaments programme, the air force is to receive 60 aircraft based on the T-50 during 2016–20. The generation of capacity to design and manufacture UAVs remains a concern. At least two batches of Israeli UAVs have been purchased for trial purposes and some are now being assembled under licence at a factory in Ekaterinburg. Two projects are now under way to develop a new strike UAV. According to Putin, some R400bn will be allocated to the development of UAVs by 2020, but this is likely to remain a problematic area for some time, as the latest UAVs now present challenges in advanced materials, microelectronics and propulsion technology.

The MoD rejected the new T-95 main battle tank under development at the Uralvagonzavod plant, and now awaits the development of the new *Armata* platform, with the hope that it will be available for procurement after 2015 (see box, p. 203). In addition to Israeli UAVs, other significant systems of foreign origin include the *Mistral* amphibious assault vessel, the first of which is now under construction in France, and the *Rys* (Iveco LMV M65) armoured vehicle, now being built at Voronezh under licence, with an initial order for over 3,000. Authoritative policy statements from Putin, Rogozin and others indicate that there is no intention of converting Russia into an arms importer of any significance, but some equipment of foreign origin will be manufactured in Russia under licence, with a maximum degree of localisation of supply.

The defence industry is still experiencing serious problems. At a meeting with Rogozin in late September 2012, Putin observed that, with regard to the industry, 'to be frank, I do not yet have an optimistic mood'. The defence industry has been starved of investment for some 20 years. It has a high proportion of obsolete equipment and renewal is costly. The domestic machine-tool industry has also severely contracted and is no longer able to manufacture many modern, advanced types, obliging arms factories to import. There are acute shortages of younger skilled manual workers and technical personnel. Even in such a dynamic sector as the radio-electronics industry, one-fifth of specialists are over retirement age, including two-thirds of all doctors of science and 55% of science PhD candidates. Overall, the average age of personnel at defence industrial enterprises is 46, and 48 in R&D organisations. Many enterprises lack modern quality-management systems. There is mounting evidence of serious problems in achieving acceptable standards of quality and reliability, exemplified by six costly failed space launches during 2011 and the first half of 2012, and the long delay in accepting the new *Bulava* ICBM into service. There are capacity constraints in some sectors, notably in air-defence systems. In order to meet strong domestic and export orders, air-defence-systems manufacturer Almaz-Antey is currently building new factories in Kirov and Nizhny Novgorod. Modernisation of the defence-industrial base will take time and it is not clear that it can be undertaken fast enough to ensure successful fulfilment of the armaments programme.

Notwithstanding the state of the defence industry, however, the volume of new arms procurement, especially of aircraft, is now increasing steadily although still modest in scale. In 2011, the Federal Service for Military-Technical Cooperation, which oversees arms exports, reported record post-Soviet deliveries of US$13.2bn (compared to US$10.4bn in 2010) and has confidently forecast a similar volume of sales in 2012. However, these data need to be treated with some caution, as annual totals do not refer only to arms transfers. Thus, the Federal Service for Military-Technical Cooperation has revealed that the export of end-product weapons represents around 60% of the total, systems and components around 20%, and spares 10%, leaving another 10% for various military services. Recent developments suggest that a slowdown, or even contraction, of Russian arms sales is now possible. Major orders have been lost, for example air-defence systems to Libya and Iran, and new contracts with Syria must be in doubt, though new orders were announced with Iraq in 2012. Sales to Algeria, Venezuela and Vietnam have helped maintain overall export volumes. But with many Russian producers under pressure to prioritise domestic orders under the armaments programme, future exports of such arms as air-defence systems, naval vessels and combat aircraft could be negatively affected.

In an uncertain economic environment, Russia faces many challenges in fulfilling its defence-modernisation plans. There may be little choice but to scale back the armaments programme or extend its realisation over a longer period. Meanwhile, in early September 2012, Rogozin revealed that work was starting on a new state armaments programme to 2025. It will be some time before details emerge, but they should indicate the extent to which military modernisation remains a top priority.

EURASIA

Military and security policy in Belarus, Central Asia and the South Caucasus is driven by a wide range of internal and external influences, including defence modernisation in Russia and a recognition of changes in approach to modern military conflict.

Belarus has sought to further deepen its defence and security ties to Russia both bilaterally and within the ongoing transformation of the Collective Security Treaty Organisation (CSTO). President Alexander Lukashenko has promoted the inclusion of

Information Warfare on the CSTO agenda in response to the use of social networks and information technology during the Arab Spring. Minsk now contributes an air-assault brigade to the CSTO Collective Rapid Reaction Forces (*Kollektivnye Sily Operativnovo Reagirovaniya*, KSOR), otherwise dominated by Russia and Kazakhstan. Lukashenko's November 2011 initiative to form a new 120,000-strong army of 'territorial defence' is loosely consistent with the idea that Minsk fears some variant of the Arab Spring, but its real intentions are not clear. The successful penetration of Belarusian air defences in July 2012 by a Swedish civilian light aircraft in a PR stunt to draw attention to human-rights issues in Belarus highlights weaknesses in the system.

Moscow's defence and security concerns in Central Asia and the South Caucasus are partly guided by anxiety over conflict in these regions, particularly in the context of Russia's continued efforts to reform and modernise its armed forces. Moscow will continue to exercise caution about being drawn into conflicts in these regions, while attempting to preserve low-cost basing rights in these countries in the face of pressure from Azerbaijan, Kyrgyzstan and Tajikistan to pay for access to bases or military facilities. Although the Russian General Staff has indicated that it considers military conflict to be more likely in Central Asia, Moscow's foreign and security policy is preoccupied with wider issues linked to US and NATO ballistic-missile defence, or maintaining its interests in the Middle East.

Afghanistan is playing a less prominent role in Central Asian security concerns, despite the planned withdrawal of NATO combat forces by 2015. There is little sign of contingency planning or increased preparedness in relation to Taliban-linked or metastasised militant activity. Kazakhstan, Kyrgyzstan, Tajikistan and Uzbekistan have agreed reverse transit deals with NATO and individual Alliance member states to allow non-lethal military equipment withdrawn from Afghanistan to pass through their territories. Moreover, Bishkek, Dushanbe and Tashkent express interest in benefitting from the drawdown by obtaining equipment donations from NATO members to boost their own defence capabilities.

Such concerns and subtle shifts in defence policy are most evident in Kazakhstan, the first country in the Commonwealth of Independent States (CIS) to issue a new military doctrine since Russia's latest version emerged in February 2010. Kazakhstan's fourth military doctrine since independence, issued on 11 October 2011, sets out a more ambitious role for the domestic defence industry to meet the procurement needs of the armed forces. The doctrine enhances the role of the General Staff to assume full control over military operations by absorbing the Committee of the Joint Chiefs of Staff, while also assigning much less significance to cooperation with NATO than the 2007 military doctrine. Such cooperation will now focus more narrowly on strengthening peacekeeping capabilities to deploy in support of UN-mandated international missions. Astana has declared the development of Kazakhstan's navy to be a state secret, and consequently all discussion on the subject with NATO is prohibited. International terrorism plays a relatively minor role in the threat-assessment element of the doctrine, while the main external threat to the state's security stems from 'socio-political instability' in a neighbouring country, which may reflect anxiety over future instability in Kyrgyzstan or Tajikistan.

Moreover, the doctrine links external and internal threats and the potential for conflict to erupt suddenly. This will drive the country's defence policy towards more flexible, better-trained and better-equipped defence and security forces. There is no evidence in the doctrine that Astana has overreacted to a suicide bombing and other terrorist incidents around Kazakhstan in 2011, or to domestic security issues. The level of investment and support offered to the domestic defence industry suggests the country is moving away from over-reliance on Russia or dependence on the CSTO or the Shanghai Cooperation Organisation (SCO) to meet its security needs. In the air-mobile forces (subordinate to the ground forces), the most combat-capable and combat-ready formation is the 37th Air Assault brigade in Taldykurgan, which is well-equipped and has a high proportion of contract personnel. It is assigned to KSOR.

Joint CIS air-defence initiatives have had a troubled record since 1995, with some members participating only on paper and others often proving reluctant to share information concerning their airspace. Recent plans suggest Moscow is adopting a more varied and regional approach. Russian defence policymakers are influenced by what they consider to be the increasing use of space for military purposes, led by the United States. Russian military analyses of the development of conflict over the past 20 years stress the use of air and space by NATO forces. Consequently, Moscow is now prioritising air defence within its new Aerospace Defence Forces (VKO), and is pursuing close regional

Uzbekistan and the troubled CSTO

An internal transformation of the Collective Security Treaty Organisation (CSTO) has been overshadowed by Tashkent's decision to suspend its membership. Uzbekistan took this step from a position of relative strength, aware of its strategic significance to others in Central Asia, and confident that it could avoid damaging its bilateral relationship with Russia.

The formal reasons for suspension, a step not provided for in the CSTO charter, note Uzbek objections to placing Afghanistan on the body's agenda and the increased level of military cooperation among its members. The former reflects Tashkent's long-standing security approach to Afghanistan, preferring bilateral over multilateral instruments, while the latter clearly relates to opposition to the 20,000-strong Collective Rapid Reaction Force (KSOR) formed in June 2009.

Tashkent had earlier objected to Russian proposals (later shelved) to open a second air base in Kyrgyz-stan in 2009, and fiercely opposed the KSOR. It withheld consent over creation of the new force, refused to participate in its structure or exercises, and questioned the legality of amending the CSTO charter to authorise KSOR to act beyond collective defence against external aggression. Tashkent therefore suspended its CSTO membership at a time when other members were preparing to face an uncertain post-2014 security environment.

Reaction to Tashkent's move was relatively muted among other members, with some urging patience and others arguing that the body may be stronger without Uzbekistan. Uzbek defence officials are confident that, whether fully in or out of the organisation, no CSTO military operations in Central Asia would prove viable without Tashkent's tacit approval.

cooperation with Belarus and Kazakhstan. This will involve creating an integrated air-defence network, exporting Russian *Pantsyr-S1* and S-300PMU and possibly S-400 SAMs as well as upgrading MiG-31 assets, continuing deliveries of *Tor-M2* air-defence systems to Belarus and enhancing the tempo of joint exercises. The interests and future development of the VKO will continue to impact on regional air-defence priorities. The 62nd meeting of the CIS Council of Defence Ministers in Kaliningrad on 5 July 2012 reinforced commitment among its members to jointly develop air defence. However, the widely varying assets and resources of these countries render such agreements largely symbolic. A Russia–Kazakhstan regional air-defence agreement is planned for 2013, which should lead to greater integration of the countries' air-defence policies and capabilities. The mainstay of Belarus and Kazakhstan's air-defence assets will likely remain the S-300PMU SAM system.

Moscow's security concerns revolve around a fresh outbreak of conflict in the South Caucasus and drive efforts to consolidate its military presence in the breakaway Georgian territories of Abkhazia and South Ossetia. Moscow officially claims it has around 3,500 total personnel at the 4th Military Base in South Ossetia and the 7th Military Base in Abkhazia, though the actual levels are likely to be higher. Russian military personnel and border guards protect South Ossetia's administrative boundary line with Georgia, following the completion in July 2012 of 18 border-control complexes for the Southern Regional Border Directorate of the Federal Security Service (FSB). Military priorities for the 4th Military Base mostly relate to improving infrastructure, such as the training range, lecture halls, gymnasium or accommodation. There are also plans to create additional military training facilities in South Ossetia to support the base, as well as to ensure that personnel follow the combat-training programme being used elsewhere in the Russian armed forces. Nonetheless, Moscow's justifications for such enhanced military presence and infrastructure in these territories are not matched by any significant increase in Georgian military capabilities. The Southern Military District is a priority area for Russian defence deployments, and many new advanced systems are deployed there first. Russia staged military exercises involving the Southern Military District in September 2012; *Kavkaz 2012* and *Vzaimodeystviye 2012* involved joint force elements in Armenia, Abkhazia and South Ossetia, and provided a fresh opportunity to test KSOR.

The OSCE Minsk Group on Nagorno-Karabakh (NK) is designed to promote a lasting settlement between Armenia and Azerbaijan; there has been limited diplomatic progress in this regard. Russia's presence in the Minsk Group reflects Moscow's concern about renewed conflict, although it continues to arm both sides. The military build-up by Azerbaijan has also been accompanied by tactical–operational improvements in its armed forces. Since April 2012, military engagements centred on the Armenian Tavash region led to the deaths of servicemen on both sides; US Secretary of State Hillary Clinton, in Armenia when the attacks started, expressed concern

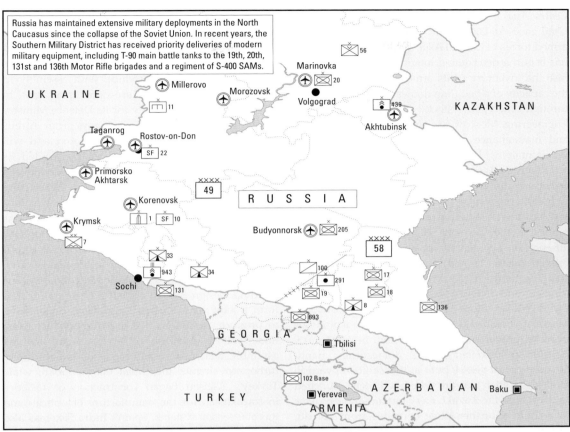

Map 6 **Military dispositions in Russia's Southern Military District**

about the possibility of escalation. In June 2012, attacks centred on Armenian defensive positions along the NK line of contact; though these skirmishes do not necessarily indicate any greater threat of imminent conflict. Baku is also implementing a new military strategy to link its increased military procurement to achieving 'operational readiness' by 2014 (the twentieth anniversary of the NK conflict), though its military reform primarily involves revamping the conscript system by redesigning the existing system of mobilisation rather than transitioning to a professional force structure. Experts believe that frontline Azeri forces suffer from low morale due to a lack of equipment, inadequate training, ill-discipline and weak unit cohesion. The Armenian armed forces' reforms focus on raising the number of contract personnel and increasing procurement levels. Yerevan's efforts to go beyond mere structural changes to address deeper issues linked to improving military manpower and training are hampered by increased levels of hazing, eroding discipline and

leadership standards, as well as a decline in the reputation of the armed forces within society. While the risk persists of both sides accidentally sliding into conflict, Baku appears to be strengthening its military options in the event diplomacy fails.

Defence economics

In Central Asia and the South Caucasus, there continues to be a lack of transparency and accountability over reported defence budgets, spending and figures on procurement. Exaggerated figures are fed by local corruption, secrecy for its own sake, and the lack of a tradition in the region's defence ministries with regard to production of reliable military statistics. These combine to present misleading and confused portrayals of both defence spending and its influence on military capability. Azerbaijan remains the leader in foreign military procurement in the South Caucasus, while Kazakhstan is leading the way in Central Asia. Some observers believe this could stimulate a regional arms race.

Central Asia

Until 2009–10, Uzbekistan maintained the strongest armed forces in Central Asia. Since then, Kazakhstan has begun a determined long-term effort to modernise the inventory of its armed forces, building on the capacity of a fledgling domestic defence industry through the joint stock company Kazakhstan Engineering. Moscow has agreed to open ten repair and maintenance centres in Kazakhstan to assist in maintaining Russian-produced equipment, and additional deals on the S-300PMU air-defence system are near completion. The scale of ambition in Astana to build a modernised military is evident from such indicators as its secretive project to boost naval capabilities in the Caspian Sea. Despite the apparent absence of a potential adversary in the Caspian region, Astana signed a memorandum of understanding between Kazakhstan Engineering, MBDA (France) and INDRA Sistemas (Spain) to produce *Exocet* MM40 Block 3 anti-ship missiles, with a range of 180km. While its longer-term aspirations in naval procurement are classified, in April 2012, Kazakhstan unveiled its first domestically manufactured patrol vessel, built at the Zenit shipyard in Uralsk (another two are scheduled to be launched in 2013), and the Kazakh navy has announced plans to acquire a further three corvettes from abroad. President Nursultan Nazarbayev has set a target for up to 70% of the modern weapons and equipment required by the country's armed forces to be manufactured domestically by 2015, though defence spending is capped at 0.9% of GDP (compared to 1% in the 2000 Military Doctrine), or US$2.27bn for 2012. This aspiration is supported by the military modernisation agenda of the 2011 Military Doctrine. Moreover, as part of its 'multi-vector policy', Astana is increasingly diversifying its international military cooperation beyond its traditional reliance on Russia for purchases and on Belarus and Ukraine for repair and maintenance. Instead it is strengthening defence ties with Turkey, France, Italy, Poland and especially Israel. Kazakhstan is the only country in the region to host a biannual arms exhibition, and KADEX 2012 was more elaborate and diverse than the first such exhibition in 2010. KADEX 2012 included around 240 international defence companies (with a notably increased presence from Israel and Turkey), and a reported US$1.8bn in arms deals were struck over the course of the exhibition. Over the past year, Kazakh officials have expressed aspirations to acquire additional capabilities in military transport, air defence, tactical UAVs, battlefield-management systems and even combat aircraft.

Astana's shift in defence procurement and industrial strategy is clearest in high-profile deals to purchase or jointly produce, with assembly in Kazakhstan, Airbus or Eurocopter platforms to enhance airlift and mobility for its Defence Ministry forces. Astana procured two C-295s from Airbus Military with delivery expected in 2013 and will purchase six more by 2018. It also expanded its Eurocopter joint venture – Eurocopter Kazakhstan Engineering, which opened in July 2012 – by ordering an additional eight EC145s for a total of 45 helicopters. Astana also wants to purchase a further 20 EC725s for Defence Ministry forces to be used across the full range of missions. Following an initial accord on vehicle overhaul announced at the end of 2011, in May 2012 Ukraine's Kharkiv Morozov Machine Building Design Bureau agreed a US$150m deal to form a joint venture with Kazakhstan Engineering to produce 100 BTR-4 APCs. Additionally, Cessna undertook to establish a service centre for the assembly, maintenance and repair of its light utility turboprop aircraft, the *Grand Caravan* 208B; while Turkey's Aselsan began construction of facilities in Kazakhstan for the manufacture of optical- and thermal-sensor systems. Spain's Indra Sistemas also began upgrading a facility to locally produce radar and maritime-surveillance systems. Other foreign procurement initiatives are increasingly featuring in Kazakh participation in international military exercises. Astana used *Peace Mission 2012* (see box, p. 213) to showcase its Turkish-procured *Cobra* infantry fighting vehicles, and its 37th Air Assault Brigade used French Samsung Thales communications equipment during CSTO exercises. The domestic defence industry is pursuing joint ventures with multiple foreign partners and is especially interested in jointly manufacturing high-technology C4ISR elements.

Kyrgyzstan and Tajikistan's armed forces depend mainly on credit for purchases or modernisation of existing systems, or on foreign military donations, though both militaries still have very limited capabilities. Their core defence budgets, US$40m and US$105m respectively, mask additional spending on paramilitary forces, particularly border guards. Neither country's armed forces undertake much in the way of real combat training, and their special forces approach moderate combat infantry standards at best. International security-assistance programmes

Peace Mission 2012

From 8–16 June 2012, the ninth Shanghai Coopera-tion Organisation (SCO) *Peace Mission* military exercise was held in northern Tajikistan. Approximately 2,000 military personnel participated in *Peace Mission 2012* from China, Kazakhstan, Kyrgyzstan, Russia and Tajiki-stan; Uzbekistan refused to participate. Tashkent also declined a request from Astana to permit Kazakh units taking part in the exercise to transit Uzbek territory. The anti-terrorist exercises were smaller than previous such events, and were marked by a parity of Chinese and Rus-sian forces.

Russian forces taking part in the exercise were drawn from the 201st Military Base headquartered in Dushanbe and air assets were deployed from the Kant Collective Security Treaty Organisation (CSTO) air base in Kyrgyzstan. Moscow essentially used forces assigned to the CSTO during the SCO exercise in order to test its logistical and air-support capabilities linked to rapid response to a future security crisis in Central Asia.

Anti-terrorist scenario-planning for the exercise relied heavily on the capacities of the Russian and Chinese de-fence ministries, with relatively little of substance added by the other participants. Observers of the exercise, how-ever, noted that the briefings and other features of *Peace Mission 2012* were strongly led by China's PLA.

Peace Mission 2012 reinforced the trend towards small-er exercises, officially designated as anti-terrorist though in appearance resembling traditional combined-arms op-erations. The exercise confirmed China's de facto leader-ship of the organisation.

The military dimension of the SCO security agenda remains under-developed, with disagreement among members about the precise requirements of SCO mili-tary capabilities. A joint SCO force has not emerged, nor have members moved to address differences in doctrine or increase the tempo of joint training. Moreover, China appears to prefer bilateral instruments in responding to any security crisis potentially damaging to its interests in Central Asia. It is thus unlikely to activate SCO routes.

---

have failed to reverse endemic internal corruption or perennial problems in discipline, unit cohesion and defence planning. The Tajik armed forces and special forces struggled to respond adequately to (and mini-mise casualties among security forces engaging) criminal groups in eastern Khorog Tajikistan in July 2012. Standards and conditions among Tajikistan's conscripts are the worst in the region, with authorities press-ganging recruits. Consequently, Bishkek and Dushanbe are keen to receive weapons or equipment donations from NATO members as combat force drawdowns in Afghanistan near, yet despite concern expressed by Moscow, NATO countries have limited discussions to equipment for infrastructure support rather than offering major weapons systems. The US requested an increase in foreign military financing and related programmes for Central Asia for 2013, particularly seeking to strengthen Tajik border secu-rity.

Frustration with Russian offers of discounted prices within the CSTO is a significant driver under-lying regional efforts to enter joint ventures with foreign defence companies or request greater levels of equipment donations. Although CSTO members can request preferential prices on purchases from Russia this rarely works in practical terms, as it goes against the interests of the Russian companies involved. Additionally, when equipment is transferred, the end

user has to explore alternative options for repair and maintenance. Official Russian sources estimate that arms sales to Central Asia account for no more than 5% of Russia's total export market. While weaker members of the CSTO may look towards Moscow for greater defence assistance, Russian spending on collective defence and peacekeeping has sharply declined from R7.7bn (US$250m) in 2010 to less than R500m (US$16.1m).

The South Caucasus

Not only are there inherent difficulties with regard to reported figures on defence budgets and defence spending in Central Asia and the South Caucasus, there are also examples of governments deliberately exaggerating them for political effect. This is further complicated by myths surrounding the defence build-up taking place in some of these countries, notably Azerbaijan. At face value, Baku's defence spending has vastly increased in recent years, rising from US$1.5bn (3.95% of GDP) in 2010 to US$3.1bn (6.2% of GDP) in 2011. In 2011, Baku signed a US$1.6bn defence deal with Tel Aviv, an indication not only of its increased spending but the trend to agree purchases in the international arms market. The deal included five *Heron* UAVs and five *Searcher* UAVs.

Baku invested an additional US$1.4bn in its defence industry in 2011 to facilitate domestic defence orders. On its own, this trend does not imply preparation for military action or an increased risk of conflict with Armenia. Baku includes spending on paramilitary forces, prosecutors' offices and even the courts, in these figures, in order to inflate them. Moreover, the types of systems and equipment being acquired are not always consistent with preparations for an assault on Nagorno-Karabakh, although Armenian sources report an increase in Azeri UAV activity close to the line of contact in that breakaway region. Azeri foreign UAV procurement can give them systems with a long-distance capability that may transcend Nagorno-Karabakh-linked operational planning. Equally, Baku's increased spending on defence involves replacing much of the ex-Soviet military systems or equipment in its inventory and, despite its 'build-up', the Azeri military currently lacks the capability to overwhelm Armenian air defences, which would render risky any operation in Nagorno-Karabakh.

Armenia's defence spending levels have stabilised at around 4% of GDP, significantly lower than Azerbaijan's steadily rising level in both percentage and absolute terms, given the disparity in the size of their economies. Yerevan's defence budget for 2013 is set to rise to 170bn drams, yet achieving a modern weapons and equipment inventory is a long way off, especially in light of corruption and the defence ministry's financial inefficiency.

The Georgian armed forces' efforts to enhance military capabilities, aimed primarily at boosting the capability of the state to defend the country's territorial integrity, continue to be hampered by a generally cautious policy among NATO members, apparently sensitive to Russian concerns about 'rearming' Tbilisi. In December 2011, the US Congress passed an act to normalise defence cooperation ties with Georgia and, though this allows the transfer of arms to Tbilisi to support territorial defence, it is closely tied to Georgia's commitment to its pledge not to use force. The impact of the Five-Day War in August 2008 and the reduction in defence spending before 2011 will hamper efforts by Tbilisi to restore combat capabilities to pre-war levels. This is unlikely to occur before 2015, while lower levels of foreign military procurement will prove ineffectual without a sustained effort to address the operational weaknesses exposed during combat with Russian and separatist units in 2008.

Armenia ARM

Armenian Dram d		2011	2012	2013
GDP	d	3.82tr	4.17tr	
	US$	10.4bn	10.6bn	
per capita	US$	3,501	3,568	
Growth	%	4.55	3.91	
Inflation	%	7.65	2.81	
Def exp [a]	d	148bn		
	US$	396m		
Def bdgt [b]	d	146bn	155bn	170bn
	US$	393m	391m	
FMA (US)	US$	2.99m	2.7m	2.7m
US$1=d		372.51	395.38	

[a] Includes imported military equipment and military pensions

[b] Includes imported military equipment, excludes military pensions

Population 2,970,495

Age	0–14	15–19	20–24	25–29	30–64	65 plus
Male	9.3%	4.1%	5.3%	4.9%	19.7%	3.7%
Female	8.1%	3.8%	5.2%	5.0%	24.6%	6.2%

Capabilities

Armenia's armed forces focus on territorial defence, given continuing tensions with neighbouring Azerbaijan. While overall military doctrine remains influenced strongly by Russian thinking, Armenia's overseas deployments, which include support to ISAF in Afghanistan, enable the troops serving in the Pul-e Khumri PRT to learn lessons from their NATO counterparts. The ISAF contribution increased in 2011. In November 2011, Armenia signed a new Individual Partnership Action Plan with NATO. While conscription continues, there is a growing cohort of professional officers. The country's armed forces are generally held to be at least competent and well-motivated. Serviceability and maintenance have been a problem for the air force, and Russia provides national air defence from a leased base. The army exercises regularly, and aims to be able to deploy and sustain a battalion-sized contingent by 2015 as part of a multi-national mission. To inform these developments, Armenia completed a Strategic Defense Review in May 2011.

ACTIVE 48,850 (Army 45,850, Air/AD Aviation Forces (Joint) 1,050, other Air Defence Forces 1,950) **Paramilitary 6,700**

Terms of service conscription 24 months.

RESERVES some mob reported, possibly 210,000 with military service within 15 years.

ORGANISATIONS BY SERVICE

Army 19,950; 25,900 conscripts (total 45,850)

FORCES BY ROLE
SPECIAL FORCES
1 SF regt

MANOEUVRE
Mechanised
1 (1st) corps (1 recce bn, 1 tk bn, 2 MR regt, 1 maint bn)
1 (2nd) corps (1 recce bn, 1 tk bn, 2 MR regt, 1 lt inf regt, 1 arty bn)
1 (3rd) corps (1 recce bn, 1 tk bn, 4 MR regt, 1 lt inf regt, 1 arty bn, 1 MRL bn, 1 sigs bn, 1 maint bn)
1 (4th) corps (4 MR regt; 1 SP arty bn; 1 sigs bn)
1 (5th) corps (with 2 fortified areas) (1 MR regt, 1 lt inf regt)
Other
1 indep MR trg bde
COMBAT SUPPORT
1 arty bde
1 AT regt
1 AD bde
2 AD regt
1 (radiotech) AD regt
1 engr regt

EQUIPMENT BY TYPE
MBT 110: 3 T-54; 5 T-55; 102 T-72
AIFV 104: 80 BMP-1; 7 BMP-1K; 5 BMP-2; 12 BRM-1K
APC (W) 136: 11 BTR-60; 100 look-a-like; 21 BTR-70; 4 BTR-80
ARTY 239
  SP 38: **122mm** 10 2S1 *Carnation*; **152mm** 28 2S3
  TOWED 131: **122mm** 69 D-30; **152mm** 62: 26 2A36; 2 D-1; 34 D-20
  MRL 51: **122mm** 47 BM-21; **273mm** 4 WM-80
  MOR 120mm 19 M120
AT • MSL 22
  SP 22: 9 9P148 *Konkurs*; 13 9P149 MT-LB *Spiral*
AD
  SAM
    SP 2K11 *Krug* (SA-4 *Ganef*); 2K12 *Kub* (SA-6 *Gainful*); 9K33 *Osa* (SA-8 *Gecko*); S-300PM (SA-10 *Grumble* C)
    TOWED S-75 *Dvina* (SA-2 *Guideline*); S-125 *Pechora* (SA-3 *Goa*)
  GUNS
    SP ZSU-23-4
    TOWED 23mm ZU-23-2
RADAR • LAND 6 SNAR-10
MSL • TACTICAL • SSM 9K72 *Elbrus* (SS-1C *Scud* B); 9K79 *Tochka* (SS-21 *Scarab*)
AEV MT-LB
ARV BREhM-D; BREM-1

Air and Air Defence Aviation Forces 1,050

1 Air & AD Joint Command

FORCES BY ROLE
GROUND ATTACK
1 sqn with Su-25/Su-25UBK *Frogfoot*

EQUIPMENT BY TYPE
AIRCRAFT 15 combat capable
  FTR (1 MiG-25 *Foxbat* in store)
  ATK 15: 13 Su-25 *Frogfoot*; 2 Su-25UBK *Frogfoot*
  TPT 3 Heavy 2 Il-76 *Candid*; **PAX** 1 A319CJ
  TRG 14: 4 L-39 *Albatros*; 10 Yak-52
HELICOPTERS
  ATK 8 Mi-24P *Hind*

ISR 4: 2 Mi-24K *Hind*; 2 Mi-24R *Hind* (cbt spt)
MRH 10 Mi-8MT (cbt spt)
C2 2 Mi-9 *Hip* G (cbt spt)
TPT • **Light** 9 PZL Mi-2 *Hoplite*

Paramilitary 6,694

Ministry of Internal Affairs

FORCES BY ROLE
MANOEUVRE
  Other
    4 paramilitary bn
EQUIPMENT BY TYPE
AIFV 55: 5 BMD-1; 44 BMP-1; 1 BMP-1K; 5 BRM-1K
APC (W) 24 BTR-60/BTR-70/BTR-152

Border Troops
Ministry of National Security
EQUIPMENT BY TYPE
AIFV 43: 5 BMD-1; 35 BMP-1; 3 BRM-1K
APC (W) 23: 5 BTR-60; 18 BTR-70

DEPLOYMENT

Legal provisions for foreign deployment:
Constitution: Codified constitution (1995, amended 2005)
Specific legislation: 'Law on Defence of the Republic of Armenia'
Decision on deployment of troops abroad: by the president, in accordance with 'Law on Defence of the Republic of Armenia' (Article 5 (2) (1). Also, under Art.55 (13) of constitution, president can call for use of armed forces (and National Assembly shall be convened). (Also Art.81 (3) of constitution.)

AFGHANISTAN
NATO • ISAF 126

LEBANON
UN • UNIFIL 1

SERBIA
NATO • KFOR 35

FOREIGN FORCES

Russia 3,303 (Gyumri, Armenia): 1 MR bde; 74 MBT; 201 ACV; 84 arty; (12 MRL; 72 SP/towed)
Military Air Forces (Yerevan, Armenia): 1 ftr sqn with 18 MiG-29 *Fulcrum*; 2 SAM bty with S-300V (SA-12 *Gladiator/Giant*); 1 SAM bty with 2K12 *Kub* (SA-6 *Gainful*)

Azerbaijan AZE

Azerbaijani New Manat m		2011	2012	2013
GDP	m	51.7bn	55.3bn	
	US$	64.8bn	71bn	
per capita	US$	6,826	7,479	
Growth	%	0.09	3.89	
Inflation	%	7.87	3.00	
Def exp	m	ε2.45bn		
	US$	ε3.1bn		
Def bdgt	m	1.33bn	1.38bn	
	US$	1.68bn	1.77bn	
FMA (US)	US$	2.99	2.70	2.70
US$1=m		0.79	0.78	

Population   9,493,600

Age	0–14	15–19	20–24	25–29	30–64	65 plus
Male	12.2%	4.5%	5.3%	4.7%	20.4%	2.4%
Female	10.5%	4.2%	5.0%	4.5%	22.4%	3.9%

Capabilities

While the armed forces have yet to successfully transition from a Soviet-era model, increasing defence expenditure has provided the opportunity to acquire some more capable military equipment. Rising oil revenues have provided the financial headroom for acquisitions, including the S-300 SAM system, but it is unclear whether the potential benefits brought by these modern systems have been felt in terms of operational capability. The armed forces still rely on conscription, and readiness within the services varies considerably between units. Peacekeeping deployments have included a small number of personnel in Afghanistan. Azerbaijan maintains defence relationships with NATO through an IPAP, and has a close relationship with Turkey. With NATO support, the Internal Troops are developing a police support unit to be available for NATO-led operations. US military assistance has included support to maritime-security operations in the Caspian Sea. The air force suffers from training and maintenance problems. The armed forces cannot organically support external deployments.

ACTIVE 66,950 (Army 56,850 Navy 2,200 Air 7,900)
Paramilitary 15,000
Terms of service 17 months, but can be extended for ground forces.

RESERVE 300,000
Reserves some mobilisation reported, 300,000 with military service within 15 years

ORGANISATIONS BY SERVICE

Army 56,850
FORCES BY ROLE
COMMAND
  5 corps HQ

MANEOEUVRE
Mechanised
4 MR bde
Light
19 MR bde
Other
1 sy bde
COMBAT SUPPORT
1 arty bde
1 arty trg bde
1 MRL bde
1 AT bde
1 engr bde
1 sigs bde
COMBAT SERVICE SUPPORT
1 log bde

EQUIPMENT BY TYPE
MBT 339: 95 T-55; 244 T-72
AIFV 111: 20 BMD-1; 43 BMP-1; 33 BMP-2; 15 BRM-1
APC 575
  APC (T) 336 MT-LB
  APC (W) 149: 10 BTR-60; 132 BTR-70; 7 BTR-80A
  PPV 90: 45 *Marauder*; 45 *Matador*
ARTY 458
  SP 69: **122mm** 46 2S1 *Carnation*; **152mm** 6 2S3 **155mm** 5 ATMOS-2000; **203mm** 12 2S7
  TOWED 207: **122mm** 129 D-30; **130mm** 36 M-46; **152mm** 42: 18 2A36; 24 D-20
  GUN/MOR 120mm 18 2S9 NONA
  MRL 70+: **122mm** 46+: 43 BM-21; 3+ IMI *Lynx*; **128mm** 12 RAK-12; **300mm** 12 9A52 *Smerch*
  MOR 120mm 112: 5 CARDOM; 107 PM-38
AT • MSL • MANPATS 9K11 *Malyutka* (AT-3 *Sagger*); 9K111 *Fagot* (AT-4 *Spigot*); 9K113 *Konkurs* (AT-5 *Spandrel*)/9K115 *Metis* (AT-7 *Saxhorn*); *Spike*-LR
AD • SAM • SP 9K35 *Strela*-10 (SA-13 *Gopher*); 2K11 *Krug* (SA-4 *Ganef*): 9K33 *Osa* (SA-8 *Gecko*)‡
MANPAD 9K32 *Strela* (SA-7 *Grail*;) 9K34 *Strela*-3; (SA-14 *Gremlin*); 9K310 *Igla*-1 (SA-16 *Gimlet*); 9K338 *Igla-S* (SA-24 *Grinch*)
MSL • SSM ε4 9M79 *Tochka* (SS-21 *Scarab*)
RADAR • LAND SNAR-1 *Long Trough*/SNAR-2/-6 *Pork Trough* (arty); *Small Fred*/*Small Yawn*/SNAR-10 *Big Fred* (veh, arty); GS-13 *Long Eye* (veh)
UAV • ISR • Medium 3 *Aerostar*
AEV MT-LB
MW *Bozena*

Navy 2,200

EQUIPMENT BY TYPE
PATROL AND COASTAL COMBATANTS 8
  CORVETTES • FS 1 *Petya II* with 2 RBU 6000 *Smerch 2*, 2 twin 76mm gun
  PSO 1 *Luga* (*Woodnik 2* Class) (FSU Project 888; additional trg role)
  PCC 3: 2 *Petrushka* (FSU *UK-3*; additional trg role); 1 *Shelon* (FSU Project 1388M)
  PB 3: 1 *Bryza* (FSU Project 722); 1 *Turk* (TUR AB 25); 1 *Poluchat* (FSU Project 368)

MINE WARFARE • MINE COUNTERMEASURES 4
  MHC 4: 2 *Yevgenya* (FSU Project 1258); 2 *Yakhont* (FSU *Sonya*)
AMPHIBIOUS 6
  LSM 3: 1 *Polnochny A* (FSU Project 770) (capacity 6 MBT; 180 troops); 2 *Polnochny B* (FSU Project 771) (capacity 6 MBT; 180 troops)
  LCU 1 *Vydra*† (FSU) (capacity either 3 AMX-30 MBT or 200 troops)
  LCM 2 T-4 (FSU)
LOGISTICS AND SUPPORT 2
  AGS 1 (FSU Project 10470)
  ARS 1 *Iva* (FSU *Vikhr*)

Air Force and Air Defence 7,900

FORCES BY ROLE
FIGHTER
  1 sqn with MiG-29 *Fulcrum*
FIGHTER/GROUND ATTACK
  1 regt with MiG-21 *Fishbed*; Su-17 *Fitter*; Su-24 *Fencer*; Su-25 *Frogfoot*; Su-25UB *Frogfoot B*
TRANSPORT
  1 sqn with An-12 *Cub*; Yak-40 *Codling*
ATTACK/TRANSPORT HELICOPTER
  1 regt with Mi-8 *Hip*; Mi-24 *Hind*; Mi-35M *Hind*; PZL Mi-2 *Hoplite*

EQUIPMENT BY TYPE
AIRCRAFT 44 combat capable
  FTR 14 MiG-29 *Fulcrum*
  FGA 11: 4 MiG-21 *Fishbed* (1 more in store); 4 Su-17 *Fitter*; 1 Su-17U *Fitter*; 2 Su-24 *Fencer*†
  ATK 19: 16 Su-25 *Frogfoot*; 3 Su-25UB *Frogfoot B*
  TPT 4: **Medium** 1 An-12 *Cub*; **Light** 3 Yak-40 *Codling*
  TRG 40: 28 L-29 *Delfin*; 12 L-39 *Albatros*
HELICOPTERS
  ATK 38: 26 Mi-24 *Hind*; 12 Mi-35M *Hind*
  TPT 20: **Medium** 13 Mi-8 *Hip*; **Light** 7 PZL Mi-2 *Hoplite*
UAV • ISR • Medium 4 *Aerostar*
AD • SAM S-75 *Dvina* (SA-2 *Guideline*); S-125 *Neva* (SA-3 *Goa*)/S-200 *Vega* (SA-5 *Gammon*) static; S-300PM/PMU2 (SA-10 *Grumble*/SA-20 *Gargoyle*)
MSL • AAM • IR R-60 (AA-8 *Aphid*); R-73 (AA-11 *Archer*)
IR/SARH R-27 (AA-10 *Alamo*)

Paramilitary ε15,000

Border Guard ε5,000
Ministry of Internal Affairs
AIFV 168 BMP-1/2
APC (W) 19 BTR-60/70/80

Coast Guard
The Coast Guard was established in 2005 as part of the State Border Service.

EQUIPMENT BY TYPE
PATROL AND COASTAL COMBATANTS 10
  PBF 6: 1 *Osa II* (FSU Project 205); 2 Silver Ships 48ft; 3 *Stenka*
  PB 4: 2 Baltic 150; 1 *Point* (US); 1 *Grif* (FSU *Zhuk*)

Militia 10,000+

Ministry of Internal Affairs
APC (W) 7 BTR-60/BTR-70/BTR-80

DEPLOYMENT

Legal provisions for foreign deployment:
Constitution: Codified constitution (1995)
Decision on deployment of troops abroad: By parliament upon proposal by president (Art. 109, No. 28)

AFGHANISTAN
NATO • ISAF 94

TERRITORY WHERE THE GOVERNMENT DOES NOT EXERCISE EFFECTIVE CONTROL

Data presented here represent an assessment of the de facto situation. Nagorno-Karabakh was part of the Azerbaijani Soviet Socialist Republic (SSR), but mostly populated by ethnic Armenians. In 1988, when inter-ethnic clashes between Armenians and Azeris erupted in Azerbaijan, the local authorities declared their intention to secede from Azerbaijan and join the Armenian SSR. Baku rejected this and armed conflict erupted. A ceasefire was brokered in 1994. All ethnic Azeris had been expelled from Nagorno-Karabakh and almost all ethnic Armenians were forced to leave Azerbaijan. Since 1994, Armenia has controlled most of Nagorno-Karabakh, and also seven adjacent regions of Azerbaijan, often called the 'occupied territories'. While Armenia provides political, economic and military support to Nagorno-Karabakh, the region has declared itself independent – although this has not been recognised by any other state, including Armenia. Azerbaijan claims, and the rest of the international community generally regards, Nagorno-Karabakh and the occupied territories as part of Azerbaijan. (See IISS *Strategic Comment*, Medvedev momentum falters in Nagorno-Karabakh, August 2011.)

Available estimates vary with reference to military holdings in Nagorno-Karabakh. Main battle tanks are usually placed at around 200–300 in number, with similar numbers for armoured combat vehicles and artillery pieces, with small numbers of fixed- and rotary-wing aviation. Available personnel number estimates are between 18,000–20,000.

Belarus BLR

Belarusian Ruble r		2011	2012	2013
GDP	r	274.3tr	490.3tr	
	US$	55.1bn	58.2bn	
per capita	US$	5,714	6,035	
Growth	%	5.34	4.30	
Inflation	%	53.23	60.19	
Def exp	r			
	US$			
Def bdgt	r	2.1tr	4.61tr	
	US$	422m	547m	
US$1=r		4,974.65	8,422.33	

Population	9,643,566

Age	0–14	15–19	20–24	25–29	30–64	65 plus
Male	7.7%	2.8%	3.9%	4.3%	23.4%	4.4%
Female	7.3%	2.7%	3.7%	4.2%	26.1%	9.5%

Capabilities

Belarus inherited the bulk of its military equipment from the Soviet Union, and Russia's influence over its military doctrine remains strong. High inflation during 2011 also adversely affected morale within the conscript-based armed forces, which have reduced in size. The military and government were embarrassed in July 2012, when a light aircraft entered Belarusian airspace in a pro-democracy protest, costing the air force commander his post. Aircrew flying hours are inadequate for a modern air force, though the target was to increase the amount by a third for 2012. Additional S-300 and *Tor*-M2 air-defence systems are also expected to be delivered. Belarusian forces exercise with their Russian counterparts regularly and could support notionally a regional joint operation with Moscow, though the actual combat capacity of its ground forces is uncertain. Belarus has sought to deepen its defence and security ties to Russia both bilaterally and within the ongoing transformation of the Collective Security Treaty Organization (CSTO). Minsk now contributes an air assault brigade to the CSTO Collective Rapid Reaction Forces. A new National Security concept was adopted in late 2010, with reforms introduced to the military's central command structure.

ACTIVE 48,000 (Army 22,500 Air 15,000 Joint 10,500) **Paramilitary 110,000**
Terms of service 9–12 months

RESERVE 289,500 (Joint 289,500 with mil service within last 5 years)

ORGANISATIONS BY SERVICE

Joint 10,500 (Centrally controlled units and MoD staff)

Army 22,500
FORCES BY ROLE
COMMAND
   2 comd HQ (West & North West)

SPECIAL FORCES

1 SF bde

MANOEUVRE

Mechanised

1 (mobile) armd inf bde

1 (mobile) mech bde

4 mech bde

COMBAT SUPPORT

2 arty bde

1 arty gp

1 MRL bde

2 MRL regt

2 SSM bde

2 AD bde

2 engr bde

2 engr regt

1 NBC regt

1 ptn bridging regt

2 sigs bde

EQUIPMENT BY TYPE

MBT 515: 446 T-72; 69 T-80

AIFV 1,111: 100 BMD-1; 875 BMP-2; 136 BRM-1

APC 264

APC (T) 72: 22 BTR-D; 50 MT-LB

APC (W) 192: 39 BTR-70; 153 BTR-80

ARTY 1,003

SP 432: **122mm** 198 2S1 *Carnation*; **152mm** 236: 108 2S3; 116 2S5; 12 2S19 *Farm*

TOWED 228: **122mm** 48 D-30; **152mm** 180: 48 2A36; 132 2A65

GUN/MOR 120mm 48 2S9 NONA

MRL 234: **122mm** 126 BM-21; **220mm** 72 9P140 *Uragan*; **300mm** 36 9A52 *Smerch*

MOR 120mm 61 2S12

AT • MSL

SP 236: 126 9P148 *Konkurs*; 110 9P149 *Shturm*

MANPATS 9K111 *Fagot* (AT-4 *Spigot*); 9K113 *Konkurs* (AT-5 *Spandrel*); 9K114 *Shturm* (AT-6 *Spiral*); 9K115 *Metis* (AT-7 *Saxhorn*)

AD • SAM • SP 350 9K37 *Buk* (SA-11 *Gadfly*); S-300V(SA-12A *Gladiator*/SA-12B *Giant*); 9K35 *Strela*-10 (SA-13 *Gopher*); 9K33 *Osa* (SA-8 *Gecko*) (700–2,100 eff.); *Tor*-M2E (SA-15 *Gauntlet*)

RADAR • LAND GS-13 *Long Eye*/SNAR-1 *Long Trough*/ SNAR-2/-6 *Pork Trough* (arty); some *Small Fred*/*Small Yawn*/ SNAR-10 *Big Fred* (veh, arty)

MSL • TACTICAL • SSM 96: 36 FROG/SS-21 *Scarab* (*Tochka*); 60 *Scud*

AEV MT-LB

VLB MTU

Air Force and Air Defence Forces 15,000

Flying hours 15 hrs/year

FORCES BY ROLE

FIGHTER

2 bases with MiG-29S/UB *Fulcrum*; Su-27P/UB *Flanker* B/C

GROUND ATTACK

2 sqn with Su-25K/UBK *Frogfoot* A/B

TRANSPORT

1 base with An-12 *Cub*; An-24 *Coke*; An-26 *Curl*; Il-76 *Candid*; Tu-134 *Crusty*

TRAINING

Some sqn with L-39 *Albatros*

ATTACK HELICOPTER

Some sqn with Mi-24 *Hind*

TRANSPORT HELICOPTER

Some (cbt spt) sqn with Mi-6 *Hook*; Mi-8 *Hip*; Mi-24K *Hind G2*; Mi-24R *Hind G1*; Mi-26 *Halo*

EQUIPMENT BY TYPE

AIRCRAFT 93 combat capable

FTR 38 MiG-29S/UB *Fulcrum*

FGA 21 Su-27P/SUB *Flanker* B/C

ATK 34 Su-25K/UBK *Frogfoot* A/B

TPT 13: **Heavy** 2 Il-76 *Candid* (+9 civ Il-76 available for mil use); **Medium** 3 An-12 *Cub*; **Light** 8: 1 An-24 *Coke*; 6 An-26 *Curl*; 1 Tu-134 *Crusty*

TRG Some L-39 *Albatros*

HELICOPTERS

ATK 49 Mi-24 *Hind*

ISR 20: 8 Mi-24K *Hind G2*; 12 Mi-24R *Hind G1*

TPT 168: **Heavy** 43: 29 Mi-6 *Hook*; 14 Mi-26 *Halo*; **Medium** 125 Mi-8 *Hip*

MSL

ASM Kh-25 (AS-10 *Karen*); Kh-29 (AS-14 *Kedge*)

ARM Kh-58 (AS-11 *Kilter*)

AAM • IR R-60 (AA-8 *Aphid*); R-73 (AA-11 *Archer*)

SARH R-27R (AA-10 *Alamo A*)

Air Defence

AD data from Uzal Baranovichi EW radar

FORCES BY ROLE

AIR DEFENCE

1 bde (2 AD bn)

EQUIPMENT BY TYPE

AD • SAM S-300PS (SA-10B *Grumble*); S-125 *Pechora* (SA-3 *Goa*); S-200 (SA-5 *Gammon*)

Paramilitary 110,000

Border Guards 12,000

Ministry of Interior

Militia 87,000

Ministry of Interior

Ministry of Interior Troops 11,000

DEPLOYMENT

LEBANON

UN • UNIFIL 5

FOREIGN FORCES

Russia: Military Air Forces: 4 SAM units with S-300 (SA-10 *Grumble* (quad))

Georgia GEO

Georgian Lari		2011	2012	2013
GDP	lari	24.2bn	26.3bn	
	US$	14.4bn	15.8bn	
per capita	US$	3,150	3,457	
Growth	%	6.95	6.54	
Inflation	%	8.54	0.16	
Def bdgt	lari	710m	651m	
	US$	421m	391m	
FMA (US)	US$	15.97m	14.4m	14.4m
US$1=lari		1.69	1.67	

Population   4,570,934

Age	0–14	15–19	20–24	25–29	30–64	65 plus
Male	8.3%	3.3%	4.1%	3.9%	21.8%	6.4%
Female	7.2%	3.1%	4.0%	4.0%	24.4%	9.7%

Capabilities

Georgia's armed forces continue to make efforts to address lessons from the conflict with Russia in 2008, while tensions with Moscow remain. The brief war revealed significant shortcomings in key areas, including anti-armour and air-defence capabilities, though performance in air defence was better. It has also acquired the Israeli *Spyder* short-range air-defence system A substantial number of Georgia's T-72 MBTs were destroyed during the short conflict. Current plans call for the small air force – comprising Soviet-era ground-attack aircraft and combat-support helicopters as well as transport and utility helicopters – to merge with the army. Georgia currently deploys personnel to ISAF in Afghanistan, and has aspirations for NATO membership. Training activity involves international forces, including the US. Moves are under way to generate a pool of four-year contract servicemen to boost professionalisation.

ACTIVE 20,650 (Army 17,750 Air 1,300 National Guard 1,600) **Paramilitary 11,700**

Terms of service conscription, 18 months

ORGANISATIONS BY SERVICE

Army 14,000; 3,750 conscript (total 17,750)

FORCES BY ROLE
SPECIAL FORCES
1 SF bde
MANOEUVRE
Light
5 inf bde
Amphibious
2 mne bn (1 cadre)
COMBAT SUPPORT
2 arty bde
1 engr bde
1 sigs bn
1 SIGINT bn
1 MP bn

COMBAT SERVICE SUPPORT
1 med bn
EQUIPMENT BY TYPE
MBT 93 T-72; (3 T-72 & 23 T-55 in store)
AIFV 63: 17 BMP-1; 45 BMP-2; 1 BRM-1K; (8 BMP-1 & 1 BMP-2 in store)
APC 137
  APC (T) 45 MT-LB; (21 MT-LB in store)
  APC (W) 92: 25 BTR-70 (1 in store); 17 BTR-80 (2 in store); 50 *Ejder* (15 in store)
ARTY 185
  SP 35: **152mm** 32 DANA; 13 2S3; 1 2S19; **203mm** 1 2S7
  TOWED 68: **122mm** 55 D-30; (3 D-30 in store); **152mm** 13: 3 2A36; 10 2A65
  MRL 122mm 37: 13 BM-21; 6 GRADLAR; 18 RM-70
  MOR 120mm 43: 13 2S12; 21 M-75; 9 M120; (1 2S12, 13 M-75 & 9 M120 in store)
AT ε50
  MSL ε10
  GUNS ε40
AD • SAM • SP 9K35 *Strela*-10 (SA-13 *Gopher*); *Spyder*
  MANPAD *Grom*; 9K32 *Strela*-2 (SA-7 *Grail*)‡; 9K36 *Strela*-3 (SA-14 *Gremlin*); 9K310 *Igla*-1 (SA-16 *Gimlet*)

Air Force 1,300 (incl 300 conscript)

1 avn base, 1 hel air base
AIRCRAFT 12 combat capable
  ATK 12: 3 Su-25 *Frogfoot*; 7 Su-25K *Frogfoot* A; 2 Su-25UB *Frogfoot* B
  TPT • Light 9: 6 An-2 *Colt*; 1 Tu-134A *Crusty* (VIP); 2 Yak-40 *Codling*
  TRG 9 L-29 *Delfin*
  UAV 1+ Hermes 450
HELICOPTERS
  TPT 29 **Medium** 17 Mi-8T *Hip* **Light** 12 Bell 205 (UH-1H *Iroquois*)
AD • SAM 1–2 bn 9K37 *Buk*-M1 (SA-11 *Gadfly*), 8 9K33 *Osa*-AK (SA-8B *Gecko*) (two bty), 6-10 9K33 *Osa*-AKM updated SAM systems.

National Guard 1,600 active reservists opcon Army

FORCES BY ROLE
MANOEUVRE
  Light
  1 inf bde

Paramilitary 11,700

Border Guard 5,400

Coast Guard

HQ at Poti. The Navy was merged with the Coast Guard in 2009 under the auspices of the Georgian Border Guard, within the Ministry of the Interior.
PATROL AND COASTAL COMBATANTS 18
  PBF 2: 1 *Kaan 33*; 1 *Kaan 20*
  PB 16: 7 *Zhuk* (3 ex-UKR); 2 *Point*; 2 *Dauntless*; 2 *Dilos* (ex-GRC); 1 *Akhmeta* (up to 20 patrol launches also in service)

AMPHIBIOUS • LANDING CRAFT • LCU 1 *Vydra* (ex-BUL)
LOGISTIC AND SUPPORT • YTL 1

Ministry of Interior Troops 6,300

DEPLOYMENT

Legal provisions for foreign deployment of armed forces:
Constitution: Codified constitution (1995)
Decision on deployment of troops abroad: By the presidency upon parliamentary approval (Art. 100)

AFGHANISTAN
NATO • ISAF 800; 1 inf bn

TERRITORY WHERE THE GOVERNMENT DOES NOT EXERCISE EFFECTIVE CONTROL

Following the August 2008 war between Russia and Georgia, the areas of Abkhazia and South Ossetia declared themselves independent. Data presented here represent the de facto situation and do not imply international recognition as sovereign states.

FOREIGN FORCES

Russia Army 6,900; 1 MR bde at Gudauta (Abkhazia); 1 MR bde at Djava/Tskhinvali (S. Ossetia)

Kazakhstan KAZ

Kazakhstani Tenge t		2011	2012	2013
GDP	t	27.3tr	30.03tr	
	US$	186.2bn	200.64bn	
per capita	US$	10,627	11,451	
Growth	%	7.50	5.47	
Inflation	%	8.33	5.04	
Def exp	t	265bn		
	US$	1.8bn		
Def bdgt	t	259bn	340bn	
	US$	1.77bn	2.27bn	
FMA (US)	US$	2.395m	1.8m	1.8m
US$1=t		146.62	149.71	

Population 17,522,010

Ethnic groups: Kazakh 51%; Russian 32%; Ukrainian 5%; German 2%; Tatar 2%; Uzbek 13%

Age	0–14	15–19	20–24	25–29	30–64	65 plus
Male	12.3%	4.2%	4.8%	4.6%	19.8%	2.3%
Female	12.1%	4.0%	4.7%	4.5%	22.2%	4.4%

Capabilities

The Soviet origins of Kazakhstan's conscript-based armed forces are still evident. There is ongoing cooperation with Russia on air defence, with discussion ongoing on the supply of the S-300PMU-1. A Russia–Kazakhstan regional air-defence agreement is planned for 2013, which should lead to greater integration of both countries' air-defence policies and capabilities. Kazakhstan also participates in military exercises by the Shanghai Cooperation Organisation (SCO) and the Collective Security Treaty Organisation (CSTO), of which it is a member. Army training is limited by Western standards, although there is a better-trained rapid-reaction force of around brigade strength. A new Military Doctrine was produced in October 2011. In the threat assessment element of the doctrine, international terrorism plays a relatively minor role, while the main external threat to the state's security stems from 'socio-political instability' in a neighbouring country. Development of the navy is a priority, and the army has substantially reorganised in recent years. The air force reportedly struggles to keep its fleet of Russian-supplied aircraft airworthy, although air-defence fighters fare better than strike aircraft. Tactical airlift is being bolstered with the purchase of the C-295, with delivery to begin in 2013. Ukraine is also emerging as a defence-industrial partner, with collaboration on armoured vehicle production.

ACTIVE 39,000 (Army 20,000 Navy 3,000 Air 12,000 MoD 4,000) Paramilitary 31,500
Terms of service 12 months

ORGANISATIONS BY SERVICE

Army 20,000
4 regional comd: Astana, East, West and Southern
FORCES BY ROLE
MANOEUVRE
  Armoured
  1 tk bde
  Mechanised
  4 mech bde
  Air Manoeuvre
  4 air aslt bde
COMBAT SUPPORT
  3 arty bde
  1 SSM unit
  3 cbt engr bde
EQUIPMENT BY TYPE
MBT 300 T-72
RECCE 100: 40 BRDM; 60 BRM
AIFV 602: 500 BMP-2; 100 BTR-80A/82A; 2 BTR-3E
APC 350
  APC (T) 150 MT-LB
  APC (W) 200: 190 BTR-80; 10 *Cobra*
ARTY 602
  SP 246: **122mm** 126: 120 2S1 *Carnation*; 6 *Semser*; **152mm** 120 2S3
  TOWED 150: **122mm** 100 D-30; **152mm** 50 2A65; (**122mm** up to 300 D-30 in store)
  GUN/MOR 120mm 25 2S9 *Anona*
  MRL 118: **122mm** 100 BM-21 *Grad*; **300mm** 18 *Lynx* (with 50 msl); (**122mm** 100 BM-21 *Grad*; **220mm** 180 9P140 *Uragan* all in store)
  MOR 63 **SP 120mm** 18 CARDOM **120mm** 45 2B11/M120

AT • MSL • MANPATS 9K111 *Fagot* (AT-4 *Spigot)*; 9K113 *Konkurs* (AT-5 *Spandrel)*; 9K115 *Metis* (AT-6 *Spiral)*
GUNS 100mm 68 MT-12/T-12
MSL • SSM 12 9K79 *Tochka* (SS-21 *Scarab)*
AEV MT-LB

Navy 3,000

PATROL AND COASTAL COMBATANTS 17
PCG 1 *Kazakhstan* with 2 quad lnchr with 3424 *Uran* (SS-N-25 *Switchblade)* AShM, 1 *Ghibka* lnchr with SA-N-10 *Gimlet* SAM
PB 16: 4 *Almaty*; 1 *Dauntless*; 3 *Sea Dolphin*; 1 *Turk* (AB25); 2 *Zhuk*; 3 *Sardar*; 2 *Saygak*

Coastal Defence

MANOEUVRE
Other
1 coastal defence bde

Air Force 12,000 (incl Air Defence)

Flying hours   100 hrs/year

FORCES BY ROLE
FIGHTER
1 sqn with MiG-29/MiG-29UB *Fulcrum*
2 sqn with MiG-31/MiG-31BM *Foxhound*
FIGHTER/GROUND ATTACK
2 sqn with MiG-27 *Flogger* D; MiG-23UB *Flogger* C
2 sqn with Su-27/Su-27UB *Flanker*
GROUND ATTACK
1 sqn with Su-25 *Frogfoot*
TRANSPORT
1 unit with Tu-134 *Crusty*; Tu-154 *Careless*,
1 sqn with An-12 *Cub*, An-26 *Curl*, An-30 *Clank*, An-72 *Coaler*
TRAINING
1 sqn with L-39 *Albatros*
ATTACK HELICOPTER
5 sqn with Mi-24V *Hind*
TRANSPORT HELICOPTER
Some sqn with Bell 205 (UH-1H); EC145; Mi-8 *Hip*; Mi-17V-5 *Hip*; Mi-26 *Halo*
AIR DEFENCE
Some regt with S-75M *Volkhov* (SA-2 *Guideline)*; S-125 *Neva* (SA-3 *Goa)*; S-300 (SA-10 *Grumble)*; 2K11 *Krug* (SA-4 *Ganef)*; S-200 *Angara* (SA-5 *Gammon)*; 2K12 *Kub* (SA-6 *Gainful)*

EQUIPMENT BY TYPE
AIRCRAFT 123 combat capable
FTR 56: 12 MiG-29 *Fulcrum*; 2 MiG-29UB *Fulcrum*; 42 MiG-31/MiG-31BM *Foxhound*
FGA 53: 24 MiG-27 *Flogger* D; 4 MiG-23UB *Flogger* C; 21 Su-27 *Flanker*; 4 Su-27UB *Flanker*
ATK 14: 12 Su-25 *Frogfoot*; 2 Su-25UB *Frogfoot*
ISR 1 An-30 *Clank*
TPT 15: **Medium** 2 An-12 *Cub*: **Light** 8; 6 An-26 *Curl*, 2 An-72 *Coaler*, 2 CN-295 ; **Light** 2 Tu-134 *Crusty*; **PAX** 1 Tu-154 *Careless*
TRG 18 L-39 *Albatros*
HELICOPTERS
ATK 40+ Mi-24V *Hind* (first 9 upgraded)

MRH 20 Mi-17V-5 *Hip*
TPT 64 **Heavy** 2 Mi-26 *Halo*; **Medium** 50 Mi-8 *Hip*; **Light** 12: 6 Bell-205 (UH-1H); 6 EC145
AD • SAM 147+
SP 47+: 20 2K12 *Kub* (SA-6 *Gainful)*; 27+ 2K11 *Krug* (SA-4 *Ganef)/S-200 Angara* (SA-5 *Gammon)*; static; S-300 (SA-10 *Grumble)*
TOWED 100 S-75M *Volkhov* (SA-2 *Guideline)*; S-125 *Neva* (SA-3 *Goa)*
MSL
ASM Kh-23 (AS-7 *Kerry)‡*; Kh-25 (AS-10 *Karen)*; Kh-29 (AS-14 *Kedge)*
ARM Kh-28 (AS-9 *Kyle)*; Kh-27 (AS-12 *Kegler)*; Kh-58 (AS-11 *Kilter)*
AAM • IR R-60 (AA-8 *Aphid)*; R-73 (AA-11 *Archer)* **IR/SARH** R-27 (AA-10 *Alamo)* **SARH** R-33 (AA-9 *Amos)* **ARH** R-77 (AA-12 *Adder* – on MiG-31BM)

Paramilitary 31,500

Government Guard 500

Internal Security Troops ε20,000
Ministry of Interior

Presidential Guard 2,000

State Border Protection Forces ε9,000
Ministry of Interior
HEL • TPT • Medium 1 Mi-171

Kyrgyzstan KGZ

Kyrgyzstani Som s		2011	2012	2013
GDP	s	273.11bn	292.4bn	
	US$	5.92bn	6.2bn	
per capita	US$	1,077	1,128	
Growth	%	5.68	1.00	
Inflation	%	16.59	2.87	
Def bdgt [a]	s	4.71bn	4.95bn	4.91bn
	US$	102m	105m	
FMA (US)	US$	1.496m	1.5m	1.5m
US$1=s		46.13	47.18	

[a] Includes expenses on the Ministry of the Interior

Population   5,496,737

Age	0–14	15–19	20–24	25–29	30–64	65 plus
Male	15.1%	4.9%	5.3%	4.7%	17.1%	1.9%
Female	14.5%	4.7%	5.2%	4.7%	18.9%	3.0%

Capabilities

Kyrgyzstan's military capability is limited and its air force has only small numbers of jet trainer and transport aircraft. Greater numbers of armed and transport helicopters are in the inventory, but maintenance problems probably mean most of these are not operationally available. Availability issues have been exacerbated by planned defence-funding cuts for 2012. Despite these weaknesses, Kyrgyzstan's armed forces participate in SCO exercises, including those on counter-terrorism. The country has also hosted SCO exercises within its training areas, indicating the ability to offer command-and-control facilities to disparate military units. However, levels of combat training in the armed forces are assessed as relatively low.

ACTIVE 10,900 (Army 8,500 Air 2,400) **Paramilitary 9,500**

Terms of service 18 months

ORGANISATIONS BY SERVICE

Army 8,500

FORCES BY ROLE
SPECIAL FORCES
 1 SF bde
MANOEUVRE
 Mechanised
 2 MR bde
 1 (mtn) MR bde
COMBAT SUPPORT
 1 arty bde
 1 AD bde
EQUIPMENT BY TYPE
MBT 150 T-72
RECCE 30 BRDM-2
AIFV 320: 230 BMP-1; 90 BMP-2
APC (W) 35: 25 BTR-70; 10 BTR-80
ARTY 246
 SP 122mm 18 2S1 *Carnation*
 TOWED 141: 100mm 18 M-1944; **122mm** 107: 72 D-30; 35 M-30 (M-1938); **152mm** 16 D-1
 GUN/MOR 120mm 12 2S9 *Anona*
 MRL 21: 122mm 15 BM-21; **220mm** 6 9P140 *Uragan*
 MOR 120mm 54: 6 2S12; 48 M-120
AT • MSL • MANPATS 26+: 26 9K11 (AT-3 *Sagger*); 9K111 (AT-4 *Spigot*); 9K113 (AT-5 *Spandrel*)
 RCL 73mm SPG-9
 GUNS 100mm 18 MT-12/T-12
AD • SAM • MANPAD 9K32 *Strela-2* (SA-7 *Grail*)‡
 GUNS 48
 SP 23mm 24 ZSU-23-4
 TOWED 57mm 24 S-60

Air Force 2,400

FORCES BY ROLE
FIGHTER
 1 regt with L-39 *Albatros**
FIGHTER/TRANSPORT
 1 (comp avn) regt with MiG-21 *Fishbed*; An-2 *Colt*; An-26 *Curl*
ATTACK/TRANSPORT HELICOPTER
 1 regt with Mi-24 *Hind*; Mi-8 *Hip*
AIR DEFENCE
 Some regt with S-125 *Pechora* (SA-3 *Goa*); S-75 *Dvina* (SA-2 *Guideline*)

EQUIPMENT BY TYPE
AIRCRAFT 33 combat capable
 FGA 29 MiG-21 *Fishbed*
 TPT • Light 6: 4 An-2 *Colt*; 2 An-26 *Curl*
 TRG 4 L-39 *Albatros**
HELICOPTERS
 ATK 2 Mi-24 *Hind*
 TPT • Medium 8 Mi-8 *Hip*
AD • SAM
 SP 2K11 *Krug* (SA-4 *Ganef*)
 TOWED S-75 *Dvina* (SA-2 *Guideline*); S-125 *Pechora* (SA-3 *Goa*)

Paramilitary 9,500

Border Guards 5,000 (KGZ conscript, RUS officers)

Interior Troops 3,500

National Guard 1,000

DEPLOYMENT

LIBERIA
UN • UNMIL 3 obs

SOUTH SUDAN
UN • UNMISS 2 obs

SUDAN
UN • UNISFA 1 obs

FOREIGN FORCES

Russia ε500 Military Air Forces: 5 Su-25 *Frogfoot*; 2 Mi-8 *Hip*

Moldova MDA

Moldovan Leu L		2011	2012	2013
GDP	L	82.2bn	90.1bn	
	US$	7bn	7.6bn	
per capita	US$	1,914	2,078	
Growth	%	6.41	3.00	
Inflation	%	7.65	5.15	
Def exp	L			
	US$			
Def bdgt [a]	L	448m	207m	221m
	US$	38m	17m	
FMA (US)	US$	1.497m	1.25m	1.25m
US$1=L		11.73	11.88	

[a] Includes military pensions

Population 3,656,843

Age	0 – 14	15 – 19	20–24	25–29	30–64	65 plus
Male	9.0%	3.6%	4.5%	4.6%	22.8%	4.0%
Female	8.5%	3.4%	4.3%	4.4%	24.4%	6.6%

Capabilities

Moldova has only a limited capacity for military operations. While its government recognises the need for military restructuring and re-equipment, adequate financial support has not been forthcoming. The conscript-based army's primary focus is on the disputed territory of Transdniestr. A Russian army garrison still remains there, as well as a peacekeeping contingent. With UK assistance, Moldova developed a Strategic Defence Review document, which was presented to the Upper Security Council in April 2011, although, given a lack of funding, implementation will prove a challenge. Moldova's air capability is limited to a small fixed- and rotary-wing transport fleet. Moldovan forces are deployed in small numbers on UN operations.

ACTIVE 5,350 (Army 3,250 Air 800 Logistic Support 1,300) **Paramilitary 2,400**

Terms of service 12 months

RESERVE 58,000 (Joint 58,000)

ORGANISATIONS BY SERVICE

Army 1,300; 1,950 conscript (total 3,250)

FORCES BY ROLE
SPECIAL FORCES
1 SF bn
MANOEUVRE
Light
3 mot inf bde
1 mot inf bn
Other
1 gd bn
COMBAT SUPPORT
1 arty bn
1 engr bn
1 NBC coy
1 sigs coy

EQUIPMENT BY TYPE
AIFV 44 BMD-1
APC 164
APC (T) 64: 9 BTR-D; 55 MT-LB **APC (W)** 100: 11 BTR-80; 89 TAB-71
ARTY 148
TOWED 69: **122mm** 17 (M-30) *M-1938*; **152mm** 52: 21 2A36; 31 D-20
GUN/MOR • **SP 120mm** 9 2S9 *Anona*
MRL 220mm 11 9P140 *Uragan*
MOR 59: **82mm** 52; **120mm** 7 M-120
AT
MSL • **MANPATS** 120: 72 9K111 *Fagot* (AT-4 *Spigot*); 21 9K113 *Konkurs* (AT-5 *Spandrel*); 27 9K114 *Shturm* (AT-6 *Spiral*)
RCL 73mm 138 SPG-9
GUNS 100mm 36 MT-12
AD • **GUNS** • **TOWED** 39: **23mm** 28 ZU-23; **57mm** 11 S-60
RADAR • **LAND** 4: 2 ARK-1; 2 SNAR-10

Air Force 800 (incl 250 conscripts)

FORCES BY ROLE
TRANSPORT
2 sqn with An-2 *Colt*; An-26 *Curl*; An-72 *Coaler*; Mi-8PS *Hip*; Yak-18
AIR DEFENCE
1 regt with S-125 *Neva* (SA-3 *Goa*)

EQUIPMENT BY TYPE
AIRCRAFT
TPT • **Light** 6: 2 An-2 *Colt*; 1 An-26 *Curl*; 2 An-72 *Coaler* 1 Yak-18
HELICOPTERS
MRH 4 Mi-17-1V *Hip* H
TPT • **Medium** 2 Mi-8PS *Hip*
AD • **SAM** 12 S-125 *Neva* (SA-3 *Goa*)

Paramilitary 2,400

Ministry of Interior

OPON 900 (riot police)

Ministry of Interior

DEPLOYMENT

Legal provisions for foreign deployment:
Constitution: Codified constitution (1994)
Decision on deployment of troops abroad: By the parliament (Art. 66)

CÔTE D'IVOIRE
UN • UNOCI 4 obs

LIBERIA
UN • UNMIL 2 obs

SERBIA
UN • UNMIK 1 obs

SOUTH SUDAN
UN • UNMISS 1; 2 obs

FOREIGN FORCES

Russia ε1,500 (including 355 peacekeepers) Military Air Forces 7 Mi-24 *Hind*/Mi-8 *Hip*
Ukraine 10 mil obs (Joint Peacekeeping Force)

Russia RUS

Russian Rouble r		2011	2012	2013
GDP	r	54.37tr	60.85tr	
	US$	1.85tr	1.95tr	
	US$a	2.38tr	2.51tr	
per capita	US$	12,981	13,683	
Growth	%	4.30	3.70	
Inflation	%	8.44	5.10	
Def exp	r	1.98tr		
	US$	67.3bn		
	US$a	86.7bn		
Def bdgt	r	1.52tr	1.86tr	2.35tr
	US$	51.6bn	59.9bn	
	US$ a	66.6bn	76.8bn	
US$1=r	MER	29.38	31.15	
	PPP	22.81	24.23	

a PPP estimate

Population   142,517,670

Ethnic groups: Tatar 4%; Ukrainian 3%; Chuvash 1%; Bashkir 1%; Belarussian 1%; Moldovan 1%; Other 8%

Age	0–14	15–19	20–24	25–29	30–64	65 plus
Male	8.1%	2.5%	3.8%	4.4%	23.6%	3.9%
Female	7.6%	2.4%	3.7%	4.3%	26.6%	9.0%

Capabilities

Russia remains a significant military power, with a sizeable nuclear arsenal. Efforts are under way to recapitalise strategic and conventional weapons inventories, though progress has been at best patchy. Defence reforms begun in 2008 continue with higher pay rates introduced at the beginning of 2012. The aim is to recruit and retain more contract personnel, though conscription remains for the moment. Some analysts believe that key elements of the reform process are largely complete, such as the initiative to transform the army towards a combined arms brigade-based structure, though adjustments are still to be made, largely in the internal formation of these units. The air force continues to receive small numbers of new aircraft, with new equipment also being delivered to the army in modest amounts. A handful of new ships are also in various stages of build or delivery to the navy. The overall equipment modernisation plan to 2020, however, could be jeopardised by the Finance Ministry's aim of curtailing proposed defence spending by 20% in the 2013–15 period.

ACTIVE 845,000 (Army 250,000 Airborne 35,000 Navy 130,000 Air 150,000 Strategic Deterrent Forces 80,000 Command and Support 200,000) **Paramilitary 519,000**

Terms of service: 12 months conscription.

RESERVE 20,000,000 (all arms)

Some 2,000,000 with service within last 5 years; Reserve obligation to age 50.

ORGANISATIONS BY SERVICE

Strategic Deterrent Forces ε80,000 (incl personnel assigned from the Navy and Air Force)

Navy
SUBMARINES • STRATEGIC • SSBN 11

3 *Kalmar* (*Delta* III) with 16 RSM-50 (SS-N-18 *Stingray*) strategic SLBM

6 *Delfin* (*Delta* IV) with 16 R-29RMU *Sineva* (SS-N-23 *Skiff*) strategic SLBM (of which 1 vessel in repair following a fire; expected return to service 2014)

1 *Akula* (*Typhoon*)† in reserve with capacity for 20 *Bulava* (SS-N-X-32) strategic SLBM (trials/testing)

1 *Borey* (sea trials completed in September 2010; commissioning delayed until 2013; *Bulava* (SS-N-X-32) SLBM not yet operational; 1 additional unit completed sea trials Oct 2012; 2 further units in build)

Strategic Rocket Force Troops
3 Rocket Armies operating silo and mobile launchers organised in 12 divs (reducing to 8). Launcher gps normally with 10 silos (6 for RS-20/SS-18), or 9 mobile lnchr, and one control centre

MSL • STRATEGIC 313

ICBM 313: 54 RS-20 (SS-18 *Satan*) (mostly mod 5, 10 MIRV per msl); 120 RS-12M (SS-25 *Sickle*) (mobile single warhead); 40 RS-18 (SS-19 *Stiletto*) (mostly mod 3, 6 MIRV per msl.); 60 RS-12M2 *Topol*-M (SS-27M1) silo-based (single warhead); 18 RS-12M2 *Topol* M (SS-27M1) road mobile (single warhead); 21 RS-24 *Yars* (SS-27M2; ε3 MIRV per msl)

Long-Range Aviation Command
FORCES BY ROLE
BOMBER
1 sqn with Tu-160 *Blackjack*
3 sqn with Tu-95MS *Bear*

EQUIPMENT BY TYPE
AIRCRAFT
LRSA 79: 16 Tu-160 *Blackjack* each with up to 12 Kh-55 SM (AS-15A/B *Kent*) nuclear ALCM; 32 Tu-95MS6 (*Bear* H-6) each with up to 6 Kh-55/SM (AS-15A/B *Kent*) nuclear ALCM; 31 Tu-95MS16 (*Bear* H-16) each with up to 16 Kh-55 (AS-15A *Kent*) nuclear ALCM; (Kh-102 likely now entering service on Tu-95MS)

Warning Forces 3rd Space and Missile Defence Army
ICBM/SLBM launch-detection capability: 3 operational satellites
RADAR (9 stations) 1 ABM engagement system located at Sofrino (Moscow). Russia leases ground-based radar stations in Baranovichi (Belarus); Balkhash (Kazakhstan); Gaballa (Azerbaijan). It also has radars on its own territory at Lekhtusi, (St Petersburg); Armavir, (southern Russia); Olenegorsk (northwest Arctic); Pechora (northwest Urals); Mishelevka (east Siberia).

MISSILE DEFENCE 2,032: 68 53T6 (ABM-3 *Gazelle*); 1,900 S-300 (SA-10 *Grumble*); 64 S-400 (SA-21 *Growler*); (32 51T6 (ABM-4 *Gorgon*) in store; possibly destroyed)

Space Forces 40,000

Formations and units to detect missile attack on the RF and its allies, to implement BMD, and to be responsible for military/dual-use spacecraft launch and control. May become part of new Air-Space Defence Command.

SATELLITES 58
  COMMUNICATIONS 25: 1 *Geizer* (*Potok*); 1 *Globus* (*Raduga*-1); 2 Mod *Globus* (*Raduga*-1M); 11 *Strela*; 7 *Rodnik* (*Gonets*-M); 3 *Meridian*
  NAVIGATION/POSITIONING/TIMING 27 GLONASS
  ELINT/SIGINT 2: 1 *Liana* (*Lotos*-S); 1 *Tselina*-2;
  EARLY WARNING 4 *Oko*

Army ε205,000 (incl 35,000 AB); ε80,000 conscript (total 285,000)

Transformation process continues; previous 6 Military Districts have been consolidated into 4 (West (HQ St Petersburg), Centre (HQ Yekaterinburg), South (HQ Rostov-on-Don) & East (HQ Khabarovsk), each with a unified Joint Strategic Command. Current plans call for the establishment of 28 new bdes (6 MR; 2 air aslt; 1 engr; 1 AD & 18 army avn), and for the restructuring of the existing MR brigades into new light, medium and heavy formations.

FORCES BY ROLE
COMMAND
  10 army HQ
SPECIAL FORCES
  7 (Spetsnaz) SF bde
  1 (AB Recce) SF regt
MANOEUVRE
  Reconnaissance
  1 recce bde
  Armoured
  4 tk bde (1 armd recce bn; 3 tk bn; 1 MR bn; 1 arty bn; 1 MRL bn; 2 AD bn; 1 engr bn; 1 EW coy; 1 NBC coy)
  Mechanised
  1 (201st) MR div
  31 MR bde (1 recce bn; 1 tk bn; 3 MR bn; 2 arty bn; 1 MRL bn; 1 AT bn; 2 AD bn; 1 engr bn; 1 EW coy; 1 NBC coy)
  2 MR bde (4−5 MR bn; 1 arty bn; 1 AD bn; 1 engr bn)
  3 (lt/mtn) MR bde (1 recce bn; 2 MR bn; 1 arty bn)
  1 (18th) MGA div (2 MGA regt; 1 arty regt; 1 tk bn; 2 AD bn)
  Air Manoeuvre
  4 (VdV) AB div (2 para/air aslt regt; 1 arty regt; 1 AD regt)
  1 (VdV) indep AB bde
  3 (army) air aslt bde
COMBAT SUPPORT
  8 arty bde
  4 MRL bde
  2 MRL regt
  1 SSM bde with *Iskander-M* (SS-26 *Stone*)
  8 SSM bde with *Tochka* (SS-21 *Scarab* — to be replaced by *Iskander-M*)
  10 AD bde

  4 engr bde
  1 MP bde

EQUIPMENT BY TYPE
MBT 2,800+: 1,500 T-72B/BA; 1,000 T-80BV/U; 300+ T-90/T-90A; (18,000 in store: 2,800 T-55; 2,500 T-62; 2,000 T-64A/B; 7,500 T-72/T-72A/B; 3,000 T-80B/BV/U; 200 T-90)
RECCE 1,200+: 100+ *Dozor*, 100+ *Tigr*, 1,000 BRDM-2/2A; (1,000+ BRDM-2 in store)
AIFV 7,360+: 700 BMD-1; 600 BMD-2; 100 BMD-3; 60+ BMD-4; 1,000 BMP-1; 3,500 BMP-2; 500+ BMP-3; 700 BRM-1K; 200+ BTR-80A/82A; (8,500 in store: 7,000 BMP-1; 1,500 BMP-2) **APC** 9,700+
  APC (T) 5,700+: some BMO-T; 700 BTR-D; 5,000 MT-LB; (2,000 MT-LB in store)
  APC (W) 4,000+ BTR-60/70/80; (4,000 BTR-60/70 in store)
ARTY 5,436+
  SP 1,820: **122mm** 400 2S1; **152mm** 1,400: 800 2S3; 150 2S5; 450 2S19; **203mm** 20 2S7; (4,050 in store: **122mm** 1,800 2S1; **152mm** 1,950: 1,000 2S3; 800 2S5; 150 2S19; **203mm** 300 2S7)
  TOWED 550: **122mm** 400 D-30; **152mm** 150 2A65; (12,215 in store: **122mm** 7,950: 4,200 D-30; 3,750 M-30 *M-1938*; **130mm** 650 M-46; **152mm** 3,575: 1,100 2A36; 600 2A65; 1,075 D-20; 700 D-1 *M-1943*; 100 ML-20 *M-1937*; **203mm** 40 B-4M)
  GUN/MOR 970+
    SP 120mm 870+: 790 2S9 NONA-S; 30 2S23 NONA-SVK; 50+ 2S34
    TOWED 120mm 100 2B16 NONA-K
  MRL 1,106+ **122mm** 800 BM-21; **220mm** 200 9P140 *Uragan*; some TOS-1A; **300mm** 106 9A52 *Smerch*; (2,920 in store: **122mm** 2,120: 1,700 BM-21; 420 9P138; **132mm** 100 BM-13; **220mm** 700 9P140 *Uragan*)
  MOR 990
    SP 240mm 20 2S4; (410 2S4 in store)
    TOWED 970+: **120mm** 970: 50+ 2B23; 920 2S12; (2,100 in store: **120mm** 1,800: 900 2S12; 900 PM-38; **160mm** 300 M-160)
AT
  MSL
    SP BMP-T with 9K120 *Ataka* (AT-9 *Spiral* 2); 9P149 with 9K114 *Shturm* (AT-6 *Spiral*); 9P157-2 with 9K123 *Khrisantema* (AT-15 *Springer*)
    MANPATS 9K11/9K14 *Malyutka* (AT-3 *Sagger*); 9K111 *Fagot* (AT-4 *Spigot*); 9K112 *Kobra* (AT-8 *Songster*); 9K113 *Konkurs* (AT-5 *Spandrel*); 9K114 *Shturm* (AT-6 *Spiral*); 9K115 *Metis* (AT-7 *Saxhorn*); 9K115-1 *Metis-M* (AT-13 *Saxhorn* 2); 9K116 *Bastion/Basnya* (AT-10 *Stabber*); 9K119 *Reflex/Svir* (AT-11 *Sniper*); 9K135 *Kornet* (AT-14 *Spriggan*)
  RCL 73mm SPG-9
  RL 105mm RPG-29
  GUNS 562+
    SP: 125mm 36+ 2S25
      TOWED 100mm 526 MT-12; (**100mm** 2,000 T-12/MT-12 in store)
AD • SAM 1,570+
  SP 1,320+: 350+ 9K37/9K317 *Buk* (SA-11 *Gadfly*); 400 9K33M3 *Osa-AKM* (SA-8 *Gecko*); 400 9K35M3 *Strela-10* (SA-13 *Gopher*); 120+ 9K330/9K331 *Tor* (SA-15 *Gauntlet*)
  SPAAGM 250+ 2K22 *Tunguska* (SA-19 *Grison*)

MANPAD *Igla-1* (SA-16 *Gimlet*); 9K38 *Igla* (SA-18 *Grouse*): 9K338 *Igla-S* (SA-24 *Grinch*); 9K34 *Strela-3* (SA-14 *Gremlin*)

GUNS

　SP 23mm ZSU-23-4

　TOWED 23mm ZU-23-2; **57mm** S-60

UAV • **Heavy** Tu-143 *Reys*; Tu-243 *Reys*/Tu-243 *Reys-D*; Tu-300 *Korshun* **Light** BLA-07; Pchela-1; Pchela-2

MSL • **SSM** 200+: 200 *Tochka* (SS-21 *Scarab*); some *Iskander-M* (SS-26 *Stone*); (some FROG in store; some *Scud* in store)

AEV BAT-2; IMR; IMR-2; IRM; MT-LB

ARV BMP-1; BREM-1/64/D/K/L; BREhM-D; BTR-50PK(B); M1977; MTP-LB; RM-G; T-54/55; VT-72A

VLB KMM; MT-55A; MTU; MTU-20; MTU-72; PMM-2

MW BMR-3M; GMX-3; MCV-2 (reported); MTK; MTK-2

Reserves

Cadre formations, on mobilisation form

MANOEUVRE

　Armoured

　1 tk bde

　Mechanised

　13 MR bde

Navy ε130,000

4 major fleet organisations (Northern Fleet, Pacific Fleet, Baltic Fleet, Black Sea) and Caspian Sea Flotilla

EQUIPMENT BY TYPE

SUBMARINES 64

　STRATEGIC • **SSBN** 11:

　　3 *Kalmar* (*Delta* III) with 16 R-29R *Volna* (SS-N-18 *Stingray*) strategic SLBM

　　6 *Delfin* (*Delta* IV) with 16 R-29RMU *Sineva* (SS-N-23 *Skiff*) strategic SLBM (of which 1 vessel in repair following a fire; expected return to service 2014)

　　1 *Akula* (*Typhoon*)† in reserve for training with capacity for 20 *Bulava* (SS-N-X-32) strategic SLBM (trials/testing - 2 more awaiting decommissioning)

　　1 *Borey* (sea trials completed in September 2010; commissioning delayed until 2013; *Bulava* (SS-N-X-32) SLBM not yet operational; 1 additional unit completed sea trials Oct 2012; 2 further units in build)

　TACTICAL 45

　SSGN 8:

　　8 *Antyey* (*Oscar* II) (of which 3 in reserve and 1 in refit) with 2 single 650mm TT each with T-65 HWT, 4 single 553mm TT with 3M45 *Granit* (SS-N-19 *Shipwreck*) AShM

　SSN 17:

　　2 *Schuka-B* (*Akula* II) with 4 single 533mm TT each with 3M10 *Granat* (SS-N-21 *Sampson*) SLCM, 4 single 650mm TT with T-65 HWT (one further boat leased to India for 10 years from 2012)

　　8 *Schuka-B* (*Akula* I) (of which 2 in reserve) with 4 single 533mm TT with 3M10 *Granat* (SS-N-21 *Sampson*) SLCM, 4 single 650mm TT with T-65 HWT

　　2 *Kondor* (*Sierra* II) with 4 single 533mm TT each with 3M10 *Granat* (SS-N-21 *Sampson*) SLCM, 4 single 650mm TT with T-65 HWT

　　1 *Barracuda* (*Sierra* I) with 4 single 533mm TT with 3M10 (SS-N-21 *Sampson*) SLCM, RPK-2 (SS-N-15 *Starfish*) and T-53 HWT, 4 single 650mm TT with RPK-7 (SS-N-16 *Stallion*) AShM and T-65 HWT

　　4 *Schuka* (*Victor* III) (of which 1 in reserve) with 4 single 533mm TT each with 3M10 *Granat* (SS-N-21 *Sampson*) SLCM, 2 single 650mm TT with T-65 HWT

　(1 *Yasen* (*Graney*) in sea trials; expected ISD 2013)

　SSK 20:

　　15 *Paltus* (*Kilo*) with 6 single 533mm TT with T-53 HWT

　　4 *Varshavyanka* (*Kilo*) with 6 single 533mm TT (3 additional vessels under construction)

　　1 *Lada* with 6 single 533mm TT (2 additional vessels in build)

　SUPPORT 8

　　SSAN 7: 1 *Orenburg* (*Delta* III Stretch); 1 *Losharik*; 2 Project 1851 (*Paltus*); 3 *Kashalot* (*Uniform*)

　　SSA 1 *Sarov*

PRINCIPAL SURFACE COMBATANTS 33

　AIRCRAFT CARRIERS • **CV** 1 *Orel* (*Kuznetsov*) with 1 12-cell VLS with 3M45 *Granit* (SS-N-19 *Shipwreck*) AShM, 4 sextuple VLS with 3K95 *Kindzhal* (SA-N-9 *Gauntlet*) SAM (capacity 18-24 Su-33 *Flanker D* FGA ac; 4 Su-25UTG *Frogfoot* ac, 15 Ka-27 *Helix* ASW hel, 2 Ka-31R *Helix* AEW hel)

　CRUISERS 5

　CGHMN 1:

　　1 *Orlan* (*Kirov*) with 10 twin VLS with 3M45 *Granit* (SS-N-19 *Shipwreck*) AShM, 2 twin lnchr with *Osa*-M (SA-N-4 *Gecko*) SAM, 12 single VLS with *Fort*/*Fort* M (SA-N-6 *Grumble*/SA-N-20 *Gargoyle*) SAM, 2 octuple VLS with 3K95 *Kindzhal* (SA-N-9 *Gauntlet*) SAM, 10 single 533mm ASTT, 1 twin 130mm gun, (capacity 3 Ka-27 *Helix* ASW hel) (2nd *Orlan* undergoing extensive refit currently non operational; expected return to service in 2017)

　CGHM 4:

　　1 *Berkot-B* (*Kara*)† (scheduled to be decommissioned), with 2 quad lnchr with *Rastrub* (SS-N-14 *Silex*) AShM/ASW, 2 twin lnchr with 4K60 *Shtorm* (SA-N-3 *Goblet*) SAM, 2 twin lnchr with *Osa*-M (SA-N-4 *Gecko*) SAM, 2 quintuple 533mm ASTT, 2 RBU 6000, 2 twin 76mm gun, (capacity 1 Ka-27 *Helix* ASW hel)

　　3 *Atlant* (*Slava*) with 8 twin lnchr with 4K80 *Bazalt* (SS-N-12 *Sandbox*) AShM, 8 octuple VLS with SA-N-6 *Grumble* SAM, 2 quintuple 533mm ASTT, 1 twin 130mm gun, (capacity 1 Ka-27 *Helix* ASW hel) (one *Atlant* entered repairs in June 2011, currently non-operational; expected return to service in 2013)

　DESTROYERS 18

　DDGHM 17:

　　8 *Sarych* (*Sovremenny*) (of which 3 in reserve) with 2 quad lnchr with 3M80 *Moskit* (SS-N-22 *Sunburn*) AShM, 2 twin lnchr with 3K90 *Uragan*/9K37 *Yezh* (SA-N-7 *Gadfly*/SA-N-12 *Grizzly*) SAM, 2 twin

533mm TT, 2 twin 130mm gun, (capacity 1 Ka-27 *Helix* ASW hel)

8 *Fregat* (*Udaloy* I) each with 2 quad lnchr with *Rastrub* (SS-N-14 *Silex*) AShM/ASW, 8 octuple VLS with 3K95 *Kindzhal* (SA-N-9 *Gauntlet* SAM), 2 quad 533mm ASTT, 2 100mm gun, (capacity 2 Ka-27 *Helix* ASW hel)

1 *Fregat* (*Udaloy* II) with 2 quad lnchr with 3M80 *Moskit* (SS-N-22 *Sunburn*) AShM, 8 octuple VLS with 3K95 *Kindzhal* (SA-N-9 *Gauntlet*) SAM, 2 CADS-N-1 CIWS with 9M311 *Kashtan* (SA-N-11 *Grison*) SAM, 10 single 533mm ASTT, 2 100mm gun, (capacity 2 Ka-27 *Helix* ASW hel)

DDGM 1:

1 *Komsomolets Ukrainy* (*Kashin* mod) with 2 quad lnchr with 3M24 *Uran* (SS-N-25 *Switchblade*) AShM, 2 twin lnchr with *Volnya* (SA-N-1 *Goa*) SAM, 5 single 533mm ASTT, 1 twin 76mm gun

FRIGATES 9

FFGHM 4:

2 *Jastreb* (*Neustrashimy*) with 2 quad lnchr with 3M24 *Uran* (SS-N-25 *Switchblade*) AShM, 4 octuple VLS with 3K95 *Kindzhal* (SA-N-9 *Gauntlet*) SAM, 4 single 533mm ASTT, 1 RBU 12000, 2 *Kashtan* (SA-N-11 *Grison*) CIWS/SAM, 1 100mm gun, (capacity 1 Ka-27 *Helix* ASW) (3rd in build, but production halted in 1997; unclear status)

1 *Steregushchiy* with 2 quad lnchr with 3M24 *Uran* (SS-N-25 *Switchblade*) AShM, 1 *Kashtan* (SA-N-11 *Grison*) CIWS/SAM, 1 100mm gun

1 *Steregushchiy* with 2 quad lnchr with 3M24 *Uran* (SS-N-25 *Switchblade*) AShM, 1 12-cell VLS with 9M96 *Redut* SAM, 1 100mm gun (5 additional vessels in build, of which one is an improved *Steregushchiy* II)

FFGM 5:

2 *Gepard* with 2 quad lnchr with 3M24 *Uran* (SS-N-25 *Switchblade*) AShM, 1 twin lnchr with *Osa*-M (SA-N-4 *Gecko*) SAM, 2 30mm CIWS, 1 76mm gun

1 *Burevestnik* (*Krivak* I mod)† with 1 quad lnchr with *Rastrub* (SS-N-14 *Silex*) AShM/ASW, 1 twin lnchr with *Osa*-M (SA-N-4 *Gecko*) SAM, 2 quad 533mm ASTT, 2 twin 76mm gun

2 *Burevestnik* M (*Krivak* II) each with 1 quad lnchr with RPK-3 *Rastrub* (SS-N-14 *Silex*) AShM/ASW, 2 twin lnchr with 10 *Osa*-M (SA-N-4 *Gecko* SAM), 2 quad 533mm ASTT, 2 RBU 6000, 2 100mm gun

PATROL AND COASTAL COMBATANTS 82

CORVETTES 47:

FSGM 15:

2 *Sivuchi* (*Dergach*) with 2 quad lnchr with 3M80 *Moskit* (SS-N-22 *Sunburn*) AShM, 1 twin lnchr with *Osa*-M (SA-N-4 *Gecko*) SAM, 1 76mm gun

12 *Ovod* (*Nanuchka* III) with 2 triple lnchr with P-120 *Malakhit* (SS-N-9 *Siren*) AShM, 1 twin lnchr with *Osa*-M (SA-N-4 *Gecko*), 1 76mm gun

1 *Ovod* (*Nanuchka* IV) with 2 triple lnchr with 3M55 *Onix* (SS-N-26) AShM, 1 twin lnchr with *Osa*-M (SA-N-4 *Gecko*), 1 76mm gun

FSM 32:

3 *Albatros* (*Grisha* III) with 1 twin lnchr with *Osa*-M (SA-N-4 *Gecko*) SAM, 2 twin 533mm ASTT, 2 RBU 6000 *Smerch* 2

21 *Albatros* (*Grisha* V) with 1 twin lnchr with *Osa*-M (SA-N-4 *Gecko*) SAM, 2 twin 533mm ASTT, 1 RBU 6000 *Smerch* 2, 1 76mm gun

8 *Parchim* II (one in reserve following a fire in 2008) with 2 quad lnchr with *Strela*-2 (SA-N-5 *Grail*) SAM, 2 twin 533mm ASTT, 2 RBU 6000 *Smerch* 2, 1 76mm gun

PATROL CRAFT 35:

PCFG 25:

6 *Molnya* (*Tarantul* II) with 2 twin lnchr with P-15M *Termit* (SS-N-2C/D *Styx*) AShM

19 *Molnya* (*Tarantul* III) with 2 twin lnchr with 3M80 *Moskit* (SS-N-22 *Sunburn*) AShM

PCM 5:

2 *Astrakhan* (*Buyan*) with some 9K310 *Igla*-1 (SA-16 *Gimlet*) SAM, 1 100mm gun (1 more vessel in build)

3 *Grachonok* with 4 9K38 *Igla* (SA-18 *Grouse*) SAM (original design was as diving tender)

PHG 4 *Vekhr* (*Matka*) with 2 single lnchr with P-15M *Termit* (SS-N-2C/D *Styx*) AShM, 1 76mm gun

PHT 1 *Sokol* (*Mukha*) with 2 quad 406mm TT, 1 76mm gun (damaged in 2007; unclear status)

MINE WARFARE • MINE COUNTERMEASURES 53

MHO 2 *Rubin* (*Gorya*) (of which one laid up in 2011 for repair)

MSO 11: 10 *Akvamaren* (*Natya*); 1 *Agat* (*Natya* II)

MSC 25: 23 *Yakhont* (*Sonya*); 2 Project 1258 (*Yevgenya*)

MHI 15: 9 *Sapfir* (*Lida*); 3 Project 696 (*Tolya*); 3 *Malakhit* (*Olya*)

AMPHIBIOUS 40

LANDING SHIPS 21

LSM 1:

1 Project 771 (*Polnochny* B) (5 more in reserve) (capacity 6 MBT; 180 troops)

LST 20:

4 *Tapir* (*Alligator*) (capacity 20 tanks; 300 troops)

12 Project 775 (*Ropucha* I) (capacity either 10 MBT and 190 troops or 24 APC (T) and 170 troops)

3 Project 775M (*Ropucha* II) (capacity either 10 MBT and 190 troops or 24 APC (T) and 170 troops)

1 *Tapir* (*Alligator* (mod)) (capacity 1 Ka-29 *Helix* B; 13 MBT; 300 troops)

LANDING CRAFT 19

LCU 5:

1 *Dyugon* (two more in build)

4 Project 11770 (*Serna*) (capacity 100 troops)

LCM 7 *Akula* (*Ondatra*) (capacity 1 MBT)

LCAC 7:

2 *Dzheryan* (*Aist*) (capacity 4 lt tk)

2 *Pomornik* (*Zubr*) (capacity 230 troops; either 3 MBT or 10 APC (T))

3 *Kalmar* (*Lebed*) (capacity 2 lt tk)

LOGISTICS AND SUPPORT 637

ABU 12: 8 *Kashtan*; 4 *Sura*

AE 2: 1 *Muna*;; 1 *Dubnyak*

AEM 3: 2 *Amga*; 1 *Lama*

AG 3: 2 *Vytegrales*; 1 *Potok*

AGB 4 *Dobrynya Mikitich*

AGE 2: 1 *Tchusovoy*; 1 *Zvezdochka* (2 more vessels under construction)

AGI 11: 2 *Alpinist*; 1 *Balzam*; 3 *Moma*; 5 *Vishnya*

AGM 1 *Marshal Nedelin*

AGOR 7: 2 *Akademik Krylov*; 2 *Sibiriyakov*, 2 *Vinograd*; 1 *Seliger*

AGS 21: 3 BGK-797; 6 *Kamenka*; 9 *Onega*; 3 *Vaygach*

AGSH 4: 1 *Samara*; 3 *Vaygach*

AGSI 52: 8 *Biya*; 25 *Finik*; 7 *Moma*; 14 *Yug*

AH 3 *Ob* †

AK 2 *Bira*

AOL 13: 2 *Dubna*; 5 *Uda*; 6 *Altay* (mod)

AOR 5 *Boris Chilikin*

AORL 3: 1 *Kaliningradneft*; 2 *Olekma*

AOS 1 *Luza*

AR 13 *Amur*

ARC 7: 4 *Emba*; 3 *Klasma*

ARS 14: 4 *Mikhail Rudnitsky*; 10 *Goryn*

AS 1 Project 2020 (*Malina*)

ASR 2: 1 *Nepal*; 1 *Alagez*

ATF 61: 2 *Baklazhan*; 5 *Katun*; 3 *Ingul*; 2 *Neftegaz*; 14 *Okhtensky*; 18 *Prometey*; 1 *Prut*; 3 *Sliva*; 13 *Sorum*

AWT 2 *Manych*

AXL 12: 10 *Petrushka*; 2 *Smolny*

YDG 15 *Bereza*

YDT 104: 40 *Flamingo*; 20 *Nyryat 2*; 28 *Yelva*; 3 *11980*; 13 *Pelym*

YGS 60 GPB-480

YO 36: 5 *Khobi*; 30 *Toplivo*; 1 *Konda*

YPB 30 *Bolva*

YPT 43: 12 *Shelon*; 31 *Poluchat*

YTB 46: 11 *Stividor*; 35 *Sidehole*

YTR 42: 27 *Pozharny*; 15 *Morkov*

Naval Aviation ε28,000

4 Fleet Air Forces; most combat aircraft previously assigned to Naval Aviation were transfered to Air Force command by end 2011.

Flying hours 60+ hrs/year

FORCES BY ROLE
FIGHTER
  2 sqn with Su-33 *Flanker* D; Su-25UTG *Frogfoot*

ANTI-SURFACE WARFARE/ISR
  2 sqn with Su-24M/MR *Fencer*

ANTI-SUBMARINE WARFARE
  2 sqn with Il-20RT *Coot A*; Il-38 *May**
  8 sqn with Ka-27/Ka-29 *Helix*
  1 sqn with Mi-14 *Haze-A*
  2 sqn with Tu-142M/MR *Bear F/J**
  1 unit forming with Ka-31R

MARITIME PATROL/ELECTRONIC WARFARE
  1 sqn with An-12 *Cub*; Be-12 *Mail**; Mi-8 *Hip*

TRANSPORT
  3 sqn with An-12 *Cub*; An-24 *Coke*; An-26 *Curl*; Tu-134

EQUIPMENT BY TYPE
AIRCRAFT 107 combat capable
  FTR 18 Su-33 *Flanker D*
  FGA 18 Su-24M *Fencer*
  ISR 4 Su-24MR *Fencer E**
  ATK 5 Su-25UTG *Frogfoot*
  ASW 27 Tu-142M/MR *Bear* F/J
  MP 35: 9 Be-12 *Mail**; 26 Il-38 *May**

EW • ELINT 7: 2 Il-20RT *Coot A*; 5 An-12 *Cub*

TPT 37 An-12 *Cub*/An-24 *Coke*/An-26 *Curl*/Tu-134

HELICOPTERS
ASW 90: 70 Ka-27 *Helix*; 20 Mi-14 *Haze-A*

AEW 2 Ka-31R *Helix*

EW 8 Mi-8 *Hip* J

SAR 62: 22 Ka-25PS *Hormone* C/Ka-27PS *Helix* D; 40 Mi-14PS *Haze C*

TPT 50 **Heavy** 10 Mi-6 *Hook*; **Medium** 40: 28 Ka-29 *Helix*; 12 Mi-8 *Hip*

MSL
ASM Kh-25 (AS-10 *Karen*); Kh-59 (AS-13 *Kingbolt*)

ARM Kh-58 (AS-11 *Kilter*); Kh-25MP (AS-12 *Kegler*)

AShM Kh-22 (AS-4 *Kitchen*)

AAM • IR R-27T/ET (AA-10B/D *Alamo*); R-60 (AA-8 *Aphid*); R-73 (AA-11 *Archer*); **SARH** R-27R/ER (AA-10A/C *Alamo*)

Coastal Defence • Naval Infantry (Marines) 9,500

FORCES BY ROLE
SPECIAL FORCES
  1 (fleet) SF bde (1 para bn, 2–3 underwater bn, 1 spt unit)
  2 (fleet) SF bde (cadre) (1 para bn, 2–3 underwater bn, 1 spt unit)

MANOEUVRE
  Mechanised
  1 indep naval inf bde
  3 indep naval inf regt

EQUIPMENT BY TYPE
MBT 160 T-55M/T-72/T-80

RECCE 60 BRDM-2 each with 9K11 (AT-3 *Sagger*)

AIFV 150+: ε150 BMP-2; BMP-3; BRM-1K

APC 750+
  APC (T) 250 MT-LB
  APC (W) 500+ BTR-60/70/80

ARTY 367
  SP 113: **122mm** 95 2S1 *Carnation*; **152mm** 18 2S3
  TOWED 122mm 45 D-30
  GUN/MOR 113
    SP 120mm 95: 20 2S23 NONA-SVK; 75 2S9 NONA-S
    TOWED 120mm 18 2B16 NONA-K
  MRL 122mm 96 9P138

AT • MSL • MANPATS 72 9K11 (AT-3 *Sagger*)/9K113 (AT-5 *Spandrel*)
  GUNS 100mm T-12

AD • SAM 320
  SP 70: 20 9K33 *Osa* (SA-8 *Gecko*); 50 Strela-1/Strela-10 (SA-9 *Gaskin*/SA-13 *Gopher* [200 eff])
  MANPAD 250 9K32 Strela-2 (SA-7 *Grail*)
  GUNS 23mm 60 ZSU-23-4

Coastal Defence Troops 2,000

(All units reserve status)

FORCES BY ROLE
MANOEUVRE
  Other
  2 coastal def bde

COMBAT SUPPORT

2 arty regt
2 SAM regt
3 AShM bty with K-300P *Bastion* (SSC-5 *Stooge*)
1 AShM bn with 3K60 *Bal* (SSC-6 *Sennight*)

EQUIPMENT BY TYPE

MBT 350 T-64
AIFV 450 BMP
APC 320
    APC (T) 40 MT-LB
    APC (W) 280 BTR-60/70/80
ARTY 400
    SP 84 **130mm** ε36 A-222 *Bereg;* **152mm** 48 2S5
    TOWED 280: **122mm** 140 D-30; **152mm** 140: 50 2A36;
    50 2A65; 40 D-20
    MRL 122mm 36 BM-21
AShM 24: 12 3K60 *Bal* (SSC-6 Sennight); 12 K-300P
Bastion (SSC-5 *Stooge*)
AD • SAM 50

Military Air Forces ε150,000 (incl conscripts — reducing to 148,000)

Flying hours   60 to 100 hrs/year (combat aircraft)
                120+ (tranpsort aircraft)

HQ at Balashikha, near Moscow. A joint CIS Unified Air Defence System covers RUS, ARM, BLR, KAZ, KGZ, TJK, TKM, UKR and UZB. The Russian Air Force is currently undergoing a period of restructuring, both in terms of general organisation as well as air base and unit structure.

FORCES BY ROLE

BOMBER

6 sqn with Tu-22M3/MR *Backfire* C
3 sqn with Tu-95MS *Bear*
1 sqn with Tu-160 *Blackjack*

FIGHTER

8 sqn with MiG-29 *Fulcrum*
3 sqn with MiG-29SMT *Fulcrum*
11 sqn with MiG-31/MiG-31BM *Foxhound*
10 sqn with Su-27 *Flanker*
4 sqn with Su-27SM2 *Flanker;* Su-30M2

FIGHTER/GROUND ATTACK

1 sqn with Su-27SM3 *Flanker;* Su-30M2

GROUND ATTACK

13 sqn with Su-24M/M2 *Fencer*
13 sqn with Su-25/Su-25SM *Frogfoot*
1 sqn with Su-34 *Fullback*

GROUND ATTACK/ISR

1 sqn with Su-24M/MR *Fencer**

ELECTRONIC WARFARE

1 sqn with Mi-8PPA *Hip*

ISR

1 sqn with MIG-25RB *Foxbat**
8 sqn with Su-24MR *Fencer**
1 flt with An-30 *Clank*

AIRBORNE EARLY WARNING & CONTROL

1 sqn with A-50/A-50U *Mainstay*

TANKER

1 sqn with Il-78/Il-78M *Midas*

TRANSPORT

7 (mixed) sqn with An-12 *Cub*/An-24 *Coke*/An-26 *Curl*/
Mi-8 *Hip*/Tu-134 *Crusty*/Tu-154 *Careless*

2 sqn with An-124 *Condor*
1 flt with An-12BK *Cub*
1 sqn with An-22 *Cock*
13 sqn with Il-76MD *Candid*

ATTACK HELICOPTER

1 sqn (forming) with Ka-52A *Hokum* B
13 sqn with Mi-24 *Hind*
2 sqn (forming) with Mi-28N *Havoc* B

TRANSPORT HELICOPTER

17 sqn with Mi-8 *Hip*/Mi-26 *Halo*

AIR DEFENCE

35 regt with S-300PS (SA-10 *Grumble*); S-300PM (SA-20
  Gargoyle)
5 regt with S-400 (SA-21 *Growler*); 96K6 *Pantsir-S1* (SA-
  22 *Greyhound*)

EQUIPMENT BY TYPE

AIRCRAFT 1,462 combat capable
  BBR 184: 105 Tu-22M3/MR *Backfire* C; 32 Tu-95MS6 *Bear;*
  31 Tu-95MS16 *Bear;* 16 Tu-160 *Blackjack*
  FTR 630: 150 MiG-29 *Fulcrum;* 40 MiG-29UB *Fulcrum;* 200
  MiG-31/31BM *Foxhound;* 200 Su-27 *Flanker;* 40 Su-27UB
  Flanker
  FGA 323: 28 MiG-29 SMT *Fulcrum;* 6 MiG-29UBT
  Fulcrum; 160 Su-24M *Fencer;* 40 Su-24M2 *Fencer;* 47
  Su-27SM2 *Flanker;* 12 Su-27SM3; 4 Su-30M2; 20 Su-34
  Fullback; 6 Su-35S
  ATK 215: 170 Su-25 *Frogfoot;* 30+ Su-25SM *Frogfoot;* 15 Su-
  25UB *Frogfoot*
  ISR 114+: 4 An-30 *Clank;* 10+ MiG-25RB *Foxbat**; 100 Su-
  24MR *Fencer**
  ELINT 22 Il-22 *Coot* B
  AEW&C 23: 19 A-50/A-50U *Mainstay;* 4 Il-76SKIP (Be-976
  - telemetry aircraft)
  C&C 6: 2 Il-76VKP; 4 Il-86VKP *Maxdome*
  TKR 20 Il-78/Il-78M *Midas*
  TPT 389: **Heavy** 136: 12 An-124 *Condor;* 6 An-22 *Cock;* 118
  Il-76MD/MF *Candid;* **Medium** 50 An-12/An-12BK *Cub;*
  Light 192: 25 An-24 *Coke;* 80 An-26 *Curl;* 15 An-72 *Coaler;*
  2 An-140; 40 L-410; 30 Tu-134 *Crusty;* **PAX** 11: 1 Tu-154
  Careless; 10 Yak-40 *Codling*
  TRG 204: 190 L-39 *Albatros;* 14 Yak-130 *Mitten*
HELICOPTERS
  ATK 378+: 12 Ka-50 *Hokum;* 21 Ka-52A *Hokum* B; 290 Mi-
  24 *Hind* D/V/P; 45+ Mi-28N *Havoc* B; 10+ Mi-35 *Hind*
  EW 60 Mi-8PPA *Hip*
  TPT 566: **Heavy** 32 Mi-26 *Halo;* **Medium** 534 Mi-17 (Mi-
  8MT) *Hip* H/Mi-8 *Hip*
  TRG 20+: 10 Ka-226; 10+ Ansat-U
UAV • ISR Some **Light** *Pchela*-1T
AD • SAM • SP 1,900+ S-300PS (SA-10 *Grumble*)/S-300PM
(SA-20 *Gargoyle*)/S-400 (SA-21 *Growler*); 96K6 *Pantsir-S1*
(SA-22 *Greyhound*)
MSL
  AAM • IR R-27T/ET (AA-10 *Alamo* B/D); R-73 (AA-11
  Archer); R-60T (AA-8 *Aphid*); **SARH** R-27R/ER (AA-10
  Alamo A/C); R-33/33S (AA-9 *Amos* A/B); **ARH** R-77/R-77-1
  (A-12 *Adder*) K-37M (AA-X-13 *Axehead*) (due to complete
  development by end 2012); **PRH** R-27P/EP (AA-10 *Alamo*
  E/F)

ARM Kh-58 (AS-11 *Kilter*); Kh-25MP (AS-12 *Kegler*); Kh-15P (AS-16 *Kickback*) Kh-31P/PM (PM entering production) (AS-17A *Krypton*)
ASM Kh-25 (AS-10 *Karen*); Kh-59/Kh-59M (AS-13 *Kingbolt*/AS-18 *Kazoo*); Kh-29 (AS-14 *Kedge*); Kh-31A/AM (AM entering production) (AS-17B *Krypton*); Kh-38 (in development)
LACM Kh-22 (AS-4 *Kitchen*); Kh-55/55SM (AS-15A/B *Kent*); Kh-101; Kh-102; Kh-555 (AS-15C *Kent*)
BOMBS • Laser-guided KAB-500; KAB-1500L; TV-guided KAB-500KR; KAB-1500KR; KAB-500OD;UPAB 1500

Russian Military Districts

Western Military District

(ex-Leningrad & Moscow Military Districts & Kaliningrad Special Region) HQ at St Petersburg

Army

FORCES BY ROLE
COMMAND
2 army HQ
SPECIAL FORCES
2 (Spetsnaz) bde
1 (AB Recce) bn
MANOEUVRE
Armoured
2 tk bde
Mechanised
6 MR bde
Air Manoeuvre
3 (VdV) AB div
COMBAT SUPPORT
2 arty bde
1 MRL bde
1 SSM bde with *Iskander-M*
2 SSM bde with *Tochka* (SS-21 *Scarab*)
2 AD bde
1 engr bde
1 MP bde

Reserves

FORCES BY ROLE
  MANOEUVRE
    Armoured
    1 tk bde
    Mechanised
    2 MR bde

Northern Fleet

EQUIPMENT BY TYPE
SUBMARINES 40
  STRATEGIC 9 SSBN (1 additional SSBN completed sea trials; Bulava SLBM not yet operational)
  TACTICAL 23: 3 SSGN; 13 SSN; 7 SSK
  SUPPORT 8: 7 SSAN (other roles); 1 SSA
PRINCIPAL SURFACE COMBATANTS 10: 1 CV; 1 CGHMN; 1 CGHM (in repair); 7 DDGHM (of which 1 in refit)
PATROL AND COASTAL COMBATANTS 12: 3 FSGM; 9 FSM

MINE WARFARE 12: 1 MHSO (in repair); 3 MSO; 8 MSC
AMPHIBIOUS 5: 4 LST; 1 LSM

Naval Aviation

FORCES BY ROLE
FIGHTER
  2 sqn with Su-33 *Flanker D*; Su-25UTG *Frogfoot*
ANTI-SUBMARINE WARFARE
  1 sqn with Il-20RT *Coot A*; Il-38 *May**; Tu-134
  3 sqn with Ka-27/Ka-29 *Helix*
  1 sqn with Tu-142M/MR *Bear F/J*

EQUIPMENT BY TYPE
AIRCRAFT
  FTR 18 Su-33 *Flanker* D
  ATK 5 Su-25UTG *Frogfoot*
  ASW 13 Tu-142M/MR *Bear* F/J
  EW • ELINT Il-20RT *Coot* A
  MP 14 Il-38 *May**
  TPT Tu-134
HELICOPTERS
  ASW Ka-27 *Helix* A
  TPT Ka-29 *Helix* B; Mi-8 *Hip*

Naval Infantry

FORCES BY ROLE
MANOEUVRE
  Mechanised
  1 naval inf regt

Coastal Defence

FORCES BY ROLE
MANOEUVRE
  Other
  1 coastal def bde with 360 MT-LB; 134 arty
COMBAT SUPPORT
  1 AD regt

Baltic Fleet

EQUIPMENT BY TYPE
SUBMARINES • TACTICAL 3 SSK: 1 *Lada*; 2 *Paltus* (*Kilo*)
PRINCIPAL SURFACE COMBATANTS 7: 2 DDGHM; 4 FFGHM; 1 FFGM
PATROL AND COASTAL COMBATANTS 21: 4 FSGM; 8 FSM; 8 PCFG; 1 PCM
MINE WARFARE • MINE COUNTERMEASURES 15: 4 MSC; 11 MHI
AMPHIBIOUS 11: 4 LST; 5 LCM; 2 LCAC

Naval Aviation

FORCES BY ROLE
ANTI-SUBMARINE WARFARE
  1 sqn with Ka-27/Ka-29 *Helix*
TRANSPORT
  1 sqn with An-24 *Coke*; An-26 *Curl*; Tu-134 *Crusty*

EQUIPMENT BY TYPE
AIRCRAFT
  TPT An-24 *Coke*/An-26 *Curl*/Tu-134 *Crusty*
HELICOPTERS
  ASW Ka-27 *Helix*
  TPT • Medium Ka-29 *Helix*

Naval Infantry

FORCES BY ROLE
MANOEUVRE
 Mechanised
 1 MR bde
 1 MR regt
 1 naval inf bde
COMBAT SUPPORT
 1 arty bde

Coastal Defence

FORCES BY ROLE
COMBAT SUPPORT
 2 arty regt
 1 AShM regt with P5/P-35 (SS-C-1B *Sepal*)

Military Air Forces

1st Air Force & Air Defence Command

(ex-6th & 16th Air Army)

FORCES BY ROLE
FIGHTER
 1 sqn with MiG-29 *Fulcrum*
 2 sqn with MiG-29SMT *Fulcrum*
 4 sqn with MiG-31 *Foxhound*
 8 sqn with Su-27/Su-27UB *Flanker*
GROUND ATTACK
 3 sqn with Su-24M/M2 *Fencer*
GROUND ATTACK/ISR
 1 sqn with Su-24M/MR *Fencer**
ISR
 1 flt with A-30 *Clank*
 1 sqn with MiG-25RB *Foxbat**
 2 sqn with Su-24MR *Fencer-E*
ELECTRONIC WARFARE
 1 sqn with Mi-8PPA *Hip*
TRANSPORT
 1 sqn with An-12 *Cub*; An-26 *Curl*; Tu-134 *Crusty*
ATTACK HELICOPTER
 6 sqn with Mi-24 *Hind*
TRANSPORT HELICOPTER
 6 sqn with Mi-8 *Hip*

EQUIPMENT BY TYPE
AIRCRAFT
 FTR 180: 20 MiG-29 *Fulcrum*; 51 MiG-31 *Foxhound*;
 109 Su-27/Su-27UB *Flanker*
 FGA 78: 28 MiG-29SMT *Fulcrum*; 6 MiG-29UBT
 Fulcrum; 44 Su-24M/M2 *Fencer*
 ISR 42+: 4 An-30 *Clank*; 10+ MiG-25RB *Foxbat** 28
 Su-24MR *Fencer**
 TPT 12 An-12/An-26/Tu-134
HELICOPTERS
 ATK 60 Mi-24 *Hind*
 EW 10 Mi-8PPA *Hip*
 TPT • Medium 60 Mi-8 *Hip*
AD • SAM 1,125 incl S-300V

Central Military District

(ex-Volga-Ural & part ex-Siberia Military Districts) HQ
at Yekaterinburg

Army

FORCES BY ROLE
COMMAND
 2 army HQ
SPECIAL FORCES
 1 (Spetsnaz) SF bde
MANOEUVRE
 Armoured
 1 tk bde
 Mechanised
 1 (201st) MR div
 7 MR bde
 Air Manoeuvre
 1 (VdV) AB bde
COMBAT SUPPORT
 1 arty bde
 1 MRL regt
 2 SSM bde with *Tochka* (SS-21 *Scarab*)
 2 AD bde
 1 engr bde

Reserves

FORCES BY ROLE
MANOEUVRE
 Mechanised
 3 MR bde

Military Air Force

2nd Air Force & Air Defence Command

(ex-5th & elm ex-14th Air Army)

FORCES BY ROLE
FIGHTER
 4 sqn with MiG-31 *Foxhound*
GROUND ATTACK
 2 sqn with Su-24 *Fencer*
ISR
 1 sqn with Su-24MR *Fencer E*
TRANSPORT
 3 sqn with An-12 *Cub*; An-24 *Coke*; Il-86; Tu-134
 Crusty; Tu-154; Mi-8 *Hip*
ATTACK HELICOPTER
 2 sqn with Mi-24 *Hind*
TRANSPORT HELICOPTER
 3 sqn with Mi-8 *Hip*/Mi-26 *Halo*

EQUIPMENT BY TYPE
AIRCRAFT
 FTR 73 MiG-31 *Foxhound*
 FGA 26 Su-24M *Fencer*
 ISR 13 Su-24MR *Fencer E*
 TPT 36 An-12/An-24 *Coke*/Tu-134 *Crusty*/Tu-154
 Careless
HELICOPTERS
 ATK 24 Mi-24 *Hind*
 TPT 46: 6 Mi-26 *Halo*; 40 Mi-8 *Hip*
AD • SAM S-300 (SA-10 *Grumble*)

Southern Military District

(ex-North Caucasus Military District — including
Trans-Caucasus Group of Forces (GRVZ)) HQ located at
Rostov-on-Don

Army

FORCES BY ROLE
COMMAND
2 army HQ
SPECIAL FORCES
2 (Spetsnaz) SF bde
MANOEUVRE
Reconnaissance
1 recce bde
Mechanised
6 MR bde
2 MR bde (Armenia)
1 MR bde (Abkhazia)
1 MR bde (South Ossetia)
3 (lt/mtn) MR bde
Air Manoeuvre
1 (VdV) AB div
1 (army) air aslt bde
COMBAT SUPPORT
1 arty bde
1 MRL bde
1 MRL regt
1 SSM bde with *Tochka* (SS-21 *Scarab*)
2 AD bde
1 engr bde

Black Sea Fleet

The RUS Fleet is leasing bases in Sevastopol and Karantinnaya Bay, and is based, jointly with UKR warships, at Streletskaya Bay.

EQUIPMENT BY TYPE
SUBMARINES • TACTICAL 1 **SSK** (also 1 *Som* (*Tango*) in reserve)
PRINCIPAL SURFACE COMBATANTS 5: 2 **CGHM**; 1 **DDGM**; 2 **FFGM**
PATROL AND COASTAL COMBATANTS 19: 4 **FSGM**; 6 **FSM**; 1 **PHM**; 5 **PCFG**; 2 **PCM**; 1 **PHT**
MINE WARFARE • MINE COUNTERMEASURES 9: 1 **MCO**; 6 **MSO**; 2 **MSC**
AMPHIBIOUS 9: 8 **LST**; 1 **LCU**

Naval Aviation

FORCES BY ROLE
FIGHTER
ANTI-SURFACE WARFARE/ISR
2 sqn with Su-24M/MR *Fencer*
ANTI-SUBMARINE WARFARE
1 sqn with Ka-27 *Helix*
1 sqn with Mi-14 *Haze*
MARITIME PATROL/ELECTRONIC WARFARE
1 sqn with An-12 *Cub*; Be-12 *Mail**; Mi-8
EQUIPMENT BY TYPE
AIRCRAFT
FGA 18 Su-24M *Fencer*
ISR 4 Su-24MR *Fencer* E
MP 9 Be-12 *Mail**
EW • ELINT An-12 *Cub*
TPT An-12; An-26
HELICOPTERS
ASW Ka-27 *Helix*
TPT • **Medium** Mi-8 *Hip* (MP/EW/Tpt)

Naval Infantry

FORCES BY ROLE
MANOEUVRE
Mechanised
1 naval inf bde

Coastal Defence

3 AShM bty with K-300P *Bastion* (SSC-5 *Stooge*)
1 bn with 3K60 *Bal* (SSC-6 *Sennight*)

Caspian Sea Flotilla

EQUIPMENT BY TYPE
PRINCIPAL SURFACE COMBATANTS 2 **FFGM**
PATROL AND COASTAL COMBATANTS 6: 2 **PCFG**; 3 **PHM**; 1 **PCM**
MINE WARFARE • MINE COUNTERMEASURES 7: 5 **MSC**; 2 **MHI**
AMPHIBIOUS 11: 2 **LCM**; 4 **LCU**; 5 **LCAC**

Military Air Force

4th Air Force & Air Defence Command
(ex 4th Air Army)
FORCES BY ROLE
FIGHTER
3 sqn with MiG-29 *Fulcrum*
1 sqn with MiG-29 *Fulcrum* (Armenia)
3 sqn with Su-27 *Flanker*
FIGHTER/GROUND ATTACK
1 sqn with Su-27SM3 *Flanker*; Su-30M2
GROUND ATTACK
4 sqn with Su-24M *Fencer*
6 sqn with Su-25 *Frogfoot*
1 sqn with Su-34 *Fullback*
ISR
2 sqn with Su-24MR *Fencer*-E
TRANSPORT
1 sqn with An-12 *Cub*/Mi-8 *Hip*
ATTACK HELICOPTER
3 sqn with Mi-24 *Hind*
2 sqn (forming) with Mi-28N *Havoc* B
TRANSPORT HELICOPTER
6 sqn with Mi-8 *Hip*/Mi-26 *Halo*
EQUIPMENT BY TYPE
AIRCRAFT
FTR 121: 63 MiG-29 *Fulcrum*; 58 Su-27 *Flanker*
FGA 84: 62 Su-24M *Fencer*; 12 Su-27SM3 *Flanker*; 2 Su-30M2; up to 8 Su-34 *Fullback*
ATK 129 Su-25 *Frogfoot*
ISR 24 Su-24MR *Fencer**
TPT 12 An-12 *Cub*
HELICOPTERS
ATK 36: 24 Mi-24 *Hind*; 12+ Mi-28N *Havoc* B
TPT 72 **Heavy** 10 Mi-26 *Halo* **Medium** 28 Mi-8 *Hip*

Eastern Military District
(ex Far East & part ex-Siberia Military Districts) HQ located at Khabarovsk

Russia and Eurasia

Army

FORCES BY ROLE
COMMAND
4 army HQ
SPECIAL FORCES
2 (Spetsnaz) SF bde
MANOEUVRE
Armoured
1 tk bde
Mechanised
10 MR bde
1 MGA div
Air Manoeuvre
2 (army) air aslt bde
COMBAT SUPPORT
4 arty bde
2 MRL bde
3 SSM bde with *Tochka* (SS-21 *Scarab*)
4 AD bde
1 engr bde

Reserves

FORCES BY ROLE
MANOEUVRE
Mechanised
8 MR bde

Pacific Fleet

EQUIPMENT BY TYPE
SUBMARINES 21
STRATEGIC 3 SSBN
TACTICAL 18: 5 SSGN; 4 SSN; 9 SSK
PRINCIPAL SURFACE COMBATANTS 9: 1 **CGHM**;
8 **DDGHM** (of which one in reserve)
PATROL AND COASTAL COMBATANTS 23: 4
FSGM; 9 **FSM**; 10 **PCFG**
MINE WARFARE 7: 2 MSO; 5 MSC
AMPHIBIOUS 4 LST

Naval Aviation FORCES BY ROLE
ANTI-SUBMARINE WARFARE
3 sqn with Ka-27/Ka-29 *Helix*
1 sqn with Il-38 *May**
1 sqn with Tu-142M/MR *Bear* F/J*
TRANSPORT
2 sqn with An-12 *Cub*; An-26 *Curl*

EQUIPMENT BY TYPE
AIRCRAFT
ASW 14 Tu-142M/MR *Bear* F/J*
MP 15 Il-38 *May**
TPT An-12 *Cub* (MR/EW); An-26 *Curl*
HELICOPTERS
ASW Ka-27 *Helix*
TPT • **Medium** Ka-29 *Helix*; Mi-8 *Hip*

Naval Infantry

FORCES BY ROLE
MANOEUVRE
Mechanised
1 naval inf bde (1 tk bn, 3 inf bn, 1 arty bn)
1 naval inf regt

Coastal Defence

FORCES BY ROLE
MANOEUVRE
Other
1 coastal def bde

Military Air Force

3rd Air Force & Air Defence Command
(ex 11th & elms 14th AF and AD Army)

FORCES BY ROLE
FIGHTER
3 sqn with MiG-29 *Fulcrum*
3 sqn with MiG-31 *Foxhound*
4 sqn with Su-27SM2 *Flanker*; Su-30M2
GROUND ATTACK
4 sqn with Su-24M/M2 *Fencer*
5 sqn with Su-25 *Frogfoot*
ISR
3 sqn with Su-24MR *Fencer-E*
TRANSPORT
2 sqn with An-12 *Cub*/An-24 *Coke*/An-26 *Curl*/Tu-134 *Crusty*/Tu-154 *Careless*
ATTACK HELICOPTER
2 sqn with Mi-24 *Hind*
1 sqn (forming) with Ka-52A *Hokum* B
TRANSPORT HELICOPTER
6 sqn with Mi-8 *Hind*/Mi-26 *Halo*

EQUIPMENT BY TYPE
AIRCRAFT
FTR 104: 60 MiG-29 *Fulcrum*; 44 MiG-31 *Foxhound*
FGA 103: 44 Su-24M *Fencer*; 10 Su-24M2 *Fencer*; 47 Su-27SM2 *Flanker*; 2 Su-30M2
ATK 72 Su-25 *Frogfoot*
ISR 28 Su-24MR *Fencer-E**
TPT 22 An-12 *Cub*/An-24 *Coke*/An-26 *Curl*; 1 Tu-134 *Crusty*; 1 Tu-154 *Careless*
HELICOPTERS
ATK 32: 8 Ka-52A *Hokum* B; 24 Mi-24 *Hind*
TPT 48 **Heavy** 4 Mi-26 *Halo* **Medium** 56 Mi-8 *Hip*
AD • **SAM** S-300P (SA-10 *Grumble*)

Direct Reporting Commands

Long-Range Aviation Command
Flying hours: 80–100 hrs/yr
FORCES BY ROLE
BOMBER
6 sqn with Tu-22M3/MR *Backfire* C
3 sqn with Tu-95MS *Bear*
1 sqn with Tu-160 *Blackjack*
EQUIPMENT BY TYPE
AIRCRAFT
BBR 184: 105 Tu-22M3/MR *Backfire* C; 32 Tu-95MS6 *Bear*; 31 Tu-95MS16 *Bear*; 16 Tu-160 *Blackjack*

Transport Aviation Command
Flying hours   60 hrs/year

FORCES BY ROLE
TRANSPORT
    2 sqn with An-124 *Condor*
    1 flt with An-12BK *Cub*
    1 sqn with An-22 *Cock*
    13 sqn with Il-76MD *Candid*

EQUIPMENT BY TYPE
AIRCRAFT • TPT 157 **Heavy** 151: 12 An-124 *Condor*;
21 An-22 *Cock* (Under MoD control); 118 Il-76MD/MF
Candid **Medium** 6 An-12BK *Cub*

Paramilitary 519,000

Federal Border Guard Service ε160,000

Directly subordinate to the president; now reportedly
all contract-based personnel

FORCES BY ROLE
10 regional directorates
MANOEUVRE
  Other
    7 frontier gp

EQUIPMENT BY TYPE
AIFV/APC (W) 1,000 BMP/BTR
ARTY • SP 90: **122mm** 2S1 *Carnation*; **120mm** 2S12;
120mm 2S9 *Anona*
PRINCIPAL SURFACE COMBATANTS
  FRIGATES • FFHM 3 *Nerey* (*Krivak* III) with 1 twin
    lnchr with *Osa*-M (SA-N-4 *Gecko*) SAM, 2 quad
    533mm TT lnchr, 2 RBU 6000 *Smerch* 2 lnchr, 1
    100mm gun (capacity 1 Ka-27 *Helix* A ASW hel)
PATROL AND COASTAL COMBATANTS 213
  CORVETTES • FSM 3: 1 *Albatros* (*Grisha* II); 2 *Albatros*
    (*Grisha* III)
  PCM 46:
    2 *Molnya* II (*Pauk* II) with 1 quad lnchr with SA-N-5
      Grail SAM, 2 twin 533mm TT lnchr, 2 RBU 1200
      lnchr, 1 76mm gun
    27 *Svetljak* (*Svetlyak*) with 1 quad lnchr with SA-N-5
      Grail SAM, 2 single 406mm TT, 1 76mm gun
    17 *Molnya* I (*Pauk* I) with 1 quad lnchr with SA-N-5
      Grail SAM, 4 single 406mm TT, 1 76mm gun
  PHT 2 *Antares* (*Muravey*)
  PCO 15: 8 Project 503 (*Alpinist*); 1 *Sprut*; 3 *Rubin*; 2
    Antur; 1 *Purga*
  PSO 4 *Komandor*
  PCC 13 *Tarantul* (*Stenka*)
  PB 51: 9 Project 14310 (*Mirazh*); 13 Type 1496; 12 *Grif*
    (*Zhuk*); 17 *Kulik*
  PBR 25: 3 *Ogonek*; 8 *Piyavka*; 5 *Shmel*; 7 *Moskit* (*Vosh*); 2
    Slepen (*Yaz*)
  PBF 54: 1 A-125; 2 *Bogomol*; 6 *Mangust*; 4 *Mustang*
    (Project 18623); 15 *Saygak*; 12 *Sobol*; 1 *Sokzhoi*; 13
    Stenka
AMPHIBIOUS • LC • LCAC 7 *Tsaplya* (used for patrol
  duties)
LOGISTICS AND SUPPORT 41
  AGB 5 *Ivan Susanin* (primarily used as patrol ships)
  AGS 2 *Yug* (primarily used as patrol ships)
  AK 8 *Neon Antonov*
  AKSL 6 *Kanin* **AO** 2: 1 *Baskunchak*; 1 Project 1510

ATF 18 *Sorum* (primarily used as patrol ships)
AIRCRAFT • TPT ε86: 70 An-24 *Coke*/An-26 *Curl*/An-72
Coaler/Il-76 *Candid*/Tu-134 *Crusty*/Yak-40 *Codling*; 16 SM-
92
HELICOPTERS: ε200 Ka-28 (Ka-27) *Helix* ASW/Mi-24
Hind Atk/Mi-26 *Halo* Spt/Mi-8 *Hip* Spt

Federal Agency for Special Construction (MOD) ε50,000

Federal Communications and Information Agency ε55,000

FORCES BY ROLE
MANOEUVRE
  Other
    4 paramilitary corps
    28 paramilitary bde

Federal Protection Service ε10,000–30,000 active

Org include elm of ground forces (mech inf bde and AB
regt)

FORCES BY ROLE
MANOEUVRE
  Mechanised
    1 mech inf regt
  Air Manoeuvre
    1 AB regt
  Other
    1 (Presidential) gd regt

Federal Security Service ε4,000 active (armed)

FORCES BY ROLE
MANOEUVRE
  Other
    Some cdo unit (including Alfa and Vympel units)

Interior Troops ε170,000

FORCES BY ROLE
7 Regional Commands: Central, Urals, North Caucasus,
Volga, Eastern, North-Western and Siberian
MANOEUVRE
  Other
    3 (55th, 59th & ODON) paramiltiary div (2–5
      paramilitary regt)
    18 (OBRON) paramilitary bde (3 mech bn, 1 mor bn)
    2 indep paramilitary bde (OBR/OSMBR)
    102 paramilitary regt/bn (incl special motorised units)
    11 (special) paramilitary unit
  Aviation
    8 sqn
COMBAT SUPPORT
  1 arty regt

EQUIPMENT BY TYPE
MBT 9
AIFV/APC (W) 1,650 BMP-1/BMP-2/BTR-80
ARTY 35
  TOWED 122mm 20 D-30
  MOR 120mm 15 PM-38

AIRCRAFT TPT 23: **Heavy** 9 Il-76 *Candid*; **Medium** 2 An-12 *Cub*; **Light** 12 An-26 *Curl*; 6 An-72 *Coaler*
HELICOPTERS • TPT 70: **Heavy** 10 Mi-26 *Halo*; **Medium** 60 Mi-8 *Hip*

Railway Troops (MOD) ε50,000

Cyber

Until 2003, activities within the cyber domain were the responsibility of the Russian SIGINT agency, FAPSI. In 2003, this agency was abolished and its responsibilities divided between the Defence Ministry and the internal security service FSB, with the latter having responsibility for investigating cyber crime. Moscow State University's Institute for Information Security Issues conducts research on technical issues including cryptography and counts the General Staff and the FSB among its clients. In March 2012, Dmitry Rogozin, deputy prime minister with responsibility for the defence industry, said Russia was considering establishing a 'Cyber Security Command' in the armed forces, though there is scant detail. The first official doctrinal statement on the role of the Russian military in cyberspace, the 'Conceptual Views on the Activity of the Russian Federation Armed Forces in Information Space', was released at the end of 2011, and described cyber force tasks with little correlation to those of equivalent commands in the West. In particular, the document contains no mention of the possibility of offensive cyber activity. The document is entirely defensive in tone, and focuses on force protection and prevention of information war, including allowing for a military role in negotiating international treaties governing information security. Following mixed performance in the information aspects of the armed conflict with Georgia in 2008, there was discussion about creating 'Information Troops', whose role would include cyber capability; but this initiative was publicly scotched by the FSB. In January 2012, then-CGS Makarov gave a different picture of the three main tasks for any new command: 'disrupting adversary information systems, including by introducing harmful software; defending our own communications and command systems'; and 'working on domestic and foreign public opinion using the media, Internet and more.' The third task is a reminder that, unlike some other nations with advanced cyber capabilities, Russia deals in cyber warfare as an integral component of information warfare.

DEPLOYMENT

ARMENIA
Army 3,214; 1 MR bde; 74 MBT; 330 AIFV; 14 APC (T)/APC (W); 68 SP/towed arty; 8 mor; 8 MRL; 1 base
Military Air Forces 1 sqn with 18 MiG-29 *Fulcrum*; 2 AD bty with S-300V (SA-12 *Gladiator/Giant*); 1 AD bty with 2K12 *Kub* (SA-6 *Gainful*); 1 air base at Yerevan

BELARUS
Strategic Deterrent Forces • Warning Forces 1 radar station at Baranovichi (*Volga* system; leased)
Navy 1 Naval Communications site

CÔTE D'IVOIRE
UN • UNOCI 9 obs

DEMOCRATIC REPUBLIC OF THE CONGO
UN • MONUSCO 28 obs

GEORGIA
Army 7,000; Abkhazia 1 MR bde; South Ossetia 1 MR bde; **Military Air Forces** some atk hel; some S-300 SAM

GULF OF ADEN
Navy 1 DDGHM; 1 AORL; 1 ATF

KAZAKHSTAN
Strategic Deterrent Forces • Warning Forces 1 radar station at Balkash (*Dnepr* system; leased)

KYRGYZSTAN
Military Air Forces ε500; 5 Su-25 *Frogfoot*; 2 Mi-8 *Hip* spt hel

LIBERIA
UN • UNMIL 4 obs

MIDDLE EAST
UN • UNTSO 3 obs

MOLDOVA/TRANSDNESTR
Army ε1,500 (including 355 peacekeepers); 2 MR bn; 100 MBT/AIFV/APC;
Military Air Forces 7 Mi-24 *Hind*; some Mi-8 *Hip*

SOUTH SUDAN
UN • UNMISS 2; 2 obs

SUDAN
UN • UNISFA 2; 1 obs

SYRIA
Army/Navy 150; 1 naval facility under renovation at Tartus

TAJIKISTAN
Army 5,000; 1 mil base with (1 201st) MR div(-); 54 T-72; 300 BMP-2/BTR-80/MT-LB; 100 2S1/2S3/2S12/9P140 *Uragan*)
Military Air Forces 5 Su-25 *Frogfoot*; 4 Mi-8 *Hip*

UKRAINE
Navy • Coastal Defence • 13,000 including Naval Infantry (Marines) 1,100; 102 AIFV/APC; 24 arty
Navy Black Sea Fleet 1 Fleet HQ located at Sevastopol:
Strategic Deterrent Forces. Warning Forces; 2 radar stations located at Sevastopol (*Dnepr* system, leased) and Mukachevo (*Dnepr* system, leased).

WESTERN SAHARA
UN • MINURSO 18 obs

Tajikistan TJK

Tajikistani Somoni Tr		2011	2012	2013
GDP	Tr	30.07bn	35.79bn	
	US$	6.52bn	7.26bn	
per capita	US$	839	935	
Growth	%	7.40	6.80	
Inflation	%	12.42	5.96	
Def bdgt [a]	Tr	674m	808m	923m
	US$	146m	164m	
FMA (US)	US$	0.75m	0.8m	1.5m
US$1=Tr		4.61	4.93	

[a] Includes defence and law enforcement expenses

Population	7,768,385

Age	0–14	15–19	20–24	25–29	30–64	65 plus
Male	17.1%	5.1%	5.5%	4.9%	15.7%	1.4%
Female	16.5%	4.9%	5.4%	4.9%	16.7%	1.9%

Capabilities

Tajikistan's military capability is limited, with internal security a primary concern. The conscript-based land force is hampered by inadequate training and poor conditions, and the air element operates only a small number of fixed and rotary-wing aircraft to support ground forces. There is little capacity to deploy other than token forces, though the Tajik military is an active participant in CSTO and SCO military exercises. Russia maintains a military base in the country, housing the 201st Motor-Rifle Division. The two countries negotiated an extension to the basing deal in October 2012. It was reported that the new agreement expires in 2042.

ACTIVE 8,800 (Army 7,300, Air Force/Air Defence 1,500) **Paramilitary 7,500**

Terms of service 24 months

ORGANISATIONS BY SERVICE

Army 7,300

FORCES BY ROLE
MANOEUVRE
  Mechanised
  3 MR bde
  Air Manoeuvre
  1 air aslt bde
COMBAT SUPPORT
  1 arty bde
  1 SAM regt
EQUIPMENT BY TYPE
MBT 37: 30 T-72; 7 T-62
AIFV 23: 8 BMP-1; 15 BMP-2
APC (W) 23 BTR-60/BTR-70/BTR-80
ARTY 23
  TOWED 122mm 10 D-30
  MRL 122mm 3 BM-21

MOR 120mm 10
AD • SAM 20+
  TOWED 20 S-75 *Dvina* (SA-2 *Guideline*); S-125 *Pechora-2M* (SA-3 *Goa*)
  MANPAD 9K32 *Strela-2* (SA-7 *Grail*)‡

Air Force/Air Defence 1,500

FORCES BY ROLE
TRANSPORT
  1 sqn with Tu-134A *Crusty*
ATTACK/TRANSPORT HELICOPTER
  1 sqn with Mi-24 *Hind*; Mi-8 *Hip*; Mi-17TM *Hip H*
EQUIPMENT BY TYPE
AIRCRAFT
  TPT • Light 1 Tu-134A *Crusty*
  TRG 4+: 4 L-39 *Albatross*; some Yak-52
HELICOPTERS
  ATK 4 Mi-24 *Hind*
  TPT • Medium 11 Mi-8 *Hip*/Mi-17TM *Hip H*

Paramilitary 7,500

Interior Troops 3,800

National Guard 1,200

Emergencies Ministry 2,500

Border Guards

FOREIGN FORCES

India Air Force: 1 Fwd Op Base located at Farkhar
Russia 5,000 Army: 1 mil base (subord Central MD) with (1 (201st) MR div(-); 54 T-72; 300 BMP-2/BTR-80/MT-LB; 100 2S1/2S3/2S12/9P140 *Uragan* • Military Air Forces: 5 Su-25 *Frogfoot*; 4 Mi-8 *Hip*

Turkmenistan TKM

Turkmen New Manat TMM		2011	2012	2013
GDP	TMM	79.98bn	95.38bn	
	US$	28.06bn	33.47bn	
per capita	US$	5,551	6,621	
Growth	%	14.65	7.97	
Inflation	%	5.28	4.31	
Def bdgt	TMM	ε599m		
	US$	ε210m		
FMA (US)	US$	0.75m	0.685m	0.685m
USD1=TMM		2.85	2.85	

Population	5,054,828

Ethnic groups: Turkmen 77%; Uzbek 9%; Russian 7%; Kazak 2%

Age	0–14	15–19	20–24	25–29	30–64	65 plus
Male	13.7%	5.4%	5.4%	4.9%	18.5%	1.8%
Female	13.4%	5.3%	5.3%	4.9%	19.2%	2.3%

Capabilities

Turkmenistan's conscript-based armed forces struggle with challenges ranging from inadequate training to spares shortages and equipment-maintenance problems. There is still almost exclusive reliance on Soviet-era equipment and doctrine. The air force has a limited number of fixed-wing combat aircraft and helicopters, though the level of availability is uncertain. There is little capability to engage in operations beyond national territory.

ACTIVE 22,000 (Army 18,500 Navy 500 Air 3,000)

Terms of service 24 months

ORGANISATIONS BY SERVICE

Army 18,500

5 Mil Districts

FORCES BY ROLE
MANOEUVRE
Mechanised
3 MR div
2 MR bde
Air Manouvre
1 air aslt bn
Other
1 MR trg div
COMBAT SUPPORT
1 arty bde
1 MRL regt
1 AT regt
1 SSM bde with *Scud*
2 SAM bde
1 engr regt

EQUIPMENT BY TYPE †
MBT 680: 10 T-90S; 670 T-72
RECCE 170 BRDM/BRDM-2
AIFV 942: 930 BMP-1/BMP-2; 12 BRM
APC (W) 829 BTR-60/BTR-70/BTR-80
ARTY 564
  SP 56: **122mm** 40 2S1 *Carnation;* **152mm** 16 2S3
  TOWED 269: **122mm** 180 D-30; **152mm** 89: 17 D-1; 72 D-20
  GUN/MOR 120mm 17 2S9 *Anona*
  MRL 131: **122mm** 65: 9 9P138; 56 BM-21; **220mm** 60 9P140 *Uragan*
  300mm 6 BM 9A52 *Smerch*
  MOR 97: **82mm** 31; **120mm** 66 PM-38
AT
  MSL • MANPATS 100 9K11 (AT-3 *Sagger*); 9K111 (AT-4 *Spigot*); 9K113 (AT-5 *Spandrel*); 9K115 (AT-6 *Spiral*)
  GUNS 100mm 72 MT-12/T-12
AD • SAM 53+
  SP 53: 40 9K33 *Osa* (SA-8 *Gecko*); 13 9K35 *Strela-10* (SA-13 *Gopher*)
  MANPAD 9K32 *Strela-2* (SA-7 *Grail*)‡
  GUNS 70
  SP 23mm 48 ZSU-23-4
  TOWED 57mm 22 S-60
MSL • SSM 10 SS-1 *Scud*

Navy 500

Intention to form a combined navy/coast guard and currently has a minor base at Turkmenbashy. Caspian Sea Flotilla (see Russia) is operating as a joint RUS, KAZ, TKM flotilla under RUS comd based at Astrakhan.

EQUIPMENT BY TYPE
PATROL AND COASTAL COMBATANTS 10
  PCFG 2 *Edermen* (RUS *Molnya*) with 4 quad lnchr with 3M24E *Uran* AShM, 1 76mm gun
  PCC 2 *Arkadag*
  PBF 5 *Grif-T*
  PB 1 *Point*

Air Force 3,000

FORCES BY ROLE
FIGHTER/GROUND ATTACK
  2 sqn with MiG-29 *Fulcrum*; MiG-29UB *Fulcrum*; Su-17 *Fitter*; Su-25MK *Frogfoot*
TRANSPORT
  1 sqn with An-26 *Curl*; Mi-8 *Hip*; Mi-24 *Hind*
TRAINING
  1 unit with Su-7B *Fitter-A*; L-39 *Albatros*
AIR DEFENCE
  Some sqn with S-75 *Dvina* (SA-2 *Guideline*); S-125 *Pechora* (SA-3 *Goa*); S-200 *Angara* (SA-5 *Gammon*)

EQUIPMENT BY TYPE
AIRCRAFT 94 combat capable
  FTR 24: 22 MiG-29 *Fulcrum*; 2 MiG-29UB *Fulcrum*
  FGA 68: 3 Su-7B *Fitter-A*; 65 Su-17 *Fitter-B*;
  ATK 2 Su-25MK *Frogfoot* (41 more being refurbished)
  TPT • Light 1 An-26 *Curl*
  TRG 7: 2 L-39 *Albatros*
HELICOPTERS
  ATK 10 Mi-24 *Hind*
  TPT • Medium 8 Mi-8 *Hip*
AD • SAM 50 S-75 *Dvina* (SA-2 *Guideline*)/S-125 *Pechora* (SA-3 *Goa*)/S-200 *Angara* (SA-5 *Gammon*)

Ukraine UKR

Ukrainian Hryvnia h		2011	2012	2013
GDP	h	1.32tr	14.4tr	
	US$	165.3bn	180.2bn	
per capita	US$	3,685	4,017	
Growth	%	5.15	3.00	
Inflation	%	7.96	1.97	
Def bdgt	h	13.2bn	16.4bn	
	US$	1.66bn	2.05bn	
FMA (US)	US$	8,982m	7,00m	7,00m
US$1=h		7.97	7.99	

Population	44,854,065

Age	0–14	15–19	20–24	25–29	30–64	65 plus
Male	7.1%	2.8%	3.7%	4.3%	23.0%	5.1%
Female	6.7%	2.7%	3.6%	4.2%	26.5%	10.4%

Capabilities

Ambitious plans to reform Ukraine's armed forces have been hampered by inadequate funding, recognised in the country's 2010 Defence White Paper. This has left the country with armed forces capable only of providing limited territorial defence. The 2006–11 defence programme was underfunded. Ambitions to end conscription by the end of 2011 were shelved, though the aim is to increase the number of contract personnel over the 2012–17 period. Ageing Soviet-era equipment increasingly needs to be replaced, for example much of the country's SAM inventory. There is at least a notional ability for limited force projection using airmobile troops. Aircraft availability and serviceability, however, remain low, as do aircrew flying hours. The air force inventory is based on aircraft inherited from the Soviet Union. Funding restrictions have constrained naval ambitions, though the programme to re-equip the fleet with a new class of corvette is proceeding slowly. The navy is also attempting to return its one *Foxtrot*-class submarine to service condition, after more than a decade of inactivity. The armed forces take part in national and multinational exercises, while also providing personnel for UN peacekeeping operations.

ACTIVE 129,950 (Army 70,750 Navy 13,950 Air 45,250) **Paramilitary 84,900**

Terms of Service Army, Air Force 18 months, Navy 2 years. Currently contract servicemen comprise about 50% of the Ukrainian armed forces.

RESERVE 1,000,000 (Joint 1,000,000)

mil service within 5 years

ORGANISATIONS BY SERVICE

Ground Forces (Army) 70,750

Transformation due to be completed by 2015.

FORCES BY ROLE:
COMMAND
  3 corps HQ
SPECIAL FORCES
  2 SF regt
MANOEUVRE
  Armoured
  2 tk bde
  Mechanised
  8 mech bde
  1 mech regt
  Air Manoeuvre
  1 AB bde
  2 air mob bde
  1 air mob regt
  Aviation
  2 avn regt
COMBAT SUPPORT
  3 arty bde
  3 MRL regt
  1 SSM bde
  3 AD regt
  4 engr regt
  1 EW regt
  1 CBRN regt
  4 sigs regt

EQUIPMENT BY TYPE
MBT 1,110: 10 T-84 *Oplot* (development complete); 1,100 T-64; (165 T-80; 600 T-72; 650 T-64; 20 T-55 all in store)
RECCE 600+ BRDM-2
AIFV 3,028: 60 BMD-1, 78 BMD-2; 994 BMP-1; 1,434 BMP-2; 4 BMP-3; 458 BRM-1K
APC 1,432
  APC (T) 44 BTR-D
  APC (W) 1,398: up to 10 BTR 4; 136 BTR-60; 857 BTR-70; 395 BTR-80
ARTY 3,351
  SP 1,226: **122mm** 600 2S1 *Carnation*; **152mm** 527: 40 2S19 *Farm*; 463 2S3; 24 2S5; **203mm** 99 2S7
  TOWED 1,065: **122mm** 371: 369 D-30; 2 (M-30) *M-1938*; **152mm** 694: 287 2A36; 185 2A65; 215 D-20; 7 ML-70
  GUN/MOR 120mm 69:
    SP 67 2S9 *Anona*
    TOWED 2 2B16 *NONA-K*
  MRL 554: **122mm** 335: 20 9P138; 315 BM-21; **132mm** 2 BM-13; **220mm** 137 9P140 *Uragan*; **300mm** 80 9A52 *Smerch*
  MOR 120mm 437: 318 2S12; 119 PM-38
AT • MSL • MANPATS AT-4 9K111 *Spigot*/AT-5 9K113 *Spandrel*/AT-6 9K114 *Spiral*
  GUNS 100mm ε500 MT-12/T-12
HELICOPTERS
  ATK 139 Mi-24 *Hind*
  TPT • Medium 38 Mi-8 *Hip*
AD • SAM • SP 435: 60 9K37 *Buk* (SA-11 *Gadfly*); ε150 9K35 *Strela*-10(SA-13 *Gopher*); 100 2K11 *Krug* (SA-4 *Ganef*); 125 9K33 *Osa* (SA-8 *Gecko*); S-300V (SA-12 *Gladiator*)
  GUNS 470:
    SP 30mm 70 2S6
    TOWED 57mm ε400 S-60
RADAR • LAND *Small Fred/Small Yawn/*SNAR-10 *Big Fred* (arty)
MSL • SSM 212: 50 FROG; 90 *Tochka* (SS-21 *Scarab*); 72 Scud-B
AEV 53 BAT-2; MT-LB
ARV BREM-2; BREM-64; T-54/T-55
VLB MTU-20

Navy 11,950; 2,000 conscript (total 13,950 incl Naval Aviation and Naval Infantry)

After intergovernmental agreement in 1997, the Russian Federation Fleet currently leases bases in Sevastopol and Karantinnaya Bays and also shares facilities jointly with Ukr warships at Streletskaya Bay. The overall serviceability of the fleet is assessed as low.

EQUIPMENT BY TYPE
SUBMARINES • TACTICAL • SSK 1 *Foxtrot* (T-641)† with 10 533mm TT (dive trials were completed in mid-2012; return to service expected in early 2013)
PRINCIPAL SURFACE COMBATANTS 1
  FRIGATES • FFHM 1 *Hetman Sagaidachny* (RUS *Krivak* III) with 1 twin lnchr with *Osa*-M (SA-N-4 *Gecko*) SAM,

2 quad 533mm ASTT with T-53 HWT, 1 100mm gun, (capacity 1 Ka-27 *Helix* ASW hel)

PATROL AND COASTAL COMBATANTS 10

CORVETTES • FSM 3 *Grisha* (II/V) with 1 twin lnchr with *Osa*-M (SA-N-4 *Gecko*) SAM, 2 twin 533mm ASTT with SAET-60 HWT, 1 to 2 RBU 6000 *Smerch 2*, 1 76mm gun

PCFGM 2 *Tarantul* II (FSU *Molnya*) with 2 twin lnchr with P-15 Termit-R (SS-N-2D *Styx*) AShM; 1 quad lnchr (manual aiming) with 9K32 *Strela*-2 (SA-N-5 *Grail*); 1 76mm gun

PHG 2 *Matka* (FSU *Vekhr*) with 2 single lnchr with P-15 Termit-M/R (SS-N-2C/D *Styx*) AShM, 1 76mm gun

PCMT 2 *Pauk* I (FSU *Molnya* II) with 1 quad lnchr (manual aiming) with 9K32 Strela-2 (SA-N-5 *Grail*) SAM, 4 single 406mm TT, 2 RBU-1200, 1 76mm gun

PB 1 *Zhuk* (FSU *Grif*)

MINE WARFARE • MINE COUNTERMEASURES 5

MHI 1 *Yevgenya* (FSU *Korund*)

MSO 2 *Natya*

MSC 2 *Sonya* (FSU *Yakhont*)

AMPHIBIOUS

LANDING SHIPS 2:

LSM 1 *Polnochny* C (capacity 6 MBT; 180 troops)

LST 1 *Ropucha* with 4 quad lnchr with 9K32 Strela-2 (SA-N-5 *Grail*) SAM, 92 mine, (capacity either 10 MBT or 190 troops; either 24 APC (T) or 170 troops)

LANDING CRAFT 3:

LCAC 1 *Pomornik* (*Zubr*) with 2 quad lnchr with 9K32 Strela-2 (SA-N-5 *Grail*) SAM, (capacity 230 troops; either 3 MBT or 10 APC (T))

LCU 2

LOGISTICS AND SUPPORT 34

ABU 1 *Shostka*

ADG 1 *Bereza*

AGI 2 *Muna*

AGF 2: 1 *Bambuk* (fitted with 2 quad lnchr with SA-N-5/8 *Grail* SAM (manual aiming)); 1 *Amur* (can also act as a spt ship for surface ships and submarines)

AGS 2: 1 *Moma* (mod); 1 *Biya*

AWT 1 *Sudak*

AXL 3 *Petrushka*

YDT 13: 1 *Yelva*; 12 other

YTM 6

YTR 2 *Pozharny*

YY 1 *Sokal*

Naval Aviation ε2,500

AIRCRAFT 10 combat capable

ASW 10 Be-12 *Mail*

TPT 16: **Medium** 5 An-12 *Cub*; **Light** 10: 1 An-24 *Coke*; 8 An-26 *Curl*; 1 Tu-134 *Crusty*; **PAX** 1 Il-18 *Coot*

HELICOPTERS

ASW 72: 28 Ka-25 *Hormone*; 2 Ka-27E *Helix*; 42 Mi-14 *Haze*

TPT • Heavy 5 Mi-6 *Hook*

Naval Infantry 3,000

FORCES BY ROLE:

MANOEUVRE

Mechanised

1 mech inf bde

COMBAT SUPPORT

1 arty bde

EQUIPMENT BY TYPE

MBT 40 T-64

AIFV 75 BMP-2

APC (W) 100: 50 BTR-70; 50 BTR-80

ARTY 90

SP • 122mm 12 2S1 *Carnation*

TOWED 36: **122mm** 18 D-30; **152mm** 18 2A36

MRL • 122mm 18 BM-21

MOR 120mm 24 2S12

Air Forces 45,250

Flying hours 40 hrs/yr

FORCES BY ROLE

FIGHTER

5 bde with MiG-29 *Fulcrum*; Su-27 *Flanker*

FIGHTER/GROUND ATTACK

2 bde with Su-24M *Fencer*; Su-25 *Frogfoot*

ISR

2 sqn with Su-24MR *Fencer*-E*

TRANSPORT

3 bde with An-24; An-26; An-30; Il-76 *Candid*; Tu-134 *Crusty*

TRAINING

Some sqn with L-39 *Albatros*

TRANSPORT HELICOPTER

Some sqn with Mi-8; Mi-9; PZL Mi-2 *Hoplite*

EQUIPMENT BY TYPE

AIRCRAFT 211 combat capable

FTR 126 MiG-29 *Fulcrum*; 36 Su-27 *Flanker*

FGA 36 Su-24 *Fencer*

ATK 36 Su-25 *Frogfoot*

ISR 26: 3 An-30 *Clank*; 23 Su-24MR *Fencer*-E*

TPT 46: **Heavy** 20 Il-76 *Candid*; **Medium** 26: 3 An-24 *Coke*; 21 An-26 *Curl*; 2 Tu-134 *Crusty*

TRG 39 L-39 *Albatros*

HELICOPTERS

C&C 4 Mi-9

TPT 34: **Medium** 31 Mi-8 *Hip*; **Light** 3 PZL Mi-2 *Hoplite*

AD • SAM 825 S-300PS (SA-10 *Grumble*)/SA-11 *Gadfly*/S-75 Volkhov (SA-2 *Guideline*) (towed)/S-125 *Pechora* (SA-3 *Goa*) (towed)/S-200V *Angara* (SA-5 *Gammon*) (static)/9K37M *Buk*-M1 (SA-11 *Gadfly*)

MSL

ASM: Kh-25 (AS-10 *Karen*); Kh-59 (AS-13 *Kingbolt*); Kh-29 (AS-14 *Kedge*);

ARM: Kh-58 (AS-11 *Kilter*); Kh-25MP (AS-12 *Kegler*); Kh-28 (AS-9 *Kyle*)

AAM • IR R-60 (AA-8 *Aphid*); R-73 (AA-11 *Archer*)

SARH R-27 (AA-10A *Alamo*)

Paramilitary

MVS ε39,900 active

(Ministry of Internal Affairs)

FORCES BY ROLE

MANOEUVRE

Other

4 paramilitary tp

COMBAT SUPPORT

1 (Internal Security) MP tp

Border Guard 45,000 active

Maritime Border Guard

The Maritime Border Guard is an independent subdivision of the State Comission for Border Guards and is not part of the navy.

FORCES BY ROLE

PATROL

4 (cutter) bde

2 rvn bde

MINE WARFARE

1 MCM sqn

TRANSPORT

3 sqn

TRANSPORT HELICOPTER

1 sqn

COMBAT SERVICE SUPPORT

1 trg div

1 (aux ships) gp

EQUIPMENT BY TYPE

PATROL AND COASTAL COMBATANTS 27

PCFT 6 *Stenka* with 4 single 406mm TT

PCT 3 *Pauk* I with 4 single 406mm TT, 2 RBU-1200, 1 76mm gun

PHT 1 *Muravey* with 2 single 406mm TT, 1 76mm gun

PB 13: 12 *Zhuk*; 1 *Orlan* (seven additional vessels under construction)

PBR 4 *Shmel*

LOGISTICS AND SUPPORT • AGF 1

AIRCRAFT • TPT Medium An-8 *Camp*; **Light** An-24 *Coke*; An-26 *Curl*; An-72 *Coaler*

HELICOPTERS • ASW: Ka-27 *Helix* A

Civil Defence Troops 9,500+ (civilian)

(Ministry of Emergency Situations)

FORCES BY ROLE

MANOEUVRE

Other

4 paramilitary bde

4 paramilitary regt

DEPLOYMENT

Legal provisions for foreign deployment:

Constitution: Codified constitution (1996)

Specific legislation: 'On the procedures to deploy Armed Forces of Ukraine units abroad' (1518-III, March 2000).

Decision on deployment of troops abroad: Parliament authorised to approve decision to provide military assistance, deploy troops abroad and allow foreign military presence in Ukraine (Art. 85, para 23); Also, in accordance with Art. 7 of the specific legislation (above), president is authorised to take a decision to deploy troops abroad and at the same time to submit a draft law to the Parliament of Ukraine for approval.

AFGHANISTAN

NATO • ISAF 25

DEMOCRATIC REPUBLIC OF THE CONGO

UN • MONUSCO 154; 14 obs; 2 atk hel sqn

LIBERIA

UN • UNMIL 277; 2 obs; 1 hel coy

MOLDOVA

10 obs

SERBIA

NATO • KFOR 149; 1 inf coy

UN • UNMIK 2 obs

SOUTH SUDAN

UN • UNMISS 3 obs

SUDAN

UN • UNISFA 2; 2 obs

FOREIGN FORCES

Russia ε13,000 Navy 1 Fleet HQ at Sevastopol; 1 indep naval inf regt; 102 AIFV/APC (T)/APC (W); 24 arty

Uzbekistan UZB

Uzbekistani Som s		2011	2012	2013
GDP	s	77.75tr	97.33tr	
	US$	45.35bn	51.62bn	
per capita	US$	1,597	1,818	
Growth	%	8.30	7.36	
Inflation	%	12.82	12.91	
Def bdgt	s	ε2.44tr		
	US$	ε1.42bn		
US$1=s		1714.34	1885.35	

Population 28,394,180

Ethnic groups: Uzbek 73%; Russian 6%; Tajik 5%; Kazakh 4%; Karakalpak 2%; Tatar 2%; Korean <1%; Ukrainian <1%

Age	0–14	15–19	20–24	25–29	30–64	65 plus
Male	13.6%	5.6%	5.6%	4.9%	18.1%	2.0%
Female	12.9%	5.5%	5.5%	4.8%	18.9%	2.7%

Capabilities

Uzbekistan's conscript-based armed forces are significantly better-equipped than those of its immediate neighbours, including Kyrgyzstan (with which it has a territorial dispute) and Turkmenistan. The army is attempting to improve its mobility in order to manage internal-security challenges. Air force flying hours are reported to be low, with significant logistical and maintenance shortcomings affecting the availability of aircraft. Uzbekistan is a member of the SCO, but suspended its membership of the CSTO in mid-2012.

ACTIVE 48,000 (Army 24,500 Air 7,500 Joint 16,000)
Paramilitary 20,000

Terms of service conscription 12 months

ORGANISATIONS BY SERVICE

Army 24,500

4 Mil Districts; 2 op comd; 1 Tashkent Comd

FORCES BY ROLE
SPECIAL FORCES
1 SF bde
MANOEUVRE
Armoured
1 tk bde
Mechanised
11 MR bde
Air Manoeuvre
1 air aslt bde
1 AB bde
Mountain
1 lt mtn inf bde
COMBAT SUPPORT
3 arty bde
1 MRL bde

EQUIPMENT BY TYPE
MBT 340: 70 T-72; 100 T-64; 170 T-62
RECCE 19: 13 BRDM-2; 6 BRM
AIFV 399: 120 BMD-1; 9 BMD-2; 270 BMP-2
APC 309
APC (T) 50 BTR-D
APC (W) 259: 24 BTR-60; 25 BTR-70; 210 BTR-80
ARTY 487+
SP 83+: **122mm** 18 2S1 *Carnation*; **152mm** 17+: 17 2S3; 2S5 (reported); **203mm** 48 2S7
TOWED 200: **122mm** 60 D-30; **152mm** 140 2A36
GUN/MOR 120mm 54 2S9 *Anona*
MRL 108: **122mm** 60: 24 9P138; 36 BM-21; **220mm** 48 9P140 *Uragan*
MOR 120mm 42: 5 2B11; 19 2S12; 18 PM-120
AT • MSL • MANPATS 9K11 (AT-3 *Sagger*); 9K111 (AT-4 *Spigot*)
GUNS 100mm 36 MT-12/T-12

Air Force 7,500

FORCES BY ROLE
FIGHTER
1 regt with MiG-29/MiG-29UB *Fulcrum*; Su-27/Su-27UB *Flanker*
FIGHTER/GROUND ATTACK
1 regt with Su-24 *Fencer*; Su-24MP *Fencer-F** (ISR)
GROUND ATTACK
1 regt with Su-25/Su-25BM *Frogfoot*; Su-17M (Su-17MZ) *Fitter* C/Su-17UM-3 (Su-17UMZ) *Fitter* G

ELINT/TRANSPORT
1 regt with An-12/An-12PP *Cub*; An-26/An-26RKR *Curl*
TRANSPORT
Some sqn with An-24 *Coke*; Tu-134 *Crusty*
TRAINING
Some sqn with L-39 *Albatros*
ATTACK/TRANSPORT HELICOPTER
1 regt with Mi-24 *Hind* (attack); Mi-26 *Halo* (tpt); Mi-8 *Hip* (aslt/tpt);
1 regt with Mi-6 *Hook* (tpt); Mi-6AYa *Hook-C* (C2)

EQUIPMENT BY TYPE
AIRCRAFT 135 combat capable
FTR 30 MiG-29/MiG-29UB *Fulcrum*
FGA 74: 26 Su-17M (Su-17MZ)/Su-17UM-3 (Su-17UMZ) *Fitter* C/G; 23 Su-24 *Fencer*; 25 Su-27/Su-27UB *Flanker*
ATK 20 Su-25/Su-25BM *Frogfoot*
EW/Tpt 26 An-12 *Cub* (med tpt)/An-12PP *Cub* (EW)
ELINT 11 Su-24MP *Fencer* F*
ELINT/Tpt 13 An-26 *Curl* (lt tpt)/An-26RKR *Curl* (ELINT)
TPT • Light 2: 1 An-24 *Coke*; 1 Tu-134 *Crusty*
TRG 5 L-39 *Albatros* (9 more in store)
HELICOPTERS
ATK 29 Mi-24 *Hind*
C2 2 Mi-6AYa *Hook-C*
TPT 79 **Heavy** 27: 26 Mi-6 *Hook*; 1 Mi-26 *Halo* **Medium** 52 Mi-8 *Hip*
AD • SAM 45
TOWED S-75 *Dvina* (SA-2 *Guideline*); S-125 *Pechora* (SA-3 *Goa*)
STATIC S-200 *Angara* (SA-5 *Gammon*)
MSL
ASM Kh-23 (AS-7 *Kerry*); Kh-25 (AS-10 *Karen*)
ARM Kh-25P (AS-12 *Kegler*); Kh -28 (AS-9 *Kyle*); Kh-58 (AS-11 *Kilter*)
AAM • IR R-60 (AA-8 *Aphid*); R-73 (AA-11 *Archer*); **IR/SARH** R-27 (AA-10 *Alamo*)

Paramilitary up to 20,000

Internal Security Troops up to 19,000
Ministry of Interior

National Guard 1,000
Ministry of Defence

FOREIGN FORCES

Germany 163; some C-160 *Transall*

Table 11 **Selected Arms Procurements and Deliveries, Russia and Eurasia**

Designation	Type	Quantity (Current)	Contract Value	Prime Nationality	Prime Contractor	Order Date	First Delivery Due (Current)	Notes
Azerbaijan (AZE)								
T-90S	MBT	n/k	n/k	RUS	Rosoboron-export	2011	n/k	Unspecified number reported ordered in 2011. Delivery status unclear
Mi-35M *Hind*	Atk Hel	24	n/k	RUS	Rosvertol	2010	2011	First 4 delivered Dec 2011; 12 delivered by Aug 2012
Mi-17-1V *Hip*	MR Hel	40	n/k	RUS	Rosvertol	2010	2010	Delivery to be complete by end 2012
Heron	ISR UAV	5	see notes	ISR	IAI	2011	n/k	Reported to be part of US$1.6bn deal that also incl AD and AShM assets
Searcher II	ISR UAV	5	see notes	ISR	IAI	2011	n/k	Reported to be part of US$1.6bn deal that also incl AD and AShM assets
Belarus (BLR)								
Tor-M2 (SA-15 *Gauntlet*)	SAM	12	n/k	RUS	Almaz-Antey	2011	2011	First bty delivered 2011; second bty due by end 2012
Kazakhstan (KGZ)								
BTR-82A	AIFV	30	n/k	RUS	n/k	n/k	2012	For airborne forces
BTR-4	APC (W)	100	US$150m	UKR/KAZ	KMDB/ Kazakhstan Engineering	2012	2012	Joint production. 10 to be built 2012; remainder in 2013
Cobra	APC(W)	n/k	n/k	TUR/KAZ	Otokar/ Kazakhstan Engineering	2012	n/k	Joint production.
S-300PS	SAM	40	n/k	RUS	Rosoboron-export	2009	n/k	To equip 10 battalions. Negotiations continue; to be drawn from Russian stock
C-295	Tpt ac	2	n/k	Int'l	EADS (CASA)	2012	2012	First delivered Nov 2012. Second due 2013. Option for 6 more
EC145	Tpt Hel	2	n/k	Int'l	Eurocopter	2012	n/k	Part of a combined order for 8 including 6 for the Ministry of Emergency Situations
Russia (RUS)								
Bulava 30 (SS-NX-30)	SLBM	n/k	n/k	RUS	n/k	n/k	n/k	Development concluding. For *Borey*-class SSBN
BTR-82A	APC (W)	n/k	n/k	RUS	n/k	n/k	n/k	Delivery in progress
Tor-M2 (SA-15 *Gauntlet*)	SAM	n/k	n/k	RUS	Almaz-Antey	n/k	n/k	Deliveries yet to begin in late 2012
Buk-M2 (SA-17 *Grizzly*)	SAM	n/k	n/k	RUS	n/k	n/k	n/k	One bde set delivered by early 2012
S-400 *Triumf* (SA-21 *Growler*)	SAM	18 battalions	n/k	RUS	n/k	n/k	2007	4 regt deployed by late 2012; fifth due early 2013
S-300V4 (SA-23 *Gladiator/ Giant*)	SAM	12	n/k	RUS	Almaz-Antey	2012	n/k	
Pantsir-S1	AD	n/k	n/k	RUS	KBP	n/k	2010	Delivery in progress to S-400 regiments
Project 955/ *Borey*-class	SSBN	3	n/k	RUS	Sevmash Shipyard	1996	2013	Lead vessel launched Feb 2008; awaiting entry into service of *Bulava* missile
Project 955A/ *Borey*-A-class	SSBN	5	n/k	RUS	Sevmash Shipyard	2012	n/k	Construction delayed by price dispute. Contract signed in May 2012, although pricing dispute continues and will be reviewed in 2015
Project 885/ *Yasen*-class	SSN	5	n/k	RUS	Sevmash Shipyard	1993	2012	First of class, *Severodvinsk*, launched Jun 2010, with expected ISD 2012
Project 636.3/ *Kilo*-class	SSK	6	n/k	RUS	n/k	2010	2013	

Table 11 **Selected Arms Procurements and Deliveries, Russia and Eurasia**

Designation	Type	Quantity (Current)	Contract Value	Prime Nationality	Prime Contractor	Order Date	First Delivery Due (Current)	Notes
Project 677/ Lada-class	SSK	3	n/k	RUS	Admiralty Shipyards	1997	2010	First launched and commissioned in 2010, but construction suspended on further 2 boats in 2011
Project 22350/ Admiral Gorshkov-class	FFGHM	6	US$400m	RUS	Severnaya Verf Shipyard	2005	2013	First vessel ISD expected Nov 2013
Project 20380/ Steregushchiy-class	FFGHM	6	n/k	RUS	Severnaya Verf Shipyard/ Komosololsk Shipyard	2001	2008	First two vessels delivered. Third and fourth vessels launched; expected ISD 2012–13
Project 20380/ Improved Steregushchiy-class	FFGHM	2	n/k	RUS	Severnaya Verf Shipyard	2011	2015	First of class laid down Feb 2012
Project 11356M/ Admiral Grigorovich-class (Krivak IV)	FFGHM	6	n/k	RUS	Yantar Shipyard	2010	2013	3 vessels in build for Black Sea Fleet. 3 more ordered, with delivery scheduled for 2015–16. First ISD expected 2013
Project 21630/ Buyan-class	FSG	3	n/k	RUS	JSC Almaz Shipbuilding	2004	2006	For Caspian flotilla. Final vessel (Mahachkala) launched Apr 2012. ISD expected by end 2012
Project 21631/ Buyan M-class	FSG	5	n/k	RUS	Zelenodolsk Shipyard	2010	n/k	For Caspian flotilla. Further vessels may be ordered
Vladivostock-class (Mistral)	LHD	2	US$1.2bn	FRA	DCNS/STX	2011	2014	Contract signed in 2011 for two vessels. A further two vessels are expected
Project 11711E/Ivan Gren-class	LST	1	n/k	RUS	Yantar Shipyard	2004	2013	Launched May 2012. Delivery currently planned for 2013. Up to four more vessels planned
Tu-160 Blackjack	Bbr ac upgrade	15	n/k	RUS	UAC (Tupolev)	2007	2012	Upgrade of Blackjack fleet, programme lagging behind orginal schedule
MiG-29K Fulcrum D	Ftr ac	24	n/k	RUS	UAC (MiG)	2012	2013	20 MiG-29K and 4 MiG-29KUB. For navy
Su-30SM	FGA ac	30	n/k	RUS	UAC (Sukhoi)	2012	2012	Delivery to commence in late 2012
Su-34 Fullback	FGA ac	32	US$864m	RUS	UAC (Sukhoi)	2008	2010	Delivery in progress, original 2013 date appears unlikley to be met
Su-34 Fullback	FGA ac	60	n/k	RUS	UAC (Sukhoi)	2012	n/k	
Su-35S Flanker	FGA ac	48	see notes	RUS	UAC (Sukhoi)	2009	2012	Part of combined order for 48 Su-35S, 12 Su-27SM3 and 4 Su-30. Worth US$2.5bn; 6 in trials late 2012
An-140	Tpt ac	11	n/k	UKR	Antonov	2011	2012	First two ac delivered 2012
Yak-130	Trg ac	55	n/k	RUS	UAC (Yakolev)	2012	2012	To replace current L-39. Delivery in progress
Ka-52 Hokum B	Atk Hel	30	n/k	RUS	Progress	2008	2009	Twin-seat version of Ka-50 Black Shark. For air force. Delivery in progress
Turkmenistan (TKM)								
T-90S	MBT	40	n/k	RUS	Rosoboron-export	2009	2009	Initial order for 10 in 2009 with additional order for 30 in 2011
Ukraine (UKR)								
BTR-4E	APC (W)	n/k	n/k	UKR	KMDB	2012	n/k	
Gaiduck-class	FFGHM	4	UAH16.2bn (US$2.01bn)	UKR	Cherno-morsky Shipbuilding	2011	2016	First keel laid down 2011. All vessels expected to be delivered by 2016
An-70	Tpt ac	5	n/k	UKR	Antonov	1991	n/k	Flight testing resumed

Chapter Six
Asia

MILITARY MODERNISATION CONTINUES

Most Asian states have been expanding their military budgets and attempting to improve their armed forces' capabilities in recent years. This is largely a result of increasing uncertainty about the future distribution of power in the region and widespread suspicions, in some cases increasing tension, among regional armed forces. While these efforts are intended to deter potential adversaries, there is substantial evidence of action-reaction dynamics taking hold and influencing regional states' military programmes.

Analysts were waiting at the end of 2012 to see what effect China's once-in-a-decade leadership change might have on the wider Asian region. New capabilities displayed in 2012 provided further evidence of China's efforts to expand the capabilities of its People's Liberation Army (PLA). The United States' 'rebalance' to the Asia-Pacific and associated Air–Sea Battle concept were both widely seen as responses to Beijing's growing power and assertiveness in the region.

Concerns about Beijing's growing assertiveness were also reflected in rising tensions over maritime disputes in the East and South China Seas. China's maritime agencies have continued to send paramilitary vessels to promote and defend its extensive but ill-defined claims in the South China Sea. Meanwhile, China finally commissioned its first aircraft carrier, the *Liaoning*, in September 2012 (see p. 252). Some Chinese commentators emphasised the significance of the *Liaoning's* commissioning in relation to the maritime disputes around China's littoral, and the *Liaoning's* commissioning certainly affected other regional states' assessments of Chinese power.

North Korea continued efforts to develop its nuclear-weapons capability and its closely related long-range missile arsenal. Japan has made significant, if incremental, capability improvements in the face of North Korea's nuclear and missile programmes and the escalation of maritime disputes. Many factors, not least the deterrent effect of the US–Japan alliance, militated against the likelihood of open conflict, but the continuing deterioration of Japan's regional strategic environment provided impetus for efforts

to implement the 'dynamic defence force' idea (see p. 266).

India's defence policy retained a substantial focus on deterring Pakistan, primarily through the larger country's nuclear-weapons capability, but its defence planners increasingly view China as a potential strategic challenge and New Delhi has continued to invest in developing its military capabilities (see p. 259).

Southeast Asian states party to the dispute in the Spratly Islands have focused on using diplomacy, particularly through the Association of Southeast Asian Nations (ASEAN) and related institutions, to constrain Chinese adventurism. Nevertheless, continuing tensions in the South China Sea have unnerved several Southeast Asian governments, contributing to a greater or lesser degree to their attempts to improve their military capabilities.

In the Philippines, a funding shortage continued to stymie armed-forces modernisation. The 2013 military modernisation budget, approved in September 2012, only provided one-third of the US$120 million which the armed forces required annually for the latest five-year modernisation programme. In April 2012, Manila requested military assistance from the United States in the form of second-hand F-16 combat aircraft, naval vessels and radar systems. However, by the following month, the potential cost of operating F-16s had apparently led to this idea's abandonment; new plans for reviving the air force's combat-fighter capability involved acquiring 12 TA-50 advanced trainers from South Korea. In May 2012, the US transferred a second former *Hamilton*-class Coast Guard cutter to the Philippine Navy. The first ship of the class to be transferred, commissioned in March 2011, was involved in a stand-off in April 2012 with Chinese maritime surveillance paramilitary vessels off the disputed Scarborough Shoal in the South China Sea. Navy plans call for the frigates to be fitted with new weapons, including *Harpoon* anti-ship missiles.

The announcement in October 2012 of a framework agreement between the Philippine government and the country's major armed opposition group, the Moro Islamic Liberation Front, raised the prospect of peace in Mindanao in the southern Philippines, where a 40-year conflict had claimed an estimated 120,000 lives and required a major counter-insurgency commitment. This development could facilitate the armed forces' reorientation towards conventional warfare. However, internal security threats from other sources, notably the New People's Army and the Abu Sayyaf Group continued, and would prevent the armed forces from abandoning their watch on domestic security in the near future.

Although a claimant in the Spratly Islands dispute, Malaysia has not been particularly affected by the growing tensions in the South China Sea and has continued to pursue close relations with China. Indeed, in September 2012, the two countries held their first bilateral 'defence and security consultation', and agreed to strengthen 'mutual exchange and cooperation' in the military sphere. Defence minister Zahid Hamidi revealed that Malaysia was considering purchasing, and possibly producing, Chinese missile systems of undisclosed type.

Nevertheless, recognition of China's growing power has been one of many factors influencing continued efforts to boost the Malaysian armed forces' capabilities. The 2013 defence budget includes a RM 2.7 billion (US$885m) 'development' component, roughly 23% more than in 2012. The defence ministry will spend most of this on the four largest current procurement projects now under way, including six locally built, 2,750 tonne DCNS *Gowind* frigates under the Littoral Combat Ship project. The current major procurement decision concerns a contract for 18 new Multi-Role Combat Aircraft. A decision is expected during 2013 between the Dassault *Rafale*, Eurofighter *Typhoon*, Saab *Gripen*, Sukhoi Su-30MKM and Boeing F/A-18E/F. Procuring the aircraft will almost certainly require a larger development budget or supplementary funding. In the meantime, critics continue to stress that expensive military acquisition programmes may not automatically translate into improved capabilities: in October 2012, Chief of Navy Admiral Tan Sri Abdul Aziz Jaafar was forced to refute rumours that the navy's two *Scorpene* submarines were still not fully operational.

Singapore's government has continued to provide the resources necessary to expand military capabilities. The Singapore Armed Forces received a steady stream of new equipment, ensuring that the city-state maintains a lead in military technology over potential regional adversaries. However, some of the most important continuing capability developments involve the low-profile enhancement of C4I capacity through the Advanced Combat Man System and the Battlefield Management System. New ISR acquisitions in 2012 included *Scan Eagle* UAVs, to be operated from navy corvettes. Singapore's defence ministry has also negotiated and maintained training and exercise arrangements with regional and international partners, and these contribute significantly to SAF capabilities. For example, in September 2012, for the first time, Singapore's air force deployed F-15SG strike aircraft and G550-AEW ISR platforms to Darwin for the annual *Pitch Black* multinational air exercise with Australia, Indonesia, New Zealand, Thailand and the US. Defence relations with the US are closer than ever. Singapore air-force detachments there are training on F-15SG and F-16C/D combat aircraft, and AH-64D and CH-47D helicopters. Meanwhile, US deployments to Singapore will expand significantly with the arrival of the first Littoral Combat Ship, planned for the second quarter of 2013.

In Thailand, the government led by Prime Minister Yingluck Shinawatra has striven to remain on equable terms with the leadership of the armed forces (which in 2006 deposed her brother, Thaksin Shinawatra). Partly for this reason, the 2013 budget, announced in May 2012, indicated that annual defence spending would rise by 7% in 2013. However, the budget increase also occurred against the backdrop of serious border clashes with Cambodia between October 2008 and May 2011, clashes on the border with Myanmar between Karen rebel units and Myanmar's army, and continuing violence in Thailand's four southernmost provinces, where an obscure conflict involving Malay–Muslim insurgents, criminal gangs, and apparently unaccountable security forces has claimed more than 5,000 lives since early 2004.

Thailand's military procurement has remained eclectic. Major projects under way during 2012 included Phase 2 of the project to acquire 12 Saab *Gripen* combat aircraft and two associated Saab 340 AEW platforms: the second Saab 340 AEW was delivered in October 2012, and the second batch of six *Gripens* is due in 2013. A related development was the award, in April 2012, of a contract to equip the aircraft carrier HTMS *Chakri Naruebet* with the Saab 9LV Mk.4 combat system and with data links for communication with the *Gripens* and AEW aircraft.

In September 2012, the Cabinet approved funding for the next major acquisition programme, which will involve procurement of two new frigates by 2018.

This supersedes the earlier priority of purchasing as many as six submarines.

Myanmar's large armed forces are dominated by the army, reflecting their long involvement in combating numerous ethnic-minority rebel armies. After coming to power in March 2011, the partially civilian government of President Thein Sein has signed ceasefires with nearly one dozen armed groups, including the United Wa State Army and the Shan State Army–South. But although the president ordered Myanmar's army, the *Tatmadaw,* to halt offensive operations against the large Kachin Independence Army (KIA) in late 2011, peace talks have failed and fighting has continued. In August 2012, the KIA claimed that more than 10,000 troops had been deployed in Kachin State and were escalating operations. (See the IISS *Armed Conflict Database* for more analysis.) It remained unclear whether the political reforms led by the president, and supported by opposition leader Aung San Suu Kyi, would lead to peace in Kachin State and other areas of ethnic-minority unrest, and to military reforms affecting the *Tatmadaw*. However, in October 2012, there was a sign of willingness by other countries to engage more directly with the *Tatmadaw* as a result of the country's rapidly improving international image, when the US invited Myanmar to participate in the next annual *Cobra Gold* exercise in Thailand, in early 2013. The *Tatmadaw* used to see the *Cobra Gold* exercises as aimed at Myanmar, so its participation – even as an observer – would be significant. Then, in November, US President Barack Obama visited Myanmar.

ASIA DEFENCE ECONOMICS

Strong economic growth in Asia during 2010 (9.51%) and much of 2011 (7.76%) (see *The Military Balance 2012*, p. 208) had slowed by early 2012 because of a deteriorating external environment and weakening internal demand. Nonetheless, the region as a whole was still expected to expand by 6.67% in 2012.

Lower US growth and the ongoing eurozone crisis limited demand for Asian exports, which

---

Australia: budget reduces, but capability improves

As part of efforts to return its overall budget to surplus in the year to 30 June 2013, the federal government announced defence-spending cuts in May 2012. Defence spending for 2012–13 was reduced to A\$24.2bn (US\$25.1bn), down from a projected A\$26.5bn (US\$27.4bn) for 2011–12. Overall, the cuts should save A\$5.45bn by the end of the 2015–16 financial year.

Most of the reduction will be achieved by deferring equipment procurement and infrastructure improvements. Crucially, a decision on purchasing the air force's first 12 F-35 Joint Strike Fighters will be delayed by two years to 2014–15. But some planned procurement, including self-propelled artillery, was simply abandoned.

The government did, however, reaffirm its commitment to building 12 new submarines in Australia, and announced an in-depth study of the various build options.

Canberra also brought the next White Paper forward a year to 2013, and published a Defence Force Posture Review in May 2012 to provide part of the context for the White Paper.

Examining Australia's evolving regional strategic environment, the Posture Review concluded that the Australian Defence Force (ADF) needed to be able to support operations in the country's northern and western approaches, as well as joint operations with partners in the Asia-Pacific and around the Indian Ocean rim. It noted that the planned reduction of Australian forces in Afghanistan, Timor Leste and the Solomon Islands provided a chance for reorientation.

The Posture Review emphasised the importance of developing joint amphibious capabilities and the 'transformational effect' this would have on the ADF. It also stressed the need to develop the defence infrastructure of northern and western Australia, including expanding the capacity of Fleet Base West near Perth and upgrading air bases to support operations by 'future combat aircraft', KC-30 tankers and P-8 maritime-patrol aircraft.

Meanwhile, capability enhancements quietly continued. In October 2011, the last four of 24 F/A-18F *Super Hornet* fighters were delivered to the air force, which also received its sixth and final *Wedgetail* AEW platform in June 2012. Four out of five KC-30 tankers were delivered before the *Pitch Black* exercise in July–August 2012. In May 2012, the defence department announced a contract for ten C-27J transport aircraft.

The navy's *Hobart*-class Air Warfare Destroyer (AWD) and *Canberra*-class Landing Helicopter Dock (LHD) projects also made headway. Work began on the first AWD in Adelaide in September 2012, with commissioning scheduled for 2016. In October 2012, the hull of the first LHD arrived in Australia: once commissioned in 2014, it will be the navy's largest-ever warship.

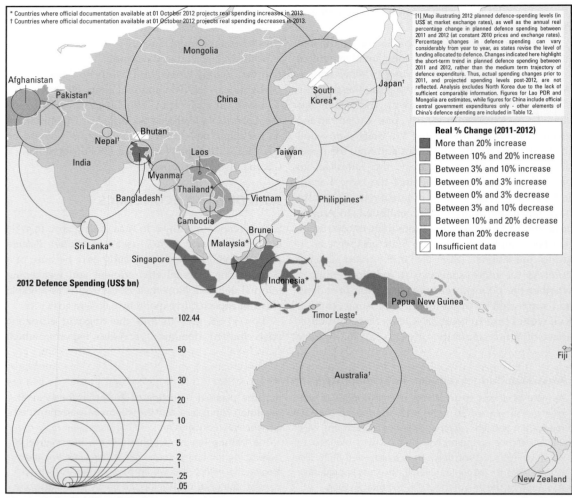

Map 7 **Asia Regional Defence Spending**[1]

particularly affected Hong Kong, Taiwan and South Korea. The withdrawal of fiscal stimulus measures implemented after 2008 in China and other Asian economies also constrained growth, as did the delayed effects of incremental monetary tightening across the region in 2011 in response to potential economic overheating and concerns over asset-price inflation.

Slowing economic growth in China and India further tempered the regional outlook. China began expansionary policy actions when the People's Bank of China cut its reserve requirements three times between May and July 2012, and lowered interest rates for the first time since 2008. However, in India, a combination of strong inflationary pressures, currency depreciation, trade deficits and rising public debt limited the government's ability to respond to

declining economic fundamentals (see India defence economics p. 261).

Overall, in the first half of 2012, Asia's growth was at its lowest rate since the 2008 financial crisis (from 2008–11 growth averaged 8.04%). Yet, as in previous years, Asia remained the global growth leader in 2012, with the Asian Development Bank forecasting the region would expand by at least two percentage points faster than the global average. Economic activity in Japan and Thailand was supported by reconstruction efforts following the March 2011 earthquake and tsunami and the October 2011 floods respectively. Higher consumer confidence and private consumption across Southeast Asia, particularly Indonesia and the Philippines, offset trade declines caused by the weakened external economic environment. High levels of capital investment in

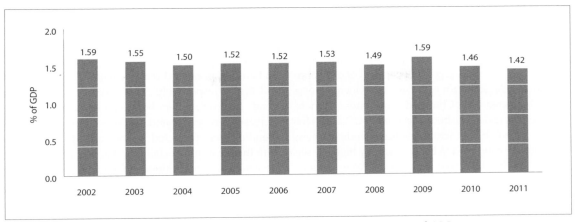

Figure 16 **East Asia and Australasia Regional Defence Expenditure** as % of GDP

the Australian mining sector, and reconstruction expenditure after flooding and Cyclone Yasi in 2011, saw 2.1% GDP growth in 2011 and a projected 3.3% for 2012. The IMF's October 2012 World Economic Outlook projected average growth rates across Asia in 2012 to be a healthy 5.18% (down from 5.46% in 2011). Falling global commodity prices, along with the reduction in aggregate demand pressures on domestic prices, served to dampen regional inflation. This was projected to average 5.54% in 2012, significantly down from 6.83% in 2011.

Defence spending trends

This resilient regional economic growth between 2010 and 2012 allowed Asian defence spending to increase strongly. Defence spending, at current prices and exchange rates, rose from US$257.42bn in 2010 to US$293.85bn in 2011, a nominal increase of 14.15%; it rose by a further 7.13% in 2012, to US$314.81bn. Of the US$20.96bn in nominal Asian spending increases between 2011 and 2012, 62.4% was accounted for by East Asia, followed by Southeast Asia (13.8%), South Asia (12.4%) and Australasia (11.4%). However, heightened currency volatility in 2010 and an inflationary spike in 2011 meant that nominal spending increases may give a distorted perspective on changes in the underlying resource levels allocated for defence. (Note: variations in nominal US dollar totals at current prices and exchange rates will in part reflect exchange rate movements and the effects of inflation, rather than the real, effective change in defence resourcing.) After discounting exchange rate and inflationary effects, defence spending in Asia rose by 3.76% in 2011, before accelerating to 4.94% in 2012 (both at constant 2010 prices and exchange rates). Overall, increases in the region's defence budgets remained broadly in line with GDP growth; defence spending as a percentage of Asian GDP remained relatively constant between 2010 and 2012, at approximately 1.41% (see bar charts in Figure 16). (Note: aggregate figures cited above will differ from those contained in *The Military Balance 2012*, in part due to a change in the composition of countries that make up the region 'Asia'. While *The Military Balance 2012* included Central Asian states under the 'Asia' chapter, in the current edition, these states have been re-allocated to the new 'Russia & Eurasia' section – see p. 199.)

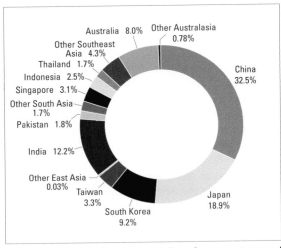

Figure 17 **Asia defence spending by country and sub-region**

East Asia

East Asia continued to dominate Asian defence spending (making up 63.9%, or just under two-thirds of the 2012 total), with spending rising in real terms by 3.63% in 2011 and 4.43% in 2012, to US$201.26bn. More than 90% of the 2011–12 East Asian increase was driven by increases in China's defence budget, where the official 2012 defence budget exceeded US$100bn for the first time (China's actual defence-spending levels, however, are estimated to be significantly higher – see p. 255). Having increased its share of Asian defence expenditure to above 30% for the first time in 2011, in 2012, China's defence budget rose by a further 8.3% in real terms (note: this refers to a percentage increase, rather than the 1.84% percentage point increase in China's share of Asian defence spending, and now accounts for some 32.5% of total Asian defence spending), and just over half (50.9%) of the East Asian sub-regional total. China's official defence budget is now around ten times higher than that of Taiwan, but Taiwan had the second-largest real increase in East Asian defence spending in 2012 (7.6%), with increased personnel costs incurred due to the country's transition towards an 'all-volunteer' force (see p. 273). South Korea's defence budget increased modestly in 2012 (1.8%), with a similar increase planned for 2013, partly to fund military pay increases (see p. 271).

Japan was the only East Asian country to reduce defence spending between 2010 and 2012; real spending was cut by 0.4% in 2012, causing the country's share of East Asian defence spending to fall below 20% of the sub-regional total. A further reduction of 1.7% is planned for 2013, reportedly the largest annual reduction in Japanese defence spending in half a century, in part due to mounting fiscal pressures stemming from the rising costs of social security and Japan's heavy debt burden (see p. 269).

South Asia

Defence spending in South Asia rose in real terms by 3.74% in 2012; at US$49.6bn, it accounted for 15.8% of total 2012 Asian defence spending. India comprised more than three-quarters of the South Asian total. Real defence spending growth slightly outpaced that seen in 2011 (4.6%), rising by 5.0% in 2012 (see India defence economics, p. 261).

Pakistan and Bangladesh also increased their defence budgets in 2012, by around 4.84% and 22.3% respectively. This followed real reductions in 2011, when spending fell by -1.8% and -5.8%. Spending in Bangladesh is projected to remain at elevated levels

in 2013, reflecting a major arms-procurement drive (see 'Selected Arms Procurements & Deliveries, Asia', p. 344).

By contrast, defence spending in Afghanistan and Sri Lanka experienced real declines in 2012, of 18.3% and 8.18% respectively. This reversed an upwards trend in 2011, when both countries experienced increases – of 57.5% and 10.7%. Sri Lankan defence spending was projected to increase again in 2013, with the government claiming that higher allocations were necessary to continue repayments on equipment acquired during the long-running civil war with the Liberation Tigers of Tamil Eelam (Tamil Tigers) that ended in 2009. Colombo said it also needed more money to maintain its heavy troop deployments across the country, particularly in the north.

Southeast Asia

Southeast Asia accounted for 11.6% of total Asian defence spending in 2012 (US$36.41bn). In line with Southeast Asia's robust economic performance, there were significant rises in real defence spending, at 7.85% in 2011 and 6.89% in 2012. Southeast Asian states also experienced some of the largest fluctuations in defence-spending levels across Asia, with large real increases seen in Vietnam (16.9% in 2012), Cambodia (8.14% in 2012) and the Philippines (37.1% in 2011 and 5.1% in 2012).

A substantial part of the Philippines' large 2011 increase stemmed from the reallocation of military retirement pensions from the Special Purpose Fund to the Department of National Defence budget. Nonetheless, the Philippines has increased funding for defence. In June 2011, the government increased military pay, partly in response to rising soft commodity-price inflation in 2010–11, while in 2012–13 capital expenditure was set to rise with Manila's planned procurement of transport aircraft, helicopters, coastal-patrol vessels and air/maritime defence systems. The 2013 coastguard budget was increased by 62% (in nominal terms), while discussions with the Italian government were continuing in late 2012 over the purchase of two *Maestrale*-class frigates. In July 2012, President Benigno Aquino announced a government proposal that around PHP100bn (US$2.3bn) be allocated to the Armed Forces of the Philippines Modernisation Programme fund, to be disbursed over five years. Of this, PHP28bn (US$640m) had already been allocated.

After almost 15 years of constrained defence spending in the wake of the 1997 Asian financial

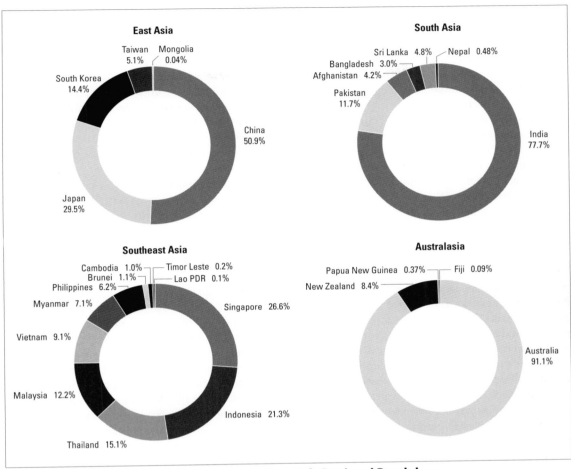

Figure 18 **Composition of Asia Defence Spending: Sub-Regional Breakdown**

crisis, Indonesia has recently been allocating more funds towards defence equipment recapitalisation, maintenance and modernisation. Indonesia increased its real defence spending significantly in 2011 (9.9%) and 2012 (33.3%), causing its share of total Southeast Asian spending to rise from 17.0% in 2010 to around 21.3% in 2012. The government expects to disburse some IDR150tr (US$17bn) on equipment procurement alone over the next 10–15 years, particularly as it modernises ageing air and naval capabilities (see pp. 264–6).

Malaysia and Thailand held their defence budgets relatively constant in local currency terms in 2012, after increasing defence spending in 2011. This stable approach meant that, after accounting for inflation, real spending fell in both countries by around 3.5%.

Singapore retained the highest defence budget in Southeast Asia in 2012 (US$9.68bn), although its 2.3% annual increases in defence spending in 2011 and 2012 was substantially below the sub-regional average (of 4.92% in 2011 and 6.94% in 2012). As a result, the city-state's defence spending as a proportion of the Southeast Asian total fell from 30.3% in 2010 to 26.6% in 2012.

Australasia

Australia announced defence-spending cuts in May 2012 (see box p. 247) as part of efforts to meet a promise by Treasurer Wayne Swan to return the federal budget to surplus in the 2012–13 financial year. Defence spending in New Zealand increased by 2.7% in real terms in 2012, as additional funds were allocated towards the development of tri-service network-centric warfare capabilities, part of the New Zealand Defence Force development programme announced by the government in October 2011.

CHINA

The *Liaoning* commissions

China's armed forces continue to develop power-projection capacity. The country's first aircraft carrier, the 50,000 tonne *Liaoning*, was commissioned in late September 2012 after a long refit, modernisation and refurbishment programme. The vessel, based on the hull of the uncompleted Soviet carrier *Varyag*, was not expected to be fully operational for at least several years, with an air group comprising combat aircraft and helicopters, and as part of a battle group viable in anything more than a low-intensity environment.

Nonetheless, China's intention to develop its aircraft-carrier capability is clear. In August–September 2012, during the vessel's tenth sea trial, observers noted poles on either side of the deck, possibly orientation markers for training pilots at sea. Prototype J-15 aircraft later landed on the carrier in November 2012. A Z-8 AEW helicopter was photographed landing on the vessel in late 2011 and images were again released in 2012 of Z-8 AEW take-offs.

The crew of the *Liaoning* is engaged in a wide range of flight-deck training. This includes hangar and flight-deck organisation, and practice marshalling with mock-ups of the developmental J-15 and dummy-guided weapons. Mock-up anti-ship missiles have been seen, suggesting that the J-15 might have a multi-role capability from the outset, unlike the Su-33, which has a purely air-defence role (see p. 254). Also, deck crew wearing a variety of coloured overalls (suggesting allocation of flight-deck tasks) have been observed working on aircraft, although it is difficult to draw precise conclusions from available imagery.

The vessels are obviously high-value targets as well as key providers of military capability, and they need protection. The Z-8 might operate in an AEW role, but it is unclear how far the PLAN has advanced towards carrier task-group operations providing protection against air and subsurface threats. A fixed-wing carrier-borne AEW aircraft, the JZY-01, is known to be under development. Since 2011, the vessel has been equipped with an active phased array radar system and the *Sea Eagle* 3D search radar and weapon systems including four 18-cell FL-3000N missile systems and two 12-tube anti-submarine rocket launchers.

Other less-publicised developments indicate the PLA's steady development of offensive military capa-bilities. For instance, in July 2012, Internet imagery revealed what appeared to be launch tubes for the DH-10 land-attack cruise missile (LACM) aboard a test vessel. The Second Artillery first deployed the ground-launched DH-10 variant in 2006–08, and an air-launched variant, under development for more than five years, is probably on the brink of entering service. While anti-ship missiles are often observed on PLAN ships, a ship-based DH-10 would be significant in terms of providing land-attack capability from the sea.

The development of two new Type-052D destroyers suggests a continuing desire to enhance blue-water capabilities. In August 2012, the first images of a Type-052D in the water appeared; observers noted 64 vertical launch-system tubes on the ship.

It is not yet clear whether the Type-052D will be built in quantity. In the past, the PLAN has constructed one or two vessels in a particular class before moving on to a more developed design. However, the last class developed, the Type-052C, included only six hulls over the past decade and, with the Type-052D perhaps reaching the technological limits of China's current shipbuilding design and construction, the PLAN may prefer to build a larger fleet of Type-052Ds over a longer period, so that early lessons can be incorporated in later batches. In combination with the Type-052Cs and other classes, these ships could form the backbone of a globally deployable destroyer fleet.

Increasingly distant deployments indicate the PLAN's growing power-projection capability. Counter-piracy patrols continue in the Gulf of Aden. These have allowed Chinese vessels to engage in cooperative maritime activities and have furthered the PLAN's knowledge of Indian Ocean ports for repairs and resupply. The patrols have also created direct contacts with otherwise remote navies, including those of European states and the US; and they have trained PLAN personnel in skills necessary for sustained distant deployments, in particular replenishment at sea.

The lack of modern replenishment ships and overseas bases is a continuing weak point on these operations. However, the launch of two new *Fuchi*-class replenishment ships in March and May 2012, doubled the number of this class of AOR.

Beijing is likely to avoid the complications inherent in establishing permanent foreign bases: it will more probably follow a 'places, not bases' strategy in forming strong relationships with key allies and partners in order to allow its naval vessels to dock, replenish and refit in key locations. There is speculation that Pakistan's Gwadar port, while it will continue to be developed largely as a commercial port, may also be used as a replenishment station for naval vessels, possibly including Chinese ships.

In July 2012, unnamed US officials reportedly said that China had test-fired a DF-41 intercontinental ballistic missile, although little information was provided. The DF-41 would, if deployed, be the first land-based missile able to reach the entire continental United States. The July test was reported to include a multiple independently targetable re-entry vehicle (MIRV), though it is unclear whether MIRVed warheads have yet been deployed on China's current longest-range ICBM, the DF-31A. This continues to be produced, with satellite imagery from 2011 suggesting that the 809 Brigade in Datong was receiving DF-31s in place of DF-21s. Taiwan's 2010 report on Chinese military power claimed that the Second Artillery had also deployed a few new DF-16 MRBMs. Within a month, China also conducted a successful test of the JL-2 ballistic missile. The JL-2 is the submarine-launched version of the DF-31 road-mobile ICBM, to be deployed on the Type-094 nuclear-ballistic-missile submarine. Successful development and deployment of the hitherto troubled JL-2 would give China a more secure second-strike deterrent, as the four Type-094 submarines currently in the water would then be able to provide continuous at-sea deterrence.

China's overseas security interests remain dominated by regional issues, including Taiwan, the Korean peninsula and disputed territories with India and in the East and South China Seas. A sign of near-sea concerns was the launch of six Type-056 corvettes within six months in 2012. The Type-056 is intended to replace the outdated *Jianghu* I-class frigates. The speed with which the Type-056 has been developed suggests it will be deployed in significant numbers to give China greater control over its coastal areas and nearby enclosed seas. The Type-056 is, in part, intended to close China's long-standing gap in anti-submarine warfare capability, which regional countries are attempting to exploit by buying attack submarines. The development of a maritime patrol aircraft (MPA) would be a major step in closing this gap, and in late 2011, photographs of a Shaanxi Y-8 MPA appeared on the Internet. Its entry into service will improve China's surveillance over its littoral and its ability to detect the growing number of submarines in the region.

Aerospace

Development continues of extra J-11 types, including an apparent strike version of the aircraft that may be designated J-16. Flight testing of two J-20 prototypes continues and a third airframe was shown publicly in October 2012. Beijing also unveiled a medium fighter design with low-observable characteristics, unofficially dubbed the J-21 or J-31 (see box below). Meanwhile, front-line deliveries of the J-10 medium fighter continue, replacing obsolescent types.

China's maritime paramilitaries

The capabilities required for contingencies in China's maritime littoral are neither long-range nor militarily advanced. Unarmed paramilitary vessels, particularly from China Marine Surveillance (CMS) and the Fisheries Law Enforcement Command (FLEC), undertake the majority of China's activities in support of Beijing's claims to sovereignty in the South China Sea. CMS vessels confronted the US-donated Philippine Navy flagship *Gregorio del Pilar* in April 2012 near the disputed feature of Scarborough Shoal, beginning a stand-off that lasted months. Although the situation subsequently eased and China did not deploy naval vessels, Beijing's firm stance and its successful use of coercive economic diplomacy (through import quotas) and coercive maritime diplomacy through the use of maritime paramilitaries underlined China's growing assertiveness over its maritime interests.

The use of maritime paramilitary forces has diverse benefits, including the demonstration of de facto sovereignty and reduction of the chance of escalation. It is perhaps for this reason that China is expanding its paramilitary forces, with 36 new vessels planned for the China Marine Surveillance force in the next five years. CMS will also receive numbers of former naval vessels; two frigates and two auxiliaries were delivered in 2012. CMS is one of five maritime paramilitary agencies and, in combination with FLEC, are the forces most often employed. Maritime Safety Administration vessels are also unarmed and its sizeable ships can often be seen in foreign ports on goodwill missions. Two other paramilitaries, the China Coast Guard and the General Administration of Customs, are limited in their capabilities and confined to internal and coastal waters.

Air force efforts to bolster long-range airlift capacity had been based on acquiring more than 30 extra Il-76s. A 2005 deal with Moscow unravelled because Russia was unable to manufacture the aircraft to the required schedule. As an interim measure, Beijing is believed to have acquired five second-hand Il-76s from Belarus. The problems encountered with Moscow over the Il-76 deal probably strengthened support for an indigenous programme, with the Xian and Shenyang aerospace companies working on a four-engine turbofan aircraft. A prototype was reportedly under construction in late 2012. Russia continues to harbour hopes of further transport aircraft sales, offering China the IL-476, a new upgraded version of the Il-76.

The failure to secure additional Il-76s may have hampered the air force's AEW and tanker plans: only five KJ-2000 AEW aircraft have been built, while the ageing H-6 (Tu-16 *Badger*) continues as the basis for the air force's small tanker fleet. Special mission aircraft also continue to be added to the inventory, with the ubiquitous Y-8 platform being used as the basis for diverse ISR applications.

Ground forces

The army still dominates PLA political structures, but many of the higher-profile procurements are now for the air force, navy and Second Artillery Corps. This reflects a gradual reorientation of the army-centred PLA. Beijing feels increasingly comfortable with the ability of its armed forces to protect its land borders.

Furthermore, the clearer delineation between the People's Armed Police (PAP) and PLA in internal security operations means the armed forces are less likely to be called out.

That said, the army is continuing to reorganise and receive substantial investment, in efforts to make it a more flexible, leaner force capable of rapid combined-arms operations. At the heart of this transformation is the 'brigadisation' process, whereby regiments and divisions have been recast as combined-arms brigades. By early 2012, PLA army aviation regiments and armoured divisions were reforming as brigades. The development of 'heavy', 'medium' and 'light' formations, along with the brigadisation process of 'create, test and adjust' is similar to the Russian experience of army reform and arguably mirrors the experiences of Western armed forces; the same can be said of the developing capabilities of the PLA ground forces, with increased emphasis on platforms capable of adapting to differing firepower, protection and mobility demands.

In 2010, Beijing purchased 11 mine-resistant ambush-protected vehicles and related technology from South African firm Mobile Land Systems. An outcome of this transfer appeared to be the Norinco 8M infantry fighting vehicle unveiled in June 2012. It is unclear whether the 8M, which has both military and police variants, will be adopted wholesale by the PLA or PAP or will remain export-oriented. However, increasing protection is also evident in

Another year, another stealthy aircraft

In September 2012, China's aerospace ambitions were again confirmed when images emerged of a twin-engine medium fighter manufactured by the Shenyang Aerospace Company, unofficially identified as either the J-21 or J-31. Unlike the *Chengdu* J-20 heavy fighter, unveiled in January 2011 and gauged by some analysts as of possibly Russian heritage, the J-21 reflects US designs, with echoes of the F-22 and the F-35. This has led to speculation of industrial espionage during its development.

As with the J-20, Beijing has yet to comment formally on the nature or specific purpose of the J-21 project. The J-21 airframe has almost all the hallmarks of a low observable design, and is missing the large canards that feature on the J-20. That said, the aft quadrant and engine nozzles do not appear optimised to minimise radar and infrared signatures, although this may reflect its prototype status.

The extent to which the structural materials used are appropriate for a low-observable design remains un-

clear, as does the degree to which the sensor suite would support stealth operations. It is widely speculated that the first aircraft could be fitted with the Russian RD-93 engine, which is being exported to China for Pakistan-bound JF-17 light fighters.

The J-21 is smaller than the J-20, and it may be intended to complement the larger aircraft. At the end of 2012, however, it remained unclear which of the services was the project's initial sponsor, or indeed whether the design began as a competitor to the J-20. The Shenyang prototype also features characteristics of a carrier-borne fighter. However, the PLAN already has a carrier-borne multi-role fighter under development, in the Shenyang J-15. The J-15 is based on the locally produced variant of the Su-27, while Chinese industry may also have benefitted from the purchase of a prototype Su-33 from Ukraine. At least five J-15 prototypes are being tested.

other areas; other Chinese infantry fighting vehicles were observed during 2012 sporting bolt-on armour.

Army equipment has been one area where the Chinese defence industry has successfully developed and marketed indigenous designs. While some retain design features from Soviet or Russian equipment, China is essentially self-sufficient in all ground-based anti-armour weapons, including laser-guided artillery projectiles and wire-guided anti-tank weapons. Armoured vehicle programmes also continue to develop, with 2012 seeing new versions of lightweight infantry fighting vehicles, armoured personnel and security vehicles produced for domestic and export markets. During the year, ZBD08 infantry fighting vehicle were issued to regular line units. Like the previous Type-04 AIFV, the Type-08 outwardly resembles a BMP-type platform, but has better armour and an improved main gun. The Type-08 chassis has also been used as the basis for a number of support variants, forming a common family of armoured vehicles in a fashion similar to the PLA's wheeled Type-09 APC and Type-05 AAV.

Defence economics

The equipment programmes outlined here, and the PLA's rapid modernisation, have been enabled by sustained double-digit annual percentage growth in defence spending over the past decade. China is now clearly the second-largest defence spender in the world. However, it is unclear whether the economic growth witnessed over the past 30 years, and therefore defence-spending growth, will continue indefinitely. The slower rate of Chinese economic growth, to 7.6% in the second quarter, may remain enviable by international standards but also suggests that China may struggle to maintain the defence-spending growth rates it has seen. The 'easy growth' China has experienced since opening up in 1979 may be over, as the population demands higher wages and the debt created during the 2008 stimulus rises (although, as a percentage of GDP, China's debt remains lower than in most developed countries). While China's military technology will continue to catch up with its more advanced rivals, the pace of improvement may be less rapid in future.

Given the rapid growth in China's military spending over the past decade, the question arises of how long it will be before China may be expected to rival the US as the world's largest defence spender. Such projections are fraught with difficulty because they rely on assumptions about future economic growth rates and the trajectories of not just China's defence spending, but also that of the US. While neither definitive nor clearly predictive, they can offer an indication.

Figure 19 shows the potential future convergence in Chinese and US defence spending, assuming that average defence-spending growth in both countries between 2001 and 2012 is maintained. If US base defence-budget spending figures contained in the FY12 defence budget request submitted to Congress (in February 2011) are extrapolated, these converge with projections of the official PLA budget in around 15 years, in 2028. If the lower US base defence spending contained in the FY13 budget request is used instead, convergence with official PLA budget projects occurs slightly sooner, in 2026. Under sequestration (see pp. 59–66), this convergence would occur earlier still, in 2025.

However, as noted each year in *The Military Balance*, official Chinese defence budget figures probably underestimate the true extent of Beijing's defence spending. Although official figures include personnel, operations and equipment expenditure, it is widely held that other military-related expenditures are omitted – such as allocations for R&D and overseas weapons purchases. A fuller account of China's true military-spending levels should also include funding allocated to the People's Armed Police (PAP). As shown in Table 12, if estimates of these additional items are included, Chinese defence spending rises by a factor of approximately 1.4–1.5 relative to officially published figures, to an estimated RMB883.3bn (US$136.7bn) using market exchange rates (MER). If these higher estimates of Chinese spending are projected into the future, convergence with US defence spending could occur as early as 2023 (if US FY13 proposed spending levels are accepted) or 2022 (if sequestration is instituted).

Of course, several factors might delay or even prevent such convergence. A lower trajectory of economic growth in China as the global economy slows, or a downshift in economic activity as the country attempts to move away from an export-oriented growth model, or economic turbulence as China attempts to modernise its fledgling financial markets and uncompetitive banking sector – these are all factors that could diminish economic growth, limiting the resources available for defence and, at the very least, delaying the date of convergence.

For example, if the average nominal defence spending increase in China slowed to 7.8% (half the

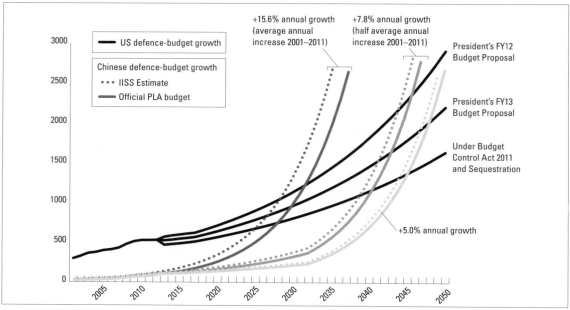

Figure 19 **China–United States Defence Expenditure Convergence 2001–2050**

15.6% average increase in nominal Chinese spending between 2001 and 2012), official PLA spending would only converge with the FY13 US base budget spending projection in 2038 (2036 under sequestration). At 5% average annual spending growth, official Chinese spending converges with the US FY13 base budget projection in 2042 (2040 under sequestration). A sharp

increase in US defence spending under a future US administration would have a similar delaying effect on convergence. Alternatively, a combination of the two could occur: US spending growth increases and Chinese spending growth reduces. The estimates provided here should thus be seen as indicative projections based on current trends; and on the

Table 12 **China Defence Budget Trends and Estimates[1] (2009–11)**

	2009	2010	2011
China GDP (RMB bn)	34,090	40,151	47,156
China GDP Growth	9.2%	10.4%	9.2%
Official Defence Budget (RMB bn)	**495.1**	**533.3**	**583.0**
Nominal % Change	18.5%	7.7%	9.3%
Real % Change	19.2%	1.8%	4.7%
Official Defence Budget as a % of Total Outlays	6.5%	5.9%	5.3%
Official Defence Budget as a % of GDP	1.45%	1.33%	1.24%
Total Estimated Defence Spending (RMB bn)	**671.8**	**753.4**	**883.3**
Nominal % Change	16.3%	12.1%	17.2%
Real % Change	17.0%	6.0%	9.1%
Total Estimated Defence Spending as a % of Total Outlays	8.8%	8.4%	8.1%
Total Estimated Defence Spending as a % of GDP	1.97%	1.88%	1.87%
Official Defence Budget (US$ bn, MER)	**72.5**	**78.7**	**90.2**
Total Estimated Defence Spending (US$ bn, MER)	**98.4**	**111.1**	**136.7**
Total Estimated Defence Spending (US$ bn, MER & PPP)	**170.0**	**178.0**	**197.9**
US$1=Y (MER)	6.83	6.78	6.46

Source: China Statistical Yearbooks (2010–2012) and Congressional Research Service, 'Conventional Arms Transfers to Developing Nations' (2002–2009, 2003–2010 and 2004–2011).
[1] Estimate figures for 2012 only available after release of the China Statistical Yearbook 2013 (in late 2013). See previous editions of The Military Balance for further details on estimates, in particular editions from 2006, p. 249 and 2010, p. 392.

balance of probabilities, any convergence is more likely to occur after 2028 rather than before, should it occur at all. It should also be noted that in considering possible convergence between China's defence-spending levels and the US base defence budget, this discussion excludes military expenditures on overseas contingency operations (OCO) allocated to operational military activities, such as those undertaken in Iraq and Afghanistan. OCO funding is by nature ad hoc and can vary considerably year by year.

China's defence industry

An ambitious upgrade of China's military technological capabilities is under way, and an array of new weapons is emerging from research and production facilities. Priorities for the new 12th Five Year Defence Plan (2011–15) were set out at the All-Army Armament Work Conference in late 2011. There were also calls to accelerate defence modernisation and close the wide technological gap with foreign defence establishments. After 15 years of reform and investment, generational improvements in strategic and conventional weapons capabilities, record corporate profits, soaring rates of patent applications and approvals and an increasingly well-qualified workforce signal a defence industry that is becoming more innovative and effective. However, structural, operational and governance problems remain – from entrenched corporate monopolies to the absence of a rules-based acquisition system.

Growing defence economy

China's defence industrial sector is enjoying a period of unprecedented expansion and creativity fuelled by generous state funding (see p. 255) and military demand. Average annual revenues from the ten leading state-owned defence corporations have expanded by around 20% since the mid-2000s. Total reported revenues from these firms came to an estimated Rmb1.477trillion (US$233bn) in 2011, according to the Study of Innovation and Technology in China run by the Institute of Global Conflict and Cooperation at the University of California. Around one-third of defence spending is on equipment expenses, according to official explanations. This includes R&D, experimentation, procurement and maintenance activities, and would make the 2012 equipment budget around Rmb220bn (US$34.8bn).

However, defence industry financial data suggest that PLA acquisitions maybe significantly greater than these official figures. Approximately one-quarter of the ten defence corporations' income, or Rmb370bn (US$58bn), is likely to derive from defence-related business, with civilian output comprising the remainder. Even accounting for modest levels of foreign arms exports, estimated at between US$1bn and US$1.4bn annually, these figures suggest that Chinese military research, development, and acquisition (RDA) spending is at least 50% higher than the official figures. Though the PLA might be the defence industry's largest source of funding, the State Administration for Science, Technology, and Industry for National Defence (SASTIND) is another major source. As the central government's defence industrial regulatory agency, SASTIND provides substantial funds for R&D as well as industrial support.

China's internal security apparatus makes up an increasing proportion of the defence and broader national-security economy. In 2010, the public security budget surpassed the official defence budget. The 2012 public security budget, at Rmb701.8bn (US$111bn), was 11.5% higher than in 2011, mirroring the rate of defence-budget growth. The public security budget encompasses law-enforcement organisations from the PAP to the court and prison systems. Most outlays are likely to go towards personnel costs rather than equipment.

Defence corporations

The strong growth and profitability of China's ten state-owned defence corporations indicates their improving efficiency. Total industry earnings in 2011 were Rmb10bn more than in 2010, representing a profit margin of 5.4% for that year. In comparison, US defence firms' estimated profit margins were around 10.5% in 2010.

There is no breakdown between civilian and military sales, but contractors have long complained that they struggle to make any profits from the PLA. This, they say, stems from old regulations limiting profit margins on military contracts to a fixed 5% on top of actual costs. PLA acquisition officials argue that contractors inflate costs. There are few performance incentives for contractors to lower costs by, for instance, more cost-effective design or manufacturing. So risk-taking and innovation are discouraged. The PLA and civilian authorities have made concerted efforts to overhaul weapons pricing, with only modest progress.

Of the six sectors that constitute China's defence industry, the ordnance industry is the largest in terms of revenue and size of workforce. The two dominant companies, China Ordnance Equipment Group (COEG) and China Ordnance Industry Group (Norinco), accounted for 40% of total defence industry revenue in 2011. However, most of their output is in commercial non-defence goods. The aviation and shipbuilding industries are the next largest sectors, with 2011 revenue of more than Rmb250bn (US$39.4bn) each, followed by the space and missile, nuclear, and defence electronics and information technology sectors.

R&D and innovation

The *China Innovative Enterprises Development Report 2011* showed that the space and missile industry spent most on R&D. The R&D expenditures of China Aerospace Science and Technology Corporation (CASTC) and China Aerospace Industry Corporation (CASIC), totalled Rmb21.5bn (US$3.4bn) in 2010, or around 10% of revenue. CASTC accounted for nearly two-thirds of this expenditure and had the third-largest R&D spend of all state-owned corporations. The shipbuilding industry had the second-highest spending, with the combined R&D of its two major corporations reaching Rmb12.4bn (US$1.96bn) in 2010, equivalent to 5% of revenue. All defence corporations have to spend at least 3% of their annual revenues on R&D by 2020.

The PLA and SASTIND also have sizeable R&D budgets. Further defence-related R&D funding can be found in other parts of the state budget, including science and technology-development programmes.

The report also provided information on state-owned corporations' patent activities. These are often used as a proxy measure of innovation. According to PLA statistics, there has been an annual 40% rise in defence-related patent applications since 2000. This increase in R&D and patent activity demonstrates the high priority that the defence authorities have placed on developing indigenous defence capabilities. A high-level review conference on the state of defence R&D in late 2011 noted a substantial boost during the 11th Five Year Plan (1996–2000) with major breakthroughs in critical bottlenecks, higher rates of converting R&D into actual production, and an improvement in the level of research talent entering the defence science and technology industries. PLA formations and defence firms have also been establishing defence laboratories to conduct both basic and applied R&D.

Obstacles to future progress

The defence industry still faces challenges that could impede progress. One is that segments of the defence industry continue to operate under socialist central planning principles. Another is a continuing lack of competitive mechanisms for awarding contracts, resulting from the defence industry's monopolistic structure. Contracts are awarded through single-sourcing mechanisms to the ten state-owned defence corporations, and competitive bidding and tendering only occur for non-combat support equipment. At the end of the 1990s, there was an effort to inject more competition by splitting into two each company in charge of a defence sub-sector, but this did little to curb this monopoly structure – seen by some analysts as the biggest single obstacle to long-term reform.

Bureaucratic fragmentation is another problem and affects critical coordination and command mechanisms within the PLA. The PLA General Armament Department (GAD), is only responsible for managing the armament needs of the ground forces, PAP and militia. The navy, air force, and Second Artillery have their own armament bureaucracies. This compartmentalised structure undermines efforts to promote joint undertakings.

A lack of coordination and bureaucratic rivalries are also evident in the PLA's four general departments. This led military authorities to establish a Strategic Planning Department (SPD) in November 2011 that would be housed within the General Staff Department. However, the GAD and General Logistics Department are reluctant to allow any diminution of their authority and influence in key management, budgetary, and planning issues. The RDA process is also plagued by compartmentalisation and linkages among relevant groups tend to be ad hoc in nature with major gaps in oversight, reporting, and information sharing.

If China's defence industry is to meet its goal of catching up by the 2020s with the advanced technologies developed and deployed by other – primarily Western – states, it will need to successfully move to a market-oriented, rules-based system. This will require a decisive break from its central planning legacy, taking a bolder approach to tackle the defence industry's underlying weaknesses. For the time being, the PLA leadership appears satisfied to continue with gradual reform and modernisation, although in select high-priority areas, such as space and missiles, there is a willingness to pursue more intensive and bolder development strategies.

INDIA

Having signed a strategic partnership with Afghanistan in late 2011 and unveiled a 'Connect Central Asia' policy in June 2012, India is clearly looking for a wider security role in its region. However, its defence policy remains dominated by concerns over China and Pakistan. In October – the fiftieth anniversary of India's border war with China – Defence Minister A. K. Antony insisted his country was now capable of 'defending every inch' of its territory. India's concern over China has a strong maritime dimension, in light of the PLA Navy's recent forays into the Indian Ocean.

Internal security remains a challenge. Prime Minister Manmohan Singh said in his 15 August 2012 independence-day speech that Maoist-inspired Naxalism was 'still a serious problem'. He also used the speech to promise to keep modernising India's armed and paramilitary forces and to provide them 'with the necessary technology and equipment'. He singled out those 'scientists and technologists who have enhanced our prestige by successfully testing the *Agni* V Missile'.

This missile was fired for the first time in April 2012. It is intended to have an operational range of more than 5,000km, taking it very close to the widely accepted 5,500km range threshold for an intercontinental ballistic missile.

Capability improvements

Armour, artillery, and ground-based air defence remain priorities in the modernisation programme, although ageing systems have often been replaced less quickly than desired; in early 2012, former army chief General V.K. Singh wrote to the prime minister raising concerns over 'deficiencies' within the army, including anti-armour and air defence. Nonetheless, India continues to improve its armoured forces: deliveries of T-90 main battle tanks continue, and the army plans to field the *Arjun* MkII. The army also plans to enhance the technology available to its infantry. The F-INSAS (Futuristic Infantry Soldier As A System) project is aimed at developing weapons, sensors, personal protection and communications to be fielded at battalion level by 2015. To modernise its ageing surface-to-air missile systems, the army plans to deploy the long-delayed indigenous *Akash* medium-range surface-to-air missile system from 2013.

Ensuring the security of sea lines of communication, energy supplies and the coast are maritime priorities. The navy also sees itself becoming a 'net security provider' to island nations in the Indian Ocean, given its activity in training exchanges, EEZ and air surveillance, as well as the provision of naval assets and refit facilities.

The navy accounts for 18% of the defence budget and has several major national procurement projects under way, including aircraft carriers, submarines, advanced surveillance systems and precision-guided weapons. To guide its modernisation, the navy is adopting a capability-based rather than threat-based approach, and has developed a 15-year plan to try to ensure development of a balanced fleet with adequate reach and combat power. The navy plans to have at least two fully operational and combat-capable carriers available at any given time. One carrier (the vintage *Viraat*) is currently operational, while boiler malfunctions during sea trials have again delayed the delivery of the *Vikramaditya* from Russia. The vessel will now not be handed over until the end of 2013. Despite these delays, 15 MiG-29K fighters have been delivered for carrier operations, and the first of an additional 29 MiG-29Ks is expected to fly in 2013. Delays in receiving steel plates and technical equipment such as diesel alternators and gearboxes mean that the launch of the first indigenous 37,500 tonne aircraft carrier, or 'Air Defence Ship', is now expected in 2013. The intended air wing is believed to comprise up to 30 aircraft. The government has approved two additional indigenous carriers. Other naval air elements are being strengthened, with delivery of P-8I maritime patrol aircraft from 2013 intended to expand surveillance capacity.

Under Project 75, six new *Scorpene*-class submarines are under construction at Mazagon Dock in Mumbai in collaboration with France's DCNS. The boats are three years late, with the first vessel now likely to be delivered in 2015 and the last in 2018.

After a twenty-year gap, India has also returned to operating nuclear-powered submarines. The Russian-built Project 971 *Akula*-II-class guided missile boat INS *Chakra* was delivered in April 2012. It is being leased for ten years, and the navy plans to use it as a training platform for the indigenous *Arihant* nuclear-powered ballistic-missile submarine. Sea trials and missile tests will reportedly take place by early 2013. Its K-15 ballistic missile, with a range of 750km, is reportedly ready to enter service. India plans to use its nuclear submarines as a key plank of its nuclear deterrent, Admiral Nirmal Verma, India's former navy chief, said at the IISS in June 2012.

Map 8 **India bolsters border dispositions**

India continues to reinforce its military capability in its border regions with Pakistan and China. The air force has over the past two to three years deployed its most capable multi-role combat aircraft, the Sukhoi Su-30MKI *Flanker*, at bases in the northeast and in the northwest, while the army established two additional mountain divisions (the 56th and 71st) and plans a mountain strike corps in the former region. *Flankers* were deployed to Tezpur and Chabua air bases in 2009 and 2011 respectively, with the type being deployed to Bhatinda and Halwara during 2012. Leh and Nyoma are likely planned forward-operating bases for the *Flanker*, with the latter being upgraded presently. Nyoma is under 15 miles from the Line of Actual Control with China. See explanatory notes p. 570 for key to symbols.

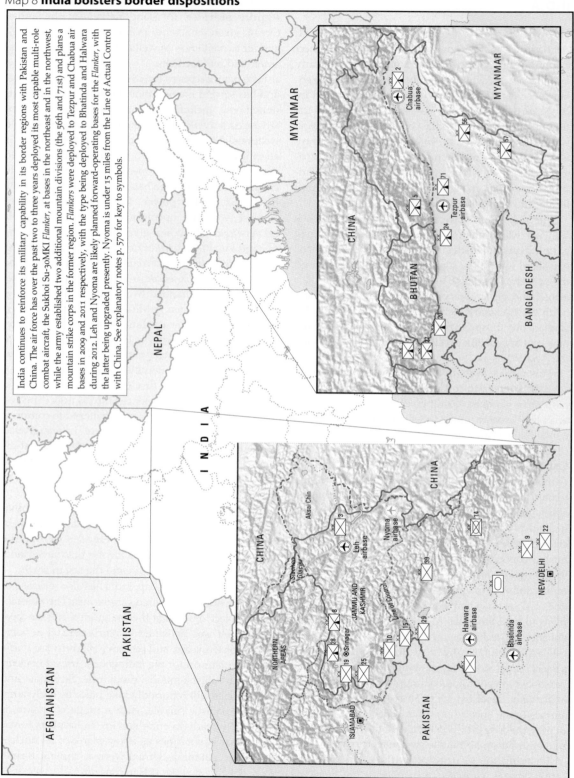

India finally selected the Dassault *Rafale* to meet the Medium Multi-Role Combat Aircraft requirement in January 2012, although contracts remained unsigned in October 2012. Air-force modernisation is particularly driven by regional concerns. Since 2011, China has unveiled two new combat aircraft exhibiting low-observable design characteristics, while the PLA air force also continued to develop and field J-10 and J-11 variants. Pakistan, meanwhile, continues to deploy more JF-17 light fighters, while also receiving its final F-16s from the US. So it is not surprising that since 2010, India's air force has based Su-30MKI *Flanker* squadrons in the east of the country near the Chinese border, and in the west close to Pakistan. The eighth front-line Su-30MKI squadron was due to form at Sirsa at the end of 2012 (see map, p. 260).

The air force also hopes to acquire at least 272 Su-30MKIs. In late 2012, there were negotiations with Russia over a new batch of 42 aircraft with improved avionics and sensors. The Su-30MKI will be joined after 2020 by a new Sukhoi aircraft developed to meet the Russian air force's PAK FA requirement; currently this bears the designation T-50 (see p. 203). As of late 2012, India had a notional requirement for 144 of the type, although this figure may change.

Delivery of the air force's ten Boeing C-17 *Globemaster* airlifters will begin in 2013, while the last of its six Lockheed Martin C-130J *Hercules* was delivered in early 2012. An order for six more was anticipated as of late 2012. In October 2012, the development phase was approved in the long-running proposal to jointly develop a Medium Transport Aircraft with Russia. India is also acquiring three EMB-145 airborne early-warning and control (AEW&C) aircraft to complement its three larger A-50EI AEW&C. Two of the three EMB-145s were due to be delivered by the end of 2012. Selection of a type to meet a further tanker-transport aircraft was also expected in late 2012.

Defence economics

The previously buoyant Indian economy stagnated in 2011 and 2012, with growth declining from 10.1% in 2010 to 6.8% in 2011 and just 4.7% in 2012 (IMF October 2012 projection). The slowdown has been spurred by declining business confidence in the face of political paralysis over economic reforms; as well as by rising inflation (8.9% and 10.3% in 2011 and 2012 respectively, due to higher oil and soft commodity prices), which dampened private consumption. Higher interest rates put in place to combat the inflationary pressures also deterred capital investment, while higher commodity prices caused a widening of the trade deficit. With deteriorating economic conditions, the government continued to run higher than expected budget deficits, of around 5.9% of GDP in FY2011/12. The diminished short-term growth prospects, faltering economic liberalisation, persistent current account and budget deficits, combined with increased risk aversion in global currency markets, caused the rupee to depreciate to record lows in 2012 – which further exacerbated inflationary pressures.

The deteriorating macroeconomic environment has affected real defence-spending levels. Higher inflation eroded much of the large nominal increases in the Indian defence budget, which was raised by 12.8% in 2011 (to INR1.71tr or US$36.1bn) and 13.2% in 2012 (to INR1.93tr or US$38.5bn). At constant 2010 prices and exchange rates, the real increase in spending was much lower – 4.6% in 2011 and 5.0% in 2012. The declining rupee has had a particularly pernicious effect. India still imports some 65% of its equipment requirements, paying for these in foreign currencies rather than in rupees, so a lower rupee has diminished the MoD's purchasing power.

Defence industry

For many years, there was little internal competition in India's defence industry. State firms dominated the sector after the Industrial Policy Resolution of 1948 prevented private Indian defence firms from entering the domestic market. Between the mid-1960s and mid-1990s, private Indian firms were limited to producing basic and intermediate components as well as spare parts. Liberalisation only came in 2001, in a national-security review following the 1999 Kargil conflict. At this time, the government permitted private organisations to hold 100% equity in defence firms, subject to licensing requirements.

But India's state defence sector remains powerful. Today it consists of nine state-owned defence corporations (called defence public-sector undertakings, or DPSUs) and 41 ordnance factories. These are run by the Department of Defence Production. Meanwhile, the state-run Defence Research and Development Organisation (DRDO) coordinates a system of some 50 state defence-research facilities.

Private sector challenges

Although legal barriers to entry have been removed, private Indian defence firms still face disadvantages compared to DPSUs. Contracts have been awarded to DPSUs without competitive bidding, and the MoD retains the right to nominate who bids for its supply contracts. Unlike private defence companies, DPSUs and ordnance factories are exempt from excise duties and pay reduced customs on imported parts. All of this effectively relegates private defence firms to providing components and ancillary support.

There is also a perception within the MoD and the armed services that the private sector lacks the technological capacity and infrastructure to undertake advanced defence projects. This creates a vicious circle: the absence of a dependable stream of government contracts deters private firms from making costly infrastructure and technical investments, which in turn reinforces perceptions that the private sector lacks production and technical capacity.

Reform measures

The Kelkar Committee on defence acquisition was tasked with identifying reforms to India's defence-industrial sector. It reported in April and November 2005. One recommendation was to develop a 15-year plan for defence acquisitions (the Long-Term Integrated Perspective Plan, LTIPP). This would improve procurement information available to private industry, giving private firms greater lead-time to more efficiently target their R&D activities, and enabling them to enter the acquisition process earlier. The LTIPP for 2012–27 was approved in April 2012.

To address the special treatment given to DPSUs, the Kelkar Committee recommended designating some private defence firms as Champions of Defence Industry (*Raksha Udyog Ratnas*, or RURs). This would give them equal status with DPSUs and ordnance factories when bidding for defence contracts, and also provide access to MoD financing for up to 80% of R&D expenses on selected weapons systems. In addition, RURs would enjoy the same tax status as DPSUs. However, in February 2010, it emerged that the MoD had scrapped this reform proposal, partly because of DPSU trade unions' concerns about potential job losses.

In 2009, the MoD amended the Defence Procurement Procedure 2008 (DPP 2008) to create a new procurement category entitled 'Buy and Make (Indian)'. This category permitted private Indian firms to establish joint ventures with foreign suppliers. Although the MoD has said it views this category as important to future defence-industrial

development, procedural complexities have meant that only two 'Make' projects have emerged.

The first Defence Production Policy (DPP) was released in January 2011. It said industry should move beyond licensed production by improving its ability to absorb technology and design weapons and components. In February 2012, the Department of Defence Production issued guidelines for joint ventures between DPSUs and private Indian defence firms, partly because some DPSUs did not have the capacity to fulfil orders.

The first public–private partnership, Mazagon Dock Pipavav, a 50:50 joint venture, was cleared in May 2012 between Mazagon Dock Ltd (MDL) and Pipavav Defence & Offshore Engineering. The government hopes that deeper collaboration between the public and private sector will enable R&D funding to be allocated more efficiently, with private-sector participation allowing DPSUs to focus more on riskier R&D activities.

However, India has yet to effectively meld its state and private defence sectors in a way that will help incubate a successful indigenous defence research base. Only 6% of India's defence budget is allocated to R&D, significantly less than in other major defence spending countries; in the US and China, for example, R&D exceeds 10% of defence spending. It is estimated that India still imports 65% of its military equipment. Much of the 35% produced locally is low-tech equipment, and only around 9% is accounted for by private industry. Of the three services, the navy has been most willing to accept the long delivery times required by domestic producers; but even here Indian industry excels mainly at the labour-intensive assembly and integration of systems, and still relies heavily on imported components.

Developing domestic defence industry

New Delhi is also trying to use offsets to channel foreign defence production through the domestic

Table 13 **India's state-owned defence corporations**

Bharat Dynamics
Bharat Earth Movers
Bharat Electronics
Hindustan Aeronautics
Garden Reach Shipbuilders & Engineers (Kolkata)
Goa Shipyard
Hindustan Shipyard
Mazagon Dock
Mishra Dhatu Nigam

Table 14 **Indian Defence Expenditure by Function (FY2010/11–FY2012/13) (INR bn)**

	FY2010/11 Outturn	FY2011/12 Revised Estimate	FY2012/13 Budget
Personnel Expenditure			
Wages and Salary Total (of which:)			
Army Personnel[1]	354.6	409.9	459.7
Navy Personnel	24.4	28.0	34.3
Air Force Personnel	61.4	63.4	73.8
Joint Personnel	**10.9**	**12.4**	**13.7**
Civilian Personnel	**50.4**	**66.1**	**64.0**
Total Personnel Expenditure (excluding pensions) (% of total)	**501.7 (32.4%)**	**579.8 (33.8%)**	**645.5 (33.3%)**
Equipment Procurement Expenditure			
Military Equipment[2] (of which:)			
Army	19.7	41.8	53.0
Navy	138.1	132.7	189.4
Air Force	161.2	188.3	237.0
Non-Military Equipment	172.1	160.0	163.3
Defence Ordnance Factories	**4.5**	**3.0**	**4.0**
Total Equipment Procurement Expenditure (% of total)	**495.6 (32.0%)**	**525.8 (30.7%)**	**646.7 (33.3%)**
Operations & Maintenance Expenditure			
Transport	27.8	33.9	30.8
Stores	213.6	228.9	250.8
Works, Repairs & Refits	82.6	88.7	87.4
Total Operations & Maintenance Expenditure (% of total)	**324.0 (20.9%)**	**351.6 (20.5%)**	**369.0 (19.0%)**
Research & Development Expenditure			
Defence Services Research & Development	51.8	53.9	60.0
Research & Development Capital Outlays	49.7	46.3	46.4
Total Research & Development (% of total)	**101.5 (6.6%)**	**100.1 (5.8%)**	**106.4 (5.5%)**
Other Expenditure			
Other Revenue Expenditure[3]	49.0	66.2	69.1
Land Acquisition and Maintenance	1.1	7.7	2.1
Military Construction	65.9	66.1	80.7
Other Capital Expenditure[3,4]	8.3	15.6	19.9
Total Other Expenditure (% of total)	**124.3 (8.0%)**	**155.5 (9.1%)**	**171.8 (8.9%)**
Total Defence Expenditure (Excluding Pensions)	**1,547**	**1,713**	**1,939**
% Change	n.a.	10.7%	13.2%
Total Governmental Outlays	21,073	23,797	27,365
% of Total Outlays	7.34%	7.20%	7.09%
GDP	75,053	86,465	est.97,700
% of GDP	2.06%	1.98%	1.99%
Total Pensions & Retirement Benefits	**373.4**	**340.0**	**390.0**
Total Defence Expenditure (Including Pensions)	**1,920**	**2,053**	**2,329**

Sources: Government of India Ministry of Finance Public Finance Statistics 2011-2012; Government of India Union Budget & Economic Survey; Government of India Ministry of Defence, International Monetary Fund

Note: Totals may vary due to rounding effects.
[1] Includes pay, allowances and expenses for the auxiliary forces.
[2] Includes expenditure on aircraft, engines, medium and heavy vehicles, as well as the naval fleet.
[3] Excludes MoD expenditure on administration, miscellaneous general services, housing, public works and financial restructuring.
[4] Includes miscellaneous capital expenditures such as procurement of rolling stock, special projects, joint staff etc.

defence sector. This idea first appeared in the Defence Procurement Procedure (DPP) 2005, which said that foreign vendors awarded contracts in excess of Rs3bn (around US$60m) under the 'Buy' and 'Buy and Make' procurement categories had to spend 30% of the order value either within India (by making FDI through joint ventures with Indian firms, or by investing in Indian R&D organisations) or by purchasing Indian defence products. For certain contracts the offset requirement was raised to 50% by DPP 2006. However, this policy has so far failed to transform the local defence-industrial base.

A major obstacle has been the 26% cap on FDI, in place since 2001. Foreign defence suppliers have been reluctant to provide advanced technology and expertise for a minority 26% stake that gives them limited influence on decision-making and grants them only a small share of any dividends. Even if a foreign vendor were willing to engage in FDI at 26% equity, it would still need to find a private Indian defence firm willing to generate the remaining 74% capital. Given the constraints faced by private Indian industry in the defence sector, few local firms are willing to take the risk of raising such large sums of capital merely to enter joint-venture arrangements.

The government has refused to raise the FDI cap, and instead has widened the list of eligible offset areas to include the civilian aerospace, training and internal security sectors. In April 2012, technology transfer was included as a new method of discharging offsets for contracts awarded under the 'Buy' procurement category. In July 2012, the marine equipment and coastal-security sectors were added to the list of eligible industrial areas, and commercial shipbuilding is also under consideration.

However, widening the set of offset activities means that foreign investment could be channelled away from the defence sector. For India's defence-industrial base to benefit in this instance, these sectors must have dual-use possibilities. In turn, this requires precisely identifying civilian technological areas with potential dual-use applicability. Guidelines agreed in late July 2012 divided responsibility over offsets. The MoD's acquisition wing is responsible for agreeing offset arrangements, while the Department of Defence Production is responsible for monitoring implementation. New Delhi also announced it was revising its penalties for non-compliance with offset agreements: vendors that failed to meet offset liabilities within two years after the completion of a procurement contract would face unlimited penalties.

INDONESIA

Indonesia's efforts to improve its armed forces' capabilities are guided by the notion of a Minimum Essential Force (MEF), developed after concern that defence-funding levels in the 2000s had fallen below acceptable levels. Political and military leaders in Jakarta recognise the need to provide more substantial defences against external threats to Indonesia's extensive maritime interests. But they are also aware of the need to avoid being entrapped in a regional arms race and unduly diverting national resources from crucial social and developmental spending.

Civilian governments in Jakarta over the past decade have found it politically expedient to expand naval and air capabilities, as this has moved resources and influence away from the army, which dominated Indonesian politics from 1966–98 under President Suharto. However, the army has sought to retain its extensive territorial structure, which acts as an apparatus for intelligence-gathering and, its critics allege, indirect political influence throughout Indonesia.

The army has also worked to keep its role in maintaining internal security. The separatist wars in Timor Leste and Aceh have been resolved, via independence and political autonomy respectively, but a separatist struggle continues in West Papua and Indonesia's armed forces are involved in suppressing this uprising.

Strategic relations

Indonesia's broad strategic alignment since the mid-1960s has been towards the West, although the country remains non-aligned. Western military sanctions during Indonesia's occupation of Timor Leste between 1975–99 significantly affected the international outlook of its political and military elites. One outcome of this is Indonesia's present reluctance to depend completely on Western sources of military equipment. This has led Jakarta to continue buying equipment from diverse sources, while using technology-transfer agreements with foreign suppliers to develop its defence industry.

During 2011–12, Indonesia reached agreement with the US on the supply of 24 F-16C/D combat aircraft. It will also maintain its Russian-supplied Su-27s and Su-30s while participating in South Korea's K-FX project to develop an advanced combat aircraft.

After a hiatus following the Australian-led military intervention in Timor Leste in 1999, defence ties with Canberra revived in the wake of the 2002 Bali terrorist attacks. In September, the two countries announced a Defence Cooperation Agreement (DCA) and Canberra said it would donate surplus C-130H transport aircraft to Jakarta. The DCA, according to Australian Defence Minister Stephen Smith, provides a framework for 'practical cooperation' in areas like counter-terrorism, humanitarian assistance and disaster relief, and intelligence- and information-sharing. It was also evident that Australia hoped to develop defence-industrial cooperation with Indonesia.

Defence economics

Indonesia's defence planning is framed by the government's Medium-Term Development Plans for 2010–14 and 2015–19, as well as by a Long-Term Plan for 2010–25. Defence planning priorities were outlined in the 2010 Decree of the Minister of Defence on the Vision and Mission of Defence Planning. Procurement requirements were detailed in the 2010–14 Defence Strategic Plan, particularly the equipment levels required for the Minimum Essential Force (MEF). Personnel levels will be maintained within the armed forces, or Tentara Nasional Indonesia (TNI), with a focus on organisational structures and policies to enable 'right sizing and zero growth'; military education and training will also be improved. The drive to attract personnel has led to ministry focus on welfare benefits relating to performance, meal allowances, healthcare, insurance, housing programmes, and special assignment allowances.

Increased budgets in the National Budget Notes of 2013 indicate a desire to improve force and equipment readiness. For instance, by 2014, ground forces' readiness is planned to reach above 80%; naval force readiness to a greater than 40% average, while air-force readiness is planned to surpass 70% on average. Current readiness status is unknown.

Defence budgeting

In August 2012, during a rare special cabinet coordination meeting at TNI Headquarters, President Susilo Bambang Yudhoyono reinforced his commitment to develop the armed forces by boosting the defence budget. In 2004, the budget amounted to IDR 21.7tr (US$2.4bn). It is now planned to reach IDR77.7tr (approximately US$8.3bn) in 2013. On average, budgets have seen 8% annual growth over the previous ten years, and this trajectory is expected to continue over the next five years.

However, while the overall defence budget as a percentage of GDP remains around 0.8%, there is debate in Indonesia about possibly raising future defence budgets to around 2% of GDP. It remains unclear if GDP growth would permit such disbursements, given other sectors of government spending, but the fact remains that meeting Jakarta's strategic concerns, as well replacing ageing weapons systems and promoting professional armed forces, will be costly.

During the Suharto era, the TNI had business interests that provided the armed forces with a source of off-budget defence funding. This practice was prohibited by legislation in 2004, and no longer remains significant.

Procurement

In a January 2012 meeting of TNI commanders, it was announced that the army would acquire 103 Leopard 2A6 tanks from Germany; a previous attempt to procure Leopards from the Netherlands collapsed. The navy (TNI-AL) plans to boost capability with an initial three (and perhaps ultimately as many as ten) South Korean Chang Bogo submarines (based on the German Type-209), which local industry will help build. In June 2012, Indonesia agreed to buy an additional Sigma-class frigate, to be assembled in Indonesia from modules made in the Netherlands. This could be the precursor to a major construction programme involving as many as 20 ships. Local industry has continued to build smaller naval vessels, including a 63m trimaran with stealth technologies and suitable for the sea-denial role.

In August, Indonesia reached agreement with China to locally produce C-705 anti-ship missiles. The navy will increase its Regional Sea Commands from two to three, while the marines will gain an additional division and will receive more BMP-3F amphibious infantry fighting vehicles.

Indonesia has operated Block 15 F-16A/Bs since the 1980s, and in November 2011 requested 24 upgraded F-16 C/Ds from the US. A month later, Jakarta ordered a further six Su-30MK2 aircraft from Russia. Air mobility will be augmented with the transfer of four refurbished C-130H Hercules transports from Australia; an MoU was signed in mid-2012. In September 2012, Indonesia took delivery of the first two of nine C-295 medium transports. It is intended that a C-295 final assembly line be established in Indonesia. Meanwhile, in September 2012, Indonesia requested eight AH-64D helicopters from the US; these will supposedly operate against maritime as well as land targets.

Defence industry

Development of the domestic defence industry is a priority for the Medium- and Long-Term Development Plans. In the latter half of 2012, parliament debated a defence industry bill aimed at improving existing strategic defence-industry concerns – notably shipbuilders PAL, aerospace firm Dirgantara Indonesia, ground forces concern Pindad, telecoms firm INTI and other smaller defence-technology companies – while boosting the sector's development more broadly.

In addition to a defence-industry policy committee, the government has established a high-level committee to determine which weapon systems will be produced domestically. Domestically produced equipment will include C-235 maritime patrol variants, Bell 212EP helicopters and naval trimarans with stealth characteristics.

Collaboration is also under way between national shipbuilders PAL and South Korea's Daewoo Shipbuilding & Marine Engineering, on the three new *Chang Bogo* submarines the navy is buying. The first will be completed in South Korea in 2015, with the remaining two units built by PAL in Surabaya, which will also assemble modules for the new *Sigma*-class frigate.

JAPAN

Tokyo's security concerns were heightened by North Korea's missile launch in April 2012 and China's expanding maritime activities. A territorial dispute with Seoul over the Takeshima/Dokdo/Liancourt islets was also reawakened by the South Korean president's flying visit there in August 2012.

The US–Japan alliance might be seen recently as relatively fragile, notably considering domestic political debates in Japan, renewed controversy over US bases on Okinawa and overall Japanese confidence in US alliance guarantees. Renewed controversy has hit US bases. But ironically, all of this comes as the alliance has been strengthening militarily, through shared projects such as ballistic-missile defence (BMD) as well as the US 'rebalance' to the Asia-Pacific.

Constrained defence resources, the perceived need to maintain a relatively autonomous defence-industrial base, and problems with political leadership further complicated the picture.

The Japan Ministry of Defense (MoD) has had several leadership changes. Former defence ministers Yasuo Ichikawa and Naoki Tanaka were removed from the post in January and June 2012. The new minister, Satoshi Morimoto, is a non-elected security expert and will also face challenges in managing the intensely political battles over defence and US bases on Okinawa. With an election likely in December, a new ministerial team was a possibility for 2013.

Strategic concerns

Tokyo was unconvinced by North Korea's protestations that its April 2012 space launch was for a purely civilian purpose. Even through the trajectory of the vehicle was expected to pass to the south, Tokyo mobilised its full range of ballistic-missile defence systems to guard against possible debris falling on Japan's southernmost islands. The Maritime Self-Defense Force (MSDF) deployed three *Aegis* destroyers in the Sea of Japan (East Sea) and East China Sea, and the Air Self-Defense Force (ASDF) deployed seven PAC-3 batteries on the mainland and in Okinawa Prefecture, along with 500 Ground Self-Defense Force (GSDF) troops. The failure of the launch meant that Japan's BMD systems were not fully tested, but the episode highlighted continuing early-warning deficiencies, as Tokyo was unable to track the full trajectory of the missile without US space-based sensors. Some conservative politicians later expressed discontent about Japan's high degree of reliance on the US for early warning, although a subsequent MoD report made clear that Japan did not have the resources to develop an autonomous capability in this area.

A more pressing long-term security preoccupation remains China's developing military capacity. China's continued maritime activity around the disputed Senkaku/Diaoyu Islands, and build-up of naval anti-access/area denial (A2/AD) capabilities, has generated concern that Beijing might seize outlying Japanese islands in a *fait accompli*. There are also fears that Beijing might be intending to displace the Japanese and US naval presence in the East China Sea and first island chain. Japanese policymakers have watched with considerable interest China's attempt to intimidate ASEAN states in the South China Sea and are keen to avoid the same happening to Japan.

Sino-Japanese tension over the Senkaku/Diaoyu Islands increased in the autumn. The Japanese government decided to purchase three of the islands from their private Japanese owner after Tokyo's nationalist governor, Shintaro Ishihara, tried to buy

Map 9 **The US rebalance to Asia**

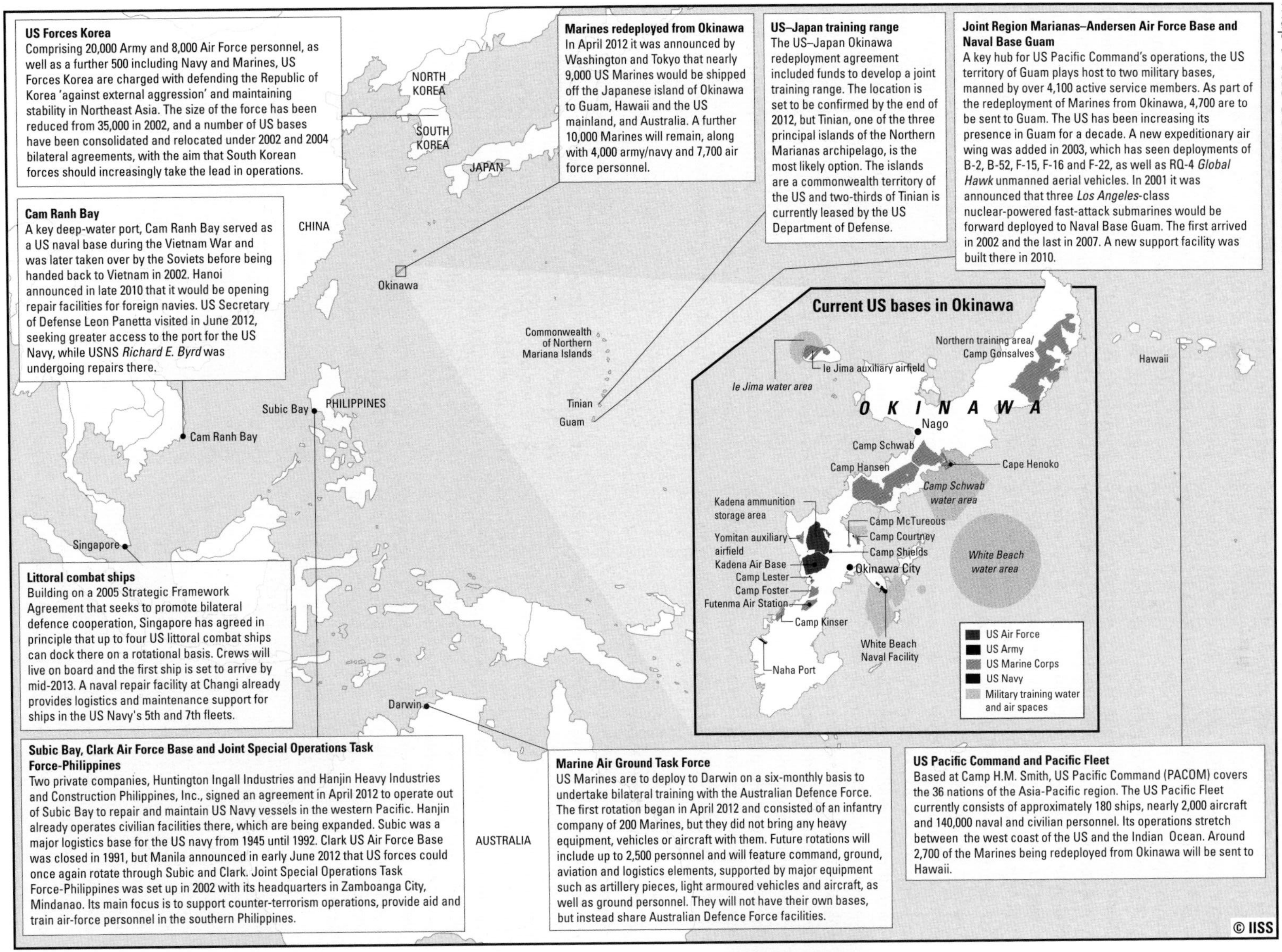

© IISS

US Forces Korea

Comprising 20,000 Army and 8,000 Air Force personnel, as well as a further 500 including Navy and Marines, US Forces Korea are charged with defending the Republic of Korea 'against external aggression' and maintaining stability in Northeast Asia. The size of the force has been reduced from 35,000 in 2002, and a number of US bases have been consolidated and relocated under 2002 and 2004 bilateral agreements, with the aim that South Korean forces should increasingly take the lead in operations.

Cam Ranh Bay

A key deep-water port, Cam Ranh Bay served as a US naval base during the Vietnam War and was later taken over by the Soviets before being handed back to Vietnam in 2002. Hanoi announced in late 2010 that it would be opening repair facilities for foreign navies. US Secretary of Defense Leon Panetta visited in June 2012, seeking greater access to the port for the US Navy, while USNS *Richard E. Byrd* was undergoing repairs there.

Littoral combat ships

Building on a 2005 Strategic Framework Agreement that seeks to promote bilateral defence cooperation, Singapore has agreed in principle that up to four US littoral combat ships can dock there on a rotational basis. Crews will live on board and the first ship is set to arrive by mid-2013. A naval repair facility at Changi already provides logistics and maintenance support for ships in the US Navy's 5th and 7th fleets.

Subic Bay, Clark Air Force Base and Joint Special Operations Task Force–Philippines

Two private companies, Huntington Ingall Industries and Hanjin Heavy Industries and Construction Philippines, Inc., signed an agreement in April 2012 to operate out of Subic Bay to repair and maintain US Navy vessels in the western Pacific. Hanjin already operates civilian facilities there, which are being expanded. Subic was a major logistics base for the US navy from 1945 until 1992. Clark US Air Force Base was closed in 1991, but Manila announced in early June 2012 that US forces could once again rotate through Subic and Clark. Joint Special Operations Task Force–Philippines was set up in 2002 with its headquarters in Zamboanga City, Mindanao. Its main focus is to support counter-terrorism operations, provide aid and train air-force personnel in the southern Philippines.

Marines redeployed from Okinawa

In April 2012 it was announced by Washington and Tokyo that nearly 9,000 US Marines would be shipped off the Japanese island of Okinawa to Guam, Hawaii and the US mainland, and Australia. A further 10,000 Marines will remain, along with 4,000 army/navy and 7,700 air force personnel.

US–Japan training range

The US–Japan Okinawa redeployment agreement included funds to develop a joint training range. The location is set to be confirmed by the end of 2012, but Tinian, one of the three principal islands of the Northern Marianas archipelago, is the most likely option. The islands are a commonwealth territory of the US and two-thirds of Tinian is currently leased by the US Department of Defense.

Joint Region Marianas–Andersen Air Force Base and Naval Base Guam

A key hub for US Pacific Command's operations, the US territory of Guam plays host to two military bases, manned by over 4,100 active service members. As part of the redeployment of Marines from Okinawa, 4,700 are to be sent to Guam. The US has been increasing its presence in Guam for a decade. A new expeditionary air wing was added in 2003, which has seen deployments of B-2, B-52, F-15, F-16 and F-22, as well as RQ-4 *Global Hawk* unmanned aerial vehicles. In 2001 it was announced that three *Los Angeles*-class nuclear-powered fast-attack submarines would be forward deployed to Naval Base Guam. The first arrived in 2002 and the last in 2007. A new support facility was built there in 2010.

Marine Air Ground Task Force

US Marines are to deploy to Darwin on a six-monthly basis to undertake bilateral training with the Australian Defence Force. The first rotation began in April 2012 and consisted of an infantry company of 200 Marines, but they did not bring any heavy equipment, vehicles or aircraft with them. Future rotations will include up to 2,500 personnel and will feature command, ground, aviation and logistics elements, supported by major equipment such as artillery pieces, light armoured vehicles and aircraft, as well as ground personnel. They will not have their own bases, but instead share Australian Defence Force facilities.

US Pacific Command and Pacific Fleet

Based at Camp H.M. Smith, US Pacific Command (PACOM) covers the 36 nations of the Asia-Pacific region. The US Pacific Fleet currently consists of approximately 180 ships, nearly 2,000 aircraft and 140,000 naval and civilian personnel. Its operations stretch between the west coast of the US and the Indian Ocean. Around 2,700 of the Marines being redeployed from Okinawa will be sent to Hawaii.

Current US bases in Okinawa

OKINAWA

Northern training area/
Camp Gonsalves

Cape Henoko

Camp Schwab water area

Nago

Ie Jima auxiliary airfield

Camp Schwab

White Beach water area

Camp Hansen

Camp McTureous
Camp Courtney
Camp Shields

Okinawa City

Ie Jima water area

Kadena ammunition storage area

Yomitan auxiliary airfield
Kadena Air Base
Camp Lester
Camp Foster
Futenma Air Station

White Beach Naval Facility

Camp Kinser

Naha Port

Legend:
- US Air Force
- US Army
- US Marine Corps
- US Navy
- Military training water and air spaces

NORTH KOREA

SOUTH KOREA

JAPAN

CHINA

Okinawa

PHILIPPINES

Subic Bay

Cam Ranh Bay

Singapore

Commonwealth of Northern Mariana Islands

Tinian

Guam

Hawaii

Darwin

AUSTRALIA

them for his municipality. Ultimately, however, Japanese policymakers had little choice in the matter, fearing the nationalist rhetoric that Ishihara's actions might have generated, and they have sought to reassure Beijing that Tokyo does not intend to stoke the bilateral dispute.

Concerns over North Korea and China led the Democratic Party of Japan (DPJ) government to try to bolster strategic ties with the US. Japanese security planners have broadly welcomed the US' rebalance towards the Asia-Pacific, and the Japanese defence debate has been dominated by discussion of the US Air–Sea Battle concept, and how the Japanese Self-Defense Forces (JSDF) can complement this with its own 'dynamic defence force' concept, adopted in December 2010's revised National Defense Programme Guidelines (see *The Military Balance 2012*, p. 220). Defence discussion has also centred on how Tokyo can deepen cooperation with the US in the fields of BMD, ISR and cyber defence.

But familiar problems beset alliance cooperation. The government has pledged to proceed with existing agreements to relocate the US Marine Corps (USMC) Futenma Air Station on Okinawa from Ginowan city to another site at Henoko. Implementation of the agreement has been held up because of opposition within Okinawa, which believes a base at Henoko will cause environmental damage and wants marines moved off the island entirely.

In a bid to break the deadlock, both governments agreed in February that the Futenma relocation would be 'delinked' from larger US base realignment plans in Okinawa prefecture, and that some USMC personnel would be redeployed to Guam. While this means that Japan and the US can now proceed with other realignments on Okinawa, the Futenma issue remains unresolved. The decision to deploy USMC MV-22 *Ospreys* to Futenma in early October compounded tensions on Okinawa. New allegations of rape levelled at two US servicemen on Okinawa that same month reminded residents of an infamous 1995 case and further inflamed the situation.

Japanese policymakers, though they noted US condemnation of the North Korean rocket launch, also recognised that little new pressure was brought to bear on Pyongyang. Similarly, Tokyo might welcome the US rebalance to the Asia-Pacific, but is aware that it means little unless the rhetoric is backed

F-35 A wins the F-X competition

Toyko's major procurement announcement in 2012 concerned its decision to finally select the Lockheed Martin F-35A to replace its F-4Js under the F-X fighter competition. The choice of the F-35A over the Eurofighter *Typhoon* and Boeing F/A-18 was controversial. Unlike the *Typhoon*, the F-35A is not strictly an air superiority fighter (the original ASDF requirement). Furthermore, it is not yet operationally capable or combat tested; its probable delivery date is not before 2020; and, with the possible exception of some cockpit work, it will give Japanese defence industry few opportunities to maintain industrial capacity in fighter production.

At ¥10bn–20bn per aircraft, the F-35A is also costly. After the full price was disclosed, some Japanese policymakers called for contract renegotiation. Nevertheless, when delivered, a fleet of 42 F-35As will provide the Air Self-Defense Force (ASDF) with a formidable fifth-generation multi-role aircraft with stealth characteristics. The importance the ASDF attaches to the stealth capabilities of the F-35A and its associated strengths in an air-defence-penetration, rather than air-superiority, role suggests an interest in developing an offensive counter-air doctrine for the ASDF.

But the F-35A is also symbolic of the problems in trying to sustain an indigenous defence production base. Japan is tentatively planning to begin full-scale development of a new fighter, the F-3, in 2016–17, with a notional in-service date in the early 2030s. Without such a programme, there is the possibility that Japan will no longer be building its own fighters or even assembling them under licence. This could mark a descent into the second-tier of defence producers, and increase dependence on the US for key platforms.

In an attempt to revitalise the industry, the government has continued to revise the ban on Japanese arms exports to countries other than the US. It was announced in 2010 that the arms export ban would be reviewed for further exemptions so Japan could look to collaborate with foreign partners on R&D. In April 2012, Japan and the UK announced a defence-cooperation agreement. This agreement was Japan's first outside those with the US. Areas of focus might include niche military technologies connected with NBC defence, maritime propulsion systems or equipment fits related to existing Japanese procurements. How much any new exemptions to the arms export ban will help boost defence industry is questionable, not least now that there are few major development opportunities in the wake of Japan's rejection of *Typhoon*.

Table 15 **Japan Defence-Related Expenditures Breakdown and Trends (2009–12)** (¥bn)

	FY 2009/10	FY 2010/11	FY 2011/12	FY 2012/13
Personnel & Provisions (% of Total)	2,077 (43.5%)	2,285 (45.8%)	2,092 (43.8%)	2,070 (43.9%)
Equipment Procurement (% of Total)	825 (17.3%)	774 (15.5%)	780 (16.3%)	757 (16.0%)
Maintenance (% of Total)	1,034 (21.7%)	1018 (20.4%)	1,071 (22.4%)	1,106 (23.5%)
Research & Development (% of Total)	120 (2.51%)	159 (3.18%)	85.1 (1.78%)	94.4 (2.0%)
Other Expenditure (of which:)				
Facility Improvements	133	134	120	100
Base Countermeasures	440	437	434	442
SACO-Related Projects	11.2	16.9	10.1	8.6
US Military Realignment	60.2	90.9	103	60
Other Miscellaneous Outlays	74.4	76	80.9	76.9
Other Expenditure Total (% of Total)	718 (15.0%)	755 (15.1%)	747 (15.6%)	687 (14.6%)
Total	4,774	4,990	4,775	4,714

Sources: *Bōei Hakusho* and *Bōei Handobukku*, various years.

Notes: Equipment procurement expenditures include the purchase of military vehicles and aircraft, and the construction of ships. Maintenance expenditures include those for housing, clothing and training.

with stronger military deployments. The US might be shifting the weight of its naval deployments to the Asia-Pacific, but for Tokyo, it is hard to see how the announced rebalance will lead to any significantly stronger US capability in the region.

Defence economics

With the Noda government pushing through austerity measures to rein in Japan's huge public debt (running at around 200% of GDP and set to rise because of an ageing population) and to help finance reconstruction after 2011's earthquake and tsunami, defence spending will fall in 2013 for the 11th consecutive year. The MoD submitted a 2013 budget request of ¥4.57tr (US$58bn), a 1.7% decrease on 2012. This represents the largest annual percentage drop in half a century and the lowest overall defence budget for nearly 20 years.

This means the JSDF has only been able to make incremental investments in new capabilities for its 'dynamic defence force' concept. However, with the government promising to protect all of Japan's seas and territories, the budget request announced in September 2012 does cover procurements relating to maritime security and the defence of outlying islands.

The MSDF has requested ¥72.3bn (US$912m) for a new 5,000 tonne anti-submarine destroyer; it will buy one extra submarine, and has started procuring the Kawasaki P-1 maritime patrol aircraft.

The GSDF has announced plans to buy four amphibious assault vehicles (AAV), costing ¥2.5bn (US$32m) – an acquisition suggesting an attempt to generate an, albeit limited, amphibious assault capa-

bility, perhaps with an eye to any contingency on Japan's outlying islands. That said, the advanced age of the equipment and the low numbers could instead indicate that the procurement is designed so that Japan can learn about amphibious operations.

The MoD is further investing around ¥21bn (US$260m) in the creation of a 100-strong cyber defence force.

NORTH KOREA

A failed North Korean space launch in April 2012 attracted international headlines and opprobrium, although a more interesting development was the unveiling of prototype road-mobile long-range ballistic missiles that same month. The 18m-long, three-stage, liquid-fuelled missiles, dubbed KN-08 by the US, were seen by some as giving North Korea intercontinental reach. In the absence of any observable test flights, however, the capability is only speculative. Six mock-ups were paraded in Pyongyang on the one-hundredth anniversary of founding father Kim Il-sung's birth. They were carried by Chinese-made transporter-erector-launchers, whose export to North Korea for military purposes was arguably banned by Security Council resolutions.

The failed 13 April launch of an 'earth-observation satellite' from a new launch site at Sohae on the west coast also took place during the week of anniversary festivities. The rocket exploded within two minutes of take-off. The launch also buried a 'Leap Day deal' signed with the US on 29 February under which North Korea was to have received 240,000 tonnes of food aid in exchange for a moratorium on nuclear and missile tests and on uranium enrichment at Yongbyon. Imagery analysis in April also showed preparations for a third nuclear test, but there were indications that China and the US eventually dissuaded Pyongyang from such a move.

Apart from the missile launch, North Korean provocations in 2012 included jamming the global positioning systems of aircraft using Seoul's main international airports, as well as those of vessels in nearby waters. This was achieved by using Soviet-made vehicle-mounted radar systems with a range of 50–100km. North Korea also continued to launch distributed denial-of-service attacks on South Korean institutions and pursue cyber infiltration against military and other government agencies.

New and old electronic warfare tools, and the propensity to use them, add to North Korea's asymmetric military capabilities. Chief among these are a plutonium stockpile sufficient for four to 12 nuclear weapons, a uranium-enrichment programme that could add fissile material for an extra one or two weapons a year, and an array of short- and medium-range ballistic missiles that could threaten targets up to 1,600km and can carry nuclear weapons if these can be made small enough. The untested *Musudan* missiles displayed in October 2010 might extend that reach to 2,400km.

North Korea also has the world's third-largest chemical-weapons arsenal and possibly also biological weapons. Other North Korean military capabilities often described as asymmetric include the world's largest special-operations force, long-range artillery targeting Seoul and other locations, and a fleet of mini-submarines.

The April space launch was apparently decreed by leader Kim Jong-il before his death on 17 December 2011. Leadership of the country and of the military immediately passed to his designated heir Kim Jong-un, thought at the time to be 28–29 years old.

Conjecture that succession to the young, untested third son might spark an internal power struggle proved to be unfounded, but the transition was not entirely smooth. On 15 July 2012, Vice Marshall Ri Yong-ho, chief of the general staff, was abruptly stripped of all his positions on the euphemistic grounds of 'ill health'. Ri was replaced as chief of staff by an unknown general, Hyon Yong-chol.

Also benefitting from Ri's departure was Kim family confidant and party official Chae Ryongo-hae, who was made a vice marshal in April and given charge of the powerful political bureau of the Korean People's Army (KPA). Appointing a civilian to the role indicated a rebalancing of power between the Korean Workers' Party and the military. Ri had reportedly resisted moves to divest the military of some of its commercial holdings.

The new leader's consolidation of control was reflected both in Ri's dismissal and in Kim's own promotion to the rank of marshall in the same month. How much his uncle Jang Song-taek and his aunt Kim Kyong-hui act as regent is unclear. Also uncertain is whether the changes in style that the young leader brought to North Korea, including public appearances with his stylish wife, portend substantive changes in policy. Agricultural reforms, including some measures that failed to take root in the past, were announced in summer 2012 and Jang travelled to China for discussions about economic development. Notwithstanding these moves, there was no doubt that the 'military first' doctrine that has underscored policy for the past decade-and-a-half remains entrenched.

SOUTH KOREA

South Korea's defence establishment is managing a complex set of priorities including balancing the requirements for robust defence against North Korea with the need to address changing regional dynamics such as the growing power-projection capabilities of China's PLA. It is busy implementing provisions of the new missile guidelines agreed with the United States in October 2012 and making preparations for the transfer of wartime operational control (OPCON) planned for December 2015, while managing the implications of a declining military manpower pool. The precise direction Seoul takes on these issues will have to be decided by a new government. After a December 2012 election, the Lee Myung-bak administration will come to the end of its term in February 2013. While it emphasised budget rationalisation and efficiency, the administration has been unable to implement structural reforms, such as force-integration proposals and greater jointness across the armed forces.

Defence policy priorities

Implementing key provisions of the long-term 'Basic Defense Reform Plan 2012–30', finalised on 29 August 2012, is a major issue. Important elements, such as the streamlining of command-and-control to give more operational authority to the Joint Chiefs of Staff, have run into opposition from within the services and the National Assembly. The reform plan also calls for upgraded maritime assets and the creation of a separate submarine command by 2015. A related development calls for the Jeju Defense Command to be restructured as a marine unit better able to meet potential regional contingencies. Finally, in order to meet rising cyber-security threats, cyber-warfare staffing is set to increase by 1,000.

Seoul also has to cope with military threats from North Korea, particularly Pyongyang's growing asymmetric strengths such as rudimentary nuclear assets, ballistic missiles, long-range artillery and special operations forces. Following the appointment of Kim Jong-un as the new North Korean leader, South Korea continues to closely monitor his hold on power, the level of his dependency on the armed forces, and the continuing defence priorities of the Korean People's Army.

South Korea's armed forces have to enhance deterrence, war-fighting and intelligence capabilities across the full range of contingencies vis-à-vis the North, while also taking into account the systematic military modernisation of key neighbouring powers.

Moreover, as the armed forces prepare for the transfer of OPCON, the South Korea–US Combined Forces Command has to be reconfigured. At the same time, Seoul's military intelligence, C4ISR, network-centric warfare, and cyber-security capabilities all require upgrades.

Incidents such as the sinking of the *Cheonan* and the shelling of Yeonpyong Island in April and November 2010 have spurred changes to rules of engagement and rapid-response procedures in the event of similar attacks. An October 2012 agreement with Washington replaced a previous bilateral understanding relating to the range and payload of South Korea's ballistic missiles. To counter the growing threat posed by North Korean ballistic missiles, the range of permitted missiles was increased to 800km, still with a 500kg payload limit; this means all of North Korea can be targeted from central South Korea. Payload limits on shorter-range missiles were raised to 2 tonnes. Simultaneously, the US agreed that UAV payloads could rise from 500kg to 2.5 tonnes.

The December 2012 presidential election is unlikely to substantively change Seoul's defence posture. Although the conservative and ruling Saenuri Party, and the more progressive Democratic United Party, have emphasised contrasting policies, whichever candidate wins the election is likely to promote enhanced confidence-building measures with the North.

Service developments

The 'Mid-Term Defense Plan 2013–17' emphasised countermeasures to North Korea's nuclear capabilities, ballistic missiles, long-range artillery and cyber attacks. The top priority lies in deploying the *Hyunmu* 2A SSM and the *Hyunmu*-3C cruise missiles after configuration tests are completed between 2012 and 2014. The ministry also stressed the need to deploy mid- and long-range surface-to-air missiles against North Korea's growing ballistic-missile inventory; the so-called L-SAM programme (a Korean *Patriot* variant) is due to begin development in 2013, with an initial cost of some US$87m. In total, the ministry plans to spend some US$5.3bn up to 2016 in meeting current military threats from the North. Critics have said, however, that by focusing on countering near-term North Korean threats, South Korea has under-emphasised some emerging risks.

The mid-term defence plan also called for the general-purpose forces to be reduced from 636,000 to 520,000 by 2022, leaving 387,000 in the ground forces; 65,000 in the air force; 40,000 in the navy; and 28,000 Marines. By 2020, the army will reduce to eight corps and 37 divisions, and fall further to six corps and 28 divisions by 2030. Meanwhile, a Mountain Brigade will be created by 2020, together with extra ATGW units and short-range UAVs. The navy has announced a range of capability developments intended to better meet North Korean and regional contingencies and has said it will establish new marine, ground-defence and attack-helicopter units.

Defence economics

Defence outlays over the next five to ten years will be driven by the need to meet threats from North Korea, modernisation imperatives, reducing the size of the armed forces, and moving to a 'leaner' and 'smarter' force. The armed forces' ability to achieve the latter two objectives depends on balanced investments between the services, given the historic army lead. As Seoul prepares for the transfer of full OPCON in 2015, some analysts think that it may be called on to shoulder an increased portion of the defence burden shared with the US. Defence exports are one area of potential growth, though South Korean firms will have to compete in an era of reducing budgets.

The 2012 defence budget amounted to US$29bn or 14.8% of the central government budget and 2.5%

of GDP. There is a growing consensus that defence spending should increase to at least 2.7% of GDP. The 'Mid-Term Defense Plan 2013–17' called for increased spending on capabilities including surface-to-surface missiles, stand-off precision-guided weapons and airborne electronic-attack systems. However, additional outlays will be constrained by annual growth rates that, due to the country's maturing economy, will likely hover around 2–3%, as well as by calls for increased social-welfare spending by presidential election candidates.

The MoD has said that some areas of defence policy and capability require particular attention. C4ISR capacities need to be improved, initiatives must be taken to enhance the 'jointness' of the armed forces, and the 2015 OPCON transfer needs to be carefully planned for. Core elements of the 'Basic Defense Reform Plan 2012–30' also have to be pursued, such as upgrading military command-and-control structures, increasing R&D spending by 7%, and enhancing cyber-warfare and information-security capabilities. In addition, the ministry wants to save around US$400m (¥31.7bn) in each year of the 2013–17 mid-term defence programme by streamlining the procurement process and other reforms. The MoD has estimated that such measures would help save US$340m in 2013, US$400m in 2014 and 2015, and $410m in 2016. It is hoped that increased financial efficiency, organisational and manpower restructuring, improved standards and processes, and outsourcing, will also help savings. Totalling US$2bn over five years, projected savings are not insignificant, but they still only amount to less than 0.7% of the 2012 defence budget.

Some 70% of the 2012 budget was allocated for force maintenance and around 30% for force modernisation; the latter is due to increase to 33% by 2017 after a reassessment of North Korea's asymmetric capabilities. If the force-modernisation programmes requested by the services are implemented during the five-year mid-term defence plan, the current level of spending, as a percentage of total government spending, would need to rise by an unlikely 8% annually. So while the defence plan requested US$5.2bn for key force modernisation, neither the National Assembly, nor the incoming administration is likely to accept this.

Procurement

Procurement programmes are dominated by service-specific priorities rather than by integrated initiatives, but Seoul's main short-term goal is to enhance deterrent capabilities in relation to Pyongyang's ballistic-missile and long-range artillery threats. There are plans to introduce the *Hyunmu*-2A surface-to-surface missile and the *Hyunmu*-3C cruise missile, as well as to develop medium- and longer-range surface-to-air missiles. The navy plans to introduce more integrated surface, submarine and naval-aviation capabilities by 2020 and has also announced plans to develop six new destroyers (KDX-IIA) with a displacement greater than the six KDX-II vessels in operation but smaller than the *Aegis*-capable KDX III. As well as its plan to inaugurate a Submarine Command by 2015, the navy will move towards procuring Type-214 submarines.

The air force has many priorities, including an airborne early-warning unit in 2017, a satellite surveillance control centre in 2019, medium- and high-altitude UAVs, as well as signals- and electronic-intelligence platforms and related systems that will improve surveillance over the Korean Peninsula, particularly after OPCON transfer in 2015.

However, air-force modernisation is dominated by the FX-3 fighter replacement programme. This is the armed forces' largest procurement programme, with a budget of some US$7.6bn for a total of 40 combat aircraft, to be introduced from 2016. Seoul is seeking to replace its ageing F-16s as well as its older F-4s. Reportedly, the latter are virtually inoperable. The three contenders for the FX-3 are Boeing's F-15SE, Lockheed Martin's F-35, and the Eurofighter *Typhoon*. The Defense Acquisition Program Administration (DAPA) has insisted that war-fighting capabilities, cost and maintenance efficiency, associated technology transfers, and interoperability will be the key criteria in the final decision. The original plan was for DAPA and the ministry to decide the winner by the end of October 2012 – a deadline that was not met.

Defence industry

Domestic defence sales amounted to US$7bn in 2011. Given force structure reductions, domestic demand is unlikely to increase significantly, so the government is keen to reorient the industry towards defence exports, which in 2011 totalled US$2.4bn. The initial goal had been US$1.6bn, with sales of the T-50 *Golden Eagle* aircraft largely responsible for beating this figure. By 2017, DAPA forecasts that South Korea's total defence exports will increase up to US$10bn. Seoul hopes that defence exports could be helped if the sector can piggyback on civilian industries such as shipbuilding; if industry can reap benefits from expertise in ground and naval weapons systems currently evenly distributed among Korean defence firms; and if industry can exploit existing export markets, particularly in niche sectors.

South Korea's aerospace industry is the least developed sector, although the co-development of the T-50 trainer and the FA-50 light fighter variants show longer-term potential. Indonesia signed a contract in May 2011 for 16 T-50s, and the Philippines selected it in August 2012. The largest potential market is in the US, where the air force's T-X trainer competition (for up to 350 aircraft) could provide a major boost to the T-50.

In naval systems, South Korea already produces *Aegis* destroyers and its own LHDs. In February 2012, Daewoo Shipbuilding won a contract to build four military oilers for the UK Royal Navy and also won a US$1.1bn contract to build four submarines for Indonesia. South Korea has established capacity in manufacturing armoured vehicles, such as the XK-2 tank and K9/10 self-propelled howitzers, which Seoul hopes to export. Lower labour costs, precision engineering, and South Korea's military experience have boosted defence-industrial prospects.

TAIWAN

Tension across the Taiwan Strait has reduced since President Ma Ying-jeou came to power in 2008, with his Kuomintang party also defeating the pro-independence Democratic Progressive Party in parliamentary elections. However, Taipei remains sensitive to the PLA's rapid modernisation. China has not ruled out the use of force should Taiwan declare formal independence.

According to the latest White Paper, Taiwan's armed forces have sought to develop into a 'small but superb, small but strong and small but smart' military through a combination of structural reforms, careful resource allocations and capability developments. The development of an all-volunteer force is a top priority, in light of a drop in the number of male citizens of military-service age and after an election promise by President Ma to phase out conscription. Other main concerns include improving ISR and asymmetric capabilities, as well as joint war-fighting capability.

The 'hard ROC' concept remains an objective, whereby the armed forces can achieve 'resolute defence and credible deterrence'. In the 2000s, the armed forces changed their definition of 'victory' in war from a complete defeat of the enemy to preventing landing forces from establishing a secure foothold, and increasing the material cost of invasion. Capability improvements were key, as were efforts to harden targets. Taipei's defence priorities are now beginning to reflect the PLA's development of anti-access/area-denial capabilities that could challenge any US ability to intervene in wartime. But Taipei acknowledges that its economy could not support a direct arms competition with Beijing, while a backlog of defence acquisitions released by the US since 2008 could strain the defence budget. The armed forces have also adapted to meet various 'unconventional security issues' by investing in humanitarian-and-disaster-relief (HA/DR) capabilities.

Capability improvements

Naval surveillance will be improved when P-3C *Orion* maritime-patrol aircraft are introduced after 2013, while E-2K *Hawkeye* early-warning aircraft have been upgraded. Air-defence and early-warning systems are being modernised under the *Po Sheng* 'Broad Victory' C4ISR programme. Meanwhile, a near billion-dollar, long-range UHF early-warning Surveillance Radar Programme (SRP) on Leshan Mountain is expected to come online in late 2012. Once operational, the Raytheon-built SRP will give Taiwan the capacity to track and monitor some ballistic and air-breathing targets inside China, as well as providing limited capability to track vessels at sea.

Leading defence R&D house Chungshan Institute of Science and Technology (CSIST) has been trying to develop UAVs for some time, but little progress has been made, mostly due to US export controls. As for space-based surveillance systems, Taiwan has run into US opposition over the development of launch vehicles, as this expertise could be applied to missile technology. Given this, Taipei's decision to proceed with long-range guided-weapons-related technologies probably resulted in Washington's refusal to cooperate on some programmes. Taiwan's security establishment has developed world-class capabilities in detecting, analysing and countering cyber intrusions from the PRC, and Taiwan has an integrated 'offensive' and 'defensive' cyber warfare apparatus.

Personnel developments

Government statistics show there were only 117,814 men of draft age in Taiwan in 2012, and this figure is expected to drop to 75,338 by 2025. After December 2011 amendments to the Act of Military Service System, Taiwan is seeking to create a smaller but more professional military with an all-volunteer force. Since voluntary service was introduced in 2003, the ratio of volunteers to conscripts has gradually increased. Now from 2013, men born on or after the 1 January 1994 will only be required to serve for four months rather than one year. Those born before 1994 but not yet called up will have to still serve one year, but will be able to choose an alternative community service until 2015. Total force levels are to reduce to 215,000 by the end of 2014, when it is intended the service will be all-volunteer.

Taiwan will have to address training regimes to ensure that those serving four months will learn adequate military skills; this will be realised through investment in the reserve formations, which remain mandatory for citizens up to 30. The move to an all-volunteer force is also likely to be costly.

Defence economics

The current and former presidents have tried unsuccessfully to set the defence budget at 3% of GDP. Defence budgets have followed an uneven trajec-tory in recent years, from US$9.6bn (2.7%) in 2009 to US$10.2bn (2.1%) in 2011 with several levels in between. In 2012, the defence budget was US$10.3bn, or 2.2% of GDP. Given shrinking national revenue and budgets, and with more than US$16bn spent on US defence acquisitions since 2008, Taiwan is unlikely to reach the goal of 3% of GDP any time soon.

The move to an all-volunteer force will further increase personnel costs, probably reducing the share for operations and maintenance. The plan to triple current salaries will cost around NT$28bn (US$1bn) – even before training, education, housing and restruc-turing are considered.

Industry and procurement

National defence priorities and local industrial capacities are integrated by the Ministry of Economic Affairs/Ministry of National Defense (MD) Industrial Cooperation Policy Guidance Council and the Executive Committee for Industrial Cooperation. Budgetary constraints and Washington's evident reluctance to sell advanced military hardware to Taiwan have prompted a gradual shift in Taiwan's procurement strategy: it now emphasises self-reliance and asymmetry.

The F-16 debate

Taiwan has been trying to buy 66 F-16C/D aircraft since 2006 to replace an ageing fleet. However, Washington has been increasingly cautious about providing state-of-the-art equipment to Taipei in recent years, not wishing to cross any 'red lines' with an increasingly influential Beijing, which still claims Taiwan as part of its territory. The last time the US sold F-16s to Taiwan was in 1992, and although the 1979 Taiwan Relations Act calls on Washington to provide Taipei with defensive weaponry, President George W. Bush cancelled annual weapons talks after 9/11. On several occasions after 2001, Taiwan was told it could not submit a letter of request (LoR) to Washington, which in turn allowed the US to claim that it could not proceed because it had not received a LoR. This was to avoid a scenario in which a Taiwanese request was refused by the US, adversely affecting future arms sales.

In early 2010, the administration of President Barack Obama authorised a US$6bn Bush-era arms package to Taiwan, including *Patriot* missiles, *Black Hawk* helicopters and communications equipment. However, like the previous administration it delayed a decision on F-16s.

Finally, under pressure from members of Congress supporting Taiwan or from defence-manufacturing US regions, the Obama administration decided in September 2011 on an alternative US$5.2bn package to help upgrade Taiwan's 146 existing F-16A/Bs with new radar, smart bombs and laser-guided equipment.

In April 2012, after more political pressure, the White House promised to give 'serious consideration' to selling new F-16s to Taiwan – although late in 2012 nothing had come of this. Proponents of the programme argue that Taiwan needs newer aircraft because it is losing its ability to counter potential threats from China. Opponents point to the high costs, limited qualitative advantage over upgraded F-16A/Bs, and the small number of runways in Taiwan – all in range of Chinese missiles – in arguing that Taiwan should spend elsewhere. Taiwan has also begun signalling that it could not afford both programmes. Reports, denied by the ministry, have also emerged claiming Taiwan could seek fewer new F-16s.

Taiwan's main aerospace research branch, Aerospace Industrial Development Corporation (AIDC), is meanwhile involved in the F-16A/B upgrade. It hopes it can develop the upgrade facility into an international F-16 maintenance centre.

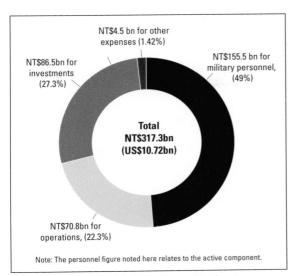

NT$4.5 bn for other expenses (1.42%)

NT$86.5bn for investments (27.3%)

NT$155.5 bn for military personnel, (49%)

Total
NT$317.3bn
(US$10.72bn)

NT$70.8bn for operations, (22.3%)

Note: The personnel figure noted here relates to the active component.

Figure 20 **Taiwan: 2012 Defence Budget Composition**

There has also been particular emphasis on dual-use technology. The MND's regulations on industrial cooperation, amended in November 2010, mean that the military is now expected to increase technology transfer to the private sector and increase cooperation with academic institutions. Most of Taiwan's advanced weapons systems are US in origin. Despite the lack of formal diplomatic ties, Taiwanese F-16A/B pilots train at Luke air force base in Arizona and on the P-3C in Florida. Since 2008, procurements from the US have included six PAC-3 systems (the first four are scheduled for 2014–2015). In conjunction with Taiwan's indigenous *Tien Kung* II (TK-2), these will improve Taiwan's BMD capacity.

The air force is set to decommission 56 *Mirage* 2000 and 45 F-5 fighters by 2020, leaving a mix of F-16A/Bs and F-CK-1 *Ching Kuo* Indigenous Defence Fighters. Alternatives to the F-16C/D remain limited. However, Aerospace Industrial Development Corporation (AIDC), which manufactured the *Ching Kuo*, is involved in a mid-life update for the aircraft, including the integration of *Tien Chien* II *Sky Sword* air-to-air missiles and TC-IIA anti-radiation missiles (under development at CSIST).

The army continues to focus on countering an amphibious attack on Taiwan and defending offshore islands. During peacetime, it spearheads major humanitarian relief efforts and anti-terrorism operations. The army signalled its intention to procure surplus US *Abrams* tanks as excess defence articles to add firepower along coastal areas, though critics said

that, given the *Abrams'* size, Taiwan should instead buy medium-weight wheeled armoured vehicles or the M109A6 *Paladin* self-propelled howitzer.

The navy has benefitted from a shift towards an asymmetric strategy to counter China, focusing on light, low-signature fast-attack missile boats for littoral defence. Since 2010, 31 *Kuang Hua* VI 70 tonne fast-attack boats equipped with *Hsiung Feng* II (HF-2) anti-ship missiles from manufacturer CSIST have been deployed in three squadrons. From 2011, the navy also began upgrading its 500 tonne *Jinn Chiang*-class patrol boats which are due to take four *Hsiung Feng* III (HF-3) ramjet-powered supersonic anti-ship missiles, touted as Taiwan's carrier killer. A new 450 tonne fast-attack corvette being developed under the *Hsun Hai* programme will be fitted with HF-2 and HF-3 launchers. In early 2012, reports emerged that Taiwan could, with foreign engineering help, embark on a domestic programme for medium-sized submarines. At present, the navy only has two combat-ready *Hai Lung* submarines. Work is ongoing to give them *Harpoon* missile capability.

In late 2010, a senior defence official confirmed rumours that CSIST was developing a longer-range HF-2E LACM to provide counterforce capability. The US denied assisting with the programme. Washington's adherence to the Missile Technology Control Regime has delayed efforts by CSIST to extend the range of its missiles and miniaturise warheads.

VIETNAM

Vietnam's defence priorities have changed over the past five years to reflect its growing maritime economy, territorial claims in the South China Sea, other regional states' military modernisation and emerging military technologies. The December 2009 Defence White Paper advocated incremental modernisation. Current priorities were outlined in January 2011 at the Communist Party's eleventh national congress. The political report delivered by the secretary-general identified armed-forces and defence-industry modernisation as key national objectives.

Its force-modernisation programme has led the military to start developing capacity to conduct operations in Vietnam's maritime domain. In September 2009, Vietnam began transferring air-force assets and personnel to the navy's 1st Regional Command,

Asia

headquartered at the northern port city of Haiphong. This is the first step towards creating a naval air arm in all five of Vietnam's naval commands. In 2012, Su-27/Su-30s started flying reconnaissance missions over the South China Sea. (see map opposite).

Strategic relations

Vietnam's participation in international defence cooperation has increased since the mid-2000s in pursuit of its foreign policy aim of 'multilateralising and diversifying' its external relations. In 2010, Vietnam raised its strategic dialogues with both China and the United States to vice-ministerial level. In September 2011, Vietnam and the US held their second Defence Policy Dialogue and signed an MoU on cooperation in low-key areas such as search and rescue (SAR) and HA/DR. Vietnam has also agreed to conduct minor passage repairs on US Military Sealift Command (MSC) vessels. The most recent repairs were conducted in the commercial port facilities at Cam Ranh Bay. Vietnam makes a distinction between official goodwill visits by naval warships, which are restricted to one per country per year, and commercial repairs. The MSC vessels are not warships and three have been serviced in Cam Ranh Bay (as well as two other vessels in two different ports).

In August 2011, at the second China–Vietnam Strategic Defence and Security Dialogue, it was agreed that military exchanges would be increased and a hotline established between the two defence ministries. China agreed to share its experiences in UN peacekeeping. China and Vietnam commenced biannual joint naval patrols in the Gulf of Tonkin in April 2006. In recent years these joint patrols have included SAR exercises. The thirteenth joint patrol, in June 2012, included communications and anti-piracy drills. The PLA Navy resumed port visits to Vietnam in November 2008 after a 17-year gap. The Vietnam People's Army (VPA) Navy made its first port call to China in June 2009 and revisited in June 2011. On 3 September 2012, both sides held their sixth defence and security consultations at vice-ministerial level.

Marine Police

Although China and Vietnam might seem to have separated their South China Sea dispute from wider bilateral relations, challenges remain in managing these simmering tensions. Use of paramilitary forces is one way that states seek to exert influence, while simultaneously seeking to manage escalation. In

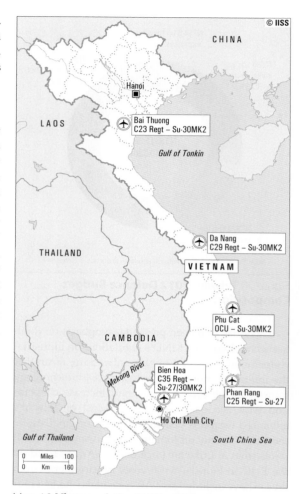

Map 10 **Vietnam's Su-27/Su-30 bases**

Vietnam's case, its Marine Police has confronted Chinese marine surveillance vessels in disputed areas. The Marine Police operates under the direction of the defence ministry and plays a role in national defence in cooperation with the navy.

In peacetime, the Marine Police has responsibility for enforcing maritime law as well as protecting Vietnam sovereignty and sovereign jurisdiction. Twenty-five of its 35 ships are in the 120–400 tonne range. Vietnam's Song Thu shipbuilding company and the Damen Group from the Netherlands have constructed ten Offshore Patrol Vessels (OPVs) in the 1,200–2,500 tonne range. Moves to increase all-weather OPVs in the 2,000 tonne range will boost capabilities, as will plans to expand the Marine Police's naval-aviation element. The first of three CASA-212-400 maritime-patrol aircraft was received in August 2012.

Defence economics

Vietnam's 2009 Defence White Paper broke new ground by releasing figures on total defence budgets from 2005–08. It was also reported that the government resolved to allocate 1.8% of GDP to the defence budget. In practice, the official defence budget has exceeded this benchmark every year, with an average 2.25% of GDP allocated to defence for the four years from 2009–12. Strong economic growth in recent years has enabled increased outlays on defence, which rose to VND55.1tr (US$2.67bn) in 2011, before increasing again to VND7otr (US$3.33bn) in 2012 – nominal increments averaging 25.6% annually.

However, Vietnam experienced one of the highest rates of inflation across Asia in 2011 (18.7%), in part because of excessive credit growth and a series of currency devaluations. Thus, at constant 2010 prices and exchange rates, Vietnamese real defence expenditure only rose by 2.7% in 2011, before growing to 16.9% in 2012, although in part this reflected the government's success in bringing down inflation. Measures to curb inflation have started to constrain economic growth (which fell to 5.9% in 2011 and is projected to drop to 5.1% in 2012). It remains to be seen if this will moderate Vietnam's defence expenditure increases. But defence spending has been prioritised: military outlays as a percentage of total government spending rose from 6.85% in 2010 to 7.72% in 2012, while defence expenditure as a percentage of GDP rose from 2.24% to 2.42% over the same period (indicating that defence-spending growth exceeded GDP growth between 2010 and 2012).

Still, Vietnam's budgetary practices remain opaque and the country does not provide a budget breakdown. One Vietnamese official has indicated that defence-budget details are only provided to the chairman of the National Defence and Security Committee. Members of the committee vote on the total figure but do not examine detailed allocations. According to informed observers, the defence minister can approach the prime minister with special extra budgetary requests, and if the funds were available these requests would be approved. Because of the lack of transparency, it is estimated that defence expenditure could be double the official figures.

Procurement and industry

Russia remains Vietnam's main provider of advanced military equipment and technology, and since 2008 the navy has taken delivery of two *Gepard*-class guided missile frigates (of four ordered) and some 400 Kh-35 *Uran*/SS-N-25 anti-ship missiles. The VPA's air-defences force took delivery of two S-300PMU-1 batteries, 200 9M311/SA-19 *Grison* missiles and four *Kolchnya* air-defence search radars. In 2010–12, the air force acquired 20 Su-30MK2V combat aircraft armed with Kh-59MK anti-ship cruise missiles. The navy received two batteries of the K-300P *Bastion* (SS-C-5 *Stooge*) coastal defence missile system.

Notable future acquisitions include six *Kilo*-class attack submarines and four Dutch *Sigma*-class corvettes. The first *Kilo* was launched in Russia on 28 August 2012, and delivery was expected by the end of 2012. The *Kilos* will likely be armed with heavy torpedoes (53-56 or TEST 76) and anti-ship missiles. The *Kilo* is capable of using the Novator *Klub* family of missiles, including the 3M54E (SS-N-27 *Sizzler*). When the *Kilo* purchase was first announced, the total cost was estimated by foreign analysts at US$1.8bn–$2.1bn. This has now risen to US$3.2bn to include armaments and Russian construction of a service and maintenance facility at Cam Ranh Bay.

Vietnam has also approached Russia and India for assistance in producing anti-ship cruise missiles and the repair and maintenance of naval vessels, and is seeking the transfer of Russian technology to help maintain its Su-30s and *Kilo*-class submarines.

Hanoi is also expected to produce two of its upcoming *Sigma*-class corvettes in-country with the assistance of the Dutch Damen Group. Between 2011–12, the Hong Ha shipbuilding company launched Vietnam's first indigenously constructed naval vessels: a 54m, 400 tonne fast patrol boat (Project TT400TP) and a 72m troop transport vessel. In February 2012, it was announced that Vietnam and Russia would jointly produce a modified *Uran* anti-ship missile in Vietnam, while in June 2012, it was announced that the Military Institute of Technology had mastered the production of a key oxidising ingredient for fuel used by Vietnam's R-17E (*Scud*) missile force.

Afghanistan AFG

New Afghan Afghani Afs		2011	2012	2013
GDP	Afs	874.67bn	1tr	
	US$	18.32bn	19.85bn	
per capita	US$	602	653	
Growth	%	5.77	5.22	
Inflation	%	11.81	6.61	
Def exp [a]	Afs	87bn		
	US$	1.82bn		
Def bdgt	Afs	119bn	106bn	
	US$	2.49bn	2.09bn	
US$1=Afs		47.76	50.55	

[a] Security expenditure. Includes expenditure on Ministry of Defence, Ministry of Interior, Ministry of Foreign Affairs, National Security Council and the General Directorate of National Security. Includes US DoD funds to Afghan Ministry of Defence & Ministry of Interior.

Population   30,419,928

Ethnic groups: Pashtun 38%; Tajik 25%; Hazara 19%; Uzbek 12%; Aimaq 4%; Baluchi 0.5%

Age	0–14	15–19	20–24	25–29	30–64	65 plus
Male	21.9%	6.1%	4.9%	3.7%	12.9%	1.2%
Female	21.2%	5.9%	4.7%	3.5%	12.6%	1.3%

Capabilities

The Afghan National Army (ANA) is fighting the Taliban alongside NATO forces while continuing to improve its capability. With the planned force structure now fully-manned, the priority is to develop combat support, logistic leadership and technical expertise. Plans call for the ANA to reach full capability as a counter-insurgency force in time for the Afghan assumption of security leadership by the end of 2014, by which time ANA units should be operating independently. Already some elements – notably the Special Forces – are highly rated by ISAF. However, many army units still require support from NATO. International training assistance continued in 2012, in the midst of concern arising from 'Green-on-blue' attacks, some of which – but not all – could be ascribed to the actions of Taliban militants. Governance shortcomings and widespread corruption undermine the army's effectiveness. There are plans to develop Afghan Air Force capability, but its effectiveness is limited by corruption. (See pp. 8–11.)

ACTIVE 190,700 (Army 184,700 Air Force 6,000)
Paramilitary 149,650

ORGANISATIONS BY SERVICE

Afghan National Army (ANA) 184,700

5 regional comd.

FORCES BY ROLE
SPECIAL FORCES
   1 spec ops div (1 SF gp; 2 cdo bde with (total: 5 cdo bn)

MANOEUVRE
   Light
   1 (201st) corps (1 cdo bn, 2 inf bde, 1 mech bde, 1 EOD coy)
   3 (207th, 209th & 215th) corps (1 cdo bn, 3 inf bde, 1 EOD coy)
   2 (203rd & 205th) corps (1 cdo bn, 4 inf bde, 1 EOD coy)
   1 (111st Capital) div (2 inf bde)
   7 rapid reaction bn (forming)
COMBAT SUPPORT
   1 sigs bn
EQUIPMENT BY TYPE
RECCE 406 M1117 ASV
APC 173
   APC (T) 173 M113A2
ARTY
   TOWED 109: **122mm** 85 D-30; **155mm** 24 M114A1
MSL • SSM SS-1 *Scud*†
MW Bozena

Afghan Air Force (AAF) 6,000

EQUIPMENT BY TYPE
AIRCRAFT
   TPT 35: **Medium** 15 G-222 (C-27A) (2 more being acquired) **Light** 20: 6 Cessna 182; 14 Cessna 208B
   TRG 2 L-39 *Albatros*†
HELICOPTERS
   ATK 11 Mi-35
   MRH 46+: 6 MD-530F; 40+ Mi-17

Paramilitary 149,650

Afghan National Police 149,650

Under control of Interior Ministry. Includes Afghan Uniformed Police (AUP), Afghan National Civil Order Police (ANCOP), Afghan Border Police (ABP) and Afghan Anti-Crime Police. (AACP)

FOREIGN FORCES

All under ISAF comd unless otherwise specified. ISAF HQ resembles a static HQ with contributing NATO countries filling identified posts.

Albania 212; 1 inf coy
Armenia 126
Australia 1,550; 1 inf BG with (1 mot inf coy; 1 armd recce sqn); elm 1 arty regt; 1 hel gp with 2 CH-47D; 1 UAV det with RQ-7B *Shadow* 200; 3 C-130J *Hercules*
Austria 3
Azerbaijan 94
Bahrain 95
Belgium 283; 6 F-16 *Fighting Falcon*
Bosnia-Herzegovina 54
Bulgaria 572; 1 mech inf coy
Canada 950; 1 inf bn (trg)
Croatia 260
Czech Republic 422 • UNAMA 1 obs
Denmark 613; 1 mech inf BG with (2 mech inf coy; 1 tk pl) • UNAMA 1 obs

El Salvador 24

Estonia 155; 1 mech inf coy; 1 mor det

Finland 136

France 2,418; 1 armd bde HQ; 2 inf BG; 1 hel bn; 1 log bn; 4 EC665 *Tiger*; 2 AS532 *Cougar*; 2 EC725AP *Caracal*; 3 *Harfang* UAV

Georgia 800; 1 inf bn

Germany 4,737; 1 div HQ; 2 inf BG; CH-53G *Stallion*; 6 *Tornado* ECR; C-160 *Transall* • UNAMA 1 obs

Greece 12

Hungary 555; 1 lt inf coy

Ireland 6

Italy 4,000; 1 mtn inf bde HQ; 3 mtn inf regt; 6 A-129 *Mangusta*; 3 CH-47; 2 RQ-1 *Predator* 2 C-27J; some C-130 • UNAMA 1 obs

Jordan *Operation Enduring Freedom – Afghanistan* 720; 1 ranger bn

Korea, Republic of 350

Latvia 40

Lithuania 221

Luxembourg 10

Macedonia, Former Yugoslav Republic of 168

Malaysia 46

Mongolia 88 • UNAMA 1 obs

Montenegro 41

Netherlands 500

New Zealand 155 • UNAMA 1 obs

Norway 145 • UNAMA 1 obs

Poland 1,800; 1 AB bde HQ; 2 inf BG; 6 Mi-24; 4 Mi-17 • UNAMA 1 obs

Portugal 141 • UNAMA 1 obs

Romania 1,762; 2 inf bn; • UNAMA 1 obs

Singapore 39

Slovakia 343

Slovenia 77

Spain 1,450; 1 AB bde

Sweden 506 • UNAMA 3 obs

Tonga 55

Turkey 1,328; 1 inf bde HQ; 2 inf bn • UNAMA 1 obs

Ukraine 25

United Arab Emirates 35

United Kingdom 9,500; 1 (4th) mech bde HQ (1 recce regt, 1 armd regt, 5 lt inf bn, 1 cdo bn, 1 arty regt; 1 engr regt); 8 AH-64D *Apache*; 5 *Lynx*; *Hermes* 450; MQ-9 *Reaper*; 6 *Sea King* HC4 8 *Tornado* GR4; 4 C-130 *Hercules*; 8 CH-47 *Chinook*; 6 *Merlin* HC3; 4 *Shadow R1* (Beech *King Air 350*)

United States 68,000; 1 corps HQ; 2 div HQ; 2 mech inf SBCT; 2 lt inf IBCT; 2 AB IBCT; 3 cbt avn bde; 1 ARNG IBCT HQ; 1 MEF with (1 RCT); F-15E *Strike Eagle*; F-16C/D *Fighting Falcon*; A-10 *Thunderbolt II*; AV-8B *Harrier*; EC-130H *Compass Call*, C-130 *Hercules*, MV-22B *Osprey*, KC-130J *Hercules*, AH-64 *Apache*; OH-58 *Kiowa*; CH-47 *Chinook*; UH-60 *Black Hawk*; HH-60 *Pave Hawk*; AH-1W *Cobra*, CH-53 *Sea Stallion*; UH-1 *Iroquois*; RQ-7B *Shadow*; MQ-1 *Predator*; MQ-9 *Reaper* (Equipment includes both ISAF and OEF-A forces) • *Operation Enduring Freedom – Afghanistan* ε7,000

Uruguay UNAMA 1 obs

Australia AUS

Australian Dollar A$		2011	2012	2013
GDP	A$	1.44tr	1.49tr	
	US$	1.49tr	1.54tr	
per capita	US$	67,679	69,950	
Growth	%	2.14	3.31	
Inflation	%	3.39	2.05	
Def exp [a]	A$	24.6bn		
	US$	25.4bn		
Def bdgt	A$	22.1bn	24.2bn	24.2bn
	US$	22.8bn	25.1bn	
US$1=A$		0.97	0.97	

[a] Including military pensions

Population   22,015,576

Age	0–14	15–19	20–24	25–29	30–64	65 plus
Male	7.1%	3.0%	3.1%	3.1%	24.8%	7.8%
Female	6.8%	2.8%	3.0%	3.1%	24.8%	10.7%

Capabilities

Australia has a strong military tradition and its relatively compact armed forces' considerable operational experience, together with the country's high levels of technological expertise, defence-industrial base, and international defence relationships (particularly with the US) contribute substantially to its military capabilities. Continuing modernisation of all three services seems likely to ensure that the sophistication of the ADF's equipment at least matches, and in many cases continues to surpass, that of nations in Australia's immediate region. Notable planned future procurement includes up to 100 F-35 Joint Strike Fighters, and new conventional submarines, while build continues on the two *Canberra*-class LHDs. ADF units benefit from high training standards and participate in regular joint-service exercises at the national, bilateral and multinational levels. The ADF trains with a view to future operational deployments in Southeast Asia and possibly further afield, as well as in defence of the Australian continent. As Canberra reduces its military commitments in Afghanistan, Solomon Islands and Timor Leste the ADF will intensify its engagement with the armed forces of states in Australia's immediate region (particularly Indonesia).

ACTIVE 57,050 (Army 28,850 Navy 14,000 Air 14,200)

RESERVE 22,650 (Army 16,650 Navy 2,000 Air 4,000)

The High-Readiness Reserve of 2,800 army and 331 airforce personnel is intended to strengthen the Australian Defence Force (ADF) with members trained to the same skill levels as the Regular Force. Integrated units are formed from a mix of reserve and regular personnel. All ADF operations are now controlled by Headquarters Joint Operations Command (HQJOC).

Asia

ORGANISATIONS BY SERVICE

Space

SATELLITES • COMMUNICATIONS 1 *Optus* C1 (dual use for civil/mil comms)

Army 28,850

Forces Command

FORCES BY ROLE
COMMAND
1 (1st) div HQ
MANOEUVRE
Reconnaissance
3 (regional force) surv unit (integrated)
Mechanised
1 (1st) mech inf bde (1 armd recce regt, 1 armd regt, 2 mech inf bn, 1 arty regt, 1 cbt engr regt, 1 sigs regt, 1 CSS bn)
Light
1 (7th) mot inf bde (1 armd recce regt, 2 mot inf bn, 1 arty regt, 1 cbt engr regt, 1 sigs sqn, 1 CSS bn)
1 (3rd) lt inf bde (1 recce regt, 1 (IMV) mot inf sqn, 2 lt inf bn, 1 AB bn, 1 arty regt, 1 cbt engr regt, 1 sigs regt, 1 CSS bn)
Aviation
1 (16th) avn bde (1 regt (2 ISR hel sqn), 1 regt (3 tpt hel sqn), 1 regt (1 spec ops hel sqn, 1 avn sqn))
COMBAT SUPPORT
1 (6th) cbt spt bde (1 STA regt (1 STA bty, 1 UAV bty, 1 CSS bty), 1 AD/FAC regt (integrated), 1 int bn)
1 EW regt
COMBAT SERVICE SUPORT
1 (17th) CSS bde (3 log bn, 3 med bn, 1 MP bn)
1 engr regt (2 (construction) engr sqn, 1 (topographic) engr sqn)

Special Operations Command

FORCES BY ROLE
SPECIAL FORCES
1 (SAS) SF regt
1 (SF Engr) SF regt
2 cdo bn
COMBAT SUPPORT
3 sigs sqn (incl 1 reserve sqn)
COMBAT SERVICE SUPPORT
1 CSS sqn

Reserve Organisations

Force Command 16,650 reservists

FORCES BY ROLE
COMMAND
1 (2nd) div HQ
MANOEUVRE Light
6 inf bde (1 recce unit, 23 inf bn, some cbt spt/CSS unit)
COMBAT SERVICE SUPPORT
2 (construction) engr regt

EQUIPMENT BY TYPE
MBT 59 M1A1 *Abrams*
AIFV 257 ASLAV-25 (all variants)
APC 1,431
  APC (T) 694: 336 M113A1 (awaiting disposal); 358 M113AS4 (73 more being upgraded)
  PPV 737 *Bushmaster* IMV
ARTY 364
  TOWED 179: **105mm** 109 L-118 Light Gun; **155mm** 70: 35 M198; 35 M777A2
  MOR 81mm 185
AT
  MSL • MANPATS 111 *Javelin*
  RCL • 84mm 1,082 *Carl Gustav*
AMPHIBIOUS 15 LCM-8 (capacity either 1 MBT or 200 troops)
HELICOPTERS
  ATK 22 EC665 *Tiger*
  TPT 104: **Heavy** 6 CH-47D *Chinook* **Medium** 57: 22 NH90 TTH (MRH90 TTH) (18 more on order); 35 S-70A *Black Hawk* **Light** 41 Bell 206B-1 *Kiowa*
UAV • ISR • Medium 8 RQ-7B *Shadow* 200
AD • SAM • MANPAD 41: 1 CRAM; 40 RBS-70
RADAR • LAND 38: 7 AN/TPQ-36 *Firefinder* (arty, mor); 31 LCMR
ARV 18+: 10 ASLAV-F; 1 ASLAV-R; 7 M88A2; M806A1
VLB 5 *Biber*
MW 11: 3 *Chubby*; 8 ST-AT/V

Navy 14,000

Fleet Comd HQ located at Stirling; Naval Systems Comd located at Canberra

EQUIPMENT BY TYPE
SUBMARINES • TACTICAL • SSK 6 *Collins* each with 6 single 533mm TT each with Mk48 *Sea Arrow* ADCAP HWT/UGM-84C *Harpoon* AShM
PRINCIPAL SURFACE COMBATANTS 12
  FRIGATES • FFGHM 12:
    4 *Adelaide* (Mod) with 1 Mk13 GMLS with RGM-84C *Harpoon* AShM/SM-2 MR SAM, 1 8 cell Mk41 VLS with RIM-162 *Evolved Sea Sparrow* SAM, 2 triple Mk32 324mm ASTT with MU90 LWT, 1 76mm gun, (capacity 2 S-70B *Seahawk* ASW hel)
    8 *Anzac* (GER MEKO 200) with 2 quad Mk141 lnchr with RGM-84C *Harpoon* AShM, 1 8 cell Mk41 VLS with RIM-162 *Evolved Sea Sparrow* SAM, 2 triple 324mm ASTT with MU90 LWT, 1 127mm gun, (capacity 1 S-70B *Seahawk* ASW hel), (capability upgrades in progress)
PATROL AND COASTAL COMBATANTS • PHSC 14 *Armidale*
MINE WARFARE • MINE COUNTERMEASURES 9
  MHO 6 *Huon*
  MSD 3
AMPHIBIOUS
  PRINCIPAL AMPHIBIOUS SHIPS 2:
    LSD 1 *Choules* (UK *Bay*) (capacity 4 LCU; 2 LCVP; 24 MBT; 350 troops)
    LSL 1 *Tobruk*; 2 LCM; 2 LCVP; 40 APC and 18 MBT; 500 troops)

LANDING CRAFT 10:

LCH 6 *Balikpapan* (capacity 3 MBT or 13 APC - 3 to decommission end-2012)

LCVP 4

LOGISTICS AND SUPPORT 24

AE 3 *Wattle*

AGSH 2 *Leeuwin*

AGS 4 *Paluma*

AORH 1 *Success*

AOR 1 *Sirius*

AOL 4 *Warrigal*

ASR 3

AX 3: 1 **AXL**; 2 **AXS**

YPT 3

Naval Aviation 1,350

FORCES BY ROLE

ANTI SUBMARINE WARFARE

1 sqn with NH-90 NFH (MRH-90); S-70B-2 *Seahawk*

TRAINING

1 sqn with AS350BA *Ecureuil*; Bell 429

EQUIPMENT BY TYPE

HELICOPTERS

ASW 18 : 2 NH-90 NFH (MRH-90) (additional ac on order); 16 S-70B-2 *Seahawk*;

TPT • Light 16: 13 AS350BA *Ecureuil*; 3 Bell 429

Air Force 14,200

Flying hours   175 hrs/year on F/A-18 *Hornet*

FORCES BY ROLE

FIGHTER/GROUND ATTACK

3 sqn with F/A-18A/B *Hornet*

2 sqn with F/A-18F *Super Hornet*

ANTI SUBMARINE WARFARE

2 sqn with AP-3C *Orion*

AIRBORNE EARLY WARNING & CONTROL

1 sqn with B-737-700 *Wedgetail*

TANKER/TRANSPORT

1 sqn with KC-30B MRTT

TRANSPORT

1 VIP sqn with B-737BBJ; CL-604 *Challenger*

1 sqn with Beech 350 *King Air*

1 sqn with C-17A *Globemaster*

1 sqn with C-130J-30 *Hercules*

TRAINING

1 sqn with Beech 350 *King Air*

2 (LIFT) sqn with *Hawk* MK127*

1 sqn with PC-9/A(F)

EQUIPMENT BY TYPE

AIRCRAFT 142 combat capable

FGA 95: 55 F/A-18A *Hornet*; 16 F/A-18B *Hornet*; 24 F/A-18F *Super Hornet*

ASW 19 AP-3C *Orion*

AEW&C 6 B-737 *Wedgetail*

TKR/TPT 5 KC-30A MRTT

TPT 42: **Heavy** 5 C-17A *Globemaster* (6th on order); **Medium** 12: (8 C-130H *Hercules* withdrawn end 2012); 12 C-130J-30 *Hercules* **Light** 16 Beech 300 *King Air* **PAX** 5: 2 B-737BBJ (VIP); 3 CL-604 *Challenger* (VIP)

TRG 95: 33 *Hawk* Mk127*; 62 PC-9/A (incl 4 PC-9/A(F) for tgt marking)

HELICOPTERS • TPT • Light 5–7 S-76 (civil contract)

RADAR • AD RADAR 8

OTH-B *Jindalee* 4

Tactical 4

MSL

AAM • IR AIM-9M/X *Sidewinder*; **IIR** AIM-9X *Sidewinder*; ASRAAM; **ARH** AIM-120 AMRAAM

ASM AGM-154 JSOW

AShM AGM-84A *Harpoon*

LACM AGM-158 JASSM

BOMBS

Conventional Mk 82 500lb GP; Mk 84 2,000lb GP; BLU-109/B 2,000lb penetrator

Laser-guided *Paveway* II/IV; Laser JDAM (being delivered)

INS/GPS guided JDAM; JDAM-ER (in development)

Paramilitary

Border Protection Command

Has responsibility for operational coordination and control of both civil and military maritime enforcement activities within Australia's Exclusive Economic Zone. The BPC is staffed by military and civilian officials from Defence, Customs, the Australian Fisheries Management Authority and the Australian Quarantine Inspection Service.

EQUIPMENT BY TYPE

PATROL AND COASTAL COMBATANTS 11

PSO 1 *Ocean Protector* with 1 hel landing platform

PCO 1 *Triton* with 1 hel landing platform

PCC 9: 1 *Ashmore Guardian*; 8 *Bay*

AIRCRAFT

TPT • Light 15: 6 BN-2B *Islander*; 1 *Commander* (AC50 *Shrike*); 5 DHC-8; 3 F-406 *Caravan II*

HELICOPTERS • TPT 2 **Medium** 1 Bell 214 **Light** 1 Bell 206L *Long Ranger*

Cyber

Canberra published a Cyber Security Strategy in 2009, and the issue featured heavily in the 2009 Defence White Paper. There is a cyber policy coordinator within the Department of the Prime Minister. A Cyber Security Operations Centre (CSOC) was established in 2010 within the Defence Signals Directorate (DSD), while CERT Australia was established in the Attorney General's Department. CSOC includes embedded representation from the Department of Defence, the Australian Security Intelligence Organisation, the Defence Intelligence Organisation, CERT Australia and the Australian Federal Police. It reports an improvement in ICT security due to improved awareness, in tandem with government efforts to implement mitigation strategies (such as updating software OS patches). Within the Department of Defence, routine Computer Network Defence is managed by the Chief Information Officer Group, which also runs the network. The function is carried out by the Australian Defence Force Computer Incident Response Team, located at the Defence Network Operations Centre. The Defence

Signals Directorate produces the Australian Government Information Security Manual, and also published details on strategies to mitigate targeted cyber intrusions.

DEPLOYMENT

Legal provisions for foreign deployment:
Constitution: Constitution (1900)
Decision on deployment of troops abroad: By Government exercising its executive power under Section 61 of the Australian Constitution.

AFGHANISTAN
NATO • ISAF 1,550; 1 inf BG with (1 mot inf coy; 1 armd recce sqn); elms 1 arty regt; 1 hel gp with 2 CH-47D; 1 UAV det with RQ-7B *Shadow* 200; 1 UAV det with *Heron*; 25 *Bushmaster* IMV

ARABIAN SEA
Combined Maritime Forces • CTF-151 1 FFGHM

EGYPT
MFO (*Operation Mazurka*) 25

IRAQ
UN • UNAMI 2 obs

MALAYSIA
Army 115; 1 inf coy (on 3-month rotational tours)
Air force 15; 1 AP-3C *Orion* (on occasion)

MIDDLE EAST
UN • UNTSO 11 obs

PAPUA NEW GUINEA
Army 38; 1 trg unit

SOLOMON ISLANDS
RAMSI (*Operation Anode*) 80; 2 inf pl; 4 OH-58 *Kiowa*; 2 S-70 *Black Hawk*; 2 *Armidale* PCC

SOUTH SUDAN
UN • UNMISS 12; 4 obs

TIMOR LESTE
ISF (*Operation Astute*) 390; 1 inf bn HQ; 2 inf coy; 1 AD bty; elm 1 cbt engr regt; 1 hel det with 4 S-70 *Black Hawk*
UN • UNMIT 4 obs

UNITED ARAB EMIRATES
Air Force 300; 1 tpt det with 3 C-130 *Hercules*; 1 MP det with 2 AP-3C *Orion* , 1 C-17A (on occasion)

FOREIGN FORCES

New Zealand Army: 9 (air navigation) trg
Singapore Air Force 230: 1 trg sqn at Pearce with PC-21 trg ac; 1 trg sqn at Oakey with 12 AS332 *Super Puma/AS532 Cougar*
United States US Pacific Command: 180; 1 SEWS at Pine Gap; 1 comms facility at NW Cape; 1 SIGINT stn at Pine Gap

Bangladesh BGD

Bangladeshi Taka Tk		2011	2012	2013
GDP	Tk	8.56tr	9.74tr	
	US$	113.86bn	118.69bn	
per capita	US$	707	737	
Growth	%	6.51	6.05	
Inflation	%	10.70	8.52	
Def exp	Tk	111bn		
	US$	1.48bn		
Def bdgt	Tk	93.2bn	122bn	129bn
	US$	1.24bn	1.49bn	
FMA (US)	US$	2.957m	1.5m	1.65m
US$1=Tk		75.16	82.02	

Population 161,083,804

Religious groups: Muslim 90%; Hindu 9%; Buddhist 1%

Age	0–14	15–19	20–24	25–29	30–64	65 plus
Male	17.1%	4.8%	4.0%	3.5%	7.8%	17.0%
Female	16.6%	5.2%	4.8%	4.3%	10.7%	18.1%

Capabilities

Bangladesh has a limited military capability. The military has previously taken a political role, which ended with the 2008 general election. In 2009, a pay dispute sparked a rebellion by a group of the Bangladesh Rifles paramilitary force, but this did not directly affect the armed forces. Inter-service cooperation is limited. International exercises during 2011–12 included drills with India and the US (the latter in the *Pacific Resilience* HA/DR exercise). Bangladesh's long record of service in UN peacekeeping missions has brought considerable operational experience. Modest efforts to improve its inventory are underway across all three services. Mid-2012 saw the country request four second hand C-130E *Hercules* from the US

ACTIVE 157,050 (Army 126,150 Navy 16,900 Air 14,000) Paramilitary 63,900

ORGANISATIONS BY SERVICE

Army 126,150
FORCES BY ROLE
COMMAND
  7 inf div HQ
SPECIAL FORCES
  1 cdo bn
MANOEUVRE
  Armoured
  1 armd bde
  6 indep armd regt
  Light
  18 inf bde
  1 (composite) bde
  Aviation
  1 avn regt (2 avn sqn)

COMBAT SUPPORT
20 arty regt
1 AD bde
1 engr bde
1 sigs bde

EQUIPMENT BY TYPE
MBT 232: 58 Type-69/Type-69G; 174 Type-59
LT TK 8 Type-62
APC 306
  APC (T) 134 MT-LB
  APC (W) 172: 155 BTR-80; 17 *Cobra*
ARTY 815+
  TOWED 343+: **105mm** 170: 56 Model 56A1; 114 Model 56/L 10A1 pack howitzer; **122mm** 111: 57 Type-54/54-1 (M-30), 54 T96 (D-30), **130mm** 62 Type-59-1 (M-46)
  MOR 472: **81mm** 11 M29A1; **82mm** 366 Type-53/87/M-31 (M-1937); **120mm** 95 MO-120-AM-50 M67/UBM 52
AT • RCL 106mm 238 M40A1
AIRCRAFT • TPT • Light 6: 5 Cessna 152; 1 PA-31T *Cheyenne*
AD • SAM
  SP FM-90
  MANPAD QW-2; HN-5A (being replaced by QW-2)
  GUNS • TOWED 164: **37mm** 132 Type-65/74 **57mm** 34 Type-59 (S-60)
AEV MT-LB
ARV T-54/T-55; Type-84
VLB MTU

Navy 16,900

Navy HQ at Dhaka

EQUIPMENT BY TYPE
PRINCIPAL SURFACE COMBATANTS • FRIGATES 5
  FFGHM 1:
    1 *Bangabandhu* (ROK *Modified Ulsan*) with 2 twin lnchr with *Otomat* Mk2 AShM, 2 triple 324mm TT, 1 76mm gun (capacity: 1 AW109E hel)
  FFG 1:
    1 *Osman* (PRC *Jianghu* I) with 2 quad lnchr with YJ-82 (C-802) AShM, 2 RBU 1200, 2 twin 100mm gun
  FF 3:
    2 *Abu Bakr*† (UK *Leopard*) with 2 twin 115mm gun
    1 *Umar Farooq*† (UK *Salisbury* – trg role) with 3 *Squid*, 1 twin 115mm gun
PATROL AND COASTAL COMBATANTS 42
  PSOH 2 *Bijoy* (UK *Castle*)
  PCFG 4 *Durdarsha* (PRC *Huangfeng*) with 4 single lnchr with HY-2 (CSS-N-2) *Silkworm* AShM
  PCO 6: 1 *Madhumati* (*Sea Dragon*); 5 *Kapatakhaya* (UK *Island*)
  PCC 3: 2 *Meghna* (fishery protection); 1 *Nirbhoy* (PRC *Hainan*) with 4 RBU 1200
  PBFG 5 *Durbar* (PRC *Hegu*) with 2 single lnchr with SY-1 AShM
  PBFT 4 *Huchuan* (PRC) with 2 single 533mm TT each with YU 1 Type-53 HWT
  PBF 4 *Titas* (ROK *Sea Dolphin*)

  PB 14: 2 *Akshay*; 1 *Barkat* (PRC *Shanghai III*); 1 *Bishkali*; 2 *Karnaphuli*; 1 *Salam* (PRC *Huangfen*); 7 *Shaheed Daulat* (PRC *Shanghai II*)
MINE WARFARE • MINE COUNTERMEASURES 5
  MSO 5: 1 *Sagar*; 4 *Shapla* (UK *River*)
AMPHIBIOUS 11
  LANDING SHIPS • LSL 1
  LANDING CRAFT 10:
    LCU 2†
    LCVP 3†
    LCM 5 *Yuchin*
LOGISTICS AND SUPPORT 11
  AOR 2 (coastal)
  AR 1†
  AG 1
  ATF 1†
  AGHS 2: 1 *Agradoot*; 1 *Anushandhan*
  AX 1 *Shaheed Ruhul Amin*
  YTM 3

Naval Aviation

EQUIPMENT BY TYPE
HELICOPTERS • TPT • Light 2 AW109E *Power*

Air Force 14,000

FORCES BY ROLE
FIGHTER
  1 sqn with MiG-29B/UB *Fulcrum*
FIGHTER/GROUND ATTACK
  1 sqn with F-7MB/FT-7B *Airguard*
  1 sqn with F-7BG/FT-7BG *Airguard*
GROUND ATTACK
  1 sqn with A-5C (Q-5III) *Fantan*; FT-6 (MiG-19UTI) *Farmer*
TRANSPORT
  1 sqn with An-32 *Club*
  1 sqn with C-130B *Hercules*
TRAINING
  1 (OCU) sqn with L-39ZA *Albatros**
  1 sqn with PT-6
TRANSPORT HELICOPTER
  2 sqn with Mi-17 *Hip* H; Mi-17-1V *Hip* H; Mi-171Sh
  1 sqn with Bell 212
  1 trg sqn with Bell 206L *Long Ranger*
EQUIPMENT BY TYPE†
AIRCRAFT 70 combat capable
  FTR 45: 10 F-7MB *Airguard*; 11 F-7BG *Airguard*; (recce capable); 5 FT-7B *Airguard*; 4 FT-7BG *Airguard*; 7 FT-6 *Farmer*; 6 MiG-29 *Fulcrum*; 2 MiG-29UB *Fulcrum*
  ATK 18 A-5C *Fantan*
  TPT 7: **Medium** 4 C-130B *Hercules*; **Light** 3 An-32 *Cline*†
  TRG 17: 7 L-39ZA *Albatros**; 10 PT-6
HELICOPTERS
  MRH 14: 12 Mi-17 *Hip* H; 2 Mi-17-1V *Hip* H (VIP)
  TPT 9: **Medium** 3 Mi-171Sh **Light** 6: 2 Bell 206L *Long Ranger*; 4 Bell 212
MSL • AAM • IR R-3 (AA-2 *Atoll*)‡; R-73 (AA-11 *Archer*); PL-5; PL-7; **SARH** R-27R (AA-10A *Alamo*)

Paramilitary 63,900

Ansars 20,000+
Security Guards

Armed Police 5,000
Rapid action force (forming)

Border Guard Bangladesh 38,000
FORCES BY ROLE
MANOEUVRE
  Other
  41 paramilitary bn

Coast Guard 900
EQUIPMENT BY TYPE
PATROL AND COASTAL COMBATANTS 9
  PB 4: 1 *Ruposhi Bangla*; 1 *Shaheed Daulat*; 2 *Shetgang*
  PBR 5 *Pabna*

DEPLOYMENTS

CÔTE D'IVOIRE
UN • UNOCI 2,170; 13 obs; 2 inf bn; 1 avn coy; 1 engr coy; 1 sigs coy; 1 fd hospital

DEMOCRATIC REPUBLIC OF THE CONGO
UN • MONUSCO 2,519; 34 obs; 2 mech inf bn; 1 avn coy; 1 hel coy(-); 1 engr coy

LEBANON
UN • UNIFIL 326; 1 FFG; 1 PCO

LIBERIA
UN • UNMIL 1,383; 11 obs; 1 inf bn; 2 engr coy; 1 MP pl; 1 sigs coy(-); 1 log coy; 1 fd hospital

SOUTH SUDAN
UN • UNMISS 278; 1 engr coy; 1 fd hospital

SUDAN
UN • UNAMID 391; 12 obs; 1 inf coy; 1 log coy

TIMOR LESTE
UN • UNMIT 3 obs

WESTERN SAHARA
UN • MINURSO 20; 7 obs; 1 fd hospital

Brunei BRN

Brunei Dollar B$		2011	2012	2013
GDP	B$	20.58bn	21.38bn	
	US$	16.36bn	16.85bn	
per capita	US$	40,713	41,225	
Growth	%	2.21	2.66	
Inflation	%	2.02	1.74	
Def bdgt	B$	514m	513m	
	US$	409m	405m	
US$1=B$			1.26	1.27

Population   408,786

Ethnic groups: Malay, Kedayan, Tutong, Belait, Bisaya, Dusun, Murut 66.3%; Chinese 11.2%; Iban, Dayak, Kelabit 6%; Other 11.8%

Age	0–14	15–19	20–24	25–29	30–64	65 plus
Male	12.9%	4.4%	4.3%	4.7%	21.8%	1.8%
Female	12.1%	4.4%	4.6%	5.1%	22.1%	1.9%

Capabilities

The small, professional Royal Brunei Armed Forces (RBAF) are an important source of employment in this oil-rich state. Despite being well-trained, they could offer little resistance on their own to a determined aggressor. However, the sultanate has long-established defence relations with the United Kingdom and Singapore, with which its forces train. It has deployed small contingents, under Malaysian command, to the Lebanon (UNIFIL) and southern Philippines (IMT).

ACTIVE 7,000 (Army 4,900 Navy 1,000 Air 1,100)
Paramilitary 2,250

RESERVE 700 (Army 700)

ORGANISATIONS BY SERVICE

Army 4,900
FORCES BY ROLE
MANOEUVRE
  Light
  3 inf bn
COMBAT SUPPORT
  1 cbt spt bn (1 armd recce sqn, 1 engr sqn)

  Reserves 700
  FORCES BY ROLE
  MANOEUVRE
    Light
    1 inf bn

EQUIPMENT BY TYPE
LT TK 20 *Scorpion* (16 to be upgraded)
APC (W) 45 VAB
ARTY • MOR 81mm 24
ARV 2 *Samson*

Navy 1,000
FORCES BY ROLE
SPECIAL FORCES
  1 SF sqn

EQUIPMENT BY TYPE

PATROL AND COASTAL COMBATANTS 11
  PSO 3 *Darussalam*
  PCC 4 *Itjihad*
  PBF 1 *Mustaed*
  PB 3 *Perwira*
AMPHIBIOUS • LANDING CRAFT • LCU 4: 2 *Teraban*;
2 *Cheverton Loadmaster*

Air Force 1,100

FORCES BY ROLE
MARITIME PATROL
  1 sqn with CN-235M
TRAINING
  1 sqn with PC-7; Bell 206B *Jet Ranger* II
TRANSPORT HELICOPTER
  1 sqn with Bell 212; Bell 214 (SAR)
  1 sqn with Bo-105
  1 sqn with S-70A *Black Hawk*
AIR DEFENCE
  1 sqn with Rapier
  1 sqn with *Mistral*
EQUIPMENT BY TYPE
AIRCRAFT
  MP 1 CN-235M
  TRG 4 PC-7
HELICOPTERS
  TPT 23 **Medium** 5: 1 Bell 214 (SAR); 4 S-70A *Black Hawk*
  Light 18: 2 Bell 206B *Jet Ranger II*; 10 Bell 212; 6 Bo-105
  (armed, 81mm rockets)
AD • SAM *Rapier*; 12 *Mistral*

Paramilitary ε2,250

Gurkha Reserve Unit 400-500

FORCES BY ROLE
MANOEUVRE
  Light
  2 inf bn (-)

Royal Brunei Police 1,750

EQUIPMENT BY TYPE
PATROL AND COASTAL COMBATANTS • PB 10: 3
Bendaharu; 7 PDB-type

DEPLOYMENT

LEBANON
UN • UNIFIL 30

PHILIPPINES
IMT 9

FOREIGN FORCES

Singapore Army: 1 trg camp with infantry units on
rotation Air Force; trg school; 1 hel det with AS 332 *Super
Puma*
United Kingdom Army: 550; 1 Gurkha bn; 1 trg unit; 1 hel
flt with 3 hel

Cambodia CAM

Cambodian Riel r		2011	2012	2013
GDP	r	52.15tr	57.54tr	
	US$	12.89bn	14.25bn	
per capita	US$	862	953	
Growth	%	7.08	6.45	
Inflation	%	5.48	3.61	
Def bdgt [a]	r	1.25tr	1.4tr	
	US$	308m	346m	
FMA (US)	US$	0.748m	0.8m	1m
US$1=r		4046.09	4039.03	

[a] Includes public security expenditure disbursed by the Ministry
of Interior. Excludes defence capital expenditure.

Population   14,952,665

Ethnic groups: Khmer 90%; Vietnamese 5%; Chinese 1%

Age	0–14	15–19	20–24	25–29	30–64	65 plus
Male	16.0%	5.2%	5.7%	5.0%	15.0%	1.8%
Female	15.9%	5.3%	5.8%	5.1%	17.2%	1.9%

Capabilities

Despite their name, which reflects Cambodia's formal status as a constitutional monarchy, and their integration, in
the early 1990s, of two non-communist resistance armies,
the Royal Cambodian Armed Forces (RCAF) are essentially the modern manifestation of the armed forces of the
former People's Republic of Kampuchea, established in
1979 following Vietnam's invasion. The army is organised
into many under-strength 'divisions', and is top-heavy
with senior officers. Minor skirmishes on the border with
Thailand since 2008 provide little indication of the RCAF's
capacity for high-intensity combat, which is probably limited.

**ACTIVE 124,300 (Army 75,000 Navy 2,800 Air 1,500
Provincial Forces 45,000) Paramilitary 67,000**

Terms of service conscription authorised but not
implemented since 1993

ORGANISATIONS BY SERVICE

Army ε75,000

6 Military Regions (incl 1 special zone for capital)

FORCES BY ROLE
SPECIAL FORCES
  1 AB/SF regt
MANOEUVRE
  Reconnaissance
  Some indep recce bn
  Armoured
  3 armd bn
  Light
  12 inf div(-)
  3 indep inf bde
  9 indep inf regt

Other
1 (70th) sy bde (4 sy bn)
17 (border) sy bn
COMBAT SUPPORT
2 arty bn
1 AD bn
4 fd engr regt
COMBAT SERVICE SUPPORT
1 (construction) engr regt
EQUIPMENT BY TYPE
MBT 200+: 50 Type-59; 150+ T-54/T-55
LT TK 20+: Type-62; 20 Type-63
RECCE 4+ BRDM-2
AIFV 70 BMP-1
APC 230+
  APC (T) M113
  APC (W) 230: 200 BTR-60/BTR-152; 30 OT-64
ARTY 428+
  TOWED 400+ **76mm** ZIS-3 (M-1942)/**122mm**
  D-30/**122mm** M-30 (M-1938)/**130mm** Type-59-I
  MRL 28+: **107mm** Type-63; **122mm** 8 BM-21; **132mm** BM-13-16 (BM-13); **140mm** 20 BM-14-16 (BM-14)
  MOR 82mm M-37; **120mm** M-43; **160mm** M-160
AT • RCL 82mm B-10; **107mm** B-11
AD
  MSL • MANPAD 50 FN-6; FN-16 (reported)
  GUNS • TOWED 14.5mm ZPU-1/ZPU-2/ZPU-4; **37mm**
  M-1939; **57mm** S-60
ARV T-54/T-55
MW Bozena; RA-140 DS

Navy ε2,800 (incl 1,500 Naval Infantry)

EQUIPMENT BY TYPE
PATROL AND COASTAL COMBATANTS 11
  PBF 2 Stenka
  PB 7: 4 (PRC 46m); 3 (PRC 20m)
  PBR 2 Kaoh Chhlam
AMPHIBIOUS • CRAFT
  LCU 1

Naval Infantry 1,500

FORCES BY ROLE
MANOEUVRE
  Light
  7 inf bn
COMBAT SUPPORT
  1 arty bn

Air Force 1,500

FORCES BY ROLE
ISR/TRAINING
  1 sqn with P-92 Echo; L-39 Albatros*
TRANSPORT
  1 VIP sqn (reporting to Council of Ministers) with An-24RV Coke; AS350 Ecureuil; AS355F2 Ecureuil II
  1 sqn with BN-2 Islander; Y-12 (II)
TRANSPORT HELICOPTER
  1 sqn with Mi-26 Halo; Mi-17 Hip H; Mi-8 Hip
EQUIPMENT BY TYPE
AIRCRAFT 5 combat capable

TPT • Light 10: 2 An-24RV Coke; 1 BN-2 Islander; 5 P-92 Echo (pilot trg/recce); 2 Y-12 (II)
TRG 5 L-39 Albatros*
HELICOPTERS
MRH 3 MI-17 Hip H
TPT 10: **Heavy** 2 Mi-26 Halo **Medium** 4 Mi-8 Hip **Light** 4: 2 AS350 Ecureuil; 2 AS355F2 Ecureuil II

Provincial Forces 45,000+

Reports of at least 1 inf regt per province, with varying numbers of inf bn (with lt wpn)

Paramilitary

Police 67,000 (including gendarmerie)

DEPLOYMENT

LEBANON
UN • UNIFIL 216; 1 engr coy

SOUTH SUDAN
UN • UNMISS 145; 3 obs; 1 MP coy; 1 fd hospital

SUDAN
UN • UNISFA 1 obs

China, People's Republic of PRC

Chinese Yuan Renminbi Y		2011	2012	2013
GDP	Y	47.16tr	52.18tr	
	US$	7.3tr	8.25tr	
	US$[a]	11.3tr	12.4tr	
per capita	US$	5,435	6,142	
Growth	%	9.24	7.83	
Inflation	%	5.42	3.01	
Def exp [c]	Y	883bn		
	US$	137bn		
	US$[a]	198bn		
Def bdgt [b]	Y	583bn	648bn	
	US$	90.2bn	102bn	
US$1=Y	MER	6.46	6.33	
	PPP	4.17	4.21	

[a] PPP estimate

[b] Official central government expenditure on national defence

[c] See p.256 for details on China defence expenditure estimates

Population 1,343,239,923

Ethnic groups: Tibetan, Uighur and other non-Han 8%

Age	0–14	15–19	20–24	25–29	30–64	65 plus
Male	9.3%	3.9%	4.6%	4.1%	25.3%	4.4%
Female	8.0%	3.4%	4.2%	3.9%	24.3%	4.7%

Capabilities

The People's Liberation Army (PLA) is engaged in a modernisation programme fuelled by the country's rapid economic development. With a fleet including modern submarines and naval escorts, more capable fighter aircraft and advanced armoured vehicles, not to mention new missiles, it is now superior to the armed forces of less developed countries in Southeast Asia. More advanced platforms and weapons are also in development, including aircraft exhibiting stealth characteristics. However, a lack of war-fighting experience (China has not been involved in a significant conflict since the war with Vietnam in 1979), questions over training and morale, and key capability weaknesses in areas such as C4ISTAR and anti-submarine warfare, mean that it remains qualitatively inferior, in some respects, to more technologically advanced armed forces in the region, such as South Korea and Japan, and lags far behind the US. Though 2012 saw China's first carrier commissioned, the country has yet to field the suite of capabilities that would enable carrier battle group operations. Nevertheless, it increasingly has the capacity to complicate US operations in China's littoral and, while defending national sovereignty remains the PLA's primary concern, increased funding is allowing it to develop limited power-projection capabilities which have been demonstrated in operational naval deployments to the western Indian Ocean in the counter-piracy role (See essay pp. 252–8).

ACTIVE 2,285,000 (Army 1,600,000 Navy 255,000 Air 300,000-330,000 Strategic Missile Forces 100,000) Paramilitary 660,000

Terms of service selective conscription; all services 2 years

RESERVE ε510,000

Overall organisation: army leadership is exercised by the four general headquarters/departments. A military region exercises direct leadership over the army units under it. The navy, air force and Second Artillery Force each have a leading body consisting of the headquarters, political department, logistics department and armaments department. These direct the military, political, logistical and equipment work of their respective troops, and take part in the command of joint operations.

ORGANISATIONS BY SERVICE

Strategic Missile Forces (100,000+)

Offensive

The Second Artillery Force organises and commands its own troops to launch nuclear counterattacks with strategic missiles and to conduct operations with conventional missiles. Org as launch bdes subordinate to 6 army-level msl bases (1 in Shenyang & Beijing MR, 1 in Jinan MR, 1 in Nanjing MR, 2 in Gunagzhou MR and 1 in Lanzhou MR). Org varies by msl type. The DF-16 MRBM is reported to be in service, but it is not yet clear which formation it has been assigned to.

FORCES BY ROLE
MISSILE
  1 ICBM bde with DF-4
  3 ICBM bde with DF-5A
  1 ICBM bde with DF-31
  2 ICBM bde with DF-31A

  1 IRBM bde with DF-3A
  1 MRBM bde with DF-21
  7 MRBM bde with DF-21A (1 bde may be transitioning to DF-31A)
  2 MRBM bde with DF-21C
  1 MRBM bde forming with DF-21D (reported)
  4 SRBM bde with DF-11A
  4 SRBM bde with DF-15
  2 SSM bde with DH-10
  2 SSM trg bde
MSL • STRATEGIC 470
  ICBM 72: ε10 DF-4 (CSS-3); ε20 DF-5A (CSS-4 Mod 2); ε12 DF-31 (CSS-9); ε30 DF-31A (CSS-9 Mod 2)
  IRBM ε2 DF-3A (CSS-2 Mod)
  MRBM 122+: some DF-16; ε80 DF-21/DF-21A (CSS-5 Mod 1/2); ε36 DF-21C (CSS-5 Mod 3); ε6 DF-21D (CSS-5 Mod 4 - ASBM) reported
  SRBM 252: ε108 DF-11A/M-11A (CSS-7 Mod 2); ε144 DF-15/M-9 (CSS-6)
  LACM ε54 CJ-10 (DH-10)

Navy

SUBMARINES • STRATEGIC • SSBN 4:
  1 *Xia* with 12 JL-1 (CSS-N-3) strategic SLBM
  3 *Jin* with up to 12 JL-2 (CSS-NX-4) strategic SLBM (operational status unknown; 3rd and 4th vessels in build)

Defensive

RADAR • STRATEGIC: some phased array radar; some detection and tracking radars (covering Central Asia and Shanxi on the northern border) located in Xinjiang province

Space

SATELLITES 52
  COMMUNICATIONS 4 *Zhongxing* (dual use telecom satellites for civ/mil comms)
  NAVIGATION/POSITIONING/TIMING 17: 2 *Beidou*-1; 5 *Beidou*-2(M); 5 *Beidou*-2(G); 5 *Beidou*-2 (IGSO)
  ISR 20: 1 *Haiyang* 2A; 17 *Yaogan Weixing* (remote sensing); 2 *Zhangguo Ziyuan* (ZY-2 - remote sensing)
  ELINT/SIGINT 11: 8 *Shijian* 6 (4 pairs - reported ELINT/SIGINT role); 3 *Shijian* 11 (reported ELINT/SIGINT role)

People's Liberation Army ε800,000; ε800,000 conscript (reductions continue) (total ε1,600,000)

7 military region comds are sub-divided into a total of 28 military districts. The army is currently in the process of converting its remaining armoured divisions into new armoured and mechanised brigades. The remaining aviation regiments are also being converted into new brigades.

FORCES BY ROLE
COMMAND
  7 mil region
  18 (Group) army HQ
SPECIAL FORCES
  7 SF unit

MANOEUVRE

Armoured
5 armd div
11 armd bde

Mechanised
7 mech inf div
2 (high alt) mech inf div
9 mech inf bde
1 (high alt) mech inf bde
2 indep mech inf regt

Light
10 mot inf div
3 (high alt) mot inf div
1 (jungle) mot inf div
19 mot inf bde
2 (high alt) mot inf bde

Amphibious
1 amph armd bde
2 amph mech div

Mountain
2 mtn inf bde

Other
1 (OPFOR) armd bde
1 mech gd div
1 lt gd div

Aviation
6 avn bde
4 avn regt
2 trg avn regt

COMBAT SUPPORT

2 arty div
17 arty bde
9 (coastal defence) AShM regt
21 AD bde
1 indep AD regt
1 engr bde
13 engr regt
5 EW regt
50 sigs regt

Reserves

FORCES BY ROLE
MANOEUVRE

Armoured
2 armd regt

Light
18 inf div
4 inf bde
3 indep inf regt

COMBAT SUPPORT

3 arty div
7 arty bde
17 AD div
8 AD bde
8 AD regt
15 engr regt
1 ptn br bde
3 ptn br regt
7 chem regt
10 sigs regt

COMBAT SERVICE SUPPORT

9 log bde
1 log regt

EQUIPMENT BY TYPE

MBT 7,430+: 4,300 Type-59/Type-59D/Type-59-II; 300 Type-79; 500 Type-88A/B; 1,000 Type-96; 800 Type-96A; 500 Type-98A/Type-99; 30+ Type-99A2

LT TK 800: 200 Type-05 AAAV (ZTD-05); 400 Type-62; 200 Type-63A

AIFV 2,150: 500 Type-04 (ZBD-04); 250 Type-05 AAAV (ZBD-05); 100 Type-08 (ZBD-08); 500 Type-86/Type-86A (WZ-501); 650 Type-92; 150 Type-92A

APC 2,900

  APC (T) 2,000: 1,650 Type-63/Type-63C; 350 Type-89

  APC (W) 900: 300 Type-09 (ZBL-09); 500 Type-92B; 100 WZ-523

ARTY 12,367+

  SP 1,821: **122mm** 1,371: 1,296 Type-70-I/Type-89/Type-07 (PLZ-07); ε75 Type-09 (PLC-09); **152mm** 324 Type-83; **155mm** 126 Type-05 (PLZ-05)

  TOWED 6,140: **122mm** 3,800 Type-54-1 (M-1938)/Type-83/Type-60 (D-74)/Type-96 (D-30); **130mm** 234 Type-59 (M-46)/Type-59-I; **152mm** 2,106 Type-54 (D-1)/Type-66 (D-20)

  GUN/MOR 50+: **120mm** 50+ Type-05 (PLL-05)

  MRL 1,770+

    SP 1,716+: **107mm** some **122mm** 1,620 Type-81/Type-89; **300mm** 96 Type-03 (PHL-03)

    TOWED • 107mm 54 Type-63

  MOR 2,586

    TOWED 81mm Type-W87; **82mm** Type-53 (M-37)/Type-67/Type-82; **100mm** Type-71 (reported); **120mm** Type-55 (incl SP); **160mm** Type-56 (M-160)

AT

  MSL

    SP 276 HJ-9 *Red Arrow* 9

    MANPATS HJ-73A/B/C; HJ-8A/C/E

  RCL 3,966: **75mm** Type-56; **82mm** Type-65 (B-10)/Type-78; **105mm** Type-75; **120mm** Type-98

  GUNS 1,888: **100mm** 1,658: 1,308 Type-73 (T-12)/Type-86; 350 Type-02 (PTL-02); **120mm** up to 230 Type-89 SP

AIRCRAFT • TPT 8 **Medium** 3 Y-8 **Light** 5 Y-7

HELICOPTERS

  ATK 42: ε30 Z-10; ε12 Z-19

  MRH 401: 22 Mi-17 *Hip* H; 33 Mi-17-V5 *Hip* H; 24 Mi-17-V7 *Hip* H; 8 SA316 *Alouette* III; 8 SA342L *Gazelle*; 80 Z-9/9B; 200 Z-9 WA; 26 Z-9W

  TPT 234 **Heavy** 21: 4 Mi-26 *Halo*; 7 SA321 *Super Frelon*; 10 Z-8 **Medium** 145: 50 Mi-8T *Hip*; 69 Mi-171; 8 Mi-172; 18 S-70C2 (S-70C) *Black Hawk* **Light** 68: 53 AS350 *Ecureuil*; 15 EC120

UAV • ISR • Heavy BZK-005; BZK-009; WZ-5 **Medium** ASN-105; ASN-206; BZK-006; **Light** ASN-104; W-50

AD

  SAM 302+:

    SP 302: 200 HQ-7A; 60 9K331 *Tor-M1* (SA-15 *Gauntlet*); 30 HQ-6D *Red Leader*; 12 HQ-16

    MANPAD HN-5A/HN-5B *Hong Nu*; FN-6/QW-1/QW-2

GUNS 7,700+

SP 25mm Type-95/Type-04; **35mm** Type-07; **37mm** Type-88

TOWED 23mm Type-80 (ZU-23-2); **25mm** Type-85; **35mm** Type-90 (GDF-002); **37mm** Type-55 (M-1939)/ Type-65/Type-74; **57mm** Type-59 (S-60); **85mm** Type-56 (KS-12); **100mm** Type-59 (KS-19)

RADAR • LAND *Cheetah*; RASIT; Type-378

MSL

AShM HY-1 (CSS-N-2) *Silkworm*; HY-2 (CSS-C-3) *Seersucker*; HY-4 (CSS-C-7) *Sadsack*

ASM KD-10

UAV • ISR • **Medium** BZK-007

ARV Type-73; Type-84; Type-85; Type-97; Type-654

VLB KMM; MTU; TMM; Type-84A

MW Type-74; Type-79; Type-81-II; Type-84

Navy ε215,000; 40,000 conscript (total 255,000)

The PLA Navy is organised into five service arms: submarine, surface, naval aviation, coastal defence and marine corps, as well as other specialised units. There are three fleets, the Beihai Fleet (North Sea), Donghai Fleet (East Sea) and Nanhai Fleet (South Sea).

EQUIPMENT BY TYPE

SUBMARINES 65

STRATEGIC • SSBN 4:

1 *Xia* (Type-092) with 12 JL-1 (CSS-N-3) strategic SLBM

3 *Jin* (Type-094) with up to 12 JL-2 (CSS-NX-4) strategic SLBM (operational status unknown; 1 additional vessels in build)

TACTICAL 61:

SSN 5:

3 *Han* (Type-091) with YJ-82 AShM, 6 single 533mm TT

2 *Shang* (Type-093) with 6 single 533mm TT (operational status unknown)

SSK 55:

12 *Kilo* (2 Project 877, 2 Project 636, 8 Project 636N) with 3M54 *Klub* (SS-N-27B *Sizzler*) ASCM; 6 single 533mm TT with up to 18 *Test-71/96* HWT

20 *Ming* (4 Type-035, 12 Type-035G, 4 Type-035B) with 8 single 533mm TT

16 *Song* (Type-039/039G) with YJ-82 (CSS-N-8) *Saccade* ASCM, 6 single 533mm TT

4 *Yuan* (Type-039A) with 6 533mm TT

3 *Yuan* II (Type-039B) with 6 533mm TT (1 additional vessel launched; expected ISD 2013)

SSB 1 *Qing* (SLBM trials)

PRINCIPAL SURFACE COMBATANTS 77

AIRCRAFT CARRIERS • CV 1

1 *Liaoning* (capacity 18-24 J-15 ac; 4 JL-9 ac; 17 Ka-28/ Ka-31/Z-8S/Z-8JH/Z-8AEW hel)

DESTROYERS 14

DDGHM 12:

4 *Hangzhou* (RUS *Sovremenny*) with 2 quad lnchr with 3M80/3M82 *Moskit* (SS-N-22 *Sunburn*) AShM, 2 3K90 *Uragan* (SA-N-7 *Grizzly*) SAM, 2 twin 533mm ASTT, 2 RBU 1000 *Smerch* 3, 2 twin 130mm gun, (capacity 1 Z-9C/Ka-28 *Helix* A hel)

2 *Luyang* (Type-052B) with 4 quad lnchr with YJ-82/83 AShM, 2 single lnchr with 3K90 *Uragan* (SA-N-7 *Grizzly*) SAM, 2 triple 324mm TT with Yu-7 LWT, 1 100mm gun, (capacity 1 Ka-28 *Helix* A hel)

3 *Luyang* II (Type-052C) with 2 quad lnchr with YJ-62 AShM, 8 sextuple VLS with HHQ-9 SAM, 2 triple 324mm TT with Yu-7 LWT, 1 100mm gun, (capacity 2 Ka-28 *Helix* A hel) (3 additional vessels; expected ISD 2013/14)

1 *Luhai* (Type-051B) with 4 quad lnchr with YJ-83 AShM, 1 octuple lnchr with HQ-7 SAM, 2 triple 324mm ASTT with Yu-7 LWT, 1 twin 100mm gun, (capacity 2 Z-9C/Ka-28 *Helix* A hel)

2 *Luhu* (Type-052) with 4 quad lnchr with YJ-82/83 AShM, 1 octuple lnchr with HQ-7 SAM, 2 triple 324mm ASTT with Yu-7 LWT, 2 FQF 2500, 1 twin 100mm gun, (capacity 2 Z-9C hel)

DDGM 2:

2 *Luzhou* (Type-051C) with 2 quad lnchr with YJ-82/83 AShM; 6 sextuple VLS with SA-N-20 *Grumble* SAM, 1 100mm gun, 1 hel landing platform

FRIGATES 62

FFGHM 29:

2 *Jiangkai* (Type-054) with 2 quad lnchr with YJ-82/83 AShM, 1 octuple lnchr with HQ-7 SAM, 2 triple 324mm TT with Yu-7 LWT, 2 RBU 1200, 1 100mm gun, (capacity 1 Ka-28 *Helix* A/Z-9C hel)

13 *Jiangkai* II (Type-054A) with 2 quad lnchr with YJ-82/83 AShM, 1 32-cell VLS with HQ-16 SAM (reported), 2 triple 324mm TT with Yu-7 LWT, 2 RBU 1200, 1 76mm gun, (capacity 1 Ka-28 *Helix* A/Z-9C hel) (3 additional vessels launched)

4 *Jiangwei* I (Type-053H2G) with 2 triple lnchr with YJ-82/83 AShM, 1 sextuple lnchr with HQ-61 (CSA-N-2) SAM, 2 RBU 1200, 1 twin 100mm gun, (capacity 2 Z-9C hel)

10 *Jiangwei* II (Type-053H3) with 2 quad lnchr with YJ-82/83 AShM, 1 octuple lnchr with HQ-7 SAM, 2 RBU 1200, 2 100mm gun, (capacity 2 Z-9C hel)

FFGH 1:

1 *Jianghu* IV (Type-053H1Q - trg role) with 1 triple lnchr with HY-2 (CSS-N-2) AShM, 4 RBU 1200, 1 100mm gun, (capacity 1 Z-9C hel)

FFGM 4:

2 *Luda* III (Type-051DT) with 4 quad lnchr with YJ-82/83 AShM, 1 octuple lnchr with HQ-7 SAM, 2 FQF 2500, 2 twin 100mm gun

2 *Luda* III (Type-051G) with 4 quad lnchr with YJ-82/83 AShM, 1 octuple lnchr with HQ-7 SAM, 2 FQF 2500, 2 triple 324mm ASTT, 2 twin 100mm gun

FFG 28:

8 *Jianghu* I (Type-053H) with 2 triple lnchr with SY-1 (CSS-N-2) AShM, 4 RBU 1200, 2 100mm gun

5 *Jianghu* II (Type-053H1) with 2 triple lnchr with HY-2 (CSS-N-2) AShM, 2 RBU 1200, 1 twin 100mm gun, (capacity 1 Z-9C hel)

3 *Jianghu* III (Type-053H2) with 4 twin lnchr with YJ-82/83 AShM, 2 RBU 1200, 2 twin 100mm gun

6 *Jianghu* V (Type-053H1G) with 2 quad lnchr with YJ-82/83 AShM, 2 RBU 1200, 2 twin 100mm gun

6 *Luda* II (Type-051) with 2 triple lnchr with HY-2 (CSS-N-2) *Seersucker* AShM, 2 triple 324mm ASTT, 2 twin 130mm gun, (mine-laying capability)

PATROL AND COASTAL COMBATANTS 211+

PCFG 76+

65+ *Houbei* (Type-022) with 2 quad lanchr with YJ-82/83 AShM

11 *Huangfen* (Type-021) with 2 twin lnchr with HY-2 (CSS-N-3) AShM

PCG 26

6 *Houjian* (Type-037/II) with 2 triple lnchr with YJ-8 (CSS-N-4) AShM

20 *Houxin* (Type-037/IG) with 2 twin lnchr with YJ-8 (CSS-N-4) AShM

PCC 75

3 *Haijui* (Type-037/I) with 4 RBU 1200

50 *Hainan* (Type-037) with ε4 RBU 1200

22 *Haiqing* (Type-037/IS) with 2 Type-87

PB 34+ *Haizui/Shanghai III* (Type-062/I)

MINE WARFARE 47

MINE COUNTERMEASURES 46

MCO 7: 6 *Wochi*; 1 *Wozang*

MSO 16 T-43

MSC 16 *Wosao*

MSD 7: 4 *Futi*-class (Type-312 - 42 more in reserve); 3 (other)

MINELAYERS • ML 1 *Wolei*

AMPHIBIOUS

PRINCIPAL AMPHIBIOUS VESSELS • LPD 2 *Yuzhao* (Type-071) (capacity 2 LCAC or 4 UCAC plus supporting vehicles; 500–800 troops; 2 hel) (1 additional vessel launched, expected ISD 2012-3)

LANDING SHIPS 85

LSM 59:

10 *Yubei* (capacity 10 tanks or 150 troops)

1 *Yudeng* (Type-073) (capacity 6 tk; 180 troops)

10 *Yuhai* (capacity 2 tk; 250 troops)

28 *Yuliang* (Type-079) (capacity 5 tk; 250 troops)

10 *Yunshu* (Type-073A) (capacity 6 tk)

LST 26:

7 *Yukan* (capacity 10 tk; 200 troops)

9 *Yuting* (capacity 10 tk; 250 troops; 2 hel)

10 *Yuting* II (capacity 4 LCVP; 10 tk; 250 troops)

LANDING CRAFT 151

LCU 120 *Yunnan*

LCM 20 *Yuchin*

LCAC 1

UCAC 10

LOGISTICS AND SUPPORT 205

AORH 5: 2 *Fuqing*; 2 *Fuchi* (2 more vessels launched; awaiting commssioning); 1 *Nanyun*

AOT 50: 7 *Danlin*; 20 *Fulin*; 2 *Shengli*; 3 *Jinyou*; 18 *Fuzhou*

AOL 5 *Guangzhou*

AS 8: 1 *Dazhi*; 5 *Dalang*; 2 *Dazhou*

ASR 1 *Dajiang* (capacity 2 Z-8)

ARS 2: 1 *Dadong*; 1 *Dadao*

AG 6: 4 *Qiongsha* (capacity 400 troops); 2 *Qiongsha* (hospital conversion)

AK 23: 2 *Yantai*; 2 *Dayun*; 6 *Danlin*; 7 *Dandao*; 6 *Hongqi*

AWT 18: 10 *Leizhou*; 8 *Fuzhou*

AGOR 5: 1 *Dahua*; 2 *Kan*; 1 *Bin Hai*; 1 *Shuguang*

AGI 1 *Dadie*

AGM 5 (space and missile tracking)

AGS 6: 5 *Yenlai*; 1 *Ganzhu*

AGB 4: 1 *Yanbing*; 3 *Yanha*

ABU 7 *Yannan*

ATF 51: 4 *Tuzhong*; 10 *Hujiu*; 1 *Daozha*; 17 *Gromovoy*; 19 *Roslavl*

AH 1 *Daishan*

AX 2: 1 *Shichang*; 1 *Daxin*

YDG 5 *Yen Pai*

MSL • AShM 72 YJ-62 (coastal defence) (3 regt)

Naval Aviation 26,000

FORCES BY ROLE

BOMBER

1 regt with H-6DU/G; Y-8X

1 regt with H-6G

FIGHTER

1 regt with J-7E

1 regt with J-8F

1 regt with J-8H

FIGHTER/GROUND ATTACK

1 regt with J-10A/S

1 regt with J-11B/BS

1 regt with Su-30MK2

ATTACK

2 regt with JH-7

3 regt with JH-7A

ELINT/ISR/AEW

1 regt with Y-8J/JB/W

MARITIME PATROL

1 regt with SH-5

TRANSPORT

1 regt with Y-7; Y-7H; Y-8

1 regt with Y-7; Y-8; Z-8; Z-9

TRAINING

1 regt with CJ-6A

2 regt with HY-7

1 regt with JL-8

1 regt with JL-9

1 regt with Mi-8 *Hip*; Z-9C

1 regt with Y-5

HELICOPTER

1 regt with Mi-8; Ka-28; Ka-31

1 regt with AS365; Ka-28; Z-8; Z-8A/JH/S

AIRCRAFT 341 combat capable

BBR 30 H-6G

FTR 72: 24 J-7E *Fishbed*; 24 J-8F *Finback*; 24 J-8H *Finback*

FGA 200: 120 JH-7/JH-7A; 28 J-10A/S; 28 J-11B/BS; 24 Su-30MK2 *Flanker*

ASW 4 SH-5

ELINT 7: 4 Y-8JB *High New 2*; 3 Y-8X

AEW&C 6: 4 Y-8J; 2 Y-8W *High New 5*

ISR 7 HZ-5

TKR 3 H-6DU

TPT 66: **Medium** 4 Y-8 **Light** 62: 50 Y-5; 4 Y-7; 6 Y-7H; 2 Yak-42

TRG 106+: 38 CJ-6; 5 HJ-5*; 21 HY-7; 14 JJ-6*; 4 JJ-7*; 12 JL-8*; 12+ JL-9

HELICOPTERS

ASW 44: 19 Ka-28 *Helix* A; 25 Z-9C

AEW 10+: 9 Ka-31; 1+ Z-8 AEW
SAR 6: 4 Z-8JH; 2 Z-8S
TPT 43 **Heavy** 35: 15 SA321 *Super Frelon*; 20 Z-8/Z-8A;
Medium 8 Mi-8 *Hip*
UAV • ISR Heavy BZK-005; **Medium** BZK-007
MSL
AAM • IR PL-5; PL-8; PL-9; R-73 (AA-11 *Archer*)
SARH PL-11 **IR/SARH** R-27 (AA-10 *Alamo*) **ARH** R-77
(AA-12 *Adder*); PL-12
ASM Kh-31A (AS-17B *Krypton*); KD-88
AShM YJ-61; YJ-8K; YJ-83K
ARM YJ-91
BOMBS
Conventional: Type-200-4/Type-200A
Laser-Guided: LS-500J
TV-Guided: KAB-500KR; KAB-1500KR

Marines ε10,000

FORCES BY ROLE
MANOEUVRE
Amphibious
2 mne bde (1 spec ops bn, 1 SF amph recce bn, 1 recce
bn, 2 tk bn, 4 mech inf bn, 1 arty bn, 1 AT/AD bn, 1
engr bn, 1 sigs bn)

EQUIPMENT BY TYPE
LT TK 124 Type-05 AAAV (ZTD-05)
APC (T) 248 Type-05 AAAV (ZBD-05)
ARTY 40+
SP 122mm 40+: 20+ Type-07; 20+ Type-89
MRL 107mm Type-63
MOR 82mm
AT
MSL • MANPATS HJ-73; HJ-8
RCL 120mm Type-98
AD • SAM • MANPAD HN-5

Air Force 300,000–330,000

The PLAAF organises its command through seven military-
region air forces (MRAF) – Shenyang, Beijing, Lanzhou,
Jinan, Nanjing, Guangzhou and Chengdu – five corps
deputy leader-grade command posts (Datong, Kunming,
Wuhan, Xian, and Fuzhou); four corps deputy leader-
grade bases (Nanning, Urumqi, Shanghai, and Dalian); and
four division leader-grade command posts (Lhasa, Hetian,
Zhangzhou, and Changchun). Each MRAF, CP, and base
is responsible for all subordinate combat organizations
(aviation, SAM, AAA, and radar) in its area of operations.
The regiments of four air divisions have been reorganised
into new brigades, and MRAF training formations have
been consolidated into three new flying academies.

Flying hours Ftr, ground attack and bbr pilots average
100–150 hrs/yr. Tpt pilots average 200+
per year. Each regt has two quotas to meet
during the year – a total number of hours,
and the percentage of flight time dedicated
to tactics trg.

FORCES BY ROLE
BOMBER
1 regt with H-6A/M
5 regt with H-6H/K with YJ-63

FIGHTER
6 regt with J-7 *Fishbed*
6 regt with J-7E *Fishbed*
3 regt with J-7G *Fishbed*
1 regt with J-8B *Finback*
2 regt with J-8F *Finback*
2 regt with J-8H *Finback*
1 regt with Su-27SK/UBK *Flanker*
6 regt with J-11/Su-27UBK
2 regt with J-11B/BS
2 bde with J-7/J-7G *Fishbed*

FIGHTER/GROUND ATTACK
3 regt with Su-30MKK *Flanker*
7 regt with J-10A/S
2 bde with J-7E *Fishbed*; J-11B/BS; Q-5D/E *Fantan*
2 bde with J-8H *Finback*; J-11B/BS; JH-7A

FIGHTER/GROUND ATTACK/ISR
2 bde with J-7E *Fishbed*; J-8H *Finback*; JZ-8F *Finback** Su-
30MKK

GROUND ATTACK
4 regt with JH-7A
4 regt with Q-5C/D/E *Fantan*

ELECTRONIC WARFARE
1 regt with Y-8CB/G/XZ
1 regt with Y-8CB/G

ISR
1 regt with JZ-8F *Finback**
1 regt with Y-8H1

AIRBORNE EARLY WARNING & CONTROL
1 regt with KJ-200; KJ-2000; Y-8T

COMBAT SEARCH & RESCUE
1 regt with Mi-171; Z-8

TANKER
1 regt with H-6U

TRANSPORT
1 (VIP) regt with B-737; CRJ-200/700
1 (VIP) regt with B-737; Tu-154M; Tu-154M/D
1 regt with Il-76MD/TD *Candid*
1 regt with Mi-17V-5; Y-7
3 regt with Y-7
2 regt with Y-8
1 regt with Y-8; Y-9

TRAINING
2 regt with J-7; JJ-7
5 bde with CJ-6/6A/6B; JL-8*; Y-5; Y-7; Z-9

TRANSPORT HELICOPTER
1 regt with AS332 *Super Puma* (VIP)

AIR DEFENCE
3 SAM div
2 mixed SAM/ADA div
9 SAM bde
2 mixed SAM/ADA bde
2 ADA bde
9 indep SAM regt
1 indep ADA regt
4 indep SAM bn

EQUIPMENT BY TYPE
AIRCRAFT 1,903 combat capable
BBR up to 82 H-6A/H/K/M

Asia

FTR 842: 216 J-7 *Fishbed*; 192 J-7E *Fishbed*; 96 J-7G *Fishbed*; 24 J-8B *Finback*; 48 J-8F *Finback*; 96 J-8H *Finback*; 95 J-11; 43 Su-27SK *Flanker*; 32 Su-27UBK *Flanker*
FGA 543+: 240+ J-10A/S; 110+ J-11B/BS *Flanker*; 120 JH-7A; 73 Su-30MKK *Flanker*
ATK 120 Q-5C/D/E *Fantan*
EW 13: 4 Y-8CB *High New 1*; 7 Y-8G *High New 3*; 2 Y-8XZ *High New 7*
ELINT 4 Tu-154M/D *Careless*
ISR 51: 24 JZ-8 *Finback**; 24 JZ-8F *Finback**; 3 Y-8H1
AEW&C 8+: 4+ KJ-200; 4 KJ-2000
C2 5: 2 B-737; 3 Y-8T *High New 4*
TKR 10 H-6U
TPT 326+ **Heavy** 15 Il-76MD/TD *Candid*; **Medium** 41+: 40 Y-8; 1+ Y-9; **Light** 239: 170 Y-5; 41 Y-7/Y-7H; 20 Y-11; 8 Y-12 **PAX** 31: 9 B-737 (VIP); 5 CRJ-200; 5 CRJ-700; 12 Tu-154M *Careless*
TRG 950: 400 CJ-6/6A/6B; 200 JJ-7*; 350 JL-8*
HELICOPTERS
 MRH 22: 20 Z-9; 2 Mi-17-V5 *Hip H*
 TPT 28+: **Heavy** 18+ Z-8 (SA321) **Medium** 10+: 6+ AS332 *Super Puma* (VIP); 4+ Mi-171
UAV • ISR • Heavy CH-1 *Chang Hong*; *Chang Kong 1*; *Firebee* **Light** *Harpy*
AD
 SAM 600+
  SP 300+: 24 HD-6D; 60+ HQ-7; 32 HQ-9; 24 HQ-12 (KS-1A); 32 S-300PMU (SA-10B *Grumble*); 64 S-300PMU1 (SA-20 *Gargoyle*); 64 S-300PMU2 (SA-20 *Gargoyle*)
  TOWED 300+ HQ-2 (SA-2) *Guideline* Towed/HQ-2A/HQ-2B(A)
 GUNS 16,000 **100mm/85mm**
MSL
 AAM • IR PL-2B‡; PL-5B/C; PL-8; R-73 (AA-11 *Archer*); **SARH** PL-11; **IR/SARH** R-27 (AA-10 *Alamo*); **ARH** PL-12; R-77 (AA-12 *Adder*)
 ASM KD-88; Kh-29 (AS-14 *Kedge*); Kh-31A/P (AS-17 *Krypton*); Kh-59 (AS-18 *Kazoo*); YJ-91 (Domestically produced Kh-31P variant)
 LACM YJ(KD)-63; CJ-10 (in development)

15th Airborne Corps

FORCES BY ROLE
SPECIAL FORCES
 1 SF unit
MANOEUVRE
 Reconnaissance
 1 recce regt
 Air Manoeuvre
 2 AB div (2 AB regt; 1 arty regt)
 1 AB div (1 AB regt; 1 arty regt)
COMBAT SUPPORT
 1 sigs gp
COMBAT SERVICE SUPPORT
 1 log gp
EQUIPMENT BY TYPE
AIFV 130+ Type-03 (ZBD-03)
ARTY 108+
 TOWED • 122mm ε54 Type-96 (D-30)
 MRL • TOWED • 107mm ε54 Type-63
 MOR • 82mm some
AT • SP some HJ-9 *Red Arrow 9*

Military Regions

This represents the geographical disposition of the PLA's group armies, fleets and air divisions within China, as opposed to a joint-service command structure. Designated Rapid Reaction Units (RRU) are indicated.

Shenyang MR (North East)

Land Forces

(Heilongjiang, Jilin, Liaoning MD)
16th Group Army
(1 armd bde, 1 mech inf bde, 2 mot inf div, 2 mot inf bde, 1 arty bde, 1 AD bde, 1 engr regt)
39th Group Army
(1 armd bde, 1 mech inf div, 2 mech inf bde, 1 mot inf div; 1 arty bde, 1 AD bde, 1 avn regt)
40th Group Army
(1 armd bde, 2 mot inf bde, 1 arty bde, 1 AD bde, 1 engr regt)
Other Forces
(1 SF unit; 1 mot inf bde; 1 EW regt)

North Sea Fleet Naval Aviation

Other Forces
(1 trg regt with CJ-6A; 1 trg regt with HY-7; 1 trg regt with Y-5)

Shenyang MRAF

1st Fighter Division
(1 ftr regt with J-11B; 1 FGA regt with J-10A; 1 ftr regt with J-8F)
11th Attack Division
(1 atk regt with JH-7A; 1 atk regt with Q-5)
16th Special Mission Division
(1 EW regt with Y-8CB/G; 1 ISR regt with JZ-8F; 1 tpt regt with Y-8)
21st Fighter Division
(1 ftr regt with J-7E; 1 ftr regt with J-8H; 1 ftr regt with J-7H)
Dalian Base
(2 FGA bde with J-7E; J-11B; Q-5)
Harbin Flying Academy
(2 trg bde with CJ-6; JL-8; Y-5; Y-7)
Other Forces
(1 (mixed) SAM/ADA bde; 1 SAM bde)

Beijing MR (North)

Land Forces

(Beijing, Tianjin Garrison, Inner Mongolia, Hebei, Shanxi MD)
27th Group Army
(1 (OPFOR) armd bde, 2 mech inf bde, 2 mot inf bde, 1 arty bde, 1 AD bde, 1 engr regt)
38th Group Army
(1 armd div, 2 mech inf div, 1 arty bde, 1 AD bde, 1 engr regt, 1 avn bde)
65th Group Army
(1 armd div, 1 mech inf div, 1 mot inf div, 1 arty bde, 1 AD bde, 1 engr regt, 1 avn bde)
Other Forces
(1 SF unit, 2 (Beijing) gd div; 1 mot inf bde; 1 ADA bde)

North Sea Fleet Naval Aviation
7th Naval Air Division
(1 trg regt with JL-9, 1 FGA regt with JH-7A)
Other Forces
(1 tpt regt with Y-7/Y-8; 1 trg regt with HY-7; 1 trg regt with JL-8)

Beijing MRAF
7th Fighter Division
(1 ftr regt with J-11; 1 ftr regt with J-7G; 1 ftr regt with J-7)
15th Fighter/Attack Division
(1 FGA regt with J-10A; 1 atk regt with Q-5C)
24th Fighter Division
(1 ftr regt with J-8F; 1 FGA regt with J-10A)
Shijiazhuang Flying Academy
(1 trg bde with CJ-6; JL-8; Y-5; Y-7)
Other Forces
(1 Flight Test Centre with J-7/J-8/J-10/JL-9/Su-30 (on rotation); 3 SAM div; 1 (mixed) SAM/ADA div)

Other Forces
34th VIP Transport Division
(1 tpt regt with B-737; CRJ200/700; 1 tpt regt with B-737; Tu-154M; Tu-154M/D; 1 tpt regt with Y-7; 1 hel regt with AS332)

Lanzhou MR (West)

Land Forces
(Ningxia, Shaanxi, Gansu, Qing-hai, Xinjiang, South Xinjiang MD)
21st Group Army
(1 armd bde, 1 mech inf bde, 1 mot inf div (RRU), 1 arty bde, 1 AD bde, 1 engr regt)
47th Group Army
(1 armd bde, 1 mech inf bde, 2 (high alt) mot inf bde, 1 arty bde, 1 AD bde, 1 engr regt)
Xinjiang MD
(1 (high alt) mech div, 2 indep mech inf regt, 3 (high alt) mot div, 1 arty bde, 1 AD bde, 1 engr regt, 1 avn bde)
Xi'an Flying Academy
(2 trg bde with CJ-6; JL-8; Y-7; Z-9)
Other Forces
(1 SF unit; 1 EW regt)

Lanzhou MRAF
6th Fighter Division
(1 ftr regt with J-11; 1 ftr regt with J-7E; 1 ftr regt with J-7)
36th Bomber Division
(1 surv regt with Y8H-1; 1 bbr regt with H-6M; 1 bbr regt with H-6H)
Urumqi Base
(2 FGA bde with J-8H; J-11B; JH-7A)
Other Forces
(1 trg regt with J-7/JJ-7; 4 trg regt with JL-8; 1 trg regt with Y-7; 1 hel trg regt with Z-9; 1 (mixed) SAM/ADA div; 1 SAM bde; 4 indep SAM regt)

Jinan MR (Centre)

Land Forces
(Shandong, Henan MD)
20th Group Army
(1 armd bde, 1 mech inf bde, 1 mot inf bde, 1 arty bde, 1 AD bde, 1 engr regt)
26th Group Army
(1 armd div, 3 mot inf bde, 1 arty bde, 1 AD bde, 1 avn regt)
54th Group Army
(1 armd bde, 2 mech inf div (RRU), 1 mech bde, 1 arty bde, 1 AD bde, 1 avn regt)
Other Forces
(1 SF unit; 1 EW regt)

North Sea Fleet
Coastal defence from DPRK border (Yalu River) to south of Lianyungang (approx 35°10′N); equates to Shenyang, Beijing and Jinan MR, and to seaward; HQ at Qingdao; support bases at Lushun, Qingdao. 9 coastal-defence districts
3 **SSBN**; 3 **SSN**; 20 **SSK**; 2 **DDGHM**; 2 **DDGM**; 5 **FFGHM**; 2 **FFGM**; 1 **FFGH**; 6 **FFG**; 1 **ML**; ε22 **PCFG/PCG**; ε28 **PCC**; 9 **LS**; ε7 **MCMV**

North Sea Fleet Naval Aviation
5th Naval Air Division
(1 FGA regt with JH-7A; 1 ftr regt with J-8F)
Other Forces
(1 EW/ISR/AEW regt with Y-8J/JB/W; 1 MP regt with SH-5; 1 hel regt with AS365; Ka-28; SA321; Z-9)

Jinan MRAF
5th Attack Division
(1 atk regt with Q-5E; 1 atk regt with JH-7A)
12th Fighter Division
(1 ftr regt with J-8B; 1 ftr regt with J-7G)
19th Fighter Division
(1 ftr regt with Su-27SK; 1 ftr regt with J-7; 1 trg regt with J-7/JJ-7)
Other Forces
(1 Flight Instructor Training Base with CJ-6; JL-8; 4 SAM bn)

Nanjing MR (East)

Land Forces
(Shanghai Garrison, Jiangsu, Zhejiang, Fujian, Jiangxi, Anhui MD)
1st Group Army
(1 armd bde, 1 amph mech div, 1 mot inf bde, 1 arty div, 1 AD bde, 1 engr regt, 1 avn bde)
12th Group Army
(1 armd div, 3 mot inf bde (1 RRU), 1 arty bde, 1 AD bde, 1 engr regt)
31st Group Army
(1 (amph) armd bde, 2 mot inf div (incl 1 RRU), 1 mot inf bde, 1 arty bde, 1 AD bde, 1 avn regt)
Other Forces
(1 SF unit)

East Sea Fleet

Coastal defence from south of Lianyungang to Dongshan (approx 35°10′N to 23°30′N); equates to Nanjing Military Region, and to seaward; HQ at Ningbo; support bases at Fujian, Zhoushan, Ningbo. 7 coastal defence districts

17 SSK; 6 DDGHM; 14 FFGHM; 11 FFG; ε34 PCFG/PCG; ε22 PCC; 27 LS; ε22 MCMV

East Sea Fleet Naval Aviation

4th Naval Aviation Division
(1 FGA regt with Su-30Mk2; 1 FGA regt with J-10A)
6th Naval Aviation Division
(2 FGA regt with JH-7; 1 bbr regt with H-6G)
Other Forces
(1 hel regt with Mi-8; Ka-28; Ka-31)

Nanjing MRAF

3rd Fighter Division
(1 ftr regt with J-7G; 1 FGA regt with J-10A; 1 FGA regt with Su-30MKK)
10th Bomber Division
(2 bbr regt with H-6H; 1 EW regt with Y-8CB/G/XZ)
14th Fighter Division
(1 ftr regt with J-11; 1 ftr regt with J-7E)
26th Special Mission Division
(1 AEW&C regt with KJ-200/KJ-2000/Y-8T; 1 CSAR regt with M-171/Z-8)
28th Attack Division
(2 atk regt with JH-7A; 1 atk regt with Q-5D/E)
32nd Fighter Division
(1 ftr regt with J-11B; 1 trg regt with J-7/JJ-7)
Shanghai Base
(2 FGA/ISR bde with J-7E; J-8H; JZ-8F; Su-30MKK)
Other Forces
(3 SAM bde; 1 ADA bde; 2 indep SAM regt)

Guangzhou MR (South)

Land Forces

(Hubei, Hunan, Guangdong, Guangxi, Hainan MD)
41st Group Army
(1 armd bde, 1 mech inf div (RRU), 1 mot inf div, 1 arty bde, 1 AD bde, 1 engr regt)
42nd Group Army
(1 armd bde, 1 amph mech div (RRU), 1 mot inf div, 1 arty div, 1 AD bde, 1 avn bde)
Other Forces
(1 SF unit; 1 mot inf bde; 1 (composite) mot inf bde (Composed of units drawn from across the PLA and deployed to Hong Kong on a rotational basis); 1 AD bde; 1 EW regt)

South Sea Fleet

Coastal defence from Dongshan (approx 23°30′N) to VNM border; equates to Guangzhou MR, and to seaward (including Paracel and Spratly Islands); HQ at Zuanjiang; support bases at Yulin, Guangzhou
1 SSBN; 2 SSN; 18 SSK; 5 DDGHM; 9 FFGHM; 12 FFG; ε42 PCFG/PCG; ε20 PCC; 2 LPD; 51 LS; ε10 MCMV

South Sea Fleet Naval Aviation

8th Naval Aviation Division
(1 FGA regt with J-11B; 1 bbr regt with H-6G; 1 ftr regt with J-7E)
9th Naval Aviation Division
(1 ftr regt with J-8H, 1 FGA regt with JH-7A)
Other Forces
(1 tpt regt with Y-7; Y-8; Z-8; Z-8JH/S; Z-9)

Guangzhou MRAF

2nd Fighter Division
(1 ftr regt with J-8H; 1 FGA regt with J-10A; 1 ftr regt with J-11)
8th Bomber Division
(1 tkr regt with H-6U; 1 bbr regt with H-6H; 1 bbr regt with H-6K)
9th Fighter Division
(1 FGA regt with J-10A; 2 ftr regt with J-7E)
13th Transport Division
(1 tpt regt with Y-8; 1 tpt regt with Y-7; 1 tpt regt with Il-76MD/TD)
18th Fighter Division
(1 ftr regt with J-7; 1 FGA regt with Su-30MKK)
Nanning Base
(2 ftr bde with J-7/J-7G *Fishbed*)
Other Forces
(4 SAM Bde, 1 ADA bde, 1 indep ADA regt)

Other Forces

Marines
(2 mne bde)
15th Airborne Corps
(3 AB div)

Chengdu MR (South-West)

Land Forces

(Chongqing Garrison, Sichuan, Guizhou, Yunnan, Tibet MD)
13th Group Army
(1 armd bde, 1 (high alt) mech inf div (RRU), 1 mot inf div, 1 arty bde, 1 AD bde, 1 engr regt, 1 avn bde)
14th Group Army
(1 armd bde, 1 (jungle) mot inf div, 1 mot inf div, 1 arty bde, 1 AD bde)
Other Forces
(1 SF unit; 1 (high alt) mech inf bde; 2 mtn inf bde; 1 EW regt)

Chengdu MRAF

4th Transport Division
(1 tpt regt with Y-8/Y-9; 1 tpt regt with Y-7; 1 tpt regt with Mi-17V-5/Y-7)
33rd Fighter Division
(1 ftr regt with J-7E; 1 ftr regt with J-11)
44th Fighter Division
(1 ftr regt with J-7; 1 FGA regt with J-10)
Other Forces
(1 (mixed) SAM/ADA bde; 3 indep SAM regt)

Paramilitary 660,000+ active

People's Armed Police ε660,000

Internal Security Forces ε400,000

FORCES BY ROLE
MANOEUVRE
Other
14 (mobile) paramilitary div
22 (mobile) indep paramilitary regt
Some (firefighting/garrison) unit

Border Defence Force (incl Coast Guard) ε260,000

FORCES BY ROLE
COMMAND
30 div HQ
MANOEUVRE
Other
110 (border) paramilitary regt
20 (marine) paramilitary regt
EQUIPMENT BY TYPE
PATROL AND COASTAL COMBATANTS 156+
PSO 2
PCO 16
PB/PBF 138+

China Marine Surveillance

Patrols China's EEZ
EQUIPMENT BY TYPE
PATROL AND COASTAL COMBATANTS 78+
PSO 9 (2 additional vessels currently refitting; expected ISD 2013)
PCO 21
PB/PBF 48+

Maritime Safety Administration (MSA)

Various tasks including aid to navigation
EQUIPMENT BY TYPE
PATROL AND COASTAL COMBATANTS 234+
PSO 4;
PCO 10;
PB 200+

Fisheries Law Enforcement Command (FLEC)

Enforces Chinese fishery regulations
EQUIPMENT BY TYPE
PATROL AND COASTAL COMBATANTS 134+
PSO 5
PCO 11
PB/PBF 118+

Cyber

The PLA has devoted much attention to information warfare over the past decade, both in terms of battlefield EW and wider, cyber-warfare capabilities. The main doctrine is the 'Integrated Network Electronic Warfare' document, which guides PLA computer-network operations and calls for the combination of network warfare and EW tools at the start of a conflict in order to paralyse (or at least degrade) an opponent's C4ISR capabilities. PLA thinking however appears to have moved beyond INEW towards a new concept of 'information confrontation' (*xinxi duikang*) which aims to integrate both electronic and non-electronic aspects of information warfare within a single command authority. This concept appears to reflect the perception of PLA information warfare pioneers such as Shen Weiguang about information warfare as an all-of-nation exercise conducted in both peace and wartime for which information sovereignty is an essential prerequisite. PLA thinking sees warfare under informationised conditions as characterised by opposing sides using complete systems of ground, naval air, space and electromagnetic forces. It aspires to link all service branches into a common operating platform that can be accessed at multiple levels of command – a system of systems to improve battlespace situational awareness. Three PLA departments – Informatisation, Strategic Planning and Training – have either been established or re-formatted to help bring about this transformation. And since 2008, major PLA military exercises, including *Kuayue 2009*, *Shiming Xingdong 2010* and *Lianhe 2011*, have all had significant cyber and information operations components that have been both offensive and defensive in nature. China's cyber assets fall under the command of two main departments of the General Staff Department (GSD). Computer network attacks and EW would, in theory, come under the 4th Department (Electronic Countermeasures), and computer network defence and intelligence gathering comes under the 3rd Department (Signals Intelligence). The 3rd Department is supported by a variety of 'militia units' comprising both military cyber-warfare personnel and civilian hackers. In July 2010, colours were presented by General Cheng Bingde, head of the PLA General Staff Department, to a new 'Information Safeguards Base' tasked with addressing cyber threats and safeguarding China's information security and infrastructure. Some PLA sources claim that the base is not an offensive cyber capability but rather is intended to bolster resilience. In 2011, the PLA said that a much-reported 'Cyber Blue Team' was a body designed to improve the PLA's 'ability to safeguard internet security'.

DEPLOYMENT

CÔTE D'IVOIRE
UN • UNOCI 6 obs

CYPRUS
UN • UNFICYP 2

DEMOCRATIC REPUBLIC OF THE CONGO
UN • MONUSCO; 218; 16 obs; 1 engr coy; 1 fd hospital

GULF OF ADEN
Navy: 2 FFGHM; 1 AORH

LEBANON
UN • UNIFIL 343; 1 engr coy; 1 fd hospital

LIBERIA
UN • UNMIL 564; 2 obs; 1 engr coy; 1 tpt coy; 1 fd hospital

MIDDLE EAST
UN • UNTSO 2 obs

SOUTH SUDAN
UN • UNMIS 347; 3 obs; 1 engr coy; 1 fd hospital

SUDAN
UN • UNAMID 323; 1 engr coy

TIMOR LESTE
UN • UNMIT 2 obs

WESTERN SAHARA
UN • MINURSO 10 obs

Fiji FJI

Fijian Dollar F$		2011	2012	2013
GDP	F$	6.81bn	7.28bn	
	US$	3.8bn	3.95bn	
per capita	US$	4,269	4,438	
Growth	%	2.08	2.04	
Inflation	%	8.68	4.75	
Def bdgt	F$	49m	48m	46m
	US$	27m	26m	
US$1=F$		1.79	1.84	

Population   890,057

Ethnic groups: Fijian 51%; Indian 44%; European/Others 5%

Age	0–14	15–19	20–24	25–29	30–64	65 plus
Male	14.6%	4.6%	4.4%	4.4%	20.3%	2.5%
Female	14.0%	4.4%	4.2%	4.2%	19.5%	2.9%

Capabilities

The Republic of Fiji Military Forces (RFMF) are small, but have substantial operational experience. They have participated in international peacekeeping missions in Lebanon, the Sinai and Iraq, operations which have also provided an important revenue source for Fiji's government. Since the 1980s, however, the RFMF has also been heavily involved in domestic politics, mounting a coup for the third time in 2006. This intervention disrupted relations with Fiji's traditional military partners, Australia and New Zealand, leading the military-controlled government to emphasise the potential of defence ties with China, India and South Korea. In January 2011, the RFMF Engineers Regiment received a gift of major civil engineering equipment from China, allowing a major expansion of its developmental role. The RFMF's small naval unit operates primarily in EEZ protection and search-and-rescue roles. Though it has operated helicopters in the past, the RFMF presently has no aircraft.

ACTIVE 3,500 (Army 3,200 Navy 300)

RESERVE ε6,000
(to age 45)

ORGANISATIONS BY SERVICE

Army 3,200 (incl 300 recalled reserves)
FORCES BY ROLE
SPECIAL FORCE
  1 spec ops coy
MANOEUVRE
  Light
  3 inf bn
COMBAT SUPPORT
  1 arty bty
  1 engr bn

Reserves 6,000
FORCES BY ROLE
MANOEUVRE
  Light
  3 inf bn
EQUIPMENT BY TYPE
ARTY 16
  TOWED 85mm 4 25-pdr (ceremonial)
  MOR 81mm 12

Navy 300
EQUIPMENT BY TYPE
PATROL AND COASTAL COMBATANTS • PB 5: 3 *Kula*; 2 *Levuka*

DEPLOYMENT

EGYPT
MFO 338; 1 inf bn

IRAQ
UN • UNAMI 277; 3 sy unit

SOUTH SUDAN
UN • UNMISS 2: 2 obs

TIMOR LESTE
UN • UNMIT 1 obs

India IND

Indian Rupee Rs		2011	2012	2013
GDP	Rs	86.46tr	97.7tr	
	US$	1.83tr	1.95tr	
per capita	US$	1,519	1,618	
Growth	%	6.84	4.86	
Inflation	%	8.86	10.25	
Def exp [a]	Rs	2.1tr		
	US$	44.3bn		
Def bdgt [a]	Rs	1.71tr	1.93tr	
	US$	36.1bn	38.5bn	
US$1=Rs		47.33	50.19	

[a] Includes military pensions & additional Ministry of Defence allocations

Population 1205073612

Religious groups: Hindu 80%; Muslim 14%; Christian 2%; Sikh 2%

Age	0–14	15–19	20–24	25–29	30–64	65 plus
Male	15.5%	5.0%	4.6%	4.3%	19.7%	2.6%
Female	13.7%	4.4%	4.2%	4.0%	18.9%	2.9%

Capabilities

India has the third-largest armed forces in the world and is making serious efforts to improve their all-round capabilities. The armed forces regularly carry out combined arms and joint-service exercises, and have joined international exercises with France, Singapore, the UK and the US, among others. All three services have wide-ranging procurement programmes aimed at modernising their inventories, although this procurement, particularly from the inefficient indigenous defence industry, has often been hampered by delay. Moscow remains the country's main foreign source of defence equipment, but New Delhi has revived procurement from Europe and has bought transport aircraft among other equipment from the United States. The air force selected the French *Rafale* as its preferred choice to meet its 126-aircraft MMRCA requirement in early 2012. Current procurement programmes, including new aircraft carriers, promise to improve India's power-projection capabilities substantially over the next decade. Acquisitions have improved mobility and extended reach, and the navy's carrier aviation capability will be bolstered by the arrival – if behind schedule – of the *Vikramaditya* from Russia. India is in the process of developing the last element of its nuclear triad with a first-generation submarine-launched ballistic missile. India is among the largest providers of personnel for UN peacekeeping operations.

ACTIVE 1,325,000 (Army 1,129,900, Navy 58,350 Air 127,200, Coast Guard 9,550) **Paramilitary 1,322,150**

RESERVE 1,155,000 (Army 960,000 Navy 55,000 Air 140,000) **Paramilitary 987,800**

Army first-line reserves (300,000) within 5 years of full time service, further 500,000 have commitment to the age of 50.

ORGANISATIONS BY SERVICE

Strategic Forces Command

Strategic Forces Command (SFC) is a tri-service command established in 2003. The commander-in-chief of SFC, a senior three-star military officer, manages and administers all strategic forces through separate army and air force chains of command.

FORCES BY ROLE
MISSILE
  1 gp with *Agni* I
  1 gp with *Agni* II
  1 gp (reported forming) with *Agni* III
  2 gp with SS-150/250 *Prithvi* I/II
EQUIPMENT BY TYPE
MSL • STRATEGIC 54
  IRBM/ICBM *Agni* V (in test)
  IRBM 24+: ε12 *Agni* I (80–100 msl); ε12 *Agni* II (20–25 msl); some *Agni* III (entering service); *Agni* IV (in test)
  SRBM 30+: ε30 SS-150 *Prithvi* I/SS-250 *Prithvi* II; some SS-350 *Dhanush* (naval testbed)
  LACM *Nirbhay* (likely nuclear capable; in development)
Some Indian Air Force assets (such as *Mirage* 2000H or Su-30MKI) may be tasked with a strategic role

Space
SATELLITES • ISR 3: 1 *Cartosat* 2A; 2 RISAT

Army 1,129,900
6 Regional Comd HQ (Northern, Western, Central, Southern, Eastern, South Western), 1 Training Comd (ARTRAC)

FORCES BY ROLE
COMMAND
  3 (strike) corps HQ
  10 (holding) corps HQ
MISSILE
  2 msl gp with *Agni* I/II
  2 msl gp with SS-150/250 *Prithvi* I/II
SPECIAL FORCES
  8 SF bn
MANOEUVRE
  Armoured
  3 armd div (2–3 armd bde, 1 SP arty bde (1 medium regt, 1 SP arty regt))
  8 indep armd bde
  Mechanised
  4 (RAPID) mech inf div (1 armd bde, 2 mech inf bde, 1 arty bde)
  2 indep mech bde
  Light
  17 inf div (2–5 inf bde, 1 arty bde)
  7 indep inf bde
  Air Manoeuvre
  1 para bde
  Mountain
  12 mtn div (3-4 mtn inf bde, 3–4 art regt)
  2 indep mtn bde
  Aviation
  14 hel sqn

COMBAT SUPPORT

3 arty div (2 arty bde (3 med art regt, 1 STA/MRL regt))
8 AD bde
2 SSM regt with PJ-10 *Brahmos*
4 engr bde

Reserve Organisations

Reserves 300,000 reservists (first- line reserve
within 5 years full time service); 500,000 reservists
(commitment until age of 50) (total 800,000)

Territorial Army 160,000 reservists (only 40,000
regular establishment)

FORCES BY ROLE
MANOEUVRE
Light
25 inf bn
COMBAT SUPPORT
20 ADA regt
COMBAT SERVICE SUPPORT
6 ecological bn
37 (non-departmental) unit (raised from government
ministries)

EQUIPMENT BY TYPE
MBT 3,274+ 124 *Arjun*; 715 T-55 (being retired); 1,950
T-72M1; 485+ T-90S; (ε1,100 various models in store)
RECCE 110 BRDM-2 with 9K111 *Fagot* (AT-4 *Spigot*)/9K113
Konkurs (AT-5 *Spandrel*); *Ferret* (used for internal security
duties along with some indigenously built armd cars)
AIFV 1,455+: 350+ BMP-1; 980 *Sarath* (BMP-2); 125 BMP-2K
APC 336+
APC (W) 157+ OT-62/OT-64;
PPV 179: 165 *Casspir*; 14 *Yukthirath* MPV (of 327 order)
ARTY 9,682+
SP 20+: **130mm** 20 M-46 *Catapult*; **152mm** 2S19 *Farm*
(reported)
TOWED 2,970+: **105mm** 1,350+: 600+ IFG Mk1/Mk2/Mk3
(being replaced); up to 700 LFG; 50 M-56 **122mm** 520
D-30; **130mm** ε600 M-46; (500 in store) **155mm** 500: ε300
FH-77B; ε200 M-46 (mod)
MRL 192: **122mm** ε150 BM-21/LRAR **214mm** 14 *Pinaka*
(non operational) **300mm** 28 9A52 *Smerch*
MOR 6,520+
SP 120mm E1
TOWED 6,520+: **81mm** 5,000+ E1 **120mm** ε1,500 AM-
50/E1 **160mm** 20 M-58 *Tampella*
AT • MSL
SP 9K111 *Fagot* (AT-4 *Spigot*); 9K113 *Konkurs* (AT-5
Spandrel)
MANPATS 9K11 *Malyutka* (AT-3 *Sagger*) (being
phased out); 9K111 *Fagot* (AT-4 *Spigot*); 9K113 *Konkurs*
(AT-5 *Spandrel*); *Milan* 2
RCL 84mm *Carl Gustav*; **106mm** 3,000+ M40A1 (10 per
inf bn)
HELICOPTERS
MRH 232: 40 *Dhruv*; 12 *Lancer*; 120 SA315B *Lama*
(*Cheetah*); 60 SA316B *Alouette III* (*Chetak*)
AD
SAM 3,300+

SP 680+: 180 2K12 *Kub* (SA-6 *Gainful*); 50+ 9K33 *Osa*
(SA-8B *Gecko*); 200 9K31 *Strela*-1 (SA-9 *Gaskin*); 250
9K35 *Strela*-10 (SA-13 *Gopher*); *Akash*
MANPAD 2,620+: 620 9K32 *Strela*-2 (SA-7 *Grail* – being
phased out)‡; 2,000+ 9K31 *Igla*-1 (SA-16 *Gimlet*); 9K38
Igla (SA-18 *Grouse*)
GUNS 2,395+
SP 155+: **23mm** 75 ZSU-23-4; ZU-23-2 (truck-mounted);
30mm 20-80 2S6 *Tunguska*
TOWED 2,240+: **20mm** Oerlikon (reported); **23mm** 320
ZU-23-2; **40mm** 1,920 L40/70
UAV • ISR • Medium 26: 14 *Nishant*; 12 *Searcher* Mk I/
Mk II
RADAR • LAND 38+: 14 AN/TPQ-37 *Firefinder*; BSR Mk.2;
24 *Cymbeline*; EL/M-2140; M113 A1GE *Green Archer* (mor);
MUFAR; *Stentor*
AMPHIBIOUS 2 LCVP
MSL
IRBM 24+: ε12 *Agni*-I (80-100 msl); ε12 *Agni*-II (20-25
msl); some *Agni*-III (successfully tested)
SRBM 30: ε30 SS-150 *Prithvi* I/SS-250 *Prithvi* II
LACM 8–10 PJ-10 *Brahmos*
AEV BMP-2; FV180
ARV T-54/T-55; VT-72B; WZT-2; WZT-3
VLB AM-50; BLG-60; BLG T-72; *Kartik*; MTU-20; MT-55;
Sarvatra
MW 910 MCV-2

Navy 58,350 (incl 7,000 Naval Avn and 1,200 Marines)

Fleet HQ New Delhi; Commands located at Mumbai,
Vishakhapatnam, Kochi & Port Blair

EQUIPMENT BY TYPE
SUBMARINES • TACTICAL 15
SSN 1 *Chakra* (RUS *Nerpa*) with 4 single 533mm TT with
3M54 *Klub* (SS-N-27 *Sizzler*) SLCM, 4 single 650mm
TT with T-65 HWT; (RUS lease agreement - under
trials; not at full OC)
SSK 14:
4 *Shishumar* (GER T-209/1500) with 8 single 533mm TT
4 *Sindhughosh* (FSU *Kilo*) with 6 single 533mm TT (of
which 2 undergoing phased refit of 3M54 *Klub* (SS-
N-27 *Sizzler*) SLCM)
6 *Sindhughosh* (FSU *Kilo*) with 6 single 533mm TT with
3M54 *Klub* (SS-N-27 Sizzler) SLCM
PRINCIPAL SURFACE COMBATANTS 21
AIRCRAFT CARRIERS • CVS 1 *Viraat* (UK *Hermes*)
(capacity 30 *Sea Harrier* FRS 1 (*Sea Harrier* FRS MK51)
FGA ac; 7 Ka-27 *Helix* ASW hel/*Sea King* Mk42B ASW
hel)
DESTROYERS 11:
DDGHM 6:
3 *Delhi* with 4 quad lnchr with 3M-24 *Uran* (SS-N-
25 *Switchblade*) AShM, 2 single lnchr with 3K90
Uragan (SA-N-7 *Gadfly*) SAM, 5 single 533mm
ASTT, 1 100mm gun, (capacity either 2 *Dhruv* hel/
Sea King Mk42A ASW hel)
3 *Shivalik* with 1 octuple VLS with 3M54 *Klub* (SS-N-
27 *Sizzler*) ASCM, 1 octuple VLS with *Barak* SAM,
6 single lnchr with 3K90 *Uragan* (SA-N-7 *Gadfly*)

SAM, 1 76mm gun, (capacity 1 *Sea King* Mk42B ASW hel)

DDGM 5:

2 *Rajput* (FSU *Kashin*) with 2 twin lnchr with R-15M *Termit M* (SS-N-2C *Styx*) AShM, 2 twin lnchr with M-1 *Volna* (SA-N-1 *Goa*) SAM, 5 single 533mm ASTT, 2 RBU 6000 *Smerch 2*, 1 76mm gun, (capacity 1 Ka-25 *Hormone*/Ka-28 *Helix A* hel)

1 *Rajput* (FSU *Kashin*) with 2 twin lnchr with PJ-10 *Brahmos* ASCM, 2 single lnchr with R-15M *Termit M* (SS-N-2C *Styx*) AShM, 2 twin lnchr with M-1 *Volna* (SA-N-1 *Goa*) SAM, 5 single 533mm ASTT, 2 RBU 6000 *Smerch 2*, 1 76mm gun, (capacity 1 Ka-25 *Hormone*/Ka-28 *Helix A* hel)

2 *Rajput* (FSU *Kashin*) with 1 octuple VLS with PJ-10 *Brahmos* ASCM, 2 twin lnchr with R-15M *Termit M* (SS-N-2C *Styx*) AShM, 2 octuple VLS with *Barak* SAM. 1 twin lnchr with M-1 *Volna* (SA-N-1 *Goa*) SAM, 5 single 533mm ASTT, 2 RBU 6000 *Smerch 2*, 1 76mm gun, (capacity 1 Ka-25 *Hormone*/Ka-28 *Helix A* hel)

FRIGATES 12:

FFGHM 11:

3 *Brahmaputra* with 4 quad lnchr with SS-N-25 *Switchblade* AShM, 1 octuple VLS with *Barak* SAM, 2 triple 324mm ASTT, 1 76mm gun, (capacity 2 SA316B *Alouette III* (*Chetak*)/*Sea King* Mk42 ASW hel)

3 *Godavari* with 4 single lnchr with R-15 *Termit M* (SS-N-2D *Styx*) AShM, 1 octuple VLS with *Barak* SAM, 2 triple 324mm ASTT, 1 76mm gun, (capacity 2 SA316B *Alouette III* (*Chetak*)/*Sea King* MK42 ASW hel)

3 *Talwar* I with 1 octuple VLS with 3M54 *Klub* (SS-N-27 *Sizzler*) AShM, 6 single lnchr with 3K90 *Uragan* (SA-N-7 *Gadfly*) SAM, 2 twin 533mm ASTT, 2 RBU 6000 *Smerch 2*, 2 CADS-N-1 *Kashtan* CIWS, 1 100mm gun, (capacity 1 *Dhruv*/Ka-31 *Helix B* AEW hel/Ka-28 *Helix A* ASW hel)

2 *Talwar* II with 1 octuple VLS with 3M54 *Klub* (SS-N-27 *Sizzler*) AShM, 6 single lnchr with 3K90 *Uragan* (SA-N-7 *Gadfly*) SAM, 2 twin 533mm ASTT, 2 RBU 6000 *Smerch 2*, 2 CADS-N-1 *Kashtan* CIWS, 1 100mm gun, (capacity 1 *Dhruv*/Ka-31 *Helix B* AEW hel/Ka-28 *Helix A* ASW hel) (1 more vessel due to commission 2013)

FFH 1:

1 *Nilgiri* with 2 triple 324mm ASTT, 2 twin 114mm gun (capacity 1 SA316B *Alouette III* (*Chetak*) hel/ *Sea King* Mk42 ASW hel)

PATROL AND COASTAL COMBATANTS 59

CORVETTES 24:

FSGM 20:

4 *Khukri* with 2 twin lnchr with R-15M *Termit M* (SS-N-2C *Styx*) AShM, 2 twin lnchr with 9K32M *Strela*-2M (SA-N-5 *Grail*) SAM, 1 76mm gun, 1 hel landing platform (for *Dhruv*/SA316 *Alouette* III (*Chetak*))

4 *Kora* with 4 quad lnchr with 3M24 *Uran* (SS-N-25 *Switchblade*) AShM, 1 quad lnchr with 9K32M

Strela-2M (SA-N-5 *Grail*) SAM, 1 76mm gun, 1 hel landing platform (for *Dhruv*/SA316 *Alouette* III (*Chetak*))

10 *Veer* (FSU *Tarantul*) with 4 single lnchr with R-15 *Termit M* (SS-N-2D *Styx*) AShM, 2 quad lnchr (manual aiming) with 9K32M *Strela*-2M (SA-N-5 *Grail*), 1 76mm gun

2 *Prabal* (mod *Veer*) each with 4 quad lnchr (16 eff.) each with 3M24 *Uran* (SS-N-25 *Switchblade*) AShM, 1 quad lnchr (manual aiming) with 9K32M *Strela*-2M (SA-N-5 *Grail*) SAM, 1 76mm gun

FSM 4:

4 *Abhay* (FSU *Pauk* II) with 1 quad lnchr (manual aiming) with 9K32M *Strela*-2M (SA-N-5 *Grail*) SAM, 2 twin 533mm ASTT, 2 RBU 1200, 1 76mm gun

PSOH 6 *Sukanya* (capacity 1 SA316 *Alouette* III (*Chetak*))

PCC 16: 10 *Car Nicobar*; 6 *Trinkat* (SDB Mk5)

PBF 8 *Super Dvora*

PB 5: 3 *Plascoa* 1300 (SPB); 2 SDB Mk3

MINE WARFARE • MINE COUNTERMEASURES 8

MSO 8 *Pondicherry* (FSU *Natya*)

AMPHIBIOUS

PRINCIPAL AMPHIBIOUS VESSELS 1

LPD 1 *Jalashwa* (US *Austin*) (capacity up to 6 med spt hel; either 9 LCM or 4 LCM and 2 LCAC; 4 LCVP; 930 troops)

LANDING SHIPS 10

LSM 5 *Kumbhir* (FSU *Polnocny* C) (capacity 5 MBT or 5 APC; 160 troops)

LST 5:

2 *Magar* (capacity 15 MBT or 8 APC or 10 trucks; 500 troops)

3 *Magar* mod (capacity 11 MBT or 8 APC or 10 trucks; 500 troops)

LANDING CRAFT • LCU 8 *Vasco de Gama* Mk2/3 LC (capacity 2 APC; 120 troops)

LOGISTICS AND SUPPORT 50

AORH 4: 1 *Aditya* (mod *Deepak*); 2 *Deepak*; 1 *Jyoti*

AOL 6

ASR 1

AWT 2

AGOR 1 *Sagardhwani*

AGHS 8 *Sandhayak*

AGS 1 *Makar*

ATF 1

AP 3 *Nicobar*

AX 4: 1 *Krishna* (UK *Leander*); 1 *Tir*; 2 AXS

YPT 1

YDT 3

YTL/YTM 15

Naval Aviation 7,000

Flying hours	125–150 hrs/year on *Sea Harrier*

FORCES BY ROLE

FIGHTER/GROUND ATTACK

1 sqn with MiG-29K/KUB *Fulcrum*

1 sqn with *Sea Harrier* FRS 1 (Mk51); *Sea Harrier* T-4N (T-60)

ANTI SUBMARINE WARFARE

4 sqn with Ka-25 *Hormone*; Ka-28 *Helix* A; SA316B *Alouette* III (*Chetak*); *Sea King* Mk42A/B

MARITIME PATROL

2 sqn with BN-2 *Islander*; Do-228-101; Il-38 *May*; Tu-142M *Bear* F

AIRBORNE EARLY WARNING & CONTROL

1 sqn with Ka-31 *Helix* B

SEARCH & RESCUE

1 sqn with SA316B *Alouette* III (*Chetak*); *Sea King* Mk42C

TRANSPORT

1 (comms) sqn with Do-228

1 sqn with HS-748M (HAL-784M)

TRAINING

1 sqn with HJT-16 MkI *Kiran*; HJT-16 MkII *Kiran* II

TRANSPORT HELICOPTER

1 sqn with UH-3H *Sea King*

ISR UAV

1 sqn with *Heron*; *Searcher* MkII

EQUIPMENT BY TYPE

AIRCRAFT 34 combat capable

FTR 15 MiG-29K/KUB *Fulcrum*

FGA 10: 8 *Sea Harrier* FRS 1 (Mk51); 2 *Sea Harrier* T-4N (T-60)

ASW 9: 5 Il-38 *May*; 4 Tu-142M *Bear* F

MP 14 Do-228-101

TPT 37: **Light** 27: 17 BN-2 *Islander*; 10 Do-228 **PAX** 10 HS-748M (HAL-784M)

TRG 12: 6 HJT-16 MkI *Kiran*; 6 HJT-16 MkII *Kiran* II

HELICOPTERS

ASW 54: 7 Ka-25 *Hormone*; 12 Ka-28 *Helix* A; 21 *Sea King* Mk42A; 14 *Sea King* Mk42B

MRH 53: 4 *Dhruv*; 26 SA316B *Alouette* III (*Chetak*); 23 SA319 *Alouette* III

AEW 9 Ka-31 *Helix* B

TPT • Medium 11: 5 *Sea King* Mk42C; up to 6 UH-3H *Sea King*

UAV • ISR 12 **Heavy** 4 *Heron* **Medium** 7 *Searcher* Mk II

MSL

AShM *Sea Eagle* (service status unclear); KH-35/*Sea Skua* (*Bear* and *May* ac cleared to fire Kh-35)

ASCM PJ-10 *Brahmos*

AAM • IR R-550 *Magic* 2/R-550 *Magic*; R-73 (AA-11 *Archer*) **IR/SARH** R-27 (AA-10 *Alamo*) **ARH** *Derby*; R-77 (AA-12 *Adder*)

Marines ε1,200 (Additional 1,000 for SPB duties)

After the Mumbai attacks, the Sagar Prahari Bal (SPB), with 80 PBF, was established to protect critical maritime infrastructure.

FORCES BY ROLE

SPECIAL FORCES

1 (marine) cdo force

MANOEUVRE

Amphibious

1 amph bde

Air Force 127,200

5 regional air comds: Western (New Delhi), South-Western (Gandhinagar), Eastern (Shillong), Central (Allahabad), Southern (Trivandrum). 2 support comds: Maintenance (Nagpur) and Training (Bangalore)

Flying hours   180 hrs/year

FORCES BY ROLE

FIGHTER

3 sqn with MiG-29 *Fulcrum*; MiG-29UB *Fulcrum*

FIGHTER/GROUND ATTACK

4 sqn with *Jaguar* IB/IS

8 sqn with MiG-21bis/*Bison*

3 sqn with MiG-21M/MF *Fishbed*

6 sqn with MiG-27ML *Flogger*

3 sqn with *Mirage* 2000E/ED (2000H/TH - secondary ECM role)

9 sqn with Su-30MKI *Flanker*

ANTI SURFACE WARFARE

1 sqn with *Jaguar* IM with *Sea Eagle* AShM

ISR

1 unit with Gulfstream IV SRA-4

AIRBORNE EARLY WARNING & CONTROL

1 sqn with EMB-145AEW; Il-76TD *Phalcon*

TANKER

1 sqn with Il-78 *Midas*

TRANSPORT

1 sqn with C-130J-30 *Hercules*

5 sqn with An-32/An-32RE *Cline*

1 (comms) sqn with B-737; B-737BBJ; EMB-135BJ

4 sqn with Do-228; HS-748

2 sqn with Il-76MD *Candid*

1 flt with HS-748

TRAINING

1 sqn with *Tejas*

Some units with An-32; Do-228; *Hawk* Mk 132*; HJT-16 *Kiran*; *Jaguar* IS/IM; MiG-21bis; MiG-21FL; MiG-21M/MF; MiG-27ML*; SA316B *Alouette* III (*Chetak*)

ATTACK HELICOPTER

2 sqn with Mi-25 *Hind*; Mi-35 *Hind*

TRANSPORT HELICOPTER

4 sqn with *Dhruv*

8 sqn with Mi-8 *Hip*

6 sqn with Mi-17/Mi-17-1V *Hip* H

1 sqn (forming) with Mi-17V-5 *Hip* H

2 sqn with SA316B *Alouette* III (*Chetak*)

1 flt with Mi-8 *Hip*

1 flt with Mi-26 *Halo*

2 flt with SA315B *Lama* (*Cheetah*)

2 flt with SA316B *Alouette* III (*Chetak*)

ISR UAV

5 sqn with *Searcher* MkII

AIR DEFENCE

25 sqn with S-125 *Pechora* (SA-3B *Goa*);

6 sqn with 9K33 *Osa*-AK (SA-8B *Gecko*);

2 sqn with *Akash*

10 flt with 9K38 Igla (SA-18 *Grouse*)

EQUIPMENT BY TYPE

AIRCRAFT 870 combat capable

FTR 63: 56 MiG-29 *Fulcrum* (inc 12 MiG-29UPG by end 2012); 7 MiG-29UB *Fulcrum*

FGA 736: 14 *Jaguar* IB; 82 *Jaguar* IS; 10 *Jaguar* IM; 31 MiG-21bis; 118 MiG-21 *Bison*; 54 MiG-21M *Fishbed*; 16 MiG-21MF *Fishbed*; 40 MiG-21U/UM *Mongol*; 127 MiG-27ML *Flogger* J2; 40 *Mirage* 2000E (2000H); 10 *Mirage* 2000ED (2000TH); 194 Su-30MKI *Flanker*

ISR 3 Gulfstream IV SRA-4

AEW&C 3: 1 EMB-145AEW (2 more on order); 2 Il-76TD *Phalcon* (1 more on order)

TKR 6 Il-78 *Midas*

TPT 238 **Heavy** 24 Il-76MD *Candid*; **Medium** 6 C-130J-30 *Hercules*; **Light** 144: 90 An-32; 15 An-32RE *Cline*; 35 Do-228; 4 EMB-135BJ; **PAX** 64: 1 B-707; 4 B-737; 3 B-737BBJ; 56 HS-748

TRG 241: 66 *Hawk* Mk132*; 120 HJT-16 MkI *Kiran*; 55 HJT-16 MkII *Kiran* II

HELICOPTERS

ATK 20 Mi-25/Mi-35 *Hind*

MRH 226+: 40+ *Dhruv* (150 on order); 72 Mi-17/Mi-17-1V *Hip* H; 6 Mi-17V-5 *Hip* H; 60 SA315B *Lama* (*Cheetah*); 48 SA316B *Alouette* III (*Chetak*)

TPT 106 **Heavy** 4 Mi-26 *Halo* **Medium** 102 Mi-8

UAV • ISR • Medium some *Searcher* MkII

AD • SAM S-125 *Pechora* (SA-3B *Goa*)

SP 9K33 *Osa*-AK (SA-8B *Gecko*); *Akash*

MANPAD 9K38 *Igla*-1 (SA-18 *Grouse*)

MSL

AAM • IR R-60 (AA-8 *Aphid*); R-73 (AA-11 *Archer*) R-550 *Magic* **IR/SARH** R-27 (AA-10 *Alamo*); **SARH** Super 530D **ARH** R-77 (AA-12 *Adder*)

AShM AM-39 *Exocet*; *Sea Eagle*

ASM AS-11; AS-11B (ATGW); Kh-29 (AS-14 *Kedge*); Kh-59 (AS-13 *Kingbolt*); Kh-59M (AS-18 *Kazoo*); Kh-31A (AS-17B *Krypton*); AS-30; AS-7 *Kerry* ‡

ARM Kh-25MP (AS-12 *Kegler*); Kh-31P (AS-17A *Krypton*)

LACM *Nirbhay* (likely nuclear capable; in development)

Coast Guard 9,550

EQUIPMENT BY TYPE

PATROL AND COASTAL COMBATANTS 76

PSOH 12: 2 *Sankalp* (additional vessels in build*)*; 4 *Samar*; 3 *Samudra*; 3 *Vishwast*

PCO 7 *Vikram*

PCC 23: 8 *Priyadarshini*; 3 *Rajshree* (5 additional vessels in build); 5 *Rani Abbakka* (7 additional vessels in build); 7 *Sarojini-Naid*

PCF 2 *Cochin* 50 (additional vessels in build)

PBF 13 *Interceptor*

PB 19: 3 *Jija Bai* mod 1; 6 *Tara Bai*; 10 (various)

AMPHBIBIOUS • LCAC 6 *Griffon 8000*

AIRCRAFT • TPT • Light 24 Do-228

HELICOPTERS • MRH 17 SA316B *Alouette* III (*Chetak*)

Paramilitary 1,322,150

Rashtriya Rifles 65,000

Ministry of Defence. 15 sector HQ

FORCES BY ROLE

MANOEUVRE

Other

65 paramilitary bn

Assam Rifles 63,900

Ministry of Home Affairs. Security within north-eastern states, mainly army-officered; better trained than BSF.

FORCES BY ROLE

Equipped to roughly same standard as an army inf bn

COMMAND

7 HQ

MANOEUVRE

Other

42 paramilitary bn

EQUIPMENT BY TYPE

ARTY • MOR 81mm 252

Border Security Force 230,000

Ministry of Home Affairs.

FORCES BY ROLE

MANOEUVRE

Other

170+ paramilitary bn

EQUIPMENT BY TYPE

Small arms, lt arty, some anti-tank weapons

ARTY • MOR 81mm 942+

AIRCRAFT • TPT some (air spt)

Central Industrial Security Force 94,350 (lightly armed security guards)

Ministry of Home Affairs. Guards public-sector locations

Central Reserve Police Force 229,700

Ministry of Home Affairs. Internal security duties, only lightly armed, deployable throughout the country

FORCES BY ROLE

MANOEUVRE

Other

125 paramilitary bn

13 (rapid action force) paramilitary bn

2 (Mahila) paramilitary bn (female)

Defence Security Corps 31,000

Provides security at Defence Ministry sites

Indo-Tibetan Border Police 36,300

Ministry of Home Affairs. Tibetan border security SF/ guerrilla warfare and high-altitude warfare specialists; 30 bn

National Security Guards 7,350

Anti-terrorism contingency deployment force, comprising elements of the armed forces, CRPF and Border Security Force

Railway Protection Forces 70,000

Sashastra Seema Bal 31,550

Guards the borders with Nepal and Bhutan

Special Frontier Force 10,000

Mainly ethnic Tibetans

Special Protection Group 3,000

Protection of ministers and senior officials

State Armed Police 450,000

For duty primarily in home state only, but can be moved to other states. Some bn with GPMG and army standard infantry weapons and equipment.

FORCES BY ROLE

MANOEUVRE

Other

24 (India Reserve Police) paramilitary bn (cdo trained)

Reserve Organisations

Civil Defence 500,000 reservists

Operate in 225 categorised towns in 32 states. Some units for NBC defence

Home Guard 487,800 reservists (515,000 authorised str)

In all states except Arunachal Pradesh and Kerala; men on reserve lists, no trg. Not armed in peacetime. Used for civil defence, rescue and fire-fighting provision in wartime; 6 bn (created to protect tea plantations in Assam)

Cyber

National agencies include the Computer and Emergency Response Team (CERT-In), which has authorised designated individuals to carry out penetration tests against infrastructure. The Defence Information Assurance and Research Agency (DIARA) is mandated to deal with cyber security-related issues of the armed services, and defence ministry has close ties with Cert-In and the National Technical Research Organisation (NTRO). All services have their own cyber security policies and CERT teams, and headquarters maintain information-security policies. The Indian Army, in 2005, raised the Army Cyber Security Establishment and, in April 2010, set up the Cyber Security Laboratory at the Military College of Telecommunications Engineering in Mhow (under the Corps of Signals). Defence is, along with finance, energy, transportation and telecoms, a critical sector where information resources need to be secured, according to the Department of Electronics and Information Technology. This department has outlined a cyber-security strategy, and, though discussions proceed, such a strategy has yet to be published.

DEPLOYMENT

AFGHANISTAN

400 (Indo-Tibetan Border Police paramilitary: Protection for road construction project)

CÔTE D'IVOIRE

UN • UNOCI 8 obs

DEMOCRATIC REPUBLIC OF THE CONGO

UN • MONUSCO 3,693; 59 obs; 3 mech inf bn; 1 inf bn; 1 hel coy; 1 fd hospital

GULF OF ADEN

Navy: 1 FFGHM

LEBANON

UN • UNIFIL 894; 1 mech inf bn; elm 1 fd hospital

SOUTH SUDAN

UN • UNMISS 1,997; 5 obs; 2 inf bn; 1 engr coy; 1 fd hospital

SUDAN

UN • UNISFA 2: 2 obs

SYRIA/ISRAEL

UN • UNDOF 191; elm 1 log bn

FOREIGN FORCES

Total numbers for UNMOGIP mission in India and Pakistan

Chile 2 obs
Croatia 8 obs
Finland 6 obs
Italy 3 obs
Korea, Republic of 7 obs
Philippines 4 obs
Sweden 5 obs
Thailand 3 obs
Uruguay 2 obs

Indonesia IDN

Indonesian Rupiah Rp		2011	2012	2013
GDP	Rp	7427.09tr	8386.89tr	
	US$	846.45bn	894.85bn	
per capita	US$	3,404	3,599	
Growth	%	6.46	6.04	
Inflation	%	5.36	4.40	
Def bdgt	Rp	51.1tr	72.5tr	77.7tr
	US$	5.82bn	7.74bn	
FMA (US)	US$	19.96m	14m	14m
US$1=Rp		8774.39	9372.35	

Population   248,645,008

Ethnic groups: Javanese 45%; Sundanese 14%; Madurese 8%; Malay 8%; Chinese 3%; Other 22%

Age	0–14	15–19	20–24	25–29	30–64	65 plus
Male	13.8%	4.5%	4.2%	4.2%	20.6%	2.8%
Female	13.3%	4.4%	4.1%	4.0%	20.7%	3.6%

Capabilities

Indonesia's army remains the country's dominant military force – a legacy of the 1940s independence struggle and the army's involvement in domestic politics. Even under civilian rule, the army's 'territorial structure' continues to deploy military personnel throughout the country down to village level. Within the army, the better-trained and -equipped Strategic Command (KOSTRAD) and Special Forces Command (KOPASSUS) units are trained for deployment nationwide and for exercises with other countries' armed forces. In West Papua, where resistance to

Indonesian rule continues, the army still deploys operationally and has faced accusations of serious human-rights abuses. Rising defence spending has permitted modest equipment purchases for all three services (particularly the air force and navy), and improved pay and allowances. The armed forces lack the capacity for significant autonomous military deployments beyond national territory, but, in July–August 2012, the air force contributed Su-27/-30 combat aircraft to the annual *Pitch Black* exercise in northern Australia for the first time.

ACTIVE 395,500 (Army 300,400 Navy 65,000 Air 30,100) **Paramilitary 281,000**

Terms of service 2 years selective conscription authorised

RESERVE 400,000

Army cadre units; numerical str n.k., obligation to age 45 for officers

ORGANISATIONS BY SERVICE

Army ε300,400

Mil Area Commands (KODAM)

13 comd (I, II, III, IV, V, VI, VII, IX, XII, XVI, XVII, Jaya & Iskandar Muda)

FORCES BY ROLE
MANOEUVRE
Mechanised
  3 armd cav bn
  6 cav bn
Light
  1 inf bde (1 cav bn, 3 inf bn)
  2 inf bde (1 cdo bn, 2 inf bn)
  5 inf bde (3 inf bn)
  45 indep inf bn
  8 cdo bn
Aviation
  1 composite avn sqn
  1 hel sqn
COMBAT SUPPORT
  12 fd arty bn
  1 AD regt (2 ADA bn, 1 SAM unit)
  6 ADA bn
  3 SAM unit
  7 cbt engr bn
COMBAT SERVICE SUPPORT
  4 construction bn

Special Forces Command (KOPASSUS)

FORCES BY ROLE
SPECIAL FORCES
  3 SF gp (total: 2 cdo/para unit, 1 CT unit, 1 int unit)

Strategic Reserve Command (KOSTRAD)

FORCES BY ROLE
COMMAND
  2 div HQ
MANOEUVRE
Mechanised
  2 armd cav bn

Light
  3 inf bde (total: 3 cdo bn; 5 inf bn)
Air Manoeuvre
  3 AB bde (3 AB bn)
COMBAT SUPPORT
  2 fd arty regt (total: 6 arty bn)
  1 arty bn
  2 AD bn
  2 cbt engr bn

EQUIPMENT BY TYPE
LT TK 350: 275 AMX-13 (partially upgraded); 15 PT-76; 60 *Scorpion* 90
RECCE 142: 55 *Ferret* (13 upgraded); 69 *Saladin* (16 upgraded); 18 VBL
AIFV 22 BMP-2
APC 541
  APC (T) 90: 75 AMX-VCI; 15 FV4333 *Stormer*
  APC (W) 459: 14 APR-1; ε150 *Anoa*; 22 *Black Fox* being delivered; 40 BTR-40; 34 BTR-50PK; 22 *Commando Ranger*; 45 FV603 *Saracen* (14 upgraded); 100 LAV-150 *Commando*; 32 VAB-VTT
  PPV *Barracuda*; *Casspir*
ARTY 1,079
  TOWED 115: **105mm** 110: KH-178; 60 M101; 50 M-56; **155mm** 5 FH-88
  MOR 955: **81mm** 800; **120mm** 135: 75 Brandt; 80 UBM 52
  MLR 70mm 9 NDL-40
AT
  MSL SS.11; 100 *Milan*; 9M14M (AT-3 *Sagger*)
  RCL 135: **106mm** 45 M40A1; **90mm** 90 M67
  RL 89mm 700 LRAC
AIRCRAFT • TPT • Light 9: 1 BN-2A *Islander*; 6 C-212 *Aviocar* (NC-212); 2 *Turbo Commander* 680
HELICOPTERS
  ATK 6 Mi-35P *Hind*
  MRH 30: 12 Bell 412 *Twin Huey* (NB-412); 18 Mi-17V5 *Hip H*
  TPT • Light 30: 8 Bell 205A; 20 Bo-105 (NBo-105); 2 EC120B *Colibri*
  TRG 12 Hughes 300C
AD
  SAM
    SP 2 *Kobra* (with 125 GROM-2 msl); TD-2000B (*Giant Bow II*)
    TOWED 93: 51 *Rapier*; 42 RBS-70
    MANPAD QW-3
  GUNS • TOWED 411: **20mm** 121 Rh 202; **23mm** *Giant Bow*; **40mm** 90 L/70; **57mm** 200 S-60
ARV 9+: 2 AMX-13; 6 AMX-VCI; 3 BREM-2; *Stormer*; T-54/T-55
VLB 12+: 10 AMX-13; *Leguan*; 2 *Stormer*

Navy ε65,000 (including Marines and Aviation)

Two fleets: East (Surabaya), West (Jakarta). It is currently planned to change to three commands: Riau (West); Papua (East); Makassar (Central). Two Forward Operating Bases at Kupang (West Timor) and Tahuna (North Sulawesi)

EQUIPMENT BY TYPE
SUBMARINES • TACTICAL • SSK 2 *Cakra*† with 8 single 533mm TT with SUT HWT
PRINCIPAL SURFACE COMBATANTS 11
FRIGATES 11
FFGHM 7
  5 *Ahmad Yani* with 2 quad Mk 141 lnchr with RGM-84A *Harpoon* AShM, 2 SIMBAD twin lnchr (manual) with *Mistral* SAM, 2 triple 324mm ASTT with Mk46 LWT, 1 76mm gun (capacity 1 Bo-105 (NBo-105) hel)
  1 *Ahmad Yani* with 2 twin-cell VLS with 3M55 *Yakhont* (SS-N-26 *Strobile*) AShM; 2 SIMBAD twin lnchr (manual) with *Mistral* SAM, 2 triple 324mm ASTT with Mk46 LWT, 1 76mm gun (capacity 1 Bo-105 (NBo-105) hel)
  1 *Hajar Dewantara* (trg role) with 2 twin lnchr with MM-38 *Exocet* AShM, 2 single 533mm ASTT with SUT HWT, (capacity 1 Bo-105 (NBo-105) hel)
FFGM 4:
  4 *Diponegoro* with 2 twin lnchr with MM-40 *Exocet* Block II AShM, 2 quad *Tetral* lnchr with *Mistral* SAM, 2 triple 324mm ASTT, 1 76mm gun, 1 hel landing platform
PATROL AND COASTAL COMBATANTS 72
CORVETTES 19:
FSGH 1:
  1 *Nala* with 2 twin lnchr with MM-38 *Exocet* AShM, 1 twin 375mm A/S mor, 1 120mm gun (capacity 1 lt hel)
FSG 2:
  2 *Fatahillah* with 2 twin lnchr with MM-38 *Exocet* AShM, 2 triple B515 *ILAS*-3/Mk32 324mm ASTT with A244/Mk46 LWT, 1 twin 375mm A/S mor, 1 120mm gun
FSM 16:
  16 *Kapitan Patimura*† (GDR *Parchim* I) with 2 quad lnchr with 9K32M *Strela*-2 (SA-N-5 *Grail*) SAM, 4 single 400mm ASTT, 2 RBU 6000 *Smerch* 2
PCFG 4 *Mandau* with 4 single lnchr with MM-38 *Exocet* AShM
PCT 4 *Singa* with 2 single 533mm TT (capability upgrade programme in progress)
PCC 8: 4 *Kakap*; 4 *Todak*
PBG 4:
  2 *Clurit* with 2 twin lnchr with C-705 AShM
  2 *Waspada* with 2 twin lnchr with MM-38 *Exocet* AShM
PB 33: 1 *Cucut*; 13 *Kobra*; 1 *Krait*; 8 *Sibarau*; 10 *Viper*
MINE WARFARE • MINE COUNTERMEASURES 11
MCO 2 *Pulau Rengat*
MSC 9 *Palau Rote*†
AMPHIBIOUS
PRINCIPAL AMPHIBIOUS VESSELS • LPD 5: 1 *Dr Soeharso* (Ex-*Tanjung Dalpele*; capacity 2 LCU/LCVP; 13 tanks; 500 troops; 2 AS332L *Super Puma*); 4 *Makassar* (capacity 2 LCU/LCVP; 13 tanks; 500 troops; 2 AS332L *Super Puma*)
LANDING SHIPS • LST 26:
  1 *Teluk Amboina* (capacity 16 tanks; 200 troops);
  12 *Teluk Gilimanuk*
  7 *Teluk Langsa* (capacity 16 tanks; 200 troops);
  6 *Teluk Semangka* (capacity 17 tanks; 200 troops)

LANDING CRAFT 54 LCU
LOGISTICS AND SUPPORT 32
AGF 1 *Multatuli*
AORLH 1 *Arun* (UK *Rover*)
AOT 3: 2 *Khobi*; 1 *Sorong*
AKSL 4
AGOR 7: 5 *Baruna Jaya*; 1 *Jalanidhi*; 1 *Burujulasad*
AGHS 1
ATF 2
AXS 2
AP 8: 1 *Tanjung Kambani* (troop transport); 2 *Tanjung Nusanive* (troop transport); 5 *Karang Pilang* (troop transport)
YTM 3

Naval Aviation ε1,000

EQUIPMENT BY TYPE
AIRCRAFT
  MP 23: 3 CN-235 MPA; 14 N-22B *Searchmaster* B; 6 N-22SL *Searchmaster* L
  TPT • Light 28: 21 C-212-200 *Aviocar*; 2 DHC-5D *Buffalo*; 3 TB-9 *Tampico*; 2 TB-10 *Tobago*
HELICOPTERS
  MRH 4 Bell 412 (NB-412) *Twin Huey*
  TPT 15: **Medium** 3 AS332L *Super Puma* (NAS322L); **Light** 12: 3 EC120B *Colibri*; 9 Bo-105 (NBo-105)

Marines ε20,000

FORCES BY ROLE
SPECIAL FORCES
  1 SF bn
MANOEUVRE
  Amphibious
  2 mne gp (1 cav regt, 3 mne bn, 1 arty regt, 1 cbt spt regt, 1 CSS regt)
  1 mne bde (3 mne bn)
EQUIPMENT BY TYPE
LT TK 55 PT-76†
RECCE 21 BRDM
AIFV 83: 24 AMX-10P; 10 AMX-10 PAC 90; 37 BMP-3F; 12 BTR-80A
AAV 10 LVTP-7A1
APC (W) 100 BTR-50P
ARTY 59+
  TOWED 50: **105mm** 22 LG1 MK II; **122mm** 28 M-38
  MRL 122mm 9 RM-70
  MOR 81mm
AD • GUNS 150: **40mm** 5 L/60/L/70; **57mm** S-60

Air Force 30,100

2 operational comd (East and West) plus trg comd.
FORCES BY ROLE
FIGHTER
  1 sqn with F-5E/F *Tiger* II
  1 sqn with F-16A/B *Fighting Falcon*
FIGHTER/GROUND ATTACK
  1 sqn with Su-27SK/SKM *Flanker*; Su-30MK/MK2 *Flanker*
  3 sqn with *Hawk* MK53*/Mk109*/Mk209*
GROUND ATTACK
  1 sqn (froming) with EMB-314 (A-29) *Super Tucano**

MARITIME PATROL
1 sqn with B-737-200; CN-235M-220 MPA
TANKER/TRANSPORT
1 sqn with C-130B/KC-130B *Hercules*
TRANSPORT
1 VIP sqn with B-737-200; C-130H/H-30 *Hercules*; L-100-30; F-27-400M *Troopship*; F-28-1000/3000; AS332L *Super Puma* (NAS332L); SA330SM *Puma* (NAS300SM)
1 sqn with C-130H/H-30 *Hercules*; L-100-30
1 sqn with C-212 *Aviocar* (NC-212)
1 sqn with CN-235M-110; F-27-400M *Troopship*
TRAINING
1 sqn with AS-202 *Bravo*
1 sqn with KT-1B; T-34C *Turbo Mentor*
1 sqn with SF-260M; SF-260W *Warrior*
TRANSPORT HELICOPTER
2 sqn with AS332L *Super Puma* (NAS332L); SA330J/L *Puma* (NAS330J/L); EC120B *Colibri*

EQUIPMENT BY TYPE
Only 45% of ac op
AIRCRAFT 69 combat capable
FTR 22: 8 F-5E *Tiger* II; 4 F-5F *Tiger* II; 7 F-16A *Fighting Falcon*; 3 F-16B *Fighting Falcon*
FGA 10: 2 Su-27SK *Flanker*; 3 Su-27SKM *Flanker*; 2 Su-30 MK *Flanker*; 3 Su-30MK2 *Flanker*
MP 5: 3 B-737-200; 2 CN-235M-220 MPA
TKR 1 KC-130B *Hercules*
TPT 39 **Medium** 15: 4 C-130B *Hercules*; 3 C-130H *Hercules*; 6 C-130H-30 *Hercules*; 2 L-100-30; **Light** 19: 2 CN-295 (7 more on order); 6 C-212 *Aviocar* (NC-212); 5 CN-235-110; 6 F-27-400M *Troopship*; **PAX** 5: 1 B-737-200; 1 B-737-800BBJ; 1 F-28-1000; 2 F-28-3000
TRG 118: 39 AS-202 *Bravo*; 4 EMB-314 (A-29) *Super Tucano** (12 more on order); 6 *Hawk* Mk53*; 7 *Hawk* Mk109*; 23 *Hawk* Mk209*; 11 KT-1B; 10 SF-260M; 7 SF-260W *Warrior*; 15 T-34C *Turbo Mentor*
HELICOPTERS
TPT 31 **Medium** 19: 10 AS332 *Super Puma* (NAS-332L) (VIP/CSAR); 1 SA330SM *Puma* (NAS330SM VIP); 4 SA330J *Puma* (NAS330J); 4 SA330L *Puma* (NAS330L) **Light** 12 EC120B *Colibri*
MSL • TACTICAL
ASM AGM-65G *Maverick*
AAM • IR AIM-9P *Sidewinder*; R-73 (AA-11 *Archer*) **IR/ SARH** R-27 (AA-10 *Alamo*)
ARM Kh-31P (AS-17A *Krypton*)

Special Forces (Paskhasau)
FORCES BY ROLE
SPECIAL FORCES
3 (PASKHASAU) SF wg (total: 6 spec ops sqn)
4 indep SF coy

Paramilitary ε281,000 active

Naval Auxiliary Service
EQUIPMENT BY TYPE
PATROL AND COASTAL COMBATANTS • PB 71: 6 *Carpentaria*; 65 *Kal Kangean*

Customs
EQUIPMENT BY TYPE
PATROL AND COASTAL COMBATANTS 65
  PBF 15
  PB 50

Marine Police
EQUIPMENT BY TYPE
PATROL AND COASTAL COMBATANTS 37
  PSO 2 *Bisma*
  PCC 5
  PBF 3 *Gagak*
  PB 27: 14 *Bango*; 13 (various)
LOGISTICS AND SUPPORT • AP 1

Police ε280,000 (including 14,000 police 'mobile bde' (BRIMOB) org in 56 coy, incl CT unit (Gegana))
EQUIPMENT BY TYPE
APC (W) 34 *Tactica*
AIRCRAFT • TPT • Light 5: 2 Beech 18; 2 C-212 *Aviocar* (NC-212); 1 *Turbo Commander 680*
HELICOPTERS • TPT • Light 22: 3 Bell 206 *Jet Ranger*; 19 Bo-105 (NBo-105)

KPLP (Coast and Seaward Defence Command)
Responsible to Military Sea Communications Agency
EQUIPMENT BY TYPE
PATROL AND COASTAL COMBATANTS 11
  PCO 2 *Arda Dedali*
  PB 9: 4 *Golok* (SAR); 5 *Kujang*
LOGISTICS AND SUPPORT • ABU 1 *Jadayat*

Reserve Organisations

Kamra People's Security ε40,000 (report for 3 weeks' basic training each year; part time police auxiliary)

DEPLOYMENT

DEMOCRATIC REPUBLIC OF THE CONGO
UN • MONUSCO 175; 17 obs; 1 engr coy

HAITI
UN • MINUSTAH 168; 1 engr coy

LEBANON
UN • UNIFIL 1,458; 1 mech inf bn; 1 MP coy; elm 1 fd hospital; 1 FFGM

LIBERIA
UN • UNMIL 1 obs

SOUTH SUDAN
UN • UNMISS 3 obs

SUDAN
UN • UNAMID 3 obs
UN • UNISFA 1: 1 obs

Japan JPN

Japanese Yen ¥		2011	2012	2013
GDP	¥	468.19tr	474.56tr	
	US$	5.87tr	5.98tr	
per capita	US$	46,087	46,951	
Growth	%	-0.76	2.22	
Inflation	%	-0.29	0.04	
Def bdgt [a]	¥	4.78tr	4.71tr	4.57tr
	US$	59.8bn	59.4bn	
US$1=¥		79.81	79.30	

[a] Includes military pensions

Population   127,368,088

Ethnic groups: Korean <1%

Age	0–14	15–19	20–24	25–29	30–64	65 plus
Male	7.0%	2.6%	2.5%	2.8%	23.5%	10.3%
Female	6.5%	2.3%	2.5%	2.9%	23.7%	13.6%

Capabilities

Japan's Self-Defense Forces (SDF) are the most modern Asian armed forces in terms of their equipment. While Japan's constitution restricts the SDF to a defensive posture, Tokyo 's 2010 National Defence Programme Guidelines set the goal of creating a 'dynamic defence force' that would be more responsive and deployable military in contrast to the 'static deterrence' of previous years. The primary objective of Japan's new defence posture will be to deter North Korea and China more effectively, but HA/DR operations, counter-piracy and counter-terrorism will also be key roles. Concern over China is driving fundamental shifts in posture, with greater weight being given to deployments in, and protection of, the country's southwestern islands. The purchase of a small number of amphibious vehicles in 2012 was also an indication of the shifting priorities of the SDF, as it begins to grapple with new roles such as opposed amphibious landing. Similarly, the laying of the keel of the first of two DDH22 helicopter carriers, will augment the capability introduced by the smaller *Hyuga*-class in 2009. However, economic and constitutional constraints will continue to hamper Japanese military modernisation in the medium term.

ACTIVE 247,450 (Ground Self-Defense Force 151,350; Maritime Self- Defense Force 45,500; Air Self-Defense Force 47,100; Central Staff 3,500) **Paramilitary 12,650**

RESERVE 56,400 (General Reserve Army (GSDF) 46,000; Ready Reserve Army (GSDF) 8,500; Navy 1,100; Air 800)

ORGANISATIONS BY SERVICE

Space

SATELLITES • ISR 4: IGS 1/3/4/5

Ground Self-Defense Force 151,350

FORCES BY ROLE
COMMAND
5 army HQ (regional comd)
SPECIAL FORCES
1 spec ops unit
MANOEUVRE
Armoured
1 armd div (1 recce bn, 3 tk regt, 1 armd inf regt, 1 avn sqn, 1 SP arty regt, 1 AD bn, 1 cbt engr bn, 1 sigs bn, 1 NBC bn, 1 log regt)
Mechanised
3 armd inf div (1 recce bn, 1 tk regt, 3–4 inf regt, 1 avn sqn, 1 SP arty regt, 1 AD bn, 1 cbt engr bn, 1 sigs bn, 1 NBC bn, 1 log regt)
2 armd inf bde (1 recce coy, 1 tk bn, 3 inf regt, 1 avn sqn, 1 SP arty bn, 1 AD coy, 1 cbt engr coy, 1 sigs coy, 1 log bn)
Light
5 inf div (1 recce bn, 1 tk bn, 3-4 inf regt, 1 avn sqn, 1 arty regt, 1 AD bn, 1 cbt engr bn, 1 sigs bn, 1 NBC bn, 1 log regt)
2 inf bde (1 recce coy, 1 tk coy, 2-3 inf regt, 1 avn sqn, 1 arty bn, 1 AD coy, 1 cbt engr coy, 1 sigs coy, 1 log bn)
1 inf bde (1 recce coy, 1 inf regt, 1 avn sqn, 1 AD bn, 1 cbt engr coy, 1 EOD coy, 1 sigs coy, 1 log bn)
Air Manoeuvre
1 AB bde (3 AB bn, 1 arty bn, 1 cbt engr coy, 1 sigs coy, 1 log bn)
1 air mob inf bde (1 recce coy, 4 inf regt, 1 avn sqn, 1 SP arty bn, 1 AD coy, 1 cbt engr coy, 1 sigs coy, 1 log bn)
Aviation
1 hel bde
5 avn gp
COMBAT SUPPORT
1 arty bde
2 arty unit (bde)
2 AD bde
4 AD gp
4 engr bde
1 engr unit
1 EW bn
5 int bn
1 MP bde
1 sigs bde
COMBAT SERVICE SUPPORT
5 log unit (bde)
5 trg bde

EQUIPMENT BY TYPE
MBT 777: 26 Type-10; 410 Type-74; 341 Type-90
RECCE 102 Type-87 (some as CBRN recce variants)
AIFV 68 Type-89
APC 817
  APC (T) 286 Type-73
  APC (W) 531: 229 Type-82; 302 Type-96
ARTY 1,776
  SP 193: **155mm** 114: 46 Type-75; 68 Type-99; **203mm** 79 M110A2
  TOWED 155mm 422 FH-70
  MRL 227mm 99 M270 MLRS

MOR 1,062
  SP 120mm 24 Type-96
  TOWED 1,038: **81mm** 624 L16 **120mm** 414

AT
  MSL
    SP 30 Type-96 MPMS
    MANPATS 1,610: 140 Type-79 *Jyu-MAT*; 440 Type-87 *Chu-MAT*; 1,030 Type-01 *LMAT*
  RCL • SP 84mm 2,712 *Carl Gustav*
  RL 89mm 200

AIRCRAFT
  TPT • Light 12: 5 MU-2 (LR-1); 7 Beech 350 *King Air* (LR-2)

HELICOPTERS
  ATK 110: 74 AH-1S *Cobra*; 10 AH-64D *Apache*; 26 OH-1
  ISR 80 OH-6D
  TPT 238 **Heavy** 55: 34 CH-47D *Chinook* (CH-47J); 21 CH-47JA *Chinook* **Medium** 33: 3 EC225LP *Super Puma MkII+* (VIP); 30 UH-60L *Black Hawk* (UH-60JA) **Light** 140 Bell-205 (UH-1J); 10 Enstrom 480B (TH-480B) (delivery by end of 2012)

AD
  SAM 700
    SP 180: 20 Type-03 *Chu-SAM*; 50 Type-81 *Tan-SAM*; 110 Type-93 *Kin-SAM*
    TOWED 160 MTM-23B I-HAWK
    MANPAD 360 Type-91 *Kin-SAM*
  GUNS • SP 35mm 52 Type-87 SP
MSL • AShM 90 Type-88
AEV Type-75
ARV 71: 46 Type-78; 25 Type-90
VLB Type-67; Type-70; Type-81; Type-91
MW Type-82; Type-92

Maritime Self-Defense Force 45,500

Surface units organised into 4 Escort Flotillas with a mix of 7–8 warships each. Bases at Yokosuka, Kure, Sasebo, Maizuru, Ominato. SSK organised into two flotillas with bases at Kure and Yokosuka. Remaining units assigned to five regional districts.

EQUIPMENT BY TYPE
SUBMARINES • TACTICAL • SSK 18:
  3 *Harushio* (incl 2 in trg role) with 6 single 533mm TT with T-89 HWT/UGM-84C *Harpoon* AShM
  11 *Oyashio* with 6 single 533mm TT with T-89 HWT/UGM-84C *Harpoon* AShM
  4 *Soryu* (AIP fitted) with 6 single 533mm TT with T-89 HWT/UGM-84C *Harpoon* AShM (additional vessels in build)

PRINCIPAL SURFACE COMBATANTS 47
  AIRCRAFT CARRIERS • CVH 2:
    2 *Hyuga* with 1 16-cell Mk41 VLS with ASROC/RIM-162/ESSM *Sea Sparrow*, 2 triple 324mm TT with Mk46 LWT, 2 20mm CIWS gun, (normal ac capacity 3 SH-60 *Seahawk* ASW hel; plus additional ac embarkation up to 7 SH-60 *Seahawk* or 7 MCH-101)
  CRUISERS • CGHM 2:
    2 *Atago* (*Aegis* Base Line 7) with 2 quad lnchr with SSM-1B AShM, 1 64-cell Mk41 VLS with SM-2 MR SAM/ASROC, 1 32-cell Mk41 VLS with SM-2 MR SAM, 2 triple 324mm ASTT with Mk46 LWT, 1 127mm gun, (capacity 1 SH-60 *Seahawk* ASW hel)

DESTROYERS 30:
  DDGHM 22:
    7 *Asagiri* with 2 quad Mk141 lnchr with RGM-84C *Harpoon* AShM, 1 octuple Mk29 lnchr with *Sea Sparrow* SAM, 2 triple 324mm ASTT with Mk46 LWT, 1 octuple Mk112 lnchr with ASROC, 1 76mm gun, (capacity 1 SH-60 *Seahawk* ASW hel)
    1 *Akizuki* with 2 quad lnchr with SS-1B AShM, 1 32-cell Mk41 VLS with ASROC/ESSM Sea Sparrow SAM, 1 triple 324mm ASTT with Mk46 LWT, 1 127mm gun (capacity 1 SH-60 *Seahawk* ASW hel)
    9 *Murasame* with 2 quad lnchr with SSM-1B AShM, 1 16-cell Mk48 VLS with RIM-7M *Sea Sparrow* SAM, 2 triple 324mm TT with Mk46 LWT, 1 16-cell Mk41 VLS with ASROC, 2 76mm gun, (capacity 1 SH-60 *Seahawk* ASW hel)
    5 *Takanami* (improved *Murasame*) with 2 quad lnchr with SSM-1B AShM, 1 32-cell Mk41 VLS with ASROC/RIM-7M/ESSM *Sea Sparrow* SAM, 2 triple 324mm TT with Mk46 LWT, 1 127mm gun, (capacity 1 SH-60 *Seahawk* ASW hel)
  DDGM 6:
    2 *Hatakaze* with 2 quad Mk141 lnchr with RGM-84C *Harpoon* AShM, 1 Mk13 GMLS with SM-1 MR SAM, 2 triple 324mm ASTT, 2 127mm gun, 1 hel landing platform
    4 *Kongou* (*Aegis* Baseline 4/5) with 2 quad Mk141 lnchr with RGM-84C *Harpoon* AShM, 1 29-cell Mk41 VLS with SM-2/3 SAM/ASROC, 1 61-cell Mk41 VLS with SM-2/3 SAM/ASROC, 2 triple 324mm ASTT, 1 127mm gun
  DDM 2:
    2 *Shirane* with 1 octuple Mk112 lnchr with ASROC, 1 octuple Mk29 lnchr with RIM-162A *Sea Sparrow* SAM, 2 triple ASTT with Mk46 LWT, 2 127mm gun, (capacity 3 SH-60 *Seahawk* ASW hel)

FRIGATES • FFGM 13:
  6 *Abukuma* with 2 quad Mk141 lnchr with RGM-84C *Harpoon* AShM, 2 triple ASTT with Mk 46 LWT, 1 Mk112 octuple lnchr with ASROC, 1 76mm gun
  7 *Hatsuyuki* with 2 quad Mk141 lnchr with RGM-84C *Harpoon* AShM, 1 octuple Mk29 lnchr with RIM-7F/M *Sea Sparrow* SAM, 2 triple ASTT with Mk46 LWT, 1 octuple Mk112 lnchr with ASROC, 1 76mm gun, (capacity 1 SH-60 *Seahawk* ASW hel)

PATROL AND COASTAL COMBATANTS 6
PBFG 6 *Hayabusa* with 4 SSM-1B AShM, 1 76mm gun

MINE WARFARE • MINE COUNTERMEASURES 33
  MCM SPT 4:
    2 *Nijma*
    2 *Uraga* with 1 hel landing platform (for MH-53E)
  MSO 25: 3 *Hirashima*; 12 *Sugashima*; 7 *Uwajima*; 3 *Yaeyama*
  MSD 4

AMPHIBIOUS
  LANDING SHIPS • LST 5:
    3 *Osumi* with 1 hel landing platform (for 2 CH-47 hel) (capacity 10 Type-90 MBT; 2 LCAC(L) ACV; 330 troops)
    2 *Yura* (capacity 70 troops)

Asia

LANDING CRAFT 19
  LCU 2 *Yusotei*
  LCM 11
  ACV 6 LCAC(L) (capacity either 1 MBT or 60 troops)
LOGISTICS AND SUPPORT 76
  AOE 5: 2 *Mashu*; 3 *Towada*
  AS 1 *Chiyoda* (submarine rescue facilities)
  ASR 1 *Chihaya*
  ARC 1 *Muroto*
  AG 2: 1 *Kurihama*; 1 *Asuka* (wpn trials)
  AGOS 2 *Hibiki*
  AGS 4: 1 *Futami*; 1 *Nichinan*; 1 *Shonan*; 1 *Suma*
  AGB 1 *Shirase*
  ATF 25
  TRG 6: 1 *Kashima*; 2 *Shimayuki*; 1 *Asagiri* with 2 triple
  ASTT with Mk46 LWT, 1 octuple Mk112 lnchr with
  ASROC, 1 Mitsubishi Type-71 ASW RL, 1 76mm gun;
  1 *Tenryu* (trg spt ship); 1 *Kurobe* (trg spt ship)
  SPT 5 *Hiuchi*
  YAC 1 *Hashidate*
  YDT 6
  YTM 16

Naval Aviation ε9,800

7 Air Groups

FORCES BY ROLE
ANTI SUBMARINE/SURFACE WARFARE
  7 sqn (shipboard/trg) with SH-60B (SH-60J)/SH-60K
  Seahawk
MARITIME PATROL
  6 sqn (incl 1 trg) with P-3C *Orion*
ELECTRONIC WARFARE
  1 sqn with EP-3 *Orion*
MINE COUNTERMEASURES
  1 sqn with MH-53E *Sea Dragon*; MCH-101
SEARCH & RESCUE
  1 sqn with *Shin Meiwa* US-1A/US-2
  2 sqn with UH-60J *Black Hawk*
TRANSPORT
  1 sqn with AW101 *Merlin* (CH-101); Beech 90 *King Air*
  (LC-90); YS-11M
TRAINING
  1 sqn with EC135 (TH-135); OH-6DA
  3 sqn with T-5; Beech 90 *King Air* (TC-90)
EQUIPMENT BY TYPE
AIRCRAFT 78 combat capable
  ASW 78 P-3C *Orion* (2 P-1 in test - additional ac on
  order)
  ELINT 5 EP-3C *Orion*
  SAR 7: 2 *Shin Meiwa* US-1A; 5 *Shin Meiwa* US-2
  TPT • Light 28: 3 YS-11M; 5 Beech 90 *King Air* (LC-90);
  20 Beech 90 *King Air* (TC-90)
  TRG 32 T-5
HELICOPTERS
  ASW 87: 49 SH-60B *Seahawk* (SH-60J); 37 SH-60K
  Seahawk; 1 USH-60K *Seahawk*
  MCM 12: 7 MH-53E *Sea Dragon*; 5 MCH-101
  ISR 4 OH-6DA
  SAR 19 UH-60J *Black Hawk*

TPT 10 **Medium** 2 AW101 *Merlin* (CH-101) (additional
ac being delivered); **Light** 8 EC135 (TH-135)

Air Self-Defense Force 47,100

Flying hours   150 hrs/year

7 cbt wg

FORCES BY ROLE
FIGHTER
  7 sqn with F-15J *Eagle*
  2 sqn with F-4EJ (F-4E) *Phantom II*
  3 sqn with Mitsubishi F-2
ELECTRONIC WARFARE
  2 sqn with Kawasaki EC-1; YS-11E
ISR
  1 sqn with RF-4EJ (RF-4E) *Phantom II**
AIRBORNE EARLY WARNING & CONTROL
  2 sqn with E-2C *Hawkeye*; E-767
SEARCH & RESCUE
  1 wg with U-125A *Peace Krypton*; MU-2 (LR-1); UH-60J
  Black Hawk
TANKER
  1 sqn with KC-767J
TRANSPORT
  1 (VIP) sqn with B-747-400
  3 sqn with C-1; C-130H *Hercules*; YS-11
  Some (liaison) sqn with Gulfstream IV (U-4); T-4*
TRAINING
  1 (aggressor) sqn with F-15J *Eagle*
TEST
  1 wg with F-15J *Eagle*; T-4*
TRANSPORT HELICOPTER
  4 flt with CH-47 *Chinook*
EQUIPMENT BY TYPE
AIRCRAFT 552 combat capable
  FTR 201 F-15J *Eagle*
  FGA 139: 76 F-2A/B; 63 F-4E *Phantom II* (F-4EJ)
  EW 3: 1 Kawasaki EC-1; 2 YS-11EA
  ISR 17: 13 RF-4E *Phantom II** (RF-4J); 4 YS-11EB
  AEW&C 17: 13 E-2C *Hawkeye*; 4 E-767
  SAR 28 U-125A *Peace Krypton*
  TKR 4 KC-767J
  TPT 66 **Medium** 16 C-130H *Hercules*; **PAX** 50: 2 B-747-
  400; 13 Beech T-400; 26 C-1; 5 Gulfstream IV (U-4); 4 YS-
  11
  TRG 248: 199 T-4*; 49 T-7
HELICOPTERS
  SAR 41 UH-60J *Black Hawk*
  TPT • Heavy 15 CH-47 *Chinook*
MSL
  ASM ASM-1 (Type-80); ASM-2 (Type-93)
  AAM • IR AAM-3 (Type-90); AIM-9 *Sidewinder*; **IIR**
  AAM-5 (Type-04); **SARH** AIM-7 *Sparrow*; **ARH** AAM-4
  (Type-99)

Air Defence

Ac control and warning. 4 wg; 28 radar sites

FORCES BY ROLE
AIR DEFENCE
  6 SAM gp (total: 24 SAM bty with MIM-104 *Patriot*)

1 (Air Base Defence) AD gp with Type-81 *Tan-SAM*; Type-91 *Kei-SAM*; M167 *Vulcan*

EQUIPMENT BY TYPE

AD • SAM

  SP Type-81 *Tan-SAM*
  TOWED 120 MIM-104 *Patriot*
  MANPAD Type-91 *Kei-SAM*
  GUNS • TOWED 20mm M167 *Vulcan*

Paramilitary 12,650

Coast Guard

Ministry of Land, Transport, Infrastructure and Tourism (no cbt role)

PATROL AND COASTAL COMBATANTS 403

  PSOH 13: 2 *Mizuho*; 1 *Shikishima*; 10 *Soya*
  PSO 28: 3 *Hida*; 1 *Izu*; 1 *Kojima* (trg); 1 *Miura*; 1 *Nojima*; 7 *Ojika*; 12 *Shiretoko*; 2 *Kunigami*
  PCO 44: 3 *Aso*; 2 *Bihoro*; 9 *Hateruma*; 14 *Natsui*; 2 *Takatori*; 14 *Teshio* (1 with ice-strengthened hull)
  PCC 21: 4 *Amani*; 17 *Tokara*
  PBF 44: 17 *Hayagumo*; 5 *Mihashi*; 14 *Raizan*; 2 *Takatsuki*; 6 *Tsuruugi*
  PB 253: 9 *Akizuki*; 4 *Asogiri*; 201 CL-Type; 15 *Hayanami*; 1 *Matsunami*; 9 *Murakumo*; 2 *Natsugiri*; 1 *Shikinami*; 3 *Shimagiri*; 4 *Yodo*; 2 *Agaki*; 2 *Katonami*

LOGISTICS AND SUPPORT 39:

  ABU 1
  AGS 12
  AKSL 9
  YAG 5
  YPC 3
  YTR 9

AIRCRAFT

  MP 2 *Falcon* 900 MPA
  ISR 2 Beech 200T
  TPT 21 **Light** 12: 10 Beech 350 *King Air* (LR-2); 1 Cessna 206 *Stationair* (U-206G); 1 YS-11A **PAX** 9: 3 CL-300; 2 Gulfstream V (MP); 4 Saab 340B

HELICOPTERS

  MRH 7 Bell 412 *Twin Huey*
  TPT 39 **Medium** 6: 4 AS332 *Super Puma*; 2 EC225 *Super Puma* **Light** 33: 5 AW139; 4 Bell 206B *Jet Ranger II*; 20 Bell 212; 4 S-76C

Cyber

The Self-Defense Forces (SDF) established a Command Control Communication Computer Systems Command in 2008. According to the government's 'Secure Japan 2009' document, the Ministry of Defense was to be involved in investigating the latest technological trends in cyber attacks. In order to analyse attacks on MOD information systems and response capabilities, government agencies were to 'study the basics of illegal access monitoring and analysis technology, cyber attack analysis technology, and active defense technology'. Further, the 'Information Security 2010' document stated that 'at the end of FY2010, a cyber planning and coordination officer (provisional title) will be stationed in the Joint Staff Office of the Ministry of Defense to enhance […] preparedness against cyber attacks'. In the

2013 defence budget, the MOD announced a ¥20 billion investment in creating a 100-strong cyber-defence force, unnamed as of late 2012, to improve the resilience of its networks and infrastructure.

DEPLOYMENT

DJIBOUTI

MSDF 200; 2 P-3C *Orion*

GULF OF ADEN & INDIAN OCEAN

MSDF: 2 DDGHM

HAITI

UN • MINUSTAH 225; 1 engr coy

SOUTH SUDAN

UN • UNMISS 271; 1 engr coy

SYRIA/ISRAEL

UN • UNDOF 31; elm 1 log bn

FOREIGN FORCES

United States US Pacific Command: 36,700

  Army 2,500; 1 HQ (9th Theater Army Area Command) at Zama

  Navy 6,750; 1 CVN; 2 CG; 8 DDG; 1 LCC; 2 MCM; 1 LHD; 2 LSD; 1 base at Sasebo; 1 base at Yokosuka

  USAF: 12,500; 1 HQ (5th Air Force) at Okinawa–Kadena AB; 1 ftr wg at Okinawa–Kadena AB (2 ftr sqn with 18 F-16C/D *Fighting Falcon* at Misawa AB); 1 ftr wg at Okinawa–Kadena AB (1 SAR sqn with 8 HH-60G *Pave Hawk*, 1 AEW sqn with 2 E-3B *Sentry*, 2 ftr sqn with total of 24 F-15C/D *Eagle*); 1 airlift wg at Yokota AB with 10 C-130E *Hercules*; 2 C-21J; 1 spec ops gp at Okinawa–Kadena AB

  USMC 14,950; 1 Marine div (3rd); 1 ftr sqn with 12 F/A-18D *Hornet*; 1 tkr sqn with 12 KC-130J *Hercules*; 2 tpt hel sqn with 12 CH-46E *Sea Knight*; 1 tpt hel sqn with 12 MV-22B *Osprey*; 3 tpt hel sqn with 10 CH-53E *Sea Stallion*

Korea, Democratic People's Republic of DPRK

North Korean Won		2011	2012
GDP*	US$		
per capita	US$		
Def exp*	won		
	US$		

US$1=won

*definitive economic data not available

Population	24,589,122

Age	0–14	15–19	20–24	25–29	30–64	65 plus
Male	11.2%	4.2%	4.2%	3.7%	22.1%	3.1%
Female	10.9%	4.1%	4.0%	3.6%	22.8%	6.2%

Capabilities

North Korea maintains the world's fourth-largest standing armed forces. However, equipment is mainly in a poor state, and training, morale and operational readiness all remain questionable. Pyongyang relies on weight of numbers and asymmetric capabilities to deter its southern neighbour, with which North Korea is still officially at war. North Korea is actively pursuing a nuclear-weapons capability, with two devices tested in 2006 and 2009, a second route to nuclearisation opened up by the uranium enrichment programme revealed in 2010, and a ballistic-missile programme that has deployed hundreds of short- and medium-range missiles. However, there is no proof that North Korea has successfully weaponised a nuclear device. The ideological 'military first' construct ensures that the armed forces will continue to have prioritised access to resources. New leader Kim Jong-un's early visits to military facilities in the first months of his tenure suggest little change in the military-first policy.

ACTIVE 1,190,000 (Army ε1,020,000 Navy 60,000 Air 110,000) **Paramilitary 189,000**

Terms of service Army 5–12 years, Navy 5–10 years Air Force 3–4 years, followed by compulsory part-time service to age 40. Thereafter service in the Worker/Peasant Red Guard to age 60.

RESERVE ε600,000 (Armed Forces ε600,000), **Paramilitary 5,700,000**

Reservists are assigned to units (see also Paramilitary)

ORGANISATIONS BY SERVICE

Strategic Forces

North Korea's *No-dong* missiles and H-5 (Il-28) bombers could in future be used to deliver nuclear warheads or bombs. At present, however, there is no conclusive evidence to suggest that North Korea has successfully produced a warhead or bomb capable of being delivered by either of these systems.

Army ε1,020,000

FORCES BY ROLE
COMMAND
  2 mech corps HQ
  9 inf corps HQ
  1 (Capital Defence) corps HQ
MANOEUVRE
  Armoured
  1 armd div
  15 armd bde
  Mechanised
  4 mech div
  Light
  27 inf div
  14 inf bde
COMBAT SUPPORT
  1 arty div
  21 arty bde

9 MRL bde
1 SSM bde with *Scud*
1 SSM bde with FROG-7
5–8 engr river crossing / amphibious regt
1 engr river crossing bde

Special Purpose Forces Command 88,000

FORCES BY ROLE
SPECIAL FORCES
  8 (Reconnaissance General Bureau) SF bn
MANOEUVRE
  Reconnaissance
  17 recce bn
  Light
  9 lt inf bde
  6 sniper bde
  Air Manoeuvre
  3 AB bde
  1 AB bn
  2 sniper bde
  Amphibious
  2 sniper bde

Reserves 600,000

FORCES BY ROLE
MANOEUVRE
  Light
  40 inf div
  18 inf bde

EQUIPMENT BY TYPE (ε)
MBT 3,500+ T-34/T-54/T-55/T-62/Type-59/*Chonma*/*Pokpoong*
LT TK 560+: 560 PT-76; M-1985
APC 2,500+
  APC (T) Type-531 (Type-63); VTT-323
  APC (W) 2,500 BTR-40/BTR-50/BTR-60/BTR-80A/BTR-152/BTR look-a-like
ARTY 21,000+
  SP/TOWED 8,500: **SP 122mm** M-1977/M-1981/M-1985/M-1991; **130mm** M-1975/M-1981/M-1991; **152mm** M-1974/M-1977; **170mm** M-1978/M-1989
  TOWED 122mm D-30/D-74/M-1931/37; **130mm** M-46; **152mm** M-1937/M-1938/M-1943
  GUN/MOR 120mm (reported)
  MRL 5,100: **107mm** Type-63; **122mm** BM-11/M-1977 (BM-21)/M-1985/M-1992/M-1993; **240mm** M-1985/M-1989/M-1991
  MOR 7,500: **82mm** M-37; **120mm** M-43; **160mm** M-43
AT • MSL
  SP 9K11 *Malyutka* (AT-3 *Sagger*)
  MANPATS 2K15 *Shmel* (AT-1 *Snapper*); 9K111 *Fagot* (AT-4 *Spigot*); 9K113 *Konkurs* (AT-5 *Spandrel*)
  RCL 82mm 1,700 B-10
AD
  SAM
    SP some 9K35 *Strela*-10 (SA-13 *Gopher*)
    MANPAD 9K310 *Igla*-1 (SA-16 *Gimlet*)/9K32 *Strela*-2 (SA-7 *Grail*)‡
  GUNS 11,000
    SP 14.5mm M-1984; **23mm** M-1992; **37mm** M-1992; **57mm** M-1985

TOWED 11,000: **14.5mm** ZPU-1/ZPU-2/ZPU-4; **23mm** ZU-23; **37mm** M-1939; **57mm** S-60; **85mm** M-1939 *KS-12*; **100mm** KS-19

MSL

SSM 64+: 24 FROG-3/FROG-5/FROG-7; KN-08 (in development); some *Musudan*; ε10 *No-dong* (ε90+ msl); 30+ *Scud*-B/*Scud*-C (ε200+ msl)

Navy ε60,000

EQUIPMENT BY TYPE

SUBMARINES • TACTICAL 72:

SSK 22 PRC Type-031/FSU *Romeo*† with 8 single 533mm TT with 14 SAET-60 HWT

SSC 30+:

28 *Sang-O*† with 2 single 533mm TT with Type-53–65 HWT;

2+ *Sang-O II* (reported) with 4 single 533mm TT with Type-53–65 HWT;

SSW 20† (some *Yugo* with 2 single 406mm TT; some *Yeono*)

PRINCIPAL SURFACE COMBATANTS 3

FRIGATES • FFG 3:

2 *Najin* with 2 single lnchr with P-15 *Termit* (SS-N-2) AShM, 2 RBU 1200, 2 100mm gun

1 *Soho* with 4 single lnchr with P-15 *Termit* (SS-N-2) AShM, 2 RBU 1200, 1 100mm gun, 1 hel landing platform (for med hel)

PATROL AND COASTAL COMBATANTS 383

PCG 18

8 *Osa* II with 2 single lnchr with P-15 *Termit* (SS-N-2) AShM

10 *Soju* with 4 single lnchr with P-15 *Termit* (SS-N-2) AShM

PCO 5: 4 *Sariwon*; 1 *Tral* with 1 85mm gun

PCC 18:

6 *Hainan* with 4 RBU 1200

12 *Taechong* with 2 RBU 1200, 1 100mm gun

PBFG 16:

4 *Huangfen* with 4 single lnchr with P-15 *Termit* (SS-N-2) AShM

6 *Komar* with 2 single lnchr with P-15 *Termit* (SS-N-2) AShM

6 *Sohung* with 2 single lnchr with P-15 *Termit* (SS-N-2) AShM

PBF 229: 54 *Chong-Jin*; 142 *Ku Song/Sin Hung/Sin Hung (mod)*; 33 *Sinpo*

PB 97

59 *Chaho*

6 *Chong-Ju* with 2 RBU 1200, 1 85mm gun

13 *Shanghai* II

19 SO-1

MINE WARFARE • MINE COUNTERMEASURES 24: 19 *Yukto* I; 5 *Yukto* II

AMPHIBIOUS

LANDING SHIPS • LSM 10 *Hantae* (capacity 3 tanks; 350 troops)

LANDING CRAFT 257:

LCPL 96 *Nampo* (capacity 35 troops)

LCM 25

LCVP 136 (capacity 50 troops)

LOGISTICS AND SUPPORT 23:

AS 8 (converted cargo ships); **ASR** 1 *Kowan*; **AGI** 14 (converted fishing vessels)

Coastal Defence

FORCES BY ROLE

COMBAT SUPPORT

2 AShM regt with HY-1 (CSS-N-2) (6 sites, and probably some mobile launchers)

EQUIPMENT BY TYPE

ARTY • TOWED 122mm M-1931/37; **152mm** M-1937 **COASTAL 130mm** M-1992; SM-4-1

MSL • AShM HY-1 (CSS-N-2); KN-01 (in development)

Air Force 110,000

4 air divs. 1st, 2nd and 3rd Air Divs (cbt) responsible for N, E and S air defence sectors respectively; 8th Air Div (trg) responsible for NE sector. The AF controls the national airline.

Flying hours 20 hrs/year on ac

FORCES BY ROLE

BOMBER

3 (lt) regt with H-5†

FIGHTER

1 regt with F-7B *Airguard*

6 regt with J-5

4 regt with J-6

5 regt with J-7

1 regt with MiG-23ML/P *Flogger*

1 regt with MiG-29 *Fulcrum*

FIGHTER/GROUND ATTACK

1 regt with Su-7 *Fitter*

GROUND ATTACK

1 regt with Su-25 *Frogfoot*

TRANSPORT

Some regt with Y-5 (to infiltrate 2 air-force sniper brigades deep into ROK rear areas), but possibly grounded; An-24 *Coke*; Il-18 *Coot*; Il-62M *Classic*; Tu-134 *Crusty*; Tu-154 *Careless*

TRAINING

Some regt with CJ-6; FT-2; MiG-21 *Fishbed*

ATTACK HELICOPTER

1 regt with Mi-24 *Hind*

TRANSPORT HELICOPTER

Some regt with Hughes 500D†; Mi-8 *Hip*/Mi-17 *Hip H*; PZL Mi-2 *Hoplite*; Z-5

AIR DEFENCE

19 bde with S-125 *Pechora* (SA-3 *Goa*); S-75 *Dvina* (SA-2 *Guideline*); S-200 *Angara* (SA-5 *Gammon*); 9K36 *Strela-3* (SA-14 *Gremlin*); 9K310 *Igla-1* (SA-16 *Gimlet*); 9K32 *Strela-2* (SA-7 *Grail*)‡; (KN-06 SAM system shown in 2010)

EQUIPMENT BY TYPE

AIRCRAFT 603 combat capable

BBR 80 H-5†

FTR 441+: 40 F-7B *Airguard*; 107 J-5; 100 J-6; 120 J-7†; 46 MiG-23ML *Flogger*; 10 MiG-23P *Flogger*; 18+ MiG-29A/S *Fulcrum*

FGA 48: 30 MiG-21bis *Fishbed*†; 18 Su-7 *Fitter*

ATK 34 Su-25 *Frogfoot*

TPT 217: **Light** 208: 6 An-24 *Coke*; 2 Tu-134 *Crusty*; ε200
Y-5 **PAX** 9: 2 Il-18 *Coot*; 2 Il-62M *Classic*; 4 Tu-154 *Careless*;
1 Tu-204-300
TRG 215: 180 CJ-6; 35 FT-2
HELICOPTERS
ATK 20 Mi-24 *Hind*
MRH 80 Hughes 500D†
TPT 202 **Medium** 63: 15 Mi-8 *Hip*/Mi-17 *Hip H*; 48 Z-5
Light 139 PZL Mi-2 *Hoplite*
UAV • ISR • Light *Pchela*-1 (*Shmel*)
AD • SAM 3400+
TOWED 312+: 179+ S-75 *Dvina* (SA-2 *Guideline*); 133
S-125 *Pechora* (SA-3 *Goa*)
STATIC/SHELTER 38 S-200 (SA-5 *Gammon*)
MANPAD 3,050+ 9K32 *Strela*-2 (SA-7 *Grail*)‡; 9K36
Strela-3 (SA-14 *Gremlin*); 9K310 *Igla*-1 (SA-16 *Gimlet*)
MSL
ASM Kh-23 (AS-7 *Kerry*); Kh-25 (AS-10 *Karen*)
AShM KN-01
AAM • IR R-3 (AA-2 *Atoll*)‡; R-60 (AA-8 *Aphid*); R-73
(AA-11 *Archer*); PL-5; PL-7; **SARH** R-23/24 (AA-7 *Apex*);
R-27R/ER (AA-10 A/C *Alamo*)

Paramilitary 189,000 active

Security Troops 189,000 (incl border guards, public safety personnel)
Ministry of Public Security

Worker/Peasant Red Guard ε5,700,000 reservists
Org on a provincial/town/village basis; comd structure is
bde–bn–coy–pl; small arms with some mor and AD guns
(but many units unarmed)

Cyber

Since the 1970s, the North Korean military (the Korean
People's Army – KPA) has maintained a modest electronic
warfare (EW) capability. As a result of strategic reviews
following *Operation Desert Storm*, the KPA established an
information warfare (IW) capability under the concept of
'electronic intelligence warfare' (EIW). Complementing
these EIW developments, the KPA is believed to have expanded its EW capabilities with the introduction of more
modern ELINT equipment, jammers and radars. In 1998,
Unit 121 was reportedly established within the Reconnaissance Bureau of the General Staff Department to undertake
offensive cyber operations. Staff are trained in North Korea
but some also receive training in Russia and China. In early
2012, activity attributed to Pyongyang included jamming
the global positioning systems of aircraft using Seoul's
main international airports, as well as those of vessels in
nearby waters for two weeks. North Korea also continued
to launch distributed denial of service attacks on South Korean institutions and pursue cyber infiltration against military and other government agencies.

Korea, Republic of ROK

South Korean Won		2011	2012	2013
GDP	won	1237.13tr	1309.38tr	
	US$	1.12tr	1.15tr	
per capita	US$	22,922	23,536	
Growth	%	3.63	2.69	
Inflation	%	4.03	2.22	
Def bdgt	won	31.4tr	33tr	34.6tr
	US$	28.3bn	29bn	
US$1=won		1108.29	1137.34	

Population   48,860,500

Age	0–14	15–19	20–24	25–29	30–64	65 plus
Male	7.9%	3.7%	3.5%	3.6%	26.5%	4.8%
Female	7.2%	3.3%	3.1%	3.2%	26.1%	7.0%

Capabilities

More than half a century of tailoring its defence posture
around the possibility of an invasion from its northern
neighbour has left South Korea with some of the best-
equipped and most capable armed forces in East Asia. But
not even this has been able to deter lethal aggression from
the north – as demonstrated by the sinking of the *Cheonan* in
March 2010, and the shelling of Yeongpyeong Island in November 2010. These attacks took Seoul by surprise, leading
to a commitment to invest in improving the South's capacity to deter and, if necessary, respond to northern aggression. At the same time, South Korea is developing broader
ambitions, building a blue-water navy and a major new naval base on Jeju island. The country has also demonstrated
a willingness to deploy forces overseas in support of international coalitions and operations. The Cheonghae Unit is a
dedicated counter-piracy task force that has operated in the
Indian Ocean since April 2009.

ACTIVE 655,000 (Army 522,000 Navy 68,000 Air
65,000) **Paramilitary 4,500**
Terms of service conscription: Army, Navy and Air Force 26
months

RESERVE 4,500,000
Reserve obligation of three days per year. First Combat
Forces (Mobilisation Reserve Forces) or Regional Combat
Forces (Homeland Defence Forces) to age 33.

Paramilitary 3,000,000
Being reorganised

ORGANISATIONS BY SERVICE

Army 522,000
FORCES BY ROLE
COMMAND
2 army HQ
8 corps HQ
1 (Capital Defence) comd HQ

SPECIAL FORCES

1 (Special Warfare) SF comd
7 SF bde

MANOEUVRE

Armoured

4 armd bde

Mechanised

6 mech inf div (1 recce bn, 1 armd bde, 2 mech inf bde, 1 fd arty bde, 1 engr bn)

Light

16 inf div (1 recce bn, 1 tk bn, 3 inf regt, 1 arty regt (4 arty bn), 1 engr bn)

2 indep inf bde

Air Manoeuvre

1 air aslt bde

Other

3 (Counter Infiltration) bde

Aviation

1 (army avn) comd

COMBAT SUPPORT

3 SSM bn
3 ADA bde
3 SAM bn with I-HAWK
2 SAM bn with *Nike Hercules*
6 engr bde
5 engr gp
1 CBRN defence bde
8 sigs bde

COMBAT SERVICE SUPPORT

4 log cpt cmd
5 sy regt

EQUIPMENT BY TYPE

MBT 2,414: 1,000 K1; 484 K1A1; 253 M48; 597 M48A5; 80 T-80U; (400 M-47 in store)

AIFV 240: 40 BMP-3; ε200 K21

APC 2,790

APC (T) 2,560: 300 Bv 206; 1,700 KIFV; 420 M113; 140 M577

APC (W) 220: 20 BTR-80; 200 KM-900/-901 (Fiat 6614)

PPV 10 *MaxxPro*

ARTY 11,038+

SP 1,353+: **155mm** 1,340: ε300 K9 *Thunder*; 1,040 M109A2 (K55/K55A1); **175mm** some M107; **203mm** 13 M110

TOWED 3,500+: **105mm** 1,700 M101/KH-178; **155mm** 1,800+ KH-179/M114/M115

MRL 185: **130mm** 156 *Kooryong*; **227mm** 29 MLRS (all ATACMS capable)

MOR 6,000: **81mm** KM-29 (M-29); **107mm** M-30

AT

MSL

SP *Spike* NLOS

MANPATS 9K115 *Metis* (AT-7 *Saxhorn*); TOW-2A

RCL **57mm**; **75mm**; **90mm** M67; **106mm** M40A2

GUNS 58

SP 90mm 50 M36

TOWED 76mm 8 M18 *Hellcat* (AT gun)

HELICOPTERS

ATK 60 AH-1F/J *Cobra*

MRH 175: 130 Hughes 500D; 45 MD-500

TPT 222 **Heavy** 23: 17 CH-47D *Chinook*; 6 MH-47E *Chinook* **Medium** 87 UH-60P *Black Hawk* **Light** 112: ε100 Bell-205 (UH-1H *Iroquois*); 12 Bo-105

AD

SAM 1,286+

SP *Chun Ma Pegasus*

TOWED 306: 158 MIM-23B I-HAWK; 48 *Patriot* PAC-2

STATIC 200 MIM-14 *Nike Hercules*

MANPAD 780+: 60 FIM-43 *Redeye*; ε200 FIM-92A *Stinger*; 350 *Javelin*; 170 *Mistral*; 9K31 *Igla-1* (SA-16 *Gimlet*)

GUNS 330+

SP 170: **20mm** ε150 KIFV *Vulcan* SPAAG; **30mm** 20 BIHO *Flying Tiger*

TOWED 160: **20mm** 60 M167 *Vulcan*; **35mm** 20 GDF-003; **40mm** 80 L/60/L/70; M1

RADAR • LAND AN/TPQ-36 *Firefinder* (arty, mor); AN/TPQ-37 *Firefinder* (arty); RASIT (veh, arty)

MSL • SSM 30 NHK-I/-II *Hyonmu*

AEV 207 M9

ARV 238: 200 K1; K288A1; M47; 38 M88A1

VLB 56 K1

Reserves

FORCES BY ROLE

COMMAND

1 army HQ

MANOEUVRE

Light

24 inf div

Navy 68,000 (incl marines)

Naval HQ (CNOROK) located at Gyeryongdae, with an Operational Cmd HQ (CINCROKFLT) located at Jinhae with three separate fleet elements; 1st Fleet Donghae (Sea of Japan (East Sea)); 2nd Fleet Pyeongtaek (West Sea/Yellow Sea); 3rd Fleet Busan (South Sea/Korea Strait); additional three flotillas (incl SF, mine warfare, amphibious and spt elements) and 1 Naval Air Wing (3 gp plus Spt gp).

EQUIPMENT BY TYPE

SUBMARINES • TACTICAL 23

SSK 12:

9 *Chang Bogo* with 8 single 533mm TT with SUT HWT

3 *Son Won-ill* (KSS-2; AIP fitted) with 8 single 533mm TT with SUT HWT (additional vessels in build)

SSC 11: 9 *Cosmos*; 2 *Dolgorae* (KSS-1) with 2 single 406mm TT

PRINCIPAL SURFACE COMBATANTS 28

CRUISERS • CGHM 2

2 *Sejong* (KDX-3) with 2 quad Mk141 lnchr with RGM-84 *Harpoon* AShM, 1 48-cell Mk41 VLS with SM-2MR SAM, 1 32-cell Mk41 VLS with SM-2MR SAM, 1 Mk49 GMLS with RIM-116, 2 triple 324mm ASTT with K745 LWT, 1 32-cell VLS with ASROC (intended for *Cheon Ryong* LACM), 1 127mm gun, (capacity 2 *Lynx* Mk99 hel); (additional vessel undergoing sea trials)

DESTROYERS • DDGHM 6:

6 *Chungmugong Yi Sun-Jhin* (KDX-2) with 2 quad Mk141 lnchr with RGM-84C *Harpoon* AShM, 2

32-cell Mk41 VLS with SM-2 MR SAM/ASROC, 2 triple 324mm ASTT with Mk46 LWT,1 127mm gun (capacity 1 *Lynx* Mk99 hel)

FRIGATES 12

FFGHM 3:

3 *Gwanggaeto Daewang* (KDX-1) with 2 quad Mk141 lnchr with RGM-84 *Harpoon* AShM, 1 16 cell Mk48 VLS with *Sea Sparrow* SAM, 2 triple 324mm ASTT with Mk46 LWT, 1 127mm gun, (capacity 1 *Lynx* Mk99 hel)

FFGM 9:

9 *Ulsan* with 2 quad Mk141 lnchr with RGM-84C *Harpoon* AShM, 2 triple 324mm ASTT with Mk46 LWT, 2 76mm gun

PATROL AND COASTAL COMBATANTS 114

CORVETTES 34

FSG 30:

9 *Gumdoksuri* with 2 twin lnchr with RGM-84 *Harpoon* AShM, 1 76mm gun (additional vessel in build)

2 *Po Hang* with 2 single lnchr with MM-38 *Exocet* AShM, 2 triple ASTT with Mk 46 LWT, 1 76mm gun

19 *Po Hang* with 2 twin lnchr with RGM-84 *Harpoon* AShM, 2 triple ASTT with Mk46 LWT, 2 76mm gun

FS 4:

4 *Dong Hae* with 2 triple ASTT with Mk46 LWT, 1 76mm gun

PBF 80 *Sea Dolphin*

MINE WARFARE 10

MINE COUNTERMEASURES 9

MHO 6 *Kan Kyeong*

MSO 3 *Yang Yang*

MINELAYERS • ML 1 *Won San*

AMPHIBIOUS

PRINCIPAL AMPHIBIOUS SHIPS 1:

LPD 1 *Dokdo* (capacity 2 LCAC; 10 tanks; 700 troops; 10 UH-60 hel)

LANDING SHIPS 6:

LST 6: 4 *Alligator* (capacity 20 tanks; 300 troops); 2 *Un Bong* (capacity 16 tanks; 200 troops)

LANDING CRAFT 41:

LCAC 5: 3 *Tsaplya* (capacity 1 MBT; 130 troops); 2 LSF-II

LCM 10 LCM-8

LCT 6

LCVP 20

LOGISTICS AND SUPPORT 24

AORH 3 *Chun Jee*

ARS 1

AG 1 *Sunjin* (trials spt)

ATS 2

AGOR 17 (civil manned, funded by the Ministry of Transport)

Naval Aviation

AIRCRAFT 8 combat capable

ASW 16: 8 P-3C *Orion*; 8 P-3CK *Orion*

TPT • Light 5 Cessna F406 *Caravan II*

HELICOPTERS

ASW 24: 11 *Lynx* Mk99; 13 *Lynx* Mk99-A

MRH 3 SA319B *Alouette III*

TPT 15 **Medium** 8 UH-60P *Black Hawk* **Light** 7 Bell 205 (UH-1H *Iroquois*)

Marines 27,000

FORCES BY ROLE

MANOEUVRE

Amphibious

2 mne div (1 recce bn, 1 tk bn, 3 mne regt, 1 amph bn, 1 arty regt, 1 engr bn)

1 mne bde

COMBAT SUPPORT

Some cbt spt unit

EQUIPMENT BY TYPE

MBT 100 50 K1A1; 50 M48

AAV 166 AAV-7A1

ARTY TOWED: 105mm; 155mm

MSL • AShM RGM-84A *Harpoon* (truck mounted)

Air Force 65,000

4 Comd (Ops, Southern Combat, Logs, Trg)

FORCES BY ROLE

FIGHTER/GROUND ATTACK

3 sqn with F-4E *Phantom* II

11 sqn with F-5E/F *Tiger* II

3 sqn with F-15K *Eagle*

10 sqn with F-16C/D *Fighting Falcon* (KF-16C/D)

ISR

1 wg with KO-1

1 sqn with RF-4C *Phantom* II*

SIGINT

1 sqn with Hawker 800RA/XP

SEARCH & RESCUE

2 sqn with AS332L *Super Puma*; Bell 412EP; HH-47D *Chinook*; HH-60P *Black Hawk*; Ka-32 *Helix* C

TRANSPORT

1 VIP sqn with B-737-300; B-747; CN-235-220; S-92A *Superhawk*; VH-60P *Black Hawk* (VIP)

3 sqn (incl 1 Spec Ops) with C-130H *Hercules*

2 sqn with CN-235M-100/220

TRAINING

2 sqn with F-5E/F *Tiger* II

1 sqn with F-16C/D *Fighting Falcon*

1 sqn with *Hawk* Mk67

4 sqn with KT-1

1 sqn with Il-103

3 sqn with T-50/TA-50 *Golden Eagle**

TRANSPORT HELICOPTER

1 sqn with UH-60P *Black Hawk* (Spec Ops)

EQUIPMENT BY TYPE

AIRCRAFT 569 combat capable

FTR 174: 142 F-5E *Tiger* II; 32 F-5F *Tiger* II

FGA 294: 70 F-4E *Phantom* II; 60 F-15K *Eagle*; 118 F-16C *Fighting Falcon* (KF-16C); 46 F-16D *Fighting Falcon* (KF-16D); (some F-4D *Phantom* II in store)

AEW&C 4 B-737 AEW

ISR 41: 4 Hawker 800RA; 20 KO-1; 17 RF-4C *Phantom* II*

SIGINT 4 Hawker 800SIG

TPT 33 **Medium** 12: 8 C-130H *Hercules*; 4 C-130H-30 *Hercules* **Light** 20: 12 CN-235M-100; 8 CN-235M-220 (incl 2 VIP) **PAX** 2: 1 B-737-300; 1 B-747

TRG 190: 15 *Hawk* Mk67*; 23 Il-103; 83 KT-1; 50 T-50 *Golden Eagle**; 9 T-50B *Black Eagle** (aerobatics); 10 TA-50 *Golden Eagle**

HELICOPTERS

SAR 16: 5 HH-47D *Chinook*; 11 HH-60P *Black Hawk*

MRH 3 Bell 412EP

TPT • Medium 30: 2 AS332L *Super Puma*; 8 Ka-32 *Helix C*; 3 S-92A *Superhawk*; 7 UH-60P *Black Hawk*; 10 VH-60P *Black Hawk* (VIP)

UAV • ISR 103+ **Medium** 3+: some *Night Intruder*; 3 *Searcher* **Light** 100 *Harpy*

MSL

ASM AGM-65A *Maverick*; AGM-84-H SLAM-ER

AShM AGM-84 *Harpoon*; AGM-130; AGM-142 *Popeye*

ARM AGM-88 *HARM*

AAM • IR AIM-9 *Sidewinder*; **IIR** AIM-9X *Sidewinder*; **SARH** AIM-7 *Sparrow*; **ARH** AIM-120B/C5 AMRAAM

Paramilitary ε4,500 active

Civilian Defence Corps 3,000,000 reservists (to age 50)

Coast Guard ε4,500

PATROL AND COASTAL COMBATANTS 50:

PSO 5: 1 *Sumjinkang*; 3 *Mazinger*; 1 *Sambongho*

PCO 16: 1 *Han Kang*; 15 *Tae Geuk*

PCC 10: 4 *Bukhansan*; 6 (430 tonne)

PB 19: 5 Hyundai Type; ε14 (various)

LOGISTICS AND SUPPORT • ARS 29

AIRCRAFT

MP 5: 1 C-212-400 MP; 4 CN-235-110 MPA

TPT • PAX 1 CL-604

HELICOPTERS

MRH 8: 6 AS365 *Dauphin* II; 1 AW139; 1 Bell 412SP

TPT • Medium 8 Ka-32 *Helix*-C

Cyber

South Korea established a Cyber Warfare Command Centre in early 2010, with over 200 personnel, in the wake of a substantial distributed denial of service attack in 2009. The new centre responds to the attention given to cyber and information security by the National Intelligence Service and the Defense Security Command. South Korea published an 'Internet White Paper' in 2009.

DEPLOYMENT

AFGHANISTAN

NATO • ISAF 350

GULF OF ADEN

Navy: 1 DDGHM

CÔTE D'IVOIRE

UN • UNOCI 2 obs

HAITI

UN • MINUSTAH 242; 1 engr coy

INDIA/PAKISTAN

UN • UNMOGIP 7 obs

LEBANON

UN • UNIFIL 352; 1 mech inf bn

LIBERIA

UN • UNMIL 1; 1 obs

SOUTH SUDAN

UN • UNMISS 6; 2 obs

SUDAN

UN • UNAMID 2

UAE

140 (trg activities at UAE Spec Ops School)

WESTERN SAHARA

UN • MINURSO 4 obs

FOREIGN FORCES

Sweden NNSC: 5 obs

Switzerland NNSC: 5 obs

United States US Pacific Command: 28,500

Army 19,200; 1 HQ (8th Army) at Seoul; 1 div HQ (2nd Inf) at Tongduchon; 1 armd HBCT with M1 *Abrams*; M2/M3 *Bradley*; M109; 1 cbt avn bde with AH-64 *Apache*; CH-47 *Chinook*; UH-60 *Black Hawk*; 1 arty (fires) bde with M270 MLRS; 1 AD bde with MIM 104 *Patriot*/FIM-92A *Avenger*

Navy 250

USAF 8,800; 1 HQ (7th Air Force) at Osan AB; 1 ftr wg at Kunsan AB (1 ftr sqn with 20 F-16C/D *Fighting Falcon*); 1 ftr wg at Kunsan AB (1 ftr sqn with 20 F-16C/D *Fighting Falcon*, 1 ftr sqn with 24 A-10C *Thunderbolt II* at Osan AB)

USMC 250

Laos LAO

New Lao Kip		2011	2012	2013
GDP	kip	66.51tr	75.38tr	
	US$	8.3bn	9.27bn	
per capita	US$	1,260	1,407	
Growth	%	8.04	8.29	
Inflation	%	7.57	5.10	
Def bdgt	kip	ε150bn	ε179bn	
	US$	ε19m	ε22m	
US$1=kip		8011.87	8132.77	

Population 6,586,266

Ethnic groups: Lao 55%; Khmou 11%; Hmong 8%

Age	0–14	15–19	20–24	25–29	30–64	65 plus
Male	18.2%	5.5%	5.0%	4.2%	15.0%	1.7%
Female	17.9%	5.6%	5.1%	4.3%	15.5%	2.0%

Capabilities

The Lao People's Armed Forces (LPAF) have considerable historical military experience from the Second Indochina War and the 1988 border war with Thailand. However, Laos is one of the world's poorest countries and the defence budget and military procurement have been extremely limited for the last 20 years. The armed forces remain closely linked to the ruling Communist Party, and their primary orientation is towards internal security, with operations continuing against Hmong rebel remnants. Contacts with the Chinese and Vietnamese armed forces continue, but the LPAF have made no international deployments and have little capacity for sustained high-intensity operations.

ACTIVE 29,100 (Army 25,600 Air 3,500) **Paramilitary 100,000**

Terms of service 18 month minimum conscription

ORGANISATIONS BY SERVICE

Army 25,600

FORCES BY ROLE
4 Mil Regions
MANOEUVRE
   Armoured
   1 armd bn
   Light
   5 inf div
   7 indep inf regt
   65 indep inf coy
   Aviation
   1 (liaison) flt
COMBAT SUPPORT
   5 arty bn
   9 ADA bn
   1 engr regt
   2 (construction) engr regt
EQUIPMENT BY TYPE
MBT 25: 15 T-54/T-55; 10 T-34/85
LT TK 10 PT-76
APC (W) 50: 30 BTR-40/BTR-60; 20 BTR-152
ARTY 62+
   TOWED 62: **105mm** 20 M101; **122mm** 20 D-30/M-30 M-1938; **130mm** 10 M-46; **155mm** 12 M114
   MOR 81mm; **82mm**; **107mm** M-1938/M-2A1; **120mm** M-43
AT • RCL 57mm M18/A1; **75mm** M20; **106mm** M40; **107mm** B-11
AD • SAM • MANPAD 9K32 *Strela-2* (SA-7 *Grail*)‡; 25 9K310 *Igla-1* (SA-16 *Gimlet*)
   GUNS
   SP 23mm ZSU-23-4
   TOWED 14.5mm ZPU-1/ZPU-4; **23mm** ZU-23; **37mm** M-1939; **57mm** S-60
ARV T-54/T-55
VLB MTU

Army Marine Section ε600

PATROL AND COASTAL COMBATANTS 52
   PBR 52
AMPHIBIOUS LCM 4

Air Force 3,500

FORCES BY ROLE
TRANSPORT
   1 sqn with An-2 *Colt*; An-26 *Curl*; An-74 *Coaler*; Y-7; Y-12; Yak-40 *Codling* (VIP)
TRAINING
   1 sqn with Yak-18 *Max*
TRANSPORT HELICOPTER
   1 sqn with Ka-32T *Helix C*; Mi-6 *Hook*; Mi-8 *Hip*; Mi-17 *Hip H*; Mi-26 *Halo*; SA360 *Dauphin*
EQUIPMENT BY TYPE
AIRCRAFT
   TPT • Light 15: 4 An-2 *Colt*; 3 An-26 *Curl*; 1 An-74 *Coaler*; 5 Y-7; 1 Y-12; 1 Yak-40 *Codling* (VIP)
   TRG 8 Yak-18 *Max*
HELICOPTERS
   MRH 12 Mi-17 *Hip H*
   TPT 15 **Heavy** 2: 1 Mi-6 *Hook*; 1 Mi-26 *Halo* **Medium** 10: 1 Ka-32T *Helix C* (5 more on order); 9 Mi-8 *Hip* **Light** 3 SA-360 *Dauphin*
MSL • AAM • IR R-3 (AA-2 *Atoll*)†

Paramilitary

Militia Self-Defence Forces 100,000+
Village 'home guard' or local defence

Malaysia MYS

Malaysian Ringgit RM		2011	2012	2013
GDP	RM	881.08bn	946.11bn	
	US$	287.94bn	307.18bn	
per capita	US$	9,868	10,527	
Growth	%	5.08	4.40	
Inflation	%	3.17	2.00	
Def exp	RM	14.4bn		
	US$	4.69bn		
Def bdgt	RM	13.8bn	13.7bn	15.3bn
	US$	4.52bn	4.45bn	
US$1=RM		3.06	3.08	

Population   29,179,952

Ethnic groups: Malay and other indigenous (Bunipatre) 64%; Chinese 27%; Indian 9%

Age	0–14	15–19	20–24	25–29	30–64	65 plus
Male	15.1%	4.5%	4.2%	4.1%	20.4%	2.4%
Female	14.3%	4.4%	4.1%	4.1%	19.7%	2.7%

Capabilities

Malaysia's armed forces have considerable historical experience of counter-insurgency. Over the last 30 years, however, substantial equipment modernisation programmes have helped to develop their capacity for external defence. Malaysian army units have deployed on UN peacekeeping operations, and the navy has achieved well-publicised successes with its anti-piracy patrols in the Gulf of Aden. There is considerable emphasis on joint-service operations.

Malaysia regularly participates in Five Power Defence Arrangements exercises. Malaysian armed forces personnel are disproportionately drawn from the Malay community; few ethnic-Chinese Malaysians and members of other ethnic minorities are drawn to military service. While this ethnic homogeneity may reinforce military morale, it may also have implications for the armed forces' capabilities (particularly because of problems recruiting sufficient technical personnel), and for the government's ability to sustain national support for military operations.

ACTIVE 109,000 (Army 80,000 Navy 14,000 Air 15,000) Paramilitary 24,600

RESERVE 51,600 (Army 50,000, Navy 1,000 Air Force 600) Paramilitary 244,700

ORGANISATIONS BY SERVICE

Army 80,000 (to be 60–70,000)

2 mil region, 4 area comd (div)

FORCES BY ROLE
SPECIAL FORCES
  1 SF bde (3 SF bn)
MANOEUVRE
  Armoured
  1 tk regt (with 5 armd bn)
  Mechanised
  5 armd regt
  1 mech inf bde (3 mech bn, 1 cbt engr sqn)
  Light
  9 inf bde (total: 36 inf bn)
  Air Manoeuvre
  1 (Rapid Deployment Force) AB bde (1 lt tk sqn, 3 AB bn,
    1 lt arty regt, 1 engr sqn)
  Aviation
  1 hel sqn
COMBAT SUPPORT
  9 arty regt
  1 arty locator regt
  1 MRL regt
  3 ADA regt
  1 cbt engr sqn
  3 fd engr regt (total: 7 cbt engr sqn, 3 engr spt sqn)
  1 int unit
  4 MP regt
  1 sigs regt
COMBAT SERVICE SUPPORT
  1 const regt

EQUIPMENT BY TYPE
MBT 48 PT-91M *Twardy*
LT TK 21 *Scorpion-90*
RECCE 296: 130 AML-60/90; 92 *Ferret* (60 mod); K216A1 (as CBRN recce); 74 SIBMAS (some †)
AIFV 44: 31 ACV300 *Adnan* (25mm *Bushmaster*); 13 ACV300 *Adnan* AGL
APC 787
  APC (T) 265: 149 ACV300 *Adnan* (incl 69 variants); 13 FV4333 *Stormer* (upgraded); 63 K-200A; 40 K-200A1

APC (W) 522: 32 *Anoa*; 300 *Condor* (incl variants); 150 LAV-150 *Commando*; 30 M3 *Panhard*; 10 VBL
ARTY 424
  TOWED 134: **105mm** 100 Model 56 pack howitzer; **155mm** 34: 12 FH-70; 22 G-5
  MRL 36 *ASTROS* II (equipped with 127mm SS-30)
  MOR 254: **81mm SP** 14: 4 K281A1; 10 ACV300-S; **120mm SP** 8 ACV-S **81mm**: 232
AT
  MSL
    SP 8 ACV300 *Baktar Shikan*; K263
    MANPATS 60+: 18 9K115 *Metis* (AT-7 *Saxhorn*); 9K115-2 *Metis*-M (AT-13 Saxhorn 2); 24 *Eryx*; 18 *Baktar Shihan* (HJ-8); C90-CRRB; SS.11
  RCL 260: **84mm** 236 *Carl Gustav*; **106mm** 24 M40
AMPHIBIOUS • LCA 165 Damen Assault Craft 540 (capacity 10 troops)
HELICOPTERS
  TPT • Light 11 AW109
AD SAM 15 *Jernas* (Rapier 2000)
  MANPAD 88+: *Anza*; HY-6 (FN-6); 40 9K38 *Igla* (SA-18 Grouse); QW-1 *Vanguard*; 48 *Starburst*;
  GUNS • TOWED 60: **35mm** 16 GDF-005; **40mm** 36 L40/70
AEV 9: 3 MID-M; 6 WZT-4
ARV 41+: *Condor*; 15 ACV300; 4 K-288A1; 22 SIBMAS
VLB 5+: *Leguan*; 5 PMCz-90

Reserves

Territorial Army
Some paramilitary forces to be incorporated into a re-organised territorial organisation.

FORCES BY ROLE
MANOEUVRE
  Light
  16 inf regt
  Other
  2 (Border) sy bde (being created from existing Territorial units)
  5 (highway) sy bn
COMBAT SUPPORT
  2 fd engr regt

Navy 14,000
3 Regional Commands; Kuantan (East Coast); Kinabalu (Borneo) & Langkawi (West Coast

EQUIPMENT BY TYPE
SUBMARINES • TACTICAL • SSK 2 *Tunku Abdul Rahman* (Scorpene) with 6 single 533mm TT for WASS *Black Shark* HWT
PRINCIPAL SURFACE COMBATANTS 10
  FRIGATES 10:
    FFGHM 2:
      2 *Lekiu* with 2 quad lnchr with MM-40 *Exocet* AShM, 1 16-cell VLS with *Sea Wolf* SAM, 2 B515 *ILAS-3* triple 324mm ASTT with *Sting Ray* LWT, (capacity 1 *Super Lynx* hel)
    FFG 2:
      2 *Kasturi* with 2 twin lnchr with MM-40 *Exocet* AShM, 1 twin 375mm A/S mor, 1 100mm gun, 1 hel landing platform

FF 6:

   6 *Kedah* (MEKO) with 1 76mm gun, 1 hel landing platform, (fitted for MM-40 *Exocet* AShM & RAM CIWS)

PATROL AND COASTAL COMBATANTS 37

  CORVETTES • FSGM 4:

   4 *Laksamana* with 3 twin lnchr with Mk 2 *Otomat* AShM, 1 quad lnchr with *Aspide* SAM, 2 B515 *ILAS*-3 triple 324mm TT with A244 LWT, 1 76mm gun

  PCFG 4 *Perdana* (*Combattante* II) with 2 single lnchr with MM-38 *Exocet* AShM

  PBG 4 *Handalan* (*Spica*-M) with 2 twin lnchr with MM-38 *Exocet* AShM

  PBF 17 *Tempur*

  PB 8: 6 *Jerong* (Lurssen 45); 2 *Sri Perlis*

MINE WARFARE • MINE COUNTERMEASURES

  MCO 4 *Mahamiru*

AMPHIBIOUS

  LANDING CRAFT 115 **LCM/LCU**

LOGISTICS AND SUPPORT 13

  AOR 2; **AG** 1; **ARS** 2; **AGS** 2; **ATG** 2; **AX** 1; **AXS** 1; **AP** 2

Naval Aviation 160

HELICOPTERS

  ASW 6 *Super Lynx 300*

  MRH 6 AS555 *Fennec*

MSL • AShM *Sea Skua*

Special Forces

FORCES BY ROLE

SPECIAL FORCES

  1 (mne cdo) SF unit

Air Force 15,000

1 Air Op HQ, 2 Air Div, 1 trg and Log Cmd, 1 Intergrated Area Def Systems HQ

Flying hours 60 hrs/year

FORCES BY ROLE

FIGHTER

  2 sqn with MiG-29/MiG-29UB *Fulcrum*

FIGHTER/GROUND ATTACK

  1 sqn with F/A-18D *Hornet*

  1 sqn with Su-30MKM *Flanker*

  2 sqn with *Hawk* Mk108*/Mk208*

FIGHTER/GROUND ATTACK/ISR

  1 sqn with F-5E/F *Tiger* II; RF-5E *Tigereye**

MARITIME PATROL

  1 sqn with Beech 200T

TANKER/TRANSPORT

  2 sqn with KC-130H *Hercules*; C-130H *Hercules*; C-130H-30 *Hercules*; Cessna 402B

TRANSPORT

  1 (VIP) sqn with A319CT; AW109; B-737-700 BBJ; BD700 *Global Express*; F-28 *Fellowship*; *Falcon* 900

  1 sqn with CN-235

TRAINING

  1 unit with PC-7; SA316 *Alouette* III

TRANSPORT HELICOPTER

  4 (tpt/SAR) sqn with S-61A-4 *Nuri*; S-61N; S-70A *Black Hawk*

AIR DEFENCE

  1 sqn with *Starburst*

SPECIAL FORCES

  1 (Air Force Commando) unit (airfield defence/SAR)

EQUIPMENT BY TYPE

AIRCRAFT 67 combat capable

  FTR 21: 8 F-5E *Tiger II*; 3 F-5F *Tiger II*; 8 MiG-29 *Fulcrum* (MiG-29N); 2 MiG-29UB *Fulcrum* (MiG-29NUB) (MiG-29 to be withdrawn from service)

  FGA 26: 8 F/A-18D *Hornet*; 18 Su-30MKM

  ISR 4 Beech 200T; 2 RF-5E *Tigereye**

  TKR 4 KC-130H *Hercules*

  TPT 32 **Medium** 10: 2 C-130H *Hercules*; 8 C-130H-30 *Hercules*; **Light** 17: 8 CN-235M-220 (incl 2 VIP); 9 Cessna 402B (2 modified for aerial survey) **PAX** 5: 1 A319CT; 1 B-737-700 BBJ; 1 BD700 *Global Express*; 1 F-28 *Fellowship*; 1 *Falcon* 900

  TRG 80: 6 *Hawk* Mk108*; 12 *Hawk* Mk208*; 8 MB-339C; 7 MD3-160 *Aero Tiga*; 30 PC-7; 17 PC-7 Mk II *Turbo Trainer*

HELICOPTERS

  MRH 17 SA316 *Alouette* III

  TPT 33 **Medium** 32: 28 S-61A-4 *Nuri*; 2 S-61N; 2 S-70A *Black Hawk* **Light** 1 AW109

UAV • ISR 3+ **Heavy** 3 *Eagle* ARV **Medium** *Aludra*

AD • SAM •MANPAD *Starburst*

MSL

  AAM • IR AIM-9 *Sidewinder*; R-73 (AA-11 *Archer*) **IR/SARH** R-27 (AA-10 *Alamo*); **SARH** AIM-7 *Sparrow*; **ARH** AIM-120C AMRAAM; R-77 (AA-12 *Adder*)

  ASM AGM-65 *Maverick*

  AShM AGM-84D *Harpoon*

Paramilitary ε24,600

Police-General Ops Force 18,000

FORCES BY ROLE

COMMAND

  5 bde HQ

SPECIAL FORCES

  1 spec ops bn

MANOEUVRE

  Other

  19 paramilitary bn

  2 (Aboriginal) paramilitary bn

  4 indep paramilitary coy

EQUIPMENT BY TYPE

RECCE ε100 S52 *Shorland*

APC (W) 170: 140 AT105 *Saxon*; ε30 SB-301

Malaysian Maritime Enforcement Agency (MMEA) ε4,500

Controls 5 Maritime Regions (Northern Peninsula; Southern Peninsula; Eastern Peninsula; Sarawak; Sabah), sub-divided into a further 18 Maritime Districts. Supported by one provisional MMEA Air Unit.

EQUIPMENT BY TYPE

PATROL AND COASTAL COMBATANTS 84:

  PSO 2 *Langkawi* with 1 hel landing platform

  PBF 12: 10 MRTP 16; 2 *Penggalang* 18

PB 70: 15 *Gagah*; 4 *Malawali*; 2 *Nusa*; 1 *Peninjau*; 5 *Ramunia*; 2 *Rhu*; 4 *Semilang*; 15 *Sipadan* (ex-*Kris/Sabah*); 8 *Icarus 1650*; 10 *Pengawal*; 4 *Penyelamat*
LOGISTICS AND SUPPORT • AX 1 *Marlin*
AIRCRAFT • MP 2 Bombardier 415MP
HELICOPTERS
  MRH 3 AS365 *Dauphin*

Marine Police 2,100

EQUIPMENT BY TYPE
PATROL AND COASTAL COMBATANTS 132
  PBF 12: 6 *Sangitan*; 6 Stan Patrol 1500
  PB/PBR 120

Police Air Unit

AIRCRAFT
  TPT • Light 17: 4 Cessna 206 *Stationair*; 6 Cessna 208 *Caravan*; 7 PC-6 *Turbo-Porter*
HELICOPTERS
  TPT • Light 3: 1 Bell 206L *Long Ranger*; 2 AS355F *Ecureuil II*

Area Security Units (R) 3,500

(Auxiliary General Ops Force)

FORCES BY ROLE
MANOEUVRE
  Other
  89 paramilitary unit

Border Scouts (R) 1,200

in Sabah, Sarawak

People's Volunteer Corps 240,000 reservists (some 17,500 armed)

RELA

Customs Service

PATROL AND COASTAL COMBATANTS 23
  PBF 10
  PB 13

DEPLOYMENT

AFGHANISTAN
NATO • ISAF 46

DEMOCRATIC REPUBLIC OF THE CONGO
UN • MONUSCO 17 obs

LEBANON
UN • UNIFIL 877; 1 mech inf bn; 1 mech inf coy

LIBERIA
UN • UNMIL 6 obs

PHILIPPINES
IMT 19

SUDAN
UN • UNAMID 11; 2 obs
UN • UNISFA 1 obs

WESTERN SAHARA
UN • MINURSO 12 obs

FOREIGN FORCES

Australia Air Force: 15 with 1 AP-3C *Orion* on occasion; Army: 115; 1 inf coy (on 3-month rotational tours)

Mongolia MNG

Mongolian Tugrik t		2011	2012	2013
GDP	t	11.09tr	13.86tr	
	US$	8.71bn	9.92bn	
per capita	US$	2,739	3,119	
Growth	%	17.51	12.67	
Inflation	%	7.68	14.15	
Def bdgt	t	103bn	ε122bn	
	US$	81m	ε87m	
FMA (US)	US$	2.996m	3m	3m
US$1=t		1273.13	1396.48	

Population 3,179,997

Ethnic groups: Khalka 80%; Kazakh 6%

Age	0–14	15–19	20–24	25–29	30–64	65 plus
Male	13.8%	4.6%	5.4%	5.0%	19.5%	1.7%
Female	13.3%	4.5%	5.3%	4.9%	19.8%	2.3%

Capabilities

Mongolia's armed forces are small and generally under-equipped. The army fields largely obsolete armoured vehicles while its air force operates only transport aircraft and helicopters. Mongolia has nevertheless contributed to international operations, and in September 2011, the defence minister announced that 850 troops would be sent to South Sudan. However, the armed forces possess no logistical capabilities for supporting and sustaining forces deployed internationally. Attempts are being made to modernise the armed forces. An annual simulation exercise, and collaboration with international partners, including China, European states, Japan, Russia and the US, ensures continued training. However, improving the equipment and capability of Mongolia's armed forces would require substantially greater investment than the defence budget currently provides.

ACTIVE 10,000 (Army 8,900 Air 800 Construction Troops 300) **Paramilitary 7,200**
Terms of service conscription: one year (males aged 18–25)

RESERVE 137,000 (Army 137,000)

ORGANISATIONS BY SERVICE

Army 5,600; 3,300 conscript (total 8,900)

FORCES BY ROLE
MANOEUVRE
  Mechanised
  6 MR regt(-)
  Light
  1 (rapid deployment) lt inf bn (2nd bn to form)

Air Manoeuvre
1 AB bn
COMBAT SUPPORT
1 arty regt
EQUIPMENT BY TYPE
MBT 370 T-54/T-55
RECCE 120 BRDM-2
AIFV 310 BMP-1
APC (W) 170: 150 BTR-60; 20 BTR-80
ARTY 570
TOWED ε300: **122mm** D-30/M-30 (M-1938); **130mm** M-46; **152mm** ML-20 (M-1937)
MRL **122mm** 130 BM-21
MOR 140: **120mm**; **160mm**; **82mm**
AT • GUNS 200: **85mm** D-44/D-48; **100mm** M-1944/MT-12
AD • SAM 2+ S-125 *Pechora* 2M (SA-3B *Goa*)
ARV T-54/T-55

Air Force 800

FORCES BY ROLE
TRANSPORT
1 sqn with An-24 *Coke*; An-26 *Curl*
ATTACK/TRANSPORT HELICOPTER
1 sqn with Mi-8 *Hip*; Mi-171
AIR DEFENCE
2 regt with S-60/ZPU-4/ZU-23
EQUIPMENT BY TYPE
AIRCRAFT • TPT • Light 3: 2 An-24 *Coke*; 1 An-26 *Curl*
HELICOPTERS
TPT • **Medium** 13: 11 Mi-8 *Hip*; 2 Mi-171
AD • GUNS • TOWED 150: **14.5mm** ZPU-4; **23mm** ZU-23; **57mm** S-60

Paramilitary 7,200 active

Border Guard 1,300; 4,700 conscript (total 6,000)

Internal Security Troops 400; 800 conscript (total 1,200)
FORCES BY ROLE
MANOEUVRE
Other
4 gd unit

Construction Troops 300

DEPLOYMENT

AFGHANISTAN
NATO • ISAF 88
UN • UNAMA 1 obs

DEMOCRATIC REPUBLIC OF THE CONGO
UN • MONUSCO 2 obs

SOUTH SUDAN
UN • UNMISS 857; 2 obs; 1 inf bn

SUDAN
UN • UNAMID 70; 1 fd hospital
UN • UNISFA 2 obs

WESTERN SAHARA
UN • MINURSO 4 obs

Myanmar MMR

Myanmar Kyat K		2011	2012	2013
GDP	K	39.72tr	44.64tr	
	US$[a]	51.44bn	54.05bn	
	US$[b]	82.68bn	89.23bn	
per capita	US$[a]	942	990	
	US$[b]	1,531	1,635	
Growth	%	5.46	6.20	
Inflation	%	3.98	5.84	
Def bdgt	K	1.86tr	1.88tr	
	US$[a]	2.41bn	2.27bn	
US$1=K	Official Rate[c]	6.4	818	
	Unofficial Rate	772.08	826.00	

[a] Calculated using the estimated unofficial rate.

[b] PPP estimate

[c] Myanmar's central bank floated the Kyat in April 2012

Population   54,584,650

Ethnic groups: Burman 68%; Shan 9%; Karen 7%; Rakhine 4%; Chinese 3+%; Other Chin, Kachin, Kayan, Lahu, Mon, Palaung, Pao, Wa, 9%

Age	0–14	15–19	20–24	25–29	30–64	65 plus
Male	14.0%	4.9%	4.8%	4.6%	19.3%	2.2%
Female	13.5%	4.7%	4.7%	4.5%	20.0%	2.8%

Capabilities

Myanmar's armed forces have, since the country's independence struggle in the 1940s, been intimately involved in domestic politics, which they still dominate despite the advent of a nominally civilian government in March 2011. Their focus has always been on holding together this ethnically-diverse state, particularly in the face of the world's longest-running insurgencies, conducted by the Karen, Kachin, Mon, Shan and other minority groups around the country's perimeter. However, ceasefires with most of the rebel groups lasted for two decades and contributed to a decline in the army's operational experience: new offensives during 2011 against ethnic-minority groups that refused to integrate with the army-controlled Border Guard Force were essentially failures. Morale among ordinary soldiers (mainly poorly-paid conscripts) is reportedly low. While the army grew substantially after the military seized power in 1988, its counter-insurgency focus means that it has remained essentially a light infantry force. Nevertheless, during the 1990s, large-scale military procurement resulted in new armoured vehicles, air-defence weapons, artillery, combat aircraft and naval vessels from China, Russia and other diverse sources coming into service. More recently, the armed forces have sponsored the growth of a substantial domestic defence industry.

ACTIVE 406,000 (Army 375,000 Navy 16,000 Air 15,000) Paramilitary 107,250

ORGANISATIONS BY SERVICE

Army ε375,000

12 regional comd, 4 regional op comd, 14 military op comd, 34 tactical op comd (TDC)

FORCES BY ROLE
MANOEUVRE
Armoured
10 armd bn
Light
10 lt inf div
100 inf bn
337 inf bn (regional comd)
COMBAT SUPPORT
7 arty bn
37 indep arty coy
7 AD bn
6 cbt engr bn
54 fd engr bn
40 int coy
45 sigs bn

EQUIPMENT BY TYPE
MBT 160: 10 T-55; 50 T-72; 100 Type-69-II
LT TK 105 Type-63 (ε60 serviceable)
RECCE 115: 45 *Ferret*; 40 Humber *Pig*; 30 Mazda
APC 361
  APC (T) 331: 26 MT-LB; 250 Type-85; 55 Type-90
  APC (W) 20 *Hino*
  PPV 10 MPV
ARTY 404+
  SP 155mm 30 B-52 NORA
  TOWED 264+: **105mm** 132: 36 M-56; 96 M101; **122mm** 100 D-30; **130mm** 16 M-46; **140mm**; **155mm** 16 *Soltam*
  MRL 30+: **107mm** 30 Type-63; **122mm** BM-21 (reported); **240mm** M-1991 (reported)
  MOR 80+: **82mm** Type-53 (M-37); **120mm** 80+: 80 *Soltam*; Type-53 (M-1943)
AT
  RCL 1,000+: **106mm** M40A1; **84mm** ε1,000 *Carl Gustav*
  GUNS 60: **57mm** 6-pdr; **76.2mm** 17-pdr
AD • **SAM** • **MANPAD** HN-5 *Hong Nu/Red Cherry* (reported); 9K310 Igla-1 (SA-16 *Gimlet*)
  GUNS 46
    SP 57mm 12 Type-80
    TOWED 34: **37mm** 24 Type-74; **40mm** 10 M1
MSL • **SSM** some *Hwasong-6* (reported)
ARV Type-72

Navy ε16,000

EQUIPMENT BY TYPE
PRINCIPAL SURFACE COMBATANTS • **FRIGATES** 3
  FFG 3:
    1 *Aung Zeya* (reported) with 2 twin lnchr with YJ-82 (C-802) AShM, 1 76mm gun
    2 *Mahar Bandoola* (PRC Type-053H1) with 2 triple lnchr with HY-2 (C-201) *Seersucker* AShM, 2 RBU 1200, 2 twin 100mm gun
PATROL AND COASTAL COMBATANTS 99
  CORVETTES • **FSG** 3 *Anawrahta* with 2 twn lnchr with YJ-82 (C-802) AShM; 1 76mm gun

PCG 6 *Houxin* with 2 twin lnchr with C-801 (CSS-N-4 *Sardine*) AShM
PCO 2 *Indaw*
PCC 9 *Hainan*
PBG 4 *Myanmar* with 2 twin lnchr with C-801 (CSS-N-4 *Sardine*) AShM
PB 18: 3 PB-90; 6 PGM 401; 6 PGM 412; 9 *Myanmar*; 3 *Swift*
PBR 57: 4 *Sagu*; 9 Y-301; 1 Y-301 (Imp); 43 (various)
AMPHIBIOUS • **CRAFT** 18: 8 LCU 10 **LCM**
LOGISTICS AND SUPPORT 18
  AOT 1; **AK** 1; **AKSL** 5; **AGS** 1; **ABU** 1; **AP** 9

Naval Infantry 800
FORCES BY ROLE
MANOEUVRE
Light
1 inf bn

Air Force ε15,000
FORCES BY ROLE
FIGHTER
3 sqn with F-7 *Airguard*; FT-7; MiG-29B *Fulcrum*; MiG-29UB *Fulcrum*
GROUND ATTACK
2 sqn with A-5M *Fantan*
TRANSPORT
1 sqn with An-12 *Cub*; F-27 *Friendship*; FH-227; PC-6A *Turbo Porter*/PC-6B *Turbo Porter*
TRAINING
2 sqn with G-4 *Super Galeb**; PC-7 Turbo Trainer*; PC-9*
1 (trg/liaison) sqn with Cessna 550 *Citation II*; Cessna 180 *Skywagon*; K-8 *Karakorum**
TRANSPORT HELICOPTER
4 sqn with Bell 205; Bell 206 *Jet Ranger*; Mi-17 *Hip H*; PZL Mi-2 *Hoplite*; PZL W-3 *Sokol*; SA316 *Alouette III*

EQUIPMENT BY TYPE
AIRCRAFT 136 combat capable
  FTR 69: 49 F-7 *Airguard*; 10 FT-7*; 8 MiG-29B *Fulcrum*; 2 MiG-29UB *Fulcrum*
  ATK 22 A-5M *Fantan*
  TPT 19 **Light** 15: 2 An-12 *Cub*; 4 Cessna 180 *Skywagon*; 1 Cessna 550 *Citation II*; 3 F-27 *Friendship*; 5 PC-6A *Turbo Porter*/PC-6B *Turbo Porter* **PAX** 4 FH-227
  TRG 45+: 12 G-4 *Super Galeb**; 12+ K-8 *Karakorum**; 12 PC-7 *Turbo Trainer**; 9 PC-9*
HELICOPTERS
  MRH 20: 11 Mi-17 *Hip H*; 9 SA316 *Alouette III*
  TPT 46: **Medium** 10 PZL W-3 *Sokol* **Light** 36: 12 Bell 205; 6 Bell 206 *Jet Ranger*; 18 PZL Mi-2 *Hoplite*
MSL • **AAM** • **IR** Pl-5; R-73 (AA-11 *Archer*) **IR/SARH** R-27 (AA-10 *Alamo*)

Paramilitary 107,250

People's Police Force 72,000

People's Militia 35,000

People's Pearl and Fishery Ministry ε250
PATROL AND COASTAL COMBATANTS • **PBR** 6 *Carpentaria*

Nepal NPL

Nepalese Rupee NR		2011	2012	2013
GDP	NR	1.37tr	1.56tr	
	US$	18.98bn	19.42bn	
per capita	US$	635	650	
Growth	%	3.88	4.63	
Inflation	%	9.61	8.31	
Def bdgt [a]	NR	19.4bn	19.1bn	17.9bn
	US$	269m	238m	
FMA (US)	US$	0.898m	0.94m	0.845m
US$1=NR		72.11	80.20	

[a] 2013 defence budget an estimate.

Population   29,890,686

Religious groups: Hindu 90%; Buddhist 5%; Muslim 3%

Age	0–14	15–19	20–24	25–29	30–64	65 plus
Male	17.1%	6.2%	5.0%	3.8%	14.8%	2.1%
Female	16.5%	6.0%	5.2%	4.4%	16.5%	2.4%

Capabilities

Nepal's army continues to struggle to integrate former Maoist insurgents following a 2006 peace accord and the subsequent transition from a monarchy to a republic. A draft national-security policy, in early 2011, focused on territorial integrity. Mobility remains a challenge for the military. The army is extensively involved in UN peace-support operations and receives training support from several countries, including the US. The Indian and British armies, and Singapore's police force, recruit personnel for their Gurkha units in Nepal.

ACTIVE 95,750 (Army 95,750) **Paramilitary 62,000**

Nepal is attempting to integrate the 23,500-strong (Maoist) People's Liberation Army (PLA) into the national army.

ORGANISATIONS BY SERVICE

Army 95,750

FORCES BY ROLE

COMMAND

6 inf div HQ

1 (valley) comd

SPECIAL FORCES

1 bde (1 SF bn, 1 AB bn , cdo bn, 1 ranger bn, 1 mech inf bn)

MANOEUVRE

Light

16 inf bde (total: 63 inf bn)

32 indep inf coy

COMBAT SUPPORT

4 arty regt

2 AD regt

4 indep AD coy

5 engr bn

EQUIPMENT BY TYPE

RECCE 40 Ferret

APC 253

APC (W) 13: 8 OT-64C; 5 WZ-551

PPV 240: 90 Casspir; 150 MPV

ARTY 109+

TOWED 39: **75mm** 6 pack; **94mm** 5 3.7in (mtn trg); **105mm** 28: 8 L118 Lt Gun; 14 Pack Howitzer (6 non-operational)

MOR 70+: **81mm**; **120mm** 70 M-43 (est 12 op)

AD • GUNS • TOWED 32+: **14.5mm** 30 Type-56 (ZPU-4); **37mm** (PRC); **40mm** 2 L/60

Air Wing 320

AIRCRAFT • TPT 4 Light 3: 1 BN-2T Islander; 2 M-28 Skytruck **PAX** 1 BAe-748

HELICOPTERS

MRH 9: 1 Dhruv; 2 Lancer; 3 Mi-17-1V Hip H; 1 SA315B Lama (Cheetah); 2 SA316B Alouette III

TPT 3 Medium 1 SA330J Super Puma **Light** 2 AS350B2/B3 Ecureuil

Paramilitary 62,000

Armed Police Force 15,000

Ministry of Home Affairs

Police Force 47,000

DEPLOYMENT

CÔTE D'IVOIRE

UN • UNOCI 1; 3 obs

DEMOCRATIC REPUBLIC OF THE CONGO

UN • MONUSCO 1,024; 24 obs; 1 inf bn; 1 engr coy

HAITI

UN • MINUSTAH 361; 1 inf bn(-)

IRAQ

UN • UNAMI 117; 1 sy unit

LEBANON

UN • UNIFIL 1,018; 1 inf bn

LIBERIA

UN • UNMIL 18; 2 obs; 1 MP sect

MIDDLE EAST

UN • UNTSO 3 obs

SOUTH SUDAN

UN • UNMISS 858; 5 obs; 1 inf bn

SUDAN

UN • UNAMID 345; 15 obs; 2 inf coy

UN • UNISFA 2; 3 obs

TIMOR LESTE

UN • UNMIT 1 obs

WESTERN SAHARA

UN • MINURSO 4 obs

FOREIGN FORCES

United Kingdom Army 280 (Gurkha trg org)

New Zealand NZL

New Zealand Dollar NZ$		2011	2012	2013
GDP	NZ$	200.81bn	209.35bn	
	US$	158.87bn	166.92bn	
per capita	US$	36,708	38,568	
Growth	%	1.35	2.23	
Inflation	%	4.03	1.88	
Def exp	NZ$	2.78bn		
	US$	2.2bn		
Def bdgt	NZ$	2.78bn	2.91bn	
	US$	2.2bn	2.32bn	
US$1=NZ$			1.26	1.25

Population   4,327,944

Ethnic groups: NZ European 58%; Maori 15%; Other European 13%; Other Polynesian 5% ; Chinese 2%; Indian 1%; Other 6%

Age	0–14	15–19	20–24	25–29	30–64	65 plus
Male	10.4%	3.7%	3.6%	3.2%	22.8%	6.1%
Female	9.9%	3.5%	3.5%	3.2%	23.0%	7.2%

Capabilities

The New Zealand Defence Force (NZDF) is small, but it draws on a strong national military tradition: New Zealand has contributed forces to almost every conflict in which the country's larger allies have been involved over the last century, and forces remain deployed overseas. Despite funding shortfalls and capability losses including the withdrawal from service of jet combat aircraft a decade ago, the NZDF is characterised by high training standards, professionalism and morale. The November 2010 Defence White Paper promised to maintain and enhance existing capabilities, and to provide some additional elements (such as short-range maritime air patrol aircraft). However, there was no promise of any significant increase to the defence budget.

ACTIVE 8,550 (Army 4,300 Navy 1,900 Air 2,350)

RESERVE 2,290 (Army 1,800 Navy 300 Air Force 190)

ORGANISATIONS BY SERVICE

Army 4,300

FORCES BY ROLE
COMMAND
  2 gp HQ
SPECIAL FORCES
  1 SF gp
MANOEUVRE
  Reconnaissance
  1 armd recce regt
  Mechanised
  1 mech inf bn (to become lt inf by end 2012)
  Light
  1 lt inf bn
COMBAT SUPPORT
  1 arty regt (2 arty bty, 1 AD tp)
  1 engr regt(-)
  1 EOD sqn
  1 MI coy
  1 MP coy
  1 sigs regt
COMBAT SERVICE SUPPORT
  2 log bn
  1 med bn
EQUIPMENT BY TYPE
AIFV 105 NZLAV-25
ARTY 74
  TOWED 105mm 24 L-118 Light Gun
  MOR 81mm 50
AT • MSL 24 *Javelin*
  RCL 84mm 42 *Carl Gustav*
AD • SAM • MANPAD 12 *Mistral*
AEV 7 NZLAV
ARV 3 LAV-R

Reserves

Territorial Force 1,800 reservists
Responsible for providing trained individuals for augmenting deployed forces
FORCES BY ROLE
COMBAT SERVICE SUPPORT
  6 (Territorial Force Regional) trg regt (reducing to 3)

Navy 1,900

Fleet HQ at Auckland
EQUIPMENT BY TYPE
PRINCIPAL SURFACE COMBATANTS • FRIGATES • FFHM 2
  2 *Anzac* with 1 8-cell Mk41 VLS with RIM-7M *Sea Sparrow* SAM, 2 triple 324mm TT, 1 Mk15 *Phalanx* CIWS gun, 1 127mm gun, (capacity 1 SH-2G (NZ) *Super Seasprite* ASW hel)
PATROL AND COASTAL COMBATANTS 6:
  PSOH 2 *Otago* (capacity 1 SH-2G *Super Seasprite* ASW hel)
  PCC 4 *Rotoiti*
AMPHIBIOUS • LANDING CRAFT • LCM 2
LOGISTICS AND SUPPORT 5
  MRV 1 *Canterbury* (capacity 4 NH90 tpt hel; 1 SH-2G *Super Seasprite* ASW hel; 2 LCM; 16 NZLAV; 14 NZLOV; 20 trucks; 250 troops)
  AO 1 *Endeavour*
  AGHS (SVY) 1 *Resolution*
  YDT/spt 1 *Manawanui*

Air Force 2,350

Flying hours   190

FORCES BY ROLE

MARITIME PATROL
1 sqn with P-3K/K2 *Orion*

TRANSPORT
1 sqn with B-757-200 (upgraded); C-130H *Hercules* (being progressively upgraded)

ANTI SUBMARINE/SURFACE WARFARE
1 (RNZAF/RNZN) sqn with SH-2G *Super Seasprite* (SH-2G(NZ))

TRAINING
1 sqn with CT-4E *Airtrainer* (leased);
1 sqn with Beech 200 *King Air* (leased);
1 (transition) hel unit with AW109; NH90

TRANSPORT HELICOPTER
1 sqn with Bell 205 (UH-1H *Iroquois*) (to be replaced by NH90)

EQUIPMENT BY TYPE

AIRCRAFT 6 combat capable
ASW 6: 3 P-3K *Orion*; 3 P-3K2 *Orion*
TPT 12 **Medium** 5 C-130H *Hercules* (being upgraded) **Light** 5 Beech 200 *King Air* (leased, to be replaced) **PAX** 2 B-757-200 (upgraded)
TRG 13 CT-4E *Airtrainer* (leased)

HELICOPTERS
ASW 5 SH-2G *Super Seasprite* (SH-2G(NZ))
TPT 22 **Medium** 4 NH90 (1 more used for spares - further 4 due by end 2013); **Light** 18: 5 AW109 (1 more used for spares); 13 Bell 205 (UH-1H *Iroquois*) (being replaced by NH90)
MSL • ASM AGM-65B/G *Maverick*

DEPLOYMENT

AFGHANISTAN
NATO • ISAF 155
UN • UNAMA 1 obs

EGYPT
MFO 28; 1 trg unit; 1 tpt unit

IRAQ
UN • UNAMI 1 obs

MIDDLE EAST
UN • UNTSO 8 obs

SOLOMON ISLANDS
RAMSI 45

SOUTH SUDAN
UN • UNMISS 1; 2 obs

TIMOR LESTE
ISF *(Operation Koru)* 27 (theatre extraction team)
UN • UNMIT 1 obs

Pakistan PAK

Pakistani Rupee Rs		2011	2012	2013
GDP	Rs	18.03tr	20.65tr	
	US$	210.22bn	230.53bn	
per capita	US$	1,105	1,211	
Growth	%	3.04	3.68	
Inflation	%	13.66	11.01	
Def exp	Rs	469bn		
	US$	5.47bn		
Def bdgt [a]	Rs	447bn	518bn	551bn
	US$	5.21bn	5.78bn	
FMA (US) [b]	US$	295m	98m	350m
US$1=Rs		85.78	89.59	

[a] Includes budget for Ministry of Defence Production

[b] FMA figure does not include the Pakistan Counter-Insurgency Capability Fund, the 2011 request for which amounted to US$1.2bn.

Population 190,291,129

Religious groups: Hindu less than 3%

Age	0–14	15–19	20–24	25–29	30–64	65 plus
Male	17.8%	5.8%	5.4%	4.5%	15.8%	2.0%
Female	16.9%	5.5%	5.0%	4.2%	14.8%	2.2%

Capabilities

Pakistan's nuclear and conventional forces have been primarily oriented and structured against a prospective threat from India. Its nuclear weapons are currently believed to be well-secured against terrorist attack. Since 2008, however, a priority for Pakistan's army has been counter-insurgency operations against Islamic insurgents in the Federally Administered Tribal Area. Militarily these have been successful, with Pakistan's forces demonstrating the ability to innovate, learn in combat, and better integrate air and land operations including precision bombing. Pakistan's air force is modernising and reducing its fighter inventory while improving its precision strike and ISTAR capabilities However, the May 2011 US helicopter-borne attack on Osama Bin Laden's compound outside Abbottabad called into question the effectiveness of Pakistan's air defences. The navy's submarine force could hamper any attacker's freedom to manoeuvre, but is too small to sustain a long campaign against enemy vessels equipped with ASW capabilities. Internationally, the navy has contributed to international efforts to counter Indian Ocean piracy, and there is a long tradition of the army contributing to UN peacekeeping operations.

ACTIVE 642,000 (Army 550,000 Navy 22,000 Air 70,000) **Paramilitary 304,000**

ORGANISATIONS BY SERVICE

Strategic Forces

Operational control rests with the National Command Authority (NCA); army and air force strategic forces are responsible for technical aspects, training and administrative control of the services' nuclear assets.

Army Strategic Forces Command 12,000-15,000

Commands all land-based strategic nuclear forces.

MSL • STRATEGIC 60

  MRBM ε30 *Ghauri/Ghauri* II (*Hatf-5*)/*Shaheen-2* (*Hatf-6* - in test)

  SRBM ε30 *Ghaznavi* (*Hatf-3* - PRC M-11)/*Shaheen-1* (*Hatf-4*);

  LACM *Babur* (*Hatf-7* - in development); Ra'ad (*Hatf-8* - in development)

  ARTY • MRL *Nasr* (*Hatf-9* - likely nuclear capable; in development)

Air Force

1-2 sqn of F-16A/B or *Mirage* 5 may be assigned a nuclear strike role

Army 550,000

FORCES BY ROLE

COMMAND

  9 corps HQ

  1 (area) comd

SPECIAL FORCES

  2 SF gp (total: 4 SF bn)

MANOEUVRE

  Armoured

  2 armd div

  7 indep armd bde

  Mechanised

  2 mech inf div

  1 indep mech bde

  Light

  18 inf div

  5 indep inf bde

  Aviation

  1 VIP avn sqn

  5 (composite) avn sqn

  10 hel sqn

COMBAT SUPPORT

  9 (corps) arty bde

  5 indep arty bde

  1 AD comd (3 AD gp (total: 8 AD bn))

  7 engr bde

EQUIPMENT BY TYPE

MBT 2,411+: ε265 MBT 2000 *Al-Khalid*; 320 T-80UD; 51 T-54/T-55; 1,100 Type-59; 400 Type-69; 275+ Type-85; (270 M48A5 in store)

APC 1,390

  APC (T) 1,260: 1,160 M113/*Talha*; ε100 Type-63

  APC (W) 120 BTR-70/BTR-80

  PPV 10 *Dingo* II

ARTY 4,607+

  SP 375: **155mm** 315: 200 M109A2; ε115 M109A5 **203mm** 60 M110/M110A2

  TOWED 1,659: **105mm** 329: 216 M101; 113 M-56; **122mm** 570: 80 D-30 (PRC); 490 Type-54 M-1938; **130mm** 410

Type-59-I; **155mm** 322: 144 M114; 148 M198; ε30 *Panter* **203mm** 28 M115

  MRL 88+ **107mm** Type-81; **122mm** 52+: 52 *Azar* (Type-83); some KRL-122 **300mm** 36 A100

  MOR 2,350+: **81mm**; **120mm** AM-50; M-61

AT

  MSL

  SP M901 TOW

  MANPATS 11,100: 10,500 HJ-8/TOW; 600 9K119 *Refleks* (AT-11 *Sniper*)

  RCL 75mm Type-52; **106mm** M40A1

  RL 89mm M20

  GUNS 85mm 200 Type-56 (D-44)

AIRCRAFT

  ISR 30 Cessna O-1E *Bird Dog*

  TPT • Light 14: 1 Beech 200 *King Air*; 1 Beech 350 *King Air*; 3 Cessna 208B; 1 Cessna 421; 1 Cessna 550 *Citation*; 1 Cessna 560 *Citation*; 2 Turbo Commander 690; 4 Y-12(II)

  TRG 90 Saab 91 *Safir* (50 obs; 40 liaison)

HELICOPTERS

  ATK 42: 25 AH-1F *Cobra* with TOW; 16 AH-1S *Cobra*; 1 Mi-24 *Hind*

  MRH 114+: 10 AS550 *Fennec*; 6 AW139; 26 Bell 412EP *Twin Huey*; 40+ Mi-17 *Hip H*; 12 SA315B *Lama*; 20 SA319 *Alouette* III

  TPT 59 **Medium** 36: 31 SA330 *Puma* ; 4 Mi-171; 1 Mi-172 **Light** 23: 5 Bell 205 (UH-1H *Iroquois*); 5 Bell 205A-1 (AB-205A-1); 13 Bell 206B *Jet Ranger* II

  TRG 22: 12 Bell 47G; 10 Hughes 300C

UAV • ISR • Light *Bravo*; *Jasoos*; *Vector*

AD

  SAM

  SP some M113 with RBS-70

  MANPAD 2,990+: 2,500 Mk1/Mk2; 60 FIM-92A *Stinger*; HN-5A; 230 *Mistral*; 200 RBS-70

  GUNS • TOWED 1,934: **14.5mm** 981; **35mm** 248 GDF-002/GDF-005 (with 134 *Skyguard* radar units); **37mm** 310 Type-55 (M-1939)/Type-65; **40mm** 50 L/60; **57mm** 144 Type-59 (S-60); **85mm** 200 Type-72 (M-1939) *KS-12*

  RADAR • LAND AN/TPQ-36 *Firefinder* (arty, mor); RASIT (veh, arty); SLC-2

  MSL

  STRATEGIC

  MRBM ε30 *Ghauri/Ghauri* II (*Hatf-5*); some *Shaheen-2* (*Hatf-6* - in test)

  SRBM ε30 *Ghaznavi* (*Hatf-3* - PRC M-11)/*Shaheen-1* (*Hatf-4*);

  LACM some *Babur* (*Hatf-7* - in development)

  TACTICAL • SRBM 105+: 105 Hatf-1; some *Abdali* (*Hatf-2*);

  ARV 117+: 65 Type-653; *Al Hadeed*; 52 M88A1; T-54/T-55

  VLB M47M; M48/60

  MW *Aardvark* Mk II

Navy 22,000 (incl ε1,400 Marines and ε2,000 Maritime Security Agency (see Paramilitary))

EQUIPMENT BY TYPE

SUBMARINES • TACTICAL 8

  SSK 5:

  2 *Hashmat* (FRA *Agosta* 70) with 4 single 533mm ASTT with F17P HWT/UGM- 84 *Harpoon* AShM

3 *Khalid* (FRA *Agosta* 90B – 1 with AIP) with 4 single 533mm ASTT with F17 Mod 2 HWT/SM-39 *Exocet* AShM

SSI 3 MG110 (SF delivery) each with 2 single 533mm TT

PRINCIPAL SURFACE COMBATANTS • FRIGATES 10

FFGHM 3:

3 *Sword* (PRC Type-054) with 2 quad lnchr with YJ-83 AShM, 1 octuple lnchr with HQ-7 SAM, 2 triple 324mm ASTT with Mk 46 LWT, 1 76mm gun, (capacity 1 Z-9C *Haitun* hel)

FFGH 4:

4 *Tariq* (UK *Amazon*) with 2 twin Mk141 lnchr with RGM-84D *Harpoon* AShM, 2 single TT with TP 45 LWT, 1 114mm gun, (capacity 1 hel)

FFHM 2:

2 *Tariq* with 1 sextuple lnchr with LY-60 (*Aspide*) SAM, 2 triple 324mm ASTT with Mk 46 LWT, 1 114mm gun, (capacity 1 hel)

FFH 1

1 *Alamgir* (US *Oliver Hazard Perry*) with 2 triple 24mm ASTT with Mk46 LWT, 1 76mm gun

PATROL AND COASTAL COMBATANTS 12

PBFG 2 *Zarrar* each with 4 single each with RGM-84 *Harpoon* AShM

PBG 4:

2 *Jalalat* II with 2 twin lnchr with C-802 (CSS-N-8 *Saccade*) AShM

2 *Jurrat* with 2 twin lnchr with C-802 (CSS-N-8 *Saccade*) AShM

PBF 4: 2 *Kaan 15*; 2 *Kaan 33*

PB 2: 1 *Larkana*; 1 *Rajshahi*

MINE WARFARE • MINE COUNTERMEASURES

MHC 3 *Munsif* (FRA *Eridan*)

AMPHIBIOUS

LANDING CRAFT • UCAC 4 Griffon 2000

LOGISTICS AND SUPPORT 11

AORH 2:

1 *Fuqing* (capacity 1 SA319 *Alouette III* utl hel)

1 *Moawin* (capacity 1 *Sea King* Mk45 ASW hel) **AOT** 3: 1 *Attock*; 2 *Gwadar*

AGS 1 *Behr Paima*

AXS 1

YTM 5

Marines ε1,400

FORCES BY ROLE

SPECIAL FORCES

1 cdo gp

Naval Aviation

AIRCRAFT 7 ac combat capable

ASW 7: 3 *Atlantic*; 4 P-3C *Orion* (additional 2-4 ac on order)

MP 6 F-27-200 MPA

TPT • PAX 1 Hawker 850XP

HELICOPTERS

ASW 12: 5 *Sea King* Mk45; 7 Z-9C *Haitun*

MRH 6 SA319B *Alouette III*

MSL • AShM AM-39 *Exocet*

Air Force 70,000

3 regional comds: Northern (Peshawar) Central (Sargodha) Southern (Masroor). The Composite Air Tpt Wg, Combat Cadres School and PAF Academy are Direct Reporting Units.

FORCES BY ROLE

FIGHTER

2 sqn with F-7P/FT-7P *Skybolt*

3 sqn with F-7PG/FT-7PG *Airguard*

1 sqn with F-16A/B *Fighting Falcon*

1 sqn with *Mirage* IIID/E (IIIOD/EP)

FIGHTER/GROUND ATTACK

1 sqn with JF-17 *Thunder* (FC-1)

1 sqn (forming) with JF-17 *Thunder* (FC-1)

1 sqn with F-16C/D Block 52 *Fighting Falcon*

3 sqn with *Mirage* 5 (5PA)

ANTI SURFACE WARFARE

1 sqn with *Mirage* 5PA2/5PA3 with AM-39 *Exocet* AShM

ELECTRONIC WARFARE/ELINT

1 sqn with *Falcon* 20F

AIRBORNE EARLY WARNING & CONTROL

1 sqn with Saab 2000; Saab 2000 *Erieye*; ZDK-03

SEARCH & RESCUE

1 sqn with Mi-171Sh (SAR/liaison)

6 sqn with SA316 *Alouette III*

TANKER

1 sqn with Il-78 Midas

TRANSPORT

1 sqn with C-130B/E *Hercules*; CN-235M-220; L-100-20

1 VIP sqn with B-707; Cessna 560XL *Citation Excel*; CN-235M-220; F-27-200 *Friendship*; Falcon 20E; Gulfstream IVSP

1 (comms) sqn with EMB-500 *Phenom 100*; Y-12 (II)

TRAINING

2 OCU sqn with F-7P/FT-7P *Skybolt*

1 OCU sqn with *Mirage* III/*Mirage* 5

1 OCU sqn with F-16A/B *Fighting Falcon*

2 sqn with K-8 *Karakourm**

2 sqn with MFI-17

2 sqn with T-37C *Tweet*

AIR DEFENCE

1 bty with CSA-1 (SA-2 *Guideline*); 9K310 *Igla*-1 (SA-16 *Gimlet*)

6 bty with *Crotale*

EQUIPMENT BY TYPE

AIRCRAFT 423 combat capable

FTR 200: 51 F-7PG *Airguard*; 75 F-7P *Skybolt*; 24 F-16A *Fighting Falcon*; 21 F-16B *Fighting Falcon* (undergoing mid-life update) 21 FT-7; 6 FT-7PG; 2 *Mirage* IIIB

FGA 174: 12 F-16C Block 52 *Fighting Falcon*; 6 F-16D Block 52 *Fighting Falcon*; 33+ JF-17 *Thunder* (FC-1 - 150+ to be acquired); 7 *Mirage* IIID (*Mirage* IIIOD); 63 *Mirage* IIIE (IIIEP); 40 *Mirage* 5 (5PA)/5PA2; 3 *Mirage* 5D (5DPA)/5DPA2; 10 *Mirage* 5PA3 (ASuW)

ISR 10 *Mirage* IIIR* (*Mirage* IIIRP)

ELINT 2 Falcon 20F

AEW&C 6: 4 Saab 2000 *Erieye*; 2 ZDK-03

TKR 4 Il-78 *Midas*

TPT 34: **Medium** 16: 5 C-130B *Hercules*; 10 C-130E *Hercules*; 1 L-100-20 **Light** 13: 1 Cessna 560XL *Citation Excel*; 4 CN-235M-220; 4 EMB-500 *Phenom 100*; 1 F-27-

200 *Friendship*; 2 Y-12 (II) **PAX** 5: 1 B-707; 1 *Falcon* 20E; 2 Gulfstream IVSP; 1 Saab 2000

TRG 143: 39 K-8 *Karakorum**; 80 MFI-17B *Mushshak*; 24 T-37C *Tweet*

HELICOPTERS

MRH 15 SA316 *Alouette III*

TPT • Medium 4 Mi-171Sh

AD • SAM 150+

TOWED 150+: 6 CSA-1 (SA-2 *Guideline*); 144 *Crotale*; some SPADA 2000

MANPAD 9K310 *Igla-1* (SA-16 *Gimlet*)

RADAR • LAND 51+: 6 AR-1 (AD radar low level); some *Condor* (AD radar high level); some FPS-89/100 (AD radar high level)

MPDR 45 MPDR/MPDR 60 MPDR 90 (AD radar low level)

TPS-43G Type-514 some (AD radar high level)

MSL

ASM: AGM-65 *Maverick*; CM-400AKG (reported); *Raptor II*

AShM AM-39 *Exocet*;

LACM *Raad* (in development)

ARM MAR-1

AAM • IR AIM-9L/P *Sidewinder*; *U-Darter*; PL-5; **SARH** *Super* 530; **ARH** PL-12 (SD-10 – likely on order for the JF-17); AIM-120C AMRAAM

Paramilitary up to 304,000 active

Coast Guard

PATROL AND COASTAL COMBATANTS 5

PBF 4

PB 1

Frontier Corps up to 65,000 (reported)

Ministry of Interior

FORCES BY ROLE

MANOEUVRE

Reconnissance

1 armd recce sqn

Other

11 paramilitary regt (total: 40 paramilitary bn)

EQUIPMENT BY TYPE

APC (W) 45 UR-416

Maritime Security Agency ε2,000

PRINCIPAL SURFACE COMBATANTS

DESTROYERS 1

DD 1 *Nazim* (US *Gearing*) with 2 triple 324mm TT, 1 twin 127mm gun

PATROL AND COASTAL COMBATANTS 15:

PCC 4 *Barkat*

PBF 5

PB 6: 2 *Subqat* (PRC *Shanghai II*); 1 *Sadaqat* (ex-PRC *Huangfen*); 3 (various)

National Guard 185,000

Incl *Janbaz* Force; *Mujahid* Force; National Cadet Corps; Women Guards

Northern Light Infantry ε12,000

FORCES BY ROLE

MANOEUVRE

Other

3 paramilitary bn

Pakistan Rangers up to 40,000

Ministry of Interior

DEPLOYMENT

CÔTE D'IVOIRE

UN • UNOCI 1,387; 10 obs; 1 inf bn; 1 engr coy; 1 tpt coy

DEMOCRATIC REPUBLIC OF THE CONGO

UN • MONUSCO 3,695; 58 obs; 3 mech inf bn; 1 inf bn; 1 hel coy

LIBERIA

UN • UNMIL 2,765; 6 obs; 3 inf bn; 2 engr coy; 1 fd hospital

SUDAN

UN • UNAMID 499; 6 obs; 1 engr coy

TIMOR LESTE

UN • UNMIT 3 obs

WESTERN SAHARA

UN • MINURSO 11 obs

FOREIGN FORCES

Unless specified, figures represent total numbers for UNMOGIP mission in India and Pakistan

Chile 2 obs

Croatia 8 obs

Finland 6 obs

Italy 3 obs

Korea, Republic of 7 obs

Philippines 4 obs

Sweden 5 obs

Thailand 3 obs

United Kingdom some (fwd mounting base) air elm located at Karachi

Uruguay 2 obs

Papua New Guinea PNG

Papua New Guinea Kina K		2011	2012	2013
GDP	K	30.17bn	34.3bn	
	US$	12.66bn	15.39bn	
per capita	US$	2,006	2,439	
Growth	%	8.91	7.67	
Inflation	%	8.45	6.84	
Def exp [a]	K	183m		
	US$	77m		
Def bdgt [a]	K	196m	229m	
	US$	82m	103m	
US$1=K		2.38	2.23	

[a] Includes defence allocations to the Public Sector Development Programme (PSDP), including funding to the Defence Division and the Defence Production Division.

Population	6,310,129					
Age	0–14	15–19	20–24	25–29	30–64	65 plus
Male	18.3%	5.3%	4.6%	4.0%	17.2%	2.0%
Female	17.7%	5.1%	4.4%	3.8%	15.9%	1.7%

Capabilities

In view of chronic funding problems, the government reduced the size of the Papua New Guinea Defence Force (PNGDF) substantially during the 2002–7 period. It is now a more compact force, including small air and naval elements, and receives financial and training support from Australia, and to a lesser extent New Zealand, France, Germany and China. Though it has engaged in internal security operations and minor regional deployments, the PNGDF would be stretched to provide comprehensive border security, let alone defend national territory, without substantial Australian support.

ACTIVE 3,100 (Army 2,500 Maritime Element 400 Air 200)

ORGANISATIONS BY SERVICE

Army ε2,500
FORCES BY ROLE
MANOEUVRE
   Light
   2 inf bn
COMBAT SUPPORT
   1 engr bn
   1 EOD unit
   1 sigs sqn
EQUIPMENT BY TYPE
ARTY • MOR 3+: **81mm**; **120mm** 3

Maritime Element ε400

1 HQ located at Port Moresby
EQUIPMENT BY TYPE
PATROL AND COASTAL COMBATANTS 4:

PB 4 *Pacific*
AMPHIBIOUS 2:
   LANDING SHIPS • **LSM** 2 *Salamaua*

Air Force 200
FORCES BY ROLE
TRANSPORT
   1 sqn with CN-235M-100; IAI-201 *Arava*
TRANSPORT HELICOPTER
   1 sqn with Bell 205 (UH-1H *Iroquois*)†
EQUIPMENT BY TYPE
AIRCRAFT • TPT • **Light** 5: 2 CN-235M-100; 3 IAI-201 *Arava*
HELICOPTERS • TPT • **Light** 4 Bell 205 (UH-1H *Iroquois*)†

DEPLOYMENT

SOLOMON ISLANDS
RAMSI 30; 1 inf pl

SOUTH SUDAN
UN • UNMISS 1 obs

FOREIGN FORCES

Australia Army 38; 1 trg unit

Philippines PHL

Philippine Peso P		2011	2012	2013
GDP	P	9.74tr	10.49tr	
	US$	224.77bn	240.66bn	
per capita	US$	2,166	2,319	
Growth	%	3.91	4.84	
Inflation	%	4.72	3.51	
Def exp [a]	P	117bn		
	US$	2.7bn		
Def bdgt [a]	P	105bn	113bn	122bn
	US$	2.42bn	2.59bn	
FMA (US)	US$	11,97bn	14,555bn	13,5bn
US$1=P		43.31	43.60	

[a] Includes military pensions

Population	103,775,002					
Age	0–14	15–19	20–24	25–29	30–64	65 plus
Male	17.5%	5.1%	4.7%	4.3%	16.6%	1.9%
Female	16.8%	4.9%	4.5%	4.2%	17.0%	2.5%

Capabilities

The Armed Forces of the Philippines (AFP), particularly the army and marines, are deployed extensively in an internal security role across the country in the face of continuing challenges from insurgent groups. Until the withdrawal of the US military presence in 1992, the Philippines had largely relied on Washington to provide for its external defence, and since then perennially low defence budgets have thwarted efforts to develop any significant capacity for conventional warfighting or deterrence. While the government of Benigno Aquino III has promised, since 2011, that it will provide a stronger military defence of its South China Sea claims, military modernisation budgets have consistently failed to provide the resources needed to fulfil the armed forces' procurement plans.

ACTIVE 125,000 (Army 86,000 Navy 24,000 Air 15,000) **Paramilitary 40,500**

RESERVE 131,000 (Army 100,000 Navy 15,000 Air 16,000) **Paramilitary 40,000 (to age 49)**

ORGANISATIONS BY SERVICE

Army 86,000
5 Area Unified Comd (joint service), 1 National Capital Region Comd
FORCES BY ROLE
SPECIAL FORCES
1 spec ops comd (1 Scout Ranger regt, 1 SF regt, 1 lt reaction bn)
MANOEUVRE
Mechanised
1 lt armd div with (3 lt armd bn; 3 lt armd coy; 4 armd cav tp; 4 mech inf bn; 1 cbt engr coy; 1 avn bn)
Light
10 div (each: 3 inf bde; 1 arty bn)
Other
1 (Presidential) gd gp
COMBAT SUPPORT
1 arty regt HQ
5 engr bde
1 int gp
1 sigs gp
EQUIPMENT BY TYPE
LT TK 7 Scorpion
AIFV 36: 2 YPR-765; 34 M113A1 FSV
APC 299
APC (T) 76: 6 ACV300; 70 M113
APC (W) 223: 77 LAV-150 Commando; 146 Simba
ARTY 254+
TOWED 214: 105mm 204 M101/M102/M-26/M-56 155mm 10 M114/M-68
MOR 40+: 81mm M-29; 107mm 40 M-30
AT • RCL 75mm M20; 90mm M67; 106mm M40A1
AIRCRAFT
TPT • Light 4: 1 Beech 80 Queen Air; 1 Cessna 170; 1 Cessna 172; 1 Cessna P206A
UAV • ISR • Medium Blue Horizon
ARV ACV-300; Samson; M578

Navy 24,000
EQUIPMENT BY TYPE
PRINCIPAL SURFACE COMBATANTS • FRIGATES
FF 1 Rajah Humabon with 3 76mm gun
PATROL AND COASTAL COMBATANTS 56
PSOH 1 Gregorio del Pilar with 1 76mm gun (US Hamilton - 2nd vessel refitting - ISD 2012)

PCF 1 Cyclone
PCO 11:
3 Emilio Jacinto with 1 76mm gun
6 Miguel Malvar with 1 76mm gun
2 Rizal with 2 76mm gun
PBF 11: 3 Conrado Yap; 8 Tomas Batilo
PB 32: 2 Aguinaldo; 22 Jose Andrada; 2 Kagitingan; 2 Point; 4 Swift Mk3
AMPHIBIOUS
LANDING SHIPS • LST 6
2 Bacolod City (Besson-class) with 1 hel landing platform (capacity 32 tanks; 150 troops)
4 Zamboanga del Sur (capacity 16 tanks; 200 troops)
LANDING CRAFT 26: 8 LCU; 2 LCVP; 16 LCM
LOGISTICS AND SUPPORT 7: AOL 2; AR 1; AK 1; AWT 2; TPT 1

Naval Aviation
AIRCRAFT • TPT • Light 6: 4 BN-2A Defender 2 Cessna 177 Cardinal
HELICOPTERS • TPT • Light 4 Bo-105

Marines 8,300
FORCES BY ROLE
MANOEUVRE
Amphibious
4 mne bde (total: 12 mne bn)
EQUIPMENT BY TYPE
APC (W) 24 LAV-300
AAV 85: 30 LVTP-5; 55 LVTP-7
ARTY 31+
TOWED 105mm 31: 23 M101; 8 M-26
MOR 107mm M-30

Air Force 15,000
FORCES BY ROLE
FIGHTER
1 sqn with S-211*
GROUND ATTACK
1 sqn with OV-10A/C Bronco*
ISR
1 sqn with Turbo Commander 690A
SEARCH & RESCUE
4 (SAR/Comms) sqn with Bell 205 (UH-1M Iroquois); AUH-76
TRANSPORT
1 sqn with C-130B/H Hercules; L-100-20
1 sqn with N-22B Nomad; N-22SL Searchmaster
1 sqn with F-27-200 MPA; F-27-500 Friendship
1 VIP sqn with F-28 Fellowship
TRAINING
1 sqn with SF-260F/TP
1 sqn with T-41B/D/K Mescalero
ATTACK HELICOPTER
1 sqn with MD-520MG
TRANSPORT HELICOPTER
1 sqn with AUH-76
1 sqn with W-3 (forming - combat utility role)
4 sqn with Bell 205 (UH-1H Iroquois)

1 (VIP) sqn with Bell 412EP *Twin Huey*; S-70A *Black Hawk* (S-70A-5)

EQUIPMENT BY TYPE

AIRCRAFT 23 combat capable

MP 2: 1 F-27-200 MPA; 1 N-22SL *Searchmaster*

ISR 11 OV-10A/C *Bronco**

TPT 9 **Medium** 5: 1 C-130B *Hercules*; 3 C-130H *Hercules*; 1 L-100-20; **Light** 3: 1 F-27-500 *Friendship*; 1 N-22B *Nomad*; 1 *Turbo Commander* 690A; **PAX** 1 F-28 *Fellowhip* (VIP)

TRG 40: 12 S-211*; 8 SF-260F; 10 SF-260TP; 10 T-41B/D/K *Mescalero*

HELICOPTERS

MRH 23: 4 W-3 *Sokol* 3 AUH-76; 3 Bell 412EP *Twin Huey*; 2 Bell 412HP *Twin Huey*; 11 MD-520MG

TPT 40 **Medium** 1: 1 S-70A *Black Hawk* (S-70A-5) **Light** 39 Bell 205 (UH-1H *Iroquois*)

UAV • ISR • Medium 2 *Blue Horizon* II

Paramilitary

Philippine National Police 40,500

Department of Interior and Local Government. 15 regional & 73 provincial comd. 62,000 auxiliaries.

EQUIPMENT BY TYPE

PATROL AND COASTAL COMBATANTS • PB 14 : 10 *Rodman* 101; 4 *Rodman* 38

AIRCRAFT

TPT • Light 5: 2 BN-2 *Islander*; 3 Lancair 320

Coast Guard

PATROL AND COASTAL COMBATANTS 57

PCO 5: 4 *San Juan*; 1 *Balsam*

PCC 2 *Tirad*

PB 50: 3 *De Haviland*; 4 *Ilocos Norte*; 1 *Palawan*; 12 PCF 50 (US *Swift* Mk1/2); 10 PCF 46; 10 PCF 65 (US *Swift* Mk3); 11 (various)

PBR 11

AMPHIBIOUS • LANDING CRAFT 2

LCM 1

LCVP 1

LOGISTICS AND SUPPORT • ABU 3

HELICOPTERS 3 SAR

Citizen Armed Force Geographical Units 50,000 reservists

MANOEUVRE

Other

56 militia bn (part-time units which can be called up for extended periods)

DEPLOYMENT

CÔTE D'IVOIRE

UN • UNOCI 3; 3 obs

HAITI

UN • MINUSTAH 157; 1 HQ coy

INDIA/PAKISTAN

UN • UNMOGIP 4 obs

LIBERIA

UN • UNMIL 116; 2 obs; 1 inf coy

SOUTH SUDAN

UN • UNMISS 3 obs

SUDAN

UN • UNISFA 1; 1 obs

SYRIA

UN • UNDOF 341; 1 inf bn

TIMOR LESTE

UN • UNMIT 2 obs

FOREIGN FORCES

Brunei IMT 9
Libya IMT 2
Malaysia IMT 19
United States US Pacific Command: 180

Singapore SGP

Singapore Dollar S$		2011	2012	2013
GDP	S$	326.83bn	339.87bn	
	US$	259.85bn	267.94bn	
per capita	US$	48,538	50,050	
Growth	%	4.89	2.08	
Inflation	%	5.25	4.47	
Def bdgt	S$	11.8bn	12.3bn	
	US$	9.36bn	9.68bn	
US$1=S$		1.26	1.27	

Population   5,353,494

Ethnic groups: Chinese 76%; Malay 15%; Indian 6%

Age	0–14	15–19	20–24	25–29	30–64	65 plus
Male	7.1%	3.9%	5.2%	5.1%	24.2%	3.5%
Female	6.8%	3.8%	5.6%	5.7%	24.8%	4.3%

Capabilities

The Singapore Armed Forces (SAF) are the best-equipped military force in Southeast Asia, and have benefitted, since the late 1960s, from steadily increasing defence spending and the gradual development of a substantial national defence industry capable of producing and modifying equipment for specific national requirements. The SAF is organised essentially along Israeli lines; the air force and navy being staffed mainly by professional personnel while, apart from a small core of regulars, the much larger army is based on conscripts and reservists. Much training is routinely carried out overseas, notably, but not only, in Australia, Brunei, Taiwan, Thailand, and the United States. The SAF also engages in multilateral exercises through the Five Power Defence Arrangements. Singapore's government has traditionally been reluctant to make public details of its strategic outlook or military doctrine, but it is widely presumed that the SAF has been developed primarily with a view to deterring near-neighbours from attacking the city-state or impinging on its vital interests (such as its water supply from Malaysian reservoirs). Since the 1990s, however, the SAF has increasingly also become involved – albeit on a relatively small-scale – in multinational peace-support operations. While these deployments have provided some operational experience, and SAF training and operational readiness are high by international standards, the army's reliance on conscripts and reservists limits its capacity for sustained operations away from Singapore.

ACTIVE 72,500 (Army 50,000 Navy 9,000 Air 13,500) **Paramilitary 75,100**

Terms of service conscription 24 months

RESERVE 312,500 (Army 300,000 Navy 5,000 Air 7,500) **Paramilitary 44,000**

Annual trg to age of 40 for army other ranks, 50 for officers

ORGANISATIONS BY SERVICE

Army 15,000; 35,000 conscript (total 50,000)

FORCES BY ROLE
SPECIAL FORCES
  1 cdo bn
MANOEUVRE
  Reconnaissance
  4 lt armd/recce bn
  Armoured
  1 armd bn
  Mechanised
  3 combined arms div (mixed active/reserve formations
    (1 recce bn, 1 armd bde, 2 inf bde (3 inf bn), 2 arty bn,
    1 AD bn, 1 engr bn, 1 sigs bn, 1 log spt cmd)
  Light
  1 rapid reaction div (mixed active/reserve formations)
    (1 inf bde, 1 air mob bde, 1 amph bde (3 amph bn), 1
    AD bn, 1 engr bn, 1 sigs bn, 1 log spt cmd)
  8 inf bn
COMBAT SUPPORT
  4 arty bn
  4 engr bn
  1 int bn
  1 CBRN coy

Reserves

9 inf bde incl in mixed active/inactive reserve formations listed above; 1 op reserve div with additional inf bde; People's Defence Force Comd (homeland defence) with inf bn 12

FORCES BY ROLE
SPECIAL FORCES
  1 cdo bn
MANOEUVRE
  Reconnaissance
  6 lt armd/recce bn
  Mechanised
  6 mech inf bn
  Light
  ε56 inf bn

COMBAT SUPPORT
  ε12 arty bn
  ε8 engr bn

EQUIPMENT BY TYPE
MBT 96 *Leopard* 2A4; (80–100 *Tempest* (upgraded *Centurion*) in store)
LT TK ε350 AMX-13 SM1
RECCE 22 AMX-10 PAC 90
AIFV 407+: 22 AMX-10P; 135 AV-81 *Terrex*; 250 IFV-25 *Bionix*; 50+ M113A1/A2 (some with 40mm AGL, some with 25mm gun)
APC 1,695+
  APC (T) 1,400+: 250 IFV-40/50; 700+ M113A1/M113A2; 400+ ATTC *Bronco*
  APC (W) 280: 250 LAV-150 *Commando*/V-200 *Commando*; 30 V-100 *Commando*
  PPV 15 *MaxxPro Dash*
ARTY 798+
  SP 155mm 54 SSPH-1 *Primus*
  TOWED 88: **105mm** (37 LG1 in store); **155mm** 88: 18 FH-2000; ε18 *Pegasus*; 52 FH-88
  MRL 227mm 18 HIMARS
  MOR 638+
  SP 90+ **81mm**; **120mm** 90: 40 on *Bronco*; 50 on M113
  TOWED 548 **81mm** 500 **120mm** 36 **M-65 160mm** 12 M-58 *Tampella*
AT • MSL • MANPATS 60: 30 *Milan*; 30 *Spike MR*
  RCL 290: **84mm** ε200 *Carl Gustav*; **106mm** 90 M40A1
AD • SAM 75+
  SP *Mistral*; RBS-70; 9K38 *Igla* (SA-18 *Grouse*) (on V-200/M-113)
  MANPAD *Mistral*; RBS-70; 9K38 *Igla* (SA-18 *Grouse*)
  GUNS 34
  SP 20mm GAI-C01
  TOWED 34 **20mm** GAI-C01; **35mm** 34 GDF (with 25 *Super-Fledermaus* fire control radar)
UAV • ISR • Light *Skylark*
RADAR • LAND AN/TPQ-36 *Firefinder*; AN/TPQ-37 *Firefinder* (arty, mor); 3 *ARTHUR* (arty)
AEV 80: 18 CET; 54 FV180; 8 M728
ARV *Bionix*; *Büffel*; LAV-150; LAV-300
VLB *Bionix*; LAB 30; *Leguan*; M2; M3; 12 M60
MW 910-MCV-2; *Trailblazer*

Navy 3,000; 1,000 conscript; ε5,000 active reservists (total 9,000)

EQUIPMENT BY TYPE
SUBMARINES • TACTICAL • SSK 5:
  3 *Challenger* with 4 single 533mm TT
  1 *Challenger* (trg role) with 4 single 533mm TT
  1 *Archer* (SWE *Västergötland*-class) (AIP fitted) with 6 single 533mm TT for *WASS Black Shark* LWT (2nd vessel expected ISD 2012)
PRINCIPAL SURFACE COMBATANTS 6:
  FRIGATES • FFGHM 6 *Formidable* with 2 quad lnchr with RGM-84 *Harpoon* AShM, 4 octuple VLS with *Aster* 15 SAM, 2 triple 324mm ASTT, 1 76mm gun, (capacity 1 S-70B *Sea Hawk* hel)

PATROL AND COASTAL COMBATANTS 35:

CORVETTES • FSGM 6 *Victory* with 2 quad Mk140 lnchr with RGM-84C *Harpoon* AShM, 2 octuple lnchr with *Barak* SAM, 2 triple 32mm ASTT, 1 76mm gun

PCO 11 *Fearless* with 2 sextuple *Sadral* lnchr with *Mistral* SAM, 1 76mm gun

PBF 6

PB 12

MINE WARFARE • MINE COUNTERMEASURES

MHC 4 *Bedok*

AMPHIBIOUS

PRINCIPAL AMPHIBIOUS SHIPS • LPD 4 *Endurance* with 2 twin lnchr with *Mistral* SAM, 1 76mm gun (capacity 2 hel; 4 LCVP; 18 MBT; 350 troops)

LANDING CRAFT 34 **LCU** 100 **LCVP**

LOGISTICS AND SUPPORT 2

AR 1 *Swift Rescue*

TRG 1

Air Force 13,500 (incl 3,000 conscript)

5 comds

FORCES BY ROLE

FIGHTER/GROUND ATTACK

2 sqn with F-5S/T *Tiger* II

1 sqn with F-15SG *Eagle*

3 sqn with F-16C/D *Fighting Falcon* (some used for ISR with pods)

ISR

1 ISR sqn with RF-5E *Tiger* II*

MARITIME PATROL/TRANSPORT

1 sqn with F-50

AIRBORNE EARLY WARNING & CONTROL

1 sqn with G550-AEW

TANKER

1 sqn with KC-135R *Stratotanker*

TANKER/TRANSPORT

1 sqn with KC-130B/H *Hercules*; C-130H *Hercules*

TRAINING

1 (France-based) sqn with A-4SU/TA-4SU *Super Skyhawk*

4 (US-based) units with AH-64D *Apache*; CH-47D *Chinook*; F-15SG: F-16C/D

1 (Australia-based) sqn with PC-21

ATTACK HELICOPTER

1 sqn with AH-64D *Apache*

TRANSPORT HELICOPTER

1 sqn with CH-47SD *Super D Chinook*

2 sqn with AS332M *Super Puma*; AS532UL *Cougar*

ISR UAV

2 sqn with *Searcher* MkII

1 sqn with *Hermes* 450

EQUIPMENT BY TYPE

AIRCRAFT 140 combat capable

FTR 29: 20 F-5S *Tiger* II; 9 F-5T *Tiger* II

FGA 84: 24 F-15SG *Eagle*; 20 F-16C *Fighting Falcon*; 40 F-16D *Fighting Falcon* (incl reserves)

ATK 14: 4 A-4SU *Super Skyhawk*; 10 TA-4SU *Super Skyhawk*

MP 5 F-50 *Maritime Enforcer**

ISR 8 RF-5E *Tiger* II*

AEW&C 4 G550-AEW

TKR 5: 1 KC-130H *Hercules*; 4 KC-135R *Stratotanker*

TKR/TPT 4 KC-130B *Hercules*

TPT 9 **Medium** 5 C-130H *Hercules* (2 ELINT); **PAX** 4 F-50

TRG 19 PC-21

HELICOPTERS

ATK 19 AH-64D *Apache*

ASW 6 S-70B *Seahawk*

TPT 40+ **Heavy** 16: 6 CH-47D *Chinook*; 10 CH-47SD *Super D Chinook* **Medium** 30: 18 AS332M *Super Puma* (incl 5 SAR); 12 AS532UL *Cougar*

TRG 5 EC120B *Colibri* (leased)

UAV • ISR 45 **Heavy** 5 *Hermes* 450 **Medium** 40 *Searcher* MkII

MSL • TACTICAL

ASM: AGM-65B/G *Maverick*; *Hellfire*

AShM AGM-84 *Harpoon*; AM-39 *Exocet*

ARM AGM-45 *Shrike*

AAM • IR AIM-9N/P *Sidewinder*; *Python 4* (reported); **IIR** AIM-9X *Sidewinder*; **SARH** AIM-7P *Sparrow*; (AIM-120C AMRAAM in store in US)

Air Defence Group

FORCES BY ROLE

MANOEUVRE

Other

4 (field def) sy sqn

Air Defence Bde

FORCES BY ROLE

AIR DEFENCE

1 ADA sqn with Oerlikon

1 AD sqn with MIM-23 HAWK

1 AD sqn with *Spyder*

Air Force Systems Bde

FORCES BY ROLE

AIR DEFENCE

1 AD sqn with radar (mobile)

1 AD sqn with LORADS

Divisional Air Def Arty Bde

Attached to army divs

FORCES BY ROLE

AIR DEFENCE

1 AD bn with *Mistral*

1 AD bn with 9K38 *Igla* (SA-18 *Grouse*)

3 AD bn with RBS-70

EQUIPMENT BY TYPE

AD • SAM

SP *Spyder*

TOWED *Mistral*; RBS-70; MIM-23 HAWK

MANPAD 9K38 *Igla* (SA-18 *Grouse*)

Paramilitary 75,100 active

Civil Defence Force 1,600 regulars; 3,200 conscript; 54,000+ volunteers; 1 construction bde (2,500 conscript) (total 61,300+); 23,000 reservists

Singapore Police Force (including Coast Guard) 8,500; 3,500 conscript; (total 12,000); 21,000 reservists

EQUIPMENT BY TYPE
PATROL AND COASTAL COMBATANTS 99
PBF 78: 10 *Shark*; 68 (various)
PB 21: 2 *Manta Ray*; 19 (various)

Singapore Gurkha Contingent (under police) 1,800

FORCES BY ROLE
MANOEUVRE
Other
6 paramilitary coy

Cyber

The Singapore Ministry of Defence has long identified the potential damage that could be caused by cyber attacks, with this concern perhaps more acute following its adoption of the Integrated Knowledge-based Command and Control (IKC2) doctrine, designed to aid the transition of Singapore's Armed Forces to a 'third generation' force. Meanwhile, Singapore established the Singapore Infocomm Technology Security Authority (SITSA) on 1 October 2009, as a division within the Internal Security Department of the Ministry of Home Affairs (MHA). Its main responsibilities will be dealing with cyber terrorism and cyber espionage, as well as operational IT security development.

DEPLOYMENT

AFGHANISTAN
NATO • ISAF 39

ARABIAN SEA & GULF OF ADEN
Combined Maritime Forces • 1 LPD

AUSTRALIA
Air force 2 trg schools – 1 with 12 AS-332 *Super Puma/ AS-532 Cougar* (flying trg) located at Oakey; 1 with PC-21 (flying trg) located at Pearce. Army: prepositioned AFVs and heavy equipment at Shoalwater Bay training area.

BRUNEI
Army 1 trg camp with infantry units on rotation
Air force 1 hel det with AS-332 *Super Puma*

FRANCE
Air force 200: 1 trg sqn with 4 A-4SU Super Skyhawk; 10 TA-4SU *Super Skyhawk*

TAIWAN
Army 3 trg camp (incl inf and arty)

THAILAND
Army 1 trg camp (arty, cbt engr)

TIMOR LESTE
UN • UNMIT 1 obs

UNITED STATES
Air force trg units at Luke AFB (AZ) with F-16 C/D; Mountain Home AFB (ID) with F-15 SG; AH-64D *Apache*

at Marana (AZ); 6+ CH-47D *Chinook* hel at Grand Prairie (TX)

FOREIGN FORCES

United States US Pacific Command: 150; 1 naval spt facility at Changi naval base; 1 USAF log spt sqn at Paya Lebar air base
UK and NZ minor support elements

Sri Lanka LKA

Sri Lankan Rupee Rs		2011	2012	2013
GDP	Rs	6.54tr	7.53tr	
	US$	59.15bn	59.77bn	
per capita	US$	2,754	2,782	
Growth	%	8.26	6.75	
Inflation	%	6.72	7.91	
Def bdgt [a]	Rs	186bn	184bn	202bn
	US$	1.68bn	1.46bn	
FMA (US)	US$	0.998m	0.5m	0.45m
US$1=Rs		110.61	125.92	

[a] Includes all funds allocated to the Ministry of Defence & Urban Development except those disbursed to the following departments: Police, Immigration & Emigration, Registration of Persons, Coast Conservation and Civil Security.

Population	21,481,334

Age	0–14	15–19	20–24	25–29	30–64	65 plus
Male	12.7%	3.9%	3.8%	4.0%	21.0%	3.5%
Female	12.2%	3.8%	3.8%	4.0%	22.7%	4.6%

Capabilities

Internal security was the main focus for Sri Lanka's armed forces, including the air force and navy, from 1983 until 2009 during the protracted campaign against the LTTE (Tamil Tigers). During the counter-insurgency campaign, the air force competently provided tactical air support to the army and navy, despite considerable losses to LTTE anti-aircraft fire. The navy fought numerous sea battles with the LTTE's naval commando units. The navy has a littoral protection capability, is equipped with fast-attack and patrol vessels, and has experience of coordinating with foreign navies in exercise scenarios. There is little capacity for force projection beyond national territory.

ACTIVE 160,900 (Army 200,000 Navy 15,000 Air 28,000) Paramilitary 62,200

RESERVE 5,500 (Army 1,100 Navy 2,400 Air Force 2,000) Paramilitary 30,400

ORGANISATIONS BY SERVICE

Army 160,000; 40,00 active reservists (recalled) (total 200,000)
Regt are bn sized

FORCES BY ROLE
COMMAND
12 div HQ
SPECIAL FORCES
1 indep SF bde
MANOEUVRE
Reconnaissance
3 armd recce regt
Armoured
1 armd bde (under strength)
Light
34 inf bde
1 cdo bde
Air Manoeuvre
1 air mob bde
COMBAT SUPPORT
9 arty regt
1 MRL bty
4 engr regt
5 sigs regt

EQUIPMENT BY TYPE
MBT 62 T-55AM2/T-55A
RECCE 15 *Saladin*
AIFV 62: 13 BMP-1; 49 BMP-2
APC 221+
  APC (T) 30+: some Type-63; 30 Type-85; some Type-89
  APC (W) 191: 25 BTR-80/BTR-80A; 31 *Buffel*; 20 Type-92; 105 *Unicorn*
ARTY 908
  TOWED 96: **122mm** 20; **130mm** 30 Type-59-I; **152mm** 46 Type-66 (D-20)
  MRL 122mm 28: 6 KRL-122; 22 RM-70 *Dana*
  MOR 784: **81mm** 520; **82mm** 209; **120mm** 55 M-43
AT • RCL 40: **105mm** ε10 M-65; **106mm** ε30 M40
  GUNS 85mm 8 Type-56 (D-44)
UAV • ISR • Medium 1 *Seeker*
RADAR • LAND 4 AN/TPQ-36 *Firefinder* (arty)
ARV 16 VT-55
VLB 2 MT-55

Navy 15,000 (incl 2,400 recalled reservists)
1 (HQ and Western comd) located at Colombo

EQUIPMENT BY TYPE
PATROL AND COASTAL COMBATANTS 138
  PSOH 1 *Sayura* (IND *Vigraha*)
  PCG 2 *Nandimithra* (ISR *Sa'ar* 4) with 3 single lnchr with 1 GII *Gabriel II* AShM, 1 76mm gun
  PCO 2: 1 *Reliance*; 1 *Sagara* (IND *Vikram*)
  PCC 1 *Jayesagara*
  PBF 87: 26 *Colombo*; 3 *Dvora*; 3 *Killer* (ROK); 6 *Shaldag*; 14 *Super Dvora* (Mk1/II/III); 3 *Simonneau*; 5 *Trinity Marine*; 27 *Wave Rider*
  PB 18: 4 *Cheverton*; 2 *Prathapa* (PRC mod *Haizhui*); 3 *Ranajaya* (PRC *Haizhui*); 1 *Ranarisi* (PRC mod *Shanghai* II); 5 *Weeraya* (PRC *Shanghai II*); 3 (various)
  PBR 27
AMPHIBIOUS
  LANDING SHIPS • LSM 1 *Yuhai* (capacity 2 tanks; 250 troops)
  LANDING CRAFT 8

  LCU 2 *Yunnan*
  LCM 2
  LCP 3 *Hansaya*
  UCAC 1 M 10 (capacity 56 troops)
LOGISTICS AND SUPPORT 2: 1 AP; 1 AX

Air Force 28,000 (incl SLAF Regt)
FORCES BY ROLE
FIGHTER
1 sqn with F-7BS/G; FT-7
FIGHTER/GROUND ATTACK
1 sqn with MiG-23UB *Flogger C*; MiG-27M *Flogger J2*
1 sqn with *Kfir* C-2/C-7/TC-2
1 sqn with K-8 *Karakoram**
TRANSPORT
1 sqn with An-32B *Cline*; C-130K *Hercules*; Cessna 421C *Golden Eagle*
1 sqn with Beech B200 *King Air*; Y-12 (II)
TRAINING
1 wg with PT-6, Cessna 150L
ATTACK HELICOPTER
1 sqn with Mi-24V *Hind* E; Mi-35P *Hind*
TRANSPORT HELICOPTER
1 sqn with Mi-17 *Hip* H
1 sqn with Bell 206A/B (incl basic trg), Bell 212
1 (VIP) sqn with Bell 212; Bell 412 *Twin Huey*
ISR UAV
1 sqn with *Blue Horizon*-2
1 sqn with *Searcher* II
MANOEUVRE
Other
1 (SLAF) sy regt

EQUIPMENT BY TYPE
AIRCRAFT 30 combat capable
  FTR 8: 3 F-7BS; 4 F-7GS; 1 FT-7
  FGA 15: 4 *Kfir* C-2; 2 *Kfir* C-7; 2 *Kfir* TC-2; 6 MiG-27M *Flogger J2*; 1 MiG-23UB *Flogger C* (conversion trg)
  TPT 23 **Medium** 2 C-130K *Hercules*; **Light** 21: 5 An-32B *Cline*; 6 Cessna 150L; 1 Cessna 421C *Golden Eagle*; 7 Y-12 (II); 2 Y-12 (IV)
  TRG 14: 7 K-8 *Karakoram**; 7 PT-6
HELICOPTERS
  ATK 11: 6 Mi-24P *Hind*; 3 Mi-24V *Hind* E; 2 Mi-35V *Hind*
  MRH 18: 6 Bell 412 *Twin Huey* (VIP); 2 Bell 412EP (VIP); 10 Mi-17 *Hip* H
  TPT • Light 12: 2 Bell 206A *Jet Ranger*; 2 Bell 206B *Jet Ranger*; 8 Bell 212
UAV • ISR • Medium 2+: some *Blue Horizon*-2; 2 *Searcher* II
AD • GUNS • TOWED 27: **40mm** 24 L/40; **94mm** 3 (3.7in)

Paramilitary ε62,200

Home Guard 13,000

National Guard ε15,000

Police Force 30,200; 1,000 (women) (total 31,200) 30,400 reservists

Ministry of Defence Special Task Force 3,000
Anti-guerrilla unit

DEPLOYMENT

DEMOCRATIC REPUBLIC OF THE CONGO
UN • MONUSCO 2 obs

HAITI
UN • MINUSTAH 861; 1 inf bn

LEBANON
UN • UNIFIL 151; 1 inf coy

SOUTH SUDAN
UN • UNMISS 2 obs

SUDAN
UN • UNISFA 1; 5 obs

WESTERN SAHARA
UN • MINURSO 1 obs

Taiwan (Republic of China) ROC

New Taiwan Dollar NT$		2011	2012	2013
GDP	NT$	13.75tr	13.99tr	
	US$	466.42bn	466.05bn	
per capita	US$	20,074	20,058	
Growth	%	4.03	1.31	
Inflation	%	1.43	2.50	
Def bdgt	NT$	286bn	310bn	
	US$	9.72bn	10.3bn	
US$1=NT$		29.47	30.01	

Population   23,234,936

Ethnic groups: Taiwanese 84%; mainland Chinese 14%

Age	0–14	15–19	20–24	25–29	30–64	65 plus
Male	7.6%	3.6%	3.5%	3.8%	26.1%	5.3%
Female	7.1%	3.4%	3.4%	3.8%	26.4%	6.0%

Capabilities

Taiwan's armed forces are well-trained and operate some advanced equipment, but their relatively small size, lack of combat experience and the age of some equipment, not to mention China's rapid and substantial military modernisation, have reduced previous military advantage. The current government has proposed transforming the military, and continues to aim to move towards an all-volunteer recruitment system. However, although compulsory basic training will remain for adult males, with the term reducing to a four-month period for those born after 1994. This could create a more professional, dedicated military, albeit at a significant cost. A reduction to 220,000 personnel is planned, resulting almost entirely from cuts to the army. The result will be a relatively small, professional force that will continue to benefit from close defence relations with the US in terms of training. However, the capacity of such a small armed forces to withstand a concerted Chinese offensive from across the Taiwan Strait is doubtful. Moreover, a growing reluctance on the part of the US to furnish Taiwan with the most advanced military equipment means that

China is rapidly closing the technology gap. Taipei is currently emphasising the procurement of early-warning and missile-defence systems to enable the island to withstand an assault for as long as possible, with the goal of buying time for US intervention.

ACTIVE 290,000 (Army 200,000 Navy 45,000 Air 45,000) Paramilitary 17,000
Terms of service 12 months

RESERVE 1,657,000 (Army 1,500,000 Navy 67,000 Air Force 90,000)
Army reservists have some obligation to age 30

ORGANISATIONS BY SERVICE

Space
SATELLITES • ISR 1 Rocsat-2

Army ε200,000 (incl MP)
FORCES BY ROLE
COMMAND
   4 defence HQ
   3 corps HQ
SPECIAL FORCES/AVIATION
   1 SF/avn comd (2 spec ops bde, 3 avn bde)
MANOEUVRE
   Armoured
   5 armd bde
   Mechanised
   1 armd inf bde
   Light
   3 mot inf bde
   25 inf bde
COMBAT SUPPORT
   1 (coastal defence) AShM bn
   3 engr group
   3 CBRN group
   3 sigs gp

Missile Command
FORCES BY ROLE
AIR DEFENCE
   2 AD/SAM gp (total: 6 SAM bn with MIM-23 HAWK; PAC-3 *Patriot*; 6 Tien Kung I *Sky Bow*/Tien Kung II *Sky Bow*)

Reserves
FORCES BY ROLE
MANOEUVRE
   Light
   7 lt inf div
EQUIPMENT BY TYPE
MBT 565: 200 M60A3; 100 M48A5; 265 M48H *Brave Tiger*
LT TK 855: 230 M24 *Chaffee* (90mm gun); 625 M41/Type-64
RECCE 48+: BIDS (CBRN recce); 48 K216A1 (CBRN recce); KM453 (CBRN recce)
AIFV 225 CM-25 (M113 with 20–30mm cannon)
APC 986
   APC (T) 686: 36 CM-32 *Yunpao*; 650 M113

APC (W) 300 LAV-150 *Commando*
ARTY 2,204
  SP 492: **105mm** 100 M108; **155mm** 318: 225 M109A2/A5; 48 M44T; 45 T-69; **203mm** 70 M110; **240mm** 4
  TOWED 1,060+: **105mm** 650 T-64 (M101); **155mm** 340+: 90 M-59; 250 T-65 (M114); M-44; XT-69 **203mm** 70 M115
  COASTAL 127mm ε50 US Mk 32 (reported)
  MRL 330: **117mm** 120 *Kung Feng* VI; **126mm** 60 *Kung Feng* III/*Kung Feng* IV; 150 RT 2000 *Thunder* (KF towed and SP)
  MOR 322+
    SP 162+: **81mm** 72+: M-29; 72 M125; **107mm** 90 M106A2
    TOWED 81mm 160 M-29; T75; **107mm** M30; **120mm** K5; XT-86
AT MSL 1,060: **SP** TOW
  MANPATS 60 *Javelin*; TOW
  RCL 500+: **90mm** M67; **106mm** 500+: 500 M40A1; Type-51
HELICOPTERS
  ATK 61 AH-1W *Cobra*
  MRH 38 OH-58D *Kiowa Warrior*
  TPT 89 **Heavy** 8 CH-47SD *Super D Chinook* **Light** 80 Bell 205 (UH-1H *Iroquois*)
  TRG 29 TH-67 *Creek*
UAV • ISR • Light *Mastiff* III
AD
  SAM 678
    SP 76: 74 FIM-92A *Avenger*; 2 M48 *Chaparral*
    TOWED up to 137: 25 MIM-104 *Patriot*; 100 MIM-23 *HAWK*; up to 6 PAC-3 *Patriot* (systems); up to 6 *Tien Kung* I *Sky Bow*/*Tien Kung* II *Sky Bow*
    MANPAD 61 FIM-92A *Stinger* (465 msl)
  GUNS 400
    SP 40mm M-42
    TOWED 20: **35mm** 20 GDF-001 (30 systems with 20 guns) **40mm** L/70
MSL • AShM *Ching Feng*
RADAR 1 TPQ-37 *Firefinder*
AEV 18 M9
ARV CM-27/A1; 37 M88A1
VLB 22 M3; M48A5

Navy 45,000

3 district; 1 (ASW) HQ located at Hualein; 1 Fleet HQ located at Tsoying; 1 New East Coast Fleet

EQUIPMENT BY TYPE
SUBMARINES • TACTICAL • SSK 4:
  2 *Hai Lung* with 6 single 533mm TT with SUT HWT
  2 *Hai Shih* (trg role) with 10 single 533mm TT (6 fwd, 4aft) with SUT HWT
PRINCIPAL SURFACE COMBATANTS 26
  CRUISERS • CGHM 4 *Keelung* (ex US *Kidd*) with 1 quad lnchr with RGM-84L *Harpoon* AShM, 2 twin Mk26 lnchr with SM-2MR SAM, 2 octuple Mk112 lnchr with ASROC, 2 127mm gun, (capacity 1 S-70 ASW hel)
  FRIGATES 22
    FFGHM 20:
      8 *Cheng Kung* with 2 quad lnchr with *Hsiung Feng* AShM, 1 Mk13 GMLS with SM-1MR SAM, 2 triple 324mm ASTT with Mk 46 LWT, 1 76mm gun, (capacity 2 S-70C ASW hel)

      6 *Chin Yang* with 1 octuple Mk112 lnchr with ASROC/RGM-84C *Harpoon* AShM, 2 triple lnchr with SM-1 MR SAM, 2 twin lnchr with SM-1 MR SAM, 2 twin 324mm ASTT with Mk 46 LWT, 1 127mm gun, (capacity 1 MD-500 hel)
      6 *Kang Ding* with 2 quad lnchr with *Hsiung Feng* AShM, 1 quad lnchr with *Sea Chaparral* SAM, 2 triple 324mm ASTT with Mk 46 LWT, 1 76mm gun, (capacity 1 S-70C ASW hel)
    FFGH 2:
      2 *Chin Yang* with 1 octuple Mk112 lnchr with ASROC/RGM-84C *Harpoon* AShM, 2 twin 324mm ASTT with Mk 46 LWT, 1 127mm gun, (capacity 1 MD-500 hel)
PATROL AND COASTAL COMBATANTS 51
  PCG 12 *Jin Chiang* with 1 quad lnchr with *Hsiung Feng* AShM
  PBG 31 *Kwang Hua* with 2 twin lnchr with *Hsiung Feng* II AShM
  PBF 8 *Ning Hai*
MINE WARFARE • MINE COUNTERMEASURES 14
  MHC 2 *Yung Jin* (US *Osprey*)
  MSC 8: 4 *Yung Chuan*; 4 *Yung Feng*
  MSO 4 *Aggressive* (Ex US)
COMMAND SHIPS • LCC 1 *Kao Hsiung*
AMPHIBIOUS
  PRINCIPAL AMPHIBIOUS SHIPS • LSD 2:
    1 *Shiu Hai* (capacity either 2 LCU or 18 LCM; 360 troops) with 1 hel landing platform
    1 *Chung Cheng* with 1 quad lnchr with *Sea Chapparal* SAM (capacity 3 LCU or 18 LCM)
  LANDING SHIPS 13
    LST 13:
      11 *Chung Hai* (capacity 16 tanks; 200 troops)
      2 *Newport* (capacity 3 LCVP, 400 troops)
  LANDING CRAFT 288: 18 LCU; 100 LCVP; 170 **LCM**
LOGISTICS AND SUPPORT 13
  AOE 1 *Wu Yi* with 1 hel landing platform
  ARS 6
  AK 3 *Wu Kang* with 1 hel landing platform (capacity 1,400 troops)
  AGOR 1 *Ta Kuan*

Marines 15,000

FORCES BY ROLE
MANOEUVRE
  Amphibious
  3 mne bde
COMBAT SUPPORT
  Some cbt spt unit

EQUIPMENT BY TYPE
AAV 204: 52 AAV-7A1; 150 LVTP-5A1
ARTY • TOWED 105mm; 155mm
AT • RCL 106mm
ARV 2 AAV-7R

Naval Aviation

FORCES BY ROLE
ANTI SUBMARINE WARFARE
  3 sqn with S-70C *Seahawk* (S-70C *Defender*)

MARITIME PATROL

2 sqn with S-2T *Tracker*

EQUIPMENT BY TYPE

AIRCRAFT 24 combat capable

ASW 24 S-2T *Tracker*

HELICOPTERS • ASW 20 S-70C *Seahawk* (S-70C *Defender*)

Air Force 55,000

Flying hours   180 hrs/year

FORCES BY ROLE

FIGHTER

3 sqn with *Mirage* 2000-5E/D (2000-5EI/DI)

FIGHTER/GROUND ATTACK

3 sqn with F-5E/F *Tiger II*

6 sqn with F-16A/B *Fighting Falcon*

5 sqn with F-CK-1A/B *Ching Kuo*

ELECTRONIC WARFARE

1 sqn with C-130HE *Tien Gian*

ISR

1 sqn with RF-5E *Tigereye*; RF-16A *Fighting Falcon*

AIRBORNE EARLY WARNING & CONTROL

1 sqn with E-2T *Hawkeye*

SEARCH & RESCUE

1 sqn with EC225; S-70C *Black Hawk*

TRANSPORT

2 sqn with C-130H *Hercules*

1 (VIP) sqn with B-727-100; B-737-800; Beech 1900; F-50

TRAINING

1 sqn with AT-3A/B *Tzu-Chung**

1 sqn with Beech 1900

1 (basic) sqn with T-34C *Turbo Mentor*

TRANSPORT HELICOPTER

1 sqn with CH-47 *Chinook*; S-70C *Black Hawk*; S-62A (VIP)

EQUIPMENT BY TYPE

AIRCRAFT 475 combat capable

FTR 290: 87 F-5E/F *Tiger II* (some in store); 146 F-16A/B *Fighting Falcon*; 10 *Mirage* 2000-5D (2000-5DI); 47 *Mirage* 2000-5E (2000-5EI)

FGA 128 F-CK-1A/B *Ching Kuo*

ISR 7 RF-5E *Tigereye*

EW 1 C-130HE *Tien Gian*

AEW&C 6 E-2T *Hawkeye*

TPT 33 **Medium** 19 C-130H *Hercules*; **Light** 10 Beech 1900

PAX 4: 1 B-737-800; 3 F-50

TRG 99: 57 AT-3A/B *Tzu-Chung**; 42 T-34C *Turbo Mentor*

HELICOPTERS

TPT 23: **Heavy** 3 CH-47 *Chinook*; **Medium** 20: 3 EC225; 1 S-62A (VIP); 16 S-70C *Black Hawk*

MSL

ASM AGM-65A *Maverick*

AShM AGM-84 *Harpoon*

ARM *Sky Sword* IIA

AAM • IR AIM-9J/P *Sidewinder*; R-550 *Magic* 2; *Shafrir*; *Sky Sword* I; **IR/ARH** MICA; **ARH** AIM-120C AMRAAM; *Sky Sword* II

AD • SAM *Antelope*

Paramilitary 17,000

Coast Guard 17,000

EQUIPMENT BY TYPE

PATROL AND COASTAL COMBATANTS 136

PSO 4: 2 *Ho Hsing*; 1 *Shun Hu* 7; 1 *Tainan*

PCO 15: 2 *Chin Hsing*; 2 *Kinmen*; 2 *Mou Hsing*; 1 *Shun Hu* 1; 2 *Shun Hu* 2/3; 4 *Taichung*; 2 *Taipei*

PBF 83 (various)

PB 34: 1 *Shun Hu* 5; 1 *Shun Hu* 6; 32 (various)

Directorate General (Customs)

EQUIPMENT BY TYPE

PATROL AND COASTAL COMBATANTS 9

PCO 1 *Yun Hsing*

PB 4 *Hai Cheng*; 4 *Hai Ying*;

Cyber

Although Taiwan has a highly developed civilian IT sector, the Taiwanese government has been relatively slow to exploit this advantage for national-defence purposes. But for the past decade, Taipei has worked on its *Po Sheng* – Broad Victory – C4ISR programme, an all-hazards defence system with a significant defence component located in the Hengshan Command Center which also houses the Tri-Service Command. The main focus of the military component of this programme is on countering PLA IW and EW attacks. Taiwanese civilian hackers are thought to be responsible for many of the viruses infecting Chinese computers but it is unclear to what extent, if at all, such activities benefit from government direction. Responsible authorities for cyber activity include the National Security Bureau (NSB), the defence ministry, and the Research, Development and Evaluation Commission (RDEC). Among other projects, the Chungshan Institute of Science and Technology (a government R&D house) plans to invest finance between 2013–2015 on a project to 'display and confirm' Taiwan's latest 'cyber offensive system'.

FOREIGN FORCES

Singapore Army: 3 trg camp (incl inf and arty)

Thailand THA

Thai Baht b		2011	2012	2013
GDP	b	10.54tr	11.47tr	
	US$	345.67bn	376.99bn	
per capita	US$	5,152	5,619	
Growth	%	0.05	5.57	
Inflation	%	3.81	3.24	
Def bdgt [a]	b	168bn	167bn	181bn
	US$	5.52bn	5.5bn	
FMA (US)	US$	1.568m	0.988m	0.988m
US$1=b		30.49	30.43	

[a] Excludes military pensions

Population   67,091,089

Ethnic and religious groups: Thai 75%; Chinese 14%; Muslim 4%

Age	0–14	15–19	20–24	25–29	30–64	65 plus
Male	10.0%	3.9%	3.8%	3.8%	23.6%	4.3%
Female	9.5%	3.8%	3.6%	3.8%	24.7%	5.2%

Capabilities

Thailand's armed forces have benefitted from substantially increased funding since reasserting their central political role in a 2006 coup. However, despite increased resources, and other positive indications such as continuing involvement in multinational exercises and significant international deployments during 2010–11, the armed forces' entanglement in domestic politics often appears to overshadow efforts to sustain and modernise operational capability. The army remains the dominant service, its commander-in-chief wielding considerably greater authority than the chief of defence force. While the army prevailed in clashes with Red-Shirt protesters in Bangkok in May 2010, the confrontation revealed potential splits in the service, particularly in light of many ordinary soldiers' origin in relatively poor northern and northeastern provinces where Red-Shirt support is strong. Subsequently, the army played a high-profile role in flood relief operations during 2011. Operations against Malay-Muslim insurgents in the three southernmost provinces continue, but ineffectively: the low-intensity war there remains stalemated. Sporadic border clashes with Cambodia in 2008–11 were essentially small-scale skirmishes involving infantry supported by mortar and artillery fire.

ACTIVE 360,850 (Army 245,000 Navy 69,850 Air 46,000) **Paramilitary 113,700**

Terms of service 2 years

RESERVE 200,000 Paramilitary 45,000

ORGANISATIONS BY SERVICE

Army 130,000; ε115,000 conscript (total 245,000)
FORCES BY ROLE
COMMAND
   4 (regional) army HQ
   3 corps HQ

SPECIAL FORCES
   1 SF div
   1 SF regt
MANOEUVRE
   Mechanised
   3 cav div
   1 armd inf div
   5 mech inf div
   Light
   3 lt inf div
   1 Rapid Reaction force (1 bn per region forming)
   Aviation
   Some hel flt
COMBAT SUPPORT
   1 arty div
   1 ADA div (6 bn)
   1 engr div
COMBAT SERVICE SUPPORT
   4 economic development div
EQUIPMENT BY TYPE
MBT 283: 53 M60A1; 125 M60A3; (50 Type-69 in store); 105 M48A5
LT TK 194: 24 M41; 104 *Scorpion* (50 in store); 66 *Stingray*
RECCE 32+: 32 S52 Mk 3; M1114 HMMWV
AIFV 96 BTR-3E1
APC 1,140
   APC (T) 880: *Bronco*; 430 M113A1/A3; 450 Type-85
   APC (W) 160: 18 *Condor*; 142 LAV-150 *Commando*
   PPV 100 *Reva*
ARTY 2,555+
   SP 155mm 26: 6 CAESAR; 20 M109A5
   TOWED 577: **105mm** 340: 24 LG1 MkII; 12 M-56; 200 M101/-Mod; 12 M102; 32 M618A2; 60 L119; **130mm** 54 Type-59-I; **155mm** 183: 42 GHN-45 A1; 48 M114; 61 M198; 32 M-71
   MRL 78: **130mm** 60 Type-85; **302mm** 18 DTI-1
   MOR 1,900
      SP 33: **81mm** 21 M125A3; **107mm** M106A3; **120mm** 12 M1064A3
      TOWED 1,867: **81mm**; **107mm** M106A1; **120mm** 12 M1064
AT
   MSL 318+
      SP 18+ M901A5 (TOW)
      MANPATS 300 M47 *Dragon*
   RCL 180: **75mm** 30 M20; **106mm** 150 M40
AIRCRAFT
   TPT • Light 19: 2 Beech 200 *King Air*; 2 Beech 1900C; 1 C-212 *Aviocar*; 10 Cessna A185E (U-17B); 2 ERJ-135LR; 2 *Jetstream* 41
   TRG 33: 11 MX-7-235 *Star Rocket*; 22 T-41B *Mescalero*
HELICOPTERS
   ATK 7 AH-1F *Cobra*
   MRH 3 Mi-17V-5 *Hip H*
   TPT 201 **Heavy** 5 CH-47D *Chinook*; **Medium** 6 UH-60L *Black Hawk* **Light** 190: 94 Bell 205 (UH-1H *Iroquois*); 28 Bell 206 *Jet Ranger*; 52 Bell 212 (AB-212); 16 Enstrom 480B
   TRG 54 Hughes 300C
UAV • ISR • Medium *Searcher*; *Searcher* II

AD • SAM
  STATIC *Aspide*
  MANPAD 36 9K338 *Igla*-S (SA-24 *Grinch*); FIM-43 *Redeye*; HN-5A
  GUNS 202+
    SP 54: **20mm** 24 M163 *Vulcan*; **40mm** 30 M1/M42 SP
    TOWED 148+: **20mm** 24 M-167 *Vulcan*; **37mm** 52 Type-74; **40mm** 48 L/70; **57mm** 24+: ε6 Type-59 (S-60); 18+ non-operational
RADAR • LAND AN/TPQ-36 *Firefinder* (arty, mor); RASIT (veh, arty)
ARV 43: 22 M88A1; 6 M88A2; 10 M113; 5 Type-653; WZT-4
VLB Type-84
MW Bozena; *Giant Viper*

Reserves

FORCES BY ROLE
COMMAND
  1 inf div HQ

Navy 44,000 (incl Naval Aviation, Marines, Coastal Defence); 25,850 conscript (total 69,850)

EQUIPMENT BY TYPE
PRINCIPAL SURFACE COMBATANTS 11
  AIRCRAFT CARRIERS • CVH 1:
    1 *Chakri Naruebet* (capacity 6 S-70B *Seahawk* ASW hel)
  FRIGATES 10
    FFGHM 2:
      2 *Naresuan* with 2 quad Mk141 lnchr with RGM-84A *Harpoon* AShM, 1 8 cell Mk41 VLS with RIM-7M *Sea Sparrow* SAM, 2 triple 324mm TT, 1 127mm gun, (capacity 1 *Super Lynx* 300 hel)
    FFGM 4:
      2 *Chao Phraya* with 4 twin lnchr with C-801 (CSS-N-4 *Sardine*) AShM, 2 twin lnchr with HQ-61 (CSA-N-2) SAM (non-operational), 2 RBU 1200, 2 twin 100mm gun
      2 *Kraburi* with 4 twin lnchr with C-801 (CSS-N-4 *Sardine*) AShM, 2 twin lnchr with HQ-61 (CSA-N-2) SAM, 2 RBU 1200, 1 twin 100mm gun, 1 hel landing platform
    FFGH 2:
      2 *Phuttha Yotfa Chulalok* (leased from US) with 1 octuple Mk112 lnchr with RGM-84C *Harpoon* AShM/ASROC, 2 twin 324mm ASTT with Mk 46 LWT, 1 127mm gun, (capacity 1 Bell 212 (AB-212) hel)
    FF 2:
      1 *Makut Rajakumarn* with 2 triple 34mm ASTT, 2 114mm gun
      1 *Pin Klao* (trg role) with 6 single 324mm ASTT, 3 76mm gun
PATROL AND COASTAL COMBATANTS 84
  CORVETTES 7:
    FSG 2 *Rattanakosin* with 2 quad Mk140 lnchr with RGM-84A *Harpoon* AShM, 1 octuple *Albatros* lnchr with *Aspide* SAM, 2 triple 324mm ASTT, 1 76mm gun

    FS 5:
      3 *Khamronsin* with 2 triple 324mm ASTT, 1 76mm gun
      2 *Tapi* with 6 single 324mm ASTT with Mk46 LWT, 1 76mm gun
  PCFG 6:
    3 *Prabparapak* with 2 single lnchr with 1 GI *Gabriel I* AShM, 1 triple lnchr with GI *Gabriel I* AShM
    3 *Ratcharit* with 2 twin lnchr with MM-38 *Exocet* AShM, 1 76mm gun
  PCO 5: 3 *Hua Hin* with 1 76mm gun; 2 *Pattani* with 1 76mm gun
  PCC 9: 3 *Chon Buri* with 2 76mm gun; 6 *Sattahip* with 1 76mm gun
  PBF 4
  PB 53: 7 T-11; 9 *Swift*; 3 T-81; 9 T-91; 3 T-210; 13 T-213; 3 T-227; 3 T-991; 3 T-994
MINE WARFARE • MINE COUNTERMEASURES 17
  MCM SPT 1 *Thalang*
  MCO 2 *Lat Ya*
  MCC 2 *Bang Rachan*
  MSR 12
AMPHIBIOUS
  PRINCIPAL AMPHIBIOUS SHIPS 1:
    LPD 1 *Anthong* with 1 76mm gun (capacity 2 hel; 19 MBT; 500 troops)
  LANDING SHIPS 2:
    LST 2 *Sichang* with 1 hel landing platform (capacity 14 MBT; 300 troops)
  LANDING CRAFT 56:
    LCU 13: 3 *Man Nok*; 6 *Mataphun* (capacity either 3–4 MBT or 250 troops); 4 *Thong Kaeo*
    LCM 24
    LCVP 12
    LCA 4
    UCAC 3 Griffon 1000TD
LOGISTICS AND SUPPORT 14
  AORH 1 *Similan* (capacity 1 hel)
  AOR 1 *Chula*
  AOL 5: 4 *Prong*; 1 *Samui*
  AWT 1
  AGOR 1
  AGS 2
  ABU 1
  TRG 1
  TPT 1

Naval Aviation 1,200

AIRCRAFT 3 combat capable
  ASW 2 P-3A *Orion* (P-3T)
  RECCE 9 *Sentry* O-2-337
  MP 1 F-27-200 MPA*
  TPT • Light 12: 7 Do-228-212*; 2 ERj-135LR; 2 F-27-400M *Troopship*; 3 N-24A *Searchmaster*; 1 UP-3A *Orion* (UP-3T)
HELICOPTERS
  ASW 8: 6 S-70B *Seahawk*; 2 *Super Lynx* 300
  TPT 13 **Medium** 2 Bell 214ST (AB-214ST) **Light** 11: 6 Bell 212 (AB-212); 5 S-76B
MSL • AShM AGM-84 *Harpoon*

Marines 23,000
FORCES BY ROLE
COMMAND
  1 mne div HQ
MANOEUVRE
  Reconnaissance
  1 recce bn
  Light
  2 inf regt (total: 6bn)
  Amphibious
  1 amph aslt bn
COMBAT SUPPORT
  1 arty regt (3 fd arty bn, 1 ADA bn)
EQUIPMENT BY TYPE
APC (W) 24 LAV-150 *Commando*
AAV 33 LVTP-7
ARTY • TOWED 48: **105mm** 36 (reported); **155mm** 12 GC-45
AT • MSL 24+
  TOWED 24 HMMWV TOW
  MANPATS M47 *Dragon*; TOW
AD • GUNS 12.7mm 14
ARV 1 AAVR-7

Air Force ε46,000
4 air divs, one flying trg school

Flying hours   100 hrs/year

FORCES BY ROLE
FIGHTER
  2 sqn with F-5E/5F *Tiger II*
  3 sqn with F-16A/B *Fighting Falcon*
  1 sqn with L-39ZA *Albatros**
FIGHTER/GROUND ATTACK
  1 sqn with *Gripen* C/D
GROUND ATTACK
  1 sqn with *Alpha Jet**
  1 sqn with AU-23A *Peacemaker*
  1 sqn with L-39ZA *Albatros**
ELINT/ISR
  1 sqn with DA42 MPP *Guardian*; IAI-201 *Arava*, *Learjet* 35A
AIRBORNE EARLY WARNING & CONTROL
  1 sqn with Saab 340 *Erieye*
TRANSPORT
  1 (Royal Flight) sqn with A310-324; A319CJ; B-737-400; BAe-748; Beech 200 *King Air*; Bell 412 *Twin Huey*
  1 sqn with ATR-72; BAe-748; Saab 340B
  1 sqn with BT-67; N-22B *Nomad*
  1 sqn with C-130H/H-30 *Hercules*
TRAINING
  1 sqn with CT-4A/B/E *Airtrainer*; T-41D *Mescalero*
TRANSPORT HELICOPTER
  2 sqn with Bell 205 (UH-1H *Iroquois*); Bell 412 *Twin Huey*
  1 sqn with Bell 412 *Twin Huey*
EQUIPMENT BY TYPE
AIRCRAFT 163 combat capable
  FTR 88: 31 F-5E *Tiger II*; 3 F-5F *Tiger II* (32 F-5E/F being upgraded); 39 F-16A *Fighting Falcon*; 15 F-16B *Fighting Falcon*
  FGA 6: 2 *Gripen* C; 4 *Gripen* D

ATK 18 AU-23A *Peacemaker*
ISR 3 DA42 MPP *Guardian*
AEW&C 1 Saab 340 *Erieye*
TPT 59 **Medium** 13: 6 C-130H *Hercules*; 6 C-130H-30 *Hercules*; 1 Saab 340B; **Light** 36: 4 ATR-72; 3 Beech 200 *King Air*; 1 Beech E90 *King Air*; 9 BT-67; 1 *Commander* 690; 2 IAI-201 *Arava*; 2 *Learjet* 35A; 14 N-22B *Nomad*; **PAX** 10: 1 A310-324; 1 A-319CJ; 2 B-737-400; 6 BAe-748
TRG 119: 19 *Alpha Jet**; 14 CT-4A *Airtrainer*; 6 CT-4B *Airtrainer*; 20 CT-4E *Airtrainer*; 32 L-39ZA *Albatros**; 20 PC-9; 8 T-41D *Mescalero*
HELICOPTERS
MRH 11: 2 Bell 412 *Twin Huey*; 2 Bell 412SP *Twin Huey*; 1 Bell 412HP *Twin Huey*; 6 Bell 412EP *Twin Huey*
TPT 23 **Medium** 3 S-92A *Super Hawk* **Light** 20 Bell 205 (UH-1H *Iroquois*)
MSL
AAM • IR AIM-9B/J *Sidewinder*; *Python* III **ARH** AIM-120 AMRAAM
ASM: AGM-65 *Maverick*

Paramilitary ε113,700 active

Border Patrol Police 41,000

Marine Police 2,200
PATROL AND COASTAL COMBATANTS 92
  PCO 1 *Srinakrin*
  PCC 2 *Hameln*
  PB 43: 1 *Burespadoongkit*; 2 *Chasanyabadee*; 3 *Cutlass*; 1 *Sriyanont*; 1 *Yokohama*; 35 (various)
  PBR 46

National Security Volunteer Corps 45,000 – Reserves

Police Aviation 500
AIRCRAFT 6 combat capable
  ATK 6 AU-23A *Peacemaker*
  TPT 16 **Light** 15: 2 CN-235; 8 PC-6 *Turbo-Porter*; 3 SC-7 3M *Skyvan*; 2 *Short* 330UTT **PAX** 1 F-50
HELICOPTERS
  MRH 6 Bell 412 *Twin Huey*
  TPT • Light 67: 27 Bell 205A; 14 Bell 206 *Jet Ranger*; 20 Bell 212 (AB-212)

Provincial Police 50,000 (incl est. 500 Special Action Force)

Thahan Phran (Hunter Soldiers) ε20,000
Volunteer irregular force
FORCES BY ROLE
MANOEUVRE
  Other
  13 paramilitary regt (total: 107 paramilitary coy)

DEPLOYMENT

Legal provisions for foreign deployment:
Constitution: In addition to the below, Government has to ensure no violation of Para 1 and 2 of Provision 190 of the Constitution of the Kingdom of Thailand, B.E. 2550

Decision on deployment of troops abroad: Depends on operation. In case of PSO or HADR, cabinet resolution endorsing deployment and defence council concurrence would constitute legislation. Legal provisions for foreign deployment generally under the Defence Act, BE 2551 (2008). Justification for overseas missions is in accordance with following sections of the Act. Provision 37, Art. 4: Minister of Defence has exclusive authority to arrange and deploy armed forces to areas considered appropriate; Provision 38, Art. 4: Employment of armed forces for peace operations shall be endorsed by council of ministers with concurrence of defence council. No terms of reference on 'the foreign deployment of forces for combat operations in [a] conventional war area are stipulated' in the Act, so deployment purpose and operation type should be clearly determined.

ARABIAN SEA & GULF OF ADEN
Combined Maritime Forces • CTF-151: 1 PCO; 1 AORH

INDIA/PAKISTAN
UN • UNMOGIP 3 obs

SUDAN
UN • UNAMID 6; 4 obs

FOREIGN FORCES

United States US Pacific Command: 120

Timor Leste TLS

US$		2011	2012	2013
GDP	US$	4.54bn	4.21bn	
per capita	US$	3,970	3,681	
Growth	%	0.05	5.57	
Inflation	%	3.81	3.24	
Def bdgt	US$	52m	64m	67m

Population	1,143,667					

Age	0–14	15–19	20–24	25–29	30–64	65 plus
Male	22.1%	5.4%	4.4%	3.4%	13.2%	1.7%
Female	20.9%	5.2%	4.5%	3.8%	13.5%	1.8%

Capabilities

The Timor Leste Defence Force was formed in 2001 from the former Falintil insurgent army. However, it soon became clear that the new force suffered from poor morale and weak discipline. In 2006, these problems culminated in the dismissal of large numbers of military personnel who had protested over poor conditions and alleged discrimination on regional lines, which precipitated the collapse of both the defence force and the national police. These circumstances forced the government to call for an international intervention; Australian-led foreign forces will draw down from November 2012 and depart by mid-2013. Meanwhile, the government has attempted to rebuild the defence force. Long-term plans outlined in the Force 2020 document, made public in 2006, call for an expanded defence force, conscription, the establishment of an air

component, and acquisition of modern weapons. In the meantime, the defence force continues to depend heavily on foreign assistance and training, notably from Australia, Portugal and Brazil.

ACTIVE 1,330 (Army 1,250 Naval Element 80)

ORGANISATIONS BY SERVICE

Army 1,250
Training began in Jan 2001 with the aim of deploying 1,500 full-time personnel and 1,500 reservists. Authorities are engaged in developing security structures with international assistance.

FORCES BY ROLE
MANOEUVRE
Light
2 inf bn
COMBAT SUPPORT
1 MP pl
COMBAT SERVICE SUPPORT
1 log spt coy

Naval Element 80
PATROL AND COASTAL COMBATANTS 7
PB 7: 2 *Albatros*; 2 *Dili*; 2 *Shanghai* II; 1 *Sea Dolphin* (ROK *Chamsur*)

DEPLOYMENT

LIBERIA
UN • UNMIL 1 obs

FOREIGN FORCES

Australia ISF (*Operation Astute*) 390; 1 bn HQ; 2 inf coy; 1 AD bty; elm 1 cbt engr regt; 1 hel det with 5 S-70A-9 (S-70A) *Black Hawk*; (mission to withdraw by April 2013) • UNMIT 4 obs
Bangladesh UNMIT 3 obs
Brazil UNMIT 3 obs
China, People's Republic of UNMIT 2 obs
Fiji UNMIT 1 obs
Nepal UNMIT 1 obs
New Zealand ISF (*Operation Koru*) 27 (theatre extraction team)
Pakistan UNMIT 3 obs
Philippines UNMIT 2 obs
Portugal UNMIT 2 obs
Sierra Leone UNMIT 1 obs
Singapore UNMIT 1 obs

Vietnam VNM

Vietnamese Dong d		2011	2012	2013
GDP	d	2535.01tr	2895.91tr	
	US$	122.72bn	137.68bn	
per capita	US$	1,341	1,504	
Growth	%	5.89	5.11	
Inflation	%	18.68	8.14	
Def bdgt	d	55.1tr	70tr	
	US$	2.67bn	3.33bn	
FMA (US)	US$	1.96m	2.315m	3m
US$1=d		20656.51	21033.48	

Population   91,519,289

Ethnic groups: Kinh 86%, Tay 2%, Thai 2%, Muong 1%, Khmer 1%, Mong 1%, Nung 1%, Hoa 1%, Dao 1%, Other 4%

Age	0–14	15–19	20–24	25–29	30–64	65 plus
Male	13.0%	4.7%	5.1%	5.0%	20.0%	2.1%
Female	11.8%	4.4%	4.8%	4.8%	20.9%	3.4%

Capabilities

Communist Vietnam has a stronger military tradition and much more operational experience than any of its Southeast Asian counterparts. Although the Vietnam People's Army (VPA) remained a central element of the political system led by the Vietnam Worker's Party, following the cessation of Soviet military aid with the end of the Cold War, the armed forces suffered from much-reduced budgets and only limited procurement. With Vietnam's rapid economic growth over the last decade, however, defence spending has increased, and particular efforts have been made to re-equip the navy and air force, apparently with a view to deterring Chinese military pressure in the disputed Spratly Islands. While Vietnam cannot hope to balance China's power on its own, acquisition of a submarine capability during the present decade with *Kilo*-class boats ordered from Russia in 2009 may complicate Beijing's naval options, as may the deployment of Su-27/-30 aircraft. The conscript-based armed forces have broad popular support, particularly in the context of current tensions with China.

ACTIVE 482,000 (Army 412,000 Navy 40,000 Air 30,000) Paramilitary 40,000

Terms of service 2 years Army and Air Defence, 3 years Air Force and Navy, specialists 3 years, some ethnic minorities 2 years

RESERVES 5,000,000

ORGANISATIONS BY SERVICE

Army ε412,000

9 Mil Regions (incl capital)

FORCES BY ROLE
COMMAND
  14 corps HQ

SPECIAL FORCES
  1 SF bde (1 AB bde, 1 demolition engr regt)
MANOEUVRE
  Armoured
  10 armd bde
  Mechanised
  3 mech inf div
  Light
  58 inf div(-)
  15 indep inf regt
COMBAT SUPPORT
  10+ arty bde
  8 engr div
  20 indep engr bde
COMBAT SERVICE SUPPORT
  10-16 economic construction div
EQUIPMENT BY TYPE
MBT 1,315: 70 T-62; 350 Type-59; 850 T-54/T-55; (45 T-34 †)
LT TK 620: 300 PT-76; 320 Type-62/Type-63
RECCE 100 BRDM-1/BRDM-2
AIFV 300 BMP-1/BMP-2
APC 1,380
  APC (T) 280: 200 M113 (to be upgraded); 80 Type-63
  APC (W) 1,100 BTR-40/BTR-50/BTR-60/BTR-152
ARTY 3,040+
  SP 30+: 152mm 30 2S3; 175mm M107
  TOWED 2,300 100mm M-1944; 105mm M101/M102; 122mm D-30/Type-54 (M-1938)/Type-60 (D-74); 130mm M-46; 152mm D-20; 155mm M114
  GUN/MOR 120mm 30 2S9 *Nona*-S (reported)
  MRL 710+: 107mm 360 Type-63; 122mm 350 BM-21; 140mm BM-14
  MOR 82mm; 120mm M-43; 160mm M-43
AT • MSL • MANPATS 9K11 (AT-3 *Sagger*)
  RCL 75mm Type-56; 82mm Type-65 (B-10); 87mm Type-51
  GUNS
    SP 100mm Su-100; 122mm Su-122
    TOWED 100mm T-12 (arty)
AD • SAM • MANPAD 9K32 *Strela*-2 (SA-7 *Grail*)‡; 9K310 *Igla*-1 (SA-16 *Gimlet*); 9K38 *Igla* (SA-18 *Grouse*)
  GUNS 12,000
    SP 23mm ZSU-23-4
    TOWED 14.5mm/30mm/37mm/57mm/85mm/100mm
MSL • SSM *Scud*-B/C (reported)

Navy ε40,000 (incl ε27,000 Naval Infantry)

EQUIPMENT BY TYPE
SUBMARINES • TACTICAL • SSI 2 *Yugo*† (DPRK)
PRINCIPAL SURFACE COMBATANTS 2
  FRIGATES • FFGM 2
    2 *Dinh Tien Hoang* (RUS *Gepard* mod) with 2 quad lnchr with Kh-35 *Uran* (SS-N-25 *Switchblade*); 1 *Palma* lnchr with *Sosna*-R SAM; 2 twin 533mm TT; 1 76mm gun
PATROL AND COASTAL COMBATANTS 66
  CORVETTES 6:
    FSG 1:
      1 BPS-500 with 2 quad lnchr with 3M24 *Uran* (SS-N-25 *Switchblade*) AShM (non-operational), 9K32 *Strela*-

2M (SA-N-5 *Grail*) SAM (manually operated), 2 twin 533mm TT, 1 RBU-1600, 1 76mm gun

FSG 5:

3 *Petya* II (FSU) with 1 quintuple 406mm ASTT, 4 RBU 6000 *Smerch* 2, 4 76mm gun

2 *Petya* III (FSU) with 1 triple 533mm ASTT, 4 RBU 2500 *Smerch* 1, 4 76mm gun

PCFGM 7:

4 *Tarantul* (FSU) with 2 twin lnchr with P-15 *Termit* (SS-N-2D *Styx*) AShM, 1 quad lnchr with SA-N-5 *Grail* SAM (manually operated), 1 76mm gun

3 *Tarantul* V with 4 quad lnchr with 3M24 *Uran* (SS-N-25 *Switchblade*) AShM; 1 quad lnchr with SA-N-5 *Grail* SAM (manually operated), 1 76mm gun

PCC 8: 6 *Svetlyak*; 2 TT-400TP

PBFG 8 *Osa* II with 4 single lnchr with 1 SS-N-2 AShM

PBFT 2 *Shershen*† (FSU) with 4 single 533mm TT

PHT 3 *Turya*† with 4 single 533mm TT

PH 2 *Turya*†

PB 26: 2 *Poluchat* (FSU); 14 *Zhuk*†; 4 *Zhuk* (mod); 6 (various)

PBR 4 *Stolkraft*

MINE WARFARE • MINE COUNTERMEASURES 13

MSO 2 *Yurka*

MSC 4 *Sonya*

MHI 2 *Yevgenya*

MSR 5 K-8

AMPHIBIOUS

LANDING SHIPS 6

LSM 3:

1 *Polnochny* A† (capacity 6 MBT; 180 troops)

2 *Polnochny* B† (capacity 6 MBT; 180 troops)

LST 3 LST-510-511 (US) (capacity 16 tanks; 200 troops)

LANDING CRAFT 30: 15 LCU; 12 LCM; 3 **LCVP**

LOGISTICS AND SUPPORT 27:

AKSL 20; **AWT** 1; **AGS** 1; **AGSH** 1; **AP** 1; **AT** 1; **SPT** 2 (floating dock)

Naval Infantry ε27,000

Navy Air Wing

FORCES BY ROLE

ASW/SAR

1 regt with EC225; Ka-28 (Ka-27PL) *Helix* A; Ka-32 *Helix* C

EQUIPMENT BY TYPE

HELICOPTERS

ASW 10 Ka-28 *Helix* A

TPT • Medium 4: 2 EC225; 2 Ka-32 *Helix* C

Air Force 30,000

3 air div, 1 tpt bde

FORCES BY ROLE

FIGHTER

4 regt with MiG-21bis *Fishbed* L; MiG-21UM *Mongol* B*

FIGHTER/GROUND ATTACK

1 regt with Su-22M3/M4/UM *Fitter* (some ISR)

1 regt with Su-27SK/Su-27UBK *Flanker*

1 regt with Su-27SK/Su-27UBK *Flanker*; Su-30MK2

1 regt with Su-30MK2

TRANSPORT

2 regt with An-2 *Colt*; An-26 *Curl*; Bell 205 (UH-1H *Iroquois*); Mi-8 *Hip*; Mi-17 *Hip* H; M-28 *Bryza*

TRAINING

1 regt with L-39 *Albatros*

1 regt with Yak-52

ATTACK/TRANSPORT HELICOPTER

1 regt with Mi-8 *Hip*; Mi-17 *Hip* H; Mi-171; Mi-24 *Hind*

AIR DEFENCE

4 ADA bde

Some (People's Regional) force (total: ε1,000 AD unit, 6 radar bde with 100 radar stn)

EQUIPMENT BY TYPE

AIRCRAFT 97 combat capable

FGA 97: 25 MiG-21bis *Fishbed* L & N; 8 MiG-21UM *Mongol* B; 30 Su-22M3/M4/UM *Fitter* (some ISR); 6 Su-27SK *Flanker*; 5 Su-27UBK *Flanker*; 23 Su-30MK2 *Flanker*

TPT • Light 18: 6 An-2 *Colt*; 12 An-26 *Curl*; 1 M-28 *Bryza*

TRG 48: 18 L-39 *Albatros*; 30 Yak-52

HELICOPTERS

ATK 26 Mi-24 *Hind*

MRH 6 Mi-17 *Hip* H

TPT 30 **Medium** 18: 14 Mi-8 *Hip*; 4 Mi-171; **Light** 12 Bell 205 (UH-1H *Iroquois*)

AD • SAM

SP 12+: 2K12 *Kub* (SA-6 *Gainful*); 12 S-300PMU1 (SA-20 *Gargoyle*)

TOWED S-75 *Dvina* (SA-2 *Guideline*); S-125 *Pechora* (SA-3 *Goa*)

MANPAD 9K32 *Strela*-2 (SA-7 *Grail*)‡; 9K310 *Igla*-1 (SA-16 *Gimlet*)

GUNS 37mm; 57mm; 85mm; 100mm; 130mm

MSL

ASM Kh-29T/L (AS-14 *Kedge*); Kh-31A (AS-17B *Krypton*); Kh-59M (AS-18 *Kazoo*)

ARM Kh-28 (AS-9 *Kyle*); Kh-31P (AS-17A *Krypton*)

AAM • IR R-3 (AA-2 *Atoll*)‡; R-60 (AA-8 *Aphid*); R-73 (AA-11 *Archer*); **IR/SARH** R-27 (AA-10 *Alamo*)

Paramilitary 40,000+ active

Border Defence Corps ε40,000

Marine Police

EQUIPMENT BY TYPE

PATROL AND COASTAL COMBATANTS 32+

PSO (1 DN-2000 in sea trials; expected ISD 2013 - one more vessel on order)

PCO 1+

PCC 3 TT-400

PBF 2 *Shershen*

PB 26: 12 TT-200; 13 TT-120; 1 other

LOGISTICS AND SUPPORT • ATF 3 (1 additional vessel in build; expected ISD early 2013)

AIRCRAFT • MP 1 C-212-400 MPA

Local Forces ε5,000,000 reservists

Incl People's Self-Defence Force (urban units), People's Militia (rural units); comprises of static and mobile cbt units, log spt and village protection pl; some arty, mor and AD guns; acts as reserve.

Asia

Table 16 **Selected Arms Procurements and Deliveries, Asia**

Designation	Type	Quantity	Contract Value	Supplier Country	Prime Contractor	Order Date	First Delivery Due	Notes
Afghanistan (AFG)								
G-222 (C-27A)	Tpt ac	2	US$287m	ITA	Fin-meccanica (Alenia Aeronautica)	2010	n/k	Additional order to original 18
Cessna 208B *Grand Caravan*	Tpt ac	26	see notes	US	Cessna	2011	2011	Part of US$88.5m order incl 6 Cessna T-182T ac. Delivery in progress
Cessna T-182T	Trg ac	6	see notes	US	Cessna	2011	n/k	Part of US$88.5m order incl 26 Cessna 208B ac
Australia (AUS)								
Bushmaster	PPV	315	n/k	FRA	Thales (Thales Australia)	2011	2012	Includes 214 extra ordered in 2012. Delivery in progress
Hobart-class	DDGHM	3	US$8bn	AUS/ESP	AWD Alliance	2007	2016	Air Warfare Destroyer programme (AWD). Delivery of vessels delayed to 2016, 2017 and 2019 respectively. Option on fourth vessel
Canberra-class	LHD	2	A$3.1bn (US$2.8bn)	AUS/ESP	Navantia	2007	2014	To replace HMAS *Tobruk* and *Kanimbla*-class. First vessel launched 2011; second in 2012
A330-200 (MRTT)	Tkr / Tpt ac	5	A$1.5bn (US$1.4 bn)	Int'l	EADS	2004	2011	(KC-30B). First ac handed over to RAAF Jun 2011. Final ac due for delivery Oct 2012
C-27J *Spartan*	Tpt ac	10	A$1.4bn (US$1.4bn)	ITA	Fin-meccanica (Alenia Aermacchi)	2012	2015	Contract price includes logistics support and training. Delivery to be completed in 2016
MH-60R *Seahawk*	ASW Hel	24	US$3bn+	US	UTC (Sikorsky)	2011	2013	To replace navy's S-70Bs. First two to be delivered Dec 2013
NH90	Tpt Hel	46	A$2bn (US$1.47bn)	Int'l	NH Industries	2005	2007	12 ordered 2005; additional 34 in 2006; 6 for navy, 40 for army. Deliveries ongoing
CH-47F *Chinook*	Tpt Hel	7	A$755m (US$670m)	US	Boeing	2010	2014	All to be operational by 2017. To replace CH-47Ds
Bangladesh (BGD)								
MBT-2000	MBT	44	Tk 12bn	PRC	NORINCO	2011	n/k	Order also includes three ARVs. Delivery to be completed in 2013
NORA B-52	Arty (155mm SP)	18	n/k	SER	Yugoimport	2011	n/k	–
n/k	FSGHM	2	US$50m	PRC	Wuchang Shipyard	2009	2012	First vessel launched Aug 2012; delivery expected by end-2012. Possibly similar to PAK *Azmat* class
n/k	PCC	5	US$42m	BGD	Khulna Shipyard	2010	2012	All vessels to be delivered by Dec 2013. Incl technology agreement with China Shipbuilding and Offshore International Corporation
F-7BGI	Ftr ac	16	n/k	PRC	AVIC (Chengdu Aircraft Corporation)	2011	2012	12 F-7BGI and four FT-7BGI; first ac delivered late 2012. Delivery to be completed in 2013
Brunei (BRN)								
S-70i	Tpt Hel	12	n/k	US	UTC (Sikorsky)	2011	2013	Option for additional ten

Table 16 **Selected Arms Procurements and Deliveries, Asia**

Designation	Type	Quantity	Contract Value	Supplier Country	Prime Contractor	Order Date	First Delivery Due	Notes
China, People's Republic of (PRC)								
JL-2 (CSS-NX-5)	SLBM	n/k	n/k	PRC	n/k	1985	2009	In development; range 8,000km. Reportedly to equip new Type-094 SSBN. ISD uncertain
Type-96A	MBT	n/k	n/k	PRC	NORINCO	n/k	n/k	Delivery in progress
Type-99A/A2	MBT	n/k	n/k	PRC	NORINCO	n/k	n/k	In limited production
Type-05 (ZBD-05)	AIFV	n/k	n/k	PRC	n/k	n/k	n/k	Amphibious assault veh family. Issued to marine and amph army units
Type-08 (ZBD-08)	AIFV	n/k	n/k	PRC	NORINCO	n/k	2011	IFV Family. Improved version of Type-04 with extra armour
Type-09 (ZBL-09)	APC (W)	n/k	n/k	PRC	n/k	n/k	n/k	8×8 APC being issued to lt mech units
Type-09 (PLL-09)	Arty (122mm SP)	n/k	n/k	PRC	n/k	n/k	n/k	ZBL-09 chassis fitted with 122mm how
Type-07 (PLZ-07)	Arty (122mm SP)	n/k	n/k	PRC	n/k	n/k	n/k	122mm tracked SP how; first displayed in public at 2009 parade
Type-09 (PLC-09)	Arty (122mm SP)	n/k	n/k	PRC	n/k	n/k	n/k	Truck-mounted 122mm how. Also referred to as AH2
Type-05 (PLZ-05)	Arty (155mm SP)	n/k	n/k	PRC	n/k	n/k	n/k	155mm tracked SP how; first displayed in public at 2009 parade
Type-03	Arty (300mm MRL)	n/k	n/k	PRC	n/k	n/k	n/k	8×8 truck-mounted MRL; also referred to as AR2
HQ-16	SAM	n/k	n/k	PRC	n/k	n/k	2011	First delivered to 39th Group Army in 2011
Type-07 (PGZ-07)	SPAAG	n/k	n/k	PRC	n/k	n/k	n/k	Twin 35mm-armed tracked SPAAG
Jin-class	SSBN	5	n/k	PRC	Huludao Shipyard	1985	2008	Type-094. Commissioning status unclear; 3 vessels believed to be in service; up to 2 more awaiting commissioning
Yuan-class	SSK	7	n/k	PRC	Wuhan Shipyard	n/k	2006	Type-039A/B
Luyang II-class	DDGHM	6	n/k	PRC	Jiangnan Shipyard	2002	2004	Type-052C. Sixth vessel launched Jun 2012.
Luyang III-class	DDGHM	2	n/k	PRC	Jiangnan Shipyard	n/k	2013	Type-052D. First vessel launched Aug 2012
Jiangkai II-class	FFGHM	16	n/k	PRC	Huangpu Shipyard/ Hudong Shipyard	2005	2008	Type-054A. 14th & 15th vessels launched 2012; expected ISD for both 2013
Type-056	FS	n/k	n/k	PRC	Huangpu Shipyard/ Hudong Shipyard/ Wuchang Shipyard	n/k	n/k	6 vessels launched by Aug 2012. Undergoing sea trials
Yuzhao-class	LPD	3	n/k	PRC	Hudong Shipyard	2006	2008	Type-071. Second vessel commissioned 2012; third launched 2011
Zubr-class	LCAC	4	US$315m	PRC/UKR	PLAN/Morye Shipyard	2010	2012	2 to be constructed in Ukraine, 2 in China. First delivered Nov 2012
J-10A/S	FGA ac	n/k	n/k	PRC	AVIC (Chengdu Aircraft Corporation)	n/k	2004	In service with PLAAF and PLANAF. Improved J-10B variant currently in flight test

Table 16 **Selected Arms Procurements and Deliveries, Asia**

Designation	Type	Quantity	Contract Value	Supplier Country	Prime Contractor	Order Date	First Delivery Due	Notes
J-11B/BS	FGA ac	n/k	n/k	PRC	AVIC (Shenyang Aircraft Corporation)	n/k	2007	Upgraded J-11; now fitted with indigenous WS-10 engines. In service with PLAAF and PLANAF
J-15A/S	FGA ac	n/k	n/k	PRC	AVIC (Shenyang Aircraft Corporation)	n/k	n/k	Production under way
JH-7A	FGA ac	n/k	n/k	PRC	AVIC (Xian Aircraft Corporation)	n/k	2004	Low-rate production likely continues
Y-9	Tpt ac	n/k	n/k	PRC	AVIC (Shaanxi Aircraft Corporation)	n/k	2012	In service with 4th PLAAF division
JL-9	Trg ac	n/k	n/k	PRC	GAIC	n/k	n/k	Delivery in progress; in service with PLANAF
Z-10	Atk Hel	n/k	n/k	PRC	Harbin	n/k	n/k	In production; in service with at least 4 army avn bde
Z-19	Atk Hel	n/k	n/k	PRC		n/k	n/k	In service with at least 2 army avn bde
Mi-171E	Tpt Hel	52	n/k	RUS	Rosoboron-export	2012	2012	8 to be delivered in 2012; remainder in 2013–14

India (IND)								
Agni V	IRBM/ICBM	n/k	n/k	IND	DRDO	n/k	2012	In development. 5,000km+ range
Prithvi II	SRBM	54	INR12.13bn	IND	Bharat Dynamics	2006	n/k	For air force
Sagarika K-15	SLBM	n/k	n/k	IND	Bharat Dynamics	1991	n/k	Test-firing programme under way. Est. 700km range with 1 tonne payload
Brahmos Block II (Land Attack)	AShM/LACM	n/k	US$1.73bn	IND/RUS	Brahmos Aerospace	2010	n/k	To equip additional 2 regiments
Nirbhay	ALCM	n/k	n/k	IND	DRDO	n/k	n/k	In development
T-90S *Bhishma*	MBT	347	US$1.23bn	IND/RUS	Avadi Heavy Vehicles	2007	n/k	Delivery in progress
Arjun Mk II	MBT	124	n/k	IND	CVRDE	2010	2014	Upgraded variant. Currently in trials. To be delivered by 2016.
Akash	SAM	36	INR12bn (US$244m)	IND	DRDO	2009	2009	To equip 2 AD squadrons.
Akash	SAM	12 bty	INR125bn (US$2.77bn)	IND	DRDO	2009	2009	To equip 3 army regiments
Akash	SAM	96	INR42.7bn	IND	DRDO	2010	n/k	To equip 6 AD squadrons. For the IAF
Medium-range SAM	SAM/AD	18 units	US$1.4bn	ISR	IAI	2009	2016	For air force. Development and procurement contract for a medium-range version of the *Barak* long-range naval AD system
Advanced Technology Vessel (ATV)	SSBN	5	n/k	IND	DRDO	n/k	2012	SSBN development programme. INS *Arihant* launched Jul 2009; expected ISD 2012. Second keel launched mid-2011
Scorpene	SSK	6	INR235.62bn	FRA/IND	DCNS	2005	2012	First delivery delayed until 2014/5. Option for a further 6 SSK
Kiev-class	CV	1	US$2.5bn	RUS	Rosoboron-export	1999	2013	*Admiral Gorshkov*. Incl 16 MiG 29 K. To be renamed INS *Vikramaditya*. Delivery delayed again, until Oct 2013, due to boiler problems

Table 16 Selected Arms Procurements and Deliveries, Asia

Designation	Type	Quantity	Contract Value	Supplier Country	Prime Contractor	Order Date	First Delivery Due	Notes
Project 71 (Indigenous Aircraft Carrier)	CV	1	US$730m	IND	Cochin Shipyard	2001	2015	To be named *Vikant*. Formerly known as Air Defence Ship (ADS). Expected ISD has slipped to 2015. Second vessel of class anticipated
Shivalik II-class	DDGHM	7	INR450bn (US$9.24 bn)	IND	Mazagon Dock/GRSE	2009	2014	Project 17A. Requires shipyard upgrade
Project 15A (*Kolkata* -class)	DDGHM	3	US$1.75bn	IND	Mazagon Dock	2000	2013	First of class launched 2006, second launched in 2009, third launched in 2010. First delivery delayed, first commissioning expected in 2013
Project 15B	DDGHM	4	US$6.5bn	IND	Mazagon Dock	2011	2017	Follow-on from *Kolkata*-class with increased stealth capabilities
Talwar II-class	FFGHM	3	US$1.5bn	RUS	Yantar Shipyard	2006	2012	Option exercised 2006. First vessel commissioned Apr 2012; second vessel completed sea trials Aug 2012; third scheduled for delivery mid-2013
Kamorta-class (Project 28)	FFGHM	4	INR70bn	IND	GRSE	2003	2012	ASW role. First of class commissioned Aug 2012; second in Oct 2012. Third in build
Saryu-class	PSOH	4	n/k	IND	Goa Shipyard	2006	2012	2 launched in 2009; third and fourth in 2010. First due to commission by end-2012
105m OPV	PSO	6	n/k	IND	Goa Shipyard	2012	n/k	For coast guard
Griffon 8000TD	LCAC	12	£34m	UK	Griffon Hoverwork	2010	2012	For coast guard. First delivered Jun 2012
Makar-class	AGS	6	INR7bn (US$127m)	IND	Alcock Ashdown	2006	2012	Catamarans. First vessel commissioned Sep 2012, second launched Mar 2010. Delivery to be completed in 2016
3M14E *Klub*-S (SS-N-27 *Sizzler*)	SLCM	28	INR8.44bn (US$182m)	RUS	Novator Design Bureau	2006	n/k	For a number of *Sindhughosh*-class SSK
Brahmos PJ-10	ASCM	n/k	US$2bn	IND/RUS	Brahmos Aerospace	2006	2010	Built jointly with RUS. For army, navy and air force. Air and submarine launch versions undergoing testing
Su-30MKI	FGA ac	140	see notes	IND/RUS	HAL/Rosoboronexport	2000	n/k	Delivered in kit form and completed in IND under licence. Part of a 1996 US$8.5bn deal for 238 Su-30. Final delivery due 2015
Su-30MKI	FGA ac	40	US$1.6bn	RUS	Rosoboronexport	2007	2008	First 4 delivered early 2008
Su-30MKI	FGA ac	42	INR150bn (US$3.3bn)	RUS	HAL/Rosoboronexport	2010	n/k	Delivery to be complete by 2016–7. 40 + 2 accident replacements. Delivery to be completed in 2017
MiG-29K *Fulcrum* D	FGA ac	29	US$1.5bn	RUS	Rosoboronexport	2010	n/k	Flight trials due to begin by end-2012
Tejas	FGA ac	20+	INR20bn (US$445m)	IND	HAL	2005	2011	Limited series production
P-8I *Poseidon*	ASW ac	8	US$2.1bn	US	Boeing	2009	2013	Deliveries due 2013–5
Il-76TD *Phalcon*	AEW&C ac	3	US$1bn	ISR/RUS	IAI	2008	2009	Option on 2003 contract exercised
EMB-145	AEW&C ac	3	US$210m	BRZ	Embraer	2008	2014	Part of a INR18bn (US$400m) AEW&C project. Ac due to enter into service with the air force in 2014
C-17A *Globemaster* III	Tpt ac	10	US$4.1bn	US	Boeing	2011	2013	Delivery to occur 2013–14
Hawk Mk132 Advanced Jet Trainer	Trg ac	57	US$780m	IND	HAL	2010	2013	40 for air force and 17 for navy. Delivery to be complete by 2016

Asia

Table 16 **Selected Arms Procurements and Deliveries, Asia**

Designation	Type	Quantity	Contract Value	Supplier Country	Prime Contractor	Order Date	First Delivery Due	Notes
PC-7 *Turbo Trainer* MkII	Trg ac	75	n/k	CHE	Pilatus	2012	2012	To replace HPT-32s. First delivery due late 2012
Dhruv	MRH Hel	245	n/k	IND	HAL	2004	2004	159 Dhruvs and 76 Dhruv-WSI. Deliveries ongoing
Mi-17V-5 *Hip*	MRH Hel	80	INR58.41bn (US$1.2bn)	RUS	Rosoboron-export	2008	2011	To be weaponised and replace current Mi-8 fleet. Final delivery due 2014
AW101 *Merlin*	Tpt Hel	12	€560m	ITA	Finmeccanica (Agusta Westland)	2010	2012	For air force VIP tpt
AGM-84 *Harpoon* Block II	AShM	24	US$170m	US	Boeing	2010	n/k	For integration on *Jaguar* maritime strike ac. Possible additional purchase of AGM-84L Block II for P-8I MPA

Indonesia (IDN)

Designation	Type	Quantity	Contract Value	Supplier Country	Prime Contractor	Order Date	First Delivery Due	Notes
Leopard 2A4	MBT	103	US$280m	GER	Rheinmetall	2012	2012	Bundeswehr surplus. Final delivery due 2014
Black Fox 6×6	AIFV	22	US$70m	ROK	Doosan DST	2009	2012	Delivery to be complete in 2013
BMP-3F	AIFV	37	US$100m	RUS	Rosoboron-export	2012	n/k	For marines; second order following deliver of 17 in Nov 2010
Marder 1A3	AIFV	50	n/k	GER	Rheinmetall	2012	n/k	
Anoa 6×6	APC (W)	31	Rp250bn	IDN	PT Pindad	2012	n/k	
CAESAR	155mm SP Arty	37	n/k	FRA	Nexter	2012	2014	All to be delivered in 2014
Type-209/1200	SSK	3	US$1.1bn	ROK/IDN	DSME/PT PAL	2012	2015	First to be built in ROK; second to be partially assembled in IDN and third to be largely built in IDN. Delivery to be completed in 2020
SIGMA 10514	FFGHM	1	US$220m	NLD	Damen Schelde Naval Shipbuilding	2012	2016	Further acquisitions are expected, with technology transfers allowing greater proportions to be built in IDN
KCR-60	PCGM	3	n/k	IDN	PT PAL	2011	n/k	Construction begun mid-2012
Clurit-class	PBG	n/k	see notes	IDN	PT Palindo Marine	2012	n/k	KCR-40. Follow on contract from initial order. Up to 14 planned. Unit cost εRp73bn (US$8m)
X3K Trimaran	PBG	4	εRp456bn (US$50m)	IDN	PT Lundin Industry Invest	2012	2012	MoU signed Nov 2010; contract signed Jan 2012. First vessel launched Aug 2012, but subsequently suffered catastrophic fire. Delivery to be completed in 2014
Su-30MK2	FGA ac	6	n/k	RUS	Rosoboron-export	2011	2012	2 ac to be delivered annually 2012–14
C-295	Tpt ac	9	US$325m	Int'l	EADS (CASA)	2012	2012	First 2 ac delivered late 2012. Final ac to be delivered mid-2014
C-130H *Hercules*	Tpt ac	4	free transfer	AUS	government transfer	2012	2012	AUS surplus aircraft
EMB-314 *Super Tucano*	Trg ac	16	US$284m	BRZ	Embraer	2010	2012	Second batch of eight ordered 2012, to be delivered in 2014
T-50 *Golden Eagle*	Trg ac	16	εUS$400m	ROK	KAI	2011	2013	Delivery to be complete in 2013
Bell 412EP	MR hel	20	US$250m	IDN	PT Dirgantara	2011	2012	Manufactured under license from Bell Helicopter
EC725 *Cougar*	Tpt Hel	6	n/k	Int'l	Eurocopter	2012	2014	To be delivered to PT Dirgantara for modification before final delivery

Table 16 **Selected Arms Procurements and Deliveries, Asia**

Designation	Type	Quantity	Contract Value	Supplier Country	Prime Contractor	Order Date	First Delivery Due	Notes
Japan (JPN)								
Theatre Missile Defence System	BMD	n/k	n/k	JPN/US	n/k	1997	n/k	Joint development with US from 1998. Programme ongoing and incl SM-3 and PAC-3 systems
Type-10	MBT	68	¥55.1bn (US$679m)	JPN	MHI	2010	2011	Final delivery due 2015
Soryu-class	SSK	6	n/k	JPN	KHI / MHI	2004	2009	Second batch may be ordered. Fourth vessels delivered. Fifth launched Oct 2011; ISD expected early 2013
22DDH	CVH	2	US$1.3bn	JPN	IHI Marine United	2010	2014	Keel of first vessel laid Jan 2012
Akizuki-class (19DD)	DDGHM	4	¥84.8bn (US$700m)	JPN	MHI	2007	2012	To replace the oldest 5 *Hatsuyuki*-class. First vessel commissioned 2012; further three ISD expected 2013–14
Hirashima-class (improved)	MSO	2	n/k	JPN	Universal Shipbuilding Corporation	n/k	2012	—
Standard Missile 3 (SM-3) Block IIA	SAM	n/k	US$1.1bn	US	Raytheon	2006	2014	Upgrade of Japanese SM-3 capabilities. Final delivery due 2016
AH-64D *Apache*	Atk Hel	13	n/k	US	Boeing	2001	2006	Up to six in *Longbow* config. Original ambition for 62 abandoned on cost grounds.
AW101 *Merlin*/ MCH-101	ASW/ MCM Hel	14	n/k	ITA/JPN/UK	Finmeccanica (Agusta Westland)/ KHI	2003	2006	For JMSDF to replace MH-53E and S-61 hel under MCH-X program
Enstrom 480B	Trg Hel	30	n/k	US	Enstrom Helicopter Corporation	2010	2010	Delivery to be complete by 2014. For JGSDF
South Korea (ROK)								
K2	MBT	Up to 400	n/k	ROK	Hyundai Rotem	2007	2013	Production delayed due to problems with engine and transmission
K21	AIFV	ε500	US$3.5m per unit	ROK	Doosan Infracore	2008	2009	Delivery resumed after accident investigation
Spike NLOS	SP AT	67	US$43m	ISR	Rafael	2011	2012	For deployment on Baengnyeong and Yeonpyeong islands
M-SAM (Multi-function Surface to Air Missile)	SAM	n/k	n/k	ROK	n/k	1998	n/k	In development. To replace current army MIM-23B HAWK SAMs.
Son Won-il-class	SSK	6	εUS$3bn	ROK	DSME	2008	2014	KSS-II (Type-214). Second batch of six. Expected ISD of first boat 2014. Delivery to be completed in 2018
KSS-III	SSK	n/k	n/k	ROK	DSME/ Hyundai Heavy Industries	2007	2017	Contract for design signed in 2007. No contract for build yet signed. Expected class to include VLS, but cost concerns have delayed progress
Sejong Daewang-class	CGHM	3	n/k	ROK	DSME	2002	2008	KDX-3. Third vessel expected to commission mid-2013
Incheon-class	FFGHM	6	KRW1.7bn (US$1.8bn)	ROK	Hyundai Heavy Industries	2006	2013	FFX. First vessel launched May 2011. Fourth and fifth vessels contracted to STX Marine
LST II	LPD	4	n/k	ROK	Hanjin Heavy Industries	2011	2014	

Asia

Table 16 **Selected Arms Procurements and Deliveries, Asia**

Designation	Type	Quantity	Contract Value	Supplier Country	Prime Contractor	Order Date	First Delivery Due	Notes
Falcon 2000LX	ELINT ac	2	n/k	FRA	Dassault	2012	n/k	To replace Hawker 800SIGs
C-130J-30 *Hercules*	Tpt ac	4	εUS$500m	US	Lockheed Martin	2011	2014	
Surion	Tpt Hel	up to 242	up to KRW8bn	ROK	KAI	2012	2013	KUH. 24 to be delivered by end-2013. All to be delivered by end-2017
Malaysia (MYS)								
AV8 *Pars* 8×8	APC (W)	257	US$559m	MYS/TUR/ UK/US	FNSS	2010	2012	Letter of intent signed Apr 2010. To include 12 variants
Second Generation Patrol Vessel (SGPV)	FF	6	RM9bn (US$2.8bn)	MYS	Boustead Naval Shipyard	2011	2017	Licence-built DCNS Gowind 100m design
A400M *Atlas*	Tpt ac	4	RM907m (US$246m)	Int'l	EADS (Airbus)	2006	2016	In development. Official unit cost US$80m. First deliveries delayed until at least 2016
EC725 *Cougar*	Tpt Hel	12	RM1.6bn (US$500m)	Int'l	Eurocopter	2010	2012	8 for air force, 4 for army. First delivery due Dec 2012. Delivery to be completed in 2013
Myanmar (MMR)								
MiG-29 *Fulcrum*	Ftr ac	20	US$570m	RUS	Rosoboron-export	2009	2011	First 6 delivered 2011. Delivery to be completed by end-2012. Aircraft variant remains to be determined
K-8 *Karakorum*	Trg ac	50	n/k	PRC	Hongdu	2009	2010	Deliveries ongoing
New Zealand (NZL)								
NH90 TTH	Tpt Hel	9	NZ$771m (US$477m)	Int'l	NH Industries	2006	2011	8 operational and 1 attrition airframe. 5 delivered by late 2012; 4 more due by end-2013
AW109	Tpt Hel	5	NZ$139m (US$109m)	ITA	Fin-meccanica (Agusta Westland)	2008	2011	First hel delivered Mar 2011. Likely to replace Bell 47G-3B *Sioux*
Pakistan (PAK)								
Hatf 8 (Raad)	ALCM	n/k	n/k	PAK	n/k	n/k	n/k	In development. Successfully test fired
Al Khalid (MBT 2000)	MBT	460	n/k	PAK	Heavy Industries Taxila	1999	2001	
Spada 2000	AD system	10	€415m	ITA	MBDA	2007	2009	Delivery in progress. Final delivery due 2013
Zulfiquar-class	FFGHM	4	see notes	PAK/PRC	Hudong-Zhonghua Shipbuilding	2005	2009	Improved version of *Jiangwei* II FF. fourth ship to be built indigenously at Karachi. Deal worth est. US$750m incl 6 Z-9EC hels. 3 vessels in service; final delivery due 2013
Azmat-class	FSG	2	n/k	PRC/PAK	Xinggang Shipyard / KS&EW	2010	2012	First vessel built in PRC and commissioned May 2012. Second built in PAK and launched Aug 2012
JF-17 (FC-1)	FGA ac	150	n/k	PAK/PRC	PAC	2006	2008	150 currently on order; plans for total order of 200–300. 26 produced in PAK by mid-2011
F-16 Block 15 *Fighting Falcon*	FGA ac upgrade	42	US$75m	TUR	TAI	2009	2014	Upgrade to Block 40 standard

Table 16 Selected Arms Procurements and Deliveries, Asia

Designation	Type	Quantity	Contract Value	Supplier Country	Prime Contractor	Order Date	First Delivery Due	Notes
Saab 2000 *Erieye*	AEW&C ac	4	SEK8.3bn (US$1.05bn)	SWE	Saab	2006	2009	Plus one tpt ac for trg. Order reduced from 6 ac.
ZDK-03 (KJ-200)	AEW&C ac	4	n/k	PAK/PRC	n/k	2008	2011	Second ac delivered early 2012

Philippines (PHL)								
SF-260F/PAF	Trg ac	18	US$13.1m	ITA	Alenia Aermacchi	2008	2010	Contract renegotiated. First 8 delivered 2010. Final delivery due 2012
C-130 Hercules	Tpt ac	2	n/k	US	Lockheed Martin	2012	2012	To be delivered by end-2012
W-3 *Sokol*	Tpt Hel	8	PHP2.8bn (US$59.8m)	ITA	Finmeccanica (PZL Świdnik)	2010	2012	First 4 delivered Feb 2012. Remainder due by Nov 2012

Singapore (SGP)								
Archer-class	SSK	2	US$127m	SWE	Kockums	2005	2011	*Archer* commissioned Dec 2011; *Swordsman* to follow
F-15SG *Eagle*	FGA ac	12	n/k	US	Boeing	2007	2010	Incl 28 GBU-10 and 56 GBU-12 PGM. Delivery to be complete in 2012
M-346 *Master*	Trg ac	12	SG$543m (US$411m)	ITA/SGP	ST Aerospace	2010	2012	To be based at Cazaux in France. Delivery to begin in 2012

Sri Lanka (LKA)								
MA60	Tpt ac	4	n/k	PRC	AVIC	2010	2011	First two delivered Oct 2011; delivery status of remaining ac unclear
Mi-171	Tpt hel	14	n/k	RUS	Rosoboron-export	2012	n/k	Part of order funded by US$300m 10-year loan from Russia

Taiwan (ROC)								
CM-32 *Yunpao*	APC (W)	up to 650	n/k	ROC	Ordnance Readiness Development Centre	2010	2011	To replace existing M113s. Delivery in progress
Patriot PAC-3	AD	Up to 6	US$6bn	US	Raytheon	2009	n/k	FMS purchase of at least 4 additional OFUs. 3 existing being upgraded PAC-2 to PAC-3
P-3C *Orion*	ASW ac	12	US$1.3bn	US	Lockheed Martin	2010	2013	Refurbished by Lockheed Martin
E-2C *Hawkeye* 2000	AEW&C ac upgrade	6	US$154m	US	Northrop Grumman	2009	2011	Upgrade from Group II config to *Hawkeye* 2000 (H2K) export config. Delivery to be completed by 2013
AH-64D Block III *Apache Longbow*	Atk Hel	30	US$2.5bn	US	Boeing	2010	2014	–
UH-60M *Black Hawk*	Tpt Hel	4	US$91.8m	US	UTC (Sikorsky)	2011	2014	To be modified to unique Taiwan configuration. Up to 60 to be procured
AGM-84L *Harpoon* Block II	AShM	60	US$89m	US	Boeing	2007	2009	For F-16s. Delivery under way
Hsiung Feng IIE	AShM	n/k	n/k	ROC	CSIST	2005	n/k	In production
Hsiung Feng III	AShM	n/k	n/k	ROC	CSIST	n/k	n/k	–

Thailand (THA)								
T-84 *Oplot*	MBT	49	US$241m	UKR	KMP	2011	2013	–

Table 16 **Selected Arms Procurements and Deliveries, Asia**

Designation	Type	Quantity	Contract Value	Supplier Country	Prime Contractor	Order Date	First Delivery Due	Notes
BTR-3E1 8x8	AIFV	102	THB4bn (US$134m)	UKR	KMDB	2007	2010	Amphibious APC. Initial order for 96 increased to 102 (including 14 for the marines)
BTR-3E1 8x8	AIFV	121	US$140m	UKR	KMDB	2011	2013	–
OPV	PSO	1	n/k	THA	Bangkok Dock	2009	2012	Built to BAE design. Launched Dec 2011; expected ISD 2013
M36 Patrol Craft	PCC	3	THB553m (US$18m)	THA	Marsun	2012	n/k	Possible further order for six more vessels
Gripen C/D	FGA ac	6	see notes	SWE	Saab	2010	2013	THB14.8bn (US$415.5m) incl one 340 Erieye
Saab 340 Erieye	AEW ac	1	see notes	SWE	Saab	2010	n/k	THB14.8bn (US$415.5m) incl 6 Gripen
EC725 Cougar	Tpt Hel	4	εUS$130m	Int'l	Eurocopter	2012	n/k	SAR configuration
AW139	MR Hel	2	n/k	ITA	Finmeccanica (Agusta Westland)	2012	2014	For army

Vietnam (VNM)								
Gepard-class	FFGM	2	n/k	RUS	Rosoboron-export	2011	n/k	Follow on order form original 2005 contract. Reportedly to be fitted for ASW
Kilo-class	SSK	6	US$1.8bn	RUS	Rosoboron-export	2009	2012	First vessel launched Aug 2012. Delivery to be completed by end-2016
n/k	PSOH	2	n/k	VNM	189 Shipbuilding Company	2011	2012	For marine police. CSB 8001 and 8002
VNREDSat-1	Sat	1	US$100m	FRA/VNM	EADS (Astrium)/ VAST	2009	2014	Remote sensing; launch delayed until 2014
DHC-6 Twin Otter	Tpt ac	6	n/k	CAN	Viking Air	2010	2012	For MP role. To be delivered 2012–14

Chapter Seven
Middle East and North Africa

CIVIL–MILITARY RELATIONS AFTER THE ARAB SPRING

The Arab uprisings of 2011 have led to a recalibration in relations between armed forces and the state across the Middle East. The magnitude of the shift varies across the region, producing a new relationship between militaries and civilian governments in places such as Tunisia and Egypt, while in other states – notably where regimes resisted the uprisings – existing structures and practices were reinforced. But despite this recalibration, there has yet to be a transformation of the fundamental basis of civil–military relations across the region.

Transitions without conflict: Tunisia and Egypt

With signs that norms of professionalism can flourish and comprehensive civilian control can eventually be established in formerly autocratic regimes, Tunisia is a relative bright spot. Its armed forces have traditionally been small by regional standards, poorly resourced and deliberately isolated from the institutions of the state. There had been dramatic growth, notably under President Zine El Abidine Ben Ali, of security services and militia controlled by the Interior Ministry and in some cases informally by the palace, which further reduced the military's political role. Unlike the Egyptian or Syrian armed forces, the Tunisian military did not have a significant institutional or informal role in the economy and has remained largely isolated from domestic politics. Although this was largely the result of Ben Ali's strategy to insulate the regime against challenges from within the military, the effect has been to allow autonomy and the development of professional norms among Tunisian officers. The military thus did not have a vested interest in the Ben Ali regime and was willing to defect from it; moreover, Tunisia's military has less to lose institutionally from democratisation than does its Egyptian counterpart. Still, the Tunisian armed forces' apolitical and professional tendencies should not be over-stated: the decision to side against the Ben Ali regime and not defend it with force was as much the result of political calculations than of professional norms. The military also retains significant autonomy and authority, reflected for example in the September 2012 conviction of a former presidential adviser for criticising the army. How much the Tunisian military will subordinate its institutions to civilian control remains to be seen. The extent to which the Tunisian military stays outside of politics is a result of historical dynamics and the Ben Ali regime's formula for sustaining political control, and not evidence of a consolidation or transformation in civilian control of the military. The Tunisian experience may, therefore, not be easily replicated in other Arab states.

Egypt has also undergone significant change, including a recalibration of the authority and responsibilities of the civilian government and armed forces. In a key development in August 2012, President Muhammad Morsi seized significant authority when he nullified constitutional rules limiting the powers of the president that had been put in place by the armed forces. At the same time, he removed Defence Minister Field Marshal Hussein Tantawi and General Sami Anan, the army chief, as well as the commanders of the navy, air force and air-defence forces. Some analysts contended that these decisions could have been driven by Tantawi's unpopularity with junior officers or even a deal with Tantawi's successor General Abdel Fatah Al-Sisi, the former head of military intelligence. Whatever the precise drivers, Morsi's actions removed some of the key leaders of the Supreme Council of the Armed Forces (SCAF).

Relations between the civilian authorities and the military, however, remain defined by a carefully negotiated bargain in which senior officers retain

Table 17 **North Africa: Active Military Strength 2013**

Algeria	130,000
Egypt	438,500
Libya	n.k
Mauritania	15,870
Morocco	195,800
Tunisia	35,800

significant leverage. Morsi's actions did not challenge the core corporate interests of the military, which entail maintaining institutional autonomy and prestige, while protecting internal cohesion (which, by many reports, has been stressed by disillusionment among junior officers over their superiors' management of the armed forces). Safeguarding control of the armed forces' significant economic assets is also a critical interest. These enterprises, from manufacturing to agriculture to service industries, are not, like the defence budget, subject to parliamentary control. They allow senior officers access to key positions and salaries. Shielding this military-run economy and the institution's autonomy and privileges from civilian control will remain a priority and there is little evidence that Morsi, or anyone else, has the ability to challenge those prerogatives in the foreseeable future. According to a June 2012 Reuters article, 'Military leaders boast that their businesses help the country. Mahmud Nasr, [then] Tantawi's assistant on financial affairs, said the army has given the state 12 billion Egyptian pounds (US$1.99 billion) since early last year.' While the senior leadership may recognise the harm done to the armed forces and its prestige by the form of direct governance seen after Mubarak's ouster, and may be willing to tolerate some personnel changes, that does not mean the generals are ready to abandon their stakes in the regime. They will continue to be important behind-the-scenes actors.

Egypt's unique geographical and political position in the region is a further complication. The armed forces and government face serious issues in balancing international pressures and incentives while accommodating domestic opinion. Most notably, it complicates efforts to sustain constructive relations with Israel and, as evident in the Morsi government's response to anti-American protests in mid-2012, with the United States. Maintaining positive relations with Washington is essential to sustain ongoing American aid, which largely benefits the Egyptian military, and for maintaining US support for International Monetary Fund assistance, which is essential to Egypt's economic and political stability. Another critical issue is the security vacuum in the Sinai Peninsula, evidenced by insurgent attacks on Israeli targets and incidents such as the killing of Egyptian border guards in August 2012, which provided the backdrop for the replacement of Tantawi and other senior leaders in the same month.

The other side of the coin: autocratic response

The changes in Egypt and Tunisia could lay a path to more fundamental changes in civil–military relations. However, in other regimes, protests have led to a reinforcement of the autocratic bargain: the armed forces' leverage increases concomitantly with the regime's reliance on coercive force to maintain order. In Bahrain, for example, authorities responded to the uprisings by increasing salaries and incentives and through symbolic steps such as awarding medals to members of armed forces. Qatar also raised military salaries, while Saudi Arabia announced bonuses and promotions for military personnel. In Jordan, where the regime has offered limited political concessions while continuing to police and monitor opposition forces to head-off the emergence of a sizeable protest movement, the king has also been attentive to the private and corporate interests of the military. In Yemen, where the armed forces remain divided in their loyalties (and still battle an insurgency in the country's south), the government has sought to reduce the influence of former President Ali Abdullah Saleh through appointments and reassignments, including the creation of a new presidential protection force. None of these methods of sustaining political control and securing the loyalty of the armed forces are novel; they are long-standing practices used by the region's authoritarian regimes.

Awaiting meaningful reform

The absence of reform of the police and other non-military security forces is a serious issue, particularly in states in transition such as Egypt and Tunisia. Lack of reform has led to cynicism within the population, but is also a broader challenge to the effective promotion of institutional change and democratic governance. There have been some personnel changes, but in both countries changes to Interior Ministry staff, or fundamental restructuring and organisational change, remain elusive even if leaders are inclined to pursue such moves. As they stand, the actions of police forces have shown, according to some observers, an alarming mixture of ineptitude, brutality and corruption. In Tunisia, there have been significant, and in some cases, serious civil disturbances since Ben Ali's ouster, especially in the centre of the country (notably the Gafsa region), but also in the wealthier coastal areas. Both Cairo and Tunis require the support of police and security forces to maintain social order and stability, but lack the political wherewithal to

Table 18 **Libya: selected militias in 2012**

Tabu Brigade
Misrata Brigade
Zintan Brigade
Zawya Brigade
Libya Shield Brigade (reportedly government-aligned)
Awfia Brigade
Rafallah Sahaty Brigade
Ansar al-Sharia
Al-Sawaiq Brigade for Protection (reportedly government-aligned)
Martyrs of Abu-Salim Brigade
Al-Qaqa Brigade (reportedly government-aligned)
Martyrs of 17 February Brigade (conflicting reports of alignment)
Other armed groups are aligned to towns and tribes

(Sources: UN Report August 2012, BBC)

promote changes that could threaten the positions and prerogative of the individuals on whom they depend. In turn, the actions of police and security forces in many cases contribute to ongoing instability and act as a rallying cry for protesters and disaffected citizens.

Security-sector reform (SSR) has been discussed in Tunisia, and non-governmental organisations have been actively promoting dialogue on such issues. However, given the long-standing entrenchment of authoritarian regimes, systematic efforts towards SSR have historically been largely unknown in the Arab world, and contemporary challenges to promoting comprehensive change are significant. In places such as Egypt, and elsewhere in the Arab world, senior officers and leaders of armed and police forces are apt to resist changes that involve incursions on internal autonomy, let alone challenges to organisational resources and individual benefits. The challenges to reform are even more acute in Libya, where militias have supplanted police forces and government in providing local security and in some cases social services, and whose leaders are fiercely protective of their status and suspicious of the national army and police.

Even if SSR programmes are developed, Libya's continuing weakness in state capacity means that Tripoli's ability to implement these remains limited. Furthermore, as in other former conflict zones, there is a need not just for SSR, but also for demobilisation, disarmament and reintegration (DDR) initiatives. Implementing DDR and SSR is particularly challenging in environments that have seen bitter fighting and the effective collapse of state structures as well as a rise in armed – and empowered – militia groups.

This scenario developed in Libya; it is now a growing concern in Syria given the continuing and increasingly bitter conflict there.

A steady stream of defections has occurred within the Syrian armed forces, but these have been limited largely to individuals or small groups and low-level personnel. Neither whole units nor a critical mass of senior officers from elite units have defected. Were they to occur, such large-scale defections could mark a turning point in the conflict, although it is uncertain what might lead to them. One possibility is that the effects of mounting losses in the civil war could fracture the military, either due to declining morale or as officers seek to secure themselves in a post-Assad Syria by aligning with the winning side. (This assumes they could be credibly assured that they would not be prosecuted by the new leadership.) At least in the conflict's early phases, the regime benefitted from an effective formula that combined long-standing methods of political control (including inducing rivalries among factions and employing sectarian bias in appointments) and its adeptness at monitoring its armed forces. These measures deterred dissent by making it more risky, and costly, to organise opposition to the regime. The fact that many of the regime's most valued forces are also those implicated in atrocities and sectarian underpinnings of the civil war is also a powerful hedge against organised defection by elite units. In the event of the regime's fall, moreover, significant challenges would likely confront a post-Assad Syria, in which the alliances among factions and armed groupings sustained by the battle against the regime would likely unravel – a prospect that means that any victory by rebel groups will likely devolve, perhaps in a manner similar to Libya, into power struggles among factions, yielding a new raft of security challenges.(See pp. 11–15 for an analysis of the war in Syria.)

REGIONAL MACROECONOMICS

The robust economic growth in the region highlighted in last year's *Military Balance* continued in 2012, with high oil prices leading to considerable inflows to oil-producing states. According to OPEC statistics, oil prices rose sharply in early 2012, reaching US$123 per barrel in March, largely stemming from tensions with Iran. Prices then declined to around US$94 per barrel within two months as concern over the future of the eurozone created uncertainty over future demand. (This period coincided with Greece's parlia-

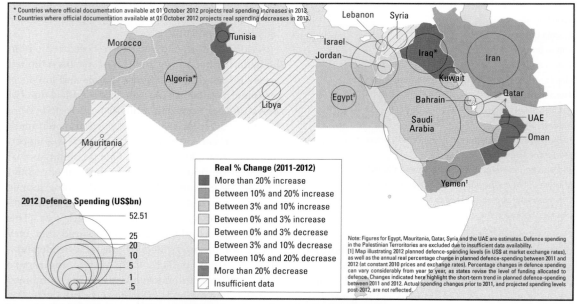

* Countries where official documentation available at 01 October 2012 projects real spending increases in 2013.
† Countries where official documentation available at 01 October 2012 projects real spending decreases in 2013.

Real % Change (2011-2012)

■	More than 20% increase
■	Between 10% and 20% increase
■	Between 3% and 10% increase
■	Between 0% and 3% increase
■	Between 0% and 3% decrease
■	Between 3% and 10% decrease
■	Between 10% and 20% decrease
■	More than 20% decrease
⧄	Insufficient data

2012 Defence Spending (US$bn)

52.51
25
20
10
5
1
.5

Note: Figures for Egypt, Mauritania, Qatar, Syria and the UAE are estimates. Defence spending in the Palestinian Territories are excluded due to insufficient data availability.
[1] Map illustrating 2012 planned defence-spending levels (in US$ at market exchange rates), as well as the annual real percentage change in planned defence-spending between 2011 and 2012 (at constant 2010 prices and exchange rates). Percentage changes in defence spending can vary considerably from year to year, as states revise the level of funding allocated to defence. Changes indicated here highlight the short-term trend in planned defence-spending between 2011 and 2012. Actual spending changes prior to 2011, and projected spending levels post-2012, are not reflected.

Map 11 **Middle East and North Africa Regional Defence Spending**[1]

mentary elections.) Prices then rebounded somewhat, reaching US$105.7 in November. Demand remained relatively robust, particularly from fast-growing emerging economies such as those in East Asia, but the price variations over the year show the degree to which prices can be affected by political factors.

High oil prices have supported the initiatives of some exporting states to boost government spending in the wake of the Arab Spring, through, for example, government subsidies and higher salaries. Such spending, intended to shore up political support in the short to medium term, may in fact put additional strain on government finances and increase exposure to fluctuations in oil prices.

According to the IMF, growth in oil-exporting states was expected to reach 6.5% in 2012, boosted by increased output from Libya after the dislocation experienced during the fighting in 2011. However, for oil importers growth was about 1.5–2%, 'reflecting the effects of social unrest and political uncertainty, weak external demand and high oil prices'. Contracting economic activity in Europe has led to a drop-off in trade, while eurozone uncertainty has also had negative effects. While the IMF predicts that growth in oil-importing states will rise to about 3.25% in 2013 as demand improves and states still undergoing transitions stabilise, these states will still have to cope with an uncertain investment environment, uncertain tourist revenues, and variable commodity prices. This

may impel governments in oil-importing states, in particular, to boost subsidies. Deteriorating economic conditions may mean governments would prefer to rein in such disbursements, but the competing imperative to maintain spending that supports stability means that governments could resist such cuts.

Defence spending

Defence budgetary transparency across the Middle East and North African region generally tends to be low, with few states providing details on the composition of defence outlays. Some states, such as Iran and Qatar, do not even publish top-line defence-spending figures on a regular basis. Opacity has increased in recent times, in part due to heightened governmental concerns over the increasingly fraught civil–military relations in the region. Civil conflicts over 2011 and 2012 in Libya, Tunisia and Syria have also increased uncertainty over the true levels of defence spending in these states. Defence-spending levels and spending trends in real terms for many states in the region thus have to be estimated (see Map 11 for IISS estimates of these trends).

Oil-exporting states are estimated to have increased real spending in 2012 by 3.6%, while non-oil-exporting states saw real spending rises of around 7.8%. Overall, defence spending in the region is estimated to have risen from US$155.9bn in 2011 to $166.4bn in 2012 (current prices and exchange rates),

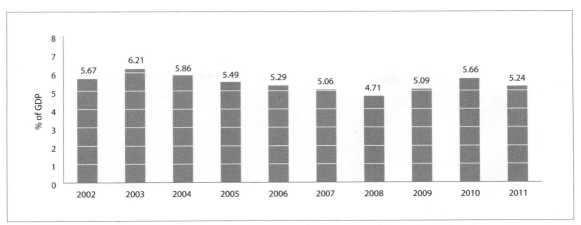

Figure 21 **Middle East and North Africa Regional Defence Expenditure** as % of GDP

a nominal increase of around 6.7%. After discounting for inflationary and exchange rate effects, the real increase in regional defence spending was an estimated 4.6% (at constant 2010 prices and exchange rates). A substantial proportion of this rise was driven by spending increases in Iraq, Kuwait, Oman and Yemen. Although Iran claimed to have doubled its defence budget for 2012, this is likely to have been achieved by reallocating spending previously included elsewhere under the rubric of defence. It is likely that spending on IRGC military construction and facilities' development projects, as well as military social-security expenditure, have now been included under the defence budget. For 2012, these items collectively amounted to around 55% of the new, higher Iranian defence budget, and make up the entire 127% increase announced in February 2012 (see Figure 22 and textbox: Estimating Iranian Defence Spending p. 359).

As in previous years, Saudi Arabia remains the top military spender in the region, accounting for 31.6% of the estimated total (See Figure 22). As noted on p. 368, high oil prices have allowed Riyadh to increase government expenditure, with a planned spend of SR690bn (US183.9bn) for 2012 (a 19% increase over 2011). Most of this has apparently been set aside for further increases in, for instance, housing, health, transport and infrastructure. But defence and security usually make up the largest share of government spending, not least because of concern over the regional security environment, especially the Iranian nuclear issue. (Detailed figures on defence spending are not published by the Saudi authorities.) Over the next few years, Riyadh is expected to commit to a substantial number of additional defence-procure-

ment schemes plus upgrades to existing equipment. As well as the purchase of additional F-15s, deals were signed to upgrade Saudi Arabia's existing inventory to the -SA configuration; contracts were signed with Boeing in 2012. Another major development was an agreement to extend the existing Saudi–British Defence Cooperation Programme. Saudi Arabia continues to try to leverage defence investments through offsets to improve training and employment prospects for Saudi nationals, as well as to boost the local defence production sector.

Saudi Arabia is not the only Gulf state concerned by uncertainty over Iran's nuclear programme and also keen to boost the domestic defence industry. The United Arab Emirates (UAE) is home to defence concerns ranging from armoured-vehicle manufacturers to shipyards and, like Saudi Arabia, sees the defence sector as a way to stimulate domestic economic activity and (in the long term) export potential. A major deal in prospect involves replacement of the UAE's ageing *Mirage* 2000 fighters. The French Dassault *Rafale* has been mentioned in connection with such a deal, though nothing has been signed. UK Prime Minister David Cameron's visit to Abu Dhabi in November 2012 was widely reported in the British press as part of an effort to interest UAE defence officials in the *Typhoon* combat aircraft. To the east, Oman is reported to be in talks with the *Typhoon*'s manufacturer, BAE Systems, over the sale of up to 12 aircraft.

Iraq is seeing more disbursements on defence items after years of economic recovery. According to the IMF, GDP rose by 8.4% in 2011 (against a regional average of 3.3%), with a projected increase of 10.2% in 2012 and 14.7% in 2013. A key priority is rebuilding the air force in terms of airframes and systems. A 2011

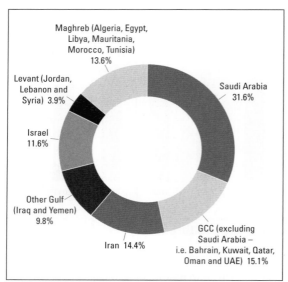

Figure 22 **Estimated MENA Defence Expenditure 2012: Sub-Regional Breakdown**

order for 12 F-16C/Ds was followed in 2012 by an order for a further 12. While US firms continue to do well, Iraq also announced orders with Russian firms. However, one large order, reportedly including attack helicopters and air-defence systems, was cancelled in November. Iraq allocated US$14.7bn, or about 15% of its budget, to security in 2011 – second only to energy, which made up 20%.

Algeria has also seen marked increases in its defence budget, with a 28% increase in real terms in 2011 followed by another 6% rise in 2012. Besides the higher equipment-procurement disbursements seen in recent years, the country also raised personnel salaries in 2011 in response to the popular discontent elsewhere in the region. Algeria is expected to further increase defence spending in 2013 to over US$10bn (compared to US$5.6bn in 2010), in part because the Ministry of Defence will assume responsibility for and restructure the Municipal Guard, which was previously under the Interior Ministry.

IRAN

Defence-industrial developments

Self-reliance is a key tenet of Iran's strategic doctrine. Motivated by ambition and experience, Iran's pre- and post-revolution leaders alike have aimed to establish an indigenous capacity to train and equip the country's armed forces and secure national interests independent of foreign support.

In the 1970s, awash with oil revenues, the Shah sought to promote Iran's regional position by creating a domestic defence industry capable of supplying its armed forces. Contracts with Western arms manufacturers were established with the concurrent aims of procuring state-of-the-art weaponry and building an indigenous weapons-production infrastructure. Western experts were imported to help operate the manufacturing lines and train Iranian specialists. The shah's military-industrialisation plans were ultimately crushed by the Islamic Revolution, after which Tehran's ties with the West were severed and defence contracts subsequently terminated.

When Iraq attacked Iran in December 1980, Tehran had few allies, fewer reliable military suppliers and a still-embryonic weapons-production infrastructure. The Islamic Republic attempted to maintain existing military equipment and produce key spare parts indigenously, but ultimately had to forge relations with willing suppliers to meet its military needs. China, North Korea and Brazil were indispensible providers of materiel that helped sustain Iran's war efforts. More importantly, these countries offered Iran licensed production and assembly facilities to support the manufacture of new weapons. Russian expertise was solicited, often illicitly, to deliver technical education and training to Iran's young military-production professionals. The industrial base and technical know-how created during and immediately after the war provided a foundation upon which a more competent and self-sufficient defence manufacturing capacity could be developed.

Iran continues to develop and expand its defence industries in a broad range of armament domains with the expressed aim of further reducing its reliance on foreign suppliers, minimising the effects of economic sanctions and highlighting the country's technological prowess. Iran now boasts that it can produce domestically a variety of light weapons, military vehicles, anti-tank and anti-ship missiles, heavy artillery rockets, short- and medium-range ballistic missiles, drones and UAVs, and light tanks and small naval vessels, though officials in Tehran reluctantly admit the country is unable to manufacture advanced weaponry such as advanced fighter jets and heavy armour.

Iran's missiles sector

Despite Tehran's prioritised investment in its defence industries over the past three decades, available evidence suggests that self-sufficiency remains an

Estimating Iranian Defence Spending

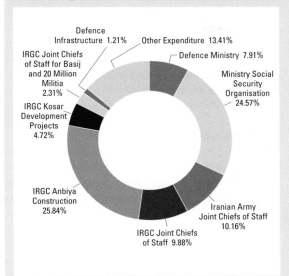

Figure 23 **Composition of Iranian Defence Spending 2012**

Trying to calculate Iranian defence spending in 2012 presents complex issues. In recent years, Tehran has not published official defence-spending figures, which has meant they have had to be estimated. In 2011 the IISS estimated that Iranian defence spending was approximately IR128tr, or around US$12bn (see *The Military Balance 2012*, p. 323).

In February 2012 President Mahmoud Ahmadinejad announced that his country was more than doubling its defence budget that year, with a 127% increase. However, he did not announce the new total figure. If the IISS estimate for 2011 spending was accurate, the announcement would have meant that the 2012 defence budget would be around IR256tr, or US$24bn (at constant 2011 exchange rates). In US dollar terms, that would place Iranian defence spending in 2012 above Israel's (US$19.4bn). But at the time of the February 2012 announcement, several analysts observed that the weakening of the Iranian economy as a result of US-led sanctions probably meant that such a large increase in defence spending was the result of a reclassification of existing spending under the rubric of defence, rather than the actual allocation of more funding.

Iranian budgetary data subsequently obtained by the IISS indicates that the official Iranian defence budget for 2012 was IR309.5tr, around 21% higher than the IR256tr calculation above. The data show that more than 50% of the budget was allocated to social-security expenses

and IRGC construction projects (see Figure 23 for details). Excluding these items would bring 2012 Iranian defence spending to IR138.9tr, a figure well within the range of the 2011 IISS estimate of IR128tr. Therefore, these may be the additional items of spending hitherto included elsewhere in the Iranian budget that have now been reclassified under defence. Indeed, if social-security expenses and IRGC construction projects were suddenly transferred to the defence budget they would increase spending by 123%, a figure very close to the 127% increase announced in February 2012.

Assuming the increase in Iranian spending was primarily the result of a budgetary reclassification, and allocating equivalent additional amounts into the IISS estimate for 2011, then in real terms Iranian defence spending declined by 10.3% between 2011 and 2012. This is because of the high levels of inflation (more than 25%) that the country experienced in 2012 through the combined effects of economic sanctions and domestic economic mismanagement.

Exchange-rate confusion

Despite the increased clarity over total Iranian defence spending, economic sanctions on Iran in 2012 have complicated international comparisons of defence spending in US dollar terms. As a result of US- and EU-led sanctions measures targeting Iran's supply of hard currency (see IISS *Strategic Survey 2012*, p. 61–74, for a case study), the Rial experienced significant volatility in 2012. For example, after the unofficial, black-market rate had progressively depreciated over the year, the Rial lost almost 60% of its value in less than a week in September, as Iranians lost confidence in the currency and dumped Rials en masse.

This volatility has made it difficult to establish the relevant exchange rate to be used for US dollar conversions of defence-spending figures. At the revised official exchange rate announced in January 2012 (US$1=12,260 rials), Iranian defence spending would amount to US$25.2bn. At the black-market rate from September 2012 (US$1=24,600 rials), it would be US$12.6bn; while at the black-market rate from October 2012 (US$1=39,000 rials), it would be US$7.9bn. Given that the IMF's October 2012 *World Economic Outlook* database uses an implied exchange rate close to that of official rate (US$1= 12,934 rials), and that the Iranian government is likely to finance its budget expenditures at around the official rate, Iranian defence-spending analysis across *The Military Balance 2013* uses the IMF rate – yielding a 2012 defence-budget figure of US$23.9bn.

elusive goal. Perhaps the achievements and limitations of Iran's domestic capabilities are best illustrated by examining its ballistic-missile industry, which began with the importation of *Scud*-B and -C missiles (dubbed locally as *Shahab*-1 and -2 respectively) in the 1980s and early 1990s, and *No-dong* missiles (renamed *Shahab*-3) in the mid- to late 1990s. At the turn of the century, Iran is judged to have established the capacity to manufacture the missile airframes, propellant tanks and other inert components, while still relying on foreign-made engines and guidance units. In 2004, engineers began modifying the *Shahab*-3 to extend its maximum range from about 900 kilometres to 1,600km. And, in support of its nascent but ambitious space programme, Iran further modified the *Shahab*-3 and added a second stage to produce its first satellite-carrier rocket, known as the *Safir*. In February 2009, the *Safir* inserted a 27 kilogramme satellite into low Earth orbit, an achievement repeated three times since.

Iran's ability to leverage available technologies and foreign-supplied components to enhance its ballistic missiles may be a harbinger of future weapons developments in other areas. Indeed, Iran appears to have upgraded the *Hawk*-I air-defence missiles received from the US in the late 1970s, as well as existing Soviet SA-5s and other weapons. Similarly, Iran is believed to have acquired a licensed production line from China for the manufacture of anti-ship missiles, including C-802, C-803, C-705 and C-401 systems, known locally as *Noor*, *Ghadr*, *Nasr* and *Ra'ad*. These missiles have been deployed on small ships, helicopters and other unique launch platforms. The creation of hybrid systems based on outdated weapons, but supplemented with modern Chinese subsystems, could surprise Iran's adversaries should war break out.

Defence organisations

In the aftermath of the Islamic Revolution, a series of purges paralysed and intimidated Iran's regular armed forces (the Artesh). But the Artesh reorganised enough to halt the invading Iraqi forces at the beginning of the Iran–Iraq war (1980–1988). After pioneering a counter-offensive which led to the recapture of the port of Khorramshahr in May 1982, the Islamic regime assigned the Artesh a secondary role in contrast to the rising Islamic Revolutionary Guard Corps (IRGC).

For more than two decades since the end of the Iran–Iraq war, the Artesh has been in an unwinnable competition with the IRGC. The constitution of the Islamic Republic underlines the division between the two military organisations: the Artesh is responsible for defending the country's borders and maintaining internal security while the IRGC is responsible for protecting the regime. The rivalry between the two military organisations is rooted in doctrinal differences, as well as unequal access to the regime's political centres of power, funding and recruitment.

The Revolutionary Guard Corps

The IRGC is effectively the regime's Praetorian Guard. It is omnipresent, interfering in the political, economic, social, military and foreign affairs of the country. Economically, its engineering and construction arm, the holding company Khatam al-Anbiya, is highly active in the construction, energy, media and communications sectors. Between 2009 and 2011 Khatam al-Anbiya was granted some US$25bn in contracts to develop Iran's oil and gas sector, according to a January 2011 report on the Artesh by the Middle East Institute. In September 2012, the IRGC was given the responsibility of confronting 'troublemakers' in the currency market who were deemed to be behind the sharp fluctuations of the Iranian rial against the US dollar.

Politically, the IRGC exercises great influence through positions of power held by former members in the cabinet; the defence, oil and interior ministries; the Defence Industries Organisation and the Majlis (the national parliament). Many senior IRGC officers serve as governors and governors-general across the country. The IRGC has unique access to Supreme Leader Ayatollah Ali Khamenei, and almost all the senior officers of his personal staff, on the Armed Forces General Command Headquarters (responsible for planning, resources, operations and logistics), are IRGC members.

Budgeting

The 125,000-strong IRGC is numerically smaller than the 350,000-strong Artesh, yet according to the Middle East Institute, the National Budget for March 2010–March 2011 allocated the IRGC the equivalent of US$5.8bn, while the Artesh received US$4.8bn. For March 2011–March 2012, military expenditure was estimated at around US$11.9bn, of which analysts estimate around US$8.9bn was allocated to the IRGC and around US$2.5bn to the Artesh, meaning that the IRGC budget was three-and-a-half times greater than that of the Artesh.

The *Military Balance 2012* estimated Iran's 2011 defence budget to be around US$12bn. Iran's economy has been grappling with the tightening sanctions imposed by the UN, EU and US over concerns about the country's nuclear programme. In spite of this, President Mahmoud Ahmadinejad reportedly raised the defence budget for March 2012–March 2013 by 127%. This would bring the defence budget to around US$24bn. In contrast, the national budget, which amounts to R5.1 quadrillion (approximately US$416bn), is about US$40bn less than the year before, due to the official devaluation of the rial.

The Artesh

In contrast, the regular armed forces are relatively apolitical and marginalised. Since 1979, the regime has attempted to change the national and apolitical character of the Artesh, with mixed results, by giving it heavy doses of indoctrination in Islamic belief and allegiance to the principle of *velayat-e-faqih* ('the rule of the jurisprudent', the central plank of Iran's theocracy), and by placing some IRGC officers in senior regular military command posts. Though its senior officers show undivided allegiance to Khamenei, informed observers believe that its rank and file do not possess such in-depth ideological conviction.

After the June 2009 presidential election, the IRGC and its paramilitary wing, the Basij, suppressed demonstrators protesting the victory of Mahmoud Ahmadinejad. There were indications in the Iranian press that the regime might order the Artesh to intervene against the protesters as well. Commanders of several regular military units, including army aviation, the air force and some training colleges, reportedly released a letter criticising the IRGC and Basij, suggesting that if unrest spiralled out of control, the regular armed forces could not necessarily be relied upon to suppress protesters.

Naval reorganisation

IRGC–Artesh rivalry can also be observed in naval matters. Both possess naval forces, which differ in terms of doctrine, structure, mission and capabilities.

After the inception of the IRGC Navy in 1985, in the midst of the Iran–Iraq War, the two navies shared overlapping responsibilities in the Persian Gulf, the Gulf of Oman and the Caspian Sea. But in 2007, Khamenei, as commander-in-chief of the Iranian Armed Forces, redefined the primary duties and operational areas of the Islamic Republic of Iran Navy (IRIN), or the regular navy, and the IRGC Navy

(IRGCN). The reorganisation gave the IRGCN sole responsibility for defence in the Persian Gulf and gave the IRIN responsibility for the Caspian Sea and the area outside the Strait of Hormuz into and beyond the Gulf of Oman.

IRGCN operational doctrine

The IRGCN concept of maritime combat is a form of guerrilla warfare. This was outlined by Rear Admiral Ashkbous Danekar in 1999, before the division of labour emerged between the IRGC and the IRIN, in an article entitled 'Operational Doctrine of the Islamic Republic of Iran Navy', published in the Artesh journal *SAFF*, produced by the Political and Ideological Organisation of the Artesh. The concept emphasises avoiding direct and sustained confrontation with the enemy, and relying instead on different layers of defence, launching surprise attacks and gaining psychological victories. For instance, Danekar wrote that Iran must capitalise on favourable Persian Gulf geography; launch amphibious and naval attacks on enemy bases and installations; use islands in the Persian Gulf to mount attacks; block oil-export routes; use anti-ship missiles and mines; conduct commando operations against enemy oil installations; use fast boats for hit-and-run missions taking advantage of islands and inlets; use the Gulf of Oman as its first line of defence; and employ offensive electronic warfare.

The biggest perceived threat to the IRGC in the Persian Gulf comes from the US Navy. Given the overwhelming conventional superiority of the US Navy, Iran instead looks to leverage asymmetric advantage. This is the cornerstone of IRGCN activities and doctrine, though it does not mean that the IRGC has abandoned modern military technology, even with the sanctions on Iran's military procurement imposed by Western countries and the UN.

Because of the IRGCN's revolutionary nature and the strong ideological support it provides, the regime favours it and considers it more politically reliable than the IRIN. This is reflected in the resources the IRGCN receives to build vessels or procure them from abroad. The IRGCN deploys fast torpedo and missile boats, shore-based anti-ship missiles, mines, flying boats, unmanned surface vessels and swimmer-delivery vehicles, though the number and precise capability of these systems is unclear.

IRGCN's acquisition and capabilities

In the years immediately after the Iran–Iraq War, the IRGC acquired some boats and weapons from China and North Korea, but under Iran's so-called 'self-suffi-ciency jihad' in arms production, in the last few years, the IRGC has made a concerted effort to reverse engi-neer, indigenously manufacture or upgrade equip-ment to add to its inventory of high-speed boats.

In 2010, the IRGCN commissioned 12 additional *Peykaap-* (North Korean design) and *Tir*-class boats with torpedo and missile capabilities and displayed *Bavar* flying boats, reportedly exhibiting stealthy char-acteristics. In August of the same year, the production lines for British-built *Bladerunner* fast boats purchased from South Africa (*Seraj*-1) and for *Zolfaqar* missile boats were simultaneously inaugurated.

In 2011, an undisclosed number of these boats were commissioned by the IRGCN. In early July 2012, during the *Great Prophet*-7 exercises, the IRGC fired its newest anti-ship missile, apparently named *Persian Gulf*. According to the commander of the IRGCN, Rear Admiral Ali Fadavi, reported in the *Jam-e-Jam* newspaper, this missile has a range of 300km and is intended for use against large surface targets.

IRIN missions and capabilities

In contrast, the 18,000-strong IRIN, with its larger surface vessels, is more of a blue-water navy, but because of perceived ideological deficiency it is in a poor position to compete with the IRGCN for resources. According to a January 2012 Middle East Institute report on the regular navy, however, there are indications that 'the IRIN is regarded more highly by Iran's populace than the IRGCN, both for its high degree of professionalism and apolitical nature'.

In line with the redefinition of the two navies' areas of operation by Khamenei, the IRIN is to form the first line of defence in the Gulf of Oman and project Iran's power beyond its shores. The IRIN, as defined by Khamenei, is to be a 'strategic navy'. Recent claims by the IRIN commander, Rear Admiral Habibollah Sayyari, and other navy officials, reported by the *Hamshahri* newspaper, suggest that the IRIN wishes to extend its reach within an area surrounded by four strategic chokepoints: the Strait of Hormuz, the Bab al-Mandab, the Strait of Malacca and the Suez Canal.

In pursuing this aim, the IRIN has enhanced its presence in international waters to expand Iran's influence and regional leverage. So far, the IRIN has dispatched several squadrons of ships (21 as of September 2012) to the Gulf of Aden and the Red Sea to conduct anti-piracy operations alongside other navies. Since 2009, the IRIN has made several

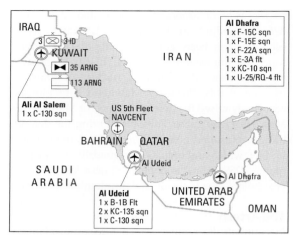

Map 12 **Key US military dispositions in the Persian Gulf**

visits to Sri Lanka, Djibouti, Oman and Saudi Arabia and its ships have transited the Suez Canal to the Mediterranean to visit Latakia in Syria.

Ambitious deployments and resources

In September 2011, Sayyari raised the prospect of expanding the IRIN's ability to operate out of area, possibly sending ships close to the Atlantic coast of the United States. Later, he announced that the IRIN plans to expand its presence in international waters near Antarctica. He reportedly said in September that 'we have the capability to hoist Iran's flag in different regions from the North Pole to the South Pole'.

However, the significance of these statements is questionable. There is currently a wide gap between the capabilities of the IRIN and its aim of becoming a strategic naval force capable of maintaining a pres-ence on the high seas. Despite IRIN efforts to main-tain and refit its ships, they suffer from obsolescence. With the exception of three Russian-made *Kilo*-class submarines and one home-made frigate (the *Jamaran*, a *Mowj*-class ship), the rest of the IRIN's seagoing ships were acquired by the shah over 40 years ago and have limited capacity for sustained operations. The same applies to the IRIN's air arm of maritime-patrol aircraft and anti-submarine helicopters.

The most substantive development with regard to inventory was the launch of the hull of a new *Mowj*-class frigate, the *Sahand*, on 18 September 2012. In 2011, the IRIN received three more *Qadir* (*Yono*-class) mini-submarines and equipped some of its frigates with a new locally produced version of the C-802 anti-ship missile. In general, the regime has given the

IRIN a subordinate defensive role compared with the IRGCN, reflecting the increasing role and influence of the IRGC in Iranian security and politics.

ISRAEL

Defence policy

Israel's strategic developments in the next few years will be influenced by two major developments: the Iranian nuclear project and the upheavals in the Middle East and North Africa in the wake of the Arab Spring. The combination of these two trends, both seen by Israel as troubling and negative, grants internal legitimacy to the policy of Benjamin Netanyahu's government of ignoring the fate of the Israeli–Palestinian peace process, effectively halted for the last four years. The international community, with the United States still in the lead, is also focused on the Iranian threat and the turmoil in some Arab states, and for now largely accepts Israel's arguments concerning the Palestinian situation. In the long term, however, this neglect might be disastrous: demographic changes could imperil the vision of a two-state solution, while the risk remains of re-emergent military conflict with the Palestinians.

The intense debate over the Iranian nuclear programme, and the surprise caused by the Arab Spring, are used by Israel's security apparatus to justify its demands for a larger security budget. The prime minister has stated recently that strategic changes in the region will dictate the allocation of more money to the Israel Defense Forces (IDF). But Netanyahu's government now faces a double challenge. After a generally successful navigation of the 2008 financial crisis, some Israeli analysts can detect signs of economic recession with, for instance, rising trade deficits in 2012. And the relative quiet until recently along the borders and in the Palestinian territories over the last three years has led many citizens to concentrate on the economy. The Israeli public is now approaching a consensus regarding the need for more investment in education and health services rather than defence, while Netanyahu stresses the need for more cutbacks.

The IDF, which is awaiting cabinet decisions on the budget before finalising its five-year plan, will also have to deal with the consequences of the ongoing debate about the enlistment of ultra-orthodox (*Haredim*) Yeshiva students, who now comprise 14% of 18-year-old men, and who are still, for the most part, excused service. As a result, the army has less manpower at its disposal than in the past. Even more troubling is the possible effect this might have on the motivation to serve among conscripts.

Iran

Israeli policymakers remain concerned by the level of development in, and possible intent of, Iran's nuclear programme. Until about 2007–08, Israel's readiness to undertake a military operation against Iranian nuclear sites was quite low, though Israeli analysts believe that matters have improved since then. Israeli decision-makers believe that a strike might delay the programme by a year or two. The US, meanwhile, believes an Israeli strike would be counterproductive because it would spur Iran into leaving the Nuclear Non-Proliferation Treaty and give Tehran an incentive to reconstitute its programme with the full weight of the economy behind it and to forgo IAEA inspections. Unsurprisingly, Israel has kept the exact amount spent on preparations for military action confidential. In 2010, it was announced that the Ministry of Defense had received an extra sum of NIS2bn (about US$600m at the time) for 'strategic issues', generally thought of as code for Iran-related planning, though this is probably just the tip of the iceberg. One could safely assume that the IDF, especially the air force, has spent some billions of dollars in the last five years on developing its capabilities with regard to Iran. A credible Israeli attack would likely require the use of more than a 100 warplanes and tankers, UAVs, electronic-warfare systems, and possibly even some ground commando units. (The use of Israel's submarine fleet, too, should not be discounted.) Israel has invested considerable sums in recent years on UAVs. It is believed, though, that the air force lacks enough tankers, deeply penetrating bombs ('bunker busters') and especially the capability to perform a damage assessment and follow-up attack – something the United States would find much easier.

Changing IDF border deployments

Israel had become used to relatively secure borders with Syria and Egypt along the Golan Heights and Sinai. In the wake of President Hosni Mubarak's ouster in Egypt, however, the security situation in Sinai has worsened, compounded by the outflow of weapons across North Africa from Libya, while Syria is in the midst of a bitter civil war. These situations provide opportunities for extremist terrorist organisations, mostly small groups affiliated with or influenced by al-Qaeda. Israel has already moved to confront this danger, which has been manifested by a few terrorist attacks across the Egyptian border since August 2011. A substantial barrier is currently being built along the Sinai border, while improvements have been made to the Golan fence. The IDF has also established a new regional brigade command along the Egyptian border, re-examined its operational plans for the Egyptian front (largely neglected during the last three decades) and is now considering re-building its Southern Corps (not to be confused with the higher level Southern Command), disbanded after the Israeli–Egyptian peace treaty.

In early August 2012, Egypt's newly elected president, Muhammad Morsi, sacked many of the country's leading generals and acquired more authority. This caused concern in Israel, as did the Egyptian dispatch of armoured vehicles (later withdrawn) into Sinai. Restrictions were placed on military deployments to Sinai under the Egypt–Israel peace treaty, though Cairo's move was generally held as a response to militant activity after Egyptian troops were reported killed in an August attack. Israeli intelligence experts do not foresee an armed conflict with Egypt in the near future, not least because of the country's economic situation and its dependence on financial and military assistance from the US. Israel is, however, preparing for the possibility of more terrorist attacks from Sinai and also an escalation in the Gaza Strip, which could lead to more tension with Egypt. The main problem with Sinai is that Israel cannot initiate pre-emptive strikes against Islamic terror groups for fear of further alienating the Egyptian regime. Work on the new barrier should be finished by early 2013. By then, it is likely that Israel will also start building a fence on the southern part of its border with Jordan. Prior to the November 2012 killing of Hamas military chief Ahmad Jabari, the Palestinian conflict was less of a cause for immediate concern, although the IDF worried about both Hamas's plans in Gaza and the possibility that a lack of progress with the Palestinian Authority would lead to violence in the West Bank.

The IDF subsequently launched *Operation Pillar of Defense* with, according to the IDF, twin objectives to 'protect Israeli civilians and to cripple the terrorist infrastructure in Gaza.' IDF statistics held that 667 rockets had hit Israeli territory between 14–20 November 2012, though the frequency of launches was diminishing. Israeli air and naval forces were heavily engaged in the campaign and as of mid-November, Israeli ground forces were positioned close to Gaza. At time of writing it was too early to reach conclusions about this latest conflict, though early lessons from the Israeli employment, and effectiveness, of its *Iron Dome* missile-defence batteries will have been carefully studied by both Hamas and Hizbullah. For the IDF, the use by Hamas of the Iranian-origin *Fajr-5* rocket placed Tel Aviv and Jerusalem within range of the Gaza Strip for the first time. The reports of accelerated funding for *Iron Dome* may owe something to this development, as well as the sheer volume of lower-range missiles launched from Gaza. Meanwhile, for Hamas, a key concern would have been – as well as the losses of both civilian and military personnel and infrastructure – the level of awareness that Israel's intelligence apparatus demonstrated over Hamas' personnel movements and infrastructure.

Will the home front become the front line?

With or without a strike against Iran, there are troubling signs that any future conflict will include both terrorist attacks against Israeli and Jewish targets abroad, as well as bombardment of Israel's population centres. The head of IDF military intelligence, General Aviv Kochavy, estimated in January 2012 that 200,000 rockets and missiles are pointed at the Israeli population. Scenarios drafted by IDF experts suggest that, in a future conflict with Iran and Hizbullah, between 200 and 500 could die on the home front. Defences have been improved: Israel now has two batteries of the *Arrow*-2 missile-defence system and five batteries of the lower-tier *Iron Dome* system, built to intercept short-range rockets. The main problem remains the medium tier between around 75–400 km. *David's Sling*, the system meant to deal with such threats, is due to become operational by 2014. So far, analysts estimate that around US$2.8bn has been spent on these three systems, 60% of that by the US. There has been some progress made with regard to early warning, with the US deploying an X-radar in the Negev; in defending the home front, mainly through more exercises and better cooperation with municipalities; and in the air force, which has boosted training for responding while bases are under bombardment. But the gaps in coverage remain substantial. It has been estimated that Israel will need 13 *Iron Dome* batteries to defend the whole country, but money has only been allocated for eight. Analysts also wonder where the army would deploy its *Iron Dome* batteries during a war: to protect the population in Tel Aviv, to defend civilian infrastructure, such as power stations, or to defend air force bases, so the planes could actually take off and respond.

The 2006 Lebanon War was a wake-up call for the IDF. In response, it has improved training for both regular army units and reserve brigades, and forces now spend time practising for combat against those launching rocket attacks, as well as for fighting in heavily populated areas. After four weeks of hesitation by the ground forces during the last war, analysts believe that in future, where appropriate, they will be rapidly dispatched inside enemy territory. On the other hand, if substantial numbers of rockets do strike Israeli civilian population centres, the leadership might feel obligated to inflict disproportionate damage on an enemy's civilian infrastructure. In any case, the army is currently preparing for asymmetric warfare against adaptive adversaries of the kind exemplified by Hizbullah. The judgement is believed to be that a conventional war against Arab armies is unlikely in the near future.

Since 2006, Israeli doctrine has emphasised the importance of defence, something neglected in the past, and there could well be a focus on international cooperation in the future. The changes across the region have already dictated the establishment of new units: battalions specialising in intelligence gathering, home-front defence, rocket interception and UAVs. Other important forces, such as the navy, have remained a generally low priority. Germany has recently signed an agreement to build a sixth submarine for Israel, to be supplied by 2018 at an estimated cost of US$400m; these submarines are believed to have the ability to launch land-attack cruise missiles as well as, perhaps, 'second strike' nuclear capabilities. But other than that, the navy has found it hard to obtain more funding, even though it says it requires NIS3bn (around US$750m) to buy ships to protect Israel's new-found gas fields in the Mediterranean.

The IDF's top budget priorities have recently included the air force, intelligence and technology, and especially cyber warfare. After years in which Israel had refused to deal with the issue publicly, a new national cyber authority was established by the prime minister in 2011 – with the Internal Security Services (known by their Hebrew acronym, SHABAK) acting as a professional instruction body, focused on defence. In the army, the C4I Branch has been put in charge of defending computer systems against cyber attack. It has been widely assumed that the Intelligence Branch has acquired responsibility for cyber attacks, although this subject remains off-limits in the Israeli press. Israel had identified some attacks on its defence IT systems over the past three years, though none appeared to be particularly sophisticated. But the growing discussion regarding the Stuxnet and Flame viruses that hit Iran might well lead Israeli defence officials to conclude that Israel should consider itself a possible target.

Defence economics

Though there were arguments between the MoD and Finance Ministry over the 2013 security budget, informed observers noted that this was not unusual, and that defence usually won out. In the wake of the 2006 war in Lebanon, the Brodet Committee concluded that the MoD's budget was in fact too small, but that it should only be increased if the ministry cut back on unnecessary expenses by NIS10bn over five years. (Military pensions are a major expense, particularly with the retirement age set at 45; in future, the retirement age for some office-based posts will gradually rise to 48.) The IDF, meanwhile, had to postpone its five-year plan, scheduled to begin in 2012, by one year as a result of the summer 2011 social protests in Israel over matters such as the high cost of housing, which led to calls to reduce the defence budget. However, as far as the government was concerned, these demands had to be set against competing imperatives arising from changing regional security dynamics.

Since 2006, the defence budget had grown in nominal terms, from NIS46bn in 2006 to NIS49bn in 2007, NIS51bn in 2008, NIS52bn in 2009, NIS53bn in 2010, NIS54bn in 2011 and NIS60bn in 2012, according to Finance Ministry data. (US$1 is now worth NIS4, compared to about NIS3.5 in 2007.) These numbers include US$3bn annually in American military assistance, as well as special additions for specific reasons, such as financing *Operation Cast Lead* in Gaza in 2009. For 2013, the MoD asked for NIS62bn, while the Finance Ministry held out for NIS55.5bn – the same as for 2012 without the extras.

The MoD, however, insists that its relative share of the budget has in fact decreased over the last two decades, while money for social sectors such as education has been increased in recent years. Some analysts think that the Finance Ministry believes the IDF is intentionally inflating threats from Iran and Hizbullah. Yuval Steinitz, the minister of finance, claimed in August that the regional arms race had virtually stopped in the 1990s and that Israel does not face any real danger of a full conventional war in

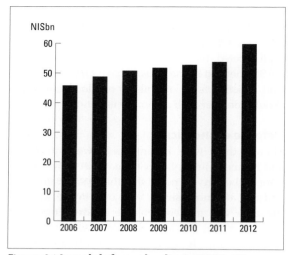

Figure 24 **Israel defence budgets 2006–12**

the next few years. This is an oversimplification, and the assessment of Israeli security experts is that the threats facing Israel have become more complex and require a much more sophisticated response by the Israeli defence and security establishment.

A large proportion of the budget is spent on salaries and pensions as well as on benefits for wounded soldiers or families of deceased soldiers. Procurement funding remain high for equipment such as F-35 aircraft, *Merkava* 4 tanks and German-built *Dolphin* submarines, while spending on unit practice, especially in the ground forces, is falling. In 2012, the army will spend only NIS1.4bn on ground-forces practice, with only NIS460m of this on reserve units. Major-General Yishai Beer, who retired last year, described the army in an interview to *Ha'aretz* in May as a 'poor family that insists on buying a 42" television screen, while it has no money for its kids' education'. Why, he said, 'did we reach the edge of an abyss this year? Because most of the budget was committed to projects, so no money was left for training; no money to buy toilet paper. Four hours of driving training for a tank driver in the regular army – that's what the troops got ahead of Lebanon 2006 … There has been a significant improvement in readiness since the end of the Lebanon war, but if we backtrack now from what we've achieved, we'll revert to 2006. A chief of staff can't send soldiers into battle without training.'

While the budget remains a troubling issue, Israel's defence industry (major parts owned by the state) provides some positive news. In 2010, Israel exported weapons worth US$7bn, its highest ever amount. The MoD has not published 2011 figures.

Analysts presume that in this year the industry suffered from the general austerity prevailing in the international arms market. The numbers are nonetheless impressive, given that in 2002, Israel exported around US$1.5bn. MoD policy, as well as the military censorship system, prevents the Israeli media from publishing many key details of arms deals. Still, it is apparent that the country's major markets are now in Asia, with India and Singapore procuring assets such as airborne early-warning systems, the US (mainly cooperation deals, where American companies buy Israeli components with Israel then making purchases in the US) and then Europe. South Korea is now also considered a growing market for the Israeli arms industry, though it remains to be seen whether there will be any effect from Israel's decision not to choose the South Korean T-50 for its training aircraft requirement. On the other hand Turkey, once considered a strategic ally and a major buyer, has faded as a market because of the tensions between the two countries.

SAUDI ARABIA

Ministry developments

Prince Salman bin Abdulaziz, half-brother of King Abdullah, was appointed minister of defence on 5 November 2011 following the death of his full brother Crown Prince Sultan. Prince Salman had little experience or understanding of defence before his appointment, though he had been a constant companion of Sultan during the last four years of his life. Salman brought to the post a reputation as a mediator and conciliator, as well as the history of a largely corruption-free 48-year governorship of Riyadh Province. Later, after the death of Interior Minister Prince Naif, Salman was promoted to crown prince and deputy prime minister on 18 June 2012, retaining the defence portfolio. This suggests both that the appointment enjoyed widespread support within the Allegiance Council (which decides the succession), and that the king is reconciled that his successor will be yet another member of the 'Sudairi Seven', the full brothers of the late King Fahd.

Salman inherited a complex portfolio at defence, even though responsibility for civil aviation has been hived off into a separate agency. There are serious security issues at a number of locations close to Saudi Arabia's borders. Salman also has to manage the activities and aspirations of armed forces which, though not starved of resources, do not always manage them effectively, and he has had to make a number of key procurement decisions. Analysts believe that he has performed reasonably well during his first months in office. His first major overseas visits, to the UK and US in April 2012, were regarded as successful: in London he met Prime Minister David Cameron (a rare occurrence for a defence minister visiting on his own) and in the US he called on President Barack Obama. In December 2011, Riyadh approved both the extension of the Saudi–British Defence Cooperation Programme (SBDCP) for a further five years and the provision of additional funds to enable the final 48 *Typhoon* aircraft to be assembled in the UK and the whole fleet to be operated and fully supported in future.

The appointment of the late Prince Sultan's eldest son Khalid as deputy defence minister was widely seen as formalising Khalid's position during the last months of his father's life, when he largely managed the minister's office and its priorities. In a separate but potentially significant move, Sultan's second son Bandar, former Saudi ambassador to the US, was appointed director general of the Saudi Intelligence Agency in July 2012 in succession to Prince Muqrin, the youngest surviving son of King Abdulaziz; the reasons are said to include Bandar's long experience in foreign affairs and the need to improve the agency's efficiency in response to the situations in Syria, Yemen, Bahrain and the Eastern Province. Muqrin was appointed to a new post as senior ministerial adviser to the king.

Regional concerns

Aside from the ever-present perceived threat from Iran, continued unrest in Syria was the most urgent security issue for Saudi Arabia in 2012. Along with other regional powers, Riyadh began the year calling on Damascus to stop attacking its own citizens and to implement the Kofi Annan peace plan. It has now moved towards much more active support of Syrian rebel forces, notably the Free Syrian Army (FSA). In late July 2012, Gulf sources were reporting that Saudi Arabia, Turkey and Qatar had established a base in Turkey to provide communications and weapons to the FSA. Riyadh's contribution is largely financial, although there have also been reports of materiel belonging to or destined for the Saudi Armed Forces being diverted to the FSA, despite generally being subject to strict end-user conditions. Riyadh does not appear to have any appetite for direct intervention in the conflict, although the longer it continues the more the Saudis will be concerned at the likelihood of instability spilling beyond Syria's borders, particularly into western Iraq.

The Saudi Arabian National Guard (SANG) continues to provide the main component of the Gulf Cooperation Council (GCC) Peninsula Shield forces deployed to Bahrain. Its stated mission was to help secure key government facilities and infrastructure, and since deployment in March 2011 it has generally kept a low profile. Saudi Arabia has urged greater integration of GCC economies and military forces on a number of occasions over the past year, most recently at the foreign ministers' meeting in May 2012. This initiative has met with resistance from other GCC members, such as Kuwait and Qatar, although discussions are continuing on establishing a customs union with Bahrain. Riyadh's concerns about the stability of its own Shia-dominated regions appear to be growing: in June 2012, a further 1,200 SANG troops were deployed to the Eastern Province, and the king reportedly ordered all forces be put on high alert, with some officers' leave cancelled.

Riyadh remains deeply concerned at continued instability in Yemen, despite brokering the resignation of former President Ali Abdullah Saleh. Concern over border security persists: though there has been little military activity since the conflict between Yemeni and Saudi forces and local tribal militias in 2009–10, border violations by smugglers and armed gangs are reported on an almost daily basis.

A Saudi diplomat seized by al-Qaeda-affiliated militants in March was still in captivity in October. The Royal Saudi Naval Force (RSNF) continues to take part in CTF150 patrol activities in the Arabian Sea, primarily counter-piracy operations.

Procurement

The government continues to invest heavily in defence equipment. The US Foreign Military Sales deal to procure 84 F-15SA aircraft and associated equipment, upgrade 70 existing aircraft, and purchase additional helicopters for the Land Forces and SANG, worth an estimated US$60bn in full-life costs, was announced and approved by Congress in 2010; the formal contract was signed in January 2012. In May, it was announced that the Royal Saudi Air Force (RSAF) would procure 22 UK-built *Hawk* 65 jet trainers, plus 55 *Pilatus* PC-21 turboprop trainers, in a deal worth some £1.9bn (US$3bn). Funds will be provided from within the 2011–16 SBDCP budget, which was approved in December 2011.

The Land Forces have shown interest in diversifying their traditional suppliers by procuring *Leopard* 2A7+ main battle tanks from Germany. The original requirement of 200, as stated in mid-2011, was reportedly increased to 600–800 in June 2012. The request remains under consideration in Berlin, where opposition to the deal has surfaced in the Defence and Foreign Ministries. The RSNF continues to aspire to upgrade or replace some of its existing vessels. Some US$20–23bn is said to be earmarked for the next phase of the Naval Expansion Programme, possibly including the acquisition of DDG-51 *Aegis* destroyers from the US, although there have been few concrete signs of deals emerging. Similarly, talks on the procurement of the Franco-Italian FREMM are as yet nowhere near conclusion. Saudi military relations with Russia have soured as a result of Moscow's continuing support for the Syrian government, and further new equipment procurement from Moscow is unlikely in the near future.

Defence economics

As noted in *The Military Balance 2012*, Saudi Arabia recovered quickly from the global financial crisis, with growth momentum re-established on the back of stronger oil prices. Riyadh has been implementing a policy of domestic fiscal expansion that has included investment in many new infrastructure projects and education schemes. Having risen 5.1% in 2010, real GDP rose a further 7.1% during 2011. However, against the somewhat surprising expectation of lower oil prices, the 2012 forecast indicated a slightly reduced growth rate of 6%.

Despite a pattern of lower oil demand through 2011 caused by the continuing global economic downturn, the effect of the Arab Spring, together with increasing geopolitical concern over the region, has left oil prices in a relatively stable, high position. For 2010, budgeted oil revenues accounted for 90.4% of total Saudi revenue but in 2011 this declined to 86%. For 2012, the Saudi government forecast suggested that oil would represent 85% of total revenue. However, given a long tradition in which the difference between the budgeted and actual price achieved for oil has often been in excess of 40%, it may be that for 2012 the government has actually been less conservative with oil-price expectations than in the past. (For 2011, the wide differential between budgeted and actual price of oil allowed the kingdom to produce a surplus of SR306bn (US$81.6bn), the second highest on record.

Government revenues of SR1.11 trillion (US$296bn) were in fact 100% in excess of budgeted levels.)

To balance the 2012 budget, Saudi Arabia would need the oil price to be maintained over US$76 per barrel. Given the consensus view that global demand for oil would increase during 2012 it is also possible that the Saudi oil-revenue forecast suggests an intention by the government to aggressively cut back oil production. This may explain why forecast total revenue for 2012 had been budgeted to decline to SR890bn (US$237bn). However, it should be remembered that from 2010 to 2012 the Saudi government ignored pressure from other OPEC members to limit oil supply in order to keep prices high. In so doing, and by adopting policies designed to augment supply and forestall possible shortages, the Saudi government acted to stabilise the oil price. The high price of oil has allowed Riyadh to dramatically increase its expenditure budget, with a planned spend of SR690bn (US$183.9bn) for 2012. This represents a 19% increase over 2011, with most apparently set aside for further increases in housing, health, transport, social welfare and infrastructure. Reducing high unemployment remains a priority.

Defence spending

Saudi Arabia has become increasingly aware of the need to further strengthen internal security and bolster its defences. The government has over the past ten years also seen the need to better develop what had been a small and relatively ineffective local defence industry. Working with many foreign-based industrial partners, Saudi-based companies are now able to provide a range of sophisticated electronics products, both materials and an increased amount of internally provided 'through-life product and maintenance support'.

No accurate and detailed figures on defence spending are published by the Saudi authorities, but analysts estimate that the kingdom's annual spend on defence procurement represents around 10% of annual GDP. With a reported 233,500 active military personnel and force numbers still growing, it is clear that Riyadh remains committed to plans to rebuild and modernise its armed forces.

Over the next few years, Riyadh is expected to commit to a substantial number of additional defence-procurement schemes plus upgrades to existing equipment. Much has already been spent on defence-infrastructure modernisation, facilities improvement and synthetics-based training. In

December 2011, a final agreement emerged for the RSAF to purchase 84 Boeing F-15SAs. The agreement with the US also included an upgrade of 70 existing F-15 aircraft. The deal was followed by agreements to extend the existing Saudi-British Defence Cooperation Programme together with provision of funding for the purchase of 22 advanced *Hawk* trainers and 55 PC-21 trainers. An additional $2.4bn funding was confirmed covering a potential 'Tranche 3' multi-role capability requirement that may emerge for the final batch of 24 aircraft within the 2008 'Salam' order for 72 *Typhoon* aircraft. The Saudi government has also signed agreements with Sikorsky to modernise and upgrade the fleet of *Black Hawk* helicopters.

Defence offsets

The Saudi government has long engaged in a policy of both direct (procurement-related) and indirect (unrelated to procurement) offset and industrial-participation programmes. The requirement can include direct participation in construction or maintenance of defence equipment or, in the case of the 'Salam' programme as originally envisaged, assembly and support. Additionally, the offset programme requirement could be biased toward job creation and industry diversification away from traditional sectors.

In general, Saudi Arabia sets no minimum threshold for offsets, although most usually the obligation will fall within a 35–40% requirement range (35% was the minimum figure established in the 1984 offset policy). Offset policy has more generally been biased toward industrialisation requirements and planned diversification of the economy. However, over the past seven years Saudi offset policy has been increasingly directed where needed to assist in specific industrial and technology ventures, encouraging supplier companies to become minority or equal partner stakeholders within private-sector companies and joint ventures. Such policies have enabled Saudi Arabia to bring in new disciplines, skills and expertise. Inward investment, technology transfer and training support are already important elements of industrialisation and diversification requirements and these can be expected to increase.

Defence offsets in Saudi Arabia

The umbrella term 'offset' is, confusingly, applied to a number of different activities. In Saudi Arabia, defence offset projects have included:

a. Establishment of companies or plants in-kingdom for direct participation in construction or maintenance of defence equipment. Examples include the creation of a number of companies in Saudi Arabia to take part in the 1980s Boeing-led *Peace Shield* air-defence project. Some of those companies are now involved in assembly and support activities under the UK's *Salam* programme to supply *Typhoon* aircraft. Annual turnover of the Saudi offset companies is currently estimated at several billion dollars.

b. Economic offset programmes aimed at importing technology, providing jobs and diversifying the Saudi economy away from oil and gas production. UK programmes in support of *Al Yamamah* and the SBDCP range from a sugar refinery to pharmaceutical plants to advanced petrochemicals. French offset programmes include glass, precious metals and smart cards; US programmes have even included the establishment of a shrimp farm. A 2009 study estimated that such projects had created more than 6,500 new job opportunities, with total sales by economic offset companies reaching US$8bn and exports about US$1.5bn.

Riyadh has also emphasised the ability to train more Saudi nationals and to bring them into management, technical and other qualified positions. For example, BAE Systems now employs more than 2,500 Saudi nationals next to 2,150 expatriates. BAE Systems is working with a number of Saudi industrial partners that employ an additional 2,000 Saudi nationals, such as Aircraft Accessories and Components, Advanced Electronics, Alsalam Aircraft and International Systems Engineering. While previous defence procurement offset requirements have seen investment in a variety of non-defence businesses, more recent inward investment has tended toward more sophisticated technology products, such as electronics and software. Training and development that locks the original equipment manufacturer into long-term partnerships with Saudi-based companies is another Saudi objective.

Algeria ALG

Algerian Dinar D		2011	2012	2013
GDP	D	14.38tr	15.95tr	
	US$	197.86bn	206.55bn	
per capita	US$	5,295	5,528	
Growth	%	2.35	2.56	
Inflation	%	4.49	8.40	
Def bdgt	D	631bn	723bn	
	US$	8.68bn	9.37bn	
US$1=D		72.70	77.20	

Population　37,367,226

Age	0–14	15–19	20–24	25–29	30–64	65 plus
Male	14.2%	4.7%	5.0%	4.9%	19.5%	2.3%
Female	13.6%	4.5%	4.8%	4.8%	19.0%	2.7%

Capabilities

Algeria's military has experience in counter-insurgency, although recent procurement has been focused on conventional weaponry for state-on-state contingencies, with which the armed forces have little familiarity. There is limited experience of tri-service joint operations, and few training exercises have focused on this issue. Nonetheless, Algeria has been a leading proponent of combined training with regional powers, partially to build capacity in neighbouring states to combat al-Qaeda in the Islamic Maghreb. Algeria, Mali, Niger and Mauritania formed a joint operation staff committee in 2010 to coordinate intelligence and operations. Algiers has conducted joint operations with Mali and, in October 2012, Algeria agreed to support an ECOWAS intervention in Mali's north. Limited combined training has occurred with the US, with SF exercises and through the International Military Education and Training programme, as well as with France, the UK and Belgium. The army maintains a division-sized rapid-reaction force, although the fact that two-thirds of the army is conscript-based reduces expertise and the ability to deploy quickly. Mobility is enhanced by a large fleet of light armoured vehicles and helicopters. A modest power-projection capability is also apparent in the transport and air tanker fleet, although given the size of the country these may be more useful for internal rather than overseas deployment. The procurement of a landing platform dock by 2015 will greatly enhance the country's naval power projection.

ACTIVE 130,000 (Army 110,000 Navy 6,000 Air 14,000) **Paramilitary 187,200**

Terms of service Conscription in army only, 18 months (6 months basic, 12 months wth regular army often involving civil projects)

RESERVE 150,000 (Army 150,000) **to age 50**

ORGANISATIONS BY SERVICE

Army 35,000; 75,000 conscript (total 110,000)

FORCES BY ROLE

6 Mil Regions; re-org into div structure on hold

MANOEUVRE

Armoured

2 (1st & 8th) armd div (3 tk regt; 1 mech regt, 1 arty gp)

1 indep armd bde

Mechanised

2 (12th & 40th) mech div (1 tk regt; 3 mech regt, 1 arty gp)

3 indep mech bde

Light

2 indep mot bde

Air Manoeuvre

1 AB div (4 para regt; 1 SF regt)

COMBAT SUPPORT

2 arty bn

7 AD bn

4 engr bn

EQUIPMENT BY TYPE

MBT 1,080: 185 T-90S; 325 T-72; 300 T-62; 270 T-54/T-55

RECCE 134: 44 AML-60; 26 BRDM-2; 64 BRDM-2M with 9M133 *Kornet* (AT-14 *Spriggan*)

AIFV 1,089: 100 BMP-3; 304 BMP-2M with 9M133 *Kornet* (AT-14 *Spriggan*); 685 BMP-1

APC 707

　APC (W) 705: 250 BTR-60; 150 BTR-80; 150 OT-64; 55 M3 Panhard; 100 *Fahd*

　PPV 2 *Marauder*

ARTY 1,019

　SP 170: **122mm** 140 2S1 *Carnation*; **152mm** 30 2S3

　TOWED 375: **122mm** 160 D-30; 25 D-74; 100 M-1931/37; 60 M-30 *M-1938*; **130mm** 10 M-46; **152mm** 20 ML-20 M-1937

　MRL 144: **122mm** 48 BM-21; **140mm** 48 BM-14/16; **240mm** 30 BM-24; **300mm** 18 9A52 *Smerch*

　MOR 330: **82mm** 150 M-37; **120mm** 120 M-1943; **160mm** 60 M-1943

AT

　MSL • MANPATS Milan; 9K133 *Kornet*-E (AT-14 *Spriggan*); 9K115-2 *Metis*-M1 (AT-13 *Saxhorn-2*); 9K11 (AT-3 *Sagger*); 9K111 (AT-4 *Spigot*); 9K113 (AT-5 *Spandrel*)

　RCL 180: **107mm** 60 B-11; **82mm** 120 B-10

　GUNS 250: **57mm** 160 ZIS-2 M-1943; **85mm** 80 D-44; **100mm** 10 T-12; (50 SU-100 SP in store)

AD

　SAM 288+

　　SP 132+: ε48 9K-33 *Osa* (SA-8 *Gecko*); ε20 9K31 *Strela*-1 (SA-9 *Gaskin*); Pantsyr S1 (SA-22 *Greyhound*)

　　MANPAD 200+: ε200 9K32 *Strela*-2 (SA-7A/B *Grail*)

　GUNS ε830

　　SP ε225 ZSU-23-4

　　TOWED ε605: **14.5mm** 100: 60 ZPU-2; 40 ZPU-4 **23mm** 100 ZU-23 **37mm** ε150 M-1939 **57mm** 75 S-60 **85mm** 20 M-1939 **KS-12 100mm** 150 KS-19 **130mm** 10 KS-30

Navy ε6,000

EQUIPMENT BY TYPE

SUBMARINES • TACTICAL • SSK 4

　2 *Kilo* (FSU *Paltus*) with 6 single 533mm TT with Test-71ME HWT

2 Improved *Kilo* (RUS *Varshavyanka*) with 6 single 533mm TT

PRINCIPAL SURFACE COMBATANTS 3

FRIGATES • FFM 3

3 *Mourad Rais* (FSU *Koni*) with 2 twin 533mm TT, 2 RBU 6000 *Smerch* 2, 2 twin 76mm gun

PATROL AND COASTAL COMBATANTS 24

CORVETTES 6

FSGM 3 *Rais Hamidou* (FSU *Nanuchka* II) with 2 quad lnchr with 3M24 *Uran* (SS-N-25 *Switchblade*) AShM, 1 twin lnchr with 9M33 *Osa*-M (SA-N-4 *Gecko*) SAM

FSG 3 *Djebel Chenona* with 2 twin lnchr with C-802 (CSS-N-8 *Saccade*) AShM, 1 76mm gun

PBFG 9 *Osa* II (3†) with 4 single lnchr with P-15 *Termit* (SS-N-2B *Styx*) AShM

PB 9 *Kebir*

AMPHIBIOUS • LS 3

LSM 1 *Polnochny* B (capacity 6 MBT; 180 troops)

LST 2 *Kalaat beni Hammad* (capacity 7 tanks; 240 troops) with 1 med hel landing platform

LOGISTICS AND SUPPORT 11

AGS 1 *El Idrissi*

AX 1 *Daxin*

YGS 2 *Ras Tara*

YPT 1 *Poluchat* I (used for SAR)

YTB 6: 1 *El Chadid*; 1 *Kader*; 4 *Mazafran*

Naval Aviation

EQUIPMENT BY TYPE
HELICOPTERS
SAR 10: 6 AW101 SAR; 4 *Super Lynx* Mk130

Coast Guard ε500

PATROL AND COASTAL COMBATANTS 55

PBF 6 *Baglietto* 20

PB 49: 6 *Baglietto Mangusta*; 12 *Jebel Antar*; 21 *Deneb*; 4 *El Mounkid*; 6 *Kebir*

LOGISTICS AND SUPPORT 8

ARL 1 *El Mourafek*

AXL 7 *El Mouderrib* (PRC *Chui-E*) (2 in reserve†)

Air Force 14,000

Flying hours   150 hrs/year

FORCES BY ROLE
FIGHTER

1 sqn with MiG-23MF/MS/U *Flogger* (possibly withdrawn)

1 sqn with MiG-25PDS/RU *Foxbat*

4 sqn with MiG-29C/UB *Fulcrum*

FIGHTER/GROUND ATTACK

2 sqn with Su-24M/MK *Fencer*

2 sqn with Su-30MKA *Flanker*

ELINT

1 sqn with Beech 1900D

MARITIME PATROL

2 sqn with Beech 200T/300 *King Air*

ISR

1 sqn with Su-24MR *Fencer* E*; MiG-25RBSh *Foxbat* D*

TANKER

1 sqn with Il-78 *Midas*

TRANSPORT

1 sqn with C-130H/H-30 *Hercules*; L-100-30

1 sqn with C-295M

1 sqn with Gulfstream IV-SP; Gulfstream V

1 sqn with Il-76MD/TD *Candid*

TRAINING

2 sqn with Z-142

1 sqn with Yak-130

2 sqn with L-39C/ZA *Albatros*

1 hel sqn with PZL Mi-2 *Hoplite*

ATTACK HELICOPTER

3 sqn with Mi-24 *Hind*

TRANSPORT HELICOPTER

1 sqn with AS355 *Ecureuil*

5 sqn with Mi-8 *Hip*; Mi-17 *Hip* H

1 sqn with Ka-27PS *Helix* D; Ka-32T *Helix*

AIR DEFENCE

3 ADA bde

3 SAM regt with S-75 *Dvina* (SA-2 *Guideline*)/S-125 *Neva* (SA-3 *Goa*)/2K12 *Kub* (SA-6 *Gainful*); S-300PMU2 (SA-20 *Gargoyle*)

EQUIPMENT BY TYPE
AIRCRAFT 125 combat capable

FTR 55: 12 MiG-25 *Foxbat*; 25 MiG-29C *Fulcrum*/MiG-29UB *Fulcrum*; 18 MiG-23MF/MS/U *Flogger* (possibly withdrawn)

FGA 62: 28 Su-30MKA; 34 Su-24M/Su-24MK *Fencer* D

ISR 8: 4 MiG-25RBSh *Foxbat* D*; 4 Su-24MR *Fencer* E*

TKR 6 Il-78 *Midas*

TPT 68 **Heavy** 12: 3 Il-76MD *Candid* B; 9 Il-76TD *Candid*; **Medium** 18: 9 C-130H *Hercules*; 7 C-130H-30 *Hercules*; 2 L-100-30; **Light** 32: 3 Beech C90B *King Air*; 5 Beech 200T *King Air*; 6 Beech 300 *King Air*; 12 Beech 1900D (electronic surv); 5 C-295M; 1 F-27 *Friendship*; **PAX** 6: 1 A340; 4 Gulfstream IV-SP; 1 Gulfstream V

TRG 99: 36 L-39ZA *Albatros*; 7 L-39C *Albatros*; 16 Yak-130; 40 Z-142

HELICOPTERS

ATK 33 Mi-24 *Hind*

SAR 3 Ka-27PS *Helix* D

MRH 3 Bell 412EP

MRH/TPT 75 Mi-8 *Hip* (med tpt)/Mi-17 *Hip* H

TPT 40 **Medium** 4 Ka-32T *Helix* **Light** 36: 8 AS355 *Ecureuil*; 28 PZL Mi-2 *Hoplite*

AD

SAM S-75 *Dvina* (SA-2 *Guideline*); S-125 *Pechora*-M (SA-3 *Goa*); 2K12 *Kvadrat* (SA-6 *Gainful*) SP; S-300PMU2 (SA-20 *Gargoyle*)

GUNS 725 **100mm/130mm/85mm**

MSL

ASM Kh-25 (AS-10 *Karen*); Kh-29 (AS-14 *Kedge*); Kh-23 (AS-7 *Kerry*); Kh-31P/A (AS-17A/B *Krypton*); Kh-59ME (AS-18 *Kazoo*)

ARM Kh-25MP (AS-12 *Kegler*)

AAM • IR R-3 (AA-2 *Atoll*)‡; R-60 (AA-8 *Aphid*); R-73 (AA-11 *Archer*); **IR/SARH** R-40/46 (AA-6 *Acrid*); R-23/24 (AA-7 *Apex*); R-27 (AA-10 *Alamo*); **ARH** R-77 (AA-12 *Adder*)

Paramilitary ε187,200

Gendarmerie 20,000

Ministry of Defence control; 6 regions

EQUIPMENT BY TYPE

RECCE AML-60/110 M-3 Panhard APC (W)
APC (W) 100 *Fahd*
HELICOPTERS • TPT • Light Some PZL Mi-2 *Hoplite*

National Security Forces 16,000

Directorate of National Security. Small arms

Republican Guard 1,200

EQUIPMENT BY TYPE

RECCE AML-60
APC (T) M-3

Legitimate Defence Groups ε150,000

Self-defence militia, communal guards (60,000)

DEPLOYMENT

DEMOCRATIC REPUBLIC OF CONGO

UN • MONUSCO 5 obs

Bahrain BHR

Bahraini Dinar D		2011	2012	2013
GDP	D	9.73bn	9.97bn	
	US$	25.87bn	26.51bn	
per capita	US$	20,723	21,236	
Growth	%	2.10	1.98	
Inflation	%	-0.42	0.59	
Def bdgt [a]	D	355m	383m	
	US$	943m	1.02bn	
FMA (US)	US$	15.461m	10m	10m
US$1=D		0.38	0.38	

[a] Includes expenditure on National Guard. Excludes arms purchases.

Population	1,248,348

Ethnic groups: Nationals 64%; Asian 13%; other Arab 10%; Iranian 8%; European 1%)

Age	0–14	15–19	20–24	25–29	30–64	65 plus
Male	10.3%	3.9%	4.9%	7.0%	33.2%	1.2%
Female	10.0%	3.4%	3.6%	4.1%	16.9%	1.4%

Capabilities

Bahrain retains moderately well-trained and -equipped forces, but their small size limits their effectiveness. While in general focused on the possibility of state-to-state conflict, their role in internal security became more apparent in 2011. With regards to its primary role, defence of the island from an amphibious invasion and/or aerial assault from Iran, Bahrain could mount a sturdy defence though it would eventually be overwhelmed by concerted operations. The kingdom therefore relies on the security umbrella offered by the Gulf Cooperation Council and the de-terrent effect provided by the presence of the US through Fifth Fleet/NAVCENT. Bahrain is a member of the GCC, and has participated in GCC military exercises. The GCC's defence obligations were invoked in 2011, reflecting the Bahraini military's inability to quench protests. Following a series of crackdowns on protesters, a state of emergency was declared and Saudi, Qatari and Emirati personnel were deployed to Bahrain as part of the GCC's Peninsula Shield force. Washington suspended arms transfers in the wake of this security crackdown, though this suspension was partially lifted in May 2012. The deployment was a tacit admission by Manama that its security forces needed assistance in the internal security role and suggested greater training and improved rules of engagement might be required for any similar future operations.

ACTIVE 8,200 (Army 6,000 Navy 700 Air 1,500)
Paramilitary 11,260

ORGANISATIONS BY SERVICE

Army 6,000

FORCES BY ROLE

SPECIAL FORCES

1 bn

MANOEUVRE

Armoured

1 armd bde(–) (1 recce bn, 2 armd bn)

Mechanised

1 inf bde (2 mech bn, 1 mot bn)

Light

1 (Amiri) gd bn

COMBAT SUPPORT

1 arty bde (1 hvy arty bty, 2 med arty bty, 1 lt arty bty, 1 MRL bty)
1 AD bn (1 ADA bty, 2 SAM bty)
1 engr coy

COMBAT SERVICE SUPPORT

1 log coy
1 tpt coy
1 med coy

EQUIPMENT BY TYPE

MBT 180 M60A3
RECCE 30: 22 AML-90; 8 S52 *Shorland*; (8 *Ferret* & 8 *Saladin* in store)
AIFV 25 YPR-765 (with 25mm)
APC 375
  APC (T) 200 M113A2
  APC (W) 120: 10 AT105 *Saxon*; 110 M3 Panhard
  PPV 55: 49 *Cobra*; 6 *Nimer-1*
ARTY 151
  SP 82: **155mm** 20 M109A5; **203mm** 62 M110A2
  TOWED 36: **105mm** 8 L118 Light Gun; **155mm** 28 M198
  MRL 227mm 9 M270 MLRS (with 30 ATACMS)
  MOR 24: **SP 120mm** 12 M113A2; **81mm** 12 L16
AT • MSL • MANPATS 75: 60 *Javelin*; 15 BGM-71A TOW
  RCL 31: **106mm** 25 M40A1; **120mm** 6 MOBAT
AD • SAM 91
  SP 7 *Crotale*
  TOWED 6 MIM-23B I-HAWK

MANPAD 78: 18 FIM-92A *Stinger*; 60 RBS-70
GUNS 24: **35mm** 12 Oerlikon; **40mm** 12 L/70
ARV 53 *Fahd* 240

Navy 700

EQUIPMENT BY TYPE
PRINCIPAL SURFACE COMBATANTS 1
  FRIGATES • FFGHM 1 *Sabha* (US *Oliver Hazard Perry*)
    with 1 Mk13 GMLS with SM-1MR SAM/RGM-84C
    Harpoon AShM, 2 triple 324mm ASTT, 1 76mm gun,
    (capacity 1 Bo-105 hel)
PATROL AND COASTAL COMBATANTS 12
  CORVETTES • FSG 2 *Al Manama* (GER Lurssen 62m)
    with 2 twin lnchr with MM-40 *Exocet* AShM, 1 76mm
    gun, 1 hel landing platform
  PCFG 4 *Ahmed el Fateh* (GER Lurssen 45m) with 2 twin
    lnchr with MM-40 *Exocet* AShM, 1 76mm gun
  PB 4: 2 *Al Jarim* (US *Swift* FPB-20); 2 *Al Riffa* (GER Lurssen
    38m)
  PBF 2 Mk V SOC
AMPHIBIOUS • CRAFT 9
  LCU 9: 1 *Loadmaster*; 4 *Mashtan*; 2 ADSB 42m
  LCVP 2 *Sea Keeper*
LOGISTICS AND SUPPORT 2
  YFL 1 *Tighatlib*
  YFU 1 *Ajeera*

Naval Aviation

EQUIPMENT BY TYPE
HELICOPTERS • TPT • Light 2 Bo-105

Air Force 1,500

FORCES BY ROLE
FIGHTER
  2 sqn with F-16C/D *Fighting Falcon*
FIGHTER/GROUND ATTACK
  1 sqn with F-5E/F *Tiger* II
TRANSPORT
  1 (Royal) flt with B-727; B-747; BAe-146; Gulfstream II;
    Gulfstream IV; Gulfstream 450; Gulfstream 550; S-92A
TRAINING
  1 sqn with *Hawk* Mk-129*
  1 sqn with T-67M *Firefly*
ATTACK HELICOPTER
  2 sqn with AH-1E/F *Cobra*; TAH-1P *Cobra*
TRANSPORT HELICOPTER
  1 sqn with Bell 212 (AB-212)
  1 sqn with UH-60M *Black Hawk*
  1 (VIP) sqn with Bo-105; S-70A *Black Hawk*; UH-60L
    Black Hawk

EQUIPMENT BY TYPE
AIRCRAFT 39 combat capable
  FTR 12: 8 F-5E *Tiger* II; 4 F-5F *Tiger* II
  FGA 21: 17 F-16C *Fighting Falcon*; 4 F-16D *Fighting Falcon*
  TPT • PAX 10: 1 B-727; 2 B-747; 1 Gulfstream II; 1
    Gulfstream IV; 1 Gulfstream 450; 1 Gulfstream 550; 3
    BAe-146
  TRG 9: 6 *Hawk* Mk-129*; 3 T-67M *Firefly*
HELICOPTERS
  ATK 28: 16 AH-1E *Cobra*; 12 AH-1F *Cobra*

TPT 27 **Medium** 13: 3 S-70A *Black Hawk*; 1 S-92A (VIP);
  1 UH-60L *Black Hawk*; 8 UH-60M *Black Hawk* **Light** 14: 11
  Bell 212 (AB-212); 3 Bo-105
  TRG 6 TAH-1P *Cobra*
MSL
  ASM AGM-65D/G *Maverick*
  AAM • IR AIM-9P *Sidewinder*; SARH AIM-7 *Sparrow*;
    ARH AIM-120 AMRAAM
  AT • MSL some TOW

Paramilitary ε11,260

Police 9,000
Ministry of Interior
HELICOPTERS
  MRH 2 Bell 412 *Twin Huey*
  ISR 2 Hughes 500
  TPT • Light 1 Bo-105

National Guard ε2,000
FORCES BY ROLE
MANOEUVRE
  Other
    3 paramilitary bn

Coast Guard ε260
Ministry of Interior
PATROL AND COASTAL COMBATANTS 52
  PBF 23: 6 *Jaris*; 6 *Saham*; 6 *Fajr*; 5 *Jarach*
  PB 29: 6 *Haris*; 1 *Al Muharraq*; 10 *Deraa* (of which 4
    Halmatic 20, 2 *Souter 20*, 4 *Rodman 20*); 10 *Saif* (of which
    4 *Fairey Sword*, 6 *Halmatic 160*); 2 *Hawar*
  AMPHIBIOUS • LANDING CRAFT • LCU 1 *Load-
    master* II
  LOGISTICS AND SUPPORT • YAG 1 *Safra*

DEPLOYMENT

AFGHANISTAN
NATO • ISAF 95

FOREIGN FORCES

Saudi Arabia GCC (SANG): Peninsula Shield ε1,000
United Kingdom Air Force 1 BAe-125 CC-3; 1 BAe-146
MKII
United States US Central Commmand: 2,100; 1 HQ (5th
Fleet)

Egypt EGY

Egyptian Pound E£		2011	2012	2013
GDP	E£	1.37tr	1.53tr	
	US$	235.72bn	255bn	
per capita	US$	2,817	3,047	
Growth	%	1.78	1.96	
Inflation	%	11.07	8.65	
Def exp	E£	20.7bn		
	US$	3.56bn		
Def bdgt	E£	25.2bn	25.3bn	26.3bn
	US$	4.33bn	4.21bn	
FMA (US)	US$	1.2974bn	1.3bn	1.3bn
US$1=E£		5.82	6.01	

Population   83,688,164

Age	0–14	15–19	20–24	25–29	30–64	65 plus
Male	16.6%	4.7%	4.6%	4.8%	17.7%	2.1%
Female	15.9%	4.5%	4.4%	4.5%	17.5%	2.6%

Capabilities

Egypt's Supreme Council for the Armed Forces (SCAF) assumed power in February 2011, after the departure of former President Hosni Mubarak. SCAF was in charge of overseeing the transition towards elections, which, in May, saw Muslim Brotherhood candidate Muhammad Morsi elected president. Morsi reinforced presidential authority in August, with his decision to retire then SCAF head Field Marshal Mohammed Tantawi, after SCAF had previously tried to limit presidential power. The armed forces remain focused on their tentative relations with the new civilian authorities, and there seems little appetite to change strategic orientation. However, the new administration's position on regional security issues, such as the Israeli-Palestinian issue, may be different from those seen in the Mubarak era. That said, Cairo still receives $1.3 billion annually in US military aid, and has long been upgrading its inventories with US systems. There is little incentive to endanger its ability to continue this process, or undermine support and maintenance agreements. That Cairo might widen its list of suppliers is not inconceivable in some capability areas, but since the two countries' Peace Vector deal in 1980, US equipment has increasingly replaced Egypt's ageing Soviet-era equipment. Though the armed forces have not been tested in large-scale combat since *Operation Desert Storm*, they maintain a regular exercise schedule including with foreign militaries (such as the *Bright Star* series). However, while training will be at a high standard for many within the military, it is harder to judge effectiveness across the entire force, given the level of conscription and the tasks that some conscripts are reported to undertake, in relation to the Egyptian armed forces' extensive domestic business and industrial interests. The attack by militants on an Egyptian military base in the Sinai peninsula, in August 2012, has resulted in their largest operational deployment since the 1991 Gulf War, and created a new security challenge for the armed forces.

ACTIVE 438,500 (Army 310,000 Navy 18,500 Air 30,000 Air Defence Command 80,000) **Paramilitary 397,000**

Terms of service 12 months–3 years (followed by refresher training over a period of up to 9 years)

RESERVE 479,000 (Army 375,000 Navy 14,000 Air 20,000 Air Defence 70,000)

ORGANISATIONS BY SERVICE

Army 90,000–120,000; 190,000–220,000 conscript (total 310,000)

FORCES BY ROLE
SPECIAL FORCES
  5 cdo gp
  1 counter-terrorist unit
MANOEUVRE
  Armoured
  4 armd div (2 armd bde, 1 mech bde, 1 arty bde)
  4 indep armd bde
  1 Republican Guard bde
  Mechanised
  8 mech div (1 armd bde, 2 mech bde, 1 arty bde)
  4 indep mech bde
  Light
  1 inf div
  2 indep inf bde
  Air Manoeuvre
  2 air mob bde
  1 para bde
COMBAT SUPPORT
  15 arty bde
  1 SSM bde with FROG-7
  1 SSM bde with *Scud*-B
  6 engr bde (3 engr bn)
  2 spec ops engr bn
  6 salvage engr bn
  24 MP bn
  18 sigs bn
COMBAT SERVICE SUPPORT
  36 log bn
  27 med bn

EQUIPMENT BY TYPE
MBT 2,497: 1,087 M1A1 *Abrams*; 300 M60A1; 850 M60A3; 260 *Ramses II* (mod T-54/55); (840 T-54/T-55 in store); (500 T-62 in store)
RECCE 412: 300 BRDM-2; 112 *Commando Scout*
AIFV 390 YPR-765 (with 25mm); (220 BMP-1 in store)
APC 3,560
  APC (T) 2,000 M113A2/YPR-765 (incl variants); (500 BTR-50/OT-62 in store)
  APC (W) 1,560: 250 BMP-600P; 250 BTR-60S; 410 *Fahd-30/TH* 390 *Fahd*; 650 *Walid*
ARTY 4,468
  SP 492: **122mm** 124 SP 122; **155mm** 368: 164 M109A2; 204 M109A5
  TOWED 962: **122mm** 526: 190 D-30M; 36 M-1931/37; 300 M-30 *M-1938*; **130mm** 420 M-46; **155mm** 16 GH-52

MRL 450: **122mm** 356: 96 BM-11; 60 BM-21; 50 *Sakr*-10; 50 *Sakr*-18; 100 *Sakr*-36; **130mm** 36 *Kooryong*; **140mm** 32 BM-14; **227mm** 26 M270 MLRS; **240mm** (48 BM-24 in store)
MOR 2,564
    SP 136: **107mm** 100: 65 M106A1; 35 M106A2 **120mm** 36 M1064A3
    81mm 50 M125A2; **82mm** 500 **120mm** 1,848: 1,800 M-1943; 48 Brandt **160mm** 30 M160
AT • MSL
    SP 262: 52 M-901, 210 YPR 765 PRAT
    MANPATS 2,100: 1,200 9K11 *Malyutka* (AT-3 *Sagger*) (incl BRDM-2); 200 *Milan*; 700 TOW-2
UAV • ISR • Heavy R4E-50 *Skyeye*
AD
  SAM
    SP 96: 50 FIM-92A *Avenger*; 26 M48 *Chaparral*; 20 9K31 *Strela*-1 (SA-9 *Gaskin*)
    MANPAD 2,764: 2,000 *Ayn al-Saqr*/9K32 *Strela*-2 (SA-7 *Grail*)‡; 164 FIM-92A *Stinger*; 600 *Igla* (SA-18 *Grouse*)
  GUNS
    SP 355: **23mm** 165: 45 *Sinai*-23; 120 ZSU-23-4; **37mm** 150; **57mm** 40 ZSU-57-2
    TOWED 700: **14.5mm** 300 ZPU-4; **23mm** 200 ZU-23-2; **57mm** 200 S-60
RADAR • LAND AN/TPQ-36 *Firefinder*; AN/TPQ-37 *Firefinder* (arty/mor)
MSL • TACTICAL • SSM 42+: 9 FROG-7; 24 *Sakr*-80; 9 *Scud*-B
ARV 355+: *Fahd* 240; GMR 3560.55; 220 M88A1; 90 M88A2; M113 ARV; 45 M578; T-54/55 ARV
VLB KMM; MTU; MTU-20
MW *Aardvark* JFSU Mk4

Navy ε8,500 (incl 2,000 Coast Guard); 10,000 conscript (total 18,500)

EQUIPMENT BY TYPE
SUBMARINES • TACTICAL • SSK 4 *Romeo*† (PRC Type-033) with 8 single 533mm TT with UGM-84C *Harpoon* AShM
PRINCIPAL SURFACE COMBATANTS 8
  FRIGATES 8:
    FFGHM 4 *Mubarak* (US *Oliver Hazard Perry*) with 1 Mk13 GMLS with RGM-84C *Harpoon* AShM/SM-1MP SAM, 1 76mm gun, (capacity 2 SH-2G *Super Seasprite* ASW hel)
    FFGH 2 *Damyat* (US *Knox*) with 1 octuple Mk16 GMLS with RGM-84C *Harpoon* AShM/ASROC, 2 twin 324mm TT, 1 127mm gun, (capacity 1 SH-2G *Super Seasprite* ASW hel)
    FFG 2 *Najim Al Zaffer* (PRC *Jianghu* I) with 2 twin lnchr with HY-2 (CSS-N-2 *Silkworm*) AShM, 2 RBU 1200
PATROL AND COASTAL COMBATANTS 55
  CORVETTES • FSGM 2
    2 *Abu Qir* (ESP *Descubierta*) with 2 quad Mk141 lnchr with RGM-84C *Harpoon* AShM, 1 octuple lnchr with *Aspide* SAM, 2 triple 324mm with *Sting Ray* LWT, 1 twin 375mm A/S mor, 1 76mm gun
  PCFG 11
    6 *Ramadan* with 4 single lnchr with *Otomat* MkII AShM, 1 76mm gun

5 *Tiger* with 2 twin lnchr with MM-38 *Exocet* AShM, 1 76mm gun
PCC 5
  5 *Hainan* (PRC – 3 more in reserve†) with 2 triple 324mm TT, 4 single RL
PBFG 18
  1 *Ezzat* (US *Ambassador* IV) with 2 quad lnchr with RGM-84L *Harpoon* Block II AShM, 1 21-cell Mk49 lnchr with RAM Block 1A SAM, 1 Mk15 Mod 21 Block 1B *Phalanx* CIWS, 1 76mm gun (3 additional vessels in build)
  4 *Hegu* (PRC – *Komar* type) with 2 single lnchr with SY-1 AShM (2 additional vessels in reserve)
  5 *October* (FSU *Komar* – 1†) with 2 single lnchr with *Otomat* MkII AShM (1 additional vessel in reserve)
  8 *Osa* I (FSU – 3†) with 4 single lnchr with P-15 *Termit* (SS-N-2A *Styx*) AShM
PBFM 4
  4 *Shershen* (FSU) with 1 9K32 *Strela*-2 (SA-N-5 *Grail*) SAM (manual aiming), 1 12-tube BM-24 MRL
PBF 7
  3 *Kaan* (TUR MRTP20) (3 additional vessels in build)
  4 *Osa* II (FSU)
PB 8
  4 *Shanghai* II (PRC)
  2 *Shershen* (FSU – 1†) with 4 single 533mm TT, 1 8-tube BM-21 MRL
  2 *Swiftships* 28 (2 additional vessels under construction)
MINE WARFARE • MINE COUNTERMEASURES 14
  MHC 5: 2 *Osprey*; 3 *Dat Assawari* (US *Swiftships*)
  MSI 2 *Safaga* (US *Swiftships*)
  MSO 7: 3 *Assiout* (FSU T-43 class); 4 *Aswan* (FSU *Yurka*)
AMPHIBIOUS 12
  LANDING SHIPS • LSM 3 *Polnochny* A (FSU) (capacity 6 MBT; 180 troops)
  LANDING CRAFT • LCU 9 *Vydra* (capacity either 3 AMX-30 MBT or 100 troops)
LOGISTICS AND SUPPORT 26
  AOT 7 *Toplivo* (1 additional in reserve)
  AE 1 *Halaib* (*Westerwald*-class)
  AKR 3 *Al Hurreya*
  ARL 1 *Shaledin* (*Luneberg*-class)
  ATA 5† *Okhtensky*
  AX 5: 1 *El Fateh*† (UK 'Z' class); 1 *El Horriya* (also used as the presidential yacht); 1 *Al Kousser*; 1 *Intishat*; 1 other
  YPT 2 *Poluchat* 1
  YDT 2

Coastal Defence

Army tps, Navy control
EQUIPMENT BY TYPE
ARTY • COASTAL 100mm; 130mm SM-4-1; **152mm**
MSL • AShM 4K87 (SSC-2B *Samlet*); *Otomat* MkII AShM

Naval Aviation

All aircraft operated by Air Force
AIRCRAFT • TPT • Light 4 Beech 1900C (Maritime Surveillance)

HELICOPTERS
ASW 14: 10 SH-2G *Super Seasprite* with Mk 46 LWT; 4 *Sea King* Mk47

MRH 5 SA342 *Gazelle*

UAV • ISR • Light 2 *Camcopter* 5.1

Coast Guard 2,000
PATROL AND COASTAL COMBATANTS 74
PBF 15: 6 *Crestitalia*; 6 *Swift Protector*; 3 *Peterson*

PB 59: 5 *Nisr*; 12 *Sea Spectre* MkIII; 9 *Swiftships*; 21 *Timsah*; 3 Type-83; 9 *Peterson*

Air Force 30,000 (incl 10,000 conscript)
FORCES BY ROLE
FIGHTER
1 sqn with F-16A/B *Fighting Falcon*

8 sqn with F-16C/D *Fighting Falcon*

6 sqn with J-7/MiG-21 *Fishbed*/MiG-21U *Mongol* A

2 sqn with *Mirage* 5D/E

1 sqn with *Mirage* 2000B/C

FIGHTER/GROUND ATTACK
2 sqn with F-4E *Phantom* II

1 sqn with *Mirage* 5E2

ANTI-SUBMARINE WARFARE
1 sqn with SH-2G *Super Seasprite*

1 sqn with *Sea King* Mk47

MARITIME PATROL
1 sqn with Beech 1900C

ELECTRONIC WARFARE
1 sqn with Beech 1900 (ELINT); *Commando* Mk2E (ECM)

ELECTRONIC WARFARE/TRANSPORT
1 sqn with C-130H/VC-130H *Hercules*

AIRBORNE EARLY WARNING
1 sqn with E-2C *Hawkeye*

SEARCH & RESCUE
1 unit with AW139

TRANSPORT
1 sqn with An-74TK-200A

1 sqn with C-130H/C-130H-30 *Hercules*

1 sqn with C-295M

1 sqn with DHC-5D *Buffalo*

1 sqn with B-707-366C; B-737-100; Beech 200 *Super King Air*; *Falcon* 20; Gulfstream III; Gulfstream IV; Gulfstream IV-SP

TRAINING
1 sqn with *Alpha Jet**

1 sqn with DHC-5 *Buffalo*

3 sqn with EMB-312 *Tucano*

1 sqn with Grob 115EG

ε6 sqn with K-8 *Karakorum**

1 sqn with L-39 *Albatros*; L-59E *Albatros**

ATTACK HELICOPTER
2 sqn with AH-64D *Apache*

2 sqn with SA-342K *Gazelle* (with HOT)

1 sqn with SA-342L *Gazelle*

TRANSPORT HELICOPTER
1 sqn with CH-47C/D *Chinook*

2 sqn with Mi-8 *Hip*

1 sqn with S-70 *Black Hawk*; UH-60A/L *Black Hawk*

UAV
Some sqn with R4E-50 *Skyeye*; Teledyne-Ryan 324 *Scarab*

EQUIPMENT BY TYPE
AIRCRAFT 589 combat capable

FTR 82: 26 F-16A *Fighting Falcon*; 6 F-16B *Fighting Falcon*; ε50 J-7

FGA 310: 29 F-4E *Phantom* II; 127 F-16C *Fighting Falcon*; 38 F-16D *Fighting Falcon*; 3 *Mirage* 2000B; 15 *Mirage* 2000C; 36 *Mirage* 5D/E; 12 *Mirage* 5E2; ε50 MiG-21 *Fishbed*/MiG-21U *Mongol* A

ELINT 2 VC-130H *Hercules*

ISR 6 *Mirage* 5R (5SDR)*

AEW&C 7 E-2C *Hawkeye*

TPT 61 **Medium** 24: 21 C-130H *Hercules*; 3 C-130H-30 *Hercules* **Light** 26: 3 An-74TK-200A (3 more on order); 1 Beech 200 *King Air*; 4 Beech 1900 (ELINT); 4 Beech 1900C; 5 C-295; 9 DHC-5D *Buffalo* **PAX** 11: 1 B-707-366C; 3 *Falcon* 20; 2 Gulfstream III; 1 Gulfstream IV; 4 Gulfstream IV-SP

TRG 329: 36 *Alpha Jet**; 54 EMB-312 *Tucano*; 74 Grob 115EG; 120 K-8 *Karakorum**; 10 L-39 *Albatros*; 35 L-59E *Albatros**

HELICOPTERS
ATK 35 AH-64D *Apache*

ASW 15: 10 SH-2G *Super Seasprite* (opcon Navy); 5 *Sea King* Mk47 (opcon Navy)

ELINT 4 *Commando* Mk2E (ECM)

MRH 72: 2 AW139 (SAR); 65 SA342K *Gazelle* (some with HOT); 5 SA342L *Gazelle* (opcon Navy)

TPT 93: **Heavy** 19: 3 CH-47C *Chinook*; 16 CH-47D *Chinook*; **Medium** 74: 2 AS-61; 24 *Commando* (of which 3 VIP); 40 Mi-8 *Hip*; 4 S-70 *Black Hawk* (VIP); 4 UH-60L *Black Hawk* (VIP)

TRG 17 UH-12E

UAV • ISR • Heavy R4E-50 *Skyeye*; Teledyne-Ryan 324 *Scarab*

MSL
ASM 245+: 80 AGM-65A *Maverick*; 123 AGM-65D *Maverick*; 12 AGM-65F *Maverick*; 30 AGM-65G *Maverick*; AGM-119 *Hellfire*; AGM-84 *Harpoon*; AM-39 *Exocet*; AS-30L HOT

ARM *Armat*; Kh-25MP (AS-12 *Kegler*)

AAM • IR R-3(AA-2 *Atoll*)‡; AIM-9FL/P *Sidewinder*; R-550 *Magic*; **SARH** AIM-7E/F/M *Sparrow*; R530

Air Defence Command 80,000 conscript; 70,000 reservists (total 150,000)
FORCES BY ROLE
AIR DEFENCE
5 AD div (geographically based) (total: 12 SAM bty with M48 *Chaparral*, 12 radar bn, 12 ADA bde (total: 100 ADA bn), 12 SAM bty with MIM-23B I-HAWK, 14 SAM bty with *Crotale*, 18 SAM bn with *Skyguard*, 110 SAM bn with S-125 *Pechora*-M (SA-3A *Goa*); 2K12 *Kub* (SA-6 *Gainful*); S-75M *Volkhov* (SA-2 *Guideline*))

EQUIPMENT BY TYPE
AD
SYSTEMS 72+: Some *Amoun* with RIM-7F *Sea Sparrow* SAM, 36+ quad SAM, *Skyguard* towed SAM, 36+ twin 35mm guns

SAM 702+

SP 130+: 24+ *Crotale*; 50+ M48 *Chaparral*; 56+ SA-6 *Gainful*

TOWED 572+: 78+ MIM-23B I-HAWK; S-75M *Volkhov* (SA-2 *Guideline*) 282+ *Skyguard*; 212+ S-125 *Pechora*-M (SA-3A *Goa*)

GUNS 1,566+

SP • 23mm 266+: 36+ *Sinai-23* (SPAAG) with *Ayn al-Saqr* MANPAD, Dassault 6SD-20S land; 230 ZSU-23-4

TOWED 57mm 600 S-60; **85mm** 400 M-1939 *KS-12*; **100mm** 300 KS-19

Paramilitary ε397,000 active

Central Security Forces 325,000

Ministry of Interior; Includes conscripts
APC (W) 100+: 100 *Hussar*; *Walid*

National Guard 60,000

Lt wpns only

FORCES BY ROLE
MANOEUVRE
Other
8 paramilitary bde (cadre) (3 paramilitary bn)

EQUIPMENT BY TYPE
APC (W) 250 *Walid*

Border Guard Forces 12,000

Ministry of Interior; lt wpns only

FORCES BY ROLE
MANOEUVRE
Other
18 Border Guard regt

DEPLOYMENT

CÔTE D'IVOIRE
UN • UNOCI 176; 1 engr coy

DEMOCRATIC REPUBLIC OF THE CONGO
UN • MONUSCO 1,000; 26 obs; 1 SF coy; 1 inf bn

LIBERIA
UN • UNMIL 7 obs

SOUTH SUDAN
UN • UNMISS 3 obs

SUDAN
UN • UNAMID 2,399; 37 obs; 2 inf bn; 1 engr coy; 1 sigs coy; 1 tpt coy

WESTERN SAHARA
UN • MINURSO 21 obs

FOREIGN FORCES

Australia MFO (*Operation Mazurka*) 25
Canada MFO 28
Colombia MFO 354; 1 inf bn
Czech Republic MFO 3
Fiji MFO 338; 1 inf bn

France MFO 2
Hungary MFO 42; 1 MP unit
Italy MFO 84; 4 coastal ptl unit
New Zealand MFO 28 1 trg unit; 1 tpt unit
Norway MFO 3
United States MFO 700; 1 ARNG inf bn; 1 spt bn (1 EOD coy, 1 medical coy, 1 hel coy)
Uruguay MFO 58 1 engr/tpt unit

Iran IRN

Iranian Rial r		2011	2012	2013
GDP	r	5457.28tr	6257.35tr	
	US$	482.43bn	483.78bn	
per capita	US$	6,117	6,134	
Growth	%	2.04	-0.94	
Inflation	%	21.50	25.20	
Def bdgt[a]	r	ε298tr	310tr	
	US$	26.4bn	23.9bn	
US$1=r			11312.00	12934.30

[a] See textbox on p. 359 for discussion of Iranian defence spending in local currency and US dollar terms.

Population   78,868,711

Ethnic groups: Persian 51%; Azeri 24%; Gilaki/Mazandarani 8%; Kurdish 7%; Arab 3%; Lur 2%; Baloch 2%; Turkman 2%

Age	0–14	15–19	20–24	25–29	30–64	65 plus
Male	12.2%	4.7%	6.0%	5.7%	19.7%	2.4%
Female	11.6%	4.5%	5.6%	5.5%	19.3%	2.7%

Capabilities

The Iranian Revolutionary Guard Corps (IRGC) is a capable organisation well-versed in a variety of different operations. There has been some division of labour between the regular armed forces and IRGC in terms of tasks and areas of responsbility Although the armed forces suffer from a generally outdated arsenal, innovative and cost-effective tactics and techniques (particularly the use of asymmetric warfare) mean that Iran is able to pose a challenge to most potential adversaries, especially its weaker neighbours. At the same time, the inability to offer effective deterrence to an advanced military such as that of the United States, may be a motivation for Iran's pursuit of dual-use nuclear programmes. Tehran claims its uranium enrichment is for a civil-energy purpose but, in conjunction with evidence of weapons-design work, it provides a potential break-out capability. A nuclear deterrent, based on its burgeoning ballistic-missile programme, would, in Tehran's view, afford Iran greater security in its relations with two of its prime antagonists, the US and Israel, and also the ability to act with greater impunity regionally. The Iran–Iraq War of the 1980s and various counter-insurgency campaigns mean the military is battle-hardened and, perhaps now true more for mid-level and senior staff, combat-experienced. Yet, its lack of modern and useable equipment means the military must rely on personnel and platform numbers rather than technology to wage war. Large numbers of small, fast-attack craft with anti-ship missiles, for instance, would be able to use swarm or hit-and-run tactics to attempt to disable much larger opponents. Similarly, army equipment may rely on numerical superiority, not sophistication, to prevent an opponent's advance. The air force's ageing fleets of US and European fighters is of limited value and many may already have been cannibalised to keep others flying. The imposition of a UN embargo on most major conventional weapons imports into Iran, in June 2010, has likely only exacerbated the debilitated state of Iran's equipment. Although Tehran has attempted, with partial success, to invigorate its domestic defence industry, it relies on foreign states for high-technology equipment, including anti-ship missiles and advanced air-defence platforms (see pp. 358–363).

ACTIVE 523,000 (Army 350,000 Islamic Revolutionary Guard Corps 125,000 Navy 18,000 Air 30,000) **Paramilitary 40,000**

Armed Forces General Staff coordinates two parallel organisations: the regular armed forces and the Revolutionary Guard Corps

RESERVE 350,000 (Army 350,000, ex-service volunteers)

ORGANISATIONS BY SERVICE

Army 130,000; 220,000 conscript (total 350,000)

FORCES BY ROLE
5 corps-level regional HQ
COMMAND
  1 cdo div HQ
  4 armd div HQ
  2 mech div HQ
  4 inf div HQ
SPECIAL FORCES
  1 cdo div (3 cdo bde)
  6 cdo bde
  1 SF bde
MANOEUVRE
  Armoured
  7 armd bde
  Mechanised
  16 mech bde
  Light
  13 inf bde
  Air Manoeuvre
  1 AB bde
  Aviation
  Some avn gp
COMBAT SUPPORT
  5 arty gp

EQUIPMENT BY TYPE
Totals incl those held by IRGC Ground Forces. Some equipment serviceability in doubt
MBT 1,663+: ε150 *Zulfiqar*; 480 T-72Z; 150 M60A1; 75+ T-62; 100 *Chieftain* Mk3/Mk5; 540 T-54/T-55/Type-59/*Safir*-74; 168 M47/M48

LT TK 80+: 80 *Scorpion*; *Towsan*
RECCE 35 EE-9 *Cascavel*
AIFV 610: 210 BMP-1; 400 BMP-2 with 9K111 *Fagot* (AT-4 *Spigot*)
APC 640+
  APC (T) 340+: 140 *Boragh* with 9K111 *Fagot* (AT-4 *Spigot*); 200 M113; BMT-2 *Cobra*
  APC (W) 300+: 300 BTR-50/BTR-60; *Rakhsh*
ARTY 8,798+
  SP 292+: **122mm** 60+: 60 2S1 *Carnation*; *Raad*-1 (*Thunder* 1) **155mm** 150+: 150 M109; *Raad*-2 (*Thunder* 2) **170mm** 30 M-1978; **175mm** 22 M107; **203mm** 30 M110
  TOWED 2,030+; **105mm** 150: 130 M101A1; 20 M-56; **122mm** 640: 540 D-30; 100 Type-54 (M-30) M-1938; **130mm** 985 M-46; **152mm** 30 D-20; **155mm** 205: 120 GHN-45; 70 M114; 15 Type-88 WAC-21; **203mm** 20 M115
  MRL 1,476+: **107mm** 1,300: 700 Type-63; 600 HASEB *Fadjr* 1; **122mm** 157: 7 BM-11; 100 BM-21; 50 *Arash/Hadid/Noor*; **240mm** 19: ε10 *Fadjr* 3; 9 M-1985; **330mm** *Fadjr* 5
  MOR 5,000: **60mm**; **81mm**; **82mm**; **107mm** M-30; **120mm** M-65
AT
  MSL • MANPATS 9K11 *Malyutka* (AT-3 *Sagger*/I-*Raad*); 9K111 *Fagot* (AT-4 *Spigot*); 9K113 *Konkurs* (AT-5 *Spandrel*/*Towsan*-1); *Saeqhe* 1; *Saeqhe* 2; *Toophan*; *Toophan* 2
  RCL 200+: **75mm** M-20; **82mm** B-10; **106mm** ε200 M-40; **107mm** B-11
AIRCRAFT • TPT 17 **Light** 16: 10 Cessna 185; 2 F-27 *Friendship*; 4 *Turbo Commander* 690 **PAX** 1 *Falcon* 20
HELICOPTERS
  ATK 50 AH-1J *Cobra*
  TPT 173: **Heavy** 20 CH-47C *Chinook*; **Medium** 25 Mi-171; **Light** 128: 68 Bell 205A (AB-205A); 10 Bell 206 *Jet Ranger* (AB-206); 50 Bell 214
UAV • ISR • Medium *Mohajer* 3/4; **Light** *Mohajer* 2; *Ababil*
AD • SAM
  SP 10+: HQ-7 (reported); 10 *Pantsyr* S-1E (SA-22 *Greyhound*)
  MANPAD 9K36 *Strela*-3 (SA-14 *Gremlin*); 9K32 *Strela*-2 (SA-7 *Grail*)‡; *Misaq* 1 (QW-1 *Vanguard*); *Misaq* 2 (QW-11); *Igla*-S (SA-24 *Grinch* - reported); HN-54
  GUNS 1,122
    SP 180: **23mm** 100 ZSU-23-4; **57mm** 80 ZSU-57-2
    TOWED 942 **14.5mm** ZPU-2; ZPU-4; **23mm** 300 ZU-23-2; **35mm** 92 *Skyguard*; **37mm** M-1939; **40mm** 50 L/70; **57mm** 200 S-60; **85mm** 300 M1939
MSL • TACTICAL • SSM ε30 CSS-8 (175 msl); *Shahin*-1/*Shahin*-2; *Nazeat*; *Oghab*
ARV 20+: BREM-1 reported; 20 *Chieftain* ARV; M578; T-54/55 ARV reported
VLB 15: 15 *Chieftain* AVLB
MW *Taftan* 1

Iranian Revolutionary Guard Corps 125,000+

Iranian Revolutionary Guard Corps Ground Forces 100,000+

Controls Basij paramilitary forces. Lightly manned in peacetime. Primary role: internal security; secondary role: external defence, in conjunction with regular armed forces.

FORCES BY ROLE
COMMAND
31 provincial corps HQ (2 in Tehran)
MANOEUVRE
Light
31 indep bde (each bde allocated 10 Basij militia bn for ops)

Iranian Revolutionary Guard Corps Naval Forces 20,000+ (incl 5,000 Marines)

FORCES BY ROLE
COMBAT SUPPORT
Some arty bty
Some AShM bty with HY-2 (CSS-C-3 *Seersucker*) AShM

EQUIPMENT BY TYPE
In addition to the vessels listed the IRGC operates a substantial number of patrol boats with a full-load displacement below 10 tonnes, including ε40 Boghammar-class vessels and small *Bavar*-class wing-in-ground effect air vehicles
PATROL AND COASTAL COMBATANTS 113
  PBFG 46:
    5 *China Cat* with 2 twin lnchr with C-701/*Kosar* AShM
    10 *Thondor* (PRC *Houdong*) with 2 twin lnchr with C-802 (CSS-N-8 *Saccade*) AShM
    25 *Peykaap II* (IPS-16 mod) with 2 single lnchr with C-701 (*Kosar*) AShM
    6 *Zolfaghar* (*Peykaap III/IPS-16 mod*) with 2 single lnchr with C-701 (*Kosar*)/C-704 (*Nasr*) AShM
  PBF 35: 15 *Peykaap I* (IPS -16); 10 *Tir* (IPS 18); ε10 *Pashe* (MIG-G-1900)
  PB ε 20 *Ghaem*
  PTG 12
AMPHIBIOUS
  LANDING SHIPS 4
    2 *Hejaz* (mine-laying capacity)
    2 MIG-S-5000
LOGISTICS AND SUPPORT • AP 3 *Naser*
MSL • TACTICAL • AShM C-701 (*Kosar*); C-704 (*Nasr*); C-802; HY-2 (CSS-C-3 *Seersucker*)

Iranian Revolutionary Guard Corps Marines 5,000+

FORCES BY ROLE
MANOEUVRE
Amphibious
1 marine bde

Iranian Revolutionary Guard Corps Air Force
Controls Iran's strategic missile force.

FORCES BY ROLE
MISSILE
ε1 bde with *Shahab*-1/2
ε1 bn with *Shahab*-3; *Ghadr*-1; *Sajjil*-2 (in devt)

EQUIPMENT BY TYPE
MISSILE • TACTICAL
  MRBM 12+: 12+ *Shahab*-3/*Ghadr*-1; some *Sajjil*-2 (in devt)

  SRBM 18+: some *Fateh* 110; 12-18 *Shahab*-1/2 (ε200–300 msl)
  SSM Some *Zelzal*

Navy 18,000
HQ at Bandar-e Abbas
EQUIPMENT BY TYPE
In addition to the vessels listed the Iranian Navy operates a substantial number of patrol boats with a full-load displacement below 10 tonnes.
SUBMARINES 29
  TACTICAL 21:
    SSK 3 *Kilo* (RUS Type 877EKM) with 6 single 533mm TT
    SSC 1 *Fateh*
    SSW 17: 16 *Qadir* with 2 single 533mm TT (additional vessels in build); 1 *Nahang*
  SDV 8: 5 *Al Sabehat* (SF insertion and mine-laying capacity); 3 other
PATROL AND COASTAL COMBATANTS 69 (+ ε50 small craft under 10 tonnes)
  CORVETTES 6:
    FSGM 1 *Jamaran* (UK Vosper Mk 5 – 2 more under construction at Bandar-e Anzali and Bandar Abbas, expected ISD 2013) with 2 twin lnchr with CSS-N-4 *Sardine* AShM, 2 lnchr with SM-1 SAM, 2 triple 324mm ASTT, 1 76mm gun, 1 hel landing platform
    FSG 4:
      3 *Alvand* (UK Vosper Mk 5) with 2 twin lnchr with CSS-N-4 *Sardine* AShM, 2 triple 324mm ASTT, 1 114mm gun
      1 *Bayandor* (US PF-103) with 2 twin lnchr with C-802 AShM, 2 triple 324mm ASTT, 2 76mm gun
    FS 1 *Bayandor* (US PF-103) with 2 76mm gun
  PCFG 14 *Kaman* (FRA *Combattante* II) with 1–2 twin lcnhr with C-802 AShM
  PBFG 8:
    ε4 Mk13 with 2 single lnchr with C-704 (*Nasr*) AShM, 2 single 324mm TT
    4 *China Cat* with 2 single lnchr with C-701 (*Kosar*) AShM
  PBF 16: 15 *Kashdom* II; 1 *M155*
  PB 22: 3 *Kayvan*; 6 MkII; 10 MkIII; 3 *Parvin*
  PTF 1 *Kajami* (semi-submersible)
  MINE WARFARE • MINE COUNTERMEASURES 5:
    MSC 3: 2 Type-292; 1 *Shahrokh* (in Caspian Sea as trg ship)
    MSI 2 *Riazi* (US *Cape*)
AMPHIBIOUS
  LANDING SHIPS 13:
    LSM 3 *Farsi* (ROK) (capacity 9 tanks; 140 troops)
    LST 4 *Hengam* (capacity 9 tanks; 225 troops)
    LSL 6 *Fouque*
  LANDING CRAFT 10:
    LCAC 7: 6 *Wellington*; 1 *Iran*
    LCT 2
    LCU 1 *Liyan 110*
LOGISTICS AND SUPPORT 47
  AB 12 *Hendijan* (also used for coastal patrol)
  AE 2 *Delvar*
  AFD 2 *Dolphin*

AG 1 *Hamzah*
AK 3 *Delvar*
AORH 3: 2 *Bandar Abbas*; 1 *Kharg*
AWT 5: 4 *Kangan*; 1 *Delvar*
AX 2 *Kialas*
YTB 17
MSL • AshM C-701 (*Kosar*); C-704 (*Nasr*); C-802/A (*Noor/ Ghader*); *Ra'ad* (reported; coastal defence)

Marines 2,600

FORCES BY ROLE
MANOEUVRE
 Amphibious
  2 marine bde

Naval Aviation 2,600

EQUIPMENT BY TYPE
AIRCRAFT 3 combat capable
 ASW 3 P-3F *Orion*
 TPT 16 Light 13: 5 Do-228; 4 F-27 *Friendship*; 4 *Turbo Commander 680* **PAX** 3 *Falcon* 20 (ELINT)
HELICOPTERS
 ASW ε10 SH-3D *Sea King*
 MCM 3 RH-53D *Sea Stallion*
 TPT • Light 17: 5 Bell 205A (AB-205A); 2 Bell 206 *JetRanger* (AB-206); 10 Bell 212 (AB-212)

Air Force 30,000 (incl 12,000 Air Defence)

FORCES BY ROLE
Serviceability probably about 60% for US ac types and about 80% for PRC/Russian ac. Includes IRGC Air Force equipment.
FIGHTER
 1 sqn with F-7M *Airguard*; JJ-7 *Mongol* A*
 2 sqn with F-14 *Tomcat*
 2 sqn with MiG-29A/UB *Fulcrum*
FIGHTER/GROUND ATTACK
 1 sqn with *Mirage* F-1E; F-5E/F *Tiger* II
 1 sqn with Su-24MK *Fencer* D
 5 sqn with F-4D/E *Phantom* II
 3 sqn with F-5E/F *Tiger* II
MARITIME PATROL
 1 sqn with P-3MP *Orion**
ISR
 1 (det) sqn with RF-4E *Phantom* II*
SEARCH & RESCUE
 Some flt with Bell-214C (AB-214C)
TANKER/TRANSPORT
 1 sqn with B-707; B-747; B-747F
TRANSPORT
 1 sqn with B-707; Falcon 50; L-1329 *Jetstar*; Bell 412
 2 sqn with C-130E/H *Hercules*
 1 sqn with F-27 *Friendship*; *Falcon* 20
 1 sqn with Il-76 *Candid*; An-140 (Iran-140 *Faraz*)
TRAINING
 1 sqn with Beech F33A/C *Bonanza*
 1 sqn with F-5B *Freedom Fighter*
 1 sqn with PC-6
 1 sqn with PC-7 *Turbo Trainer*
 Some units with EMB-312 *Tucano*; MFI-17 *Mushshak*; TB-21 *Trinidad*; TB-200 *Tobago*

TRANSPORT HELICOPTER
 1 sqn with CH-47 *Chinook*
 Some units with Bell 206A *JetRanger* (AB-206A); *Shabaviz* 2-75; *Shabaviz* 2061
AIR DEFENCE
 16 bn with MIM-23B I-HAWK/*Shahin*
 5 sqn with FM-80 (*Crotale*); *Rapier*; *Tigercat*; S-75M *Volkhov* (SA-2 *Guideline*); S-200 *Angara* (SA-5 *Gammon*); FIM-92A *Stinger*; 9K32 *Strela*-2 (SA-7 *Grail*)‡; 9K331 *Tor*-M1 (SA-15 *Gauntlet*) (reported)

EQUIPMENT BY TYPE
AIRCRAFT 334 combat capable
 FTR 184+: 20 F-5B *Freedom Fighter*; 55+ F-5E *Tiger* II/F-5F *Tiger* II; 24 F-7M *Airguard*; 43 F-14 *Tomcat*; 36 MiG-29A/U/UB *Fulcrum*; up to 6 *Azarakhsh* reported
 FGA 111: 65 F-4D/E *Phantom* II; 10 *Mirage* F-1E; 30 Su-24MK *Fencer* D; up to 6 *Saegheh* reported
 ATK 13: 7 Su-25K *Frogfoot*; 3 Su-25T *Frogfoot*; 3 Su-25UBK *Frogfoot*
 ASW 5 P-3MP *Orion*
 ISR: 6+ RF-4E *Phantom* II*
 TKR/TPT 3: ε1 B-707; ε2 B-747
 TPT 117: **Heavy** 12 Il-76 *Candid*; **Medium** ε19 C-130E/H *Hercules*; **Light** 75: 11 An-74TK-200; 5 An-140 (Iran-140 *Faraz*) (45 projected); 10 F-27 *Friendship*; 1 L-1329 *Jetstar*; 10 PC-6B *Turbo Porter*; 8 TB-21 *Trinidad*; 4 TB-200 *Tobago*; 3 *Turbo Commander* 680; 14 Y-7; 9 Y-12; **PAX** 11: 2 B-707; 1 B-747; 4 B-747F; 1 *Falcon* 20; 3 *Falcon* 50
 TRG 151: 25 Beech F33A/C *Bonanza*; 15 EMB-312 *Tucano*; 15 JJ-7*; 25 MFI-17 *Mushshak*; 12 *Parastu*; 15 PC-6; 35 PC-7 *Turbo Trainer*; 9 T-33
HELICOPTERS
 MRH 32: 30 Bell 214C (AB-214C); 2 Bell 412
 TPT 4+: **Heavy** 2+ CH-47 *Chinook*; **Light** 2+: 2 Bell 206A *Jet Ranger* (AB-206A); some *Shabaviz* 2-75 (indigenous versions in production); some *Shabaviz* 2061
 AD • SAM 529+: 250 FM-80 (*Crotale*); 30 *Rapier*; 15 *Tigercat*; 150+ MIM-23B I-HAWK/*Shahin*; 45 S-75 *Dvina* (SA-2 *Guideline*); 10 S-200 *Angara* (SA-5 *Gammon*); 29 9K331 *Tor*-M1 (SA-15 *Gauntlet*) (reported)
  MANPAD FIM-92A *Stinger*; 9K32 *Strela*-2 (SA-7 *Grail*)‡
  GUNS • TOWED 23mm ZU-23; **37mm** Oerlikon
MSL
 ASM AGM-65A *Maverick*; Kh-25 (AS-10 *Karen*); Kh-29 (AS-14 *Kedge*); C-801K AShM
 ARM Kh-58 (AS-11 *Kilter*)
 AAM • IR PL-2A‡; PL-7; R-60 (AA-8 *Aphid*); R-73 (AA-11 *Archer*): AIM-9 *Sidewinder*; **IR/SARH** R-27 (AA-10 *Alamo*) **SARH** AIM-54 *Phoenix*†; AIM-7 *Sparrow*

Air Defence Command

Established to co-ordinate army, air force and IRGC air-defence assets. Precise composition unclear.

Paramilitary 40,000–60,000

Law-Enforcement Forces 40,000–60,000 (border and security troops); 450,000 on mobilisation (incl conscripts)

Part of armed forces in wartime
PATROL AND COASTAL COMBATANTS • PB ε 90

AIRCRAFT • TPT: 2 *Iran-140*; some Cessna 185/Cessna 310

HELICOPTERS • UTL ε24 AB-205 (Bell 205)/AB-206 (Bell 206) *Jet Ranger*

Basij Resistance Force up to ε1,000,000 on mobilisation

Paramilitary militia, with claimed membership of 12.6 million; perhaps 1 million combat capable; in the process of closer integration with IRGC Ground Forces.

FORCES BY ROLE
MANOEUVRE
Other
2,500 militia bn (claimed, limited permanent membership)

Cyber

Iran is believed to have a developed capacity for cyber operations. The precise relationship of groups such as the 'Iranian Cyber Army' to regime and military organisations is unclear, but the former has launched hacking attacks against a number of foreign organisations. In 2011, it was reported by state-sponsored media that Iran was stepping up its cyber defences and conducting exercises in this area, and that Iran was establishing its own cyber command. In 2011/2012, Tehran established a Joint Chiefs of Staff Cyber Command with emphasis on thwarting attacks against Iranian nuclear facilities. In June 2012, the head of the Civil Defence Organisation announced that plans to develop a cyber-defence strategy were under way.

DEPLOYMENT

GULF OF ADEN AND SOMALI BASIN
Navy: 1 FSG; 1 AORH

SUDAN
UN • UNAMID 2 obs

Iraq IRQ

Iraqi Dinar D		2011	2012	2013
GDP	D	133.65tr	152.25tr	
	US$	114.23bn	130.57bn	
per capita	US$	3,670	4,194	
Growth	%	8.86	10.17	
Inflation	%	5.60	6.00	
Def bdgt [a]	D	14.1tr	17.2tr	19.9tr
	US$	12bn	14.7bn	
US$1=D		1170.00	1166.00	

[a] Defence and security budget

Population   31,129,225

Ethnic and religious groups: Arab 75–80% (of which Shi'a Muslim 55%, Sunni Muslim 45%) Kurdish 20–25%

Age	0–14	15–19	20–24	25–29	30–64	65 plus
Male	19.1%	5.3%	4.7%	4.6%	15.5%	1.4%
Female	18.5%	5.1%	4.6%	4.5%	15.1%	1.7%

Capabilities

In conjunction with the police and other security services, the Iraqi Army's prime role is to provide internal security. The speed with which the Iraqi Army was reconstituted after 2003 meant that up to 70% of old, pre-regime-change officers were eventually reintegrated into the new officer corps. To counter this, Iraq's ruling elite have inserted so-called *dimaj* officers into the senior ranks of the military. These political appointments were either militia leaders or had no military experience at all. Beyond political interference, a broad set of problems continue to plague the Iraqi Army and need to be addressed for it to fulfil its new responsibilities. The first involves weaknesses in management, logistics and strategic planning. The unwillingness of senior military officials to delegate responsibility down the chain of command also stifles innovation and independent decision-making at a junior level. The withdrawal of all US troops and NATO trainers has greatly reduced external training assistance and mentoring. In spite of inefficiencies and politicisation, Iraq's security forces have been able to impose a rough order on the country since the departure of western forces. However, the forces are still growing in terms of their ability to provide effective security in areas such as airspace and border security, while the continuation of a terrorist campaign by Sunni and al-Qaeda insurgents points to continuing deficiencies across wider security-force tactics and leadership.

ACTIVE 271,400 (Army 193,400 Navy 3,600 Air 5,050 Support 69,350) Ministry of Interior 531,000

ORGANISATIONS BY SERVICE

Military Forces

Figures for Iraqi security forces reflect ongoing changes in organisation and manpower.

Army 193,400
FORCES BY ROLE
SPECIAL FORCES
2 SF bde
MANOEUVRE
Armoured
1 armd div (3 armd bde, 1 lt mech bde, 1 engr bn, 1 sigs regt, 1 log bde)
Light
8 mot div (4 mot inf bde, 1 engr bn, 1 sigs regt, 1 log bde)
2 mot div (3 mot inf bde, 1 engr bn, 1 sigs regt, 1 log bde)
1 inf div (1 mech bde, 2 inf bde, 1 air mob bde, 1 engr bn, 1 sigs regt, 1 log bde)
1 inf div (4 lt inf bde, 1 engr bn, 1 sigs regt, 1 log bde)
1 inf div (3 lt inf bde, 1 engr bn, 1 sigs regt, 1 log bde)
2 (presidential) mot bde
1 (Baghdad) indep mot bde
Aviation
1 sqn with Bell 205 (UH-1H *Huey* II)
1 sqn with Bell 206; OH-58C *Kiowa*

1 sqn with Bell T407
3 sqn with Mi-17 *Hip* H; Mi-171
1 sqn with SA342M *Gazelle*

EQUIPMENT BY TYPE
MBT 336+: 140 M1A1 *Abrams*; 120+ T-72; 76 T-55;
RECCE 73: 18 BRDM 2; 35 EE-9 *Cascavel*; 20 *Fuchs* NBC
AIFV 120: 100 BMP-1; 20 BTR-4
APC 2,799+
  APC (T) 605+: 100 FV 103 *Spartan*; 400+ M113A2; 61
  MT-LB; 44 *Talha*
  APC (W) 860: 570 *Akrep/Scorpion*; 60 AT-105 *Saxon*; 100
  BTR-80; 10 *Cobra*; 50 M3 Panhard; 60 *Mohafiz*; 10 VCR-
  TT
  PPV 1,334: 12 *Barracuda*; 600 *Dzik-3*; 607 ILAV *Cougar*;
  115 *Mamba*
ARTY 1,386+
  SP 48+: **152mm** 18+ Type-83; **155mm** 30: 6 M109A1; 24
  M109A5
  TOWED 138+: **130mm** 18+ M-46; **155mm** 120 M198
  MLRS 122mm some BM-21
  MOR 1,200: **81mm** 650 M252; **120mm** 550 M120
ARV 215+: 180 BREM; 35+ M88A1/2; T-54/55 ARV; Type-
653; VT-55A
HELICOPTERS
  MRH 30+: 26 Mi-17 *Hip* H; 4+ SA342 *Gazelle*
  ISR 10 OH-58C *Kiowa*
  TPT 37: **Medium** 8 Mi-171Sh; **Light** 29: 16 Bell 205
  (UH-1H *Huey* II); 10 Bell 206B3 *Jet Ranger*; 3 Bell T407

Navy 3,600

Iraqi Coastal Defence Force (ICDF)
EQUIPMENT BY TYPE
PATROL AND COASTAL COMBATANTS 29+:
  PCO 2 *RiverHawk*
  PCC 4 *Fateh* (ITA *Diciotti*)
  PB 17: 9 *Swiftships* 35 (6 additional vessels under
  construction); 5 *Predator* (PRC-27m); 3 *Al Faw*
  PBR 6: 2 Type-200; 4 Type-2010
LOGISTICS AND SUPPORT • AG 1 *Al Shams* (also
used for offshore patrol)

Iraqi Air Force 5,050
FORCES BY ROLE
ISR
  1 sqn with CH-2000 *Sama*; SB7L-360 *Seeker*
  1 sqn with Cessna 208B *Grand Caravan*; Cessna AC-
  208B *Combat Caravan**
  1 sqn with Beech 350 *King Air*
TRANSPORT
  1 sqn with An-32B *Cline*
  1 sqn with C-130E/J-30 *Hercules*
TRAINING
  1 sqn with Cessna 172, Cessna 208B
  1 sqn with Lasta-95
  1 sqn with T-6A
EQUIPMENT BY TYPE
AIRCRAFT 3 combat capable
  ISR 5: 3 Cessna AC-208B *Combat Caravan**; 2 SB7L-360
  Seeker

TPT 32: **Medium;** 10: 3 C-130E *Hercules*; 1 C-130J-30
Hercules; 6 An-32B *Cline* **Light** 22: 6 Beech 350 *King Air*;
8 Cessna 208B *Grand Caravan*; 8 Cessna 172
TRG 33+: 8 CH-2000 *Sama*; 10+ *Lasta-95*; 15 T-6A
MSL
  ASM AGM-114 *Hellfire*

Ministry of Interior Forces 531,000

Iraqi Police Service 302,000 (incl Highway Patrol)

Iraqi Federal Police 44,000

Facilities Protection Service 95,000

Border Enforcement 60,000

Oil Police 30,000

FOREIGN FORCES
Australia UNAMI 2 obs
Fiji UNAMI 277; 3 sy unit
Jordan UNAMI 2 obs
Nepal UNAMI 117; 1 sy unit
New Zealand UNAMI 1 obs

Israel ISR

New Israeli Shekel NS		2011	2012	2013
GDP	NS	871.83bn	908.9bn	
	US$	243.65bn	246.78bn	
per capita	US$	32,098	32,511	
Growth	%	4.61	2.95	
Inflation	%	3.45	1.66	
Def bdgt	NS	54.1bn	60bn	
	US$	15.1bn	16.3bn	
FMA (US)	US$	2.994bn	3.075bn	3.1bn
US$1=NS		3.58	3.68	

Population 7,590,758

Age	0–14	15–19	20–24	25–29	30–64	65 plus
Male	14.1%	4.1%	3.9%	3.8%	19.7%	4.5%
Female	13.4%	3.9%	3.7%	3.6%	19.3%	5.8%

Capabilities

The Israel Defence Forces (IDF) remain the most capable
in the region, with the motivation, equipment and training to considerably overmatch the conventional capability of other regional armed forces. Though the changing
strategic environment arising from the Arab Spring will
concern Israeli planners, they are currently able to contain
the military threats posed by Hamas and Hizbullah. Many
of the lessons of the unsuccessful 2006 war against Hizbullah in Lebanon appear to have been addressed. *Operation
Cast Lead* against Hamas in Gaza in 2008–09 demonstrated

a high degree of combined-arms and air–land cooperation as well as advances in ISR and command capabilities, albeit against an enemy significantly less capable than Hizbullah. In a war against the rearmed Hizbullah, the IDF could probably only partially neutralise the rocket and missile threat to Israel, but the capability of its forces to damage Hizbullah's organisation and infrastructure may have a deterrent effect. Israeli efforts to defend against the rocket threat were validated during a short rocket offensive by Hamas in March 2012. The *Iron Dome* missile system and Israeli counter-strikes were successful. And Israel is one of the few countries in the world with a credible civil-defence capability, which further reduces civilian casualties. But an all-out 'rocket war' waged from both Lebanon and Gaza would be more difficult to counter. Although Israel has the capability to attack some nuclear and ballistic missile facilities in Iran, it would probably be insufficient to inflict lasting damage on their programmes. Israel continues to develop missile-defence capacities beyond those of *Iron Dome*, with *Arrow*, *Hawk* and *Patriot* also in service. In late 2012, Israel conducted a major missile-defence exercise with the US, *Exercise Austere Challenge*. The emergence of unanticipated Hamas systems, such as the Iranian-origin *Fajr*-5 rocket, first launched from Gaza during November 2012, has complicated Israeli planning, with Tel Aviv and Jerusalem now in range of Gaza, adding urgency to *Iron Dome* development and deployment.

ACTIVE 176,500 (Army 133,000 Navy 9,500 Air 34,000) Paramilitary 8,000

RESERVE 465,000 (Army 400,000 Navy 10,000 Air 55,000)

Terms of service officers 48 months, other ranks 36 months, women 24 months (Jews and Druze only; Christians, Circassians and Muslims may volunteer). Annual trg as cbt reservists to age 40 (some specialists to age 54) for male other ranks, 38 (or marriage/pregnancy) for women

ORGANISATIONS BY SERVICE

Strategic Forces
Israel is widely believed to have a nuclear capability – delivery means include ac, *Jericho* 1 SRBM and *Jericho* 2 IRBM

FORCES BY ROLE
MISSILE
　3 sqn with *Jericho* 1/2
EQUIPMENT BY TYPE
MSL • STRATEGIC
　IRBM: *Jericho* 2
　SRBM: *Jericho* 1
WARHEADS up to 200 nuclear warheads

Strategic Defences
FORCES BY ROLE
AIR DEFENCE
　3 bty with *Arrow/Arrow* 2 ATBM with *Green Pine/Super Green Pine* radar and *Citrus Tree* command post.
　5 bty with *Iron Dome*

　17 bty with MIM-23B I-HAWK
　6 bty with MIM-104 *Patriot*

Space
SATELLITES • IMAGERY 4: 3 *Ofeq* (5, 7 & 9); 1 TecSAR-1 (*Polaris*)

Army 26,000; 107,000 conscript; (total 133,000)
Organisation and structure of formations may vary according to op situations. Equipment includes that required for reserve forces on mobilisation.

FORCES BY ROLE
COMMAND
　3 (regional comd) corps HQ
　2 armd div HQ
　4 (territorial) inf div HQ
SPECIAL FORCES
　3 SF bn
MANOEUVRE
　Reconnaissance
　1 indep recce bn
　Armoured
　3 armd bde (1 armd recce coy, 3 armd bn, 1 AT coy, 1 cbt engr bn)
　Mechanised
　3 mech inf bde (3 mech inf bn, 1 cbt spt bn,1 sigs coy)
　1 mech inf bde (6 mech inf bn)
　1 indep mech inf bn
　Light
　1 indep inf bn
　Air Manoeuvre
　1 para bde (3 para bn,1 cbt spt bn. 1 sigs coy)
　Other
　1 armd trg bde (3 armd bn)
COMBAT SUPPORT
　3 arty bde
　3 engr bn
　1 EOD coy
　1 CBRN bn
　3 int bn
　2 MP bn

Reserves 400,000+ on mobilisation
FORCES BY ROLE
COMMAND
　5 armd div HQ
　1 AB div HQ
MANOEUVRE
　Armoured
　13 armd bde
　Mechanised
　8 mech inf bde
　Light
　14 (territorial/regional) inf bde
　Air Manoeuvre
　4 para bde
　Mountain
　1 mtn inf bn
COMBAT SUPPORT
　4 arty bde

COMBAT SERVICE SUPPORT

6 log unit

EQUIPMENT BY TYPE

MBT 480: ε160 *Merkava* MkII; ε160 *Merkava* MkIII; ε160 *Merkava* MkIV (ε440 *Merkava* Mk1; ε290 *Merkava* MkII; ε270 *Merkava* MkIII; ε140 *Merkava* MkIV; 111 *Magach-7*; 711 M60/M60A1/M60A3 all in store)

RECCE 308: ε300 RBY-1 RAMTA; ε8 Tpz-1 *Fuchs* (NBC)

APC 1,265

APC (T) 1,165: ε65 *Namer*; ε200 *Achzarit* (modified T-55 chassis); 500 M113A2; ε400 *Nagmachon* (Centurion chassis); *Nakpadon* (5,000 M-113A1/A2 in store)

APC (W) 100 *Ze'ev*

ARTY 530

SP 250: **155mm** 250 M109A5 (**155mm** 148 L-33; 30 M109A1; 50 M-50; **175mm** 36 M107; **203mm** 36 M110 all in store)

TOWED (**122mm** 5 D-30; **130mm** 100 M-46; **155mm** 171: 40 M-46; 50 M-68/M-71; 81 M-839P/M-845P all in store)

MRL 30: **227mm** 30 M270 MLRS (**122mm** 58 BM-21; **160mm** 50 LAR-160; **227mm** 30 M270 MLRS; **240mm** 36 BM-24; **290mm** 20 LAR-290 all in store)

MOR 250 81mm 250 (**81mm** 1,100; **120mm** 650 **160mm** 18 Soltam M-66 all in store)

AT • MSL

SP M113 with *Spike*; *Spike* NLOS

MANPATS IMI MAPATS; *Spike* MR/LR/ER

AD • SAM

SP 20 *Machbet*

MANPAD FIM-92A *Stinger*

RADAR • LAND AN/PPS-15 (arty); AN/TPQ-37 *Firefinder* (arty); EL/M-2140 (veh)

MSL 100

STRATEGIC ε100 *Jericho* 1 SRBM/*Jericho* 2 IRBM

TACTICAL • SSM (7 *Lance* in store)

AEV D9R; *Puma*

ARV Centurion Mk2; *Eyal*; *Merkava*; M88A1; M113 ARV

VLB *Alligator* MAB; M48/60; MTU

Navy 7,000; 2,500 conscript (total 9,500)

EQUIPMENT BY TYPE

SUBMARINES • TACTICAL • SSK 3 *Dolphin* (GER Type-212 variant) with 6 single 533mm TT with UGM-84C *Harpoon* AShM/HWT, 4 single 650mm TT (3 additional vessels under construction; ISD expected at rate of one boat per year from 2013 until 2015)

PATROL AND COASTAL COMBATANTS 59

CORVETTES • FSGHM 3 *Eilat* (*Sa'ar* 5) with 2 quad Mk140 lnchr with RGM-84C *Harpoon* AShM, 2 32-cell VLS with *Barak* SAM, 2 triple 324mm TT with Mk 46 LWT, 1 76mm gun (capacity either 1 AS565SA *Panther* ASW hel)

PCGM 8 *Hetz* (*Sa'ar* 4.5) with 6 single lnchr with *Gabriel* II AShM, 2 twin Mk140 lnchr with RGM-84C *Harpoon* AShM, 1 16-32-cell Mk56 VLS with *Barak* SAM, 1 76mm gun

PCG 2 *Reshef* (*Sa'ar* 4) with 4–6 single lnchr with *Gabriel* II AShM, 1 twin or quad Mk140 lnchr with RGM-84C *Harpoon* AShM, 2 triple 324mm TT

PBFT 13: 9 *Super Dvora* MkI with 2 single 324mm TT with Mk 46 LWT (AShM may also be fitted); 4 *Super Dvora* MkII with 2 single 324mm TT with Mk 46 LWT (AShM may also be fitted)

PBT 15 *Dabur* with 2 single 324mm TT with Mk 46 LWT

PBF 18: 5 *Shaldag*; 3 *Stingray*; 10 *Super Dvora* MK III (AShM & TT may be fitted)

AMPHIBIOUS • LANDING CRAFT • LCT 3: 1 *Ashdod*; 2 others

LOGISTICS AND SUPPORT 3

AG 2 *Bat Yam* (ex German Type-T45)

AX 1 *Queshet*

Naval Commandos ε300

Air Force 34,000

Responsible for Air and Space Coordination

FORCES BY ROLE

FIGHTER & FIGHTER/GROUND ATTACK

1 sqn with F-15A/B/D *Eagle*

1 sqn with F-15B/C/D *Eagle*

1 sqn with F-15I *Ra'am*

7 sqn with F-16A/B/C/D *Fighting Falcon*

4 sqn with F-16I *Sufa*

(3 sqn with A-4N *Skyhawk*/F-4 *Phantom II*/*Kfir* C-7 in reserve)

ANTI-SUBMARINE WARFARE

1 sqn with AS565SA *Panther* (missions flown by IAF but with non-rated aircrew)

MARITIME PATROL/TANKER/TRANSPORT

1 sqn with IAI-1124 *Seascan*; KC-707

ELECTRONIC WARFARE

2 sqn with RC-12D *Guardrail*; Beech A36 *Bonanza* (*Hofit*); Beech 200 *King Air*; Beech 200T *King Air*; Beech 200CT *King Air*

AIRBORNE EARLY WARNING & CONTROL

1 sqn with Gulfstream G550 *Eitam*; Gulfstream G550 *Shavit*

TANKER/TRANSPORT

2 sqn with C-130E/H *Hercules*; KC-130H *Hercules*

TRAINING

1 OPFOR sqn with F-16A/B *Fighting Falcon*

1 sqn with A-4N/TA-4H/TA-4J *Skyhawk*

ATTACK HELICOPTER

1 sqn with AH-1E/F *Cobra*

1 sqn with AH-64A *Apache*

1 sqn with AH-64D *Apache*

TRANSPORT HELICOPTER

2 sqn with CH-53D *Sea Stallion*

2 sqn with S-70A *Black Hawk*; UH-60A *Black Hawk*

1 medevac unit with CH-53D *Sea Stallion*

UAV

1 ISR sqn with *Hermes* 450

1 ISR sqn with *Searcher* MkII

1 ISR sqn with *Heron* (*Shoval*); *Heron* TP (*Eitan*)

AIR DEFENCE

3 bty with *Arrow*/*Arrow* 2

5 bty with *Iron Dome*

17 bty with MIM-23 I-HAWK

6 bty with MIM-104 *Patriot*

EQUIPMENT BY TYPE

AIRCRAFT 441 combat capable

FTR 143: 16 F-15A *Eagle*; 6 F-15B *Eagle*; 17 F-15C *Eagle*; 11 F-15D *Eagle*; 77 F-16A *Fighting Falcon*; 16 F-16B *Fighting Falcon*

FGA 252: 25 F-15I *Ra'am*; 78 F-16C *Fighting Falcon*; 49 F-16D *Fighting Falcon*; 100 F-16I *Sufa*

ATK 46: 20 A-4N *Skyhawk*; 10 TA-4H *Skyhawk*; 16 TA-4J *Skyhawk*

FTR/FGA/ATK (200+ A-4N *Skyhawk*/F-4 *Phantom* II/F-15A *Eagle*/F-16A/B *Fighting Falcon*/*Kfir* C-7 in store)

MP 3 IAI-1124 *Seascan*

ISR 6 RC-12D *Guardrail*

ELINT 4: 1 EC-707; 3 Gulfstream G550 *Shavit*

AEW 4: 2 B-707 *Phalcon*; 2 Gulfstream G550 *Eitam* (1 more on order)

TKR/TPT 9: 2 KC-130H *Hercules*; 7 KC-707

TPT 60: **Medium** 13: 5 C-130E *Hercules*; 8 C-130H *Hercules*; **Light** 47: 3 AT-802 *Air Tractor*; 9 Beech 200 *King Air*; 8 Beech 200T *King Air*; 5 Beech 200CT *King Air*; 22 Beech A36 *Bonanza* (*Hofit*)

TRG 37: 17 Grob G-120; 20 T-6A

HELICOPTERS

ATK 77: 33 AH-1E/F *Cobra*; 27 AH-64A *Apache*; 17 AH-64D *Apache* (*Sarat*)

ASW 7 AS565SA *Panther* (missions flown by IAF but with non-rated aircrew)

ISR 12 OH-58B *Kiowa*

TPT 188: **Heavy** 26 CH-53D *Sea Stallion*; **Medium** 49: 39 S-70A *Black Hawk*; 10 UH-60A *Black Hawk*; **Light** 6 Bell 206 *JetRanger*

UAV • ISR 25+: **Heavy** 4+: *Hermes* 450; *Hermes* 900; *Heron* (*Shoval*); 3 *Heron* TP (*Eitan*); RQ-5A *Hunter*; **Medium** 22 *Searcher* MkII (22+ in store); **Light** *Harpy*

AD

SAM 24+: 24 *Arrow*/*Arrow* 2; some *Iron Dome*; some MIM-104 *Patriot*; some MIM-23 I-HAWK

GUNS 920

SP 165: **20mm** 105 M163 Machbet *Vulcan*; **23mm** 60 ZSU-23-4

TOWED 755: **23mm** 150 ZU-23; **20mm/37mm** 455 M167 *Vulcan* towed 20mm/M-1939 towed 37mm/TCM-20 towed 20mm; **40mm** 150 L/70

MSL

ASM AGM-114 *Hellfire*; AGM-62B *Walleye*; AGM-65 *Maverick*; Popeye I/Popeye II; Delilah AL

AAM • IR AIM-9 *Sidewinder*; *Python* 4; **IIR** *Python* 5; **ARH** *Derby*; AIM-120C AMRAAM

BOMB • PGM • JDAM GBU-31; *Spice, Lizard, Opher, Griffon*

Airfield Defence 3,000 active (15,000 reservists)

Paramilitary ε8,000

Border Police ε8,000

Cyber

Israel is widely reported to have developed capacity for cyber operations. Some reporting has highlighted a 'Unit 8200' believed responsible for ELINT, and reportedly cyber, operations. The IDF's Intelligence and C4I Corps are also concerned with cyber-related activity, with the C4I Corps having telecommunications and EW within its purview. According to the IDF, 'The IDF cyber staff was established [in early 2011], and works to recruit qualified soldiers building an integrative body that will cooperate with other technologically-affiliated units.' The IDF has, it says, 'been engaged in cyber activity consistently and relentlessly, gathering intelligence and defending its own cyber space. Additionally if necessary the cyber space will be used to execute attacks and intelligence operations.' In early 2012, the Israel National Cyber Bureau (INCB) was created in the prime minister's office, to develop technology, human resources and international collaboration. In late October 2012, the INCB and the MoD's Directorate for Research and Development announced a dual cyber-security programme, called MASAD, 'to promote R&D projects that serve both civilian and defense goals at the national level'.

FOREIGN FORCES

UNTSO unless specified. Figures represent total numbers for mission in Israel, Syria & Lebanon

Argentina 3 obs

Australia 11 obs

Austria 6 obs

Belgium 2 obs

Canada 8 obs • 9 (*Operation Proteus*) USSC

Chile 3 obs

China 2 obs

Denmark 11 obs

Estonia 1 obs

Finland 17 obs

France 2 obs

Ireland 11 obs

Italy 7 obs

Malawi 1 obs

Nepal 3 obs

Netherlands 11 obs

New Zealand 8 obs

Norway 12 obs

Russia 3 obs

Serbia 1 obs

Slovakia 2 obs

Slovenia 3 obs

Sweden 8 obs

Switzerland 11 obs

United States 2 obs • US European Command; 1 AN/TPY-2 X-band radar at Nevatim

Jordan JOR

Jordanian Dinar D		2011	2012	2013
GDP	D	20.48bn	22.23bn	
	US$	28.88bn	31.35bn	
per capita	US$	4,437	4,816	
Growth	%	2.59	3.00	
Inflation	%	4.41	4.51	
Def exp	D	951m		
	US$	1.34bn		
Def bdgt ª	D	971m	1.03bn	
	US$	1.37bn	1.45bn	
FMA (US)	US$	299.4m	300m	300m
US$1=D		0.71	0.71	

ª Excludes expenditure on public order and safety

Population   6,508,887

Ethnic groups: Palestinian ε50–60%

Age	0–14	15–19	20–24	25–29	30–64	65 plus
Male	18.0%	5.5%	4.9%	4.3%	15.8%	2.4%
Female	16.9%	5.2%	4.6%	4.2%	15.7%	2.5%

Capabilities

Long-standing political accommodation with Israel means that the country does not face a major external threat. Its main roles are border and internal security. Jordanian forces are well-trained, especially their aircrew, and regular exercises take place with foreign air forces. Jordan's fully professional armed forces are capable of combat and contributing to international expeditionary operations, as demonstrated by the deployment of Jordanian fighter aircraft to escort Jordanian C-130s flying humanitarian aid to Libya. Jordanian SF are well-trained and highly regarded, have served alongside ISAF forces in Afghanistan and participate in various UN missions. The country has developed a bespoke SF training centre, and regularly plays host to various SF contingents, affording its own forces opportunity to develop their own capability.

ACTIVE 100,500 (Army 88,000 Navy 500 Air 12,000) **Paramilitary 10,000**

RESERVE 65,000 (Army 60,000 Joint 5,000)

ORGANISATIONS BY SERVICE

Army 88,000

Jordan has reorganised from a divisional structure to four commands (Northern, Central, Eastern and Southern), a strategic reserve and a special operations command. The strategic reserve still has a divisional structure, and special operations command is responsible for counter-terrorism and unconventional operations. The Royal Guard also comes under this command.

FORCES BY ROLE

SPECIAL FORCES

1 spec ops bde (2 SF bn, 2 AB bn, 1 AB arty bn, 1 psyops unit)

MANOEUVRE

Armoured

1 (strategic reserve) armd div (3 armd bde, 1 arty bde, 1 AD bde)

1 armd bde

Mechanised

5 mech bde

Light

3 lt inf bde

COMBAT SUPPORT

3 arty bde

3 AD bde

EQUIPMENT BY TYPE

MBT 752: 390 CR1 *Challenger* 1 (*Al Hussein*); 274 FV4030/2 *Khalid*; 88 M60 *Phoenix*; (292 *Tariq Centurion*; 115 M60A1A3; 23 M47/M48A5 in store)

LT TK (19 *Scorpion*; in store)

RECCE 153: 103 *Scimitar*; 50 *Ferret*

AIFV 472: 31 BMP-2; 321 *Ratel*-20; ε120 YPR-765

APC 450+

　APC (T) 400+: 100 M113A1; 300 M113A2 Mk1J; some *Temsah*

　PPV 50: 25 *Marauder*; 25 *Matador*

ARTY 1,339

　SP 468: **105mm** 30 M-52; **155mm** 290: 270 M109A1/A2; 20 M-44; **203mm** 148 M110A2

　TOWED 100: **105mm** 72: 54 M102; 18 MOBAT; **155mm** 28: 10 M-1/M-59; 18 M114; **203mm** (4 M115 in store)

　MRL 227mm 12 HIMARS (with 432 guided msl)

　MOR 759:

　　SP 81mm 50

　　TOWED 709: **81mm** 359; **107mm** 50 M-30; **120mm** 300 Brandt

AT • MSL 975

　SP 115: 70 M901; 45 YPR-765 with *Milan*

　MANPATS 860: 30 *Javelin* (116 msl); 310 M47 *Dragon*; 320 TOW/TOW-2A; 200 9K123 *Kornet* (AT-14 *Spriggan* with 2,000 msl)

　RL 112mm 2,300 APILAS

AD

　SAM 930+

　　SP 140: 92 9K35 *Strela*-10 (SA-13 *Gopher*); 48 9K33 *Osa*-M (SA-8 *Gecko*)

　　MANPAD 790+: 250 FIM-43 *Redeye*; 9K32M *Strela*-2M (SA-7B *Grail*); 300 9K36 *Strela*-3 (SA-14 *Gremlin*); 240 9K310 *Igla*-1 (SA-16 *Gimlet*); 9K38 *Igla/Igla*-1 (SA-18 *Grouse*)

　GUNS • SP 356: **20mm** 100 M163 *Vulcan*; **23mm** 40 ZSU-23-4; **40mm** 216 M-42 (not all op)

RADAR • LAND 7 AN/TPQ-36 *Firefinder*/AN/TPQ-37 *Firefinder* (arty, mor)

ARV 137+: *Al Monjed*; 55 *Chieftain* ARV; *Centurion Mk2*; 20 M47; 32 M88A1; 30 M578; YPR-806

MW 12 *Aardvark* Mk2

Navy ε500

EQUIPMENT BY TYPE
PATROL AND COASTAL COMBATANTS 7 (+ 10 patrol boats under 10 tonnes)
PB 7: 3 *Al Hussein* (UK Vosper 30m); 4 *Abdullah (US Dauntless)*

Air Force 12,000

Flying hours   180 hrs/year

FORCES BY ROLE
FIGHTER
1 sqn with F-16A/B ADF *Fighting Falcon*
FIGHTER/GROUND ATTACK
1 sqn with F-5E/F *Tiger* II
2 sqn with F-16AM/BM *Fighting Falcon*
FIGHTER/GROUND ATTACK/ISR
1 sqn with F-5E/F *Tiger* II
ISR
1 unit with *Seeker* SB7L
ISR/TRANSPORT HELICOPTER
1 (spec ops) sqn wth SA 2-37B; AS350B3; EC635; UH-60L *Black Hawk*
TRANSPORT
1 sqn with Il-76MF; C-130E/H *Hercules*; CN-235; Cessna 208B
1 (Royal) flt with S-70A *Black Hawk*; UH-60A *Black Hawk*
TRAINING
1 OCU with F-5E *Tiger* II
1 sqn with C-101 *Aviojet*
1 sqn with T-67M *Firefly*
1 sqn with AS350B3; Bell 205 (UH-1H *Iroquois*); Hughes 500
ATTACK HELICOPTER
2 sqn with AH-1F *Cobra* (with TOW)
TRANSPORT HELICOPTER
2 sqn with AS332M *Super Puma*; Bell 205 (UH-1H *Iroquois*)
AIR DEFENCE
1 comd (5–6 bty with PAC-2 *Patriot*; 5 bty with MIM-2BB Phase III I-HAWK; 6 bty with *Skyguard/Aspide*)

EQUIPMENT BY TYPE
AIRCRAFT 85 combat capable
FTR 46: 30 F-5E/F *Tiger* II; 16 F-16A/B ADF *Fighting Falcon*
FGA 39 F-16AM/BM *Fighting Falcon*; (15 *Mirage* F-1C (F-1CJ); 15 *Mirage* F-1E (F-1EJ) all in store)
ISR 1 SA 2-37B
TPT 17: **Heavy** 2 Il-76MF *Candid*; **Medium** 6: 4 C-130H *Hercules*; 2 C-130E *Hercules*; **Light** 9: 2 C-295M; 2 CN-235; 5 Cessna 208B
TRG 26: 16 T-67M *Firefly*; 10 C-101 *Aviojet*
HELICOPTERS
ATK 25 AH-1F *Cobra* (TOW)
MRH 13 EC635 (Tpt/SAR)
TPT 75: **Medium** 25: 12 AS332M *Super Puma*; 3 S-70A *Black Hawk*; 2 UH-60A *Black Hawk*; 8 UH-60L *Black Hawk*; **Light** 50: 36 Bell 205 (UH-1H *Iroquois*); 8 Hughes 500D; 6 AS350B3
AD • SAM 64: 24 MIM-23B Phase III I-HAWK; 40 PAC-2 *Patriot*

MSL
ASM AGM-65D *Maverick*; BGM-71 TOW
AAM • IR AIM-9J/N/P *Sidewinder*; R-550 *Magic*; **SARH** AIM-7 *Sparrow*; R530; **ARH** AIM-120C AMRAAM

Paramilitary 10,000 active

Public Security Directorate ε10,000 active
Ministry of Interior
FORCES BY ROLE
MANOEUVRE
Other
1 security bde
EQUIPMENT BY TYPE
LT TK: *Scorpion*
APC (W) 55+: 25+ EE-11 *Urutu*; 30 FV603 *Saracen*

Reserve Organisations 60,000 reservists
FORCES BY ROLE
MANOEUVRE
Armoured
1 Royal Guard armd div with (3 armd bde, 1 arty bde, 1 AD bde)

Civil Militia 'People's Army' ε35,000 reservists
Men 16–65, women 16–45

DEPLOYMENT

AFGHANISTAN
Operation Enduring Freedom- Afghanistan 720; 1 ranger bn

CÔTE D'IVOIRE
UN • UNOCI 1,067; 7 obs; 1 SF coy; 1 inf bn

DEMOCRATIC REPUBLIC OF THE CONGO
UN • MONUSCO 220; 26 obs; 1 SF coy; 1 fd hospital

HAITI
UN • MINUSTAH 252; 1 inf coy

IRAQ
UN • UNAMI 2 obs

LIBERIA
UN • UNMIL 120; 4 obs; 1 fd hospital

SOUTH SUDAN
UN • UNMISS 4; 4 obs

SUDAN
UN • UNAMID 11; 12 obs

Kuwait KWT

Kuwaiti Dinar D		2011	2012	2013
GDP	D	44.41bn	48.54bn	
	US$	160.98bn	174.63bn	
per capita	US$	60,832	65,990	
Growth	%	8.16	6.35	
Inflation	%	4.75	4.29	
Def bdgt	D	1.12bn	1.28bn	
	US$	4.07bn	4.62bn	
US$1=D		0.28	0.28	

Population 2,646,314

Ethnic groups: Nationals 35%; other Arab 35%; South Asian 9%; Iranian 4%; other 17%

Age	0–14	15–19	20–24	25–29	30–64	65 plus
Male	13.4%	3.4%	5.1%	7.7%	28.2%	1.0%
Female	12.3%	3.1%	3.9%	4.5%	16.3%	1.1%

Capabilities

Kuwait's military has been transformed since its failure to prevent or deter an Iraqi invasion in 1991. A more professional officer corps now exists, with better training, greater joint force capabilities and a higher state of readiness. However, the force remains too small to deter a resolute threat from its larger neighbours, and hence the country relies on its membership of the GCC and relationship with the US to guarantee its security. A close defence relationship with the US has afforded Kuwait access to high-technology weapons systems and combined training exercises. This has allowed Kuwait to develop a professional, relatively well-equipped, land-focused force. The US maintains large bases in the country, until recently preoccupied with managing the drawdown of personnel and equipment from Iraq; the US retains substantial forces in Kuwait. The navy is small, with patrol boats capable of ensuring maritime security within and defence against small flotillas entering Kuwaiti waters. The air force regularly deploys aircraft to GCC air exercises and flew humanitarian flights during 2011 to bring injured Libyans to Kuwait.

ACTIVE 15,500 (Army 11,000 Navy 2,000 Air 2,500)
Paramilitary 7,100
Terms of service voluntary

RESERVE 23,700 (Joint 23,700)
Terms of service obligation to age 40; 1 month annual trg

ORGANISATIONS BY SERVICE

Army 11,000

FORCES BY ROLE
SPECIAL FORCES
1 SF unit (forming)
MANOEUVRE
Reconnaissance
1 mech/recce bde

Armoured
3 armd bde
Mechanised
2 mech inf bde
Light
1 cdo bn
Other
1 (Amiri) gd bde
COMBAT SUPPORT
1 arty bde
1 engr bde
1 MP bn
COMBAT SERVICE SUPPORT
1 log gp
1 fd hospital

Reserve

FORCES BY ROLE
MANOEUVRE
Mechanised
1 bde

EQUIPMENT BY TYPE
MBT 293: 218 M1A2 *Abrams*; 75 M-84 (75 more in store)
RECCE 11 TPz-1 *Fuchs*
AIFV 432: 76 BMP-2; 120 BMP-3; 236 *Desert Warrior*† (incl variants)
APC 260
  APC (T) 260: 230 M113A2; 30 M577
  APC (W) (40 TH 390 *Fahd* in store)
ARTY 218
  SP 155mm 106: 37 M109A3; 18 (AMX) Mk F3; 51 PLZ45; (18 AU-F-1 in store)
  MRL 300mm 27 9A52 *Smerch*
  MOR 78: **81mm** 60; **107mm** 6 M-30; **120mm** ε12 RT-F1
AT • MSL 118+
  SP 74: 66 HMMWV TOW; 8 M901
  MANPATS 44+: 44 TOW-2; M47 *Dragon*
  RCL 84mm ε200 *Carl Gustav*
AD • SAM 60+
  STATIC/SHELTER 12 *Aspide*
  MANPAD 48 *Starburst*; *Stinger*
  GUNS • TOWED 35mm 12+ Oerlikon
ARV 24+: 24 M88A1/2; Type-653A; *Warrior*
MW *Aardvark* Mk2

Navy ε2,000 (incl 500 Coast Guard)

EQUIPMENT BY TYPE
PATROL AND COASTAL COMBATANTS 17
  PCFG 2:
    1 *Al Sanbouk* (GER Lurssen TNC-45) with 2 twin lnchr with MM-40 *Exocet* AShM, 1 76mm gun
    1 *Istiqlal* (GER Lurssen FPB-57) with 2 twin lnchr with MM-40 *Exocet* AShM, 1 76mm gun
  PBF 7 *Al Nokatha* (US Mk V *Pegasus*) (a further 3 on order; ISD by end-2013)
  PBG 8 *Um Almaradim* (FRA P-37 BRL) with 2 twin lnchr with *Sea Skua* AShM, 1 sextuple lnchr (lnchr only)
LOGISTICS AND SUPPORT • AG 1 *Sawahil*

Air Force 2,500

Flying hours   210 hrs/year

FORCES BY ROLE
FIGHTER/GROUND ATTACK
  2 sqn with F/A-18C/D *Hornet*
TRANSPORT
  1 sqn with L-100-30
TRAINING
  1 unit with EMB-312 *Tucano* (*Tucano* Mk52)*; *Hawk* Mk64*
ATTACK HELICOPTER
  1 sqn with AH-64D *Apache*
  1 atk/trg sqn with SA342 *Gazelle* with HOT
TRANSPORT HELICOPTER
  1 sqn with AS532 *Cougar*; SA330 *Puma*; S-92
AIR DEFENCE
  1 comd (5–6 SAM bty with PAC-2 *Patriot*; 5 SAM bty with MIM-23B I-HAWK Phase III; 6 SAM bty with *Skyguard/Aspide*)

EQUIPMENT BY TYPE
AIRCRAFT 66 combat capable
  FGA 39: 31 F/A-18C *Hornet*; 8 F/A-18D *Hornet*
  TPT • Medium 3 L-100-30
  TRG 27: 11 *Hawk* Mk64*; 16 EMB-312 *Tucano* (*Tucano* Mk52)*
HELICOPTERS
  ATK 16 AH-64D *Apache*
  MRH 13 SA342 *Gazelle* with HOT
  TPT 13: **Medium** 3 AS532 *Cougar*; 7 SA330 *Puma*; 3 S-92
MSL
  ASM AGM-65G *Maverick*; AGM-84A *Harpoon*; AGM-114K *Hellfire*
  AAM • IR AIM-9L *Sidewinder*; R-550 *Magic*; **SARH** AIM-7F *Sparrow*; **ARH** AIM-120C7 AMRAAM
SAM 76: 40 PAC-2 *Patriot*; 24 MIM-23B I-HAWK Phase III; 12 *Skyguard/Aspide*

Paramilitary ε7,100 active

National Guard ε6,600 active

FORCES BY ROLE
SPECIAL FORCES
  1 SF bn
MANOEUVRE
  Reconnaissance
  1 armd car bn
  Other
  3 security bn
COMBAT SUPPORT
  1 MP bn
EQUIPMENT BY TYPE
RECCE 20 VBL
APC (W) 97+: 5+ *Desert Chameleon*; 70 *Pandur*; 22 S600 (incl variants)
ARV *Pandur*

Coast Guard 500

PATROL AND COASTAL COMBATANTS 32
  PBF 12 *Manta*
  PB 20: 3 *Al Shaheed*; 4 *Inttisar* (Austal 31.5m); 3 *Kassir* (Austal 22m); 10 *Subahi*

AMPHIBIOUS • LANDING CRAFT • LCU 4: 2 *Al Tahaddy*; 1 *Saffar*; 1 other
LOGISTICS AND SUPPORT • AG 1 *Sawahil*

FOREIGN FORCES

United Kingdom Army 35
United States United States Central Command: 23,000; 1 HBCT; 1 ARNG cbt avn bde; 1 ARNG spt bde; 2 AD bty with total of 16 PAC-3 *Patriot*; elm 1 (APS) HBCT eqpt set.

Lebanon LBN

Lebanese Pound LP		2011	2012	2013
GDP	LP	58.85tr	62.96tr	
	US$	39.04bn	41.77bn	
per capita	US$	9,429	10,089	
Growth	%	1.50	2.00	
Inflation	%	4.99	6.51	
Def bdgt	LP	1.69tr	1.73tr	
	US$	1.12bn	1.15bn	
FMA (US)	US$	74.9m	75m	75m
US$1=LP		1507.49	1507.52	

Population   4,140,289

Ethnic and religious groups: Christian 30%; Druze 6%; Armenian 4%, excl ε300,000 Syrians and ε350,000 Palestinian refugees

Age	0–14	15–19	20–24	25–29	30–64	65 plus
Male	11.5%	4.4%	4.7%	4.5%	19.6%	4.2%
Female	11.0%	4.2%	4.6%	4.4%	21.8%	5.0%

Capabilities

The most capable armed forces in Lebanon are those of Hizbullah. These have extensively rearmed since the 2006 war with Israel and have sufficient rockets and missiles to pose a significant threat to most Israeli territory. Although it could not prevent an attack by the modernised Israeli forces, Hizbollah has continued to develop its forces, fortifications and military infrastructure to impose significant costs on any Israeli ground incursion. Its armed forces are more than capable of protecting its political position within Lebanon, where it is now part of the government. It will be concerned that the civil war in Syria may reduce its external military support from that country and Iran. It will have watched closely Hamas's rocket launch tactics in November 2012, as well as the Israeli tactical response and *Iron Dome* capabilities. Meanwhile, the Lebanese regular military is able to meet basic internal-security requirements for those parts of the state not controlled by Hizbullah. But they are not capable of countering Hizbullah influence and activity, and have been unable to contain sectarian violence apparently overspilling from the conflict in Syria. In recent years, the army has seen a number of inventory modernisation drives, such as that to re-equip its APC fleet with modernised ex-US M113s. The armed forces have also benefitted from US security assistance, with initiatives including counter-terrorism training in 2011, and have received donations of equipment from UNIFIL, the UN force in Lebanon.

ACTIVE 60,000 (Army 56,600 Navy 1,800 Air 1,600) Paramilitary 20,000

The number of troops can increase to 291,750 if conscripts are recalled.

ORGANISATIONS BY SERVICE

Army 56,600

FORCES BY ROLE

5 regional comd (Beirut, Bekaa Valley, Mount Lebanon, North, South)

SPECIAL FORCES
1 cdo regt

MANOEUVRE
Armoured
Mechanised
11 mech inf bde
Air Manoeuvre
1 AB regt
Amphibious
1 mne cdo regt
Other
1 Presidential Guard bde
5 intervention regt
2 border sy regt

COMBAT SUPPORT
2 arty regt
1 cbt spt bde (1 engr rgt, 1 AT regt, 1 sigs regt)
1 MP bde

COMBAT SERVICE SUPPORT
1 log bde
1 med regt
1 construction regt

EQUIPMENT BY TYPE
MBT 324: 92 M48A1/A5; 185 T-54; 47 T-55
RECCE 55 AML
AIFV 16 AIFV-B-C25
APC 1,330
  APC (T) 1,244 M113A1/A2 (incl variants)
  APC (W) 86 VAB VCT
ARTY 487
  TOWED 201: **105mm** 13 M101A1; **122mm** 35: 9 D-30; 26 M-30 M-1938; **130mm** 15 M-46; **155mm** 97: 18 M114A1; 106 M198; 14 Model-50
  MRL **122mm** 11 BM-21
  MOR 275: **81mm** 134; **82mm** 112; **120mm** 29 Brandt
AT
  MSL • MANPATS 38: 26 *Milan*; 12 TOW
  RCL **106mm** 113 M40A1
  RL **73mm** 11 M-50; **90mm** 8 M-69
AD
  SAM • MANPAD 83 9K32 *Strela*-2/2M (SA-7A *Grail*/SA-7B *Grail*)‡
  GUNS • TOWED 77: **20mm** 20; **23mm** 57 ZU-23
ARV M113 ARV; T-54/55 ARV reported
VLB MTU-72 reported

MW Bozena
UAV • ISR • **Medium** 8 *Mohajer 4*

Navy 1,800

EQUIPMENT BY TYPE

In addition to the vessels listed, the Lebanese Navy operates a further 22 vessels with a full-load displacement below ten tonnes.

PATROL AND COASTAL COMBATANTS 13
  PCC 1 *Trablous*
  PB 11: 1 *Aamchit* (GER *Bremen*); 1 *Al Kalamoun* (FRA *Avel Gwarlarn*); 7 *Tripoli* (UK *Attacker/Tracker* Mk 2); 1 *Naquora* (GER *Bremen*); 1 *Tabarja* (GER *Bergen*)
  PBF 1
AMPHIBIOUS • LANDING CRAFT • LCT 2 *Sour* (FRA *Edic* – capacity 8 APC; 96 troops)

Air Force 1,600

4 air bases

FORCES BY ROLE
FIGHTER/GROUND ATTACK
1 sqn with *Hunter* Mk6/Mk9/T66; Cessna AC-208 *Combat Caravan**
ATTACK HELICOPTER
1 sqn with SA342L *Gazelle*
TRANSPORT HELICOPTER
4 sqn with Bell 205 (UH-1H)
1 sqn with AS330/IAR330SM *Puma*
1 trg sqn with R-44 *Raven* II

EQUIPMENT BY TYPE
AIRCRAFT 7 combat capable
  FGA 4: 3 *Hunter* Mk6/Mk9; 1 *Hunter* T66
  ISR 1 Cessna AC-208 *Combat Caravan**
  TRG (3 *Bulldog*; could be refurbished)
HELICOPTERS
  MRH 9: 1 AW139; 8 SA342L *Gazelle* (plus 5 unserviceable – could be refurbished); (5 SA316 *Alouette III* unserviceable – 3 could be refurbished); (1 SA318 *Alouette II* unserviceable – could be refurbished)
  TPT 29: **Medium** 13: 3 S-61N (fire fighting); 10 AS330/IAR330 *Puma*; **Light** 16: 12 Bell 205 (UH-1H *Huey*) (11 more unserviceable); 4 R-44 *Raven* II (basic trg); (7 Bell 212 unserviceable – 6 could be refurbished)

Paramilitary ε20,000 active

Internal Security Force ε20,000

Ministry of Interior

FORCES BY ROLE
Other Combat Forces
1 (police) judicial unit
1 regional sy coy
1 Beirut Gendarmerie coy

EQUIPMENT BY TYPE
APC (W) 60 V-200 *Chaimite*

Customs

PATROL AND COASTAL COMBATANTS 7
  PB 7: 5 *Aztec*; 2 *Tracker*

FOREIGN FORCES

Unless specified, figures refer to UNTSO and represent total numbers for the mission in Israel, Syria & Lebanon.

Argentina 3 obs
Armenia UNIFIL 1
Australia 11 obs
Austria 6 obs • UNIFIL 151: 1 log bn
Bangladesh UNIFIL 326: 1 FFG; 1 PCO
Belarus UNIFIL 5
Belgium 2 obs • UNIFIL 100: 1 engr coy
Brazil UNIFIL 268 1 FFGHM
Brunei UNIFIL 30
Cambodia UNIFIL 216: 1 engr coy
Canada 8 obs (*Op Jade*)
Chile 3 obs
China, People's Republic of 2 obs • UNIFIL 343: 1 engr bn; 1 fd hospital
Croatia UNIFIL 1
Cyprus UNIFIL 1
Denmark 11 obs
El Salvador UNIFIL 52: 1 inf pl
Estonia 1 obs
Finland 17 obs • UNIFIL 177; 1 inf coy
France 2 obs • UNIFIL 902: 1 armd cav BG; *Leclerc*; AMX-10P; PVP; VAB; CAESAR; AU-F1; *Mistral*
Germany UNIFIL 153: 2 PC; 1 SPT
Ghana UNIFIL 872: 1 mech inf bn
Greece UNIFIL 51: 1 PB
Guatemala UNIFIL 3
Hungary UNIFIL 4
India UNIFIL 894: 1 mech inf bn; elm 1 fd hospital
Indonesia UNIFIL 1,458: 1 mech inf bn; 1 MP coy; elm 1 fd hospital; 1 FFGM
Ireland 11 obs • UNIFIL 354 1 inf bn(-)
Italy 7 obs • UNIFIL 1,150: 1 armd bde HQ; 1 armd recce bn; 1 hel sqn; 1 sigs coy; 1 CIMIC coy
Kenya UNIFIL 1
Korea, Republic of UNIFIL 352: 1 mech inf bn
Luxembourg UNIFIL 3
Macedonia, Former Yugoslav Republic of UNIFIL 1
Malaysia UNIFIL 877: 1 mech inf bn
Malawi 1 obs
Nepal 3 obs • UNIFIL 1,018: 1 inf bn
Netherlands 11 obs
New Zealand 8 obs
Nigeria UNIFIL 1
Norway 12 obs
Qatar UNIFIL 3
Russia 3 obs
Serbia 1 obs • UNIFIL 5
Sierra Leone UNIFIL 2
Slovakia 2 obs
Slovenia 3 obs • UNIFIL 14; 1 inf pl
Spain UNIFIL 977: 1 mech inf bde HQ; 1 armd inf bn
Sri Lanka UNIFIL 151: 1 inf coy

Sweden 8 obs
Switzerland 11 obs
Tanzania UNIFIL 159; 2 MP coy
Turkey UNIFIL 452: 1 engr coy; 1 FFGH
United States 2 obs

Libya LBY

Libyan Dinar D		2011	2012	2013
GDP	D	43.69bn	107.98bn	
	US$	35.7bn	85.11bn	
per capita	US$	6,360	15,162	
Growth	%	-59.69	121.90	
Inflation	%	15.90	9.99	
Def bdgt	D		3.77bn	
	US$		2.97bn	
FMA (US)	US$	0.25m	0.15m	0.15m
US$1=D		1.22	1.27	

Population	5,613,380

Age	0–14	15–19	20–24	25–29	30–64	65 plus
Male	14.2%	4.8%	5.2%	5.6%	20.3%	2.0%
Female	13.5%	4.5%	4.7%	4.9%	18.7%	1.9%

Capabilities

Although the National Transitional Council is acting as the interim government, it is not clear that it has any meaningful authority over the forces of the former rebels. These consist of a large number of 'brigades', most of which have little formal structure of command and control and vary in size from tens of personnel to several thousand. These include the relatively cohesive and capable 'Misrata Brigade' and the externally trained 'Tripoli Brigade'. Some of these groups are reportedly aligned with the authorities in Tripoli; the allegiance of others is less clear. There has been little progress in developing concerted DDR programmes. Several hundred foreign advisers, many from Qatar, assisted the rebel forces during the war. It is not clear how many, if any, remain. Although only a proportion of Gadhafi-regime weapons were destroyed in the fighting, the rebels are mostly infantry mounted in 4×4 'technical' vehicles, largely armed with anti-aircraft cannon. Although it is possible to estimate remaining warships and military aircraft (many were destroyed during the air campaign), it is not clear if Libya retains any credible air or maritime capability.

ACTIVE not known

RESERVE not known

ORGANISATIONS BY SERVICE

Army not known

FORCES BY ROLE

The old Libyan army effectively ceased to exist as an organised force during the 2011 civil war. The new transitional government controls a small number of formations. A tank company and artillery battery appear extant, but there is no evidence of their use of any other combat support.

EQUIPMENT BY TYPE

Much equipment was damaged or destroyed during the civil war. It is not yet clear how much of Libya's previous holdings are still operational and available to the new government.

MBT some: T-72; T-62; T-55
RECCE some: BRDM-2; EE-9 *Cascavel*
AIFV some: BMP-1; BMD
APC
  APC (T) some: M113; BTR-50/BTR-60
  APC (W) some: EE-11 *Urutu*; OT-62/OT-64
ARTY
  SP some: **122mm** 2S1 *Carnation*; **152mm**: 2S3; M-77 *Dana*; **155mm** M109; VCA 155 *Palmaria*
  TOWED some: **105mm** M101; **122mm** D-30; D-74; **130mm** M-46; **152mm** M-1937
  MRL some: **107mm** Type-63; **122mm** BM-11; BM-21; RM-70 *Dana*
  MOR some: **82mm**; **120mm** M-43; **160mm** M-160
AT • MSL
  SP some 9P122 BRDM-2 *Sagger*
  MANPATS some: 9K11 *Maljutka* (AT-3 *Sagger*); 9K11 *Fagot* (AT-4 *Spigot*); 9K113 *Konkurs* (AT-5 *Spandrel*); *Milan*
  RCL some: **106mm** M40A1; **84mm** *Carl Gustav*
AD • SAM • SP: *Crotale* (quad); 9K32 *Strela*-2 (SA-7 *Grail*)‡; 9K35 *Strela*-10 (SA-13 *Gopher*); 9K31 *Strela*-1 (SA-9 *Gaskin*); 9K338 *Igla*-S (SA-24 *Grinch*)
  GUNS
  SP 23mm some ZSU-23-4
  TOWED: **14.5mm** some ZPU-2; **30mm** M-53/59; **40mm** L/70; **57mm** S-60
RADAR • LAND RASIT (veh, arty)
MSL • TACTICAL • SSM some: FROG-7; *Scud*-B
ARV T-54/55 ARV

Navy (incl Coast Guard) not known

EQUIPMENT BY TYPE

SUBMARINES • TACTICAL • SSK 2 *Khyber*† (FSU *Foxtrot*) each with 10 533mm TT (6 fwd, 4 aft)
PRINCIPAL SURFACE COMBATANTS 1
  FRIGATES • FFGM 1 *Al Hani*† (FSU *Koni*) with 2 twin lnchr (with P-15 *Termit*-M (SS-N-2C *Styx*) AShM, 1 twin lnchr with 9K33 *Osa*-M (SA-N-4 *Gecko*) SAM, 2 twin 406mm ASTT with USET-95 Type-40 LWT, 1 RBU 6000 *Smerch 2*, 2 twin 76mm gun
PATROL AND COASTAL COMBATANTS 11
  CORVETTES • FSGM 1 *Tariq Ibin Ziyad* (FSU *Nanuchka* II) with 4 single lnchr with P-15 *Termit*-M (SS-N-2C *Styx*) AShM, 1 twin lnchr with SA-N-4 *Gecko* SAM
  PBFG 10:
    4 *Al Zuara* (FSU *Osa* II) with 4 single lnchr with P-15 *Termit*-M (SS-N-2C *Styx*) AShM
    6 *Sharaba* (FRA *Combattante* II) with 4 single lnchr with *Otomat* Mk2 AShM, 1 76mm gun
MINE WARFARE • MINE COUNTERMEASURES 4
  MSO 4 *Ras al Gelais* (FSU *Natya*)

AMPHIBIOUS 7
  LANDING SHIPS • LST 2 *Ibn Harissa* (capacity 1 SA316B *Alouette* III hel; 11 MBT; 240 troops)
  LANDING CRAFT 5
    LCAC 2 *Slingsby* SAH 2200
    LCT 3† *C107*
LOGISTICS AND SUPPORT 21:
  AFD 2
  AG 10 *El Temsah*
  ARS 1 *Al Munjed* (YUG *Spasilac*)
  YDT 1 *Al Manoud* (FSU *Yelva*)
  YTB 7

Coastal Defence

EQUIPMENT BY TYPE
PBF 6 *Bigliari*

Naval Aviation

EQUIPMENT BY TYPE
HELICOPTERS • TPT • Heavy SA321 *Super Frelon* (air force assets)

Air Force not known

EQUIPMENT BY TYPE

A small number of aircraft inherited from the previous regime continue to be operated, though the air force needs to be rebuilt.

AIRCRAFT
  FTR some: MiG-23 *Flogger*; MiG-23U *Flogger*; MiG-25 *Foxbat*; MiG-25U *Foxbat*
  FGA some: MiG-21 *Fishbed*; MiG-23BN *Flogger H*; *Mirage* 5DP30; *Mirage* F-1A (F-1AD); *Mirage* F-1B (F-1BD); *Mirage* F-1E (F-1ED); Su-17M-2 *Fitter D*; Su-20 *Fitter C*; Su-24MK *Fencer D*
  ISR some MiG-25R *Foxbat*
  TPT some: **Heavy**: An-124 *Condor*; Il-76 *Candid*; **Medium**: C-130H *Hercules*; G-222; L-100-20; L-100-30; **Light**: An-26 *Curl*; L-410 *Turbolet*
  TRG: G-2 *Galeb*; L-39ZO *Albatros*; SF-260WL *Warrior**
HELICOPTERS
  ATK: Mi-25 *Hind D*; Mi-35 *Hind*
  MRH SA316 *Alouette* III
  MRH/TPT Mi-8 *Hip* (med tpt)/Mi-17 *Hip H*
  TPT: **Heavy** CH-47C *Chinook*; **Light**: Bell 206 *Jet Ranger* (AB-206); PZL Mi-2 *Hoplite*
MSL
  ASM Kh-23 (AS-7 *Kerry*); 9M17 (AT-2 *Swatter*)
  ARM Kh-28 (AS-9 *Kyle*); Kh-58 (AS-11 *Kilter*)
  AAM • IR AAM R-3 (AA-2 *Atoll*)‡; R-60 (AA-8 *Aphid*); R-550 *Magic* **IR/SARH AAM** R-40/46 (AA-6 *Acrid*); R-23/24 (AA-7 *Apex*); R530

Air Defence Command

Senezh (C2 system, degraded by air strikes in 2011)

FORCES BY ROLE
AIR DEFENCE
  Equipment includes 2K12 *Kub* (SA-6 *Gainful*)/9K33 *Osa* (SA-8 *Gecko*); S-125 *Pechora* (SA-3 *Goa*); S-75 *Volkhov* (SA-2 *Guideline*); S-200 *Angara* (SA-5 *Gammon*)

EQUIPMENT BY TYPE
AD
  SAM some:
    SP 2K12 *Kub* (SA-6 *Gainful*)/9K33 *Osa* (SA-8 *Gecko*)
    TOWED S-75 *Volkhov* (SA-2 *Guideline*)
    STATIC S-200 *Angara* (SA-5A *Gammon*); S-125 *Pechora* (SA-3 *Goa*)
  GUNS some

DEPLOYMENT

PHILIPPINES
IMT 2 obs

Mauritania MRT

Mauritanian Ouguiya OM		2011	2012	2013
GDP	OM	1.18tr	1.22tr	
	US$	4.2bn	4.1bn	
per capita	US$	1,250	1,221	
Growth	%	3.95	5.30	
Inflation	%	5.69	5.90	
Def exp	OM	ε30.1bn		
	US$	ε107m		
US$1=OM		280.86	296.75	
Population	3,359,185			

Age	0–14	15–19	20–24	25–29	30–64	65 plus
Male	20.1%	5.3%	4.5%	3.8%	13.0%	1.5%
Female	20.0%	5.4%	4.8%	4.2%	15.4%	2.0%

Capabilities

While Mauritania's armed forces may be able to cope with some internal-security contingencies, a lack of transport aircraft means the military lacks mobility and deployability across the country's extensive territory. Force readiness appears low, with little combat experience. Much of the military's equipment is outdated. Investment in new equipment is sporadic and often lacks direction, although a focus on the air force and navy since the 1990s has marginally improved resource-protection capabilities and light transport. Patrol craft donated by the EU have been key to the navy's improvement, but also highlight the lack of funds available for military modernisation. Mauritania's capabilities are inadequate to secure its territory and resources; combined with the perceived regional threat from al-Qaeda in the Islamic Maghreb; this has encouraged the US to provide training to the armed forces through the *Flintlock* Joint Combined Exchange Training progamme, as part of the Trans-Sahara Counterterrorism Initiative. In late 2012, Mauritanian personnel took part in the *Seaborder* 2012 international maritime exercise CPX in Algeria.

ACTIVE 15,850 (Army 15,000 Navy 600 Air 250)
Paramilitary 5,000
Terms of service conscription 24 months authorised

ORGANISATIONS BY SERVICE

Army 15,000
FORCES BY ROLE
6 mil regions
MANOEUVRE
  Reconnaissance
  1 armd recce sqn
  Armoured
  1 armd bn
  Light
  7 mot inf bn
  8 (garrison) inf bn
  Air Manoeuvre
  1 cdo/para bn
  Other
  2 (camel corps) bn
  1 gd bn
COMBAT SUPPORT
  3 arty bn
  4 ADA bty
  1 engr coy
EQUIPMENT BY TYPE
MBT 35 T-54/T-55
RECCE 70: 20 AML-60; 40 AML-90; 10 *Saladin*
APC
  APC (W) 25: 5 FV603 *Saracen*; ε20 M3 Panhard
ARTY 194
  TOWED 80: **105mm** 36 HM-2/M-101A1; **122mm** 44: 20 D-30; 24 D-74
  MOR 114: **60mm** 24; **81mm** 60; **120mm** 30 Brandt
AT • MSL • MANPATS 24 *Milan*
  RCL 114: **75mm** ε24 M20; **106mm** ε90 M40A1
AD • SAM 104
    SP ε4 SA-9 *Gaskin* (reported)
    MANPAD ε100 9K32 *Strela-2* (SA-7 *Grail*)‡
  GUNS • TOWED 82: **14.5mm** 28: 16 ZPU-2; 12 ZPU-4; **23mm** 20 ZU-23-2; **37mm** 10 M-1939; **57mm** 12 S-60; **100mm** 12 KS-19
ARV T-54/55 ARV reported

Navy ε600
EQUIPMENT BY TYPE
PATROL AND COASTAL COMBATANTS 16
  PCO 1 *Voum-Legleita*
  PCC 5: 1 *Abourbekr Ben Amer* (FRA OPV 54); 1 *Arguin*; 2 *Conjera*; 1 *Limam El Hidran* (PRC *Huangpu*)
  PB 10: 1 *El Nasr* (FRA *Patra*); 4 *Mandovi*; 1 *Yacoub Ould Rajel*; 2 *Rodman 55M*; 2 *Saeta-12*

Air Force 250
EQUIPMENT BY TYPE
AIRCRAFT
  TPT 7: **Light** 6: 2 BN-2 *Defender*; 2 PA-31T *Cheyenne* II; 2 Y-12(II); **PAX** 1 Basler BT-67
  TRG 8: 4 EMB-312 *Tucano*; 4 SF-260E
HELICOPTERS
  MRH 3: 1 SA313B *Alouette* II; 2 Z-9

Middle East and North Africa

Paramilitary ε5,000 active

Gendarmerie ε3,000

Ministry of Interior

FORCES BY ROLE
MANOEUVRE
  Other
    6 regional sy coy

National Guard 2,000

Ministry of Interior
Aux   1,000

Customs

PATROL AND COASTAL COMBATANTS • PB 2: 1
Dah Ould Bah (FRA *Amgram* 14); 1 *Yaboub Ould Rajel* (FRA
RTB 18)

Morocco MOR

Moroccan Dirham D		2011	2012	2013
GDP	D	803.16bn	847.72bn	
	US$	99.28bn	97.17bn	
per capita	US$	3,073	3,007	
Growth	%	4.85	2.87	
Inflation	%	0.91	2.20	
Def bdgt	D	27bn	29.4bn	
	US$	3.34bn	3.37bn	
FMA (US)	US$	8.98m	8m	≥8m
US$1=D		8.09	8.72	

Population	32,309,239					
Age	0–14	15–19	20–24	25–29	30–64	65 plus
Male	13.9%	4.6%	4.5%	4.5%	18.8%	2.8%
Female	13.5%	4.6%	4.6%	4.7%	20.0%	3.4%

Capabilities

Morocco's armed forces are well-trained, enjoying a good relationship with the US and French militaries. The armed forces have gained extensive experience in counter-insurgency operations in difficult conditions in the Western Sahara. This has given them expertise in desert warfare and combined air–land operational experience, although there is little capability to launch tri-service operations. The country has taken part in many peacekeeping operations, providing overseas experience for thousands of its troops. However, there has been little experience in state-on-state warfare. The military is relatively mobile, relying on mechanised infantry, supported by a modest fleet of medium-lift, fixed-wing transport aircraft and various transport helicopters. Air force equipment is ageing, with the bulk of the combat fleet procured in the 1970s and 1980s, although this has been partially rectified by last delivery, in 2012, of 24 F-16s. This is a tangible benefit of the closer relationship with the US since the early 2000s, amid a shared concern over non-state threats. The navy has traditionally been the least favoured and used of the three services, with a moderately sized but ageing fleet of patrol and coastal craft that is incapable of preventing fast-boat smuggling across the Mediterranean. Nonetheless, more significant investment is now being seen in the fleet, with three SIGMA frigates delivered and a FREMM destroyer pending, which will provide a much-improved sea-control capability.

ACTIVE 195,800 (Army 175,000 Navy 7,800 Air 13,000) Paramilitary 50,000
Terms of service conscription 18 months authorised; most enlisted personnel are volunteers

RESERVE 150,000 (Army 150,000)
Terms of service obligation to age 50

ORGANISATIONS BY SERVICE

Army ε75,000; 100,000 conscript (total 175,000)

FORCES BY ROLE
2 comd (Northern Zone, Southern Zone)
MANOEUVRE
  Armoured
    12 armd bn
  Mechanised
    3 mech inf bde
  Mechanised/Light
    8 mech/mot inf regt (2–3 bn)
  Light
    1 lt sy bde
    3 (camel corps) mot inf bn
    35 lt inf bn
    4 cdo unit
  Air Manoeuvre
    2 para bde
    2 AB bn
  Mountain
    1 mtn inf bn
COMBAT SUPPORT
  11 arty bn
  7 engr bn
  1 AD bn

Royal Guard 1,500

FORCES BY ROLE
MANOEUVRE
  Other
    1 gd bn
    1 cav sqn

EQUIPMENT BY TYPE
MBT 380: 40 T-72, 220 M60A1; 120 M60A3; (ε200 M48A5 in store)
LT TK 116: 5 AMX-13; 111 SK-105 *Kuerassier*
RECCE 384: 38 AML-60-7; 190 AML-90; 80 AMX-10RC; 40 EBR-75; 16 *Eland*; 20 M1114 HMMWV
AIFV 70: 10 AMX-10P; 30 MK III-20 *Ratel*-20; 30 MK III-90 *Ratel*-90
APC 851
  APC (T) 486: 400 M113A1/A2; 86 M577A2

APC (W) 365: 45 VAB VCI; 320 VAB VTT

ARTY 2,141

SP 282: **105mm** 5 Mk 61; **155mm** 217: 84 M109A1/A1B; 43 M109A2; 90 (AMX) Mk F3; **203mm** 60 M110

TOWED 118: **105mm** 50: 30 L118 Light Gun; 20 M101; **130mm** 18 M-46; **155mm** 50: 30 FH-70; 20 M114

MRL 35 BM-21

MOR 1,706

SP 56: **106mm** 32–36 M106A2; **120mm** 20 (VAB APC)

TOWED 1,650: **81mm** 1,100 Expal model LN; **120mm** 550 Brandt

AT • MSL 790

SP 80 M-901

MANPATS 710: 40 9K11 *Malyutka* (AT-3 *Sagger*); 440 M47 *Dragon*; 80 *Milan*; 150 TOW

RCL **106mm** 350 M40A1

RL **89mm** 200 M20

GUNS 36

SP **100mm** 8 SU-100

TOWED **90mm** 28 M-56

UAV • Heavy R4E-50 *Skyeye*

AD • SAM 119

SP 49: 12 2K22M *Tunguska*-M (SA-19 *Grison*) SPAAGM; 37 M-48 *Chaparral*

MANPAD 70 9K32 *Strela*-2 (SA-7 *Grail*)‡

GUNS 407

SP 60 M-163 *Vulcan*

TOWED 347: **14.5mm** 200: 150-180 ZPU-2; 20 ZPU-4; **20mm** 40 M-167 *Vulcan*; **23mm** 75-90 ZU-23-2; **100mm** 17 KS-19

RADAR • LAND: RASIT (veh, arty)

ARV 48+: 10 *Greif*; 18 M88A1; M578; 20 VAB-ECH

Navy 7,800 (incl 1,500 Marines)

EQUIPMENT BY TYPE

PRINCIPAL SURFACE COMBATANTS

FRIGATES 5

FFGHM 3 SIGMA with 4 single lnchr with MM-40 *Exocet* Block II AShM, 2 sextuple lnchr with MICA SAM, 2 triple 324 mm ASTT with Mu-90 LWT, 1 76mm gun (capacity 1 AS565SA *Panther*)

FFGH 2 *Mohammed V* (FRA *Floreal*) with 2 single lnchr with MM-38 *Exocet* AShM, 1 76mm gun (can be fitted with *Simbad* SAM if 20mm guns replaced) (capacity 1 AS565SA *Panther*)

PATROL AND COASTAL COMBATANTS 50

CORVETTES • FSGM 1

1 *Lt Col Errhamani* (ESP *Descubierto*) with 2 twin lnchr with MM-38 *Exocet* AShM, 1 octuple *Albatros* lnchr with *Aspide* SAM, 2 triple 324mm ASTT with Mk 46 LWT, 1 76mm gun

PSO 1 *Bin an Zaran* (OPV 70) with 1 76mm gun

PCG 4 *Cdt El Khattabi* (ESP *Lazaga* 58m) with 4 single lnchr with MM-40 *Exocet* AShM, 1 76mm gun

PCO 5 *Rais Bargach* (under control of fisheries dept)

PCC 12:

4 *El Hahiq* (DNK *Osprey* 55, incl 2 with customs)

6 *LV Rabhi* (ESP 58m B-200D)

2 *Okba* (FRA PR-72) each with 1 76mm gun

PB 27: 6 *El Wacil* (FRA P-32); 10 VCSM (RPB 20); 10 *Rodman* 101; 1 other *(UK Bird)*

AMPHIBIOUS 6

LANDING SHIPS 4:

LSM 3 *Ben Aicha* (FRA *Champlain* BATRAL) (capacity 7 tanks; 140 troops)

LST 1 *Sidi Mohammed Ben Abdallah* (US *Newport*) (capacity 3 LCVP; 400 troops)

LANDING CRAFT 2:

LCM 1 CTM (FRA CTM-5)

LCU 1 *Lt Malghah*† (FRA *Edic*)

LOGISTICS AND SUPPORT 5

AGOR 1 (US lease); AK 2; AX 1 *Essaouira*; YDT 1

Marines 1,500

FORCES BY ROLE

MANOEUVRE

Amphibious

2 naval inf bn

Naval Aviation

EQUIPMENT BY TYPE

HELICOPTERS • ASW/ASUW 3 AS565SA *Panther*

Air Force 13,000

Flying hours 100 hrs/year on *Mirage* F-1/F-5E/F *Tiger II*/F-16C/D *Fighting Falcon*

FORCES BY ROLE

FIGHTER/GROUND ATTACK

2 sqn with F-5E/F-5F *Tiger* II

1 sqn (2 more sqn forming) with F-16C/D *Fighting Falcon*

1 sqn with *Mirage* F-1C (F-1CH)

1 sqn with *Mirage* F-1E (F-1EH)

ELECTRONIC WARFARE

1 sqn with EC-130H *Hercules*; *Falcon* 20 (ELINT)

MARITIME PATROL

1 flt with Do-28

TANKER/TRANSPORT

1 sqn with C-130/KC-130H *Hercules*

TRANSPORT

1 sqn with CN-235

1 VIP sqn with B-737BBJ; Beech 200/300 *King Air*; *Falcon* 50; Gulfstream II/III/V-SP

TRAINING

1 sqn with *Alpha Jet**

ATTACK HELICOPTER

1 sqn with SA342L *Gazelle* (Some with HOT)

TRANSPORT HELICOPTER

1 sqn with Bell 205A (AB-205A); Bell 206 *Jet Ranger* (AB-206); Bell 212 (AB-212)

1 sqn with CH-47D *Chinook*

1 sqn with SA330 *Puma*

EQUIPMENT BY TYPE

AIRCRAFT 92 combat capable

FTR 22: 19 F-5E *Tiger* II; 3 F-5F *Tiger* II

FGA 51: 16 F-16C *Fighting Falcon*; 8 F-16D *Fighting Falcon*; 16 *Mirage* F-1C (F-1CH); 11 *Mirage* F-1E (F-1EH)

ELINT 1 EC-130H *Hercules*

TKR/TPT 2 KC-130H *Hercules*

TPT 49: **Medium** 15: 2 C-27J *Spartan* (2 more on order); 13 C-130H *Hercules*; **Light** 21: 4 Beech 100 *King Air*; 2 Beech 200 *King Air*; 1 Beech 200C *King Air*; 2 Beech 300 *King Air*; 3 Beech 350 *King Air*; 7 CN-235; 2 Do-28; **PAX** 9: 1 B-737BBJ; 2 *Falcon* 20; 2 *Falcon* 20 (ELINT); 1 *Falcon* 50 (VIP); 1 *Gulfstream* II (VIP); 1 *Gulfstream* III; 1 *Gulfstream* V-SP

TRG 64: 12 AS-202 *Bravo*; 19 *Alpha Jet**; 2 CAP-10; 8 T-6C *Texan*; 9 T-34C *Turbo Mentor*; 14 T-37B *Tweet*

HELICOPTERS

MRH 19 SA342L *Gazelle* (7 with HOT, 12 with cannon)

TPT 70: **Heavy** 7 CH-47D *Chinook*; **Medium** 24 SA330 *Puma*; **Light** 39: 25 Bell 205A (AB-205A); 11 Bell 206 *Jet Ranger* (AB-206); 3 Bell 212 (AB-212)

MSL

AAM • IR AIM-9B/D/J *Sidewinder*; R-550 *Magic*; **IIR** (AIM-9X *Sidewinder* on order); **SARH** R530; **ARH** (AIM-120 AMRAAM on order)

ASM AGM-62B *Walleye* (for F-5E); HOT

Paramilitary 50,000 active

Gendarmerie Royale 20,000

FORCES BY ROLE

MANOEUVRE

Air Manoeuvre

1 para sqn

Other

1 paramilitary bde

4 (mobile) paramilitary gp

1 coast guard unit

TRANSPORT HELICOPTER

1 sqn

EQUIPMENT BY TYPE

PATROL AND COASTAL COMBATANTS • PB 33

AIRCRAFT • TRG 2 R-235 *Guerrier*

HELICOPTERS

MRH 14: 3 SA315B *Lama*; 2 S316 *Alouette* III; 3 SA318 *Alouette* II; 6 SA342K *Gazelle*

TPT 8: **Medium** 6 SA330 *Puma*; **Light** 2 SA360 *Dauphin*

Force Auxiliaire 30,000 (incl 5,000 Mobile Intervention Corps)

Customs/Coast Guard

PATROL AND COASTAL COMBATANTS • PB 49: 4 *Erraid*; 18 *Arcor* 46; 15 *Arcor* 53; 12 (other SAR craft)

DEPLOYMENT

CÔTE D'IVOIRE

UN • UNOCI 726; 1 inf bn

DEMOCRATIC REPUBLIC OF THE CONGO

UN • MONUSCO 849; 6 obs; 1 mech inf bn; 1 fd hospital

SERBIA

NATO • KFOR 168; 1 inf coy

Oman OMN

Omani Rial R		2011	2012	2013
GDP	R	27.95bn	30.75bn	
	US$	72.68bn	79.97bn	
per capita	US$	23,520	25,879	
Growth	%	5.44	4.95	
Inflation	%	4.03	3.25	
Def bdgt	R	1.65bn	2.59bn	
	US$	4.29bn	6.72bn	
FMA (US)	US$	13m	8m	≥ 8m
US$1=R		0.38	0.38	

Population   3,090,150

Expatriates: 27%

Age	0–14	15–19	20–24	25–29	30–64	65 plus
Male	15.8%	5.2%	5.5%	6.2%	20.5%	1.6%
Female	15.0%	4.9%	4.8%	4.8%	14.0%	1.6%

Capabilities

Oman's armed forces are relatively capable and, although small in comparison to larger regional neighbours, the military is well-staffed given the country's population, with a strong history of cooperation and training with the UK armed forces. It retains an effective inventory handled by well-trained personnel. Despite a lack of war-fighting experience, it maintains a good state of readiness. The armed forces have remained well-funded. This has ensured a steady flow of new equipment, primarily from the UK and the US, to maintain military effectiveness. Although focused on territorial defence, there is some versatility of roles within the military, with a special forces and small amphibious capability, a relatively high proportion of airlift and modest sea-lift and the Royal Guard brigade, which reports directly to the sultan and carries out internal security and ceremonial functions. Oman is in the market for around 12 new combat aircraft, with discussion focused the Eurofighter *Typhoon*. However, there are also capability gaps, such as anti-submarine warfare, and greater training and equipment (particularly ISR systems) are required to cope more effectively with security issues such as smuggling across the Strait of Hormuz. Oman is a GCC member.

ACTIVE 42,600 (Army 25,000 Navy 4,200 Air 5,000 Foreign Forces 2,000 Royal Household 6,400) **Paramilitary 4,400**

ORGANISATIONS BY SERVICE

Army 25,000

FORCES BY ROLE

(Regt are bn size)

MANOEUVRE

Armoured

1 armd bde (2 armd regt, 1 recce regt)

Light

1 inf bde (5 inf regt, 1 arty regt, 1 fd engr regt, 1 engr regt, 1 sigs regt)

1 inf bde (3 inf regt, 2 arty regt)

1 indep inf coy (Musandam Security Force)

Air Manoeuvre

1 AB regt

COMBAT SUPPORT

1 ADA regt (2 ADA bty)

COMBAT SERVICE SUPPORT

1 tpt regt

EQUIPMENT BY TYPE

MBT 117: 38 CR2 *Challenger* 2; 6 M60A1; 73 M60A3

LT TK 37 *Scorpion*

RECCE 137: 13 *Sultan*; 124 VBL

APC 206

  APC (T) 16: 6 FV 103 *Spartan*; 10 FV4333 *Stormer*

  APC (W) 190: 175 *Piranha* (incl variants); 15 AT-105 *Saxon*

ARTY 233

  SP 155mm 24 G-6

  TOWED 108: **105mm** 42 ROF lt; **122mm** 30 D-30; **130mm** 24: 12 M-46; 12 Type-59-I; **155mm** 12 FH-70

  MOR 101: **81mm** 69; **107mm** 20 M-30; **120mm** 12 Brandt

AT • MSL 88

  SP 8 VBL (TOW)

  MANPATS 80: 30 *Javelin*; 32 *Milan*; 18 TOW/TOW-2A

AD • SAM 74+

  SP 20: up to 12 *Pantsyr* S1E SPAAGM; 8 *Mistral* 2

  MANPAD 54: 20 *Javelin*; 34 9K32 *Strela-2* (SA-7 Grail)‡

  GUNS 26: **23mm** 4 ZU-23-2; **35mm** 10 GDF-005 (with *Skyguard*); **40mm** 12 L/60 (Towed)

ARV 11: 4 *Challenger*; 2 M88A1; 2 *Piranha*; 3 *Samson*

Navy 4,200

EQUIPMENT BY TYPE

SUBMARINES • SDV 2 Mk 8

PRIMARY SURFACE COMBATANTS 1

  FFGHM 1 *Al-Shamikh* with 2 quadruple lnchr with MM-40 *Exocet* Block III AShM, 2 sextuple lnchr with VL MICA SAM, 1 76mm gun (two additional vessels under construction; ISD 2013)

PATROL AND COASTAL COMBATANTS 13

  CORVETTES • FSGM 2

    2 *Qahir Al Amwaj* with 2 quad lnchr with MM-40 *Exocet* AShM, 1 octuple lnchr with *Crotale* SAM, 2 triple 324mm TT (to be fitted), 1 76mm gun, 1 hel landing platform

  PCFG 4 *Dhofar* with 2 quad lnchr with MM-40 *Exocet* AShM, 1 76mm gun

  PCC 3 *Al Bushra* (FRA P-400) with 4 single 406mm TT, 1 76mm gun

  PB 4 *Seeb* (UK Vosper 25m, under 100 tonnes)

AMPHIBIOUS 6

  LANDING SHIPS • LST 1 *Nasr el Bahr* (with hel deck) (capacity 7 tanks; 240 troops)

  LANDING CRAFT 5: 1 LCU; 3 LCM; 1 LCT

LOGISTICS AND SUPPORT 7

  AK 1 *Al Sultana*

  AKSH 1 *Fulk Al Salamaf*

  AGHS 1

AP 2 *Shinas* (commercial tpt - auxiliary military role only) (capacity 56 veh; 200 tps)

AX 1 *Al Mabrukah* (with hel deck, also used in OPV role)

AXS 1 *Shabab Oman*

Air Force 5,000

FORCES BY ROLE

FIGHTER/GROUND ATTACK

1 sqn with F-16C/D Block 50 *Fighting Falcon*

1 sqn with *Hawk* Mk103; *Hawk* Mk203

2 sqn with *Jaguar* S (OS)/*Jaguar* B (OB)

TRANSPORT

1 sqn with C-130H/J-30 *Hercules*

1 sqn with SC.7 3M *Skyvan* (radar-equipped, for MP)

TRAINING

1 sqn with MFI-17B *Mushshak*; PC-9*; Bell 206 (AB-206) *Jet Ranger*

TRANSPORT HELICOPTER

3 (med) sqn with Bell 205 (AB-205); Bell 212 (AB-212); *Super Lynx* Mk300 (maritime/SAR)

AIR DEFENCE

2 sqn with *Rapier*; *Blindfire*; S713 *Martello*

EQUIPMENT BY TYPE

AIRCRAFT 54 combat capable

  FGA 26: 8 F-16C Block 50 *Fighting Falcon*; 4 F-16D Block 50 *Fighting Falcon*; 12 *Jaguar* S (OS); 2 *Jaguar* B (OB)

  TPT 13: **Medium** 4: 3 C-130H *Hercules*; 1 C-130J-30 *Hercules*; **Light** 7 SC.7 3M *Skyvan* (radar-equipped, for MP); **PAX** 2 A320-300

  TRG 36: 4 *Hawk* Mk103*; 12 *Hawk* Mk203*; 8 MFI-17B *Mushshak*; 12 PC-9*

HELICOPTERS

  MRH 15 *Super Lynx* Mk300 (maritime/SAR)

  TPT 35 **Medium** 10 NH90 TTH (10 more on order); **Light** 25: 19 Bell 205 (AB-205); 3 Bell 206 (AB-206) *Jet Ranger*; 3 Bell 212 (AB-212)

AD • SAM 40 *Rapier*

RADAR • LAND 6+: 6 *Blindfire*; S713 *Martello*

MSL

  AAM • IR AIM-9N/M/P *Sidewinder*; **ARH** AIM-120C AMRAAM

  ASM 20 AGM-84D *Harpoon*; AGM-65 *Maverick*

Royal Household 6,400

(incl HQ staff)

FORCES BY ROLE

SPECIAL FORCES

2 SF regt

Royal Guard bde 5,000

FORCES BY ROLE

MANOEUVRE

  Light

    1 gd bde (2 gd regt, 1 armd sqn, 1 cbt spt bn)

EQUIPMENT BY TYPE

LT TK (9 VBC-90 in store)

RECCE 9 *Centauro* MGS

APC (W) 73: ε50 Type-92; 14 VAB VCI; 9 VAB VDAA

ARTY • MRL 122mm 6 Type-90A

AT • MSL • MANPATS *Milan*

AD • SAM • MANPAD 14 *Javelin*
GUNS • SP 9: 20mm 9 VAB VDAA

Royal Yacht Squadron 150
PATROL AND COASTAL COMBATANTS • MISC BOATS/CRAFT • DHOW 1 *Zinat Al Bihaar*
LOGISTICS AND SUPPORT 3
   AP 1 *Fulk Al Salamah* (also veh tpt) with up to 2 AS332 *Super Puma* hel
   YAC 2: 1 *Al Said*; 1 (Royal Dhow)

Royal Flight 250
AIRCRAFT • TPT • PAX 5: 2 B-747SP; 1 DC-8-73CF; 2 Gulfstream IV
HELICOPTERS • TPT • Medium 6: 3 SA330 (AS330) *Puma*; 2 AS332F *Super Puma*; 1 AS332L *Super Puma*

Paramilitary 4,400 active

Tribal Home Guard 4,000
org in teams of ε100

Police Coast Guard 400
PATROL AND COASTAL COMBATANTS 56
   PCO 2 *Haras*
   PBF 23: 20 *Cougar Enforcer 33*; 3 Mk V *Pegasus*
   PB 31: 5 *Vosper 75*; 1 CG27; 3 CG29; 1 P1903; 14 *Rodman 58*; 2 D59116; 5 *Zahra*

Police Air Wing
AIRCRAFT • TPT • Light 4: 1 BN-2T *Turbine Islander*; 2 CN-235M; 1 Do-228
HELICOPTERS • TPT • Light 5: 2 Bell 205A; 3 Bell 214ST (AB-214ST)

FOREIGN FORCES
United Kingdom Army 30; Navy 20; Air Force 30; 1 *Tristar* tkr; 1 *Sentinel*

Palestinian Autonomous Areas of Gaza and Jericho PA

New Israeli Shekel NS		2011	2012	2013
GDP	US$			
per capita	US$			
Growth	%			
Inflation	%			

*definitive economic data unavailable

US$1=NS		3.55	3.89

Age	0–14	15–19	20–24	25–29	30–64	65 plus
Male	19.8%	5.7%	5.3%	4.1%	14.7%	1.4%
Female	18.7%	5.5%	5.0%	3.9%	14.0%	1.9%

Capabilities
The Palestinian Authority's National Security Force is a paramilitary organisation intended to provide internal security support within Gaza and the West Bank. Its writ only runs in the West Bank, where it has proved capable of maintaining internal security. It would have little effect against any Israeli incursion. Since 2007, the Gaza strip has been run by Hamas. The Izz ad-Din al-Qassam Brigades, Hamas's military wing, is seen by the organisation as its best-trained and most disciplined force. It has a strong well-developed rocket artillery capability, including manufacturing, development and testing, but this is increasingly countered by Israel's *Iron Dome* missile-defence system. It is seeking to improved its command-and-control structure, the acquisition of better weapons and the creation of a training programme. The revolution in Egypt has reduced security in the Sinai. Smuggling tunnels continue to function between Sinai and Gaza, which likely benefit military holdings in the territory. In the November 2012 hostilities, Iranian-developed *Fajr*-5 rockets were fired, putting Tel Aviv and Jerusalem within range of rocket fire. Israel's military actions, meanwhile, will have degraded the command-and-control, as well as physical infrastructure, of Hamas forces.

ACTIVE 0 Paramilitary 56,000
Precise personnel strength figures for the various Palestinian groups are not known

ORGANISATIONS BY SERVICE
There are few data available on the status of the organisations mentioned below. Following internal fighting in June 2007, Gaza is under the de facto control of Hamas, while the West Bank is controlled by the Palestinian Authority.

Paramilitary

National Forces ε56,000 (reported)
GENERAL SECURITY
Presidential security 3,000
SF 1,200
Police 9,000
Preventative Security n.k.
Civil Defence 1,000

AD • SAM • MANPAD 9K32 *Strela*-2 (SA-7 *Grail*)‡

The **al-Aqsa Brigades** profess loyalty to the Fatah group that dominates the Palestinian Authority. The strength of this group is not known.

Hamas groupings include internal-security groupings such as the **Executive Force** (est strength: 10–12,000; major equipment include: artillery rockets, mortars, SALW) and the **al-Qassam Brigades** (est strength: 10,000; major equipment include: mines and IEDs, artillery rockets, mortars, SALW)

Qatar QTR

Qatari Riyal R		2011	2012	2013
GDP	R	631.61bn	671.82bn	
	US$	173.52bn	184.57bn	
per capita	US$	88,912	94,574	
Growth	%	14.12	6.29	
Inflation	%	1.92	2.02	
Def exp	R	ε12.6bn		
	US$	ε3.46bn		
US$1=R			3.64	3.64

Population   1,951,591

Ethnic groups: Nationals 25%; Expatriates 75% of which Indian 18%; Iranian 10%; Pakistani 18%

Age	0–14	15–19	20–24	25–29	30–64	65 plus
Male	6.4%	2.8%	7.8%	12.5%	46.7%	0.5%
Female	6.2%	1.6%	2.2%	3.1%	10.0%	0.3%

Capabilities

Qatar maintains a small military with limited capability, although its equipment is relatively modern and its forces are well-trained and motivated. As with other small Gulf states, Qatar relies on its international alliances, primarily with the US and through the GCC, to guarantee its security. However, a high proportion of government spending goes to defence, so the Qatari military has been able to maintain an adequate defence capability despite its small size. Some equipment, particularly main battle tanks and fast missile craft, are ageing, but high-technology weapons, such as *Exocet* anti-ship missiles, make these platforms capable of fulfilling their primary role of border and maritime security. The armed forces suffer from a number of capability gaps, particularly in air defence, and the age of some equipment may hamper its ability to perform in high-tempo operations. In late 2012, Qatar requested the sale of *Patriot* and THAAD missile-defence batteries from the US. It had earlier requested for 24 AH-64 *Apache* attack helicopters and 12 UH-60M *Black Hawk* utility helicopters. The air force has seen investment in recent years, with the arrival of C-17 transports, which – along with *Mirage* 2000 aircraft – were deployed on operations over Libya, in 2011, to enforce UNSCR 1973. Later that year, the chief of staff also admitted that Qatar deployed 'hundreds' of ground troops to conduct liaison duties.

ACTIVE 11,800 (Army 8,500 Navy 1,800 Air 1,500)

ORGANISATIONS BY SERVICE

Army 8,500

FORCES BY ROLE
SPECIAL FORCES
   1 SF coy
MANOEUVRE
   Armoured
   1 armd bde (1 tk bn, 1 mech inf bn, 1 AT bn, 1 mor sqn)

Mechanised
3 mech inf bn
Light
1 (Royal Guard) bde (3 inf regt)
COMBAT SUPPORT
   1 fd arty bn
EQUIPMENT BY TYPE
MBT 30 AMX-30
RECCE 68: 12 AMX-10RC; 20 EE-9 *Cascavel*; 12 *Ferret*; 8 V-150 *Chaimite*; 16 VBL
AIFV 40 AMX-10P
APC 226
   APC (T) 30 AMX-VCI
   APC (W) 196: 36 *Piranha* II; 160 VAB
ARTY 89
   SP 155mm 28 (AMX) Mk F3
   TOWED 155mm 12 G-5
   MRL 4 ASTROS II
   MOR 45
      SP • 81mm 4 VAB VPM 81
      81mm 26 L16
      120mm 15 *Brandt*
AT • MSL 148
   SP 24 VAB VCAC HOT
   MANPATS 124: 24 HOT; 100 *Milan*
   RCL 84mm ε40 *Carl Gustav*
ARV 3: 1 AMX-30D; 2 *Piranha*

Navy 1,800 (incl Marine Police)

EQUIPMENT BY TYPE
PATROL AND COASTAL COMBATANTS 10
   PCFG 7:
      4 *Barzan* (UK *Vita*) with 2 quad lnchr with MM-40 *Exocet* AShM, 1 sextuple lnchr with *Mistral* SAM, 1 76mm gun
      3 *Damsah* (FRA *Combattante* III) with 2 quad lnchr with MM-40 *Exocet* AShM, 1 76mm gun
   PB 3 Q-31 series (Marine Police)
AMPHIBIOUS • LANDING CRAFT • LCT 1 *Rabha* (capacity 3 MBT; 110 troops)

Marine Police

EQUIPMENT BY TYPE
PATROL AND COASTAL COMBATANTS 11
   PBF 4 DV 15
   PB 7: 4 *Crestitalia* MV-45; 3 *Halmatic* M160

Coastal Defence

FORCES BY ROLE
MISSILE
   1 bty with 3 quad lnchr with MM-40 *Exocet* AShM
EQUIPMENT BY TYPE
MSL • AShM Some MM-40 *Exocet* AShM

Air Force 1,500

FORCES BY ROLE
FIGHTER/GROUND ATTACK
   1 sqn with *Alpha Jet**
   1 sqn with *Mirage* 2000ED; *Mirage* 2000D

TRANSPORT
1 sqn with C-17A; C-130J-30
1 sqn with A-340; B-707; B-727; *Falcon* 900

ATTACK HELICOPTER
1 ASuW sqn with *Commando* Mk3 with *Exocet*
1 sqn with SA341 *Gazelle*; SA342L *Gazelle* with HOT

TRANSPORT HELICOPTER
1 sqn with *Commando* Mk2A; *Commando* Mk2C
1 sqn with AW139

EQUIPMENT BY TYPE
AIRCRAFT 18 combat capable
FGA 12: 9 *Mirage* 2000ED; 3 *Mirage* 2000D
TPT 12: **Heavy** 2 C-17A *Globemaster*; **Medium** 4 C-130J-30
Hercules; **PAX** 6: 1 A340; 2 B-707; 1 B-727; 2 *Falcon* 900
TRG 6 *Alpha Jet**
HELICOPTERS
ASuW 8 *Commando* Mk3
MRH 31: 18 AW139 (3 more being delivered); 2 SA341
Gazelle; 11 SA342L *Gazelle*
TPT • Medium 4: 3 *Commando* Mk2A; 1 *Commando* Mk2C
AD • SAM 75: 24 *Mistral*
SP 9 *Roland* II
MANPAD 42: 10 *Blowpipe*; 12 FIM-92A *Stinger*; 20 9K32
Strela-2 (SA-7 Grail)‡
MSL
ASM AM-39 *Exocet*; *Apache*; HOT
AAM • IR R-550 *Magic* 2; **ARH** *Mica*

DEPLOYMENT

LEBANON
UN • UNIFIL 3

FOREIGN FORCES

United Kingdom Air Force: 4 C-130J
United States US Central Command: 600; elm 1 (APS)
HBCT set; USAF CAOC

Saudi Arabia SAU

Saudi Riyal R		2011	2012	2013
GDP	R	2.24tr	2.46tr	
	US$	597.09bn	657.05bn	
per capita	US$	22,502	24,762	
Growth	%	7.06	5.97	
Inflation	%	4.98	4.91	
Def exp [a]	R	182bn		
	US$	48.5bn		
US$1=R		3.75	3.75	

[a] Defence and security budget

Population   26,534,504

Ethnic groups: Nationals 73% of which Bedouin up to 10%, Shi'a 6%, Expatriates 27% of which Asians 20%, Arabs 6%, Africans 1%, Europeans <1%

Age	0–14	15–19	20–24	25–29	30–64	65 plus
Male	14.7%	5.0%	5.6%	6.0%	21.8%	1.6%
Female	14.0%	4.6%	4.6%	4.6%	16.0%	1.4%

Capabilities

Saudi Arabia has the best-equipped military forces in the Gulf region, and is a GCC member. The Saudi inventory is generally more modern and better maintained than its neighbours'. However, coordination and cooperation between the regular armed forces remains poor and decision-making at the highest levels is hampered by inter-service competition as well as the age and infirmity of senior ministers. Air force priorities are air defence and deterrence, not expeditionary air operations. The same is true of the less well-equipped naval forces. The land forces are configured militarily and geographically to meet threats such as instability at key borders. The ability of the armed forces to effectively utilise their advanced inventory was questioned by operations against Houthi rebels in late 2009 and early 2010; these appeared to demonstrate the capabilities of the air force, but land forces reportedly struggled to fight effectively in the mountainous terrain of the south. Saudi Arabia relies on overseas partners to ultimately guarantee its security in the face of any substantial threats and to assist its military development. The Saudi armed forces retain a good relationship with overseas militaries, in particular the US, the UK and France, which affords combined training possibilities as well as access to equipment. The country's air-defence network is extensive and highly capable. Meanwhile, the armed forces require a range of lift to be able to deploy across the country. Capability in this area is good, meaning a moderate power-projection capability exists. In November 2012, Saudi Arabia requested the sale of 20 C-130J airlifters and 5 KC-130J tankers, which would constitute an upgrade to its existing C-130H fleet. However, sealift is inadequate to sustain a large force overseas for any period of time. The national guard was the primary contributor to the Peninsula Shield force that entered Bahrain in March 2011, but given the proximity of the island to the country, no significant support or sustainment is necessary.

ACTIVE 233,500 (Army 75,000 Navy 13,500 Air 20,000 Air Defence 16,000 Industrial Security Force 9,000 National Guard 100,000) **Paramilitary 15,500**

ORGANISATIONS BY SERVICE

Army 75,000
FORCES BY ROLE
MANOEUVRE
Armoured
4 armd bde (1 recce coy, 3 tk bn, 1 mech bn, 1 fd arty bn, 1 AD bn, 1 AT bn,1 engr coy, 1 log bn, 1 maint coy, 1 med coy)
Mechanised
5 mech bde (1 recce coy, 1 tk bn, 3 mech bn, 1 fd arty bn, 1 AD bn, 1 AT bn, 1 engr coy, 1 log bn, 1 maint coy, 1 med coy)
Light
1 (Royal Guard) regt (3 lt inf bn)
Air Manoeuvre
1 AB bde (2 AB bn, 3 SF coy)
Aviation
1 comd (1 atk hel bde, 1 tpt hel bde)
COMBAT SUPPORT
1 arty bde (5 fd arty bn, 2 MRL bn, 1 msl bn)

EQUIPMENT BY TYPE
MBT 600: 200 M1A2 *Abrams* (115 more in store); 400 M60A3; (145 AMX-30 in store)
RECCE 300 AML-60/AML-90
AIFV 780: 380 AMX-10P; 400 M2 *Bradley*
APC 1,423
  APC (T) 1,200 M113A1/A2/A3 (incl variants)
  APC (W) 150 M3 Panhard; (ε40 AF-40-8-1 *Al-Fahd* in store)
  PPV 73 *Aravis*
ARTY 909
  SP 155mm 224: 60 AU-F-1; 110 M109A1B/A2; 54 PLZ-45
  TOWED 50: **105mm** (100 M101/M102 in store); **155mm** 50 M114 (60 M198 in store); **203mm** (8 M115 in store)
  MRL 60 ASTROS II
  MOR 437
    SP 220: **81mm** 70; **107mm** 150 M30
    TOWED 217: **81mm/107mm** 70 incl M30 **120mm** 147: 110 Brandt; 37 M12-1535
AT • MSL 2,240+
  SP 290+: 90+ AMX-10P (HOT); 200 VCC-1 *ITOW*
  MANPATS 1950: 1,000 M47 *Dragon*; 950 TOW-2A
  RCL 450: **84mm** 300 *Carl Gustav*; **106mm** 50 M40A1; **90mm** 100 M67
  RL 112mm ε200 APILAS
AD • SAM 1,000+
  SP *Crotale*
  MANPAD 1,000: 500 FIM-43 *Redeye*; 500 FIM-92A *Stinger*
RADAR • LAND AN/TPQ-36 *Firefinder*/AN/TPQ-37 *Firefinder* (arty, mor)
MSL • TACTICAL • SSM 10+ CSS-2 (40 msl)
AEV 15 M728
ARV 283+: 8 ACV ARV; AMX-10EHC; 55 AMX-30D; *Leclerc* ARV; 130 M88A1; 90 M578
VLB 10 AMX-30
MW *Aardvark* Mk2

HELICOPTERS
ATK 12 AH-64 *Apache*
MRH 21: 6 AS365N *Dauphin 2* (medevac); 15 Bell 406CS *Combat Scout*
TPT • Medium 58: 12 S-70A-1 *Desert Hawk*; 22 UH-60A *Black Hawk* (4 medevac); 24 UH-60L *Black Hawk*

Navy 13,500
Navy HQ at Riyadh; Eastern Fleet HQ at Jubail; Western Fleet HQ at Jeddah

EQUIPMENT BY TYPE
PRINCIPAL SURFACE COMBATANTS 7
  DESTROYERS • DDGHM 3 *Al Riyadh* with 2 quad lnchr with MM-40 *Exocet* Block II AShM, 2 8-cell VLS with *Aster* 15 SAM, 4 single 533mm TT with F17P HWT, 1 76mm gun (capacity 1 AS365N *Dauphin 2* hel)
  FRIGATES • FFGHM 4 *Madina* (FRA F-2000) with 2 quad lnchr with *Otomat* Mk 2 AShM, 1 octuple lnchr with *Crotale* SAM, 4 single 533mm ASTT with F17P HWT, 1 100mm gun (capacity 1 AS365N *Dauphin 2* hel)
PATROL AND COASTAL COMBATANTS 69
  CORVETTES • FSG 4 *Badr* (US *Tacoma*) with 2 quad Mk140 lnchr with RGM-84C *Harpoon* AShM, 2 triple 324mm ASTT with Mk 46 LWT, 1 76mm gun
  PCFG 9 *Al Siddiq* (US 58m) with 2 twin Mk140 lnchr with RGM-84C *Harpoon* AShM, 1 76mm gun
  PB 56: 17 (US *Halter Marine*); 39 *Simmoneau 51*
MINE WARFARE • MINE COUNTERMEASURES 7
  MCC 4 *Addriyah* (US MSC-322)
  MHC 3 *Al Jawf* (UK *Sandown*)
AMPHIBIOUS 8
  LCU 4 *1610* (capacity 120 troops)
  LCM 4 *LCM 6* (capacity 80 troops)
LOGISTICS AND SUPPORT 17
  AORH 2 *Boraida* (mod FRA *Durance*) (capacity either 2 AS365F *Dauphin 2* hel or 1 AS332C *Super Puma*)
  YAC 2
  YTB 2
  YTM 11 *Radhwa*

Naval Aviation
HELICOPTERS
  MRH 34: 6 AS365N *Dauphin 2*; 15 AS565 with AS-15TT AShM; 13 Bell 406CS *Combat Scout*
  TPT • Medium 12 AS332B/F *Super Puma* with AM-39 *Exocet* AShM

Marines 3,000
FORCES BY ROLE
MANOEUVRE
Amphibious
1 inf regt with (2 inf bn)

EQUIPMENT BY TYPE
APC (W) 140 BMP-600P

Air Force 20,000
FORCES BY ROLE
FIGHTER
1 sqn with F-15S *Eagle*
4 sqn with F-15C/D *Eagle*
FIGHTER/GROUND ATTACK
2 sqn with F-15S *Eagle*

3 sqn with *Tornado* IDS; *Tornado* GR1A

2 sqn with *Typhoon*

AIRBORNE EARLY WARNING & CONTROL/TANKER

1 sqn with E-3A *Sentry*; KE-3A

ELINT

1 sqn with RE-3A/B

TANKER/TRANSPORT

1 sqn with KC-130H *Hercules* (tkr/tpt)

1 sqn forming with A330 MRTT

TRANSPORT

3 sqn with C-130H *Hercules*; C-130H-30 *Hercules*; CN-235; L-100-30HS (hospital ac)

TRAINING

3 sqn with *Hawk* Mk65*; *Hawk* Mk65A*

1 sqn with *Jetstream* Mk31

1 sqn with Cessna 172; MFI-17 *Mushshak*

2 sqn with PC-9

TRANSPORT HELICOPTER

4 sqn with AS532 *Cougar* (CSAR); Bell 212 (AB-212); Bell 412 (AB-412) *Twin Huey* (SAR): AS-61A-4

EQUIPMENT BY TYPE

AIRCRAFT 296 combat capable

FTR 81: 56 F-15C *Eagle*; 25 F-15D *Eagle*

FGA 165: 71 F-15S *Eagle*; 70 Tornado IDS; 24 *Typhoon*

ISR 10 Tornado GR1A*

AEW&C 5 E-3A *Sentry*

ELINT 3: 2 RE-3A; 1 RE-3B

TKR/TPT 10: 3 A330 MRTT (5 more on order); 7 KC-130H *Hercules*

TKR 7 KE-3A

TPT 54 **Medium** 36: 30 C-130H *Hercules*; 3 C-130H-30 *Hercules*; 3 L-100-30; **Light** 18: 13 Cessna 172; 4 CN-235; 1 *Jetstream* Mk31

TRG 100: 24 *Hawk* Mk65* (incl aerobatic team); 16 *Hawk* Mk65A*; 20 MFI-17 *Mushshak*; 40 PC-9

HELICOPTERS

MRH 15 Bell 412 (AB-412) *Twin Huey* (SAR)

TPT 30: **Medium** 10 AS532 *Cougar* (CSAR); **Light** 20 Bell 212 (AB-212)

MSL

ASM AGM-65 *Maverick*

AShM *Sea Eagle*

LACM *Storm Shadow*

ARM ALARM

AAM • **IR** AIM-9P/L/X *Sidewinder*; **SARH** AIM-7 *Sparrow*; AIM-7M *Sparrow*; **ARH** AIM-120 AMRAAM

Royal Flt

AIRCRAFT • **TPT** 24; **Medium** 8: 5 C-130H *Hercules*; 3 L-100-30; **Light** 3: 1 Cessna 310; 2 Learjet 35; **PAX** 13: 1 A340; 1 B-737-200; 2 B-737BBJ; 2 B-747SP; 4 BAe-125-800; 2 Gulfstream III; 1 Gulfstream IV

HELICOPTERS • **TPT** 3+; **Medium** 3: 2 AS-61; 1 S-70 *Black Hawk*; **Light** Some Bell 212 (AB-212)

Air Defence Forces 16,000

FORCES BY ROLE

AIR DEFENCE

16 bty with PAC-2; 17 bty with *Shahine*/AMX-30SA; 16 bty with MIM-23B I-HAWK; 73 units (static defence) with *Crotale/Shahine*

EQUIPMENT BY TYPE

AD • SAM 1,805

SP 581: 40 *Crotale*; 400 FIM-92A *Avenger*; 73 *Shahine*; 68 *Crotale/Shahine*

TOWED 224: 128 MIM-23B I-HAWK; 96 PAC-2

MANPAD 500 FIM-43 *Redeye*

NAVAL 500 *Mistral*

GUNS 1,070

SP 942: **20mm** 92 M163 *Vulcan*; **30mm** 850 AMX-30SA

TOWED 128: **35mm** 128 GDF *Oerlikon*; **40mm** (150 L/70 in store)

RADARS • AD RADAR 80: 17 AN/FPS-117; 28 AN/TPS-43; AN/TPS-59; 35 AN/TPS-63; AN/TPS-70

Industrial Security Force 9,000+

The force is part of a new security system that will incorporate surveillance and crisis management.

National Guard 75,000 active; 25,000 (tribal levies) (total 100,000)

FORCES BY ROLE

MANOEUVRE

Mechanised

4 mech bde (4 combined arms bn, 1 SP arty bn)

Light

5 inf bde (3 combined arms bn, 1 arty bn, 1 log bn)

Other

1 (ceremonial) cav sqn

EQUIPMENT BY TYPE

RECCE 450 LAV-25 *Coyote*

AIFV 1,117 IFV-25

APC • APC (W) 1,410: 1,120 *Piranha II*; 290 V-150 *Commando* (810 in store)

ARTY 208+

SP 155mm 100 CAESAR (32 more on order)

TOWED 108: **105mm** 50 M102; **155mm** 58 M198

MOR 81mm

AT • MSL • MANPATS 116+: 116 TOW-2A (2,000 msl); M47 *Dragon*

RCL • 106mm M40A1

AD • GUNS • TOWED 160: **20mm** 30 M167 *Vulcan*; **90mm** 130 M2

ARV LAV-R ARV; V-150 ARV; *Piranha* ARV reported

Paramilitary 15,500+ active

Border Guard 10,500

FORCES BY ROLE

Subordinate to Ministry of Interior. HQ in Riyadh. 9 subordinate regional commands

MANOEUVRE

Other

Some mobile def (long range patrol/spt) units

2 border def (patrol) units

12 infrastructure def units

18 harbour def units

Some coastal def units

COMBAT SUPPORT

Some MP units

Coast Guard 4,500

EQUIPMENT BY TYPE
PATROL AND COASTAL COMBATANTS 14 (100+ small patrol boats are also in service)
  PBF 6: 4 *Al Jouf*; 2 *Sea Guard*
  PB 8: 6 *StanPatrol 2606*; 2 *Al Jubatel*
AMPHIBIOUS • LANDING CRAFT 8: 3 **UCAC**; 5 **LCAC** *Griffin 8000*
LOGISTICS AND SUPPORT 4: 1 **AXL**; 3 **AO**

General Civil Defence Administration Units

HELICOPTERS • TPT • Medium 10 Boeing Vertol 107

Special Security Force 500

APC (W): UR-416

DEPLOYMENT

BAHRAIN
GCC • *Peninsula Shield* ε1,000 (SANG)

FOREIGN FORCES

United States US Central Command: 270

---

significant losses of armour, while the air force has also lost some combat aircraft and helicopters. The navy remained largely untouched. The nominal pre-war strength of the army has likely been reduced by half: the result of a combination of defections, desertions and casualties. The most capable and most reliable of those remaining are the mainly Alawite Special Forces, the Republican Guard, and the elite 3rd and 4th divisions: perhaps 50,000 troops in total. The army was complemented by police, various security and intelligence agencies and irregular, locally raised, pro-regime militia. The strength of these organisations was impossible to estimate. (See pp. 11–15.)

ACTIVE 178,000 (Army 110,000 Navy 5,000 Air 27,000 Air Defence 36,000) **Paramilitary n.k.**

RESERVE 314,000 (Army 280,000 Navy 4,000 Air 10,000 Air Defence 20,000)
Terms of service conscription, 30 months

ORGANISATIONS BY SERVICE

Army ε110,000 (incl conscripts)

FORCES BY ROLE
Most formations are now understrength. Some brigades are reported to have been disbanded because of either political unreliablity or heavy casualties.
COMMAND
  3 corps HQ
SPECIAL FORCES
  2 SF div (total: 10 SF gp)
MANOEUVRE
  Armoured
  7 armd div (3 armd bde, 1 mech bde, 1 arty bde)
  1 (Republican Guard) armd div (3 armd bde, 1 mech bde, 2 sy regt, 1 arty bde)
  1 indep tk regt
  Mechanised
  3 mech div (1 armd bde, 2 mech bde, 1 arty bde)
  Light
  4 indep inf bde
  5 (Border Guard) lt inf bde (under command of the General Security Directorate for border sy)
COMBAT SUPPORT
  2 arty bde
  2 AT bde
  1 SSM bde (3 SSM bn with FROG-7)
  1 SSM bde (3 SSM bn with SS-21)
  1 SSM bde (3 SSM bn with *Scud*-B/C)

Reserves

FORCES BY ROLE
COMMAND
  1 armd div HQ
MANOEUVRE
  Armoured
  4 armd bde
  2 tk regt
  Light
  31 inf regt
COMBAT SUPPORT
  3 arty regt

Syria SYR

Syrian Pound S£		2011	2012	2013
GDP	S£			
	US$			
per capita	US$			
Growth	%			
Inflation	%			
Def exp	S£			
	US$			
Def bdgt	S£	ε130bn	ε243bn	
	US$	ε2.68bn	ε3.52bn	
US$1=S£		ε48.51	ε69.21	

*definitive economic data unavailable

Population 22,530,746

Age	0–14	15–19	20–24	25–29	30–64	65 plus
Male	17.7%	5.5%	5.3%	4.7%	15.8%	1.7%
Female	16.8%	5.2%	5.1%	4.5%	15.5%	2.1%

Capabilities

Syria was wracked by civil war throughout the course of 2012, with anti-regime elements controlling large areas of countryside, but with most urban areas under government control. The rebels represented disparate groups, appearing largely self-organising Syrians, though a small number of jihadis were also fighting the government. They lacked coherent military command, and were, in the main, lightly armed, though they had captured and used some armour, and successfully used both roadside bombs and suicide bombs. The army has borne the brunt of the fighting with

EQUIPMENT BY TYPE

Equipment numbers represent pre-war holdings, and have been significantly attrited during the civil war.

MBT 4,950: 1,500–1,700 T-72 T-72M; 1,000 T-62K/T-62M; 2,250 T-55/T-55MV (some in store)

RECCE 590 BRDM-2

AIFV up to 2,450 BMP-1/BMP-2/BMP-3

APC (W) 1,500: 500 BTR-152; 1,000 BTR-50/BTR-60/BTR-70

ARTY up to 3,440+

    SP 500+: **122mm** 450+: 400 2S1 *Carnation* (*Gvosdik*); 50+ D-30 (mounted on T34/85 chassis); **152mm** 50 2S3 (*Akatsiya*)

    TOWED 2,030: **122mm** 1,150: 500 D-30; 150 (M-30) M1938; 500 in store (no given designation); **130mm** 700-800 M-46; **152mm** 70 D-20/ML-20 M1937; **180mm** 10 S23

    MRL up to 500: **107mm** up to 200 Type-63; **122mm** up to 300 BM-21 (*Grad*)

    MOR 410+: **82mm**; **120mm** circa 400 M-1943; **160mm** M-160 (hundreds); **240mm** up to 10 M-240

AT • MSL 2,600

    SP 410 9P133 BRDM-2 *Sagger*

    MANPATS 2190+: 150 AT-4 9K111 *Spigot*; 40 AT-5 9K113 *Spandrel*; AT-7 9K115 *Saxhorn*; 800 AT-10 9K116 *Stabber*; 1,000 AT-14 9M133 *Kornet*; 200 Milan

    RL 105mm RPG-29

AD

    SAM 4,184+

        SP 84: 14 9K33 *Osa* (SA-8 *Gecko*); 20 9K31 *Strela*-1 (SA-9 *Gaskin*); 20 9K37 *Buk* (SA-11 *Gadfly*); 30 9K35 *Strela*-10 (SA-13 *Gopher*); 96K6 *Pantsir*-S1 (SA-22 *Greyhound*); 9K317 *Buk*-M2 (SA-17 *Grizzly*)

        MANPAD 9K32 *Strela*-2 (SA-7 *Grail*)‡; 9K38 *Igla* (SA-18 *Grouse*); 9K36 *Strela*-3 (SA-14 *Gremlin*); 9K338 *Igla*-S (SA-24 *Grinch*)

    GUNS 1,225+

        SP ZSU-23-4

        TOWED 23mm 600 ZU-23; **37mm** M-1939; **57mm** 600 S-60; **100mm** 25 KS-19

MSL • TACTICAL • SSM 84+: 18 *Scud-B/Scud-C/Scud-D*; 30 look-a-like; 18 FROG-7; 18+ SS-21 *Tochka* (*Scarab*)

ARV BREM-1 reported; T-54/55

VLB MTU; MTU-20

UAV • ISR • Medium Mohajer 3/4 **Light** Ababil

Navy ε5,000

EQUIPMENT BY TYPE

PATROL AND COASTAL COMBATANTS 32:

    CORVETTES • FS 2 *Petya* III (1†) with 1 triple 533mm ASTT with SAET-60 HWT, 4 RBU 2500 *Smerch* 1†, 2 twin 76mm gun

    PBFG 22

        16 *Osa* I/II with 4 single lnchr with P-15M *Termit*-M (SS-N-2C *Styx*) AShM

        6 *Tir* with 2 single lnchr with C-802 (CSS-N-8 *Saccade*) AShM

    PB 8 *Zhuk*

MINE WARFARE • MINE COUNTERMEASURES 7:

    MHC 1 *Sonya*

    MSO 1 *Natya*

    MSI 5 *Yevgenya*

AMPHIBIOUS • LANDING SHIPS • LSM 3 *Polnochny* B (capacity 6 MBT; 180 troops)

LOGISTICS AND SUPPORT • AX 1 *Al Assad*

Coastal Defence

FORCES BY ROLE

COMBAT SUPPORT

    1 (coastal defence) AShM bde with P-35 (SS-C-1B *Sepal*); P-15M *Termit*-R SS-C-3 *Styx*; C-802; K-300P *Bastion* (SS-C-5 *Stooge*)

EQUIPMENT BY TYPE

MSL • AShM 10+: 4 P-35 (SS-C-1B *Sepal*); 6 P-15M *Termit*-R (SS-C-3 *Styx*); C-802; K-300P *Bastion* (SS-C-5 *Stooge*)

Naval Aviation

HELICOPTER

    ASW 13: 2 Ka-28 *Helix A* (air force manned); 11 Mi-14 *Haze*

Air Force ε27,000

Flying hours 15 to 25 hrs/year on FGA/ftr; 50 hrs/year on MBB-223 *Flamingo* trg ac (pre-war levels)

FORCES BY ROLE

FIGHTER

    2 sqn with MiG-23 MF/ML/UM *Flogger*

    2 sqn with MiG-25/MiG-25R/MiG-25U *Foxbat* (non-operational)

    2 sqn with MiG-29A/U *Fulcrum*

FIGHTER/GROUND ATTACK

    6 sqn with MiG-21MF/bis *Fishbed*; MiG-21U *Mongol A*

    2 sqn with MiG-23BN/UB *Flogger*

    4 sqn with Su-22 *Fitter* D

    1 sqn with Su-24 *Fencer*

TRANSPORT

    1 sqn with An-24 *Coke*; An-26 *Curl*; Il-76 *Candid*

    1 sqn with *Falcon* 20; *Falcon* 900

    1 sqn with Tu-134B-3

    1 sqn with Yak-40 *Codling*

TRAINING

    1 sqn with L-39 *Albatros**

ATTACK HELICOPTER

    3 sqn with Mi-25 *Hind* D

    2 sqn with SA342L *Gazelle*

TRANSPORT HELICOPTER

    6 sqn with Mi-8 *Hip*/Mi-17 *Hip* H

EQUIPMENT BY TYPE

The level of readiness of a significant element of the air force's combat aircraft inventory is likely poor. Equipment numbers represent pre-war holdings, and have been significantly attrited during the civil war.

AIRCRAFT 365 combat capable

    FTR 85: 50 MiG-23MF/ML/UM *Flogger*; 35 MiG-29A/U *Fulcrum*; (30 MiG-25 *Foxbat* non-operational); (2 MiG-25U *Foxbat* non-operational)

    FGA 240: 105 MiG-21MF/bis *Fishbed*; 15 MiG-21U *Mongol* A; 50 MiG-23BN/UB *Flogger*; 50 Su-22 *Fitter* D; 20 Su-24 *Fencer*

    ISR (8 MiG-25R *Foxbat** non-operational)

TPT 23: **Heavy** 3 Il-76 *Candid*; **Light** 13: 1 An-24 *Coke*; 6 An-26 *Curl*; 2 PA-31 *Navajo*; 4 Yak-40 *Codling*; **PAX** 7: 2 *Falcon* 20; 1 *Falcon* 900; 4 Tu-134B-3
TRG 81: 40 L-39 *Albatros**; 35 MBB-223 *Flamingo* (basic); 6 MFI-17 *Mushshak*
HELICOPTERS
ATK 33 Mi-25 *Hind* D
MRH 70: 40 Mi-17 *Hip* H; 30 SA342L *Gazelle*
TPT • Medium 40 Mi-8 *Hip*
MSL
AAM • IR R-3 (AA-2 *Atoll*)‡; R-60 (AA-8 *Aphid*); R-73 (AA-11 *Archer*); **IR/SARH** R-40/46 (AA-6 *Acrid*); R-23/24 (AA-7 *Apex*); R-27 (AA-10 *Alamo*)
ASM Kh-25 (AS-7 *Kerry*); HOT
ARM Kh-31P (AS-17A *Krypton*)

Air Defence Command ε36,000

FORCES BY ROLE
AIR DEFENCE
2 AD div (total: 25 AD bde (total: 150 SAM bty with S-125 *Pechora* (SA-3 *Goa*); 2K12 *Kub* (SA-6 *Gainful*); S-75 *Dvina* (SA-2 *Guideline*); some ADA bty with 9K32 *Strela-2/M* (SA-7A *Grail*/SA-7B *Grail*)‡)
2 AD regt (2 SAM bn with (2 SAM bty with S-200 *Angara* (SA-5 *Gammon*))

EQUIPMENT BY TYPE
AD • SAM 4,707
SP 195 2K12 *Kub* (SA-6 *Gainful*)
TOWED 468: 320 S-72 *Dvina* (SA-2 *Guideline*); 148 S-125 *Pechora* (SA-3 *Goa*)
STATIC/SHELTER 44 S-200 *Angara* (SA-5 *Gammon*)
MANPAD 4,000 9K32 *Strela-2/2M* (SA-7A *Grail*/SA-7B *Grail*)‡

Paramilitary not known

Gendarmerie
Ministry of Interior

Popular Committees
Local security organisations

Shabbiha Militia
Pro-government militia

FOREIGN FORCES

UNTSO unless specified. UNTSO figures represent total numbers for mission in Israel, Syria and Lebanon.
Argentina 3 obs
Australia 11 obs
Austria 6 obs • UNDOF 374; elm 1 inf bn
Belgium 2 obs
Canada 8 obs • UNDOF 3
Chile 3 obs
China, People's Republic of 2 obs
Croatia UNDOF 95; 1 inf coy
Denmark 11 obs
Estonia 1 obs
Finland 17 obs
France 2 obs
India UNDOF 191; elm 1 log bn
Ireland 11 obs
Italy 7 obs
Japan UNDOF 31; elm 1 log bn
Malawi 1 obs
Nepal 3 obs
Netherlands 11 obs
New Zealand 8 obs
Norway 12 obs
Philippines UNDOF 343; 1 inf bn
Russia 3 obs • Army/Navy 150, naval facility reportedly under renovation at Tartus
Serbia 1 obs
Slovakia 2 obs
Slovenia 3 obs
Sweden 8 obs
Switzerland 11 obs
United States 2 obs

Tunisia TUN

Tunisian Dinar D		2011	2012	2013
GDP	D	64.75bn	70.4bn	
	US$	45.99bn	44.7bn	
per capita	US$	4,285	4,165	
Growth	%	-1.80	2.70	
Inflation	%	3.53	5.00	
Def exp	D		1.9bn	
	US$		1.21bn	
FMA (US)	US$	17.1m	17.5m	≥ 15m
US$1=D		1.41	1.57	

Population	10,732,900

Age	0–14	15–19	20–24	25–29	30–64	65 plus
Male	11.9%	4.3%	4.3%	4.4%	21.2%	3.7%
Female	11.2%	4.2%	4.3%	4.6%	22.0%	3.9%

Capabilities

Small and relatively poorly equipped by regional standards, Tunisia's armed forces are reliant on conscripts, and much of the equipment across the three services is outdated and, in some cases, approaching obsolescence. In terms of internal security, the military's role is limited as the National Guard, arguably better-trained and designed to act as a counterbalance to the armed forces, takes the lead on domestic stability. Nonetheless, the army was integral to the 'Jasmine Revolution' of January–February 2011, as it refused to fire on protesters and verbally leant its support to the demonstrations. The military was also utilised during the Libyan uprising in 2011, with the army and air force able to patrol the borders relatively successfully and the navy competently dealing with migrant flows and search-and-rescue operations in Tunisian waters. Tunisia's armed forces were well-suited to these constabulary roles, with

Middle East and North Africa

more traditional military roles, such as high-tempo war fighting, largely beyond their current capabilities. Military modernisation programmes may be undermined by the 2011 revolution. As such, the country will most probably continue to rely on surplus stocks of US, French and Italian equipment for its arsenal.

ACTIVE 35,800 (Army 27,000 Navy 4,800 Air 4,000)
Paramilitary 12,000

Terms of service 12 months selective

ORGANISATIONS BY SERVICE

Army 5,000; 22,000 conscript (total 27,000)
FORCES BY ROLE
SPECIAL FORCES
1 SF bde
1 (Sahara) SF bde
MANOEUVRE
Reconnaissance
1 recce regt
Mechanised
3 mech bde (1 armd regt, 2 mech inf regt, 1 arty regt, 1 AD regt, 1 engr regt, 1 sigs regt, 1 log gp)
COMBAT SUPPORT
1 engr regt
EQUIPMENT BY TYPE
MBT 84: 30 M60A1; 54 M60A3
LT TK 48 SK-105 *Kuerassier*
RECCE 60: 40 AML-90; 20 *Saladin*
APC 268
  APC (T) 140 M113A1/A2
  APC (W) 128: 18 EE-11 *Urutu*; 110 Fiat 6614
ARTY 276
  TOWED 115: **105mm** 48 M101A1/A2; **155mm** 67: 12 M114A1; 55 M198
  MOR 161: **81mm** 95; **107mm** 48 (some SP); **120mm** 18 Brandt
AT • MSL 590
  SP 35 M901 ITV TOW
  MANPATS 555: 500 *Milan*; 55 TOW
  RL 89mm 600: 300 LRAC; 300 M20
AD • SAM 86
  SP 26 M48 *Chaparral*
  MANPAD 60 RBS-70
  GUNS 127
  SP 40mm 12 M-42
  TOWED 115: **20mm** 100 M-55; **37mm** 15 Type-55 (M-1939)/Type-65
RADAR • LAND RASIT (veh, arty)
AEV 2 *Greif*
ARV 3 *Greif*; 6 M88A1

Navy ε4,800
EQUIPMENT BY TYPE
PATROL AND COASTAL COMBATANTS 25
  PCFG 3 *La Galite* (FRA *Combattante* III) with 2 quad Mk140 lnchr with MM-40 *Exocet* AShM, 1 76mm gun
  PCG 3 *Bizerte* (FRA P-48) with 8 SS 12M AShM

  PCF 6 *Albatros* (GER Type-143B) with 2 single 533mm TT, 2 76mm guns
  PB 13: 3 *Utique* (mod PRC *Haizhui* II); 4 *Istiklal*; 6 *V Series*
LOGISTICS AND SUPPORT 7:
  ABU 3
  AGS 1
  AWT 1
  AX 1 *Salambo* (US *Conrad*, survey)
  YTB 1

Air Force 4,000
FORCES BY ROLE
FIGHTER/GROUND ATTACK
1 sqn with F-5E/F-5F *Tiger* II
TRANSPORT
1 sqn with C-130B *Hercules*; C-130H *Hercules*; G-222; L-410 *Turbolet*
1 liaison unit with S-208A
TRAINING
2 sqn with L-59 *Albatros**; MB-326B; SF-260
1 sqn with MB-326K; MB-326L
TRANSPORT HELICOPTER
2 sqn with AS350B *Ecureuil*; AS365 *Dauphin* 2; AB-205 (Bell 205); SA313; SA316 *Alouette* III; UH-1H *Iroquois*; UH-1N *Iroquois*
1 sqn with HH-3E
EQUIPMENT BY TYPE
AIRCRAFT 24 combat capable
  FTR 12: 10 F-5E *Tiger* II; 2 F-5F *Tiger* II
  ATK 3 MB-326K
  TPT 17: **Medium** 12: 6 C-130B *Hercules*; 1 C-130H *Hercules*; 5 G-222; **Light** 5: 3 L-410 *Turbolet*; 2 S-208A
  TRG 30: 9 L-59 *Albatros**; 4 MB-326B; 3 MB-326L; 14 SF-260
HELICOPTERS
  MRH 10: 1 AS365 *Dauphin* 2; 6 SA313; 3 SA316 *Alouette* III
  SAR 11 HH-3 *Sea King*
  TPT • Light 33: 6 AS350B *Ecureuil*; 15 Bell 205 (AB-205); 10 Bell 205 (UH-1H *Iroquois*); 2 Bell 212 (UH-1N *Iroquois*)
MSL • AAM • IR AIM-9P *Sidewinder*

Paramilitary 12,000

National Guard 12,000
Ministry of Interior
PATROL AND COASTAL COMBATANTS 21
  PCC 6 *Kondor* I (GDR)
  PCI 15: 5 *Bremse* (GDR); 4 *Gabes*; 4 *Rodman 38*; 2 *Socomena*
  HELICOPTERS • MRH 8 SA318 *Alouette* II/SA319 *Alouette* III

DEPLOYMENT

CÔTE D'IVOIRE
UN • UNOCI 3; 7 obs

DEMOCRATIC REPUBLIC OF THE CONGO
UN • MONUSCO 31 obs

United Arab Emirates UAE

Emirati Dirham D		2011	2012	2013
GDP	D	1.26tr	1.33tr	
	US$	341.96bn	361.91bn	
per capita	US$	64,347	68,101	
Growth	%	5.19	4.04	
Inflation	%	0.88	0.71	
Def bdgt[a]	D	34.2bn		
	US$	9.32bn		
US$1=D		3.67	3.67	

[a] Excludes extra-budgetary equipment procurement funding

Population 5,314,317

Ethnic groups: Nationals 24%; Expatriates 76% of which Indian 30%, Pakistani 20%; other Arab 12%; other Asian 10%; UK 2%; other European 1%

Age	0–14	15–19	20–24	25–29	30–64	65 plus
Male	10.5%	2.9%	5.4%	10.7%	38.6%	0.6%
Female	10.0%	2.4%	3.3%	4.1%	11.2%	0.3%

Capabilities

The UAE maintains a capable military. Although objectively small in personnel numbers, the armed forces comprise a relatively large percentage of the population (about 1%), and maintain an extensive array of high-quality equipment. Arms purchases will continue in the near future, particularly for the navy, which is undetaking a far-reaching modernisation. In common with other regional states, and perhaps in line with regional threat perceptions, the UAE has expanded its air-defence capabilities with purchases in recent years of *Patriot* missile systems. In late 2012, the UAE requested the sale of THAAD systems from the US. It is a GCC member. However, the UAE comprises seven separate emirates joined in a federation, each retaining influence within the overall command structure through regional commands, essentially nominally independent forces maintained by three emirates (in 1976, the Abu Dhabi Defence Force became the Western Command, the Dubai Defence Force became the Central Command and the Ras al-Khaimah Mobile Force became the Northern Command). Although under the aegis of the federal Union Defence Force, this situation leads to greater autonomy and influence from these emirates on procurement and organisation. The country was one of the leading proponents of Arab participation in operations in Libya in 2011, sending six F-16s and six *Mirage* fighter aircraft in support.

ACTIVE 51,000 (Army 44,000 Navy 2,500 Air 4,500)

The Union Defence Force and the armed forces of the UAE (Abu Dhabi, Dubai, Ras al-Khaimah, Fujairah, Ajman, Umm al-Qawayn and Sharjah) were formally merged in 1976 and headquartered in Abu Dhabi. Dubai still maintains independent forces, as do other emirates to a lesser degree.

ORGANISATIONS BY SERVICE

Army 44,000 (incl Dubai 15,000)
FORCES BY ROLE
GHQ Abu Dhabi
MANOEUVRE
Armoured
1 armd bde
Mechanised
3 mech bde
Light
2 inf bde
Aviation
1 bde with AH-64D *Apache*; CH-47F Chinook; UH-60L/M *Black Hawk*
Other
1 Royal Guard bde
COMBAT SUPPORT
1 arty bde (3 arty regt)
1 engr gp

Dubai Independent Forces
FORCES BY ROLE
MANOEUVRE
Mechanised
2 mech inf bde
EQUIPMENT BY TYPE
MBT 471: 390 *Leclerc*; 36 OF-40 Mk2 (*Lion*); 45 AMX-30
LT TK 76 *Scorpion*
RECCE 105: 49 AML-90; 24 VBL; 32 TPz-1 *Fuchs* (NBC); (20 *Ferret* in store); (20 *Saladin* in store)
AIFV 605: 15 AMX-10P; 590 BMP-3
APC 892
  APC (T) 136 AAPC (incl 53 engr plus other variants)
  APC (W) 756: 90 BTR-3U *Guardian*; 120 EE-11 *Urutu*; 370 M-3 Panhard; 80 VCR (incl variants); 20 VAB
  PPV 76 RG-31 *Nyala*
ARV 46
ARTY 561+
  SP 155mm 221: 78 G-6; 125 M-109A3; 18 Mk F3
  TOWED 93: **105mm** 73 ROF lt; **130mm** 20 Type-59-I
  MRL 92+: **70mm** 18 LAU-97; **122mm** 48+: 48 Firos-25 (est 24 op); Type-90 (reported); **227mm** 20 HIMARS being delivered; **300mm** 6 9A52 *Smerch*
  MOR 155: **81mm** 134: 20 Brandt; 114 L16; **120mm** 21 Brandt
AT • MSL 305+
  SP 20 HOT
  MANPATS 285+: 30 HOT; 230 *Milan*; 25 TOW; (*Vigilant* in store)
  RCL 262: **84mm** 250 *Carl Gustav*; **106mm** 12 M-40
AD • SAM • MANPAD 40+: 20+ *Blowpipe*; 20 *Mistral*
  GUNS 62
    SP 20mm 42 M3 VDAA
    TOWED 30mm 20 GCF-BM2
MSL • TACTICAL • SSM 6 *Scud*-B (up to 20 msl)
AEV 53 ACV-AESV
ARV 143: 8 ACV-AESV Recovery; 4 AMX-30D; 85 BREM-L; 46 *Leclerc* ARV

HELICOPTERS

ATK 30 AH-64D *Apache*
TPT 45 **Heavy** 4 CH-47F *Chinook* **Medium** 41: 11 UH-60L *Black Hawk*; 30 UH-60M *Black Hawk*

Navy ε2,500

EQUIPMENT BY TYPE
SUBMARINES • SWIMMER DELIVERY VEHICLES ε10
PATROL AND COASTAL COMBATANTS 19
CORVETTES 5
    FSGHM 2:
      1 *Baynunah* with 2 quadruple lnchr with MM-40 *Exocet* Block III AShM, 1 8-cell Mk 56 VLS with RIM-162 ESSM SAM, 1 21-cell MR49 lnchr with RIM 116B SAM, 1 76mm gun (five additional vessels under construction)
      1 *Abu Dhabi* with 2 quad lnchr with MM-40 *Exocet* Block III AShM, 1 76mm gun
    FSGM 2:
      2 *Muray Jib* (GER Lurssen 62m) with 2 quad lnchr with MM-40 *Exocet* AShM, 1 octuple lnchr with *Crotale* SAM, 1 76mm gun, 1 hel landing platform
    PCFGM 2 *Mubarraz* (GER Lurssen 45m) with 2 twin lnchr with MM-40 *Exocet* AShM, 1 sextuple lnchr with *Mistral* SAM, 1 76mm gun
    PCFG 6 *Ban Yas* (GER Lurssen TNC-45) with 2 twin lnchr with MM-40 *Exocet* AShM, 1 76mm gun
    PB 6 *Ardhana* (UK Vosper 33m)
MINE WARFARE • MINE COUNTERMEASURES 2:
    MHO 2 *Al Murjan* (*Frankenthal*-class Type-332)
AMPHIBIOUS • LANDING CRAFT 28
    LCP 16: 12 *Ghannatha* (capacity 40 troops; currently undergoing modernisation to include weapons mounts); 4 (Fast Supply Vessel multi-purpose
    LCU 5: 3 *Al Feyi* (capacity 56 troops); 2 (capacity 40 troops and additional vehicles)
    LCT 7
LOGISTICS AND SUPPORT 4: 1 **YDT**; 1 **YTB**; 2 **YTM**

Naval Aviation

AIRCRAFT • TPT • Light 2 Learjet 35A
HELICOPTERS
    ASW 7 AS332F *Super Puma* (5 in ASuW role)
    MRH 11: 7 AS565 *Panther*; 4 SA316 *Alouette* III

Air Force 4,500

Flying hours 110 hrs/year

FORCES BY ROLE
FIGHTER/GROUND ATTACK
    3 sqn with F-16E/F Block 60 *Fighting Falcon*
    3 sqn with *Mirage* 2000-9DAD/EAD/RAD
GROUND ATTACK
    1 sqn with AT802 *Air Tractor*
SEARCH & RESCUE
    2 flt with AW109K2; AW139
TRANSPORT
    1 sqn with C-130H/C-130H-30 *Hercules*; L-100-30
    1 sqn with CN-235M-100

    1 (Spec Ops) sqn with AS365F *Dauphin* 2; AS550C3 *Fennec*; AW139; Cessna 208B *Grand Caravan*; CH-47C *Chinook*; DHC-6-300 *Twin Otter*
TRAINING
    1 sqn with Grob 115TA
    1 sqn with *Hawk* Mk63A/C*
    1 sqn with *Hawk* Mk102*
    1 sqn with PC-7 *Turbo Trainer*
TRANSPORT HELICOPTER
    1 sqn with Bell 412 *Twin Huey*

EQUIPMENT BY TYPE
AIRCRAFT 193 combat capable
    FGA 139: 54 F-16E Block 60 *Fighting Falcon* (*Desert Eagle*); 25 F-16F Block 60 *Fighting Falcon* (13 to remain in US for trg); 16 *Mirage* 2000-9DAD; 44 *Mirage* 2000-9EAD
    ISR 7 *Mirage* 2000 RAD*
    AEW&C 1 Saab 340 *Erieye*
    TPT 49: **Heavy** 6 C-17 *Globemaster* III; **Medium** 6: 3 C-130H *Hercules*; 1 C-130H-30 *Hercules*; 2 L-100-30; **Light** 37: 2 Beech 350 *King Air*; 8 Cessna 208B *Grand Caravan*; 7 CN-235M-100; 1 DHC-6-300 *Twin Otter*; 4 DHC-8 *Dash* 8 (MP); 15 AT802 *Air Tractor*
    TRG 74: 12 Grob 115TA; 20 *Hawk* Mk63A/C*; 12 *Hawk* Mk102*; 30 PC-7 *Turbo Trainer*
HELICOPTERS
    MRH 31: 4 AS365F *Dauphin* 2 (VIP); 18 AS550C3 *Fennec*; 9 Bell 412 *Twin Huey*
    TPT 35: **Heavy** 12 CH-47C *Chinook* (SF); **Light** 12: 3 AW109K2; 8 AW139 (incl 2 VIP); 1 Bell 407
MSL
    AAM • IR AIM-9L *Sidewinder*; R-550 *Magic*; **IIR/ARH** Mica; **ARH** AIM-120 AMRAAM
    ASM AGM-65G *Maverick*; AGM-114 *Hellfire*; Hydra-70; Hakeem 1/2/3 (A/B) HOT
    ARM AGM-88 HARM
    LACM *Black Shaheen* (*Storm Shadow*/SCALP EG variant)

Air Defence

FORCES BY ROLE
AIR DEFENCE
    2 AD bde (3 bn with MIM-23B I-HAWK,)
    3 (short range) AD bn with *Crotale*; *Mistral*; *Rapier*; RB-70; *Javelin*; 9K38 Igla (SA-18 *Grouse*)

EQUIPMENT BY TYPE
AD • SAM
    SP *Crotale*; RB-70
    TOWED MIM-23B I-HAWK; *Rapier*
    MANPAD *Javelin*; 9K38 Igla (SA-18 *Grouse*)
    NAVAL *Mistral*

Paramilitary

Coast Guard

Ministry of Interior
PATROL AND COASTAL COMBATANTS 53
    PBF 9: 6 *Baglietto* GC23; 3 *Baglietto* 59
    PB 50: 2 *Protector*; 16 (US Camcraft 65); 5 (US Camcraft 77); 6 *Watercraft* 45; 12 *Halmatic Work*; 9 *Al Saber* (a further 3 are in build; ISD by 2013)

UAE National Infrastructure Authority

PATROL AND COASTAL COMBATANTS
PBF 20 MRTP 16 (a further 14 are in build)

DEPLOYMENT

AFGHANISTAN
NATO • ISAF 35

FOREIGN FORCES

Australia 313; 1 tpt det with 3 C-130 *Hercules*; 1 MP det with 2 AP-3C *Orion*
France 800: 1 (Foreign Legion) BG (2 recce sqn, 2 inf sqn, 1 aty bty, 1 engr coy); 6 *Rafale*, 1 KC-135F
South Korea: 140 (trg activities at UAE Spec Ops School)
United States: 175; 2 bty with MIM-104 *Patriot*

Yemen, Republic of YEM

Yemeni Rial R		2011	2012	2013
GDP	R	7.22tr	7.8tr	
	US$	33.76bn	36.37bn	
per capita	US$	1,363	1,468	
Growth	%	-10.48	-1.94	
Inflation	%	19.54	14.96	
Def bdgt	R	287bn	350bn	357bn
	US$	1.34bn	1.63bn	
FMA (US)	US$	19.96m	20m	20m
US$1=R		213.80	214.33	

Population   24,771,809

Ethnic groups: Majority Arab, some African and South Asian

Age	0–14	15–19	20–24	25–29	30–64	65 plus
Male	21.7%	5.7%	5.0%	4.4%	12.7%	1.2%
Female	20.9%	5.5%	4.9%	4.2%	12.4%	1.4%

Capabilities

Yemen's armed forces are under-equipped, poorly-trained, and, in light of events since 2011, have problems with morale across the force. Despite a relatively high level of defence spending compared to GDP, the country's underdeveloped economic status means that the state is unable to exercise full control over internal security. An autonomous enclave, established by al-Qaeda in the Arabian Peninsula insurgents in the southern province of Abyan in 2011, was overrun by the military in June 2012, although some militants were reportedly displaced to other areas. The army is the best-equipped of the services, but still relies on Soviet-era equipment. The importance of tribal ties within Yemen, combined with a conscription service that was reintroduced in 2007, highlights the difficulties facing the military in encouraging loyalty to the armed forces and morale. This was compounded, in early 2011, by the instability that beset the country as part of the Arab Spring, as a number of high-ranking military officers deserted the president, defections were reported across military units and, in certain cases, loyal military units exchanged fire with defectors. A military reshuffle in April 2012 and restructure in August 2012, whereby a new Presidential Protection Force was formed that is financially and administratively independent of the military, was an attempt to resolve the issues with loyalty. The Yemeni air force and navy are unable to fulfil their core roles of defending territorial sovereignty, with insufficient equipment and training. Given the size of the country, air-lift is almost non-existent, leading to severe problems in rapid internal military deployments. Some of the combat aircraft, meanwhile – particularly the aged MiG-21s – are unreliable. The navy's Chinese-supplied *Hounan*-class patrol boats may well be unserviceable and, while international maritime forces on counter-piracy duties do liaise with representatives from the Yemeni coast guard, the rest of the small naval force faces challenges in monitoring and securing the country's extensive coastline.

ACTIVE 66,700 (Army 60,000 Navy 1,700 Air Force 3,000, Air Defence 2,000) **Paramilitary 71,200**
Terms of service conscription, 2 years

ORGANISATIONS BY SERVICE

Army 60,000 (incl conscripts)
FORCES BY ROLE
COMMAND
  1 (1st) armd div HQ
  1 mtn div HQ
SPECIAL FORCES
  1 SF bde
MANOEUVRE
  Armoured
  6 armd bde
  4 (Republican Guard) armd bde
  Mechanised
  6 mech bde
  3 (Republican Guard) armd bde
  Light
  19+ inf bde
  Air Manoeuvre
  2 cdo/AB bde
  Mountain
  5 mtn inf bde
  Other
  1 (Presidential Protection) gd force (1 armd bde, (1 Republican Guard) armd bde, 2 (Republican Guard) sy bde)
COMBAT SUPPORT
  3 arty bde
  1 SSM bde
  2 AD bn
EQUIPMENT BY TYPE
MBT 866: 50 M60A1; 70 T-72; 66 T-80; 200 T-62; 450 T-54/T-55; 30 T-34
RECCE 130+: 80 AML-90; 50 BRDM-2; *Ratel*
AIFV 200: 100 BMP-1; 100 BMP-2
APC 258
  APC (T) 60 M113A2
  APC (W) 180: 60 BTR-40; 100 BTR-60; 20 BTR-152; (470 BTR-40/BTR-60/BTR-152 in store)
  PPV 18 YLAV *Cougar*

ARTY 1,307

SP 122mm 25 2S1 *Carnation*

TOWED 310: **105mm** 25 M101A1; **122mm** 200: 130 D-30; 30 M-1931/37; 40 M-30 M-1938; **130mm** 60 M-46; **152mm** 10 D-20; **155mm** 15 M114

COASTAL 130mm 36 SM-4-1

MRL 294: **122mm** 280 BM-21 (150 op); **140mm** 14 BM-14

MOR 642: **81mm** 250; **82mm** 144 M-43; **107mm** 12; **120mm** 136; **160mm** ε100

AT

MSL • MANPATS 71: 35 9K11 *Malyutka* (AT-3 *Sagger*); 24 M47 *Dragon*; 12 TOW

RCL 75mm M-20; **82mm** B-10; **107mm** B-11

GUNS 50+

SP 100mm 30 SU-100

TOWED 20+: **85mm** D-44; **100mm** 20 M-1944

AD

SAM ε800

SP 9K31 *Strela-1* (SA-9 *Gaskin*); 9K35 *Strela-10* (SA-13 *Gopher*)

MANPAD 9K32 *Strela-2* (SA-7 *Grail*)‡; 9K36 *Strela-3* (SA-14 *Gremlin*)

GUNS 530

SP 70: **20mm** 20 M163 *Vulcan*; **23mm** 50 ZSU-23-4

TOWED 460: **20mm** 50 M167 *Vulcan*; **23mm** 100 ZU-23-2; **37mm** 150 M-1939; **57mm** 120 S-60; **85mm** 40 M-1939 *KS-12*

MSL • TACTICAL • SSM 28: 12 FROG-7; 10 SS-21 *Scarab* (*Tochka*); 6 *Scud*-B (ε33 msl)

ARV T-54/55 reported

VLB MTU reported

Navy 1,700

EQUIPMENT BY TYPE

PATROL AND COASTAL COMBATANTS 22

PCO 1 *Tarantul*† with 2 twin lnchr (fitted for P-15 *Termit*-M (SS-N-2C *Styx*) AShM)

PBF 6 *Baklan*

PB 15: 3 *Hounan*† with 4 single lnchr (fitted for C-801 (CSS-N-4 *Sardine*) AShM); 10 P-1000 (Austal 37.5m); 2 *Zhak* (FSU *Osa* II) (1†)

MINE WARFARE • MINE COUNTERMEASURES 1: **MSO** 1 *Natya* (FSU)

AMPHIBIOUS

LANDING SHIPS • LSM 1 NS-722 (capacity 5 MBT; 110 troops)

LANDING CRAFT • LCU 3 *Deba*

LOGISTICS AND SUPPORT 2: 1 **AFD**; 1 **AGS**

Air Force 3,000

FORCES BY ROLE

FIGHTER

3 sqn with F-5E *Tiger* II; MiG-21 *Fishbed*; MiG-29SMT/MiG-29UBT *Fulcrum*

FIGHTER/GROUND ATTACK

1 sqn with Su-22 *Fitter* D/Su-22UMS *Fitter* G

MARTIME PATROL

1 unit with DHC-8 MPA

TRANSPORT

1 sqn with An-12 *Cub*; An-26 *Curl*; C-130H *Hercules*; Il-76 *Candid*

ATTACK/TRANSPORT HELICOPTER

3 sqn with Bell 205 (UH-1H); Bell 212; Ka-27; Mi-8 *Hip*; Mi-17 *Hip* H; Mi14PS; Mi-35 *Hind*

EQUIPMENT BY TYPE

AIRCRAFT 79 combat capable

FTR 10 F-5E *Tiger* II

FGA 69: 15 MiG-21 *Fishbed*; 4 MiG-21U *Mongol* A*; 15 MiG-29SMT *Fulcrum*; 1 MiG-29UBT; 30 Su-22 *Fitter* D; 4 Su-22UM3 *Fitter* G

MP 2 DHC-8 MPA

TPT 11: **Heavy** 3 Il-76 *Candid*; **Medium** 4: 2 An-12 *Cub*; 2 C-130H *Hercules*; **Light** 4 An-26 *Curl*

TRG 36: 24 L-39C; 12 Z-242

HELICOPTERS

ATK 8 Mi-35 *Hind*

ASW 1 Ka-27 (tpt role)

MRH 10 Mi-17 *Hip* H

TPT 26: **Medium** 9 Mi-8 *Hip*; **Light** 6: 2 Bell 212; 4 Bell 205 (UH-1H)

Air Defence 2,000

AD • SAM:

SP 2K12 *Kub* (SA-6 *Gainful*); 9K31 *Strela-1* (SA-9 *Gaskin*); 9K35 *Strela-10* (SA-13 *Gopher*)

TOWED S-75 *Dvina* (SA-2 *Guideline*); S-125 *Pechora* (SA-3 *Goa*)

MANPAD 9K32 *Strela-2* (SA-7 *Grail*); 9K36 *Strela-3* (SA-14 *Gremlin*)

MSL • IR R-3 (AA-2 *Atoll*)‡; R-60 (AA-8 *Aphid*); AIM-9 *Sidewinder*; **IR/SARH** R-27 (AA-10 *Alamo*)

Paramilitary 71,200+

Ministry of the Interior Forces 50,000

Tribal Levies 20,000+

Yemeni Coast Guard Authority ε1,200

PATROL AND COASTAL COMBATANTS 12

PBF 4 *Archangel* (US)

PB 10: 2 *Marine Patrol*; 8 various

DEPLOYMENT

COTE D'IVOIRE

UN • UNOCI 8 obs

DEMOCRATIC REPUBLIC OF 8THE CONGO

UN • MONUSCO 6 obs

LIBERIA

UN • UNMIL 1

SOUTH SUDAN

UN • UNMISS 2; 6 obs

SUDAN

UN • UNAMID 5; 33 obs

WESTERN SAHARA

UN • MINURSO 10 obs

Table 19 **Selected Arms Procurements and Deliveries, Middle East and North Africa**

Designation	Type	Quantity (Current)	Contract Value	Prime Nationality	Prime Contractor	Order Date	First Delivery Due (Current)	Notes
Algeria (ALG)								
T-90S	MBT	120	εUS$470m	RUS	Rosoboron-export	2011	n/k	Follow-on order following delivery of original 180
Fuchs 2	APC(W)	54	n/k	GER	Rheinmetall	2011	2013	
S-300PMU-2	SAM	32	US$1bn	RUS	Rosoboron-export	2006	2008	Eight bty
Pantsir-S1	AD	38	US$500m	RUS	Rosoboron-export	2006	2010	Delivery under way
Tigr (*Steregushchiy*)	FFGHM	2	n/k	RUS	USC	2011	n/k	Project 20380
MEKO A200	FFGHM	2	see notes	GER	TKMS	2012	2016	Part of US$3.3bn (€2.5bn) deal including 6 Super Lynx 300 hel
n/k	LPD	1	ε€400m	ITA	Fincantieri	2011	2015	8,800 tonne FLD reported
Su-30MKA	FGA ac	16	US$1bn	RUS	Rosoboron-export	2010	2011	Delivery status unclear
Super Lynx 300	MRH Hel	6	see notes	ITA	Finmeccanica (Agusta Westland)	2012	n/k	Part of US$3.3bn (€2.5bn) deal including 2 MEKO A200 FFGHM
Bahrain (BHR)								
Arma 6×6	APC(W)	ε60-80	US$63.2m	TUR	Otokar	2011	2012	For national guard. Follow-on order to initial 2010 contract
Egypt (EGY)								
Ambassador Mk III	PCFG	4	US$1.3bn	US	VT Halter Marine	2008	2011	Phase II of the Fast Missile Craft (FMC) project
n/k	PCC	4	US$20.2m	US	Swiftships	2011	n/k	Delivery to be complete by 2014
n/k	PBF	6	n/k	TUR	Yonca-Onuk Shipyard	2010	2011	Three delivered by Aug 2012
F-16C/D *Fighting Falcon*	FGA ac	20	n/k	US	Lockheed Martin	2010	n/k	16 F-16C and four F-16D. To be complete by 2013
C-295	Tpt ac	3	n/k	Int'l	EADS (CASA)	2012	n/k	Second contract, following delivery of initial order in 2011
Anka	ISR UAV	10	n/k	TUR	TAI	2012	n/k	
Iran (IRN)								
Mowj-class	FSG	3	n/k	IRN	Marine Industries Group	2006	2010	Second vessel launched at Bandar Anzali, on Caspian Sea, in 2012
Iraq (IRQ)								
M113A2	APC (T)	440	US$31m	UK/US	BAE Systems/ Anniston Army Depot	2012	n/k	Refurbished ex-US Army models
MT-LB	APC(T)	500	€150m	BLG	Terem	2012	n/k	
BTR-4	APC (W)	420	US$2.5bn	UKR	KMDB	2010	n/k	Contract value includes 6 An-32 tpt ac
Al Basra-class	PCC	2	US$86m	US	River Hawk Fast Sea Frames	2010	2012	Delivery scheduled for late 2012
F-16C/D *Fighting Falcon* Block 52	FGA ac	18	n/k	US	Lockheed Martin	2011	2014	Initial order for 18 in 2011, with additional 18 ordered 2012. 24 C and 12 D models. Delivery to be completed in 2018
C-130J-30 *Super Hercules*	Tpt ac	6	US$433.1m	US	Lockheed Martin	2009	2012	First delivered late 2012

Table 19 **Selected Arms Procurements and Deliveries, Middle East and North Africa**

Designation	Type	Quantity (Current)	Contract Value	Prime Nationality	Prime Contractor	Order Date	First Delivery Due (Current)	Notes
EC635	Tpt Hel	24	€360m (US$490m)	Int'l	Eurocopter	2009	2011	Cost incl. training and maintenance. First delivery reported mid-2011
Bell 407	Tpt Hel	27	US$60.3m	US	Textron (Bell Helicopters)	2009	n/k	For army, AR-407 configuration. FMS contract
Israel (ISR)								
Arrow 2	ATBM/ BMD	n/k	undisclosed	ISR/US	IAI	2008	n/k	Number and cost undisclosed
Merkava MkIV	MBT	up to 400	n/k	ISR	MANTAK	2001	2003	Further production delayed by engine problems until 2013
Dolphin-class (Type-800)	SSK	3	€1.4bn (US$1.7bn)	GER	TKMS (HDW)	2006	2012	With Air-Independent Propulsion (AIP) system. First handed over May 2012
F-35A Lightning II	FGA ac	20	US$2.75bn	US	Lockheed Martin	2010	2016	Option for a further 75
C-130J-30 Hercules	Tpt ac	3	US$233.1m	US	Lockheed Martin	2010	2013	First 3 of up to 9 to be ordered under the FMS programme
M-346 Master	Trg ac	30	US$1bn	ITA	Finmeccanica (Alenia Aeronautica)	2012	2014	Part of a deal under which Italy agrees to purchase US$1bn of military equipment from Israeli suppliers
Hermes 900	ISR UAV	3	US$50m	ISR	Elbit Systems	2010	2011	Price includes additional Hermes-450 UAVs. First delivered 2011
Jordan (JOR)								
YPR-765	AIFV	510	n/k	NLD	Government transfer	2010	2010	Order includes 69 M577s and unknown number of YPR-806s. Deliveries to be complete by 2014
M109A2	Arty (155mm SP)	121	n/k	NLD	Government transfer	2010	2010	Deliveries to be complete by 2014
Kuwait (KWT)								
MK V	PBF	10	US$461m	US	USMI	2009	n/k	For navy. Final del due 2013
KC-130J	Tkr ac	3	US$245m	US	Lockheed Martin	2010	2013	Deliveries to be complete in early 2014
Mauritania (MRT)								
EMB-314 Super Tucano	Trg ac	4	n/k	BRZ	Embraer	2012	2012	First two delivered Oct 2012
Morocco (MOR)								
M1A1SA Abrams	MBT	200	US$1bn	US	General Dynamics	2012	2012	Refitted ex-US Army vehicles. Order includes 10 M88A2 ARVs
Mohammed VI-class	DDGHM	1	€470m (US$676m)	FRA/ITA	DCNS	2008	2013	FREMM. Launched Sep 2011; delivery delayed until 2013
Bin an Zaran-class	PSO	4	US$140m	FRA	STX Shipbuilding	2008	2011	OPV-70. First vessel delivered 2011
Oman (OMN)								
Al-Shamikh-class	FFG	3	£400m (US$785m)	UK	BAE Systems (Maritime)	2007	2012	Project Khareef. Delivery delayed
Fearless-class	PCO	4	US$880m (€535m)	SGP	ST Engineering (ST Marine)	2012	2015	

Table 19 **Selected Arms Procurements and Deliveries, Middle East and North Africa**

Designation	Type	Quantity (Current)	Contract Value	Prime Nationality	Prime Contractor	Order Date	First Delivery Due (Current)	Notes
Rodman 101	PB	3	€12m	ESP	Rodman Polyships	2012	2013	For coastal police
C-130J-30 *Hercules*	Tpt ac	2	n/k	US	Lockheed Martin	2010	2013	Delivery due in 2013 and 2014
C-295	Tpt ac	8	n/k	Int'l	EADS (CASA)	2012	2013	For air force. 5 in tpt and 3 in MP configuration
NH90 TTH	Tpt Hel	20	n/k	Int'l	NH Industries	2004	2010	10 delivered by mid-2012
Qatar (QTR)								
MRTP 34	PBF	3	n/k	TUR	Yonca-Onuk Shipyard	2012	n/k	
MRTP 16	PBF	3	n/k	TUR	Yonca-Onuk Shipyard	2012	n/k	
AW139	MRH Hel	3	n/k	ITA	Finmeccanica (Agusta Westland)	2011	n/k	
Saudi Arabia (SAU)								
LAV II	APC (W)	724	US$2.2bn	US	General Dynamics (GDLS)	2009	2011	For national guard
CAESAR	Arty (155mm SP)	132	n/k	FRA	Nexter	2006	2010	For national guard. 100 delivered 2010–11. Additional order for 32 signed in 2012 for delivery by end-2014
Patriot Advanced Capability (PAC) 3	AD System upgrade	n/k	US$1.7bn	US	Raytheon	2011	n/k	Incl. ground-systems, training package and support equipment
Typhoon	FGA ac	72	GB£4.43bn (US$8.9bn)	Int'l	Eurofighter GmbH	2005	2008	Project Salam. First 24 delivered by Sept 2011. Original plan to final assemble remaining 48 in SAU dropped
A330 MRTT	Tkr / Tpt ac	6	US$600m	FRA	EADS	2008	2011	Delivery in progress
Saab 2000 *Erieye*	AEW&C ac	1	US$670m	SWE	Saab	2010	n/k	
F-15E *Strike Eagle*	FGA ac	84	US$11.4bn	US	Boeing	2012	n/k	F-15SA variant. Part of a package incl F-15S upgrades, AH-64 and AH-6i helicopters that could total US$24bn
F-15S *Eagle*	FGA ac upg	68	n/k	US	Boeing	2012	n/k	Upgrade to F-15SA standard. Part of a package incl F-15S upgrades, AH-64 and AH-6i helicopters that could total US$24bn
PC-21	Trg ac	55	n/k	CHE	Pilatus	2012	2014	To replace PC-9s
Hawk Mk132 Advanced Jet Trainer	Trg ac	22	n/k	UK	BAE Systems	2012	n/k	
MD530F	MRH Hel	12	US$40.7m	US	MD Helicopters	2012	2013	All to be delivered in 2013
UH-60M *Black Hawk*	Tpt Hel	24	n/k	US	UTC (Sikorsky)	2012	n/k	For national guard
Syria (SYR)								
Buk-M2 (SA-17 *Grizzly*)	SAM	n/k	US$200m	RUS	Rosoboron-export	2007	n/k	Some delivered
Yak-130	Trg ac	36	US$550m	RUS	Rosoboron-export	2012	n/k	Contract status uncertain

Table 19 **Selected Arms Procurements and Deliveries, Middle East and North Africa**

Designation	Type	Quantity (Current)	Contract Value	Prime Nationality	Prime Contractor	Order Date	First Delivery Due (Current)	Notes
Tunisia (TUN)								
C-130J *Hercules*	Tpt ac	2	n/k	US	Lockheed Martin	2010	2013	To be delivered 2013–4
United Arab Emirates (UAE)								
Agrab (*Scorpion*) 120mm MMS	Arty (120mm SP Mor)	48	AED390m (US$106m)	RSA/ SGP/UAE/ UK	IGG	2007	n/k	Delivery status unclear
Agrab Mk2 (*Scorpion*) MMS	Arty (120mm SP Mor)	72	US$214m	RSA/ SGP/UAE/ UK	IGG	2011	n/k	
Patriot Advanced Capability (PAC) 3	AD System	10 fire units, 172 msl	US$3.3bn	US	Raytheon	2008	2012	To replace HAWK. First bty delivered 2012
Abu Dhabi-class	FFGHM	1	n/k	ITA	Fincantieri	2009	2012	Delivery scheduled for late 2012
Baynunah-class	FSGHM	6	AED3bn (US$820m)	FRA/UAE	ADSB	2003	2011	Fourth vessel launched Feb 2012. Delivery expected to be complete by 2014
Ganthoot-class	FS	2	AED430m (US$117m)	ITA	Fincantieri	2009	2012	Both vessels launched 2012. Delivery scheduled for late 2012/ early 2013
Ghannatha II-class	PBFG	12	AED935m	SWE/UAE	Swedeship Marine/ADSB	2009	n/k	3 to be built in Sweden; remaining 9 in UAE. First UAE-built vessel launched Jul 2012
Al Saber-class	PB	12	AED127m (US$34.6m)	UAE	ADSB	2008	2011	For coast guard
MRTP16	PB	34	AED460m	TUR/UAE	Yonca-Onuk Shipyard/ADSB	2009	2010	First 12 to be built in Turkey; remaining 22 in UAE. 20 delivered by Aug 2012
Saab 340 *Erieye*	AEW ac	2	Skr1.5bn (US$234m)	SWE	Saab	2009	2011	First delivered Apr 2011
A330 MRTT	Tkr / Tpt ac	3	n/k	Int'l	EADS	2008	2012	First delivered 2012; other 2 due by end-2012. Order for 3 more possible
PC-21	Trg ac	25	Fr500m ($492.4m)	CHE	Pilatus Aircraft	2009	2011	First aircraft flew in 2011. Deliveries under way
UH-60M *Black Hawk*	Tpt Hel	14	US$171m	US	UTC (Sikorsky)	2009	n/k	To be delivered by end-2012
UH-60M *Black Hawk*	Tpt Hel	26	n/k	US	UTC (Sikorsky)	2008	2010	16 delivered by end 2011; up to 23 to be upgraded with *Battle Hawk* kits

Chapter Eight
Latin America and the Caribbean

Drugs and insecurity

The most significant security problem for states in the Caribbean and Latin America is the threat to law and order posed by transnational non-state groups engaged in narcotics trafficking and other criminal activity. In 2012, for example, Mexico remained gripped by the activities of narco-criminal organisations; according to President Felipe Calderón, criminals there have 'started to control territories and cities'. In some states, the armed forces remained deployed on law-enforcement tasks, and the effect that such deployments can have on the missions, organisation and inventories of military forces as well as on their readiness to undertake traditional tasks – such as territorial defence or manoeuvre warfare – continued to provoke debate.

Washington remained concerned about the drug route linking cocaine producers in South America to the US via Central America, where countries still lacked the capacity to effectively counter transnational trafficking organisations. Central American nations have, however, looked to improve domestic security capacities in recent years by developing military and security capabilities – such as moves to boost surveillance – and policy coordination through, for example, the Central American Integration System (SICA). The Central American Security Commission – a subsidiary body of SICA with country representatives at the vice-ministerial level – said in May that regional police training and improvements to the justice system, prisons and intelligence capacities would be the first areas addressed as part of SICA's anti-drug strategy. US$80 million in funding support was to come from Spain and the EU.

The regional US security assistance initiative, *Operation Martillo,* began in January 2012. It aimed to target narcotics-trafficking networks and intercept ships and aircraft moving illicit narcotics in coastal waters and airspace. All seven Central American nations are taking part, with assistance from Colombia, Mexico and Canada, among others. Maritime operations constitute the bulk of the effort (the US military estimates that 80% of the cocaine trafficked from the region to the US transits regional

waters at some point). Some 32 tonnes of cocaine were seized in the first four months of *Operation Martillo* while drug trafficking by air fell by 60–70%, according to Washington. The operation has been accompanied by an increase in US operations in Central America, notably along the Atlantic coast of Honduras, with the remote Mosquito Coast vulnerable to the activities of drug traffickers. Mexican drug cartels and their allies reportedly receive some drug shipments from South America in this area.

The US has deployed personnel to Soto Cano airbase in Honduras for some years (as Joint Task Force Bravo) for capacity-building, counter-narcotics and HADR tasks, and in 2012 established three Forward Operating Bases (Mocoron, El Aguacate and Puerto Castilla) to support local counter-narcotic operations; the US presence at these locations included Drug Enforcement Administration (DEA) and State Department personnel and resources. In August, a similar structure was established on Guatemala's Pacific coast. Here, around 200 marines and four UH-1N *Huey* helicopters arrived as *Detachment Martillo* in Guatemala City. After arriving in August, the unit patrolled Guatemala's littoral waters, reporting suspicious activity though not, according to a US Marine Corps spokesman, directly apprehending suspects; it departed in October. In Honduras, US personnel took part in a number of joint US–Honduran counter-narcotics operations. One of these, in May 2012, reportedly led to four people being shot. According to the State Department in August, 'a preliminary Honduran military report suggests that it may have been a case of mistaken identity'. Incidents like this have provoked tension with the local population and, after the May shootings, residents of the Mosquito Coast region protested against the US presence. The DEA denied claims that its officers were responsible, saying they did not use their weapons during the operation.

SOUTHCOM's chief, Air Force General Douglas Fraser, said that insufficient assets meant that only about 30% of detected traffickers were likely to be intercepted. In an attempt to fill this gap, particularly to increase persistent surveillance, Washington might deploy more unmanned aerial vehicles (UAVs). A report by the *Los Angeles Times* in June said that the US Department of Homeland Security had plans to expand the use of UAVs over the waters of the Caribbean and the Gulf of Mexico. The air force announced in the same month that some of the systems withdrawn from combat operations overseas would be assigned tasks in the region, responding to requests by SOUTHCOM for more intelligence and surveillance assets.

Operation Martillo fills a gap in the military capabilities of Central American countries, notably in surveillance capacities and equipment suitable for use in littoral waters. Countries in the violent northern triangle area – Honduras, Guatemala and El Salvador – lack resources for significant procurements related to counter-narcotic activities. Indeed, US donations of small boats and other hardware represent the bulk of new acquisitions. But the head of El Salvador's Joint Chiefs of Staff, General César Acosta, announced that his force would 'operate with what we have', highlighting the refurbishment of three Cessna A-37B aircraft for counter-narcotic missions. The Honduran air force announced a similar arrangement for six of its EMB312/T-27 *Tucanos*, with the support of Embraer technicians.

States in South America are procuring surveillance systems likely to be of use in combating criminal and narcotics-smuggling networks. Colombia and Peru, two of the largest coca producers in the world, plan to deploy new radar systems to monitor coastal waters. Colombian Defence Minister Juan Carlos Pinzón announced in August the purchase of 11 'radar systems' to reinforce the Pacific coast against drug traffickers, though he did not specify the origin, type or cost of the equipment. Meanwhile, the authorities in Lima continue to face low-level violence from Shining Path insurgents based predominantly in the remote coca-growing areas of the Apurimac, Ene and Mantaro river valley area. When a Shining Path faction kidnapped workers from a gas company in April, several members of the security forces were killed in rescue attempts and the hunt for the perpetrators. Amid criticism of the security forces for failing to locate two missing members of the National Police, Peru's defence and interior ministers resigned. A further reshuffle in July, this time prompted by protests against a mining project in the Cajamarca region, again saw the defence portfolio change hands.

Brazil has inked several counter-narcotic partnership agreements with its neighbours, indicative of its increased role in the region's fight against drug

Colombia: peace negotiations begin

In October 2012, Colombian government negotiators met representatives of the Revolutionary Armed Forces of Colombia (FARC) in Norway. Though an earlier attempt at a peaceful settlement of the long-running insurgency failed in 2002, Colombia's President Juan Manuel Santos was reported as saying that this time there is 'a real opportunity to end the conflict'.

FARC remains active in Colombia, and killings continue to be ascribed to them. There are also continued security and military operations designed to counter the threat FARC's actions pose to state authority. But a number of senior FARC leaders have been killed in recent years, and disputes and disagreements at the top of the group, as well as FARC's nebulous international and regional ties, were made clear by analysis of computers captured during the Colombian Army raid across the border in Ecuador in 2008 in which FARC leader 'Raúl Reyes' was killed (this analysis was published in an IISS Strategic Dossier, *The FARC Files: Venezuela, Ecuador and the Secret Archive of 'Raúl Reyes'*). Political and military pressure on the group led some analysts to conclude that there was a risk

FARC would fragment, which would make any future negotiations more problematic.

Impetus was given to the peace process from unexpected quarters, notably a change in attitude in Caracas, where Venezuela's President Hugo Chávez was reported in the *Guardian* as saying that the conflict 'needs a political solution'. In April 2012, FARC leader 'Timoshenko' had announced in Havana that the group had abandoned disarmament and demobilisation as preconditions for talks. In September, after preliminary negotiations with Colombian representatives in Havana, 'Timoshenko' said that the agreed talks in Oslo aimed to achieve 'lasting, democratic and just peace'. The Colombian government has experience conducting nationwide DDR programmes, notably the demobilisation process for former members of the Autodefensas Unidas de Colombia (AUC) between 2003 and 2006 (see the 2009 ICTJ report *Transitional Justice and DDR: The Case of Colombia*). Before considering any form of DDR for FARC fighters and the national debate this would stimulate, however, substantial challenges will have to be overcome in negotiations for a political solution to the insurgency.

producers and other criminal gangs. In 2011, Brasília and Lima signed an agreement allowing Brazilian agents to enter Peruvian territory to destroy coca plantations and cocaine laboratories. In April 2012, the Joint Chiefs of Staff of Brazil, Colombia and Peru agreed to share intelligence on counter-narcotics and to begin joint training in surveillance and night combat operations. These partnerships are separate from the *Ágata* military operations periodically mounted by Brazil (see Brazil, p. 425), but bolster regional efforts to combat drug gangs. Another major coca producer, Bolivia, joined the list of Latin American countries which have sent their army into the streets to help counter a crime wave. President Evo Morales dispatched 2,300 soldiers to the country's four main cities in response to protests against increasing drug-related homicides and kidnappings.

Concern over increasing drug-related violence helped influence Chile's new National Security and Defence Strategy, presented to Congress in June. The document stated that Chile faced new global and interconnected challenges, including drug trafficking, organised crime and terrorism, as well as established threats such as that to territorial integrity. It introduced a new concept called *seguridad ampliada*, or 'amplified security', which includes five criteria: 'protection of people, the correlation between security and development, complementarity between security and defence, international cooperation as an impera-

tive, and security as public policy'. This led some Chilean legislators, led by the president of the Senate, Camilo Escalona, to criticise the document, saying it attributed some law-enforcement roles to the armed forces. This criticism led the government to withdraw the document, although it had already been publicly presented by President Sebastián Piñera, and had even been distributed to neighbouring governments. In August, the Defence Ministry announced it was preparing a new version and that the one presented in June was just a 'draft'.

The episode highlighted the political sensitivity within the region of mooting a law-enforcement role for the armed forces in the fight against narcotics-smuggling and organised crime. Such deployments have taken place in Colombia, Bolivia, El Salvador, Guatemala, Honduras, Mexico and Peru, and sporadically in Brazil and Venezuela, while Ecuador announced plans for 'urban brigades' in an attempt to reduce drug-related violence in the cities.

Mexico's drug war: military effects

As of late 2012, close to 60,000 Mexican army, navy and air force personnel were committed to the fight against transnational narco-trafficking groups in the country. Mexico's armed forces have been at the forefront of the effort, although Calderón's attempt to modify Mexico's National Security Law to provide the armed forces with a legal framework for their

Regional naval OPV programmes

Maritime procurement in Latin America has been categorised in recent years by a focus on offshore patrol vessels (PSO/Hs). Argentina, Chile and Colombia have all invested in a Fassmer design, the OPV 80 programme, with varying success. In Argentina, where it is known as the *Patrulleros de Alta Mar* project, five vessels have been on order since 2009, but the project was briefly suspended a year later. In Chile, two have been delivered as the *Piloto Pardo*-class (in service with the navy's Coast Guard) and in Colombia the first of the *20 de Julio*-class has been commissioned with a second ordered in 2012. Brazil has followed this trend for Latin American OPVs with its 2012 decision to pick up Trinidad's three unwanted *Port of Spain*-class vessels from BAE Systems, while Venezuela's long-running POVZEE and BVL programmes each saw the delivery of their fourth boat in 2012, completing the navy's *Guaiqueri*-class and the Coast Guard's *Guaicamacuto*-class. Mexico, meanwhile, has taken delivery of four *Oaxaca*-class OPVs over the past 10 years, and even one

of the UK's *River*-class PSOs, the HMS *Clyde*, is stationed in the region as the Falkland Islands' patrol ship.

The spate of PSO procurements in Latin America reflects the security priorities of the various armed services. The threat of inter-state warfare is low (despite occasional militaristic rhetoric between Venezuela and Colombia), and hence war-fighting vessels are largely unnecessary. Rather, navies are increasingly occupied with constabulary roles, from counter-narcotics to anti-trafficking operations. Offshore patrol vessels, which are ocean-going and able to operate for two to three weeks at a time, offer the ability to project law enforcement further beyond the shores. They are only lightly armed, with one 76mm gun as the primary armament at most, as they are highly unlikely to require anti-ship missiles to confront an opponent that is more than probably civilian. They also offer flexibility: their size means they can often carry a helicopter for surveillance and support, and many will have RIBs for boarding operations.

internal security role was unsuccessful. President-elect Enrique Peña Nieto, due to take office in December 2012, has signalled his determination to continue a security-led fight against narcotics trafficking and other criminal organisations but that a change of strategy is needed. He said in July that he wanted to establish a 'national gendarmerie', expand the Federal Police and tackle corruption within police forces.

Established groups, such as the Gulf, Sinaloa, Milenio, Juarez and Tijuana cartels, are still focused on trafficking illegal drugs into the US, which provides the majority of their income. Others, however, have evolved to dominate criminal activities inside Mexico. A new generation of enforcer groups with paramilitary-like capabilities have emerged, such as the Zetas, Cartel de Jalisco Nueva Generación (CJNG), and the Caballeros Templarios. Their activities include drug trafficking, kidnapping, extortion, human trafficking, fuel smuggling, counterfeiting and vehicle theft. Internal rivalry, and the arrest or death of leaders, fractured some groups, increasing the breadth and geographical scale of security problems for the government, which has come close to losing control over parts of the country.

Access to light weapons, grenades and ammunition in both the United States and Guatemala, and the relative ease with which these are smuggled into Mexico, has increased these groups' capacity for violence. Some, such as the Zetas, Caballeros Templarios and the CJNG, are, analysts believe, now able to stand up platoon- and even company-sized formations equipped with light weapons, improvised light artillery, light armour and command and control networks. In some areas of the country, such as Chihuahua, Michoacán, Guerrero, Veracruz, Tamaulipas, Coahuila and Nuevo Leon, civilian authorities have been taken over or deeply penetrated by criminal groups.

Large-scale military operations to support the civilian authorities and restore law and order have been launched in all these states, with varying success. Tasks include establishing roadside checkpoints and augmenting local or state police forces. Most army units used have been drawn from infantry, military police, Special Forces battalions and motorised cavalry regiments though, at times, artillery regiments and mortar units were deployed in an infantry role. The navy's new marine battalions were deployed inland; they are used mostly for short-term operations.

During 2010 and 2011, in some of the worst affected areas such as Veracruz and Tamaulipas, the armed forces replaced entire police forces due to high levels of corruption. Efforts by the federal government to undertake nationwide police reforms, in which over 2,000 state and municipal police departments would be consolidated into 32 large state-level forces, have not been approved by Congress. Federal Police numbers, meanwhile, have risen significantly, from 6,500 in 2006 to 37,000 in 2012, while mobility and technological capabilities have been boosted with the acquisition of *Black Hawk* helicopters, unmanned aerial vehicles, C4ISR systems and light armoured vehicles.

Internal security actions have led the armed forces to consider changes to their organisation, doctrine, training and equipment. Mexico's conventional military capability has traditionally focused on internal security and disaster-relief capabilities. The country lacks an external threat, and the military is barred by a non-interventionist foreign policy from participating in foreign deployments, including international peacekeeping operations.

Army doctrine was redrafted in 2007 to emphasise special operations and urban and counter-guerrilla warfare. To enable this shift, most battalion- and brigade-size conventional exercises were suspended between 2007 and 2012. Training activities now focus on section-, platoon- or company-sized operations in scenarios that include urban warfare, convoy protection, roadside checkpoints, counter-intelligence, and the restoration of law and order in small towns. Equipment requirements have also been modified. Mobility in urban areas was a challenge with the army's standard tactical vehicle, the HMMWV, proving too wide and slow for urban operations. As a consequence, the army took delivery of 250 Oshkosh *SandCat* light armoured vehicles in 2011 specifically for the law-enforcement role; the force had earlier, from 2008, bought 1,320 4×4 pickup trucks. In 2011, the army established four mobile forensic units and began to establish 13 'strategic control outposts' – checkpoints on roads identified as critical to drug and weapons smuggling. These outposts comprise a platoon- or company-sized formation around fixed infrastructure equipped with surveillance and detection equipment for screening large numbers of vehicles.

Since 2008, Mexico has received around US$1.6bn in security assistance – in the form of equipment and training – from the US under The Mérida Initiative. Initial focus on equipment provision has now shifted towards training and capacity-building programmes. Mérida funding has provided the Federal Police with seven UH-60M *Black Hawks* and the navy with four CN235MP *Persuader* maritime patrol aircraft and three UH-60M *Black Hawks*. The army received detection equipment and the air force received eight Bell 412 helicopters.

REGIONAL DEFENCE ECONOMICS

Regional macroeconomics

After South America's relatively strong economic performance in 2011, when regional economic output expanded by 4.8%, growth slowed to a projected 2.9% in 2012. This reflected, in part, the lagged effects of the fiscal- or monetary-policy tightening measures undertaken by South American states earlier in 2011 (see *The Military Balance 2012*, p. 365, for the impact of Brazilian policy-tightening measures in 2011 on the economy and on defence spending). These measures were adopted due to fears over rising domestic inflation and the general deterioration in the external economic environment over the course of 2011 and 2012 as weakened US growth, renewed financial-market disruption in Europe, and the slowdown in Asian growth rates in 2012 tempered global and hence South American economic activity. Of particular significance has been the gradual deceleration in China, which over the past decade has imported large quantities of raw materials and industrial base metals. If this slowdown continues, it could mean significant falls in commodity prices. Real growth in several commodity-exporting countries (such as Argentina, Bolivia, Ecuador, Paraguay and Venezuela) was projected to decrease in 2012 relative to the elevated levels seen in 2011, although in some of these states (for example, Argentina and Venezuela), high levels of government spending provided additional demand support.

External economic and financial stress, particularly in the eurozone, increased risk aversion in global financial markets, resulting in diminished capital inflows into South America relative to recent years (significantly, however, these flows did not reverse direction). The reduced inflows provided greater space for policymakers to respond with monetary easing from August 2011. For example, between August 2011 and October 2012, Brazil reduced its policy rate by more than 500 basis points, or 5%. However, the rising proportion of non-performing loans in several economies after the rapid credit growth seen in recent years tempered these policy actions' effect on the real economies of the region. In any case, output gaps (the difference between actual and potential output) across the region are close to zero, indicating that South American economies are operating close to or at full capacity; and that structural reforms, rather than expansionary policies, are becoming more important in order to achieve sustained future growth. Economic activity remained subdued in Central America and the Caribbean, in part because these economies are heavily linked to the economic performance of advanced economies, particularly the United States, but also because they remain hamstrung by high levels of public debt due to low levels of revenue collection.

Defence spending

Moderating economic growth and increased uncertainty over global economic prospects meant that

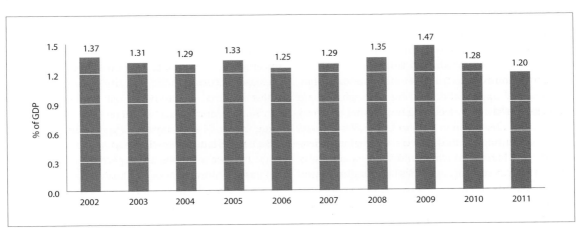

Figure 25 **Latin America and the Caribbean Regional Defence Expenditure** as % of GDP

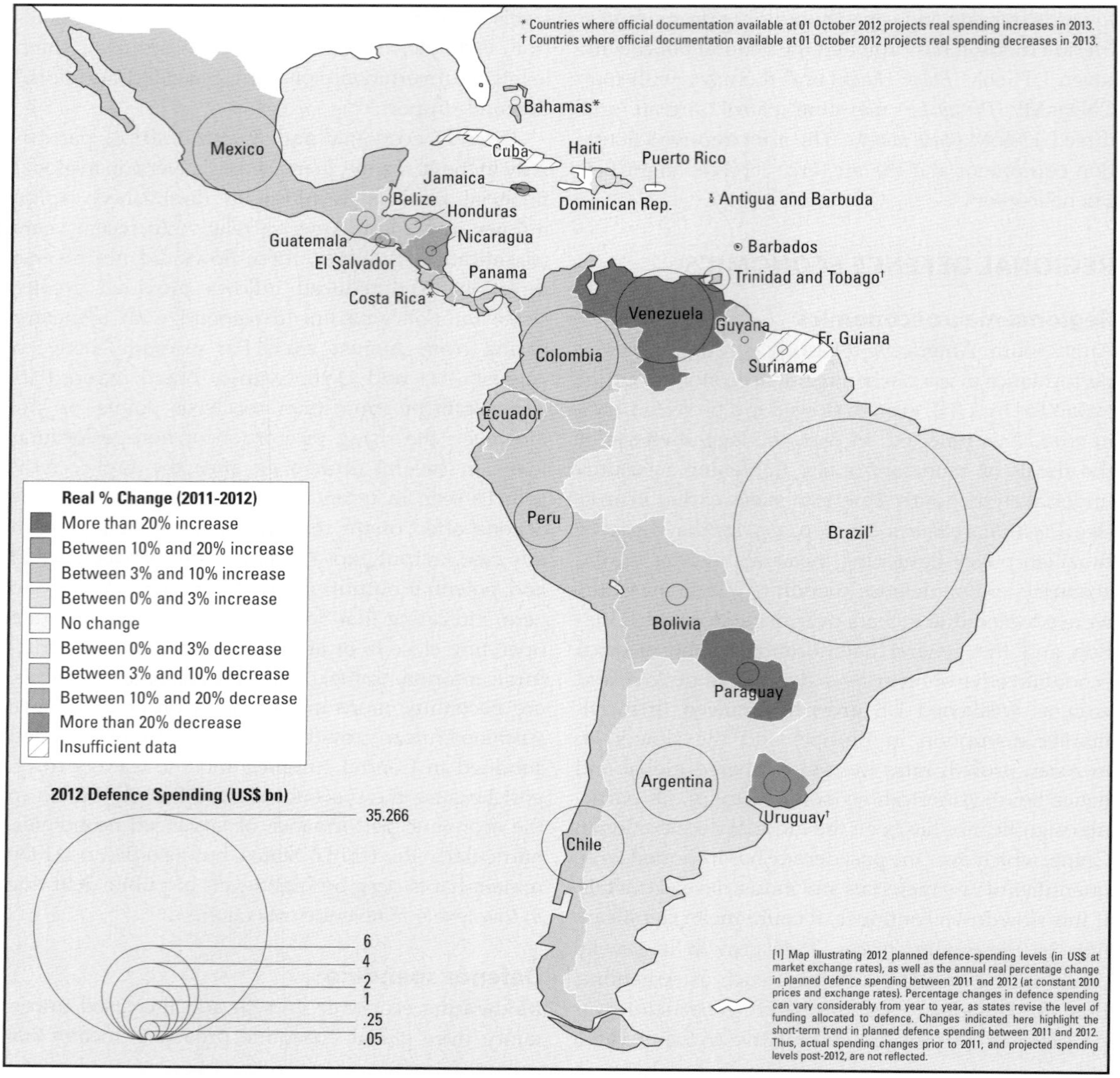

* Countries where official documentation available at 01 October 2012 projects real spending increases in 2013.
† Countries where official documentation available at 01 October 2012 projects real spending decreases in 2013.

Mexico

Bahamas*

Cuba   Haiti   Puerto Rico

Jamaica   Antigua and Barbuda
Belize   Dominican Rep.
Honduras
Guatemala   Nicaragua
El Salvador   Panama   Barbados
Costa Rica*   Trinidad and Tobago†

Venezuela   Guyana   Fr. Guiana
Colombia   Suriname

Ecuador

Real % Change (2011-2012)

- More than 20% increase
- Between 10% and 20% increase
- Between 3% and 10% increase
- Between 0% and 3% increase
- No change
- Between 0% and 3% decrease
- Between 3% and 10% decrease
- Between 10% and 20% decrease
- More than 20% decrease
- Insufficient data

Peru   Brazil†

Bolivia

Paraguay

2012 Defence Spending (US$ bn)

35.266

6
4
2
1
.25
.05

Argentina   Uruguay†

Chile

[1] Map illustrating 2012 planned defence-spending levels (in US$ at market exchange rates), as well as the annual real percentage change in planned defence spending between 2011 and 2012 (at constant 2010 prices and exchange rates). Percentage changes in defence spending can vary considerably from year to year, as states revise the level of funding allocated to defence. Changes indicated here highlight the short-term trend in planned defence spending between 2011 and 2012. Thus, actual spending changes prior to 2011, and projected spending levels post-2012, are not reflected.

Map 13 **Latin America and the Caribbean Regional Defence Spending[1]**

Latin American states were more cautious about expanding defence spending in 2012.

Higher than expected rates of inflation and substantial currency appreciation during 2011 pushed up total regional defence spending in nominal terms by 10.9%, from US$62.0bn in 2010 to US$68.8bn in 2011. After discounting for these effects, the region experienced a 0.68% real reduction in defence spending in 2011. In 2012, as several currencies in the region depreciated relative to their 2011 highs, the rate of nominal regional spending growth (in US dollar terms) decelerated to 3.08%, reaching a total of US$70.9bn. Real defence spending grew by 3.86%, despite the

moderation in economic growth and increased uncertainty over global economic prospects. Real increases occurred in the majority of Latin American states in 2012, including Brazil (1.5%), Colombia (4.5%) and Mexico (4.2%). There were exceptionally large increases in Venezuela (34.0%) and Paraguay (28.4%), the latter following a 41.5% real increase in 2011. Further increases are expected in Paraguay in 2013 as the country raises military pay and continues to modernise its forces, with planned purchases of combat aircraft, radar systems, armoured vehicles and patrol vessels. Nevertheless, Paraguay remains only the 15th largest defence spender in the region,

Defence spending transparency and synchronisation in Latin America

In December 2010, the members of UNASUR's South American Defence Council began talks on adopting a common regional methodology for calculating defence spending, as well as exploring potential mechanisms for monitoring defence expenditure. Discussions continued over the course of 2011 to develop an action plan for 2012 to include sharing information on military procurement, expenditure and other security issues. Momentum on defence-spending transparency was led by a committee consisting of Chile, Ecuador and Peru. In January 2012, six of UNASUR's 12 member countries – Argentina, Chile, Colombia, Ecuador, Paraguay and Uruguay – formally agreed to share defence expenditure information for the 2006–10 period. By May 2012, the remaining six states – Bolivia, Brazil, Guyana, Peru, Suriname and Venezuela – had also agreed to contribute their defence statistics. (Mexico and Panama, which only have observer status within UNASUR, did not contribute their spending figures).

The information was collated and analysed by UN-ASUR's Centre for Strategic Defence Studies (Centro de Estudios Estratégicos), with a final report presented at the UNASUR Ministerial Meeting in Asunción, Paraguay in June 2012. It is not known precisely how much detail on military expenditure states were prepared to divulge. For example, as part of defence treaties with Russia, Iran and Cuba, Venezuela receives military assistance and credit for equipment purchases, while Colombia receives funds from the US under the 'Plan Colombia' programme. It is also unclear if the information provided by states was independently audited or verified, or whether the defence statistics would eventually be made publicly available. Nonetheless, increased transparency on military spending is seen as an important confidence-building measure for the region, with the UN general secretary for disarmament's representative characterising UNASUR's efforts as 'an exercise in transparency unseen in any other region of the world'.

with levels slightly below those of neighbouring Bolivia. The increase in Venezuela, coming after an 8.2% real reduction in spending in 2011, was in part due to higher funding allocations for military wages announced by President Hugo Chávez a month after his re-election in October 2012 and backdated to April 2012. Military pay for all ranks was raised by around 40%, in a move widely regarded as overdue by the services as the country continued to experience annual inflation rates in excess of 20%.

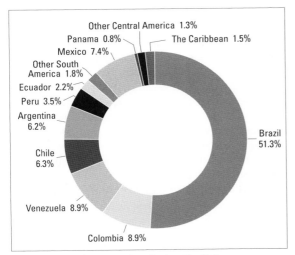

Figure 26 **Latin America & the Caribbean Defence Spending by Country & Sub-Region**

Brazil retained its position as the largest defence spender in the region, although its 1.5% rate of real defence-spending growth in 2012 was well below the regional average of 4.4%. As a result of strong spending increments elsewhere, Brazil's share of regional spending in 2012 declined to just above half the regional total (51.3%, down from 56.3% in 2010). Collectively, the region's top five defence spenders (Brazil, Colombia, Mexico, Venezuela and Chile) made up just over 80% of total regional spending, with the next five (Argentina, Peru, Ecuador, Panama and Uruguay) accounting for a further 15.5%. Overall, spending in South America rose by 4.02% in 2012, while Central America saw an even larger 4.25% real increase after strong increments in Nicaragua (18.2%), Panama (6.5%) and Costa Rica (5.2%). Planned defence spending grew at the lowest rate in the Caribbean (1.4%) due to the sub-region's high degree of indebtedness, although the substantial reductions seen in 2011 were reversed in 2012 with significant real increases in spending in Antigua and Barbuda (7.4%) and Barbados (20.1%).

Regional defence-industrial organisation and defence industries

In recent years, Latin American countries have on balance allocated relatively low levels of resources to defence, primarily due to decades of economic dislocations, from the Latin American debt crisis of the 1980s and early 1990s, to the slow growth and intermittent economic turbulence caused by periodic currency crises in the mid-1990s and early 2000s. As a result, equipment inventories across the region are increasingly in need of replacement and modernisation, and regional defence-industrial development has been restricted.

High levels of commodities-driven growth since the mid-2000s, however, have led to increased governmental receipts, significantly improving the fiscal balances of many Latin American states. There is also an appreciation of the need to diversify regional economies away from extractive and primary industries towards more technology-intensive, tertiary sectors. This has renewed regional ambitions to re-industrialise economies in high value-added areas such as defence. Governments are increasing expenditure on research and development, providing greater funding for domestic defence programmes rather than resorting to foreign 'off-the-shelf' purchases, and engaging in collaborative defence-industrial arrangements with both developed and emerging countries.

Brazil's FX2 fighter programme: defence-industrial collaboration

The Dassault *Rafale,* Saab *Gripen* NG and Boeing F/A-18 E/F *Super Hornet* are still vying for Brazil's protracted FX2 fighter competition. An initial order for 36 could lead to the purchase of 100 aircraft. Estimates of the total value of the initial 36-fighter deal vary between $4–9 billion, though the competition may be worth up to double this when follow-on orders, long-term maintenance and service contracts, ancillary contracts and spare parts are factored in. Following diplomatic lobbying and offers of technology transfer when France's then-President Nicolas Sarkozy visited Brazil in 2009, Dassault was viewed by some as favourite. However, President Luiz Inácio Lula da Silva's outgoing government declined to take a final decision, and the new administration of President Dilma Rousseff opted to review all three offers, before deciding to defer a decision until mid-2012 – in part because funds previously allocated for defence procurement were suspended in 2011 because of budgetary constraints (see *The Military Balance 2012,* p. 365).

Presidential and other high-level US visits to Brazil in 2011 were followed in April 2012 by meetings between President Dilma Rousseff, President Barack Obama, US Secretary of State Hillary Clinton and US Defense Secretary Leon Panetta. With the competition for the FX2 fighter replacement contract still open, the US has put diplomatic muscle behind Boeing's bid, while Boeing and other US firms have signed a raft of agreements with local defence industry. On a visit to Brazil in April 2012, Panetta said that the US would permit significant technology transfers 'only reserved for our closest allies and partners' if Boeing won the competition. Boeing has increased its local partnerships in order to meet Brazil's high industrial-offset requirements. It established a Brazil office in São Paolo in October 2011, and in March 2012 it signed two agreements to develop advanced avionics with Elbit Systems' Brazilian subsidiary, AEL Sistemas. Following Panetta's April visit, Boeing announced a collaboration with Embraer in areas of aircraft safety, efficiency and operational costs, and that it would establish an aerospace research facility (called Boeing Research and Technology – Brazil) in São Paolo later in the year. In May 2012, Boeing and Northrop Grumman (a producer of F/A-18E/F components) signed a Memorandum of Agreement with Brazil's RCS Precision Machining & Maintenance and GNS Industry & Trade. In June, Boeing signed a collaboration arrangement with Embraer to share technical expertise for the joint development, marketing and sales of Embraer's KC-390 transport/tanker.

Swedish firm Saab, another competitor for the FX2 contract, has also been actively promoting broad defence-industrial cooperation with Brazil. In May 2011, Saab opened the Swedish–Brazilian Centre of Research and Innovation in São Bernardo de Campo, aimed at strengthening Brazil's domestic research sector. In March 2012, Saab bolstered its arrangements with AEL Sistemas, which provides a variety of support services for *Gripen* avionics. In May, Saab announced a 15% stake in Brazilian defence-aerospace engineering firm Akaer, after five years of cooperation on *Gripen* NG design.

In mid-2012, Brazil announced that a final decision on the FX2 programme would again be delayed due to the deterioration of its macroeconomic environment in 2011–12. But Brasília realises a decision is necessary: Defence Minister Celso Amorim said in September 2011 that Brazil needed to finalise its selection due to its ageing fighter fleet. The FX2 programme is seen as the foundation of Brazil's future advanced aerospace industry, and as part of the deal, Brazil has laid down significant technology-transfer and local-participation requirements in order to develop its defence-industrial base. However, it appears that, in light of economic uncertainty and perceived inadequacies in the offset proposals thus far submitted, Brasília is prepared to hold out for better terms.

Foreign penetration of South American defence markets

Foreign defence companies have made considerable effort to penetrating Brazil's defence market, by far the largest in the region. Brazil makes up over 50% of total Latin American regional defence spending, and has a rapidly expanding economy and a number of major procurement programmes. To accelerate its defence-industrial transformation and raise defence production capacity, Brazil has placed considerable emphasis on establishing industrial partnerships with advanced suppliers, and foreign defence companies have increased their engagement with domestic firms to meet Brazil's defence-offset requirements. A number have opened subsidiary offices, or taken stakes in local defence-related firms.

Brazil has already benefitted from technology-transfer relationships with French defence firms relating to its conventional- and nuclear-powered submarine programmes, and as noted above, the US would allow the transfer of advanced technology to Brazil should Boeing win the FX2 fighter competition (see box, p. 422). But foreign defence-industrial interest is not limited to the major FX2 and submarine programmes.

European missile house MBDA, for example, has stepped up its collaboration with local Brazilian firms, notably Avibras Indústria Aeroespacial and Mectron-Engenharia (Indústria e Comércio), on Brazil's $40m Block I MM40 *Exocet* renovation and maintenance programme, and in April 2012, the navy successfully test fired a re-engined missile. Israeli defence firms remain active in the Brazilian market, particularly following a 2010 confidentiality agreement in which Brazil undertook not to transfer classified technologies to third parties. The UAV market has proved particularly fruitful, with a 2011 joint venture between AEL Sistemas and Embraer Defesa e Seguranca – Embraer's defence and security division, which acquired a 25% stake in AEL as part of the agreement – to develop, produce and support the *Hermes* 450 under a joint entity called Harpia Sistemas. Other deals have seen AEL Sistemas supply avionics for Embraer's *Super Tucano* and KC-390 programmes. Together with another Elbit subsidiary, Elisra Electronic Systems, AEL is involved in upgrading, between 2013–17, the Air Force's AMX A-1 FGA aircraft, a deal which includes jamming equipment from Israel's state-owned Rafael Advanced Defense Systems. Rafael itself expanded into the Brazilian defence sector in April 2012, acquiring a 40% share in Gespi Aeronautics.

South Africa's Denel Dynamics and Brazilian defence firms Mectron-Engenharia, Avibras Indústria Aeroespacial and Opto Electronics have been jointly pursuing a $120m research and development programme for the *A-Darter* 5th generation air-to-air missile (due to be delivered in 2013) since 2007, and are looking to expand this collaboration to other areas. Over the course of 2012, Brazil raised the prospect of enhanced defence-industrial cooperation with a number of other states. In February, Amorim visited India, where he discussed potential cooperation over the manufacture, training and maintenance of *Scorpene* submarines. He later visited Italy, where Defence Minister Giampaolo Di Paola stressed Italy's interest in working with Brazil to jointly generate

Regional update:

- In February 2012, Paraguay announced the selection of Embraer's EMB-314 *Super Tucano* as its future combat aircraft.
- In January 2012, Brazil and Colombia signed a defence-industrial and training agreement which included the establishment of a commission to explore the potential for bilateral collaboration in the fields of armoured vehicles, cyber security and UAVs. The two states are seeking to jointly develop a riverine patrol vessel by 2015.
- In May 2012, the Brazilian Navy signed a contract to purchase four PAF-L lightweight riverine patrol vessels from Colombia.
- Brazil and Cuba are exploring the possibility of deepening their defence-industrial relations and moving towards close collaboration in defence, aviation and security industries, following the formal establishment in January 2012 of training exchanges between the two.
- In July 2012, Argentina and Venezuela signed a bilateral defence-cooperation agreement that included science, technological development and military manufacturing.
- Brazil and Argentina agreed a Mechanism for Strategic Dialogue (MDPEVM), which had its first meeting in April 2012.
- In April, South Korea and Peru signed an MoU to develop defence and security cooperation. Peru is reported to be considering purchasing 20 South Korean KT-1 training aircraft.

Brazil's requirements under its PROSUPER surface fleet programme (see p. 425).

Other regional markets are also targeted by foreign defence firms. In June 2012, EADS entered a manufacturing partnership agreement with Chile's national aeronautical enterprise ENAER (Empresa Nacional de Aeronáutica), which manufactures the T-35 *Pillan* trainer. Analysts believe that EADS could restructure ENAER, in consultation with the Chilean air force, to create a new company better able to meet air-force requirements for equipment manufacture and aircraft servicing. In return, the partnership will enable EADS to take advantage of lower manufacturing costs and boost EADS' regional market access.

In July 2012, Argentina and China renewed an existing memorandum of understanding during a visit by Argentine Defence Minister Arturo Puricelli to Beijing. The MoU provided for increased defence-industrial collaboration between Argentina's state-owned aircraft manufacturer Fábrica Argentina de Aviones (FAdeA) and the China National Aero-Technology Import & Export Corporation (CATIC), which are seeking to establish a production facility for CATIC's Z-11 light multi-purpose helicopter in Cordoba, Argentina. In March 2012, FAdeA announced a partnership with Germany's Grob Aircraft AG to produce a minimum of 100 IA-63 *Pampa* and AT-63 *Pampa* II advanced training and combat aircraft (see below).

These foreign partnership arrangements provide development opportunities for local defence firms, and are aimed at better enabling them to meet domestic-procurement requirements as well as to improve export prospects. As part of the process, governments are raising offset requirements for foreign participation in domestic markets to increase technology transfer. They are also incentivising the growth of their domestic defence manufacturing bases by amending domestic legislation (see p. 427) and by supporting export drives.

Intra-regional defence industrial collaboration and procurement

Intra-regional procurement and defence-industrial cooperation are also increasing. Much is centred on Brazil; many regional states view involvement in its KC-390 and EMB-314 *Super Tucano* programmes as an opportunity to internationalise their own defence industries. In turn, Brazil views defence collaboration with other states as a way to position its defence

industry for future regional sales and to increase regional defence-manufacturing capacity.

The KC-390 tanker/transport aircraft programme, for example, incorporates neighbouring countries into its manufacturing supply chains. In April 2011, Argentina and Brazil signed a contract to jointly manufacture the aircraft; Argentina will act as a junior partner and subcontractor to Embraer, establishing an assembly line in Argentina to produce several structural components for the aircraft. FAdeA will build the tail cone, cargo-ramp door, spoilers and nose-wheel landing-gear door. The programme also involves the Colombian and Chilean aerospace sectors; the former plans to invest $70–$80m to build an industrial area in the eastern coastal city of Buenaventura to produce the cockpits.

In April 2012, Brazil and Argentina agreed to expand areas of collaboration to include the joint production of UAVs using technology developed by Israel's Elbit Systems. Argentina is also looking to Brazil to assist in the production of *A-Darter* air-to-air missiles, which Brazil is developing with South Africa; has asked Brazil to recondition its MM-38 and MM-40 *Exocet* missiles to increase their lifespan, as well as to accelerate delivery to Argentina of *Guaraní* armoured vehicles, jointly developed by Brazil's Army Technology Centre and Italy's Iveco.

South American countries have also agreed to strengthen multilateral defence-industrial ties, and plans for multinational projects in primary basic training aircraft (the UNASUR I project) and UAVs were agreed in November 2011 by UNASUR defence ministers. Progress in 2012 centred on planning and coordination. Buenos Aires has driven the UNASUR I initiative, perhaps as a means to boost its defence-aerospace industry (the project working group was based in Córdoba, where FAdeA is headquartered). Puricelli said that UNASUR I would standardise advanced training for pilots in South America, given the ageing aircraft on which many currently train. Some analysts are discussing the possibility that Buenos Aires could transform its ongoing project for a basic training aircraft, the IA-73, into the UNASUR I, possibly as a way of boosting its domestic industry. The IA-73 is a joint development between Chile and Argentina to replace T-35A/B *Pillán* basic trainers; production is due to begin in 2013. The AT-63 *Pampa* II, the IA-73 and the UNASUR I projects are all in line with the country's attempts to boost its aerospace industry, jump-started in 2009 when the government took over FAdeA, until then owned by Lockheed Martin.

BRAZIL

Brazil's defence policy remains focused on the protection and surveillance of its borders, particularly its jungle border regions and substantial offshore oil reserves. This is broadly in line with the aspirations of its 2008 National Defence Strategy (NDS) (see *The Military Balance 2011*, p. 345). But the army has made little progress in its 'rebalance' toward Brazil's western borders in the Amazon, a priority area for the NDS, though the armed forces continue to conduct security operations in the region against drugs and arms trafficking. In a speech in April 2012, Amorim made it clear that Brazil does not feel threatened by any of its neighbours, but noted the potential interference of 'a power from outside the region' as a key concern, a reflection of unfounded but long-enduring Brazilian military anxieties about a foreign invasion of the Amazon.

Submarine programmes

The NDS noted as a priority the development of a capability to build and operate nuclear-powered submarines. A large segment of the 2012 procurement budget, some R$2.4bn (US$1.3bn), has been allocated to the Submarine Development Programme (PROSUB). A deal signed with France in 2008 includes the construction of one nuclear-powered and four conventionally-powered submarines in partnership with French shipbuilder DCNS. On 6 July 2012, the design stage of the nuclear-powered submarine formally began with a ceremony in São Paulo; the submarine is due to enter service in 2023. DCNS is assisting in the design and construction of the non-nuclear portions of the nuclear submarine. In February, Brazil claimed it had mastered the nuclear fuel cycle necessary to power the vessel, with the inauguration of a Uranium Hexafluoride Production Unit (USEXA) in Sorocaba, São Paulo. Some 80% of the equipment is reportedly of Brazilian manufacture. According to the NDS, nuclear-powered submarines are vital for 'sea-denial' capabilities aimed at, in the first instance, 'proactive defense of the oil platforms' (p. 20). The PROSUB programme is also aimed at protecting the Atlantic, or 'Blue Amazon', coast, as well as Brazil's oil reserves. It was the programme least affected by the belt-tightening applied to major Brazilian procurement programmes in 2011 and 2012 (see *The Military Balance 2012*, pp. 366–7). Construction of the conventional-powered *Scorpene* submarines continues.

The programme has other motivations. The NDS noted a desire for Brazil 'to reach its deserved spot in the world' (p. 8). It also noted Brazil's 'strategic need to develop and master nuclear technology' (p. 12). This national strategic objective led Congress to approve, in July, the creation of a publicly owned company, Amazônia Azul Tecnologias de Defesa (Amazul), with the stated aim of sponsoring research and business initiatives in areas of nuclear technology related to PROSUB. Indeed, Brazil's Defence White Book, launched in November 2012, identifies nuclear-submarine development as a key driver of national technological progress more broadly, alongside the defence of trade routes, free navigation of national territorial waters and protection of natural resources.

Brazil's Defence White Book

The first National Defence White Book was presented to Congress in July. It outlines the main procurement and policy priorities for the armed forces, restating Brazil's commitment to non-intervention: Brazil's foreign policy 'emphasises its immediate geopolitical surrounding, constituted by South America, the South Atlantic and the western coast of Africa'.

The book mentions 'new themes' in international security, specifically citing the 'global problem of drugs', bio-piracy, cyber threats, international terrorism and tensions over scarce resources, among others. It does not, however, outline which are the most important. It states clearly Brazil's ambitions for a force-projection capability to support its aspiration for great-power status. The strategy it outlines to increase projection capabilities seems to indicate that the country will continue to oppose interventions justified by the 'right to protect', except where there is a clear UN Security Council mandate. The document also states the necessity of a 'capacity for power projection aiming at the eventual participation' in UN-authorised operations. It also deals with the controversial involvement of the armed forces in law-enforcement operations, stating that missions should be temporary and in a specific geographical area, and that decisions to intervene are to be made by the president. It also states that law-enforcement interventions should only happen once the traditional instruments designed 'to preserve public order have been depleted'.

The Amazon

Two ambitious wide-area surveillance programmes to monitor the Amazon and the Atlantic coast were approved in 2012. One, the Integrated Border Monitoring System (SISFRON) to secure Brazil's western borders from trafficking groups, is expected to cost around R$12bn (US$6.5bn) over ten years, and will be composed of radar stations, satellites, land systems and unmanned aerial vehicles. On 31 July 2012, the army opened the bidding process for a pilot project for radar stations in the city of Dourados, in Mato Grosso do Sul, along the borders with Bolivia and Paraguay. The plan is for SISFRON to link with the Management System of the Blue Amazon (SisGAAz), an Atlantic monitoring system currently being designed by Atech, a defence and aerospace technology company in which Embraer has a 50% stake. The two programmes will, according to military planners, be complementary, enabling security and armed forces to rapidly respond to threats across large tracts of Brazil's territory.

The armed forces have stepped up large-scale security operations to combat armed narcotics- and weapons-trafficking groups in western border areas. Brasília is increasingly concerned by the drug problem, and both Roussef and her predecessor Luis Inácio Lula da Silva launched a series of operations, codenamed *Ágata*, to combat narcotics smuggling. Five have been carried out since June 2011. *Ágata 4*, in May 2012, was the largest joint operation ever carried out in Brazil's sparsely populated northern region: 8,500 personnel operated along 5,500 kilometres of jungle border in Amazonas state. In July, an even larger force, composed of 17,000 army, navy and air force personnel, was deployed to the southwestern border region near Uruguay, Argentina, Paraguay and Bolivia. A sixth *Ágata* operation took place in late-year. These operations were part of Brazil's Strategic Border Plan, which also includes a permanent law-enforcement operation, *Operation Sentinel*, led by the Ministry of Justice. Some 115 tonnes of cocaine and marijuana were seized during the first three *Ágata* operations, 14 times more than the amount apprehended in the first half of 2011, while air force A-29 *Super Tucanos* were used to destroy clandestine airstrips along the border.

The armed forces have, however, been slower to implement the 'Protected Amazon' initiative to increase their presence in that region. Two new Special Border Platoons (PEFs) were established in the Amazon, bringing the total number to 23, far short of the planned total of 49. The R$8.5m (US$4.6m) cost of each PEF might have contributed to the delay. The chief of the Joint Staffs, General José Carlos de Nardi, announced in February 2012 that the air force would soon move aircraft to the Amazon, though details were scant.

Cyber security

A cyber attack on Brazilian government and military websites in June 2011, allegedly committed by the LulzSec group, prompted the government to buy a new anti-virus system and cyber-attack simulator, reportedly able to stage 25 different attack scenarios, in January 2012 at a cost of some R$6m (US$3.3m). The Federal Police (PF), focused on internal law-enforcement missions ranging from countering money laundering to fighting organised crime in mainly poor areas, opened a 24-hour cyber-crime monitoring centre with an eye to the forthcoming 2014 FIFA World Cup and 2016 Summer Olympic Games. The army's Center for Cyber Defence (CDCiber), established in 2010, was unprepared for the June 2011 attacks. CDCiber announced its first large-scale mission to protect network security during the Rio+20 international climate conference in June 2012, an occasion that passed without incident.

Brazil has seen frequent and audacious cyber attacks, one of which disabled the presidency website on the day of Roussef's inauguration in 2010. In June 2011, around the same time of the attack on civilian government websites, a group called Fatal Error Crew highlighted the armed forces' vulnerability to cyber attack by stealing personal data of 1,000 military personnel. During 2011, cyber attacks in Brazil increased threefold, with 400,000 recorded incidents, according to Brazil's civilian Computer Emergency Response Team. Nearly two years after the creation of CDCiber, the top cyber-security authority in the Brazilian Armed Forces, General Antonino Santos Guerra, admitted in February 2012 that the country only had a 'minimum' level of preparedness to defend against theft and large-scale cyber attacks such as those of June 2011, but he hoped the new cyber-attack simulator would improve readiness. He expressly denied that Brazil was worried about cyber attacks or cyber espionage by other states.

Domestic deployments

In June, the army ended its 1,700-strong occupation of the Alemão and Penha *favela* complexes in Rio de Janeiro, where a 'Pacification Force' had been deployed since November 2010 to expel organised-crime groups. Security in these areas was transferred to the Military Police, which since 2008 has occupied other large slums in the city as part of the 'Pacifying Police Unit' (UPPs) programme, designed to expel militias connected to organised crime. Prior to the withdrawal, however, the army reported an increase in attacks. A few weeks after the army pulled out, a policewoman was killed in the Alemão; the first death in service of a UPP member. There has been debate over perceived risks in prolonged military involvement in police missions. Critics point to the view, shared by some *favela* dwellers, that soldiers could be more likely to use force than the police.

In May, the Rousseff administration established a Truth Commission to investigate human-rights violations. The president, a former leftist guerrilla who had been tortured under the 1964–85 military regime, had managed to overcome suspicions in the military after her electoral victory in 2010. But the situation deteriorated ahead of the commission's official launch. A group of retired military officers published a letter on 16 February criticising comments made by the minister of the Human Rights Secretariat, in which she raised the possibility of legal action against members of the armed forces suspected of involvement in abuses during the dictatorship. The group also accused Rousseff of governing for just 'a portion of the population'. In response, according to reports in the Brazilian press, Rousseff ordered Amorim and the chiefs of staff to reprimand the group and even considered imprisoning one of the authors. The retired officers eventually published a note disavowing the earlier letter. Members of the Naval Club, a Rio de Janeiro-based cultural organisation connected to the armed forces, created a 'parallel commission' designed to scrutinise the conclusions of the Truth Commission. Dissatisfaction is believed greatest among retired commanders fearful that Rousseff could investigate armed forces' archives and ignore the Amnesty Law, passed during the final phase of the dictatorship.

Defence economics

The defence budget has continued the upward trajectory observed since 2004, but remains subject to emergency restrictions (see *The Military Balance 2012*, p. 367). The government says these measures are necessary due to reduced fiscal income resulting from a slowdown in Brazil's economic growth since 2010. Tax revenue from the crucial mining sector fell by 67% in the first half of 2012, compared to the same period in 2011. With revenue sources slowing down, the government's primary surplus fell 14.1% year on year in the six months to June 2012, sparking fears that its aim for a 3.1% surplus in the year would remain unfulfilled. The slowdown forced the government to reduce its forecast for total tax revenue in 2012 by R\$13.3bn (US\$7.2bn), from R\$890bn (US\$484bn) to R\$876.7bn (US\$477bn).

The government has restricted governmental outlays for the last two years, and the level announced in February 2012 was R\$55bn (US\$29.9bn), slightly higher than the R\$50bn (US\$27.2bn) for 2011. In both years, the Ministry of Defence was among the worst affected, with R\$3.3bn (US\$1.8bn) frozen. In June 2012, however, the MoD was given a R\$1.5bn investment line as part of the government's Accelerated Growth Program (AGP), designed to stimulate the economy. The defence industry is a particular target for the AGP as it is seen as having the potential to drive innovation throughout the economy and boost exports.

The bulk of AGP resources allocated to defence, some R\$939.6m (US\$511m), were for the purchase of 4,170 transport vehicles. Some R\$342m (US\$186m) went towards renewing the army's obsolete fleet of armoured vehicles with the purchase of 40 amphibious *Guaranis*, produced by Iveco in Minas Gerais state, while 30 *Astros* 2020 MLRS – an update of the *Astros* II produced by Brazil's Avibrás – were bought for R\$246m (US\$134m).

The defence industry received a further boost from legislation introducing special incentives and reducing taxes on the sector. Under the Special Taxation Regime for the Defence Industry (Regime Especial Tributário para a Indústria de Defesa), 'strategic defence companies' will be exempt from three key taxes: the Pis/Pasep and Cofins, both charged to companies, and the IPI, charged on industrialised products. The exemptions benefit Brazilian defence companies' intermediate industrial suppliers, equipment and imports and exports. The law also allows the government to conduct public auctions for priority defence products. 'Strategic defence companies' must have an administrative structure based in the country and more than two-thirds of voting shares held by Brazilian nationals. According to the Brazilian army, 186 companies currently qualify. One of the main aims of the law was to level the playing field between national and imported defence products, which are exempt from import taxes. This tax

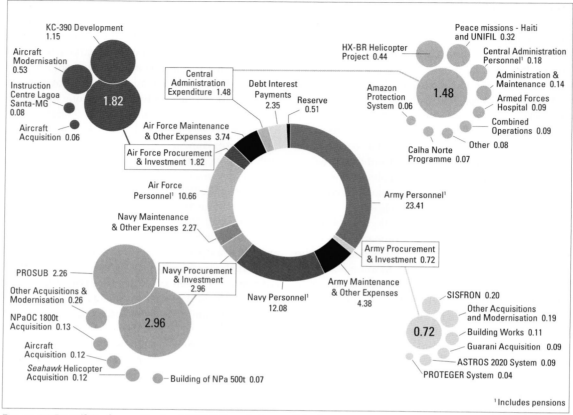

Figure 27 **Brazil Defence Budget 2013 Breakdown (Rbn)**

asymmetry contributed to a US$1.9bn trade deficit in defence products from 2000–10.

The new rules were greeted by the Federation of Industries of São Paulo State (FIESP) – the most powerful industry association in Brazil – as a step in the right direction. However, the organisation's president, Rubens Barbosa, said the law did not address the taxes in place on the final sale from industry to government. The exemptions apply primarily to intermediate supplies and industrial equipment, not the final products. Moreover, according to FIESP, a rule that 70% of a company's profits must come exclusively from the defence sector discourages the development of technologies with both civil and military uses, leaving companies dependent on government purchases. Finally, FIESP argues that defence procurement remains inconsistent. The cutbacks on defence expenditure since 2010 have delayed projects and increased industrial uncertainty. In response, the administration has developed a Plan for Coordination and Defence Equipments (Plano de Articulação e Equipamentos de Defesa), which establishes procure-

ment priorities until 2031; this is expected to be released by the end of 2012.

Procurement programmes

Brazil aspires to develop a force-projection capability consistent with global-power status, with new ships, submarines, surveillance systems (SisGAAz and SISFRON) and the long-delayed FX2 fighter programme (see above, p. 425, and box, p. 422) all part of procurement aims. A total of R$40bn (US$22bn) in medium- to long-term investments have been announced in recent years, according to Brazil's defence industry association (Associação Brasileira das Indústrias de Materiais de Defesa e Segurança, ABIMDE), expected to rise to R$100bn (US$54bn) over the next 20 years. But delays to the release of procurement funds in 2011–12 show that these ambitions remain uncertain. In April 2012, Amorim told the Senate that defence spending should approximate that of the other BRIC nations. Russia, China and India, he said, spend on average 2.4% of GDP on defence, in contrast to Brazil's 1.5%. Although the total amount had grown by nearly R$20bn (US$11bn) over the five years since 2008, resources were, he said, still insufficient to cover military procurement requirements.

One large project still to see funding disbursed is PROSUPER, the domestic construction of five ocean-patrol boats, five frigates and a logistics support vessel for the navy. The project was suspended in early 2011, despite extensive interest by foreign companies. With defence of the 'Blue Amazon' high on the agenda, the navy filled a gap in coastal capabilities with the acquisition of three ocean patrol vessels from BAE Systems in the second half of 2012, at a cost of R$365m (US$199m).

One significant development was Boeing's partnership with Brazil's Embraer, announced in June, to improve safety and efficiency in commercial aerospace projects and to supply weapons systems for the A-29 *Super Tucano* light attack aircraft. The two companies also agreed to share technical knowledge that would benefit the KC-390 tanker/transport aircraft programme. The KC-390 and the *Super Tucano* are two of Brazil's most successful defence exports. The KC-390 has been ordered by Argentina, Chile, Colombia, the Czech Republic and Portugal, as well as by Brazil, while nine countries in Latin America, Africa and Southeast Asia have ordered the *Super Tucano*, with six receiving deliveries. One of Brasília's aims with the AGP stimulus package is to create more success stories like Embraer. The expectation surrounding Brazil's defence ambitions and its growing international influence have already brought a number of newcomers to the sector. The ABIMDE association saw a 35% rise in members from 2009–11.

Nevertheless, the steady growth of the domestic defence industry hinges on the health of the overall economy, and on how much Brazil sees state-of-the-art military hardware as necessary to sustain its international political ambitions. The absence of a conventional strategic threat in the region and, more recently, slow economic growth contribute to a reluctance to make defence spending a priority.

VENEZUELA

The display in July of the *Arpia* UAV, believed to have been developed as part of a 2007 Venezuela–Iran agreement to build UAVs, was a notable development. The year also saw further equipment-procurement and technical-training agreements between Venezuela and Russia. Military equipment continued to arrive from Russia as part of deals agreed in previous years and procurement continued to focus on military equipment designed mainly for conventional warfare. A Venezuelan delegation that visited Moscow in June negotiated an additional line of credit.

The main threats to Venezuela's security, however, come from its border areas – particularly the border with Colombia – in the form of drug trafficking. In March, Caracas announced *Operation Sentinel,* with a planned deployment of up to 15,000 troops on Venezuela's 4,500km borders with Brazil, Colombia and Guyana, to respond to the growth in drug gangs using Venezuelan territory to move drugs produced in Colombia. President Hugo Chávez is also worried about the growing number of homicides that might be connected to Colombian drug organisations operating inside Venezuela. Caracas showed willingness to cooperate with Bogotá over border security after 23 Colombian soldiers were killed by FARC rebels in two attacks near the frontier. On at least one occasion, on 21 May in Guajira, Colombian authorities said they were able to determine that the guerrillas had crossed the border from Venezuela. In contrast to previous years, Caracas expressed support for Bogotá and deployed 3,000 troops to the area, in addition to those already earmarked for the *Sentinel* deployment.

Chávez bolsters his position

Chávez, who graduated from the Venezuelan military academy in 1975, is aware that his army contemporaries are dwindling in number; his fellow graduates from the 1970s are starting to retire, leaving him without some of his most trusted men inside the military. Moreover, much media attention has recently been devoted to Chávez's health. He has been battling cancer for some years, and has visited Cuba for treatment on several occasions and faced a presidential election on 7 October 2012, in which he was victorious.

In April 2012, on the anniversary of a failed 2002 coup attempt against him, and immediately before another trip to Cuba's clinics, Chávez announced the establishment of an 'anti-coup command' (*comando especial antigolpe*) tasked with preventing anti-governmental moves by the 'bourgeoisie', long one of the principal targets – along with the 'imperial' United States – of Chávez's rhetoric. In the preceding six months, he had promoted to key positions two of his former co-conspirators in his own failed 1992 coup. One, Diosdado Cabello, became vice-president of the governing United Socialist Party (PSUV) in December 2011, and shortly thereafter president of the National Assembly; another, General Henry Rangel Silva, was promoted to defence minister in January 2012. Rangel Silva had told the Venezuelan newspaper *Últimas Noticias* that the military was 'married' to Chávez's political project and that the armed forces would not accept an opposition victory in the presidential election.

Chávez has been attempting to reinforce his position within the armed forces with new organisations, appointments and procurements. But his actions have also heightened divisions between his supporters and opponents. One of the most sensitive issues relates to the involvement of Cuban authorities in Venezuela's armed forces. According to a charge levelled in April by Venezuelan politician María Corina Machado, the 'Linkage and Cooperation Group' (GRUCE), led by Cuban General Ermio Hernández Rodríguez, frequently intervenes in the formulation of strategic documents, weapons acquisitions and officer education. Machado also claimed that the armed forces were working on 'Plan Sucre', a Cuban-assisted programme to shift the country's military doctrine towards irregular warfare should Venezuela suffer foreign invasion; presently this role is primarily played by the Bolivarian Militia.

The Bolivarian Militia

Chávez's establishment of the militia is another element of his 'coup-proofing' strategy. The militia is intended to comprise public-sector employees, students (especially those from military schools), and members of local councils, all officially affiliated with the PSUV. Militia operations are directed by the president through the Strategic Operational Command and, while it was ostensibly established to address a fear of external invasion, the militia is seen as the regime's insurance policy.

The militia gained official status as an arm of the military services in 2009, and is believed to be mostly a reserve force, with a full planned strength of 125,000 registered members. It is composed of two formations: the Territorial Militia, formed by volunteers registered with their local Bolivarian Militia, and the Combatant Corps, organised and trained by the General Command of the Bolivarian Militia. While reports by opposition media and legislators indicate that at least part of this contingent is trained in guerrilla tactics and the use of small arms and light weapons, the effectiveness of this training

– and the degree of special-to-arm and continuation training that these militia receive – is harder to gauge. This is particularly important in the context of an announcement by Chávez in early 2012 that some of the Russian-manufactured T-72 tanks delivered to Venezuela would go to equip a Bolivarian Militia tank battalion. It was unclear at time of writing whether the militia would assume the training, maintenance and storage liabilities associated with such equipment, or whether the regular armed forces would undertake these on the militia's behalf.

Defence economics

Ahead of the October elections, Chávez boosted government spending, particularly on major infrastructure and development projects as well as on social expenditure. Governmental outlays increased by 43% in nominal terms in 2012, reaching VEB297.8bn (US$57.2bn). Increased public infrastructure spending and a housing boom spurred growth in the construction sector, which expanded by 29.6% overall (with state construction activity alone increasing by 56.6% compared to the first quarter of 2011), although this overall increase masked a 10.6% contraction in private-sector construction activity. According to estimates by Bank of America Merrill Lynch, public spending on social programmes rose to VEB81.2bn (US$15.6bn) in the first quarter of 2012 compared to the same period in 2011 (a real terms increase of 17%). The Defence Ministry enjoyed the single-largest funding increase: the 2012 defence budget presented to the National Assembly in October 2011 was VEB21.3bn (US$6.09bn), a 108.2% jump over the VEB10.2bn (US$4.38bn) officially allocated in 2011 and some 7% of the entire 2012 budget – although with domestic inflation running at over 30%, the increase in real spending was closer to 60%. At least part of the increase stems from a 40% rise in military salaries announced by Chávez in October 2012. Opposition lawmakers had previously criticised Chávez for prioritising expensive military procurement programmes and postponing personnel salary increases. Venezuelan NGO Transparencia Venezuela, which conducts annual budget analyses, asserted that the procurement budget was seven times that allocated to internal law enforcement.

Defence procurement

Procurement/investment funding detailed in the budget amounts to VEB8.6bn (US$1.65bn) although, in common with previous years, new funding was also allocated during the year. August saw the defence minister announce a new $4bn line of credit from Moscow. Rangel Silva also specified an extra $1bn for the 'modernisation of the navy's infantry, the maintenance of Sukhois and the construction of a factory for military radios'. The timeframe in which the money will be spent remains unclear, but it was reported that the credits will be released in two equal amounts in 2012 and 2013. In addition, Venezuela has made extensive use of off-budget discretionary mechanisms to channel defence funding, via para-fiscal entities (which disburse revenues not covered by the legislative process) such as the Fondo de Desarrollo Nacional (FONDEN, or National Development Fund, created in 2005). This has been used to finance the building of ammunition and light-weapons plants, and the acquisition of coastal patrol vessels, fixed- and rotary-wing aviation, radar and electro-optic systems, as well as the construction of facilities for equipment maintenance, repair and overhaul. FONDEN has also disbursed funds for training and logistics support. In April 2012, the Fitch ratings agency estimated that extra-budgetary entities such as FONDEN, Venezuela's state-owned oil company PDVSA, the Joint China-Venezuela Fund (FCCV) and another long-term financing agreement between Venezuela and China accounted for 57% of central government outlays in 2011.

As in previous years, equipment from Russia, China and Iran comprised the majority of Venezuela's procurement programmes in 2012. It is believed that the new Russian credit line will be used for arms acquisitions and the maintenance of Russian-made Sukhoi aircraft (Venezuela has over 20 Su-30s) and helicopters (possibly Mi-17s). Some funding will also be used to purchase a further 50 T-72s, in addition to the 92 delivered in April 2011. The Girardot rifle factory being built with Russian assistance in Aragua state is key to plans for the Bolivarian Militia. At a visit to the plant, operated by the Venezuelan Military Industries Company Ltd (CAVIM), on 13 June, Chávez announced it had already produced 3,000 AK-103 assault rifles and that it would eventually be able to make 25,000 rifles per year. Chávez also announced in July that he remained interested in acquiring the Su-35 multi-role combat aircraft in 'coming years'. On 24 May, Chávez referred to the crucial role Russia now plays in his ambitious procurement programmes, saying that 'without Russia's support we wouldn't have the military power we now have'.

December 2011 saw another $4bn credit agreement, this time with China, now by far the largest external source of finance for Chávez's housing and infrastructure projects. In July 2012, Chávez announced that $500m of the loan would be spent on an unknown number of Chinese amphibious vehicles. The Chinese deal sparked criticism from the opposition, since it was secured with oil: PDVSA was to send 430,000 barrels a day of crude to China (during the first half of 2012 it was able to send just 410,000 a day). The opposition says it is unclear how the money is being spent and how much the country still owes China. During the election campaign, opposition candidate Henrique Capriles said he would scrap such deals if elected, saving $6.7bn annually.

Iran is another strategic defence partner. Although Venezuelan authorities state that the *Arpia* UAV displayed on 5 July is an indigenous system, it closely resembles the Iranian *Mohajer* 2 and is thought to be a product of this partnership, dating back to the 2007 agreement. (Chávez says that the programme includes 'inputs' from China and Russia.) CAVIM says that each *Arpia* system consists of a mobile control station, one launcher, and three air vehicles. The Spanish newspaper *ABC* claimed on 11 June 2012 that it had access to documents from an investigation by the attorney general of New York revealing that Venezuela paid $28m to Iran's Aerospace Industries Organizations (AIO), through Commerzbank in Frankfurt, to purchase up to 12 UAVs and construct a factory at Maracay air force base. The article also raised the possibility that the UAV programme might be a cover for a secret project of unknown design, due to the high contract value in relation to the number of air vehicles purchased, though the contract value could include Iranian technical support and training. The *Arpia*'s parade appearance a few weeks after the *ABC* article appeared suggests that CAVIM was happy to publicise the project. Though Chávez and CAVIM say that the UAVs only carry cameras and are intended for non-military tasks (including surveillance and reconnaissance), there have been conflicting media reports based on leaked documents, and the government has not specified the precise cost or which contract elements have involved foreign participation.

Antigua and Barbuda ATG

East Caribbean Dollar EC$		2011	2012	2013
GDP	EC$	3.02bn	3.17bn	
	US$	1.12bn	1.17bn	
per capita	US$	12,582	13,143	
Growth	%	-5.48	1.02	
Inflation	%	3.46	3.85	
Def bdgt	EC$	16m	18m	
	US$	6m	7m	
US$1=EC$		2.70	2.70	

Population   89,018

Age	0–14	15–19	20–24	25–29	30–64	65 plus
Male	12.8%	4.4%	3.8%	3.4%	20.0%	3.0%
Female	12.4%	4.4%	4.0%	3.9%	23.9%	4.0%

Capabilities

Due to the overall size and equipment of the force – notably the lack of an air component – it lacks broad military capability or international deployment capacity. Key duties include internal security, counter-narcotics and HA/DR tasks. Despite this, small numbers of personnel have contributed to PKO in both Haiti and Grenada. It is an active participant in regional security initiatives, and, in 2011, hosted the *Tradewinds* exercise, focusing on PKO and counter-illicit trafficking, including US and other regional states.

ACTIVE 180 (Army 130 Navy 50)
(all services form combined Antigua and Barbuda Defence Force)

RESERVE 80 (Joint 80)

ORGANISATIONS BY SERVICE

Army 130

Navy 50
EQUIPMENT BY TYPE
PATROL AND COASTAL COMBATANTS • PB 2: 1 *Dauntless*; 1 *Swift*

FOREIGN FORCES

United States US Strategic Command: 1 detection and tracking radar at Antigua Air Station

Argentina ARG

Argentine Peso P		2011	2012	2013
GDP	P	1.84tr	2.2tr	
	US$	444.61bn	474.81bn	
per capita	US$	10,538	11,253	
Growth	%	8.87	2.59	
Inflation	%	9.78	9.86	
Def bdgt[a]	P	16.8bn	19.7bn	
	US$	4.07bn	4.26bn	
US$1=P		4.14	4.62	

[a] Excludes funds allocated to Interior Security

Population   42,192,494

Age	0–14	15–19	20–24	25–29	30–64	65 plus
Male	12.9%	4.0%	4.1%	3.8%	19.8%	4.6%
Female	12.3%	3.9%	3.9%	3.8%	20.2%	6.5%

Capabilities

The military remains structured predominantly for conventional state-on-state conflict, despite a reduction in tensions with neighbouring states in recent years. There is also a growing emphasis on counter-narcotics operations. The armed forces are going through a period of reform, though an intended complementary re-equipment programme has suffered from inadequate funding. During the course of the last 12 months, the government has also renewed its political campaign to try to wrest sovereignty of the Falklands Islands from the UK. Armed forces restructuring is intended to trade overall quantity for improved capability, since substantial elements of the military's equipment inventory is increasingly aged and in need of replacement. Army procurement projects include the upgrade of its TAM medium tank along with replacement of elements of its light armoured vehicles fleet. The navy continues to harbour ambitions to revamp some of its fleet, and to upgrade naval aviation, where it operates a number of mature types. The air force is also faced with an ageing inventory with its combat fleet dependent on *Mirage/Dagger* and *Skyhawk* aircraft. The armed forces have a modest capacity for power projection with limited amphibious and tactical airlift capability. Morale within the services is likely to be at least adequate.

ACTIVE 73,100 (Army 38,500 Navy 20,000 Air 14,600) Paramilitary 31,250

ORGANISATIONS BY SERVICE

Army 38,500; 7,000 civilian
Regt and gp are usually bn-sized
FORCES BY ROLE
SPECIAL FORCES
  1 SF gp
MANOEUVRE
  Mechanised
  1 (1st) div (1 armd bde (4 tk regt, 1 mech inf regt, 1 SP arty gp, 1 cbt engr bn, 1 int coy, 1 sigs coy, 1 log coy),

1 jungle bde (3 jungle inf regt, 1 arty gp, 1 engr bn, 1 int coy, 1 sigs coy, 1 log coy, 1 med coy), 2 engr bn, 1 sigs bn, 1 log coy)

1 (3rd) div (1 mech bde (1 armd recce regt, 1 tk regt, 2 mech inf regt,1 SP arty gp, 1 cbt engr bn, 1 int coy, 1 sigs coy, 1 log coy), 1 mech bde (1 armd recce tp, 1 tk regt, 2 mech inf regt, 1 SP arty gp, 1 cbt engr bn, 1 int coy, 1 sigs coy, 1 log coy), 1 int bn, 1 sigs bn, 1 log coy)

1 (Rapid Deployment) force (1 armd bde (1 recce sqn, 3 tk regt, 1 mech inf regt, 1 SP arty gp, 1 cbt engr coy, 1 int coy, 1 sigs coy, 1 log coy), 1 mech bde (1 armd recce regt, 3 mech inf regt, 1 arty gp, 1 cbt engr coy, 1 int coy, 1 sigs coy,1 log coy), 1 AB bde (1 recce tp, 2 para regt, 1 arty gp, 1 cbt engr coy, 1 sigs coy, 1 log coy), 1 AD gp (2 AD bn))

Light

1 mot cav regt (presidential escort)

Air Manoeuvre

1 air aslt regt

Mountain

1 (2nd) div (2 mtn inf bde (1 armd recce regt, 3 mtn inf regt, 2 arty gp, 1 cbt engr bn, 1 sigs coy, 1 log coy), 1 mtn inf bde (1 armd recce bn, 2 mtn inf regt, 1 jungle inf regt, 2 arty gp, 1 cbt engr bn, 1 construction coy, 1 log coy), 1 AD gp, 1 sigs bn)

Aviation

1 avn gp (bde)

COMBAT SUPPORT

1 arty gp (bn)

1 engr bn

1 sigs gp (1 EW bn, 1 sigs bn, 1 maint bn)

1 sigs bn

1 sigs coy

COMBAT SERVICE SUPPORT

5 maint bn

EQUIPMENT BY TYPE

MBT 213: 207 TAM, 6 TAM S21

LT TK 123: 112 SK-105A1 *Kuerassier;* 6 SK-105A2 *Kuerassier;* 5 *Patagón*

RECCE 81: 47 AML-90; 34 M1025A2 HMMWV

AIFV 377: 263 VCTP (incl variants); 114 M113A2 (20mm cannon)

APC (T) 294: 70 M113 A1-ACAV; 224 M113A2

ARTY 1,103

SP 155mm 37: 20 Mk F3; 17 VCA 155 *Palmaria*

TOWED 179: **105mm** 70 M-56 (Oto Melara); **155mm** 109: 25 M-77 *CITEFA*/M-81 *CITEFA*; 84 SOFMA L-33

MRL 105mm 4 SLAM *Pampero*

MOR 883: **81mm** 492; **120mm** 353 *Brandt*

SP 38: 25 M106A2; 13 TAM-VCTM

AT

MSL • SP 3 HMMWV with total of 18 TOW-2A

RCL 150 M-1968

RL 78mm MARA

AIRCRAFT

ISR 1+ OV-1D *Mohawk*

TPT 18 Medium 3 G-222; **Light** 15: 1 Beech 80 *Queen Air*; 1 C-212-200 *Aviocar*; 3 Cessna 207 *Stationair*; 1 Cessna 500 *Citation* (survey); 2 DHC-6 *Twin Otter*; 3 SA-226 *Merlin IIIA*; 3 SA-226AT *Merlin IVA*; 1 Sabreliner 75A (*Gaviao* 75A)

TRG 5 T-41 *Mescalero*

HELICOPTERS

MRH 4 SA315B *Lama*

TPT 51 **Medium** 3 AS332B *Super Puma* **Light** 43: 1 Bell 212; 30 Bell 205 (UH-1H *Iroquois* - 6 armed); 3 Bell 206B3; 9 UH-1H-II *Huey* II

TRG 8 UH-12E

AD

SAM 6 RBS -70

GUNS • TOWED 411: **20mm** 230 GAI-B01; **30mm** 21 HS L81; **35mm** 12 GDF Oerlikon (*Skyguard* fire control); **40mm** 148: 24 L/60 training, 40 in store; 76 L/60; 8 L/70

RADAR • AD RADAR 11: 5 Cardion AN/TPS-44; 6 *Skyguard*

LAND 18+: M113 A1GE *Green Archer* (mor); 18 RATRAS (veh, arty)

ARV *Greif*

Navy 20,000; 7,200 civilian

Commands: Surface Fleet, Submarines, Naval Avn, Marines

EQUIPMENT BY TYPE

SUBMARINES • TACTICAL • SSK 3:

1 *Salta* (GER T-209/1200) with 8 single 533mm TT with Mk 37/SST-4 HWT

2 *Santa Cruz* (GER TR-1700) with 6 single 533mm TT with SST-4 HWT

PRINCIPAL SURFACE COMBATANTS 11

DESTROYERS 5:

DDGHM 4 *Almirante Brown* (GER MEKO 360) with 2 quad lnchr with MM-40 *Exocet* AShM, 2 triple B515 *ILAS*-3 324mm with A244 LWT, 1 127mm gun, (capacity 1 AS555 *Fennec*/SA316B *Alouette* III hel)

DDH 1 *Hercules* (UK Type-42 - utilised as a fast troop transport ship), with 1 114mm gun, (capacity 1 SH-3H *Sea King* hel)

FRIGATES • FFGHM 6:

6 *Espora* (GER MEKO 140) with 2 twin lnchr with MM-38 *Exocet* AShM, 2 triple B515 *ILAS*-3 324mm ASTT with A244 LWT, 1 76mm gun (capacity either 1 SA319 *Alouette* III hel or 1 AS555 *Fennec* hel)

PATROL AND COASTAL COMBATANTS 17

CORVETTES • FSG 3 *Drummond* (FRA A-69) with 2 twin lnchr with MM-38 *Exocet* AShM, 2 triple Mk32 324mm ASTT with A244 LWT, 1 100mm gun

PSO 3:

2 *Irigoyen* (US *Cherokee* AT);

1 *Teniente Olivieri* (ex-US oilfield tug)

PCO 3:

2 *Murature* (US *King* - trg/river patrol role) with 3 105mm gun

1 *Sobral* (US *Sotoyomo* AT)

PCGT 1 *Interpida* (GER Lurssen 45m) with 2 single lnchr with MM-38 *Exocet* AShM, 2 single 533mm TT with SST-4 HWT, 1 76mm gun

PCT 1 *Interpida* (GER Lurssen 45m) with 2 single 533mm TT with SST-4 HWT, 1 76mm gun

PB 6: 4 *Baradero* (*Dabur*); 2 *Point*

AMPHIBIOUS 18 LCVP

LOGISTICS AND SUPPORT 12

AOR 1 *Patagonia* (FRA *Durance*) with 1 hel platform

Latin America and the Caribbean

AORL 1 *Ingeniero Julio Krause*
AK 3 *Costa Sur*
AGOR 1 *Commodoro Rivadavia*
AGHS 1 *Puerto Deseado* (ice breaking capability, used for polar research)
AGB 1 *Almirante Irizar*
ABU 3 *Red*
AXS 1 *Libertad* (held in custody in Ghana in late 2012 owing to an international dispute over debt default)

Naval Aviation 2,000

AIRCRAFT 23 combat capable
  FGA 2 *Super Etendard* (9 more in store)
  ATK 1 *AU-23 Turbo-Porter*
  ASW 10: 4 S-2T *Tracker*; 6 P-3B *Orion*
  TPT 9 **Light** 7 Beech 200F/M *King Air* **PAX** 2 F-28 *Fellowship*
  TRG 10 T-34C *Turbo Mentor**
HELICOPTERS
  ASW 6 SH-3H (ASH-3H) *Sea King*
  MRH 4 AS555 *Fennec*
  TPT • Medium 2 UH-3H *Sea King*
MSL
  AAM • IR AAM R-550 *Magic*
  ASM AS-25K CITEFA *Martin Pescador*‡
  AShM AM-39 *Exocet*

Marines 2,500

FORCES BY ROLE
MANOEUVRE
  Amphibious
  1 (fleet) force (1 cdo gp, 1 (AAV) amph bn, 1 mne bn, 1 arty bn, 1 ADA bn)
  1 (fleet) force (2 mne bn, 2 navy det)
  1 force (1 mne bn)
EQUIPMENT BY TYPE
RECCE 52: 12 ERC-90F *Sagaie*; 40 M1097 HMMWV
APC (W) 24 Panhard VCR
AAV 17: 10 LARC-5; 7 LVTP-7
ARTY 100
  TOWED 105mm 18: 6 M101; 12 Model 56 pack howitzer
  MOR 82: 70 **81mm**; 12 **120mm**
AT
  MSL • MANPATS 50 *Cobra*/RB-53 *Bantam*
  RCL 105mm 30 M-1974 FMK-1
  RL 89mm 60 M-20
AD
  SAM 6 RBS-70
  GUNS 30mm 10 HS-816; **35mm** GDF-001

ARV AAVR7 Air Force 14,600; 6,900 civilian

4 Major Comds – Air Operations, Personnel, Air Regions, Logistics, 8 air bde

Air Operations Command

FORCES BY ROLE
FIGHTER/GROUND ATTACK
  1 sqn with *Mirage* IIID/E (*Mirage* IIIDA/EA)
  1 sqn with *Nesher* S/T (*Dagger* A/B)

GROUND ATTACK
  2 sqn with A-4/OA-4 (A-4AR/OA-4AR) *Skyhawk*
  2 (tac air) sqn with IA-58 *Pucara*; EMB-312 *Tucano* (on loan for border surv/interdiction)
ISR
  1 sqn with Learjet 35A
SEARCH & RESCUE/TRANSPORT HELICOPTER
  2 sqn with Bell 212; Bell 212 (UH-1N); SA-315B *Lama*
TANKER/TRANSPORT
  1 sqn with C-130B/E/H *Hercules*; KC-130H *Hercules*; L-100-30
TRANSPORT
  1 sqn with B-707
  1 sqn with DHC-6 *Twin Otter*; Saab 340
  1 sqn with F-27 *Friendship*
  1 sqn with F-28 *Fellowship*; Learjet 60
  1 (Pres) flt with B-757-23ER; S-70A *Black Hawk*, S-76B
TRAINING
  1 sqn with AT-63 *Pampa*
  1 sqn with EMB-312 *Tucano*
  1 sqn with T-34 *Mentor*
  1 sqn with Hughes 369
TRANSPORT HELICOPTER
  1 sqn with Bell 205 (UH-1H *Iroquois*)
  3 sqn with Hughes 369; MD-500; MD500D
EQUIPMENT BY TYPE
AIRCRAFT 108 combat capable
  FGA 18: 8 *Mirage* IIID/E (*Mirage* IIIDA/EA*)*; 7 *Nesher* S (*Dagger* A), 3 *Nesher* T (*Dagger* B);
  ATK 64: 30 A-4 (A-4AR) *Skyhawk*; 4 OA-4 (OA-4AR) *Skyhawk*; 21 IA-58 *Pucara*; 9 IA-58M *Pucara*
  ELINT 1 Cessna 210
  TKR 2 KC-130H *Hercules*
  TPT 37: **Medium** 7: 1 C-130B *Hercules*; 1 C-130E *Hercules*; 4 C-130H *Hercules*; 1 L-100-30 **Light** 22: 1 Cessna 310; 8 DHC-6 *Twin Otter*; 4 F-27 *Friendship*; 4 Learjet 35A (test and calibration); 1 Learjet 60; 4 Saab 340 **PAX** 8: 1 B-757-23ER; 7 F-28 *Fellowship*
  TRG 69: 20 AT-63 *Pampa** (LIFT); 19 EMB-312 *Tucano*; 6 EMB-312 *Tucano** (LIFT) (on loan from Brazil); 24 T-34 *Mentor*
HELICOPTERS
  MRH 25: 15 *Hughes* 369; 3 MD-500; 4 MD-500D; 3 SA315B *Lama*
  TPT 10 **Medium** 3: 2 Mi-171E (3 more on order); 1 S-70A *Black Hawk* **Light** 8: 7 Bell 212; 1 S-76B
MSL
  AAM • IR AIM-9L *Sidewinder*; R-550 *Magic*; *Shafrir* II ‡
AD
  GUNS 88: **20mm**: 86 Oerlikon/Rh-202 with 9 Elta EL/M-2106 radar; **35mm**: 2 Oerlikon GDF-001 with *Skyguard* radar
RADAR 6: 5 AN/TPS-43; 1 BPS-1000

Paramilitary 31,250

Gendarmerie 18,000

Ministry of Interior

FORCES BY ROLE

COMMAND
  5 regional comd
MANOEUVRE
  Other
  16 paramilitary bn
EQUIPMENT BY TYPE
RECCE S52 *Shorland*
APC (W) 87: 47 *Grenadier*; 40 UR-416
ARTY • MOR 81mm
AIRCRAFT
  TPT • Light 12: 3 Cessna 152; 3 Cessna 206; 1 Cessna 336; 1 PA-28 *Cherokee*; 2 PC-6B *Turbo-Porter*; 2 PC-12
HELICOPTERS
  MRH 2 MD-500C
  TPT • Light 16: 5 Bell 205 (UH-1H *Iroquois*); 7 AS350 *Ecureuil*; 1 EC135; 3 R-44 *Raven* II
  TRG 1 S-300C

Prefectura Naval (Coast Guard) 13,250

PATROL AND COASTAL COMBATANTS 55
  PCO 6: 1 *Delfin*; 5 *Mantilla* (F30 *Halcón*)
  PCC 1 *Mandubi*
  PB 47: 1 *Dorado*; 25 *Estrellemar*; 2 *Lynch* (US *Cape*); 18 *Mar del Plata* (Z-28); 1 *Surel*
  PBR 1 *Tonina*
LOGISTICS & SUPPORT • AX 4
AIRCRAFT
  TPT • Light 5 C-212 *Aviocar*
HELICOPTERS
  SAR 3 AS565MA *Panther*
  MRH 1 AS365 *Dauphin 2*
  TPT 4 **Medium** 2 SA330L (AS330L) *Puma* **Light** 2 AS355 *Ecureuil* II
  TRG 4 S-300C

DEPLOYMENT

CYPRUS
UN • UNFICYP 265; 2 inf coy; 1 hel pl; 2 Bell 212

HAITI
UN • MINUSTAH 723; 1 inf bn; 1 hel coy; 1 spt coy; 1 fd hospital

MIDDLE EAST
UN • UNTSO 3 obs

WESTERN SAHARA
UN • MINURSO 3 obs

Bahamas BHS

Bahamian Dollar B$		2011	2012	2013
GDP	B$	7.79bn	8.25bn	
	US$	7.79bn	8.25bn	
per capita	US$	24,638	26,093	
Growth	%	1.63	2.50	
Inflation	%	2.50	2.00	
Def exp	B$	50m		
	US$	50m		
Def bdgt	B$	51m	57m	64m
	US$	51m	57m	
FMA (US)	US$			
US$1=B$		1.00	1.00	

Population   316,182

Age	0–14	15–19	20–24	25–29	30–64	65 plus
Male	12.2%	4.5%	4.3%	3.9%	21.5%	2.5%
Female	11.8%	4.4%	4.2%	3.8%	22.8%	4.0%

Capabilities

The Bahamas Defence Force is a coast guard-type organisation with some amphibious capability provided by attached infantry battalion; it has a limited territorial defence role, but has not engaged in active combat in the past 30 years. The country is a regular participant in the US Southcom-sponsored *Tradewinds* exercise series.

ACTIVE 850

ORGANISATIONS BY SERVICE

Royal Bahamian Defence Force 850

FORCES BY ROLE
MANOEUVRE
  Amphibious
  1 mne coy (incl marines with internal and base security duties)
EQUIPMENT BY TYPE
PATROL AND COASTAL COMBATANTS 10 (additional 8 patrol boats under 10 tonnes)
  PCC 2 *Bahamas*
  PB 8: 2 *Dauntless*; 1 *Eleuthera*; 1 *Protector*; 2 Sea Ark 12m; 2 Sea Ark 15m
AIRCRAFT • TPT • Light 3: 1 Beech A350 *King Air*; 1 Cessna 208 *Caravan*; 1 P-68 *Observer*

FOREIGN FORCES

Guyana Navy: Base located at New Providence Island

Barbados BRB

Barbados Dollar B$		2011	2012	2013
GDP	B$	8.63bn	9.07bn	
	US$	4.31bn	4.53bn	
per capita	US$	14,979	15,744	
Growth	%	0.56	0.70	
Inflation	%	9.43	8.16	
Def bdgt	B$	61m	76m	
	US$	30m	38m	
US$1=B$		2.00	2.00	

a Defence & security expenditure

Population	287,733

Age	0–14	15–19	20–24	25–29	30–64	65 plus
Male	9.4%	3.3%	3.7%	3.7%	24.4%	3.9%
Female	9.4%	3.3%	3.6%	3.7%	25.6%	6.1%

Capabilities

The Barbados Defence Force is a small coast guard- and constabulary-style force with a very limited regional deployment capability for PKO within the Caribbean. Its primary role has been to provide support to the Royal Barbados Police Force and to participate in disaster-relief efforts. In recent years, it has suffered from recruitment problems. The country is a regular participant in the US Southcom-sponsored *Tradewinds* exercise series, hosting the 2012 iteration.

ACTIVE 610 (Army 500 Navy 110)

RESERVE 430 (Joint 430)

ORGANISATIONS BY SERVICE

Army 500

FORCES BY ROLE
MANOEUVRE
Light
1 inf bn (cadre)

Navy 110

HQ located at HMBS Pelican, Spring Garden
EQUIPMENT BY TYPE
PATROL AND COASTAL COMBATANTS • PB 6: 1 *Dauntless*; 2 *Enterprise*; 3 *Trident* (Damen Stan Patrol 4207)
LOGISTICS & SUPPORT • AX 1

Belize BLZ

Belize Dollar BZ$		2011	2012	2013
GDP	BZ$	2.89bn	3.04bn	
	US$	1.45bn	1.52bn	
per capita	US$	4,425	4,638	
Growth	%	1.96	2.29	
Inflation	%	1.49	2.18	
Def bdgt[a]		31m	32m	
	US$	16m	16m	
FMA (US)	US$	0.2m	0.2m	0.85m
US$1=BZ$		2.00	2.00	

a Excludes funds allocated to Coast Guard

Population	327,719

Age	0–14	15–19	20–24	25–29	30–64	65 plus
Male	18.5%	5.6%	5.2%	4.5%	15.2%	1.7%
Female	17.8%	5.4%	5.0%	4.3%	15.0%	1.9%

Capabilities

The Belize Defence Force has both national sovereignty and internal-security roles, principally countering narcotics smuggling. It also deployed combat engineers to assist Haiti in 2010. Although well-trained in jungle operations, the size of Belize, and the relatively small size of the BDF, means that its capabilities are limited to countering relatively minor threats. British infantry units used training areas in Belize for jungle training until this was halted in 2011; however, some British units, generally at company-level, still train in-country.

ACTIVE ε1,050 (Army ε1,050)

RESERVE 700 (Joint 700)

ORGANISATIONS BY SERVICE

Army ε1,050

FORCES BY ROLE
MANOEUVRE
Light
3 inf bn (each 3 inf coy)
COMBAT SERVICE SUPPORT
1 spt gp
EQUIPMENT BY TYPE
MOR 81mm 6
RCL 84mm 8 *Carl Gustav*

Air Wing

EQUIPMENT BY TYPE
AIRCRAFT
TPT • Light 3: 1 BN-2A *Defender*; 1 BN-2B *Defender*; 1 Cessna 182 *Skylane*
TRG 1 T-67M-200 *Firefly*

Reserve

FORCES BY ROLE
MANOEUVRE
Light
3 inf coy

FOREIGN FORCES

United Kingdom Army 10

Bolivia BOL

Bolivian Boliviano B		2011	2012	2013
GDP	B	166.13bn	183.5bn	
	US$	24.06bn	26,75bn	
per capita	US$	2,338	2,600	
Growth	%	5.17	5.00	
Inflation	%	9.88	4.75	
Def bdgt	B	2.05bn	2.3bn	
	US$	298m	336m	
US$1=B		6.90	6.86	

Population	10,290,003

Age	0–14	15–19	20–24	25–29	30–64	65 plus
Male	17.4%	5.2%	4.9%	4.5%	15.3%	2.1%
Female	16.8%	5.1%	4.8%	4.5%	16.7%	2.6%

Capabilities

The Bolivian military is in the midst of restructuring. The armed forces are tasked with providing territorial integrity and renewed emphasis on border security. Drug trafficking is a significant concern for the Bolivian government, with emphasis being placed on improving the military's ability to counter the narcotics trade. The military has no credible independent power-projection capacity, and such a capability would be contrary to the government's stated defence policy. The army and air force are receiving new or upgraded equipment, though in small numbers. Notable purchases include six Chinese H425 medium transport helicopters for the army, which will provide the service with an organic rotary-wing capacity. Deliveries are due 2012–13. China was also the source of the air force's six K-8VB jet trainer and light attack aircraft, delivery of which was completed in 2011. Tactical airlift is provided by a variety of aircraft, including a handful of C-130 *Hercules*. The armed forces have taken part in recent UN peacekeeping missions.

**ACTIVE 46,100 (Army 34,800 Navy 4,800 Air 6,500)
Paramilitary 37,100**

ORGANISATIONS BY SERVICE

Army 9,800; 25,000 conscript (total 34,800)

FORCES BY ROLE
COMMAND
6 mil region HQ
10 div HQ

SPECIAL FORCES
3 SF regt
MANOEUVRE
Reconnaissance
1 mot cav gp
Armoured
1 armd bn
Mechanised
1 mech cav regt
2 mech inf regt
Light
1 (aslt) cav gp
5 (horsed) cav gp
3 mot inf regt
21 inf regt
1 (Presidential Guard) inf regt
Air Manoeuvre
2 AB regt (bn)
Aviation
2 avn coy
COMBAT SUPPORT
6 arty regt (bn)
1 ADA regt
6 engr bn
1 MP bn
1 sigs bn
COMBAT SERVICE SUPPORT
2 log bn
EQUIPMENT BY TYPE
LT TK 54: 36 SK-105A1 *Kuerassier*; 18 SK-105A2 *Kuerassier*
RECCE 24 EE-9 *Cascavel*
APC 152+
  APC (T) 87+: 50+ M113, 37 M9 half-track
  APC (W) 61: 24 EE-11 *Urutu*; 22 MOWAG *Roland*; 15 V-100 *Commando*
ARTY 311+
  TOWED 61: **105mm** 25 M101A1; **122mm** 36 M-30 (M-1938)
  MOR 250+: **81mm** 250 M29; Type-W87; **107mm** M30; **120mm** M120
AT • MSL• MANPATS 50+ HJ-8 (2 SP on *Koyak*)
  RCL 106mm M40A1; **90mm** M67
  RL 89mm 200+ M20
AIRCRAFT
  TPT • Light 3: 1 Beech 90 *King Air*; 1 C-212 *Aviocar*; 1 Cessna 210 *Centurion*
AD • GUNS • TOWED 37mm 18 Type-65
ARV 4 4K-4FA-SB20 *Greif*; M578

Navy 4,800

Organised into six naval districts with HQ located at Puerto Guayaramerín

EQUIPMENT BY TYPE
PATROL AND COASTAL COMBATANTS • PBR 3: 1 *Santa Cruz*; 2 others (additional five patrol boats and 30-40 small craft under 10 tonnes)
LOGISTICS AND SUPPORT 19:
  AH 2
  YFL 10 (river transports)
  AG 7

Marines 1,700 (incl 1,000 Naval Military Police)

FORCES BY ROLE

MANOEUVRE

Mechanised

1 mech inf bn

Amphibious

6 mne bn (1 in each Naval District)

COMBAT SUPPORT

4 (naval) MP bn

Air Force 6,500 (incl conscripts)

FORCES BY ROLE

GROUND ATTACK

2 sqn with AT-33AN *Shooting Star*

1 sqn with K-8WB *Karakorum*

ISR

1 sqn with Cessna 206; Cessna 402; Learjet 25B/25D (secondary VIP role)

SEARCH & RESCUE

1 sqn with AS332B *Super Puma*; AS350B3 *Ecureuil*; EC145

TRANSPORT

1 sqn with BAe-146-100; CV-580; MA60

1 (TAB) sqn with C-130A *Hercules*; DC-10

1 sqn with C-130B/H *Hercules*

1 sqn with F-27-400M *Troopship*

1 (VIP) sqn with Beech 90 *King Air*; Beech 200 *King Air* Beech 1900; *Falcon* 900EX; *Sabreliner* 60

6 sqn with Cessna 152/206; IAI-201 *Arava*; PA-32 *Saratoga*; PA-34 *Seneca*

TRAINING

1 sqn with DA40; T-25

1 sqn with Cessna 152/172

1 sqn with PC-7 *Turbo Trainer*

1 hel sqn with R-44 *Raven* II

TRANSPORT HELICOPTER

1 (anti-drug) sqn with Bell 205 (UH-1H *Iroquois*)

AIR DEFENCE

1 regt with Oerlikon; Type-65

EQUIPMENT BY TYPE

AIRCRAFT 39 combat capable

ATK 15 AT-33AN *Shooting Star*

TPT 81: **Medium** 4: 1 C-130A *Hercules*; 2 C-130B *Hercules*; 1 C-130H *Hercules* **Light** 68: 1 *Aero-Commander* 690; 3 Beech 90 *King Air*; 2 Beech 200 *King Air*; 1 Beech 1900; 3 C-212-100; 10 Cessna 152; 2 Cessna 172; 19 Cessna 206; 1 Cessna 402; 1 CV-580; 9 DA40; 3 F-27-400M *Troopship*; 4 IAI-201 *Arava*; 2 Learjet 25B/D; 2 MA60; 1 PA-32 *Saratoga*; 3 PA-34 *Seneca*; 1 *Sabreliner* 60 **PAX** 9: 1 B-737-200; 5 BAe-146-100; 2 DC-10; 1 *Falcon* 900EX (VIP)

TRG 24:; 6 K-8W *Karakorum**; 6 T-25; 18 PC-7 *Turbo Trainer**

HELICOPTERS

MRH 1 SA316 *Alouette* III

TPT 29 **Medium** 1 AS332B *Super Puma* **Light** 28: 2 AS350B3 *Ecureuil*; 19 Bell 205 (UH-1H *Iroquois*); 1 EC145 (2nd due by end 2012); 6 R-44 *Raven* II

AD•GUNS 18+: **20mm** Oerlikon; **37mm** 18 Type-65

Paramilitary 37,100+

National Police 31,100+

FORCES BY ROLE

MANOEUVRE

Other

27 frontier sy unit

9 paramilitary bde

2 (rapid action) paramilitary regt

Narcotics Police 6,000+

FOE (700) - Special Operations Forces

DEPLOYMENT

CÔTE D'IVOIRE

UN • UNOCI 3 obs

DEMOCRATIC REPUBLIC OF THE CONGO

UN • MONUSCO 9 obs

HAITI

UN • MINUSTAH 209; 1 mech inf coy

LIBERIA

UN • UNMIL 1; 2 obs

SOUTH SUDAN

UN • UNMISS 3 obs

SUDAN

UN • UNISFA 1; 3 obs

Brazil BRZ

Brazilian Real R		2011	2012	2013
GDP	R	4.14tr	4.46tr	
	US$	2.49tr	2.43tr	
per capita	US$	12,492	12,191	
Growth	%	2.73	1.47	
Inflation	%	6.64	5.23	
Def exp[a]	R	61.2bn		
	US$	36.8bn		
Def bdgt[a]	R	60.2bn	64.8bn	66.4bn
	US$	36.2bn	35.3bn	
US$1=R		1.66	1.84	

[a] Includes military pensions

Population   199,321,413

Age	0–14	15–19	20–24	25–29	30–64	65 plus
Male	12.6%	4.3%	4.3%	4.4%	20.8%	3.0%
Female	12.1%	4.1%	4.2%	4.4%	21.8%	4.1%

Capabilities

As South America's most capable military power, Brazil continues to develop its armed forces, with ambitions to enhance its power projection capability. A 2012 defence white paper built on the 2008 National Defence Strategy. Emerging areas highlighted by both included concerns of cyber security while the white paper also reinforced the importance Brazil attaches to its defence-industrial base, including securing technology access in defence procurements from the international community. The security of the vast Amazon region and the associated coastal waters remains a priority for the government as part of the military's broader role of assuring territorial integrity. Substantial recapitalisation of the equipment inventory is required to fully support the ambitions of the National Defence Strategy and the white paper. The army is in the midst of improving its heavy armour and protected mobility, while the navy is looking to develop its amphibious and blue water capabilities. The air force is again trying to update its combat aircraft fleet, with a decision on a fighter purchase expected now to be made by 2013. Airlift capabilities will be enhanced with the delivery of the KC-390 from domestic manufacturer Embraer. The type selected would provide a successor to the F-5. Emblematic of the navy's long-term blue water ambition, and the government's intent to see the country take a more global role commensurate with its economic strength, is the country's submarine development programme, intended to see conventional and nuclear-powered submarines enter service. The military exercises regularly, also participating in international exercises.

ACTIVE 318,500 (Army 190,000 Navy 59,000 Air 69,500) Paramilitary 395,000

RESERVE 1,340,000
Terms of service 12 months (can be extended to 18)

ORGANISATIONS BY SERVICE

Army 120,000; 70,000 conscript (total 190,000)
FORCES BY ROLE
COMMAND
7 mil comd HQ
12 mil region HQ
7 div HQ (2 with regional HQ)
SPECIAL FORCES
1 SF bde (1 SF bn, 1 cdo bn)
1 SF coy
MANOEUVRE
Reconaissance
3 mech cav regt
Armoured
2 (5th & 6th) armd bde (1 mech cav sqn, 2 armd bn, 2 armd inf bn, 1 SP arty bn, 1 engr bn, 1 sigs coy, 1 log bn)
Mechanised
3 (1st, 2nd & 4th) mech cav bde (1 armd cav bn, 3 mech cav bn, 1 arty bn, 1 engr coy, 1 sigs coy, 1 log bn)
1 (3rd) mech cav bde (1 armd cav bn, 2 mech cav bn, 1 arty bn, 1 engr coy, 1 sigs coy, 1 log bn)
Light
1 (3rd) mot inf bde (1 mech cav sqn, 2 mot inf bn, 1 inf bn, 1 arty bn, 1 engr coy, 1 sigs coy, 1 log bn)
1 (4th) mot inf bde (1 mech cav sqn, 1 mot inf bn, 1 inf bn, 1 mtn inf bn, 1 arty bn, 1 sigs coy, 1 log bn)

1 (7th) mot inf bde (3 mot inf bn, 1 arty bn)
1 (8th) mot inf bde (1 mech cav sqn, 3 mot inf bn, 1 arty bn, 1 log bn)
1 (10th) mot inf bde (1 mech cav sqn, 4 mot inf bn, 1 inf coy, 1 arty bn, 1 engr coy, 1 sigs coy)
1 (13th) mot inf bde (1 mot inf bn, 2 inf bn, 1 inf coy, 1 arty bn)
1 (14th) mot inf bde (1 mech cav sqn, 3 inf bn, 1 arty bn)
1 (15th) mot inf bde (3 mot inf bn, 1 arty bn, 1 engr coy, 1 log bn)
1 (11th) lt inf bde (1 mech cav regt, 3 inf bn, 1 arty bn, 1 engr coy, 1 sigs coy, 1 MP coy, 1 log bn)
11 inf bde
Air Manoeuvre
1 AB bde (1 cav sqn, 3 AB bn, 1 arty bn, 1 engr coy, 1 sigs coy, 1 log bn)
1 (12th) air mob bde (1 cav sqn, 3 air mob bn, 1 arty bn, 1 engr coy, 1 sigs coy, 1 log bn)
Jungle
1 (1st) jungle inf bde (1 mech cav sqn, 2 jungle inf bn, 1 arty bn)
3 (2nd, 16th & 17th) jungle inf bde (3 jungle inf bn)
1 (23rd) jungle inf bde (1 cav sqn, 4 jungle inf bn, 1 arty bn, 1 sigs coy, 1 log bn)
2 jungle inf bn
Other
1 (9th) mot trg bde (3 mot inf bn, 1 arty bn, 1 log bn)
1 (18th) sy bde (total 2 sy bn, 2 sy coy)
1 sy bn
7 sy coy
3 gd cav regt
1 gd inf bn
Aviation
1 avn bde (3 hel bn, 1 maint bn)
1 hel bn
COMBAT SUPPORT
3 SP arty bn
6 fd arty bn
1 MRL bn
1 ADA bde (5 ADA bn)
6 engr bn
1 EW coy
1 int coy
6 MP bn
3 MP coy
4 sigs bn
2 sigs coy
COMBAT SERVICE SUPPORT
1 engr gp (1 engr bn, 4 construction bn)
1 engr gp (4 construction bn, 1 construction coy)
2 construction bn
5 log bn
1 tpt bn
4 spt bn
EQUIPMENT BY TYPE
MBT 439: 128 *Leopard* 1A1BE; 220 *Leopard* 1A5BR; 91 M60A3/TTS
LT TK 152 M41B/C
RECCE 408 EE-9 *Cascavel*
APC 807

APC (T) 584 M113
APC (W) 223 EE-11 *Urutu*
ARTY 1,805
　SP 109: **105mm** 72 M7/108; **155mm** 37 M109A3
　TOWED 431
　　105mm 336: 233 M101/M102; 40 L-118 *Light Gun*; 63
　　Model 56 pack howitzer
　　155mm 95 M114
　MRL 20+: **70mm** SBAT-70; 20 ASTROS II
　MOR 1,245: **81mm** 1,168: 453 Royal Ordnance L-16, 715
　M936 AGR; **120mm** 77 M2
AT
　MSL • MANPATS 30: 18 *Eryx*; 12 *Milan*
　RCL 343: **106mm** 194 M40A1; **84mm** 149 *Carl Gustav*
HELICOPTERS
　MRH 49: 32 AS565 *Panther* (HM-1); 17 AS550U2 *Fennec*
　(HA-1 - armed)
　TPT 29 **Heavy** 2 EC725 *Super Cougar* (HM-4); **Medium**
　12: 8 AS532 *Cougar* (HM-3); 4 S-70A-36 *Black Hawk* (HM-
　2) **Light** 15 AS350 LI *Ecureuil* (HA-1)
AD
　MANPAD 53 9K38 *Igla* (SA-18 *Grouse*)
　GUNS 66: **35mm** 39 GDF-001 towed (some with *Super
　Fledermaus* radar); **40mm** 27 L/70 (some with BOFI)
　RADAR: 5 SABER M60
　AEV 4+: *Greif*; HART; 4+ *Leopard* 1; M578
　VLB 4+: XLP-10; 4 *Leopard* 1

Navy 59,000

FORCES BY ROLE
Organised into 9 districts with HQ I Rio de Janeiro, HQ II
Salvador, HQ III Natal, HQ IV Belém, HQ V Rio Grande,
HQ VI Ladario, HQ VII Brasilia, HQ VIII Sao Paulo, HQ
IX Manaus

EQUIPMENT BY TYPE
SUBMARINES • TACTICAL • SSK 5:
　4 *Tupi* (GER T-209/1400) with 8 single 533mm TT with
　MK 24 *Tigerfish* HWT
　1 *Tikuna* with 8 single 533mm TT with MK 24 *Tigerfish*
　HWT
PRINCIPAL SURFACE COMBATANTS 15
　AIRCRAFT CARRIERS • CV 1:
　　1 *Sao Paulo* (FRA *Clemenceau*) (capacity 15–18 A-4
　　Skyhawk atk ac; 4–6 SH-3D/A *Sea King* ASW hel; 3
　　AS355F/AS350BA *Ecureuil* hel; 2 AS532 *Cougar* hel)
　DESTROYERS • DDGHM 3
　　3 *Greenhaigh* (UK *Broadsword*, 1 low readiness) with 4
　　single lnchr with MM-40 *Exocet* AShM, 2 sextuple
　　lnchr with *Sea Wolf* SAM, 6 single 324mm ASTT with
　　Mk 46 LWT, (capacity 2 *Super Lynx* Mk21A hel)
　FRIGATES 11:
　　FFGHM 6 *Niteroi* with 2 twin lnchr with MM-40 *Exocet*
　　AShM, 1 octuple *Albatros* lnchr with *Aspide* SAM, 2
　　triple 324mm ASTT with Mk 46 LWT, 1 twin 375mm
　　A/S mor, 1 115mm gun, (capacity 1 *Super Lynx*
　　Mk21A hel)
　　FFGH 5:
　　　4 *Inhauma* with 2 twin lnchr with MM-40 *Exocet*
　　　AShM, 2 triple 324mm ASTT with Mk 46 LWT, 1
　　　115mm gun, (1 *Super Lynx* Mk21A hel)

　　　1 *Barroso* with 2 twin lnchr with MM-40 *Exocet*
　　　AShM, 2 triple 324mm ASTT with Mk 46 LWT, 1
　　　115mm gun, (capacity 1 *Super Lynx* Mk21A hel)
PATROL AND COASTAL COMBATANTS 44
　PSO 1 *Amazonas* (2 more vessels on order)
　PCO 7: 4 *Bracui* (UK *River*); 2 *Imperial Marinheiro* with 1
　76mm gun; 1 *Parnaiba* with 1 hel landing platform
　PCC 3 *Macaé* (4 additional vessels on order)
　PCR 5: 2 *Pedro Teixeira*; 3 *Roraima*
　PB 28: 12 *Grajau*; 6 *Marlim*; 6 *Piratini*; 4 *Tracker*
　(Marine Police)
MINE WARFARE • MINE COUNTERMEASURES •
MSC 6 *Aratu* (GER *Schutze*)
AMPHIBIOUS
　PRINCIPAL AMPHIBIOUS SHIPS • LSD 2:
　　2 *Ceara* (US *Thomaston*) (capacity either 21 LCM or 6
　　LCU; 345 troops)
　LANDING SHIPS 3:
　　LST 1 *Mattoso Maia* (US *Newport*) (capacity 3 LCVP; 1
　　LCPL; 400 troops)
　　LSLH 2: 1 *Garcia D'Avila* (UK *Sir Galahad*) (capacity 1
　　hel; 16 MBT; 340 troops); 1 *Almirante Saboia* (UK *Sir
　　Bedivere*) (capacity 1 med hel; 18 MBT; 340 troops)
　LANDING CRAFT 27: 3 LCU; 8 LCVP; 16 LCM
LOGISTICS AND SUPPORT 42
　AOR 2: 1 *Gastao Motta*; 1 *Marajo*
　ASR 1 *Felinto Perry* (NOR *Wildrake*)
　AG 2: 1 (troop carrier); 1 (river spt)
　AH 5: 2 *Oswaldo Cruz*; 1 *Dr Montenegro*; 1 *Tenente
　Maximianol*; 1 *Soares de Meirelles*
　AK 5
　AGOB 2: 1 *Ary Rongel*; 1 *Almirante Maximiano*
　AGSH 1 *Sirius*
　AGS 6: 1 *Aspirante Moura*; 1 *Cruzeiro do Sul*; 1 *Antares*; 3
　Amorim Do Valle (UK *Rover*)
　ABU 6: 1 *Almirante Graca Aranah* (lighthouse tender); 4
　Comandante Varella; 1 *Faroleiro Mario Seixas*
　ATF 5: 3 *Tritao*; 2 *Almirante Guihem*
　AP 2: 1 *Paraguassu*; 1 *Piraim* (river transports)
　AX 1 *Brasil*
　AXL 3 *Nascimento*
　AXS 1

Naval Aviation 2,500

FORCES BY ROLE
GROUND ATTACK
　1 sqn with AF-1 (A-4/4M) *Skyhawk*; AF-1 (TA-4/4M)
　Skyhawk
ANTI SURFACE WARFARE
　1 sqn with *Super Lynx* Mk21A
ANTI SUBMARINE WARFARE
　1 sqn with SH-3G/H *Sea King*; S-70B *Seahawk* (MH-16)
TRAINING
　1 sqn with Bell 206B3 *Jet Ranger* III
TRANSPORT HELICOPTER
　1 sqn with AS332 *Super Puma*; AS532 *Cougar*
　4 sqn with AS350 *Ecureuil* (armed); AS355 *Ecureuil* II
　(armed)

EQUIPMENT BY TYPE

AIRCRAFT 12 combat capable

ATK 9 AF-1 (A-4/4M) *Skyhawk*; 3 AF-1A (TA-4/4M) *Skyhawk*

HELICOPTERS

ASW 18: 12 *Super Lynx* Mk21A; 4 SH-3G/H *Sea King*; 2 S-70B *Seahawk* (MH-16 - 2 more to be delivered)

TPT 50: **Heavy** 2 EC725 *Super Cougar* (UH-15); **Medium** 7: 5 AS332 *Super Puma*; 2 AS532 *Cougar* **Light** 41: 18 AS350 *Ecureuil* (armed); 8 AS355 *Ecureuil* II (armed); 15 Bell 206B3 *Jet Ranger* III

MSL • AShM: AM-39 *Exocet; Sea Skua*

Marines 15,000

FORCES BY ROLE

SPECIAL FORCES

1 SF bn

MANOEUVRE

Amphibious

1 (Fleet Force) div (1 comd bn, 3 inf bn, 1 arty gp)

8+ (regional) mne gp

3 mne inf bn

COMBAT SUPPORT

1 engr bn

EQUIPMENT BY TYPE

LT TK 18 SK-105 *Kuerassier*

APC 45

APC (T) 30 M113

APC (W) 15 *Piranha* IIIC (additional 15 on order)

AAV 25: 13 AAV-7A1; 12 LVTP-7

ARTY 59

TOWED 41: **105mm** 33: 18 L118 Light Gun; 15 M101; **155mm** 8 M114

MOR 18 **81mm**

AT

MSL• **MANPATS** RB-56 *Bill*

RL 89mm M20

AD • GUNS 40mm 6 L/70 (with BOFI)

AEV 1 AAVR7

Air Force 69,500

Brazilian air space is divided into 7 air regions, each of which is responsible for its designated air bases. Air assets are divided among four designated air forces (I, II, III & V) for operations (IV Air Force temporarily deactivated).

FORCES BY ROLE

FIGHTER

1 gp with *Mirage* 2000B/C

4 sqn with F-5EM/FM *Tiger* II

FIGHTER/GROUND ATTACK

2 sqn with AMX (A-1A/B)

GROUND ATTACK/ISR

4 sqn with EMB-314 *Super Tucano* (A-29A/B)*

MARITIME PATROL

1 sqn with EMB-111 (P-95A/P-95B)/P-3AM *Orion*

3 sqn with EMB-111 (P-95A/P-95B)

ISR

1 sqn with AMX-R (RA-1)*

1 sqn with Learjet 35 (R-35A); EMB-110B (R-95)

AIRBORNE EARLY WARNING & CONTROL

1 sqn with EMB-145RS (R-99); EMB-145SA (E-99)

TANKER/TRANSPORT

1 sqn with C-130H/KC-130H *Hercules*

TANKER

1 sqn with KC-137

TRANSPORT

1 VIP sqn with A319 (VC-1A); EMB-190 (VC-2); AS332M *Super Puma* (VH-34); AS355 *Ecureuil* II (VH-55); EC635 (VH-35)

1 VIP sqn with EMB-135BJ (VC-99B); ERJ-135LR (VC-99C); ERJ-145LR (VC-99A); Learjet 35A (VU-35); Learjet 55C (VU-55C)

2 sqn with C-130E/H *Hercules*

2 sqn with C-295M (C-105A)

7 (regional) sqn with Cessna 208/208B (C-98); Cessna 208-G1000 (C-98A); EMB-110 (C-95); EMB-120 (C-97)

1 sqn with ERJ-145 (C-99A)

1 sqn with EMB-120RT (VC-97), EMB-121 (VU-9)

TRAINING

1 sqn with EMB-110 (C-95)

2 sqn with EMB-312 *Tucano* (T-27) (incl 1 air show sqn)

1 sqn with T-25A/C

ATTACK HELICOPTER

1 sqn with Mi-35M *Hind* (AH-2)

TRANSPORT HELICOPTER

1 sqn with AS332M *Super Puma* (H-34)

1 sqn with AS350B *Ecureuil* (H-50); AS355 *Ecureuil* II (H-55)

1 sqn with Bell 205 (H-1H); EC725 *Super Cougar* (H-36)

2 sqn with UH-60L *Black Hawk* (H-60L)

ISR UAV

1 sqn with *Hermes* 450

EQUIPMENT BY TYPE

AIRCRAFT 234 combat aircraft

FTR 57: 6 F-5E *Tiger* II; 51 F-5EM/FM *Tiger* II

FGA 61: 38 AMX (A-1); 11 AMX-T (A-1B); 12 *Mirage* 2000B/C

ASW 9 P-3AM *Orion* (delivery in progress)

MP 19: 10 EMB-111 (P-95A *Bandeirulha*)*; 9 EMB-111 (P-95B *Bandeirulha*)*

ISR: 8: 4 AMX-R (RA-1)*; 4 EMB-110B (R-95)

ELINT 6: 3 EMB-145RS (R-99); 3 Learjet 35A (R-35A)

AEW&C 5 EMB-145SA (E-99)

SAR 5: 4 EMB-110 (SC-95B), 1 SC-130E *Hercules*

TKR/TPT 5: 2 KC-130H; 3 KC-137 (1 more in store)

TPT 199 **Medium** 20: 4 C-130E *Hercules*; 16 C-130H *Hercules*; **Light** 172: 12 C-295M (C-105A); 7 Cessna 208 (C-98); 9 Cessna 208B (C-98); 13 Cessna 208-G1000 (C-98A); 53 EMB-110 (C-95A/B/C/M); 16 EMB-120 (C-97); 4 EMB-120RT (VC-97); 5 EMB-121 (VU-9); 7 EMB-135BJ (VC-99B); 3 EMB-201R *Ipanema* (G-19); 2 EMB-202A *Ipanema* (G-19A); 2 ERJ-135LR (VC-99C); 7 ERJ-145 (C-99A); 1 ERJ-145LR (VC-99A); 9 Learjet 35A (VU-35); 1 Learjet 55C (VU-55); 9 PA-34 *Seneca* (U-7); 12 U-42 *Regente* **PAX** 7: 1 A319 (VC-1A); 2 EMB-190 (VC-2); 4 Hawker 800XP (EU-93A- calibration)

TRG 270: 105 EMB-312 *Tucano* (T-27); 39 EMB-314 *Super Tucano* (A-29A)*; 45 EMB-314 *Super Tucano* (A-29B)*; 81 T-25A/C

HELICOPTERS

ATK 9 Mi-35M *Hind* (AH-2 - 3 more due by end 2012)
TPT 82: **Heavy** 2 EC725 *Super Cougar* (H-36) **Medium** 26: 10 AS332M *Super Puma* (H-34/VH-34); 16 UH-60L *Black Hawk* (H-60L) **Light** 54: 24 AS350B *Ecureuil* (H-50); 4 AS355 *Ecureuil II* (H-55/VH-55); 24 Bell 205 (H-1H); 2 EC635 (VH-35)
UAV • ISR • Heavy *Hermes* 450
MSL • AAM • IR MAA-1 *Piranha*; *Magic* 2; *Python* III; **SARH** *Super 530F* **ARH** *Derby*
ARM MAR-1 (in development)

Paramilitary 395,000 opcon Army

Public Security Forces 395,000

State police organisation technically under army control. However, military control is reducing, with authority reverting to individual states.

EQUIPMENT BY TYPE

UAV • ISR • Heavy 3 *Heron* (deployed by Federal Police for Amazon and border patrols)

Cyber

Cyber was a key component of the 2008 National Defence Strategy and was a theme of the July 2012 Defence White Book. The Federal Police (PF), focused on internal law enforcement, has opened a 24-hour cyber-crime monitoring centre with an eye to the forthcoming 2014 World Cup and 2016 Olympic Games. In 2011, the army inaugurated Brazil's cyber-defence centre (CDCiber) to coordinate the existing activities of the army, navy and air force. The centre can reportedly also run simulation software and conduct threat analysis. CDCiber announced its first large-scale mission to protect network security during the Rio +20 international climate conference in June 2012. But cyber attacks and attempted attacks have increased. In February 2012, Brazil's military cyber chief said that the country only had a 'minimum' level of preparedness to defend against theft and large-scale cyber attacks, such as a large cyber attack on government websites in June 2011, but he hoped a new anti-virus system and cyber-attack simulator, bought in January 2012, would improve readiness.

DEPLOYMENT

CÔTE D'IVOIRE
UN • UNOCI 3; 4 obs

CYPRUS
UN • UNFICYP 1

HAITI
UN • MINUSTAH 1,894; 2 inf bn; 1 engr coy

LEBANON
UN • UNIFIL 268; 1 FFGHM

LIBERIA
UN • UNMIL 2; 2 obs

SOUTH SUDAN
UN • UNMISS 3; 5 obs

SUDAN
UN • UNISFA 2; 1 obs

TIMOR LESTE
UN • UNMIT 3 obs

WESTERN SAHARA
UN • MINURSO 10 obs

Chile CHL

Chilean Peso pCh		2011	2012	2013
GDP	pCh	120.16tr	129.42tr	
	US$	248.43bn	268.28bn	
per capita	US$	14,556	15,719	
Growth	%	5.92	4.96	
Inflation	%	3.34	3.11	
Def exp	pCh	2.06tr		
	US$	4.25bn		
Def bdgt	pCh	2.03tr	2.08tr	
	US$	4.21bn	4.31bn	
FMA (US)	US$	0.75m		
US$1=pCh		483.67	482.41	

Population   17,067,369

Age	0–14	15–19	20–24	25–29	30–64	65 plus
Male	10.9%	4.2%	4.4%	4.0%	21.8%	3.9%
Female	10.5%	4.0%	4.2%	3.9%	22.8%	5.5%

Capabilities

Assuring sovereignty and the territorial integrity of the state are the core roles of the country's military. The services have been the focus of restructuring and re-equipment projects. The army has shifted to a brigade structure with an increased emphasis on mobility, while its heavy armour inventory has been bolstered by the acquisition of second-hand *Leopard* 2s. Second-hand purchases have also been used to revamp the navy's frigate inventory over the past ten years. A mix of surplus and new-build F-16s have been acquired since 2005 to improve the air force's combat aircraft fleet. The country has an amphibious assault capability built around its marine corps. The air force has a modest tactical airlift fleet, though its overall operational reach has been improved by the acquisition of three KC-135 tanker aircraft. The services train regularly on a national basis, and also participate routinely in military exercises with international and regional partners. Morale amongst the services is generally held to be high. The country has a significant interest in Antarctic security.

ACTIVE 59,050 (Army 35,000 Navy 16,300 Air 7,750)
Paramilitary 44,700

Terms of service Army 1 year, Navy and Air Force 22 months. Voluntary since 2005

RESERVE 40,000 (Army 40,000)

ORGANISATIONS BY SERVICE

Space
SATELLITES
ISR 1 SSOT (Sistema Satelital del la Observación del la Tierra)

Army 24,000; 11,000 conscript (total 35,000)
6 military administrative regions.

FORCES BY ROLE
Currently being reorganised into 4 armd, 2 mot, 2 mtn and 1 SF brigade. Standard regt/gp are single bn strength, reinforced regt comprise multiple bn.

COMMAND
6 div HQ

SPECIAL FORCES
1 SF bde (1 SF bn, 1 (mtn) SF Gp, 1 para bn, 1 cdo coy, 1 log coy)
2 cdo coy

MANOEUVRE
Reconnaissance
1 armd recce pl
3 cav sqn
4 recce pl

Armoured
3 (1st, 2nd & 3rd) armd bde (1 armd recce pl, 1 armd cav gp, 1 mech inf bn, 1 arty gp, 1 AT coy, 1 engr coy, 1 sigs coy)
1 (4th) armd bde (1 armd recce pl, 1 armd cav gp, 1 mech inf bn, 1 arty gp, 1 engr coy)

Mechanised
1 (1st) mech inf regt

Light
1 (1st) reinforced regt (1 mot inf bn, 1 arty gp, 2 AT coy, 1 engr bn)
1 (4th) reinforced regt (1 mot inf bn, 1 MRL gp, 1 mor coy, 1 AT coy, 1 engr bn)
1 (5th) reinforced regt (1 armd cav gp, 1 mech inf coy, 1 arty gp, 1 engr coy)
1 (7th) reinforced regt (1 mot inf bn, 1 arty gp, 1 sigs coy)
1 (10th) reinforced regt (1 mot inf bn, 1 AT coy, 1 engr bn, 1 sigs bn)
2 (11th & 24th) reinforced mot inf regt (1 mot inf bn, 1 arty gp, 1 AT coy)
1 (14th) reinforced mot inf regt (1 mot inf bn, 1 sigs coy, 1 AT coy)
7 mot inf regt

Mountain
1 (3rd) reinforced mtn regt (1 mtn inf bn, 1 arty gp, 1 engr coy)
1 (9th) reinforced mtn regt (1 mtn inf bn, 1 engr bn)
1 (17th) reinforced mtn regt (1 mtn inf bn, 1 engr coy)
2 mtn inf regt

Aviation
1 avn bde (1 tpt avn bn, 1 hel bn, 1 maint bn, 1 spt bn, 1 log coy)

COMBAT SUPPORT
3 arty regt
1 engr regt
2 sigs regt
1 int regt
1 MP bn

COMBAT SERVICE SUPPORT
1 log div (2 log regt)
4 log regt
6 log coy
1 maint div (1 maint regt)

EQUIPMENT BY TYPE
MBT 253: 122 *Leopard 1*; 131 *Leopard 2A4*
AIFV 191: 173 *Marder*; 18 YPR-765
APC 426
  APC (T) 247 M113A1/A2
  APC (W) 179 Cardoen *Piranha*
ARTY 1,005
  SP 155mm 24 M109A3
  TOWED 233: **105mm** 193: 89 M101; 104 Mod 56; **155mm** 40 M-68
  MRL 160mm 12 LAR-160
  MOR 734:
    81mm 650: 300 M-29; 150 Soltam; 200 FAMAE; **120mm** 170: 110 FAMAE; 60 Soltam M-65
    SP 120mm 84: 36 FAMAE (on *Piranha* 6x6); 48 M-5L1A
AT
  MSL• MANPATS 55 *Spike*
  RCL 106mm M40A1; **84mm** *Carl Gustav*
AIRCRAFT
  TPT • Light 8: 2 C-212 *Aviocar*; 3 Cessna 208 *Caravan*; 3 CN-235
HELICOPTERS
  ISR 9 MD-530F *Lifter* (armed)
  TPT 17 **Medium** 12: 8 AS532AL *Cougar*; 4 SA330 *Puma*
  Light 5: 4 AS350B3 *Ecureuil*; 1 AS355F *Ecureuil II*
AD
  SAM 24:
  MANPAD 24 *Mistral*
  GUNS 41:
  SP 16: **20mm** 16 *Piranha*/TCM-20
  TOWED 25: **20mm** 25 M167 *Vulcan*
AEV 8 *Leopard 1*
ARV 21 *Leopard 1*
VLB 13 *Leopard 1*
MW 3 *Leopard 1*

Navy 15,500; 800 conscript (total 16,300)
5 Naval Zones; 1st Naval Zone and main HQ at Valparaiso; 2nd Naval Zone at Talcahuano; 3rd Naval Zone at Punta Arenas; 4th Naval Zone at Iquique; 5th Naval Zone at Puerto Montt

EQUIPMENT BY TYPE
SUBMARINES • TACTICAL • SSK 4:
  2 *O'Higgins* (*Scorpene*) with 6 single 533mm TT with A-184 *Black Shark* HWT/SUT HWT/SM-39 *Exocet* AShM
  2 *Thompson* (GER T-209/1300) with 8 single 533mm TT with SUT HWT
PRINCIPAL SURFACE COMBATANTS 8
  DESTROYERS • DDGHM 1 *Almirante Williams* (UK Type-22) with 2 quad Mk141 lnchr with RGM-84 *Harpoon* AShM, 2 octuple VLS with *Barak* SAM; 2 triple

324mm ASTT with Mk46 LWT, 1 76mm gun (capacity
1 AS532SC *Cougar*)

FRIGATES 7:
FFGHM 5:
3 *Almirante Cochrane* (UK *Duke*-class Type-23) with 2
quad Mk141 lnchr with RGM-84C *Harpoon* AShM,
1 32-cell VLS with *Sea Wolf* SAM, 2 twin 324mm
ASTT with Mk46 Mod 2 LWT, 1 114mm gun,
(capacity 1 AS-532SC *Cougar*)
2 *Almirante Riveros* (NLD *Karel Doorman*-class) with 2
quad lnchr with RGM-84 *Harpoon* AShM, 1 octuple
Mk48 lnchr with RIM-7P *Sea Sparrow* SAM, 4
single Mk32 Mod 9 324mm ASTT with Mk46 Mod
5 HWT, 1 76mm gun, (capacity 1 AS532SC *Cougar*)
FFGM 2:
2 *Almirante Lattore* (NLD *Jacob Van Heemskerck*-class)
with 2 quad Mk141 lnchr with RGM-84 *Harpoon*
AShM, 1 Mk13 GMLS with SM-1MR SAM, 1
octuple Mk48 lnchr with RIM-7P *Sea Sparrow*
SAM, 2 twin 324mm ASTT with Mk46 LWT

PATROL AND COASTAL COMBATANTS 13
PCG 7:
3 *Casma* (ISR *Sa'ar* 4) with 4 GI *Gabriel I* AShM, 2 76mm
gun
4 *Tiger* (GER Type-148) with 4 single lnchr with MM-40
Exocet AShM, 1 76mm gun
PCO 6 *Micalvi*

AMPHIBIOUS
PRINCIPAL AMPHIBIOUS SHIPS
LPD 1 *Sargento Aldea* (FRA *Foudre*)
LANDING SHIPS 4
LSM 2 *Elicura*
LST 2 *Maipo* (FRA *Batral* - capacity 7 tanks; 140 troops)
LANDING CRAFT 3
LCT 1 CDIC (for use in *Sargento Aldea*)
LCM 2 (for use in *Sargento Aldea*)
LOGISTICS AND SUPPORT 9:
ABU 1 *George Slight Marshall*
AOR 2: 1 *Almirante Montt*; 1 *Araucano*
AGP 1 *Almirante* (also used as general spt ship)
AGS 1 Type 1200 (ice strengthened hull, ex-CAN)
ATF 2 *Veritas*
AP 1 *Aguiles*
AXS 1 *Esmeralda*
MSL • AShM MM-38 *Exocet*

Naval Aviation 600

AIRCRAFT 22 combat capable
ASW 5: 2 C-295ASW *Persuader*; 3 P-3ACH *Orion*
MP 4: 1 C-295MPA *Persuader*; 3 EMB-111 *Bandeirante**
ISR 7 Cessna O-2A *Skymaster**
TPT • Light 3 C-212A *Aviocar*
TRG 7 PC-7 *Turbo Trainer**
HELICOPTERS
ASW 5 AS532SC *Cougar*
MRH 9: 8 AS365 *Dauphin*;1 Bell 412HP
TPT 12 Medium 2 AS332L *Super Puma* (SAR) **Light**
10: 5 Bell 206 *Jet Ranger*; 5 Bo-105S
MSL • AShM AM-39 *Exocet*

Marines 3,600

FORCES BY ROLE
MANOEUVRE
Amphibious
1 amph bn
4 mne gp
(total: 4 inf bn, 4 fd arty bty, 1 SSM bty (Excalibur
Central Defence System), 4 ADA bty, 2 trg bn)
7 sy det (1 per naval zone)
EQUIPMENT BY TYPE
LT TK 15 *Scorpion*
APC (W) 25 MOWAG *Roland*
ARTY 26
TOWED 18: 105mm 4 KH-178; **155mm** 14 G-5
MOR 8 81mm
AD • SAM • SP 18: 4 M998 HMMWV; 4 M1151A
HMMWV; 10 M1097 HMMWV *Avenger*

Coast Guard

Integral part of the Navy
PATROL AND COASTAL COMBATANTS 43+
PSOH 2 *Piloto Pardo* (1 additional vessel in build)
PBF 1+ *Archangel*
PB 40: 18 *Alacalufe* (*Protector*-class); 8 *Grumete Diaz*
(*Dabor*-class); 6 *Pelluhue*; 5 *Archangel*; 2 *Maullin*; 1 *Ona*

Air Force 7,300; 450 conscript (total 7,750)

Flying hours   100 hrs/year

FORCES BY ROLE
FIGHTER
1 sqn with F-5E/F *Tiger* III+
2 sqn with F-16AM/BM *Fighting Falcon*
FIGHTER/GROUND ATTACK
1 sqn with F-16C/D Block 50 *Fighting Falcon* (*Puma*)
ISR
1 (photo) flt with; DHC-6-300 *Twin Otter*; Learjet 35A
AIRBORNE EARLY WARNING
1 flt with B-707 *Phalcon*
TANKER/TRANSPORT
1 sqn with B-737-300; C-130B/H *Hercules*; KC-135
TRANSPORT
3 sqn with Bell 205 (UH-1H *Iroquois*); C-212-200/300
Aviocar; Cessna O-2A; Cessna 525 *Citation CJ1*; DHC-
6-100/300 *Twin Otter*; PA-28-236 *Dakota*; Bell 205 (UH-
1H *Iroquois*)
1 VIP flt with B-737-500 (VIP); Gulfstream IV
TRAINING
1 sqn with EMB-314 *Super Tucano**
1 sqn with PA-28-236 *Dakota*; T-35A/B *Pillan*
TRANSPORT HELICOPTER
1 sqn with Bell 205 (UH-1H *Iroquois*); Bell 206B (trg); Bell
412 *Twin Huey*; Bo-105CBS-4; S-70A *Black Hawk*
AIR DEFENCE
1 AD regt (5 AD sqn) with *Mygale*; Mistral; M163/M167
Vulcan; GDF-005; *Oerlikon*; *Crotale*
EQUIPMENT BY TYPE
AIRCRAFT 79 combat capable
FTR 48: 12 F-5E/F *Tigre* III+; 29 F-16AM *Fighting Falcon*;
7 F-16BM *Fighting Falcon*

FGA 10: 6 F-16C Block 50 *Fighting Falcon*; 4 F-16D Block 50 *Fighting Falcon*

ATK 9 C-101CC *Aviojet* (A-36 *Halcón*)

ISR 2 Cessna O-2A

AEW&C 1 B-707 *Phalcon*

TKR 3 KC-135

TPT 38: **Medium** 3: 1 C-130B *Hercules*; 2 C-130H *Hercules*; **Light** 31: 2 C-212-200 *Aviocar*; 1 C-212-300 *Aviocar*; 4 Cessna 525 *Citation CJ1*; 3 DHC-6-100 *Twin Otter*; 7 DHC-6-300 *Twin Otter*; 2 Learjet 35A; 11 PA-28-236 *Dakota* **PAX** 4: 1 B-737-300; 1 B-737-500; 1 B-767-300ER; 1 Gulfstream IV

TRG 42: 12 EMB-314 *Super Turano**; 30 T-35A/B *Pillan*

HELICOPTERS

MRH 12 Bell 412EP *Twin Huey*

TPT 19: **Medium** 1 S-70A *Black Hawk*; **Light** 16: 13 Bell 205 (UH-1H *Iroquois*); 5 Bell 206B (trg); 2 BK-117; 1 Bo-105CBS-4

AD

SYSTEMS *Mygale*

SAM *Mistral*

SP 5 *Crotale*

GUNS • TOWED 20mm M163/M167 *Vulcan*; **35mm** GDF-005 Oerlikon

MSL

AAM • IR AIM-9J/M *Sidewinder*; *Python* III; *Python* IV; *Shafrir*‡; **ARH** AIM-120C AMRAAM; *Derby*

ASM AGM-65G *Maverick*

BOMBS JDAM; *Paveway* II

Paramilitary 44,700

Carabineros 44,700

Ministry of Defence; 15 zones, 36 districts, 179 *comisaria*

EQUIPMENT BY TYPE

APC (W) 20 MOWAG *Roland* **MOR 60mm; 81mm**

AIRCRAFT

TPT • Light 4: 1 Beech 200 *King Air*; 1 Cessna 208; 1 Cessna 550 *Citation* V; 1 PA-31T *Cheyenne* II

HELICOPTERS • TPT • Light 14: 4 AW109E *Power*; 1 Bell 206 *Jet Ranger*; 2 BK 117; 5 Bo-105; 2 EC135

Cyber

The Joint Staff coordinates cyber-security policies for the Ministry of Defense and the Armed Forces. Each service has a cyber-security organisation within their security structure. The Ministry of Interior and Public Security (Internal Affairs) is the national coordination authority for cyber security and is currently developing a National Cyber Security Strategy.

DEPLOYMENT

Legal provisions for foreign deployment:

Constitution: Constitution (1980, since amended)

Decision on deployment of troops abroad: Article 63, number 13 of the Constitution, concerning matters of law, states that the procedures for foreign deployment are a matter that must be established by law by Congress. Law Number 19.067 regulates matters concerning the foreign deployment of Chilean troops and deployment of foreign troops in Chile. It states that the government needs to request congressional approval.

BOSNIA-HERZEGOVINA

EU • EUFOR • *Operation Althea* 22

CYPRUS

UN • UNFICYP 15

HAITI

UN • MINUSTAH 498; 1 inf bn; 1mne coy(-); 1 hel coy; elm 1 engr coy

INDIA/PAKISTAN

UN • UNMOGIP 2 obs

MIDDLE EAST

UN • UNTSO 3 obs

Colombia COL

Colombian Peso pC		2011	2012	2013
GDP	pC	615.73tr	658.11tr	
	US$	327.63bn	365.4bn	
per capita	US$	7,242	8,077	
Growth	%	5.91	4.25	
Inflation	%	3.42	3.21	
Def exp[a]	pC	10.6tr		
	US$	5.63bn		
Def bdgt[a]	pC	10.3tr	11tr	
	US$	5.48bn	6.13bn	
FMA (US)	US$	47.9m	37m	30m
US$1=pC		1879.36	1801.07	

[a] Excludes decentralised expenditures & expenditure on National Police

Population	45,239,079

Age	0–14	15–19	20–24	25–29	30–64	65 plus
Male	13.4%	4.7%	4.6%	4.1%	19.9%	2.6%
Female	12.8%	4.6%	4.5%	4.1%	21.0%	3.7%

Capabilities

Colombia's security and defence requirements are dominated by two tasks: counter-insurgency and counter-narcotics. The state continues to wage a campaign against the FARC (Fuerzas Armadas Revolucionarias de Colombia), a conflict now in its fifth decade, with the armed services focused near wholly on counter-insurgency operations. In 2012, peace talks with FARC were announced. Colombia also enjoys considerable support from the US, both in terms of training and equipment provision, to try to bolster its counter-narcotics effort. Army special forces have received US training, while the air force operates a large fleet of US helicopter types to provide tactical mobility for the army. Fixed-wing tactical transport has also been enhanced, while the air force has, in recent years, upgraded and received additional *Kfir* fighters. The air force took part in the US *Red Flag* exercises in 2012. The navy has a littoral warfare capacity only. Morale in the air force and navy is at least adequate, similarly within the army's special forces. Given the concentration on counter-insurgency, the military has little ability to project power.

ACTIVE 281,400 (Army 221,500, Navy 46,150 Air 13,750) **Paramilitary 159,000**

RESERVE 61,900 (Army 54,700 Navy 4,800 Air 1,200 Joint 1,200)

ORGANISATIONS BY SERVICE

Army 221,500

FORCES BY ROLE
SPECIAL FORCES
1 SF bde (2 SF bn)
1 anti-terrorist SF bn
MANOEUVRE
Mechanised
1 (1st) div (1 (2nd) mech bde (2 mech inf bn, 1 mtn inf bn, 1 engr bn, 1 MP bn, 1 cbt spt bn, 1 log bn, 1 Gaula anti-kidnap gp); 1 (10th) mech bde (1 (med) tk bn, 1 mech cav bn, 1 mech inf bn, 1 mtn inf bn, 1 fd arty bn, 1 engr bn, 1 cbt spt bn, 2 Gaula anti-kidnap gp); 2 sy bn; 1 log bn)
Light
1 (2nd) div (1 (5th) lt inf bde (3 lt inf bn, 1 fd arty bn, 1 AD bn, 1 engr bn, 1 cbt spt bn, 1 Gaula anti-kidnap gp); 1 (30th) lt inf bde (1 cav recce bn, 2 lt inf bn, 1 sy bn, 1 arty bn, 1 engr bn, 1 cbt spt bn, 1 log bn); 1 rapid reaction force (3 mobile sy bde, 1 fixed sy bde))
1 (3rd) div (1 (3rd) lt inf bde (2 lt inf bn, 1 mtn inf bn, 1 COIN bn, 1 arty bn, 1 engr bn, 1 cbt spt bn, 1 MP bn, 1 log bn, 1 Gaula anti-kidnap gp); 1 (23rd) lt inf bde (1 cav gp, 1 lt inf bn, 1 jungle inf bn, 1 cbt spt bn, 1 log bn); 1 (29th) mtn bde (1 mtn inf bn, 1 lt inf bn, 2 COIN bn, 1 cbt spt bn, 1 log bn); 2 rapid reaction force (total: 7 mobile sy bde))
1 (4th) div (1 (7th) air mob bde (2 air mob inf bn, 1 lt inf bn, 1 COIN bn, 1 engr bn, 1 cbt spt bn, 1 log bn, 1 Gaula anti-kidnap gp); 1 (22nd) jungle bde (1 air mob inf bn, 1 lt inf bn, 1 jungle inf bn, 1 COIN bn, 1 cbt spt bn, 1 log bn); 1 (31st) jungle bde (1 lt inf bn, 1 jungle inf bn))
1 (5th) div (1 (6th) lt inf bde (2 lt inf bn,1 mtn inf bn, 2 COIN bn, 1 cbt spt bn, 1 log bn, 1 Gaula anti-kidnap gp); 1 (8th) lt inf bde (1 lt inf bn, 1 mtn inf bn, 1 arty bn, 1 engr bn, 1 cbt spt bn, 1 Gaula anti-kidnap gp); 1 (9th) lt inf bde (1 SF bn, 2 lt inf bn, 1 arty bn, 1 COIN bn, 1 cbt spt bn, 1 sy bn, 1 log bn, 1 Gaula anti-kidnap gp); 1 (13th) lt inf bde (2 cav recce bn, 1 airmob inf bn, 3 lt inf bn, 1 COIN bn, 1 arty bn, 1 engr bn, 1 cbt spt bn, 2 MP bn, 1 log bn, 2 Gaula anti-kidnap gp); 1 rapid reaction force (3 mobile sy bde))
1 (6th) div (1 (12th) lt inf bde (2 lt inf bn, 2 jungle inf bn, 1 COIN bn, 1 engr bn, 1 cbt spt bn, 1 Gaula anti-kidnap gp); 1 (13th) mobile sy bde (4 COIN bn); 1 (26th) jungle bde (1 lt jungle inf bn, 1 COIN bn, 1 cbt spt bn);

1 (27th) lt inf bde (2 lt inf bn, 1 jungle inf bn, 1 sy bn, 1 arty bn, 1 cbt spt bn, 1 log bn))
1 (7th) div (1 (4th) lt inf bde (1 cav recce bn, 3 lt inf bn, 1 sy bn, 1 arty bn, 1 engr bn, 1 MP bn, 1 cbt spt bn, 1 log bn); 1 (11th) lt inf bde (2 lt inf bn, 1 sy bn, 1 engr bn, 1 cbt spt bn); 1 (14th) lt inf bde (2 lt inf bn, 1 sy bn, 1 engr bn, 1 cbt spt bn, 1 log bn); 1 (15th) jungle bde (1 ilt inf bn, 1 COIN bn, 1 engr bn, 1 log bn); 1 (17th) lt inf bde (2 lt inf bn, 1 COIN bn, 1 engr bn, 1 cbt spt bn, 1 log bn); 1 rapid reaction force (1 (11th) mobile sy bde (3 COIN bn)))
1 (8th) div (1 (16th) lt inf bde (1 mech cav recce bn, 1 lt inf bn, 1 log bn, 1 Gaula anti-kidnap gp); 1 (18th) lt inf bde (1 air mob gp, 1 sy bn, 1 arty bn, 1 engr bn, 1 cbt spt bn, 1 log bn); 1 (28th) jungle bde (2 inf, 2 COIN, 1 cbt spt bn); 1 rapid reaction force (1 (5th) mobile sy bde (3 COIN bn); 1 (31st) mobile sy bde (5 COIN bn)))
3 COIN mobile bde (each: 4 COIN bn, 1 cbt spt bn)
Other
1 indep counter-narcotics bde (3 counter-narcotics bn, 1 spt bn)
1 indep rapid reaction force (1 SF bde; 3 mobile sy bde)
Aviation
1 air aslt div (1 (25th) bde (4 hel bn; 5 avn bn; 1 avn log bn)
COMBAT SUPPORT
1 cbt engr bde (1 SF engr bn, 1 (emergency response) engr bn, 1 EOD bn, 1 construction bn, 1 demining bn, 1 maint bn)
1 int bde (2 SIGINT bn, 1 kog bn, 1 maint bn)
COMBAT SERVICE SUPPORT
2 spt/log bde (each: 1 spt bn, 1 maint bn, 1 supply bn, 1 tpt bn, 1 medical bn, 1 log bn)

EQUIPMENT BY TYPE
RECCE 222: 119 EE-9 *Cascavel*; 6 M8 (anti-riot vehicle); 8 M8 with TOW; 39 M1117 *Guardian*; 50 VCL
APC 114
  APC (T) 54: 28 M113A1 (TPM-113A1); 26 M113A2 (TPM-113A2)
  APC (W) 56 EE-11 *Urutu*
  PPV 4 RG-31 *Nyala*
ARTY 710
  TOWED 121: **105mm** 106: 20 LG1 MkIII; 86 M101; **155mm** 15 155/52 APU SBT-1
  MOR 589: **81mm** 141: 125 M1; 16 M125A1 (SP) **107mm** 148 M2; **120mm** 300: 210 *Brandt*, 38 HY12; 52 AM50
AT
  MSL• SP 8+: 8 TOW; *Nimrod*
   MANPATS 10+: 10 TOW; *Spike*-ER; APILAS
  RCL 106mm 63 M40A1
  RL 15+: **89mm** 15 M20; **90mm** C-90C; **106mm** SR-106
AD
  SAM • TOWED 3 *Skyguard/Sparrow*
  GUNS 39+
   SP 12.7mm 18 M8/M55
   TOWED 21+: **35mm** GDF Oerlikon; **40mm** 21 M1A1 (with 7 *Eagle Eye* radar)
AIRCRAFT
  ELINT 3: 2 Beech B200 *King Air*; 1 Beech *King Air* 350

TPT • **Light** 22: 2 An-32B; 2 Beech 350 *King Air*; 2 Beech 200 *King Air* (Medevac); 1 Beech C90 *King Air*; 2 C-212 *Aviocar* (Medevac); 1 CV-580; 1 Cessna 206; 6 Cessna 208B *Grand Caravan*; 2 PA-34 *Seneca*; 3 *Turbo Commander 695A*

HELICOPTERS
MRH 22: 8 Mi-17-1V *Hip*; 9 Mi-17MD; 5 Mi-17V-5 *Hip*
TPT 105 **Medium** 44 UH-60L *Black Hawk* **Light** 60: 29 Bell 205 (UH-1H *Iroquois*); 27 Bell 212 (UH-1N *Twin Huey*)

Navy 46,150; (incl 7,200 conscript)

HQ (Tri-Service Unified Eastern Command HQ) located at Puerto Carreño

EQUIPMENT BY TYPE
SUBMARINES • TACTICAL • SSK 4:
2 *Pijao* (GER T-209/1200) each with 8 single 533mm TT each with HWT
2 *Intrepido* (GER T-206A) each with 8 single 533mm TT each with HWT

PRINCIPAL SURFACE COMBATANTS 4
FRIGATES • FFG 4 *Almirante Padilla* (undergoing modernisation programme) with 2 twin lnchr with MM-40 *Exocet* AShM, 2 twin *Simbad* lnchr with *Mistral* SAM, 2 triple B515 *ILAS-3* 324mm ASTT each with A244 LWT, 1 76mm gun, (capacity 1 Bo-105/AS555SN *Fennec* hel)

PATROL AND COASTAL COMBATANTS 56
PSOH 1 *20 de Julio* (1 additional vessel in build)
PCO 2: 1 *Reliance* with 1 hel landing platform; 1 *San Andres*
PCC 2: 1 *Espartana* (ESP *Cormoran*); 1 *Lazaga*
PCR 16: 3 *Arauca*; 2 *Nodriza* (PAF-VII/VIII); 8 *Nodriza* (PAF-II) with hel landing platform; 3 LPR-40 (additional vessels on order)
PBF 1 *Quitasueño* (US *Asheville*) with 1 76mm gun
PB 13: 1 *11 de Noviembre* (CPV-40); 2 *Castillo Y Rada* (*Swiftships* 105); 2 *Jaime Gomez*; 2 *José Maria Palas* (*Swiftships* 110); 4 *Point*; 2 *Toledo*
PBR 21: 7 *Diligente*; 3 *Swiftships*; 9 *Tenerife*; 2 PAF-L

AMPHIBIOUS 10
LCM 3 LCM-8 (there are more than 200 small assault RHIBs also in service)
LCU 7 *Morrosquillo* (LCU 1466)

LOGISTICS AND SUPPORT 8
AG 2 *Luneburg* (ex-GER, depot ship for patrol vessels)
AGOR 2 *Providencia*
AGP 1 *Inirida*
AGS 1 *Gorgona*
ABU 1 *Quindio*
AXS 1 *Gloria*

Naval Aviation 146
AIRCRAFT
MP 3 CN-235 MPA *Persuader*
ISR 1 PA-31 *Navajo* (upgraded for ISR)
TPT • Light 9: 1 C-212 (Medevac); 4 Cessna 206; 2 Cessna 208 *Caravan*; 1 PA-31 *Navajo*; 1 PA-34 *Seneca*
HELICOPTERS
MRH 6: 2 AS555SN *Fennec*; 4 Bell 412 *Twin Huey*
TPT • Light 10: 1 Bell 212; 6 Bell 212 (UH-1N); 1 BK 117; 2 Bo-105

Marines 27,000

FORCES BY ROLE
SPECIAL FORCES
1 SF bde (forming)
1 SF bn
2 (river) SF gp
MANOEUVRE
Amphibious
1 mne bde (3 mne bn, 2 COIN bn, 1 comd/spt bn)
1 rvn bde (3 mne bn)
1 rvn bde (3 mne bn, 3 mne aslt bn, 1 comd/spt bn)
1 rvn bde (4 mne bn)
COMBAT SERVICE SUPPORT
1 log bde (forming)
1 trg bde (3 trg bn)

EQUIPMENT BY TYPE
APC (W) 8 BTR-80A
ARTY • MOR • 81mm 20

Air Force 13,750

6 Combat Air Commands (CACOM) plus CACOM 7 (former Oriental Air Group) responsible for air ops in specific geographic area. Flts can be deployed or 'loaned' to a different CACOM

FORCES BY ROLE
FIGHTER/GROUND ATTACK/ISR
1 sqn with A-37B/OA-37B *Dragonfly*
1 sqn with AC-47T; Hughes 369
1 sqn with EMB-312 *Tucano**
2 sqn with EMB-314 *Super Tucano** (A-29)
1 sqn with *Kfir* C-10/C-12/TC-12
EW/ELINT
2 sqn with Beech 350 *King Air*; Cessna 208; Cessna 560; C-26B *Metroliner*; SA-2-37
MARITIME PATROL/SEARCH & RESCUE
1 sqn with Bell 212, EMB-110P1 (C-95)
TRANSPORT
1 (Presidential) sqn with B-707 Tkr; B-727; B-737BBJ; EMB *Legacy* 600; KC-767; Bell 212; Bell 412; F-28 *Fellowship*
1 sqn with C-130B/H *Hercules*; C-295M
1 sqn with Beech C90 *King Air*; C-212; CN-235M; Do-328; IAI *Arava*
TRAINING
1 (primary trg) sqn with Bell 205 (UH-1H *Iroquois*); PA-42 *Cheyenne*
1 (basic trg) sqn with T-34 *Mentor*
1 sqn with T-37B
2 hel sqn with Bell 206B3
HELICOPTER
1 sqn with AH-60L *Arpia III*
1 sqn with UH-60L *Black Hawk* (CSAR)
1 sqn with MD500; Bell 205 (UH-1H)
1 sqn with Hughes 369
1 sqn with Bell 205 (UH-1H); Hughes 369
1 sqn with Bell 206B3; Hughes 369

EQUIPMENT BY TYPE
AIRCRAFT 82 combat capable
FGA 23: 10 *Kfir* C-10; 10 *Kfir* C-12; 3 *Kfir* TC-12

ATK 20: 4 A-37B *Dragonfly*; 8 OA-37B *Dragonfly*; 8 AC-47T *Spooky* (*Fantasma*)

ISR 13: 1 C-26B *Metroliner*; 5 Cessna 560 *Citation* V; 6 Schweizer SA-2-37; 1 Beech C90 *King Air*

ELINT 3: 1 Beech 350 *King Air*; 2 Cessna 208 *Grand Caravan*

TKR/TPT 2: 1 B-707 Tkr; 1 KC-767

TPT 70: **Medium** 7: 4 C-130B *Hercules* (3 more in store); 3 C-130H *Hercules*; **Light** 58: 5 ATR-42; 2 ATR-72′ 2 Beech 300 *King Air*; 5 Beech 350C *King Air*; 2 Beech C90 *King Air*; 4 C-212; 4 C-295M; 1 Cessna 182R; 12 Cessna 208B (medevac); 1 Cessna 337G; 1 Cessna 337H; 1 Cessna 550; 3 CN-235M; 6 Do-328; 2 EMB-110P1 (C-95); 1 EMB-170-100LR; 1 IAI-201 *Arava*; 1 L-410UVP *Turbolet*; 2 PA-42 *Cheyenne*; 2 Turbo Commander 695 **PAX** 5: 1 B-727; 1 B-737BBJ; EMB *Legacy* 600; 1 F-28-1000 *Fellowship*; 1 F-28-3000 *Fellowship*

TRG 77+: 14 EMB-312 *Tucano**; 25 EMB-314 *Super Tucano* (A-29)*; 8+ Lancair *Synergy* (T-90 - 17 more on order); 10 T-34 *Mentor*; 20 T-37B

HELICOPTERS

ISR 20 OH-58 *Kiowa*

MRH 17: 12 AH-60L *Arpia* III; 2 Bell 412 *Twin Huey*; 2 Hughes 500M; 1 MD-500E

TPT 55 **Medium** 10: 8 UH-60A *Black Hawk* (6 being upgraded to UH-60L); 4 UH-60L *Black Hawk* **Light** 45: 22 Bell 205 (UH-1H *Iroquois*); 12 Bell 206B3 *JetRanger III*; 11 Bell 212

MSL • IR *Python* III; R530 **ARH** Derby

Paramilitary 159,000

National Police Force 159,000

AIRCRAFT

ELINT 3: 1 Cessna 208B, 2 C-26B *Metroliner*

TPT • Light 29: 15 AT-802; 1 ATR-42; 3 Beech 200 *King Air*; 3 Beech 300 *King Air*; 2 Beech 1900; 1 Beech C99; 4 BT-67; 5 C-26 *Metroliner*; 2 Cessna 152; 3 Cessna 172; 7 Cessna 206; 5 Cessna 208 Caravan; 2 DHC 6 *Twin Otter*; 4 PA-31 *Navajo*

HELICOPTERS

MRH 4: 1 Bell 412EP; 1 MD-500D; 2 Hughes 369

TPT 53 **Medium** 7 UH-60L *Black Hawk* **Light** 46: 25 Bell 205 (UH-1H-II *Huey II*); 3 Bell 206B; 7 Bell 206L *Long Ranger*; 10 Bell 212; 1 Bell 407

DEPLOYMENT

EGYPT

MFO 354; 1 inf bn

FOREIGN FORCES

United States US Southern Command: 60

Costa Rica CRI

Costa Rican Colon C		2011	2012	2013
GDP	C	20.74tr	22.93tr	
	US$	40.95bn	44.88bn	
per capita	US$	8,832	9,680	
Growth	%	4.16	4.80	
Inflation	%	4.88	4.61	
Def exp	C	137bn		
	US$	271m		
Sy Bdgt[a]	C	158bn	175bn	202bn
	US$	312m	343m	
FMA (US)	US$	0.349m	0.315m	1.4m
US$1=C		506.40	510.79	

[a] No armed forces. Paramilitary budget

Population   4,636,348

Age	0–14	15–19	20–24	25–29	30–64	65 plus
Male	12.4%	4.6%	4.7%	4.7%	20.9%	3.0%
Female	11.8%	4.4%	4.6%	4.5%	21.0%	3.5%

Capabilities

Military forces were constitutionally abolished in 1949. Costa Rica relies on a series of moderately-sized para-military-style organisations for assistance in internal security and regional peacekeeping operations. Some force elements, such as the special operations unit, have received training in some capability areas by outside states including the US.

Paramilitary 9,800

ORGANISATIONS BY SERVICE

Paramilitary 9,800

Civil Guard 4,500

FORCES BY ROLE

SPECIAL FORCES

1 spec ops unit

MANOEUVRE

Other

1 (tac) police *comisaria*

6 (provincial) paramilitary *comisaria*

7 (urban) paramilitary *comisaria*

Border Police 2,500

FORCES BY ROLE

MANOEUVRE

Other

2 (border) sy comd (8 comisaria)

Coast Guard Unit 400

EQUIPMENT BY TYPE

PATROL AND COASTAL COMBATANTS 8:

PB 8: 2 *Cabo Blanco* (US *Swift* 65); 1 *Isla del Coco* (US *Swift* 105); 3 *Point*; 1 *Primera Dama* (US *Swift* 42); 1 *Puerto Quebos* (US *Swift* 36)

Air Surveillance Unit 400
AIRCRAFT • TPT • Light 10: 4 Cessna T210 *Centurion*; 4 Cessna U206G *Stationair*; 1 DHC-7 *Caribou*; 2 PA-31 *Navajo*; 2 PA-34 *Seneca*
HELICOPTERS • MRH 2 MD-500E

Rural Guard 2,000
Ministry of Government and Police. Small arms only
FORCES BY ROLE
MANOEUVRE
　Other
　　8 paramilitary comd

Cuba CUB

Cuban Peso P		2011	2012	2013
GDP	P			
	US$			
per capita	US$			
Growth	%			
Inflation	%			
Def bdgt[a]	P	ε2.21bn	ε2.3bn	
	US$	ε96m	ε99m	
US$=P		23.15	23.15	

*definitive economic data unavailable

[a] Defence & internal order

Population	11,075,244					
Age	0–14	15–19	20–24	25–29	30–64	65 plus
Male	9.2%	3.3%	3.9%	3.4%	24.6%	5.4%
Female	8.7%	3.1%	3.7%	3.3%	24.9%	6.5%

Capabilities

Numerically the strongest in the Caribbean, the effectiveness of the Cuban armed forces is restricted by their largely outdated equipment holdings and maintenance problems resulting largely from US sanctions on Cuba. They have focused on a national-defence role after the end of the Cold War, and lack recent experience of either combat or significant operational deployment. They do, however, retain strong ties with some regional militaries, particularly Venezuela, and have deployed advisors and medical personnel to these countries.

ACTIVE 49,000 (Army 38,000 Navy 3,000 Air 8,000)
Paramilitary 26,500
Terms of service 2 years

RESERVE 39,000 (Army 39,000) **Paramilitary 1,120,000**
Ready Reserves (serve 45 days per year) to fill out Active and Reserve units; see also Paramilitary.

ORGANISATIONS BY SERVICE

Army ε38,000
FORCES BY ROLE
COMMAND
　3 regional comd HQ
　3 army comd HQ
MANOEUVRE
　Armoured
　up to 5 armd bde
　Mechanised
　9 mech inf bde (1 armd regt, 3 mech inf regt, 1 arty regt, 1 ADA regt)
　Light
　1 (frontier) bde
　Air Manoeuvre
　1 AB bde
COMBAT SUPPORT
　1 ADA regt
　1 SAM bde

Reserves 39,000
FORCES BY ROLE
MANOEUVRE
　Light
　　14 inf bde
EQUIPMENT BY TYPE†
MBT ε900 T-34/T-54/T-55/T-62
LT TK PT-76
RECCE BRDM-1/2
AIFV ε 50 BMP-1
APC • APC (W) ε500 BTR-152/BTR-40/BTR-50/BTR-60
ARTY 1,730+
　SP 40 2S1 *Carnation* **122mm**/2S3 **152mm**
　TOWED 500 **152mm** D-1/**122mm** D-30/**152mm** M-1937/**122mm** M-30/**130mm** M-46/**76mm** ZIS-3 M-1942
　MRL SP 175 **140mm** BM-14/**122mm** BM-21
　MOR 1,000 **120mm** M-38/**82mm** M-41/**120mm** M-43/**82mm** M-43
　STATIC 15 **122mm** 15 JS-2M (hy tk)
AT
　MSL • MANPATS 2K16 *Shmel* (AT-1 *Snapper*); 9K11 Malyutka (AT-3 9K11 *Sagger*)
　GUNS 700+: **100mm** 100 SU-100 SP; **85mm** D-44; **57mm** 600 M-1943
AD • SAM
　SP 200+: 200 9K35 *Strela*-10 (SA-13 *Gopher*); 2K12 *Kub* (SA-6 *Gainful*); 9K33 *Osa* (SA-8 *Gecko*); 9K31 *Strela*-1 (SA-9 *Gaskin*)
　MANPAD 9K36 *Strela*-3 (SA-14 *Gremlin*); 9K310 *Igla*-1 (SA-16 *Gimlet*); 9K32 *Strela*-2 (SA-7 *Grail*)‡
　GUNS 400
　　SP 57mm ZSU-57-2 SP/**23mm** ZSU-23-4 SP/**30mm** BTR-60P SP
　　TOWED 100mm KS-19/M-1939/**85mm** KS-12/**57mm** S-60/**37mm** M-1939/**30mm** M-53/**23mm** ZU-23

Navy ε3,000

Western Comd HQ at Cabanas; Eastern Comd HQ at Holquin

EQUIPMENT BY TYPE
PATROL AND COASTAL COMBATANTS 8
  PSO 1 *Type 390* with two single P-15M *Termit* (SS-N-2C *Styx*) AShM
  PCM 1 *Pauk* II† (FSU) with 1 quad lnchr (manual aiming) with 9K32 *Strela*-2 (SA-N-5 *Grail* SAM), 4 single ASTT, 2 RBU 1200, 1 76mm gun
  PBF 6 *Osa* II† (FSU) each with 4 single lnchr (for P-15 *Termit* (SS-N-2B *Styx*) AShM – missiles removed to coastal defence units)
MINE WARFARE AND MINE COUNTERMEASURES 5
  MHI 3 *Yevgenya*† (FSU)
  MSC 2 *Sonya*† (FSU)
LOGISTICS AND SUPPORT 3
  AG 1
  ABU 1
  AX 1

Coastal Defence

ARTY • TOWED 122mm M-1931/37; **130mm** M-46; **152mm** M-1937
MSL• AShM 2+: *Bandera* IV (reported); 2 P-15 *Rubezh* (SSC-3 *Styx*)

Naval Infantry 550+

FORCES BY ROLE
MANOEUVRE
  Amphibious
  2 amph aslt bn

Anti-aircraft Defence and Revolutionary Air Force ε8,000 (incl conscripts)

Air assets divided between Western Air Zone and Eastern Air Zone

Flying hours   50 hrs/year

FORCES BY ROLE
FIGHTER/GROUND ATTACK
  3 sqn with MiG-21ML *Fishbed*; MiG-23ML/MF/UM *Flogger*; MiG-29A/UB *Fulcrum*
TRANSPORT
  1 (VIP) tpt sqn with An-24 *Coke*; Mi-8P *Hip*; Yak-40
ATTACK HELICOPTER
  2 sqn with Mi-17 *Hip H*; Mi-35 *Hind*
TRAINING
  2 (tac trg) sqn with L-39C *Albatros* (basic); Z-142 (primary)

EQUIPMENT BY TYPE
AIRCRAFT 45 combat capable
  FTR 33: 16 MiG-23ML *Flogger*; 4 MiG-23MF *Flogger*; 4 MiG-23U *Flogger*; 4 MiG-23UM *Flogger*; 2 MiG-29A *Fulcrum*; 3 MiG-29UB *Fulcrum* (6 MiG-15UTI *Midget*; 4+ MiG-17 *Fresco*; 4 MiG-23MF *Flogger*; 6 MiG-23ML *Flogger*; 2 MiG-23UM *Flogger*; 2 MiG-29 *Fulcrum* in store)
  FGA 12: 4 MiG-21ML *Fishbed*; 8 MiG-21U *Mongol A* (up to 70 MiG-21bis *Fishbed*; 30 MiG-21F *Fishbed*; 28 MiG-

21PFM *Fishbed*; 7 MiG-21UM *Fishbed*; 20 MiG-23BN *Flogger* in store)
  ISR 1 An-30 *Clank*
  TPT 11: **Heavy** 2 Il-76 *Candid*; **Light** 9: 1 An-2 *Colt*; 3 An-24 *Coke*; 2 An-32 *Cline*; 3 Yak-40 (8 An-2 *Colt*; 18 An-26 *Curl* in store)
  TRG 45: 25 L-39 *Albatros*; 20 Z-326 *Trener Master*
HELICOPTERS
  ATK 4 Mi-35 *Hind* (8 more in store)
  ASW (5 Mi-14 in store)
  MRH 8 Mi-17 *Hip H* (12 more in store)
  TPT • Medium 2 Mi-8P *Hip*
AD • SAM SA-3 *Goa*; SA-2 *Guideline* towed
MSL
  AAM • IR R-3 ‡ (AA-2 *Atoll*); R-60 (AA-8 *Aphid*); R-73 (AA-11 *Archer*); **IR/SARH** R-23/24 ‡ (AA-7 *Apex*); R-27 (AA-10 *Alamo*)
  ASM Kh-23 (AS-7 *Kerry*)‡

Paramilitary 26,500 active

State Security 20,000

Ministry of Interior

Border Guards 6,500

Ministry of Interior
PATROL AND COASTAL COMBATANTS 20
  PCC: 2 *Stenka*
  PB 18 *Zhuk*

Youth Labour Army 70,000 reservists

Civil Defence Force 50,000 reservists

Territorial Militia ε1,000,000 reservists

FOREIGN FORCES

United States US Southern Command: 950 at Guantánamo Bay

Dominican Republic DOM

Dominican Peso pRD		2011	2012	2013
GDP	pRD	2.12tr	2.38tr	
	US$	55.75bn	59.13bn	
per capita	US$	5,526	5,861	
Growth	%	4.48	4.04	
Inflation	%	8.46	4.09	
Def bdgt	pRD	8.74bn	9.6bn	
	US$	230m	238m	
US$1=pRD		38.01	40.30	

Population   10,088,598

Age	0–14	15–19	20–24	25–29	30–64	65 plus
Male	14.7%	4.9%	4.6%	4.2%	19.1%	3.1%
Female	14.2%	4.7%	4.4%	4.0%	18.4%	3.6%

Capabilities

Lacking a credible external threat, the Dominican military is primarily focused on internal paramilitary duties and counter-narcotics operations. A sizeable proportion of the army is deployed on the Haitian border to bolster security. Heavy equipment holdings are minimal and serviceability is questionable. Under the US SOUTHCOM-managed Caribbean Basin Security Initiative (the Secure Seas programme), the Dominican Republic received two *Defender*-class sub-10-tonne patrol vessels in 2012.

ACTIVE 24,500 (Army 15,000 Navy 4,000 Air 5,500)
Paramilitary 15,000

ORGANISATIONS BY SERVICE

Army 15,000

5 Defence Zones

FORCES BY ROLE
SPECIAL FORCES
  3 SF bn
MANOEUVRE
  Mechanised
  1 armd bn
  Light
  1 (2nd) inf bde (4 inf bn, 1 mtn inf bn)
  2 (1st & 3rd) inf bde (3 inf bn)
  2 (4th & 5th) inf bde (2 inf bn)
  1 (6th) inf bde (1 inf bn)
  Air Manoeuvre
  1 air cav bde (1 cdo bn, 1 (6th) mtn regt, 1 hel sqn with Bell 205 (op by Air Force); OH-58 *Kiowa*; R-22; R-44 *Raven* II)
  Other
  1 (Presidential Guard) gd regt
  1 (MoD) sy bn
COMBAT SUPPORT
  2 arty bn
  1 engr bn

EQUIPMENT BY TYPE
LT TK 12 M41B (76mm)
APC (W) 8 LAV-150 *Commando*
ARTY 104
  TOWED 105mm 16: 4 M101; 12 *Reinosa* 105/26
  MOR 88: **81mm** 60 M1; **107mm** 4 M-30; **120mm** 24 Expal Model L
AT
  RCL 106mm 20 M40A1
  GUNS 37mm 20 M3
HELICOPTERS
  ISR 8: 4 OH-58A *Kiowa*; 4 OH-58C *Kiowa*
  TPT • Light 6: 4 R-22; 2 R-44 *Raven II*

Navy 4,000

HQ located at Santo Domingo

FORCES BY ROLE
SPECIAL FORCES
  1 (SEAL) SF unit

MANOEUVRE
  Amphibious
  1 mne sy unit
EQUIPMENT BY TYPE
PATROL AND COASTAL COMBATANTS 19
  PCO 2 *Balsam*
  PCC 2 *Tortuguero* (US ABU)
  PB 15: 2 *Altair* (Swiftships 35m); 4 *Bellatrix* (US Sewart Seacraft); 2 *Canopus*; 4 *Hamal* (Damen Stan 1505); 3 *Point*
AMPHIBIOUS 1 *Neyba* (US LCU 1675)
LOGISTICS AND SUPPORT 11
  AG 9
  AT 1
  YFD 1

Air Force 5,500

Flying hours   60 hrs/year

FORCES BY ROLE
GROUND ATTACK
  1 sqn with EMB-314 *Super Tucano**
SEARCH & RESCUE
  1 sqn with Bell 205 (UH-1H *Huey II*); Bell 205 (UH-1H *Iroquois*); Bell 430 (VIP); OH-58 *Kiowa* (CH-136); S-333
TRANSPORT
  1 sqn with C-212-400 *Aviocar*; PA-31 *Navajo*
TRAINING
  1 sqn with T-35B *Pillan*
AIR DEFENCE
  1 ADA bn with 20mm guns

EQUIPMENT BY TYPE
AIRCRAFT 8 combat capable
  ISR 1 AMT-200 *Super Ximango*
  TPT • Light 12: 3 C-212-400 *Aviocar*; 1 Cessna 172; 1 Cessna 182; 1 Cessna 206; 1 Cessna 207; 1 *Commander* 690; 3 EA-100; 1 PA-31 *Navajo*
  TRG 14: 8 EMB-314 *Super Tucano**; 6 T-35B *Pillan*
HELICOPTERS
  ISR 9 OH-58 *Kiowa* (CH-136)
  TPT • Light 16: 8 Bell 205 (UH-1H *Huey* II); 5 Bell 205 (UH-1H *Iroquois*); 1 Bell 430 (VIP); 2 S-333
AD • GUNS 20mm 4

Paramilitary 15,000

National Police 15,000

Ecuador ECU

US Dollar $[a]		2011	2012	2013
GDP	US$	66.47bn	70.84bn	
per capita	US$	4,366	4,653	
Growth	%	7.78	4.05	
Inflation	%	4.48	5.05	
Def bdgt	US$	1.51bn	1.51bn	
FMA (US)	US$	0.499m	0.45m	0.45m

[a] The US dollar was adopted as the official currency in 2000

Population   15,223,680

Age	0–14	15–19	20–24	25–29	30–64	65 plus
Male	15.1%	4.9%	4.5%	4.2%	17.9%	3.2%
Female	14.5%	4.8%	4.5%	4.2%	18.9%	3.4%

Capabilities

Border security has long been a priority and a source of friction for the state. Clashes with Peru in the 1990s were only resolved in 1998 with a peace treaty. In recent years there has been tension with Colombia over their shared border and the impact of Colombia's conflict with FARC rebels. A border incursion by Colombian forces in 2008 resulted in a military shake-up. Defence policy is predicated on guaranteeing sovereignty and the territorial integrity of the state, with the desire for the military to also participate in international peacekeeping. The army is coming toward the end of a period of change, which included relocating units to reflect tensions with Colombia, along with renewed emphasis on border security. The services exercise regularly, with the army and navy also participating in international exercises. Much of the services' inventory is ageing, with acquisitions often second-hand. The air force, in 2011, purchased 12 ex-South African Air Force *Cheetah* fighter aircraft, while the navy's frigates were bought from Chile. The military has no genuine capacity for sustained power projection beyond national borders.

ACTIVE 58,000 (Army 46,500 Navy 7,300 Air 4,200)
Paramilitary 500

Terms of Service conscription 1 year, selective

RESERVE 118,000 (Joint 118,000)

Ages 18–55

ORGANISATIONS BY SERVICE

Army 46,500

FORCES BY ROLE
gp are bn sized.
COMMAND
  4 div HQ
SPECIAL FORCES
  1 (9th) SF bde (3 SF gp; 1 SF sqn, 1 para bn,1 sigs sqn, 1 log comd)

MANOEUVRE
  Mechanised
  1 (11th) armd cav bde (3 armd cav gp, 1 mech inf bn, 1 SP arty gp, 1 engr gp)
  1 (5th) inf bde (1 SF sqn, 2 mech cav gp, 2 inf bn, 1 cbt engr coy, 1 sigs coy, 1 log coy)
  Light
  1 (1st) inf bde (1 SF sqn, 1 armd cav gp, 1 armd recce sqn, 3 inf bn, 1 med coy)
  1 (3rd) inf bde (1 SF gp, 1 mech cav gp, 1 inf bn, 1 arty gp, 1 hvy mor coy, 1 cbt engr coy, 1 sigs coy, 1 log coy)
  1 (7th) inf bde (1 SF sqn, 1 armd recce sqn, 1 mech cav gp, 3 inf bn, 1 jungle bn, 1 arty gp, 1 cbt engr coy, 1 sigs coy, 1 log coy, 1 med coy)
  1 (13th) inf bde (1 SF sqn, 1 armd recce sqn, 1 mot cav gp, 3 inf bn, 1 arty gp, 1 hvy mor coy, 1 cbt engr coy, 1sigs coy, 1 log coy)
  Jungle
  2 (17th & 21st) jungle bde (3 jungle bn, 1 cbt engr coy, 1 sigs coy, 1 log coy)
  1 (19th) jungle bde (3 jungle bn, 1 jungle trg bn, 1 cbt engr coy, 1 sigs coy, 1 log coy)
  Aviation
  1 (15th) avn bde (2 tpt avn gp, 2 hel gp, 1 mixed avn gp)
COMBAT SUPPORT
  1 (27th) arty bde (1 SP arty gp, 1 MRL gp, 1 ADA gp, 1 cbt engr coy, 1 sigs coy, 1 log coy)
  1 ADA gp
  1 (23rd) engr bde (3 engr bn)
  2 indep MP coy
  1 indep sigs coy
COMBAT SERVICE SUPPORT
  1 (25th) log bde
  2 log bn
  2 indep med coy

EQUIPMENT BY TYPE
LT TK 24 AMX-13
RECCE 67: 25 AML-90; 10 EE-3 *Jararaca*; 32 EE-9 *Cascavel*
APC 123
  APC (T) 95: 80 AMX-VCI; 15 M113
  APC (W) 28: 18 EE-11 *Urutu*; 10 UR-416
ARTY 541+
  SP 155mm 5 (AMX) Mk F3
  TOWED 100: **105mm** 78: 30 M101; 24 M2A2; 24 Model 56 pack howitzer; **155mm** 22: 12 M114; 10 M198
  MRL 24: 18 122mm BM-21, 6 RM-70
  MOR 412+: **81mm** 400 M-29; **107mm** M-30 (4.2in); **160mm** 12 M-66 Soltam
AT
  RCL 404: **106mm** 24 M40A1; **90mm** 380 M67
AIRCRAFT
  TPT • Light 17: 1 Beech 200 *King Air*; 2 C-212; 2 CN-235; 4 Cessna 172; 2 Cessna 206; 1 Cessna 500 *Citation I*; 4 IAI-201 *Arava*; 1 PC-6B *Turbo-Porter*
  TRG 4: 2 MX-7-235 *Star Rocket*; 2 T-41D *Mescalero*
HELICOPTERS
  MRH 26: 6 Mi-17-1V *Hip*; 3 SA315B *Lama*; 18 SA342L *Gazelle* (13 with HOT for anti-armour role)
  TPT 10 **Medium** 7: 5 AS332B *Super Puma*; 2 Mi-171E; (3

SA330 *Puma* in store) **Light** 2 AS350B *Ecureuil*; 2 AS350B2 *Ecureuil*

AD

SAM • MANPAD 185+: 75 *Blowpipe*; 20+ 9K32 *Strela-2* (SA-7 *Grail*)‡; 90 9K38 *Igla* (SA-18 *Grouse*)

GUNS 240

SP 44 M163 *Vulcan*

TOWED 196: **14.5mm** 128 ZPU-1/-2; **20mm** 38: 28 M-1935, 10 M167 *Vulcan*; **40mm** 30 L/70/M1A1

Navy 7,300 (incl Naval Aviation, Marines and Coast Guard)

EQUIPMENT BY TYPE
SUBMARINES • TACTICAL • SSK 2:
2 *Shyri*† (GER T-209/1300, undergoing refit in Chile) each with 8 single 533mm TT each with SUT HWT

PRINCIPAL SURFACE COMBATANTS 2

FRIGATES 2:

FFGHM 1 *Presidente Eloy Alfaro*† (ex-UK *Leander* batch II) with 4 single lnchr with MM-40 *Exocet* AShM, 3 twin lnchr with *Mistral* SAM, 1 twin 114mm gun, (capacity 1 Bell 206B *Jet Ranger II* hel)

FFGH 1 *Condell* (mod UK *Leander*) with 4 single lnchr with MM-40 *Exocet* AShM, 2 triple ASTT with Mk 46 LWT, 1 twin 114mm gun, (capacity 1 Bell 206B *Jet Ranger II* hel)

PATROL AND COASTAL COMBATANTS 9

CORVETTES • FSGM 6 *Esmeraldas* (4†) with 2 triple lnchr with MM-40 *Exocet* AShM, 1 quad lnchr with *Aspide* SAM, 2 triple B515 *ILAS-3* 324mm with A244 LWT (removed from two vessels), 1 76mm gun, 1 hel landing platform (upgrade programme ongoing)

PCFG 3 *Quito* (GER Lurssen TNC-45 45m) with 4 single lnchr with MM-38 *Exocet* AShM, 1 76mm gun (upgrade programme ongoing)

LOGISTICS AND SUPPORT 13

AE 1

AG 1

AGOS 1 *Orion*

AGS 1

AK 1

AOL 1 *Taurus*

ATF 2

AWT 2

AXS 1

YFD 2 *Rio Napo* (US *ARD 12*)

Naval Aviation 380

AIRCRAFT

MP 1 CN-235-300M

ISR 3: 2 Beech 200T *King Air*; 1 Beech 300 *Catpass King Air*

TPT • Light 3: 1 Beech 200 *King Air*; 1 Beech 300 *King Air*; 1 CN-235-100

TRG 6: 2 T-34C *Turbo Mentor*; 4 T-35B *Pillan*

HELICOPTERS

TPT • Light 9: 3 Bell 206A; 3 Bell 206B; 1 Bell 230; 2 Bell 430

UAV • ISR 6: **Heavy** 2 *Heron* **Medium** 4 *Searcher* Mk.II

Marines 2,150

FORCES BY ROLE
SPECIAL FORCES
1 cdo unit
MANOEUVRE
Amphibious
5 mne bn (on garrison duties)
EQUIPMENT BY TYPE
ARTY • MOR 32+ 60mm/81mm/120mm
AD • SAM • MANPAD 64 *Mistral*/9K38 *Igla* (SA-18 *Grouse*)

Air Force 4,200

Operational Command

FORCES BY ROLE
FIGHTER
1 sqn with *Cheetah* C/D; *Mirage* 50DV/EV
FIGHTER/GROUND ATTACK
2 sqn with EMB-314 *Super Tucano**
1 sqn with *Kfir* C.10 (CE); *Kfir* C-2; *Kfir* TC-2

Military Air Transport Group

FORCES BY ROLE
SEARCH & RESCUE/TRANSPORT HELICOPTER
1 sqn with Bell 206B *Jet Ranger II*
1 sqn with *Dhruv*; PA-34 *Seneca*
TRANSPORT
1 sqn with C-130/H *Hercules*; L-100-30
1 sqn with HS-748
1 sqn with DHC-6-300 *Twin Otter*
1 sqn with B-727; EMB-135BJ *Legacy* 600; F-28 *Fellowship*; *Sabreliner* 40/60
TRAINING
1 sqn with Cessna 150/206; DA20-C1; MXP-650; T-34C *Turbo Mentor*

EQUIPMENT BY TYPE
AIRCRAFT 48 combat capable
FGA 31: 10 *Cheetah* C; 2 *Cheetah* D; 4 *Kfir* C.2; 7 *Kfir* C.10 (CE); 2 *Kfir* TC.2; 3 *Mirage* 50DV; 3 *Mirage* 50EV
TPT 37 **Medium** 4: 2 C-130B *Hercules*; 1 C-130H *Hercules*; 1 L-100-30; **Light** 21: 1 Beech E90 *King Air*; 7 Cessna 150; 1 Cessna 206; 3 DHC-6 *Twin Otter*; 1 EMB-135BJ *Legacy* 600; 2 EMB-170; 1 EMB-190; 1 MXP-650; 2 *Sabreliner* 40; 1 *Sabreliner* 60; 1 PA-34 *Seneca* **PAX** 12: 2 A320; 3 B-727; 1 F-28 *Fellowship*; 6 HS-748
TRG 35: 6 DA20-C1; 17 EMB-314 *Super Tucano**; 12 T-34C *Turbo Mentor*
HELICOPTERS
MRH 8: 2 AS550C3 *Fennec*; 6 *Dhruv*
TPT • Light 8 Bell 206B *Jet Ranger II*
MSL • AAM • IR 60 *Python* III; 50 *Python* IV; R-550 *Magic*; *Shafrir*‡ **SARH** Super 530
AD
MSL
SAM 7 M48 *Chaparral*
SP 6 9K33 *Osa* (SA-8 *Gecko*)
MANPAD 185+: 75 *Blowpipe*; 9K32 *Strela-2* (SA-7 *Grail*)‡; 20 9K310 *Igla-1* (SA-16 *Gimlet*); 90 9K38 *Igla* (SA-18 *Grouse*)

GUNS
SP 20mm 28 M35

TOWED 64: **23mm** 34 ZU-23; **35mm** 30 GDF-002 (twin)

RADAR: 2 CFTC gap fillers; 2 CETC 2D

Paramilitary
All police forces; 39,500

Police Air Service
HELICOPTERS •

ISR 3 MD530F

TPT • **Light** 6: 2 AS350B *Ecureuil*; 1 Bell 206B *Jet Ranger*; 3 R-44

Coast Guard 500
PATROL AND COASTAL COMBATANTS 19

PCC 3 *Isla Fernandina* (*Vigilante*)

PB 8: 2 10 *de Agosto*; 2 *Espada*; 1 *Isla Isabela*; 2 *Manta* (GER Lurssen 36m); 1 *Point*

PBR 8: 2 *Río Esmeraldas*; 6 *Rio Puyango*

DEPLOYMENT

CÔTE D'IVOIRE
UN • UNOCI 1 obs

HAITI
UN • MINUSTAH 67; elm 1 engr coy

LIBERIA
UN • UNMIL 1; 2 obs

SOUTH SUDAN
UN • UNMISS 4 obs

SUDAN
UN • UNISFA 1 obs

El Salvador SLV

El Salvador Colon C		2011	2012	2013
GDP	C	22.76bn	23.99bn	
	US$	200bn	214bn	
per capita	US$	3,737	3,939	
Growth	%	1.40	1.50	
Inflation	%	3.58	4.00	
Def bdgt	C	1.28bn	1.29bn	
	US$	146m	144m	
FMA (US)	US$	1.25m	1.25m	1.8m
US$1=C		8.79	8.93	

Population	6,090,646

Age	0–14	15–19	20–24	25–29	30–64	65 plus
Male	15.3%	5.7%	4.8%	3.9%	15.7%	2.9%
Female	14.5%	5.5%	4.9%	4.2%	19.1%	3.6%

Capabilities

Since the end of the country's civil war in 1992, the Salvadorian military has been dramatically reduced in size. Despite this, El Salvador has been able to deploy small forces to both Iraq, where its forces were reportedly well-regarded by its coalition partners, and Afghanistan. Challenges for the armed forces include boosting professionalisation, and tackling organised crime and narcotics-trafficking. In 2009, high crime rates led the government to deploy the army in support of the police, deploying in high-crime areas as well as border zones.

ACTIVE 15,300 (Army 13,850 Navy 700 Air 750)
Paramilitary 17,000
Terms of Service conscription 18 months voluntary

RESERVE 9,900 (Joint 9,900)

ORGANISATIONS BY SERVICE

Army 9,850; 4,000 conscript (total 13,850)
FORCES BY ROLE
SPECIAL FORCES
   1 spec ops gp (1 SF coy, 1 para bn, 1 (naval inf) coy)
MANOEUVRE
   Reconnaissance
   1 armd cav regt (2 armd cav bn)
   Light
   6 inf bde (3 inf bn)
   Other
   1 (special) sy bde (2 border gd bn, 2 MP bn)
COMBAT SUPPORT
   1 arty bde (2 fd arty bn, 1 AD bn)
   1 engr comd (2 engr bn)
EQUIPMENT BY TYPE
RECCE 5 AML-90; 4 (in store)
APC (W) 38: 30 M37B1 *Cashuat* (mod); 8 UR-416
ARTY 217+
   TOWED 105mm 54: 36 M102; 18 M-56 (FRY)
   MOR 163+: **81mm** 151 M29; **120mm** 12+: (M-74 in store); 12 UBM 52
AT
   RCL 399: **106mm** 20 M40A1 (incl 16 SP); **90mm** 379 M67
AD • **GUNS** 35: **20mm** 31 M-55; 4 TCM-20

Navy 700 (incl some 90 Naval Inf and SF)
EQUIPMENT BY TYPE
PATROL AND COASTAL COMBATANTS 11
   PCO 1 *Balsam*
   PB 10: 3 *Camcraft* (30m); 1 *Point*; 1 *Swiftships* 77; 1 *Swiftships* 65; 4 Type-44 (ex-USCG)
AMPHIBIOUS • **LANDING CRAFT**
   LCM 4

Naval Inf (SF Commandos) 90
FORCES BY ROLE
SPECIAL FORCES
   1 SF coy

Air Force 750 (incl 200 Air Defence)

Flying hours   90 hrs/year on A-37 *Dragonfly*

FORCES BY ROLE
FIGHTER/GROUND ATTACK/ISR
1 sqn with A-37B *Dragonfly*; O-2A *Skymaster**
TRANSPORT
1 sqn with BT-67; Cessna 210 *Centurion*; Cessna 337G; Commander 114; IAI-202 *Arava*; SA-226T *Merlin IIIB*
TRAINING
1 sqn with R-235GT *Guerrier*; T-35 *Pillan*; T-41D *Mescalero*; TH-300
TRANSPORT HELICOPTER
1 sqn with Bell 205 (UH-1H *Iroquois*); Bell 407; Bell 412EP *Twin Huey*; MD-500E; UH-1M *Iroquois*

EQUIPMENT BY TYPE
AIRCRAFT 16 combat capable
ATK 4 A-37B *Dragonfly*
ISR 11: 6 O-2A/B *Skymaster**; 5 OA-37B *Dragonfly**
TPT • Light 10: 2 BT-67; 2 Cessna 210 *Centurion*; 1 Cessna 337G *Skymaster*; 1 Commander 114; 3 IAI-201 *Arava*; 1 SA-226T *Merlin IIIB*
TRG 11: 5 R-235GT *Guerrier*; 5 T-35 *Pillan*; 1 T-41D *Mescalero*
HELICOPTERS
MRH 13: 4 Bell 412EP *Twin Huey*; 7 MD-500E; 2 UH-1M *Iroquois*
TPT• Light 19: 18 Bell-205 (UH-1H *Iroquois*) (incl 4 SAR); 1 Bell 407 (VIP tpt, govt owned)
TRG 5 TH-300
MSL • AAM • IR *Shafrir* ‡

Paramilitary 17,000

National Civilian Police 17,000

Ministry of Public Security
AIRCRAFT
ISR 1 O-2A *Skymaster*
TPT • Light 1 Cessna 310
HELICOPTERS
MRH 2 MD-520N
TPT • Light 3: 1 Bell 205 (UH-1H *Iroquois*); 2 R-44 *Raven* II

DEPLOYMENT

AFGHANISTAN
NATO • ISAF 24

CÔTE D'IVOIRE
UN • UNOCI 3 obs

LEBANON
UN • UNIFIL 52; 1 inf pl

LIBERIA
UN • UNMIL 2 obs

SOUTH SUDAN
UN • UNMISS 2 obs
UN • UNISFA 1 obs

WESTERN SAHARA
UN • MINURSO 3 obs

FOREIGN FORCES

United States US Southern Command: 1 Forward Operating Location (Military, DEA, USCG and Customs personnel)

Guatemala GUA

Guatemalan Quetzal q		2011	2012	2013
GDP	q	365.14bn	393.72bn	
	US$	46.9bn	50.3bn	
per capita	US$	3,326	3,568	
Growth	%	3.87	3.10	
Inflation	%	6.22	3.93	
Def bdgt	q	1.55bn	1.61bn	
	US$	200m	206m	
FMA (US)	US$	0.499m	0.5m	0.75m
US$1=q		7.79	7.83	

Population   14,099,032

Age	0–14	15–19	20–24	25–29	30–64	65 plus
Male	19.0%	6.0%	5.2%	4.1%	13.2%	1.9%
Female	18.3%	5.9%	5.2%	4.3%	14.8%	2.2%

Capabilities

The peace accords that ended the Guatemalan civil war in 1996 mandated both a reduction in the size of the military, and an exclusive focus on external threats. As a result of these restrictions, manpower levels have fallen by about one-third and procurement of new equipment has been limited. Rising levels of organised crime and narcotics-trafficking have led the current administration to seek to reverse this trend, with proposed increases to the defence budget linked to new procurement and recruitment drives. As well as combating criminality, the armed forces retain a focus on participation in international operations as well as HA/DR tasks. Given the level of transnational organised criminality and narcotics-trafficking in Central America, Guatemala's armed forces engage in close cooperation with forces from Mexico, El Salvador and Honduras.

ACTIVE 17,300 (Army 15,550 Navy 900 Air 850)
Paramilitary 25,000

RESERVE 63,850 (Navy 650 Air 900 Armed Forces 62,300)

(National Armed Forces are combined; the army provides log spt for navy and air force)

ORGANISATIONS BY SERVICE

Army 15,550
15 Military Zones

FORCES BY ROLE
SPECIAL FORCES
  1 SF bde (1 SF bn, 1 trg bn)
  1 SF bde (1 SF coy, 1 ranger bn)
MANOEUVRE
  Light
  1 (strategic reserve) mech bde (1 inf bn, 1 cav regt, 1 log coy)
  6 inf bde (1 inf bn)
  Air Manoeuvre
  1 AB bde with (2 AB bn)
  Other
  1 (Presidential) gd bde (1 gd bn, 1 MP bn, 1 CSS coy)
COMBAT SUPPORT
  1 engr comd (1 engr bn, 1 construction bn)
  2 MP bde with (1 MP bn)

Reserves

FORCES BY ROLE
MANOEUVRE
  Light
  ε19 inf bn
EQUIPMENT BY TYPE
RECCE (7 M8 in store)
APC 47
  APC (T) 10 M113 (5 more in store)
  APC (W) 37: 30 Armadillo; 7 V-100 Commando
ARTY 149
  TOWED 105mm 76: 12 M101; 8 M102; 56 M-56
  MOR 73: 81mm 55 M1 **107mm** (12 M-30 in store)
  120mm 18 ECIA
AT
  RCL 120+: 105mm 64 M-1974 FMK-1 (ARG); **106mm** 56 M40A1; **75mm** M20
AD • GUNS • TOWED 32: **20mm** 16 GAI-D01; 16 M-55

Navy 900

EQUIPMENT BY TYPE
PATROL AND COASTAL COMBATANTS 10
  PB 10: 6 Cutlass; 1 Dauntless; 1 Kukulkan (US Broadsword 32m); 2 Sewart
AMPHIBIOUS • LANDING CRAFT • LCP 2 Machete
LOGISTICS AND SUPPORT • AXS 3

Marines 650 reservists

FORCES BY ROLE
MANOEUVRE
  Amphibious
  2 mne bn (-)

Air Force 850

2 Air Comd
FORCES BY ROLE
FIGHTER/GROUND ATTACK/ISR
  1 sqn with A-37B Dragonfly
  1 sqn with PC-7 Turbo Trainer*
TRANSPORT
  1 sqn with BT-67; Beech 90/100/200/300 King Air; IAI-201 Arava

  1 (tactical support) sqn with Cessna 206; PA-31 Navajo
TRAINING
  1 sqn with Cessna R172K Hawk XP; T-35B Pillan
TRANSPORT HELICOPTER
  1 sqn with Bell 206 Jet Ranger; Bell 212 (armed); Bell 412 Twin Huey (armed); UH-1H Iroquois
EQUIPMENT BY TYPE
Serviceability of ac is less than 50%
AIRCRAFT 9 combat capable
  ATK 2 A-37B Dragonfly
  TPT • Light 26: 5 Beech 90 King Air; 1 Beech 100 King Air; 1 Beech 200 King Air; 2 Beech 300 King Air; 4 BT-67; 2 Cessna 206; 1 Cessna 208B; 5 Cessna R172K Hawk XP; 4 IAI-201 Arava; 1 PA-31 Navajo
  TRG 11: 7 PC-7 Turbo Trainer*; 4 T-35B Pillan
HELICOPTERS
  MRH 2 Bell 412 Twin Huey (armed)
  TPT • Light 18: 2 Bell 205 (UH-1H Iroquois); 9 Bell 206 Jet Ranger; 7 Bell 212 (armed)

Tactical Security Group

Air Military Police

Paramilitary 25,000 active

National Civil Police 25,000

FORCES BY ROLE
SPECIAL FORCES
  1 SF bn
MANOEUVRE
  Other
  1 (integrated task force) paramilitary unit (incl mil and treasury police)

DEPLOYMENT

CÔTE D'IVOIRE
UN • UNOCI 5 obs

DEMOCRATIC REPUBLIC OF THE CONGO
UN • MONUSCO 150; 1 obs; 1 SF coy

HAITI
UN • MINUSTAH 138; 1 MP coy

LEBANON
UN • UNIFIL 3

SOUTH SUDAN
UN • UNMISS 2; 3 obs

SUDAN
UN • UNISFA 1; 2 obs

Guyana GUY

Guyanese Dollar G$		2011	2012	2013
GDP	G$	525.67bn	574.57bn	
	US$	2.58bn	2.79bn	
per capita	US$	3,478	3,761	
Growth	%	5.44	3.66	
Inflation	%	4.96	2.96	
Def bdgt	G$	6.16bn	6.32bn	
	US$	30m	31m	
US$1=G$		203.99	206.09	

Population   741,908

Age	0–14	15–19	20–24	25–29	30–64	65 plus
Male	15.8%	5.8%	4.7%	3.8%	17.7%	2.0%
Female	15.3%	5.5%	4.4%	3.4%	18.7%	2.9%

Capabilities

The country has a very limited military capability based on the Guyana Defence Force which also undertakes paramilitary and policing tasks. Border issues with Venezuela and Suriname have, in the past, been the focus of security concerns.

ACTIVE 1,100 (Army 900 Navy 100 Air 100)

Active numbers combined Guyana Defence Force

RESERVE 670 (Army 500 Navy 170)

ORGANISATIONS BY SERVICE

Army 900

FORCES BY ROLE
SPECIAL FORCES
  1 SF coy
MANOEUVRE
  Light
  1 inf bn
  Other
  1 (Presidential) gd bn
COMBAT SUPPORT
  1 arty coy
  1 (spt wpn) cbt spt coy
  1 engr coy
EQUIPMENT BY TYPE
RECCE 9: 6 EE-9 *Cascavel* (reported); 3 S52 *Shorland*
ARTY 54
  TOWED 130mm 6 M-46†
  MOR 48: 81mm 12 L16A1; **82mm** 18 M-43; **120mm** 18 M-43

Navy 100

EQUIPMENT BY TYPE
PATROL AND COASTAL COMBATANTS 5
  PCO 1 *Essequibo* (ex-UK *River*)
  PB 4 *Barracuda*

Air Force 100

FORCES BY ROLE
TRANSPORT
  1 unit with Bell 206; Cessna 206; Y-12 (II)
EQUIPMENT BY TYPE
AIRCRAFT • TPT • **Light** 2: 1 Cessna 206; 1 Y-12 (II)
HELICOPTERS
  MRH 1 Bell 412 *Twin Huey*†
  TPT • Light 2 Bell 206

Haiti HTI

Haitian Gourde G		2011	2012	2013
GDP	G	297.69bn	328.81bn	
	US$	7.39bn	7.9bn	
per capita	US$	754	806	
Growth	%	5.59	4.50	
Inflation	%	7.39	6.72	
FMA (US)	US$	1.597m	–	1.6m
US$1=G		40.29	41.65	

Population   9,801,664

Age	0–14	15–19	20–24	25–29	30–64	65 plus
Male	17.7%	5.7%	5.0%	4.3%	15.2%	1.8%
Female	17.6%	5.7%	5.0%	4.3%	15.6%	2.2%

Capabilities

No active armed forces. On 1 June 2004, following a period of armed conflict, the United Nations established a multinational stabilisation mission in Haiti (MINUSTAH). Continuing tensions with MINUSTAH, following the 2010 earthquake and the 2011 cholera outbreak, have led to calls for national armed forces to be re-established, however. Following his election in 2011, President Martelly asked international donors for US$95m to fund a new 3,500-strong army. Mindful of the history of armed forces in Haiti, it is anticipated that this might start with the creation of an engineering unit capable of deploying within Haiti.

Paramilitary 50

ORGANISATIONS BY SERVICE

Paramilitary 50

Coast Guard ε50

EQUIPMENT BY TYPE
PATROL AND COASTAL COMBATANTS • PB 5
  Dauntless

FOREIGN FORCES

Argentina 723; 1 inf bn; 1 avn coy; 1 spt coy; 1 fd hospital
Bolivia 209; 1 inf coy
Brazil 1,894; 2 inf bn; 1 engr coy
Canada 5
Chile 498; 1 inf bn; mne coy (-); 1 avn coy; elm 1 engr coy

Ecuador 67; elm 1 engr coy
France 3
Guatemala 138; 1 MP coy
Indonesia 168: 1 engr coy
Japan 225; 1 engr coy
Jordan 252; 1 inf coy
Korea, Republic of 242; 1 engr coy
Nepal 361; 2 inf coy
Paraguay 162; 1 engr coy
Peru 372; 1 inf coy
Philippines 157; 1 HQ coy
Sri Lanka 861; 1 inf bn
United States 8
Uruguay 957; 2 inf bn; 1 mne coy, 1 avn sect

Honduras HND

Honduran Lempira L			2011	2012	2013
GDP		L	329.66bn	356.92bn	
		US$	17.37bn	18.18bn	
per capita		US$	2,094	2,191	
Growth		%	3.62	3.83	
Inflation		%	6.76	5.79	
Def bdgt[a]		L	2.68bn	2.94bn	
		US$	141m	150m	
FMA (US)		US$	0.998m	1m	3m
US$1=L			18.98	19.63	

[a] Excludes military pensions

Population 8,296,693

Age	0–14	15–19	20–24	25–29	30–64	65 plus
Male	18.4%	5.7%	5.1%	4.5%	14.9%	1.7%
Female	17.7%	5.5%	4.9%	4.3%	15.2%	2.1%

Capabilities

Prior to the coup of 2009, the administration of President Zelaya had appeared to have achieved some success in improving the conditions, morale and professionalism of the Honduran armed forces. However, although recruitment levels improved, the declared target of a 15,000-strong military was never achieved. In 2011, the Honduran military began to be deployed in a paramilitary role, in conjunction with the police, in order to combat organised crime and narcotics-trafficking.

ACTIVE 12,000 (Army 8,300 Navy 1,400 Air 2,300)
Paramilitary 8,000

RESERVE 60,000 (Joint 60,000; Ex-servicemen registered)

ORGANISATIONS BY SERVICE

Army 8,300
6 Military Zones

FORCES BY ROLE
SPECIAL FORCES
1 (special tac) SF gp (1 SF bn, 1 inf/AB bn)
MANOEUVRE
Mechanised
1 armd cav regt (1 recce sqn, 1 lt tk sqn, 2 mech bn, 1 arty bty, 1 ADA bty)
Light
3 inf bde (3 inf bn, 1 arty bn)
1 inf bde (3 inf bn)
Other
1 (Presidential) gd coy
COMBAT SUPPORT
1 engr bn

Reserves

FORCES BY ROLE
MANOEUVRE
Light
1 inf bde

EQUIPMENT BY TYPE
LT TK 12 Scorpion
RECCE 57: 13 RBY-1; 40 Saladin; 3 Scimitar; 1 Sultan
ARTY 118+
TOWED 28: **105mm:** 24 M102; **155mm:** 4 M198
MOR 90+: **60mm; 81mm; 120mm** 60 FMK-2; **160mm** 30 M-66
AT • RCL 170: **106mm** 50 M40A1; **84mm** 120 Carl Gustav
AD • GUNS 48: **20mm** 24 M55A2; 24 TCM-20

Navy 1,400
EQUIPMENT BY TYPE
PATROL AND COASTAL COMBATANTS 15
PB 15: 1 Chameleon (Swiftships 85); 1 Tegucilgalpa (US Guardian 32m); 4 Guanaja; 3 Guaymuras (Swiftships 105); 5 Nacaome (Swiftships 65); 1 Rio Coco (US PB Mk III)
AMPHIBIOUS • LANDING CRAFT 3
LCU 1 Punta Caxinas
LCM 2

Marines 830
FORCES BY ROLE
MANOEUVRE
Amphibious
1 mne bn

Air Force 2,300
FORCES BY ROLE
FIGHTER/GROUND ATTACK
1 sqn with A-37B Dragonfly
1 sqn with F-5E/F Tiger II
GROUND ATTACK/ISR/TRAINING
1 unit with Cessna 182 Skylane; EMB-312 Tucano; MXT-7-180 Star Rocket
TRANSPORT
1 sqn with C-130A Hercules; Cessna 185/210; IAI-201 Arava; PA-42 Cheyenne
1 VIP flt with PA-31 Navajo; Bell 412SP Twin Huey
TRANSPORT HELICOPTER
1 sqn with Bell 205 (UH-1H Iroquois); Bell 412SP Twin Huey

EQUIPMENT BY TYPE
AIRCRAFT 17 combat capable
  FTR 11: 9 F-5E *Tiger* II†; 2 F-5F *Tiger* II†
  ATK 6 A-37B *Dragonfly*
  TPT 8 **Medium** 1 C-130A *Hercules* **Light** 7: 2 Cessna 182 *Skylane*; 1 Cessna 185; 1 Cessna 210; 1 IAI-201 *Arava*; 1 PA-31 *Navajo*; 1 PA-42 *Cheyenne*
  TRG 16: 9 EMB-312 *Tucano*; 7 MXT-7-180 *Star Rocket*
HELICOPTERS
  MRH 7: 5 Bell 412SP *Twin Huey*; 2 Hughes 500
  TPT • **Light** 2 Bell 205 (UH-1H *Iroquois*)
MSL • **AAM** • **IR** *Shafrir*‡

Paramilitary 8,000

Public Security Forces 8,000
Ministry of Public Security and Defence; 11 regional comd

DEPLOYMENT

WESTERN SAHARA
UN • MINURSO 12 obs

FOREIGN FORCES

United States US Southern Command: 360; 1 avn bn with CH-47 *Chinook*; UH-60 *Black Hawk*

Jamaica JAM

Jamaican Dollar J$		2011	2012	2013
GDP	J$	1.24tr	1.35tr	
	US$	14.49bn	15.26bn	
per capita	US$	5,015	5,282	
Growth	%	1.27	0.89	
Inflation	%	7.53	7.26	
Def bdgt	J$	11.9bn	10.9bn	
	US$	139m	124m	
US$1=J$			85.70	88.21

Population   2,889,187

Age	0–14	15–19	20–24	25–29	30–64	65 plus
Male	15.0%	5.6%	5.3%	4.5%	15.6%	3.4%
Female	14.5%	5.5%	5.3%	4.7%	16.2%	4.2%

Capabilities

The primary mission of the Jamaican Defence Forces is to provide assistance to the Jamaica Constabulary in its activities against organised crime; a role that has proven controversial domestically. It receives support from the Canadian Armed Forces, most tangibly in the deployment of a small number of CH-146 helicopters for SAR missions.

ACTIVE 2,830 (Army 2,500 Coast Guard 190 Air 140)
(combined Jamaican Defence Force)

RESERVE 980 (Army 900 Navy 60 Air 20)

ORGANISATIONS BY SERVICE

Army 2,500
FORCES BY ROLE
MANOEUVRE
  Light
  2 inf bn
COMBAT SUPPORT
  1 engr regt (4 engr sqn)
COMBAT SERVICE SUPPORT
  1 log bn
EQUIPMENT BY TYPE
APC (W) 4 LAV-150 *Commando*
MOR 81mm 12 L16A1

Reserves
FORCES BY ROLE
MANOEUVRE
  Light
  1 inf bn

Coast Guard 190
EQUIPMENT BY TYPE
PATROL AND COASTAL COMBATANTS 11
  PBF 3
  PB 8: 3 *Cornwall* (Damen Stan 4207); 4 *Dauntless*; 1 *Paul Bogle* (US 31m)

Air Wing 140
Plus National Reserve
FORCES BY ROLE
MARITIME PATROL/TRANSPORT
  1 flt with BN-2A *Defender*; Cessna 210M *Centurion*
SEARCH & RESCUE/TRANSPORT HELICOPTER
  1 flt with Bell 407
  1 flt with Bell 412EP
TRAINING
  1 unit with Bell 206B-3; DA-40-180FP *Diamond Star*
EQUIPMENT BY TYPE
AIRCRAFT
  TPT • **Light** 4: 1 BN-2A *Defender*; 1 Cessna 210M *Centurion*; 2 DA40-180FP *Diamond Star*
HELICOPTERS
  MRH 3 Bell 412EP
  TPT • **Light** 5: 2 Bell 206B-3 *Jet Ranger*; 3 Bell 407

FOREIGN FORCES

Canada *Operation Jaguar*: 65 (SAR spt)

Mexico MEX

Mexican Peso NP		2011	2012	2013
GDP	NP	14.34tr	15.67tr	
	US$	1.15tr	1.16tr	
per capita	US$	10,002	10,089	
Growth	%	3.94	3.78	
Inflation	%	3.40	3.95	
Def bdgt[a]	NP	62.8bn	68.9bn	
	US$	5.05bn	5.11bn	
FMA (US)	US$	7.98m	7m	7m
US$1=NP		12.42	13.47	

[a] National security expenditure

Population   114,975,406

Age	0–14	15–19	20–24	25–29	30–64	65 plus
Male	14.2%	4.7%	4.4%	4.0%	18.5%	3.4%
Female	13.6%	4.6%	4.5%	4.2%	20.6%	4.2%

Capabilities

Mexico's armed forces are continuing to adapt to the country's identified national-security priorities; combating organised crime and countering the narcotics trade. Operations against drug cartels have become the army's primary activity, involving about a quarter of its active strength at any given time. In a similar vein, the navy and air force have both prioritised procurement of ISR and transport platforms. Although it retains a theoretical national-defence role as an asymmetric guerrilla force, the army does not train for conventional warfare and its equipment holdings are very limited in this regard. The 2007–12 defence reform plan has tried to address outstanding personnel problems relating to training and morale, notably by increasing pay and benefits, in order to tackle a long-standing problem of desertions. The armed forces are constitutionally disbarred from international deployment except in wartime, but have still been involved in HA/DR operations in the US and Caribbean.

ACTIVE 270,250 (Army 200,000 Navy 58,500 Air 11,750) Paramilitary 59,500

RESERVE 87,350 (National Military Service)

ORGANISATIONS BY SERVICE

Army 200,000

12 regions (total: 46 army zones). The army consists of one manoeurvre corps (1st), with three inf bde and one armd bde, one SF corps, one AB corps and one MP corps. Command-and-control functions have been redesigned and decentralised, allowing greater independence for each of the 12 Military Region commanders and establishing C4 units in every region.

FORCES BY ROLE

SPECIAL FORCES
3 SF bde (12 SF bn)
1 amph SF bde (5 SF bn)

MANOEUVRE

Reconnaissance
3 armd bde (2 armd recce bn, 2 lt armd recce bn, 1 (Canon) AT gp)
3 armd recce regt
2 lt armd recce regt
25 mot recce regt

Light
1 (1st) armd corps (1 armd bde (2 armd recce bn, 2 lt armd recce bn, 1 (Canon) AT gp), 3 inf/rapid reaction bde (each: 3 inf bn, 1 arty regt, 1 (Canon) AT gp), 1 cbt engr bde (3 engr bn))
3 indep lt inf bde (2 lt inf bn, 1 (Canon) AT gp)
106 indep inf bn
25 indep inf coy

Air Manoeuvre
1 para bde with (1 (GAFE) SF gp, 3 bn, 1 (Canon) AT gp)

Other
1 (Presidential) gd corps (1 SF gp, 1 mech inf bde (2 inf bn, 1 aslt bn) 1 mne bn (Navy), 1 cbt engr bn, 1 MP bde (3 bn, 1 special ops anti-riot coy))

COMBAT SUPPORT
6 indep arty regt
2 MP bde (3 MP bn)

EQUIPMENT BY TYPE

RECCE 237: 124 ERC-90F1 *Lynx* (4 trg); 40 M8; 41 MAC-1; 32 VBL

APC 706
  APC (T) 472: 398 DNC-1 (mod AMX-VCI); 40 HWK-11; 34 M5A1 half-track
  APC (W) 234: 95 BDX; 25 DN-4; 19 DN-5 *Toro*; 26 LAV-150 ST; 25 MOWAG *Roland*; 44 VCR (3 amb; 5 cmd post)

ARTY 1,390
  TOWED 123: **105mm** 123: 40 M101; 40 M-56; 16 M2A1; 14 M-3; 13 NORINCO M-90
  MOR 1,267: **81mm** 400 M1, 400 *Brandt*, 300 SB
  120mm 167: 75 *Brandt*; 60 M-65; 32 RT61

AT
  MSL • SP 8 *Milan* (VBL)
  RCL 1,187+
    SP 106mm M40A1
    106mm M40A1
  GUNS 37mm 30 M3

AD
  GUNS 80
    TOWED 12.7mm 40 M-55; **20mm** 40 GAI-B01
    ARV 3 M-32 *Recovery Sherman*

Navy 58,500

HQ at Acapulco; HQ (exercise) at Vera Cruz. Two Fleet Commands: Gulf (6 zones), Pacific (11 zones)

EQUIPMENT BY TYPE

PRINCIPAL SURFACE COMBATANTS 7
  FRIGATES 7:
    FFGHM 4 *Allende* (US *Knox*) with 1 octuple Mk16 lnchr with ASROC/RGM-84C *Harpoon* AShM, 1 Mk25

GMLS with *Sea Sparrow* SAM, 2 twin 324mm ASTT with Mk46 LWT, 1 127mm gun, (capacity 1 MD-902 hel)

FF 3:

1 *Quetzalcoatl* with 2 twin 127mm gun, 1 hel landing platform

2 *Bravo* (US *Bronstein*) with 1 octuple Mk112 lnchr with ASROC, 2 triple 324mm ASTT with Mk46 LWT, 1 twin 76mm gun, 1 hel landing platform

PATROL AND COASTAL COMBATANTS 124

PSOH 4 *Oaxaca* with 1 76mm gun (capacity 1 AS-565MB *Panther* hel)

PCOH 17:

4 *Durango* (capacity 1 Bo-105 hel)

4 *Holzinger* (capacity 1 MD-902 *Explorer*)

3 *Sierra* (capacity 1 MD-902 *Explorer*)

6 *Uribe* (ESP *Halcon*) (capacity 1 Bo-105 hel)

PCO 10 *Leandro Valle* (US *Auk* MSF) with 1 76mm gun (being withdrawn from service; to be replaced with 4 additional *Oaxaca*-class)

PCG 2 *Huracan* (ISR *Aliya*) with 4 single lnchr with *Gabriel* II AShM, 1 *Phalanx* CIWS

PCC 2 *Democrata*

PBF 74: 6 *Acuario*; 2 *Acuario B*; 4 *Isla* (US *Halter*); 48 *Polaris* (SWE CB90); 14 *Polaris II* (SWE IC 16M; 1 additional vessel under construction)

PB 15: 10 *Azteca*; 3 *Cabo* (US *Cape Higgon*); 2 *Punta* (US *Point*)

AMPHIBIOUS • LS • LST 3: 2 *Papaloapan* (US *Newport*); 1 *Panuco*† (ex US LST-1152)

LOGISTICS AND SUPPORT 18

AK 3: 1 *Tarasco*; 1 *Rio Suchiate*; 1 *Montes Azules* (can also be used as landing ship; 1 additional vessel under construction)

AGOR 3: 2 *Robert D. Conrad*; 1 *Humboldt*

AGS 8: 4 *Arrecife*; 1 *Onjuku*; 1 *Rio Hondo*; 1 *Rio Tuxpan*; 1 *Moctezuma II* (also used as AXS)

AX 3: 1 *Manuel Azuela*; 2 *Huasteco* (also serve as troop transport, supply and hospital ships)

AXS 1 *Cuauhtemoc*

Naval Aviation 1,250

FORCES BY ROLE
MARITIME PATROL

5 sqn with Cessna 404 *Titan*; MX-7 *Star Rocket*; Lancair IV-P

1 sqn with CASA 212PM *Aviocar**; CN-235-300 MPA *Persuader*

1 sqn with L-90 *Redigo*

TRANSPORT

1 sqn with An-32B *Cline*

1 (VIP) sqn with DHC-8 *Dash 8*; Learjet 24; *Turbo Commander* 1000

TRANSPORT HELICOPTER

2 sqn with AS555 *Fennec*; AS-565MB *Panther*; MD-902; PZL Mi-2 *Hoplite*

2 sqn with Bo-105 CBS-5

5 sqn with Mi-17-1V/V-5 *Hip*

EQUIPMENT BY TYPE
AIRCRAFT 7 combat capable

ISR 7 CASA 212PM *Aviocar**

MR 6 CN-235-300 MPA *Persuader*

TPT • Light 23: 3 An-32B *Cline*; 4 C-295M; 1 Cessna 404 *Titan*; 1 DHC-8 *Dash 8*; 6 Lancair IV-P; 3 Learjet 24; 5 *Turbo Commander* 1000

TRG 15: 3 L-90TP *Redigo*; 4 MX-7 *Star Rocket*; 8 Z-242L

HELICOPTERS

MRH 29: 2 AS555 *Fennec*; 4 MD-500E; 22 Mi-17-1V *Hip*; 1 Mi-17-V5 *Hip*

SAR 4 AS565MB *Panther*

TPT 23 **Medium** 3 UH-60M *Black Hawk*; **Light** 20: 11 Bo-105 CBS-5; 6 MD-902 (SAR role); 2 PZL Mi-2 *Hoplite*; 1 R-44

Marines 21,500 (Expanding to 26,560)

FORCES BY ROLE
SPECIAL FORCES

3 SF unit

MANOEUVRE

Light

32 inf bn(-)

Air Manoeuvre

1 AB bn

Amphibious

2 amph bde

Other

1 (Presidential) gd bn (included in army Presidential Guard corps above)

COMBAT SERVICE SUPPORT

2 CSS bn

EQUIPMENT BY TYPE
APC (W) 29: 3 BTR-60 (APC-60); 26 BTR-70 (APC-70)

ARTY 122

TOWED 105mm 16 M-56

MRL 122mm 6 Firos-25

MOR 60mm/81mm 100

RCL 106mm M-40A1

AD • SAM • MANPAD 5+ 9K38 *Igla* (SA-18 *Grouse*)

Air Force 11,750

FORCES BY ROLE
FIGHTER

1 sqn with F-5E/F *Tiger* II

GROUND ATTACK/ISR

4 sqn with PC-7*

1 sqn with PC-7*/PC-9M

ISR/AEW

1 sqn with EMB-145AEW *Erieye*; EMB-145RS; SA-2-37B; SA-227-BC *Metro* III (C-26B)

TRANSPORT

1 sqn with IAI-201 *Arava*; C-295M; PC-6B

1 squadron with B-727; Beech 90

1 sqn with C-27J *Spartan*; C-130E/K *Hercules*; L-100-30

6 (liaison) sqn with Cessna 182/206

1 (anti-narcotic spraying) sqn with Bell 206; Cessna T206H;

1 (Presidential) gp with AS332L *Super Puma*; B-737; B-757; EC225; Gulfstream III; Learjet 35A; Learjet 36A; *Turbo Commander* 680

1 (VIP) gp with B-737; Beech 200 *King Air*; Cessna 500
   Citation; L-1329 *Jetstar 8*; S-70A-24

TRAINING
   1 sqn with Beech F-33C *Bonanza*
   1 sqn with PC-7*
   1 sqn with SF-260EU
   1 sqn (forming) with T-6C *Texan* II
   1 unit with PC-7*

TRANSPORT HELICOPTER
   1 sqn with Bell 206B; Bell 212; S-65 Yas'ur 2000
   3 sqn with Bell 206B; Bell 212
   1 sqn with MD-530F/MG
   1 sqn with Mi-8T; Mi-17; Mi-26T
   1 sqn with AS532L *Cougar*; Bell 412EP *Twin Huey*;
      S-70A-24 *Black Hawk*

ISR UAV
   1 unit with *Hermes* 450; *Skylark* Mk.I

EQUIPMENT BY TYPE
AIRCRAFT 76 combat capable
   FTR 10: 8 F-5E *Tiger* II; 2 F-5F *Tiger* II
   ISR 6: 2 SA-2-37A; 4 SA-227-BC *Metro III* (C-26B)
   ELINT 2 EMB-145RS
   AEW&C 1 EMB-145AEW *Erieye*
   TPT 120 **Medium** 12: 4 C-27J *Spartan*; 3 C-130E *Hercules*;
      2 C-130K *Hercules*; 2 C-130K-30 *Hercules*; 1 L-100-30
      Light 100: 2 Beech 90 *King Air*; 1 Beech 200 *King Air*;
      6 C-295M (4 more due by end 2012); 59 Cessna 182;
      3 Cessna 206; 8 Cessna T206H; 1 Cessna 500 *Citation*;
      3 IAI-101B *Arava*; 2 IAI 102 *Arava*; 6 IAI-202 *Arava*; 1
      L-1329 *Jetstar 8*; 2 Learjet 35A; 1 Learjet 36; 4 PC-6B; 1
      Turbo Commander 680; **PAX** 8: 3 B-727; 2 B-737; 1 B-757; 2
      Gulfstream III
   TRG 122: 20 Beech F33C *Bonanza*; 64 PC-7*; 2 PC-9M*; 7
      PT-17; 25 SF-260EU; 4 T-6C *Texan* II
HELICOPTERS
   MRH 31: 11 Bell 412EP *Twin Huey*; 20 Mi-17 *Hip H*
   ISR 14: 5 MD-530MF; 9 MD-530MG
   TPT 107 **Heavy** 7: 2 EC725 *Super Cougar*; 1 Mi-26T *Halo*;
      4 S-65C *Yas'ur* 2000 **Medium** 22: 3 AS332L *Super Puma*; 2
      AS532UL *Cougar* (on loan); 2 EC225 (VIP); 8 Mi-8T *Hip*;
      6 S-70A-24 *Black Hawk* **Light** 79: 45 Bell 206; 13 Bell 206B
      Jet Ranger II; 7 Bell 206L; 14 Bell 212
UAV • ISR 4 **Medium** 2 *Hermes* 450 **Light** 2 *Skylark* Mk.I
MSL • AAM • IR AIM-9J *Sidewinder*

Paramilitary 59,500

Federal Police 37,000
Public Security Secretariat
AIRCRAFT
   TPT 13 **Light** 7: 2 CN-235M; 2 Cessna 182 *Skylane*; 1
      Cessna 500 *Citation*; 2 Turbo Commander 695 **PAX** 6: 4
      B-727; 1 *Falcon* 20; 1 Gulfstream II
HELICOPTERS
   MRH 3 Mi-17 *Hip H*
   TPT 24 **Medium** 10: 1 SA330J *Puma*; 6 UH-60L *Black
      Hawk*; 3 UH-60M *Black Hawk* **Light** 14: 2 AS350B
      Ecureuil; 1 AS355 *Ecureuil* II; 6 Bell 206B; 5 EC-120
UAV • ISR • Light 2 S4 *Ehécatl*

Federal Ministerial Police 4,500
HELICOPTERS
TPT • Light 35: 18 Bell 205 (UH-1H); 7 Bell 212; 10
Schweizer 333

Rural Defense Militia 18,000
FORCES BY ROLE
   MANOEUVRE Light
   13 inf unit
   13 (horsed) cav unit

Nicaragua NIC

Nicaraguan Gold Cordoba Co		2011	2012	2013
GDP	Co	163.64bn	184.35bn	
	US$	7.3bn	7.83bn	
per capita	US$	1,275	1,367	
Growth	%	4.65	3.70	
Inflation	%	7.38	8.16	
Def bdgt	Co	1.21bn	1.55bn	
	US$	54m	66m	
FMA (US)	US$	0.339m	0.339m	0.339m
US$1=Co		22.43	23.55	

Population	5,727,707

Age	0–14	15–19	20–24	25–29	30–64	65 plus
Male	15.7%	6.0%	5.3%	4.3%	15.4%	2.1%
Female	15.1%	5.9%	5.4%	4.6%	17.5%	2.5%

Capabilities

The Nicaraguan military is dispersed geographically
around the country in order to provide assistance to bor-
der- and internal-security operations, with a central reserve focused on a single mechanised brigade. It has also
added specialised units focused on disaster relief and illegal logging in 2010 and 2012. Other new units are under discussion, with a focus on new marine and land force
contingents flexible enough to tackle the geographically-
diverse challenges posed by drug-traffickers. Major equipment is almost entirely of a Cold War vintage, but has seen
some recent modernisation and refurbishment.

ACTIVE 12,000 (Army 10,000 Navy 800 Air 1,200)
Terms of service voluntary, 18–36 months

ORGANISATIONS BY SERVICE

Army ε10,000
FORCES BY ROLE
SPECIAL FORCES
   1 SF bde with (2 SF bn)
MANOEUVRE
   Mechanised
   1 mech inf bde with (1 armd recce bn, 1 tk bn, 1 mech
      inf bn, 1 arty bn, 1 MRL bn, 1 AT coy)
   Light
   1 regional comd with (3 lt inf bn)

4 regional comd with (2 lt inf bn)
2 indep lt inf bn
Other
1 comd regt with (1 inf bn, 1 sy bn, 1 int unit, 1 sigs bn)
COMBAT SUPPORT
1 engr bn
COMBAT SERVICE SUPPORT
1 med bn
1 tpt regt
EQUIPMENT BY TYPE
MBT 62 T-55 (65 more in store)
LT TK 10 PT-76 in store
RECCE 20 BRDM-2
APC (W) 86: 41 BTR-152 (61 more in store); 45 BTR-60 (15 more in store)
ARTY 800
   TOWED 42: **122mm** 12 D-30; **152mm** 30 D-20 in store
   MRL 151: **107mm** 33 Type-63: **122mm** 118: 18 BM-21; 100 GRAD 1P (BM-21P) (single-tube rocket launcher, man portable)
   MOR 607: **82mm** 579; **120mm** 24 M-43: **160mm** 4 M-160 in store
AT
   MSL
      SP 12 BRDM-2 *Sagger*
      MANPATS AT-3 9K11 *Sagger*
   RCL 82mm B-10
   GUNS 371: **100mm** 24 M-1944; **57mm** 264 ZIS-2 *M-1943*; 90 in store; **76mm** 83 ZIS-3
AD • SAM • MANPAD 200+ 9K36 *Strela*-3 (SA-14 *Gremlin*); 9K310 *Igla*-1 (SA-16 *Gimlet*); 9K32 *Strela*-2 (SA-7 *Grail*)‡
AEV T-54/T-55
VLB TMM-3

Navy ε800

EQUIPMENT BY TYPE
PATROL AND COASTAL COMBATANTS • PB 8: 3 *Dabur*; 4 *Rodman 101*, 1 *Zhuk*

Air Force 1,200

FORCES BY ROLE
TRANSPORT
   1 sqn with An-26 *Curl*; Beech 90 *King Air*; Cessna U206; Cessna 404 *Titan* (VIP)
TRAINING
   1 unit with Cessna 172; PA-18 *Super Cub*; PA-28 *Cherokee*
TRANSPORT HELICOPTER
   1 sqn with Mi-17 *Hip* H (VIP/tpt/armed)
AIR DEFENCE
   1 gp with ZU-23; C3-*Morigla* M1
EQUIPMENT BY TYPE
AIRCRAFT
   TPT • Light 7: 3 An-26 *Curl*; 1 Beech 90 *King Air*; 1 Cessna 172; 1 Cessna U206; 1 Cessna 404 *Titan* (VIP); 2 PA-28 *Cherokee*
   TRG 2 PA-18 *Super Cub*
HELICOPTERS
   MRH 8:7 Mi-17 *Hip* H (armed)†; 1 Mi-17 *Hip* H (VIP)
   TPT • Medium 2 Mi-171E
AD • GUNS 36: 18 ZU-23; 18 C3-*Morigla* M1
MSL • ASM AT-2 *Swatter*

Panama PAN

Panamanian Balboa B		2011	2012	2013
GDP	B	30.57bn	34.82bn	
	US$	30.57bn	34.82bn	
per capita	US$	8,709	9,920	
Growth	%	10.58	8.48	
Inflation	%	5.88	6.00	
Def bdgt[a]	B	490m	548m	
	US$	490m	548m	
FMA (US)	US$	2.096m	1.84m	2.8m
US$1=B		1.00	1.00	

[a] Public security expenditure

Population   3,510,045

Age	0–14	15–19	20–24	25–29	30–64	65 plus
Male	14.4%	4.6%	4.3%	4.0%	19.7%	3.4%
Female	13.8%	4.4%	4.1%	3.9%	19.4%	4.0%

Capabilities

The Panamanian armed forces were abolished in 1990. A police force and an air/naval coast guard organisation were retained for low-level security activities. Panama would rely on its close relationship with the United States in the face of any more significant threat.

Paramilitary 12,000

ORGANISATIONS BY SERVICE

Paramilitary 12,000

National Police Force 11,000
No hy mil eqpt, small arms only
FORCES BY ROLE
SPECIAL FORCES
   1 SF unit (reported)
MANOEUVRE
   Other
   1 (presidential) gd bn (-)
   8 paramilitary coy
   18 police coy
COMBAT SUPPORT
   1 MP bn

National Aeronaval Service ε1,000
FORCES BY ROLE
TRANSPORT
   1 sqn with C-212M *Aviocar*; Cessna 210; PA-31 *Navajo*; PA-34 *Seneca*
   1 (Presidential) flt with ERJ-135BJ; S-76C
TRAINING
   1 unit with Cessna 152; Cessna 172; T-35D *Pillan*
TRANSPORT HELICOPTER
   1 sqn with Bell 205; Bell 205 (UH-1H *Iroquois*); Bell 212; Bell 407; Bell 412; EC145; MD-500E

EQUIPMENT BY TYPE
PATROL AND COASTAL COMBATANTS 23
  PCO 1 *Independencia* (US *Balsam* class)
  PB 22: 3 *Chiriqui* (US); 1 *Escudo de Veraguas*; 1 *Naos*; 1 *Negrita*†; 2 *Panama*; 2 *Panquiaco* (UK Vosper 31.5m); 5 *Tres De Noviembre* (US *Point*), 1 *Taboga*; 2 *Saettia*; 4 *Type 200*
LOGISTICS AND SUPPORT 5
  AG 2
  YAG 2: 1 *Nombre de Dios* (US MSB 5); 1 *Isla Paridas*
  YO 1 *Flamenco*
AIRCRAFT
  TPT • Light 12: 5 C-212M *Aviocar*; 1 Cessna 152, 1 Cessna 172; 1 Cessna 210; 1 ERJ-135BJ; 1 PA-31 *Navajo*; 2 PA-34 *Seneca*
  TRG 6 T-35D *Pillan*
HELICOPTERS
  MRH 3: 2 Bell 412; 1 MD-500E
  TPT • Light 21: 2 Bell 205; 13 Bell 205 (UH-1H *Iroquois*); 2 Bell 212; 2 Bell 407; 1 EC145; 1 S-76C

Paraguay PRY

Paraguayan Guarani Pg		2011	2012	2013
GDP	Pg	108.79tr	115.95tr	
	US$	24.08bn	26.09bn	
per capita	US$	3,681	3,988	
Growth	%	4.34	-1.50	
Inflation	%	6.58	4.97	
Def bdgt	Pg	1.05tr	1.46tr	
	US$	233m	330m	
FMA (US)	US$	0.399m	0.35m	0.35m
US$1=Pg		4518.05	4444.47	

Population   6,541,591

Age	0–14	15–19	20–24	25–29	30–64	65 plus
Male	14.0%	5.5%	5.0%	4.2%	18.5%	2.9%
Female	13.6%	5.4%	5.0%	4.3%	18.2%	3.4%

Capabilities

The potential re-emergence of a territorial dispute with Bolivia over the Chaco region is one of the country's present security concerns. This is contributing to increased interest in renewing elements of the military's equipment inventory, much of which is obsolete. The army continues to use very old land systems, while the air force has a small number of light counter-insurgency aircraft and a variety of utility and tactical transport aircraft. Though land-locked, the country supports a naval force of mainly river patrol craft, reflecting the importance of its river systems. The military has no capacity for power projection. The services train regularly.

ACTIVE 10,650 (Army 7,600 Navy 1,950 Air 1,100)
Paramilitary 14,800
Terms of service 12 months Navy 2 years

RESERVE 164,500 (Joint 164,500)

ORGANISATIONS BY SERVICE

Army 6,100; 1,500 conscript (total 7,600)

Much of the Paraguayan army is maintained in a cadre state during peacetime; the nominal inf and cav divs are effectively only at coy strength. Active gp/regt are usually coy sized.

FORCES BY ROLE
MANOEUVRE
  Reconnaissance
  1 armd cav sqn
  Light
  3 inf corps (total: 6 inf div (-), 3 cav div (-), 6 arty bty)
  Other
  1 (Presidential) gd regt (1 SF bn, 1 inf bn, 1 sy bn, 1 log gp)
COMBAT SUPPORT
  1 arty bde with (2 arty gp, 1 ADA gp)
  1 engr bde with (1 engr regt, 3 construction regt)
  1 sigs bn

Reserves
MANOEUVRE
  Light
  14 inf regt (cadre)
  4 cav regt (cadre)
EQUIPMENT BY TYPE
MBT 3 M4A3 *Sherman*
LT TK 12 M3A1 *Stuart* (6†)
RECCE 28 EE-9 *Cascavel*
APC (T) 20 M9 half-track
APC (W) 12 EE-11 *Urutu*
ARTY 94
  TOWED 105mm 14 M101
  MOR 81mm 80
AT
  RCL 75mm M20
AD • GUNS 19:
  SP 20mm 3 M-9
  TOWED 16: 40mm 10 M1A1, 6 L/60

Navy 1,100; 850 conscript (total 1,950)
EQUIPMENT BY TYPE
PATROL AND COASTAL COMBATANTS 20
  PCR 4: 1 *Itaipú*; 2 *Nanawa*†; 1 *Paraguay*† with 2 twin 120mm gun, 3 76mm gun
  PBR 16: 1 *Capitan Cabral*; 2 *Capitan Ortiz* (ROC *Hai Ou*); 2 *Novatec*; 6 *Type 701*; 5 others
AMPHIBIOUS 3 LCVP
LOGISTICS AND SUPPORT • AKSL 1 (also serves as river transport)

Naval Aviation 100
FORCES BY ROLE
TRANSPORT
  1 (liaison) sqn with Cessna 150; Cessna 210 *Centurion*; Cessna 310; Cessna 401
TRANSPORT HELICOPTER
  1 sqn with AS350 *Ecureuil* (HB350 *Esquilo*); Bell 47 (OH-13 *Sioux*)

EQUIPMENT BY TYPE
AIRCRAFT • TPT • Light 6: 2 Cessna 150; 1 Cessna 210 *Centurion;* 2 Cessna 310; 1 Cessna 401
HELICOPTERS
 TPT • Light 2 AS350 *Ecureuil* (HB350 *Esquilo*)
 TRG 1 Bell 47 (OH-13 *Sioux*)

Marines 700; 200 conscript (total 900)
FORCES BY ROLE
MANOEUVRE
 Amphibious
 3 mne bn(-)

Air Force 900; 200 conscript (total 1,100)
FORCES BY ROLE
GROUND ATTACK/ISR
 1 sqn with EMB-312 *Tucano**
TRANSPORT
 1 gp with B-707; C-212-200/400 *Aviocar;* DHC-6 *Twin Otter*
 1 VIP gp with Beech 58 *Baron;* Bell 427; Cessna U206 *Stationair;* Cessna 208B *Grand Caravan;* Cessna 210 *Centurion;* Cessna 402B; PA-32R *Saratoga* (EMB-721C *Sertanejo*); PZL-104 *Wilga 80*
TRAINING
 1 sqn with T-25 *Universal;* T-35A/B *Pillan*
TRANSPORT HELICOPTER
 1 gp with AS350 *Ecureuil* (HB-350 *Esquilo*); Bell 205 (UH-1H *Iroquois*)
EQUIPMENT BY TYPE
AIRCRAFT 6 combat capable
 TPT • Light 19: 1 Beech 58 *Baron;* 4 C-212-200 *Aviocar;* 2 C-212-400 *Aviocar;* 2 Cessna 208B *Grand Caravan;* 1 Cessna 210 *Centurion;* 1 Cessna 310; 2 Cessna 402B; 2 Cessna U206 *Stationair;* 1 DHC-6 *Twin Otter;* 1 PA-32R *Saratoga* (EMB-721C *Sertanejo*); 2 PZL-104 *Wilga 80*
 TRG 22: 6 EMB-312 *Tucano**; 6 T-25 *Universal;* 7 T-35A *Pillan;* 3 T-35B *Pillan*
HELICOPTERS • TPT • Light 10: 3 AS350 *Ecureuil* (HB-350 *Esquilo*); 6 Bell 205 (UH-1H *Iroquois*); 1 Bell 427 (VIP)

Paramilitary 14,800

Special Police Service 10,800; 4,000 conscript (total 14,800)

DEPLOYMENT

CÔTE D'IVOIRE
UN • UNOCI 2; 7 obs
CYPRUS
UN • UNFICYP 14
DEMOCRATIC REPUBLIC OF THE CONGO
UN • MONUSCO 17 obs
HAITI
UN • MINUSTAH 162; 1 engr coy
LIBERIA
UN • UNMIL 1; 3 obs
SOUTH SUDAN
UN • UNMISS 3 obs
SUDAN
UN • UNISFA 1 obs
WESTERN SAHARA
UN • MINURSO 5 obs

Peru PER

Peruvian Nuevo Sol NS		2011	2012	2013
GDP	NS	486.55bn	528.27bn	
	US$	177.19bn	200.29bn	
per capita	US$	5,996	6,778	
Growth	%	6.91	6.05	
Inflation	%	3.37	3.68	
Def exp	NS	5.59bn		
	US$	2.03bn		
Def bdgt	NS	6.04bn	6.42bn	
	US$	2.2bn	2.43bn	
FMA (US)	US$	3.5m	1.98m	1.98m
US$1=NS		2.75	2.64	

Population 29,549,517

Age	0–14	15–19	20–24	25–29	30–64	65 plus
Male	14.3%	5.1%	4.7%	4.0%	18.2%	3.1%
Female	13.8%	5.0%	4.7%	4.2%	19.5%	3.4%

Capabilities

The armed forces have been involved in a decades-long conflict with *Shining Path* leftist guerrillas, which has influenced strongly the focus of the armed services, particularly the army. Territorial disputes have, in the past, also lead to clashes, most notably with Ecuador in 1995. The government has a military modernisation programme intended to shape the forces to better meet its perceived future security requirements. The air force is well-equipped by regional standards, and is upgrading some of its primary platforms, including the MiG-29. Internal security remains the army's focus, and this is reflected by the age of much of its conventional equipment. Similarly, the navy's acquisition ambitions have, in recent years, been curtailed by funding restrictions. All three services train regularly, while also participating in multinational exercises. The air force has a reasonable tactical airlift capability, though it has no aerial refuelling capacity, while the navy has a modest amphibious operations role.

ACTIVE 115,000 (Army 74,000 Navy 24,000 Air 17,000) **Paramilitary 77,000**

RESERVE 188,000 (Army 188,000) **Paramilitary 7,000**

ORGANISATIONS BY SERVICE

Army 74,000

4 mil region

FORCES BY ROLE

SPECIAL FORCES

1 (1st) SF bde (4 cdo bn, 1 airmob arty gp, 1 MP Coy, 1 cbt spt bn)

1 (3rd) SF bde (3 cdo bn, 1 airmob arty gp, 1 MP coy)

1 SF gp (regional troops)

MANOEUVRE

Armoured

1 (3rd) armd bde (2 tk bn, 1 armd inf bn, 1 arty gp, 1 AT coy, 1 AD gp, 1 engr bn, 1 cbt spt bn)

1 (9th) armd bde (forming - 1 tk bn)

Mechanised

1 (3rd) armd cav bde (3 mech cav bn, 1 mot inf bn, 1 arty gp, 1 AD gp, 1 engr bn, 1 cbt spt bn)

1 (1st) cav bde (4 mech cav bn, 1 MP coy, 1 cbt spt bn)

Light

2 (2nd & 31st) mot inf bde (3 mot inf bn, 1 arty gp, 1 MP coy, 1 log bn)

3 (1st, 7th & 32nd) inf bde (3 inf bn, 1 MP coy, 1 cbt spt bn)

Mountain

1 (4th) mtn bde (1 armd regt, 3 mot inf bn, 1 arty gp, 1 MP coy, 1 cbt spt bn)

1 (5th) mtn bde (1 armd regt, 2 mot inf bn, 3 jungle coy, 1 arty gp, 1 MP coy, 1 cbt spt bn)

Jungle

1 (5th) jungle inf bde (1 SF gp, 3 jungle bn, 3 jungle coy, 1 jungle arty gp, 1 AT coy, 1 AD gp, 1 jungle engr bn)

1 (6th) jungle inf bde (4 jungle bn, 1 engr bn, 1 MP coy, 1 cbt spt bn)

Other

1 (18th) armd trg bde (1 mech cav regt, 1 armd regt, 2 tk bn, 1 armd inf bn, 1 engr bn, 1 MP coy, 1 cbt spt bn)

Aviation

1 (1st) avn bde (1 atk hel/recce hel bn, 1 avn bn, 2 aslt hel/tpt hel bn)

COMBAT SUPPORT

1 (1st) arty bde (4 arty gp, 2 AD gp, 1 sigs gp)

1 (3rd) arty bde (4 arty gp, 1 AD gp, 1 sigs gp)

1 AD gp (regional troops)

1 (22nd) engr bde (3 engr bn, 1 demining coy)

EQUIPMENT BY TYPE

MBT 165: 165 T-55; (75† in store)

LT TK 96 AMX-13

RECCE 95: 30 BRDM-2; 15 Fiat 6616; 50 M9A1

APC 299

APC (T) 120 M113A1

APC (W) 179: 150 UR-416; 25 Fiat 6614; 4 *Repontec*

ARTY 998

SP • 155mm 12 M109A2

TOWED 290

105mm 152: 44 M101; 24 M2A1; 60 M-56; 24 Model 56 pack howitzer; **122mm**; 36 D-30; **130mm** 36 M-46; **155mm** 66: 36 M114, 30 Model 50

MRL • 122mm 22 BM-21 *Grad*

MOR 674+

SP 107mm 24 M106A1

TOWED 650+ **81mm/107mm** 350; **120mm** 300+ Brandt/Expal Model L

AT

MSL 860

SP 22 M1165A2 HMMWV with 9K135 *Kornet* E (AT-14)

MANPATS 838: 350 9K11 *Malyutka* (AT-3 *Sagger*)/HJ-73C, 244 9K135 *Kornet* E (AT-14), 244 *Spike*-ER

RCL 106mm M40A1

AIRCRAFT

TPT • Light 16: 2 An-28 *Cash*; 3 An-32B *Cline*; 1 Beech 350 *King Air*; 1 Beech 1900D; 4 Cessna 152; 1 Cessna 208 *Caravan I*; 2 Cessna U206 *Stationair*; 1 PA-31T *Cheyenne II*; 1 PA-34 *Seneca*

TRG 4 IL-103

HELICOPTERS

MRH 8 Mi-17 *Hip H*

TPT 20 **Heavy** 1 Mi-26T *Halo* (2 more in store) **Medium** 6 Mi-171Sh **Light** 13: 2 AW109K2; 9 PZL Mi-2 *Hoplite*; 2 R-44

TRG 5 F-28F

AD

SAM • MANPAD 298+: 70 9K36 *Strela*-3 (SA-14 *Gremlin*); 128 9K310 *Igla*-1 (SA-16 *Gimlet*); 100+ 9K32 *Strela*-2 (SA-7 *Grail*)‡

GUNS 165

SP 23mm 35 ZSU-23-4

TOWED 23mm 130: 80 ZU-23-2; 50 ZU-23

ARV M578

Navy 24,000 (incl 1,000 Coast Guard)

Commands: Pacific, Lake Titicaca, Amazon River

EQUIPMENT BY TYPE

SUBMARINES • TACTICAL • SSK 6:

6 *Angamos* (GER T-209/1200 – 2 in refit/reserve) with 6 single 533mm TT with A-185 HWT

PRINCIPAL SURFACE COMBATANTS 9

CRUISERS • CG 1 *Almirante Grau* (NLD *De Ruyter*) with 8 single lnchr with *Otomat* Mk2 AShM, 4 twin 152mm gun

FRIGATES • FFGHM 8:

4 *Aguirre* (ITA *Lupo*) with 8 single lnchr with *Otomat* Mk2 AShM, 1 octuple Mk29 lnchr with RIM-7P *Sea Sparrow* SAM, 2 triple 324mm ASTT with A244 LWT, 1 127mm gun, (capacity 1 Bell 212 (AB-212)/SH-3D *Sea King*)

4 *Carvajal* (mod ITA *Lupo*) with 8 single lnchr with *Otomat* Mk2 AShM, 1 octuple *Albatros* lnchr with *Aspide* SAM, 2 triple 324mm ASTT with A244 LWT, 1 127mm gun, (capacity 1 Bell 212 (AB-212)/SH-3D *Sea King*)

PATROL AND COASTAL COMBATANTS 14

CORVETTES • FSG 6 *Velarde* (FRA PR-72 64m) with 4 single lnchr with MM-38 *Exocet* AShM, 1 76mm gun

PCR 5:

2 *Amazonas* with 1 76mm gun

1 *Manuel Clavero* (1 additional vessel in build)

2 *Marañon* with 2 76mm gun

PBR 3 *Punta Malpelo*

AMPHIBIOUS

LANDING SHIPS • LST 4 *Paita* (capacity 395 troops)
(US *Terrebonne Parish*)
LANDING CRAFT • LCAC 2 Griffon 2000TD (capacity
22 troops)

LOGISTICS AND SUPPORT 14

AFD 3
AGS 4: 1 *Carrasco*; 2 (coastal survey vessels); 1 (river
survey vessel for the upper Amazon)
AH 2 (1 also used for riverine surveillance)
AOR 1 *Mollendo*
AOT 2
AXS 1
YPT 1

Naval Aviation ε800

FORCES BY ROLE
MARITIME PATROL
  1 sqn with Beech 200T; Bell 212 ASW (AB-212 ASW);
  F-27 *Friendship*; F-60; SH-3D *Sea King*
TRANSPORT
  1 flt with An-32B *Cline*; Cessna 206
TRAINING
  1 sqn with F-28F; T-34C *Turbo Mentor*
TRANSPORT HELICOPTER
  1 (liaison) sqn with Bell 206B *Jet Ranger II*; Mi-8 *Hip*

EQUIPMENT BY TYPE
AIRCRAFT
  MP 8: 4 Beech 200T; 4 F-60
  ELINT 1 F-27 *Friendship*
  TPT • Light 4: 3 An-32B *Cline*; 1 Cessna 206
  TRG 5 T-34C *Turbo Mentor*
HELICOPTERS
  ASW 5: 2 Bell 212 ASW (AB-212 ASW); 3 SH-3D *Sea
  King*
  TPT 11 Medium 8: 2 Mi-8 *Hip*; 6 UH-3H *Sea KIng*;
  Light 3 Bell 206B *Jet Ranger II*
  TRG 5 F-28F
MSL • AShM AM-39 *Exocet*

Marines 4,000

FORCES BY ROLE
SPECIAL FORCES
  1 cdo gp
MANOEUVRE
  Light
  2 inf bn
  1 inf gp
  Amphibious
  1 mne bde (1 SF gp, 1 recce bn, 2 inf bn, 1 amph bn, 1
  arty gp)
  Jungle
  1 jungle inf bn

EQUIPMENT BY TYPE
APC (W) 35+: 20 BMR-600; V-100 *Commando*; 15 V-200
Chaimite
ARTY 18+
  TOWED 122mm D-30
  MOR 18+: 81mm; 120mm ε18
  RCL 84mm *Carl Gustav*; **106mm** M40A1

AD • GUNS 20mm SP (twin)

Air Force 17,000

Divided into five regions – North, Lima, South, Central and
Amazon.

FORCES BY ROLE
FIGHTER
  1 sqn with MiG-29S/SE *Fulcrum* C; MiG-29UB *Fulcrum* B
FIGHTER/GROUND ATTACK
  1 sqn with *Mirage* 2000E/ED (2000P/DP)
  2 sqn with A-37B *Dragonfly*
  1 sqn with Su-25A *Frogfoot* A†; Su-25UB *Frogfoot* B†
ISR
  1 (photo-survey) sqn with *Commander* 690; Learjet 36A;
  SA-227-BC *Metro* III (C-26B)
TRANSPORT
  1 sqn with B-737; An-32 *Cline*
  1 sqn with DHC-6 *Twin Otter*; DHC-6-400 *Twin Otter*;
  PC-6 *Turbo-Porter*
  1 sqn with L-100-20
TRAINING
  2 (drug interdiction) sqn with EMB-312 *Tucano*
  1 sqn with MB-339A*
  1 sqn with Z-242
  1 hel sqn with Schweizer 300C
ATTACK HELICOPTER
  1 sqn with Mi-25/Mi-35P *Hind*
TRANSPORT HELICOPTER
  1 sqn with Mi-17 *Hip H*
  1 sqn with Bell 206 *Jet Ranger*; Bell 212 (AB-212); Bell 412
  Twin Huey
  1 sqn with Bo-105C/LS
AIR DEFENCE
  6 bn with S-125 *Pechora* (SA-3 *Goa*)

EQUIPMENT BY TYPE
AIRCRAFT 78 combat capable
  FTR 20: 15 MiG-29S *Fulcrum* C; 3 MiG-29SE *Fulcrum C*
  (8 upgraded to SMP standard by end 2012); 2 MiG-29UB
  Fulcrum B
  FGA 12: 2 *Mirage* 2000ED (M-2000DP); 10 *Mirage* 2000E
  (2000P) (some†)
  ATK 36: 18 A-37B *Dragonfly*; 10 Su-25A *Frogfoot* A†; 8 Su-
  25UB *Frogfoot* B†
  ISR 6: 2 Learjet 36A; 4 SA-227-BC *Metro* III (C-26B)
  TPT 17: **Medium** 2 L-100-20; **Light** 11: 4 An-32 *Cline*; 1
  Commander 690; 3 DHC-6 *Twin Otter*; 2 DHC-6-400 *Twin
  Otter* (further 10 on order); 1 PC-6 *Turbo-Porter*; **PAX** 4
  B-737
  TRG 49: 19 EMB-312 *Tucano*; 10 MB-339A*; 6 T-41A
  Mescalero/T-41D *Mescalero*; 14 Z-242
HELICOPTERS
  ATK 18: 16 Mi-25 *Hind* D; 2 Mi-35P *Hind* E
  MRH 21: 2 Bell 412 *Twin Huey*; 19 Mi-17 *Hip* H
  TPT • Light 21: 8 Bell 206 *Jet Ranger*; 6 Bell 212 (AB-212);
  1 Bo-105C; 6 Bo-105LS
  TRG 5 Schweizer 300C
AD
  SAM 100+: S-125 *Pechora* (SA-3 *Goa*); 100+ *Javelin*

MSL
AAM • IR R-3 (AA-2 *Atoll*)‡; R-60 (AA-8 *Aphid*)‡; R-73 (AA-11 *Archer*); R-550 *Magic*; **IR/SARH** R-27 (AA-10 *Alamo*) **ARH** R-77 (AA-12 *Adder*)
ASM AS-30; Kh-29L (AS-14 *Kedge*)
ARM Kh-58 (AS-11 *Kilter*)

Paramilitary • National Police 77,000 (100,000 reported)

EQUIPMENT BY TYPE
APC (W) 100 MOWAG *Roland*

General Police 43,000

Security Police 21,000

Technical Police 13,000

Coast Guard 1,000

Personnel included as part of Navy

EQUIPMENT BY TYPE
PATROL AND COASTAL COMBATANTS 27
　PCC 5 *Rio Nepena*
　PB 10: 6 *Dauntless*; 1 *Río Chira*; 3 *Río Santa*
　PBR 12: 10 *Zorritos*; 1 *Rio Viru*; 1 *Rio Canete*
AIRCRAFT
　TPT • Light 3: 1 DHC-6 *Twin Otter*; 2 F-27 *Friendship*

Rondas Campesinas ε7,000 gp

Peasant self-defence force. Perhaps 7,000 rondas 'gp', up to pl strength, some with small arms. Deployed mainly in emergency zone.

DEPLOYMENT

CÔTE D'IVOIRE
UN • UNOCI 3 obs

DEMOCRATIC REPUBLIC OF THE CONGO
UN • MONUSCO 7 obs

HAITI
UN • MINUSTAH 372; 1 inf coy

LIBERIA
UN • UNMIL 2; 2 obs

SOUTH SUDAN
UN • UNMISS 2 obs

SUDAN
UN • UNISFA 1; 2 obs

WESTERN SAHARA
UN • MINURSO 2 obs

Suriname SUR

Suriname Dollar srd		2011	2012	2013
GDP	srd	15.02bn	16.81bn	
	US$	4.55bn	5.09bn	
per capita	US$	8,123	9,087	
Growth	%	4.15	4.00	
Inflation	%	17.72	6.24	
Def bdgt	srd	ε134m		
	US$	ε41m		
US$1=srd		3.30	3.30	

Population　560,157

Age	0–14	15–19	20–24	25–29	30–64	65 plus
Male	13.5%	4.3%	4.0%	4.7%	20.5%	2.7%
Female	12.9%	4.3%	4.1%	4.8%	20.6%	3.6%

Capabilities

While assuring sovereignty and territorial integrity are its fundamental roles, the nation's small armed forces would struggle to fulfil either were they ever to face a concerted attack. The army is the largest of the three services, with naval and air units having a very limited capability.

ACTIVE 1,840 (Army 1,400 Navy 240 Air 200)
(All services form part of the army)

ORGANISATIONS BY SERVICE

Army 1,400

FORCES BY ROLE
MANOEUVRE
　Mechanised
　1 mech cav sqn
　Light
　1 inf bn (4 coy)
COMBAT SUPPORT
　1 MP bn (coy)

EQUIPMENT BY TYPE
RECCE 6 EE-9 *Cascavel*
APC (W) 15 EE-11 *Urutu*
MOR 81mm 6
RCL 106mm: M40A1

Navy ε240

EQUIPMENT BY TYPE
PATROL AND COASTAL COMBATANTS 10
　PB 5: 3 *Rodman* 101†; 2 others
　PBR 5 *Rodman* 55M

Air Force ε200

EQUIPMENT BY TYPE
AIRCRAFT 4 combat capable
　MP 1 C-212-400 *Aviocar**
　TPT • Light 2: 1 BN-2 *Defender**; 1 Cessna 182
　TRG 1 PC-7 *Turbo Trainer**

Trinidad and Tobago TTO

Trinidad and Tobago Dollar TT$		2011	2012	2013
GDP	TT$	143.94bn	151.97bn	
	US$	22.58bn	23.84bn	
per capita	US$	18,412	19,439	
Growth	%	-1.48	0.74	
Inflation	%	5.10	9.98	
Def exp	TT$	2.42bn		
	US$	379m		
Def bdgt	TT$	2.59bn	2.84bn	2.55bn
	US$	406m	446m	
US$1=TT$		6.38	6.38	

Population   1,226,383

Age	0–14	15–19	20–24	25–29	30–64	65 plus
Male	9.9%	3.4%	4.1%	5.2%	24.4%	3.8%
Female	9.5%	3.1%	3.8%	4.9%	23.1%	5.0%

Capabilities

The Trinidad and Tobago Defence Force faces no external threat, and is primarily tasked with counter-narcotic, border-surveillance and disaster-management roles, though security forces are also preoccupied by issues arising from the flow in weapons and ammunition. The planned purchase of 3 OPVs was cancelled in 2010. According to the Chief of Defence in 2012, the country plans to work with its regional counterparts to enhance levels of interoperability across regional armed forces.

ACTIVE 4,050 (Army 3,000 Coast Guard 1,050)
(All services form the Trinidad and Tobago Defence Force)

ORGANISATIONS BY SERVICE

Army ε3,000

FORCES BY ROLE
SPECIAL FORCES
  1 SF unit
MANOEUVRE
  Light
  2 inf bn
COMBAT SUPPORT
  1 engr bn
COMBAT SERVICE SUPPORT
  1 log bn
EQUIPMENT BY TYPE
MOR 6: **81mm** L16A1
AT
  RCL 84mm ε24 Carl Gustav

Coast Guard 1,050

FORCES BY ROLE
COMMAND
  1 mne HQ

EQUIPMENT BY TYPE
PATROL AND COASTAL COMBATANTS 20
  PCO 1 Nelson (UK Island)
  PB 19: 2 Gasper Grande; 1 Matelot; 4 Plymouth; 4 Point; 6 Scarlet Ibis (Austal 30m); 2 Wasp; (1 Cascadura (SWE Karlskrona 40m) non-operational)

Air Wing 50

AIRCRAFT
  TPT • **Light** 2 SA-227 Metro III (C-26)
HELICOPTERS
  MRH 2 AW139
  TPT • **Light** 1 S-76

Uruguay URY

Uruguayan Peso pU		2011	2012	2013
GDP	pU	902.16bn	1.04tr	
	US$	46.71bn	49.72bn	
per capita	US$	14,085	14,992	
Growth	%	5.70	3.50	
Inflation	%	8.09	7.90	
Def bdgt	pU	9.34bn	9.34bn	9.55bn
	US$	484m	447m	
FMA (US)	US$	0.399m		
US$1=pU		19.31	20.91	

Population   3,316,328

Age	0–14	15–19	20–24	25–29	30–64	65 plus
Male	11.1%	4.1%	3.9%	3.5%	20.1%	5.5%
Female	10.7%	4.0%	3.8%	3.4%	21.4%	8.3%

Capabilities

Along with the basic aims of assuring sovereignty and territorial integrity, the military has in recent years taken on peacekeeping missions, most notably in Haiti. In regional terms, the military provides a competent force, though much of the services' equipment inventory is second-hand. Air force ambitions to purchase a light fighter aircraft have yet to come to fruition, with limited funding hampering its aims. The air force is focused on the counter-insurgency role, with a limited tactical airlift capacity. The military trains regularly, and on a joint basis, as well as participating in multinational exercises. The country has little ability for independent power projection.

ACTIVE 24,650 (Army 16,250 Navy 5,400 Air 3,000)
Paramilitary 800

ORGANISATIONS BY SERVICE

Army 16,250

Uruguayan units are sub-standard size, mostly around 30%. Div are at most bde size, while bn are of reinforced coy strength. Regts are also coy size, some bn size, with the largest formation being the 2nd armd cav regt.

FORCES BY ROLE
COMMAND
4 mil region/div HQ
MANOEUVRE
Mechanised
2 armd regt
1 armd cav regt
5 mech cav regt
8 mech inf regt
Light
1 mot inf bn
5 inf bn
Air Manoeuvre
1 para bn
COMBAT SUPPORT
1 (strategic reserve) arty regt
5 fd arty gp
1 AD gp
1 (1st) engr bde (2 engr bn)
4 cbt engr bn

EQUIPMENT BY TYPE
MBT 15 TI-67
LT TK 38: 16 M24 *Chaffee*; 22 M41A1UR
RECCE 110: 15 EE-9 *Cascavel*; 48 GAZ-39371 *Vodnik*; 47 OT-93;
AIFV 18 BMP-1
APC 176:
APC (T) 29: 24 M113A1UR; 3 M-93 (MT-LB); 2 PTS
APC (W) 147: 54 *Condor*; 53 OT-64: 40 MOWAG *Piranha*
ARTY 185
SP 122mm 6 2S1 *Carnation*
TOWED 44: **105mm** 36: 28 M101A1; 8 M-102; **155mm** 8 M114A1
MOR 135: **81mm** 91: 35 M1, 56 LN; **120mm** 44 SL
AT
MSL • MANPATS 15 *Milan*
RCL 69: **106mm** 69 M40A1
UAV • ISR • Light 1 *Charrua*
AD • GUNS • TOWED 14: **20mm** 14: 6 M167 *Vulcan*; 8 TCM-20 (w/Elta M-2016 radar)
AEV MT-LB

Navy 5,400 (incl 1,800 Prefectura Naval Coast Guard)

HQ at Montevideo

EQUIPMENT BY TYPE
PRINCIPAL SURFACE COMBATANTS • FRIGATES 2:
FF 2 *Uruguay* (PRT *Joao Belo*) with 2 triple 324mm ASTT with Mk46 LWT, 2 100mm gun
PATROL AND COASTAL COMBATANTS 30
PB 30: 3 *15 de Noviembre* (FRA *Vigilante* 42m); 2 *Colonia* (US *Cape*); 1 *Paysandu*; 12 (various); 9 *Type 44* (coast guard); 3 *PS* (coast guard)
MINE WARFARE • MINE COUNTERMEASURES 3:
MSO 3 *Temerario* (*Kondor* II)
AMPHIBIOUS 3: 2 **LCVP**; 1 **LCM**
LOGISTICS AND SUPPORT 9
ARS 1 *Vanguardia*
AR 1 *Artigas* (GER *Freiburg*, general spt ship)
AG 1 *Maldonado*

AGHS 2: 1 *Helgoland*; 1 *Triestre*
ABU 2
AXS 2

Naval Aviation 210

FORCES BY ROLE
ANTI SUBMARINE WARFARE
1 flt with Beech 200T*; *Jetstream* Mk2
SEARCH & RESCUE/TRANPSORT HELICOPTER
1 sqn with AS350B2 *Ecureuil* (*Esquilo*); Bo-105M; *Wessex* HC2/Mk60
TRANSPORT/TRAINING
1 flt with T-34C *Turbo Mentor*

EQUIPMENT BY TYPE
AIRCRAFT 1 combat capable
MP 2 *Jetstream* Mk2
ISR 1 Beech 200T*
TRG 2 T-34C *Turbo Mentor*
HELICOPTERS
MRH 6 Bo-105M
TPT 2 **Medium** 1 *Wessex* HC2/Mk60 **Light** 1 AS350B2 *Ecureuil* (*Esquilo*)

Naval Infantry 450

FORCES BY ROLE
MANOEUVRE
Amphibious
1 mne bn(-)

Air Force 3,000

Flying hours   120 hrs/year

FORCES BY ROLE
FIGHTER/GROUND ATTACK
1 sqn with A-37B *Dragonfly*
1 sqn with IA-58B *Pucará*
ISR
1 flt with EMB-110 *Bandeirante*
TRANSPORT
1 sqn with C-130B *Hercules*; C-212 *Aviocar*; EMB-110C *Bandeirante*; EMB-120 *Brasilia*
1 (liaison) sqn with Cessna 206H; T-41D
1 (liaison) flt with Cessna 206H
TRAINING
1 sqn with PC-7U *Turbo Trainer*
1 sqn with Beech 58 *Baron* (UB-58); SF-260EU
TRANSPORT HELICOPTER
1 sqn with AS365 *Dauphin*; Bell 205 (UH-1H *Iroquois*); Bell 212

EQUIPMENT BY TYPE
AIRCRAFT 15 combat capable
ATK 15: 10 A-37B *Dragonfly*; 5 IA-58B *Pucará*
ISR 1 EMB-110 *Bandeirante*
TPT 21 **Medium** 2 C-130B *Hercules*; **Light** 18: 2 Beech 58 *Baron* (UB-58); 4 C-212 *Aviocar*; 9 Cessna 206H; 2 EMB-110C *Bandeirante*; 1 EMB-120 *Brasilia*
TRG 21: 5 PC-7U *Turbo Trainer*; 12 SF-260 EU; 4 T-41D *Mescalero*
HELICOPTERS
MRH 1 AS365 *Dauphin*
TPT • Light 10: 6 Bell 205 (UH-1H *Iroquois*); 4 Bell 212

Paramilitary 800

Guardia de Coraceros 350 (under Interior Ministry)

Guardia de Granaderos 450

DEPLOYMENT

CÔTE D'IVOIRE
UN • UNOCI 2 obs

DEMOCRATIC REPUBLIC OF THE CONGO
UN • MONUC 1,160; 37 obs; 1 inf bn; 2 mne coy; 1 hel flt; 1 engr coy(-)

EGYPT
MFO 58; 1 engr/tpt unit

HAITI
UN • MINUSTAH 957; 2 inf bn; 1 mne coy, 2 spt coy

INDIA/PAKISTAN
UN • UNMOGIP 2 obs

SUDAN
UN • UNISFA 1

WESTERN SAHARA
UN • MINURSO 1 obs

Venezuela VEN

Venezuelan Bolivar Fuerte Bs		2011	2012	2013
GDP	Bs	1.36tr	1.76tr	
	US$	316.43bn	337.98bn	
per capita	US$	11,282	12,050	
Growth	%	4.18	5.75	
Inflation	%	26.09	23.25	
Def bdgt[a]	Bs	10.2bn	21.3bn	
	US$[b]	4.38bn	6.09bn	
US$1=Bs		4.29	5.21	

[a] Includes estimated value of Russia credit provided for arms procurement, excludes defence funding derived from the National Development Fund (FONDEN).

[b] Current US dollar defence-spending figures should be treated with caution when compared to spending in previous years, due to effects of currency revaluation in recent years.

Population	28,047,938					
Age	0–14	15–19	20–24	25–29	30–64	65 plus
Male	14.8%	4.9%	4.5%	4.0%	18.7%	2.5%
Female	14.2%	4.9%	4.5%	4.1%	19.8%	3.1%

Capabilities

The armed forces are tasked with protecting the sovereignty of the state and assuring territorial integrity. During the course of 2012, there were repeated suggestions that the Bolivarian Militia were to receive further military equipment. The military is in the process of receiving modern equipment, predominantly from Russia, to bolster its conventional capacity. In the Su-30MKV2, the air force has arguably the most capable multi-role fighter aircraft presently in the region, while the army received the T-72BV main battle tank beginning in 2011, and the navy might be a recipient of Kilo-class submarines. The Chavez regime has, however, replaced senior military officials on several occasions, and the level of political interference may have a corrosive effect on morale. The military trains regularly and there is an increasing focus on joint training. The air force has a tactical airlift capability, while an ageing KC-137 may remain in service providing air-refuelling (see pp. 429–431).

ACTIVE 115,000 (Army 63,000 Navy 17,500 Air 11,500 National Guard 23,000)
Terms of service 30 months selective, varies by region for all services

RESERVE 8,000 (Army 8,000)

ORGANISATIONS BY SERVICE

Army ε63,000
FORCES BY ROLE
MANOEUVRE
  Armoured
  1 (4th) armd div (1 armd bde, 1 lt armd bde, 1 AB bde, 1 arty bde, 1 AD bde)
  Mechanised
  1 (9th) mot cav div (1 mot cav bde, 1 ranger bde, 1 sy bde)
  Light
  1 (1st) inf div (1 SF bn, 1 armd bde, 1 mech inf bde, 1 ranger bde, 1 inf bde, 1 arty unit, 1 ADA bty, 1 spt unit)
  1 (2nd) inf div (1 mech inf bde, 1 inf bde, 1 mtn inf bde, 1 AD bty)
  1 (3rd) inf div (1 inf bde, 1 ranger bde, 1 sigs bde, 1 MP bde)
  Jungle
  1 (5th) inf div (1 SF bn, 1 cav sqn, 2 jungle inf bde, 1 engr bn)
  Aviation
  1 avn comd (1 tpt avn bn, 1 atk hel bn, 1 ISR avn bn)
COMBAT SUPPORT
  1 cbt engr corps with (3 engr regt)
COMBAT SERVICE SUPPORT
  1 log comd with (2 log regt)

Reserve Organisations 8,000
FORCES BY ROLE
MANOEUVRE
  Armoured
  1 armd bn
  Light
  4 inf bn
  1 ranger bn
COMBAT SUPPORT
  1 arty bn
  2 engr regt

EQUIPMENT BY TYPE
MBT 173: 81 AMX-30V; 92 T-72M1M
LT TK 109: 31 AMX-13; 78 *Scorpion* 90
RECCE 441: 42 *Dragoon* 300 LFV2; 10 TPz-1 *Fuchs* (CBRN);
79 V-100/-150; 310 UR-53AR50 *Tiuna*
AIFV 159: 123 BMP-3 (incl variants); 36 BTR-80A
APC 81
  APC (T) 45: 25 AMX-VCI; 12 VCI-PC; 8 VACI-TB
  APC (W) 36 *Dragoon* 300
ARTY 515+
  SP 60: **152mm** 48 2S19 (replacing Mk F3s) **155mm** 12
  (AMX) Mk F3
  TOWED 92: **105mm** 80: 40 M101; 40 Model 56 pack
  howitzer; **155mm** 12 M114
  MRL 56: **122mm** 24 BM-21 **160mm** 20 LAR SP (LAR-160);
  300mm 12 9A52 *Smerch*
  GUN/MOR 120mm 13 2S23 NONA-SVK
  MOR 294+: **81mm** 165; **120mm** 84: 60 Brandt; 48 2S12
    SP 21+: **81mm** 21 *Dragoon* 300PM; AMX-VTT
AT
  MSL • MANPATS 24 IMI MAPATS
  RCL 106mm 175 M40A1
  GUNS 76mm 75 M18 *Hellcat*
AD
  MANPAD RBS-70; *Mistral*
  GUNS 206+
    SP 23mm ε200 ZSU-23-2 **40mm** 6+ AMX-13 *Rafaga*
    TOWED 40mm M1; L/70
RADAR • LAND RASIT (veh, arty)
AIRCRAFT
  TPT • Light 28: 1 Beech 90 *King Air*; 1 Beech 200 *King Air*;
  1 Beech 300 *King Air*; 1 Cessna 172; 6 Cessna 182 *Skylane*;
  2 Cessna 206; 2 Cessna 207 *Stationair*; 1 IAI-201 *Arava*; 2
  IAI-202 *Arava*; 11 M-28 *Skytruck*
HELICOPTERS
  ATK 10 Mi-35M2 *Hind*
  MRH 33: 10 Bell 412EP; 2 Bell 412SP; 21 Mi-17V-5 *Hip* H
  TPT 9 **Heavy** 3 Mi-26T2 *Halo*; **Medium** 2 AS-61D; **Light**
  4: 3 Bell 206B *Jet Ranger*, 1 Bell 206L-3 *Long Ranger* II
  ARV 5: 3 AMX-30D; 2 *Dragoon* 300RV; *Samson*
  VLB *Leguan*

Navy ε14,300; ε3,200 conscript (total 17,500)

EQUIPMENT BY TYPE
SUBMARINES • TACTICAL • SSK 2:
  2 *Sabalo* (GER T-209/1300) with 8 single 533mm TT with
  SST-4 HWT
PRINCIPAL SURFACE COMBATANTS • FRIGATES 6
  FFGHM 6 *Mariscal Sucre* (ITA mod *Lupo*) with 8 single
  lnchr with *Otomat* Mk2 AShM, 1 octuple *Albatros* lnchr
  with *Aspide* SAM, 2 triple 324mm ASTT with A244
  LWT, 1 127mm gun, (capacity 1 Bell 212 (AB-212) hel)
PATROL AND COASTAL COMBATANTS 10
  PSOH 4 *Guaiqueri* with 1 76mm gun
  PBG 3 *Federación* (UK Vosper 37m) with 2 single lnchr
  with *Otomat* Mk2 AShM
  PB 3 *Constitucion* (UK Vosper 37m) with 1 76mm gun
AMPHIBIOUS
  LANDING SHIPS • LST 4 *Capana* (capacity 12 tanks;
  200 troops) (FSU *Alligator*)

  LANDING CRAFT 5:
    LCM 1
    LCVP 1
    LCU 2 *Margarita* (river comd)
    LCAC 1 Griffon 2000TD
LOGISTICS AND SUPPORT 6
  AORH 1
  AGOR 1 *Punta Brava*
  AGS 2
  ATF 1
  AXS 1

Naval Aviation 500

FORCES BY ROLE
ANTI SUBMARINE WARFARE
  1 sqn with Bell 212 (AB-212)
MARITIME PATROL
  1 flt with C-212-200 MPA
TRANSPORT
  1 sqn with Beech 200 *King Air*; C-212 *Aviocar*; *Turbo Commander* 980C
TRAINING
  1 hel sqn with Bell 206B *Jet Ranger II*; Bell TH-57A *Sea Ranger*
TRANSPORT HELICOPTER
  1 sqn with Bell 412EP *Twin Huey*; Mi-17V-5 *Hip* H
EQUIPMENT BY TYPE
AIRCRAFT 3 combat capable
  MP 3 C-212-200 MPA*
  TPT • Light 7: 1 Beech C90 *King Air*; 1 Beech 200 *King Air*; 4 C-212 *Aviocar*; 1 *Turbo Commander* 980C
HELICOPTERS
  ASW 5 Bell 212 ASW (AB-212 ASW)
  MRH 12: 6 Bell 412EP *Twin Huey*; 6 Mi-17V-5 *Hip*
  TPT • Light 1 Bell 206B *Jet Ranger II* (trg)
  TRG 1 Bell TH-57A *Sea Ranger*

Marines ε7,000

FORCES BY ROLE
COMMAND
  1 div HQ
SPECIAL FORCES
  1 Spec Ops bde
MANOEUVRE
  Amphibious
  1 (rvn) mne bde
  2 (landing) mne bde
COMBAT SUPPORT
  1 arty gp (3 arty bty, 1 AD bn)
  1 cbt engr bn
  1 MP bde
  1 sigs bn
COMBAT SERVICE SUPPORT
  1 log bn

EQUIPMENT BY TYPE
APC (W) 32 EE-11 *Urutu*
AAV 11 LVTP-7 (to be mod to -7A1)
ARTY • TOWED 105mm 18 M-56
  MOR 120mm 12 *Brandt*
AD • GUNS • SP 40mm 6 M-42

AD • SAM RBS-70
AT • AT-4 *Skip*
    RCL 84mm M3 *Carl Gustav*; **106mm** M40A1
AEV 1 AAVR7

Coast Guard 1,000

EQUIPMENT BY TYPE
PATROL AND COASTAL COMBATANTS 48
    PSOH 3 *Guaicamacuto* with 1 76 mm gun, (capacity 1
        Bell 212 (AB-212) hel) (1 additional vessel in build)
    PB 20: 1 *Dianca*; 12 *Gavion*; 1 *Pagalo*; 4 *Petrel* (US *Point*);
        2 *Protector*
    PBR 25: 18 *Constancia* (used by Marines); 2 *Guaicapuro*;
        2 *Manaure* (used by Marines); 3 *Terepaima* (*Cougar*)
        (used by Marines)
LOGISTICS AND SUPPORT 5
    AG 2 *Los Tanques* (salvage ship)
    AKSL 1
    AP 2

Air Force 11,500

Flying hours   155 hrs/year

FORCES BY ROLE
FIGHTER/GROUND ATTACK
    1 sqn with F-5 *Freedom Fighter* (VF-5)
    2 sqn with F-16A/B *Fighting Falcon*
    4 sqn with Su-30MKV *Flanker*
    1 sqn with K-8W *Karakorum**
GROUND ATTACK/ISR
    1 sqn with K-8W *Karakorum**
    1 sqn with EMB-312 *Tucano**
ELECTRONIC WARFARE
    1 sqn with *Falcon* 20DC; SA-227 *Metro III* (C-26B)
TANKER/TRANSPORT
    1 sqn with C-130H *Hercules*/KC-137
TRANSPORT
    1 sqn with A319CJ; B-737
    4 sqn with Cessna T206H; Cessna 750
    1 sqn with Cessna 500/550/551; *Falcon* 20F; *Falcon* 900
    1 sqn with G-222; Short 360 *Sherpa*
TRAINING
    1 sqn with Cessna 182N; SF-260E
    1 sqn with EMB-312 *Tucano**
TRANSPORT HELICOPTER
    1 VIP sqn with AS532UL *Cougar*; Mi-172
    3 sqn with AS332B *Super Puma*; AS532 *Cougar*
    2 sqn with Mi-17 *Hip H*
AIR DEFENCE
    3 bty with 9K330 *Tor-M1* (reported); *Barak*

EQUIPMENT BY TYPE
AIRCRAFT 99 combat capable

FTR 31: 5 F-5 *Freedom Fighter* (VF-5), 4 F-5B *Freedom
    Fighter* (NF-5B); 1 CF-5D *Freedom Fighter* (VF-5D); 17
    F-16A *Fighting Falcon*; 4 F-16B *Fighting Falcon*
FGA 24 Su-30MKV
EW 4: 2 *Falcon* 20DC; 2 SA-227 *Metro III* (C-26B)
TKR 1 KC-137
TPT 66 **Medium** 9: 6 C-130H *Hercules*; 1 G-222; 2 Y-8;
    Light 52: 5 Beech 200 *King Air*; 2 Beech 350 *King Air*; 10
    Cessna 182N *Skylane*; 12 Cessna 206 *Stationair*; 4 Cessna
    208B *Caravan*; 1 Cessna 500 *Citation I*; 3 Cessna 550
    Citation II; 1 Cessna 551; 1 Cessna 750 *Citation X*; 11 Quad
    City *Challenger* II; 2 Short 360 *Sherpa*; **PAX** 5: 1 A319CJ; 1
    B-737; 1 *Falcon* 20F; 2 *Falcon* 900
TRG 47: 18 EMB-312 *Tucano**; 17 K-8W *Karakorum** ; 12
    SF-260E
HELICOPTERS
    MRH 8 Mi-17 (Mi-17VS) *Hip* H
    TPT • Medium 15: 3 AS332B *Super Puma*; 8 AS532
    Cougar; 2 AS532UL *Cougar*; 2 Mi-172 (VIP)
AD
    SAM 40+: 12 9K330 *Tor-M1* (reported); 10+ *Barak*; 18
    S-125 *Pechora* (SA-3 *Goa*)
    MANPAD 200 9K338 *Igla-S* (SA-24 *Grinch*); ADAMS;
    Mistral
    GUNS • TOWED 228+: **20mm**: 114 TCM-20; **35mm**;
    40mm 114 L/70
RADARS • LAND *Flycatcher*
MSL
    AAM • IR AIM-9L/P *Sidewinder*; R-73 (AA-11 *Archer*);
    PL-5E; *Python* 4; R-27T/ET (AA-10 *Alamo*) **SARH** R-27R/
    ER (AA-10 *Alamo*); **ARH** R-77(AA-12 *Adder*)
    ASM Kh-29L/T (AS-14 *Kedge*); Kh-31A/P (AS-17 *Krypton*);
    Kh-59M (AS-18 *Kazoo*)
    AshM AM-39 *Exocet*

National Guard (Fuerzas Armadas de Cooperacion) 23,000

(Internal sy, customs) 9 regional comd
APC (W) 44: 24 Fiat 6614; 20 UR-416
MOR 50 **81mm**
PATROL AND COASTAL COMBATANTS • PB 34: 12
Protector; 12 *Punta*; 10 *Rio Orinoco II*
AIRCRAFT
    TPT • Light 34: 1 Beech 55 *Baron*; 1 Beech 80 *Queen
    Air*; 1 Beech 90 *King Air*; 1 Beech 200C *Super King Air*;
    3 Cessna 152 *Aerobat*; 2 Cessna 172; 2 Cessna 402C; 4
    Cessna U206 *Stationair*; 6 DA42 MPP; 1 IAI-201 *Arava*; 12
    M-28 *Skytruck*
    TRG 3: 1 PZL 106 *Kruk*; 2 PLZ M2-6 *Isquierka*
HELICOPTERS
    MRH 13: 8 Bell 412EP; 5 Mi-17V-5 *Hip* H
    TPT • Light 20: 9 AS355F *Ecureuil* II; 4 AW109; 6 Bell
    206B/L *Jet Ranger/Long Ranger*; 1 Bell 212 (AB 212);
    TRG 5 F-280C

Table 20 **Selected Arms Procurements and Deliveries, Latin America and the Caribbean**

Designation	Type	Quantity (Current)	Contract Value	Prime Nationality	Prime Contractor	Order Date	First Delivery Due (Current)	Notes
Argentina (ARG)								
OPV 80	PSOH	4	ARS619m (US$145m)	ARG/GER	Astillero Rio Santiago	2009	2012	Patrulleros de Alta Mar (PAM). Based on Fassmer OPV 80 design. Project suspended, then resumed in 2010
AT-63 *Pampa* II	Trg ac	10	n/k	ARG	n/k	n/k	2012	First 4 delivered to Cruz del Sur aerobatic team in 2012
Mi-171E	Tpt Hel	3	n/k	RUS	Rosoboron-export	2011	n/k	Exercised option from previous US$27m Mi-171E contract
Bell 206	Tpt Hel	20	see notes	ITA	n/k	2011	n/k	20 ex-Carabinieri hels to be delivered in exchange for 3 surplus ARG G-222s
Bolivia (BOL)								
H425	MR Hel	6	US$108m	PRC	Harbin	2011	n/k	Paid for by US$300m PRC government loan
EC145	Tpt Hel	2	n/k	Int'l	Eurocopter	2012	2012	First delivered Aug 2012. Second expected late 2012
MA60	Tpt ac	2	n/k	PRC	AVIC	2011	n/k	Paid for by US$300m PRC government loan
Brazil (BRZ)								
VBTP-MR *Guarani*	APC (W)	Up to 2,044	R6bn (€2.5bn)	BRZ/ITA	IVECO Latin America	2009	2012	First pre-production models delivered 2012. Serial production to commence 2013, with delivery to be complete by 2030
ASTROS 2020	MRL	30	R246m	BRZ	Avibras	2012	n/k	
SN-BR (Submarino Nuclear Brasileiro)	SSN	1	see notes	BRZ	DCNS	2009	2025	Part of €6.7bn (US$8.3bn) naval programme. Contract covers work on the non-nuclear sections of the submarine
S-BR (Submarino Brasileiro, *Scorpene*-class)	SSK	4	see notes	FRA	DCNS	2009	2017	Part of €6.7bn (US$8.3bn) naval programme. To be built by Itaguaí Construções Navais (JV between DCNS and Odebrecht). Delivery to be completed 2022
n/k	PSO	3	£133m	UK	BAE Systems (Maritime)	2012	2012	Originally ordered in 2007 as *Port-of-Spain*-class for Trinidad & Tobago. First vessel delivered Jun 2012. Second and third vessels due Dec 2012 and Apr 2013
Macaé (NAPA 500)	PCC	7	n/k	BRZ/FRA	1st batch: INACE/CMN 2nd batch: EISA	2006	2009	2 delivered by late 2012; third due by end 2012
PAF-L (light)	PBR	4	US$1.6m	COL	Cotecmar shipyard	2012	n/k	
Aviso Hidroceano-gráfico Fluvial	AGHS	4	n/k	BRZ	INACE	2011	2012	Riverine hydrographic vessels. First delivered Jul 2012. Final delivery due Nov 2012
P-3A *Orion*	ASW ac upgrade	8	US$401m	Int'l	EADS (CASA)	2005	2011	Upgrade to P-3AM. Option on ninth ac
A-*Darter*	AAM	n/k	ZAR1bn (US$143m)	BRZ/RSA	Denel	2007	2013	Missile firings continued during 2011. Delivery of production standard missiles due to begin 2013. Programme led by SA's Denel Dynamics
Mi-35M *Hind* (AH-2 *Sabre*)	Atk Hel	12	US$150–300m	RUS	Rosoboron-export	2008	2010	Contract value incl spares and trg. Nine delivered by mid-2012
EC725 *Super Cougar*	Tpt Hel	50	US$2bn	Int'l	EADS (EADS Brazil)	2008	2010	First three built in FRA. Remainder being manufactured in BRZ by Helibras. Delivery in progress

Table 20 **Selected Arms Procurements and Deliveries, Latin America and the Caribbean**

Designation	Type	Quantity (Current)	Contract Value	Prime Nationality	Prime Contractor	Order Date	First Delivery Due (Current)	Notes
S-70B Seahawk	ASW Hel	4	US$195m			2009	2012	Option for 2 more. To replace SH-3A/B *Sea King* hels. First 2 delivered Jul 2012
AS365K Panther	MRH Hel	34	R376m (US$215m)	Int'l	EADS (Brazil)	2009	2011	To be manufactured in BRZ by Helibras. Final delivery due 2021
Heron-1	ISR UAV	14	US$350m	ISR	IAI	2009	2010	For federal police
Hermes 450	ISR UAV	n/k	n/k	ISR	Elbit Systems	2011	2011	Delivery to be complete in 2012
Chile (CHL)								
Piloto Pardo-class	PSO	4	n/k	CHL/GER	ASMAR	2005	2008	Fassmer OPV 80 design. First two in service with coast guard
C-295 MPA/ASW	MP/ASW ac	3	US$120m	Int'l	EADS (CASA)	2007	n/k	For navy. 1 C-295 MPA; 2 C-295 ASW. Cost incl ASM and torp. Option for a further 5 MPA. MPA ac delivered Apr 2010; first ASW ac delivered Apr 2011
Hermes 900	ISR UAV	3	US$40m	ISR	Elbit Systems	2011	n/k	
Colombia (COL)								
Po Hang-class	FS	1	free transfer	ROK	n/k	2011	2012	Delivery status unclear
20 de Julio-class	PSO	1	n/k	COL	Cotecmar shipyard	2011	n/k	OPV-80. Second order
PAF-L (light)	PBR	10	n/k	COL	Cotecmar shipyard	n/k	2010	2 delivered in 2010; subsequent delivery status unclear
Ecuador (ECU)								
Shyri (Type-209/1300)	SSK upgrade	2	US$120m	CHL	ASMAR/DCNS	2008	2012	SLEP. Modernisation of first boat delayed by Chilean tsunami in 2010; second boat expected to be complete by 2014.
DA20 C1	Trg ac	12	n/k	CAN	Diamond Aircraft	2012	2012	To replace Cessna 150s. First 6 delivered Mar 2012
AS550C3 Fennec	MR Hel	7	n/k	Int'l	Eurocopter	2010	2012	Part of combined 9 hel contract with 2 AS350B2s which were delivered Dec 2011. First 2 delivered Sep 2012
El Salvador (SLV)								
MD500E	MR Hel	3	US$7.3m	US	MD Helicopters	2012	2012	First delivery due late 2012
Mexico (MEX)								
Tenochtitlan-class	PB	2	US$18m	NLD	Damen Schelde Naval Shipbuilding	n/k	2012	Damen Stan 4207 design
EC725 *Super Cougar*	Tpt Hel	6	€620m	Int'l	Eurocopter (Eurocopter de Mexico)	2009	2011	For tpt and civil sy missions
EC725 *Super Cougar*	Tpt Hel	6	n/k	Int'l	Eurocopter (Eurocopter de Mexico)	2010	2013	Follow-on from similar order signed in 2009
MEXSAT	Sat	3	US$1bn	US	Boeing	2010	2012	MEXSAT-3 due for launch late 2012. MEXSAT-1 to follow 2013–14
C-295M	Tpt ac	5	US$175m	Int'l	EADS	2011	2011	1 for air force; 4 for navy. First delivered Dec 2011
T-6C+ *Texan*	Trg ac	6	n/k	US	Hawker Beechcraft	2012	2012	To replace air force PC-7 fleet. First 2 due for delivery early 2012

Table 20 **Selected Arms Procurements and Deliveries, Latin America and the Caribbean**

Designation	Type	Quantity (Current)	Contract Value	Prime Nationality	Prime Contractor	Order Date	First Delivery Due (Current)	Notes
Peru (PER)								
Clavero-class	PCC	2	n/k	PER	SIMA Peru	n/k	2010	Second of class (Putumayo) expected to be commissioned 2013
Griffon 2000TD	UCAC	5	n/k	UK	Griffon Hoverwork	2012	n/k	For navy
DHC-6-400 Twin Otter	Tpt ac	12	n/k	CAN	Viking Air	2010	2011	Delivery in progress
UH-3H Sea King	Tpt Hel	6	US$6m	US	n/k	2009	n/k	Ex-US stock. Likely to be for SAR. First 2 delivered Dec 2010
Trinidad and Tobago (TTO)								
AW139	MRH Hel	4	US$348m	ITA	Fin-meccanica (Agusta Westland)	2009	2011	For air guard. Contract inc trg & log spt for 5 yrs
Venezuela (VEN)								
T-72M1M	MBT	100	n/k	RUS	n/k	2012	n/k	Part of US$4bn RUS loan agreement
Y-8	Tpt ac	8	n/k	PRC	AVIC	2011	2012	First 2 delivered Nov 2012
Mi-28NE Havoc	Atk Hel	10	n/k	RUS	Rosvertol	2010	2012	For army

Chapter Nine
Sub-Saharan Africa

Conflict and insecurity continue to dominate the defence and security debate across much of the continent. Since the fall of the Gadhafi regime in Libya in 2011, weaponry, mercenaries and armed groups have spread across the Sahel region. Some of the Tuareg tribesmen who rose up against the Malian government in January 2012, for example, had returned from fighting in Libya in possession of relatively sophisticated arms. The government's weak handling of this rebellion led to a coup in March, and the subsequent takeover of northern Mali by Islamists. In November 2012, the African Union (AU) approved the deployment of 3,300 troops, led by the Western African regional grouping ECOWAS, to help the Malian government regain control of its territory, but the details of the intervention were still being discussed. Islamist groups also caused growing concern in Algeria, Mauritania, Niger and particularly Nigeria, where the Boko Haram sect continued its bombing campaign.

Meanwhile, more established security crises continue to sap development progress and state resources across the continent. Conflict continues in the eastern Democratic Republic of the Congo (DRC) and Somalia, between the Sudans, as well as in areas straddling national boundaries, exemplified by the persistent and destructive presence of the Lord's Resistance Army (LRA) in parts of Uganda, the DRC, South Sudan and the Central African Republic (CAR).

Other rebel fighters continued to harass civilian populations in the North and South Kivu regions of eastern DRC. This year, well-known groups such as the Democratic Liberation Forces of Rwanda (FDLR) and the National Congress for the Defence of the People (CNDP) were joined by a new militia: M23. This group formed in April and May 2012, when several hundred former CNDP fighters integrated into the Congolese Army defected, claiming a breach of the peace agreement, signed on 23 March 2009, that brought them into the army. Rwanda and Uganda both denied a leaked UN report that accused them of backing M23, but the diplomatic ramifications had yet to play themselves out by year's end. Uganda threatened to pull out of UN peacekeeping missions in light of the allegations, and the country's prime minister announced in parliament, in November, that his government would withdraw Ugandan troops from Somalia, though it was unclear whether Kampala would act on this threat.

Military roles and capabilities

The longstanding desire to aid 'African solutions to African problems' is, for the West, perhaps bolstered by the continent's seemingly intractable security problems; few states outside Africa seem willing to deploy military force in any other fashion than a focused and limited one, while the continent's states generally retain limited (albeit developing) capability to plan complex missions, and deploy and sustain forces. External states have provided increased help with training programmes, organisational reform, and financial and material resources. But debate continues about the utility of such assistance. Despite counter-terrorist training provided to some of Mali's armed forces, for instance, they still rapidly lost control of the country's north.

Developing effective and enduring security structures is a long-term task, requiring enduring assistance programmes designed to grow forces from within. As such, programmes to train and equip troops are increasingly undertaken in conjunction with training in areas such as the rule of law. Meanwhile, organisational initiatives are not confined to ministries: the development of NCO and junior officer training is recognised as a key part of force effectiveness and institutional development more broadly. Additionally, African states are, often with donor assistance, paying more attention to matters that affect troops' welfare, such as pay, conditions and pensions. For the future development of continental armed forces, assistance in improving these issues relating to 'force health' are at least as important (and perhaps more important in the long term) as capability-relevant or mission-specific training assistance.

Some African armed forces, such as Uganda, are restructuring with ambitions to become comparatively modern, responsive forces equipped to high standards. Others retain small forces that have changed little in size or capability since the 1960s. For many states, territorial defence, support of the civilian authorities, internal security or police support remain central tasks. Several African countries take part in peacekeeping operations, and have strong professional training and military cultures, as well as modernising inventories and organisations. But few are able to independently deploy or sustain forces in strength beyond their immediate regions. Where there is personnel and equipment capacity, maintaining these at the required level of readiness is often a material and financial challenge. Few states are yet willing to gear their defence planning, budgeting and training towards generating forces useful in sustained missions.

Armed forces and police units deployed tend to be drawn from existing organisations, and structures and procurements are not necessarily geared towards producing capabilities for sustained overseas deployment. Defence and security reforms, and force-development plans, are mainly driven by domestic requirements. For instance, scarce resources may be earmarked for static garrisons or territorial defence. Further, states that suffer conflict and insurgency may develop capabilities, such as counter-insurgency, that would be useful abroad. But, instead, these forces may be deployed internally, or in support of police forces. In Nigeria, for instance, the army has been involved in tackling the threat from the Boko Haram terrorist group. Deployments like these have the potential to dilute the training and procurement requirements of armed forces, taking them away from core missions. Deployments abroad (such as on UN operations) are tasks for some, but these ambitions do not usually shape organisation and doctrine.

In recent unrest in Côte d'Ivoire, Guinea Bissau and Mali, armed forces played a role traditional for some African armed forces – as actors in domestic politics, forces designed to bolster ruling elites, or to preserve financial or other benefits. In these circumstances, where accountability to government might be recent or uncertain, or where close ties exist between government and armed forces, leaders might channel scarce resources to units designed to support regimes, such as presidential guards. Reforming security structures could help to alleviate such concerns, but historical and cultural factors can hinder implementation of uniform approaches to security sector reform (SSR).

CONTINENTAL SECURITY INITIATIVES

Harmonising continental SSR programmes

Better harmonisation of the increasing number of SSR programmes implemented across the continent requires understanding of the cultural, linguistic and colonial background of each nation and region. For instance, there are different institutional, organisational, bureaucratic and legal and security arrangements in Francophone, Anglophone and Lusophone Africa. Shared SSR policy frameworks could build on the experiences of individual states by, for instance, extending SSR theory and practice to Francophone countries or by less-intrusive forms of experience-sharing. For SSR programmes to really work in Francophone Africa, practitioners are recognising that, beyond sharing a common language, the majority of Francophone African states share a common institutional and organisational heritage. Across the continent, institutional variations matter, and have to be understood and incorporated into SSR policy and practice.

Organisations and decision-making
Francophone countries tend to have centralised presidential systems, with security bureaucracies reporting to the president. Anglophone countries initially inherited the tradition of parliamentary government, but a similar centralised system has gradually evolved, so in both areas the executive branch has gained prominence over parliament, in practical, if not necessarily constitutional, terms. Within the last ten years, almost all Anglophone countries have started to initiate structural and policy review processes, such as defence reviews, national security reviews or White Papers. Further, defence ministries in these states are organised along Western lines, where armed forces' commanders work with a civilian bureaucracy. This distinction between civil and military functions is not widespread in Francophone ministries of defence: on the contrary, these defence ministries are usually administered by the military. Furthermore, there are substantial differences between Francophone and Anglophone Africa in the organisation and purpose of police and other security forces.

Accountability and oversight
In recent years, Anglophone countries have witnessed moves designed to increase the accountability of their security forces. There have been initiatives to ensure

that defence ministries are relatively independent of the armed forces; parliamentary oversight, accountability to audit bodies, ombudsmen and other institutions such as human-rights commissions have all been introduced.

SSR has been actively promoted in countries like Sierra Leone and Ghana. There has also been some cross-fertilisation of experiences among Anglophone countries, while the South African model of democratic control over the armed forces has provided demonstration effect. But the mechanisms of 'horizontal' accountability – to audit bodies, ombudsmen, human-rights commissions etc. – remain weak, and military forces have been more affected than police. Nevertheless, security governance has been improving in some Anglophone countries in recent years.

Francophone African countries, by contrast, are often presented as not having experienced significant transformation in security governance – as evidenced by the military seizing, or assisting in the seizure of, power in Côte d'Ivoire, the CAR, Mauritania, Niger and Mali. However, the situation is not that straightforward. Often, differences in the level of transformation are a function of institutional and organisational factors peculiar to the evolution of these states' security structures. There have been some reforms. Senegal, for instance, is enhancing the control and oversight role of the parliament. It is not that states are necessarily resistant to reform; rather that reform has to be tailored to the historical, cultural and institutional frameworks in existence: one size does not fit all.

The African Standby Force

Regional economic communities are still pursuing the establishment of an African Standby Force (ASF) under overall AU command and control. As noted in recent editions of *The Military Balance*, this is the means by which the AU aims eventually to meet the demands of African security. The idea is to generate 6,500-strong deployable units across a force comprising the Southern Africa Standby Force; the ECOWAS Standby Force; the central African ECCAS Standby Force; the North African Regional Capability; and the East African Standby Force. These combined forces were originally due to be operationally capable in 2010. Documents now show 2010 as the date for initial operating capability, which some of the regional forces have now declared. Full operational capability for the whole ASF concept is now planned for 2015,

with a continent-wide rapid reaction capability due to be tested by December 2014. Though there is a need to be able to act anywhere on the continent, it is unclear whether the initiatives currently promoted are shaped and resourced to meet this requirement. However, some national armed forces, as well as the continent's security institutions and international partners, have begun to demonstrate flexible and innovative approaches.

Various 'road maps' have been designed by the AU to help the development of these standby forces, and there has been some progress in developing capacity. A series of command-post exercises and field-training exercises was held in 2009–10. These exercises and the AU's overall *Amani Africa* exercises have led to developments in doctrine, policies and procedures. They also sparked the realisation that progress was lacking in areas such as training standards and in reducing military dominance in headquarters' staffs. The AU had intended for these to be composed of staff from civilian and police contingents, as well as military personnel.

Less prescription, more regional freedom
Increasing the complexity of the standby force concept might reflect the continent's security demands, but may also delay its effective delivery. The AU has set the parameters within which the force may operate, but does not have the authority over the regional bodies to impose a uniform process and structure. As noted in the IISS *Strategic Survey 2012* (p. 60), this has permitted regional organisations to follow different paths in developing their standby forces. But the AU could still drive its agenda by building on the willingness of regional organisations to deploy troops for regional contingencies. ECOWAS, for example, launched initiatives in West Africa following the coups and unrest in Guinea Bissau and Mali. Another example is the deployment of EASF troops to Somalia, which the AU views as the first operational deployment of a regional standby force.

Further, in rapidly evolving crises, the formal structures thus far envisaged might not always allow sufficient flexibility. Reactive ad hoc responses may be more suitable. One example is the AU-led Regional Cooperation Initiative against the LRA, launched in March 2012, and due to eventually field a 5,000-strong set of task forces drawn from the CAR, DRC, South Sudan and Uganda. According to the AU, by September 2012, the following contingents had been assigned: 2,000 troops from Uganda; 500 from

Table 21 **Selected seizures of weapons exiting Libya, 2011**

Date of seizure	Place of seizure	Pistols	Assault rifles	Light machine guns	Heavy machine guns	Rocket launchers	Grenades	Military explosives	Ammunition
24 May 2011	Mauritania (Malian border)		X						X
12 June 2011	Niger (Arlit)							X	
20 June 2011	Algeria (Libyan border)	X	X	X	X	X			X
03 September 2011	Algeria (Libyan border)		X						X
15 September 2011	Niger (Aïr region)		X	X		X			X
02 October 2011	Algeria (Libyan border)					X		X	X
06 November 2011	Niger (Libyan border)		X			X			
06 November 2011	Niger (Arlit)		X	X	X	X	X		X
08 November 2011	Morocco (Laâyoune)		X						X
09 November 2011	Algeria (Libyan border)	X	X				X		X

South Sudan; and 350 out of an eventual 450-strong contingent from the CAR. (Discussions were ongoing with the DRC about its contingent.) This ad hoc development is important in that it brings together countries from different economic communities, transcending the 'boundaries' seen within the regional standby forces. Another example was the re-badging of Kenyan forces in Somalia under AMISOM (see p. 482), boosting that mission's military capacity.

CONTINENTAL SECURITY CRISES

Wider African effects of Libya's civil war

Many of the illicit arms in Africa have come from collapsing regimes. The Libyan civil war of February–October 2011 that ended Muammar Gadhafi's 42-year rule resulted in the same transfer of weapons from state to civilian control. However, Libya's pre-war arsenal was larger than usual, and coalition air-strikes left some stockpiles damaged and unsecured. Foreign members of the Libyan armed forces also returned to neighbouring states, such as Mali and Niger.

As detailed in *The Military Balance 2011* (pp. 320–1), Libya's armed forces were among the most heavily equipped in Africa before the war; and defections during it released large quantities of weapons into the hands of rebel forces and civilians. Coalition air-strikes added to the proliferation of weapons by damaging military sites and blasting open weapons- and ammunition-storage facilities, each of which facilitated widespread looting. Perhaps more seriously from the regional perspective, Tuareg and other forces (many of whom had been paid to join the defence of the regime in early 2011) fled Libya for their homelands. In the face of the threat of reprisals by rebel forces and the Libyan population, some 5,000 or more fighters abandoned Libya for Mali and Niger. Importantly, as illustrated in Table 21, they took with them a range of military materiel, including assault rifles, vehicle-mounted heavy machine guns, rocket launchers, ammunition and explosives.

It is impossible to gauge the number of weapons to have exited Libya, because the true extent of the pre-war Libyan government arsenal of small and man-portable arms is unknown, and because it is unclear which specific weapons fleeing forces could access. That the Sahara/Sahel region is scantily administered also means the interceptions and seizures listed in Table 21 probably represent just a small percentage of the total number of weapons to leave Libya in the civil war's aftermath. (The UN Panel of Experts on Libya notes various actors were involved, including former regime officials, small-scale traffickers and foreign armed groups.) In fact, it is almost certain that weapons and ammunition continue to be transported into and through neighbouring countries because of poor state control of the region.

Many ethnic Tuaregs from Mali had taken refuge in Libya after a failed rebellion in their country in 2008. They fought as mercenaries alongside Libyan government forces until the fall of the Gadhafi regime left them unwelcome in Libya, whereupon they returned home armed to a country already destabilised by the growing presence of al-Qaeda in the Islamic Maghreb (AQIM). Forming a new National Movement for the Liberation of Azawad (MNLA) in October 2011, the Tuaregs resumed their earlier rebellion, engaging the Malian military in clashes in January 2012, in which the army was sometimes forced to withdraw due to ammunition shortages. Frustrated military officers staged a coup in Bamako in March, and before ECOWAS could persuade them to make way for a transitional civilian government in April, Islamist group Ansar Dine had exploited the chaos to install sharia law in parts of northern Mali. Between them, Ansar Dine and Tuareg rebels now control much of northern Mali.

Libya's weapons fallout has not been restricted to Mali. Niger has proved a significant transit route for Libyan weapons, as has Algeria and, to a lesser extent, Chad and Egypt. In June 2011, Nigerien forces intercepted a convoy transporting 650 kilogrammes of Semtex-H and 335 detonators from Libya. Reliable reports also suggest the Darfur separatist group, the Justice and Equality Movement (JEM), returned to Sudan from the Libyan town of Kufrah in September 2011, bringing Libyan weapons and ammunition with them.

The potential proliferation of man-portable air-defence systems (MANPADS) is a major concern. Estimates suggest that Libya had imported as many as 20,000 systems before 2011. Multinational observers conclude that around 5,000 have since been secured, but some 15,000 remain unaccounted for. The weapons are sufficiently small and light to be concealed and transported without detection, and pose a severe risk of use in terrorist attacks. Military explosives pose a similar risk, particularly given the increasing activities of Islamist terrorist groups in sub-Saharan Africa, such as Boko Haram in Nigeria. The true extent of weapons proliferation from Libya is yet to be fully realised. However, it is important to recognise that the Libyan arsenal is finite. Although large quantities of weapons, ammunition and related materiel have been injected into the trans-Saharan arms market, that market – Africa's largest conveyor of illicit weapons – existed before the Libyan crisis and will continue to flourish unless governments are able to extend national control over large tracts of scantily administered territory and curtail trafficking in all commodities.

Islamist extremism spreads

Islamist militants have taken advantage of weak governments and ineffective security forces, tapping into religious and socio-economic grievances in Mali, Mauritania, Niger and Nigeria. As noted above, weapons from Libya have boosted some of their capabilities. It has been reported that some Libyan weapons have made their way into the hands of Boko Haram militants operating in the predominantly Muslim north of Nigeria. Security experts say there is evidence that Boko Haram members have been receiving weapons and training from Islamist groups such as AQIM and al-Shabaab.

In mid-2011, the Nigerian government formed a Joint Task Force (JTF), comprising personnel from the armed forces, police and the Department of State Security, to pursue *Operation Restore Order* to combat the Islamist group. Since then, security forces have arrested and killed dozens of Boko Haram operatives. However, in November 2012, Amnesty International accused the JTF of human-rights violations. 'Hundreds of people accused of links to Boko Haram have been arbitrarily detained without charge or trial; others have been extrajudicially executed or subjected to enforced disappearance,' Amnesty reported. Nigeria denied these allegations. However, combating the activities of such groups is undoubtedly difficult for armed and security forces suddenly confronted with a new threat of a complexity that few will have addressed before.

Cautious progress in Somalia

Having forced al-Shabaab Islamists to withdraw from the Somali capital, Mogadishu, in August 2011, AMISOM and other troops loyal to the Transitional Federal Government (TFG) have been gradually re-establishing control over other parts of the country. Although al-Shabaab remained in control of large swathes of the south, Ethiopian troops (together with Somali troops and personnel from the moderate Sufi militia Ahlu Sunna Wal Jama'a) drove the Islamists from Beledweyne in December 2011, Baidoa in February 2012, and El Burr in March, while AMISOM forces captured the strategic town of Afgoye in May and the port of Merca in August. Al-Shabaab lost its last urban stronghold when it was expelled from the major southern port of Kismayo in October 2012. As well as depriving al-Shabaab of access to the sea, Kismayo had been used by them to gain revenues from the export of charcoal, as well as import weapons. Meanwhile, AMISOM and TFG forces consolidated control over Mogadishu, where

Mali – what sort of intervention?

In late 2012, initiatives to intervene in Mali gained traction, given continued international and regional preoccupation that the security crisis in Mali could constitute a regional or even international threat. It was compounded by fears that terrorist groups could further secure their current foothold in the ungoverned space of Mali's north. 12 October saw the UN Security Council pass a resolution requiring ECOWAS, the AU and other partners to submit a detailed plan for the deployment of a military mission within 45 days. On 11 November, ECOWAS leaders adopted a concept of operations for the deployment of an African-lead peacekeeping force to Mali. Initial discussions focused on a possible 3,300-strong deployment. International support for this mission was immediately forthcoming, with France, Germany, Italy, Poland and Spain announcing, on 15 November, willingness 'to contribute to a possible training mission to support the Malian armed forces, in line with the [EU] Foreign Affairs Council's conclusions of the 15th of October.' ECOWAS forces will likely deploy any necessary combat power alongside Malian troops, while foreign assistance will likely prove useful in terms of providing financial, intelligence, logistic and training support. African armed forces do not lack deployable combat power in the form of infantry units; enabling these forces to deploy, move and sustain, as well as plan and execute effective and integrated operations that will be effective over a wide geographic area, will remain the focus of external support.

in August, Somalia's first functioning parliament in 20 years was sworn in.

Five years after its first arrival in Mogadishu, the AMISOM force has been bolstered by additional troop rotations from long-time contributors Uganda and Burundi, as well as a new contingent from Djibouti. Kenyan troops entered southern Somalia in October 2011 on *Operation Linda Nchi,* in the wake of kidnappings and bomb attacks on Kenyan soil attributed to al-Shabaab forces. One month later, Ethiopian forces advanced in the Mudug, Hiraan and Galguduud regions. Ethiopian troops were reported to have pulled back from towns in central Somalia in June 2012, 'but officials said they would remain in the country until the TFG had organised itself to fend off any hostile attacks and until all parties had ratified the constitution'. (See IISS *Strategic Survey 2012*, pp. 285–6.) On the Ethiopians' second tour of duty in Somalia in 2012, both Addis Ababa and the AU reportedly stressed that Ethiopian troops will

eventually hand over to AMISOM, after a new elected government has safely taken the reins from the interim administration. Kenyan forces, meanwhile, announced plans to expand beyond their positions in the far south of the country.

Military efforts were boosted by United Nations Security Council Resolution 2036, passed in February 2012. This increased AMISOM maximum strength from 12,000 to 17,731, made up of troops and formed police units. But late in the year, AMISOM's new troop levels were called into question. Rwanda and Uganda both denied a leaked UN report that accused them of backing the M23 rebels in the eastern DRC. Uganda threatened to pull out of UN peacekeeping missions in light of the allegations, and the country's prime minister announced in parliament in November that his government would withdraw Ugandan troops from Somalia. It was unclear whether Kampala would actually carry out this threat.

Resolution 2036 said that 'AMISOM shall be authorised to take all necessary measures as appropriate in those sectors in coordination with the Somali security forces to reduce the threat posed by al-Shabaab and other armed opposition groups in order to establish conditions for effective and legitimate governance across Somalia'. The resolution also targeted the charcoal trade that al-Shabaab has relied on for funding, asking member states to 'take all necessary measures' to prevent charcoal exports. Importantly, the resolution also enabled the Kenyan contingent to be re-hatted under AMISOM, bolstering AMISOM's troop strength in the south. The Kenyans were formally brought into AMISOM in June, and were instrumental in the October capture of Kismayo, advancing north towards the port city.

AMISOM advances

Constant military pressure on al-Shabaab by AMISOM led to the group being pushed out of sectors of Mogadishu. The group was by now liable to surveillance from assets such as unmanned aerial vehicles (UAVs), deployed from bases in the region. Though the US previously said that the UAVs would be used for surveillance, 'in June 2012, Washington confirmed that the US had been taking 'direct action' against al-Shabaab.' (IISS *Strategic Survey 2012*, p. 286.) April 2012 saw AMISOM troops deploy outside Mogadishu for the first time, when 100 Burundian and Ugandan troops deployed as an advance force (of an intended 2,500-strong contingent) to be co-located with Ethiopian troops.

Kenyan forces in the south made significant and deliberate advances in 2012. The methodical town-by-town advance of Kenyan and Somali forces from the south enabled artillery and air support to be deployed effectively in advance of each move, and also allowed Kenya's vehicle-dependent logistics train to keep up with advancing troops. Integrated planning, with AMISOM and its partner organisations, would have also enabled relevant surveillance and air assets to keep track of friendly forces and assist effective command and control. (It was widely reported that Kenya had been seeking *Raven* hand-launched tactical UAVs.) It was a stated aim of the Kenyan defence ministry to secure Kismayo in late 2012, an objective achieved, at the end of September, after al-Shabaab withdrew – after initially resisting – from the city in the wake of a two-pronged offensive, combining a limited beach landing in the north of the city, and a landward approach from the south by Kenyan and Somali forces. Some reports noted columns of al-Shabaab personnel departing; others pointed to personnel dispersing among the population of the city. The advance on Kismayo was well-planned.

AMISOM and Somali forces' capabilities have been boosted by the local knowledge and additional combat power of allied forces like the Ras Kamboni Brigade. But they have also received improved training. AMISOM has an established base at the Jazeera training camp in Mogadishu, primarily for Somali forces. According to an August 2011 article by the *New York Times*, some of this training (again at camps in Mogadishu) is provided by foreign defence contractors. Somali troops are also trained by the European Union's Training Mission at the Bihanga military camp in Uganda, with the first contingent arriving in the town of Entebbe in August 2010.

This mission has to overcome several challenges, according to the EU. One is that up to 80% of the intake could be illiterate; another is that the clan system makes forming mixed units difficult; yet another is the previous absence of a working command-and-control system within Somali forces (who previously were only paid intermittently). The training regime at Bihanga consists of recruit and NCO training, and staff training for company commanders, company staffs and junior officers. Additional military skills include battlefield first aid, fighting in built-up areas (FIBUA) and mine and IED awareness.

These latter two areas show how training requirements have changed in response to operational demands. Over the years of AMISOM

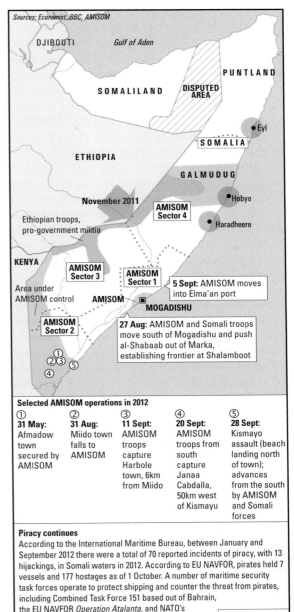

Map 14 **Somalia**

operations in Mogadishu, deployed forces have had to develop skills in patrolling on foot in conjunction with armour, as well as counter-IED, first-aid and communications skills. In August 2012, the 'Amani Peace Support Operations Village' was inaugurated; this is a FIBUA complex at the International Peace Support Training Centre in Nairobi, Kenya, which reflects regional urban terrain. The camp was opened by the commander of the Djibouti-based US Combined Joint Task Force–Horn of Africa. It has been supported by Canada, the US and the UK, in a reflection of the importance these states place on increasing the capacity of regional and Somali forces to counter al-Shabaab. In March 2012, the US was also training Ugandan personnel in 'counter-terrorism combat engineering', in a bid to establish three companies forming the basis of a Field Engineer Regiment capable of deployment to Somalia.

Some AMISOM officers have been trained in international humanitarian law prior to deployment to Somalia, in an effort to generate and maintain support for the AMISOM effort among the civilian population. Counter-battery fire was reportedly banned by AMISOM forces in Mogadishu, who have also – according to the January 2012 *AMISOM Review* – 'issued clear guidelines on the use of mortar and artillery and established no-fire zones within [Mogadishu]'. The longer foreign forces stay in Somalia, the more their areas of control expand, and the more they become responsible for helping establish the nascent Somali state – meanwhile assuming responsibility for security and service provision. Therefore, popular support will remain critical.

Though al-Shabaab has been defeated in combat engagements, it still possesses substantial territory in Somalia, and considerable equipment and personnel. As long as al-Shabaab maintains the ability to fund its activities, organise and communicate effectively, it is possible it could still exert pressure on AMISOM and pro-government forces by asymmetric, as well as conventional military, means.

Developing South Sudan's security forces

Sudan and the nascent state of South Sudan pulled back from the brink of all-out war in April 2012, and after months of internationally mediated negotiations, signed deals on oil transportation and a demilitarised buffer zone. However, the two nations' dispute over the oil-rich region of Abyei remained unresolved, and each still accuses the other of harbouring hostile rebel groups on its soil.

South Sudan's first year of existence was a difficult one. It became an independent state on 9 July 2011 without having fully resolved issues over the control of oil or the demarcation of its 1,800km border with its northern neighbour, Sudan. This has led to military confrontations in the border region between Juba's Sudan People's Liberation Army (SPLA) and

the Sudanese Armed Forces (SAF). Insurgent groups in South Sudan, backed by Khartoum and seeking to topple the Juba government, have launched periodic attacks against SPLA installations in Unity and Upper Nile states. Inter-tribal fighting, particularly in Jonglei state, has resulted in unprecedented levels of violence, placing additional strain on the SPLA and the South Sudan Police Service (SSPS).

At the same time, South Sudan's security forces are undergoing a reform and development process to enhance their ability to respond to current and future threats. The SPLA is aiming to transform from a once-factionalised guerrilla force to a standing army. (A proposal to rename the SPLA the South Sudan Defence Forces has not been enacted.) The SSPS, formed after the signing of the 2005 Comprehensive Peace Agreement (CPA) between the two halves of Sudan, needs improvements in capacity, discipline and equipment. Since 2005, South Sudan's Ministry of the Interior (MoI) has established a handful of other security organs, including a South Sudan wildlife service, prisons service, fire brigade, and customs force. Many of these, likewise, suffer from poorly trained officers and a lack of funding.

SPLA

The SPLA was the armed wing of the Sudan People's Liberation Movement (SPLM), and has become South Sudan's armed forces now the SPLM is in government in Juba. It currently has nine deployable divisions, which are assigned to specific sectors throughout South Sudan. Though the SPLA does not have any comprehensive personnel database to account for its soldiers – and the state's disarmament, demobilisation, and reintegration (DDR) programme has not managed to generate such a database – its force is estimated to number just over 200,000 troops, more than twice the size of all its other security forces combined. In 2011, the SPLA designed a blueprint for transformation called 'Objective Force 2017' which outlined the structure and composition it wished to have by 2017. Within this framework, the SPLA intends to downsize its force to 120,000 through a nationwide DDR programme, primarily funded by the international community. However, amid budgetary constraints and ad hoc recruitment drives, the DDR programme is only likely to yield marginal results during the next couple of years. Moreover, continuous reintegration of former Khartoum-backed rebel militia groups that accept amnesty agreements with Juba further inflates the SPLA's size.

During the CPA period, from 2005 until independence in 2011, South Sudan was prohibited from procuring military equipment. Despite the ban, it imported large quantities of small arms, light weapons and ammunition, as well as long-range artillery systems and tanks from Ukraine, via covert arrangements with some of its neighbours. In 2007, South Sudan signed a contract with Russia's Kazan Helicopters worth US$75 million for the purchase of nine Mi-17V-5 transport helicopters and one Mi-172 variant. For now, the helicopters fulfil a transport and reconnaissance role, but they can be fitted with machine guns and rocket pads.

When South Sudan gained its independence, the CPA expired, along with its ban on the transfer of lethal equipment to South Sudan. The US, likewise, lifted its arms embargo on South Sudan in January 2012, although it remains US policy not to supply lethal equipment. However, since 2005, the US has spent about US$275m on SPLA training and facilities. The EU arms embargo on South Sudan is the only existing legal framework prohibiting the transfer of lethal equipment to the country. Small Arms Survey estimates that the SPLA has about 250,000 small arms. These consist primarily of pistols, assault rifles, light and heavy machine guns, grenade launchers, multiple calibre recoilless rifles, anti-tank weapons, 60mm, 82mm, and 120mm mortars, 23mm anti-aircraft guns, and SA-7b man-portable air-defence systems (MANPADS).

SSPS and other organised forces

The SSPS was formed after the 2005 CPA to provide internal security in South Sudan. It was an amalgamation of police from SAF-controlled towns, SPLA soldiers who were transferred over to the police service, and demobilised SPLA soldiers. Today, despite efforts from donors to build its capacity, the SSPS remains poorly trained and inadequately funded, and, in most cases, defers to the SPLA for provision of South Sudan's internal security.

With support from international donors, the SSPS has opened training centres to replace much of its ageing force. The SSPS has approximately 50,000 officers on its payroll, but in common with the SPLA, eventually plans to slowly downsize rather than to introduce a DDR campaign. This would involve disbursing salaries in decreasing increments after retirement. Until recently, the SSPS was poorly armed, requiring that officers either purchase weapons from local traders or use their family's weapons.

In 2010, South Sudan purchased 40,500 Russian-manufactured AKM assault rifles from Ukraine. The MoI supplied 30,300 of these to the SSPS, with the remainder going to other security forces. SSPS officers possess another 20,000 weapons or so that are not registered with the police.

There are around 40,000 personnel belonging to the newly formed 'armed' security organs (such as the wildlife service, prisons service and so on), but only half of these personnel are armed.

Like the SPLA, the SSPS and its affiliate security providers have rudimentary recording and accounting mechanisms, which hampers the SSPS's ability to manage large numbers of its forces and their weapons stockpiles, both in and outside town centres. However, with support from the Nairobi-based Regional Centre on Small Arms (RECSA), the South Sudan Bureau for Community Security and Small Arms Control (BCSSAC) is leading a US Department of State-funded initiative to mark the 40,500 AKM rifles that were supplied in 2010. The bureau has also marked an additional 1,400 weapons from old police stockpiles in two of South Sudan's ten states, and is awaiting further funding to continue the programme elsewhere. For now, all marked weapons have been recorded manually, but RECSA intends to provide a software database to the bureau by the end of 2012. With support from Germany, in 2012, the bureau also established an Arms and Ammunition Working Group consisting of representatives from the SPLA, SSPS, wildlife service, prison service, and fire brigade to develop strategies for improving physical security and stockpile-management practices and dealing with surplus arms and ammunition.

Sub-Saharan Africa defence economics

There has been relatively robust growth across the region, which the IMF calculates should reach 5.25% in 2012–13. Meanwhile, regional inflation has slowed in the year, with an easing of food- and fuel-price inflation compared to that seen in 2011.

But the continental variations noted in last year's *Military Balance* remain. Low-income states are benefitting most from this increase, due in the main to their relative insulation from the shock of the global economic crises. However, drought and political instability are undermining growth in Mali and Guinea Bissau, while political instability in South Sudan and Somalia continue to negatively affect those states' prospects. Conflict in Somalia has long been a drag on northeast African growth prospects.

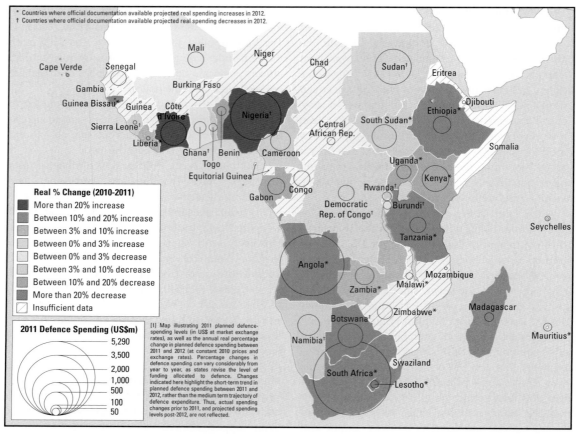

Map 15 **Sub-Saharan Africa Regional Defence Spending**[1]

Despite some success in 2012 in loosening Islamist group al-Shabaab's hold on Somalia (see p. 481), that country's prospects remain uncertain. The negative effect that Somalia's conflict has recently had on tourism in Kenya's northeast has not been reversed either.

Conflict has held back economic growth in Africa's newest state, South Sudan. Its economy depends heavily on oil production, but this was shut down only six months after independence, because of a dispute over transit fees for using a pipeline owned by its northern neighbour, Sudan, and other issues relating to competing territorial claims. Repeated outbreaks of fighting with Sudan continued late into the year. It was only in September that the two countries signed a deal making it possible for the South to resume oil exports through Sudan's pipeline, and not until November did Juba announce that it was ready to resume oil production. As noted by the IMF, institutional weakness and poor infrastructure are but two of South Sudan's sizeable economic and

political challenges. The continuing conflict is also a drain on its human resources, stymieing attempts to diversify and develop educational opportunities, as well as attempts to downsize the armed forces. As planned defence spending increased in real terms by 5.4% in 2012, even as the economy contracted by around 50% due to the shut-down in oil production, South Sudan had one of the highest levels of defence spending as a percentage of GDP in the world in 2012, rising from 3.05% in 2011 to 4.7% in 2012.

Meanwhile, the situation for middle-income countries is less favourable, given their closer integration into the global economy. South Africa, for instance, continues to experience sluggish growth, although the IMF reports that improved revenues from trade within the Southern African Customs Union (SACU) is helping to improve the four smaller SACU states' fiscal positions.

With commodity prices projected to remain soft, the near-term outlook for the region remains positive, but should world prices for, say, foodstuffs rise

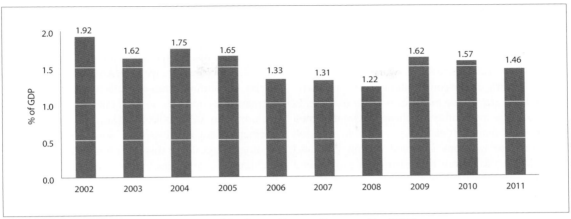

Figure 28 **Sub-Saharan Africa Regional Defence Expenditure** as % of GDP

significantly, stresses could increase in countries and regions going through poor harvests. That said, some states such as Angola and Congo should, the IMF says, be able to run fiscal surpluses. Whether states like these will divert greater resources towards armed forces or procurements remains to be seen, though with defence-spending plans across the continent still viewed through prism of security imperatives, it is certainly possible. As shown in last year's *Military Balance* (p. 419) states often have the means to find resources for advanced capabilities when directed.

Many procurements agreed in 2012 focused not on equipment such as tanks, but rather on capabilities with a dual-use potential for either military or security purposes. This can be seen through the purchase of patrol vessels by Nigeria and Mauritius which, though certainly capable of carrying out military tasks, are perhaps as intended for the constabulary role associated with counter-piracy activities. Other states continue to acquire and integrate capabilities long lacking on the continent, namely medium airlift. African states have long possessed transport aircraft capable of carrying personnel; carrying heavy equipment, or small vehicles, has long been harder and reliant on international assistance. The C-295 purchases seen in Ghana and Cameroon are emblematic of greater attention to this requirement by African states willing to deploy personnel on operations on the continent.

Africa's arms trade

The African wars of the 1990s shaped current international understanding of illicit arms flows on the continent. Major arms traffickers exploited the political collapse of the Soviet Union and economic chaos in post-Soviet states, exporting arms and ammunition to fuel a host of 'resource' wars in states such as Angola, Liberia and Sierra Leone. Conflict spillover and porous borders, in turn, led to the recirculation of illicit weapons, which has since blighted efforts to contain arms proliferation in Africa.

The primary vectors in the illicit African arms trade have always been African governments themselves, whether by supplying weapons in neighbouring conflicts, arming local populations or cascading weapons from insecure national stockpiles. Even in the 1990s, when the role of international arms traffickers received great attention, it was primarily African governments that orchestrated the supply of weapons into conflicts such as the DRC, Liberia, Rwanda and Sierra Leone.

Today, many African governments continue to supply weapons and ammunition to proxy forces in neighbouring states. In the past year alone, national governments have supplied large quantities of weapons to non-state groups in Côte d'Ivoire, the DRC and South Sudan. They do so with increasing sophistication. Recently documented cases involve military-orchestrated, cross-border supply operations; the rearming of foreign insurgent forces on domestic territory; the systematic removal of weapon serial numbers; and the repackaging of ammunition to conceal its origins.

In these cases, the legal and illicit arms markets are seamlessly linked, because states often supply new materiel directly onto illicit markets. This is particularly the case with ammunition, which, unlike weapons, is a consumable good. Ammunition manufactured as late as 2010 and 2011 is in widespread circulation on many African illicit markets – suggesting it has taken less than two years for ammunition manufactured abroad to be shipped to the continent and taken from a national government before appearing on illicit markets. For these reasons, changes in the legal market (legal transfers to African governments) have a direct bearing on the composition of illicit markets.

The legal arms trade in Africa is far from static. In the 1990s, the availability of cheap Soviet-designed weapons led many African governments to abandon NATO-calibre weapons supplied during the Cold War. NATO 7.62×51mm rifle cartridges proliferated in Africa, due to the Cold War supply of NATO rifles such as the Belgian FN FAL and German H&K G3. The smaller, NATO 5.56×45mm assault-rifle cartridge never gained such popularity, primarily because African armed forces favoured (and continue to favour) the rugged and reliable Kalashnikov-pattern assault rifle, which is chambered for the Soviet 7.62×39mm cartridge. Armed rebel and insurgent movements, likewise, adopted Soviet-calibre weapons, primarily because of ease of access, whether through capture, black-market acquisition or supply by state parties.

Over the past decade, China, which is a major producer of Soviet-calibre weaponry, has come to dominate the legal African arms market, offering cheap or offset deals. Today, indicating the rapidity with which weapons exit the legal African market, a majority of newer weapons on illicit markets are of Chinese manufacture, such as the Type-56 assault rifle. The current predominance of Chinese weaponry is not the only major change in the market. Field investigations by the UK-based group Conflict Armament Research reveal the previously unrealised, and rapidly growing, role of new suppliers, including Sudan and Iran.

Sudan increasingly acts as a regional arms supply and redistribution centre. Its activities include the provision of largely Chinese-made weapons and ammunition in regional conflicts, including to the embargoed region of Darfur and to proxy forces operating in South Sudan. In these cases, the government has tried to conceal its involvement, with the systematic removal of identifying marks on Chinese weapons and the use of unmarked ammunition packaging. Further afield, Sudan-manufactured ammunition is now a fast-growing component of trafficked weaponry, extending to illicit markets in countries as far from Sudan as the West African states of Côte d'Ivoire, Burkina Faso and Mali. The illicit redistribution of this ammunition involves land and air shipments, including to embargoed countries.

In parallel with these developments, Conflict Armament Research has also examined Iran's hitherto unrealised weapon footprint in Africa, which appears to be expanding. Iran-manufactured ammunition increasingly circulates on illicit markets across Africa, including in Côte d'Ivoire, Darfur, DRC, Guinea, northern Kenya, Libya and South Sudan. Initial findings suggest that this illicit trade runs into many millions of cartridges, with Iranian ammunition comprising as much as 80% of illicit market totals in some regions. Since March 2007, Iran has been under a UN Security Council embargo, which prohibits its export of weapons and related materiel.

Both Iran and Sudan have a record of providing destabilising materiel support to non-state armed groups. In Iran's case, this support has extended to supplying weapons to Hizbullah-aligned factions in Sinai and, potentially, to groups operating in Gaza; recent reports suggest that the territory of Sudan has been used as a transit route for such shipments. There is also some correlation between the distribution of Iranian and Sudanese ammunition on illicit markets in East and West Africa, which may suggest Sudanese involvement in the supply of Iranian materiel. In October 2012, Khartoum blamed Israel for an aerial attack on the Yarmouk arms factory in the Sudanese capital's south – which Israel neither confirmed nor denied. Reporters said Israel suspected that weapons from the factory were being smuggled to Gaza.

Taken as a whole, these indicators suggest an evolving market that is increasingly dominated by arms and ammunition supplied by states that have expressed little interest in curtailing arms exports to unstable regions – including China, Iran and African weapon-manufacturing states, such as Sudan. This arguably leaves the international community little leverage to control the flow of weapons entering the Sahara, which suggests that consideration will increasingly need to be given to strategies to control illicit arms flows within regions.

SOUTH AFRICA

South African defence thinking continues to be hampered by the absence of coherent foreign or national-security policy planning, or a clearly defined concept of national interest. South African security analysts view the 1996 White Paper on Defence and the 1998 Defence Review as generally flawed documents that have been overtaken by events, perhaps most significantly by South Africa's growing continental security engagement since 2001.

This engagement has come without any strategic context. The deployment to Burundi in 2001 followed a commitment by former President Nelson Mandela without the prior knowledge of his successor. The result was a decade-long deployment of a battalion-strength contingent with a small helicopter force. The deployment of a battalion to the Comoros in 2006 was agreed by the foreign ministry without consulting the defence department. The dispatch of a close-protection and training detachment to the CAR in 2007 remains unexplained, while the deployment of a frigate to the Mozambique Channel in early 2011 came in reaction to unexpected pirate attacks in that area, after earlier requests to join anti-piracy operations were not taken up. Most recently, on 27 September, President Zuma agreed, in principle, to provide troops for peacekeeping in Mali, despite the army being overstretched by the demands of foreign deployments and border security duties.

To compound the situation, the treasury only provides limited funding for such deployments. Similarly, the cabinet transferred border and key-point security to the police, and closed down the army's rear-area security system without any discussion of the implications this might have – before choosing to return border security to the armed forces, without restoring the funding.

The result of this inchoate handling of defence is that the South African National Defence Force (SANDF) is underfunded, as noted in previous editions of The Military Balance, and over-committed. It has too few troops to meet operational commitments, lacks the funds to train and properly maintain equipment, cannot replace obsolete equipment and cannot close critical capability gaps. The problem is aggravated when key acquisition projects are held up (the truck procurement Project Vistula) or even summarily cancelled (Project Continent for A400M transport aircraft) without clear explanation and without proper evaluation of the long-term consequences.

Defence Review 2012

The current Defence Review is an attempt to correct these deficiencies. It was established with a clear instruction to not take account of budgetary considerations that so bedevilled the 1998 review. In common with other defence reviews seen in, for instance, the US and UK , the 2012 review is intended to provide a dispassionate assessment of what capabilities will be needed over the next 30 years: costings and inevitable trade-offs will follow.

In the absence of South African foreign or national-security policies, it uses as its starting point what South Africa is actually doing. The 1998 review side-stepped regional security interests; this review accepts the reality of South African involvement in regional security matters and proposes a level of ambition for this role: two sustained medium-scale (battalion group, air and naval support) long-term deployments, three smaller short-term deployments, and short-notice crisis-response capability. It further argues for a future capacity to sustain a long-term brigade-level deployment.

This is in line with current deployments, but may not be sufficient to match South Africa's ambition to keep the chairmanship of the African Union (AU) Commission and to win a permanent seat on the UN Security Council. South Africa's Nkosazana Dlamini-Zuma replaced Gabon's Jean Ping as chair of the AU Commission in October 2012. However, AU officials have rather pointedly said that South Africa has fewer troops assigned to continental peace missions than Burundi.

The Defence Review gives the government a statement of these and other tasks that should be addressed by the SANDF, and a broad idea of the 'level of effort' required if each is to be successfully executed. It will be for the cabinet to prioritise and allocate funds accordingly.

The previous defence minister, Lindiwe Sisulu, argued strongly and repeatedly for adequate funding, and her successor, Nosiviwe Mapisa-Nqakula, has indicated she will follow suit. Soon after taking office, she also asked for a list of urgent issues facing the defence forces, and advice on what quick interventions could be made in cases like these. But, it is far from clear that the cabinet will provide either the required funding or cut back the commitments. There is a real concern among the military leadership that cabinet might fail to adequately address the issue.

Doctrine

Basic strategic and operational concepts and doctrines remain unchanged: South Africa will attempt to head off crises by diplomatic means within a regional or multilateral context if at all possible. It has committed to participating in SADC standby brigade operations, albeit with the proviso that units already engaged in

AU or UN operations will not be available, effectively ruling out a major army contribution.

If military action does become necessary, the Defence Review says that operations will be conducted by balanced forces tailored for each mission, with focused objectives and limited duration, and with emphasis on high-mobility operations. Again, the preference remains a multinational approach, but the review accepts that autonomous operations may become necessary. The review has adopted the concept of joint, inter-agency, inter-departmental and multinational operations first developed in the army's 2006 'Vision 2020' documents.

SANDF

A major focus of the Defence Review is to undo the consequences of the 're-engineering' carried out in 1998–9 by management consultants, which is now generally accepted by South African analysts to have had a deleterious effect. The re-engineering saw the end of South Africa's divisional formations, and led to units being organised according to their generalised type of equipment holding. Key aspects now identified for reversal include moving from the 'type formations' back to functional military structures (brigades, wings and navy squadrons), returning to normal command and staff systems and relationships, and devolving authority, responsibility and accountability back to unit commanders.

The proposed army structure is essentially similar to that of South African Army Vision 2020, except that the 'contingency brigade' will become a division with airborne, air-landed and sea-landed brigades. A mechanised division will form the core deterrent force; a motorised division will provide forces for longer-term deployments; and, in war, for rear-area protection. All three will comprise regular and reserve units.

The air force will move to functional wings grouped according to the missions to be performed by their units (e.g. fighter, transport, etc). Some analysts have assessed the structure in the draft Defence Review document – released in April 2012 – as rather irrational. For instance, maritime functions will apparently be split between two wings, while there will be two ISR wings. But these issues will probably be cleared up in the actual restructuring process. The navy will form frigate, submarine, patrol and support squadrons.

Accompanying this are recommendations for a total overhaul of officer and NCO systems, from recruitment through education and training to career management. There will be sharper focus on command, leadership and support in the operational environment. These changes are also intended to lead to a restructuring of the overall recruiting system for both regular and reserve personnel.

The Defence Review is intended to go to the security cluster, other members of the wider cabinet and parliament before the end of this year. However, at the time of writing this seemed unlikely given a major ANC elective congress, from 16-20 December 2012, for which parliament was expected to rise early. In this case, the review will be circulated among the relevant bodies early in 2013, after which it will go to the SANDF for implementation. The key question is whether the government will provide the necessary funding.

Readiness

While training remains adequate to allow operational deployments, readiness is severely compromised by shortfalls in key personnel categories and by poor serviceability of vehicles and equipment. The latter is a function of the shortage of technical personnel and funding, but also a result of poor discipline.

Discipline remains a major problem, as evidenced by the continuing dispute over unionisation noted in last year's *Military Balance*. The Defence Review recommends returning to a military disciplinary/legal model like that seen in many other armed forces, but that alone will not suffice. Real discipline demands professional respect among the ranks, and that is undermined by the continued tendency, say informed observers, to promote and appoint on the basis of party-political, race and gender considerations rather than competence. This is perceived negatively by junior officers, NCOs and other ranks, undermining respect for senior officers and making it more difficult to enforce discipline.

Defence economics

The defence budget was cut drastically after the end of hostilities along the Namibian–Angolan border in 1989, falling by 50% over the next decade from US$3.84 billion in 1989–90 to US$1.49bn in 1999–2000. The effect of this fall was aggravated by the need to keep as many troops deployed for internal security as were previously deployed in Namibia. The bulk of the cuts thus fell on capital projects. Internal deployments declined after 1995, but, from 2001, commitments to continental peace-support operations expanded.

Table 22 **South African Defence Budget by Programme, 2008–2014**

Rand m	2008	2009	2010	Revised Budget 2011	Budget 2012	Revised Budget 2012	Budget 2013	Budget 2014
Administration	2,480	2,881	3,427	3,718	3,730	3,820	4,040	4,262
Landward Defence	7,487	8,909	9,983	11,328	12,686	12,313	13,751	14,253
Air Defence	8,019	8,056	6,059	6,355	6,749	7,118	7,204	7,709
Maritime Defence	1,837	2,011	2,180	2,564	2,551	2,862	2,755	3,198
Military Health Support	2,177	2,483	2,770	3,244	3,316	3,496	3,515	3,692
Defence Intelligence	507	600	631	661	709	712	740	778
Joint Support	3,380	3,461	3,936	4,143	5,077	4,816	4,977	5,236
Force Employment	1,914	1,924	1,909	2,332	2,670	2,748	2,959	3,200
Total	**27,801**	**30,325**	**32,389**	**34,349**	**37,492**	**37,888**	**39,944**	**42,332**

Source: South African Defence Budget, April 2012; Adjusted Defence Budget Vote, October 2012

The defence budget declined from 4.3% of GDP in 1989–90 to 1.3% in 1999–2000 and today stands at 1.12%, despite several years of lobbying by the parliamentary defence committee for an emergency increase to 1.7%. The budget picked up somewhat after 1999 to fund 'strategic defence packages', the capital portion of the budget rising from 12.5% in 1998–99 to 35% in 2006–07, but this has fallen to 10% as increased operational tempo and higher salaries have overtaken relatively small budget increases.

By way of comparison, South Africa allocated R38.37bn (US$5.2bn) to defence in 2010–11, with R60.89bn (US$8.3bn) to the police, R107.48bn (US$14.6bn) to local government and housing, R113.8bn (US$15.5bn) to health, R144.68bn (US$19.7bn) to social protection and R195.48bn (US$26.6bn) to education. This is understandable given the development challenges in the country, but is not keeping up with the armed forces' ever-escalating operational commitments. Government allocated just under R5bn since 2005 to recapitalise state-owned defence group Denel. This requirement arose largely because inadequate defence funding had been preventing the SANDF from placing orders, which hampered export efforts.

Acquisition projects
Tight funding has made a coherent and logically phased acquisition programme impossible to implement, leaving the SANDF with some critical gaps, such as insufficient ships and shipboard helicopters, the lack of a maritime surveillance/patrol aircraft, and the lack of adequate airlift or sealift. Current airlift capacity is inadequate even to support forces already deployed. There is also an urgent need to acquire ground-forces equipment that will enable the army to perform border-patrol tasks.

But there are projects, albeit delayed, to address these gaps. The most urgent are *Project Biro* (for OPVs and IPVs) and *Project Saucepan* (maritime-surveillance aircraft), with others addressing light- and medium-airlift requirements. Future projects will include support and sealift vessels. The project to acquire heavy/long-range transport/tanker aircraft (A400M) was cancelled in 2010 under circumstances that are still unclear.

Other gaps mainly involve the replacement of old equipment, and there are projects, again mostly delayed for lack of funding, to meet requirements. One likely to proceed is *Project Hoefyster*, which is likely to see some 260 *Badger* ICVs replace part of the 30-year-old *Ratel* fleet. The Defence Review recommends that this go ahead, and that it should do so in parallel with the acquisition of new APCs and tactical logistic vehicles. The review also recommends funding and acquisition of the long-range 105mm gun currently in development.

Defence-industrial relationships
The relationship between the SANDF and the defence industry is generally sound, though fragile. This is partly because of lack of funding for major SANDF orders, and partly as a result of actions by acquisition agency Armscor that some analysts have seen as counterproductive. Among those have been the shift to quarterly, instead of monthly, tender-board meetings and making demands in respect of local ownership and black economic-empowerment levels. Acquisition decisions have also been criticised as taking too long to move through the system.

The review proposes that the present Armscor and Defence Acquisition Division be replaced by a Defence Matériel Organisation to streamline processes. It also argues for a shift to long-term, multi-year funding for major acquisition projects, as well as making long-term requirements more visible to industry. It proposes moving from a simple 'local or foreign' distinction towards four categories of recognised defence companies: South African (51% SA-owned), partly South African (26%), South African-based (plant in South Africa) and foreign. The intention is that projects considered 'sovereign' or of 'strategic importance' will be awarded, insofar as is practical, to companies in that order. It further supports international partnerships and joint ventures such as that with Brazil for the *A-Darter* short-range air-to-air missile, and that with the UAE for the manufacture there of guided weapons.

The review further argues for greater government support for defence exports. Exports have grown usefully, from R1.03bn (US$223m) in 1997 to R9.2bn (US$1.3bn) in 2011, but there is room for expansion with government support. That will also, however, depend, to an extent, on renewed local acquisition, as armed forces can tend to be reluctant to acquire equipment that is not in service with the home country's forces.

The reduction in acquisition spending by the SANDF has seen the defence industry shrink, leaving only two major wholly South African groups, state-owned Denel and Reutech, and two other large entities, DSD Protected Mobility and the avionics house ATE. Among the foreign companies that have acquired stakes in, or control of, South African companies are BAE, EADS, Rheinmetall, Saab and Thales.

Angola ANG

New Angolan Kwanza AOA		2011	2012	2013
GDP	AOA	9.78tr	11.1tr	
	US$	104.3bn	114.8bn	
per capita	US$	5,776	6,358	
Growth	%	3.92	6.83	
Inflation	%	13.50	10.75	
Def bdgt	AOA	340bn	396bn	
	US$	3.63bn	4.09bn	
USD1=AOA		93.78	96.69	

Population 18,056,072

Ethnic groups: Ovimbundu 37%; Kimbundu 25%; Bakongo 13%

Age	0–14	15–19	20–24	25–29	30–64	65 plus
Male	22.4%	5.7%	4.6%	3.8%	12.8%	1.3%
Female	21.5%	5.5%	4.4%	3.7%	12.8%	1.6%

Capabilities

After decades of focus on counter-insurgency resulting from the conflict with UNITA, the military is now going through a period of episodic restructuring while trying to cope with an ageing and sometimes obsolescent equipment inventory. The role of the armed forces is to ensure national sovereignty and territorial integrity, the importance of which is underscored by the oil and mineral wealth enjoyed by the country. Secessionist groups continue activity in the province of Cabinda. While the majority of the state's military inventory is of Russian origin, defence ties with China have been growing in recent years. The army and the navy remain of regional significance in terms of size, while a very much smaller navy operates only a handful of patrol craft. The military trains regularly, and also participates in multinational exercises. While on paper the air force constitutes a considerable regional force, including the Su-27 and the Su-24, the combat availability and serviceability of much of its aircraft is questionable. It does retain a tactical airlift capability, and in the Il-76 airlifter also has the capacity for longer-range transport missions.

ACTIVE 107,000 (Army 100,000 Navy 1,000 Air 6,000) Paramilitary 10,000

ORGANISATIONS BY SERVICE

Army 100,000

FORCES BY ROLE
MANOEUVRE
  Armoured
  1 tk bde
  Light
  1 SF bde
  1 (1st) div (1 mot inf bde, 2 inf bde)
  1 (2nd) div (3 mot inf bde, 3 inf bde, 1 arty regt)
  1 (3rd) div (2 mot inf bde, 3 inf bde)
  1 (4th) div (1 tk regt, 5 mot inf bde, 2 inf bde, 1 engr bde)
  1 (5th) div (2 inf bde)
  1 (6th) div (3 inf bde, 1 engr bde)
COMBAT SUPPORT
  Some engr units
COMBAT SERVICE SUPPORT
  Some log units
EQUIPMENT BY TYPE †
MBT 300+: ε200 T-54/T-55; 50 T-62; 50 T-72; T-80/T-84 (reported)
RECCE 600 BRDM-2
AIFV 250+: 250 BMP-1/BMP-2; BMD-3
APC (W) ε170 BTR-152/BTR-60/BTR-80
ARTY 1,408+
  SP 16+: **122mm** 2S1 *Carnation*; **152mm** 4 2S3; **203mm** 12 2S7
  TOWED 552: **122mm** 500 D-30; **130mm** 48 M-46; **152mm** 4 D-20
  MRL 90+: **122mm** 90: 50 BM-21; 40 RM-70 *Dana*; **240mm** BM-24
  MOR 750: **82mm** 250; **120mm** 500
AT • MSL • MANPATS 9K11 (AT-3 *Sagger*)
  RCL 500: 400 **82mm** B-10/**107mm** B-11 †; **106mm** 100†
  GUNS • SP 100mm SU-100†
AD • SAM • MANPAD 500 9K32 *Strela*-2 (SA-7 *Grail*)‡; 9K36 *Strela*-3 (SA-14 *Gremlin*); 9K 310 *Igla*-1 (SA-16 *Gimlet*)
  GUNS • TOWED 450+: **14.5mm** ZPU-4; **23mm** ZU-23-2; **37mm** M-1939; **57mm** S-60
ARV T-54/T-55
MW Bozena

Navy ε1,000

EQUIPMENT BY TYPE
PATROL AND COASTAL COMBATANTS 19
  PCC 5 *Rei Bula Matadi*
  PBF 5 PVC-170
  PB 9: 4 *Mandume*; 5 *Comandante Imperial Santana*

Coastal Defence

EQUIPMENT BY TYPE
MSL • AShM SS-C-1B *Sepal* (at Luanda)

Air Force/Air Defence 6,000

FORCES BY ROLE
FIGHTER
  1 sqn with MiG-21bis/MF *Fishbed*
  1 sqn with Su-27/Su-27UB *Flanker*
FIGHTER/GROUND ATTACK
  1 sqn with MiG-23BN/ML/UB *Flogger*
  1 sqn with Su-22 *Fitter D*
  1 sqn with Su-24 *Fencer*
  1 sqn with Su-25 *Frogfoot*
MARITIME PATROL
  1 sqn with F-27-200 MPA; C-212 *Aviocar*
TRANSPORT
  3 sqn with An-12 *Cub*; An-26 *Curl*; An-32 *Cline*; An-72 *Coaler*; BN-2A *Islander*; C-212 *Aviocar*; Do-28D *Skyservant*; EMB-135BJ *Legacy* 600 (VIP); Il-76TD *Candid*
TRAINING
  1 sqn with EMB-312 *Tucano*

1 sqn with L-29 *Delfin*; L-39 *Albatros*
1 sqn with PC-7 *Turbo Trainer*; PC-9*
1 sqn with Z-142

ATTACK HELICOPTER
2 sqn with Mi-24/Mi-35 *Hind*; SA342M *Gazelle* (with HOT)

TRANSPORT HELICOPTER
2 sqn with AS565; SA316 *Alouette III* (IAR-316) (incl trg)
1 sqn with Bell 212
1 sqn with Mi-8 *Hip*; Mi-17 *Hip H*

AIR DEFENCE
5 bn/10 bty with S-125 *Pechora* (SA-3 *Goa*); 9K35 *Strela-10* (SA-13 *Gopher*)†; 2K12 *Kub* (SA-6 *Gainful*); 9K33 *Osa* (SA-8 *Gecko*); 9K31 *Strela-1* (SA-9 *Gaskin*); S-75M *Volkhov* (SA-2 *Guideline*)

EQUIPMENT BY TYPE†

AIRCRAFT 94 combat capable
FTR 24: 6 Su-27/Su-27UB *Flanker*; 18 MiG-23ML *Flogger*
FGA 53: 20 MiG-21bis/MF *Fishbed*; 8 MiG-23BN/UB *Flogger*; 13 Su-22 *Fitter D*; 12 Su-24 *Fencer*
ATK 10: 8 Su-25 *Frogfoot*; 2 Su-25UB *Frogfoot*
ELINT 1 B-707
TPT 50: **Heavy** 4 Il-76TD *Candid*; **Medium** 6 An-12 *Cub* **Light** 40: 12 An-26 *Curl*; 3 An-32 *Cline*; 8 An-72 *Coaler*; 8 BN-2A *Islander*; 3 C-212-200 *Aviocar*; 4 C-212-300M *Aviocar*; 1 Do-28D *Skyservant*; 1 EMB-135BJ *Legacy* 600 (VIP)
TRG 39: 13 EMB-312 *Tucano*; 3 EMB-314 *Super Tucano** (3 more on order) 6 L-29 *Delfin*; 2 L-39C *Albatros*; 5 PC-7 *Turbo Trainer*; 4 PC-9*; 6 Z-142

HELICOPTERS
ATK 44: 22 Mi-24 *Hind*; 22 Mi-35 *Hind*
MRH 26: 8 AS565 *Panther*; 10 SA316 *Alouette III* (IAR-316) (incl trg); 8 SA342M *Gazelle*
MRH/TPT 27 Mi-8 *Hip*/Mi-17 *Hip H*
TPT • **Light** 8 Bell 212

AD • **SAM** 122
SP 70: 10 9K35 *Strela-10* (SA-13 *Gopher*)†; 25 2K12 *Kub* (SA-6 *Gainful*); 15 9K33 *Osa* (SA-8 *Gecko*); 20 9K31 *Strela-1* (SA-9 *Gaskin*)
TOWED 52: 40 S-75M *Volkhov* (SA-2 *Guideline*)‡; 12 S-125 *Pechora* (SA-3 *Goa*)

MSL
ASM AT-2 *Swatter*; HOT
ARM Kh-28 (AS-9 *Kyle*)
AAM • **IR** R-3 (AA-2 *Atoll*)‡; R-60 (AA-8 *Aphid*); R-73 (AA-11 *Archer*) **IR/SARH** R-23/24 (AA-7 *Apex*)‡

Paramilitary 10,000

Rapid-Reaction Police 10,000

Benin BEN

CFA Franc BCEAO fr		2011	2012	2013
GDP	fr	3.44tr	3.76tr	
	US$	7.3bn	7.54bn	
per capita	US$	761	786	
Growth	%	3.53	3.47	
Inflation	%	2.74	6.87	
Def bdgt	fr	34.9bn		
	US$	74m		
US$1=fr		471.84	498.40	

Population 9,598,787

Age	0–14	15–19	20–24	25–29	30–64	65 plus
Male	22.7%	5.5%	4.6%	3.9%	12.4%	1.1%
Female	21.8%	5.3%	4.4%	3.8%	13.0%	1.6%

Capabilities

The country fields a small military, dominated numerically by the army, with the navy and air force limited to providing a handful of platforms for transport and surveillance and in-shore patrol respectively. In the case of the latter, the service has been looking to France to provide additional coastal patrol craft, while the air force has acquired two LH-10 ultra-light aircraft. Piracy in the Gulf of Guinea is likely acting as a prompt to the country's renewed interest in maritime patrol. The army is predominantly a light infantry force, focused on tasks such as border security and peacekeeping.

ACTIVE 6,950 (Army 6,500 Navy 200 Air 250)
Paramilitary 2,500
Terms of service conscription (selective), 18 months

ORGANISATIONS BY SERVICE

Army 6,500

FORCES BY ROLE
MANOEUVRE
Armoured
2 armd sqn
Light
1 (rapid reaction) mot inf bn
8 inf bn
Air Manoeuvre
1 AB bn
COMBAT SUPPORT
1 arty bn
1 engr bn
1 sigs bn
COMBAT SERVICE SUPPORT
1 log bn
1 spt bn

EQUIPMENT BY TYPE
LT TK 18 PT-76 (op status uncertain)
RECCE 31: 14 BRDM-2; 7 M-8; 10 VBL
APC (T): 22 M-113

ARTY 16+
   TOWED 105mm 16: 12 L118 Light Gun; 4 M101
   MOR 81mm
AT • RL 89mm LRAC

Navy ε200

EQUIPMENT BY TYPE
PATROL AND COASTAL COMBATANTS
   PB 5: 2 *Matelot Brice Kpomasse* (ex-PRC); 3 FPB 98

Air Force 250

AIRCRAFT
   TPT 8 **Light** 4: 1 *Commander* 500B†; 1 DHC-6 *Twin Otter*†; 2 Do-28D *Skyservant*† **PAX** 4: 2 B-727; 2 HS-748†
   TRG 2 LH-10 *Ellipse*
HELICOPTERS
   TPT • Light 5: 4 AW109BA; 1 AS350B *Ecureuil*†

Paramilitary 2,500

Gendarmerie 2,500

FORCES BY ROLE
MANOEUVRE
   OTHER
      4 (mobile) paramilitary coy

DEPLOYMENT

CÔTE D'IVOIRE
UN • UNOCI 450; 14 obs; 1 inf bn

DEMOCRATIC REPUBLIC OF THE CONGO
UN • MONUSCO 428; 8 obs; 1 inf bn

LIBERIA
UN • UNMIL 1; 2 obs

SOUTH SUDAN
UN • UNMISS 2 obs

SUDAN
UN • UNISFA 1; 3 obs

Botswana BWA

Botswana Pula P		2011	2012	2013
GDP	P	120.5bn	138.9bn	
	US$	17.7bn	17.6bn	
per capita	US$	8,437	8,389	
Growth	%	5.09	3.82	
Inflation	%	8.46	7.52	
Def bdgt ª	P	3.68bn	3.68bn	
	US$	540m	467m	
FMA (US)	US$	0.339m	0.200m	0.200m
US$1=P		6.82	7.87	

ª Defence, Justice and Security Budget

Population   2,098,018

Age	0–14	15–19	20–24	25–29	30–64	65 plus
Male	17.1%	5.6%	5.3%	5.0%	15.9%	1.6%
Female	16.4%	5.5%	5.5%	5.2%	14.5%	2.4%

Capabilities

The armed forces are land-dominated, with a small air contingent. The main task is territorial integrity, increasingly coupled with involvement in regional peacekeeping missions. Ground forces have also been used for anti-poaching operations. The land force is developing a limited mechanized capability. Its air combat capacity is provided by the CF-5, an obsolescent design, but one which is adequate mostly for the limited roles it is tasked with. While the country is land-locked, its river systems justify the operation of a small number of patrol craft. The air force provides tactical airlift. Training is regular, with the military also participating in regional military exercises. Its personnel were deployed alongside the South African military to restore order following unrest in Lesotho in the late 1990s. The operations centre for the Southern African Standby Force is located in Gabarone.

ACTIVE 9,000 (Army 8,500 Air 500) **Paramilitary 1,500**

ORGANISATIONS BY SERVICE

Army 8,500
FORCES BY ROLE
MANOEUVRE
   Armoured
   1 armd bde (-)
   Light
   2 inf bde (1 armd recce regt, 4 inf bn, 1 cdo unit, 2 ADA regt, 1 engr regt, 1 log bn)
COMBAT SUPPORT
   1 arty bde
   1 AD bde (-)
   1 engr coy
   1 sigs coy

COMBAT SERVICE SUPPORT
  1 log gp

EQUIPMENT BY TYPE
LT TK 55: ε30 SK-105 *Kuerassier*; 25 *Scorpion*
RECCE 72+: RAM-V-1; ε8 RAM-V-2; 64 VBL
APC 156
  APC (T) 6 FV 103 *Spartan*
  APC (W) 150: 50 BTR-60; 50 LAV-150 *Commando* (some with 90mm gun); 50 MOWAG *Piranha* III
ARTY 46
  TOWED 30: **105mm** 18: 12 L-118 Light Gun; 6 Model 56 pack howitzer; **155mm** 12 Soltam
  MOR 28: **81mm** 22; **120mm** 6 M-43
AT
  MSL 6+
    SP V-150 TOW
    MANPATS 6 TOW
  RCL 84mm 30 *Carl Gustav*
AD • SAM • MANPAD 27: 5 *Javelin*; 10 9K310 *Igla-1* (SA-16 *Gimlet*); 12 9K32 *Strela-2* (SA-7 *Grail*)‡
  GUNS • TOWED 20mm 7 M167 *Vulcan*
ARV *Greif*; M578

Air Wing 500

FORCES BY ROLE
FIGHTER/GROUND ATTACK
  1 sqn with F-5A *Freedom Fighter*; F-5D *Tiger II*
ISR
  1 sqn with O-2 *Skymaster*
TRANSPORT
  2 sqn with BD-700 *Global Express*; BN-2A/B *Defender**; Beech 200 *Super King Air* (VIP); C-130B *Hercules*; C-212-300 *Aviocar*; CN-235M-100
TRAINING
  1 sqn with PC-7 *Turbo Trainer**
TRANSPORT HELICOPTER
  1 sqn with AS350B *Ecureuil*; Bell 412EP/SP *Twin Huey*

EQUIPMENT BY TYPE
AIRCRAFT 33 combat capable
  FTR 14: 9 F-5A *Freedom Fighter*; 5 F-5D *Tiger II*
  ISR 5 O-2 *Skymaster*
  TPT 19: **Medium** 3 C-130B *Hercules*; **Light** 15: 4 BN-2 *Defender**; 6 BN-2B *Defender**; 1 Beech 200 *King Air* (VIP); 2 C-212-300 *Aviocar*; 2 CN-235M-100 **PAX** 1 BD700 *Global Express*
  TRG 9: 4 PC-7 *Turbo Trainer**; 5 PC-7Mk II* (delivery by early 2013)
HELICOPTERS
  MRH 7: 2 Bell 412EP *Twin Huey*; 5 Bell 412SP *Twin Huey*
  TPT • Light 8 AS350B *Ecureuil*

Paramilitary 1,500

Police Mobile Unit 1,500 (org in territorial coy)

Burkina Faso BFA

CFA Franc BCEAO fr		2011	2012	2013
GDP	fr	4.81tr	5.32tr	
	US$	10.2bn	10.27bn	
per capita	US$	590	594	
Growth	%	4.16	6.99	
Inflation	%	2.75	3.00	
Def bdgt	fr	ε62.4bn		
	US$	ε132m		
US$1=fr		471.45	518.02	

Population   17,275,115

Age	0–14	15–19	20–24	25–29	30–64	65 plus
Male	22.9%	5.5%	4.6%	3.8%	12.1%	1.0%
Female	22.8%	5.4%	4.5%	3.7%	12.3%	1.5%

Capabilities

The army was involved in the social unrest that troubled the state during the first half of 2011, with protests at barracks in several cities. The aftermath of the upheaval saw the government introduce reform in the army, along with a reported reshuffle of senior officers. The three-month long disturbances, partly at least down to pay and the cost of food, places a question-mark over government-military relations. The army is predominantly infantry, with a limited number of light armoured vehicles. It does provide infantry for UN peacekeeping missions. The small air force has a limited fixed-wing light-attack and transport capacity, with firepower provided by the Mi-35. The acquisition of the *Super Tucano* could also bolster its close air support capability. France provides military training and there are growing ties with the US. The country is a partner in the US Africa Contingency Operations Training and Assistance (ACOTA) programme, and is part of the US's Trans-Sahara Counterterrorism Partnership.

ACTIVE 11,200 (Army 6,400 Air 600 Gendarmerie 4,200) **Paramilitary 250**

ORGANISATIONS BY SERVICE

Army 6,400

Three military regions. In 2011, several regiments were disbanded and merged into other formations, including the new 24th and 34th *régiments interarmes*.

FORCES BY ROLE
MANOEUVRE
  Mechanised
  1 cbd arms regt
  Light
  1 cbd arms regt
  6 inf regt
  Air Manoeuvre
  1 AB regt

COMBAT SUPPORT
1 arty bn (2 arty tp)
1 engr bn

EQUIPMENT BY TYPE
RECCE 83: 19 AML-60/AML-90; 24 EE-9 *Cascavel*; 30 *Ferret*; 2 M20; 8 M8
APC (W) 13 M3 Panhard
ARTY 18+
TOWED 14: **105mm** 8 M101; **122mm** 6
MRL 107mm ε4 Type-63
MOR 81mm Brandt
AT
RCL 75mm Type-52 (M20); **84mm** *Carl Gustav*
RL 89mm LRAC; M20
AD • SAM • MANPAD 9K32 *Strela-2* (SA-7 *Grail‡*)
GUNS • TOWED 42: **14.5mm** 30 ZPU; **20mm** 12 TCM-20

Air Force 600

FORCES BY ROLE
GROUND ATTACK/TRAINING
1 sqn with SF-260WL *Warrior**; Embraer EMB-314 *Super Tucano**
TRANSPORT
1 sqn with AT-802 *Air Tractor*; B-727 (VIP); Beech 200 *King Air*; CN-235-220; PA-34 *Seneca*
ATTACK/TRANSPORT HELICOPTER
1 sqn with AS350 *Ecureuil*; Mi-8 *Hip*; Mi-17 *Hip* H; Mi-35 *Hind*

EQUIPMENT BY TYPE
AIRCRAFT 5 combat capable
TPT 6 Light 5: 1 AT-802 *Air Tractor*; 2 Beech 200 *King Air*; 1 CN-235-220; 1 PA-34 *Seneca* **PAX** 1 B-727 (VIP)
TRG 5: 3 EMB-314 *Super Tucano**; 2 SF-260WL *Warrior**
HELICOPTERS
ATK 2 Mi-35 *Hind*
MRH 2 Mi-17 *Hip* H
TPT 2 Medium 1 Mi-8 *Hip* **Light** 1 AS350 *Ecureuil*

Gendarmerie 4,200

Paramilitary 250

People's Militia (R) 45,000 reservists (trained)

Security Company 250

DEPLOYMENT

DEMOCRATIC REPUBLIC OF THE CONGO
UN • MONUSCO 8 obs

SUDAN
UN • UNAMID 805; 10 obs; 1 inf bn

Burundi BDI

Burundi Franc fr		2011	2012	2013
GDP	fr	2.97tr	3.57tr	
	US$	2.36bn	2.53bn	
per capita	US$	224	240	
Growth	%	4.19	4.20	
Inflation	%	14.89	14.65	
Def bdgt	fr	79.7bn	89.6bn	
	US$	63m	64m	
US$1=fr		1260.89	1409.41	

Population   10,557,259
Ethnic groups: Hutu 85%; Tutsi 14%

Age	0–14	15–19	20–24	25–29	30–64	65 plus
Male	23.0%	5.3%	4.5%	3.8%	11.9%	1.0%
Female	22.8%	5.3%	4.5%	3.8%	12.5%	1.5%

Capabilities

Burundi's military is overwhelmingly a land force consisting predominantly of infantry, supported by some light armour. There is a notional air unit with a handful of light aircraft and helicopters. Border security and counter-insurgency are the main roles for the army. In recent years, the country has deployed both military and police personnel to AMISOM's mission in Somalia, gaining valuable experience in combat as well as specialist military skills.

ACTIVE 20,000 (Army 20,000) **Paramilitary 31,050**
DDR efforts continue, while activities directed at professionalising the security forces have taken place, some sponsored by BNUB, the UN mission.

ORGANISATIONS BY SERVICE

Army 20,000

FORCES BY ROLE
MANOEUVRE
Mechanised
2 lt armd bn (sqn)
Light
7 inf bn
Some indep inf coy
COMBAT SUPPORT
1 arty bn
1 AD bn 1 engr bn

Reserves

FORCES BY ROLE
MANOEUVRE
Light
10 inf bn (reported)
EQUIPMENT BY TYPE
RECCE 55: 6 AML-60; 12 AML-90; 30 BRDM-2; 7 S52 *Shorland*

APC (W) 57: 10 BTR 80; 20 BTR-40; 9 M3 Panhard; 12 RG-31 *Nyala*; 6 *Walid*

ARTY 120
  TOWED 122mm 18 D-30
  MRL 122mm 12 BM-21
  MOR 90: 82mm 15 M-43; 120mm ε75

AT
  MSL • MANPATS *Milan* (reported)
  RCL 75mm 60 Type-52 (M-20)
  RL 83mm RL-83 *Blindicide*

AD • SAM • MANPAD ε30 9K32 *Strela*-2 (SA-7 *Grail*)‡
  GUNS • TOWED 150+: 14.5mm 15 ZPU-4; 135+ 23mm ZU-23/37mm Type-55 (M-1939)

Air Wing 200
AIRCRAFT 1 combat capable
  TPT 4 Light 2 Cessna 150L†; PAX 2 DC-3
  TRG 1 SF-260W *Warrior**
HELICOPTERS
  ATK 2 Mi-24 *Hind*
  MRH 2 SA342L *Gazelle*
  TPT • Medium (2 Mi-8 *Hip* non-op)

Paramilitary 31,050

Marine Police 50
16 territorial districts
PATROL AND COASTAL COMBATANTS 3
  PHT 3 *Huchuan*†
AMPHIBIOUS • LCT 1
LOGISTICS AND SUPPORT • AG 1

General Administration of State Security ε1,000

Local Defence Militia ε30,000

DEPLOYMENT

CENTRAL AFRICAN REPUBLIC
ECCAS • MICOPAX 5

SOMALIA
AU • AMISOM 4,800; 5 inf bn

SUDAN
UN • UNAMID 2; 8 obs
UN • UNISFA 1 obs

FOREIGN FORCES
All forces part of BNUB unless otherwise stated.
Switzerland 1 obs

Cameroon CMR

CFA Franc BEAC fr		2011	2012	2013
GDP	fr	11.91tr	12.7tr	
	US$	25.65bn	24.51bn	
per capita	US$	1,274	1,267	
Growth	%	4.20	4.70	
Inflation	%	2.94	3.00	
Def bdgt	fr	164bn		
	US$	353m		
US$1=fr		464.26	518.05	

Population   20,129,878

Age	0–14	15–19	20–24	25–29	30–64	65 plus
Male	20.3%	5.3%	5.0%	4.3%	13.7%	1.5%
Female	20.0%	5.2%	4.9%	4.2%	13.7%	1.8%

Capabilities

The ability to meet the potential for regional instability (the country shares borders with six states) and internal security are tasks for Cameroon's armed forces. Piracy has, in recent years, also emerged as a threat. A long-running territorial dispute with Nigeria was settled in 2006, though the territory in question, the Bakassi Peninsula, continues to provide security challenges. Land forces are predominantly infantry supported by light vehicles, while the air force operates jet trainers in the ground-attack role. It has a small number of tactical airlift aircraft, supplemented by a handful of utility helicopters. The navy operates both blue water and coastal patrol craft, with concerns over piracy providing the impetus for recent acquisitions. The military has occasionally participated in multinational exercises. It has no ability for power projection beyond its immediate borders.

ACTIVE 14,200 (Army 12,500 Navy 1,300 Air 400)
Paramilitary 9,000

ORGANISATIONS BY SERVICE

Army 12,500
3 Mil Regions
FORCES BY ROLE
MANOEUVRE
  Light
  1 rapid reaction bde (1 armd recce bn, 1 AB bn, 1 amph bn)
  5 mot inf bde (2 mot inf bn, 1 spt bn)
  3 (rapid reaction) inf bn (under comd of mil regions)
  Air Manoeuvre
  1 cdo/AB bn
  Other
  1 (Presidential Guard) gd bn
COMBAT SUPPORT
  1 arty regt (5 arty bty)
  1 AD regt (6 AD bty)
  1 engr regt

EQUIPMENT BY TYPE
RECCE 65: 31 AML-90; 6 AMX-10RC; 15 *Ferret*; 8 M-8; 5 VBL
AIFV 22: 8 LAV-150 *Commando* with 20mm gun; 14 LAV-150 *Commando* with 90mm gun
APC 33
  APC (T) 12 M3 half-track
  APC (W) 21 LAV-150 *Commando*
ARTY 112+
  SP 18 ATMOS 2000
  TOWED 58: **75mm** 6 M-116 pack; **105mm** 20 M-101; **130mm** 24: 12 Model 1982 gun 82 (reported); 12 Type-59 (M-46); **155mm** 8 I1
  MRL 122mm 20 BM-21
  MOR 16+: **81mm** (some SP); **120mm** 16 Brandt
AT • MSL 49
  SP 24 TOW (on Jeeps)
  MANPATS 25 *Milan*
  RCL 53: **106mm** 40 M-40A2; **75mm** 13 Type-52 (M-20)
  RL 89mm LRAC
AD • GUNS • TOWED 54: **14.5mm** 18 Type-58 (ZPU-2); **35mm** 18 GDF-002; **37mm** 18 Type-63

Navy ε1,300
HQ located at Douala
EQUIPMENT BY TYPE
PATROL AND COASTAL COMBATANTS 11
  PCC 2: 1 *Bakassi* (FRA P-48); 1 *L'Audacieux* (FRA P-48)
  PB 7: 2 *Rodman 101*; 4 *Rodman 46*; 1 *Quartier Maître Alfred Motto*
  PBR 2 *Swift-38*
AMPHIBIOUS • LCU 2 *Yunnan*

Air Force 300-400
FORCES BY ROLE
FIGHTER/GROUND ATTACK
  1 sqn with MB-326K; *Alpha Jet**†
TRANSPORT
  1 sqn with C-130H/H-30 *Hercules*; DHC-4 *Caribou*; DHC-5D *Buffalo*; IAI-201 *Arava*; PA-23 *Aztec*
  1 VIP unit with AS332 *Super Puma*; AS365 *Dauphin 2*; Bell 206B *Jet Ranger*; Gulfstream III
TRAINING
  1 unit with *Tetras*
ATTACK HELICOPTER
  1 sqn with SA342 *Gazelle* (with HOT)
TRANSPORT HELICOPTER
  1 sqn with Bell 206L-3; Bell 412; SA319 *Alouette* III
EQUIPMENT BY TYPE
AIRCRAFT 9 combat capable
  ATK 5: 1 MB-326K *Impala* I; 4 MB-326K *Impala* II
  TPT 18 **Medium** 3: 2 C-130 *Hercules*; 1 C-130H-30 *Hercules* **Light** 14: 1 DHC-4 *Caribou*; 1 DHC-5D *Buffalo*; 1 IAI-201 *Arava*; 2 J.300 *Joker*; 2 PA-23 *Aztec*; 7 *Tetras* **PAX** 1 Gulfstream III
  TRG 4 *Alpha Jet**†
HELICOPTERS
  MRH 8: 1 AS365 *Dauphin 2*; 1 Bell 412 *Twin Huey*; 2 SA319 *Alouette* III; 4 SA342 *Gazelle* (with HOT)
  TPT 7 **Medium** 4: 2 AS332 *Super Puma*; 2 SA330J *Puma* **Light** 3: 2 Bell 206B *Jet Ranger*; 1 Bell 206L-3 *Long Ranger*

Paramilitary 9,000

Gendarmerie 9,000
FORCES BY ROLE
MANOEUVRE
  Reconnaissance
  3 (regional spt) paramilitary gp

DEPLOYMENT

CENTRAL AFRICAN REPUBLIC
ECCAS • MICOPAX 19

DEMOCRATIC REPUBLIC OF THE CONGO
UN • MONUSCO 5 obs

Cape Verde CPV

Cape Verde Escudo E		2011	2012	2013
GDP	E	150.8bn	162.68bn	
	US$	1.9bn	1.87bn	
per capita	US$	3,629	3,572	
Growth	%	5.05	4.29	
Inflation	%	4.47	2.09	
Def bdgt	E	722m		
	US$	9m		
US$1=E		79.25	87.09	

Population   523,568

Age	0–14	15–19	20–24	25–29	30–64	65 plus
Male	16.0%	5.7%	5.3%	4.6%	14.8%	2.0%
Female	15.9%	5.7%	5.4%	4.6%	16.7%	3.3%

Capabilities

The armed forces maintain limited forces with restricted force-projection capacities, driven by policy preoccupations with maritime security in the country's littoral.

ACTIVE 1,200 (Army 1,000 Coast Guard 100 Air 100)
Terms of service conscription (selective)

ORGANISATIONS BY SERVICE

Army 1,000
FORCES BY ROLE
MANOEUVRE
  Light
  2 inf bn (gp)
COMBAT SUPPORT
  1 engr bn
EQUIPMENT BY TYPE
RECCE 10 BRDM-2
ARTY 42
  TOWED 24: **75mm** 12; **76mm** 12

MOR 18: **82mm** 12; **120mm** 6 M-1943
AT • **RL 89mm** (3.5in)
AD • **SAM** • **MANPAD** 50 SA-7 *Grail*‡
GUNS • **TOWED** 30: **14.5mm** 18 ZPU-1; **23mm** 12 ZU-23

Coast Guard ε100

PATROL AND COASTAL COMBATANTS 5
PCC 2: 1 *Guardião*; 1 *Kondor I*
PB 2: 1 *Espadarte*; 1 *Tainha* (PRC-27m)
PBF 1 *Archangel*

Air Force up to 100

FORCES BY ROLE
MARITIME PATROL
1 sqn with C-212 *Aviocar*; Do-228

EQUIPMENT BY TYPE
AIRCRAFT • **TPT** • **Light** 5: 1 C-212 *Aviocar*; 1 Do-228; 3
An-26 *Curl*†

Central African Republic CAR

CFA Franc BEAC fr		2011	2012	2013
GDP	fr	1.04tr	1.12tr	
	US$	2.2bn	2.17bn	
per capita	US$	435	429	
Growth	%	3.30	4.10	
Inflation	%	1.20	6.85	
Def bdgt	fr	ε25.5bn		
	US$	ε54m		
US$1=fr		471.81	517.95	

Population   5,057,208

Age	0–14	15–19	20–24	25–29	30–64	65 plus
Male	20.6%	5.4%	4.9%	4.1%	13.1%	1.5%
Female	20.3%	5.3%	4.8%	4.1%	13.8%	2.2%

Capabilities

The stability of the state remains fragile. A combined EU peacekeeping mission to the CAR and Chad was succeeded by a UN force, deployment of which, in turn, concluded at the end of 2010. The military has no capacity for operations other than for internal security. It has no navy, but has some light craft for river patrol, while its small air force has a handful of transport and utility aircraft.

ACTIVE 2,150 (Army 2,000 Air 150) **Paramilitary 1,000**

Terms of service conscription (selective), 2 years; reserve obligation thereafter, term n.k.

ORGANISATIONS BY SERVICE

Army ε2,000

FORCES BY ROLE
MANOEUVRE
Mechanised
1 mech bn

Light
1 inf bn
Other
1 (Republican Guard) gd regt (3 gd bn)
1 intervention and spt bn
COMBAT SUPPORT
1 engr bn
COMBAT SERVICE SUPPORT
1 spt bn
EQUIPMENT BY TYPE
MBT 3 T-55†
RECCE 9: 8 *Ferret*†; 1 BRDM-2
AIFV 18 *Ratel*
APC (W) 39+: 4 BTR-152†; 25+ TPK 4.20 VSC ACMAT†; 10+ VAB†
ARTY • **MOR** 12+: **81mm**†; **120mm** 12 M-1943†
AT • **RCL 106mm** 14 M40†
RL 89mm LRAC†
PATROL AND COASTAL COMBATANTS 9 PBR†

Air Force 150

EQUIPMENT BY TYPE
AIRCRAFT • **TPT** 7 **Medium** 1 C-130A *Hercules* **Light** 6: 3 BN-2 *Islander*; 1 Cessna 172RJ *Skyhawk*; 2 J.300 *Joker*
HELICOPTERS
TPT • **Light** 1 AS350 *Ecureuil*

Paramilitary

Gendarmerie ε1,000

FORCES BY ROLE
MANOEUVRE
Other
8 paramilitary bde
3 (Regional Legion) paramilitary units

FOREIGN FORCES

Burundi MICOPAX 5
Cameroon MICOPAX 19
Chad MICOPAX 117
Congo MICOPAX 123
Democratic Republic of the Congo MICOPAX 118
France MICOPAX 7 • *Operation Boali* 230; 1 inf coy; 1 spt det
Gabon MICOPAX 160

Chad CHA

CFA Franc BEAC fr		2011	2012	2013
GDP	fr	4.41tr	5.04tr	
	US$	9.35bn	9.72bn	
per capita	US$	852	886	
Growth	%	1.76	7.32	
Inflation	%	1.89	5.50	
Def bdgt	fr	ε63.7bn		
	US$	ε135m		
FMA (US)	US$	0.399m	0.200m	-
US$1=fr		471.45	518.03	

Population   10,975,648

Age	0–14	15–19	20–24	25–29	30–64	65 plus
Male	23.1%	5.5%	4.2%	3.5%	10.4%	1.2%
Female	22.5%	5.7%	4.8%	4.1%	13.1%	1.7%

Capabilities

The first decade of this century saw Chad struggling with insurgency as well as conflict with Sudan, which provided a base for some of the rebels. The country was the subject of a combined EU peacekeeping mission to the Central African Republic and Chad until succeeded by a UN force, deployment of which concluded at the end of 2010. The state's military capacity is limited to internal security and border disputes, though the armed forces' ability to deal with significant challenges in either area is questionable. The land forces struggle with obsolescent equipment, the operational readiness of much of which is poor. The small air force was bolstered by the acquisition of a few Su-25s for ground attack and Mi-24 *Hind* combat-support helicopters. It has a very limited air transport capacity. The military has no ability for power projection.

ACTIVE 25,350 (Army 17,000–20,000 Air 350 Republican Guard 5,000) **Paramilitary 9,500**

Terms of service conscription authorised

ORGANISATIONS BY SERVICE

Army ε17,000–20,000 (being reorganised)

7 Mil Regions

FORCES BY ROLE
MANOEUVRE
Armoured
1 armd bn
Light
7 inf bn
COMBAT SUPPORT
1 arty bn
1 engr bn
1 sigs bn
COMBAT SERVICE SUPPORT
1 log gp

EQUIPMENT BY TYPE
MBT 60 T-55
RECCE 256: 132 AML-60/AML-90; ε100 BRDM-2; 20 EE-9 *Cascavel*; 4 ERC-90F *Sagaie*
AIFV 92: 83 BMP-1; 9 LAV-150 *Commando* (with 90mm gun)
APC (W) 52: 24 BTR-80; 8 BTR-3E; ε20 BTR-60
ARTY 7+
SP **122mm** 2 2S1 *Carnation*
TOWED **105mm** 5 M2
MOR **81mm** some; **120mm** AM-50
AT • MSL • MANPATS *Eryx*; *Milan*
RCL **106mm** M40A1
RL **112mm** APILAS; **89mm** LRAC
AD • GUNS • TOWED 14.5mm ZPU-1/ZPU-2/ZPU-4; **23mm** ZU-23

Air Force 350

FORCES BY ROLE
GROUND ATTACK
1 unit with PC-7; PC-9*; SF-260WL *Warrior**; Su-25 *Frogfoot*
TRANSPORT
1 sqn with An-26 *Curl*; C-130H-30 *Hercules*; Mi-17 *Hip* H; Mi-171
1 (Presidential) Flt with B-737BBJ; Beech 1900; DC-9-87; Gulfstream II
ATTACK HELICOPTER
1 sqn with AS550C *Fennec*; Mi-24V *Hind*; SA316 *Alouette* III

EQUIPMENT BY TYPE
AIRCRAFT 11 combat capable
ATK 8: 6 Su-25 *Frogfoot*; 2 Su-25UB *Frogfoot* B
TPT 8: **Medium** 1 C-130H-30 *Hercules* **Light** 4: 3 An-26 *Curl*; 1 Beech 1900 **PAX** 3: 1 B-737BBJ; 1 DC-9-87; 1 Gulfstream II
TRG 4: 2 PC-7 (only 1*); 1 PC-9 *Turbo Trainer**; 1 SF-260WL *Warrior**
HELICOPTERS
ATK 3 Mi-24V *Hind*
MRH 11: 6 AS550C *Fennec*; 3 Mi-17 *Hip* H; 2 SA316 *Alouette* III
TPT • Medium 2 Mi-171

Paramilitary 9,500 active

Republican Guard 5,000

Gendarmerie 4,500

DEPLOYMENT

CENTRAL AFRICAN REPUBLIC
ECCAS • MICOPAX 117

CÔTE D'IVOIRE
UN • UNOCI 1; 4 obs

FOREIGN FORCES

France *Operation Epervier* 950; 1 armd cav BG; 1 air unit with 3 *Mirage* 2000C; 2 C-160 *Transall*; 1 CN-235M; 1 C-135FR; 1 hel det with 4 SA330 *Puma*

Congo COG

CFA Franc BEAC fr		2011	2012	2013
GDP	fr	6.81tr	7.12tr	
	US$	14.44bn	13.74bn	
per capita	US$	3,307	3,147	
Growth	%	3.42	4.93	
Inflation	%	1.77	5.15	
Def bdgt	fr	ε108bn		
	US$	ε229m		
US$1=fr		471.43	518.00	

Population	4,366,266

Age	0–14	15–19	20–24	25–29	30–64	65 plus
Male	22.8%	5.6%	4.7%	3.8%	11.8%	1.1%
Female	22.5%	5.6%	4.6%	3.7%	12.1%	1.6%

Capabilities

The Congo's armed forces have struggled to recover from the brief, but devastating, civil war in the late 1990s. The presence of unofficial militias during that period led to a confusing DDR process, with a lack of clarity, even now, on the defence payroll and the proliferation of small arms in the country. Given the integration of militias into the military, training is inadequate and the level of professionalism low. This is despite a defence budget that fares relatively well in comparison to immediate neighbours and has no major procurement programmes. The armed forces' remaining equipment is often outdated or beyond repair. The air force is effectively grounded for lack of spares and serviceable equipment, and the navy is little more than a riverine force despite the need for maritime security on the country's small coastline.

ACTIVE 10,000 (Army 8,000 Navy 800 Air 1,200) **Paramilitary 2,000**

ORGANISATIONS BY SERVICE

Army 8,000
FORCES BY ROLE
MANOEUVRE
Armoured
2 armd bn
Light
2 inf bn (gp) each with (1 lt tk tp, 1 arty bty)
1 inf bn
Air Manoeuvre
1 cdo/AB bn

COMBAT SUPPORT
1 arty gp (with MRL)
1 engr bn
EQUIPMENT BY TYPE†
MBT 40+: 25 T-54/T-55; 15 Type-59; T-34 in store
LT TK 13: 3 PT-76; 10 Type-62
RECCE 25 BRDM-1/BRDM-2
APC (W) 68+: 20 BTR-152; 30 BTR-60; 18 *Mamba*; M3 Panhard
ARTY 66+
    SP 122mm 3 2S1 *Carnation*
    TOWED 25+: **76mm** ZIS-3 *M-1942*; **100mm** 10 M-1944; **122mm** 10 D-30; **130mm** 5 M-46; **152mm** D-20
    MRL 10+: **122mm** 10 BM-21; **122mm** BM-14/**140mm** BM-16
    MOR 28+: **82mm**; **120mm** 28 M-43
AT • **RCL 57mm** M18
    GUNS 57mm 5 ZIS-2 *M-1943*
AD • **GUNS** 28+
    SP 23mm ZSU-23-4
    TOWED 14.5mm ZPU-2/ZPU-4; **37mm** 28 M-1939; **57mm** S-60; **100mm** KS-19

Navy ε800
EQUIPMENT BY TYPE
PATROL AND COASTAL COMBATANTS 8
    PCC 4 *Février*
    PBR 4

Air Force 1,200†
FORCES BY ROLE
FIGHTER/GROUND ATTACK
1 sqn with *Mirage* F-1AZ
TRANSPORT
1 sqn with An-24 *Coke*; An-32 *Cline*
ATTACK/TRANSPORT HELICOPTER
1 sqn with Mi-8 *Hip*; Mi-35P *Hind*
EQUIPMENT BY TYPE†
AIRCRAFT
    FGA 2 *Mirage* F-1AZ
    TPT • **Light** 2: 1 An-24 *Coke*; 2 An-32 *Cline*
HELICOPTERS†
    ATK (2 Mi-35P *Hind* in store)
    TPT • **Medium** (3 Mi-8 *Hip* in store)
MSL • **AAM** • **IR** R-3 (AA-2 *Atoll*)‡

Paramilitary 2,000 active

Gendarmerie 2,000
FORCES BY ROLE
MANOEUVRE
Other
20 paramilitary coy

Presidential Guard some
FORCES BY ROLE
MANOEUVRE
Other
1 paramilitary bn

DEPLOYMENT

CENTRAL AFRICAN REPUBLIC
ECCAS • MICOPAX 123

Côte D'Ivoire CIV

CFA Franc BCEAO fr		2011	2012	2013
GDP	fr	11.36tr	12.57tr	
	US$	24.10bn	24.27bn	
per capita	US$	1,098	1,106	
Growth	%	-4.73	8.13	
Inflation	%	4.90	2.00	
Def bdgt[a]	fr	277bn	324bn	
	US$	587m	625m	
US$1=fr		471.43	518.05	

[a] Defence, order and security expenses.

Population   21,952,093

Age	0–14	15–19	20–24	25–29	30–64	65 plus
Male	19.8%	5.5%	5.1%	4.3%	14.4%	1.5%
Female	19.5%	5.5%	5.0%	4.2%	13.6%	1.6%

Capabilities

A UN arms embargo remains in place until at least the end of April 2013, as a result of a civil war that began in 2002. The embargo was enacted in 2004. Recent elections may eventually result in increasing political stability, though the intial result was conflict between forces loyal to the incumbent, Laurent Gbagbo, and Alassane Ouattara. This is partly reflected in the decision by the UN, in April 2012, to exempt military training and advice from the broader embargo. The army is being formed from personnel from both sides of the conflict, a task that poses obvious challenges. A naval unit with patrol craft exists, at least on paper, but the serviceability of the vessels is uncertain. A small number of helicopters constitute the only air capability.

ACTIVE ε40,000 target

RESERVE n.k.

In October 2011, President Ouattara announced the formation of the Forces Armées Nationale de Côte d'Ivoire. It is reported that these will consist of 29,000 ex-CIV military forces, 9,000 ex-Forces Nouvelles troops and 2,000 volunteers. Moves to restructure and reform the armed forces continue.

ORGANISATIONS BY SERVICE

Army n.k.
EQUIPMENT BY TYPE
MBT 10 T-55†
LT TK 5 AMX-13
RECCE 34: 15 AML-60/AML-90; 13 BRDM-2; 6 ERC-90F4 *Sagaie*
AIFV 10 BMP-1/BMP-2†

APC (W) 41: 12 M3 Panhard; 13 VAB; 6 BTR-80
ARTY 36+
   TOWED 4+: **105mm** 4 M-1950; **122mm** (reported)
   MRL 122mm 6 BM-21
   MOR 26+: **81mm**; **82mm** 10 M-37; **120mm** 16 AM-50
AT • MSL • MANPATS 9K113 *Konkurs* (AT-5 *Spandrel*) (reported); 9K133 *Kornet* (AT-14 *Spriggan*) (reported)
   RCL 106mm ε12 M40A1
   RL 89mm LRAC
AD • SAM • MANPAD 9K32 *Strela*-2 (SA-7 *Grail*)‡ (reported)
   GUNS 21+
     SP 20mm 6 M3 VDAA
     TOWED 15+: **20mm** 10; **23mm** ZU-23-2; **40mm** 5 L/60
VLB MTU
AIRCRAFT • TPT 1 An-12†

Navy ε900
EQUIPMENT BY TYPE
PATROL AND COASTAL COMBATANTS 3
   PB 1 *Intrepide* † (FRA *Patra*)
   PBR 2 *Rodman* (fishery protection duties)
AMPHIBIOUS
   LCM 2 *Aby* †
   LSM 1 *L'elephant* †

Air Force n.k.
EQUIPMENT BY TYPE†
HELICOPTERS
ATK 1 Mi-24 (reported)
TPT • Medium 3 SA330L *Puma* (IAR-330L)† **PAX** 1 B-727

Paramilitary n.k.

Republican Guard unk
APC (W): 4 *Mamba*

Gendarmerie n.k.
APC (W): some VAB
PATROL AND COASTAL COMBATANTS 4 PB

Militia n.k.

FOREIGN FORCES

All forces part of UNOCI unless otherwise stated.
Bangladesh 2,170; 13 obs; 2 inf bn; 1 avn coy; 1 engr coy; 1 sigs coy; 1 fd hospital
Benin 428; 8 obs; 1 inf bn
Bolivia 3 obs
Brazil 3; 4 obs
Chad 1; 4 obs
China, People's Republic of 6 obs
Ecuador 1 obs
Egypt 176; 1 engr coy
El Salvador 3 obs
Ethiopia 1 obs
France 6 • *Operation Licorne* 450; 1 armd cav BG; 1 hel unit with 3 SA330 *Puma*
Gambia 3 obs

Ghana 507; 6 obs; 1 inf bn; 1 hel coy; 1 fd hospital
Guatemala 5 obs
Guinea 3 obs
India 8 obs
Ireland 2 obs
Jordan 1,067; 7 obs; 1 SF coy; 1 inf bn
Korea, Republic of 2 obs
Malawi 861; 3 obs; 1 inf bn
Moldova 4 obs
Morocco 726; 1 inf bn
Namibia 2 obs
Nepal 1; 3 obs
Niger 935; 4 obs; 1 inf bn
Nigeria 64; 6 obs; 1 fd hospital
Pakistan 1,387; 10 obs; 1 inf bn; 1 engr coy; 1 tpt coy
Paraguay 2; 7 obs
Peru 3 obs
Philippines 3; 3 obs
Poland 2 obs
Romania 4 obs
Russia 9 obs
Senegal 523; 13 obs; 1 inf bn
Serbia 3 obs
Tanzania 2; 2 obs
Togo 525; 7 obs; 1 inf bn
Tunisia 3; 7 obs
Uganda 2; 5 obs
Uruguay 2 obs
Yemen, Republic of 2; 8 obs
Zimbabwe 2 obs

Democratic Republic of the Congo DRC

Congolese Franc fr		2011	2012	2013
GDP	fr	14.42tr	16.45tr	
	US$	15.71bn	17.7bn	
per capita	US$	213	240	
Growth	%	6.88	7.11	
Inflation	%	15.54	10.45	
Def bdgt	fr	203bn	213bn	
	US$	221m	229m	
FMA (US)	US$	0.3m	-	0.2m
US$1=fr		918.02	929.57	

Population   73,599,190

Age	0–14	15–19	20–24	25–29	30–64	65 plus
Male	22.1%	5.8%	4.8%	3.9%	12.2%	1.1%
Female	21.8%	5.8%	4.8%	3.8%	12.5%	1.5%

Capabilities

The Democratic Republic of the Congo ostensibly retains the largest armed forces in the Central African region.

However, given the vast size of the country and the parlous state of their training, morale and equipment, the forces are unable to provide security throughout the DRC. The DRC has suffered the most protracted war in the post-Cold War era, driven by ethnic and political division, and catalysed by international involvement and natural resources. For this reason, it is unsurprising that much military equipment is in a poor state of repair and the armed forces, which have since incorporated a number of non-state armed groups, struggle with a variety of loyalties. The latest manifestation of this latter factor was a defection by several hundred soldiers in the east of the country, dubbed the M23 group, in April 2012. This group demonstrated their capability by capturing the eastern city of Goma in November 2012. The military is heavily dominated by land forces; the air force retains a limited combat capability of mostly Soviet-origin aircraft, but the navy is wholly inadequate to secure the country's small coastline and acts as a riverine force. Given the challenges facing the armed forces, the DRC will continue to rely on international peacekeeping deployments for security, in the shape of MONUSCO. International partners, including Belgium, US AFRICOM and MONUSCO have trained personnel.

ACTIVE ε134,250 (Central Staffs ε14,000, Army 103,000 Republican Guard 8,000 Navy 6,700 Air 2,550)

ORGANISATIONS BY SERVICE

Army (Forces du Terre) ε103,000

The DRC has eleven Military Regions. In 2011, all brigades in North and South Kivu provinces were consolidated into 27 new regiments, the latest in a sequence of re-organisations designed to integrate non-state armed groups. The actual combat effectiveness of many formations is doubtful.

FORCES BY ROLE
MANOEUVRE
  Light
  6 (integrated) inf bde
  3+ inf bde (non-integrated)
  27 inf regt
COMBAT SUPPORT
  1 arty regt
  1 MP bn

EQUIPMENT BY TYPE†
(includes Republican Guard eqpt)
MBT 149: 12–17 Type-59 †; 32 T-55; 100 T-72
LT TK 40: 10 PT-76; 30 Type-62† (reportedly being refurbished)
RECCE up to 52: up to 17 AML-60; 14 AML-90; 19 EE-9 *Cascavel*; 2 RAM-V-2
AIFV 20 BMP-1
APC 138:
  APC (T) 3 BTR-50
  APC (W) 135: 30-70 BTR-60PB; 58 M3 Panhard†; 7 TH 390 *Fahd*
ARTY 520+
  SP 16: **122mm** 6 2S1 *Carnation* **152mm** 10 2S3

TOWED 119: **122mm** 77 (M-30) M-1938/D-30/Type-60; **130mm** 42 Type-59 (M-46)/Type-59 I
MRL 57: **107mm** 12 Type-63; **122mm** 24 BM-21; **128mm** 6 M-51; **130mm** 3 Type-82; **132mm** 12
MOR 328+: **81mm** 100; **82mm** 200; **107mm** M-30; **120mm** 28: 18; 10 Brandt
AT • RCL 36+: **57mm** M18; **73mm** 10; **75mm** 10 M20; **106mm** 16 M40A1
GUNS **85mm** 10 Type-56 (D-44)
AD • SAM • MANPAD 20 9K32 *Strela*-2 (SA-7 *Grail*)‡
GUNS • TOWED 114: **14.5mm** 12 ZPU-4; **37mm** 52 M-1939; **40mm** ε50 L/60† (probably out of service)

Republican Guard 8,000
FORCES BY ROLE
MANOEUVRE
Armoured
1 armd regt
Light
3 gd bde
COMBAT SUPPORT
1 arty regt

Navy 6,700 (incl infantry and marines)
EQUIPMENT BY TYPE
PATROL AND COASTAL COMBATANTS 16
PB 16: 1 *Shanghai* II; ε15 various (all under 50ft)

Air Force 2,550
AIRCRAFT 5 combat capable
FTR 2: 1 MiG-23MS *Flogger*; 1 MiG-23UB *Flogger C*
ATK 3 Su-25 *Frogfoot*
TPT 6 **Medium** 1 C-130H *Hercules* **Light** 3 An-26 *Curl*
PAX 2 B-727
HELICOPTERS
ATK 9: 4 Mi-24 *Hind*; 5 Mi-24V *Hind*
TPT 4 **Heavy** 1 Mi-26 *Halo* (non op) **Medium** 3: 1 AS332L *Super Puma*; 2 Mi-8 *Hip*

Paramilitary

National Police Force
incl Rapid Intervention Police (National and Provincial forces)

People's Defence Force

DEPLOYMENT

CENTRAL AFRICAN REPUBLIC
ECCAS • MICOPAX 118

FOREIGN FORCES
All part of MONUSCO unless otherwise specified.
Algeria 5 obs
Austria EUSEC RD Congo 1
Bangladesh 2,519; 34 obs; 2 mech inf bn; 1 avn coy; 1 hel coy(-); 1 engr coy
Belgium 21; 4 obs; 1 avn flt • EUSEC RD Congo 4
Benin 450; 14 obs; 1 inf bn

Bolivia 9 obs
Bosnia and Herzegovina 5 obs
Burkina Faso 8 obs
Cameroon 5 obs
Canada (*Operation Crocodile*) 8 obs
China, People's Republic of 218; 16 obs; 1 engr coy; 1 fd hospital
Czech Republic 3 obs
Egypt 1,000; 26 obs; 1 inf bn; 1 SF coy
France 5 obs • EUSEC RD Congo 10
Germany EUSEC RD Congo 3
Ghana 461; 26 obs; 1 mech inf bn(-)
Guatemala 150; 1 obs; 1 SF coy
Hungary EUSEC RD Congo 2
India 3,693; 59 obs; 3 mech inf bn; 1 inf bn; 1 hel coy; 1 fd hospital
Indonesia 175; 17 obs; 1 engr coy
Ireland 3 obs
Jordan 220; 26 obs; 1 SF coy; 1 fd hospital
Kenya 24 obs
Luxembourg EUSEC RD Congo 1
Malawi 10 obs
Malaysia 17 obs
Mali 16 obs
Mongolia 2 obs
Morocco 849; 6 obs; 1 mech inf bn; 1 fd hospital
Mozambique 1 obs
Nepal 1,024; 24 obs; 1 inf bn; 1 engr coy
Netherlands EUSEC RD Congo 3
Niger 16 obs
Nigeria 29 obs
Norway 1 obs
Pakistan 3,695; 58 obs; 3 mech inf bn; 1 inf bn; 1 hel coy
Paraguay 17 obs
Peru 7 obs
Poland 2 obs
Portugal EUSEC RD Congo 2
Romania 22 obs
Russia 28 obs
Senegal 22 obs
Serbia 6; 2 obs
South Africa (*Operation Mistral*) 1,201; 19 obs; 1 inf bn; 1 avn coy; 1 engr coy
Sri Lanka 2 obs
Sweden 5 obs
Switzerland 4 obs
Tanzania 2 obs
Tunisia 31 obs
Ukraine 154: 14 obs; 2 atk hel sqn
United Kingdom 4 obs • EUSEC RD Congo 4
United States 3 obs
Uruguay 1,160; 37 obs; 1 inf bn; 2 mne coy; 1 hel flt; 1 engr coy
Yemen, Republic of 6 obs
Zambia 17 obs

Djibouti DJB

Djiboutian Franc fr		2011	2012	2013
GDP	fr	220.22bn	241.67bn	
	US$	1.24bn	1.36bn	
per capita	US$	1,601	1,756	
Growth	%	4.49	4.82	
Inflation	%	5.07	4.70	
Def bdgt	fr	ε1.72bn		
	US$	ε10m		
FMA (US)	US$	1.996m	1.5m	1m
US$1=fr		177.74	177.70	

Population   774,389

Ethnic groups: Somali 60%; Afar 35%

Age	0–14	15–19	20–24	25–29	30–64	65 plus
Male	17.2%	5.4%	5.0%	4.0%	13.1%	1.5%
Female	17.1%	5.7%	5.9%	5.2%	18.0%	1.9%

Djibouti has a small military almost entirely dominated by the army, reflecting the state's size and population. The country's security is informally bolstered by the presence of French and US troops. Clashes with the Eritrean military, in 2008, demonstrated the superior nature of the Djiboutian forces' training and skills, but also highlighted the fact that the small military would be unable to counter the larger, if less well-equipped forces of its neighbours. The army has concentrated on mobility in its equipment purchases, suitable for patrol duties but ill-suited for armoured warfare. The 2008 border clashes at least temporarily swelled the ranks of the Djiboutian army, with retired personnel being recalled, but the military's size and capabilities are much reduced since the 1990s Afar insurgency. Nonetheless, that period has afforded the Djiboutian armed forces with counter-insurgency experience, with those and other skills retained through a busy exercise schedule and intensive training regime. Djibouti deployed to Somalia as part of AMISOM; 100 troops were deployed to Mogadishu from December 2011, and expanded their presence to Baladweyne in mid-2012. A close relationship with French forces stationed in Djibouti ensures access to combined training.

ACTIVE 10,450 (Army 8,000 Navy 200 Air 250 Gendarmerie 2,000) National Security Force 2,500

ORGANISATIONS BY SERVICE

Army ε8,000

FORCES BY ROLE

4 military districts (Tadjourah, Dikhil, Ali-Sabieh and Obock)

MANOEUVRE

Mechanised

1 armd regt (1 recce sqn, 3 armd sqn, 1 (anti-smuggling) sy coy)

Light

4 inf regt (3-4 inf coy, 1 spt coy)

1 rapid reaction regt (4 inf coy, 1 spt coy)

Other

1 (Republican Guard) gd regt (1 sy sqn, 1 (close protection) sy sqn, 1 cbt spt sqn (1 recce pl, 1 armd pl, 1 arty pl), 1 spt sqn)

COMBAT SUPPORT

1 arty regt

1 demining coy

1 sigs regt

1 CIS sect

COMBAT SERVICE SUPPORT

1 log regt

1 maint coy

EQUIPMENT BY TYPE

RECCE 39: 4 AML-60†; 15 VBL; 16-20 *Ratel*

APC (W) 20: 8 BTR -80; 12 BTR-60†

ARTY 96

  TOWED 122mm 6 D-30

  MOR 45: **81mm** 25; **120mm** 20 Brandt

AT

  RCL 106mm 16 M40A1

  RL 89mm LRAC

AD • GUNS 15+

  SP 20mm 5 M693

  TOWED 10: **23mm** 5 ZU-23; **40mm** 5 L/70

Navy ε200

EQUIPMENT BY TYPE

PATROL AND COASTAL COMBATANTS 12

  PBF 2 Battalion-17

  PB 10: 1 *Plascoa*; 2 Sea Ark 1739; 1 *Swari*; 6 others

AMPHIBIOUS • LCM 1 CTM

Air Force 250

EQUIPMENT BY TYPE

AIRCRAFT

  TPT • Light 3: 1 Cessna U206G *Stationair*; 1 Cessna 208 *Caravan*; 1 L-410UVP *Turbolet*

HELICOPTERS

  ATK (1 Mi-35 *Hind* in store)

  MRH 1 Mi-17 *Hip* H

  TPT 2 **Medium** (1 Mi-8 *Hip* in store) **Light** 2 AS355F *Ecureuil* II

Gendarmerie 2,000 +

Ministry of Defence

FORCES BY ROLE

MANOEUVRE

Other

1 paramilitary bn

EQUIPMENT BY TYPE

PATROL AND COASTAL COMBATANTS 1 PB

Paramilitary ε2,500

National Security Force ε2,500

Ministry of Interior

DEPLOYMENT

SOMALIA

AU • AMISOM 850; 1 inf bn

WESTERN SAHARA

UN • MINURSO 1 obs

FOREIGN FORCES

France

Army 1,050: 1 (Marine) combined arms regt (2 recce sqn, 2 inf coy, 1 arty bty, 1 engr coy); 1 hel det with 2 SA330 *Puma*; 2 SA342 *Gazelle*

Navy 100: 1 LCT

Air Force 250: 1 air sqn with 7 *Mirage* 2000C/D; 1 C-160 *Transall*; 2 SA330 *Puma*; 1 AS555 *Fennec*

Japan 200; 2 P-3C

United States US Africa Command: 1,200; 1 naval air base

Equatorial Guinea EQG

CFA Franc BEAC fr		2011	2012	2013
GDP	fr	9.24tr	10.7tr	
	US$	19.59bn	20.65bn	
per capita	US$	28,557	30,102	
Growth	%	7.80	5.67	
Inflation	%	6.29	5.42	
Def exp	fr	ε3.8bn		
	US$	ε8m		
US$1=fr		471.88	518.04	

Population 685,991

Age	0–14	15–19	20–24	25–29	30–64	65 plus
Male	21.0%	5.3%	4.5%	3.8%	13.3%	1.8%
Female	20.3%	5.1%	4.4%	3.7%	14.4%	2.3%

Capabilities

The country's armed forces are dominated by the army, with smaller naval and air components. Equipment is of Soviet or Russian origin, and some fixed- and rotary-wing aircraft may be operated by contractors. Maritime-security concerns in the Gulf of Guinea have resulted in increased emphasis on bolstering its limited coastal patrol capacity. The army's primary role is internal security, while the military has no ability to project power beyond the nation's borders.

ACTIVE 1,320 (Army 1,100 Navy 120 Air 100)

ORGANISATIONS BY SERVICE

Army 1,100

FORCES BY ROLE
MANOEUVRE
Light
3 inf bn (-)

EQUIPMENT BY TYPE
MBT 3 T-55
RECCE 6 BRDM-2
AIFV 20 BMP-1
APC (W) 10 BTR-152

Navy ε120

EQUIPMENT BY TYPE
PATROL AND COASTAL COMBATANTS 10
PSOH 1 *Bata* with 1 76mm gun
PCC 2 OPV 62
PB 7: 1 *Daphne*; 2 *Estuario de Muni*; 2 *Shaldag II*; 2 *Zhuk*
LOGISTICS AND SUPPORT
AKRH 1 *Capitan David Eyama Angue Osa* with 1 76 mm gun

Air Force 100

EQUIPMENT BY TYPE
AIRCRAFT 4 combat capable
ATK 4: 2 Su-25 *Frogfoot*; 2 Su-25UB *Frogfoot* B
TPT 4 Light 3: 1 An-32B *Cline*; 2 An-72 *Coaler*; PAX 1 *Falcon* 900 (VIP)
TRG 2 L-39C *Albatros*
HELICOPTERS
ATK 5 Mi-24P/V *Hind*
MRH 1 Mi-17 *Hip* H
TPT 4 Heavy 1 Mi-26 *Halo*; Medium 1 Ka-29 *Helix* Light 2 Enstrom 480

Paramilitary

Guardia Civil

FORCES BY ROLE
MANOEUVRE
Other
2 paramilitary coy

Coast Guard

PATROL AND COASTAL COMBATANTS • PB 1†

Eritrea ERI

Eritrean Nakfa ERN		2011	2012	2013
GDP	ERN	40.11bn	47.79bn	
	US$	2.61bn	3.11bn	
per capita	US$	429	511	
Growth	%	8.72	7.54	
Inflation	%	13.34	12.26	
Def exp	ERN	ε1.2bn		
	US$	ε78m		
USD1=ERN		15.37	15.37	

Population 6,086,495

Ethnic groups: Tigrinya 50%; Tigre and Kunama 40%; Afar; Saho 3%

Age	0–14	15–19	20–24	25–29	30–64	65 plus
Male	21.0%	5.4%	4.5%	3.8%	13.1%	1.6%
Female	20.7%	5.4%	4.5%	3.9%	14.0%	2.0%

Capabilities

Asmara has a high level of defence spending relative to total government expenditure, which allows it to maintain a large standing army (albeit largely conscripted) and an arsenal stocked with outdated but numerous weapons platforms. However, the age of some of the weapons in Eritrea's armed forces will render many of them obsolete and it is likely that the platforms will be slowly cannibalised for parts, to keep the majority running. The armed forces lack effective transport capabilities, although, as the primary focus of the military is defence of its border with Ethiopia, this does not prevent it from acting as an effective deterrent. The Eritrean military appears to have been relatively successful in adapting from being an insurgent army in the 1980s to a standing military. However, the armed forces are still, slowly, formalising lines of command and organisation. Attempts to demobilise tens of thousands of fighters from the early 2000s have been scuppered by continued tensions with Ethiopia. Although the military is heavily dominated by the army, there has been investment in the nascent air force to produce a regionally comparable fighter wing. However, it still lacks experienced and trained pilots, meaning that its ageing fighter aircraft will either have to be flown by foreign pilots, as they were in the late 1990s, or risk being outnumbered and outmatched by adversaries.

ACTIVE 201,750 (Army 200,000 Navy 1,400 Air 350)
Terms of service 16 months (4 month mil trg)

RESERVE 120,000 (Army ε120,000)

ORGANISATIONS BY SERVICE

Army ε200,000

Heavily cadreised

FORCES BY ROLE
COMMAND
  4 corps HQ
MANOEUVRE
  Mechanised
  1 mech bde
  Light
  19 inf div
  1 cdo div

Reserve ε120,000

FORCES BY ROLE
  MANOEUVRE
    Light
    1 inf div

EQUIPMENT BY TYPE
MBT 270 T-54/T-55
RECCE 40 BRDM-1/BRDM-2
AIFV 15 BMP-1
APC • APC (W) 25 BTR-152 APC (W)/BTR-60 APC (W)
ARTY 208+
  SP 45: **122mm** 32 2S1 *Carnation*; **152mm** 13 2S5
  TOWED 19+: **122mm** D-30; **130mm** 19 M-46

MRL 44: **122mm** 35 BM-21; **220mm** 9 BM-27/9P140 *Uragan*
MOR 120mm/160mm 100+
AT
  MSL • MANPATS 200 AT-3 9K11 *Sagger*/AT-5 9K113 *Spandrel*
  GUNS 85mm D-44
AD • SAM • MANPAD 9K32 *Strela-2* (SA-7 *Grail*)‡
  GUNS 70+
    SP 23mm ZSU-23-4
    TOWED 23mm ZU-23
ARV T-54/T-55 reported
VLB MTU reported

Navy 1,400

HQ located at Massawa

EQUIPMENT BY TYPE
PATROL AND COASTAL COMBATANTS 12
  PBF 9: 5 *Battalion*-17; 4 *Super Dvora*
  PB 3 Swiftships
AMPHIBIOUS 3
  LS • LST 2: 1 *Chamo*† (Ministry of Transport); 1 *Ashdod*†
  LC • LCU 1 T-4†

Air Force ε350

FORCES BY ROLE
FIGHTER/GROUND ATTACK
  1 sqn with MiG-29/MiG-29SMT/MiG-29UB *Fulcrum*
  1 sqn with Su-27/Su-27UBK *Flanker*
TRANSPORT
  1 sqn with Y-12(II)
TRAINING
  1 sqn with L-90 *Redigo*
  1 sqn with MB-339CE*
TRANSPORT HELICOPTER
  1 sqn with Bell 412 *Twin Huey*
  1 sqn with Mi-17 *Hip H*

EQUIPMENT BY TYPE
AIRCRAFT 20 combat capable
  FTR 6: 4 MiG-29 *Fulcrum*; 2 MiG-29UB *Fulcrum*;
  FGA 10: 2 MiG-29SMT *Fulcrum*; 5 Su-27 *Flanker*; 3 Su-27UBK *Flanker*
  TPT • Light 5: 1 Beech 200 *King Air*; 4 Y-12(II)
  TRG 12: 8 L-90 *Redigo*; 4 MB-339CE*
HELICOPTERS
  MRH 8: 4 Bell 412 *Twin Huey* (AB-412); 4 Mi-17 *Hip H*
  MSL
    AAM • IR R-60 (AA-8 *Aphid*); R-73 (AA-11 *Archer*) **IR/SARH** R-27 (AA-10 *Alamo*)

Ethiopia ETH

Ethiopian Birr EB		2011	2012	2013
GDP	EB	511.16bn	725.83bn	
	US$	31.72bn	41.89bn	
per capita	US$	348	459	
Growth	%	7.50	7.00	
Inflation	%	33.06	22.94	
Def bdgt	EB	4.4bn	6.5bn	
	US$	273m	375m	
FMA (US)	US$	2.0m	0.843m	-
US$1=EB		16.12	17.33	

Population   91,195,675

Ethnic groups: Oromo 40%; Amhara and Tigrean 32%; Sidamo 9%; Shankella 6%; Somali 6%; Afar 4%

Age	0–14	15–19	20–24	25–29	30–64	65 plus
Male	22.3%	5.3%	4.5%	3.8%	12.5%	1.3%
Female	22.3%	5.4%	4.6%	3.8%	12.7%	1.5%

Capabilities

Ethiopia maintains the Horn of Africa's and one of sub-Saharan Africa's most effective militaries. The country has benefitted from investment in newly procured equipment over the past decade. Like its neighbour Eritrea, its armed forces evolved from a guerrilla force in the 1990s, and had a rationalisation and demobilisation process prevented by the conflict between the two countries. The serviceability of older fighter aircraft and the army's main battle tanks, in particular, is in question. Nonetheless, the history of conflict faced by the Ethiopian military, from its insurgent roots to its state-based warfare against Eritrea, invasions of Somalia in 2006 and 2011, and deployment against Ogaden insurgents in the southeast of the country, has produced a battle-hardened and experienced corps. This has ensured a good level of readiness for the forces and demonstrated its limited power-projection capabilities. Ethiopia has had an increasingly close relationship with Israel, China and the US, which are providing some training and, in the case of the US, has offered guidance on force structure. However, arms procurement remains largely focused on former Soviet countries, with a June 2011 deal with Ukraine for more than 200 T-72 tanks a sign of both the continued reliance on Soviet-era equipment and the need for updated heavy armour. The air force maintains only a modest lift capacity, which limits, to some extent, the deployability of the forces both within the large land area of Ethiopia and, more definitely, overseas. Addis Ababa is home to the African Union secretariat, and also much of the machinery concerning policy development of the African Standby Force concept.

ACTIVE 138,000 (Army 135,000 Air 3,000)

ORGANISATIONS BY SERVICE

Army 135,000

4 Mil Regional Commands (Northern, Western, Central, and Eastern) each acting as corps HQ

FORCES BY ROLE
MANOEUVRE
Light
1 (Agazi Cdo) SF comd
1 (Northern) corps (1 mech div, 4 inf div)
1 (Western) corps (1 mech div, 3 inf div)
1 (Central) corps (1 mech div, 5 inf div)
1 (Eastern) corps (1 mech div, 5 inf div)
EQUIPMENT BY TYPE
MBT 446+: 246+ T-54/T-55/T-62; 200 T-72 being delivered
RECCE/AIFV/APC (W) ε450 BRDM/BMP/BTR-60/BTR-152/Type-89
ARTY 460+
  SP 10+: **122mm** 2S1 *Carnation*; **152mm** 10 2S19 *Farm*
  TOWED 400+: **122mm** ε400 D-30/M-1938 (M-30) M-1938; **130mm** M-46
  MRL 122mm ε50 BM-21
  MOR 81mm M1/M29; **82mm** M-1937; **120mm** M-1944
AT • MSL • MANPATS 9K11 *Malyutka* (AT-3 *Sagger*); 9K111 *Fagot* (AT-4 *Spigot*)
  RCL 82mm B-10; **107mm** B-11
  GUNS 85mm εD-44
AD • SAM ε370
  TOWED S-75 *Dvina* (SA-2 *Guideline*) S-125 *Pechora* (SA-3 *Goa*)
  MANPAD 9K32 *Strela*-2 (SA-7 *Grail*)‡
  GUNS
    SP 23mm ZSU-23-4
    TOWED 23mm ZU-23; **37mm** M-1939; **57mm** S-60
ARV T-54/T-55 reported
VLB MTU reported
MW Bozena

Air Force 3,000

FORCES BY ROLE
FIGHTER/GROUND ATTACK
1 sqn with MiG-21MF *Fishbed* J†; MiG-21UM *Mongol* B†
1 sqn with Su-27/Su-27UB *Flanker*
TRANSPORT
1 sqn with An-12 *Cub*; An-26 *Curl*; An-32 *Cline*; C-130B *Hercules*; DHC-6 *Twin Otter*; L-100-30; Yak-40 *Codling* (VIP)
TRAINING
1 sqn with L-39 *Albatros*
1 sqn with SF-260
ATTACK/TRANSPORT HELICOPTER
2 sqn with Mi-24/Mi-35 *Hind*; Mi-8 *Hip*; Mi-17 *Hip* H; SA316 *Alouette* III
EQUIPMENT BY TYPE
AIRCRAFT 26 combat capable
  FGA 26: 15 MiG-21MF *Fishbed* J/MiG-21UM *Mongol* B†; 8 Su-27 *Flanker*; 3 Su-27UB *Flanker*
  TPT 10 **Medium** 7: 3 An-12 *Cub*; 2 C-130B *Hercules*; 2 L-100-30 **Light** 4: 1 An-26 *Curl*; 1 An-32 *Cline*; 1 DHC-6 *Twin Otter*; 1 Yak-40 *Codling* (VIP)
  TRG 16: 12 L-39 *Albatros*; 4 SF-260
HELICOPTERS
  ATK 18: 15 Mi-24 *Hind*; 3 Mi-35 *Hind*
  MRH 7: 1 AW139; 6 SA316 *Alouette* III
  MRH/TPT 12 Mi-8 *Hip*/Mi-17 *Hip* H

MSL
AAM • IR R-3 (AA-2 *Atoll*)‡; R-60 (AA-8 *Aphid*); R-73 (AA-11 *Archer*) **IR/SARH** R-23/R-24 (AA-7 *Apex*) R-27 (AA-10 *Alamo*)

DEPLOYMENT

COTE D'IVOIRE
UN • UNOCI 1 obs

LIBERIA
UN • UNMIL 4; 9 obs

SOMALIA
Army Some

SUDAN
UN • UNAMID 1,946; 16 obs; 1 recce coy; 2 inf bn; 1 hel coy; 1 log coy; 1 tpt coy
UN • UNISFA 3,799; 87 obs; 2 mech inf bn; 1 inf bn; 2 arty coy; 1 engr coy; 1 fd hospital

FOREIGN FORCES

United States some MQ-9 *Reaper*

Gabon GAB

CFA Franc BEAC fr		2011	2012	2013
GDP	fr	7.91tr	8.32tr	
	US$	15.97bn	16.8bn	
per capita	US$	9,930	10,446	
Growth	%	6.64	6.11	
Inflation	%	1.26	2.30	
Def bdgtª	fr	125bn		
	US$	253m		
FMA (US)	US$	0.200m		
US$1=fr		495.28	495.29	

ª Includes funds allocated to Republican Guard

Population	1,608,321					
Age	0–14	15–19	20–24	25–29	30–64	65 plus
Male	21.2%	5.4%	4.8%	4.0%	12.8%	1.6%
Female	21.0%	5.4%	4.7%	4.0%	12.9%	2.2%

Capabilities

The country has benefitted from the long-term presence of French troops, acting as a security guarantor, while oil revenues have allowed the government to support, in regional terms, capable armed forces. The army is reasonably well-equipped, while the navy has a coastal-patrol and fishery-protection role. It also maintains an amphibious landing ship. The air force's combat capability was increased with the acquisition of six ex-South African Air Force *Mirage* F1s.

ACTIVE 4,700 (Army 3,200 Navy 500 Air 1,000)
Paramilitary 2,000

ORGANISATIONS BY SERVICE

Army 3,200
Republican Guard under direct presidential control
FORCES BY ROLE
MANOEUVRE
 Light
 1 (Republican Guard) gd gp (bn)
  (1 armd/recce coy, 3 inf coy, 1 arty bty, 1 ADA bty)
 8 inf coy
 Air Manoeuvre
 1 cdo/AB coy
COMBAT SUPPORT
 1 engr coy
EQUIPMENT BY TYPE
RECCE 70: 24 AML-60/AML-90; 12 EE-3 *Jararaca*; 14 EE-9 *Cascavel*; 6 ERC-90F4 *Sagaie*; 14 VBL
AIFV 12 EE-11 *Urutu* (with 20mm gun)
APC (W) 28+: 9 LAV-150 *Commando*; 6 Type-92 (reported); 12 VXB-170; M-3 Panhard; 1 *Pandur* (Testing)
ARTY 51
 TOWED 105mm 4 M-101
 MRL 140mm 8 *Teruel*
 MOR 39: **81mm** 35; **120mm** 4 Brandt
AT • MSL • MANPATS 4 *Milan*
 RCL 106mm M40A1
 RL 89mm LRAC
AD • GUNS 41
 SP 20mm 4 ERC-20
 TOWED 37: **23mm** 24 ZU-23-2; **37mm** 10 M-1939; **40mm** 3 L/70

Navy ε500
HQ located at Port Gentil
EQUIPMENT BY TYPE
PATROL AND COASTAL COMBATANTS 15
 PCC 2 *General Ba'Oumar* (FRA P-400)
 PBFG 1 *Patra* with 4 SS 12M AShM
 PB 12: 4 *Port Gentil* (FRA VCSM); 4 RPB 20; 4 Rodman 66
AMPHIBIOUS 13
 LANDING SHIPS • LST 1 *President Omar Bongo* (FRA *Batral*) (capacity 1 LCVP; 7 MBT; 140 troops) with 1 hel landing platform
 LANDING CRAFT • LCVP 12

Air Force 1,000
FORCES BY ROLE
FIGHTER/GROUND ATTACK
 1 sqn with *Mirage* 5G/5DG; *Mirage* 5E2; *Mirage* F-1AZ
TRANSPORT
 1 (Republican Guard) sqn with AS332 *Super Puma*; ATR-42F; *Falcon* 900; Gulfstream IV-SP
 1 sqn with C-130H *Hercules*; CN-235M-100
TRAINING
 1 (Republican Guard) sqn with T-34 *Turbo Mentor*
ATTACK/TRANSPORT HELICOPTER
 1 sqn with Bell 412 *Twin Huey* (AB-412); SA330C/H *Puma*; SA342M *Gazelle*

EQUIPMENT BY TYPE
AIRCRAFT 14 combat capable
　FGA 14: 4 *Mirage* 5E2; 2 *Mirage* 5G (*Mirage* 5); 2 *Mirage* 5DG (*Mirage* 5D); 6 *Mirage* F-1AZ
　MP (1 EMB-111* in store)
　TPT 5 **Medium** 1 C-130H *Hercules*; (1 L-100-30 in store); **Light** 2: 1 ATR-42F; 1 CN-235M-100; **PAX** 2: 1 *Falcon* 900; 1 Gulfstream IV-SP
　TRG 3 T-34 *Turbo Mentor*; (4 CM-170 *Magister* in store)
HELICOPTERS
　MRH 2: 1 Bell 412 *Twin Huey* (AB-412); 1 SA342M *Gazelle* (2 SA342L *Gazelle* in store)
　TPT 5 **Medium** 4: 1 AS332 *Super Puma*; 3 SA330C/H *Puma* **Light** 1 EC135

Paramilitary 2,000

Gendarmerie 2,000

FORCES BY ROLE
MANOEUVRE
　Armoured
　2 armd sqn
　Other
　3 paramilitary bde 11 paramilitary coy
　Aviation
　1 unit with AS350 *Ecureuil*; AS355 *Ecureuil* II
EQUIPMENT BY TYPE
　HELICOPTERS • TPT • Light 4: 2 AS350 *Ecureuil*; 2 AS355 *Ecureuil* II

DEPLOYMENT

CENTRAL AFRICAN REPUBLIC
ECCAS • MICOPAX 160

FOREIGN FORCES

France • **Army** 762; 1 recce pl with ERC-90F1 *Lynx*; 1 (Marine) inf bn; 4 SA330 *Puma*

Capabilities

The country has a small army supported by an air and marine unit. Its forces have been deployed in support of UN missions, and recieve training assistance from the US.

ACTIVE 800 (Army 800)

ORGANISATIONS BY SERVICE

Gambian National Army 800

FORCES BY ROLE
MANOEUVRE
　Light
　2 inf bn
　Other
　1 (Presidential Guard) gd coy
COMBAT SUPPORT
　1 engr sqn

Marine Unit ε70

EQUIPMENT BY TYPE
PATROL AND COASTAL COMBATANTS 9
PBF 2 Rodman 55
PB 7: 1 *Bolong Kanta*†; 2 *Fatimah* I; 4 *Taipei* (ROC *Hai Ou*)

Air Wing

EQUIPMENT BY TYPE
AIRCRAFT
　TPT 6 **Light** 2 AT-802A *Air Tractor* **PAX** 4: 1 B-727; 1 CL-601; 2 Il-62M *Classic* (VIP)

DEPLOYMENT

CÔTE D'IVOIRE
UN • UNOCI 3 obs

LIBERIA
UN • UNMIL 2 obs

SUDAN
UN • UNAMID 202; 1 inf coy

Gambia GAM

Gambian Dalasi D		2011	2012	2013
GDP	D	28.64bn	29.46bn	
	US$	0.98bn	0.94bn	
per capita	US$	532	511	
Growth	%	3.26	-1.62	
Inflation	%	4.80	4.69	
Def bdgt	D	ε189m		
	US$	ε6m		
US$1=D			29.31	31.34

Population	1,840,454					

Age	0–14	15–19	20–24	25–29	30–64	65 plus
Male	19.9%	5.5%	5.0%	4.2%	13.4%	1.5%
Female	19.7%	5.6%	5.1%	4.4%	14.0%	1.7%

Ghana GHA

Ghanaian New Cedi C		2011	2012	2013
GDP	C	59.26bn	73.92bn	
	US$	38.39bn	40.12bn	
per capita	US$	1,287	1,627	
Growth	%	14.38	8.18	
Inflation	%	8.73	9.82	
Def bdgt	C	198m	201m	259m
	US$	128m	109m	
FMA (US)	US$	0.449m	0.35m	0.35m
US$1=C			1.54	1.84

Population	24,652,402					

Age	0–14	15–19	20–24	25–29	30–64	65 plus
Male	19.5%	5.0%	4.4%	4.0%	14.6%	1.9%
Female	19.4%	4.9%	4.6%	4.2%	15.4%	2.1%

Capabilities

In common with other regional militaries, the Ghanaian armed forces are intended to conduct internal security and peacekeeping operations. They are both well-trained and well-funded, with several new equipment programmes undertaken to modernise key capabilities such as airlift and coastal patrol, as part of a concerted long-term modernisation plan. The latter is in order to better meet the challenge of piracy. The small air force is built around the tactical transport role, with a handful of jet trainers available for light attack.

ACTIVE 15,500 (Army 11,500 Navy 2,000 Air 2,000)

ORGANISATIONS BY SERVICE

Army 11,500

FORCES BY ROLE
COMMAND
2 comd HQ
MANOEUVRE
Reconnaissance
1 armd recce regt (3 recce sqn)
Light
1 (rapid reaction) mot inf bn
6 inf bn
Air Manoeuvre
2 AB coy
COMBAT SUPPORT
1 arty regt (1 arty bty, 2 mor bty)
1 fd engr regt (bn)
1 sigs regt
1 sigs sqn
COMBAT SERVICE SUPPORT
1 log gp
1 tpt coy
2 maint coy
1 med coy
1 trg bn

EQUIPMENT BY TYPE
RECCE 3 EE-9 *Cascavel*
AIFV 39: 24 *Ratel* FSC-90; 15 *Ratel-20*
APC (W) 50 *Piranha*
ARTY 84
TOWED 122mm 6 D-30
MOR 78: **81mm** 50; **120mm** 28 *Tampella*
AT • RCL 84mm 50 *Carl Gustav*
AD • SAM • MANPAD 9K32 *Strela*-2 (SA-7 *Grail*)‡
GUNS • TOWED 8+: **14.5mm** 4+: 4 ZPU-2; ZPU-4; **23mm** 4 ZU-23-2
ARV *Piranha* reported

Navy 2,000

Naval HQ located at Accra; Western HQ located at Sekondi; Eastern HQ located at Tema

EQUIPMENT BY TYPE
PATROL AND COASTAL COMBATANTS 14
  PCO 2 *Anzole* (US)

PCC 10: 2 *Achimota* (GER Lurssen 57m); 2 *Dzata* (GER Lurssen 45m); 2 *Yaa Asantewa* (GER *Gepard*); 4 *Snake* (PRC 47m)
PBF 1 *Stephen Otu* (ROK *Sea Dolphin*)
PB 1 *David Hansen* (US)

Air Force 2,000

FORCES BY ROLE
GROUND ATTACK
1 sqn with K-8 *Karakorum**; L-39ZO*: MB-326K; MB-339A*
ISR
1 unit with DA-42
TRANSPORT
1 sqn with BN-2 *Defender*; Cessna 172; F-27 *Friendship*; F-28 *Fellowship* (VIP)
TRANSPORT HELICOPTER
1 sqn with AW109A; Bell 412SP *Twin Huey*; Mi-17V-5 *Hip* H; SA319 *Alouette* III

EQUIPMENT BY TYPE†
AIRCRAFT 13 combat capable
  FGA 3 MB-326K
  TPT 14 **Light** 13: 1 BN-2 *Defender*; 2 C-295; 3 Cessna 172; 3 DA-42; 4 F-27 *Friendship* **PAX** 1 F-28 *Fellowship* (VIP)
  TRG 10: 6 K-8 *Karakorum**; 2 L-39ZO*; 2 MB-339A*
HELICOPTERS
  MRH 6: 1 Bell 412SP *Twin Huey*; 3 Mi-17V-5 *Hip* H; 2 SA319 *Alouette* III
  TPT • Light 2 AW109A

DEPLOYMENT

CÔTE D'IVOIRE
UN • UNOCI 507; 6 obs; 1 inf bn; 1 hel coy; 1 fd hospital

DEMOCRATIC REPUBLIC OF THE CONGO
UN • MONUSCO 461; 26 obs; 1 mech inf bn

LEBANON
UN • UNIFIL 872; 1 inf bn

LIBERIA
UN • UNMIL 708; 8 obs; 1 inf bn

SIERRA LEONE
IMATT 1

SOUTH SUDAN
UN • UNMISS 1

SUDAN
UN • UNAMID 7; 6 obs
UN • UNISFA 2; 3 obs

WESTERN SAHARA
UN • MINURSO 6; 10 obs

Guinea GUI

Guinean Franc fr		2011	2012	2013
GDP	fr	33.7tr	40.49tr	
	US$	5.17bn	5.74bn	
per capita	US$	475	527	
Growth	%	3.91	4.79	
Inflation	%	21.35	14.69	
Def bdgt	fr	ε275bn		
	US$	ε42m		
US$1=fr		6517.73	7049.78	

Population   10,884,958

Age	0–14	15–19	20–24	25–29	30–64	65 plus
Male	21.4%	5.3%	4.5%	3.8%	13.5%	1.6%
Female	21.0%	5.2%	4.4%	3.7%	13.7%	2.0%

Capabilities

The heavily politicised nature of Guinea's armed forces has undermined their professionalism and quality. Much of their inventory of ageing equipment is likely unserviceable.

ACTIVE 9,700 (Army 8,500 Navy 400 Air 800)
Paramilitary 2,600
Terms of service conscription, 2 years

ORGANISATIONS BY SERVICE

Army 8,500

FORCES BY ROLE
MANOEUVRE
  Armoured
  1 armd bn
  Light
  1 SF bn
  5 inf bn
  1 ranger bn
  1 cdo bn
  Air Manoeuvre
  1 air mob bn
  Other
  1 (Presidential Guard) gd bn
COMBAT SUPPORT
  1 arty bn
  1 AD bn
  1 engr bn
EQUIPMENT BY TYPE
MBT 38: 8 T-54; 30 T-34
LT TK 15 PT-76
RECCE 27: 2 AML-90; 25 BRDM-1/BRDM-2
APC (W) 40: 16 BTR-40; 10 BTR-50; 8 BTR-60; 6 BTR-152
ARTY 47+
  TOWED 24: **122mm** 12 M-1931/37; **130 mm** 12 M-46
  MRL 220mm 3 BM-27/9P140 *Uragan*
  MOR 20+: **82mm** M-43; **120mm** 20 M-1943/M-38

AT • MSL • MANPATS 9K11 *Malyutka* (AT-3 *Sagger*); 9M113 *Konkurs* (AT-5 *Spandrel*)
  RCL 82mm B-10
  GUNS 6+: **57mm** ZIS-2 *M-1943*; **85mm** 6 D-44
AD • SAM • MANPAD 9K32 *Strela*-2 (SA-7 *Grail*) ‡
  GUNS • TOWED 24+: **30mm** M-53 (twin); **37mm** 8 M-1939; **57mm** 12 Type-59 (S-60); **100mm** 4 KS-19
ARV T-54/T-55 reported

Navy ε400

EQUIPMENT BY TYPE
PATROL AND COASTAL COMBATANTS 4 • **PB** 2 Swiftships†; 2 *Zhuk*†

Air Force 800

EQUIPMENT BY TYPE†
AIRCRAFT
  FGA (3 MiG-21 *Fishbed* non-op)
  TPT • Light 2 An-2 *Colt*
HELICOPTERS
  ATK 4 Mi-24 *Hind*
  MRH 5: 2 MD-500MD; 2 Mi-17-1V *Hip* H; 1 SA342K *Gazelle*
  TPT 2 **Medium** 1 SA330 *Puma*†; **Light** 1 AS350B *Ecureuil*
MSL
  AAM • IR R-3 (AA-2 *Atoll*)‡

Paramilitary 2,600 active

Gendarmerie 1,000

Republican Guard 1,600

People's Militia 7,000 reservists

DEPLOYMENT

CÔTE D'IVOIRE
UN • UNOCI 3 obs

SOUTH SUDAN
UN • UNMISS 1 obs

SUDAN
UN • UNISFA 2 obs

WESTERN SAHARA
UN • MINURSO 4 obs

Guinea Bissau GNB

CFA Franc BCEAO fr		2011	2012	2013
GDP	fr	456.65bn	458.15bn	
	US$	0.97bn	0.88bn	
per capita	US$	596	540	
Growth	%	5.34	-2.81	
Inflation	%	5.05	5.00	
Def bdgt	fr	9.52bn	13bn	
	US$	20m	25m	
US$1=fr		471.26	518.27	

Population   1,628,603

Age	0–14	15–19	20–24	25–29	30–64	65 plus
Male	20.1%	5.3%	4.7%	4.0%	13.4%	1.3%
Female	20.1%	5.4%	4.8%	4.1%	14.9%	1.9%

Capabilities

The level of capability and professionalism of the heavily politicised Guinea Bissau armed forces is uncertain. Attempts to improve this suffered a setback after the EU Security Sector Reform Mission withdrew in August 2010, though it had started to lay the groundwork for reform, with elements such as a military census. Angola's MISSANG mission left in 2012. ECOWAS states then deployed a mission, and are now working with the government on an SSR road map. Most of the equipment holdings are unserviceable.

ACTIVE ε4,450 (Army ε4,000 (numbers reducing) Navy 350 Air 100) Gendarmerie 2,000
Terms of service conscription (selective).
Manpower and eqpt totals should be treated with caution. Recent governments have envisaged reducing the armed forces. A number of draft laws to restructure the armed services and police have been produced.

ORGANISATIONS BY SERVICE

Army ε4,000 (numbers reducing)
FORCES BY ROLE
MANOEUVRE
Reconnaissance
1 recce coy
Armoured
1 armd bn (sqn)
Light
5 inf bn
COMBAT SUPPORT
1 arty bn
1 engr coy
EQUIPMENT BY TYPE
MBT 10 T-34
LT TK 15 PT-76
RECCE 10 BRDM-2
APC (W) 55: 35 BTR-40/BTR-60; 20 Type-56 (BTR-152)

ARTY 26+
TOWED 122mm 18 D-30/*M-1938*
MOR 8+: 82mm M-43; **120mm** 8 M-1943
AT
RCL 75mm Type-52 (M20); **82mm** B-10
RL 89mm M20
GUNS 85mm 8 D-44
AD • SAM • MANPAD 9K32 *Strela*-2 (SA-7 *Grail*)‡
GUNS • TOWED 34: **23mm** 18 ZU-23; **37mm** 6 M-1939; **57mm** 10 S-60

Navy ε350
EQUIPMENT BY TYPE
PATROL AND COASTAL COMBATANTS • PB 2 *Alfeite†*

Air Force 100
EQUIPMENT BY TYPE
HELICOPTERS • MRH 1 SA-319 *Alouette* III†

Paramilitary 2,000 active
Gendarmerie 2,000

FOREIGN FORCES
Nigeria ECOMIB 160
Senegal ECOMIB 200

Kenya KEN

Kenyan Shilling sh		2011	2012	2013
GDP	sh	3.02tr	3.5tr	
	US$	34.06bn	41.84bn	
per capita	US$	792	973	
Growth	%	4.38	5.13	
Inflation	%	14.00	9.97	
Def bdgt	sh	55.9bn	78.6bn	64.3bn
	US$	629m	940m	
FMA (US)	US$	0.998m	1.5m	1.096m
US$1=sh		88.81	83.61	

Population   43,013,341
Ethnic groups: Kikuyu ε22–32%

Age	0–14	15–19	20–24	25–29	30–64	65 plus
Male	21.3%	4.9%	4.7%	4.4%	13.3%	1.2%
Female	21.2%	4.9%	4.7%	4.4%	13.4%	1.5%

Capabilities

Kenya's armed forces moved into southern Somalia in October 2010 in an action against al-Shabaab militants, *Operation Linda Nchi*, with ground units supported by the air force involved. Some foreign logistic support was reportedly required, at least initially. As of mid-2012, fighting continued, with Kenyan and Somali government forces under the banner of the African Union Mission continuing to engage with al-Shabaab fighters. The military action has led to civil disturbances among some of Kenya's own Muslim population. In regional terms, the military remains capable, but is beginning to suffer as a result of the ageing core elements of its inventory. More modern combat aircraft and heavy armour would go some way to addressing this area of weakness. The air force can provide tactical airlift, and as the operation in Somalia suggests, the country has the ability to project power, albeit on a limited basis, beyond its own territory. Morale among the services is held to be good. The military regularly takes part in international exercises.

ACTIVE 24,120 (Army 20,000 Navy 1,600 Air 2,500)
Paramilitary 5,000
(incl HQ staff)

ORGANISATIONS BY SERVICE

Army 20,000
FORCES BY ROLE
MANOEUVRE
Armoured
1 armd bde (1 armd recce bn, 2 armd bn)
Light
1 spec ops bn
1 ranger bn
1 inf bde (3 inf bn)
1 inf bde (2 inf bn)
1 indep inf bn
Air Manoeuvre
1 air cav bn
1 AB bn
COMBAT SUPPORT
1 arty bde (2 arty bn, 1 mor bty)
1 ADA bn
1 engr bde (2 engr bn)
EQUIPMENT BY TYPE
MBT 78 Vickers Mk 3
RECCE 92: 72 AML-60/AML-90; 12 *Ferret*; 8 S52 *Shorland*
APC 84+
  APC (W) 84: 52 UR-416; 32 Type-92 (reported); (10 M3 Panhard in store)
  PPV *Puma* M26-15
ARTY 110
  TOWED 105mm 48: 8 Model 56 pack howitzer; 40 Light Gun
  MOR 62: **81mm** 50; **120mm** 12 Brandt
AT • MSL • MANPATS 54: 40 *Milan*; 14 *Swingfire*
  RCL 84mm 80 *Carl Gustav*
AD • GUNS • TOWED 94: **20mm** 81: 11 Oerlikon; ε70 TCM-20; **40mm** 13 L/70
ARV 7 Vickers ARV
MW *Bozena*
HELICOPTERS
  ATK 3 Mi-28NE *Havoc* (reported)
  MRH 37+: 2 Hughes 500D†; 12 Hughes 500M†; 10 Hughes 500MD *Scout Defender*† (with TOW); 10 Hughes 500ME†; 3 Z-9W

Navy 1,600 (incl 120 marines)
EQUIPMENT BY TYPE
PATROL AND COASTAL COMBATANTS 7
  PCO 1 *Jasiri* (to be fitted with 1 76 mm gun)
  PCFG 2 *Nyayo* with 2 twin lnchr with *Otomat* AShM, 1 76mm gun
  PCC 3: 1 *Arambe* (FRA P400); 2 *Shujaa* with 1 76mm gun
  PBF 1 *Archangel*
AMPHIBIOUS • LCM 2 *Galana*
LOGISTICS AND SUPPORT • AP 2

Air Force 2,500
FORCES BY ROLE
FIGHTER/GROUND ATTACK
  2 sqn with F-5E/F *Tiger* II
TRANSPORT
  Some sqn with DHC-5D *Buffalo*†; DHC-8†; F-70† (VIP); Y-12(II)†
TRAINING
  Some sqn with *Bulldog* 103/*Bulldog* 127†; EMB-312 *Tucano*†*; *Hawk* Mk52†*; Hughes 500D†
TRANSPORT HELICOPTER
  1 sqn with SA330 *Puma*†
EQUIPMENT BY TYPE†
AIRCRAFT 38 combat capable
  FTR 22: 18 F-5E *Tiger* II; 4 F-5F *Tiger* II
  TPT 18 **Light** 17: 4 DHC-5D *Buffalo*†; 3 DHC-8†; 10 Y-12(II)†; (6 Do-28D-2† in store); **PAX** 1 F-70† (VIP)
  TRG 24: 8 Bulldog 103/127†; 11 EMB-312 *Tucano*†*; 5 *Hawk* Mk52†*
HELICOPTERS
  TPT • Medium 13: 2 Mi-171; 11 SA330 *Puma*†
MSL
  AAM • IR AIM-9 *Sidewinder*
  ASM AGM-65 *Maverick*; TOW

Paramilitary 5,000

Police General Service Unit 5,000
PATROL AND COASTAL COMBATANTS • PB 5 (2 on Lake Victoria)

Air Wing
AIRCRAFT • TPT 7 *Cessna*
HELICOPTERS
  TPT • Light 1 Bell 206L *Long Ranger*
  TRG 2 Bell 47G

DEPLOYMENT

DEMOCRATIC REPUBLIC OF THE CONGO
UN • MONUSCO 24 obs

LEBANON
UN • UNIFIL 1

SOMALIA
AU • AMISOM 3,150: 3 inf bn

SOUTH SUDAN
UN • UNMISS 692; 3 obs; 1 inf bn

SUDAN
UN • UNAMID 77; 3 obs; 1 MP coy

UGANDA
EU • EUTM 12

FOREIGN FORCES

United Kingdom Army 52

Lesotho LSO

Lesotho Loti M		2011	2012	2013
GDP	M	18.08bn	20.43bn	
	US$	2.49bn	2.62bn	
per capita	US$	1,290	1,357	
Growth	%	4.93	4.26	
Inflation	%	5.57	5.35	
Def bdgt	M	361m	607m	1.02bn
	US$	50m	78m	
US$1=M		7.26	7.80	

Population   1,930,493

Age	0–14	15–19	20–24	25–29	30–64	65 plus
Male	16.8%	5.0%	5.0%	5.0%	14.9%	2.6%
Female	16.7%	5.3%	5.7%	5.7%	14.6%	2.7%

Capabilities

The land-locked nation's small military is charged with protecting territorial integrity and sovereignty, though South Africa in effect acts as a guarantor of this. Most military personnel are in infantry units, supported by light vehicles, and a small number of tactical transport aircraft and utility helicopters.

ACTIVE 2,000 (Army 2,000)

ORGANISATIONS BY SERVICE

Army ε2,000

FORCES BY ROLE
MANOEUVRE
  Reconnaissance
  1 recce coy
  Light
  7 inf coy
  Aviation
  1 sqn
COMBAT SUPPORT
  1 arty bty (-)
  1 spt coy (with mor)
EQUIPMENT BY TYPE
RECCE 22: 4 AML-90; 10 RBY-1; 8 S52 *Shorland*
ARTY 12
  TOWED 105mm 2
  MOR 81mm 10
AT • RCL 106mm 6 M40

Air Wing 110
AIRCRAFT
  TPT • **Light** 3: 2 C-212-300 *Aviocar*; 1 GA-8 *Airvan*
HELICOPTERS
  MRH 3: 1 Bell 412 *Twin Huey*; 2 Bell 412EP *Twin Huey*
  TPT • **Light** 2: 1 Bell 206 *Jet Ranger*; 1 Bo-105LSA-3

DEPLOYMENT

SUDAN
UN • UNAMID 1; 2 obs

Liberia LBR

Liberian Dollar L$		2010	2011	2012
GDP	L$	113bn	132bn	
	US$	1.55bn	1.77bn	
per capita	US$	399	455	
Growth	%	8.17	9.00	
Inflation	%	8.49	6.6	
Def bdgt	L$	925m	1.17bn	
	US$	13m	16m	
FMA (US)	US$	7.17m	6.5m	
US$1=L$		72.06	72.75	

Population   3,786,764
Ethnic groups: Americo-Liberians 5%

Age	0–14	15–19	20–24	25–29	30–64	65 plus
Male	16.7%	4.9%	4.9%	4.9%	15.2%	2.7%
Female	16.6%	5.2%	5.6%	5.7%	14.9%	2.7%

Capabilities

Essentially a new force created after the country's 1980s and 1990s civil wars, the Armed Forces of Liberia have, since 2006, gradually developed a nascent defence capacity. However, this force is unable to deliver security throughout the country, and hence Monrovia still relies on the presence of UNMIL for stabilisation. The AFL has no ability to project power beyond its borders, and little ability to do so within areas of the country. There is no air force, and the only maritime security is provided by a small coast guard, reactivated in 2010, equipped entirely with rigid-hulled inflatable boats. The military aims to be fully operational by 2014 – the first combat mission was launched in October 2012, patrolling the country's southeastern border to prevent cross-border insurgency movements – but even then it will struggle to guarantee security in an unstable region.

ACTIVE 2,050 (Army 2,000, Coast Guard 50)

ORGANISATIONS BY SERVICE

Army 2,000

FORCES BY ROLE
MANOEUVRE
  Light
  1 (23rd) inf bde with (2 inf bn, 1 engr coy, 1 MP coy)

COMBAT SERVICE SUPPORT

1 trg unit (forming)

Coast Guard 50

10 craft (8 *Zodiac* and 2 *Defender*) under 10t FLD

FOREIGN FORCES

All under UNMIL comd unless otherwise specified

Bangladesh 1,383; 11 obs; 1 inf bn; 2 engr coy; 1 MP coy; 1 sigs coy; 1 log coy; 1 fd hospital

Benin 1; 2 obs

Bolivia 1; 2 obs

Brazil 2; 2 obs

Bulgaria 2 obs

China, People's Republic of 564; 2 obs; 1 engr coy; 1 tpt coy; 1 fd hospital

Croatia 2

Denmark 2; 3 obs

Ecuador 1; 2 obs

Egypt 7 obs

El Salvador 2 obs

Ethiopia 4; 9 obs

Finland 2

France 1

Gambia 2 obs

Ghana 708; 8 obs; 1 inf bn

Indonesia 1 obs

Jordan 120; 4 obs; 1 fd hospital

Korea, Republic of 1; 1 obs

Kyrgyzstan 3 obs

Malaysia 6 obs

Mali 1 obs

Moldova 2 obs

Montenegro 2 obs

Namibia 3; 1 obs

Nepal 18; 2 obs; 1 MP sect

Niger 1 obs

Nigeria 1,561; 12 obs; 2 inf bn; 1 sigs coy

Pakistan 2,765; 6 obs; 3 inf bn; 2 engr coy; 1 fd hospital

Paraguay 1; 3 obs

Peru 2; 2 obs

Philippines 116; 2 obs; 1 inf coy

Poland 2 obs

Romania 2 obs

Russia 4 obs

Senegal 2; 1 obs

Serbia 4 obs

Togo 1; 2 obs

Ukraine 277; 2 obs; 1 hel coy

United States 6; 4 obs

Yemen, Republic of 1

Zambia 3 obs

Zimbabwe 1 obs

Madagascar MDG

Malagsy Ariary fr		2011	2012	2013
GDP	fr	20.04tr	21.98tr	
	US$	9.90bn	10.05bn	
per capita	US$	450	457	
Growth	%	1.81	1.90	
Inflation	%	10.02	6.45	
Def bdgt	fr	146bn		
	US$	72m		
US$1=fr		2024.40	2186.42	

Population 22,005,222

Age	0–14	15–19	20–24	25–29	30–64	65 plus
Male	20.9%	5.6%	4.7%	3.9%	13.4%	1.4%
Female	20.5%	5.5%	4.7%	3.9%	13.7%	1.7%

Capabilities

Political stability has, in recent years, eluded the country, with elements of the military involved in unrest. A mutiny by some troops, in July 2012, resulted in the temporary closure of the airport. The army is the dominant force, supported by small air and naval units, neither of which have substantive combat capacity. The state has no power-projection capability.

ACTIVE 13,500 (Army 12,500 Navy 500 Air 500)

Paramilitary 8,100

Terms of service conscription (incl for civil purposes) 18 months

ORGANISATIONS BY SERVICE

Army 12,500+

FORCES BY ROLE

MANOEUVRE

Light

2 (intervention) inf regt

10 (regional) inf regt

COMBAT SUPPORT

1 arty regt

1 ADA regt

3 engr regt

1 sigs regt

COMBAT SERVICE SUPPORT

1 log regt

EQUIPMENT BY TYPE

LT TK 12 PT-76

RECCE 73: ε35 BRDM-2; 10 *Ferret*; ε20 M3A1; 8 M8

APC (T) ε30 M3A1 half-track

ARTY 25+

TOWED 17: **105mm** 5 M101; **122mm** 12 D-30

MOR 8+: **82mm** M-37; **120mm** 8 M-43

AT • RCL 106mm M40A1

RL **89mm** LRAC

AD • GUNS • TOWED 70: **14.5mm** 50 ZPU-4; **37mm** 20 Type-55 (M-1939)

Navy 500 (incl some 100 Marines)

EQUIPMENT BY TYPE
PATROL AND COASTAL COMBATANTS 7
  PCC 1 *Chamois*
  PB 6 (USCG)
AMPHIBIOUS • LCT 1 (FRA *Edic*)
LOGISTICS AND SUPPORT
  YT 3 *Aigrette*
  YTB 1 *Trozona*

Air Force 500

FORCES BY ROLE
TRANSPORT
  1 sqn with An-26 *Curl*; Yak-40 *Codling* (VIP)
  1 (liaison) sqn with Cessna 310; Cessna 337 *Skymaster*;
    PA-23 *Aztec*
TRAINING
  1 sqn with Cessna 172; J.300 *Joker*; *Tetras*
TRANSPORT HELICOPTER
  1 sqn with SA318C *Alouette* II

EQUIPMENT BY TYPE
AIRCRAFT • TPT 16 Light 14: 1 An-26 *Curl*; 4 Cessna 172; 1 Cessna 310; 2 Cessna 337 *Skymaster*; 2 J.300 *Joker*; 1 PA-23 *Aztec*; 1 *Tetras*; 2 Yak-40 *Codling* (VIP) **PAX** 2 B-737
HELICOPTERS
  MRH 4 SA318C *Alouette* II

Paramilitary 8,100

Gendarmerie 8,100
PATROL AND COASTAL COMBATANTS • 5 PB

Malawi MWI

Malawian Kwacha K		2011	2012	2013
GDP	K	879.77bn	1.06tr	
	US$	5.61bn	4.49bn	
per capita	US$	344	275	
Growth	%	4.35	4.31	
Inflation	%	7.62	17.72	
Def bdgt	K	6.7bn	7.94bn	8.62bn
	US$	43m	34m	
US$1=K		156.91	236.97	

Population   16,323,044

Age	0–14	15–19	20–24	25–29	30–64	65 plus
Male	22.5%	5.5%	4.7%	4.0%	11.9%	1.1%
Female	22.4%	5.5%	4.8%	4.1%	11.9%	1.5%

Capabilities

The military's role is to ensure the sovereignty and territorial integrity of the state, with the country's armed forces also involved in supporting UN missions. The country shares its borders with numerous states, and in recent years there has been friction with Mozambique over the use of the Zambezi river. The army is the largest force, consisting mainly of infantry supported by light armoured vehicles. The air wing provides transport for the army, with a small naval unit on Lake Malawi. The military has no capacity for power projection. The army exercises regularly, and also participates in multinational exercises.

ACTIVE 5,300 (Army 5,300) **Paramilitary 1,500**

ORGANISATIONS BY SERVICE

Army 5,300
FORCES BY ROLE
COMMAND
  2 bde HQ
MANOEUVRE
  Light
  4 inf bn
  Air Manoeuvre
  1 para bn
COMBAT SUPPORT
  1 (general) bn (1+ mne coy, 1 armd recce sqn, 2 lt arty bty, 1 engr unit)
COMBAT SERVICE SUPPORT
  8 log coy

EQUIPMENT BY TYPE
Less than 20% serviceability
RECCE 41: 13 *Eland*; 20 FV721 *Fox*; 8 *Ferret*
ARTY 17
  TOWED 105mm 9 lt
  MOR 81mm 8 L16
AD • SAM • MANPAD 15 *Blowpipe*
  GUNS • TOWED 14.5mm 40 ZPU-4

Navy 220
EQUIPMENT BY TYPE
PATROL AND COASTAL COMBATANTS • PB 1 *Kasungu†*

Air Wing 200
EQUIPMENT BY TYPE
AIRCRAFT • TPT 2 Light 1 Do-228; **PAX** 1 *Falcon* 900EX
HELICOPTERS • TPT 3 Medium 2: 1 AS532UL *Cougar*; 1 SA330H *Puma* **Light** 1 AS350L *Ecureuil*

Paramilitary 1,500

Mobile Police Force 1,500
RECCE 8 S52 *Shorland*
AIRCRAFT
  TPT • Light 4: 3 BN-2T *Defender* (border patrol); 1 SC.7 3M *Skyvan*
HELICOPTERS • MRH 2 AS365 *Dauphin* 2

DEPLOYMENT

CÔTE D'IVOIRE
UN • UNOCI 861; 3 obs; 1 inf bn

DEMOCRATIC REPUBLIC OF THE CONGO
UN • MONUSCO 10 obs

MIDDLE EAST
UN • UNTSO 1 obs

SUDAN
UN • UNAMID 1 obs

WESTERN SAHARA
UN • MINURSO 3 obs

Mali MLI

CFA Franc BCEAO fr		2011	2012	2013
GDP	fr	5tr	4.97tr	
	US$	10.61bn	9.60bn	
per capita	US$	685	620	
Growth	%	2.73	-4.49	
Inflation	%	3.05	7.25	
Def bdgt	fr	ε107bn		
	US$	ε227m		
FMA (US)	US$	0.2m	0.2m	
US$1=fr		471.44	517.99	

Population   15,494,466

Ethnic groups: Tuareg 6–10%

Age	0–14	15–19	20–24	25–29	30–64	65 plus
Male	24.0%	5.1%	3.9%	3.0%	11.2%	1.5%
Female	23.8%	5.4%	4.5%	3.8%	12.2%	1.5%

Capabilities

Mali's armed forces suffer from low morale, politicisation and outdated equipment. A *coup d'état*, launched in March 2012, was largely inspired by the army's failing campaign against Tuareg and Islamist rebels in the north of the country. The coup was led by junior officers and failed to galvanise the military, and a declaration of an independent state of Azawad took place in April 2012. The northern rebellion not only exposed the frailties of the Malian armed forces, reliant on ageing Soviet-era equipment, but also exacerbated them, as many of the ground forces' armoured vehicles were captured by the insurgents. This has left the military in a parlous state, with little capability to speak of. The coup has further limited the ability of the military to modernise through international isolation, with a shipment of former Soviet armoured personnel carriers being shipped from Bulgaria impounded by Guinea in August 2012. Given Mali's geography, the army dominates the armed forces. The small air force was intermittently capable of delivering limited strike capabilities through its two fighter aircraft and four attack helicopters, but it is unclear how much of this equipment has been captured by rebels. The navy is a riverine service equipped with vessels of questionable serviceability. Owing to its obvious shortcomings and the threat of transnational non-state armed groups, the Malian military has been a recipient of US training through the Trans-Sahara Counterterrorism Partnership. This has not addressed the fundamental lack of combat capability available to the armed forces, who will likely receive additional support, training and assistance in 2013, should the mooted ECOWAS force deploy to the country to subdue insurgents in the north.

ACTIVE 7,350 (Army 7,350) **Paramilitary 4,800 Militia 3,000**

ORGANISATIONS BY SERVICE

Army ε7,350

FORCES BY ROLE
Six of the army's infantry regiments were deployed in areas now overrun by Tuareg and Islamist rebels, and are now likely to exist in fragmentary form at best.
MANOEUVRE
Armoured
1 armd regt
Light
5 mot inf regt
6 mot inf regt(-)
Air Manoeuvre
1 AB regt
COMBAT SUPPORT
2 arty regt
3 AD bty
1 engr bn

EQUIPMENT BY TYPE†
Some of this equipment has been lost to rebel groups in the north, and a substantial part of what remains is not serviceable.
MBT 33: 12 T-54/T-55; 21 T-34
LT TK 18 Type-62
RECCE 64 BRDM-2
APC (W) 84: 44 BTR-60; 30 BTR-40; 10 BTR-152
ARTY 46+
  TOWED 14+: **100mm** 6 M-1944; **122mm** 8 D-30; **130mm** M-46 (reported)
  MRL 122mm 2 BM-21
  MOR 30+: **82mm** 6 M-43; **120mm** 30 M-43
AT • MSL • MANPATS AT-3 9K11 *Sagger*
  GUNS 85mm 6 D-44
AD • SAM 12+
  TOWED 12+ S-125 *Pechora* (SA-3 *Goa*)
  MANPAD 9K32 *Strela*-2 (SA-7 *Grail*)‡
  GUNS • TOWED 12: **37mm** 6 M-1939; **57mm** 6 S-60
ARV T-54/T-55 reported

Navy 50

EQUIPMENT BY TYPE
PATROL AND COASTAL COMBATANTS 3 PBR†

Air Force 400

FORCES BY ROLE
FIGHTER
  1 sqn with MiG-21MF *Fishbed*; MiG-21UM *Mongol B*
TRANSPORT
  1 sqn with An-24 *Coke*; An-26 *Curl*; BN-2 *Islander*; BT-67

TRAINING
1 sqn with L-29 *Delfin*; SF-260WL *Warrior**; *Tetras*
TRANSPORT HELICOPTER
1 sqn with Mi-8 *Hip*; Mi-24D *Hind*; Z-9
EQUIPMENT BY TYPE
AIRCRAFT 4 combat capable
FGA 2: 1 MiG-21MF *Fishbed*; 1 MiG-21UM *Mongol B*
TPT • **Light** 10: 1 An-24 *Coke*; 2 An-26 *Curl*; 1 BT-67; 2 BN-2 *Islander*; 4 *Tetras*
TRG 8: 6 L-29 *Delfin*; 2 SF-260WL *Warrior**
HELICOPTERS
ATK 4 Mi-24D *Hind*
MRH 1 Z-9
TPT 1 **Medium** 1 Mi-8 *Hip* **Light** (1 AS350 *Ecureuil* in store)

Paramilitary 4,800 active

Gendarmerie 1,800

FORCES BY ROLE
MANOEUVRE
Other
8 paramilitary coy

Republican Guard 2,000

National Police 1,000

Militia 3,000

DEPLOYMENT

DEMOCRATIC REPUBLIC OF THE CONGO
UN • MONUSCO 16 obs

LIBERIA
UN • UNMIL 1 obs

SOUTH SUDAN
UN • UNMISS 1 obs

SUDAN
UN • UNAMID 1 obs

TERRITORY WHERE THE GOVERNMENT DOES NOT EXERCISE EFFECTIVE CONTROL

Data presented here represent the de facto situation.

The Tuareg National Movement for the Liberation of Aza-wad (MNLA) declared the unilateral independence of the three northeastern provinces of Gao, Kidal and Timbuktu, after driving out government forces in March 2012. Control of these provinces is now disputed between the MNLA and Islamist groups Ansar Dine and the Movement for Unity and Jihad in West Africa (MUJAO), both of which are reportedly linked to al-Qaeda in the Islamic Maghreb (AQIM).

Mauritius MUS

Mauritian Rupee R		2011	2012	2013
GDP	R	323.46bn	347.17bn	
	US$	11.27bn	11.93bn	
per capita	US$	8,583	9,085	
Growth	%	4.14	3.37	
Inflation	%	6.54	4.48	
Def bdgt[a]	R	1.77bn	2.15bn	2.59bn
	US$	62m	74m	
US$1=R		28.71	29.10	

[a] Defence and Home Affairs Budget

Population   1,313,095

Age	0–14	15–19	20–24	25–29	30–64	65 plus
Male	11.0%	4.0%	4.0%	3.6%	23.5%	3.1%
Female	10.6%	3.9%	3.9%	3.5%	24.2%	4.6%

Capabilities

The country has no standing armed forces, but the Special Mobile Force, part of the police force, is tasked with providing internal and external security. The coast guard operates a number of patrol craft including one blue water patrol ship.

ACTIVE NIL Paramilitary 2,500

ORGANISATIONS BY SERVICE

Paramilitary 2,500

Special Mobile Force ε1,750

FORCES BY ROLE
MANOEUVRE
Reconnaissance
2 recce coy
Light
5 (rifle) mot inf coy
COMBAT SUPPORT
1 engr sqn
COMBAT SERVICE SUPPORT
1 spt pl
EQUIPMENT BY TYPE
RECCE 4 *Shorland*
AIFV 2 VAB (with 20mm gun)
APC (W) 16: 7 *Tactica*; 9 VAB
ARTY • **MOR 81mm** 2
AT • **RL 89mm** 4 LRAC

Coast Guard ε800

PATROL AND COASTAL COMBATANTS 5
PSOH 1 *Vigilant* (capacity 1 hel) (CAN *Guardian* design)
PB 4: 1 P-2000; 1 SDB-Mk3; 2 *Zhuk* (FSU)
AIRCRAFT • **TPT** • **Light** 3: 1 BN-2T *Defender*; 2 Do-228-101

Police Air Wing
HELICOPTERS
MRH 5: 1 *Dhruv*; 4 SA316 *Alouette* III
TPT • **Light** 1 AS355 *Ecureuil* II

Mozambique MOZ

Mozambique New Metical M		2011	2012	2013
GDP	M	365.33bn	414.38bn	
	US$	12.57bn	14.64bn	
per capita	US$	535	623	
Growth	%	7.32	7.50	
Inflation	%	10.35	3.00	
Def bdgt	M	ε2.02bn		
	US$	ε70m		
US$1=M		29.06	28.30	

Population 23,515,934

Age	0–14	15–19	20–24	25–29	30–64	65 plus
Male	23.0%	5.7%	4.3%	3.1%	11.2%	1.4%
Female	22.8%	5.8%	4.9%	3.7%	12.5%	1.6%

Capabilities

In recent years, the government has raised concerns over marine piracy and people-trafficking as additional tasks for the military, beyond assuring territorial integrity. The extent to which the country's armed forces are capable of meeting any of these tasks remains in question, given the poor state generally of its military. Budget constraints have severely limited the military's ability to address areas of weakness, leaving it partly dependent on cascaded defence equipment from other nations. There are growing ties with China in the defence sphere.

ACTIVE 11,200 (Army 10,000 Navy 200 Air 1,000)
Terms of service conscription, 2 years

ORGANISATIONS BY SERVICE

Army ε9,000–10,000
FORCES BY ROLE
SPECIAL FORCES
3 SF bn
MANOEUVRE
Light
7 inf bn
COMBAT SUPPORT
2-3 arty bn
2 engr bn
COMBAT SERVICE SUPPORT
1 log bn
EQUIPMENT BY TYPE†
Equipment at estimated 10% or less serviceability
MBT 60+ T-54
RECCE 30 BRDM-1/BRDM-2
AIFV 40 BMP-1

APC (W) 260: 160 BTR-60; 100 BTR-152
PPV 11 *Casspir*
ARTY 126
TOWED 62; **100mm** 20 M-1944; **105mm** 12 M-101; **122mm** 12 D-30; **130mm** 6 M-46; **152mm** 12 D-1
MRL 122mm 12 BM-21
MOR 52: **82mm** 40 M-43; **120mm** 12 M-43
AT • **MSL** • **MANPATS** 290: 20 AT-3 9K11 *Sagger*; 120 in store; 12 AT-4 9K111 *Spigot*; 138 in store
RCL 75mm; **82mm** B-10; **107mm** 24 B-12
GUNS 85mm 18: 6 D-48; 12 Type-56 (D-44)
AD • **SAM** • **MANPAD** 250: 20 9K32 *Strela*-2 (SA-7 *Grail*)‡; 230 in store
GUNS 330+
SP 57mm 20 ZSU-57-2
TOWED 310+: **20mm** M-55; **23mm** 120 ZU-23-2; **37mm** 100: 90 M-1939; 10 in store; **57mm** 90: 60 S-60; 30 in store

Navy ε200
EQUIPMENT BY TYPE
PATROL AND COASTAL COMBATANTS • **PB** 1 *Conejera*

Air Force 1,000
FORCES BY ROLE
TRANSPORT
1 sqn with An-26 *Curl*; FTB-337G *Milirole*
ATTACK/TRANSPORT HELICOPTER
1 sqn with Mi-24 *Hind*†
AIR DEFENCE
Some bty with S-75 *Dvina* (SA-2 *Guideline*)†‡
EQUIPMENT BY TYPE
AIRCRAFT
FGA (some MiG-21bis *Fishbed* L & N non-op)
ISR 3 FTB-337G *Milirole*
TPT • **Light** 2 An-26 *Curl*; (4 PA-32 *Cherokee* non-op)
HELICOPTERS
ATK 2 Mi-24 *Hind*†
TPT • **Medium** (2 Mi-8 *Hip* non-op)
AD • **SAM** (10+ S-125 *Pechora* SA-3 *Goa* non-op)‡
TOWED: S-75 *Dvina* (SA-2 *Guideline*)† ‡

DEPLOYMENT

SUDAN
UN • UNISFA 1 obs

Namibia NAM

Namibian Dollar N$		2011	2012	2013
GDP	N$	89.79bn	99.61bn	
	US$	12.53bn	12.15bn	
per capita	US$	5,785	5,610	
Growth	%	4.86	4.04	
Inflation	%	5.75	6.68	
Def bdgt	N$	3.01bn	3.13bn	
	US$	421m	381m	
US$1=N$			7.16	8.20

Population   2,165,828

Age	0–14	15–19	20–24	25–29	30–64	65 plus
Male	16.9%	6.0%	5.6%	5.1%	14.9%	1.8%
Female	16.5%	5.9%	5.5%	4.9%	14.4%	2.4%

Capabilities

The military is tasked with providing territorial integrity, supporting civil authorities and participating in peace-support operations. A Strategic Plan was issued in 2009 aimed at supporting the government's Vision 2030. Improving mobility remains a priority in terms of both land vehicles and air transport. Namibian forces take part in multinational exercises. They also have been involved in United Nations and African Union deployments. The military has no independent ability to project power beyond national territory. China has emerged as the main source of combat aircraft with the air force operating a squadron each of F-7 fighter and K-8 jet trainer/light attack aircraft.

ACTIVE 9,200 (Army 9,000 Navy 200) **Paramilitary 6,000**

ORGANISATIONS BY SERVICE

Army 9,000

FORCES BY ROLE
MANOEUVRE
Light
6 inf bn
Other
1 (Presidential Guard) gd bn
COMBAT SUPPORT
1 cbt spt bde with (1 arty regt)
1 AT regt
1 AD regt
COMBAT SERVICE SUPPORT
1 log bde
EQUIPMENT BY TYPE
MBT T-54/T-55†; T-34†
RECCE 12 BRDM-2
APC (W) 60: 10 BTR-60; 20 *Casspir*; 30 *Wolf Turbo* 2
ARTY 69
TOWED 140mm 24 G2

MRL 122mm 5 BM-21
MOR 40: **81mm**; **82mm**
AT • RCL 82mm B-10
GUNS 12+: **57mm**; **76mm** 12 ZIS-3
AD • SAM • MANPAD 74 9K32 *Strela-2* (SA-7 *Grail*)‡
GUNS 65
SP 23mm 15 *Zumlac*
TOWED 14.5mm 50 ZPU-4
ARV T-54/T-55 reported

Navy ε200

Fishery protection, part of the Ministry of Fisheries
EQUIPMENT BY TYPE
PATROL AND COASTAL COMBATANTS 8
PSO 1 *Elephant*
PCO 3: 2 *Nathanael Maxwilili*; 1 *Tobias Hainyenko*
PCC 1 *Oryx*
PB 3: 1 *Brendan Simbwaye*; 2 *Marlim*
LOGISTICS AND SUPPORT • AGOR 4
AIRCRAFT • TPT • Light 1 F406 *Caravan II*
HELICOPTERS • TPT • Medium 1 S-61L

Air Force

FORCES BY ROLE
FIGHTER/GROUND ATTACK
1 sqn with MiG-23 *Flogger* (reported); F-7 (F-7NM); FT-7 (FT-7NG)
ISR
1 sqn with O-2A *Skymaster*
TRANSPORT
Some sqn with An-26 *Curl*; *Falcon* 900; Learjet 36; Y-12
TRAINING
1 sqn with K-8 *Karakorum**
ATTACK/TRANSPORT HELICOPTER
1 sqn with *Chetak*; *Cheetah*; Mi-25 *Hind* D; Mi-8 *Hip*; Z-9
EQUIPMENT BY TYPE
AIRCRAFT 14 combat capable
FTR 10: 8 F-7 (F-7NM); 2 FT-7 (FT-7NG)
ISR 5 O-2A *Skymaster*
TPT 6: **Light** 5: 2 An-26 *Curl*; 1 Learjet 36; 2 Y-12; **PAX** 1 *Falcon* 900
TRG 4+ K-8 *Karakorum**
HELICOPTERS
ATK 2 Mi-25 *Hind* D
MRH 2 H425
TPT 5 **Medium** 1 Mi-8 *Hip*; **Light** 4: 3 *Chetak*: 1 *Cheetah*

Paramilitary 6,000

Police Force • Special Field Force 6,000 (incl Border Guard and Special Reserve Force)

DEPLOYMENT

CÔTE D'IVOIRE
UN • UNOCI 2 obs

LIBERIA
UN • UNMIL 3; 1 obs

SOUTH SUDAN
UN • UNMISS 1 obs

SUDAN
UN • UNAMID 1; 7 obs
UN • UNISFA 1 obs

Niger NER

CFA Franc BCEAO fr		2011	2012	2013
GDP	fr	2.84tr	3.4tr	
	US$	6.02bn	6.56bn	
per capita	US$	368	401	
Growth	%	2.29	14.46	
Inflation	%	2.94	4.50	
Def bdgt	fr	ε23.4bn		
	US$	ε50m		
US$1=fr			471.47	518.05

Population   16,344,687

Ethnic groups: Tuareg 8-10%

Age	0–14	15–19	20–24	25–29	30–64	65 plus
Male	25.3%	5.0%	3.9%	3.2%	11.5%	1.3%
Female	24.8%	5.1%	4.0%	3.3%	11.2%	1.3%

Capabilities

The Nigerien military is smaller, less well-funded and less equipped than almost all of its neighbours. It retains limited capability to deliver security, relying heavily on reconnaissance vehicles to deliver mobility and flexibility. However, given the size of the country and the lack of any significant aerial lift, the armed forces struggle to project their influence throughout Niger and are unable to deploy independently, or with any substantial force, beyond the country's borders. Nonetheless, Niger has participated in international peacekeeping missions, deploying battalion-sized forces. The military is heavily politicised, and, although control was civilianised in 1999, it retains significant political influence and another *coup d'état* was launched in 2010, leading to a year-long military junta. Two Tuareg rebellions in the north of the country in the 1990s and 2000s have ensured some experience of counterinsurgency tactics, but capabilities remain limited. As such, the EU launched the two-year EUCAP SAHEL Niger programme in August 2012, which will initially focus on training Nigerien military and security personnel. The mission aims to build capacity to combat non-state armed groups in the Sahel region. The US also includes Niger in its Trans-Sahara Counterterrorism Partnership programme.

ACTIVE 5,300 (Army 5,200 Air 100) **Paramilitary 5,400**

Terms of service selective conscription (2 year)

ORGANISATIONS BY SERVICE

Army 5,200

3 Mil Districts

FORCES BY ROLE
MANOEUVRE
  Reconnaissance
  4 armd recce sqn
  Light
  7 inf coy
  Air Manoeuvre
  2 AB coy
COMBAT SUPPORT
  1 AD coy
  1 engr coy
COMBAT SERVICE SUPPORT
  1 log gp
EQUIPMENT BY TYPE
RECCE 132: 35 AML-20/AML-60; 90 AML-90; 7 VBL
APC (W) 22 M-3 Panhard
ARTY • MOR 40: 81mm 19 Brandt; 82mm 17; 120mm 4 Brandt
AT • RCL 14: 75mm 6 M-20; 106mm 8 M-40
  RL 89mm 36 LRAC
AD • GUNS 39
  SP 10 M3 VDAA
  TOWED 20mm 29

Air Force 100

EQUIPMENT BY TYPE
AIRCRAFT
  ISR 2 DA42 MPP *Twin Star*
  TPT 5 **Medium** 1 C-130H *Hercules*; **Light** 3: 1 An-26 *Curl*; 1 Do-28; 1 Do-228-201; **PAX** 1 B-737-200 (VIP)
HELICOPTERS
  MRH 2 Mi-17 *Hip H*

Paramilitary 5,400

Gendarmerie 1,400

Republican Guard 2,500

National Police 1,500

DEPLOYMENT

CÔTE D'IVOIRE
UN • UNOCI 935; 4 obs; 1 inf bn

DEMOCRATIC REPUBLIC OF THE CONGO
UN • MONUSCO 16 obs

LIBERIA
UN • UNMIL 1 obs

Nigeria NGA

Nigerian Naira N		2011	2012	2013
GDP	N	37.75tr	43.56tr	
	US$	244.05bn	272.55bn	
per capita	US$	1,435	1,602	
Growth	%	7.36	7.07	
Inflation	%	10.84	11.45	
Def bdgt	N	348bn	326bn	
	US$	2.25bn	2.04bn	
FMA (US)	US$	1.212m	1.0m	1.0m
US$1=N		154.70	159.82	

Population   170,123,740

Ethnic groups: North (Hausa and Fulani) South-west (Yoruba) South-east (Ibo); these tribes make up ε65% of population

Age	0–14	15–19	20–24	25–29	30–64	65 plus
Male	22.5%	5.3%	4.6%	3.9%	12.6%	1.4%
Female	21.4%	5.1%	4.4%	3.8%	13.5%	1.6%

Capabilities

Nigeria retains the best-funded and -equipped forces in West Africa. Nonetheless, it suffers from endemic corruption, poor serviceability of its equipment and questionable loyalty among ground-level units. On paper, it maintains the broadest spectrum of capabilities in the region, but, in reality, much of its equipment is unfit to be deployed for prolonged periods of time. Misappropriation and misallocation of funding, under decades of military rule until the 2000s, led to a deterioration in the serviceability of much of Nigeria's equipment. Procurement decisions have arguably not focused on the primary threats to Nigeria, favouring instead equipment designed for state-to-state warfare rather than counter-insurgency roles. These trends have been reversed somewhat in recent years, as refit and repair programmes have attempted to return some of Nigeria's moribund equipment to a useable status. Equally, given the challenges faced by Niger Delta militants and West African pirates, procurement is currently focused on the navy, with offshore patrol vessels, coastal patrol craft and fast patrol boats among the highest priorities. Nevertheless, the difficulties the Nigerian military has faced when tasked with subduing the threat from the Islamist Boko Haram group in the north of the country reflects the lack of effective counter-insurgency and intelligence-gathering capabilities.

ACTIVE 80,000 (Army 62,000 Navy 8,000 Air 10,000)
Paramilitary 82,000

Reserves planned, none org

ORGANISATIONS BY SERVICE

Army 62,000

FORCES BY ROLE
MANOEUVRE
   Armoured
   1 (3rd) armd div (1 recce bn, 2 armd bde, 1 arty bde, 1 engr bde)
   Mechanised
   2 (1st & 2nd) mech div (1 recce bn, 1 mech bde, 1 mot inf bde, 1 arty bde, 1 engr bn)
   Light
   1 (81st) composite div (1 mech bde)
   1 (82nd) composite div (1 recce bde, 2 mot inf bde, 1 amph bde, 1 AB bn, 1 arty bde, 1 engr bde)
   Other
   1 (Presidential Guard) gd bde with (2 gd bn)
COMBAT SUPPORT
   1 AD regt

EQUIPMENT BY TYPE
MBT 276: 176 Vickers Mk 3; 100 T-55†
LT TK 157 Scorpion
RECCE 452: 90 AML-60; 40 AML-90; 70 EE-9 Cascavel; 50 FV721 Fox; 20 Saladin Mk2; 72 VBL (reported); 110 Cobra
APC 484+
   APC (T) 317: 250 4K-7FA Steyr; 67 MT-LB
   APC (W) 167+: 10 FV603 Saracen; 110 Piranha; 47 BTR-3U; EE-11 Urutu (reported)
ARTY 506
   SP 155mm 39 VCA 155 Palmaria
   TOWED 112: **105mm** 50 M-56; **122mm** 31 D-30/D-74; **130mm** 7 M-46; **155mm** 24 FH-77B in store
   MRL 122mm 25 APR-21
   MOR 330+: **81mm** 200; **82mm** 100; **120mm** 30+
AT • MSL • MANPATS Swingfire
   RCL 84mm Carl Gustav; **106mm** M-40A1
AD • SAM 164
   SP 16 Roland
   MANPAD 148: 48 Blowpipe ε100 9K32 Strela-2 (SA-7 Grail)‡
   GUNS 90+
   SP 30 ZSU-23-4
   TOWED 60+: **20mm** 60+; **23mm** ZU-23; **40mm** L/70
RADAR • LAND: some RASIT (veh, arty)
ARV 17: 2 Greif; 15 Vickers ARV
VLB MTU-20; VAB

Navy 8,000 (incl Coast Guard)

Western Comd HQ located at Apapa; Eastern Comd HQ located at Calabar;

EQUIPMENT BY TYPE
PRINCIPAL SURFACE COMBATANTS 1
   FRIGATES • FFGHM 1 Aradu (GER MEKO 360) with 8 single lnchr with Otomat AShM, 1 octuple Albatros lnchr with Aspide SAM, 2 triple STWS 1B 324mm ASTT with A244 LWT, 1 127mm gun, (capacity 1 Lynx Mk89 hel)
PATROL AND COASTAL COMBATANTS 94
   CORVETTES • FSM 1 Enymiri (UK Vosper Mk 9) with 1 triple lnchr with Seacat SAM, 1 twin 375mm A/S mor, 1 76mm gun
   PSOH 1 Thunder (US Hamilton) with 1 76 mm gun

PCFG 1 *Ayam* (FRA *Combattante*) with 2 twin lnchr with MM-38 *Exocet* AShM, 1 76mm gun (additional 2 vessels†)

PCO 4 *Balsam* (buoy tenders (US))

PCC 3 *Ekpe* (GER Lurssen 57m - 2†) with 1 76mm gun

PBF 22: 21 *Manta* (Suncraft 17m); 1 *Shaldag* II

PB 62: 40 Suncraft 12m; 15 *Stingray* (Suncraft 16m); 2 *Sea Eagle* (Suncraft 38m); 2 *Town*; 2 *Yola*; 1 *Andoni* (a further 150 small patrol craft under 10 tonnes FLD may be in operation)

MINE WARFARE • MINE COUNTERMEASURES 2: **MCC** 2 *Ohue* (mod ITA *Lerici*)

AMPHIBIOUS 5

LS • LST 1 *Ambe* (capacity 5 tanks; 220 troops) (GER)

LC • LCVP 4 *Stingray 20*

LOGISTICS AND SUPPORT 5

AGHS 1

YTL 4

Naval Aviation

HELICOPTERS

MRH 2 AW139 (AB-139)

TPT • Light 3 AW109E *Power*†

Air Force 10,000

FORCES BY ROLE

Very limited op capability

FIGHTER/GROUND ATTACK

1 sqn with F-7 (F-7NI); FT-7 (FT-NI)

MARITIME PATROL

1 sqn with ATR-42MP; Do-128D-6 *Turbo SkyServant*; Do-228-100/200

TRANSPORT

2 sqn with C-130H *Hercules*; C-130H-30 *Hercules*; G-222

1 (Presidential) flt with B-727; B-737BBJ; BAe-125-800; Do-228-200; *Falcon 7X*; *Falcon 900*; Gulfstream IV/V

TRAINING

1 unit with *Air Beetle*†;

1 unit with *Alpha Jet**

1 unit with L-39 *Albatros*†*; MB-339A*

1 hel unit with Mi-34 *Hermit* (trg);

ATTACK/TRANSPORT HELICOPTER

2 sqn with AW109LUH; Mi-24/Mi-35 *Hind*†

EQUIPMENT BY TYPE†

AIRCRAFT 54 combat capable

FTR 15: 12 F-7 (F-7NI); 3 FT-7 (FT-NI)

MP 2 ATR-42 MP

TPT 30: **Medium** 5: 1 C-130H *Hercules* (4 more in store†); 1 C-130H-30 *Hercules* (2 more in store); 3 G-222† (2 more in store†); **Light** 16: 1 Cessna 550 *Citation*; 8 Do-128D-6 *Turbo SkyServant*; 1 Do-228-100; 6 Do-228-200 (incl 2 VIP); **PAX** 9: 1 B-727; 1 B-737BBJ; 1 BAe 125-800; 2 *Falcon 7X*; 2 *Falcon 900*; 1 Gulfstream IV; 1 Gulfstream V

TRG 107: 58 *Air Beetle*† (up to 20 awaiting repair); 14 *Alpha Jet**; 23 L-39 *Albatros*†*; 12 MB-339AN* (all being upgraded)

HELICOPTERS

ATK 9: 2 Mi-24P *Hind*; 2 Mi-24V *Hind*; 5 Mi-35 *Hind*

MRH 6 AW109LUH

TPT 7: **Medium** 2 AS332 *Super Puma* (4 AS332 *Super Puma* in store) **Light** 1 AW109

TRG 5 Mi-34 *Hermit*†

MSL • AAM • IR R-3 (AA-2 *Atoll*)‡; PL-9C

Paramilitary ε82,000

Coast Guard

Port Security Police ε2,000

PATROL AND COASTAL COMBATANTS • MISC BOATS/CRAFT 60+ boats

AMPHIBIOUS 5+ ACV

Security and Civil Defence Corps • Police 80,000

APC (W) 70+: 70+ AT105 *Saxon*†; UR-416

AIRCRAFT • TPT • Light 4: 1 Cessna 500 *Citation I*; 2 PA-31 *Navajo*; 1 PA-31-350 *Navajo Chieftain*

HELICOPTERS • TPT • Light 4: 2 Bell 212 (AB-212); 2 Bell 222 (AB-222)

DEPLOYMENT

CÔTE D'IVOIRE

UN • UNOCI 64; 6 obs; 1 fd hospital

DEMOCRATIC REPUBLIC OF THE CONGO

UN • MONUSCO 29 obs

GUINEA BISSAU

ECOWAS • ECOMIB 160

LEBANON

UN • UNIFIL 1

LIBERIA

UN • UNMIL 1,561; 12 obs; 2 inf bn; 1 sigs coy

SOUTH SUDAN

UN • UNMISS 4; 4 obs

SUDAN

UN • UNAMID 3,318; 14 obs; 4 inf bn

UN • UNISFA 3 obs

WESTERN SAHARA

UN • MINURSO 7 obs

Rwanda RWA

Rwandan Franc fr		2011	2012	2013
GDP	fr	3.8tr	4.4tr	
	US$	6.33bn	6.95bn	
per capita	US$	542	595	
Growth	%	8.58	7.70	
Inflation	%	5.67	7.00	
Def bdgt	fr	44.1bn	46.4bn	51.7bn
	US$	73m	73m	
FMA (US)	US$	0.3m	0.2m	0.2m
US$1=fr		600.33	633.22	

Population   11,689,696

Ethnic groups: Hutu 80%; Tutsi 19%

Age	0–14	15–19	20–24	25–29	30–64	65 plus
Male	21.4%	4.9%	4.7%	4.4%	13.5%	1.0%
Female	21.1%	4.9%	4.8%	4.4%	13.6%	1.5%

Capabilities

While fielding a comparatively large army in numerical terms, Rwanda's units are lightly equipped, with little mechanisation. A small number of helicopters constitute the air force. The land forces have been involved in combat operations in the Democratic Republic of the Congo as recently as 2009, when a joint operation was conducted with the DRC to combat Democratic Forces for the Liberation of Rwanda rebels. While the stated aim of the military is to defend territorial integrity and national sovereignty, the nature of the armed forces means it would struggle to achieve this against a well-armed and focused opponent. In terms of COIN operations, however, the Rwandan military has, in the past, proved effective. The army regularly takes part in multinational exercises.

ACTIVE 33,000 (Army 32,000 Air 1,000) **Paramilitary 2,000**

ORGANISATIONS BY SERVICE

Army 32,000

FORCES BY ROLE
MANOEUVRE
Light
2 cdo bn
4 inf div (3 inf bde)
COMBAT SUPPORT
1 arty bde
EQUIPMENT BY TYPE
MBT 24 T-54/T-55 **RECCE** 106: ε90 AML-60/AML-90/AML-245; 16 VBL
AIFV 35+: BMP; 15 Ratel-90; 20 Ratel-60
APC 56+
  APC (W) 20+: BTR; Buffalo (M3 Panhard); 20 Type-92 (reported)

PPV 36 RG-31 Nyala
ARTY 155+
  TOWED 35+: **105mm** 29 Type-54 (D-1); **122mm** 6 D-30; **152mm†**
  MRL 122mm 5 RM-70 Dana
  MOR 115: **81mm; 82mm; 120mm**
AD • SAM • MANPAD 9K32 Strela-2 (SA-7 Grail)‡
  GUNS ε150: **14.5mm; 23mm; 37mm**
ARV T-54/T-55 reported

Air Force ε1,000

FORCES BY ROLE
ATTACK/TRANSPORT HELICOPTER
1 sqn with Mi-17/Mi-17MD/Mi-17V-5/Mi-17-1V Hip H; Mi-24P/V Hind
EQUIPMENT BY TYPE
HELICOPTERS
  ATK 5: 2 Mi-24V Hind E; 3 Mi-24P Hind
  MRH 10: 1 AW139; 4 Mi-17 Hip H; 1 Mi-17MD Hip H; 1 Mi-17V-5 Hip H; 3 Mi-17-1V Hip H
  TPT • Light 1 AW109S

Paramilitary

Local Defence Forces ε2,000

DEPLOYMENT

SOUTH SUDAN
UN • UNMISS 857; 2 obs

SUDAN
UN • UNAMID 3,238; 10 obs; 4 inf bn
UN • UNISFA 2; 2 obs

Senegal SEN

CFA Franc BCEAO fr		2011	2012	2013
GDP	fr	6.82tr	7.23tr	
	US$	14.46bn	13.95bn	
per capita	US$	1,115	1,076	
Growth	%	2.62	3.69	
Inflation	%	3.41	2.26	
Def bdgt	fr	ε98.8bn		
	US$	ε210m		
FMA (US)	US$	0.399m	0.325m	0.325m
US$1=fr		471.44	518.01	

Population   12,969,606

Ethnic groups: Wolof 36%; Fulani 17%; Serer 17%; Toucouleur 9%; Man-dingo 9%; Diola 9% (of which 30-60% in Casamance)

Age	0–14	15–19	20–24	25–29	30–64	65 plus
Male	21.6%	5.5%	4.7%	3.8%	11.4%	1.3%
Female	21.4%	5.5%	4.9%	4.2%	14.1%	1.6%

Capabilities

Senegal maintains a moderate defence capacity that is tailored towards, although not entirely sufficient to cope with, the primary security threats the country faces, namely the Casamancais separatist insurgency. A close defence relationship with France ensures regular training, but, fundamentally, the Sengalese armed forces lack funding and equipment. However, they did deploy limited formed units to Guinea Bissau as part of the ECOWAS mission. Procurement has traditionally favoured the army, with a priority on armoured vehicles. The navy retains a small patrol fleet and limited amphibious capability, much of which is either second-hand or ageing, or, in some cases, both. The air force, meanwhile, retains very limited capability, with just two combat, rotary-wing aircraft, and the rest of the fleet dedicated to personnel transport and training.

ACTIVE 13,600 (Army 11,900 Navy 950 Air 750)
Paramilitary 5,000

Terms of service conscription, 2 years selective

ORGANISATIONS BY SERVICE

Army 11,900 (incl conscripts)

7 Mil Zone HQ

FORCES BY ROLE
MANOEUVRE
  Reconnaissance
  4 armd recce bn
  Light
  1 cdo bn
  6 inf bn
  Air Manoeuvre
  1 AB bn
  Other
  1 (Presidential Guard) horse cav bn
COMBAT SUPPORT
  1 arty bn
  1 engr bn
  1 sigs bn
COMBAT SERVICE SUPPORT
  3 construction coy
  1 log bn
  1 med bn
  1 trg bn

EQUIPMENT BY TYPE
RECCE 118: 30 AML-60; 74 AML-90; 10 M8; 4 M20
APC 36+
  APC (T) 12 M3 half-track
  APC (W) 24: 16 M3 Panhard; 8 *Casspir*
ARTY 28
  TOWED 12: **105mm** 6 HM-2/M-101; **155mm** ε6 Model-50
  MOR 16: **81mm** 8 Brandt; **120mm** 8 Brandt
AT • MSL • MANPATS 4 *Milan*
  RL 89mm 31 LRAC
AD • GUNS • TOWED 33: **20mm** 21 M-693; **40mm** 12 L/60

Navy (incl Coast Guard) 950

EQUIPMENT BY TYPE
PATROL AND COASTAL COMBATANTS 12
  PCC 4: 1 *Fouta* (DNK *Osprey*); 1 *Njambour* (FRA SFCN 59m) with 2 76mm gun; 2 *Saint Louis*† (PR-48)
  PB 8: 2 *Alioune Samb*; 4 *Alphonse Faye* (2 operated by Fisheries Protection Directorate, 2 by Customs Service); 1 *Conejera*; 1 *Senegal II*
AMPHIBIOUS • LANDING CRAFT 6
  LCT 3: 1 *Edic*; 2 *Edic 700*
  LCM 3
LOGISTICS AND SUPPORT 3
  AG 1
  YAG 1 Archangel
  YTM 1

Air Force 750

FORCES BY ROLE
MARITIME PATROL/SEARCH & RESCUE
  1 sqn with C-212 *Aviocar*; Bell 205 (UH-1H *Iroquois*)
ISR
  1 unit with BN-2T *Islander* (anti-smuggling patrols)
TRANSPORT
  1 sqn with B-727-200 (VIP); F-27-400M *Troopship*
TRAINING
  1 sqn with R-235 *Guerrier**; TB-30 *Epsilon*
ATTACK/TRANSPORT HELICOPTER
  1 sqn with AS355F *Ecureuil II*; Bell 206; Mi-35P *Hind*; Mi-171Sh

EQUIPMENT BY TYPE
AIRCRAFT 1 combat capable
  TPT 9: **Light** 7: 1 BN-2T *Islander* (govt owned, mil op); 1 C-212-100 *Aviocar*; 2 Beech B200 *King Air*; 3 F-27-400M *Troopship* (3 more in store); **PAX** 2: 1 A319; 1 B-727-200 (VIP)
  TRG 3: 1 R-235 *Guerrier**; 2 TB-30 *Epsilon*
HELICOPTERS
  ATK 2 Mi-35P *Hind*
  TPT 8 **Medium** 2 Mi-171Sh **Light** 6: 1 AS355F *Ecureuil II*; 1 Bell 205 (UH-1H *Iroquois*); 2 Bell 206; 2 Mi-2 *Hoplite*

Paramilitary 5,000

Gendarmerie 5,000
APC (W) 12 VXB-170

Customs
PATROL AND COASTAL COMBATANTS • PB 2 VCSM

DEPLOYMENT

CÔTE D'IVOIRE
UN • UNOCI 523; 13 obs; 1 inf bn

DEMOCRATIC REPUBLIC OF THE CONGO
UN • MONUSCO 22 obs

GUINEA BISSAU
ECOWAS • ECOMIB 200

LIBERIA
UN • UNMIL 2; 1 obs

SOUTH SUDAN
UN • UNMISS 4; 3 obs

SUDAN
UN • UNAMID 827; 8 obs; 1 inf bn

FOREIGN FORCES

France 350; 1 *Atlantique*; 1 C-160 *Transall*

Seychelles SYC

Seychelles Rupee SR		2011	2012	2013
GDP	SR	12.6bn	13.67bn	
	US$	1.02bn	0.97bn	
per capita	US$	11,330	10,775	
Growth	%	5.11	3.01	
Inflation	%	2.56	7.49	
Def bdgt[a]	SR	ε292m		
	US$	ε24m		
US$1=SR		12.39	14.07	

[a] Includes Ministry of Defence capital expenditure

Population	90,024

Age	0–14	15–19	20–24	25–29	30–64	65 plus
Male	11.0%	3.8%	4.0%	4.4%	25.1%	2.7%
Female	10.5%	3.6%	3.6%	3.9%	23.0%	4.5%

Capabilities

Piracy has become a primary concern for the People's Defence Forces, with the coast guard and the air force engaged. The former element of the defence forces is expanding to meet the challenge of piracy, with equipment being donated or offered by concerned nations, including India. The air force's DHC-6 will be supplemented by a Dornier 228. The Seychelles' special forces unit is also involved anti-piracy operations, while an infantry unit is tasked with internal security. The military, given its size and nature, has no power-projection capability. The US continues to operate MQ-9 *Reaper* UAVs from the country in order to contribute to counter-piracy activities in the Indian Ocean.

ACTIVE 420 (Land Forces 200; Coast Guard 200; Air Force 20)

ORGANISATIONS BY SERVICE

People's Defence Force

Land Forces 200
FORCES BY ROLE
SPECIAL FORCES
1 SF unit

MANOEUVRE
Light
1 inf coy
Other
1 sy unit
COMBAT SUPPORT
1 MP unit
EQUIPMENT BY TYPE†
RECCE 6 BRDM-2†
ARTY• MOR 82mm 6 M-43†
AD • SAM • MANPAD 10 9K32 *Strela*-2 (SA-7 *Grail*) ‡
GUNS • TOWED 14.5mm ZPU-2†; ZPU-4†; 37mm M-1939†

Coast Guard 200 (incl 80 Marines)
EQUIPMENT BY TYPE
PATROL AND COASTAL COMBATANTS 8
PCC 2: 1 *Andromache* (ITA *Pichiotti* 42m); 1 *Topaz*
PB 6: 2 *Aries*; 1 *Junon*; 2 *Rodman 101*; 1 *Fortune* (UK *Tyne*)
AMPHIBIOUS • LCT 1 *Cinq Juin* (govt owned but civilian op)

Air Force 20
EQUIPMENT BY TYPE
AIRCRAFT
TPT • Light 5: 3 DHC-6-320 *Twin Otter*; 2 Y-12

FOREIGN FORCES

United States US Africa Command: some MQ-9 *Reaper* UAV

Sierra Leone SLE

Sierra Leonean Leone L		2011	2012	2013
GDP	L	12.7tr	17.03tr	
	US$	2.92bn	3.82bn	
per capita	US$	532	696	
Growth	%	6.01	21.29	
Inflation	%	18.46	13.70	
Def bdgt	L	54.3bn	57bn	62.7bn
	US$	12m	13m	
US$1=L		4356.24	4454.91	

Population	5,485,998

Age	0–14	15–19	20–24	25–29	30–64	65 plus
Male	20.8%	4.9%	4.4%	3.8%	13.1%	1.6%
Female	21.1%	5.1%	4.7%	4.1%	14.4%	2.1%

Capabilities

The Sierra Leonean Armed Forces are poorly funded and lack any significant combat capability. Since the devastation of the civil war in the 1990s, there has been little procurement to fill the capability gap left by the conflict. The armed forces' aerial capabilities are largely moribund and the ground forces lack serviceable vehicles. The maritime force has been rejuvenated somewhat by a donated coastal patrol craft and patrol boats, but remains very much a brown-water force. Arguably, the armed forces are currently equipped for the primary roles they face, namely internal security, and benefitted from an intensive UK training regime in the 2000s. However, should any more significant internal or external threat emerge, it is unlikely that the armed forces would be able to sustain an armed campaign and defeat a committed insurgent group or well-trained adversary. The dispatch of a battalion to serve with AMISOM in Somalia will likely lead to improvements in planning and tactics.

ACTIVE 10,500 (Joint 10,500)

ORGANISATIONS BY SERVICE

Armed Forces 10,500

FORCES BY ROLE
MANOEUVRE
Light
3 inf bde (total: 12 inf bn)
EQUIPMENT BY TYPE
ARTY • MOR 31: **81mm** ε27; **82mm** 2; **120mm** 2
AT • RCL 84mm *Carl Gustav*
HELICOPTERS • MRH/TPT 2 Mi-17 *Hip* H/Mi-8 *Hip*†
AD • GUNS 7: **12.7mm** 4; **14.5mm** 3

Navy ε200

EQUIPMENT BY TYPE
PATROL AND COASTAL COMBATANTS • PB 1
Shanghai III

DEPLOYMENT

LEBANON
UN • UNIFIL 2

SOMALIA
AU • AMISOM 850; 1 inf bn

SUDAN
UN • UNAMID 135; 6 obs; 1 recce coy
UN • UNISFA 3 obs

TIMOR LESTE
UN • UNMIT 1 obs

FOREIGN FORCES

Canada IMATT 10
Ghana IMATT 1
United Kingdom IMATT 21

Somalia SOM

Somali Shilling sh		2011	2012	2013
GDP*	US$			
per capita	US$			

*Definitive economic data unavailable

US$1=sh		1650.33	1661.50	
Population	10,085,638			

Age	0–14	15–19	20–24	25–29	30–64	65 plus
Male	22.6%	4.8%	4.5%	3.5%	13.6%	1.0%
Female	22.5%	4.8%	4.6%	3.7%	13.2%	1.4%

Capabilities

Militia forces and armed groups operate within the country, while Somaliland and Puntland have their own militias. Heavy equipment is in poor repair or inoperable. In the past, government forces were largely ad hoc troops gathered along clan lines by warlords within the government when required. An internationally backed attempt to forge a standing army has produced a nascent force trained by the African Union Mission in Somalia (AMISOM) and private security companies. Somali army troops are trained either at Mogadishu airport, or, in greater numbers, at Uganda's Bihanga training camp. This training, by an EU mission, led to some four multi-clan battalions graduating in 2012, prior to redeployment to Somalia. In some cases, Somali National Government (SNG) forces have also been accompanied by allied militias. Puntland's forces were officially absorbed by the then-TFG in 2007, but conflict with Somaliland later that year led to a new command being created in 2008. The most significant other armed group within Somalia is the insurgent al-Shabaab group, which also relies on small arms, light weapons and technicals. In 2012, it withdrew from its positions in Mogadishu in a self-declared 'tactical retreat' before being ousted from its primary revenue-generating hub of Kismayo in September 2012. Despite this, al-Shabaab remains capable of challenging the SNG's authority in southern Somalia.

ORGANISATIONS BY SERVICE

Army ε3,200

FORCES BY ROLE
MANOEUVRE
Light
Some cdo unit
2 inf bde (total: 6 inf bn)

FOREIGN FORCES

Burundi AMISOM 4,800; 5 inf bn
Djibouti AMISOM 850; 1 inf bn
Ethiopia some
Kenya AMISOM 3,150; 3 inf bn

Sierra Leone AMISOM 850; 1 inf bn
Uganda AMISOM 6,700; 6 inf bn

TERRITORY WHERE THE RECOGNISED AUTHORITY (TFG) DOES NOT EXERCISE EFFECTIVE CONTROL

Data presented here represent the de facto situation. This does not imply international recognition as a sovereign state.

Somaliland

Population   3.5m

Militia unit strengths are not known. Equipment numbers are generalised assessments; most of this equipment is in poor repair or inoperable.

ORGANISATIONS BY SERVICE

Army ε15,000

FORCES BY ROLE
MANOUEVRE
  Armoured
  2 armd bde
  Mechanised
  1 mech inf bde
  Light
  14 inf bde
COMBAT SUPPORT
  2 arty bde
COMBAT SERVICE SUPPORT
  1 spt bn

EQUIPMENT BY TYPE †
MBT 33: M47; T54/55
RECCE BTR-50; Panhard AML 90; BRDM-2
APC(W) 15-20 Fiat 6614
ARTY 69
  TOWED 122mm 12 D-30
  MOR MRL: 8-12 BM21
  45: **81mm; 120mm**
AT
  RCL 106mm 16 M40A1
AD
  GUNS some†
  TOWED 20mm; 23mm ZU-23

Coast Guard ε350

Ministry of the Interior
EQUIPMENT BY TYPE
PATROL AND COASTAL COMBATANTS 26
  PB 7 *Dolphin 26*
  PBR 19

Puntland

Armed Forces ε5–10,000; coastguard

South Africa RSA

South African Rand R		2011	2012	2013
GDP	R	2.96tr	3.21tr	
	US$	408.69bn	390.92bn	
per capita	US$	8,373	8,009	
Growth	%	3.12	2.59	
Inflation	%	5.00	5.64	
Def bdgt	R	34.3bn	37.9bn	39.9bn
	US$	4.74bn	4.62bn	
FMA (US)	US$	0.798m	0.7m	0.7m
US$1=R		7.25	8.20	

Population   48,810,427

Age	0–14	15–19	20–24	25–29	30–64	65 plus
Male	14.3%	5.0%	5.6%	5.4%	17.1%	2.4%
Female	14.2%	5.0%	5.4%	4.9%	17.3%	3.5%

Capabilities

The country remains militarily the most capable in the region, despite financial and structural problems with its armed forces. The air force and navy have been the focus of a re-equipment programme, though they have also reduced in size. Maritime security as a result of piracy is a growing concern, and the navy, in recent years, has dispatched vessels on counter-piracy missions in the Mozambique channel. The military has the ability for power projection, limited by the amount of tactical airlift (South Africa withdrew from the A400M programme), and by the impact of funding constraints on the army. The military deploys regularly on peacekeeping missions, and is a participant in multinational exercises. The country is undergoing a Defence Review process, which will likely lead to force-structure recommendations. (see essay pp. 488–492.)

ACTIVE 62,100 (Army 37,150 Navy 6,250 Air 10,650 South African Military Health Service 8,050)

RESERVE 15,050 (Army 12,250 Navy 850 Air 850 South African Military Health Service Reserve 1,100)

ORGANISATIONS BY SERVICE

Army 37,150
FORCES BY ROLE
Formations under direct command and control of SANDF Chief of Joint Operations: 9 Joint Operational Tactical HQs, troops are provided when necessary by permanent and reserve force units from all services and SF Bde. A new army structure is planned with 2 divisions (1 mechanised, 1 motorised) with 10 bdes (1 armd, 1 mech, 7 motorised and 1 rapid reaction). Training, Support and Land Commands are also planned, while Divisional HQ is to be re-established.
COMMAND
  2 bde HQ

SPECIAL FORCES
  1 SF bde (2 SF bn(-))
MANOEUVRE
  Reconnaissance
  1 armd recce bn
  Armoured
  1 tk bn
  Mechanised
  2 mech inf bn
  Light
  10 mot inf bn (1 bn roles as AB, 1 as amph)
COMBAT SUPPORT
  1 arty bn
  1 ADA bn
  1 engr regt
COMBAT SERVICE SUPPORT
  2 maint units
  1 construction bn

Reserve 12,250 reservists (under strength)

FORCES BY ROLE
MANOEUVRE
  Reconnaissance
  2 armd recce bn
  1 recce bn
  Armoured
  3 tk bn
  Mechanised
  6 mech inf bn
  Light
  16 mot inf bn (1 bn roles as AB, 1 as amph)
  3 lt inf bn (converting to mot inf)
  Air Manoeuvre
  1 AB bn
  COMBAT SUPPORT
  7 arty regt
  4 AD regt
  2 engr regt

EQUIPMENT BY TYPE
MBT 34 *Olifant* 1A (133 *Olifant* 1B in store)
RECCE 82 *Rooikat*-76 (94 in store)
AIFV 534 *Ratel*-20 Mk III-20/*Ratel*-60 Mk III-60/*Ratel*-90 Mk III-90 FSV 90
PPV 810: 370 *Casspir*; 440 *Mamba*
ARTY 1,255
  SP 155mm 2 G-6 (41 in store)
  TOWED 140mm (75 G2 in store); **155mm** 6 G-5 (66 in store)
  MRL 127mm 21: (26 *Valkiri* Mk I in store) (24 tube)); 21 *Valkiri* Mk II MARS *Bataleur* (40 tube); (4 in store (40 tube))
  MOR 1,226: **81mm** 1,190 (incl some SP); **120mm** 36
AT • MSL • MANPATS 59: 16 ZT-3 *Swift* (36 in store); 43 *Milan* ADT/ER
  RCL 106mm 100 M-40A1 (some SP)
  RL 92mm FT-5
AD • GUNS 76
  SP 23mm 36 *Zumlac*
  TOWED 35mm 40 GDF-002

RADAR • LAND ESR 220 *Kameelperd*; 2 Thales *Page*
ARV *Gemsbok*
VLB *Leguan*
UAV • ISR • Light up to 4 *Vulture*

Navy 6,250

Fleet HQ and Naval base located at Simon's Town; Naval stations located at Durban and Port Elizabeth

EQUIPMENT BY TYPE
SUBMARINES • TACTICAL • SSK 3 *Heroine* (Type-209) with 8 533mm TT (of which one cyclically in reserve/refit)
PRINCIPAL SURFACE COMBATANTS • FRIGATES 4:
  FFGHM 4 *Valour* (MEKO A200) with 2 quad lnchr with MM-40 *Exocet* AShM (upgrade to Block III planned); 2 octuple VLS with *Umkhonto*-IR naval SAM, 1 76mm gun (capacity 1 *Super Lynx* 300 hel)
PATROL AND COASTAL COMBATANTS 6
  PCC 3 *Warrior* (ISR *Reshef*) with 2 76mm gun
  PB 3 *Tobie*
MINE WARFARE • MINE COUNTERMEASURES 2
  MHC 2 *River* (GER *Navors*) (Limited operational roles; training and dive support); (additional vessel in reserve)
AMPHIBIOUS • LCU 6 *Lima*
LOGISTICS AND SUPPORT 8
  AORH 1 *Drakensberg* (capacity 4 LCU; 100 troops)
  AGOS 1 (use for Antarctic survey, privately operated for Dept of Environment)
  AGHS 1 *Protea* (UK *Hecla*)
  YTM 5

Air Force 10,650

Air Force office, Pretoria, and 4 op gps
Command & Control: 2 Airspace Control Sectors, 1 Mobile Deployment Wg
1 Air Force Command Post

FORCES BY ROLE
FIGHTER/GROUND ATTACK
  1 sqn with *Gripen* C/D (JAS-39C/D)
TRANSPORT
  1 (VIP) sqn with B-737 BBJ; Cessna 550 *Citation II*; *Falcon* 50; *Falcon* 900;
  1 sqn with BT-67 (C-47TP)
  2 sqn with C-130B/BZ *Hercules*; C-212; Cessna 185; CN-235
  9 (AF Reserve) sqn with ε130 private lt tpt ac
TRAINING
  1 (Lead-in Ftr Trg) sqn with *Hawk* Mk120*
ATTACK HELICOPTER
  1 (cbt spt) sqn with AH-2 *Rooivalk*
TRANSPORT HELICOPTER
  4 (mixed) sqn with *Oryx*; BK-117; A109UH

EQUIPMENT BY TYPE
AIRCRAFT 50 combat capable
  FGA 34: 25 *Gripen* C (JAS-39C); 9 *Gripen* D (JAS-39D)
  TPT 53 **Medium** 7 C-130B/BZ *Hercules*; **Light** 42: 3 Beech 200C *King Air*; 1 Beech 300 *King Air*; 10 BT-67 (C-47TP - 5 maritime, 3 tpt, 2 EW); 2 C-212-200 *Aviocar*; 2 C-212-300 *Aviocar*; 10 Cessna 185; 11 Cessna 208 *Caravan*;

2 Cessna 550 *Citation II*; 1 PC-12; **PAX** 4: 1 B-737 BBJ; 2 *Falcon* 50; 1 *Falcon* 900
TRG 74: 24 *Hawk* Mk120*; 50 PC-7 Mk II *Astra*
HELICOPTERS
ATK 11 AH-2 *Rooivalk* (Only 5 in service as of late 2012)
MRH 4 *Super Lynx* 300
TPT 76 **Medium** 39 *Oryx*; **Light** 37: 29 AW-109; 8 BK-117
UAV • ISR • Medium *Seeker II*
MSL •AAM • IR V3C *Darter* **IIR** IRIS-T

Ground Defence

FORCES BY ROLE
MANOEUVRE
Other
12 sy sqn (SAAF regt)
EQUIPMENT BY TYPE
2 Radar (static) located at Ellisras and Mariepskop; 2 (mobile long-range); 4 (tactical mobile). Radar air control sectors located at Pretoria, Hoedspruit

South African Military Health Service 8,050; ε1,100 reservists (total 9,150)

DEPLOYMENT

DEMOCRATIC REPUBLIC OF THE CONGO
UN • MONUSCO • *Operation Mistral* 1,201; 19 obs; 1 inf bn; 1 avn coy (air med evacuation team, air base control det); 1 engr coy

MOZAMBIQUE CHANNEL
Navy • 1 FFGHM

SUDAN
UN • UNAMID • *Operation Cordite* 802; 12 obs; 1 inf bn

South Sudan

South Sudanese Pound ssp		2011	2012	2013
GDP	ssp	52.48bn	33.76bn	
	US$	17.47bn	11.45bn	
per capita	US$	1,644	1,078	
Growth	%	1.44	-54.98	
Inflation	%	47.31	54.83	
Def exp	ssp	1.07bn		
	US$	355m		
Def bdgt	ssp	1.6bn	2.42bn	2.54bn
	US$	533m	537m	
US$1=ssp		3.00	4.50	

Population   10,625,176

Ethnic and religious groups: Muslim 70% mainly in North; Christian10% mainly in South; 52% mainly in South; Arab 39% mainly in North

Age	0–14	15–19	20–24	25–29	30–64	65 plus
Male	23.8%	5.8%	4.5%	3.6%	11.9%	1.2%
Female	22.7%	5.0%	4.2%	3.7%	12.6%	0.9%

Capabilities

Reflecting their origin as insurgent forces, the state's military overwhelmingly consists of infantry, with some armour and a small air capability. Security concerns are dominated by continuing friction with Sudan. Ukraine and China have been sources of equipment, and there has been international assistance in establishing the foundations of a security structure, such as NCO academies. There are also plans to downsize armed personnel numbers, though the demands of ongoing conflict mean that DDR and SSR remain haphazardly applied. A process to draft a national security policy began in September 2012 (see p. 484).

ACTIVE 210,000 (Army 210,000)

Terms of service unknown

ORGANISATIONS BY SERVICE

Army ε210,000

FORCES BY ROLE
MANOEUVRE
Light
9 inf div
EQUIPMENT BY TYPE
MBT 110+: Some T-55; 110 T-72
ARTY 69+
SP 24 **122mm** 12 2S1 **152mm** 12 2S3
MRL • 122mm 15 BM-21
MOR 82mm 30+

Air Force

EQUIPMENT BY TYPE
AIRCRAFT • TPT • Light 1 Beech 1900
HELICOPTERS
MRH 9 Mi-17 *Hip* H
TPT • Medium 1 Mi-172 (VIP)

FOREIGN FORCES

All UNMISS, unless otherwise indicated
Australia 12; 4 obs
Bangladesh 278; 1 engr coy; 1 fd hospital
Benin 2 obs
Bolivia 3 obs
Brazil 3; 5 obs
Cambodia 145; 3 obs; 1 MP coy; 1 fd hospital
Canada 5; 5 obs
China, People's Republic of 347; 3 obs; 1 engr coy; 1 fd hospital
Denmark 10; 2 obs
Ecuador 4 obs
Egypt 3 obs
El Salvador 2 obs
Fiji 2; 2 obs
Germany 8; 8 obs
Ghana 1
Guatemala 2; 3 obs
Guinea 1 obs
India 1,997; 5 obs; 2 inf bn; 1 engr coy; 1 fd hospital

Indonesia 3 obs
Italy 1 obs
Japan 271; 1 engr coy
Jordan 4; 4 obs
Kenya 692; 3 obs; 1 inf bn
Korea, Republic of 6; 2 obs
Kyrgyzstan 2 obs
Mali 1 obs
Moldova 1; 2 obs
Mongolia 857; 2 obs; 1 inf bn
Namibia 1 obs
Nepal 858; 5 obs; 1 inf bn
New Zealand 1; 2 obs
Nigeria 4; 4 obs
Norway 12; 4 obs
Papua New Guinea 1 obs
Paraguay 3 obs
Peru 2 obs
Philippines 3 obs
Poland 2 obs
Romania 2; 4 obs
Russia 2; 2 obs
Rwanda 857; 2 obs; 1 inf bn
Senegal 4; 3 obs
Sri Lanka 2 obs
Sweden 4; 3 obs
Switzerland 2; 2 obs
Tanzania 4 obs
Timor-Leste 1 obs
Ukraine 3 obs
United Kingdom 3; 1 obs
United States 5
Yemen 2; 6 obs
Zambia 3; 2 obs
Zimbabwe 2 obs

Sudan SDN

Sudanese Pound sdg		2011	2012	2013
GDP	sdg	170.66bn	190.53bn	
	US$	64bn	51.58bn	
per capita	US$	1,871	1,508	
Growth	%	-4.49	-11.24	
Inflation	%	18.27	28.62	
Def exp	sdg	ε3.1bn		
	US$	ε1.16bn		
US$1=sdg		2.67	3.69	

Population   34,206,710

Ethnic and religious groups: Muslim 70% mainly in North; Christian 10% mainly in South; 52% mainly in South; Arab 39% mainly in North

Age	0–14	15–19	20–24	25–29	30–64	65 plus
Male	21.4%	5.6%	4.6%	3.8%	13.3%	1.8%
Female	20.6%	5.1%	4.5%	3.9%	13.9%	1.5%

Capabilities

The military was, for two decades, focused on a civil war in the then-south of the country, which resulted in partition in 2011 and the creation of South Sudan. Tensions between the two countries, however, continue, with the Sudanese military involved in clashes with rebels in the south of the country. The military operates a mix of Russian and Chinese equipment. In regional terms, the services are reasonably well-equipped, although some of the land systems are obsolescent in Western terms. The air force, though relatively small, fields several comparatively modern combat types, including the MiG-29 and Su-25. Tactical airlift is provided by a variety of transport types. The navy is limited to littoral and river patrol. The country likely has the capacity for limited regional power projection, though its primary military focus remains South Sudan and counter-insurgency. The military has not participated in any multi-national exercises.

ACTIVE 244,300 (Army 240,000 Navy 1,300 Air 3,000) **Paramilitary 20,000**
Terms of service conscription (males 18–30) 2 years

RESERVE NIL Paramilitary 85,000

ORGANISATIONS BY SERVICE

Army ε240,000
FORCES BY ROLE
SPECIAL FORCES
  5 SF coy
MANOEUVRE
  Reconnaissance
  1 indep recce bde
  Armoured
  1 armd div
  Mechanised
  1 mech inf div
  1 indep mech inf bde
  Light
  6 inf div
  7 indep inf bde
  Air Manoeuvre
  1 AB div
  Other
  1 (Border Guard) sy bde
COMBAT SUPPORT
  3 indep arty bde
  1 engr div (9 engr bn)
EQUIPMENT BY TYPE
MBT 390: 20 M-60A3; 60 Type-59/Type-59D; 300 T-54/T-55; 10 *Al-Bashier* (Type-85-IIM)
LT TK 115: 70 Type-62; 45 Type-63
RECCE 238: 6 AML-90; 60 BRDM-1/BRDM-2; 50–80 *Ferret*; 42 M1114 HMMWV; 30–50 *Saladin*
AIFV 84+: 75 BMP-1/BMP-2; 2+ BTR-3; 7 BTR-80A
APC 412
  APC (T) 66: 36 M-113; 20-30 BTR-50

Sub-Saharan Africa

APC (W) 346: 55–80 V-150 *Commando*; 10 BTR 70; 50–80 BTR-152; 20 OT-62; 50 OT-64; 96 *Walid*; 10 Type-92 (reported)

ARTY 778+

SP 20: **122mm** 10 2S1 *Carnation*; **155mm** 10 (AMX) Mk F3

TOWED 123+ **105mm** 20 M101; **122mm** 16+: 16 D-30; D-74; M-30; **130mm** 75 M-46/Type-59-I; 12 M114A1

MRL 635: **107mm** 477 Type-63; **122mm** 158: 90 BM-21; 50 *Saqr*; 18 Type-81

MOR 81mm; **82mm**; **120mm** AM-49; M-43

AT • MSL • MANPATS 4+: 4 *Swingfire*; 9K11 *Malyutka* (AT-3 *Sagger*)

RCL 106mm 40 M40A1

GUNS 40+: 40 **76mm** ZIS-3/**100mm** M-1944; **85mm** D-44

AD • SAM • MANPAD 54 9K32 *Strela*-2 ‡ (SA-7 *Grail*)

GUNS 996+

SP 20: **20mm** 8 M-163 *Vulcan*; 12 M3 VDAA

TOWED 976+: 740+ **14.5mm** ZPU-2/**14.5mm** ZPU-4/**37mm** Type-63/**57mm** S-60/**85mm** M-1944; **20mm** 16 M-167 *Vulcan*; **23mm** 50 ZU-23-2; **37mm** 110: 80 M-1939; 30 unserviceable; **40mm** 60

RADAR • LAND RASIT (veh, arty)

Navy 1,300

HQ located at Port Sudan

EQUIPMENT BY TYPE

PATROL AND COASTAL COMBATANTS 4

PBR 4 *Kurmuk*

AMPHIBIOUS • LANDING CRAFT 7

LCT 2 *Sobat*

LCVP 5

LOGISTICS AND SUPPORT 2

AG *1*

AWT 1 *Baraka*

Air Force 3,000

FORCES BY ROLE

FIGHTER

2 sqn with MiG-29SE/UB *Fulcrum*

GROUND ATTACK

1 sqn with A-5 *Fantan*

1 sqn with Su-25/Su-25UB *Frogfoot*

TRANSPORT

Some sqn with An-26 *Curl** (modified for bombing); An-30 *Clank*; An-32 *Cline*; An-72 *Coaler*; An-74TK-200/300; C-130H *Hercules*; Il-76 *Candid*; Y-8

1 VIP unit with *Falcon* 20F; *Falcon* 50; *Falcon* 900; F-27; Il-62M *Classic*

TRAINING

1 sqn with K-8 *Karakorum**

ATTACK HELICOPTER

2 sqn with Mi-24/Mi-24P/Mi-24V/Mi-35P *Hind*

TRANSPORT HELICOPTER

2 sqn with Mi-8 *Hip*; Mi-17 *Hip* H; Mi-171

AIR DEFENCE

5 bty with S-75 *Dvina* (SA-2 *Guideline*) ‡

EQUIPMENT BY TYPE

AIRCRAFT 60 combat capable

FTR 22: 20 MiG-29SE *Fulcrum*; 2 MiG-29UB *Fulcrum*

ATK 26: 15 A-5 *Fantan*; 9 Su-25 *Frogfoot*; 2 Su-25UB *Frogfoot* B

ISR 2 An-30 *Clank*

TPT 23 **Heavy** 1 Il-76 *Candid*; **Medium** 6: 4 C-130H *Hercules*; 2 Y-8; **Light** 12: 1 An-26 *Curl** (modified for bombing); 2 An-32 *Cline*; 2 An-72 *Coaler*; 4 An-74TK-200; 2 An-74TK-300; 1 F-27 (VIP); **PAX** 4: 1 *Falcon* 20F (VIP); 1 *Falcon* 50 (VIP); 1 Falcon 900; 1 Il-62M *Classic*

TRG 15: 12 K-8 *Karakorum**; 3 UTVA-75

HELICOPTERS

ATK 28: 13 Mi-24 *Hind*; 2 Mi-24P *Hind*; 7 Mi-24V *Hind* E; 6 Mi-35P *Hind*

MRH ε5 Mi-17 *Hip* H

TPT 16 **Medium** 15: 13 Mi-8 *Hip*; 2 Mi-171; **Light** 1 Bell 205

AD • SAM • TOWED: 90 S-75 *Dvina* (SA-2 *Guideline*) ‡

MSL • AAM • IR R-3 (AA-2 *Atoll*)‡; R-60 (AA-8 *Aphid*)); R-73 (AA-11 *Archer*) **IR/SARH** R-23/24 (AA-7 *Apex*) **ARH** R-77 (AA-12 *Adder*)

Paramilitary 20,000

Popular Defence Force 20,000 (org in bn 1,000); 85,000 reservists (total 102,500)

mil wing of National Islamic Front

FOREIGN FORCES

All UNAMID, unless otherwise indicated

Bangladesh 391; 12 obs; 1 inf coy; 1 log coy

Benin UNISFA 1; 3 obs **Bolivia** UNISFA 1; 3 obs

Brazil UNISFA 2; 1 obs

Burkina Faso 805; 10 obs; 1 inf bn

Burundi 2; 8 obs • UNISFA 1 obs

Cambodia UNISFA 1 obs

China, People's Republic of 323; 1 engr coy

Ecuador UNISFA 1 obs

Egypt 2,399; 37 obs; 2 inf bn; 1 engr coy; 1 sigs coy; 1 tpt coy • UNISFA 11; 4 obs

El Salvador UNISFA 1 obs

Ethiopia 1,946 16 obs; 1 recce coy; 2 inf bn; 1 hel coy; 1 log coy; 1 tpt coy • UNISFA 3,799; 87 obs; 2 mech inf bn; 1 inf bn; 2 arty coy; 1 engr coy; 1 fd hospital

Gambia 202; 1 obs; 1 inf coy

Germany 10

Ghana 7; 6 obs • UNISFA 2; 3 obs

Guatemala UNISFA 1; 2 obs

Guinea UNISFA 2 obs

India UNISFA 2; 2 obs

Indonesia 3 obs • UNISFA 1; 1 obs

Iran 2 obs

Jordan 11; 12 obs

Kenya 77; 3 obs; 1 MP coy

Kyrgyzstan UNISFA 1 obs

Lesotho 1; 2 obs

Malawi 1 obs

Malaysia 11; 2 obs • UNISFA 1 obs

Mali 1 obs

Mongolia 70; 1 fd hospital • UNISFA 2 obs
Mozambique UNISFA 1 obs
Namibia 1; 7 obs • UNISFA 1 obs
Nepal 345; 15 obs; 2 inf coy • UNISFA 2; 3 obs
Netherlands 1
Nigeria 3,318; 14 obs; 4 inf bn • UNISFA 3 obs
Pakistan 499; 6 obs; 1 engr coy
Paraguay UNISFA 1 obs
Palau 1; 1 obs
Peru UNISFA 1; 2 obs
Philippines UNISFA 1; 1 obs
Russia UNISFA 2; 1 obs
Rwanda 3,238; 10 obs; 4 inf bn • UNISFA 2; 2 obs
Senegal 827; 8 obs; 1 inf bn
Sierra Leone 135; 6 obs; 1 recce coy • UNISFA 3 obs
South Africa 802; 12 obs; 1 inf bn
Sri Lanka UNISFA 1; 5 obs
Tanzania 890; 20 obs; 1 inf bn • UNISFA 1; 1 obs
Thailand 6; 4 obs
Togo 7 obs
Uganda 1 obs
Ukraine UNISFA 2; 2 obs
Uruguay UNISFA 1
Yemen, Republic of 5; 33 obs • UNISFA 2 obs
Zambia 1; 3 obs • UNISFA 1 obs
Zimbabwe 1; 3 obs • UNISFA 1; 2 obs

cerns with piracy, and clashes between Christians and Muslims within its own population. One focus for violence is Zanzibar, a semi-autonomous island territory of the country. In keeping with many other countries in the region, the military's ability to revamp an ageing equipment inventory is limited by a lack of finance. This is particularly acute in the air force. The emerging problem of piracy has focused attention on its naval capability, and its lack of overall capacity to independently meet such a challenge. It has looked to jointly address anti-piracy tasks with South Africa and Mozambique. A small tactical transport fleet provides some intra-theatre mobility but the state has no ability to project power independently beyond its own territory. In recent years, it has regularly taken part in multinational exercises.

ACTIVE 27,000 (Army 23,000 Navy 1,000 Air 3,000)
Paramilitary 1,400
Terms of service incl civil duties, 2 years

RESERVE 80,000 (Joint 80,000)

ORGANISATIONS BY SERVICE

Army ε23,000
FORCES BY ROLE
MANOEUVRE
  Armoured
  1 tk bde
  Light
  5 inf bde
COMBAT SUPPORT
  4 arty bn
  1 mor bn
  2 AT bn
  2 ADA bn
  1 engr regt (bn)
COMBAT SERVICE SUPPORT
  1 log gp
EQUIPMENT BY TYPE†
MBT 45: 30 T-54/T-55; 15 Type-59
LT TK 55: 30 *Scorpion*; 25 Type-62
RECCE 10 BRDM-2
APC (W) 14: ε10 BTR-40/BTR-152; 4 Type-92 (reported)
ARTY 378
  TOWED 170: **76mm** ε40 ZIS-3; **122mm** 100: 20 D-30; 80 Type-54-1 (M-30) *M-1938*; **130mm** 30 Type-59-I
  MRL **122mm** 58 BM-21
  MOR 150: **82mm** 100 M-43; **120mm** 50 M-43
AT • RCL **75mm** Type-52 (M-20)
  GUNS **85mm** 75 Type-56 (D-44)

Navy ε1,000
EQUIPMENT BY TYPE
PATROL AND COASTAL COMBATANTS 8
  PHT 2 *Huchuan* each with 2 533mm ASTT
  PB 6: 2 *Ngunguri*; 2 *Shanghai* II (PRC); 2 VT 23m
AMPHIBIOUS • LCU 2 *Yuchin*

Tanzania TZA

Tanzanian Shilling sh		2011	2012	2013
GDP	sh	37.53tr	44.71tr	
	US$	23.85bn	27.98bn	
per capita	US$	508	596	
Growth	%	6.45	6.51	
Inflation	%	12.69	15.65	
Def exp	sh	448bn		
	US$	285m		
Def bdgt[a]	sh	358bn	415bn	531bn
	US$	228m	260m	
FMA (US)	US$	0.2m	0.2m	0.2m
US$1=sh		1573.64	1597.96	

[a] Excludes expenditure on Ministry of Defence administration and National Service

Population 46,912,768

Age	0–14	15–19	20–24	25–29	30–64	65 plus
Male	22.7%	5.2%	4.5%	3.9%	12.2%	1.3%
Female	22.3%	5.2%	4.5%	3.9%	12.7%	1.6%

Capabilities

While Tanzania has enjoyed comparative stability, security concerns remain with some of its neighbours, particularly problems in the Democratic Republic of the Congo, con-

Air Defence Command ε3,000

FORCES BY ROLE
FIGHTER
3 sqn with F-6/FT-6; F-7/FT-7; FT-5; K-8 *Karakorum**
TRANSPORT
1 sqn with Cessna 404 *Titan*; DHC-5D *Buffalo*; F-28 *Fellowship*; F-50; Gulfstream G550; Y-12 (II)
TRANSPORT HELICOPTER
1 sqn with Bell 205 (AB-205); Bell 412 *Twin Huey*
EQUIPMENT BY TYPE†
Few air defence assets serviceable.
AIRCRAFT 22 combat capable
   FTR 16: 10 J-6; 6 J-7
   TPT 12: **Medium** 2 Y-8; **Light** 7: 2 Cessna 404 *Titan*; 3 DHC-5D *Buffalo*; 2 Y-12(II); **PAX** 3: 1 F-28 *Fellowship*; 1 F-50; 1 Gulfstream G550
   TRG 9: 3 FT-5 (JJ-5); 6 K-8 *Karakorum**
HELICOPTERS
   MRH 2 Bell 412 *Twin Huey*
   TPT • Light 1 Bell 205 (AB-205)
AD
   SAM 160:
      SP 20 2K12 *Kub* (SA-6 *Gainful*)†; 20 S-125 *Pechora* (SA-3 *Goa*)†
      MANPAD 120 9K32 *Strela-2* (SA-7 *Grail*)‡
   GUNS 200
      TOWED 14.5mm 40 ZPU-2/ZPU-4†; **23mm** 40 ZU-23; **37mm** 120 M-1939

Paramilitary 1,400 active

Police Field Force 1,400

18 sub-units incl Police Marine Unit

Air Wing

AIRCRAFT • TPT • Light 1 Cessna U206 *Stationair*
HELICOPTERS
   TPT • Light 4: 2 Bell 206A *Jet Ranger* (AB-206A); 2 Bell 206L *Long Ranger*
   TRG 2 Bell 47G (AB-47G)/Bell 47G2

Marine Unit 100

PATROL AND COASTAL COMBATANTS • MISC BOATS/CRAFT: some boats

DEPLOYMENT

CÔTE D'IVOIRE
UN • UNOCI 2; 2 obs

DEMOCRATIC REPUBLIC OF THE CONGO
UN • MONUSCO 2 obs

LEBANON
UN • UNIFIL 159; 2 MP coy

SOUTH SUDAN
UN • UNMISS 4 obs

SUDAN
UN • UNAMID 890; 20 obs; 1 inf bn
UN • UNISFA 1; 1 obs

Togo TGO

CFA Franc BCEAO fr		2011	2012	2013
GDP	fr	1.74tr	1.88tr	
	US$	3.7bn	3.62bn	
per capita	US$	532	520	
Growth	%	4.87	5.03	
Inflation	%	3.56	2.47	
Def bdgt	fr	27.8bn		
	US$	59m		
US$1=fr		471.15	518.60	

Population   6,961,049

Age	0–14	15–19	20–24	25–29	30–64	65 plus
Male	20.5%	5.2%	4.8%	4.2%	13.5%	1.4%
Female	20.4%	5.2%	4.9%	4.2%	13.9%	1.8%

Capabilities

Facing few external or internal threats, the Togolese armed forces are adequate for the internal-security roles for which they might be used. The army is relatively small, fielding a limited light armour capability. The air force and navy are similarly constrained by limited equipment, although, in contrast to other regional states, it is generally well maintained and serviceable. Given the size of the country, there is little requirement for airlift. Togo receives training assistance from France, with occasional visits and support from the US Navy. One possible challenge is the growing trend of piracy in the Gulf of Guinea, for which the Togolese Navy is ill-equipped. The seizure of a Greek-owned oil tanker in Togolese waters, in August 2012, by Nigerian pirates was indicative of the increasing incidence of armed robbery on the seas and the inability of the tiny Togolese Navy to prevent such cross-border attacks. With little funding to launch an aggressive procurement campaign, Togo is relatively powerless to control the development of piracy in its waters.

ACTIVE 8,550 (Army 8,100 Navy 200 Air 250)
Paramilitary 750

Terms of service conscription, 2 years (selective)

ORGANISATIONS BY SERVICE

Army 8,100+

FORCES BY ROLE
MANOEUVRE
   Reconnaissance
   1 armd recce regt
   Light
   2 cbd arms regt
   2 inf regt
   1 rapid reaction force
   Air Manoeuvre
   1 cdo/para regt (3 cdo/para coy)

Other

1 (Presidential Guard) gd regt (1 gd bn, 1 cdo bn, 2 indep gd coy)

COMBAT SUPPORT

1 spt regt (1 fd arty bty, 2 ADA bty, 1 engr/log/tpt bn)

EQUIPMENT BY TYPE

MBT 2 T-54/T-55

LT TK 9 *Scorpion*

RECCE 61: 3 AML-60; 7 AML-90; 36 EE-9 *Cascavel*; 3 M-20; 4 M-3A1; 6 M-8; 2 VBL

AIFV 20 BMP-2

APC (W) 30 UR-416

ARTY 30

  SP 122mm 6

  TOWED 105mm 4 HM-2

  MOR 82mm 20 M-43

AT • RCL 22: **75mm** 12 Type-52 (M-20)/Type-56; **82mm** 10 Type-65 (B-10)

  GUNS 57mm 5 ZIS-2

AD • GUNS • TOWED 43 **14.5mm** 38 ZPU-4; **37mm** 5 M-1939

Navy ε200 (incl Marine Infantry unit)

EQUIPMENT BY TYPE

PATROL AND COASTAL COMBATANTS • PB 2 *Kara* (FRA *Esterel*)

Air Force 250

FORCES BY ROLE

FIGHTER/GROUND ATTACK

  1 sqn with *Alpha Jet**; EMB-326G*

TRANSPORT

  1 sqn with Beech 200 *King Air*

  1 VIP unit with DC-8; F-28-1000

TRAINING

  1 sqn with TB-30 *Epsilon**

TRANSPORT HELICOPTER

  1 sqn with SA315 *Lama*; SA316 *Alouette* III; SA319 *Alouette* III

EQUIPMENT BY TYPE†

AIRCRAFT 10 combat capable

  TPT 5 **Light** 2 Beech 200 *King Air*; **PAX** 3: 1 DC-8; 2 F-28-1000 (VIP)

  TRG 10: 3 *Alpha Jet**; 4 EMB-326G *; 3 TB-30 *Epsilon**

HELICOPTERS

  MRH 4: 2 SA315 *Lama*; 1 SA316 *Alouette* III; 1 SA319 *Alouette* III

  TPT • Medium (1 SA-330 *Puma* in store)

Paramilitary 750

Gendarmerie 750

Ministry of Interior

FORCES BY ROLE

2 reg sections

MANOEUVRE

  Other

  1 (mobile) paramilitary sqn

DEPLOYMENT

CÔTE D'IVOIRE

UN • UNOCI 525; 7 obs; 1 inf bn

LIBERIA

UN • UNMIL 1; 2 obs

SUDAN

UN • UNAMID 7 obs

Uganda UGA

Ugandan Shilling Ush		2011	2012	2013
GDP	Ush	43.96tr	51.54tr	
	US$	17.43bn	20.46bn	
per capita	US$	518	608	
Growth	%	5.10	4.19	
Inflation	%	18.68	14.58	
Def bdgt	Ush	457bn	532bn	622bn
	US$	181m	211m	
FMA (US)	US$	0.3m	0.2m	0.2m
US$1=Ush		2522.70	2518.71	

Population 33,640,833

Age	0–14	15–19	20–24	25–29	30–64	65 plus
Male	24.5%	5.8%	4.7%	3.7%	10.1%	1.0%
Female	24.6%	5.9%	4.8%	3.7%	10.2%	1.2%

Capabilities

Uganda's armed forces are relatively large and well-equipped. They have, in recent years, seen some advanced capability acquisitions, boosting military capacity, particularly in the air force. Ugandan forces have been deployed to Somalia as part of the AMISOM force since 2007, and in that time will have gained valuable combat experience in terms of planning and tactics, such as in counter-IED and urban patrolling on foot and with armour. The armed forces have a good standard of training, and the country has a number of training facilities, one of which is used by the European Union to train Somali security forces.

ACTIVE 45,000 (Ugandan People's Defence Force 45,000) **Paramilitary 1,800**

ORGANISATIONS BY SERVICE

Ugandan People's Defence Force ε40,000–45,000

FORCES BY ROLE

MANOEUVRE

  Armoured

  1 armd bde

  Light

  1 cdo bn

  5 inf div (total: 16 inf bde)

  Other

  1 (Presidential Guard) mot bde

COMBAT SUPPORT

1 arty bde
2 AD bn

EQUIPMENT BY TYPE†

MBT 195: 185 T-54/T-55; 10 T-72
LT TK ε20 PT-76
RECCE 46: 40 *Eland*; 6 *Ferret*
AIFV 31 BMP-2
APC (W) 79: 15 BTR-60; 20 *Buffel*; 40 *Mamba*; 4 OT-64
ARTY 333+
  SP 155mm 6 ATMOS 2000
  TOWED 243+: **76mm** ZIS-3; **122mm** M-30; **130mm** 221; **155mm** 4 G-5; 18 M-839
  MRL 6+: **107mm** (12-tube); **122mm** 6+: BM-21; 6 RM-70
  MOR 78+: **81mm** L16; **82mm** M-43; **120mm** 78 *Soltam*
AD • SAM • MANPAD 200+: 200 9K32 *Strela*-2 (SA-7 *Grail*)‡; 9K310 *Igla*-1 (SA-16 *Gimlet*)
  GUNS • TOWED 20+: **14.5mm** ZPU-1/ZPU-2/ZPU-4; **37mm** 20 M-1939
ARV T-54/T-55 reported
VLB MTU reported
MW *Chubby*

Air Wing

FORCES BY ROLE

FIGHTER/GROUND ATTACK
  1 sqn with MiG-21bis *Fishbed*; MiG-21U/UM *Mongol A/B*; Su-30MK2
TRANSPORT
  1 unit with Y-12
  1 VIP unit with Gulfstream 550; L-100-30
TRAINING
  1 unit with L-39 *Albatros*†*
ATTACK/TRANSPORT HELICOPTER
  1 sqn with Bell 206 *Jet Ranger*; Bell 412 *Twin Huey*; Mi-17 *Hip H*; Mi-24 *Hind*; Mi-172 (VIP)

EQUIPMENT BY TYPE

AIRCRAFT 16 combat capable
  FGA 13: 5 MiG-21bis *Fishbed*; 1 MiG-21U *Mongol A*; 1 MiG-21UM *Mongol B*; 6 Su-30MK2
  TPT 4 **Medium** 1 L-100-30; **Light** 2 Y-12; **PAX** 1 Gulfstream 550
  TRG 3 L-39 *Albatros*†*
HELICOPTERS
  ATK 1 Mi-24 *Hind* (2 more non-op)
  MRH 5: 2 Bell 412 *Twin Huey*; 3 Mi-17 *Hip H* (1 more non-op)
  TPT 4: **Medium** 1 Mi-172 (VIP); **Light** 3 Bell 206 *Jet Ranger*
MISSILE
  AAM • IR R-73 (AA-11 *Archer*); **SARH** R-27 (AA-10 *Alamo*); **ARH** (AA-12 *Adder*) (reported)
  ARM Kh-31P (AS-17A *Krypton*) (reported)

Paramilitary ε1,800 active

Border Defence Unit ε600

Equipped with small arms only

Police Air Wing ε800

HELICOPTERS • TPT • Light 1 Bell 206 *Jet Ranger*

Marines ε400

PATROL AND COASTAL COMBATANTS 8 PBR

Local Militia Forces

Amuka Group ε3,000; ε7,000 (reported under trg) (total 10,000)

DEPLOYMENT

CÔTE D'IVOIRE
UN • UNOCI 2; 5 obs

SOMALIA
AU • AMISOM 6,700; 8 inf bn

SUDAN
UN • UNAMID 1 obs

FOREIGN FORCES

(all EUTM, unless otherwise indicated)
Belgium 5
Cyprus 1
France 37
Germany 3
Hungary 4
Ireland 5
Italy 15
Kenya 12
Malta 7
Portugal 17
Spain 38
Sweden 7
UK 3

Zambia ZMB

Zambian Kwacha K		2011	2012	2013
GDP	K	93.35tr	104.44tr	
	US$	19.21bn	20.68bn	
per capita	US$	1,390	1,497	
Growth	%	6.57	6.47	
Inflation	%	8.66	6.39	
Def bdgt	K	1.49tr	1.65tr	
	US$	306m	326m	
US$1=K			4860.68	5049.63

Population   13,817,479

Age	0–14	15–19	20–24	25–29	30–64	65 plus
Male	23.2%	5.5%	4.5%	3.9%	11.8%	1.0%
Female	23.0%	5.5%	4.6%	3.9%	11.7%	1.4%

Capabilities

Territorial integrity, border security and a commitment to international peacekeeping operations are tenets of the country's military. In common with many of the armed forces of the continent, the Zambian military struggles with obsolescent equipment, limited funding, and the challenges of maintaining ageing weapons systems. The army provides forces for UN peacekeeping while the country also supports the African Standby Force. As a land-locked nation, there is no navy, though a small number of light patrol craft are retained. The air force has a very limited tactical air transport capability, but the military has no independent capacity for power projection. The services have been occasional participants in international exercises.

ACTIVE 15,100 (Army 13,500 Air 1,600) Paramilitary 1,400

RESERVE 3,000 (Army 3,000)

ORGANISATIONS BY SERVICE

Army 13,500
FORCES BY ROLE
COMMAND
3 bde HQ
SPECIAL FORCES
1 cdo bn
MANOEUVRE
Armoured
1 armd regt (1 tk bn, 1 armd recce regt)
Light
6 inf bn
COMBAT SUPPORT
1 arty regt (2 fd arty bn, 1 MRL bn)
1 engr regt
EQUIPMENT BY TYPE
Some equipment†
MBT 30: 20 Type-59; 10 T-55
LT TK 30 PT-76
RECCE 70 BRDM-1/BRDM-2 (ε30 serviceable)
APC (W) 33: 20 BTR-70; 13 BTR-60
ARTY 182
    TOWED 61: **105mm** 18 Model 56 pack howitzer; **122mm** 25 D-30; **130mm** 18 M-46
    MRL 122mm 30 BM-21 (ε12 serviceable)
    MOR 91: **81mm** 55; **82mm** 24; **120mm** 12
AT • MSL • MANPATS AT-3 9K11 Sagger
    RCL 12+: **57mm** 12 M-18; **75mm** M-20; **84mm** Carl Gustav
AD • SAM • MANPAD 9K32 Strela-2 (SA-7 Grail)‡
    GUNS • TOWED 136: **20mm** 50 M-55 (triple); **37mm** 40 M-1939; **57mm** ε30 S-60; **85mm** 16 M-1939 KS-12
ARV T-54/T-55 reported

Reserve 3,000
FORCES BY ROLE
MANOEUVRE
    Light
    3 inf bn

Air Force 1,600
FORCES BY ROLE
FIGHTER/GROUND ATTACK
1 sqn with K-8 Karakorum*

1 sqn with MiG-21MF Fishbed J†; MiG-21U Mongol A
TRANSPORT
1 sqn with MA60; Y-12(II); Y-12(IV); Y-12E
1 (VIP) unit with AW139; CL-604; HS-748
1 (liaison) sqn with Do-28
TRAINING
2 sqn with MB-326GB; MFI-15 Safari
TRANSPORT HELICOPTER
1 sqn with Mi-17 Hip H
1 (liaison) sqn with Bell 47G; Bell 205 (UH-1H Iroquois/AB-205)
AIR DEFENCE
3 bty with S-125 Pechora (SA-3 Goa)
EQUIPMENT BY TYPE†
Very low serviceability.
AIRCRAFT 25 combat capable
    FGA 10: 8 MiG-21MF Fishbed J; 2 MiG-21U Mongol A
    TPT 23: **Light** 21: 5 Do-28; 2 MA60; 4 Y-12(II); 5 Y-12(IV); 5 Y-12E; **PAX** 2: 1 Cl-604; 1 HS-748
    TRG 41: 15 K-8 Karakourm*; 10 MB-326GB; 10 MFI-15 Safari; 6 SF-260TW (being delivered)
HELICOPTERS
    MRH 5: 1 AW139; 4 Mi-17 Hip H
    TPT • Light 13: 10 Bell 205 (UH-1H Iroquois/AB-205); 3 Bell 212
    TRG 5 Bell 47G
AD • SAM S-125 Pechora (SA-3 Goa)
MSL • ASM AT-3 Sagger
AAM • IR R-3 (AA-2 Atoll)‡; PL-2; Python 3

Paramilitary 1,400

Police Mobile Unit 700
FORCES BY ROLE
MANOEUVRE
    Other
    1 police bn (4 police coy)

Police Paramilitary Unit 700
FORCES BY ROLE
MANOEUVRE
    Other
    1 paramilitary bn (3 paramilitary coy)

DEPLOYMENT

DEMOCRATIC REPUBLIC OF THE CONGO
UN • MONUSCO 17 obs

LIBERIA
UN • UNMIL 3 obs

SOUTH SUDAN
UN • UNMISS 3; 2 obs

SUDAN
UN • UNAMID 1; 3 obs
UN • UNISFA 1 obs

Zimbabwe ZWE

Zimbabwe Dollar Z$		2011	2012	2013
GDP	Z$	9.46bn	10.8bn	
	US$	9.46bn	10.8bn	
per capita	US$	750	856	
Growth	%	9.38	5.02	
Inflation	%	3.47	4.95	
Def bdgt	Z$	74.7bn	120bn	130bn
	US$	198m	318m	
US$1=Z$		376.30	376.30	

Population   12,619,600

Age	0–14	15–19	20–24	25–29	30–64	65 plus
Male	20.5%	6.1%	4.9%	4.3%	11.4%	1.5%
Female	20.1%	6.0%	5.5%	5.3%	12.2%	2.2%

Capabilities

Economic problems have, in recent years, further eroded the country's already limited military capabilities. The military's task is notionally to defend the nation's independence, sovereignty and territorial integrity, all of which would likely be beyond it in the face of a committed aggressor. A substantial force was sent to the Democratic Republic of the Congo between 1998–2002 with upward of 10,000 deployed, though whether this could now be replicated is debatable. The armed forces have taken part intermittently in multinational training exercises. China has been the source of defence equipment for the limited procurement that the country has been able to undertake. The EU and the US have an arms embargo in place.

ACTIVE 29,000 (Army 25,000 Air 4,000) **Paramilitary 21,800**

ORGANISATIONS BY SERVICE

Army ε25,000
FORCES BY ROLE
COMMAND
 1 SF bde HQ
 1 mech bde HQ
 5 inf bde HQ
MANOEUVRE
 Armoured
 1 armd sqn
 Mechanised
 1 mech inf bn
 Light
 15 inf bn
 1 cdo bn
 Air Manoeuvre
 1 para bn
 Other
 3 gd bn
 1 (Presidential Guard) gd gp

COMBAT SUPPORT
 1 arty bde
 1 fd arty regt
 1 AD regt
 2 engr regt
EQUIPMENT BY TYPE
MBT 40: 30 Type-59†; 10 Type-69†
RECCE 100: 20 Eland; 15 Ferret†; 80 EE-9 Cascavel (90mm)
APC 85
 APC (T) 30: 8 Type-63; 22 VTT-323
 APC (W) 55 TPK 4.20 VSC ACMAT
ARTY 242
 TOWED 122mm 20: 4 D-30; 16 Type-60 (D-74)
 MRL 76: **107mm** 16 Type-63; **122mm** 60 RM-70 Dana
 MOR 146: **81mm/82mm** ε140; **120mm** 6 M-43
AD • SAM • MANPAD 30 9K32 Strela-2 (SA-7 Grail) ‡
 GUNS • TOWED 116: **14.5mm** 36 ZPU-1/ZPU-2/ZPU-4; **23mm** 45 ZU-23; **37mm** 35 M-1939
ARV T-54/T-55 reported
VLB MTU reported

Air Force 4,000

Flying hours   100 hrs/year

FORCES BY ROLE
FIGHTER
 1 sqn with F-7II†; FT-7†
FIGHTER/GROUND ATTACK
 1 sqn with K-8 Karakorum*
 (1 sqn Hawker Hunter in store)
GROUND ATTACK/ISR
 1 sqn with Cessna 337/O-2A Skymaster*
ISR/TRAINING
 1 sqn with SF-260F/M; SF-260TP*; SF-260W Warrior*
TRANSPORT
 1 sqn with BN-2 Islander; CASA 212-200 Aviocar (VIP)
ATTACK/TRANSPORT HELICOPTER
 1 sqn with Mi-35 Hind; Mi-35P Hind (liaison); SA316 Alouette III; AS532UL Cougar (VIP)
 1 trg sqn with Bell 412 Twin Huey, SA316 Alouette III
AIR DEFENCE
 1 sqn

EQUIPMENT BY TYPE
AIRCRAFT 46 combat capable
 FTR 9: 7 F-7II†; 2 FT-7†
 FGA (12 Hawker Hunter in store)
 ISR 2 O-2A Skymaster
 TPT • Light 26: 5 BN-2 Islander; 8 C-212-200 Aviocar (VIP - 2 more in store); 13 Cessna 337 Skymaster*; (10 C-47 Skytrain in store)
 TRG 35: 11 K-8 Karakorum*; 5 SF-260M; 8 SF-260TP*; 5 SF-260W Warrior*; 6 SF-260F
HELICOPTERS
 ATK 6: 4 Mi-35 Hind; 2 Mi-35P Hind
 MRH 10: 8 Bell 412 Twin Huey; 2 SA316 Alouette III
 TPT • Medium 2 AS-532UL Cougar (VIP)
 MSL • AAM • IR PL-2; PL-5

AD • **GUNS 100mm** (not deployed); **37mm** (not deployed); **57mm** (not deployed)

Paramilitary 21,800

Zimbabwe Republic Police Force 19,500

incl Air Wg

Police Support Unit 2,300

PATROL AND COASTAL COMBATANTS • **PB** 5: 3 *Rodman* 38; 2 *Rodman* 46 (five *Rodman* 790 are also operated, under 10 tonnes FLD)

DEPLOYMENT

CÔTE D'IVOIRE
UN • UNOCI 2 obs

LIBERIA
UN • UNMIL 1 obs

SOUTH SUDAN
UN • UNAMID 1; 3 obs

SUDAN
UN • UNAMID 1; 2 obs

Table 23 **Selected Arms Procurements and Deliveries, Sub-Saharan Africa**

Designation	Type	Quantity	Contract Value	Prime Nationality	Prime Contractor	Order Date	First Delivery Due	Notes
Angola (ANG)								
EMB-314 *Super Tucano*	Trg ac	6	n/k	BRZ	Embraer	2012	2012	First 3 due for delivery 2012; 3 more in 2013
Botswana (BWA)								
PC-7 *Turbo Trainer Mk II*	Trg ac	5	n/k	CHE	Pilatus	2011	n/k	To replace current PC-7s. Delivery to be complete by 2013
Cameroon (CMR)								
CN-235	Tpt ac	1	n/k	Int'l	EADS (Airbus)	2012	n/k	
Equatorial Guinea (EQG)								
Barroso-class	PSO	1	n/k	BRZ	EMGEPRON	2010	n/k	Delivery status unclear
Ethiopia (ETH)								
T-72	MBT	c. 200	εUS$100m	UKR	Ukrspecexport	2011	2012	
Ghana (GHA)								
DA42 MPP	ISR ac	2	€11.75m	CAN	Diamond Aircraft	2011	n/k	
Mi-171Sh	MR hel	4	ε€64m	RUS	Rosoboronexport	2011	2012	Delivery status unclear
Kenya (KEN)								
Puma M26-15	PPV	150	US$20m	RSA	OTT Technologies	2010	2011	In service by late 2011
Mi-28NE *Havoc*	Atk hel	16	n/k	RUS	Rosoboronexport	2011	2012	First 3 of an order of 16 reported delivered Jan 2012
Mauritius (MUS)								
75m OPV	PCO	1	US$58.5m	IND	GRSE	2012	2014	Financed by $100m Indian credit line obtained in 2005
Nigeria (NGA)								
95m OPV	PSOH	2	US$42m	PRC	CSIC	2012	2015	To be armed with one 76mm gun. First to be built in China; 50% of second to be built in Nigeria. Both due for delivery 2015
OPV	PSOH	2	US$200–250m	IND	Pipavav Defence and Offshore Engineering	2012	2015	To be delivered by early 2015. Option for a further two vessels.
Andoni-class	PCC	2	n/k	NGA	Nigerian Naval Dockyard	2007	2012	Seaward Defence Boat programme. First of class commissioned May 2012. Second in build; delivery due 2013
Shaldag-class	PBF	3	N80m (US$19m)	ISR	Israel Shipyards	2012	n/k	
24m Patrol Craft	PB	3	n/k	FRA	OCEA	2012	2012	P175, P176 & P177. First vessel began sea trials Mar 2012
n/k	PB	6	N993.5m	AUS	Suncraft	2012	n/k	
South Africa (RSA)								
A-*Darter*	AAM	n/k	n/k	Int'l	Denel	2007	2013	Integration on *Gripen* completed mid-2011 following a series of test firings. Production delivery due to begin in 2013

Chapter Ten
Country comparisons – force levels and economics

Table 24 **Selected Training Activity 2012**

Date	Title	Location	Aim	Principal Participants
North America (US and Canada)				
23 Jan–02 Feb 2012	*RED FLAG 12-1*	US	Air cbt ex	KSA, ROK, US
24 Jan–13 Feb	*IRON FIST*	US	Amphib ex	JPN, US
20 Jan–12 Feb 2012	*BOLD ALLIGATOR*	US	Amphib ex	AUS, CAN, ESP, FRA, ITA, NLD, NZL, UK, US
28 Feb–16 Mar 2012	*RED FLAG 12-2*	US	Air cbt ex	AUS, UK, US
02–09 May 2012	*ARDENT SENTRY*	CAN, US	MACA CPX, FTX	CAN, US
07–22 Jun 2012	*RED FLAG ALASKA 12-2*	US	Air cbt ex	GER, JPN, POL, US
16–27 Jul 2012	*RED FLAG 12-4*	US	Air cbt ex	COL, UAE, US
01–26 Aug 2012	*NANOOK 2012*	CAN	Disaster-relief ex	CAN
02–17 Aug 2012	*RED FLAG ALASKA 12-3*	US	Air cbt ex	AUS, UK, US
03–20 Oct 2012	*RED FLAG ALASKA 13-1*	US	Air cbt ex	FIN, NATO, ROK, SGP, TUR, US
09–22 Oct 2012	*TASK GROUP EX*	CAN	Interop ex	CAN, US
24–26 Oct 2012	*n.k.*	US	Air interop ex	CHL, US
Europe				
26–27 Jan 2012	*FELLOWSHIP 2012*	Atlantic Ocean	Sub NAVEX	UK, US
14–22 Mar 2012	*COLD RESPONSE*	NOR	FTX (cold-weather trg)	BEL, CAN, FRA, NLD, NOR, SWE, UK, US
14–26 Feb 2012	*PROUD MANTA*	Ionian Sea	ASW ex	CAN, ESP, FRA, GER, GRC, ITA, NLD, NOR, TUR, UK, US
27 Mar–05 Apr 2012	*LION EFFORT*	SWE	Air Ex (*Gripen* users)	CZE, HUN, RSA, SWE, THA (obs)
06–24 Apr 2012	*BLACKSEAFOR*	Black Sea	NAVEX	ROM, TUR, UKR
12–26 Apr 2012	*JOINT WARRIOR 12-1*	UK	NAVEX	CAN, DNK, FRA, GER, NLD, NOR, UK, US
16–27 Apr 2012	*FRISIAN FLAG*	NLD	Air ex	BEL, FIN, GER, NATO, NLD, POL, SWE, UK, US
02–15 May 2012	*STEADFAST JOIST*	NOR	CPX	NATO members
07–30 May 2012	*PHOENIX EXPRESS*	GRC	NAVEX	ALG, CRO, EGY, GRC, ITA, LIB, MOR, ESP, TUN, TUR, US
19–29 May 2012	*COOPERATIVE LANCER/ COOPERATIVE LONGBOW*	FYROM	PKO ex	NATO, PfP states
26 May–10 Jun 2012	*IMMEDIATE RESPONSE*	CRO	FTX	ALB, BIH, CRO, MNE, SVN, US
29 May–08 Jun 2012	*TIGER MEET*	NOR	Air cbt ex	BEL, CHE, GER, HUN, ITA, NATO, NOR, POR, TUR, UK, US
02–22 Jun 2012	*VIKING EXPRESS*	NOR	FTX	BEL, NOR
04–23 Jun 2012	*BALTOPS*	Baltic Sea	NAVEX	EST, LTU, LVA, US
10–22 Jun 2012	*SABRE STRIKE*	LVA	Interop FTX	CAN, EST, FIN, FRA, LAT, LTU, UK, US
11–22 Jun 2012	*ANATOLIAN EAGLE 2*	TUR	Air interop ex	ESP, JOR, KSA, NATO, PAK, TUR, UAE
11–22 Jun 2012	*EUROPEAN GUARDIAN*	AUT	EDA C-IED FTX	AUT, LUX
12–26 Jun 2012	*STEADFAST COBALT*	GER	NRF Interop ex	NATO Member, PfP states
18–22 Jun 2012	*CANALE*	Mediterranean Sea	MSO, SAREX	ALG, FRA, ITA, LIB, MOR, MTA, TUN
23–30 Jun 2012	*BREEZE*	BLG	NAVEX	BLG, FRA, GER, GRC, TUR, US
05–18 Jul 2012	*HOT BLADE*	POR	EDA Hel trg ex	AUT, BEL, FIN, GER, NLD, LUX, POR, SWE, UK
09–23 Jul 2012	*SEA BREEZE*	UKR	MSO ex	ALG, AZE, BEL, CAN, GEO, GER, ISR, MOL, QTR, SWE, TUR, UAE, UKR, US
12–24 Aug 2012	*BLACKSEAFOR*	Black Sea	NAVEX	BLG, ROM, RUS, TUR, UKR
21–25 Aug 2012	*NORTHERN EAGLE*	NOR	NAVEX	NOR, RUS, US
02–30 Sep 2012	*JACKAL STONE*	CRO	SOF ex	CRO, CZE, EST, ITA, LVA, LTU, NOR, POL, ROM, SVK, US
05–21 Sep 2012	*RAMSTEIN ROVER*	CZE	NATO FAC ex	CZE, GER, SVK, TUR, US
06–20 Sep 2012	*COMBINED ENDEAVOR*	GER	C4 interop ex	NATO, PfP states
18 Sep–05 Oct 2012	*GREEN BLADE*	BEL	EDA Hel trg ex	AUT, BEL, ESP, GER, IRL, ITA, LUX
24 Sep–07 Oct 2012	*NOBLE MARINER*	Mediterranean Sea	NRF NAVEX	DNK, FRA, GER, ITA, POR, SVN, TUR, UK, US
01–09 Oct 2012	*COUGAR*	ALB	Amphib ex	ALB, FRA, UK

Table 24 **Selected Training Activity 2012**

Date	Title	Location	Aim	Principal Participants
15–26 Oct 2012	*STEADFAST NOON*	NLD	Air ex	BEL, GER, ITA, NLD, UK, US
17–26 Oct 2012	*CORSICAN LION*	Mediterranean Sea	NAVEX	FRA, UK
17–30 Oct 2012	*BOLD DRAGON*	NLD, POL	NATO JTF CPX	NATO states
01–11 Oct 2012	*JOINT WARRIOR 12-2*	UK	NAVEX	UK, US
01–08 Nov 2012	*CUTLASS EXPRESS*	Indian Ocean	Counter-piracy NAVEX	DJB, MUS, MOZ, NLD, SYC, TZA, UGA, US
01–08 Nov 2012	*STEADFAST JUNCTURE*	EST, NOR, UK	NRF CPX	NATO states
Russia and Eurasia				
09–17 May 2012	*POMOR*	RUS, NOR	NAVEX	NOR, RUS
08–14 Jun 2012	*PEACE MISSION*	TAJ	SCO CT ex	PRC, KAZ, KGZ, RUS, TAJ
25 Jun–3 Jul 2012	*FRUKUS*	RUS	MSO ex	FRA, RUS, UK, US
07–13 Jul 2012	*ALDASPAN (Scimitar)*	KAZ	CPX	KAZ, RUS
05 Sep 2012	*n.k.*	TKM	NAVEX	TKM
06–21 Sep 2012	*STEPPE EAGLE*	KAZ	PSO ex	CHE (obs), FRA (obs), GER (obs), ITA (obs), KAZ, KGZ (obs), LTU (obs), TAJ, UK, UKR (obs), US
15–19 Sep 2012	*VZAIMODEISTVIYE (Interaction)*	ARM	CSTO KSOR ex	CSTO member states
17–23 Sep 2011	*KAVKAZ (Caucasus)*	RUS	Southern MD CPX/FTX	RUS
21–29 Sep 2012	*SELENGA*	RUS	FTX	MNG, RUS
08–17 Oct 2012	*NERUSIMOYE BRATSVO (Unbreakable Brotherhood)*	KAZ	PKO ex	ARM, BEL, KAZ, KGZ, RUS, TAJ
10–12 Oct 2012	*CLEAR SKY*	KGZ, KAZ, RUS, TAJ	AD ex	KGZ, KAZ, RUS, TAJ
Asia				
06–22 Jan 2012	*THUNDER WARRIOR*	NZL	Arty ex	NZL, SGP
07–17 Feb 2012	*COBRA GOLD*	THA	PSO ex	IDN, MYS, JAP, ROK, SGP, THA, US
13–24 Feb 2012	*COPE NORTH*	Guam	Air ex	AUS, JPN, US
20 Feb–04 Mar 2012	*GARUDA SHAKTI*	IND	CT EX	IDN, IND
27 Feb–09 Mar 2012	*KEY RESOLVE*	ROK	CPX	ROK, US
27 Feb–06 Mar 2012	*MALAPURA 2012*	SGP	NAVEX	MYS, SGP
01–30 Mar 2012	*BOLD KURUKSHETRA*	IND	Armd trg ex	IND, SGP
01 Mar–30 Apr 2012	*FOAL EAGLE*	ROK	FTX	ROK, US
05–15 Mar 2012	*YUDH ABHYAS*	IND	Army FTX	IND, US
12–23 Mar 2012	*COPE TIGER (2)*	THA	Air ex	SGP, THA, US
09–16 Apr 2012	*MALABAR 2012*	IND	NAVEX	IND, US
16–27 Apr 2012	*BALIKATAN*	PHL	HADR ex	PHL, US
18 Apr–21 May 2012	*PANZER STRIKE*	GER	Armd trg ex	GER, SGP
22–28 Apr 2012	*n.k.*	PRC	NAVEX	PRC, RUS
23–26 Apr 2012	*CORPAT*	IND	NAVEX	IND, THA
23 Apr–5 May 2012	*BERSAMA SHIELD*	MAL, SGP, South China Sea	FPDA NAVEX	AUS, MYS, NZL, SGP, UK
07–16 Apr 2012	*MALABAR 12*	IND	NAVEX	IND, US
01 May–11 Aug 2012	*PACIFIC PARTNERSHIP*	CAM, IDN, PHL, VNM	Civil-assistance ex	AUS, CAN, CHL, JPN, MAL, PERU, NLD, NZL, SGP, ROK, THA
09–10 Jun 2012	*JIMEX-12*	JPN	NAVEX	IND, JPN
27 Jun–04 Aug 2012	*RIMPAC 2012*	US PACOM	Interop ex	AUS, CAN, CHL, COL, FRA, IND, JAP, MYS, MEX, NLD, NZL, PERU, PHL, ROK, RUS, SGP, THA, TONGA, UK, US
27 Jul–16 Aug 2012	*PITCH BLACK*	AUS	Air cbt ex	AUS, IDN, NZL, SGP, THA, US
12–23 Aug 2012	*KHAAN QUEST*	MNG	PKO ex	AUS, CAN, MNG, NZL, ROK, US

Table 24 **Selected Training Activity 2012**

Date	Title	Location	Aim	Principal Participants
21–31 Aug 2012	*ULCHI FREEDOM GUARDIAN*	ROK	Interop ex	ROK, US
27 Aug–03 Sep 2012	*SEACAT*	SGP	CT ex	BRN, IDN, PHL, SGP, THA, US
29 Aug–15 Sep 2012	*KAKADU*	AUS	NAVEX	AUS, BRN, JAP, NZL, SGP, THA
15 Sep–05 Oct 2012	*MATILDA*	AUS	Armd trg	AUS, SGP
17–19 Sep 2012	*SINGAROO*	AUS	NAVEX	AUS, SGP
22 Sep–24 Nov 2012	*WALLABY*	AUS	Air/land cbt ex	AUS, SGP
01–20 Oct 2023	*GROWLER*	AUS	EA air ex	AUS, US
08–18 Oct 2012	*PHIBLEX 2013*	PHL	Amphib ex	PHL, US
08–24 Oct 2012	*SUMAN PROTECTOR*	SGP	FPDA CJTF/HADR ex	AUS, MYS, NZL, SGP, UK
10–17 Oct 2012	*EXERCISE CROCODILO*	TLS	FTX	TLS, US
10–24 Oct 2012	*TIGER SHAKTI*	MYS	COIN CPX	IND, MYS
12–26 Oct 2012	*CROIX DU SUD*	New Caledonia	NEO/HADR FTX	AUS, CAN, FJI, FRA, NZL, PNG, Tonga, UK, US, Vanuatu
15–18 Oct 2012	*LION ZEAL*	NZL	Interop ex	NZL, SGP
15–19 Oct 2012	*ALBATROS AUSINDO*	AUS	Air Surv ex	AUS, IDN
16 Oct–04 Nov 2012	*DARING WARRIOR*	US	Arty ex (HIMARS)	SGP, US
05–16 Nov 2012	*KEEN SWORD*	JPN	FTX	JPN, US
30 Oct–09 Nov 2012	*ORIENT SHIELD 2012*	JPN	Armd trg	JPN, US
Middle East and North Africa				
16–29 Jan 2012	*GREEN SHIELD*	KSA	Air ex	FRA, KSA
05–09 Feb 2012	*STAKENET*	Persian Gulf	NAVEX (CTF-152)	KUW, UK, US
08–18 Apr 2012	*INITIAL LINK*	BAH	Air ex	BAH, EGY, JOR, KSA, KWT, OMN, PAK, TUR, UAE, US
17–27 Apr 2012	*AFRICAN LION*	MOR	CPX, FTX	MOR, US
Apr 2012	*n.k.*	KWT	Medevac ex	KWT, US
29–30 Apr 2012	*ISLANDS OF LOYALTY*	UAE	Interop ex (Peninsula Shield)	GCC states
02 May 2012	*GULF 2012*	UAE	FTX	FRA, UAE
April–May 2012	*ARABIAN SHARK*	Gulf of Oman	ASW ex	KSA, PAK, UK, US
15–29 May 2012	*EAGER LION*	JOR	FTX	AUS, BAH, BRN, EGY, ESP, FRA, ITA, IRQ, JOR, KSA, KUW, LEB, PAK, QTR, ROM, UAE, UK, US
22–24 May 2012	*MEDLITE*	TUN	Medical ex	TUN, US
27–30 May 2012	*PEACE SHIELD 1*	UAE	GCC Jt Ops trg	QTR, UAE
02–04 Jul 2012	*HAWKS UNION*	UAE	Air trg ex	BHR, UAE
02–04 Jul 2012	*GREAT PROPHET 7*	IRN	AD ex	IRN
15–18 Sep 2012	*MORJAN 13*	KSA	NAVEX	EGY, KSA
16–27 Sep 2012	*IMCMEX12*	Persian Gulf	Mine clearing ex	30 states incl. AUS, CAN, DJB,FRA, ITA, JAP, JOR, NOR, NZL, UK, US, YEM
25–27 Sep 2012	*SEABORDER*	ALG	MSO ex	ALG, ESP, FRA, LIB, MTA, MAU, MOR, POR, TUN
Sep 2012	*SHAHEEN STAR*	UAE	Air ex	UAE, UK
Sep 2012	*n.k.*	Persian Gulf	SAR ex	IRQ, KUW (Coast Guard), US (Coast Guard)
14–16 Oct 2012	*SWORDS OF GLORY*	BAH	MOBEX	BAH, Peninsula Shield forces
21 Oct–11 Nov 2012	*AUSTERE CHALLENGE 12*	ISR	AD Ex	ISR, US
29–31 Oct 2012	*n.k.*	IRN	Cbt readiness ex (ground/air)	IRN
13–17 Nov 2012	*n.k.*	IRN	AD ex	IRN
Latin America and the Carribean				
01–09 Mar 2012	*FUSED RESPONSE*	GUY	Interop ex	GUY, US
14–29 May 2012	*UNITAS PACIFIC*	PER	NAVEX	CHL, COL, ECU, MEX, PER, US
04–31 Jun 2012	*NEW HORIZONS*	PER	Medical ex	PER, US

Table 24 **Selected Training Activity 2012**

Date	Title	Location	Aim	Principal Participants
06–14 Jun 2012	*FUERZAS COMANDO*	COL	SOF, Police FTX	BAH, BLZ, BRZ, CAN, CHL, COL, CRI, DOM, ECU, GUA, GUY, HON, JAM, MEX, PAN, PRY, PER, SLV, TTO, US, URY
14–24 Jun 2012	*TRADEWINDS*	BRB	Interop ex	ATG, BRB, BAH, BLZ, CAN, DOM, GUY, HTI, JAM, SUR, TTO, US
06–16 Aug 2012	*PANAMAX*	PAN, US	Infrastucture-protection ex	BLZ, BRZ, CAN, CHL, COL, DOM, ECU, GUA, HND, MEX, NIC, PAN, PRY, PER, SLV, US
03–13 Sep 2012	*UNITAS PARTNERSHIP OF THE AMERICAS*	US	NAVEX	ARG, BRZ, CAN, CHL, COL, ECU, PER, PRY, URY
17–28 Sep 2012	*UNITAS ATLANTIC*	US, Caribbean Sea	NAVEX	BRZ, CAN, COL, DOM, MEX, UK, US
15–19 Oct 2012	*SOLIDARIDAD*	ARG	HADR ex	ARG, CHL
04–16 Nov 2012	*CRUZEX*	BRZ	Air CPX	ARG, BRZ, CAN, CHL, ECU, FRA, PER, SWE, UK, URY, US, VEN

Sub-Saharan Africa

Date	Title	Location	Aim	Principal Participants
07–15 Feb 2012	*ATLAS ACCORD 2012*	Mali	Logistics ex	ALG, BFA, CAN, MLI, NER, SEN, TUN, UGA, US
24–29 Feb 2012	*OBANGAME EXPRESS*	Gulf of Guinea	NAVEX	CAM, COG, GAB, EQG, ESP, GHA, NGA, STP, TGO, US
05–16 Mar 2012	*MED ACCORD CENTRAL*	GAB	Medical ex	GAB, US
05–23 Mar 2012	*EXERCISE GOOD HOPE*	RSA	NAVEX	GER, RSA
09–23 Mar 2012	*APF 12-1*	GHA	Air-mobility trg ex	BEN, GHA, NGA, SEN, TOG, US
18–27 Jun 2012	*AFRICA ENDEAVOR*	CAM	Comms interop ex	36 nations incl. BFA, CAM, CAN, EGY, ETH, GAB, GHA, LSO, MAL, MRT, NLD, SEN, UGA, US
26 Jun–19 Jul 2012	*WESTERN ACCORD*	SEN	HADR, Int, PKO, FTX	BFA, GAM, GUI, SEN, US
01–17 Aug 2012	*SOUTHERN ACCORD*	BWA	HADR/PKO ex	BWA, US
06–14 Aug 2012	*MEDLITE*	BWA	Air med evac ex	BWA, US
06–13 Sep 2012	*EASTERN ACCORD*	TZA	CT trg, FTX	ANG, BWA, RSA, ZWE
07–07 Sep 2012	*EXERCISE UHURU*	RSA	PSO CPX	BOT, MAL, RSA, ZAM (obs), ZIM (obs)
28 Sep–09 Oct 2012	*EXERCISE ATLASUR IX*	RSA	NAVEX	ARG, BRZ, URY, RSA
22–26 Oct 2012	*IBSAMAR*	RSA	NAVEX	BRZ, IND, RSA
29 Oct–09 Nov 2012	*NJIWA*	ETH	AU ASF Police/Civ ex	AU members, EU and other international reps
01–08 Nov 2012	*CUTLASS EXPRESS*	DJB, TZA	NAVEX	DJB, MUS, MOZ, SEY, TZA, UGA, US

Table 25 International Comparisons of Defence Expenditure and Military Manpower

(Current US$ m)	Defence Spending current US$ m			Defence Spending per capita US$			Defence Spending % of GDP			Number in Armed Forces (000)	Estimated Reservists (000)	Paramilitary (000)
	2010	2011	2012	2010	2011	2012	2010	2011	2012	2013	2013	2013
North America												
Canada	19,142	20,081	18,355	567	590	535	1.21	1.15	1.04	66	31	0
United States	690,900	687,000	645,700	2,241	2,205	2,057	4.76	4.56	4.12	1,520	810	0
Total	710,042	707,081	664,055	2,076	2,046	1,907	4.41	4.21	3.81	1,586	841	0
Europe												
Albania[a]	182	196	229	61	65	76	1.56	1.51	1.85	14	0	1
Austria[b]	2,687	2,843	3,160	327	346	384	0.71	0.68	0.81	23	176	0
Belgium[a]	5,246	5,521	4,771	503	529	457	1.12	1.07	1.00	33	0	1
Bosnia & Herzegovina	220	250	232	48	64	60	1.33	1.38	1.40	11	0	0
Bulgaria[a]	832	758	666	116	107	95	1.75	1.42	1.31	31	303	16
Croatia[a]	917	969	816	204	216	182	1.51	1.55	1.42	19	21	3
Cyprus	498	308	258	452	274	227	2.15	1.24	1.15	12	50	1
Czech Republic[a]	2,657	2,448	2,177	260	240	214	1.39	1.14	1.12	24	0	3
Denmark[a]	4,505	4,519	4,371	817	817	789	1.45	1.36	1.41	16	54	0
Estonia[a]	330	389	434	255	303	340	1.72	1.75	2.03	6	30	0
Finland	3,589	3,979	3,596	683	757	683	1.50	1.51	1.45	22	354	3
France[a]	51,978	53,493	48,121	803	819	733	2.03	1.93	1.86	229	30	103
Germany[a]	45,875	48,184	40,356	562	591	496	1.40	1.34	1.20	196	40	0
Greece[a]	7,913	6,431	7,616	736	598	707	2.60	2.15	2.99	144	217	4
Hungary[a]	1,349	1,381	1,029	135	138	103	1.04	0.98	0.80	27	44	12
Iceland	n.a.	n.a.	n.a.	n.a.	n.a.	n.a.	n.a.	n.a.	n.a.	0	0	0
Ireland[k]	989	963	1,131	214	206	239	0.48	0.44	0.55	9	5	0
Italy[a]	28,663	30,251	23,631	472	496	386	1.40	1.38	1.19	181	18	186
Latvia[a]	270	289	259	122	131	118	1.14	1.02	0.95	5	8	0
Lithuania[a]	334	351	322	94	99	91	0.92	0.82	0.78	12	7	12
Luxembourg[a]	266	280	258	535	556	508	0.48	0.47	0.47	1	0	1
Macedonia (FYROM)	139	134	136	67	65	65	1.52	1.26	1.33	8	5	0
Malta[k]	59	56	52	144	137	128	0.71	0.63	0.62	2	0	0
Montenegro[k]	75	52	53	112	79	80	1.86	1.15	1.22	2	0	10
Netherlands[a]	11,223	11,348	10,439	677	681	624	1.44	1.35	1.36	37	3	6

Table 25 **International Comparisons of Defence Expenditure and Military Manpower**

(Current US$ m)	Defence Spending current US$ m			Defence Spending per capita US$			Defence Spending % of GDP			Number in Armed Forces (000)	Estimated Reservists (000)	Paramilitary (000)
	2010	2011	2012	2010	2011	2012	2010	2011	2012	2013	2013	2013
Norway[a]	6,494	7,232	6,850	1,389	1,541	1,455	1.57	1.49	1.37	24	45	0
Poland[a]	8,483	8,907	8,640	221	232	225	1.81	1.73	1.84	96	0	22
Portugal[a]	3,685	3,615	2,599	343	336	241	1.61	1.52	1.23	43	212	48
Romania[a]	2,079	2,380	2,176	95	109	100	1.29	1.25	1.27	71	45	80
Serbia	844	974	820	115	133	113	2.21	2.25	2.21	28	50	0
Slovakia[a]	1,138	1,066	1,012	208	195	185	1.30	1.11	1.11	16	0	0
Slovenia[a]	772	665	568	386	333	284	1.62	1.32	1.25	8	2	5
Spain[a]	14,747	13,996	11,782	317	299	250	1.05	0.95	0.88	136	32	80
Sweden[k]	5,604	5,975	5,788	618	657	636	1.22	1.10	1.11	21	0	1
Switzerland[b]	4,111	4,944	4,759	539	630	600	0.78	0.75	0.76	23	157	0
Turkey[a]	14,082	14,467	16,954	181	184	213	1.92	1.87	2.17	511	379	102
United Kingdom[a]	60,310	63,583	64,080	967	1,014	1,016	2.68	2.62	2.63	166	81	0
Total	**293,143**	**303,197**	**280,142**	**478**	**493**	**454**	**1.63**	**1.54**	**1.52**	**2,206**	**2,367**	**699**
Russia and Eurasia												
Armenia[q]	379	396	394	128	133	133	4.05	3.86	3.73	49	210	7
Azerbaijan	1,502	1,682	1,777	161	179	187	2.76	2.59	2.50	67	300	15
Belarus	725	422	547	75	44	57	1.33	0.76	0.94	48	290	110
Georgia	374	436	405	81	95	89	3.21	3.04	2.56	21	0	12
Kazakhstan	1,481	1,804	2,273	87	104	130	1.01	0.97	1.13	39	0	32
Kyrgyzstan	23	104	106	4	19	19	0.49	1.75	1.72	11	0	10
Moldova	17	21	19	5	6	5	0.30	0.30	0.25	5	58	2
Russia[z]	41,949	51,594	59,851	468	362	420	4.41	2.79	3.06	845	20,000	519
Tajikistan	138	147	165	18	19	21	2.45	2.25	2.27	9	0	8
Turkmenistan*	200	n.k.	n.k.	41	n.k.	n.k.	1.00	n.k.	n.k.	22	0	0
Ukraine[f]	n.a.	1,666	2,057	n.a.	37	46	n.a.	1.01	1.14	130	1,000	85
Uzbekistan*	1,422	n.k.	n.k.	51	n.k.	n.k.	3.65	n.k.	n.k.	48	0	20
Total**	**49,130**	**59,901**	**69,272**	**177**	**213**	**246**	**2.50**	**2.46**	**2.67**	**1,293**	**21,857**	**818**
Asia												
Afghanistan[x]	1,374	1,822	2,092	47	61	69	8.98	9.95	10.54	191	0	150
Australia	23,634	25,444	25,093	1,098	1,169	1,140	1.92	1.71	1.63	57	23	0

Table 25 International Comparisons of Defence Expenditure and Military Manpower

(Current US$ m)	Defence Spending current US$ m			Defence Spending per capita US$			Defence Spending % of GDP			Number in Armed Forces (000)	Estimated Reservists (000)	Paramilitary (000)
	2010	2011	2012	2010	2011	2012	2010	2011	2012	2013	2013	2013
Bangladesh	1,237	1,478	1,492	8	9	9	1.18	1.30	1.26	157	0	64
Brunei	351	409	405	889	1,017	990	2.88	2.50	2.40	7	1	2
Cambodia[u]	287	309	347	20	21	23	2.55	2.40	2.44	124	0	67
China[y]	76,361	90,221	102,436	57	67	76	1.30	1.24	1.24	2,285	510	660
Fiji	25	27	26	29	31	29	0.82	0.72	0.65	4	6	0
India[k]	33,550	36,115	38,538	29	30	32	2.05	1.98	1.98	1,325	1,155	1,322
Indonesia	4,647	5,844	7,741	19	24	31	0.66	0.69	0.87	396	400	281
Japan[r]	54,357	59,834	59,443	426	469	467	1.00	1.02	0.99	247	56	13
Korea, North	n.k.	n.k.	n.k.	n.k.	n.k.	n.k.	n.k.	n.k.	n.k.	1,190	600	189
Korea, South	25,069	28,335	28,978	515	581	593	2.48	2.54	2.52	655	4,500	5
Lao PDR[d]	16	19	22	3	3	3	0.25	0.23	0.24	29	0	100
Malaysia	3,651	4,693	4,453	129	163	153	1.54	1.63	1.45	109	52	25
Mongolia[d]	55	84	90	18	27	28	0.88	0.96	0.91	10	137	7
Myanmar	1,762	2,415	2,273	33	45	42	4.91	4.69	4.21	406	0	107
Nepal	240	270	239	8	9	8	1.52	1.42	1.23	96	0	62
New Zealand	2,043	2,199	2,321	480	512	536	1.46	1.38	1.39	9	2	0
Pakistan[m]	5,599	5,468	5,878	30	29	31	3.24	2.60	2.55	642	0	304
Papua New Guinea[n]	47	77	103	8	12	16	0.50	0.61	0.67	3	0	0
Philippines[b]	2,431	2,702	2,609	24	27	25	1.22	1.20	1.08	125	131	41
Singapore	8,111	9,362	9,680	1,578	1,784	1,808	3.64	3.60	3.61	73	313	75
Sri Lanka[l]	1,529	1,684	1,464	73	79	68	3.09	2.85	2.45	161	6	62
Taiwan	8,772	9,717	10,316	381	419	444	2.03	2.08	2.21	290	1,657	17
Thailand[k]	4,807	5,522	5,503	72	83	82	1.52	1.60	1.46	361	200	114
Timor Leste	54	53	64	49	47	56	1.20	1.16	1.52	1	0	0
Vietnam	2,600	2,669	3,330	29	29	36	2.54	2.18	2.42	482	5,000	40
Total	**262,611**	**296,769**	**314,937**	**69**	**78**	**81**	**1.46**	**1.42**	**1.41**	**9,434**	**14,748**	**3,706**
Middle East and North Africa												
Algeria	5,591	8,680	9,367	162	237	251	3.59	4.39	4.54	130	150	187
Bahrain[p]	736	959	1,028	624	789	824	3.27	3.71	3.88	8	0	11

Table 25 International Comparisons of Defence Expenditure and Military Manpower

(Current US$ m)	Defence Spending current US$ m			Defence Spending per capita US$			Defence Spending % of GDP			Number in Armed Forces (000)	Estimated Reservists (000)	Paramilitary (000)
	2010	2011	2012	2010	2011	2012	2010	2011	2012	2013	2013	2013
Egypt	4,129	3,561	5,510	51	43	66	1.94	1.51	2.16	439	479	397
Iran^c	27,283	26,359	23,932	355	338	303	6.61	5.46	4.95	523	350	40
Iraq^f	n.a.	12,028	14,727	n.a.	396	473	n.a.	10.53	11.28	271	0	531
Israel	15,169	18,112	19,366	2,063	2,424	2,551	6.97	7.43	7.85	177	465	8
Jordan^h	1,425	1,669	1,750	222	256	269	5.42	5.78	5.58	101	65	10
Kuwait	4,654	4,070	4,616	1,830	1,568	1,744	3.53	2.53	2.64	16	24	7
Lebanon	1,247	1,193	1,223	302	288	296	3.20	3.06	2.93	60	0	20
Libya*	2,540	n.k.	2,971	393	n.k.	529	3.62	n.k.	3.49	n.k.	n.k.	n.k.
Mauritania*	107	n.k.	n.k.	34	n.k.	n.k.	3.02	n.k.	n.k.	16	0	5
Morocco	3,172	3,352	3,374	100	105	104	3.51	3.38	3.47	196	150	50
Oman	4,189	4,304	6,731	1,412	1,422	2,178	7.28	5.92	8.42	43	0	4
Palestinian Authority	n.k.	n.k.	n.k.	n.k.	n.k.	n.k.	n.k.	n.k.	n.k.	0	0	56
Qatar	3,117	3,457	n.k.	1,813	1,869	n.k.	2.45	1.99	1.87	12	0	16
Saudi Arabia^d	45,171	48,531	52,510	1,755	1,857	1,979	10.10	8.13	7.99	234	314	0
Syrian Arab Republic*	2,296	n.k.	n.k.	103	n.k.	n.k.	3.94	n.k.	n.k.	178	0	12
Tunisia	535	n.k.	1,224	51	n.k.	114	1.22	n.k.	2.74	36	0	0
UAE*^d	16,057	9,320	n.k.	3,227	1,810	n.k.	5.32	2.73	n.k.	51	0	0
Yemen	1,452	1,363	1,654	62	56	67	4.62	4.04	4.55	67	0	71
Total**	143,056	153,781	166,379	376	397	423	5.66	5.24	5.29	2,555	1,997	1,426
Latin America and Caribbean												
Antigua and Barbuda	5	6	7	53	67	74	0.37	0.53	0.56	0	0	0
Argentina^i	2,971	4,067	4,260	72	97	101	0.81	0.91	0.90	73	0	31
Bahamas, The	47	50	57	152	161	179	0.62	0.65	0.69	1	0	0
Barbados^f	33	30	38	117	106	132	0.82	0.70	0.84	1	0	0
Belize^j	16	16	16	52	49	50	1.16	1.10	1.07	1	1	0
Bolivia	316	298	336	32	29	33	1.64	1.24	1.26	46	0	37
Brazil^b	33,385	36,822	35,266	166	186	177	1.61	1.48	1.45	318	1,340	395
Chile^b	3,731	4,254	4,310	223	251	253	1.87	1.71	1.61	59	40	45
Colombia^g	5,324	5,626	6,164	120	126	136	1.87	1.72	1.69	281	62	159
Costa Rica	213	271	343	47	59	74	0.60	0.66	0.76	0	0	10

Table 25 **International Comparisons of Defence Expenditure and Military Manpower**

(Current US$ m)	Defence Spending current US$ m			Defence Spending per capita US$			Defence Spending % of GDP			Number in Armed Forces (000)	Estimated Reservists (000)	Paramilitary (000)
	2010	2011	2012	2010	2011	2012	2010	2011	2012	2013	2013	2013
Cuba^e	89	96	99	8	9	9	n.a.	n.a.	n.a.	49	39	27
Dominican Republic	232	230	238	23	23	24	0.45	0.41	0.40	25	0	15
Ecuador	1,512	1,506	1,509	102	100	99	2.61	2.27	2.13	58	118	1
El Salvador	135	147	145	22	24	24	0.64	0.65	0.61	15	10	17
Guatemala	156	200	206	11	14	15	0.39	0.43	0.41	17	64	25
Guyana	31	30	31	41	41	41	1.38	1.17	1.10	1	1	0
Haiti	2	2	0	0	0	0	0.02	0.02	0.00	0	0	0
Honduras^k	136	142	151	17	17	18	0.90	0.82	0.83	12	60	8
Jamaica	115	139	124	40	49	43	0.87	0.96	0.81	3	1	0
Mexico^v	5,410	5,059	5,119	48	44	45	0.52	0.44	0.44	270	87	60
Nicaragua	44	54	66	8	10	12	0.68	0.74	0.85	12	0	0
Panama^w	325	493	550	95	142	157	1.24	1.61	1.58	0	0	12
Paraguay	157	234	330	25	36	50	0.90	0.97	1.26	11	165	15
Peru	1,264	2,034	2,436	44	70	82	0.83	1.15	1.22	115	188	77
Suriname*	50	59	n.k.	91	107	n.k.	1.33	1.31	n.k.	2	0	0
Trinidad and Tobago	170	379	446	138	309	364	0.84	1.68	1.87	4	0	0
Uruguay	423	484	447	128	146	135	1.07	1.04	0.90	25	0	1
Venezuela^o	4,244	4,384	6,089	156	159	217	1.77	1.39	1.80	115	8	0
Total**	**60,534**	**67,113**	**68,848**	**103**	**115**	**116**	**1.28**	**1.20**	**1.20**	**1,515**	**2,183**	**933**
Sub-Saharan Africa												
Angola	3,719	3,628	4,092	218	207	227	4.52	3.48	3.56	107	0	10
Benin	75	74	n.k.	8	8	n.k.	1.17	1.01	n.k.	7	0	3
Botswana	620	540	468	306	261	223	4.25	3.05	2.65	9	0	2
Burkina Faso*	124	n.k.	n.k.	8	n.k.	n.k.	1.43	n.k.	n.k.	11	0	0
Burundi	56	63	64	6	6	6	3.84	2.68	2.51	20	0	31
Cameroon	339	353	n.k.	18	18	n.k.	1.54	1.38	n.k.	14	0	9
Cape Verde	8	9	n.k.	16	18	n.k.	0.49	0.48	n.k.	1	0	0
Central African Republic*	51	n.k.	n.k.	10	n.k.	n.k.	2.60	n.k.	n.k.	2	0	1
Chad*	222	n.k.	n.k.	21	n.k.	n.k.	2.65	n.k.	n.k.	25	0	10
Congo*	214	n.k.	n.k.	52	n.k.	n.k.	1.82	n.k.	n.k.	10	0	2

Table 25 International Comparisons of Defence Expenditure and Military Manpower

(Current US$ m)	Defence Spending current US$ m			Defence Spending per capita US$			Defence Spending % of GDP			Number in Armed Forces (000)	Estimated Reservists (000)	Paramilitary (000)
	2010	2011	2012	2010	2011	2012	2010	2011	2012	2013	2013	2013
Cote d'Ivoire	337	587	625	16	27	28	1.50	2.44	2.57	n.k.	n.k.	n.k.
Democratic Republic of Congo	195	221	229	3	52	52	1.51	1.41	1.29	134	0	3
Djibouti*	12	n.k.	n.k.	16	n.k.	n.k.	1.04	n.k.	n.k.	10	0	0
Equatorial Guinea*	8	8	n.k.	12	12	n.k.	0.05	0.04	n.k.	1	0	0
Eritrea*	80	n.k.	n.k.	14	n.k.	n.k.	3.69	n.k.	n.k.	202	120	0
Ethiopia	309	275	376	4	3	4	1.18	0.87	0.90	138	0	0
Gabon	246	254	n.k.	159	161	n.k.	1.91	1.59	n.k.	5	0	2
Gambia, The*	7	6	n.k.	4	4	n.k.	0.65	0.66	n.k.	1	0	0
Ghana	124	129	110	5	5	4	0.39	0.34	0.27	16	0	0
Guinea*	48	n.k.	n.k.	5	n.k.	n.k.	1.03	n.k.	n.k.	10	0	3
Guinea Bissau	25	20	25	16	13	15	3.02	2.08	2.84	4	0	2
Kenya	690	630	942	17	15	22	2.23	1.85	2.25	24	0	5
Lesotho	47	50	78	24	26	40	2.06	2.00	2.97	2	0	0
Liberia	17	20	22	5	5	6	1.69	1.29	1.26	2	0	0
Madagascar	56	72	n.k.	3	3	n.k.	0.64	0.73	n.k.	14	0	8
Malawi	325	43	34	21	3	2	6.13	0.76	0.75	5	0	2
Mali	205	226	n.k.	15	15	n.k.	2.22	2.13	n.k.	7	0	5
Mauritius	34	62	74	26	47	56	0.36	0.55	0.62	0	0	3
Mozambique*	61	n.k.	n.k.	3	n.k	n.k.	0.64	n.k.	n.k.	11	0	0
Namibia	343	421	381	161	196	176	3.03	3.36	3.14	9	0	6
Niger*	46	50	n.k.	3	3	n.k.	0.86	0.82	n.k.	5	0	5
Nigeria	1,520	2,251	2,043	9	14	12	0.76	0.92	0.75	80	0	82
Rwanda	74	74	73	7	6	6	1.34	1.17	1.06	33	0	2
Senegal*	172	210	n.k.	14	17	n.k.	1.36	1.45	n.k.	14	0	5
Seychelles[d]	22	24	21	244	264	231	2.54	2.32	2.14	0	0	0
Sierra Leone	12	12	13	2	2	2	0.66	0.43	0.33	11	0	0
Somalia	n.a	n.a	n.a	n.a	n.a	n.a	n.a	n.a	n.a	3	0	0
South Africa	4,265	5,291	5,076	87	108	104	1.18	1.29	1.30	62	0	16
South Sudan	469	355	537	n.a.	35	51	n.a.	2.03	4.69	210	0	0
Sudan	1,082	1,163	n.k.	25	35	n.k.	1.65	1.82	n.k.	244	0	20

Country

Table 25 International Comparisons of Defence Expenditure and Military Manpower

(Current US$ m)	Defence Spending current US$ m			Defence Spending per capita US$			Defence Spending % of GDP			Number in Armed Forces (000)	Estimated Reservists (000)	Paramilitary (000)
	2010	2011	2012	2010	2011	2012	2010	2011	2012	2013	2013	2013
Tanzania	218	285	260	5	6	6	1.06	1.19	0.93	27	80	1
Togo	56	59	n.k.	8	9	n.k.	1.79	1.60	n.k.	9	0	1
Uganda	212	182	212	6	6	6	1.35	1.04	1.03	45	0	2
Zambia	251	306	326	19	23	24	1.57	1.59	1.58	15	3	1
Zimbabwe	199	198	318	17	16	25	2.66	2.10	2.95	29	0	22
Total**	17,194	18,902	19,162	20	22	21	1.57	1.46	1.44	1,590	203	261
Summary												
North America	710,042	707,081	664,055	2,076	2,046	1,907	4.41	4.21	3.81	1,586	841	0
Europe	293,143	303,197	280,142	478	493	454	1.63	1.54	1.52	2,206	2,367	699
Russia and Eurasia	49,130	59,901	69,272	177	213	246	2.50	2.46	2.67	1,293	20,000	519
Asia	262,611	296,769	314,937	69	78	81	1.46	1.42	1.41	9,434	14,748	3,706
Middle East and North Africa	143,056	153,781	166,379	376	397	423	5.66	5.24	5.29	2,555	1,997	1,426
Latin America & The Carribean	60,534	67,113	68,848	103	115	116	1.28	1.20	1.20	1,515	2,183	933
Sub-Saharan Africa	17,194	18,902	19,162	20	22	21	1.57	1.46	1.44	1,590	203	261
Global totals	1,535,710	1,606,744	1,582,794	224	232	226	2.46	2.31	2.23	21,767	42,542	7,805

* Estimates

** Totals include defence spending estimates for states where insufficient official information is available, in order to enable approximate comparisons of regional defence spending between years.

a NATO definition used for 2010 and 2011 figures. As 2012 NATO figures were unavailable at time of printing, official defence budget figures for 2012 have been used instead. Caution should thus be exercised when comparing 2012 figures against those of previous years.

b Includes military pensions

c 2011 figure an estimate

d 2012 figure an estimate

e Defence & internal order

f Defence & security expenditure. Comparable figures for 2010 unavailable.

g Excludes decentralised expenditures & expenditure on National Police

h Excludes expenditure on public order and safety

i Excludes funds allocated to Interior Security

j Excludes funds allocated to Coast Guard

k Excludes military pensions

l Includes all funds allocated to the Ministry of Defence & Urban Development except those disbursed to the following departments: Police, Immigration & Emigration, Registration of Persons, Coast Conservation and Civil Security.

m Includes budget for Ministry of Defence Production

n Includes defence allocations to the Public Sector Development Programme (PSDP), including funding to the Defence Division and the Defence Production Division.

o Includes estimated value of Russian credit provided for arms procurement, excludes defence funding derived from the National Development Fund (FONDEN). Current US dollar defence spending figures should be treated with caution when compared to spending in previous years, due to effects of currency revaluation in recent years.

p Includes expenditure on National Guard. Excludes arms purchases

q Includes imported military equipment, excludes military pensions

r Includes military pensions, excludes expenditure on US military realignment and SACO-related projects

s Includes military pensions. Excludes Non-MoD Elements of Turkish defence spending, on procurement, the gendarmerie and coast guard.

t Includes military pensions. Net Cash Requirement figures. These will differ from official figures based on Resource Accounting & Budgeting.

u Includes public security expenditure disbursed by the Ministry of Interior. Excludes defence capital expenditure.

w National security expenditure

w Public security expenditure

x Security expenditure. Includes expenditure on Ministry of Defence, Ministry of Interior, Ministry of Foreign Affairs, National Security Council and the General Directorate of National Security. Includes US DoD funds to Afghan Ministry of Defence & Ministry of Interior.

y Includes official central government expenditure only. See page 256 for 2010 & 2011 defence expenditure estimates.

z 'Official Budget' only at market exchange rates - excludes extra-budgetary funds

Table 26 **Arms Deliveries to Developing Nations** Leading Recipients in 2011

(current US$m)	
1 Saudi Arabia	2,800
2 India	2,700
3 Pakistan	1,800
4 UAE	1,700
5 Venezuela	1,700
6 China	1,500
7 Taiwan	1,300
8 Egypt	1,300
9 Morocco	1,300
10 Algeria	1,000

Table 27 **Arms Transfer Agreements with Developing Nations** Leading Recipients in 2011

(current US$m)	
1 Saudi Arabia	33,700
2 India	6,900
3 UAE	4,500
4 Israel	4,100
5 Indonesia	2,100
6 China	1,900
7 Taiwan	1,600
8 Egypt	1,500
9 Oman	1,500
10 Algeria	1,100

Table 28 **Global Arms Deliveries** Leading Suppliers in 2011

(current US$m)	
1 United States	16,160
2 Russia	8,700
3 UK	3,000
4 Israel	1,800
5 France	1,700
6 Italy	1,700
7 Germany	1,600
8 Spain	1,500
9 China	1,300
10 Sweden	1,200
11 Canada	1,000

Table 29 **Global Arms Transfer Agreements** Leading Suppliers in 2011

(current US$m)	
1 United States	66,274
2 Russia	4,800
3 France	4,400
4 China	2,100
5 South Korea	1,500
6 Italy	1,200
7 Ukraine	1,100
8 Turkey	800
9 Spain	500
10 UK	400
11 Israel	400

Table 30 **Value of Global Arms Transfer Agreements and Market Share by Supplier, 2004–11** (constant 2011US$m – % *in italics*)

	Total	Russia		US		UK		France		Germany		Italy		All Other European		China		Others	
2004	51,054	10,629	*20.82*	14,939	*29.26*	5,073	*9.94*	3,503	*6.86*	4,952	*9.7*	483	*0.95*	6,281	*12.3*	1,208	*2.37*	3,986	*7.81*
2005	52,338	9,727	*18.58*	14,010	*26.77*	3,358	*6.42*	7,295	*13.94*	2,316	*4.42*	1,737	*3.32*	8,569	*16.37*	3,126	*5.97*	2,200	*4.2*
2006	64,505	17,236	*26.72*	17,275	*26.78*	4,589	*7.11*	8,618	*13.36*	3,134	*4.86*	1,343	*2.08*	6,267	*9.72*	2,238	*3.47*	3,805	*5.9*
2007	66,338	11,312	*17.05*	25,768	*38.84*	10,333	*15.58*	2,393	*3.61*	1,958	*2.95*	1,523	*2.3*	7,287	*10.99*	2,719	*4.1*	3,045	*4.59*
2008	70,567	6,939	*9.83*	38,187	*54.11*	315	*0.45*	3,995	*5.66*	5,782	*8.19*	4,310	*6.11*	5,572	*7.9*	2,208	*3.13*	3,259	*4.62*
2009	67,765	13,760	*20.3*	22,762	*33.59*	1,448	*2.14*	9,932	*14.66*	3,724	*5.5*	1,655	*2.44*	6,725	*9.92*	2,586	*3.82*	5,173	*7.63*
2010	44,508	8,921	*20.04*	21,394	*48.07*	1,521	*3.42*	1,825	*4.1*	101	*0.23*	1,926	*4.33*	4,258	*9.57*	1,622	*3.64*	2,940	*6.61*
2011	85,274	4,800	*5.63*	66,274	*77.72*	400	*0.47*	4,400	*5.16*	100	*0.12*	1,200	*1.41*	3,300	*3.87*	2,100	*2.46*	2,700	*3.17*

Table 31 **Value of Global Arms Deliveries and Market Share by Supplier, 2004–11** (constant 2011US$m – % *in italics*)

	Total	Russia		US		UK		France		Germany		Italy		All Other European		China		Others	
2004	41,805	6,764	*16.18*	14,023	*33.55*	3,865	*9.25*	6,764	*16.18*	2,416	*5.78*	242	*0.58*	2,899	*6.93*	1,087	*2.6*	3,744	*8.96*
2005	36,898	4,516	*12.24*	13,623	*36.92*	4,284	*11.61*	3,126	*8.47*	2,200	*5.96*	1,158	*3.14*	3,590	*9.73*	1,158	*3.14*	3,242	*8.79*
2006	39,286	7,051	*17.95*	13,768	*35.05*	5,484	*13.96*	2,015	*5.13*	2,686	*6.84*	448	*1.14*	3,693	*9.4*	1,679	*4.27*	2,462	*6.27*
2007	37,848	5,656	*14.94*	13,375	*35.34*	2,393	*6.32*	2,719	*7.18*	3,263	*8.62*	761	*2.01*	4,351	*11.5*	1,849	*4.89*	3,481	*9.2*
2008	40,073	6,939	*17.32*	12,528	*31.26*	2,418	*6.03*	1,892	*4.72*	3,890	*9.71*	841	*2.1*	5,887	*14.69*	2,313	*5.77*	3,364	*8.4*
2009	41,403	5,794	*13.99*	14,711	*35.53*	2,586	*6.25*	1,345	*3.25*	3,104	*7.5*	828	*2*	6,311	*15.24*	1,759	*4.25*	4,966	*11.99*
2010	41,234	6,995	*16.96*	12,138	*29.44*	2,839	*6.88*	1,723	*4.18*	2,534	*6.15*	1,217	*2.95*	5,779	*14.01*	2,940	*7.13*	5,069	*12.29*
2011	44,260	8,700	*19.66*	16,160	*36.51*	3,000	*6.78*	1,700	*3.84*	1,600	*3.62*	1,700	*3.84*	6,200	*14.01*	1,300	*2.94*	3,900	*8.81*

US DoD Price Deflator. All data rounded to nearest $100m. Source: Richard F. Grimmett, *Conventional Arms Transfers to Developing Nations 2004–2011* (Washington DC: Congressional Research Service)

Table 32 Arms Deliveries to Middle East and North Africa by Supplier, 2004–11

(current US$m)

2004–07	US	Russia	China	Major West European*	All other European	Others	Total
Algeria		900	200				1,100
Bahrain	200			100			300
Egypt	5,700	300	400	-	400		6,800
Iran		500	200		-	200	900
Iraq	200	100	-	100	300	100	800
Israel	5,700	100			-		5,800
Jordan	600	100			-	-	700
Kuwait	1,500		-				1,500
Lebanon							-
Libya		200			200		400
Morocco	100	100		-		100	300
Oman	700			300			1,000
Qatar							-
Saudi Arabia	4,300	-	200	9,900	100	100	14,600
Syria		500	300			300	1,100
Tunisia							-
UAE	600	200		4,000	400		5,200
Yemen		400			100	100	600

2008–2011	US	Russia	China	Major West European*	All other European	Others	Total
Algeria		4,700	400	300			5,400
Bahrain							-
Egypt	3,900	300	400		200		4,800
Iran		200			-	-	200
Iraq	2,600	300		300	100	100	3,400
Israel	3,800	200			-		4,000
Jordan	900	100	100		300	-	1,400
Kuwait	1,300	100	100				1,500
Lebanon	200					100	300
Libya		100		300	-		400
Morocco	1,000	-	500	200	400	-	2,100
Oman	200			500			700
Qatar				200			200
Saudi Arabia	5,900		700	3,300	300	-	10,200
Syria	-	2,000	400		100	200	2,700
Tunisia							-
UAE	2,000	300	100	600	300		3,300
Yemen		100			200	100	400

* Major Western European includes, France, Germany, Italy, UK

All data rounded to nearest $100m

Source: Richard F. Grimmett, *Conventional Arms Transfers to Developing Nations 2004-2011*
(Washington DC: Congressional Research Service)

PART TWO
Explanatory Notes

The Military Balance is updated each year to provide an accurate assessment of the military forces and defence expenditures of 171 countries and territories. Each edition contributes to the provision of a unique compilation of data and information, enabling the reader to discern trends through the examination of editions as far back as 1959. The data in the current edition are accurate according to IISS assessments as at November 2012, unless specified. Inclusion of a territory, country or state in *The Military Balance* does not imply legal recognition or indicate support for any government.

GENERAL ARRANGEMENT AND CONTENTS

The Editor's Foreword contains a summary of the book and general comment on defence matters.

Part I of *The Military Balance* comprises the regional trends, military capabilities and defence economics data for countries grouped by region. Thus, North America includes the US and Canada. Regional groupings are preceded by a short introduction describing the military issues facing the region. Essays at the front of the book analyse important defence trends or debates. Tables analyse aspects of defence activity including salient comparative analyses, selected major training exercises, international defence expenditure and the international arms trade.

Part II comprises reference material.

Maps include selected deployments in Afghanistan, the war in Syria, military dispositions in Russia's Southern Military District, and competing claims in the South China Sea.

The loose Chart of Conflict is updated for 2012 to show data on recent and current armed conflicts.

USING THE MILITARY BALANCE

The country entries in *The Military Balance* are an assessment of the personnel strengths and equipment holdings of the world's armed forces. Qualitative assessment is enabled by relating data, both quantitative and economic, to textual comment, as well as through close reference to qualitative judgements applied to inventory data. The strengths of forces and the numbers of weapons held are based on the most accurate data available or, failing that, on the best estimate that can be made. In estimating a country's total capabilities, old equipment may be counted where it is considered that it may still be deployable.

The data presented each year reflect judgements based on information available to the IISS at the time the book is compiled. Where information differs from previous editions, this is mainly because of changes in national forces, but it is sometimes because the IISS has reassessed the evidence supporting past entries. Given this, care must be taken in constructing time-series comparisons from information given in successive editions.

ABBREVIATIONS AND DEFINITIONS

The large quantity of data in *The Military Balance* has been compressed into a portable volume by the extensive employment of abbreviations. An essential tool is therefore the list of abbreviations for data sections, which appears on page 567. The abbreviations may be either singular or plural; for example, 'elm' means 'element' or 'elements'. The qualification 'some' is used to indicate that while the IISS assesses that a country maintains a capability, a precise inventory is unavailable at time of press. 'About' means the total could be higher than given. In financial data, '$' refers to US dollars unless otherwise stated; billion (bn) signifies 1,000 million (m).

Within the country entries, a number of caveats are employed to aid the reader in assessing military capabilities. The * symbol is used to denote aircraft counted by the IISS as combat capable (see 'Air Forces', below); † is used when the IISS assesses that the serviceability of equipment is in doubt; and ‡ is used to denote equipment judged obsolescent (weapons whose basic design is more than four decades old and which have not been significantly upgraded within the past decade); these latter two qualitative judgements should not be taken to imply that such equipment cannot be used.

COUNTRY ENTRIES

Information on each country is shown in a standard format, although the differing availability of information and differences in nomenclature result in some variations. Country entries include economic, demographic and military data. Population figures are based on demographic statistics taken from the US Census Bureau. Data on

Reference

ethnic and religious minorities are also provided in some country entries. Military data include manpower, length of conscript service where relevant, outline organisation, number of formations and units, and an inventory of the major equipment of each service. Details of national forces stationed abroad and of foreign forces stationed within the given country are also provided.

ARMS PROCUREMENTS AND DELIVERIES

Tables at the end of the regional texts show selected arms procurements (contracts and, in selected cases, major development programmes that may not yet be at contract stage) and deliveries listed by country buyer, together with additional information including, if known, the country supplier, cost, prime contractor and the date on which the first delivery was due to be made. While every effort has been made to ensure accuracy, some transactions may not be fulfilled or may differ – for instance in quantity – from those reported. The information is arranged in the following order: land; sea; air.

DEFENCE ECONOMICS

Country entries include defence expenditures, selected economic performance indicators and demographic aggregates. There are also international comparisons of defence expenditure and military manpower, giving expenditure figures for the past three years in per capita terms and as a % of GDP. The aim is to provide an accurate measure of military expenditure and the allocation of economic resources to defence. All country entries are subject to revision each year as new information, particularly regarding defence expenditure, becomes available. The information is necessarily selective.

Individual country entries show economic performance over the past two years, and current demographic data. Where these data are unavailable, information from the last available year is provided. Where possible, official defence budgets for the current and previous two years are shown, as well as an estimate of actual defence expenditures for those countries where true defence expenditure is thought to be higher than official budget figures suggest. Estimates of actual defence expenditure, however, are only made for those countries where there are sufficient data to justify such a measurement. Therefore, there will be several countries listed in *The Military Balance* for which only an official defence budget figure is provided but where, in reality, true defence-related expenditure is almost certainly higher.

All financial data in the country entries are shown both in national currency and US dollars at current year – not constant – prices. US-dollar conversions are generally, but not invariably, calculated from the exchange rates listed

in the entry. In some cases a US-dollar purchasing power parity (PPP) rate is used in preference to official or market exchange rates and this is indicated in each case.

Definitions of terms

Despite efforts by NATO and the UN to develop a standardised definition of military expenditure, many countries prefer to use their own definitions (which are often not made public). In order to present a comprehensive picture, *The Military Balance* lists three different measures of military-related spending data.

- For most countries, an official defence-budget figure is provided.
- For those countries where other military-related outlays, over and above the defence budget, are known or can be reasonably estimated, an additional measurement referred to as defence expenditure is also provided. Defence expenditure figures will naturally be higher than official budget figures, depending on the range of additional factors included.
- For NATO countries, an official defence-budget figure as well as a measure of defence expenditure (calculated using NATO's definition) is quoted.

NATO's definition of military expenditure, the most comprehensive, is defined as the cash outlays of central or federal governments to meet the costs of national armed forces. The term 'armed forces' includes strategic, land, naval, air, command, administration and support forces. It also includes other forces if these forces are trained, structured and equipped to support defence forces and are realistically deployable. Defence expenditures are reported in four categories: Operating Costs, Procurement and Construction, Research and Development (R&D) and Other Expenditure. Operating Costs include salaries and pensions for military and civilian personnel; the cost of maintaining and training units, service organisations, headquarters and support elements; and the cost of servicing and repairing military equipment and infrastructure. Procurement and Construction expenditure covers national equipment and infrastructure spending, as well as common infrastructure programmes. R&D is defence expenditure up to the point at which new equipment can be put in service, regardless of whether new equipment is actually procured. Foreign Military Aid (FMA) contributions are also noted.

For many non-NATO countries the issue of transparency in reporting military budgets is fundamental. Not every UN member state reports defence-budget data (even fewer real defence expenditures) to their electorates, the

UN, the IMF or other multinational organisations. In the case of governments with a proven record of transparency, official figures generally conform to the standardised definition of defence budgeting, as adopted by the UN, and consistency problems are not usually a major issue. The IISS cites official defence budgets as reported by either national governments, the UN, the OSCE or the IMF.

For those countries where the official defence-budget figure is considered to be an incomplete measure of total military-related spending, and appropriate additional data are available, the IISS will use data from a variety of sources to arrive at a more accurate estimate of true defence expenditure. The most frequent instances of budgetary manipulation or falsification typically involve equipment procurement, R&D, defence-industrial investment, covert weapons programmes, pensions for retired military and civilian personnel, paramilitary forces and non-budgetary sources of revenue for the military arising from ownership of industrial, property and land assets.

Percentage changes in defence spending are referred to in either nominal or real terms. Nominal terms relate to the percentage change in numerical spending figures, and do not account for the impact of price changes (i.e. inflation) on defence spending. By contrast, real terms account for inflationary effects, and may thus be considered a more accurate representation of change over time.

The principal sources for national economic statistics cited in the country entries are the IMF, the Organisation for Economic Cooperation and Development (OECD), the World Bank and three regional banks (the Inter-American, Asian and African Development Banks). For some countries, basic economic data are difficult to obtain. The Gross Domestic Product (GDP) figures are nominal (current) values at market prices. GDP growth is real, not nominal, growth, and inflation is the year-on-year change in consumer prices. Dollar exchange rates are annual averages for the year indicated, except 2011 where the average exchange rate from 1 January to 1 November is used.

Calculating exchange rates

Typically, but not invariably, the exchange rates shown in the country entries are also used to calculate GDP and defence budget and expenditure dollar conversions. Where they are not used, it is because the use of exchange rate dollar conversions can misrepresent both GDP and defence expenditure. For some countries, PPP rather than market exchange rates are sometimes used for dollar conversions of both GDP and defence expenditures. Where PPP is used, it is annotated accordingly.

The arguments for using PPP are strongest for Russia and China. Both the UN and IMF have issued caveats concerning the reliability of official economic statistics on transitional economies, particularly those of Russia,

some Eastern European and Central Asian countries. Non-reporting, lags in the publication of current statistics and frequent revisions of recent data (not always accompanied by timely revision of previously published figures in the same series) pose transparency and consistency problems. Another problem arises with certain transitional economies whose productive capabilities are similar to those of developed economies, but where cost and price structures are often much lower than world levels. No specific PPP rate exists for the military sector, and its use for this purpose should be treated with caution. Furthermore, there is no definitive guide as to which elements of military spending should be calculated using the limited PPP rates available. The figures presented here are only intended to illustrate a range of possible outcomes depending on which input variables are used.

Arms trade

The source for data on the global and regional arms trade is the US Congressional Research Service (CRS). It is accepted that these data may vary in some cases from national declarations of defence exports, which is due, in part, to differences in the publication times of the various sets of data and national definitions of military-related equipment.

GENERAL DEFENCE DATA

Manpower

The 'Active' total comprises all servicemen and women on full-time duty (including conscripts and long-term assignments from the Reserves). When a gendarmerie or equivalent is under control of the MoD, they may be included in the active total. Under the heading 'Terms of Service', only the length of conscript service is shown; where service is voluntary there is no entry. 'Reserve' describes formations and units not fully manned or operational in peacetime, but which can be mobilised by recalling reservists in an emergency. Unless otherwise indicated, the 'Reserves' entry includes all reservists committed to rejoining the armed forces in an emergency, except when national reserve service obligations following conscription last almost a lifetime. Some countries have more than one category of 'Reserves', often kept at varying degrees of readiness. Where possible, these differences are denoted using the national descriptive title, but always under the heading of 'Reserves' to distinguish them from full-time active forces. All manpower figures are rounded to the nearest 50 personnel, except for organisations with under 500 personnel, where figures are rounded to the nearest 10.

Other forces

Many countries maintain forces whose training, organisation, equipment and control suggest they may be used to

Reference

support or replace regular military forces; these are called 'paramilitary' in this volume. They include some forces, for instance in the maritime domain, which may have a constabulary role. These are detailed after the military forces of each country, but their manpower is not normally included in the Armed Forces totals at the start of each entry. Home Guard units are counted as paramilitary.

Non-state groups

The Military Balance includes detail on selected non-state groups that pose a militarily significant challenge to state and international security. This information appears in the essays and relevant regional chapters. Non-subscribers can purchase the list online. Further detailed information may be obtained from the IISS Transnational Threats and Political Risk programme *(www.iiss.org/research)* and the Armed Conflict Database *(http://www.iiss.org/acd)*.

Cyber

Each year, *The Military Balance* includes increasing detail on selected national cyber capacities, particularly those under the control of, or designed to fulfil the requirements of, defence organisations. Capabilities are not assessed by reference to equipment numbers. Rather, national organisations, legislation, national security strategies etc. are noted, where appropriate, in an indication of the level of effort states are directing in this area. Generally, civil organisations are not traced here, though in some cases these organisations could be established with dual civil–

Units and formation strength

Company	100–200
Battalion	500–1,000
Brigade	3,000–5,000
Division	15,000–20,000
Corps or Army	50,000–100,000

military roles. Moreover, it should be assumed that any state with a modern telecommunications infrastructure has the ability to engage in – at the very minimum – monitoring of telecommunications or cyber traffic.

Forces by role and equipment by type

Quantities are shown by function (according to each nation's employment) and type, and represent what are believed to be total holdings, including active and reserve operational and training units. Inventory totals for missile systems – such as surface-to-surface missiles (SSM), surface-to-air missiles (SAM) and anti-tank guided weapons (ATGW) – relate to launchers and not to missiles. Equipment held 'in store' – that is, held in reserve and not assigned to either active or reserve units – is not counted in the main inventory totals. However, aircraft in excess of unit establishment holdings, held to allow for repair and modification or immediate replacement, are not shown 'in store'.

Land force organisation

A typical land force organisation could be (in order of decreasing size): army group; army or corps; division; brigade; unit and sub-unit.

Formations: These normally consist of varying combinations of units of several arms and services. Several brigades (groups of several combat units and dedicated command, CS and CSS elements) may combine into a division, several divisions into a corps or army, and several corps or armies into an army group.

Battalion: The smallest grouping capable of independent operations. Battalions typically contain integral combat command support, combat service support and limited combat support. The majority of personnel are of one arm or service.

Company: A subdivision of a battalion, which normally has 3–5 companies. Companies are normally subdivided further into platoons, of between about 12 and about 35 soldiers, which are then organised as vehicle crews and/or dismountable sections or squads.

National variations of terminology: The manpower strength, equipment holdings and organisation of formations such as brigades and divisions vary from country to country. For instance, some armies use the term 'regiment' to mean brigade-sized groupings of several battalions, usually with integral combat support and combat service support, while in others the term regiment is used for battalion-sized units; 'squadron' can be used as an alternative term for company; 'battery' is often used by artillery units; and 'troop' is sometimes used when referring to platoons.

Principal Land force definitions

The Military Balance *translates national military terminology for unit and formation sizes so that, for example the 'kandaks'* *of the Afghan National Army are shown as 'battalions'. National designations, however, are used where possible: for example* *'motor rifle' and 'armoured cavalry'.* The Military Balance *categorises forces by role, to make comparison of forces easier and* *more consistent.*

Forces by role

Command: it is assumed that all combined arms formations and single arms units have an integral HQ with a communication capability. Free-standing formation HQs and signals units/formations are detailed.

Special Forces (SF): SF are elite forces specially trained and equipped for unconventional warfare and operations in enemy-controlled battlespace. Many are employed in counter-terrorist roles.

Manoeuvre: combat units and formations capable of maneouvering include:

Reconnaissance: combat units and formations whose primary purpose is to gain information.

Armoured: armoured formations use Armoured Fighting Vehicles (AFVs) to provide mounted close combat capability. These usually provide the most effective opposition to other armoured forces. Armoured forces' utility can be restricted in complex and difficult terrain. Their principal weapon is the main battle tank (MBT) and they present the greatest logistic and deployment challenges.

Mechanised: mechanised formations also use armoured vehicles, but in lighter combinations, with more medium and light armoured vehicles than armoured formations, and with fewer, if any, tanks. They have less mounted firepower and protection, but can usually deploy more infantry than armoured formations. They are more deployable than armoured forces over operational and strategic distances.

Light: the principal weapon of light formations is dismounted infantry. Light formations may have few, if any, organic armoured vehicles. This reduces tactical mobility in open country, but they can move through and occupy complex and difficult terrain that armoured and mechanised forces can only penetrate with difficulty. Light forces are air-portable, aiding operational and strategic mobility. Their organic firepower is limited compared to armoured or mechanised forces and they protect themselves by dispersion, concealment or fortification. They have little capacity for manoeuvre in contact with the enemy. Some armies have 'motorised' light forces by equipping them with soft-skinned vehicles. As these cannot conduct mounted manoeuvre in contact with the enemy, they are still classified as light forces.

Air Manoeuvre: national designations may be inconsistent but usually 'airborne' and 'parachute' formations are optimised for delivery by transport aircraft, including by parachute, whilst 'airmobile' and 'air assault' formations are optimised for delivery by transport helicopters. Some formations may be capable of both roles and may or may not have integral aviation. Once delivered by air, they exhibit the strengths and weaknesses of light forces.

Aviation: organic army units and formations equipped with helicopters and/or fixed-wing aircraft.

Amphibious: amphibious forces are trained and equipped to land from the sea, and may also be capable of ship-to-shore movement by helicopter.

Mountain: formations and units trained and equipped to operate in mountainous terrain.

Other Forces: other categories for manoeuvre forces exist. For example, specifically trained and equipped 'jungle' or 'counter-insurgency' brigades found in some Latin American states. Also, security units such as 'Presidential Guards' and deployable manoeuvre units or formations permanently employed in training or demonstration tasks.

Combat Support (CS): CS supports combat units and formations to enable them to fight and manoeuvre. This includes artillery, engineers, air defence, intelligence, EOD and other CS not integral to manoeuvre formations.

Combat Service Support (CSS): CSS includes logistic, maintenance, medical, personnel administration capabilities and provision and maintenance of water, rations, power and supply routes. Combat support and combat service support organic to formations is shown with those formations. For example, brigade supply and maintenance battalions would be listed as part of the brigade.

Equipment by type

Definitions of land weapons and equipment have been revised. Weapon and armoured-vehicle categories remain based on those used in the Conventional Forces in Europe Treaty, but categories have been added and revised to reflect new developments in armoured vehicles. The considerable diversity of armies and their role, as well as the large number of irregular forces, make it impossible to apply obsolescence criteria to land equipment.

Light Weapons: light weapons include all small arms, machine guns, grenades and grenade launchers and unguided man-portable anti-armour and support weapons, such as the ubiquitous RPG. These weapons have proliferated so much and are sufficiently easy to manufacture or copy that listing them would be impracticable. It should be assumed that all soldiers and officers carry a personal small arm.

Crew Served Weapons: crew-served recoilless rifles, man-portable ATGW, MANPADS and mortars of greater than 80mm calibre are listed, but the high degree of proliferation and local manufacture of many of these weapons means that estimates of numbers held may not be reliable.

Armored Fighting Vehicles (AFVs):

Main Battle Tank (MBT): armoured, tracked combat vehicles, weighing at least 16.5 metric tonnes unladen, that may be armed with a turret-mounted gun of at least 75mm calibre. Wheeled combat vehicles that meet the latter two criteria are considered MBTs.

Reconnaissance: combat vehicles designed and equipped to facilitate reconniassance operations. Some reconnaissance vehicles are unarmoured.

Armoured Infantry Fighting Vehicle (AIFV): armoured combat vehicles designed and equipped to transport an infantry squad, armed with an integral/organic cannon of at least 20mm calibre.

Armoured Personnel Carrier (APC): lightly armoured combat vehicles designed and equipped to transport an infantry squad and armed with integral/organic weapons of less than 20mm calibre.

Protected Patrol Vehicle (PPV): role-specific armoured vehicles designed to protect troops from small arms, RPG and roadside bomb threats. Most have little or no cross-country mobility and are not designed for combined-arms manoeuvre. Protection levels and weights can vary.

Artillery: weapons (including guns, howitzers, gun/howitzers, multiple-rocket launchers, mortars and gun/mortars) with a calibre greater than 100mm for artillery pieces and 80mm and above for mortars, capable of engaging ground targets with indirect fire.

Anti-Tank (AT): guns, guided weapons and recoilless rifles designed to engage armoured vehicles and battlefield hardened targets.

Air Defence (AD): guns and missiles designed to engage fixed-wing, rotary-wing and unmanned aircraft.

CS and CSS Equipment: includes bespoke military systems, such as assault bridging, engineer tanks, armoured recovery vehicles and armoured ambulances. Civilian equipment, such as civil engineering equipment used by engineers and civilian medical equipment, is excluded.

Deployments

The Military Balance mainly lists permanent bases and operational deployments including peacekeeping operations, which are often discussed in the text for each regional section. Information in the country data files details deployments of troops and military observers and, where available, the role and equipment of deployed units.

Training activity

Selected exercises, which involve military elements from two or more states and are designed to improve interoperability or test new doctrine, forces or equipment, are detailed in tabular format. (Exceptions may be made for particularly important exercises held by single states which indicate novel capability developments or involve newly inducted equipment.)

LAND FORCES

The land data section has been revised to improve understanding of the combined-arms capabilities of modern land forces. Armies fight by integrating combat arms that engage the enemy in direct fire and close combat, classically infantry and armour, with combat support (CS) such as engineers and artillery. Medical and logistic capabilities are provided by combat service support (CSS).

Land forces are generally structured into formations, units and sub-units. Most armies achieve flexibility by adopting a modular approach which enables grouping for specific operations, or phases within them. So organisation is as important a factor as equipment in assessing armies' operational effectiveness. However, while most land forces are part of armies, there are exceptions. In some countries,

Principal Naval Equipment Definitions

To aid comparison between fleets, the following definitions, which do not conform to national definitions, are used:

Submarines: all vessels equipped for military operations and designed to operate primarily under water. Submarines with a dived displacement below 250 tonnes are classified as midget submarines; those below 500 tonnes are coastal submarines. Those vessels with submarine-launched ballistic missiles are listed under 'Strategic Nuclear Forces' as well as under the navy.

Principal surface combatants: all surface ships primarily designed for operations on the high seas, either as escorts or primary ships in a task force. These vessels usually have an FLD above 1,500 tonnes. Such ships will have offensive ship-to-ship capabilities and may include anti-submarine-warfare and/ or anti-air capabilities. Principal surface combatants include aircraft carriers (including helicopter carriers), cruisers (with an FLD above 9,750 tonnes), destroyers (with an FLD above 4,500 tonnes) and frigates (with an FLD above 1,500 tonnes).

Patrol and coastal combatants: all surface vessels designed for coastal or inshore operations, in an escort, protective or patrol role. These vessels include corvettes, which usually have an FLD between 500 and 1,500 tonnes and are distinguished from other patrol vessels by their heavier armaments, often including ship-to-ship and/or ship-to-air missiles. Also included in this category are offshore patrol ships, with a FLD greater than 1,500 tonnes, patrol craft, which have a full-load displacement between 250 and 1,500 tonnes and patrol boats with an FLD between ten and 250 tonnes. Fast patrol craft or boats have a top speed greater than 35 knots.

Mine warfare vessels: all surface vessels configured primarily for mine laying or countermeasures. Countermeasures vessels are either: sweepers, which are designed to locate and destroy mines in a maritime area; hunters, which are designed to locate and destroy individual mines; or countermeasures vessels, which combine both roles.

Amphibious vessels: all vessels designed to transport personnel and/or equipment on to unprepared shorelines. Such vessels are classified as amphibious-assault vessels, which can embark fixed-wing and/or rotary-wing air assets as well as landing craft; landing platforms, which can embark rotary-wing aircraft as well as landing craft; landing ships, which are amphibious vessels capable of ocean passage; and landing craft, which are smaller vessels designed to transport personnel and equipment from a larger vessel to land or across small stretches of water. Landing ships have a hold; landing craft are open vessels.

Reference

amphibious forces are part of the navy and airborne forces are part of the air forces. An increasing number of units and formations are part of joint organisations.

NAVAL FORCES

Classifying naval vessels according to role is increasingly complex. A post-war consensus on primary surface combatants revolved around a distinction between independently operating cruisers, air-defence escorts (destroyers) and anti-submarine-warfare escorts (frigates). However, new ships are increasingly performing a range of roles; the littoral combat ship produced by the US, for example, is a frigate-sized vessel that carries surface-to-air missiles and can be reconfigured for anti-submarine warfare, anti-surface warfare or a mine countermeasures role. For this reason, The Military Balance has drawn up a classification system based on full-load displacement (FLD) rather than a role that will allow for greater international comparisons of navies through their tonnage. Older vessels will still often retain the primary role suggested by their type, but in more modern ships, this will decreasingly be the case. This classification system thus does not assist comparison based on other important capabilities, such as command systems, but eases comparisons across international naval fleets.

Given this system, The Military Balance designation will not necessarily conform to national definitions.

AIR FORCES

Aircraft listed in The Military Balance as combat capable are assessed as being equipped to deliver air-to-air or air-to-surface ordnance. The definition includes aircraft designated by type as bomber, fighter, fighter ground attack, ground attack, and anti-submarine warfare. Other aircraft considered to be combat capable are marked with an asterisk (*). Operational groupings of air forces are shown where known. Squadron aircraft strengths vary with aircraft types and from country to country.

When assessing missile ranges, The Military Balance uses the following range indicators: Short-Range Ballistic Missile (SRBM), less than 1,000km; Medium-Range Ballistic Missile (MRBM), 1,000–3,000km; Intermediate-Range Ballistic Missiles (IRBM), 3,000–5,000km; Intercontinental Ballistic Missiles (ICBM), over 5,000km.

ATTRIBUTION AND ACKNOWLEDGEMENTS

The International Institute for Strategic Studies owes no allegiance to any government, group of governments, or any political or other organisation. Its assessments are its own, based on the material available to it from a wide variety of sources. The cooperation of governments of all listed countries has been sought and, in many cases, received. However, some data in The Military Balance are estimates. Care is taken to ensure that these data are as accurate and free from bias as possible. The Institute owes a considerable debt to a number of its own members, consultants and all those who help compile and check material. The Director-General and Chief Executive and staff of the Institute assume full responsibility for the data and judgements in this book. Comments and suggestions on the data and textual material contained within the book, as well as

---

Principal Naval Equipment Definitions (continued)

Auxiliary vessels: all ocean-going surface vessels performing an auxiliary military role, supporting combat ships or operations. Such vessels are either very lightly armed or unarmed. These generally fulfil five roles: under way replenishment (such as tankers and oilers); logistics (such as cargo ships); maintenance (such as cable-repair ships or buoy tenders); research (such as survey ships); and special purpose (such as intelligence-collection ships and ocean-going tugs).

Yard craft/miscellaneous vessels: all surface vessels performing a support role in coastal waters or to ships not in service. These vessels often have harbour roles, such as tugs and tenders. Other miscellaneous craft, such as royal yachts, are also included here.

Weapons systems: weapons are listed in the following order: land-attack missiles, ship-to-ship missiles, surface-to-air missiles, torpedo tubes, anti-submarine weapons, guns and aircraft. Missiles with a range less than 5km and guns with a calibre less than 76mm are generally not included, unless for some lightly armed minor combatants.

Organisations: naval groupings such as fleets and squadrons frequently change and are shown only where doing so would add to qualitative judgements.

Principal Aviation Equipment Definitions

Countries regularly use military aircraft in a variety of roles, determined by platform equipment, weapons and systems fit, as well as crew training. The Military Balance *uses the following main definitions as a guide.*

Type and Role Definitions

Bomber (Bbr): comparatively large platforms intended for the delivery of air-to-surface ordnance. Long-range bombers are those which have an un-refuelled combat radius of greater than 5,000km with a maximum weapons payload in excess of 10,000kg. Medium bombers have a range of between 1,000–5,000km. Bbr units are units equipped with bomber aircraft for the air-to-surface role.

Fighter (Ftr): this term covers aircraft designed primarily for air-to-air combat, with the associated sensors, weapons and performance. It may include a limited air-to-surface capability. Ftr units are equipped with aircraft intended to provide air superiority, which may have a secondary and limited air-to-surface capability.

Fighter/Ground Attack (FGA): indicates a multi-role fighter-size platform with a significant air-to-surface capability, potentially including maritime attack, and some air-to-air capacity. FGA units are multi-role units equipped with aircraft capable of air-to-air and air-to-surface attack.

Ground Attack (Atk): is used to describe aircraft designed solely for the air-to-surface task, with limited or no air-to-air capability. Atk units are equipped with fixed-wing aircraft to undertake air-to-surface missions.

Attack Helicopter (Atk Hel): rotary platforms designed for delivery of air-to-surface weapons, and fitted with an integrated fire control system.

Anti-Submarine Warfare (ASW): fixed- and rotary-wing platforms designed to locate and engage submarines, many with a secondary anti-surface-warfare capacity. ASW units are equipped with fixed- or rotary-wing aircraft for anti-submarine missions.

Anti-Surface Warfare (ASuW): ASuW units are equipped with fixed- or rotary-wing aircraft intended for anti-surface-warfare missions.

Maritime Patrol (MP): fixed-wing aircraft and unmanned aerial vehicles (UAVs) intended for maritime surface surveillance, which may possess an anti-surface-warfare capability. MP units are equipped with fixed-wing aircraft or UAVs intended for maritime surveillance. May also have an ASuW/ASW capability.

Electronic Warfare (EW): fixed- and rotary-wing aircraft and UAVs intended for electronic countermeasures. EW units are equipped with fixed- or rotary-wing aircraft or UAVs used for electronic countermeasures.

Intelligence/Surveillance/Reconnaissance (ISR): fixed- and rotary-wing aircraft and UAVs intended to provide radar, visible light, or infrared imagery, or a mix thereof. ISR units are equipped with fixed- or rotary-wing aircraft or UAVs intended for the ISR role.

Combat/Intelligence/Surveillance/Reconnaissance (CISR): is used to describe those UAVs which have the capability to deliver air-to-surface weapons, as well as undertaking ISR tasks. CISR units are equipped with armed UAVs for the ISR and air-to-surface missions.

COMINT/ELINT/SIGINT: fixed and rotary-wing platforms and UAVs capable of gathering electronic (ELINT), communication (COMINT) or signals intelligence (SIGINT). COMINT units are equipped with fixed- or rotary-wing aircraft or UAVs intended for the communications-intelligence task. ELINT units are equipped with fixed- or rotary-wing aircraft or UAVs used for gathering electronic intelligence. SIGINT units are equipped with fixed- or rotary-wing aircraft or UAVs used to collect signals intelligence.

Principal Aviation Equipment Definitions (continued)

Airborne Early Warning (& Control) (AEW (&C)): Fixed- and rotary-wing platforms capable of providing airborne early warning, with a varying degree of onboard command and control depending on the platform. AEW&C units are equipped with fixed- or rotary-wing aircraft to provide airborne early warning and command and control.

Search and Rescue (SAR): units are equipped with fixed- or rotary-wing aircraft used to recover military personnel or civilians.

Combat Search and Rescue (CSAR): units are equipped with armed fixed- or rotary-wing aircraft for recovery of personnel from hostile territory.

Tanker (Tkr): Fixed- and rotary-wing aircraft designed for air-to-air re-fuelling. Tkr units are equipped with fixed- or rotary-wing aircraft used for air-to-air refuelling.

Tanker Transport (Tkr/Tpt): describes those platforms capable of both air-to-air refuelling and military airlift.

Transport (Tpt): Fixed- or rotary-wing aircraft intended for military airlift. Light transport aircraft are categorised as having a maximum payload of up to 11,340kg, medium up to 27,215kg, and heavy above 27,215kg. Medium transport helicopters have an internal payload of up to 4,535kg; heavy transport helicopters greater than 4,535kg. PAX aircraft are platforms are platforms generally unsuited for transporting cargo on the main deck. Tpt units are equipped with fixed- or rotary-wing platforms to transport personnel or cargo.

Trainer (Trg): A fixed- or rotary-wing aircraft designed primarily for the training role, some also have the capacity to carry light to medium ordnance. Trg units are equipped with fixed- or rotary-wing training aircraft intended for pilot or other aircrew training.

Multi-role helicopter (MRH): Rotary-wing platforms designed to carry out a variety of military tasks including light transport, armed reconnaissance and battlefield support.

Unmanned Aerial Vehicles (UAVs): Remotely piloted or controlled unmanned fixed- or rotary-wing systems. Light UAVs are those weighing between 20–150kg; medium are those from 150kg–600kg; and large are those weighing more than 600kg.

Reference

Table 33 **List of Abbreviations for Data Sections**

– part of unit is detached/less than
* combat capable
" unit with overstated title/ship class nickname
+ unit reinforced/more than
< under 100 tonnes
† serviceability in doubt
‡ obsolete
ε estimated

AAA anti-aircraft artillery
AAB Advisory and Assistance Brigade
AAM air-to-air missile
AAV amphibious assault vehicle
AB airborne
ABM anti-ballistic missile
ABU sea-going buoy tender
ac aircraft
ACCS Air Command and Control System
ACM advanced cruise missile
ACP airborne command post
ACV air cushion vehicle/armoured combat vehicle
AD air defence
ADA air defence artillery
adj adjusted
AE auxiliary, ammunition carrier
AEV armoured engineer vehicle
AEW airborne early warning
AF Air Force
AFB Air Force Base/Station
AFS logistics ship
AG misc auxiliary
AGB icebreaker
AGF command ship
AGHS hydrographic survey vessel
AGI intelligence collection vessel
AGL automatic grenade launcher
AGM air-to-ground missile/missile range instrumentation ship
AGOR oceanographic research vessel
AGOS oceanographic surveillance vessel
AGS survey ship
AH hospital ship
AIFV armoured infantry fighting vehicle
AIP air independent propulsion
AK cargo ship
aka also known as
AKL cargo ship (light)
AKR roll-on/roll-off cargo ship

AKSL stores ship (light)
ALARM air-launched anti-radiation missile
ALCM air-launched cruise missile
amph amphibious/amphibian
AMRAAM advanced medium-range air-to-air missile
AO oiler
AOE fast combat support ship
AOR fleet replenishment oiler with RAS capability
AORH oiler with hel capacity
AORL replenishment oiler (light)
AORLH oiler light with hel deck
AOT oiler transport
AP armour-piercing/anti-personnel/transport
APC armoured personnel carrier
AR repair ship
ARC cable repair ship
ARG amphibious ready group
ARH active radar homing
ARL airborne reconnaissance low
ARM anti-radiation missile
armd armoured
ARS rescue and salvage ship
ARSV armoured reconnaissance/surveillance vehicle
arty artillery
ARV armoured recovery vehicle
AS anti-submarine/submarine tender
ASaC airborne surveillance and control
ASCM Anti-ship cruise missile
AShM anti-ship missile
aslt assault
ASM air-to-surface missile
ASR submarine rescue craft
ASROC anti-submarine rocket
ASTOR airborne stand-off radar
ASTOVL advanced short take-off and vertical landing
ASTROS II artillery saturation rocket system
ASTT anti-submarine torpedo tube
ASW anti-submarine warfare
ASuW anti-surface warfare
AT tug/anti-tank
ATACMS army tactical missile system
ATBM anti-tactical ballistic missile
ATF tug, ocean going
ATGW anti-tank guided weapon

ATK attack/ground attack
ATP advanced targeting pod
ATTC all terrain tracked carrier
AV armoured vehicle
AVB aviation logistic support ship
avn aviation
AWACS airborne warning and control system
AWT water tanker
AX training craft
AXL training craft (light)
AXS training craft (sail)
BA budget authority (US)
Bbr bomber
BCT brigade combat team
bde brigade
bdgt budget
BfSB battlefield surveillance brigade
BG battle group
BMD ballistic missile defence
BMEWS ballistic missile early warning system
bn battalion/billion
BSB brigade support battalion
BSTB brigade special troops battalion
bty battery
C2 command and control
CAB combat aviation brigade
CALCM conventional air-launched cruise missile
CAS close air support
casevac casualty evacuation
cav cavalry
cbt combat
CBU cluster bomb unit
CBRNE chemical, biological, radiological, nuclear, explosive
CCS command and control systems
cdo commando
CERT conputer emergency response team
CET combat engineer tractor
CFE Conventional Armed Forces in Europe
C/G/H/M/N/L cruiser/guided missile/with hangar/with missile/nuclear-powered/light
CISR Combat ISR
CIMIC civil–military cooperation
CIWS close-in weapons system
CLOS command-to-line-of-sight
COIN counter insurgency

comb combined/combination

comd command

COMINT communications intelligence

comms communications

coy company

CPV crew protected vehicle

CPX command post exercise

CS combat support

CSAR combat search and rescue

CSS combat service support

C-RAM counter rocket, artillery and mortar

CT counter terrorism

CTOL conventional take off and landing

CV/H/L/N/S aircraft carrier/helicopter/light/nuclear powered/VSTOL

CW chemical warfare/weapons

DD/G/H/M destroyer/with AShM/with hangar/with SAM

DDS dry deck shelter

def defence

demob demobilised

det detachment

div division

dom domestic

DSCS defense satellite communications system

ECM electronic countermeasures

ECR electronic combat and reconnaissance

EELV evolved expendable launch vehicle

ELINT electronic intelligence

elm element/s

engr engineer

EOD explosive ordnance disposal

eqpt equipment

ESG expeditionary strike group

ESM electronic support measures

est estimate(d)

EW electronic warfare

EWSP electronic warfare self protection

excl excludes/excluding

exp expenditure

FAC forward air control

fd field

FF/G/H/M frigate/with AShM/with hangar/with SAM

FGA fighter ground attack

FLD full-load displacement

flt flight

FMA Foreign Military Assistance

FMTV family of medium transport vehicles

FROG free rocket over ground

FS/G/H/M corvette/with AShM/with hangar/with SAM

FSSG force service support group

FSTA future strategic tanker aircraft

Ftr fighter

FTX field training exercise

FW fixed-wing

FY fiscal year

GBAD ground-based air defence

GBU guided bomb unit

gd guard

GDP gross domestic product

GEODSS ground-based electro-optical deep space surveillance system

GMLS guided missile launch system

GMLRS guided multiple-launch rocket system

GNP gross national product

gp group

GPS global positioning system

GW guided weapon

HARM high-speed anti-radiation missile

HBCT heavy brigade combat team

hel helicopter

HIMARS high-mobility artillery rocket system

HMMWV high-mobility multi-purpose wheeled vehicle

HMTV high-mobility tactical vehicle

HOT high-subsonic optically teleguided

how howitzer

HQ headquarters

HUMINT human intelligence

HWT heavyweight torpedo

hy heavy

IBCT infantry brigade combat team

IBU inshore boat unit

ICBM inter-continental ballistic missile

IFV infantry fighting vehicle

IMET international military education and training

IMINT imagery intelligence

imp improved

IMV infantry mobility vehicle

incl includes/including

indep independent

inf infantry

INS inertial navigation system

int intelligence

IR infrared

IIR imaging infrared

IRBM intermediate-range ballistic missile

IRLS infrared line scan

ISD in-service date

ISR intelligence, surveillance and reconnaissance

ISTAR intelligence, surveillance, target acquisition and reconnaissance

JDAM joint direct attack munition

JSF Joint Strike Fighter

JSTARS joint surveillance target attack radar system

LACV light armoured combat vehicle

LACM land-attack cruise missile

LAMPS light airborne multi-purpose system

LANTIRN low-altitude navigation and targeting infrared system night

LAV light armoured vehicle

LAW light anti-tank weapon

LC/A/AC/D/H/M/PA/PL/T/U/VP landing craft/assault/air cushion/dock/heavy/medium/personnel air cushion/personnel large/tank/utility/vehicles and personnel

LCC amphibious command ship

LFV light forces vehicles

LGB laser-guided bomb

LHA landing ship assault

LHD amphibious assault ship

LIFT lead-in ftr trainer

LKA amphibious cargo ship

lnchr launcher

log logistic

LORADS long-range radar display system

LP/D/H landing platform/dock/helicopter

LRAR long-range artillery rocket

LRSA long-range strike/attack

LS/D/L/LH/M/T landing ship/dock/logistic/logistic helicopter/medium/tank

Lt light

LWT lightweight torpedo

maint maintenance

MAMBA mobile artillery monitoring battlefield radar

MANPADS man portable air-defence system

MANPATS man portable anti-tank system

MARDIV marine division

MAW marine aviation wing

MBT main battle tank

MC/C/I/O mine countermeasure coastal/inshore/ocean

MCD mine countermeasure diving support

MCLOS manual CLOS

MCM mine countermeasures

MCMV mine countermeasures vessel

MD military district

MDT mine diving tender

MEADS medium extended air-defence system

MEB marine expeditionary brigade

mech mechanised

med medium / medical

medevac medical evacuation

MEF marine expeditionary force

MEU marine expeditionary unit

MFO multinational force and observers

MGA machine gun artillery

MH/C/D/I/O mine hunter/coastal/drone/inshore/ocean

MI military intelligence

mil military

MIRV multiple independently targetable re-entry vehicle

MIUW mobile inshore undersea warfare

mk mark (model number)

ML minelayer

MLRS multiple-launch rocket system

MLU mid-life update

mne marine

mob mobilisation/mobile

mod modified/modification

mor mortar

mot motorised/motor

MP maritime patrol/military police

MPA maritime patrol aircraft

MPS marine prepositioning squadron

MR maritime reconnaissance/motor rifle

MRAP mine-resistant ambush-protected

MRAAM medium-range air-to-air missile

MRBM medium-range ballistic missile

MRL multiple rocket launcher

MRTT multi-role tanker transport

MS/A/C/D/I/O/R mine sweeper/auxiliary/coastal/drone/inshore/ocean

msl missile

MSTAR man-portable surveillance and target acquisition radar

Mtn mountain

MW mine warfare

NAEW NATO Airborne Early Warning & Control Force

n.a. not applicable

n.k. not known

NBC nuclear biological chemical

NCO non-commissioned officer

nm nautical mile

nuc nuclear

O & M operations and maintenance

obs observation/observer

OCU operational conversion unit

op/ops operational/operations

OPFOR opposition training force

org organised/organisation

OTH/-B over-the-horizon/backscatter (radar)

OTHR/T over-the-horizon radar/targeting

PAAMS principal anti-air missile system

PAC *Patriot* advanced capability

para paratroop/parachute

PAX passenger/passenger transport aircraft

PB/C/F/I/R patrol boat/coastal/fast/inshore/riverine

PC/C/F/G/H/I/M/O/R/T patrol craft/coastal with AShM/fast/guided missile/with hangar/inshore/with CIWS missile or SAM/offshore/riverine/torpedo

PDMS point defence missile system

pdr pounder

pers personnel

PG/G/GF/H patrol gunboat/guided missile/fast attack craft/hydrofoil

PGM precision-guided munitions

PH/G/M/T patrol hydrofoil/with AShM/missile/torpedo

pl platoon

PKO peacekeeping operations

PPP purchasing-power parity

PPV protected patrol vehicle

PR photo-reconnaissance

PRH passive radar-homing

prepo pre-positioned

PSO/H offshore patrol vessel over 1,500 tonnes/with hangar

ptn pontoon bridging

PTRL/SURV patrol/surveillance

qd quadrillion

R&D research and development

RAM rolling airframe missile

RAS replenishment at sea

RCL recoilless launcher / ramped craft logistic

RCWS remote controlled weapon station

RCT regimental combat team

recce reconnaissance

regt regiment

RIB rigid inflatable boat

RL rocket launcher

ro-ro roll-on, roll-off

RPAS remotely piloted air system

RPV remotely piloted vehicle

RRC/F/U rapid-reaction corps/force/unit

RSTA reconnaissance, surveillance and target acquisition

RV re-entry vehicle

rvn riverine

SACLOS semi-automatic CLOS

SAM surface-to-air missile

SAR search and rescue

SARH semi-active radar homing

sat satellite

SBCT Stryker brigade combat team

SDV swimmer delivery vehicles

SEAD suppression of enemy air defence

SEWS satellite early warning station

SF special forces

SHORAD short-range air defence

SIGINT signals intelligence

sigs signals

SLAM stand-off land-attack missile

SLBM submarine-launched ballistic missile

SLCM submarine-launched cruise missile

SLEP service life extension programme

SMAW shoulder-launched multi-purpose assault weapon

SOC special operations capable

SP self propelled

Spec Ops special operations

SPAAGM Self-propelled anti-aircraft gun and missile system

spt support

sqn squadron

SRBM short-range ballistic missile

SS submarine

SSAN submersible auxiliary support vessel (nuclear)

SSBN nuclear-powered ballistic-missile submarine

SSC coastal submarine

SSG guided missile submarine

SSGN nuclear-powered guided missile submarine

SSK attack submarine with ASW capability (hunter-killer)

SSM surface-to-surface missile

SSN nuclear-powered attack submarine

SSP attack submarine with air-independent propulsion

SSW midget submarine

START Strategic Arms Reduction Talks/Treaty

STO(V)L short take-off and (vertical) landing

str strength

SUGW surface-to-underwater GW

SURV surveillance

SUT surface and underwater target

sy security

t tonnes

tac tactical

temp temporary

THAAD theatre high altitude area defence

tk tank

tkr tanker

TLAM *Tomahawk* land-attack missile

TLE treaty-limited equipment (CFE)

TMD theatre missile defence

torp torpedo

TOW tube launched optically wire guided

tpt transport

tr trillion

trg training

TRV torpedo recovery vehicle

TT torpedo tube

UAV unmanned aerial vehicle

UCAV unmanned combat air vehicle

URG under-way replenishment group

USGW underwater to surface guided weapon

utl utility

UUV unmanned undersea vehicle

V(/S)TOL vertical(/short) take-off and landing

veh vehicle

VLB vehicle launched bridge

VLS vertical launch system

VSHORAD very short-range air defence

VSRAD very short-range air defence

wg wing

WLIC Inland construction tenders

WMD weapon(s) of mass destruction

WTGB US Coast Guard Icebreaker tugs

YAC royal yacht

YAG yard craft, miscellaneous

YDG degaussing

YDT diving tender

YFB ferry boat

YFL launch

YFRT range support tenders

YTB harbour tug

YTL light harbour tug

YTM medium harbour tug

YPT torpedo recovery vessel

YTR firefighting vessel

YY general yard craft

Key to map symbols

Unit size		Unit role indicator					
Army		SF		Air Assault		Intelligence	MI
Corps		Armoured Cavalry/ Reconnaissance		Air Mobile		Military Police	MP
Division		Reconnaissance		Amphibious		Air Defence	SF
Brigade		Battlefield surveillance		Mountain		NBC	
Regiment		Armoured/Tank		Aviation		Signals	
Battalion		Combined Arms		Helicopter		Combat Support	CS
Company		Armoured Infantry		Artillery		Logistics	
Platoon		Mechanised		MRL		Maintenance	
		Motorised		Air Defence		Medical	
		Infantry		SAM		Transport	
		Airborne		Combat Engineer		Combat Service Support	CSS
				EW	EW	Airbase	
						Naval base	

Table 34 **Index of Country/Territory Abbreviations**

AFG	Afghanistan	GAM	Gambia	NPL	Nepal
ALB	Albania	GEO	Georgia	NZL	New Zealand
ALG	Algeria	GER	Germany	OMN	Oman
ANG	Angola	GF	French Guiana	PT	Palestinian Territories
ARG	Argentina	GHA	Ghana	PAN	Panama
ARM	Armenia	GIB	Gibraltar	PAK	Pakistan
ATG	Antigua and Barbuda	GNB	Guinea Bissau	PER	Peru
AUS	Australia	GRC	Greece	PHL	Philippines
AUT	Austria	GRL	Greenland	POL	Poland
AZE	Azerbaijan	GUA	Guatemala	PNG	Papua New Guinea
BDI	Burundi	GUI	Guinea	PRC	China, People's Republic of
BEL	Belgium	GUY	Guyana	PRT	Portugal
BEN	Benin	HND	Honduras	PRY	Paraguay
BFA	Burkina Faso	HTI	Haiti	PYF	French Polynesia
BGD	Bangladesh	HUN	Hungary	QTR	Qatar
BHR	Bahrain	ISL	Iceland	ROC	Taiwan (Republic of China)
BHS	Bahamas	ISR	Israel	ROK	Korea, Republic of
BIH	Bosnia–Herzegovina	IDN	Indonesia	ROM	Romania
BIOT	British Indian Ocean Territory	IND	India	RSA	South Africa
BLG	Bulgaria	IRL	Ireland	RUS	Russia
BLR	Belarus	IRN	Iran	RWA	Rwanda
BLZ	Belize	IRQ	Iraq	SAU	Saudi Arabia
BOL	Bolivia	ITA	Italy	SDN	Sudan
BRB	Barbados	JAM	Jamaica	SEN	Senegal
BRN	Brunei	JOR	Jordan	SER	Serbia
BRZ	Brazil	JPN	Japan	SGP	Singapore
BWA	Botswana	KAZ	Kazakhstan	SLB	Solomon Islands
CAM	Cambodia	KEN	Kenya	SLE	Sierra Leone
CAN	Canada	KGZ	Kyrgyzstan	SLV	El Salvador
CAR	Central African Republic	KWT	Kuwait	SOM	Somali Republic
CHA	Chad	LAO	Laos	SSD	South Sudan
CHE	Switzerland	LBN	Lebanon	STP	São Tomé and Príncipe
CHL	Chile	LBR	Liberia	SUR	Suriname
CIV	Côte d'Ivoire	LBY	Libya	SVK	Slovakia
CMR	Cameroon	LKA	Sri Lanka	SVN	Slovenia
COG	Congo	LSO	Lesotho	SWE	Sweden
COL	Colombia	LTU	Lithuania	SYC	Seychelles
CPV	Cape Verde	LUX	Luxembourg	SYR	Syria
CRI	Costa Rica	LVA	Latvia	TGO	Togo
CRO	Croatia	MDA	Moldova	THA	Thailand
CUB	Cuba	MDG	Madagascar	TJK	Tajikistan
CYP	Cyprus	MEX	Mexico	TLS	Timor Leste
CZE	Czech Republic	MHL	Marshall Islands	TTO	Trinidad and Tobago
DJB	Djibouti	MLI	Mali	TKM	Turkmenistan
DNK	Denmark	MLT	Malta	TUN	Tunisia
DOM	Dominican Republic	MMR	Myanmar	TUR	Turkey
DPRK	Korea, Democratic People's Republic of	MNE	Montenegro	TZA	Tanzania
DRC	Democratic Republic of the Congo	MNG	Mongolia	UAE	United Arab Emirates
ECU	Ecuador	MOR	Morocco	UGA	Uganda
EGY	Egypt	MOZ	Mozambique	UK	United Kingdom
EQG	Equitorial Guinea	MRT	Mauritania	UKR	Ukraine
ERI	Eritrea	MUS	Mauritius	URY	Uruguay
ESP	Spain	MWI	Malawi	US	United States
EST	Estonia	MYS	Malaysia	UZB	Uzbekistan
ETH	Ethiopia	NAM	Namibia	VEN	Venezuela
FIN	Finland	NCL	New Caledonia	VNM	Vietnam
FLK	Falkland Islands	NER	Niger	YEM	Yemen
FJI	Fiji	NGA	Nigeria	ZMB	Zambia
FRA	France	NIC	Nicaragua	ZWE	Zimbabwe
FYROM	Macedonia, Former Yugoslav Republic of	NLD	Netherlands		
GAB	Gabon	NOR	Norway		

Table 35 **Index of Countries and Territories**